Library and Book Trade Almanac™

formerly **The Bowker Annual**

2019 | 64th Edition

Library and Book Trade Almanac™

formerly **The Bowker Annual**

2019 | 64th Edition

Editor John B. Bryans

Information Today, Inc.

Published by Information Today, Inc.

International Standard Book Number 978-1-57387-554-7
International Standard Serial Number 2150-5446
Library of Congress Catalog Card Number 55-12434

Information Today, Inc.
143 Old Marlton Pike
Medford, NJ 08055-8750
Phone: 800-300-9868 (customer service)
800-409-4929 (editorial queries)
Fax: 609-654-4309
E-mail (orders): custserv@infotoday.com
Web Site: http://www.infotoday.com

Printed and bound in the United States of America

Contents

Part 1
Reports from the Field

Special Reports

Federal Agency and Federal Library Reports

National Association and Organization Reports

International Reports

Part 2
Legislation, Funding, and Grants

Legislation

Funding Programs and Grant-Making Agencies

Part 3
Library/Information Science Education, Placement, and Salaries

Part 4
Research and Statistics

Library Research and Statistics

Book Trade Research and Statistics

Part 5
Reference Information

Ready Reference

Distinguished Books

Part 6
Directory of Organizations

Directory of Library and Related Organizations

Directory of Book Trade and Related Organizations

Preface and Acknowledgments

In keeping with its annual mission, this 2019 64th edition of *Library and Book Trade Almanac* looks at the year gone by, reporting on and updating industry facts, figures, activities, and trends. As *LBTA* staff and contributors surveyed a mountain of 2018 data to produce the volume, we were impressed by both the number and the nature of the nuggets, rocks, and boulders of information cascading down. There's space enough to mention just a few of them here.

The ink-on-paper book appears to be the Comeback Kid of entertainment media: battle-scarred, but still standing, uniquely influential despite the talk (in some cases the reality) of shortened attention spans; the rise of social media, blogs, and gaming culture; and an explosion of audio and video content, not to mention e-books. Although not all publication formats or Book Industry Study Group (BISAC) categories will benefit equally from renewed public embrace of print books, the reports featured in "Book Trade Research and Statistics" in Part 4 demonstrate general stability of output and pricing in the market.

It's exciting to see so many exceptional and diverse books being published, bought, and borrowed across all formats. Along with the authors whose names we expect, scores of lesser-known and emerging scribes were celebrated for their efforts in 2018. The "Distinguished Books" section in Part 5 (which includes an extensive listing of literary prize winners) offers plenty of hope for fledgling writers and somewhat less for small and new publishers that aspire to remain independent. Acquisition-minded conglomerates continue to dominate the book publishing industry, though unless you can discern the hundreds of divisions and imprints of the top five or six publishers—Penguin Random House alone boasts nearly 275 imprints—you might not know it. (While not all lists in this section include publisher and imprint/division information, those that do—for instance, "The Year's Notable Books" from ALA's Reference and User Services Association—are instructive.)

Few *LBTA* readers will be surprised to hear that politics dominated the bestseller lists in 2018, with nonfiction titles about President Trump, his staff, and administration by Michael Wolff and Bob Woodward leading a crowded field, bookended on the fiction side by a blockbuster political thriller from James Patterson and Bill Clinton. These megabestsellers, along with every other book published in 2018, were eclipsed by Michelle Obama's *Becoming*, which was already the publishing story of the year when it hit bookstore shelves in November. (See our listings of "Top Ten Bestselling Books of 2018.")

Libraries are always at the heart of the coverage in *LBTA,* and among our chief concerns this cycle are, one, the steadily mounting pressure on them to do more with (even) less due to funding shortfalls, and, two, the Trump administration's continuing effort to eliminate federal agencies that support libraries, museums, and other educational and cultural institutions and programs. The table on page 232, showing just four of the agencies and offices on the Trump chopping block, is an eye-opener. Fortunately, as the table indicates, Congress has so far ignored the proposed budget cuts and maintained funding through 2019. Legislators who held the line should be commended, and, more importantly, all representatives should hear from their constituents who support strong federal library funding into the future.

For additional reporting on these and related issues be sure to see, in Part 2, "Legislation and Regulations Affecting Libraries in 2018," by Kathi Kromer and Shawnda Hines of ALA's Washington office. And for an enlightening and timely primer for those seeking to grasp and navigate the twists and turns around library funding and tax policy, don't miss John Chrastka's special report, "The Funding Disconnect: How State and Local Tax Revenues Will Impact the Library of Tomorrow."

Following the Chrastka report is Barbie E. Keiser's in-depth piece "Libraries Support Scholarship In (and Beyond) the Ivory Tower." As Keiser writes in her introduction, "Innovations being advanced by librarians today are not only extending the traditional role of the library but assuring that great ideas can flourish beyond the institution and, indeed, beyond academia." She backs up this assertion with a wealth of outside-the-box thinking and advice that warrant the attention of librarians, researchers, scholars, university leaders and administrators, faculty and other educators, scholarly publishers, and lifelong learners.

I would like to thank the contributors to this edition of *LBTA* for delivering everything they promised and sometimes a good deal more. There could be no annual volume without them. I particularly wish to acknowledge Shawnda Hines, George Aulisio, Bette-Lee Fox, Connie Harbison, Steve Zalusky, and Liz Page. In addition to bringing remarkable expertise and professionalism to the almanac, each of these individuals did something to bolster the editor's faith in humanity.

The skill and dedication my *LBTA* team members Christine McNaull, Sonya Manes, Nan Badgett, and Owen O'Donnell bring to the project are inspiring and indispensable. They have my gratitude. And, finally, to our readers, thank you for perusing and using this reference. Please drop me a line at jbryans@infotoday.com and let me know how we can make it more useful and relevant to your work.

John B. Bryans
Editor

Part 1
Reports from the Field

Special Reports

The Funding Disconnect: How State and Local Tax Revenues Will Impact the Library of Tomorrow

John Chrastka

The revenue model for funding public libraries that exists today is largely based on a Progressive Era notion that the government should play a positive role in people's lives and livelihoods.[1] The existence of institutions like public libraries, schools, and museums—as well as the continuation of services like public safety, parks, and health departments—are rooted in a philosophy of government in which taxation-funded cooperative services improve society overall. Public institutions like these are, to a large extent, funded by taxes levied in relatively small geographies that overlap with other taxing jurisdictions.

Local tax schemes vary greatly across the country. Some authorities levy taxes on residential, commercial, and agricultural property; some collect sales, use, or excise taxes; others tax income; while still others use fees and licenses as a core component of their revenue. For public libraries, local property taxes are often the primary source of funding, despite the limited definition of "taxable property." According to the nonpartisan Institute on Taxation and Economic Policy, "[t]oday, a state's property tax base typically includes only a subset of total wealth: primarily homes and business real estate and, in some states, cars and business property other than real estate. Wealth in the form of business equity, stocks, bonds, patents, copyrights, savings, and other intangible assets is not generally taxed by any level of government."[2]

While the library industry pays a great deal of advocacy attention to federal funding for the Institute of Museum and Library Services (IMLS), most funding for public libraries comes from local or state taxes. In many places, as much as 86 percent of the funding that supports the entire operation of the library is raised in an area as narrow as a single zip code.[3] Funding support for libraries by state and federal government is a relatively recent development in the history of libraries in

John Chrastka is executive director of EveryLibrary, a political action committee for libraries, and the EveryLibrary Institute, a nonprofit research and training organization focused on the future of library funding. He is a former board president of the Berwyn (IL) Public Library and Reaching Across Illinois Library System (RAILS). Previously, he was a partner in AssociaDirect, was director for Membership Development at the American Library Association, and was a cofounder of the educational technology start-up ClassMap. Chrastka is coauthor, with Patrick "PC" Sweeney, of the books, *Winning Elections and Influencing Politicians for Library Funding* and *Before the Ballot: Building Political Support for Library Funding*.

the United States.[4] With few exceptions, federal and state aid for libraries is allocated through programmatic grants or on a per capita basis.

The current hyperpartisan political environment has spawned renewed debate on what the government's "legitimate" or "necessary" role is in supporting libraries.[5] The debate is not only about how much tax money should be allocated, but about what the appropriate role, if any, there is at all three levels of government in providing funding. At this writing, the debate is most engaged at the local level, and it's essential that libraries understand the political, economic, and social considerations that drive local funding decisions. Yet library leaders who aspire to shape the funding conversation into the future must also keep abreast of current and emerging public and tax policy issues *nationally* and speak authoritatively about the legitimate taxpayer-funded role public libraries have in education, community development, economic growth, and livability. All sides of the political narrative need to hear from library leaders about what a modest tax investment does to create more interesting, thriving, and prosperous communities.

State and Local Funding Pressures

Because of tremendous and often changing internal and external pressures on library budgets, it is important to look at recent trends in tax and public policy in order to forecast revenues. Internal pressures come from the library leaders and staff driven to fulfill their mission. External constraints come on a local level in the form of tax caps, abatements, and rollbacks that programmatically decrease or constrain revenue. These tax caps and rollbacks can directly affect a library's budget as well as the local government services ecosystem the library participates in. External budgetary pressures, coming from increased costs or decreased revenues, are often rooted in larger policy debates such as minimum wage increases, pension obligations, and healthcare costs.

Tax Policy Divisions

Debates over property tax policies are generally divided along progressive, limited government, and libertarian lines. According to the Tax Foundation, a conservative think tank, 46 states and the District of Columbia have "adopted some form of property tax limitation regime, ranging from provisions which strictly control property tax revenues to regimes so lax as to be functionally irrelevant."[6] Progressives tend to view government services as a necessary and important part of the fabric of our society that must be paid for—provided there are fail-safes to avoid pricing people out of their own homes. Limited government-minded voters tend to look to tax caps as a way create sensible constraints on the growth of government. The libertarian perspective sees low taxes as a way to protect taxpayers from government overreach.

These are foundational beliefs about taxes and taxation, and there are significant differences in the vocabulary and worldview among the factions. The tension inherent in these different approaches impacts libraries, and library leaders need to understand how to navigate them. In his groundbreaking work *The Three Languages of Politics*, Cato Institute Fellow Arnold Kling notes:

> In politics, I claim that progressives, conservatives, and libertarians are like tribes speaking different languages. The language that resonates with one tribe does not connect with the others. As a result, political discussions do not lead to agreement. Instead, most political commentary serves to increase polarization. The points that people make do not open the minds of people on the other side. They serve to close the minds of the people on one's own side.[7]

Funding Caps

In many states, property tax caps and rollbacks put persistent negative pressure on library budgets. From the Headlee Amendment in Michigan, TABOR and Gallagher in Colorado, and others around the country, library boards lack the authority and discretion to raise new revenue to meet current obligations or provide for future services under tax caps that require district libraries to go to voters in order to increase their operating funding by as little as one dollar.[8,9] Rollbacks force library leaders to construct and propose override ballot measures or face automatic budget cuts. Tax caps, rollbacks, abatements, assessment limits, homestead exemptions, differential assessments, and even balanced budget amendments are often proposed by taxpayer rights groups as a way to find relief from perceived high taxes. They are also popular tools used by antitax and antigovernment groups to shrink the overall size and scope of government services.

In the 2018 midterm elections, North Carolina voters approved an income tax amendment that lowers the maximum state income tax rate from 10 to 7 percent.[10] Florida narrowly avoided a massive new homestead exemption cap when the vote on "Constitutional Amendment 1" fell short of 60 percent.[11] In Indiana, voters approved "Public Question 1" to enshrine a balanced budget in the state constitution and require a supermajority of both houses to override any spending limits. According to the National Conference of State Legislatures, nearly every state currently has a requirement to balance their budget in state statutes.[12] The definitions of what constitutes the "budget" vary widely. In some states, the balanced portion of the budget is operating expenditures only. In other states, the requirements to override the provisions render the entire policy moot.

As a matter of public policy, a balanced budget amendment seems like good government. However, if a state is constitutionally prohibited from borrowing money or issuing debt, measures like Indiana's "Public Question 1" will force spending cuts and shrink government during a budget crisis with no functional way to avoid a potentially catastrophic impact on services.[13] State aid for libraries and government services will be negatively impacted. Tax caps and rollbacks may become even more popular as the impact of the 2017 federal Tax Cuts and Jobs Act is felt by filers.

The Minimum Wage Debate

The "Fight for $15" minimum wage movement is gathering momentum, and minimum wage increases are being enacted at all levels at an increasing pace.[14] In some cases, these are legislatively enacted increases; in others, voters are enacting new laws through the ballot box. In 2018 voters in Missouri and Arkansas enacted phased-in increases. States like New York and California have regional variations in their minimum wage levels.[15,16]

Public and academic library workers are generally eligible to receive these wage hikes, so base pay is going up for government workers across the board. The tension for library leaders is that while wages are increasing, revenue for independent districts is capped. The same is true for municipal department libraries that find themselves among a number of departments competing for limited revenue to pay these new wages. Unless taxes are raised or government workers are exempted from these laws, minimum wage increases will create an unfunded mandate on library budgets.

Pension Costs

The impact of pension obligations on library budgets varies from state to state and from plan to plan. Most public libraries participate in a local or statewide pension plan for their employees. The financial stability of such systems is well beyond the control or influence of local library leadership. Ideally, pension plans are properly funded, and future obligations do not outstrip current revenues; however, there are pension systems in this country that are wildly out of balance.[17] While certain individual libraries may be in those plans, it is the regional impact of underfunded pension systems that is the most concerning. When nearby towns, cities, and counties (in some cases, even states) make significant cuts to current services to pay off their pension obligations, libraries often have to pick up the slack, working to provide "standard" services on top of additional burdens like healthcare applications, providing access to healthy food, and immigration support.[18]

Divided State Government

Following the 2018 midterms, Minnesota is the only state with a split legislature, Democrats having taken back the House and Republicans narrowly holding the Senate. According to the National Conference of State Legislatures, in the remaining states (not including Nebraska, with its unicameral legislature) both chambers are held by the same majority party.[19] In a similar way, only 13 states have divided legislative and executive powers. In 2019, Republicans hold the House, Senate, and governor's mansion in 22 states, and Democrats have equivalent control in 14. Referring to what is commonly called a trifecta, *Governing* magazine notes that "[w]hile one-party dominance tends to mean that legislation moves faster, that hasn't always meant better fiscal policy."[20]

It is vital for library leaders to understand the political and budgetary priorities of the party in power. If the single party in powers' political philosophy does not support libraries, then asking to increase funding for your state library agency or *any* new appropriations is going to be very difficult. It is critical for leaders to consider how to reframe the political and policy language used to describe library services when there is a significant disconnect between their vocabulary and that of elected officials. A change in the language used to describe services can make a lasting impact on the receptiveness of government funders. *Governing* magazine predicts that "states with new Democratic trifectas will focus on policies such as expanding the sales tax base, increasing income tax rates for high-income earners, and restoring tax breaks eliminated by federal tax reform."

New Sources of Revenue

There are four ways to raise revenue for school and public libraries, and only one is by directly increasing the tax rate. The other three methods focus on closing tax loopholes, stabilizing the revenue cycle, and including libraries as eligible entities in new tax systems.

Library leaders must understand how tax loopholes are being exploited in order to help correct unfair practices and ensure their own funding base. In some states, big-box retailers are using a tax loophole known as a "dark store" exemption to reduce their property taxes. The dark store exemption is, at its core, a progressive tax policy.[21] If a store is closed, or "dark," it is not generating revenue for the company, and therefore its valuation is less, and its tax burden should be lowered. What makes this loophole pernicious is that big-box retailers and property owners are applying for exemptions even while their stores are open for business. The argument being advanced is that the value of the property is less than that of a comparable building because a purpose-built big-box store cannot be readily sold and repurposed. Creating and exploiting a loophole like this upend the intent of the code, drives down tax collections, and forces a shift in the tax burden from retail to residential properties.[22]

Looking ahead to 2020, California residents will vote on the Schools and Local Communities Funding Act, a proposed state constitutional amendment that would reindex parcel (property) taxes on commercial properties while "guaranteeing existing protections for residential property and agricultural land."[23] If enacted, the act is projected to bring in $11 billion in new revenue annually for local government services and schools. The coalition advancing the legislation is large and multifaceted, including organized labor, educational stakeholders, municipal officials, and government watchdog groups. Libraries in California stand to directly benefit from the amendment. Across the country, it is critically important for library leaders to be engaged in similar self-preservatory coalitions in order to meet their legitimate future revenue needs.

The same is true for school libraries. In 2018 voters in 12 states considered new education-related ballot measures. The impact of these state-level proposals would have included hundreds of billions of dollars in new state-level funding for education. Voters in Utah turned down their statewide advisory measure supporting a new tax on motor fuel that would have allocated 30 percent to infrastructure spending and 70 percent to education. "Question #1" specifically named school library programs as eligible entities for the new funding.[24]

Progressive education coalitions regularly bring new funding measures like Utah's Question #1 directly to voters. State library associations and school library organizations should be at the table as early as possible in order to get school library programs and certified school librarian positions into the funding proposals. The Utah Library Association and Utah Educational Library Media Association (UELMA) joined an existing coalition that included 501c3 nonprofits, 501c4 political action committees, and labor unions in order to help advance Question #1.[25] Schools, libraries, and their representative organizations have the most at stake in putting school libraries into these state ballot measures, and it is incumbent upon library leaders to show up and make it happen.

State-level endowments, or trust funds, are another potential source of stable funding for libraries. Numerous local library foundations have endowments or trusts set up for the long-term benefit of specific libraries. Endowments and trusts for libraries are not common at the state level, except for Wisconsin and Ohio, which have trust funds for school and public libraries respectively. Only one state, Wyoming, has recently established a state-supported library endowment fund. The state legislature in New Mexico is considering a new endowment for rural libraries this legislative session.[26] A state endowment for libraries is not a silver bullet but can provide budgetary relief in unstable times and create new equities among libraries and districts.

In 2016 the Brookings Institution encouraged states to create permanent trust funds using severance taxes from oil and gas extraction in order to help smooth out the boom-and-bust nature of revenue collection from this volatile industry.[27] In 2018 in Georgia, 82 percent of voters approved a ballot measure to create the Georgia Outdoor Stewardship Trust Fund,[28] through which a portion of sales tax on outdoor recreational equipment will be dedicated to conserving lands that protect drinking water sources and water quality. Could library leaders make the case for directing a portion of current or new state taxes on certain types of purchases, resources, behaviors, and/or income to establish and maintain similar funds for libraries?

In 2018 Maryland voters amended the state constitution to dedicate certain gaming revenues to education, and to create an education "lock box" to ensure that tax revenues would only be used for education and not siphoned off to other priorities.[29] The governor is advocating that a portion of the funds be used as construction grants to schools and districts.[30] These new approaches by related public institutions and service providers should serve as inspiration for library leaders. If voters are willing to consider and approve new permanent trust funds for green spaces, recreation, and quality of life, and to authorize innovative ways to ensure the permanency and stability of educational funding, might they also engage a policy discussion about library funding?

For libraries to continue to serve students and the public, new sources of revenue must be found. One emerging source is sales taxes and fees from legalized marijuana. Over $11 billion in legal cannabis and cannabis-related products were sold in 2017, creating a significant revenue stream in states that have legalized recreational marijuana use. In 2018 Michigan became the tenth state to legalize when voters passed "Proposition 1."[31] Another 20 states have already legalized some type of medical use, which is often a precursor to recreational use. Colorado collected $250 million in sales taxes and fees from the sale of cannabis products in 2017 alone. Library leaders need to engage state ballot-measure proponents and legislators early on regarding how libraries and education can and should benefit from marijuana tax policy.

According to data compiled in December 2018 by *Governing* magazine, every state except Indiana saw a drop in tax revenues compared with the year prior. This ranged from -3.4 percent in Ohio to -41 percent in California.[32] The true impact of the 2017 Tax Cuts and Jobs Act (TCJA) is only now beginning to be felt by taxpayers and policymakers. The TCJA reduces federal tax revenue by $1.9 trillion over a decade by cutting personal income taxes and estate taxes, by reducing corporate tax rates, and by creating significant new exemptions and loopholes benefiting the wealthy. Although the purported goal is to spur spending and economic growth, the country is not remotely on track to make up for the lost tax revenue. As a result, the government's ability to service the current national debt, pay for mandatory programs and personnel, and respond to national emergencies over the next ten years will rely on new debt and cuts to discretionary program budgets.

Under TCJA the individual deductions for state and local taxes (SALT), which had been a core part of the federal tax code since 1913, have been limited.[33] Likewise, while the whole dollar amount of automatic deductions for filers has increased, the ability to itemize deductions above a certain threshold has been severely curtailed. While personal charitable contributions have long been an important itemized deduction for taxpayers, under TCJA charitable giving has been disincentivized from a tax perspective. Leaders at the National Council of Non-Profits are projecting as much as a $13 billion decline in charitable giving annually as a result of this change.[34]

Cutting taxes and limiting deductions are together a core principle of the Trump Administration and of the 115th Congress. They consider it highly advantageous to shift responsibility for government services from Washington, D.C., to the states and localities, and to cut the overall scope of government services. Conservative organizations and think tanks including the Heritage Foundation and the American Enterprise Institute have been promoting policies that limit the size and scope of government for decades, with varying success. Today, they have the ear of the administration.[35]

By capping SALT deductions, the federal government is using tax policy to force higher-taxing states to justify their tax levels to local voters. Come tax time, an increasing number of Americans are likely to perceive their local and state taxes as too high, and rather than turning to Washington, these property owners and voters will seek relief from municipal and state government. States, counties, municipalities, and districts could respond by cutting property taxes. This has happened before, though many governments are loath to make such cuts—especially now, with a strong economy and many state and local programs, projects, and rainy-day funds in need of replenishment following the Great Recession.[36] What are the implications for libraries as districts or municipal departments if voters and elected officials look to enact or expand exemptions, abatements, balanced budget amendments, and homestead provisions in state legislatures or directly at the ballot box?

Throughout the country, free public libraries are generally seen as a component of the basic package of local government services.[37] The services provided by state libraries, state and regional systems, and consortia exist within an approach to public policy that looks to address inequitable local services with state and federal aid. The jewel of public library services is Interlibrary Loan. At its core, ILL is a 50-year-long experiment in tax equalization.[38] Libraries have succeeded in creating a powerful and effective tax equalization scheme by moving materials from relatively rich places to relatively poorer places, and by cooperatively purchasing access to collections and services across legal jurisdictions. Can that system, which provides a modicum of equity to every library user, survive in the political and revenue climate to come?

"Wake Up the Nation: Public Libraries, Policy Making, and Political Discourse," a 2011 *Library Quarterly* article by Paul Jaeger, John Bertot, and Ursula Gorham, identified significant deficits in how library leaders engage political considerations and in the policy-making processes that "shape the funding, activities, and roles of libraries in society . . ."[39] According to the authors, "if libraries are to be able to effectively advocate for the interests of their institutions, patrons, and communities, researchers need to more strongly engage problems of politics and policy-making that impact libraries." They state that "in short, our scholarship and professional literature tends to focus on services and meeting user needs and is nearly devoid of considering the policies and politics that frame how public libraries serve their communities." Unfortunately, the article's call to action has gone largely unheeded.

In 2019 and beyond, pressure on state and local governments will continue to mount as federal program allocations are reduced across all parts of the discretionary budget. Library budgets will be increasingly squeezed as external factors like wages, pensions, and healthcare collide with tax policies that seek to constrain government or limit the burden of local taxes. For libraries to thrive, library leaders must dedicate themselves to understanding and anticipating these factors and to creating innovative, revenue-focused solutions to the formidable budget and service challenges that lie ahead.

Notes

1. Christopher J. Cyphers, *The National Civic Federation and the Making of a New Liberalism* (Westport, CT: Greenwood Publishing, 2002).
2. "Who Pays? A Distributional Analysis of the Tax Systems in All 50 States," last modified October 2018, Institute on Taxation and Economic Policy (ITEP), https://itep.org/wp-content/uploads/whopays-ITEP-2018.pdf.
3. OCLC and The American Library Association, "From Awareness to Funding Summary Report Voter Perceptions and Support of Public Libraries in 2018: Summary Report," (Dublin, OH: OCLC), https://www.oclc.org/content/dam/oclc/reports/awareness-to-funding-2018/2018_From_Awareness_to_Funding_Report.pdf.
4. Edward G. Holley and Robert F. Schremser, *Library Services and Construction Act: An Historical Overview from the Viewpoint of Major Participants* (Greenwich, CT: JAI Press, 1983).
5. John Chrastka, "What a Renewed Federalism Means for Libraries," *Library Quarterly* 87, no. 4 (2017): 342–349, https://www.journals.uchicago.edu/doi/abs/10.1086/693491?journalCode=lq.
6. Jared Walczak, "Property Tax Limitation Regimes: A Primer," Tax Foundation, last modified April 23, 2018, https://taxfoundation.org/property-tax-limitation-regimes-primer/.
7. Arnold King, "The Three Languages of Politics: Talking across the Political Divides," CATO Institute, last modified 2017, https://cdn.cato.org/libertarianismdotorg/books/ThreeLanguagesOfPolitics.pdf.
8. "Policy Basics: Taxpayer Bill of Rights (TABOR)," Center on Budget and Policy Priorities, last modified June 26, 2017, https://www.cbpp.org/research/state-budget-and-tax/policy-basics-taxpayer-bill-of-rights-tabor.
9. Michigan State Budget Office, accessed February 20, 2019, https://www.michigan.gov/budget/0,4538,7-157-21338-153206--F,00.html.

10. Associated Press, "NC Voters OK Voter ID, Tax Cap, Crime Victims, Hunting Amendments." *13WLOS News*, last modified November 6, 2018, https://wlos.com/news/election/nc-voters-reject-amendments-to-increase-legislators-say-over-elections-board-makeup.
11. Elizabeth Koh and Samantha J. Gross, "Here's How Floridians Noted on the 12 Constitutional Amendments," *Miami Herald*, last modified November 6, 2018, https://www.miamiherald.com/news/politics-government/election/article220679075.html.
12. National Conference of State Legislatures, "State Balanced Budget Provisions," last modified October 2010, http://www.ncsl.org/research/fiscal-policy/state-balanced-budget-requirements-provisions-and.aspx.
13. Richard Kogan, "Constitutional Balanced Budget Amendment Poses Serious Risks Would Likely Make Recessions Longer and Deeper, Could Harm Social Security and Other Trust Funds," Center on Budget and Policy Priorities, last modified March 16, 2016, https://www.cbpp.org/research/federal-budget/constitutional-balanced-budget-amendment-poses-serious-risks.
14. Fight for Fifteen, "Fight for Fifteen," accessed February 20, 2019, https://fightfor15.org/.
15. Natasha Vaughn, "NY's Minimum Wage: How It Is Affecting Workers and Businesses," *Democrat and Chronicle*, last modified April 19, 2018, https://www.democratandchronicle.com/story/news/politics/albany/2018/04/19/nys-minimum-wage-how-affecting-workers-and-businesses/521919002/.
16. Michael Reich, Sylvia Allegretto, and Claire Montialoux, "Effects of a $15 Minimum Wage in California and Fresno," Center on Wage and Employment Dynamics, last modified January 2017, http://irle.berkeley.edu/files/2017/Effects-of-a-15-Minimum-Wage-in-California-and-Fresno.pdf.
17. "National Data," Public Plans Data, last modified December 18, 2018, https://publicplansdata.org/quick-facts/national/.
18. Paul Jaeger and Lindsay Sarin, "The Politically Engaged Public Library: Admitting and Embracing the Political Nature of Libraries and Their Goals," *Public Library Quarterly* 35 no. 4 (2016): 325–330, https://doi.org/10.1080/01616846.2016.1245005.
19. "NCSL State Vote," National Conference on State Legislatures (NCSL), last modified 2018, http://www.ncsl.org/research/elections-and-campaigns/statevote-2018-state-legislative-races-and-ballot-measures.aspx.
20. Liz Farmer, "What Polarized Government Means for Tax Policy in 2019," *Governing*, last modified February 6, 2019, http://www.governing.com/topics/finance/gov-polarized-states-tax-policy.html.
21. Laura Bliss, "After the Retail Apocalypse, Prepare for the Property Tax Meltdown," *CityLab*, last modified November 14, 2018, https://www.citylab.com/equity/2018/11/property-tax-dark-store-theory-retail-apocalypse-walmart/574123/.
22. Michael J. Bologna, "2019 Outlook: Lowes, Wal-Mart Property Tax Loophole Under Scrutiny in Wisconsin," Bloomberg, BNA, last modified December 24, 2018, https://www.bna.com/2019-outlook-lowes-n57982094850/.
23. "California Schools and Local Communities Funding Act," *Schools and Communities First*, accessed February 20, 2019, https://schoolsandcommunitiesfirst.org/about/.
24. "Ballot Proposal," *Our Schools Now*, accessed February 20, 2019, https://ourschoolsnow.com/ballot/.
25. Rebekah Cummings, "Utah Library Association (ULA) Supports Passage of Question #1 to Fund School Libraries and Public Education," Utah Library Association, last modified September 27, 2018, http://ula.org/content/2018/09/utah-library-association-ula-supports-passage-of-question-1-to-fund-school-libraries-and-public-education/.

26. Lisa Peet, "Artist, Senator Propose $50M Endowment for Rural NM Libraries," *Library Journal*, last modified August 7, 2018, https://www.libraryjournal.com/?detailStory=180806-Endowment-for-Rural-NM-Libraries.
27. Devashree Saha and Mark Muro, "Permanent Trust Funds: Funding Economic Change with Fracking Revenues," the Brookings Institution, last modified April 19, 2016, https://www.brookings.edu/research/permanent-trust-funds-funding-economic-change-with-fracking-revenues/.
28. Joseph Bishop-Henchman, Jared Walczak, and Katherine Loughead, "Results of 2018 State and Local Tax Ballot Initiatives," Tax Foundation, last modified November 6, 2018, https://taxfoundation.org/2018-state-tax-ballot-results/.
29. "Maryland Question 1, Gambling Revenue Dedicated to Education Lockbox Amendment (2018)," *BallotOpedia*, accessed February 20, 2019, https://ballotpedia.org/Maryland_Question_1,_Gambling_Revenue_Dedicated_to_Education_Lockbox_Amendment_(2018).
30. Danielle E. Gaines, "With Education Lockbox Funding on the Way, Hogan Adds School Construction Promise to Mix," *Maryland Matters*, last modified December 11, 2018, https://www.marylandmatters.org/2018/12/11/with-education-lockbox-funding-on-the-way-hogan-adds-school-construction-promise-to-mix/.
31. Craig Giammona, "Marijuana Legalization: A Budding Industry," *Quicktake*, Bloomberg BNA, last modified November 8, 2018, https://www.bloomberg.com/quicktake/marijuana-legalization.
32. Liz Farmer, "State Revenues Take a Hit," *Governing*, last modified January 24, 2019, http://www.governing.com/topics/finance/gov-state-revenues-take-hit.html.
33. Amelia Josephson, "Changes to State and Local Tax Deduction—Explained," *SmartAsset*, last modified January 30, 2019, https://smartasset.com/taxes/trumps-plan-to-eliminate-the-state-and-local-tax-deduction-explained.
34. National Council of Nonprofits, "Federal Tax Law—Tax Cuts & Jobs Act," accessed February 20, 2019, https://www.councilofnonprofits.org/trends-policy-issues/federal-tax-law-tax-cuts-jobs-act.
35. The Heritage Foundation, "Trump Administration Embraces Heritage Foundation Policy Recommendations," last modified January 3, 2018, https://www.heritage.org/impact/trump-administration-embraces-heritage-foundation-policy-recommendations.
36. Barb Rosewicz, Jonathan Moody, and Daniel Newman, "States Make More Progress Rebuilding Rainy Day Funds," the Pew Charitable Trusts, last modified August 29, 2018, https://www.pewtrusts.org/en/research-and-analysis/articles/2018/08/29/states-make-more-progress-rebuilding-rainy-day-funds.
37. Daniel Akst, 2012, "Today's Public Libraries: Public Places of Excellence, Education and Innovation," *Carnegie Reporter* 6, no. 4 (2012), https://www.carnegie.org/publications/carnegie-reporter-vol-6no-4/.
38. John Chrastka, "Teaching Political Literacy," in *Re-Envisioning the MLS: Perspectives on the Future of Library and Information Science Education*, edited by Johnna Percell, Lindsay C. Sarin, Paul T. Jaeger, and John Carlo Bertot (Bingley, UK: Emerald Publishing Limited, 2018).
39. Paul T. Jaeger, John Carlo Bertot, and Ursula Gorham, "Wake Up the Nation: Public Libraries, Policy Making, and Political Discourse," *Library Quarterly* 83, no. 1 (2013): 61–72, http://www.jstor.org/stable/10.1086/668582.

Libraries Support Scholarship In (and Beyond) the Ivory Tower

Barbie E. Keiser

Providing researchers with access to their institution's collections, obtaining materials from other institutions when requested, is the role academic librarians have played since the middle ages. Throughout the last century, libraries assumed the responsibility for improving the ability of researchers to discover and acquire relevant material from an ever-expanding set of diverse sources, which then had to be cited properly.

Traditionally involved behind the scenes, academic libraries are increasingly taking on new responsibilities supporting scholarly output, including helping individual researchers and institutions manage content for posterity and shaping the image and reputation of both by promoting research efforts within academia and beyond. For most libraries this is simply an extension of what they have always done; for others it's meant taking on new roles, often adding staff. Success for these ventures requires doubling down on collaborative partnerships with individuals and organizations within and outside the institution.

Over the past four decades, increased costs for resources (print and online) and advances in technology, including Web-based, cloud-based, and open-source tools and platforms, have influenced what libraries do, how they do it, and for whom. Corresponding changes at the institutional level and within society-at-large affect how the researcher approaches a project today, relying on more frequent and wider interactions with colleagues in other faculties, universities, and business entities, often located abroad. These changes have allowed academic libraries to create a roadmap that guides the vision and mission of their schools, capitalizing on the skills of current staff while planning for future skills acquisition through training and hiring.

This report takes note of the impact of these changes at the intersection of libraries and publishing and presents examples of academic libraries taking advantage of the opportunities, highlighting proactive efforts by library staff to improve discovery and dissemination of scholarly publications through modern methods. Innovations being advanced by librarians today are not only extending the traditional role of the library, but assuring that great ideas can flourish beyond the institution and, indeed, beyond academia.

Change Is the New Normal

Libraries (and librarians) are resilient—far more so, it seems, than other entities. The shift from print to digital has left many organizations struggling while

Barbie E. Keiser is an information resources management consultant located in the metro–Washington, D.C., area. Familiar with the information needs and concerns of organizations, she works closely with clients to develop suitable and correct information strategies. Barbie has a unique blend of hands-on experience in helping transform the technologic know-how of an organization into productivity and profitability. A frequent speaker at library, information, and business conferences worldwide, Barbie writes a column for *ONLINE Searcher*.

academic libraries have made successful transformations. Three societal changes have had enormous impact on institutions of all types and sizes:

1 Engaging on Social Media

While they may be comfortable engaging on social media with friends and family, it's taken a while for many academics to embrace the use of social media for scholarly purposes. Newer platforms integrate conversation with publications that are often grouped by project, allowing scholars to maintain a dialog with those conducting related research and to identify potential future collaborators / co-authors. Some academic communities, for example, ResearchGate, are broad-based while others may be limited to a single subject; some may be the choice of the researcher while others are selected as "preferred" by their institution, serving as encouragement for the reluctant researcher to participate along with colleagues they already know.

Libraries were early adopters of social media, first to deliver announcements of events and programs and later to maintain a dialog with students and faculty. A university's office of scholarly communication may have originated its own blog, but it's often maintained by a librarian.

2 Embracing the Team

Management theories often conflict with one another, but there is no doubt that projects and organizations benefit when individuals collaborate, sharing perspectives and expertise. How this is accomplished—through formal partnerships or informal team efforts, in-person or virtually—is of little consequence, though a mix of approaches is advisable. Research is improved when researchers work together, rather than in isolation, and social media allows scholars to identify partners likely to further their work. Many grant agencies are making partnerships a requirement of funding and project design because of the beneficial outcomes observed through collaborations.

The solo librarian learns the importance of partnerships from Day One, but all librarians understand that they must work with faculty and departments within the institution in order to achieve their goals for student learning and scholarship. Teams of librarians work together to ensure optimal service delivery within their libraries and among libraries across multiple campuses. In some cases, this is a matter of necessity, with too few professionals working on too many projects to be able to complete each to perfection. The most successful teams work toward common goals that are aligned with institutional priorities.

3 Eliminating Barriers

Linked to the two societal changes identified above is the recognition that barriers impede scholarly progress. All research is improved when contributions emanate from diverse viewpoints. National boundaries can be transcended using social media; online scholarly communities can flourish by ignoring subject-specific boundaries. Removing geographic barriers has benefits, as evidenced by the relocation of subject specialists into academic departments and the rise of the embedded librarian to enhance collaboration in scholarly research.

Interdisciplinary teamwork is essential in today's organization, with each member contributing a complementary set of skills, experience, and knowledge. These teams ignore traditional departmental silos to further common goals and complete specific projects more efficiently. Diverse perspectives, approaches, and collaborations are pushing the frontiers of research, advancing "fundamental understanding or to solve problems whose solutions are beyond the scope of a single discipline or area of research practice" (Committee on Facilitating Interdisciplinary Research 2004:2).

Since the 1970s, interdisciplinary studies have expanded, in kind as well as number, and today there is added respect for interdisciplinary learning (Newell and Klein 1996). Fortunately, academic librarians are seen to possess the core competencies necessary for productive interdisciplinary research: expertise in conducting research, communicating, and interacting with others (Larson, Landers, and Begg 2011:39). Libraries are using these skill sets to shape their own futures to the benefit of individual institutions as well as scholarship overall.

Overcoming the boundary that's been established between academia and the mainstream is another challenge being met by academic libraries today, as they help researchers "translate" academic prose to writing that is better understood and appreciated by the public. An example is the Harvard Business School Working Knowledge website,[1] which connects practitioners and thought leaders with business management concepts contained in faculty research, cases, books, and working papers they might not otherwise encounter.

The Early Career Academic

Just as libraries recognize that the needs of first-year college students are distinct from those of upperclassmen, and have reoriented services to better serve them, librarians realize that early-career academics need specialized support for their scholarship. The first few years as a post-doc are the most productive years of an academic when scholars are formulating big ideas about their subject area specialization, in need of mentors and collaborators for their research efforts. The newly minted Ph.D. is eager to publish as that is a requirement for those seeking promotion/tenure. Today, the choice of where to publish for maximum impact within a subject area/domain, as well as exposure beyond, is confusing and changing, as are the ways in which academics team with one another.

The New Faculty Academy at the State University of New York at Buffalo (UB) is an example of a program targeting early career scholars. UB's office of the vice provost recently identified challenges faced by incoming faculty and asked deans and department chairpersons to nominate new faculty to participate in a collaborative effort of the university's libraries and its Center for Education Innovation. The project consisted of two tracks: Teaching and Writing/Publishing. During the Fall 2018 and Spring 2019 semesters, those in the Writing/Publishing cohort participated in a series of workshops led by librarians, the director of the writing center, and professors. Topics addressed during the workshops included scholarly publishing, data, and copyright issues; preparing manuscripts/grants; and tips and tricks for research. The Academy will conclude with a celebration event that gives participants an opportunity to present and showcase learning outcomes applied to individual projects.

As scholars progress in their careers they will find the research library less important for traditional discovery and document delivery, increasingly turning to it as a source of open access (OA) journals, for data management services, and to amplify their voices beyond the university (Tay 2014).

The Modern Scholarly Communication Ecosystem

A confluence of forces has led to systemic changes in scholarly communication, and the transformation is nowhere near complete. The new publishing landscape embraces "publishing as a service," with e-pub platforms that support the scholar and whose lists of services get longer each year. Scholars also benefit from electronic search of all content that might take hours to accomplish using print libraries (Peters 2007).

The proliferation of social media and its impact on transparency have long been established. The expansive nature of the inquiry process that is used by scholars to seek a range of opinions, thoughts, and studies is enhanced through the use of social media, adding a layer of less formal exploration atop their traditional approach to research. Scholarship has also benefited from the shift toward greater openness along with the platforms and discovery tools that make OA possible. The availability of digital resources, multiple avenues for finding versions of a work through its development (e.g., preprints, working papers), and the tools to mine treatises make possible complex research projects involving big data and text analysis.

Librarian support for faculty access to a wide variety of materials was necessitated by increased costs of access to scholarly research and facilitated by the new technologies. The explosion of sources and formats available for access has renewed a need for guidance concerning

1. The process of conducting research, developing ideas, and communicating informally with other scholars and scientists
2. The process of preparing, shaping, and communicating to a group of colleagues what will become formal research results
3. The ultimate formal product that is distributed for use by others (Thorin 2006:221)

Information professionals can contribute much to each step, but the final output will be significantly enhanced by partnering with experienced faculty as mentors who can help to identify potential grant opportunities or other funding to support the research effort, for example, and writing centers whose staff can help the scholar tailor an article for targeted communication vehicles.

Academic libraries today are assisting faculty at each stage of the scholarly publication life cycle (creation, evaluation, publication, dissemination and access, preservation, and reuse), with no two approaching the situation in the same manner. Librarians who once may have simply consulted *Literary Market Place*, or a list of top ten journals in a field to advise patrons where to publish, today find the options staggering, with multiple analytic tools employed to determine the best fit. There is little doubt that additional avenues for scholars' publications and exposure will emerge in the future as scholars navigate multiple options for engaging with others, wrestle to decouple their articles from journals, and negotiate the right to disseminate their own work.

The Rise of the Scholarly Communication Librarian

In the past, the scholarly communication function might have been located in the provost's office as part of an advisory team dealing with the press or legal issues. As institutions take a holistic approach to scholarship, the office of scholarly communication increasingly is situated within the library. Librarians are taking responsibility—formally recognized by the institution—for repositories, open access publishing, intellectual property rights (copyright, institutional, and authors' rights), and more. Searching any online jobs board for "scholarly communication librarian" will pull up a number of open positions. Despite the common job title, no two of these employment opportunities are likely to list an identical set of job functions or requirements.

While not every college has a dedicated office of scholarly communication, many of the associated functions are likely carried out in the library. Not all academic libraries have a "scholarly communication librarian" position on staff; rather, they distribute aspects of the function throughout the library. Large research libraries may have several individuals working in the office of scholarly communication; in most instances this is an office of one. To accomplish anything, collaboration is essential. Scholarly communication is a team effort with many librarians contributing and collaborating with offices throughout the institution.

Collaboration Is Made Easier through Co-Location

The role of the library as a storage space for collections began diminishing rapidly around the turn of the 21st century, as academic libraries made greater use of off-site storage facilities. We now see an effort by institutions to be a space that accommodates individual users, and teams, and acts as a hive of social activity. This is an environment designed to produce research that transcends boundaries.

The "library as place," featuring physical spaces with preprogrammed areas and services defined by librarians, is undergoing transformation into an open and flexible architecture that better facilitates user-directed learning. This user-centered approach is also reflected in the "library as platform." Today's digital libraries are designed to enhance personal work efforts, supporting collaboration and community building.

Evidence of change in the physical library can be seen in new construction and reconfiguration of existing buildings to incorporate related entities, making it easier for users to access related services. At many institutions, departments responsible for supporting faculty development (i.e., instructional teaching and learning) are already located in the library. At other institutions, writing centers that shoulder the responsibility for readying a dissertation for publication, including providing copy-editing services to the Ph.D. candidate, have taken up residence within or adjacent to the library. Such is the case at Elon University's Belk Library, which brought Academic Advising and the Office of Disabilities Resources into a newly renovated and expanded library space.

North Carolina State University (NCSU) is creating an academic success center in its D. H. Hill Library as part of a physical and spiritual renovation. Here, multiple entities partner on formal and informal projects designed to support the work of student scholars as well as faculty. David Woodbury, department head, Learning Spaces and Services, has described efforts to transform his library into a venue for talk—drawing researchers into the space, for example, by partnering with the office of undergraduate research for students' lightning talks concerning their research projects.[2]

More than ever before, the library is used for informal meetups of peers around scholar-adjacent subjects, including groups eager to learn more about R programming, GIS, visualization tools, copyright, and digital scholarship. "For one, the library is a comfortable setting open more hours than other areas and departments on campus . . . There is something to be said for being open when other departments are not." The NCSU library acts "as a catalyst or incubator for groups" across disciplines. It takes a holistic approach to understanding what the university has to offer. After all, the "library is accustomed to solving problems," with a staff "trained to know about all sorts of issues." Getting people to the organization on campus that can help them is normal routine for librarians, who have a "service model for owning problems."

The Library as Publisher

As Ann Okerson and Alex Holzman note in *The Once and Future of Library Publishing*, several university presses originated as library-driven efforts during the second half of the 19th century, including Cornell University Press, University of California, Johns Hopkins University, and the University of North Carolina at Chapel Hill (Okerson and Holzman 2015:2–3). Many of these universities' libraries are now at the forefront of digital publishing efforts for their institutions, such as Project MUSE, which began in 1995 as a collaboration between Johns Hopkins University Press and the Milton S. Eisenhower Library at Johns Hopkins University.

Funding of new university presses slowed after the 1960s, with very few startups in North America in the 1990s, specifically. Since then we've witnessed their resurgence, with several recently announced closures more than offset by the launch of collaborative efforts between university presses and libraries, along with library publishing programs that support OA publishing.

Many university presses are challenged financially or have management issues that make the shift to digital impossible, forcing them to rethink their participation in the publishing industry going forward. The economics of traditional publishing, in combination with a cultural embrace of digital texts, has caused many university presses to downsize their printing efforts, limiting the number of titles published and sometimes discontinuing the publication of books in favor of journals (or vice versa). In many instances, titles and lists have been sold to commercial publishers or scholarly/professional societies. Some university presses have turned to their libraries for assistance in reconfiguring workflows in the digital era.

The academic library has been at the forefront of adapting to digital publishing, including OA. When university publishing efforts are not located within the library, they benefit from cooperation and partnership with the library. At many institutions, multiple publishing efforts are afoot outside the university press but with little coordination. The library's experience working across disciplinary boundaries helps the institution assure compliance with generally accepted practices for observing intellectual property rights, branding, and exemplary practices in terms of archiving and accessibility.

Libraries are a logical venue for university publishing efforts. Until the late 1970s, courses on printing and publishing appeared as part of the library school curriculum; several accredited master's programs are now adding them back into the curriculum as electives. Traditionally, libraries have been early adopters of technology—as in the creation of online catalogs and the introduction of bibliographic (and later full-text) databases—in a way that traditional university publishers, until relatively recently, have not been.

As experienced purchasers and users of publisher/vendor products, librarians have keen insight regarding potential shortcomings and enhancements that would improve users' experience. Through the 1990s, libraries experimented by digitizing special collections and have responsibly managed those collections ever since. Finally, librarians' understanding of the importance of keywords and metadata for information retrieval makes the academic library eminently qualified to take on the responsibilities of university publisher, providing sustainable access to scholarly research produced by their institution.

The advent of OA has been a driving force in library publishing, as exemplified by Kansas State University Libraries' 2007 launch of New Prairies Press, a home for scholarly journals, monographs, and conference proceedings across disciplines. According to research conducted by Lauren Collister and Timothy Deliyannides, directors of the office of scholarly communication and publishing at the University of Pittsburgh, "75 percent of academic research libraries either offer or plan to offer publishing services, particularly self-publishing through open access" (Cruz and Fleming 2015).

As of January 2019, 35 university presses report to libraries, according to the Association of University Presses (AUPresses), an increase of five since 2016. For some, this is an administrative reporting function, as is the case at the University of Utah Press (UUP). Rick Anderson, associate dean for collections and scholarly communication in the J. Willard Marriott Library at the University of Utah, characterizes UUP as a subsidiary relationship rather than a collaboration (Anderson 2017).

For others, it's a matter of the library and publisher joining forces to create something new. At the University of Virginia, for example, the high cost of textbooks—as well as the expense incurred by any library that strives to provide broad student and faculty access to academic journals—led to a new partnership between the university library and University of Virginia Press. "Called 'Aperio,' the new digital publishing partnership . . . employs the latest technology to produce what's called 'open access' to research, scholarship and other educational materials—eventually including textbooks" (Bromley 2019:n.p.). Meantime, Columbia University Libraries lets its call for partnering take center stage on its Scholarly Communication portal as it seeks to work with faculty and students on online journals and other communication projects they characterize as playing "at the borders of currently canonized fields."[3]

Academic-Led Publishing Day is a global digital event designed "to highlight and foster discussions about how members of the scholarly community can develop and support academic-led publishing initiatives."[4] Academic-Led Publishing Day, held in February 2019, brought together stakeholders in the future of scholarly publishing. The site retains a series of on-demand recordings to the day's webinars and panel discussions, a link to the Twitter feed (#AcWriChat), plus a series of blogs and resources that will benefit any institution considering how to participate in, or fund, an academic-led publishing program.

A Laura Bush 21st Century Research Grant was awarded by the Institute of Museum and Library Services (IMLS) in 2016 to develop a library publishing curriculum. The four modules released in 2018 address the competencies required in library publishing: Content, Impact, Policy, and Sustainability.[5]

The Institutional Repository

The beginning of the 21st century witnessed a surge of interest in eliminating the silos that exist within an institution, thereby more effectively managing the knowledge throughout an organization. The prevalence of institutional repositories (IR) parallels other changes in publishing, including the rise of open source and access, affecting the ease with which intellectual property is shared. Consider the following:

- For the academic institution, the IR aids in the control of its intellectual property while improving researcher productivity and interdisciplinary collaboration.
- Faculty wants to have its work read, recognized, and used. The IR exposes research through search engines to a worldwide audience that can cite the material responsibly, giving the institution and the researcher greater visibility within, and even beyond, a given field.
- The library can leverage the IR to reposition itself within the academic institution, raising its profile by assuming new responsibilities related to IR development and management. Academic libraries at doctoral-granting universities specify the provision of an institutional repository as one of the top three functions they provide (Wolff-Eisenberg 2017:55).

The IR supports an author's publishing activities from the start of the research effort, providing preprint version control, managing the publication and its underlying data, and ensuring archival stability. Many early efforts—for instance,

Research Papers in Economics (RePEc)—serve to maintain the record and are recognized today as authentic repositories for their given fields.

These IRs developed, in part, in response to the open archives initiative (OAI). The potential for interoperability across OAI-compliant platforms meant that the IR could be included in federated searches. Hosted solutions eliminated some of the reservations concerning IT support that previously deterred many libraries from taking on responsibility for IRs. Additional factors that encouraged libraries to consider the role they would play in the development of IRs include

- Rising subscription costs for access to serials (print and online) to which their professors contribute as authors or peer reviewers
- Changes in the methods and platforms used for document delivery services, along with the rising costs of document delivery
- The expertise of librarians in managing digital material over time, assuring that each object has appropriate metadata to enable users to find it

Initial OAI experiments were limited in scope by subject or focus on a particular type of publication (e.g., preprints), serving as a prototype for later more wide-ranging efforts. Ultimately, e-print repositories became easier to build and manage, as born-digital materials required no intermediary steps for digitization.

The institutional repository accrues benefits to the institution by engaging the academic community; enhancing scholarly collaboration; improving the quality of teaching and scholarship through sharing; allowing the institution (often, the library) to collect and organize digital information for long-term preservation; and promoting the institution's reputation, along with individual expertise and impact of research within a field that contribute to today's performance metrics.

University IRs are seen benefiting individual faculty by

- Expanding discovery of their work via search engines that crawl the IR, increasing access to material that would otherwise be difficult to obtain, and offering worldwide visibility for authors and their projects
- Supporting a variety of data and multiple media formats, such as working papers, pre- and post-prints, learning objects, reports, presentations, posters, audio, video, and more
- Archiving backlisted titles for faculty use in their teaching and scholarly pursuits
- Automatically feeding the necessary data into a comprehensive faculty profiling system, removing the need to manually update multiple systems

Open source tools are making it easier for more libraries to consider spearheading IR efforts at their universities. An example is Duke University's open-access, online depository.[6] Relying on VIVO, an open source research networking tool developed at Cornell University and now part of DuraSpace, Duke faculty uses the system to publish and archive their scholarly work, "allowing readers from around the world to view these works for free."

Dealing with Resistance

Libraries face challenges locating and harvesting content from multiple departments that ought to be included in the institution's repository. A far more efficient way to get the corpus of work by researchers into such a repository is to have it uploaded within normal research workflows, with technology capturing as much as possible automatically, prompting the researcher as appropriate, with additional assistance provided by library staff when necessary. Again, the key to success is partnering—in this case, with the IT department.

Academic researchers have been known to resist new approaches and procedures, and many do not see depositing their work in an IR as their responsibility. Librarians seeking to change this mindset have found that, first and foremost, they must make the deposit process quick and easy. Libraries are utilizing tried-and-true tactics for getting targeted messages to researchers, such as advising scholars on copyright issues (and how to negotiate the right to self-archive), as is so crucial to participation in online scholarly communities.

Proven strategies that encourage scholars to deposit their work in IRs include

- Aligning the "ask" by stressing direct links between faculty actions and the institution's vision and mission statements relating to research support and scholarly publishing.
- Targeting disciplines that are strategically important to the institution, prolific professors, those who request to participate, and those viewed as role models by others. It's likely to take less effort to convince these individuals to participate, and early successes with these scholars can be used to encourage others to participate.
- Addressing author rights issues, making the IR a "best case" solution for authors.
- Relating material uploads to wider access and use, contributing to updated performance measures regarding promotion and tenure.
- Raising faculty awareness of the institution's OA policy, utilizing multiple methods and media to get the word out, and tailoring the message for specific settings and readerships.

Some libraries cover IR-related topics in scholarly communication blog posts, newsletters, and articles appearing on a dedicated section of the library website, consistently emphasizing why depositing work in the IR is important to the individual as well as the institution. Other libraries develop LibGuides that address distinct topics and activities associated with depositing scholarly works, creating "how-to" online tutorials for each step in the process. The topic may also be covered in a workshop—targeted by discipline—with personal offers of assistance by library staff provided as follow-up.

Research Data Services (RDS)

Data-intensive research requires that the institutional repository not only contain published research outputs, but the underlying data associated with it. Responsibly maintaining linked datasets and making data available is important to the research community. The academic library ensures that the research data services (RDS) it provides comports with institutional research policies, as well as the requirements of funding agencies for securing the data, respecting privacy by protecting personal information. The library that uses data-sharing platforms is now responsible for making sure that data from its institution is contributed to responsible data platforms, made available to researchers everywhere (e.g., Figshare).

RDS extend beyond digital curation and storage. Academic libraries are increasingly assuming responsibilities not only for data needs assessment, planning, management, curation, and governance, but also for training students and faculty about data-related literacy issues, including data quality and citation. The duties associated with data stewardship may require skills that library staff does not currently possess, but most academic libraries are finding ways to partner with individuals and groups on campus in order to assure the institution becomes more data savvy. Many are considering a data librarian for their next strategic hire.

Reaching Beyond the Scholarly Community

It's vitally important to make digital scholarship open and accessible to individuals outside academia, to nonexperts and policymakers alike. In addition to helping scholars orient their writing toward academic publications, libraries are assisting in making this work comprehensible to laypersons / the general public. This is particularly important for conveying scientific research (without an agenda) and communicating statistical data often illustrated with intricate graphics, compliments of data visualization tools, that can be easily misinterpreted. Small efforts can make all the difference. Exemplary practices include the following:

1. Every scholarly work needs a properly written abstract that gives readers a clear indication of what they will find in the text. Librarians are encouraging scholars to create two abstracts—one for academic publications and another suitable for the mainstream press.
2. Accompanying each scholarly work with a press release that is designed to get picked up by an editor in the general press, with the library assembling a list of likely publications and the necessary contact information. Decisions about the placement of these pieces are just as complicated as those regarding scholarly publication.
3. Finding reviews of similar works can help the scholar identify potential reviewers for their publications.
4. Just as librarians assist scholars as they create posters summarizing their research for conferences and exhibitions, they are now working with academics to create infographics that portray the key facts of their projects.
5. Libraries with radio programs or podcasts interview scholars about their work, creating audio files that the academics can host on their own websites.
6. It's not too far-fetched to assume that librarians will soon be recommending scientific comics and conceptual animation similar to the work done by Sci Ani.[7]

Research Information Management (RIM)

Materials deposited in and available through the IR are only a part of the researcher's profile. Today's libraries are also aggregating, curating, and utilizing metadata about research activities to present a profile of the institution and the individual researcher. Research information management (RIM) "intersects with many aspects of traditional library services" (e.g., information discovery, acquisition, dissemination) and activities associated with scholarly analysis (Bryant et al. 2017:6).

RIM holds all of the elements that tell the story of a faculty member, acting as a c.v. that is linked to publications, datasets, patents, grants, and project reports, listing courses the professor has taught, professional affiliations and collaborations, academic honors and service awards, and media reports that form the basis of a comprehensive personal profile. They not only capture research outputs but serve as indicators of the impact that research has had over time.

RIM systems serve as the basis for academic reviews, grant and award management systems, and researcher profiles, supporting open access deposit and discovery of locally produced research (publications + datasets) for reuse. They are used both for internal reporting and external research assessment.

Analytics that Build Reputations

Metrics are of growing importance to every institution, and the university is no exception. Global university rankings take years to reflect significant movement up or down; performance by discipline or within a geographic region (e.g., continent, nation, province, state) is a better basis on which to compare institutions. Because metrics may be used as a foundation for communicating a message, and as part of a school's effort to shape its image as well as the rationale for requests for strategic funds, universities are being more selective as they identify measures that accurately portray the institution at its best.

Oversimplified and misused metrics that purport to evaluate the work of researchers, projects, journals, or institutions can obscure the true value of research. It's vital that an institution analyze data collected, use that analysis to compare its research with that of other institutions, and devise a strategy for improving performance.

In recent years, metrics concerning scholarly publications have undergone a revolution. New tools have given us ways and measures that peer beyond the journal publication, the individual article, and the author to truly understand the impact a project's research is having within a discipline and across disciplines. Who is conducting what type of research and the pace of discoveries being made, analyzed in scholarly publications and discussed at conferences and within online communities of experts, contribute to a comprehensive portrayal of the research landscape. These considerations are having an impact on the criteria used by entities that publish annual rankings, such as the recent announcement by *U.S. News and World Report* that it is considering a new ranking that measures faculty productivity to evaluate a law school's scholarly impact (Morse 2019).

The granular level of today's performance indicators permits big data analysis to compare individuals within a department, across departments, or with faculty at other institutions. These metrics were once used to help researchers decide where to publish, but they now contribute to performance measures used by institutions for faculty promotion and tenure purposes.

Academic citations can take years to appear in peer-reviewed journals. Non-traditional metrics, or altmetrics, provide additional and quicker means to demonstrate the extent of influence a researcher has on targeted audiences. Among these indicators are social media reads, mentions, tweets, and scores; news mentions, peer reviews within scholarly communities; record of attention, exposure, engagement, discussion, and sharing; numbers of grants awarded and total funding dollars; and broader societal influence. These factors contribute to a 360-degree view of an individual's work and impact

- As a signifier of productivity and research quality
- Contributing to intellectual discussion and debate
- As evidence of expertise within a field
- In influencing policy and initiating/supporting societal change

While some institutions are eliminating tenure altogether, all have recognized that academic standards need to change. Criteria used to determine tenure and promotion beyond publishing in journals with a high impact factor are being employed, with institutions increasingly valuing interdisciplinary and collaborative work, along with recognizing non-peer-reviewed contributions.

Success Strategies for Academic Libraries' Participation in Scholarly Research

According to the S+R Faculty Survey 2015, approximately 40 percent of faculty is highly dependent on their academic library for the research they conduct (Wolff-Eisenberg, Rod, and Schonfeld 2016:65). With scholars increasingly able to conduct their research online, outside their institution's library, the size of a library's collection is less important than it once was (Wolff-Eisenberg 2017:61). Libraries are considering how they will refocus their efforts in relation to scholarship as well as how to convey the rationale for this transition to the academic community.

The type of assistance provided to scholars—how librarians work with faculty, consistently, throughout the scholarly publication lifecycle—is different at each institution. Multiple factors contribute to the decision as to the path each takes. Making certain that the contribution is recognized by faculty and the administration requires a new set of measures that values the scholarly collaboration and the library's scholarly community-building efforts; a strategic plan for expanding the library's role in the institution's scholarly communication program; "new" methods of working with scholars on pilot projects that can then be offered more broadly; new physical and virtual environments that enhance the collaborative process; and a concerted effort to reduce impediments faced by scholars at every stage.

For any academic library that seeks to ensure the success of its scholars, these five strategies can be used as a starting point:

1 Make your institution's scholarly research effort a true collaboration

Where partnerships benefit the individual players in the arrangement, collaborators work together toward a shared goal. As no single entity has all the skills necessary for a comprehensive scholarly research program, cooperation is required if the effort is to be successful. In addition to working with faculty on their research projects and publications, the library should initiate collaborative efforts with university presses, writing centers, research institutes, and information technology (IT) departments.

Scholarly research programs should enable collaborations among individual researchers by offering networking opportunities that cross departmental boundaries and are designed to further their research projects. Beyond the institution, scholarly research programs must share research with as wide an audience as possible, furthering global and interdisciplinary scholarship.

To be effective, all the players must understand the strategic vision of the institution with regard to scholarly research, appreciating the importance of the effort to the institution's future viability. Constant reminders through scholarly communication blogs and connections between an activity and the vision will need to be emphasized, repeated at each workshop to ensure participation.

2 Develop a plan for acquiring the skills current staff lacks

Academic librarians are already active participants in the conduct of scholarly research. Many of their efforts may not be recognized as specific to scholarship; they may be subsumed within larger programs, or viewed as routine. Libraries should review all the activities performed by staff to identify those who contribute substantially to research at their institutions. Renaming/rebranding activities to reflect a scholarly research focus may help the library determine gaps in its ability to contribute to the institution's larger scholarly research effort.

With knowledge of the skill sets available at their universities and armed with an understanding of institutional priorities related to scholarly research, librarians can identify missing skills. Careful consideration should be given to how librarians will acquire what's needed to empower their institution's scholarly research effort, which may include staff training, hiring to fill new positions, and alliances with external entities. This strategic approach to human resource planning should be aligned with the institution's goals and objectives for scholarly research, synchronizing the acquisition of necessary skills to the timetable and milestones for the university's research effort.

3 Experiment with "new" methods for working with scholars and extending your reach

Academic librarians should be sure that multiple channels are used to communicate the institution's scholarly research initiative throughout the university. A comprehensive review of interactions between the library and scholars may unearth opportunities not yet realized.

Successful library programs being offered in support of the institution's scholars should be extended to other colleges and universities. This can be achieved through promoting the library's scholarly blogs, webinars, and podcasts to the wider community of scholars and through opening the institution's seminars, workshops, and conferences to all. Expertise of library staff should be showcased in both library and scholarly research / digital scholarship journals and at conferences targeting the scholarly research community and library/information professionals.

4 Co-locate scholarly research collaborators in or adjacent to the library

Libraries already appreciate the benefits of proximity, as is evident in the embedded librarian model. Teams working on aspects of scholarly research programs benefit from being located near one another. Co-locating entities involved in scholarship helps users who now do not have to be referred to another office situated across the campus, eliminating another barrier to scholarship.

5 Make it easy

The surest way to get faculty to use the full range of scholarly communication services a library offers is to be certain that these are the services they need and that participation is easy. Designing the systems, platforms, and processes alongside the scholars, testing the unique requirements of different faculties (sciences, social sciences, humanities), and being willing to make adjustments along the way guarantees that the library's IR, RDS, and RIM efforts are used and appreciated.

Libraries will be successful players in their institutions' scholarly research efforts if they make technology decisions with flexibility in mind. Open scholarship requires tools that are easy to use and facilitate the flow of ideas while preserving scholarly work for posterity. The initiatives described in this report honor the dual roles of the library to assure access and preservation while placing a renewed and vital emphasis on scholarly research, publication, and communication.

Bibliography

Anderson, R. 2017. "Another Perspective on Library-Press 'Partnerships.'" In *Scholarly Kitchen*. Wheat Ridge, CO: Society for Scholarly Publishing. Available at https://scholarlykitchen.sspnet.org/2017/07/19/revisiting-two-perspectives-library-based-university-presses/.

Appleton, L. 2019. "Positioning the Academic Library within the Institution: Structures and Challenges." *New Review of Academic Librarianship*. DOI: https://doi.org/10.1080/13614533.2019.1582078.

Bromley, A. E. 2019. "UVA Library, UVA Press Partner to Make Original Scholarship Freely Available." *UVA Today*. February 11. Charlottesville: University of Virginia. Available at https://news.virginia.edu/content/uva-library-uva-press-partner-make-original-scholarship-freely-available.

Bryant, R., et al. 2017. *Research Information Management: Defining RIM and the Library's Role*. Dublin, OH: OCLC Research. DOI: https://doi.org/10.25333/C3NK88.

Collister, L. B., T. S. Deliyannides, and S. Dyas-Correia. 2014. "The Library as Publisher."

Serials Librarian, 66:1–4, 20–29. DOI: https://doi.org/10.1080/0361526X.2014.879524.

Committee on Facilitating Interdisciplinary Research, Committee on Science, Engineering, and Public Policy. 2004. *Facilitating Interdisciplinary Research*. National Academies. Washington, D.C.: National Academy Press, available at https://www.nsf.gov/od/oia/additional_resources/interdisciplinary_research/definition.jsp.

Cruz, L., and R. Fleming. 2015. "Partnerships: The Engaged University and Library Publishing." *OCLC Systems and Services: International Digital Library Perspectives* 31(4): 196–203. DOI: https://doi.org/10.1108/OCLC-02-2014-0017.

Ferguson, C. L. (Contributor). 2017. "Open Educational Resources and Institutional Repositories." *Serials Review* 43:1, 34–38. DOI: https://doi.org/10.1080/00987913.2016.1274219.

Finlay, C., A. Tsou, and C. Sugimoto. 2015. "Scholarly Communication as a Core Competency: Prevalence, Activities, and Concepts of Scholarly Communication Librarianship as Shown through Job Advertisements." *Journal of Librarianship and Scholarly Communication* 3(1): eP1236. Available at http://dx.doi.org/10.7710/2162-3309.1236.

Hardy R., and C. Oppenheim. 2004. "Research on University Presses: An Overview of UK University Presses." *Publishing Research Quarterly* 20(2): 18. DOI: https://doi.org/10.1007/s12109-004-0021-2.

Houghton, J. W., C. Steele, and M. Henty. 2004. "Research Practices and Scholarly Communication in the Digital Environment." *Learned Publishing* 17:231–249.

Jump, P. 2013. "UCL Presses Ahead with Open Access." London, UK: *Times Higher Education*. December 19. Available at https://www.timeshighereducation.com/news/ucl-presses-ahead-with-open-access/2009926.article.

Kaufman, P. 2012. "Let's Get Cozy: Evolving Collaborations in the 21st Century." *Journal of Library Administration* 52:1, 53–69. Available at https://doi.org/10.1080/01930826.2011.629962.

Larson, E. L., T. F. Landers, and M. D. Begg. 2011. "Building Interdisciplinary Research Models: A Didactic Course to Prepare Interdisciplinary Scholars and Faculty." *Clinical and Translational Science* 4:38–41. DOI: https://doi.org/10.1111/j.1752-8062.2010.00258.x.

Morse, R. 2019. "U.S. News Considers Evaluating Law School Scholarly Impact." *U.S. News and World Report*. February 13. Available at https://www.usnews.

com/education/blogs/college-rankings-blog/articles/2019-02-13/us-news-considers-evaluating-law-school-scholarly-impact.

Nagra, K. A. 2012. "Building Institutional Repositories in the Academic Libraries." *Community and Junior College Libraries* 18:3–4, 137–150. DOI: https://doi.org/10.1080/02763915.2012.799028.

Nemati-Anaraki, L., and M. Tavassoli-Farahi. 2018. "Scholarly Communication through Institutional Repositories: Proposing a Practical Model." *Collection and Curation* (37): 1, 9–17. DOI: https://doi.org/10.1108/CC-01-2018-002.

Neal, J. G. 2002. "Symbiosis or Alienation." *Journal of Library Administration* 35:1–2, 5–18. DOI: https://doi.org/10.1300/J111v35n01_02.

Newell, W., and J. Klein. 1996. "Interdisciplinary Studies into the 21st Century." *Journal of General Education* 45(2): 152–169. Available at http://www.jstor.org/stable/27797297.

Okerson, A., and A. Holzman. *The Once and Future of Library Publishing*. Washington, D.C.: Council on Library and Information Resources (CLIR). July 2015. Available at https://www.clir.org/pubs/reports/pub166/.

Peters P. 2007. "Redefining Scholarly Publishing as a Service Industry." *Journal of Electronic Publishing* 10(3). DOI: https://doi.org/10.3998/3336451.0010.309.

Pomerantz, J., and G. Marchionini. 2007. "The Digital Library as Place." *Journal of Documentation* 63(4): 505–533. DOI: http://dx.doi.org.proxy1.library.jhu.edu/10.1108/00220410710758995.

Soria, Krista M., Jan Fransen, and Shane Nackerud. 2017. "Beyond Books: The Extended Academic Benefits of Library Use for First-Year College Students." *College and Research Libraries* 78 (1, special issue) (April). Available at https://crl.acrl.org/index.php/crl/article/view/16564. DOI: https://doi.org/10.5860/crl.v78i1.16564.

Tay, A. 2014. "How Academic Libraries May Change When Open Access Becomes the Norm." *Musings about Librarianship*. August. Available at http://musingsaboutlibrarianship.blogspot.com/2014/08/how-academic-libraries-may-change-when.html.

Tenopir, C., B. Birch, and S. Allard. 2012. "Academic Libraries and Research Data Services: Current Practices and Plans for the Future." June. Chicago: Association of College and Research Libraries. Available at http://www.ala.org/acrl/sites/ala.org.acrl/files/content/publications/whitepapers/Tenopir_Birch_Allard.pdf.

Thorin, S. E. 2006. "Global Changes in Scholarly Communication." In *eLearning and Digital Publishing*. Edited by H. S. Ching, P. W. T. Poon, and C. McNaught. Computer Supported Cooperative Work, vol 33. Dordrecht: Springer. Available at https://doi.org/10.1007/1-4020-3651-5_12.

Van de Sompel, H. et al. 2004. "Rethinking Scholarly Communication: Building the System That Scholars Deserve." *D-Lib Magazine* 10, no. 9 (September). Available at http://www.dlib.org/dlib/september04/vandesompel/09vandesompel.html.

Watkinson, C. 2016. "Why Marriage Matters: A North American Perspective on Press/Library Partnerships." *Learned Publishing* 29:342–347. DOI: https://doi.org/10.1002/leap.1044.

Wolff-Eisenberg, C. 2017. *US Library Survey* 2016. New York: Ithaka S+R. DOI: https://doi.org/10.18665/sr.303066.

Wolff-Eisenberg, C, A. B. Rod, and R. C. Schonfeld. 2016. *US Faculty Survey 2015*. New York: Ithaka S+R. DOI: https://doi.org/10.18665/sr.277685.

Websites Referenced

1. https://hbswk.hbs.edu
2. https://www.lib.ncsu.edu/events/undergraduate-research-slam
3. https://scholcomm.columbia.edu/services.html
4. https://academicledpublishingday.com
5. The curriculum is available through the Educopia Institute, https://educopia.org/library-publishing-curriculum
6. https://library.duke.edu/find/scholarly
7. https://sciani.com

Federal Agency and Federal Library Reports

Library of Congress

10 First St. S.E., Washington, DC 20540
202-707-5000
World Wide Web http://www.loc.gov

Carla Hayden
Librarian of Congress

The Library of Congress is the largest library in the world, with more than 168 million items in various languages, disciplines, and formats. As the world's largest repository of knowledge and creativity, the library's mission is to engage, inspire, and inform the United States Congress and the American people with a universal and enduring source of knowledge and creativity.

The library's collections are housed in its three buildings on Capitol Hill and in climate-controlled facilities for books at Fort Meade, Maryland. Its audiovisual materials are held at the Packard Campus for Audio-Visual Conservation in Culpeper, Virginia. The library also provides global access to its resources through its website, http://www.loc.gov.

Highlights of 2018

In fiscal year (FY) 2018, from October 2017 to September 2018, the Library of Congress

- Responded to more than 1 million reference requests from Congress, the public, and other federal agencies
- Through the U.S. Copyright Office, issued over 560,000 registrations and recorded 21,668 copyright ownership transfer documents containing more than 750,000 titles
- Circulated nearly 21 million copies of braille, audio, and large print items to over 972,526 blind and physically handicapped reader accounts
- Circulated more than 958,000 items for use inside and outside the Library
- Performed 10.2 million preservation actions on items in the Library's physical collections

- Recorded a total of 168,291,642 items in the collections, including
  - 24,600,488 cataloged books in the Library of Congress classification system
  - 14,959,404 items in the nonclassified print collections, including books in large type and raised characters, incunabula (books printed before 1501), monographs and serials, music, bound newspapers, pamphlets, technical reports and other print material
  - 128,731,750 items in the nonclassified (special) collections, including
    - 4,019,643 audio materials (discs, tapes, talking books and other recorded formats)
    - 72,512,459 manuscripts
    - 5,608,003 maps
    - 17,250,956 microforms
    - 1,834,690 moving images
    - 8,248,563 items of sheet music
    - 3,449,194 other (including machine-readable items)
    - 15,733,020 visual materials, including 14,942,941 photographs, 109,307 posters, and 680,772 prints and drawings
- Welcomed over 1.9 million on-site visitors and recorded 114 million visits and 497.9 million page views on the Library's Web properties
- Employed 3,096 permanent staff members
- Operated with a total FY 2018 appropriation of $669.9 million, including the authority to spend $49.9 million in offsetting receipts

Carla Hayden, longtime chief executive of the Enoch Pratt Free Library system in Baltimore and a former president of the American Library Association, began the third year of a renewable 10-year term as the 14th librarian of congress.

Serving Congress

The Library of Congress was established in 1800 to provide resources to members of Congress for use in their work. The Joint Committee on the Library—the oldest continuing joint committee of the U.S. Congress—was created through legislation signed by President John Adams on April 24, 1800, legislation that also created a library for the nation's lawmakers and provided for its congressional oversight. The unique collaboration between these two institutions has allowed both to serve the nation for more than two centuries.

In FY 2018 the Library supported members of Congress, their staffs, and constituents in a variety of ways, from providing reference, research, and analysis on key issues to supplying surplus books to congressional districts. The Library also continued to implement new technologies to make the legislative process more accessible and transparent to the public.

Legislative Support

The Congressional Research Service (CRS) in the Library of Congress provides the nation's legislature with research, analysis, and information of the highest quality to support its legislative, oversight, and representational duties. The work of CRS is nonpartisan, objective, confidential, and authoritative. In FY 2018 CRS responded to 62,000 congressional requests. The CRS website for Congress, CRS.gov, drew approximately 1.5 million views, including more than 560,000 views of the service's reports and general-distribution products.

CRS examines pressing legislative issues facing Congress; identifies and assesses policy options; and provides analysis, consultation, and briefings to support Congress throughout the legislative process across the full range of public policy issues.

Copyright Law and Policy

The U.S. Copyright Office, headed by the register of copyrights, administers the nation's copyright laws for the advancement of the public good and the benefit of authors and users of creative works. The register's duties under the Copyright Act include registering creative works, recording information about copyright ownership and implementing certain statutory licenses. The register and her staff also provide expert impartial assistance to Congress, the courts, and executive branch agencies on questions of domestic and international copyright law and policy.

In FY 2018 the office continued assisting Congress in a number of ways, including engaging in studies and important copyright-related litigation matters, conducting regulatory activities aimed at administering the Copyright Act overall, and advising the executive branch by participating in foreign copyright law and policy matters. The office assisted Congress with the landmark Music Modernization Act, which will transform music licensing and address how federal law can interact with pre-1972 sound recordings.

Other Services to Congress

The Library reached out to Congress to ensure both new and returning members, as well as new committee chairs and ranking members, were aware of the full range of its collections, programs, and services. During FY 2018 the Congressional Relations Office (CRO) received and answered nearly 26,500 telephone and e-mail inquiries, sent nearly 140,000 outreach e-mails to congressional offices regarding Library services and programming, and assisted members of Congress in hosting 138 events at the Library.

Collections

In FY 2018 the Library's collections grew to 168,291,642 physical items in various formats. The Library added more than 1.3 million items to its collections during the year through purchase, gift, exchange, or transfer from other government agencies.

The U.S. Copyright office transferred a total of 736,833 works with an estimated value of $47,591,986 to the Library's collections in FY 2018; 294,066 of the transferred items were received from publishers under the mandatory deposit provision of the law. Of those deposits, receipts via eDeposits include 1,825 e-books and 95,716 e-serial issues for a total of 28,566,944 digital files.

The Acquisitions and Bibliographic Access Directorate (ABA) acquired 980,413 items for the Library's collections through various methods, including purchase and exchange. In addition, ABA facilitated the acquisition of 354,628 collection items through solicited gifts to the Collections and Services Directorate. With the acquisition of additional items through means such as transfers from other government agencies, a total of more than 1.3 million items were added to the collections.

The Library's six overseas offices (located in Cairo, Islamabad, Jakarta, Nairobi, New Delhi and Rio de Janeiro) acquired, cataloged, and preserved materials from their collecting areas. In FY 2018 those offices acquired 204,464 items for the Library's collections. They also acquired 329,015 collection items, on a cost-recovery basis, for more than 100 customers, chiefly U.S. libraries, that participated in the Cooperative Acquisitions Program.

Collection Development

The Collection Development Office (CDO) directly supports the Library's strategic goal of acquiring and maintaining a universal collection of knowledge and the record of America's creativity to meet the needs of Congress, researchers, and the American public. It ensures that the Library's analog and digital collections reflect the breadth and depth of knowledge published in all media, languages, and regions of the world.

During FY 2018 CDO continued to cyclically review and update the Library's collections policy statements and associated supplementary guidelines. It facilitated the customization of 14 different foreign acquisitions approval plans, including those for China, Germany, Japan, and the United Kingdom. Also, as part of its focus on foreign newspapers, it issued a report, *LC's Foreign Newspapers Holdings: Discovery Challenges and Recommended Actions.*

Preservation

Preserving the Library's holdings and the information they contain is a critical part of the institution's mission. The Preservation Directorate continued to assess and treat collections using established technologies, practices and procedures to reduce risks to these materials. It also engaged in scientific research to explore new approaches to preservation.

In FY 2018 the directorate performed 10.2 million preservation actions on items in the Library's collections, including books, serials, prints, photographs, audiovisual, and other items. During the fiscal year 117,399 items were bound into new library bindings; 33,845 were treated or repaired in conservation labs; protective containers or housings were given to 19,973 items; and 193,977 book equivalents and 1,214,800 sheets were deacidified. Staff surveyed the preservation needs of 879,812 items from the Library's general and special collections, including books, photographs, maps, audiovisual materials and other formats, monitored over 240 environmental data loggers, and continued to play a key role in the Library's security and emergency-response programs.

To protect information at risk from deterioration, staff reformatted original media to keep its informational content available. To that end, 8,366,896 pages were microfilmed, including 6,220,450 produced for the custodial divisions and 2,146,446 microfilmed by the Library's overseas offices. Digital transformation was an important focus for the year. The Preservation Reformatting Division (PRD) completed the foreign newspaper digitization pilot program, worked with the newly created Digital Collections Management and Services Division to develop and improve digital-stewardship practices and initiated its transition plan for a fully digital preservation reformatting program. Digital reformatting activities increased substantially. PRD's tangible media program reformatted 2,677 items and a combined total of 37,775,299 files, copying from obsolescent digital media and transferring them to storage servers managed by the Office of the Chief Information Officer. Furthermore, PRD's programs for creating digital facsimiles of general collection monographs increased their output by over 30 percent, for a total of 118,562 pages.

The Conservation Division completed major conservation projects concerning, for example, unique records of American history and folklife, rare musical instruments and music manuscripts, and artifacts dating to the dawn of writing. The Conservation Division, the Collections Management Division, and the Preservation Research and Testing Division worked collaboratively with the Architect of the Capitol on a number of renovation, design, and construction projects to enhance the storage and security of the Library's collections.

National Film Registry

It is estimated that half the films produced before 1950 and 80 to 90 percent of those made before 1920 are gone forever. The library is working with many organizations to prevent further losses. Under the terms of the National Film Preservation Act of 1988, the librarian of congress—with advice from the National Film Preservation Board—began selecting 25 films annually for the National Film Registry to be preserved for all time. Films are chosen for their cultural, historical, or aesthetic significance.

On December 12, 2018, the librarian of congress announced the following additions to the National Film Registry, bringing the total of films on the list to 750.

Bad Day at Black Rock (1955)
Broadcast News (1987)
Brokeback Mountain (2005)
Cinderella (1950)
Days of Wine and Roses (1962)
Dixon-Wanamaker Expedition to Crow Agency (1908)
Eve's Bayou (1997)
The Girl without a Soul (1917)
Hair Piece: A Film for Nappy-Headed People (1984)
Hearts and Minds (1974)
Hud (1963)
The Informer (1935)
Jurassic Park (1993)

The Lady from Shanghai (1947)
Leave Her to Heaven (1945)
Monterey Pop (1968)
My Fair Lady (1964)
The Navigator (1924)
On the Town (1949)
One-Eyed Jacks (1961)
Pickup on South Street (1953)
Rebecca (1940)
The Shining (1980)
Smoke Signals (1998)
Something Good—Negro Kiss (1898)

National Recordings Registry

The National Recording Preservation Act of 2000 mandates the preservation of the nation's historic sound recordings, many of which are at risk of deterioration. It directs the librarian of congress to name sound recordings of aesthetic, historical, or cultural value to the National Recording Registry, to establish an advisory National Recording Preservation Board, and to create and implement a national plan to assure the long-term preservation and accessibility of the nation's audio heritage.

On March 21, 2018, the librarian announced the addition of the following 25 sound recordings to the National Recording Registry, bringing the total to 500.

"Dream Melody Intermezzo: Naughty Marietta" (single), Victor Herbert and his Orchestra (1911)

Standing Rock Preservation Recordings, George Herzog and Members of the Yanktoni Tribe (1928)

"Lamento Borincano" (single), Canario y Su Grupo (1930)

"Sitting on Top of the World" (single), Mississippi Sheiks (1930)

The Complete Beethoven Piano Sonatas (album), Artur Schnabel (1932–1935)

"If I Didn't Care" (single), The Ink Spots (1939)

Proceedings of the United Nations Conference on International Organization (4/25/45 to 6/26/45)

"Folk Songs of the Hills" (album), Merle Travis (1946)

"How I Got Over" (single), Clara Ward and the Ward Singers (1950)

"(We're Gonna) Rock Around the Clock" (single), Bill Haley and His Comets (1954)

Calypso (album), Harry Belafonte (1956)

"I Left My Heart in San Francisco" (single), Tony Bennett (1962)

"King Biscuit Time" (radio), Sonny Boy Williamson II and others (1965)

"My Girl" (single), The Temptations (1964)

The Sound of Music (soundtrack), Various (1965)

"Alice's Restaurant Massacree" (single), Arlo Guthrie (1967)

New Sounds in Electronic Music (album), Steve Reich, Richard Maxfield, Pauline Oliveros (1967)

An Evening with Groucho (album), Groucho Marx (1972)

Rumours (album), Fleetwood Mac (1977)

"The Gambler" (single), Kenny Rogers (1978)

"Le Freak" (single), Chic (1978)

"Footloose" (single), Kenny Loggins (1984)

Raising Hell (album), Run-DMC (1986)

"Rhythm Is Gonna Get You" (single), Gloria Estefan and the Miami Sound Machine (1987)

Yo-Yo Ma Premieres Concertos for Violoncello and Orchestra (album), Various (1996)

Access

The Library makes its multiformat collections publicly available in its multiple reading rooms and research centers on Capitol Hill and at the National Audio-Visual Conservation Center in Culpeper, Virginia, and through its website. By cataloging its holdings in English and other languages, the Library provides bibliographic access to its vast and growing collections. Through shared and cooperative cataloging, the Library helps the nation's libraries provide better access to their collections.

Visitors to all Library buildings on Capitol Hill totaled 1.9 million in FY 2018. Of these, a record 1.6 million visited the Thomas Jefferson Building. The Library's Great Hall and exhibitions remained open to the public on federal holidays, with the exception of Thanksgiving, Christmas, and New Year's Day. The Visitor Engagement Office and its corps of 340 volunteers led 8,100 guided tours and answered over 345,000 inquiries.

Reference

During FY 2018 the Library continued to fulfill its role as the premier research library for Congress and the nation. More than 70,000 new reader-identification cards were issued—a significant increase over FY 2017. Library staff responded to more than 360,000 reference requests. More than 103,000 of these requests were received online, including queries handled through the Ask a Librarian service. The Library circulated 900,000 physical items through its research centers. Over 32,136 items were circulated off-site to authorized borrowers. A total of 688,974 full-text items were downloaded from the subscription databases in FY 2018. A total of 45,292 requests were received and filled for items stored off-site at Fort Meade, Cabin Branch, and Landover.

Cataloging

The Library managed 50,706,616 MARC records in its Integrated Library System during the year. The Library cataloged 305,955 new works in addition to 1.3 million manuscript items on 253,463 bibliographic records. The Cataloging in Publication program cataloged 57,573 titles and the Electronic Cataloging in Publication E-book Program prepared cataloging, in advance of publication, for 20,252 e-books and e-serials. The Library established 290,439 name and series authorities, 2,221 subject headings and 2,100 new Library of Congress Classification numbers.

The Dewey Program, which supports libraries worldwide that classify their titles in Dewey Decimal Classification (DDC), assigned DDC to 119,094 titles. In 2018 the Library's curatorial divisions created 75 new Encoded Archival Description finding aids online. As a result, researchers can now access 69,119,990 archival items in the Library's collections.

Website and Social Media

The Library's website, loc.gov, provides users with access to the institution's unparalleled resources, such as its online catalogs; selected collections in various formats; copyright, legal, and legislative information; exhibitions; and videos and podcasts of events. In FY 2018 the website recorded more than 114 million visits and 497.9 million page views. The Office of the Chief Information Officer (OCIO) collaborated with the Congressional Research Service (CRS), the Law Library, and Congress to complete 16 major releases of congress.gov, the online database of U.S. Congress legislative information. Each release included functionality and content enhancements developed using extensive user feedback.

Each month of FY 2018 the library streamed videos of concerts, lectures, and other events on YouTube and Facebook. In addition to 42 livestreamed events the Library made 632 videos available on YouTube that were liked 38,501 times and viewed 5.6 million times. The channel gained 22,490 subscribers during the year. The Library also made public 410 webcasts which were viewed 297,707 times.

The Library's Podcast account features selected podcasts, historical films from Library collections, and video and audio recordings from collections and of events at the Library. During FY 2018 the Library added 19 files to iTunes podcasts, gaining 6,920 new subscriptions, 98,132 new visitors, and 124,071 consumptions. Since its launch in 2009, the Library has added 3,985 files to its podcast account, attracting 860,687 visitors and 219,943 subscriptions with a total consumption of 4.25 million files.

Photo enthusiasts continued to not only access but also help identify Library photos from the early 1900s through the photo-sharing project on Flickr. During the fiscal year, the Library added 2,432 photos to its Flickr account, bringing the total to 32,287. Over the account's lifetime, the Library has accumulated 70,173 followers and 304.8 million image views.

In addition to its main Facebook site, the Library offers Facebook pages for the Law Library, the American Folklife Center, Performing Arts, the National Library Service for the Blind and Physically Handicapped, the Veterans History Project, and the Library's international collections. During FY 2018 the Library posted 3,087 times on those pages, gained 37,251 followers, received 274,701 likes, and earned 77.8 million impressions. Library Facebook accounts have a total of 508,432 followers, and posts have received a combined 328.9 million lifetime impressions.

At the end of FY 2018 the Library maintained 11 public-facing and two Congressional Research Service protected accounts on Twitter for members of Congress and congressional staff. The public-facing accounts issued 8,765 tweets during the fiscal year, gaining 117,402 retweets and 6,475 replies. The public accounts also gained 155,658 followers (for a total of 1.5 million followers) and made 58.6 million impressions.

The Library's Pinterest account features content from the Library's collections as well as events, National Book Festival posters and items from the Library's shop. During FY 2018 the Library created two new boards and gained 2,348 followers. To date, the account has 65 boards, 1,814 pins, 16,914 followers, and 25,119 saves.

The Library maintains 17 blogs that serve as a vehicle for curators and subject-matter experts to share their collection discoveries and to engage with users. During the fiscal year the Library published 1,139 posts, which drew 2.84 million views for a lifetime total of nearly 14.3 million views. The Library also maintains a Medium account, featuring reposts from Library blogs, the *Library of Congress Magazine*, and the *Gazette*. In FY 2018 the account added 42 posts and added 2,581 followers for a total of 35,767.

The Library's Instagram account continued to share images from current events, concerts, and exhibitions. The Instagram account added 13,882 new followers for a total of 35,931 at the end of FY 2018.

Promoting Creativity, Scholarship, and Lifelong Learning

The Library of Congress collections chronicle centuries of human creativity—a rich, diverse, and enduring source of knowledge for the American public and scholars around the world. During FY 2018 the Library promoted creativity and cultural literacy through hundreds of public programs including concerts, exhibitions, film screenings, lectures, symposia, and poetry readings.

The Library is a catalyst for promoting scholarship through the John W. Kluge Center and the American Folklife Center, which offer fellowship opportunities in various disciplines and publications that showcase the Library's unparalleled collections.

Each year the Library publishes books, calendars, and other printed products featuring its vast content. Library publications in print can be purchased in bookstores nationwide and from the Library Shop. Among the titles published in FY 2018 were *America's Greatest Library: An Illustrated History of the Library of Congress* by John Y. Cole and *Drawn to Purpose: American Women Illustrators and Cartoonists* by Martha H. Kennedy.

In addition to its fellowships, research services, and collections access, the Library of Congress promotes lifelong learning and literacy through its Center for the Book, which assists the nation's teachers in engaging students through the use of primary resources in the classroom. The Center for the Book was established by Congress in 1977 to "stimulate public interest in books and reading." A public–private partnership, the center sponsors educational programs that reach readers of all ages through its affiliated state centers, through collaborations with nonprofit reading promotion partners, and through the Young Readers Center and Poetry and Literature Center. The center also maintains and updates the Library's literacy-promotion website, Read.gov, and manages the authors' program for the National Book Festival.

The mission of the Library's Educational Outreach and Young Readers Center unit is to inform, inspire, and engage learners. Learners include visitors to the Young Readers Center—children, parents, caregivers, and educators—as well as classroom teachers and students who may never visit the Library in person.

Through its Teaching with Primary Sources (TPS) program, the Library provides educators across the grade spectrum and the curriculum with high-quality professional-development programs and classroom materials. These opportunities and tools help teachers effectively use primary sources from the Library's digital collections. In FY 2018 TPS consortium members and Educational Outreach staff engaged nearly 10,000 teachers in face-to-face and online programs in 329 congressional districts. More than 72,069 teachers viewed and/or downloaded online curricula or apps / online interactives developed by consortium partners.

The Library's website for teachers, loc.gov/teachers, remains an active hub for its educator audience. The site, which provides teacher resources on a wide range of topics as well as free professional development, was visited more than 5 million times in FY 2018.

Celebrating Achievement: Library Honors and Awards

Throughout the year, the Library of Congress celebrates the achievements of the nation's creative and scholarly communities. Through these awards and prizes, the world's greatest repository of human creativity honors those who have advanced and embodied the ideals of individuality, conviction, dedication, scholarship, and lifelong learning. Some examples follow.

Library of Congress Prize for American Fiction

The prize honors an American literary writer whose body of work is distinguished not only for its mastery of the art but also for its originality of thought and imagination. The Library awarded the prize to Annie Proulx at the National Book Festival on September 1, 2018. Proulx is the author of the Pulitzer Prize–winning novel *The Shipping News* and the short story *Brokeback Mountain*.

Poet Laureate Consultant in Poetry

Tracy K. Smith was appointed to a second term as the Library's 22nd poet laureate consultant in poetry. Smith, a Pulitzer Prize–winning poet and a professor at Princeton University, is the author of three books of poetry, including *Life on Mars*, winner of the 2012 Pulitzer Prize for Poetry; *Duende*, winner of the 2006 James Laughlin Award and the 2008 Essence Literary Award; and *The Body's Question*, winner of the Cave Canem Poetry Prize. Smith is also the author of a memoir, *Ordinary Light*, a finalist for the 2015 National Book Award. In her second term, Smith expanded her outreach efforts to rural communities and unveiled a new anthology, *American Journal: Fifty Poems for Our Time.*

Gershwin Prize for Popular Song

On September 24, 2018, Carla Hayden announced the husband-and-wife team Emilio and Gloria Estefan as the 2018 recipients of the Library of Congress Gershwin Prize for Popular Song. Named for George and Ira Gershwin, the prize honors a living music artist's lifetime achievement in promoting song to enhance cultural understanding; entertaining and informing audiences; and inspiring new generations. This decade's previous Gershwin Prize recipients are Tony Bennett, Smokey Robinson, Willie Nelson, Billy Joel, Carole King, the songwriting duo of Burt Bacharach and the late Hal David, and Sir Paul McCartney.

The honorees represent two historic firsts for the prize—the first time it has been awarded to a married couple or to musicians-songwriters of Hispanic descent. Married since 1978, the Cuban-American couple started their rise to fame in 1985 with the Miami Sound Machine, a band that blended Latin and pop rhythms. Among their iconic hits were "Conga," "Turn the Beat Around," "Get on Your Feet," and "Rhythm Is Gonna Get You," which in March was named to the National Recording Registry.

The Estefans were both named BMI's "Songwriter of the Year" and have collected 26 Grammy Awards between them. Their life story and music were showcased in the Tony Award–nominated Broadway musical "On Your Feet!," which they executive produced. Among their numerous awards, the Estefans received the Presidential Medal of Freedom, the nation's highest civilian honor.

John W. Kluge Prize for Achievement in the Study of Humanity

The $1 million John W. Kluge prize recognizes individuals whose outstanding scholarship in the humanities and social sciences has shaped public affairs and civil society. In 2018 the prize was awarded to Drew Gilpin Faust—historian, university president, and author of the Bancroft Prize–winning book *This Republic of Suffering: Death and the American Civil War*. A renowned Civil War historian, Faust's other works include *The Creation of Confederate Nationalism: Ideology and Identity in the Civil War South*, *Southern Stories: Slaveholders in Peace and War*, and *Mothers of Invention: Women of the Slaveholding South in the American Civil War*.

Literacy Awards

Created and sponsored by philanthropist David M. Rubenstein, the Library of Congress Literacy Awards seek to reward organizations that have done exemplary, innovative, and easily replicable work over a sustained period of time to promote literacy in the United States and abroad. The 2018 winners were

David M. Rubenstein Prize ($150,000)

Washington, D.C.–based Reading Is Fundamental works to create a literate America by inspiring a passion for reading among all children. The organization, founded in 1966, has distributed over 415 million books and affected the lives of more than 40 million children.

The American Prize ($50,000)

East Side Community School is a 6–12th-grade Title I public school in New York City. The school has created and sustained an independent reading program in which students read, on average, over 40 books a year to improve literacy skills and foster a love of reading.

International Prize ($50,000)

Instituto Pedagógico para Problemas del Lenguaje of Mexico City is a nonprofit organization founded 50 years ago dedicated to supporting deaf children and children with language and learning disabilities, primarily from impoverished families, through educational programs and after-school support.

Library of Congress Additional Sources of Information

Library of Congress website	www.loc.gov
Main phone number	202-707-5000
Reading room hours and locations	www.loc.gov/rr/ 202-707-6400
General reference	www.loc.gov/rr/askalib/ 202-707-3399 TTY 202-707-4210
Visitor information	www.loc.gov/visit/ 202-707-8000 TTY 202-707-6200
Exhibitions	www.loc.gov/exhibits/ 202-707-4604
Copyright information	www.copyright.gov 202-707-3000
Copyright hotline (to order forms)	202-707-9100
Library catalogs	www.catalog.loc.gov/
Cataloging information	www.loc.gov/aba/
Services for the Blind and Physically Handicapped	www.loc.gov/nls/ 202-707-5100 TDD 202-707-0744
Literacy promotion	www.read.gov
Teachers page	www.loc.gov/teachers/
Legislative information	www.Congress.gov
Library of Congress Shop (credit card orders)	888-682-3557 www.loc.gov/shop

Federal Library and Information Network

Laurie Neider
Executive Director

Summary

During fiscal year (FY) 2018 the Federal Library Information Network (FEDLINK) continued its mission to achieve better utilization of federal library and information resources by providing the most cost-effective and efficient administrative mechanism for providing necessary services and materials to federal libraries and information centers. FEDLINK also served as a forum for discussion of federal library and information policies, programs and procedures, to help inform Congress, federal agencies, and others concerned with libraries and information centers.

FEDLINK Executive Report

FEDLINK's Advisory Board (FAB) focused its bimonthly meetings on a variety of broad federal information issues including administrative issues related to streamlining the FEDLINK-assisted acquisition model. The FAB also created FEDLINK's new Federal Library Leadership Working group to provide a forum for leadership to share best practices and discuss creative solutions to common problems, establishing a consolidated voice that advocates for the interests of federal libraries, and building a strong and sustainable future for federal libraries through collaboration, advocacy, and innovation.

FEDLINK held its 2018 Spring Expo, "Driving Innovation in Federal Libraries: Best Practices, Key Metrics & Technology," which featured keynote sessions on strategic planning presented by Richard Reyes-Gavilan, executive director, D.C. Public Library and Sue Baughman, deputy executive director of the Association of Research Libraries.

FEDLINK Working Group Highlights

FEDLINK Awards Committee

To honor the many innovative ways federal libraries, librarians, and library technicians fulfill the information demands of government, business, research, scholarly communities and the American public, the Awards Committee administered a series of national awards for federal librarianship.

The following organizations and individuals were recipients of the FY 2017 Awards, awarded in FY 2018.

2017 Federal Library/Information Center of the Year

Large Library/Information Center (with a staff of 11 or more federal and/or contract employees): The U.S. Army Engineer Research and Development Center Library (ERDC) at Vicksburg, Mississippi

Small Library/Information Center (with a staff of 10 or fewer federal and/or contract employees): The U.S. Environmental Protection Agency (EPA) Library at Research Triangle Park, North Carolina

2017 Federal Librarian of the Year

Edward J. Poletti, chief of Learning Resources at the Central Arkansas Veterans Healthcare System, John L. McClellan Memorial Veterans Hospital in Little Rock, Arkansas

2017 Federal Library Technician of the Year

Ozella Lee Gates, library technician at Dwight D. Eisenhower Army Medical Command in Fort Gordon, Georgia

FEDLINK American Indian Libraries Initiative (AILI)

AILI focused on joining broader American Indian library and museum efforts, built collaborations both inside and outside of the federal government, and made resources more available to tribal libraries and universities. In addition to presentations at national and international conferences, AILI's effort to update FEDLINK's Revolving Fund legislation to allow American Indian tribal governments to have access to FEDLINK services was added to the Consolidated Appropriations Act, 2018 (Public Law 115-141).

FEDLINK Education Working Group

During FY 2018 the FEDLINK Education Working Group, in concert with FEDLINK staff and working groups, sponsored seminars, and workshops, and brokered conferences for more than 800 members of the federal library and information center community. The working group also sponsored a series of orientations to libraries and information centers to provide the opportunity for federal librarians to become acquainted with a variety of institutions and collections in the Washington, D.C., area.

FEDLINK Research and Metrics Working Group

The FEDLINK Research and Metrics Working issued a revised research agenda for the federal information community and identified its initiatives to investigate current trends and issues facing the information community and integrate that investigation using relevant metrics, data sets, analysis, training, and education. The working group offered a series of educational programs on identifying and presenting usage statistics and metrics to agency management.

FEDLINK Program Offices

FEDLINK Publications and Education Office

FEDLINK continued to develop targeted resources to support the FEDLINK program, including business and marketing plans, promotional materials, and development of supporting materials for both exposition programs and all working group events and publications. In FY 2017 FEDLINK continued its publication program as a digital communication provider and used its community listservs for outreach on critical advocacy and program information to more than 2,000 electronic subscribers.

FEDLINK Contracts and Network Operations

FEDLINK provided assisted acquisition services to the federal information community by procuring publications in a wide variety of formats (print and electronic journals, print and electronic books, sound recordings, audiovisual materials, items via document delivery and interlibrary loan, and access to databases of full text, indices, abstracts, and a variety of other data) and library support services (cataloging and related technical processing services, staffing support, information management, resource sharing, integrated library systems, digitization, digital archiving, and preservation services). Through interagency agreements (IAA), FEDLINK's contractors and network staff members worked on behalf of federal agencies with more than 90 vendors to conduct competitions, issue orders, and resolve issues with vendors.

In FY 2018 FEDLINK initiated a review of its business model to increase efficiencies throughout its processes and workflows. FEDLINK also awarded four new Indefinite Delivery/Indefinite Quantity (IDIQ) contracts for Serials Subscription Services and issued a Request for Proposal (RFP) to solicit offers for multiple IDIQ contracts for the procurement of electronic information resources. FEDLINK promoted these services at two national conferences: Special Libraries Association and Computers in Libraries.

FEDLINK Fiscal Operations

FEDLINK continued to enhance its fiscal operations while providing its members with $63.1 million in Transfer Pay services, $4.4 million in Direct Pay services, and an estimated $134 million in the Direct Express services, saving federal agencies around $40 million in vendor volume discounts and approximately $54 million more in cost avoidance.

FEDLINK Fees

The final budget for FY 2018 held membership fees steady for 6.75 percent on Transfer Pay service dollars. Direct Pay fees remained at FY 2009 levels, as did Direct Express fees of 0.75 percent for all participating commercial online information services vendors.

Accounts Receivable and Member Services

FEDLINK processed registrations from federal libraries, information centers, and other federal offices for a total of 223 signed IAAs and more than 1,834 IAA amendments for agencies that added, adjusted, or ended service funding. FEDLINK executed service requests by generating 4,993 delivery orders that FEDLINK Contract staff issued to vendors.

Transfer Pay Accounts Payable Services

FEDLINK continued to maintain open accounts for five prior years to pay invoices for members. FEDLINK completed closing of the FY 2013. Statements were issued to members for the current year and prior years.

Direct Express Services

The FEDLINK Direct Express Program includes 69 vendors offering database retrieval services. The program is set up to provide customers procurement and payment options similar to GSA in which the vendors pay a quarterly service fee to FEDLINK based on customer billings for usage.

Budget, Revenue, and Risks Reserves

In FY 2018 FEDLINK Fee Revenue was approximately $215,000 higher than FY 2017. The expenditures for FY 2017 were approximately $612,000 lower than FY 2017. FEDLINK's Reserve requirement for FY 2018 continues to be solvent. The program holds reserves for (1) mandatory requirements for shutdown and bankruptcy risks; (2) continuity of operations requirements for mission-essential systems; and (3) compliance risk mitigation initiatives.

National Agricultural Library

U.S. Department of Agriculture, Agricultural Research Service
Abraham Lincoln Bldg., 10301 Baltimore Ave., Beltsville, MD 20705-2351
E-mail agref@nal.usda.gov
World Wide Web https://www.nal.usda.gov

Paul Wester
Director

The U.S. Department of Agriculture's National Agricultural Library (NAL) is one of the world's largest and most accessible agricultural research libraries, offering service directly to the public either on-site in Beltsville, Maryland, or via its website, https://www.nal.usda.gov.

The library was established in 1862 at the same time as the U.S. Department of Agriculture (USDA). It became a national library in 1962, when Congress established it as the primary agricultural information resource of the United States (7 USCS § 3125a). Congress assigned to the library the responsibilities to

- Acquire, preserve, and manage information resources relating to agriculture and allied sciences
- Organize agricultural information products and services and provide them within the United States and internationally
- Plan, coordinate, and evaluate information and library needs relating to agricultural research and education
- Cooperate with and coordinate efforts toward development of a comprehensive agricultural library and information network
- Coordinate the development of specialized subject information services among the agricultural and library information communities

NAL is located in Beltsville, Maryland, near Washington, D.C., on the grounds of USDA's Henry A. Wallace Beltsville Agricultural Research Center. Its 14-story Abraham Lincoln Building is named in honor of the president who created the Department of Agriculture and signed several of the major U.S. laws affecting agriculture.

The library employs about 100 librarians, information specialists, computer specialists, administrators, and clerical personnel, supplemented by about 50 contract staff and cooperators from NAL partnering organizations.

NAL's reputation as one of the world's foremost agricultural libraries is supported and burnished by its expert staff, ongoing leadership in delivering information services, expanding collaborations with other U.S. and international agricultural research and information organizations, and its extensive collection of agricultural information, searchable through AGRICOLA (AGRICultural On-Line Access), the library's bibliographic database.

In 2012 NAL reorganized to better align its functions with its overall strategic plan, which includes simplified access to all NAL content, expansion of digital content, and the integration of scientific data sets and discovery tools.

The Collection

The NAL collection dates to the congressionally approved 1839 purchase of books for the Agricultural Division of the Patent Office, predating the 1862 establishment of USDA itself. Today NAL provides access to billions of pages of agricultural information—an immense collection of scientific books, journals, audiovisuals, reports, theses, artifacts, and images—and to a widening array of digital media, as well as databases and other information resources germane to the broad reach of agriculture-related sciences.

The library's collection contains more than 8 million items, dating from the 15th century to the present, including the most complete repository of USDA publications and the world's most extensive set of materials on the history of U.S. agriculture. Publications are selected for the collection based on the National Agricultural Library Collection Development Policy.

Building the Collection

NAL is the only U.S. national library with a legislated mandate to collect in the following disciplines: plant and animal health, welfare, and production; agricultural economics, products, and education; aquaculture; forestry; rural sociology and rural life; family and consumer science; and food science, safety, and nutrition. In addition to collecting as comprehensively as possible in these core subject areas, NAL collects extensively in many related subjects, such as biology, bioinformatics, biochemistry, chemistry, entomology, environmental science, genetics, invasive species, meteorology, natural resources, physics, soil science, sustainability, water quality, and zoology. The library has primary responsibility for collecting and retaining publications issued by USDA and its agencies. As well, NAL collects publications from around the world.

Special Collections

The NAL Special Collections program emphasizes access to and preservation of rare and unique materials documenting the history of agriculture and related sciences. Items in the library's special collections include rare books, manuscripts, nursery and seed trade catalogs, posters, objects, photographs, and other rare materials documenting agricultural subjects. Materials date from the 1500s to the present and include many international sources. Detailed information about these special collections is available on the NAL website at https://specialcollections.nal.usda.gov.

Special collections of note include the following:

- The U.S. Department of Agriculture History Collection (https://specialcollections.nal.usda.gov/usda-history-collection-introductionindex), assembled over 80 years by USDA historians, includes letters, memoranda, reports, and papers of USDA officials, as well as photographs, oral histories, and clippings covering the activities of the department from its founding through the early 1990s.

- The U.S. Department of Agriculture Pomological Watercolor Collection (http://usdawatercolors.nal.usda.gov) includes more than 7,000 detailed, botanically accurate watercolor illustrations of fruit and nut varieties developed by growers or introduced by USDA plant explorers. Created between 1886 and the 1940s, the watercolors served as official documentation of the work of the Office of the Pomologist and were used to create chromolithographs in publications distributed widely by the department. Although created for scientific accuracy, the works are artistic treasures in their own right. The full collection has been digitized and is now available online.
- The Henry G. Gilbert Nursery and Seed Trade Catalog Collection (https://specialcollections.nal.usda.gov/guide-collections/henry-g-gilbert-nursery-and-seed-trade-catalog-collection), begun in 1904 by USDA economic botanist Percy L. Ricker, has grown to comprise more than 200,000 U.S. and foreign catalogs. The earliest items date from the late 1700s, but the collection is strongest from the 1890s to the present. Researchers commonly use the collection to document the introduction of plants to the United States, study economic trends, and illustrate early developments in American landscape design.
- The Rare Book Collection (https://specialcollections.nal.usda.gov/guide-collections/rare-book-collection) highlights agriculture's printed historical record. It covers a wide variety of subjects but is particularly strong in botany, natural history, zoology, and entomology. International in scope, the collection documents early agricultural practices in Britain and Europe, as well as the Americas. Of particular note are the more than 300 books by or about Carl Linnaeus, the "father of taxonomy," including a rare first edition of his 1735 work, *Systema Naturae*.

Manuscript collections (https://specialcollections.nal.usda.gov/guide-collections/index-manuscript-collections), now numbering more than 400, document the story of American agriculture and its influence on the world.

NAL continues to digitize these and other unique materials to share them broadly via its website and has published detailed indexes to the content of many manuscript collections to improve discovery. AGRICOLA, NAL's catalog, includes bibliographic entries for special collection items, manuscripts, and rare books. The library provides in-house research and reference services for its special collections and offers fee-based duplication services.

Preservation/Digitization

NAL is committed to the preservation of its print and nonprint collections. It continues to monitor and improve the environmental quality of its stacks to extend the longevity of all materials in the collection. The library has instituted a long-term strategy to ensure the growing body of agricultural information is systematically identified, preserved, and archived.

NAL's digital conversion program has resulted in a growing digital collection of USDA publications and many non-USDA historical materials not restricted by copyright. NAL is in the midst of a large-scale project to digitize agricultural literature and provide online access to the general public. Important and distinctive items were selected from the NAL collection, with an initial focus on USDA-issued publications and nursery and seed trade catalogs. In 2014 NAL digitized and created citation information for 38,698 items. Publications are accessible at https://archive.org/details/usdanationalagriculturallibrary and in the NALDC.

Library Services

Reference Services

NAL serves the agricultural information needs of customers through a combination of Web-based and traditional library services, including reference, document delivery, and information centers. The NAL website offers access to a wide variety of full-text resources, as well as online access to reference and document delivery services.

The main reading room in the library's Beltsville facility features a walk-up service desk, access to an array of digital information resources (including full-text scientific journals), current periodicals, and an on-site request service for materials from NAL's collection. Services are available 8:30 to 4:30 Monday through Friday, except federal holidays.

NAL's reference services are accessible online using the Ask a Question form on the NAL web pages; by use of e-mail addressed to agref@ars.usda.gov; by telephone at 301-504-5755; or by mail to Research Services, National Agricultural Library ARS/USDA, 10301 Baltimore Avenue, Beltsville, MD 20705. Requesters receive assistance from Research Services staff in all areas and aspects of agriculture, but staff particularly answer questions, provide research guidance, and make presentations on topics not addressed by the seven subject-focused information centers of the library.

Information Centers

NAL's seven information centers are reliable sources of comprehensive, science-based information on key aspects of U.S. agriculture, providing timely, accurate, and in-depth coverage of their specialized subject areas. Their expert staff offers extensive Web-based information resources and advanced reference services:

- The Alternative Farming Systems Information Center (AFSIC) (https://www.nal.usda.gov/afsic) specializes in identifying and accessing information relating to farming methods that maintain the health and productivity of the entire farming enterprise, including natural resources. This focus includes sustainable and alternative agricultural systems, crops, and livestock.
- The Animal Welfare Information Center (AWIC) (https://www.nal.usda.gov/awic) provides scientific information and referrals to help ensure the proper care and treatment of animals used in biomedical research, testing, teaching, and exhibitions, and by animal dealers. Among its varied outreach activities, the center conducts workshops for researchers on meeting the information requirements of the Animal Welfare Act.

- The Food and Nutrition Information Center (FNIC) (https://www.nal.usda.gov/fnic) provides credible, accurate, and practical resources for nutrition and health professionals, educators, government personnel, and consumers. FNIC maintains a staff of registered dietitians who can answer questions on food and human nutrition.
- The Food Safety Research Information Office (FSRIO) (https://www.nal.usda.gov/fsrio) delivers information on publicly funded—and, to the extent possible, privately funded—food safety research initiatives. The Research Projects Database provides more than 12,000 active food safety research projects in a searchable database of U.S. and international agencies. The Research Publications Feed offers access to real-time updates of peer reviewed publications in food safety.
- The National Invasive Species Information Center (NISIC) (https://www.nal.usda.gov/nisic) delivers accessible, accurate, referenced, up-to-date, and comprehensive information on invasive species drawn from federal, state, local, and international sources.
- The Rural Information Center (RIC) (https://www.nal.usda.gov/ric) assists local officials, organizations, businesses, and rural residents working to maintain the vitality of rural areas. It collects and disseminates information on such diverse topics as community economic development, small business development, health care, finance, housing, environment, quality of life, community leadership, and education.
- The Water and Agriculture Information Center (WAIC) (https://www.nal.usda.gov/waic) collects, organizes, and communicates scientific findings, educational methodologies, and public policy issues related to water and agriculture.

In addition to these information centers, NAL manages the popular Nutrition.gov website (http://www.nutrition.gov) in collaboration with other USDA agencies and the Department of Health and Human Services. This site provides evidence-based nutrition information for the general consumer and highlights the latest in nutrition news and tools from across federal government agencies. A team of registered dietitians at NAL's Food and Nutrition Information Center maintains Nutrition.gov and answers questions on food and nutrition issues.

Document Delivery Services

NAL's document delivery operation responds to thousands of requests each year from USDA employees and from libraries and organizations around the world. NAL uses the Relais Enterprise document request and delivery system to support document delivery. With Relais fully integrated with the Voyager library system, with DigiTop, and with other Open-URL and ISO ILL- compliant systems, NAL customers can request materials or check on the status of their requests via the Web, and the needed materials can easily be delivered electronically. Document requests can also be submitted via OCLC (NAL's symbol is AGL) and DOCLINE (NAL's libid is MDUNAL). Visit https://www.nal.usda.gov/services/request.shtml for details.

Digital Products

The NAL websites, which encompass nearly all the content and services described here, collectively receive millions of page views per month from people seeking agricultural information.

AGRICOLA

AGRICOLA comprises an online catalog of NAL collections, and the article citation database delivers worldwide access to agricultural information through its searchable Web interface (http://agricola.nal.usda.gov). Alternatively, users can access AGRICOLA on a fee basis through several commercial vendors, or they can subscribe to the complete AGRICOLA file, also on a fee basis, directly from the library by e-mailing AgricolaPublishers@ars.usda.gov.

The AGRICOLA database covers materials in all formats, including printed works from the 15th century onward. Its records describe publications and resources encompassing all aspects of agriculture and allied disciplines. AGRICOLA, updated daily, includes the following two components:

- NAL Public Access Catalog, containing more than 1 million citations to books, audiovisual materials, serial titles, and other materials in the NAL collection. (The catalog also contains some bibliographic records for items cataloged by other libraries but not held in the NAL collection.)
- NAL Article Citation Database, consisting of more than 5 million citations to journal articles, book chapters, reports, and reprints. NAL has implemented automated indexing/text analytics software to produce its Article Citation Database. This application combines semantic analysis, machine learning, and human rules to automatically assign subject terms to journal articles.

DigiTop

DigiTop, USDA's Digital Desktop Library, delivers the full text of thousands of journals and hundreds of newspapers worldwide, provides 17 agriculturally significant citation databases, supplies a range of digital reference resources, and offers focused, personalized services. Navigator is a component of DigiTop that allows cross-searching of multiple bibliographic databases. This system includes AGRICOLA; AGRIS; BIOSIS; CAB Abstracts; Fish, Fisheries, and Aquatic Biodiversity Worldwide; Food Science and Technology Abstracts; GEOBASE; GeoRef; MEDLINE; Wildlife and Ecology Studies Worldwide; Scopus; and Zoological Record. DigiTop is available to on-site visitors and to the entire USDA workforce worldwide—more than 100,000 people—around the clock. NAL staff provides help desk and reference services, continuous user education, and training for DigiTop users.

Ag Data Commons

The newly released Ag Data Commons' mission is to serve as USDA's single-point-of-access to open agricultural research data. Its catalog with nearly 1,300 records is a gateway to data from large ongoing USDA research programs, including those listed below. Its repository also publishes and preserves data files from many studies. Standardized records describe datasets in detail and link them with corresponding journal publications. The goal of the Ag Data Commons is to enable data reuse for bigger, better science and decision-making. https://data.nal.usda.gov.

The Ag Data Commons uses a customized version of the open-source DKAN software, which is compliant with U.S. Project Open Data standards for federal agencies. The system includes both a catalog function describing the data and pointing to its online location, and a repository holding and publishing data not otherwise available.

Specialized data services provided by the National Agricultural Library include the following:

- USDA Food Composition Database—https://ndb.nal.usda.gov
- I5K Workspace@NAL—https://i5k.nal.usda.gov
- Life Cycle Assessment Commons (LCA Commons)—https://www.lcacommons.gov
- Dr. Duke's Phytochemical and Ethnobotanical Databases—https://phytochem.nal.usda.gov
- Long-Term Agroecosystem Research (LTAR)—https://ltar.nal.usda.gov
- Geospatial Data Catalog (GeoData)—https://geodata.nal.usda.gov

NALDC

The National Agricultural Library Digital Collections (NALDC) (https://naldc.nal.usda.gov/naldc/home.xhtml) offers easy access to collection materials available in digital format. NALDC offers rich searching, browsing, and retrieval of digital materials and collections, and provides reliable, long-term online access to selected publications. NALDC includes historical publications, U.S. Department of Agriculture (USDA) research, and more.

The scope of NALDC includes items published by the U.S. Department of Agriculture (USDA) and clearly intended for public consumption, scholarly, and peer-reviewed research outcomes authored by USDA employees while working for USDA, and other items selected in accordance with the subjects identified in the NAL Collection Development Policy.

PubAg

PubAg (https://pubag.nal.usda.gov) contains full-text articles authored by USDA employees and citations to the peer-reviewed journal literature of agriculture. These citations have been enriched through subject analysis and application of terms from NALT (NAL's Agricultural Thesaurus). They also contain links to the full text at publisher websites and other locations.

PubAg was launched originally in late 2014 and was upgraded in 2017 to include the following features: a spell checker to improve users' search quality; a type-ahead feature to suggest search terms; the ability to select records for actions such as formatting citations, printing, e-mailing records and sending them to a reference manager; filtering retrieved results by journal name, publication year, or subject term; and providing access to a publicly available Application Programming Interface (API); and an Advanced Search function.

National Agricultural Library Thesaurus (English and Spanish)

NAL is known for its expertise in developing and using a thesaurus, or controlled vocabulary, a critical component of effective digital information systems. The National Agricultural Library Thesaurus (NALT) (https://agclass.nal.usda.gov/agt.shtml) is a hierarchical vocabulary of agricultural and biological terms organized according to 17 subject categories. It comprises primarily biological nomenclature, with additional terminology supporting the physical and social sciences.

The 2018 edition is the 17th edition of NALT, issued in December 2017. It contains more than 135,000 terms and nearly 5,618 definitions. Taxonomic terms from every biological kingdom were expanded in this edition, along with common names of species. Plant species were added following taxonomic verification by the Germplasm Resources Information Network (GRIN). Semi-controlled vocabulary of the National Forest Service Library, USDA, was mapped to NALT, and many forest- and timber-related terms are included in this edition. Other subject areas expanded include terms in agricultural technology, cell biology, food sciences, chemistry, plant diseases, enzymes, health, pathology, and geological time scales.

NALT continues to be available as Linked Open Data. NAL can now connect its vocabulary to other linked data vocabularies, which, in turn, will connect NALT to the larger semantic Web. Such interconnections will help programmers create meaningful relationships that will make it easier to locate related content.

Associated with NALT, the NAL Glossary provides definitions of agricultural terms. The 2018 edition contains 5,618 definitions, ranging across agriculture and its many ancillary subjects, an increase of 396 definitions from last year. Most definitions are composed by NALT staff. (Suggestions for new terms or definitions can be sent by e-mail to agref@ars.usda.gov.)

NAL publishes Spanish-language versions of the thesaurus and glossary, which carry the names *Tesauro Agrícola* and *Glosario,* respectively. Both are updated concurrently with the annual release of the English-language version. The 2018 edition of the Spanish-language version of NALT contains more than 110,000 terms and 5,618 definitions.

The thesaurus and glossary are primarily used for indexing and for improving the retrieval of agricultural information, but they can also be used by students (from fifth grade up), teachers, writers, translators, and others who are seeking precise definitions of words from the agricultural sciences. Users can download all four publications—English and Spanish thesaurus and glossary—in both machine-readable (MARC, RDF-SKOS, and XML) and human-readable (doc, pdf) formats at https://agclass.nal.usda.gov/download.shtml.

Networks of Cooperation

The NAL collection and information resources are supplemented by networks of cooperation with other institutions, including arrangements with agricultural libraries at U.S. land-grant universities, other U.S. national libraries, agricultural libraries in other countries, and libraries of the United Nations and other international organizations.

AgNIC

Agriculture Network Information Collaborative (AgNIC) is a voluntary alliance of member institutions, mostly U.S. land-grant university libraries, dedicated to enhancing collective information and services among the members and their partners for all those seeking agricultural information over the Internet.

More information about AgNIC and its activities can be found at https://www.agnic.org.

USAIN

The United States Agricultural Information Network (USAIN) is a professional membership organization that provides a forum for members to discuss food and agricultural issues, and seeks to take a leadership role in the formation of a national information policy as related to food and agriculture. Central to its mission is cooperation with and support of the National Agricultural Library.

Learn more about USAIN at https://usain.org/.

AgLaw

Agricultural Law Information Partnership (AgLaw) is a collaboration between the National Agricultural Library, National Agricultural Law Center (NALC), and the Center for Agriculture and Food Systems (CAFS) at the Vermont Law School. The Partnership supports the dissemination of agricultural and food law information to consumers, researchers, and legal professionals. Agricultural law is defined broadly to include land-based agriculture, food and fiber production and systems, aquaculture, and energy issues.

Explore the AgLaw Partnership at https://www.nal.usda.gov/aglaw/agricultural-law-information-partnership.

AGLINET

Through the Agricultural Libraries Network (AGLINET), NAL serves as the U.S. node of an international agricultural information system that brings together agricultural libraries with strong regional or country coverage and other specialized collections. NAL functions as a gateway to U.S. agricultural libraries and resources, fulfilling requests for information via reciprocal agreements with several other libraries, information centers, and consortia. As an AGLINET member, NAL agrees to provide low-cost interlibrary loan and photocopy service to other AGLINET libraries. Most materials requested through AGLINET are delivered digitally, although reproductions via fiche or photocopy are used when appropriate. AGLINET is administered by the Food and Agriculture Organization of the United Nations.

Information Management and Information Technology

Over the past quarter century, NAL has applied increasingly sophisticated information technology to support the ever more complex and demanding information needs of researchers, practitioners, policymakers, and the general public. Technological developments spearheaded by the library date back to the 1940s and 1950s, when NAL Director Ralph Shaw invented "electronic machines" such as the photo charger, rapid selector, and photo clerk. Over the years NAL has made numerous technological improvements, from automating collections information to delivering full-text and image collections digitally on the Internet.

NAL has fully implemented the Voyager integrated library management system from Ex Libris, Ltd. The system supports ordering, receiving, and invoice processing for purchases; creating and maintaining indexing and cataloging records for AGRICOLA; circulating print holdings; and providing a Web-based online catalog for public searching and browsing of the collection. In addition, the system is fully integrated with an automated interlibrary loan and document delivery system by Relais International that streamlines services and provides desktop delivery of needed materials.

National Library of Medicine

8600 Rockville Pike, Bethesda, MD 20894
301-496-6308, 888-346-3656, fax 301-496-4450
E-mail publicinfo@nlm.nih.gov
World Wide Web http://www.nlm.nih.gov

Jody Nurik
Acting Director, Office of Communications and Public Liaison

One of the 27 Institutes and Centers of the National Institutes of Health (NIH), the National Library of Medicine (NLM) is a recognized leader in computational health sciences research and the world's largest biomedical library.

Through its cutting-edge research, information systems, collections, and training programs, NLM plays an essential role in catalyzing basic biomedical science and data-driven discovery. NLM acquires, organizes, and delivers up-to-date biomedical information across the United States and around the globe. Millions of scientists, health professionals, and members of the public use NLM's electronic information sources billions of times each year. NLM makes research results available for translation into new treatments, products, and practices; provides useful decision support for health professionals and patients; and supports disaster and emergency preparedness and response.

Leveraging its 182-year history of organizing and curating the biomedical literature, NLM has expanded to other knowledge resources, particularly data, providing leadership in the acquisition and analysis of data for discovery, as well as training of biomedical data scientists.

Delivering Reliable, High-Quality Biomedical and Health Information Services

NLM continues to expand the quantity and range of high-quality information available to scientists, health professionals, and the public. Advances in Fiscal Year (FY) 2018 included

- Indexing of approximately 1.3 million new journal articles for PubMed, NLM's most heavily used database, which contained records for 28.9 million articles in biomedical and life sciences journals at the end of FY 2018.
- Growth in PubMed Central, the digital archive of full-text biomedical literature, which included more than 5.1 million research articles at the end of FY 2018, including those produced by researchers funded by NIH, ten other federal government agencies, and private research funders.
- Expansion of ClinicalTrials.gov, the world's largest clinical trials registry, to include approximately 287,000 registered studies and summary results for more than 33,000 studies, including many not elsewhere published.
- Enhancement of Genetics Home Reference to provides consumer-level information on more than 2,700 genetic conditions and genes to an average of nearly 2 million visitors per month.

- Expanded dbGaP, a genotypes and phenotypes database, which connects individual-level genomic data with individual-level clinical information, by 23 percent to more than 1,100 studies involving more than 2 million people. dbGaP provides access to studies that investigate the interaction between genotypes and phenotypes, for both individual-level genomic data and genomic summary results. Following changes to data management procedures under the NIH Genomic Data Sharing Policy, dbGaP allows unrestricted access to summary-level genomic results from most NIH-supported genomic studies.
- Continued growth of PubChem, an archive of chemical and biological data on small molecules; PubChem contained information on more than 96 million unique chemical structures and more than 1 million bioassays at the end of FY 2018.
- Expansion by 23 percent of the RefSeq database of integrated, nonredundant, well-annotated reference sequences, which are essential to identifying and documenting genetic variations that affect human health, to over 173 million records, including more than 121 million protein records from over 84,000 organisms.
- Global Unique Device Identification Database, the NLM portal for medical device records, includes FDA unique identifiers and registration information for more than 1.8 million medical devices, supporting improvements in care and patient safety. In FY 2018 NLM added new versioning data elements to AccessGUDID records and upgraded the application program interface (API). AccessGUDID received 6.6 million application programming interface (API) calls from computer systems accessing the resource and more than 360,000 downloads of the AccessGUDID dataset.
- More than 156 million API calls to MedlinePlus Connect from health IT and EHR (Electronic Heath Record) systems requesting patient-specific delivery of consumer health information from MedlinePlus

NLM continues expanding access to its rare and unique historical collections through digitization partnerships with outside organizations, which complement the ongoing internal scanning and digitization work of the NLM staff. In FY 2018 NLM's external partners provided over 12,000 digitized manuscript pages scanned from 15 of our archival collections. During the same year, NLM digitized more than 3,900 printed historical books totaling nearly half a million pages, almost 3,000 prints and photographs, and 605 audiovisual titles, adding that content to NLM's Digital Collections, a free online archive of biomedical books, images, and videos.

NLM is exploring advanced cloud implementations with several of its resources, including Access GUDID and PubMed Labs.

Promoting Public Awareness and Access to Information

NLM offers direct-to-consumer information resources in plain language, such as MedlinePlus, which includes information about disease, conditions, and wellness issues. In FY 2018 the number of health topics covered in English and Spanish reached 1,020. MedlinePlus information is also available through MedlinePlus Connect, which works with electronic health record systems to bring information to patients and health care providers at the point of entry in healthcare systems. Websites focused on consumer health information related to the environment, drug information, genetics, and specific populations are also offered.

NLM uses multiple channels to reach the public, including direct contact, consumer-friendly websites, and social media and human networks that reach out to communities. NLM also uses technological approaches, such as with hackathons that use NLM resources to address specific information problems. Hackathons are events for computer programmers and other professionals to collaborate on software projects. In FY 2018 NLM funded more than 300 outreach projects across the country to enhance awareness and access to health information and to address health literacy issues.

NLM uses exhibitions, the media, and new technologies in its efforts to reach underserved populations and promote interest among young people in science, medicine, and technology. NLM continues to expand its successful traveling exhibitions program, which is a cost-efficient way to extend access to NLM resources around the world, including international locales for access by U.S. Armed Forces.

In FY 2018 with public-private partnerships, NLM's traveling exhibitions appeared in 186 institutions in 165 towns and cities in 42 states and two other countries. Examples include Graphic Medicine: Ill-Conceived and Well-Drawn; Native Voices: Native Peoples' Concepts of Health and Illness; For All the People: A Century of Citizen Action in Health Care Reform; and Opening Doors: Contemporary African American Academic Surgeons.

In collaboration with NIH Institutes and Centers and other partners, NLM produces NIH MedlinePlus magazine, in print and online, in English and Spanish. The magazine is distributed to 70,000 subscribers, as well as to medical offices, health science libraries, Congress, the media, federally supported community health centers, select hospital emergency and waiting rooms, and other locations nationwide. In FY 2018 NLM and NIH partnered with the National Hispanic Medical Association and enhanced its online Web presence with interactive content, animations, quizzes, and tutorials to extend the distribution of the magazine to previously underserved populations.

Research and Development for Advanced Information Systems, Standards, and Research Tools

NLM's advanced information services have long benefited from its intramural research and development (R&D) programs and from its efforts in promoting and supporting health data standards. Collectively, these efforts have led to major advances in the ways high-volume information and data are collected, structured, standardized, mined, and delivered. The Library conducts advanced R&D on different aspects of biomedical informatics through the Lister Hill National Center for Biomedical Communications (LHC) and the National Center for Biotechnology Information (NCBI), both of which were established by Congress.

NLM conducts and supports R&D in such areas as the development and dissemination of health data standards; the capture, processing, dissemination, and use of high-quality imaging data; medical language processing; high-speed access to biomedical information; advanced technology for emergency and disaster management; and analysis of large databases of clinical and administrative data to determine their usefulness in predicting patient outcomes and in validating findings from relatively small prospective clinical research studies.

In the area of natural language processing, NLM conducts research involving language resources and innovative algorithms. NLM develops tools to help advance the fields of natural language understanding and biomedical text mining and applies them to indexing and information retrieval. Projects include the UMLS (Unified Medical Language System), Medical Text Indexer (MTI), SemRep (Semantic Knowledge Representation Project), MetaMap, and MetaMap Lite, which is an easy-to-use, customizable tool for identifying medical symptoms, findings, risk factors, treatments, and diagnoses in free text narrative.

Leveraging extensive machine-learning experience and field-based projects in processing clinical images from parasites to lungs, NLM advances analytical tools that are applied in image analysis research. In FY 2018 NLM scientists applied machine-learning techniques known as deep learning, or deep neural networks, to develop a new research area, Visual Question Answering (VQA), for answering questions about images. One notable application of this automation is describing their environment and answering questions asked by visually impaired people. NLM is developing approaches to clinical and biomedical VQA to facilitate automation of VQA for medical training and decision support. NLM developed a collection of images and Q&A's accepted for publication in *Scientific Data*–Nature. Deep learning techniques are being applied with a dataset of de-identified skin photographs to help classify skin diseases. Also, deep learning improved performance in two ongoing projects: automated classification of chest X-rays in the field to detect patients with active tuberculosis, and automated detection and counting of parasitic cells in NLM's malaria screener smartphone application for malaria detection in the field. It is also applied in two new image analysis projects. In collaboration with the National Eye Institute (NEI), NLM scientists are studying a set of 51,700 retinal photographs to identify and measure the size of the lesions associated with diagnosing and managing retinal diabetes and age-related macular degeneration. These techniques make it easier to assess the effect of treatments in clinical care and research drug trials. Enabled by innovative deep learning approaches, NLM's Consumer Health Information and Question Answering system provides personalized answers from reliable resources to consumers' health-related questions.

NLM also conducts R&D on the representation, integration, and retrieval of molecular biology data and biomedical literature, in addition to providing an integrated genomic information resource consisting of more than 40 databases for biomedical researchers at NIH and around the world. These databases range from data on human genetic variation and viral pathogens, to information on genetic tests. NLM's development of large-scale data integration techniques with advanced information systems is key to its expanding ability to support the accelerated pace of research made possible by new technologies, such as next-generation DNA sequencing, microarrays, and small molecule screening. NLM's GenBank, in collaboration with partners in the United Kingdom and Japan, is the world's largest annotated collection of publicly available DNA sequences, with 209 million sequences from more than 420,000 different species. NLM's Web services provide the information and analytic tools for researchers to accelerate the rate of genomic discovery and facilitate the translation of basic science advances into new diagnostics and treatments.

As part of the National Action Plan for Combating Antibiotic-Resistant Bacteria, NLM collaborates with the Federal Drug Administration (FDA), the Centers for Disease Control and Prevention, and the United States Department of Agriculture, and other agencies and organizations, to maintain a database of whole genome sequencing (WGS) data for antibiotic-resistant bacteria, along with tools to facilitate analyses of such data. The database provides an important resource for surveillance and research into the mechanisms underlying the emergence of antibacterial resistance. This program builds upon a successful collaborative project among these same agencies to use WGS to more quickly and accurately identify and investigate outbreaks of disease caused by foodborne bacterial pathogens, such as listeria and salmonella.

The computational biology research that is rooted in complex analyses of richly annotated genomics data resources has yielded important discoveries and health advances. In FY 2018 NLM researchers collaborated with the National Eye Institute (NEI) in research to assist in the diagnosis and screening of age-related macular degeneration (AMD). By leveraging cutting-edge, deep-learning techniques and repurposing "big" imaging data from a major AMD clinical trial, the researchers developed a novel data-driven approach (called DeepSeeNet) for autonomous AMD diagnosis with performance exceeding that of human retinal specialists. NLM researchers also collaborated with a group in Freiburg, Germany, to complete a quest lasting more than two decades to characterize the molecular causes of hyperIgE syndrome, which was first characterized clinically in 1966. Two additional genes were identified, CARD11 and ZNF341. Since both genes frequently are also dysregulated in cancer, the findings about rare primary immunodeficiencies have implications for understanding the developmental pathways of cancer as well as immunology, and show promise for advancing the diagnosis and treatment of each. Other research projects included a study demonstrating the capability of MiCld, a pathogen identification tool, in identifying multiple pathogens present in the same sample. Working together with NIH's Clinical Center, the researchers will move forward with a Phase III study to assess use of the tool to identify pathogens in patient urine samples.

NLM has been a major force in health data standards for more than 30 years. In close collaboration with the Office of the National Coordinator for Health Information Technology within the U.S. Department of Health and Human Services and with support from the Centers for Medicare & Medicaid Services, the Veterans Health Administration, and FDA, NLM develops, funds, and disseminates the clinical terminologies designated as U.S. standards to promote the interoperability of electronic health records (EHRs) and health information exchange. This includes three standard vocabularies—LOINC (for identifying tests and measurements), RxNorm (for identifying drugs), and SNOMED CT (for identifying problems, organisms, and many other special items). The goal is to ensure that EHR data created in one system can be transmitted, interpreted, and aggregated appropriately in other systems to support health care, public health, and research. NLM produces tools that help EHR developers and users implement these standards and makes them available in multiple formats, including via APIs. Importantly, NLM's support allows key standards to be used free of charge in U.S. health care, public health, biomedical research, and product development.

NLM's Unified Medical Language System (UMLS) resources connect standard clinical terminologies to billing codes and more than 120 other important biomedical vocabularies, such as those used in information retrieval and gene annotation. By linking many different names for the same concepts and by providing associated natural language processing tools, UMLS resources help computer programs to interpret biomedical text and health data correctly in NIH-funded research, in commercial product development, and in many electronic information services, including those produced by NLM.

In addition, RxNorm is a widely used drug terminology developed by NLM and used for electronic prescription and exchange of drug information. NLM has developed a graphical user interface (RxNav) and APIs to facilitate access by researchers, industry, and the public. In FY 2018 these drug APIs received one billion queries. Recent developments include a locally installable version of the APIs, integration of MED-RT in RxClass and better interoperability of RxNorm with the new SNOMED CT model for medicinal products.

Extramural Programs

NLM funds extramural research, resource, and workforce development grants that build important foundations in biomedical informatics and data science bringing the methods and concepts of computational, informational, quantitative, social/behavioral, and engineering sciences to bear on problems related to basic biomedical/behavioral research, health care, public health, and consumer use of health-related information. In addition to grants for basic and applied research, predoctoral and postdoctoral training, and career transition, NLM offers unique resource grant programs that support biomedical knowledge resource development. To accomplish its extramural goals, NLM offers grants in five general categories: research project grants and supplements; training and fellowships; career transition; information resource awards; and small business grants. NLM also provides management oversight for a selection of informatics or data science grants funded by the NIH Common Fund, including NIH pioneer and early innovation awards, a transformational research award, predoctoral data science research training, and a digital curation award.

Informatics Workforce and Resources for Biomedicine and Health

Many of today's informatics researchers and health information technology leaders are graduates of NLM-funded university-based training programs in biomedical informatics. As of July 2017 NLM supported research training in biomedical informatics and data science at 16 active university-based programs, training more than 2,000 individuals each year, including 14 trainees emphasizing environmental exposures funded by NIEHS. In 2018 grant supplements were awarded to NLM's university-based training programs to foster curriculum sharing with other NIH-funded training programs, minority-serving institutions, and Information

Schools, and for providing high school and undergraduate students with summer research experiences in areas of biomedical informatics and data science. NLM also supports individual predoctoral fellowships via the National Research Service Awards (NRSA) program; two new awards were made in this program in FY 2018. Two career transition programs are offered to NLM's trainees and others ready to launch their informatics research careers; six career transition awards were made in FY 2018. Taken together, NLM's commitment to training and career transition in FY 2018 represented 33 percent of its extramural grants budget.

In FY 2018 the National Network of Libraries of Medicine (NNLM) launched a new Biomedical and Health Research Data Management Training Program for Librarians. The program provides basic knowledge and skills for librarians interested in helping customers manage their research data through an introduction to data issues and policies in support of developing and implementing or enhancing research data management services. Approximately 70 librarians have been trained since its launch.

Biomedical Informatics Research

NLM's research project grants (RPGs) support pioneering research and development to advance knowledge in biomedical informatics and data science. Complementing mission-oriented initiatives at other institutes and centers at NIH, NLM research grant programs support investigator-initiated innovation in both basic and applied research ranging from small proof-of-concept projects to larger, sustained collaborations, creating and testing approaches and tools that will be valuable to more than one domain of interest. For example, in 2018 NLM supported grant supplements to four investigators to explore methods that can speed research in the NIH HEAL initiative. In 2018 NLM launched a new grant program with focus on computational approaches to digital curation at scale. The first awards will be made in early FY 2019.

In FY 2018 NLM issued 33 new RPGs, including six exploratory/developmental awards. Awards reflect current and expanding investments in data science as well as investment in data science applications for patients. Several of the new awards address data analytic topics, including collaborative filtering for improved information retrieval, 360-degree automated characterization of the built environment, and evidence-based communication of numbers in health. New awards in translational bioinformatics focus on reconstruction and modeling of dynamical molecular networks, inference of molecular mechanisms of complex disease, and panomic analytics for microbiome data. In support of the NIH Next Generation Researcher initiative, NLM awarded new research project support to eight early-stage investigators.

NLM sets aside funds to support small business innovation and research and technology transfer (SBIR/STTR). In FY 2018 NLM met its required set-aside by funding five new SBIR/STTR awards; NLM's allocation of funds for SBIR/STTR was more than $1 million. The new projects center on decision support for real-time trauma resuscitation, a block-chain enabled health care network for population health data, and a home-based monitoring system for children with cerebral palsy.

Reaching More People More Ways

In 2017 NLM issued its first new data science funding announcement, Data Science Research: Personal Health Libraries for Consumers and Patients. Three awards were made in 2017: focused application of data science methods for improving patient and caregiver engagement, personal health records for individuals with multiple chronic conditions and for youth leaving foster care. In 2018 five new awards were made in this program in areas such as Spanish-language smart phone access to health information, personalized Web service for epilepsy patients, and personalized health maps for patients with diabetes.

Research Management and Support (RMS)

RMS activities provide administrative, budgetary, logistical, and scientific support for basic library services, intramural research programs, and the review, award, and monitoring of research grants and training awards. RMS functions also include strategic planning, coordination, and evaluation of NLM's programs, regulatory compliance, policy development, and international coordination and liaison with other federal agencies, Congress, and the public. These activities are conducted by the NLM Director and immediate staff, as well as NLM personnel from the Office of Extramural Programs, the Office of Administrative Management, the Office of Health Information Programs Development, and the Office of Communications and Public Liaison.

NLM Strategic Plan

In FY 2018 NLM released the NLM Strategic Plan 2017–2027: A Platform for Biomedical Discovery and Data-Powered Health, which will further position the Library to carry out its congressionally mandated mission and support the important work of NIH by creating a future in which data and information transform and accelerate biomedical discovery and improve health and health care. Developed with input from hundreds of stakeholders and advisers, including librarians, informatics professionals, biomedical and data scientists, clinicians, public health specialists, NLM staff, and the public at large, the strategic plan charts a pathway towards NLM's third century.

The strategic plan focuses on three essential, interdependent goals that will help guide the Library's priorities over the next ten years as it pursues its mission of collecting and integrating an expanding set of information resources and enables them to be analyzed by tools emerging from the informatics and data science research front. Those goals are to

1. accelerate discovery and advance health through data-driven research;
2. reach more people in more ways through enhanced dissemination and engagement; and
3. build a workforce for data-driven research and health.

NLM leadership is implementing the plan, with the overarching goal of improving and enhancing the Library's research and services.

The NLM Strategic Plan 2017–2027: A Platform for Biomedical Discovery and Data-Powered Health can be found at https://www.nlm.nih.gov/pubs/plan/lrp17/NLM_StrategicReport2017_2027.html.

Administration

The director of NLM, Patricia Flatley Brennan, R.N., Ph.D., is guided in matters of policy by a Board of Regents consisting of ten appointed and nine ex officio members.

United States Government Publishing Office

732 North Capitol St. N.W., Washington, DC 20401
World Wide Web http://www.gpo.gov

Gary Somerset

Chief Public Relations Officer
202-512-1957, e-mail gsomerset@gpo.gov

The U.S. Government Printing Office (GPO) was created when President James Buchanan signed Joint Resolution 25 on June 23, 1860. GPO opened its doors for business nine months later on March 4, 1861, the same day Abraham Lincoln took the oath of office to become the 16th president of the United States. On that day GPO began operation in buildings purchased by Congress, at the same address it occupies today.

A historic moment occurred for GPO in December 2014, when President Barack Obama signed into law a bill changing the agency's name to the U.S. Government Publishing Office. The new name reflects the increasingly prominent role that GPO plays in providing access to government information in digital formats through GPO's govinfo (govinfo.gov), apps, e-books, and related technologies. The information needs of Congress, federal agencies, and the public have evolved beyond only print, and GPO has transformed itself to meet its customers' needs.

Under Title 44 of the United States Code, GPO is responsible for the production and distribution of information products for all three branches of the federal government. These include the official publications of Congress, federal agencies, and the courts. Today GPO provides products in print and a variety of digital forms, all of which are born digital. In addition, GPO produces passports for the Department of State and secure credentials for many government agencies. As the federal government's official resource for gathering, producing, cataloging, providing access to, and preserving published information in all forms, GPO has disseminated millions of publications to the public. GPO's Superintendent of Documents and its Library Services and Content Management (LSCM) organizations administer and manage the four programs required by Title 44:

- The Federal Depository Library Program (FDLP)
- Cataloging and indexing (C&I)
- Distributing government publications to the International Exchange Service
- The By-Law Program, under which certain government publications are distributed to members of Congress and to other government agencies as mandated by law

The Federal Depository Library Program (FDLP) dates back to 1813, when Congress first authorized legislation to ensure the provision of certain congressional documents to selected universities, historical societies, and state libraries. At that time, the secretary of state was responsible for distributing publications. In 1857 the secretary of the interior assumed oversight of printing and the designation of depositories. In the Printing Act of 1895 the governance of the depository program was transferred to the Office of the Superintendent of Documents at

GPO. Duties remained largely unchanged until 1993, when Public Law 103-40, the Government Printing Office Electronic Information Access Enhancement Act, amended GPO's duties to not only provide public access to printed publications but to Internet-accessible publications as well.

Two centuries after the start of FDLP, the program continues to serve a vital need of the public through the partnership with federal depository libraries located in nearly every congressional district. GPO is obviously a much different agency in the digital age than it was years ago. While its name has changed, its mission—"Keeping America Informed"—is as important and relevant as ever. The FDLP and GPO's information dissemination programs are examples of the agency's long-standing commitment to permanent public access to U.S. government information.

Working with Key Stakeholders: The Libraries in the FDLP

GPO on the GO

Once again, in fiscal year (FY) 2018 GPO staff placed a special emphasis on connecting with our key stakeholders, the federal depository libraries, and we continued our visits to libraries around the country. This is part of our commitment to better support and engage with librarians and library staff at our 1,150 participating libraries in the FDLP. The purpose of these visits is to meet with staff, provide FDLP consultation services, answer questions, and offer advice and support on any topic related to the administration and management of a depository. In FY 2018 we visited 25 states and 166 libraries.

Disaster Preparedness and Response

During FY 2018 GPO created a Disaster Response Plan to assist depository libraries affected by disasters. The plan includes procedures for communicating with depositories and their regionals prior to and following disasters to better assist them with managing temporary closures and the development of the *What to do if . . .* series of information sheets to assist depositories dealing with damage to their collections. Additionally, GPO hosted four paneled webinars featuring members of the depository community who have dealt with disasters. These included fires, floods, weather disasters, theft, and planning and preparation. The panels' efforts and participation in these webinars are truly appreciated.

Partnerships with Federal Depository Libraries

Since 1997 GPO has developed strategic partnerships with federal depository libraries and other federal agencies to increase access to electronic federal information. These partnerships include cataloging, preservation, digital content, and digital access.

In FY 2018 GPO

- Completed adding bibliographic records for print versions of the Bureau of Mine's *Reports of Investigations from the University of Colorado*. Four thousand four hundred ninety-two records were added during FY 2018.

- Completed work to add bibliographic records from the University of Montana for 12 SuDoc classes.
- Added bibliographic records for electronic versions of the USGS series from the Colorado School of Mines:
  - Professional Papers: 1,430
  - Water Supply Papers: 680
  - USGS Circulars: 223
- Added 183 bibliographic records for publications from the WPA from the University of Kentucky.
- Added 6,556 records for FRASER (partnership with the Federal Reserve Bank of St. Louis).

Twenty libraries became Preservation Stewards:

- Wise Law Library of the University of Colorado Boulder: *United States Statutes at Large, United States Reports, Federal Register, United States Code, Revised Statutes, Kappler's Journal of the Continental Congress*
- Indiana State Library: *Official Gazette of the United States Patent Office*
- University of South Carolina: publications from the Department of Education and its predecessors, the *Annals of Congress, Register of Debates in Congress,* the *Congressional Globe*, and the *Congressional Record*
- U.S. Merchant Marine Academy: publications related to the Merchant Marines
- Law Library for San Bernardino County: *Public Papers of the Presidents*, Proclamations and Executive Orders: Herbert Hoover, and *Proceedings of the United States Senate in the Impeachment Trial of William Jefferson Clinton*
- University of Maine: *Public Papers of the Presidents*
- University of Rhode Island: publications from NOAA
- University of Washington, Gallagher Law Library: *Unites States Statutes at Large*
- Queens Borough Public Library: *Public Papers of the Presidents* and *Handbook of North American Indians*
- Oklahoma State University: publications from the Agricultural Research Service and the Bureau of Indian Affairs
- University of Kansas: Congressional hearings
- Arkansas State University–Jonesboro: NASA Technical Reports
- University of Virginia Library: publications from the Department of State
- North Dakota State University Libraries: *Public Papers of the Presidents* and the *War of the Rebellion* (series 1)
- University of Minnesota Libraries: United States Congressional Serial Set
- University of Maine School of Law Garbrecht Law Library: *United States Reports*

- Rittenberg Library, St. John's University School of Law: Congressional hearings from the 100th Congress through the 103rd Congress
- State Law Library of Mississippi: *United States Reports, United States Statutes at Large*, and *Public Papers of the Presidents*
- Colorado School of Mines, Arthur Lakes Library: Publications from the USGS, Bureau of Mines, ERDA, and Department of Energy
- Department of the Interior Library: Department of the Interior annual reports

Two libraries became Digital Content Contributors:

- University of Florida: various titles
- Oklahoma State University: *Kappler's Indian Laws and Treaties*

One library became a Digital Access Partner:

- Cleveland Public Library: hosting a digitized version of the *First United States Army: Report of Operations*

FDLP Academy

GPO's FDLP Academy is the FDLP community's source for training opportunities, events, webinars, and webcasts. In FY 2018 the FDLP Academy hosted 85 webinars, with more than 10,214 combined registrants.

FDLP Academy Training Repository

In FY 2018 GPO staff migrated the FDLP Academy webinar archive to a new platform, the FDLP Academy Training Repository, in order to improve the user interface and allow for greater searching and browsing capability.

Access the new FDLP Academy Training Repository at https://www.fdlp.gov/fdlp-academy/fdlp-academy-training-repository.

Features include

- A search field
- Subject and agency tags to assist in finding training by subject or presentations by federal agencies
- Recordings in MP4 format (no longer requiring a plug-in to view)
- Sorting options by date and title
- Conference recordings and webinar recordings in one location

FDLP Coordinator Certificate Program

The FDLP Coordinator Certificate Program provides in-depth, virtual classes on managing depository collections in compliance with the Legal Requirements and

Program Regulations of the FDLP. A total of 88 participants—41 participants in the spring 2018 cohort and 47 participants in the fall 2017 cohort—received a certificate of completion from the FDLP Coordinator Certificate Program in FY 2018. Since its inception in 2015, 170 FDLP community members have completed the program.

FDLP LibGuides

FDLP LibGuides is a service provided by GPO for depository libraries and the public. Guides are created by LSCM staff on a variety of topics, including those requested by the community. All guides are available for free use by the community. Libraries and agencies can also submit their own guides for inclusion on the FDLP LibGuides Community page.

In FY 2018 FDLP LibGuides had more than 4,900 views to the 19 guides offered. There are eight new guides in the queue that the FDLP LibGuides team is working to add to the collection on topics such as elections and voting, volcanoes, and the FDLP Web Archive. Forty Community Guides have been submitted in ten Subject areas.

Cataloging Record Distribution Program

The Cataloging Record Distribution Program provides GPO-produced catalog records to participating federal depository libraries, at no cost to the libraries, through a contract with MARCIVE, Inc. Currently, 185 federal depository libraries, or 16 percent of all depositories, are participating in the program.

govinfo

GPO's govinfo (govinfo.gov) provides free online access to official publications from the three branches of the federal government. The content in govinfo is available in multiple formats including PDF, XML, audio, and photographs. govinfo provides access to digitized historical content and serial publications that are updated daily. GPO adds content to govinfo regularly and continuously implements enhancements to system functionality. govinfo offers the public access to approximately 50 collections of government information, and more than 10 million documents are indexed by the govinfo search engine.

GPO staff has continued work to increase content in govinfo in FY 2018. Here are a few highlights of the new content available:

- GPO, in cooperation with the Library of Congress, has completed the digitization of all the historical issues of the bound *Congressional Record* dating back to 1873. The final release, which covered 1873–1890, was completed and made available on January 3, 2018.
- GPO, in cooperation with the National Archives' Office of the Federal Register (OFR), completed the release of the digitized issues of the *Federal Register*. The final release, which covers 1936–present, was April 11, 2018.

- In collaboration with the Office of the Legislative Counsel of the U.S. House of Representatives, the Office of the Legislative Counsel of the U.S. Senate, the Clerk of the House, and the Secretary of the Senate, GPO made select Statute Compilations available as a pilot on govinfo. These publications are compilations of public laws that either do not appear in the U.S. Code or that have been classified to a title of the U.S. Code that has not been enacted into positive law. Each Statute Compilation incorporates the amendments made to the underlying statute since it was originally enacted. An initial set of 40 compilations is now available, and additional Statute Compilations will be added to this collection over time.
- New Series of Precedents of the U.S. House of Representatives—H. Doc. 115-62—*Precedents of the U.S. House of Representatives* (2017 series), Volume 1, Chapters 1–4.
- H. Doc. 108-226—*Asian and Pacific Islander Americans in Congress*, 1900–2017—available in PDF and ePub formats.
- CFR Index and Finding Aids 2018.
- *Budget of the U.S. Government, Fiscal Year 2019.*
- New landing page for easy access to the Senate Journal.
- *Congressional Directory and Congressional Pictorial Directory for the 115th Congress.*

GPO continues to work with Digital Content Contributor partners to add digitized content to govinfo, including:

- *Indian Affairs: Laws and Treaties* (completed and edited by Charles J. Kappler): This is a compilation containing U.S. treaties, laws, and executive orders pertaining to Native American Indian tribes. The volumes cover U.S. government treaties with Native Americans from 1778–1883 (Volume II) and U.S. laws and executive orders concerning Native Americans from 1871–1970 (Volumes I, III–VII). A supplement compiling Code of Federal Regulations related to Native Americans was published in 1975. The volumes were digitized by the Edmon Low Library at the Oklahoma State University.
- Panama Canal–related publications: This year we completed the collection of Panama Canal–related publications from our partner, the University of Florida. In this final ingest, over 670 packages were added.

GPO has also awarded a contract for the audit and certification of FDsys/govinfo under the ISO 16363:2012 standard. The kick-off meeting for the contract was held in January, and the audit began on June 18. GPO completed Stage 1 of the audit in August 2018 and began Stage 2 in fall 2018. GPO anticipates becoming the first federal agency to become ISO 16363 certified in FY 2019.

Web Archiving

GPO continues to harvest digital publications and websites, thereby advancing FDLP collection development efforts.

In FY 2018 GPO

- Increased the size of the FDLP Web Archive collection to 17.1 TB, with 139 million URLs crawled.
- Increased website collections available on the FDLP Web Archive on Archive-It to 165 and 211 records available through the CGP.

National Bibliographic Records Inventory Initiative

Through the National Bibliographic Records Inventory Initiative (NBRII), GPO is

1. Identifying fugitive U.S. government publications (e.g., published federal agency materials within the scope of the FDLP and the Cataloging and Indexing Program for which agencies have not notified GPO of publication or provided GPO copies) and pre-1976 titles not in the CGP that fall within GPO's program responsibilities
2. Inventorying historical publications at GPO

In FY 2018 work continued on a variety of projects and tasks to identify and catalog fugitive and historic material for inclusion in the CGP, including the transcription of Historic Shelflist.

Catalog of U.S. Government Publications

The Catalog of U.S. Government Publications (CGP) (catalog.gpo.gov) is the finding tool for locating publications produced by the federal government, both current and historic. Students, researchers, community leaders, and anyone who needs to find information published by the U.S. government can get help from a great online resource. You can access library catalog records on a wide range of topics including defense, citizenship, U.S. laws, health, science, and more from CGP. There are also direct links to the documents—unless the publication exists only in print. People who need or prefer a print document can learn where to find the nearest federal depository library from the CGP. The CGP even has a feature called MetaLib that lets you research and retrieve reports, articles, and citations by searching across multiple U.S. government databases at once. What's more, there's a collection of U.S. government e-books from a variety of federal agencies, all free to access.

There were nearly 29 million (28,807,616) successful searches of the CGP in FY 2018.

A new service was launched in October 2017 to provide sets of bibliographic records from the CGP free of charge on a monthly basis via the GPO's CGP on GitHub repository site. This program replaced the GPO Cataloging Data Subscription Service. The CGP on GitHub datasets contain records produced by GPO staff according to national standards such as Resource Description and Access (RDA) and Anglo-American Cataloging Rules (AACR2) and include GPO Historic Shelflist project brief bibliographic records and other retrospective records.

The MARC records are available in both UTF-8 character-set (Unicode compliant) and MARC-8 character-set. A description of the record sets is provided in a readme file.

FDLP eXchange

The FDLP eXchange was launched in June 2018, creating an automated process to support the exchange of depository publications nationwide and to facilitate communication among federal depository libraries.

In regions that have adopted the application as part of their disposition process, selective depositories can enter offers for review by their regional depositories. When the regional selective has completed its review, unneeded materials move on to review by other selectives in the region. Materials not claimed by the regional or other selectives in the region move on to be offered nationally if the library has chosen to offer materials outside their region. All libraries can post needs and receive notification when their need matches another library's offer.

Libraries in regions that have not adopted FDLP eXchange for their disposition process may still use FDLP eXchange to offer materials nationally after they have been offered within their region and remain unclaimed. These libraries may also post needs to receive notification when their need matches another library's offer.

GPO provides access to a variety of training and informational resources on the new tool, such as

- Templates to upload Needs and Offers
- Recorded training webinars
- Tutorial task-based videos
- QuickStart Guides with screenshots and explanations
- Frequently asked questions
- Tips of the Week

New Classification Guidelines

Newly revised Classification Guidelines for the Superintendent of Documents (SuDocs) classification system were launched in August 2018. These new guidelines are a revision of the 1993 *GPO Classification Manual*. The system was originally developed in the late 1890s at GPO to classify and organize U.S. government publications by government author.

The Classification Guidelines are born-digital; this online format greatly expands access and facilitates subsequent updates.

Features include

- Updated SuDocs examples used in each section link to CGP catalog records.
- The Table of Contents structure lets the user preview and expand each topic and navigate directly to individual sections and sub-sections.

- The "Resources" section links to reference sources used in researching classification numbers.
- The guidance described represents the current and authoritative version of SuDocs classification rules.
- The format is print-friendly, and individual articles can be e-mailed.

National Technical Information Service

U.S. Department of Commerce, Alexandria, VA 22312

Wayne Strickland

Acting Associate Director, Office of Program Management

The National Technical Information Service (NTIS) is the nation's largest and most comprehensive source of government-funded scientific, technical, engineering, and business information produced or sponsored by U.S. and international government sources. NTIS is a federal agency within the U.S. Department of Commerce.

NTIS maintains a permanent archive of this declassified information for researchers, businesses, and the public to access quickly and easily. Release of the information is intended to promote U.S. economic growth and development and to increase U.S. competitiveness in the world market.

The NTIS collection of more than 2.5 million titles contains products available in various formats. Such information includes reports describing research conducted or sponsored by federal agencies and their contractors; statistical and business information; multimedia training programs; databases developed by federal agencies; and technical reports prepared by research organizations worldwide. NTIS maintains a permanent repository of its information products.

More than 200 U.S. government agencies contribute to the NTIS collection, including the National Aeronautics and Space Administration; the Environmental Protection Agency; the Departments of Agriculture, Commerce, Defense, Energy, Health and Human Services, Homeland Security, Interior, Labor, Treasury, Veterans Affairs, Housing and Urban Development, Education, and Transportation; and numerous other agencies.

NTIS on the Web

NTIS offers Web-based access to federal information and data on scientific, business and technical research products at http://www.ntis.gov.

NTIS Database

The NTIS Database offers unparalleled bibliographic coverage of U.S. government and worldwide government-sponsored research information products acquired by NTIS since 1964. Its contents represent hundreds of billions of research dollars and cover a range of important topics including agriculture, biotechnology, business, communication, energy, engineering, the environment, health and safety, medicine, research and development, science, space, technology, and transportation.

The NTIS Database can be leased directly from NTIS and can also be accessed through several commercial services. To lease the NTIS Database directly from NTIS, contact the NTIS Office of Program Management at 800-553-6847.

NTIS National Technical Reports Library

As of 2018 the National Technical Reports Library (NTRL) contains approximately 3 million publications, which includes 970,000 documents (representing 3.2 terabytes of data) that have been digitized for online distribution. For publication records, which do not yet include a downloadable document, NTIS will (upon request) convert the archived paper documentation into a publicly available, online digital format. Collectively, the entire clearinghouse process, bibliographic information, and online dissemination are provided at no charge to the public.

Through its stewardship of NTRL, which extends back to the 1950s, NTIS recognizes both its public responsibility as well as the continued desire within research, academic, and government communities to access this vast clearinghouse of historic government research and technical information.

Not surprisingly, today's NTRL program has migrated online after decades as a paper-based collection. NTIS was originally called the Publication Board as established in 1945. In 1964 NTIS set a new precedent by designing the first major computerized database of scientific and technical information. In the 1990s, NTIS began digitizing full-text copies of publications. In 2009 NTIS released its first online subscription service, which provided full-text, downloadable documents. In 2016 NTIS removed its cost-recovery subscription service and began providing free, public access to the entire NTRL clearinghouse.

The current NTRL collection spans a wide variety of topics, which include categories for Aeronautics, Chemistry, Energy, Environmental, Health Care, Library and Information Sciences, Mathematics, Medicine and Biology, Physics, and Transportation—to name a few. In total there are 39 major subject categories and 375 subcategories. On a weekly basis NTIS updates the NTRL database, and approximately 30,000 reports are added each year to the NTRL electronic clearinghouse.

Regarding legal authorities, Chapter 23 of Title 15 of the United States Code (15 U.S.C. 1151–1157) codified NTIS's basic authority to operate a permanent clearinghouse of scientific and technical information. This chapter also established NTIS's authority to charge fees for its products and services and to recover all costs through such fees "to the extent feasible." This authority was restated in the National Technical Information Act of 1988, codified as 15 U.S.C. 3704b. That act gave NTIS the authority to enter into joint ventures and declared the clearinghouse to be a permanent federal function that could not be eliminated or privatized without congressional approval.

The American Technology Preeminence Act of 1992 (Public Law 102-245): (1) required all costs associated with bibliographic control to be recovered by fees; (2) required agencies to make copies of their scientific and technical reports available to NTIS; and (3) directed NTIS to focus on developing new electronic methods and media for disseminating information.

Since NTIS discontinued its cost-recovery efforts in 2016 for NTRL (which historically utilized a fee-based subscription model), NTIS has been providing the public NTRL service for free while continuously exploring alternative funding models and partnerships to minimize operating loss and maintain this valued U.S. government-sponsored collection. In recent years, NTIS succeeded in cost-saving efforts that helped dramatically lower operating losses. In fiscal year (FY) 2019 and FY 2020 NTIS will move NTRL into a cloud infrastructure in order to further reduce costs.

Key NTIS/NTRL Contacts

Phone

Program Assistants	800-553-6847
8:30 A.M.–5:00 P.M. eastern time, Monday–Friday	703-605-6000

Fax

24 hours a day, seven days a week	703-605-6900

To verify receipt of fax, call 703-605-6090,
7:00 A.M.–5:00 P.M. eastern time, Monday–Friday

Mail

National Technical Information Service
5301 Shawnee Rd.
Alexandria, VA 22312

National Archives and Records Administration

700 Pennsylvania Ave. N.W., Washington, DC 20408
1-86-NARA-NARA or 1-866-272-6272
World Wide Web https://www.archives.gov

The National Archives and Records Administration (NARA), an independent federal agency, is the nation's record keeper. NARA safeguards and preserves the important records of all three branches of the federal government so that the people can discover, use, and learn from this documentary heritage. NARA ensures continuing access to records that document the rights of American citizens, the actions of government officials, and the history of the nation.

NARA carries out its mission through a national network of archives and records centers stretching from Boston to San Francisco and Atlanta to Seattle, in addition to 13 presidential libraries that document administrations back to that of Herbert Hoover—a total of 44 facilities nationwide.

The agency includes the National Historical Publications and Records Commission (NHPRC), the grant-making arm of NARA; the Office of the Federal Register, which publishes the official records of the actions of the government; the Information Security Oversight Office (ISOO), which oversees the government's classification programs; the National Declassification Center (NDC), which is streamlining the declassification process; and the Office of Government Information Services (OGIS), which reviews agencies' Freedom of Information Act (FOIA) administration and practices.

NARA also assists federal agencies, the courts, and Congress in documenting their activities by providing records storage, offering reference service, administering records management programs, scheduling records, and retiring noncurrent records to federal records centers. NARA also provides training, advice, and guidance on many issues relating to records management.

NARA's constituents and stakeholders include educators and their students at all levels, a history-minded public, family historians, the media, the archival community, and a broad spectrum of professional associations and researchers in such fields as history, political science, law, library and information services, and genealogy.

The size and breadth of NARA's holdings are staggering. NARA's electronic records holdings amount to nearly 700 terabytes of data, which includes the 2000 and 2010 census questionnaire images. This consists of records that were "born digital" and managed in a digital form throughout their life cycle.

In addition, NARA maintains traditional holdings that will be converted to digital form for preservation purposes and to ensure access to them far into the future. This, along with the ever-growing quantity of "born digital" records, creates a big data challenge for NARA and the federal government.

NARA's current traditional holdings include more than 13 billion pages, 40 million photographs, 600,000 artifacts, and 300,000 reels of motion picture films. In addition, 18 Federal Records Centers (FRCs), located around the country, provide storage for about 26 million cubic feet of noncurrent records for 200 federal agencies.

NARA issued its Strategic Plan for fiscal years (FY) 2018 through 2022, which sets its long-term objectives. It has four strategic goals: Make Access Happen, Connect with Customers, Maximize NARA's Value to the Nation, and Build Our Future through Our People. Specific initiatives are under way at NARA to reach each goal.

Records and Access

Information Security Oversight Office

The Information Security Oversight Office (ISOO) is responsible to the president for policy and oversight of the government-wide security classification system, the National Industrial Security Program, and the emerging federal policy on "controlled unclassified information" (CUI). ISOO receives policy and program guidance from the assistant to the president for national security affairs and National Security Council staff in the Executive Office of the President.

ISOO oversees the security classification programs (classification, safeguarding, and declassification) in both government and industry. It is also responsible for exercising NARA's authorities and responsibilities as the executive agent for controlled unclassified information. ISOO contributes materially to the effective implementation of the government-wide security classification program and has a direct impact on the performance of thousands of government employees and contract personnel who work with classified national security information. For more information on ISOO, visit archives.gov/isoo.

National Declassification Center

In December 2009 Executive Order 13526 established the National Declassification Center (NDC) within the National Archives to address declassification of classified federal government records. The focus of this effort was to promote transparency and accountability of records created by the Executive Branch of the U.S. government.

NDC led a process that streamlined the declassification review processes for classified historical records and eliminated a 350-million-page backlog at the National Archives. The NDC is committed to completing QA on all accessioned classified records no later than one year after they have been transferred to our custody. To date they have met that goal for records received annually from 2014 through 2016. To facilitate public access to these records, the NDC established an "Indexing on Demand" process that allows a researcher to request priority indexing and release for eligible record series.

The NDC also processes requests for classified records under the Freedom of Information Act (FOIA) and Mandatory Review Provisions of Executive Order 13526 (MDR). To respond to these requests, the NDC works closely with other agencies to ensure exempted records are reviewed by the appropriate equity agency, then processes declassified and redacted records for release. For more information about NDC, go to archives.gov/declassification.

Office of Government Information Services

As the FOIA Ombudsman, OGIS educates stakeholders about the FOIA process, resolves disputes, and assesses agency compliance.

The Open Government Act of 2007 created OGIS within the National Archives. The statute requires that OGIS offer mediation services to help resolve FOIA disputes and review agency FOIA policies and procedures. FOIA also charges OGIS with identifying methods to improve compliance with the statute.

The OGIS director chairs the FOIA Federal Advisory Committee. The Committee brings together FOIA experts from inside and outside of government to identify major issues with the implementation of FOIA and develop consensus solutions. The OGIS director also serves as the co-chair of the Chief FOIA Officers Council.

For more information about OGIS, visit archives.gov/ogis or follow OGIS on Twitter @FOIA_Ombuds.

Electronic Records Archives

NARA uses the Electronic Records Archives (ERA) system to take in and store electronic records from the White House, Congress, and agencies across the federal government. In addition, since 2012, NARA has required all federal agencies to use ERA to submit records schedules to NARA for approval by the Archivist of the United States. The adoption of ERA by federal agencies and the use of ERA to support the transfer of electronic presidential records have led to the transfer of increasing volumes of electronic records to NARA for preservation and eventual access through its public access portal, the National Archives Catalog (NAC).

NARA has launched a new system, ERA 2.0, to update and enhance the agency's capabilities to meet the ever-expanding challenges in preserving born-electronic records and digitized material. ERA 2.0 uses cloud services for greater scalability in terms of storage and computer processing to increase NARA's ability to preserve and provide access to greater amounts of digital material over time. The ERA 2.0 system consists of three major components: a digital processing environment, a digital object repository, and a business object management component. The processing component provides the capability to upload digital material of all types, gives staff a variety of software tools for verification and processing, supports the creation and editing of metadata, and allows users to submit packages of processed digital material to the repository component for preservation. The repository supports the capability to ingest processed digital material to provide for safe archival storage, delivers advanced staff search and discovery capabilities, provides digital material for further processing for preservation, and makes copies of records available for public access through the NAC. The business object management component, slated for deployment in late 2020, will provide a redesign of the online forms and approval workflows used by NARA and federal agencies to schedule and transfer records to NARA. For more information about ERA, see archives.gov/era.

Applied Research Division

NARA's Applied Research Division serves as the agency's center for advanced and applied research capabilities in the fields of computer science, engineering, and archival science. The division's staff conducts research on new technologies, both to be aware of new types of electronic record formats that will need to be preserved and to evaluate new technologies that might be incorporated into electronic records management and preservation systems at NARA to increase their effectiveness. The staff also helps NARA managers and employees acquire the knowledge and skills they need to function effectively in e-government through presentations on new technologies. For more information, visit archives.gov/applied-research.

NARA's Website

The online entrance to the National Archives is archives.gov, which provides the most widely available means of electronic access to information about and services available from NARA. Links to various sections provide help to the particular needs of researchers, including veterans and their families, educators and students, and the general public—as well as records managers, journalists, historians, and members of Congress.

The NARA website provides the following:

- Directions on how to contact NARA and conduct research at its facilities around the country
- Direct access to certain archived electronic records at archives.gov/aad
- Digital copies of selected archived documents
- A contact form, at archives.gov/contact, for customer questions, reference requests, comments, and complaints
- Electronic versions of *Federal Register* publications
- Online exhibits
- Selected articles on U.S. history from *Prologue* (archives.gov/publications/prologue), the agency's quarterly magazine
- Classroom resources for students and teachers at archives.gov/education
- Online tools such as eVetRecs (archives.gov/veterans/military-service-records), which allows veterans and their next-of-kin to complete and print, for mail-in submission, requests for their military service records

Copies of military pension records from the American Revolution through World War I, census pages, land files, court records, and microfilm publications can be ordered online at archives.gov/shop. Researchers can also submit reference questions about various research topics online. Across NARA's entire Web presence, in FY 2018 NARA welcomed 37 million Web users and received more than 127 million page views on its websites.

Public Access Projects

NARA's Office of Innovation is responsible for oversight of the digitization of NARA's holdings and for ensuring public access through the National Archives Catalog (catalog.archives.gov). The Office of Innovation is constantly developing improved tools, techniques, and workflows to accelerate access. In FY 2018 over 18 million pages were added to the National Archives Catalog resulting in a total of over 53 million pages available to the public. A key advance in improving NARA's capacity to accelerate access was groundbreaking work with the use of specialized portable storage devices (Amazon snowballs). Using these devices allowed NARA to move the images and metadata from nearly 600 hard drives into the catalog during FY 2018. In the coming years the Office of Innovation will continue to find new ways to improve digitization and access as we work toward our strategic goal of 500 million pages available in the catalog by the end of FY 2024 (for more information see https://www.archives.gov/about/plans-reports/strategic-plan).

Engagement with "citizen archivists" also represents a critical component to improving access. In FY 2018 over 122,000 pages were enhanced by the public through tagging, transcribing, and commenting. These additions from the public help make NARA's holdings more discoverable to researchers through the addition of critical metadata and transcribed text.

The History Hub (History.gov) is another tool that helps expand access to the nation's history and to NARA's holdings. After registering on the History Hub, individuals can submit questions about U.S. History; the platform allows responses from NARA staff, staff at other participating cultural heritage organizations such as the Library of Congress, and the public. This crowdsourced platform helps eliminate the silos that exists between information residing at different organizations and allows researchers, citizen historians, and archival professionals to more easily find answers to the questions they have.

Social Media

NARA uses multiple social media platforms to increase access to the records in its holdings, which is at the heart of its mission. The main goals of social media at NARA are to increase awareness about archival holdings and programs and to enrich the agency's relationship with the public through conversations about its services and holdings. In addition to expanding access, use of social media creates a more collaborative work environment and increases communication and knowledge sharing both within NARA and externally with other federal agencies.

The National Archives has 18 blogs, including one by the Archivist of the United States. NARA also offers historical videos from its holdings and videos of recent public events on the agency's ten YouTube channels. The agency shares photographs and documents from its collections through Flickr Commons. Across the country, more than 200 NARA staff contribute actively to the agency's 130 social media accounts, including Facebook, Twitter, Tumblr, Instagram, and others.

Followers can also use Really Simple Syndication (RSS) feeds of the "Document for Today" feature, NARA news, and press releases. Several mobile apps and e-books have been developed and are available free of charge in the iTunes store and Android Market for Today's Document, DocsTeach, and recent exhibits.

Social media also allow NARA's researchers, friends, and the public to become citizen archivists by tagging, sharing, and transcribing documents. For more information, go to archives.gov/citizen-archivist.

Additional information about NARA's social media projects is available at archives.gov/social-media.

National Archives Museum

The National Archives Museum, a set of interconnected resources made possible by a public–private partnership between NARA and the National Archives Foundation, provides a variety of ways to explore the power and importance of the nation's records.

The Rotunda for the Charters of Freedom at the National Archives Building in Washington, D.C., is the centerpiece of the National Archives Museum. On display are the Declaration of Independence, the Constitution, and the Bill of Rights—known collectively as the Charters of Freedom. The Public Vaults is a 9,000-square-foot permanent exhibition that conveys the feeling of going beyond the walls of the Rotunda and into the stacks and vaults of the working archives. Dozens of individual exhibits, many of them interactive, reveal the breadth and variety of NARA's holdings.

Complementing the Public Vaults, the Lawrence F. O'Brien Gallery hosts a changing array of topical exhibits based on National Archives records. The 290-seat William G. McGowan Theater is a showplace for NARA's extensive audiovisual holdings and serves as a forum for lectures and discussions.

An expanded museum shop opened in 2012, and a new exhibition gallery and visitor orientation plaza opened in 2013. The David M. Rubenstein Gallery houses a permanent interactive exhibit, "Records of Rights," which documents the struggles and debates over civil rights and liberties throughout American history. The Rubenstein Gallery is also the new home for a 1297 copy of the Magna Carta, owned by Rubenstein.

Inside the Boeing Learning Center, the ReSource Room is an access point for teachers and parents to explore documents found in the exhibits and to use NARA records as teaching tools. The center's Constitution-in-Action Learning Lab is designed to provide an intense field trip adventure for middle and high school students that links to curriculum in the classroom.

DocsTeach (docsteach.org) is an education website designed to provide instruction to teachers in the best practices of teaching with primary sources. Using documents in NARA's holdings as teachable resources, DocsTeach strongly supports civic literacy. This tool gives all teachers access to primary sources, instruction in best practices, and opportunities to interact with their counterparts across the nation.

When developing the DocsTeach site, the agency established an online community that served as a virtual meeting place for NARA's education team and colleagues from schools, institutions, and organizations nationwide to collaborate and share innovative ideas and best practices for this online resource.

The National Archives' New York City field office is located in the Alexander Hamilton U.S. Custom House at the southern tip of Manhattan. There, NARA has a large research center as well as diverse educational and program activities offered for free in the Learning Center. The new Learning Center incorporates many of the resources and activities found in the Washington, D.C., building but also includes New York–specific offerings.

At its Kansas City, Missouri, field office at 400 West Pershing Road, NARA also has a welcome center, changing exhibitions, workshops, and other public programs.

A set of web pages now makes the National Archives Museum available anywhere. An illustrated history of the Charters of Freedom can be found there, as well as information on educational programs, special events, and current exhibits at the National Archives.

Those traveling to Washington can bypass the public line during peak tourist season by making online reservations at recreation.gov. For more information, see "The National Archives Museum" at archives.gov/museum. An online version of the "Records of Rights" exhibition is available at recordsofrights.org.

NARA facilities hosted about 3.9 million physical visitors in FY 2018, of which approximately three million were headed to exhibits. More than a million visited the National Archives Museum in Washington, D.C.

National Archives Research Centers

At the Robert M. Warner Research Center in the National Archives Building in Washington, D.C., and the Steny Hoyer Research Center at the National Archives at College Park, Maryland, researchers can consult with staff experts on federal records held in each building and submit requests to examine original documents.

The Warner Research Center holds approximately 275,000 rolls of microfilmed records, documenting military service prior to World War I, immigration into the United States, the federal census, the U.S. Congress, federal courts in the District of Columbia, the Bureau of Indian Affairs, and the Freedmen's Bureau. The center also contains an extensive, ever-expanding system of reference reports, helping researchers conduct research in federal documents.

Executive branch records housed in the National Archives Building include those of the Bureau of Indian Affairs and of civilian agencies responsible for maritime affairs. Military records in this building include records of the Army before World War I and the Navy and Marine Corps before World War II. In addition, the National Archives Building holds many records relating to the federal government's interaction with individuals; these are often consulted for genealogical research.

The Hoyer Research Center in College Park holds textual records of civilian agencies from 1789; investigative records and military holdings that include records from the Army and Army Air Forces dating from World War I and Navy, Marine Corps, intelligence, defense-related, and seized enemy records dating from World War II. In addition to textual records, special media records include motion pictures, still photographs and posters, sound recordings, maps, architectural drawings, aerial photographs, and electronic records. A research room for accessioned microfilm holds records of the Department of State's Berlin Document Center and other World War II–era captured documents.

Field Archives

NARA has 12 field archives where the public can do research. They are located in or near Boston, New York, Philadelphia, Atlanta, Chicago, St. Louis, Kansas City, Fort Worth, Denver, Riverside (California), San Francisco, and Seattle. Archived records of significance, as well as, in some locations, immigration records, are available for use by the public in these field archives.

Presidential Libraries

NARA operates the libraries and museums of the 13 most recent U.S. presidents, beginning with Herbert Hoover, whose library is in West Branch, Iowa, and maintains the presidential records of the Obama Administration. The others are Franklin D. Roosevelt, Hyde Park, New York; Harry S. Truman, Independence, Missouri; Dwight D. Eisenhower, Abilene, Kansas; John F. Kennedy, Boston; Lyndon Baines Johnson, Austin; Richard Nixon, Yorba Linda, California; Gerald R. Ford, Ann Arbor (library) and Grand Rapids (museum), Michigan; Jimmy Carter, Atlanta; Ronald Reagan, Simi Valley, California; George Bush, College Station, Texas; William J. Clinton, Little Rock; and George W. Bush, Dallas. Unlike other Presidential Libraries administered by NARA, the Barack Obama Presidential Library will be a fully digital library. After the records are digitized, NARA will store and preserve the original materials in an existing NARA facility that meets NARA's standards for archival storage. Staff at that location will be responsible for caring for the records and artifacts. Currently, the Obama administration materials are housed in a temporary facility in Hoffman Estates, IL, which is not open to the public.

In FY 2018 more than two million people visited exhibits in the presidential library museums. At archives.gov/presidential-libraries, visitors can learn about the presidential library system as a whole and link to individual library websites to learn about the lives of the presidents and the times in which they served.

Federal Records Centers Program

NARA also serves federal agencies, the courts, and Congress by providing records storage, reference service, lifecycle management, and guidance on many issues relating to records management.

A network of 18 Federal Records Centers (FRCs) stores approximately 27 million cubic feet (about 69 billion pages) of noncurrent records for 200 agencies. In FY 2018 these records centers replied to nearly ten million requests for information and records, including more than 1.5 million requests for information regarding military and civilian service records provided by the National Personnel Records Center in St. Louis.

The Federal Records Centers Program is nationwide. NARA has records centers in or near Atlanta; Boston; Chicago; Dayton; Denver; Fort Worth; Kansas City; Miamisburg, Ohio; Lee's Summit, Missouri; Lenexa, Kansas; Philadelphia; Pittsfield, Massachusetts; Riverside, California; St. Louis; San Francisco; Seattle; Suitland, Maryland; and Valmeyer, Illinois.

Genealogy Research

Genealogy research brings hundreds of thousands of people to NARA facilities every year. In its holdings NARA has census records dating back to 1790, records dealing with immigration, land and pension records, and passenger lists from ships arriving from all over the world.

NARA is often considered the first stop in searching for one's ancestry, at its facilities in the Washington, D.C., area or one of its 12 field centers around the country. At these locations, NARA staff offers genealogy workshops to show the public how to look through documents dating back to the Revolutionary period.

NARA also offers an annual Genealogy Fair, which is now a "virtual" event at which NARA staff provides tips and techniques for researching genealogy records at the National Archives. Lectures are designed for experienced genealogy professionals and novices alike.

NARA also maintains close relationships with genealogical associations as well as organizations such as Ancestry.com and Fold3, which can be accessed without charge at any NARA location.

The National Archives has the census schedules on microfilm available from 1790 to 1940. (Most of the 1890 Census was destroyed in a Department of Commerce fire, although partial records are available for some states.)

Archives Library Information Center

The Archives Library Information Center (ALIC) provides access to information on American history and government, archival administration, information management, and government documents. ALIC is located in the National Archives at College Park. Customers also can visit ALIC on the Internet at archives.gov/research/alic, where they will find "Reference at Your Desk" Internet links, staff-compiled bibliographies and publications, and an online library catalog. ALIC can be reached by telephone at 301-837-3415.

Government Documents

Government publications are generally available to researchers at many of the 1,250 congressionally designated federal depository libraries throughout the nation. A record set of these publications also is part of NARA's archival holdings. Publications of the U.S. Government (Record Group 287) is a collection of selected publications of government agencies, arranged by the SuDoc classification system devised by the Office of the Superintendent of Documents, U.S. Government Publishing Office (GPO).

The core of the collection is a library established in 1895 by GPO's Public Documents Division. By 1972, when NARA acquired the library, it included official publications dating from the early years of the federal government and selected publications produced for and by federal government agencies. Since 1972 the 25,000-cubic-foot collection has been augmented periodically with accessions of government publications selected by the Office of the Superintendent of Documents as a byproduct of its cataloging activity. As with the federal depository library collections, the holdings in NARA's Record Group 287 comprise only a portion of all U.S. government publications.

NARA Publications

Historically NARA has published guides and indexes to various portions of its archival holdings. Many of these are still in print, though the most up-to-date information about NARA holdings now is available almost exclusively through online searches at archives.gov. The agency also publishes informational leaflets and brochures.

Some publications appear on NARA's website, at archives.gov/publications/online, and many are available from NARA's Customer Service Center in College Park, by calling 800-234-8861 or 866-272-6272 (in the Washington, D.C., area, 301-837-2000) or faxing 301-837-0483. The NARA website's publications homepage (archives.gov/publications) provides more detailed information about available publications and ordering.

General-interest books about NARA and its holdings that will appeal to anyone with an interest in U.S. history, exhibition catalogs, and facsimiles of certain documents are published by the National Archives Foundation. They are for sale at the foundation's myArchives Store in NARA's downtown Washington building and via the NARA website's eStore page at myarchivesstore.org.

Federal Register

The *Federal Register* is the daily gazette of the U.S. government, containing presidential documents, proposed and final federal regulations, and public notices of federal agencies. It is published by the Office of the Federal Register and printed and distributed by GPO. The two agencies collaborate in the same way to produce the annual revisions of the *Code of Federal Regulations* (*CFR*). Free access to the full text of the electronic version of the *Federal Register* and CFR, and to an unofficial, daily-updated electronic *CFR* (the *e-CFR*), is available via fdsys.gov. Federal Register documents scheduled for future publication are available for public inspection at the Office of the Federal Register (800 North Capitol St. N.W., Washington, DC 20002) or online at the electronic Public Inspection Desk (federalregister.gov/public-inspection). Federalregister.gov provides access to proposed rules, and rules published in the *Federal Register* are open for public comment (the website federalregister.gov and the multiagency website regulations.gov also provide means to comment on these documents).

The full catalog of other Federal Register publications is posted at http://www.ofr.gov and includes the *Compilation of Presidential Documents, Public Papers of the Presidents*, slip laws, *United States Statutes at Large*, and the *United States Government Manual*. Printed or microfiche editions of Federal Register publications also are maintained at federal depository libraries (gpo.gov/libraries).

The Public Law Electronic Notification Service (PENS) is a free subscription e-mail service for notification of recently enacted public laws. Varied subscriptions to the daily *Federal Register* are available from federalregister.gov. Additional information about Federal Register programs appears on Facebook (facebook.com/federalregister) and Twitter (@FedRegister).

The Office of the Federal Register also publishes information about its ministerial responsibilities associated with the operation of the Electoral College and ratification of constitutional amendments and provides access to related records. Publication information concerning laws, regulations, and presidential documents and services is available from the Office of the Federal Register (telephone 202-741-6070). Information on Federal Register finding aids, the Electoral College, and constitutional amendments is available through archives.gov/federal-register.

Publications can be ordered by contacting GPO at bookstore.gpo.gov, or by toll-free telephone at 866-512-1800. To submit orders by fax or by mail, see bookstore.gpo.gov/help/index.jsp.

Grants

The National Historical Publications and Records Commission (NHPRC) is the national grants program of the National Archives. The Archivist of the United States chairs the commission and makes grants on its recommendation. NHPRC's 14 other members represent the president (two appointees), the Supreme Court, the Senate and House of Representatives, the departments of State and Defense, the Librarian of Congress, the American Association for State and Local History, the American Historical Association, the Association for Documentary Editing, the National Association of Government Archives and Records Administrators, the Organization of American Historians, and the Society of American Archivists.

The commission's mission is to provide opportunities for the American people to discover and use records that increase understanding of the nation's democracy, history, and culture. Through leadership initiatives, grants, and fostering the creation of new tools and methods, the commission connects the work of the National Archives to the work of the nation's archives. NHPRC grants help archives, universities, historical societies, professional organizations, and other nonprofit organizations to establish or strengthen archival programs, improve training and techniques, preserve and process records collections, and provide access to them through finding aids, digitization of collections, and documentary editions of the papers of significant historical figures and movements in American history. The commission works in partnership with a national network of state archives and state historical records advisory boards to develop a national archival infrastructure. For more information about the Commission, visit archives.gov/nhprc. For more information about the projects it supports, go to facebook.com/nhprc.

Administration

The head of NARA is David S. Ferriero, who was appointed Archivist of the United States in 2009 by President Obama. As of February 28, 2019, the agency employed 2,731 people working at NARA locations around the country.

National Center for Education Statistics

U.S. Department of Education, Institute of Education Sciences
Potomac Center Plaza, 550 12th St. S.W., 4th fl., Washington, DC 20202

Samuel Barbett and Christopher A. Cody
Academic Libraries, Integrated Postsecondary Education Data System

Maura Spiegelman
School Library Media Centers, Schools and Staffing Survey/National Teacher and Principal Survey

In an effort to collect and disseminate more complete statistical information about libraries, the National Center for Education Statistics (NCES) initiated a formal library statistics program in 1989 that included surveys on academic libraries, school library media centers, public libraries, and state libraries. At the end of December 2006, the Public Libraries Survey and the State Library Agencies Survey were officially transferred to the Institute of Museum and Library Services (IMLS). The Academic Libraries Survey and the School Library Media Centers Survey continued to be administered and funded by NCES. However, the School Library Media Centers Survey was incorporated into the School and Staffing Survey (SASS), and the Academic Libraries Survey was incorporated into the Integrated Postsecondary Education Data System (IPEDS).

The library surveys conducted by NCES are designed to provide comprehensive nationwide data on the status of libraries. Federal, state, and local officials, professional associations, and local practitioners use these surveys for planning, evaluating, and making policy. These data are also available to researchers and educators.

Past information about elementary and secondary public school library media centers is available on the School and Staffing Survey website, http://nces.ed.gov/surveys/sass/. The Library Statistics Program's website, http://nces.ed.gov/surveys/libraries, provides links to data search tools, data files, survey definitions, and survey designs for the complete Academic Libraries Survey files from 1996 to 2012. The IPEDS Academic Libraries Information Center, http://nces.ed.gov/ipeds/Section/Alscenter, contains current survey definitions and designs, and the IPEDS Use the Data Website at https://nces.ed.gov/ipeds/Home/UseTheData contains complete data files for the Academic Libraries component beginning in 2014. The two library surveys conducted by NCES are described below.

Academic Libraries

The IPEDS Academic Libraries (AL) component provides descriptive statistics from academic libraries in the 50 states, the District of Columbia, and, if applicable, other U.S. jurisdictions (Guam, the Commonwealth of the Northern Mariana Islands, Puerto Rico, and the U.S. Virgin Islands).

NCES surveyed academic libraries on a three-year cycle between 1966 and 1988. From 1988 to 1998, AL was a component of IPEDS collected on a two-year cycle. From 2000 to 2012, the Academic Libraries Survey (ALS) separated from

IPEDS but remained on a two-year cycle as part of the Library Statistics Program. During this time period, IPEDS and ALS data were still linked by the identification codes of the postsecondary education institutions. In aggregate, these data provide an overview of the status of academic libraries nationally and by state. Beginning with the 2014–2015 collection cycle, AL was reintegrated back into IPEDS, and the AL component became a mandatory, annual survey for all degree-granting Title IV institutions. It was at this time, many questions from the 2012 ALS collections and services sections were removed or revised and survey questions related to library staff were moved to the IPEDS Human Resources (HR) component.

The AL survey collects data on libraries in the entire universe of degree-granting Title IV postsecondary institutions using a Web-based data collection system. The survey component collects counts of books, serials, media, and databases, both in physical and electronic formats. Additionally, academic libraries report on interlibrary loan services. Institutions with reported total library expenditures over zero or institutions that have access to a library collection are required to report collections data, while those with expenditures equal to or greater than $100,000 are required to report collections and detailed expenditures data. Academic libraries report expenditures for salaries, wages, and fringe benefits, if paid from the library budget; materials and services expenditures; operations and maintenance expenditures; and total expenditures.

For the final 2012 ALS data collection, a First Look report, "Academic Libraries: 2012" (NCES 2014-038), was released on the NCES website in February 2014, as were the final data file and documentation for the 2012 ALS (NCES 2014-039). NCES also has a Web-based peer analysis tool for AL called "Compare Academic Libraries" (https://nces.ed.gov/surveys/libraries/compare/) using AL 2012 data. Beginning with the 2014–2015 IPEDS collection cycle, the following First Look reports were released for Academic Libraries:

- "Enrollment and Employees in Postsecondary Institutions, Fall 2014; and Financial Statistics and Academic Libraries, Fiscal Year 2014" (NCES 2016-005)
- "Enrollment and Employees in Postsecondary Institutions, Fall 2015; and Financial Statistics and Academic Libraries, Fiscal Year 2015" (NCES 2017-024)
- "Enrollment and Employees in Postsecondary Institutions, Fall 2016; and Financial Statistics and Academic Libraries, Fiscal Year 2016" (NCES 2018-002)
- "Enrollment and Employees in Postsecondary Institutions, Fall 2017; and Financial Statistics and Academic Libraries, Fiscal Year 2017" (NCES 2019-021)

Finally, AL data from 2014 and on are available via the IPEDS Use the Data website (https://nces.ed.gov/ipeds/Home/UseTheData). Academic library statistics information can be obtained from Christopher A. Cody, Integrated Postsecondary Education Data System, e-mail IPEDS@ed.gov.

School Library Media Centers

National surveys of school library media centers in elementary and secondary schools in the United States were conducted in 1958, 1962, 1974, 1978, and 1986, 1993–1994, 1999–2000, 2003–2004, 2007–2008, and 2011–2012.

NCES, with the assistance of the U.S. Bureau of the Census, conducted the School Library Media Center Survey as part of the Schools and Staffing Survey (SASS). SASS is the nation's largest sample survey of teachers, schools, and principals in K–12 public and private schools. Data from the school library media center questionnaire provide a national picture of public school library staffing, collections, expenditures, technology, and services. Results from the 2011–2012 survey can be found in "Characteristics of Public Elementary and Secondary School Library Media Centers in the United States: Results from the 2011–12 Schools and Staffing Survey" (NCES 2013–315).

NCES also published a historical report about school libraries titled *Fifty Years of Supporting Children's Learning: A History of Public School Libraries and Federal Legislation from 1953–2000* (NCES 2005-311). Drawn from more than 50 sources, this report gives descriptive data about public school libraries since 1953. Along with key characteristics of school libraries, the report also presents national and regional standards, and federal legislation affecting school library media centers. Data from sample surveys are provided at the national, regional, and school levels, and by state.

NCES has recently redesigned the Schools and Staffing Survey into the National Teacher and Principal Survey (NTPS). NTPS will focus on teachers, principals, and the schools in which they work. The redesigned study collects counts of the number of school library media centers. The first NTPS (2015–2016) is currently in the field for data collection. Results will be available in summer of 2017.

Additional information on school library media center statistics can be obtained from Maura Spiegelman, e-mail maura.spiegelman@ed.gov.

NCES has included some library-oriented questions relevant to the library usage and skills of the parent and the teacher instruments of the new Early Childhood Longitudinal Study (ECLS). For additional information, visit http://nces.ed.gov/ecls. Library items also appear in National Household Education Survey (NHES) instruments. For more information about that survey, visit http://nces.ed.gov/nhes.

NCES included a questionnaire about high school library media centers in the Education Longitudinal Study of 2002 (ELS: 2002). This survey collected data from tenth graders about their schools, their school library media centers, their communities, and their home life. The report, "School Library Media Centers: Selected Results from the Education Longitudinal Study of 2002" (ELS: 2002) (NCES 2005-302), is available on the NCES website. For more information about this survey, visit http://nces.ed.gov/surveys/els2002.

How to Obtain Printed and Electronic Products

Reports are currently published in the First Look format. First Look reports consist of a short collection of tables presenting state and national totals, a survey description, and data highlights. NCES also publishes separate, more in-depth studies analyzing these data.

Internet Access

Many NCES publications (including out-of-print publications) and edited raw data files from the library surveys are available for viewing or downloading at no charge through the Electronic Catalog on the NCES website at http://nces.ed.gov/pubsearch.

Ordering Printed Products

Many NCES publications are also available in printed format. To order one free copy of recent NCES reports, contact the Education Publications Center (ED Pubs) at http://www.edpubs.org, by e-mail at edpubs@edpubs.ed.gov, by toll-free telephone at 877-4-ED-PUBS (1-877-433-7827) or TTY/TDD 877-576-7734, by fax at 703-605-6794, or by mail at ED Pubs, P.O. Box 22207, Alexandria, VA 22304.

Many publications are available through the Education Resources Information Clearinghouse (ERIC) system. For more information on services and products, visit the EDRS website at http://www.eric.ed.gov.

Out-of-print publications and data files may be available through the NCES Electronic Catalog on the NCES website at http://nces.ed.gov/pubsearch or through one of the 1,250 federal depository libraries throughout the United States (see http://catalog.gpo.gov/fdlpdir/FDLPdir.jsp). Use the NCES publication number included in the citations for publications and data files to quickly locate items in the NCES Electronic Catalog. Use the GPO number to locate items in a federal depository library.

Defense Technical Information Center

Fort Belvoir, VA 22060
World Wide Web http://www.dtic.mil

The Defense Technical Information Center (DTIC) plays a critical role in enabling the Department of Defense to meet emerging technology challenges and maintain our military's technological edge. DTIC marked fourteen years as a DoD field activity in 2018. The renewal of its field activity charter reaffirmed DTIC's position as DoD's central scientific, research, and engineering information support activity for the under secretary of defense for research and engineering (USD[R&E]). DTIC is responsible for developing, coordinating, and enabling a strong scientific and technical information (STINFO) program for USD(R&E) and the Department of Defense (DoD) scientific & technical (S&T) enterprise. In this role, DTIC sets policy for scientific and technical information (STI) exchanges for the research and engineering (R&E) community. DTIC's aim is to maximize the availability, use, and collaboration of technical information and products resulting from Defense-funded technical activities while ensuring restrictions to safeguard national security, export control, and intellectual property rights.

Since its inception in 1945, DTIC has served as a vital link in the transfer of defense-related information. The center offers engineers, researchers, scientists, information professionals, and those in laboratories, universities, and the acquisition field access to approximately four million research records. DTIC's mission is to aggregate and fuse science and technology data in order to rapidly, accurately, and reliably deliver the knowledge needed to develop the next generation of technologies to support our service members and help assure national security. As a DoD field activity, DTIC is under the office of the USD(R&E).

In 2013 DTIC saw the approval and signing of DoD Instruction 3200.12, "DoD Scientific and Technical Information Program (STIP)." The instruction establishes policy and responsibilities and proposes procedures for DTIC to carry out STIP. The instruction outlines the vital role played by DTIC in collecting, indexing, cataloging, and providing storage for scientific and technical information obtained from DoD components and their contractors, non-DoD organizations, and foreign sources.

The instruction reiterates that DoD should sustain a coordinated program to manage scientific and technical (S&T) information, which will maximize resources while eliminating duplication of efforts by the reuse of DoD research, development, test, and evaluation investments and assets. DoDI 3200.12 can be found on the DoD Issuances website (http://www.esd.whs.mil/Portals/54/Documents/DD/issuances/dodm/320014vol1_2014.pdf).

In 2014 DoD Manual 3200.14, Volume 2, "Principles and Operational Parameters of the DoD Scientific and Technical Information Program (STIP): Information Analysis Centers (IACs)," was updated. The DoD establishes IACs to acquire, digest, analyze, evaluate, synthesize, store, publish, and distribute STI and engineering data in a clearly defined specialized field or subject area of significant DoD interest or concern. Additionally, IACs provide advisory and other user services to their authorized user community. This volume describes the DoD IAC Program and implements its policy, principles, and concepts for procedural functions. This volume is available at http://www.esd.whs.mil/Portals/54/Documents/DD/issuances/dodm/320014vol2.pdf?ver=2017-11-21-114027-747.

Early in 2015 the Defense Acquisition Regulation Supplement clause on Electronic Submission of Technical Reports was updated to require electronic submissions instead of paper copies of approved final scientific or technical reports of research funded by the DoD. This reaffirms the requirement for all final scientific and technical reports on DoD funded research to be submitted to DTIC.

Reaching Customers

DTIC offers its suite of services to a diverse population within the defense community. Because of the nature of the information it handles, some of DTIC's products are only accessible to the federal government and its contractors. While DTIC also has a public website and search, there are advantages to accessing the secured sites. These value-added services include having research performed by trained information professionals and having access to limited (not publicly available) information. More information about who is eligible to access DTIC's suite of products can be found at http://www.dtic.mil/dtic/registration/registration.html.

In addition to individuals in the DoD and federal sectors, DTIC's registered customers can also be found in academia, the intelligence community, military schools, foreign governments (for example, via negotiated agreements with Australia, Canada, France, Germany, the Netherlands, the Republic of Korea, and the United Kingdom).

Who uses DTIC information? Among its more than 25,000 registered users are

- Acquisition instructors
- Active duty military personnel
- Congressional staff
- DoD contractors
- Faculty and students at military schools
- Historians
- Information professionals/librarians
- Logistics management specialists
- Small business owners
- Security managers
- Researchers
- Software engineers and developers

Resources

DTIC's holdings include technical reports on completed research; research summaries of planned, ongoing, and completed work; independent research and development summaries; defense technology transfer agreements; DoD planning documents; DoD directives and instructions; conference proceedings; security classification guides; command histories; and special collections that date back to World War II. DoD-funded researchers are required to search DTIC's collections to ensure that they do not undertake unnecessary or redundant research. The general public can access "unclassified, unlimited" information, including many full-text downloadable documents, through the public DTIC website at http://www.dtic.mil. The information on the site is free of charge, and no registration is required.

Information Sources

DTIC information is derived from many sources, including DoD organizations (civilian and military) and contractors; U.S. government organizations and their contractors; nonprofit organizations working on DoD scientific, research, and engineering activities; academia; and foreign governments. DTIC accepts information in print, nonprint (CDs and DVDs), and electronically over the Web. DTIC gets information from the defense community, for the defense community, on defense topics and more. Having a full range of science and technology and research and development information within the DTIC collection ensures that technological innovations are linked to defense development and acquisition efforts. New research projects can begin with the highest level of information available. This avoids duplication of effort, maximizing the use of DoD project dollars and saving taxpayer dollars.

Creating Tools for DoD

DTIC continues to play a key role in DoD by producing collaboration tools (often not available to the public) to help the defense research and engineering community work in a secure environment. In order to utilize many of these websites, individuals must be eligible to access DTIC's products.

The culture of DoD has encouraged communities to keep their projects closely held. But, in a more networked world, the defense work force needs the tools that will help them create, share, and reuse knowledge developed both within DoD and by its external partners (industry and academia, for example). DTIC has made strides in creating and hosting sites aimed at enhancing the ability of DoD to connect internally and externally. In addition, DTIC is working to map relationships to enable users to access the life cycle of research projects from planning to final results. DTIC employs technology to verify and validate information submitted and improve user confidence in DoD research documentation.

The Research and Engineering (R&E) Gateway provides the means to connect the acquisition enterprise (DoD Labs); Federally Funded Research and Development

Centers (FFRDCs); Program Executive Offices; Acquisition, Technology, and Logistics (AT&L); and Combatant Commands (CCMDs). In an access-controlled environment, all DTIC's unclassified assets, tools, and community interaction capabilities foster innovation, competition, and identification of solutions. DoD conducts research at its 60+ labs, in the FFRDC's, in DTIC's Information Analysis Centers (IACs) through contracts and grants, and across more than a dozen distinct priority area communities of interest. This work is available through the R&E Gateway. In addition, the R&E Gateway offers access to official defense scientific and technical information, collaborative tools, and subject matter experts. The gateway helps the defense S&T community build on past work, collaborate on current projects, and avoid duplication of effort. With better connections within DoD, the development and delivery of technologies to the armed forces can be accelerated. The R&E Gateway is the entry point to DTIC's suite of tools. Some of the tools within the gateway are

- DTIC Collection Search—This tool aids in the quick discovery of public and access-controlled DoD research projects and documents, as well as people (subject matter experts), places (organizations), and content (past and current research) from DoDTechSpace. DTIC continually works to enable additional features within our search capabilities and from commercial partners to improve information discovery and relevance.
- DoDTechipedia—Designed by DTIC in 2008, DoDTechipedia was one of the first DoD scientific and technical wikis. A secure online system, it facilitates transparency and communication among DoD scientists, engineers, program managers, and the armed forces. It helps members of the DoD S&T community collaborate and identify solutions for technology challenges. Among its numerous features are interest area pages for DoD personnel and DoD contractors to work together on challenges and solutions.
- DoDTechSpace—A social business tool, DoDTechSpace is a place for DTIC's customers to collaborate, share, find, and post information. It connects the defense research and engineering community, DoD laboratories, and other DoD agencies, while providing current and next-generation researchers with advanced Web 2.0 tools. Offering real-time discussions on capability needs and solutions, events, and people, this collaborative environment can support community activities, social networking, lessons learned, and discussions.
- DoD Budget Tools—DTIC publishes searchable congressional budget data shortly after its release and offers both public and access-controlled sites to review and analyze DoD research and engineering funding data. The center posts reports from the House and Senate committees that oversee the DoD budget information, all of which can be found on the public site http://www.dtic.mil/congressional_budget. DTIC posts this reformatted budget data within days of its release on the THOMAS legislative information website operated by the Library of Congress. The budget data is thoroughly checked prior to posting, ensuring its accuracy and reliability.
- Defense Innovation Marketplace—The Defense Innovation Marketplace was launched in late 2011 and continues to be used as an online resource (both

public and access-controlled) for "connecting industry with government customers." Creation of this site was a direct result of the "Better Buying Power" initiative within DoD, which called for the department to deliver better value by improving the way it was doing business. In short, industry submits information about DoD-related ideas and projects, which helps DoD to see what industry is working on. The site helps the department plan acquisitions and see what gaps are being encountered in research.

All these tools are available through the R&E Gateway at https://www.dtic.mil. Links are also available through DTIC's public website at http://www.dtic.mil.

DoD Information Analysis Centers (IACs)

Established under DoD Instruction 3200.14, DoD Information Analysis Centers (IACs) serve as a vital resource in providing timely, relevant information directly to users when and where it is needed. IACs serve as a bridge between the service members and the acquisition/research community, providing essential technical analysis and data support to a diverse customer base, to include the Combatant Commands (CCMDs), the Office of the Secretary of Defense, Defense Agencies, and the military services. IACs actively partner and collaborate with Defense R&E focus groups and communities of interest in specialized fields and specific technologies. The IACs create and maintain comprehensive knowledge analysis centers that include historical, technical, scientific, and other data and information collected worldwide. They are staffed with scientists, engineers, and information specialists to provide research and analysis to customers with diverse, complex, and challenging requirements. IAC operations directly support our service members and play an ongoing and critical role in solving key CCMD operational issues such as cybersecurity, unmanned aerial vehicle visual/audible signature reduction, and improvements to the ballistic resistance of body armor.

The IAC Program Management Office at DTIC performs contract acquisition, management, and operational support for IAC contract operations and the technical information that is generated through research and studies. At a time of shrinking budgets and increasing responsibility, IACs are a valuable resource for accessing scientific and technical information culled from efforts to solve new and historic challenges. Direct IAC customer support activities such as Technical Area Task (TAT) order processing, Basic Center Operations (BCO) support, Defense Finance and Accounting Service (DFAS) activities, and contracting/acquisition-related activities are funded in part through partnerships with the Defense R&E community and the annual collection of customer reimbursements for shared direct costs in accordance with the IAC Reimbursable Review Board (IRRB) recommendations, with OSD-COMPT and Office of General Counsel concurrence. This represents the maximum cost sharing with IAC customers allowable, per guidance from the OSD Office of General Counsel. Annual IAC efforts and accomplishments are dependent on the level of participation and collaboration by the R&E community at large. More information on the IACs is available at http://iac.dtic.mil.

Expanding Free Training Opportunities

Webinars have been mainstays of the opportunities offered to DTIC registered users to learn about DTIC's products and services. "DoDTechipedia 101" webinars provide information about the DoD wiki. DTIC has also produced online tutorials to help individuals learn how to use the wiki's key features.

"DTIC Boot Camp: S&T Resources for the DoD Community" offers hands-on training (at DTIC headquarters), including sessions about the center's numerous resources as well as instruction on document submission. This interactive one-day workshop is held monthly for users. DTIC users can request additional training sessions at DTIC headquarters or at their own locations.

DoD Scientific and Technical Information (STINFO) training can be held at DTIC or off-site and provides instruction on the management and conduct of an organizational STINFO program.

Public Access to Federally Funded Research

DTIC is in a leading role for the DoD's efforts to implement public access to published journal articles and digital data from research funded by taxpayers. In this role, DTIC is actively working with partners across the services, components, other federal agencies, and publishers.

DTIC protects and preserves DoD's multi-billion-dollar investment in research, which empowers the acquisition enterprise through innovative tools, information systems, and decision support capabilities. DTIC is uniquely positioned to support and unleash the value of DoD's R&D portfolio.

Education Resources

National Library of Education

Knowledge Utilization Division
National Center for Education Evaluation and Regional Assistance
Institute of Education Sciences, U.S. Department of Education
400 Maryland Ave. S.W., Washington, DC 20202
World Wide Web https://ies.ed.gov/ncee/projects/nle

The U.S. Department of Education's National Library of Education (NLE), created in 1994, is the primary resource center for education information in the federal government, serving the research needs of the Department of Education, the education community, and the public. NLE resides in the National Center for Education Evaluation and Regional Assistance, Institute of Education Sciences.

NLE was created by Public Law 103-227, the Educational Research, Development, Dissemination, and Improvement Act of 1994, and reauthorized under Public Law 107-279, the Education Sciences Reform Act of 2002. The act outlines four primary functions of NLE:

- Collect and archive information, including products and publications developed through, or supported by, the Institute of Education Sciences; and other relevant and useful education-related research, statistics, and evaluation materials and other information, projects, and publications that are consistent with scientifically valid research or the priorities and mission of the institute, and developed by the department, other federal agencies, or entities
- Provide a central location within the federal government for information about education
- Provide comprehensive reference services on matters relating to education to employees of the Department of Education and its contractors and grantees, other federal employees, and the public
- Promote greater cooperation and resource sharing among providers and repositories of education information in the United States

NLE works closely with the Education Resources Information Center (ERIC). ERIC collects and archives information and provides a central location within the federal government for information about education. Because ERIC serves as the major public program, it is covered separately. [See "Education Resources Information Center" beginning on page 101—*Ed.*]

The primary responsibility of NLE is to provide information services to agency staff and contractors, the general public, other government agencies, and other libraries. Located in the agency's headquarters building in Washington, D.C., the library houses current and historical collections and archives of information on education issues, research, statistics, and policy; there is a special emphasis on agency publications and contractor reports, as well as current and historical federal education legislation.

NLE's primary customer base includes about 4,000 department staff nationwide; department contractors performing research; education organizations and media; and academic, special, and government libraries.

Collections

The focus of NLE's collection is on education issues, with an emphasis on research and policy, with some materials on related topics including law, public policy, economics, urban affairs, sociology, history, philosophy, psychology, and cognitive development. In addition to current materials, the collection has books dating from the early 19th century, including approximately 800 books on education research in the United States and more than 25,000 historical textbooks. Some of these books were donated to the library by Henry Barnard, the first U.S. commissioner of education.

NLE maintains collections of historical documents associated with its parent agency, the U.S. Department of Education, having a complete collection of ERIC microfiche; research reports reviewed by the What Works Clearinghouse and special panels; and publications of or relating to the department's predecessor agencies, including the National Institute of Education and the U.S. Office of Education in the Department of Health, Education, and Welfare. These collections include reports, studies, manuals, statistical publications, speeches, and policy papers. NLE also serves as a selective federal depository library under the U.S. Government Publishing Office program.

Services

NLE provides reference and other information services, including legislative reference and statistical information services, to department staff, to the education community at large, and to the general public, as well as offering document delivery services to department staff and interlibrary loan services to other libraries and government agencies.

Contact Information

The U.S. Department of Education Research Library can be contacted by e-mail at askalibrarian@ed.gov. The library's reference desk is available by telephone from 9 A.M. to 5 P.M. weekdays, except federal holidays, at 800-424-1616 (toll free) or 202-205-5015, and by fax at 202-401-0547. For the hearing-impaired, the toll-free number for the Federal Relay Service is 800-877-8339.

Located in the department's headquarters building at 400 Maryland Ave. S.W., the library is open to researchers by appointment from 9 A.M. to 5 P.M. weekdays, except federal holidays.

Education Resources Information Center

Knowledge Utilization Division
National Center for Education Evaluation and Regional Assistance
Institute of Education Sciences, U.S. Department of Education
550 12th St., S.W., Washington, DC 20208
World Wide Web https://eric.ed.gov

Erin Pollard

Program Officer, ERIC
202-245-8344, e-mail erin.pollard@ed.gov

The Education Resources Information Center (ERIC) is the world's largest and most frequently used digital library of education resources. Since its inception in 1966, ERIC has added over 1.7 million records of journal articles, reports, and other materials. About 1 million records are for peer-reviewed work, and 400,000 records have free full text available to download from ERIC. Each ERIC bibliographic record contains an abstract of a journal article or gray literature document (for example, a technical report or conference paper), along with an abstract, audience, type of report, information on the assessment used, location where the research was conducted, and descriptors that work as keywords to guide users to relevant results.

Background

ERIC is a free, online database of education research that serves over 12 million users each year. With more than 50 years of service to the public, ERIC is one of the oldest programs in the U.S. Department of Education. As the world's largest education resource, it is distinguished by two hallmarks: free dissemination of bibliographic records, and the collection of gray literature such as research conference papers and government contractor reports.

The authorizing legislation for ERIC is part of the Education Sciences Reform Act of 2002, Public Law 107-279. This legislation envisioned ERIC subject areas or topics (previously covered by the ERIC Clearinghouses) as part of the totality of enhanced information dissemination to be conducted by the Institute of Education Sciences. In addition, information dissemination includes material on closing the achievement gap and on educational practices that improve academic achievement and promote learning.

Mission of ERIC

ERIC undertakes five major activities:

- *Pursues good sources.* ERIC reviews journal issues and publications from education-focused programs, organizations, and agencies to locate research in the field of education. A unique feature of ERIC is the inclusion of "gray literature," such as work from nonprofits, advocacy organizations, government agencies, or other sources that are typically not indexed by commercial databases. ERIC currently provides content from 1,984 sources, including 1,177 journals and 807 organizations and agencies. Ninety-eight percent of ERIC's journals are peer reviewed.

- *Works to make research publicly available.* ERIC negotiates with publishers to make as much of its content as freely available as possible. For example, ERIC contains 335 journals and 622 gray literature sources that allow full-text to be downloaded for free. ERIC also links to freely available content on the publisher's website for 185 journals and 126 nonjournal sources. There are over 75,000 full-text, peer-reviewed articles available for free download. Of these, 860 peer-reviewed journal articles are available as result of the IES Public Access Policy.
- *Creates records with supporting information so users know if resources are a good fit.* ERIC creates about 48,000 records per year that provide users with information about each article. Information in the record includes an abstract, audience, type of report, information on the assessment used, location where the research was conducted, and descriptors that work as keywords to guide users to relevant results. The metadata gives users the information they need to quickly see if the article will be relevant and useful to them.
- *Powers search engines with ERIC metadata to help users find good research, wherever they are searching.* ERIC shares its metadata with the public to enable search engines, academic databases, and other information providers to power their searches with ERIC data.
- *Integrates with other federally funded resources.* As applicable, ERIC records are linked with other federally funded resources, including What Works Clearinghouse study pages, Institute of Education Sciences grant abstracts, and links to federal websites. These interrelationships provide additional information and assist users in finding relevant and valuable IES resources.

Selection Standards

The selection policy provides that all materials added to the ERIC database are rigorous and relevant sources of research directly related to the field of education. The majority of journals indexed in ERIC are peer-reviewed, and peer-reviewed status is indicated for all journals indexed since 2004, when this data began to be documented by the ERIC system. The peer review status for nonjournals is indicated for all sources with a documented peer review process. The collection scope includes early childhood education through higher education, vocational education, and special education; it includes teacher education, education administration, assessment and evaluation, counseling, information technology, and the academic areas of reading, mathematics, science, environmental education, languages, and social studies.

To be considered for selection, all submissions must be in digital format and accompanied by author permission for dissemination. For individual document submissions, authors (copyright holders) can upload materials through a link on the ERIC website. Journal publishers, associations, and other entities with multiple documents also submit electronic content following guidance and instructions consistent with provider agreements from ERIC.

ERIC Users

About 12 million users search the ERIC website and download more than 7 million full-text documents each year from users all over the world. Approximately half of ERIC's users are driven from a commercial search engine, while 40 percent are driven from academic search engines.

ERIC can be reached toll-free by telephone at 800-LET-ERIC (800-538-3742), Monday through Friday, 9 A.M. to 7 P.M. eastern time. Questions can also be transmitted via the message box on the "Contact Us" page on the ERIC website.

National Association and Organization Reports

American Library Association

50 E. Huron St., Chicago, IL 60611
800-545-2433
World Wide Web http://www.ala.org

Loida Garcia-Febo
President

The American Library Association (ALA) was founded in 1876 in Philadelphia and later chartered in the Commonwealth of Massachusetts. ALA has approximately 59,000 members, including librarians, library trustees, and other interested people from every state and many nations. The association serves public, state, school, and academic libraries, as well as special libraries for people working in government, prisons, and other institutions.

ALA's mission is "to provide leadership for the development, promotion, and improvement of library and information services and the profession of librarianship in order to enhance learning and ensure access to information for all."

ALA is governed by an elected council, which is its policymaking body, and an executive board, which acts for the council in the administration of established policies and programs. In this context, the executive board is the body that manages the affairs of the association, delegating management of its day-to-day operation to the executive director.

ALA is home to 11 membership divisions, each focused on a type of library or library function. They are the American Association of School Librarians (AASL), the Association for Library Collections and Technical Services (ALCTS), the Association for Library Service to Children (ALSC), the Association of College and Research Libraries (ACRL), the Association of Specialized, Government, and Cooperative Library Agencies (ASGCLA), the Library and Information Technology Association (LITA), the Public Library Association (PLA), the Library Leadership and Management Association (LLAMA), the Reference and User Services Association (RUSA), United for Libraries, and the Young Adult Library Services Association (YALSA).

ALA also hosts 20 roundtables for members who share interests that lie outside the scope of any of the divisions. A network of affiliates, chapters, and other organizations enables ALA to reach a broad audience.

Key action areas include advocacy for libraries and the profession, diversity, education and lifelong learning, equitable access to information and library services, intellectual freedom, literacy, organizational excellence, and transforming libraries.

ALA offices address the broad interests and issues of concern to ALA members. They track issues and provide information, services, and products for members and the public. Current ALA offices are the Chapter Relations Office (CRO), the Communications and Marketing Office (CMO), the Development Office, the Office of ALA Governance, the International Relations Office (IRO), the Library and Research Center (LARC), the Office for Accreditation, the Office for Diversity, Literacy and Outreach Services (ODLOS), the Office for Human Resource Development and Recruitment (HRDR), the Office for Intellectual Freedom (OIF), the Office for Library Advocacy (OLA), the Public Programs Office (PPO), Publishing, and the Washington Office. ASGCLA is a new division, the result of a merger between the Association of Specialized & Cooperative Library Agencies (ASCLA) and the Federal and Armed Forces Round Table (FAFLRT).

ALA's headquarters is in Chicago. ALA's Washington Office is in Washington, D.C., and United for Libraries is in Exton, Pennsylvania. ALA also has an editorial office for *Choice*, a review journal for academic libraries, in Middletown, Connecticut.

ALA is a 501(c)(3) charitable and educational organization.

Leadership and Strategic Planning

Loida Garcia-Febo, international library consultant and president of Information New Wave in Brooklyn, New York, was inaugurated as ALA president at the 2018 Annual Conference in New Orleans, Louisiana. Garcia-Febo focused on a theme of "Libraries = Strong Communities," a national advocacy effort aimed at highlighting the value of academic, public, and school libraries, during her presidential year. Her key initiatives included a tour of six U.S. cities to call attention to the significant role libraries of all types play within their communities. She also advanced her commitment to wellness by joining members of the ALA Workplace Wellness Advisory Committee in relaunching the ALA–Allied Professional Association's Workplace Wellness website. Other efforts included unveiling resources to ALA's international membership, renewing the ALA's Advocacy University, a video series to teach storytelling for advocacy to library advocates, and providing another video series to help library workers embed equity, diversity, and inclusion into the services they provide. Garcia-Febo is the first ALA president invited to speak at the European Union Parliament; she spoke about her national library tour and the Libraries Ready to Code project.

Wanda Brown, director of Library Services at the C. G. O'Kelly Library, Winston-Salem State University, Winston-Salem, North Carolina, was elected ALA president-elect in the 2018 election and will be inaugurated as ALA president at the 2019 Annual Conference in Washington, D.C.

Other ALA officers include past-president James Neal, University Librarian Emeritus, Columbia University; treasurer, Susan H. Hildreth, University of Washington Information School; and executive director, Mary W. Ghikas. Ghikas became interim executive director in August 2017 upon the retirement of Keith

Michael Fiels, who had served as executive director since 2002. Ghikas was named executive director in January 2018.

The following individuals serve on the Executive Board along with the officers:

Trevor A. Dawes, University of Delaware Library; Karen Downing, University of Michigan Library; Tamika Barnes, Georgia State University Library; Ed Garcia, Cranston Public Library; Maria Taesil Hudson McCauley, Cambridge Public Library; Andrew K. Pace, Community Development, OCLC; Lessa Kanani'opua Pelayo-Lozada, Palos Verdes Library District; and Patricia M. Wong, Santa Monica Public Library.

Highlights of the Year

Academic Libraries

The ACRL Board of Directors added a core commitment to equity, diversity, and inclusion (EDI) to the association's strategic Plan for Excellence. The core commitment to EDI provides an opportunity to further examine and develop support in these critical areas.

The ACRL Board of Directors approved a revision of the association's *Standards for Libraries in Higher Education* (SLHE) in 2018. SLHE, adopted in 2004 and previously revised in 2011, is designed to guide academic libraries in advancing and sustaining their role as partners in educating students, achieving their institutions' missions, and positioning libraries as leaders in assessment and continuous improvement on their campuses.

ACRL selected the team of Rebecca R. Kennison (principal, K|N Consultants Ltd.) and Nancy L. Maron (founder, BlueSky to BluePrint, LLC) to design, develop, and deliver a new report on effective and promising practices within the research environment and scholarly communication system and identify areas where further research is needed. The researchers will look to include the perspectives of historically underrepresented communities to expand the profession's understanding of these environments and systems.

ACRL announced the publication of the six-volume *Framing Information Literacy: Teaching Grounded in Theory, Pedagogy, and Practice*, book number 73 in ACRL's Publications in Librarianship series. Edited by Mary K. Oberlies and Janna Mattson, these books are collections of lesson plans grounded in learning theory, each volume devoted to one of the six frames of the ACRL Framework for Information Literacy for Higher Education.

In addition, ACRL published *2017 Academic Library Trends and Statistics*, the latest in a series of annual publications that describe the collections, staffing, expenditures, and service activities of academic libraries in all Carnegie classifications.

Advocacy, Washington, D.C.

Federal funding for libraries continues to progress in a positive direction following a months-long campaign by ALA library advocates in conjunction with the ALA Washington Office. In late August, the full Senate approved its funding package with increases for library priorities including Institute of Museum and Library

Services, National Library of Medicine, Library of Congress, and Career and Technical Education while providing level funding for the Library Services and Technology Act, Innovative Approaches to Literacy, and Striving Readers. Many of these programs were targeted for elimination by the Trump administration earlier this year (for the second straight year).

ALA issued several statements in response to a variety of issues affecting libraries: praising the introduction of the Marrakesh Treaty Implementation Act; speaking in favor of a bill to modernize the Federal Depository Library Program (FDLP); advocating for leveraging the federal E-Rate program to improve broadband access in tribal and rural areas; and releasing a joint statement with ALA's Gay, Lesbian, Bisexual, and Transgender Round Table (GLBTRT) in response to proposals to rescind Lesbian, Gay, Bisexual, Transgender, and Queer (LGBTQ) federal civil rights protections.

ALA president James Neal (2017–2018) and American Association of School Librarians (AASL) president Steven Yates (2017–2018) released a statement supporting the efforts of Florida Association for Media in Education (FAME) and Florida Library Association to provide safe and accessible learning spaces for students and learners of all ages.

Neal also released a statement critical of the separation of refugee children from their parents and caregivers seeking asylum along the southwest border of the United States.

For 2018 National Library Week, the Washington Office and then-ALA president Jim Neal hosted events to showcase the role of libraries in providing Internet connectivity and advancing the new workforce through innovation and entrepreneurship.

On National Library Legislative Day, May 7–8, 2018, hundreds of library supporters convened in Washington, D.C., to meet with their members of Congress to rally support for library issues and policies.

Disaster Relief

Thanks to hundreds of donors contributing $80,000 toward relief, 20 libraries in Puerto Rico and the U.S. Virgin Islands received grants to assist in recovery from the damage wrought by Hurricanes Irma and Maria last year.

Thirteen libraries in Puerto Rico and seven libraries in the U.S. Virgin Islands were awarded $4,000 grants from ALA. Grant recipients were school, public, and academic libraries.

Also, ALA and its chapters in North Carolina, South Carolina, and Virginia worked to assist libraries affected by Hurricane Florence. Support efforts involved most Atlantic Seaboard libraries in serving as a lifeline for residents in dire need of FEMA and insurance forms, access to electrical power, Internet access, heat, or important information about storm relief and recovery efforts.

In January 2018 ALA president-elect Loida Garcia-Febo visited damaged libraries in Puerto Rico and provided resources to libraries in need.

Conferences and Workshops

2018 Midwinter Meeting

ALA hosted its 2018 Midwinter Meeting & Exhibits in Denver at the Colorado Convention Center and nearby locations for national discussions on the transformative role of libraries. The conference was attended by more than 8,000 librarians, library workers, and library supporters, including more than 2,600 U.S. exhibitors.

For the second year, the Symposium on the Future of Libraries produced a collection of more than 40 daily and concurrent sessions, many of which were dedicated to community-centric resources in education, technology, diversity and inclusion, government, and social justice. The Symposium also included the popular News You Can Use and ALA Masters Series.

Library advocacy and future-focused sessions were delivered through the Libraries Transform–Libraries Lead message. Transformation was a key focus of training and other events related to ALA's national public awareness campaign, Libraries Transform.

#BlackLivesMatters cofounder Patrisse Cullors opened the Midwinter Meeting, along with #1000blackgirlbooks founder Marley Dias.

TV personality Bill Nye and his co-author on the three-book series *Jack and the Geniuses*, Gregory Mone, inspired the audience with their tremendous passion for science and their assertion that being a critical thinker will get us all safely to the future.

"Are libraries neutral? Have they ever been? Should they be?" was the topic up for debate at the ALA President's Program. The program, moderated by ALA president James Neal (2017–2018), featured a sprawling discussion in which multiple definitions of neutrality were proposed, and various positions were argued for and against. The rhetoric was lively and occasionally prickly on the stage, in the audience, and on social media.

The exhibit floor opened to an excited group of attendees waiting to interact with more than 400 companies and organizations highlighting the latest products, services, technologies, and titles. The Now Showing stage unveiled diverse films and documentaries, while the Book Buzz Theater and PopTop live stages were at the ready with hundreds of publishers and authors on hand to sign books and give away stacks of advance reading copies (ARCs).

An exuberant crowd of librarians attended the highly anticipated 2018 ALA Youth Media Awards, which includes the Caldecott and Newbery medals, the Coretta Scott King Book Award, and the Printz Award. Winners and honorees are selected by committees composed of librarians and other literature and media experts. Hundreds attended the live event, and many thousands more watched via live webcast. ALA's book and media award announcements are now consolidated at Midwinter as the RUSA Book and Media Awards, including the announcement of the winners of the Andrew Carnegie Medals for Excellence in Fiction and Nonfiction.

ALA Council adopted the statement "Net Neutrality: An Intellectual Freedom Issue." Written by the ALA Intellectual Freedom Committee, the document affirms that Net Neutrality is essential to the promotion and practice of intellectual freedom and the free exercise of democracy. The Council also adopted a Library Bill of Rights interpretation that emphasizes the role art plays in libraries and states that libraries should present a broad spectrum of viewpoints in developing art exhibits and programs.

ALA 2018 Annual Conference

ALA hosted its 2018 ALA Annual Conference & Exhibition June 21–26, in New Orleans. The conference was attended by more than 17,500 librarians, library workers, and library supporters (including more than 5,100 exhibitors) from across the world.

The conference officially opened with great excitement when former first lady Michelle Obama, who discussed her book *Becoming*, took the stage. Mrs. Obama was interviewed on stage by Dr. Carla Hayden, the 14th Librarian of Congress. Hayden is the first woman and first African American to lead the national library and was nominated to the position by President Barack Obama in February 2016—and confirmed by the U.S. Senate in July 2016.

Other notable speakers included actors Viola Davis, who presented her new children's book, *Corduroy Takes a Bow*, and Sally Field, who presented her memoir, *In Pieces*. Both books were released in fall 2018.

James Neal, the 2017–2018 ALA president, hosted the ALA President's Program. He welcomed as his special guests Pulitzer Prize winners Tracy K. Smith, the 22nd United States Poet Laureate Consultant in Poetry and author of *Wade in the Water*; and journalist, filmmaker, and CEO of Define American, Jose Antonio Vargas, who discussed his book, *Dear America: Notes of an Undocumented Citizen*.

The Auditorium Speaker Series featured presidential historian Doris Kearns Goodwin, author of *Leadership: In Turbulent Times*; Jonathan Eig, author of *Ali: A Life*; and Robert Fieseler, author of *Tinderbox: The Untold Story of the Up Stairs Lounge Fire and the Rise of Gay Liberation*. All gave captivating presentations on their respective works. Champion slam poet Gayle Danley rounded out the exciting speaker roster when she performed stirring poems for a captivated audience.

More than 1,700 programs and more than 2,500 events took place at the Ernest N. Morial Convention Center and nearby locations. Much of the program content focused on ALA's four strategic directions: advocacy; information policy; professional and leadership development; and equity, diversity, and inclusion.

Librarian of Congress Carla Hayden and the tenth archivist of the United States, David S. Ferriero, were particularly welcomed by an audience of librarians and library workers when they presented "The Librarian and the Archivist: The Importance of Collecting Physical Information and Materials in the Digital Age."

Immediately following the Michelle Obama presentation, a ribbon-cutting officially opened the exhibit floor with more than 750 companies and organizations showcasing the latest technologies, titles, services, and products. The floor offered live stages—the Graphic Novels and Gaming Stage, the PopTop Stage, the What's Cooking @ ALA Demonstration Stage, and the Book Buzz Theater—that produced informative entertainment and allowed attendees to engage with top authors from the graphic novel, cooking, and pop culture genres. At Now Showing @ ALA, writer, actor, and director Emilio Estevez offered an advance screening of his new film *The Public*. The film also stars Estevez, Alec Baldwin, Taylor Schilling, and Jeffrey Wright and centers on the regular patrons of downtown Cincinnati's public library, many of whom are homeless and marginalized, and their interactions with the library staff who have built emotional connections with them. When a bitter Arctic blast hits the city, the patrons turn the library into a homeless shelter by staging a sit-in, which escalates into a police standoff. A Q&A with Estevez moderated by Ryan J. Dowd, executive director of Hesed House Shelter, followed the screening.

James Neal, president from 2017 to 2018, inaugurated newly elected ALA president Loida Garcia-Febo at the final event of the conference. Garcia-Febo communicated a special focus on the library's contribution to communities and the necessary support by ALA to the many librarians and library workers. She also launched "Libraries=Strong Communities," a national advocacy effort aimed at highlighting the value of academic, public, and school libraries.

ALA's Libraries Ready to Code initiative, sponsored by Google, released the beta version of the Libraries Ready to Code Collection, a cache of resources developed, tested, and curated by libraries, for libraries to create, implement, and enhance their computer science (CS) programming for youth.

AASL announced its 2018 Best Apps and Best Websites for Teaching & Learning. These technology resources are chosen for their ability to foster the qualities of innovation, creativity, active participation, and collaboration and for their support of AASL's *National School Library Standards*.

ALSC Institute

The ALSC National Institute, "All Aboard! Embracing Advocacy and Inclusion," was held September 27–29 in Cincinnati, Ohio. More than 400 children's librarians and educators attended the event, which featured authors Brian Selznick and David Serlin presenting the Closing General Session on September 29.

LITA Forum

The LITA Forum was held November 8–10 in Minneapolis, Minnesota. It featured 60 sessions, including active learning and discussion-based activities. The keynote speakers were Dorothea Salo, faculty associate in the iSchool at the University of Wisconsin at Madison, and Nancy Sims, Copyright Program Librarian, University of Minnesota Libraries. Preconferences included "Build Your Own National Digital Library," "Cybersecurity and Privacy in Libraries and for Librarians," and "Through the Looking Glass: Overcoming Self-Centered Design."

PLA 2018 National Conference

The PLA 2018 National Conference, "Imagine the Possibilities," was held March 20–24 in Philadelphia. Approximately 7,873 public library professionals, exhibitors, speakers, and supporters registered to attend the nation's largest conference dedicated to connecting and supporting the educational needs of public library professionals and stakeholders.

Held with the theme "Imagine the Possibilities," the event focused on advocacy; funding; consumer health information; Equity, Diversity, and Inclusion; family engagement through libraries; and digital literacy. PLA's Big Idea Series included inspiring talks with best-selling *Eat, Pray, Love* author Elizabeth Gilbert; corporate executive Steve Pemberton; and author, policy advocate, and director of Columbia University's Poliak Center for the Study of First Amendment Issues, Tim Wu.

Former U.S. deputy attorney general Sally Q. Yates headlined the event's Opening Session. Yates's remarks emphasized the invaluable role that libraries play within their communities as gateways to truth and protectors of our nation's democracy.

PLA 2018 served as a platform for several PLA national announcements. A new national study on voter perceptions of libraries was unveiled. The PLA, ALA, and OCLC released *From Awareness to Funding: Voter Perceptions and Support of Public Libraries in 2018*. The research updates OCLC's seminal 2008 study that explored voter perceptions, use, and attitudes toward public libraries, librarians, and library funding.

PLA also announced a new partnership with tech startup Short Édition's Short Story Dispenser. First launched in France, Short Story Dispensers offer readers an opportunity to randomly select a one-, three-, or five-minute story with a push of a button. The PLA and Short Edition are bringing this new technology to a select group of libraries including Akron–Summit County (Ohio) Public Library; Free Library of Philadelphia (Pennsylvania); Richland Library (Columbia, South Carolina); and Wichita (Kansas) Public Library.

Book Fairs

The fifth annual Sharjah International Book Fair/ALA Library Conference was held in Sharjah, United Arab Emirates, November 6–8. The professional development event hosted 300 library experts from 18 countries who gathered to discuss the strategic shifts that will define the next generation of library services.

The 19th year of collaboration between ALA and the Guadalajara Book Fair provided the opportunity for 150 ALA members to attend the 31st Guadalajara International Book Fair at the end of November.

Upcoming Conferences

ACRL 2019, "Recasting the Narrative," will be held April 10–13 in Cleveland, Ohio. The AASL National Conference & Exhibition will be held November 14–16, 2019, in Louisville, Kentucky.

Key Initiatives and Accomplishments

Communications and Marketing

Stephanie M. Hlywak was named ALA's new director of Communications and Marketing. Hlywak comes to ALA from the Muscular Dystrophy Association, where she served as national director of content marketing. At ALA she will lead the ALA Communications and Marketing Office, a reorganized unit of ALA bringing together the Public Awareness Office—including press relations, social media, and public information—with an increased focus on marketing. She joins ALA's management team, with the intent of strengthening consistent internal and external communications across the association.

In the area of Media Relations, more than 26,400 articles mentioned ALA during 2018. Total circulation was more than 12.1 billion. (Circulation rate is calculated using the number of articles/mentions multiplied by the monthly unique visitors for each media outlet's website.)

There was a large volume of media articles and mentions for all the various events taking place during National Library Week, including the release of the ALA *State of America's Libraries* report and the Top Ten List of the Most Challenged Books, as well as National Library Workers Day, National Bookmobile Day, Take Action for Libraries Day, and School Library Month.

Money Smart Week efforts included reaching out to print, television, and radio outlets. In addition, the Web press kit was updated with resources offered by libraries and an interactive map tracking Money Smart events. An article was written for the ALA's public website, I Love Libraries, showing how libraries were promoting Money Smart Week.

Equity, Diversity, and Inclusion

ALA president Loida Garcia-Febo released a statement affirming the association's commitment to providing library professionals with resources that support equity, diversity, and inclusion (EDI). She invited library professions seeking to make their working environments, collections, and services more inclusive to avail themselves of EDI resources offered by the ALA's Office for Diversity, Literacy, and Outreach Services.

The third National Joint Conference of Librarians of Color (JCLC), held September 26–30 at the Albuquerque Convention Center in New Mexico, celebrated the achievements of individuals from each of the American Library Association's ethnic affiliate associations, including the American Indian Library Association (AILA), the Asian/Pacific American Librarians Association (APALA), the Black Caucus of the American Library Association (BCALA), the Chinese American Librarians Association (CALA), and the National Association to Promote Library and Information Services to Latinos and the Spanish Speaking (Reforma). The conference was highlighted by the JCLC 2018 Scholarships and Awards Gala on September 28, with hundreds of participants attending the night of pride, local cuisine, and music. Honors included the JCLC Advocacy Awards, Distinguished Service Awards, Author Awards and scholarships, and the JCLC Legacy Awards and Rising Leader Awards.

In June ODLOS announced the recipients of the 2018–2019 Diversity Research Grant. These grants financially assist researchers in completing a project that is closely tied to equity, diversity, and/or inclusion in the library and information sciences field.

Art Aids Art and the eKhaya eKasi Art and Education Center in Khayelitsha, South Africa; the Athens Housing Authority, University of Georgia College of Education, and Parkview Community in Athens, Georgia; and the Uni Project in

New York City were selected to receive books as part of the 2018 Coretta Scott King Book Donation Grant program.

Alexandra Rivera (2001 Spectrum Scholar) was the 2018 recipient of the ALA's Equality Award and the first Spectrum Scholar to receive this honor.

Thanks to support from the ALA Development Office and a match opportunity from an anonymous donor, Spectrum raised $29,985 during the 2017 ALA Annual Campaign (November 1–December 31, 2017) as part of its year-long celebration of the Spectrum 20th Anniversary.

The 2017–2018 Spectrum Scholars participated in the 20th Spectrum Leadership Institute held in conjunction with the 2018 Annual Conference in New Orleans.

ODLOS trainings and presentations included a talk by Jody Gray at "Diversity Retreat: Advancing the Conversation on Inclusion," sponsored by the Pennsylvania State University Libraries. Gray also facilitated a racial healing circle at the Truth, Racial Healing, and Transformation Great Stories Club Pilot Project Orientation organized by the Public Programs Office. She also presented at "Tolerance Is Not Enough: Libraries Respond to Hate," sponsored by the Northeast Ohio Regional Library System.

Gray and Kristin Lahurd provided a half-day Equity, Diversity, and Inclusion in Libraries Consultation at the Mount Prospect (Illinois) Public Library.

Information Policy and Technology

In a panel hosted by the ALA on Capitol Hill, tribal librarians and rural telecom experts advocated for leveraging the federal E-rate program to improve broadband access in tribal and rural areas. The discussion, moderated by National Museum of the American Indian librarian Elayne Silversmith, focused on how broadband connectivity and telecommunications infrastructure in tribal and rural regions advances education, provides economic opportunity, and can close the digital divide.

Intellectual Freedom

Office for Intellectual Freedom Director Jamie LaRue joined Office for Library Advocacy director Marci Merola to present two Advocacy Bootcamps in April.

OIF deputy director Deborah Caldwell-Stone presented the John Swan Lecture for the Vermont Library Association on April 10, speaking on the topic of "Library Privacy in an Age of Surveillance Capitalism." On April 20, OIF assistant director Kristin Pekoll presented an Advocacy Bootcamp, with Marci Merola, for the Michigan Library Association.

LaRue participated in a Zoom panel on OIF and Freedom to Read Foundation (FTRF) for the San Jose University MLIS program on April 18, and then traveled to Boston on April 21–22 to participate in an 80-person symposium of librarians and journalists, supported by an IMLS grant proposal, called "Know News: Engaging with Mis- and Disinformation."

OIF director Jamie LaRue appeared on Chicago radio station WCPT-AM on July 11 to discuss the AASL's new toolkit, "Defending Intellectual Freedom: LGBTQ+ Materials in School Libraries."

From July 28 through August 1, LaRue presented on three topics for the Research Institute for Public Libraries conference in Atlanta, Georgia. LaRue spoke on "Assessing Community Needs," "Telling the Library Story," and "Data Use for Strategic Planning, Management, and Communication with Stakeholders." On August 3 LaRue presented a talk on library privacy to the Colorado Association of Libraries' Public Libraries Division. LaRue then co-presented a webinar with Colorado State Library's Sharon Morris on "Managing the Talent: A Holistic Look at Personnel Management," for Library Leadership and Management Association on August 15 and led a presentation on intellectual freedom issues for the Zion Benton Public Library's staff day on August 16.

OIF assistant director Kristin Pekoll presented "Raise the Volume on Banned Book Week Programs" for a Facebook Live event on August 22.

On June 19 the "Choose Privacy Week" microsite, managed by OIF and the Intellectual Freedom Committee Privacy Subcommittee, was rebranded as "Choose Privacy Every Day" and given a new look and a new URL address, https://chooseprivacyeveryday.org. The changes emphasize the importance of preserving patron privacy and data security in today's libraries every day of the year.

The release of the Top 10 Most Challenged Books of 2017 and unveiling of the Banned Books Week 2018 theme was another success this year, due to the coordination of multiple ALA offices and departments—including the Public Awareness Office, Graphics, American Libraries, ITTS, Production Services, Booklist, and Print Services—and experimentation with media platforms to engage members.

Platforms included an infographic of the Top 10 book covers, the Top 10 video, a Facebook Live event where users posed thoughtful questions to LaRue, and a Top 10 toolkit.

The Banned Books Week Coalition, which included ALA and the Freedom to Read Foundation, announced the theme for Banned Books Week 2018: "Banning Books Silences Stories. Speak Out!" The new Banned Books Week line of offerings was made available through the ALA Store and included digital downloads, mini-posters, buttons, and bumper stickers. The OIF-published Field Report described 91 censorship incidents from 2017, ranging from books and displays to hate crimes and programs.

Libraries Transform®

Libraries Transform®, a public awareness and advocacy campaign designed to create a national conversation about libraries, expanded to more than 10,900 participating libraries and supporters in 2018. The campaign developed new downloadable tools including new "Because" statements on topics including family engagement, privacy, digital media, and inclusive literature. Based on the success of the program, the ALA Executive Board voted in 2017 to extend it through 2020.

Library Services to Children

Every Child Ready to Read—Toolkit for Serving Early Childhood Educators was published by ALSC and PLA in 2017. The toolkit is aimed at public library staff as a how-to manual for training early childhood educators. Libraries are taking a proactive approach toward engaging parents and caregivers in supporting the early literacy development of their children, and Every Child Ready to Read @ Your Library® program is an excellent tool to ensure libraries' success. These were two of the key findings of a study released in November 2017, by Dr. Susan B. Neuman, a professor of childhood education and literacy development at New York University.

ALSC's Quicklists Committee developed Comforting Reads for Difficult Times as a resource to help adults comfort children and youth in distress due to situations like a loved one's death by suicide, tragedy, or catastrophic illness. The list includes books on these topics and others including depression, bullying, and natural disasters, as well as links to support organizations.

National Celebrations and Observances

Teen Tech Week was celebrated March 4–10 with the theme "Libraries are for Creating." The theme encourages teens to take advantage of all the great digital tools offered through the library to become content creators, and to leverage library resources to share out their creations.

The theme of National Library Week 2018 was "Libraries Lead." American Ballet Theatre principal dancer Misty Copeland served as 2018 National Library Week Honorary Chair.

April 10 was National Library Workers Day (NLWD), a time to recognize library professionals for their expertise and leadership skills in transforming lives and communities through education and lifelong learning. The day also reminds the public that library workers serve as community compasses that lead users to endless opportunities for engagement, enrichment, and development.

During National Library Week on National Bookmobile Day, April 11, the Office for Diversity, Literacy and Outreach Services and the Communications and Marketing Office worked with the Association of Bookmobile and Outreach Services to celebrate our nation's bookmobiles and the dedicated library professionals who provide this valuable and essential service to their communities every day. Social media highlights included post reach on National Bookmobile Day 2018 at 2,566, compared with 943 in 2017.

Jason Reynolds, author of *Ghost, Patina, Long Way Down,* and *Miles Morales: Spider-Man*, served as the national spokesperson for the 2018 celebration of School Library Month (SLM). Observed in April and sponsored by the American Association of School Librarians (AASL), School Library Month celebrates school libraries as approachable, equitable, and personalized learning environments necessary for every student's well-rounded education.

As part of the implementation of its new *National School Library Standards*, AASL launched a video storytelling campaign. With Every Standard Tells a Story, school library professionals can submit their own narratives on how school libraries transform teaching and learning for real people in real places through examples of the things they already do every day that meet the AASL Standards.

Choose Privacy Week (May 1–8), which promotes the importance of individual privacy rights and celebrates libraries and librarians' unique role in protecting privacy, was celebrated with the theme "Big Data Is Watching You" and focused on the growing threat of big data analytics, especially in a time when technology, mobile computing, social media, and the growing adoption of "big data" analytics pose new threats to everyone's right to privacy.

Preservation Week® April 22–28 focused on cooking and community archiving, and food writer, independent scholar, culinary historian, and historical interpreter Michael W. Twitty served as honorary chair.

From April 21–28 more than 1,000 libraries participated in Money Smart Week®, a public awareness campaign designed to help consumers better manage their personal finances.

On April 30 hundreds of libraries across the country celebrated Día, a national library program that fosters literacy for children of all backgrounds.

ALA and hundreds of libraries celebrated June as GLBT Book Month™, a nationwide celebration of the authors and writings that reflect the lives and experiences of the gay, lesbian, bisexual, and transgender community.

ALA teamed up with The Incredibles to encourage K–12 students to sign up for a free library card during Library Card Sign-Up Month in September.

During Banned Books Week (September 23–29), readers were encouraged to raise their voices in support of the freedom to read by participating in engaging activities, which included a Facebook Live event, "6 Ways to Express Your Inner Activist for Banned Books Week," and the Dear Banned Author letter-writing campaign, which encouraged readers to write to, tweet, or e-mail banned or challenged authors, sharing how their stories have impacted lives.

"It's Written in the Stars . . . READ" was the theme for this year's Teen Read Week celebration, which took place October 7–13. Teen Read Week is generously supported in part by the Dollar General Literacy Foundation. Library staff, afterschool providers, and educators can use this theme to encourage teens to think and read outside of the box, as well as seek out fantasy, science fiction, and other out-of- this-world reads.

Professional and Leadership Development

Thirty-eight mid-career librarians participated in Leading to the Future, ALA's sixth four-day immersive leadership development program for future library leaders. Led by ALA past-president Maureen Sullivan and library and leadership consultant Kathryn Deiss, the ALA Leadership Institute is designed to help participants develop and practice their leadership skills in areas critical to the future of the libraries they lead.

ALA's JobLIST Placement and Career Development Center offered complimentary career counseling sessions during the ALA 2018 Annual Conference in New Orleans. Career development coach Caitlin Williams, Ph.D., worked with individuals and organizations to create and implement professional development initiatives. She focused on helping professionals leverage their talents in ways that truly make a difference.

Public Libraries

PLA held a short fiction contest as part of the Fostering Creative Community Connections (FCCC) project, which seeks to promote reading and literary joy through public libraries. The project is funded by the John S. and James L. Knight Foundation and managed by the PLA, in partnership with community publisher Short Édition.

PLA unveiled eight new interest groups in the online community platform, ALA Connect. ALA Connect is a site where members of ALA meet and mingle virtually, discuss library-related topics and issues, share ideas, collaborate in communities, and come together to do the work of the Association.

PLA released a free promotional toolkit designed to help libraries raise awareness of family engagement through libraries. This new resource can be used to supplement libraries' marketing, fundraising, community relations, and political advocacy work.

Constance Wu, star of the film *Crazy Rich Asians*, was featured in three new video Public Service Announcements (PSAs) promoting the transformative resources available at libraries. In the PSAs, Wu shares her love of libraries and explains how they advance inclusion and education for people of all backgrounds.

PLA unveiled a new model for its Leadership Development Initiative. Developed by 21 select library leaders, the PLA Leadership Model describes the work, methods, and core values of leadership in a public library context. In alignment with the association's strategic goals of Transformation and Leadership, this model advances public libraries' shift from an organizational focus to a community focus and supports leadership that reflects the needs of the community.

As part of its ongoing work to support the public library's role in creating healthy communities, PLA offered funding and resources for libraries to help more Americans enroll in affordable health insurance. PLA partnered with the Robert Wood Johnson Foundation (RWJF) and Community Catalyst to address a shortened period for enrolling in the Affordable Care Act (ACA) marketplace and reduced funding for enrollment navigators.

Through its new initiative "Promoting Health Communities: Libraries Connecting You to Coverage," PLA issued mini-grants to support up to 120 U.S. public libraries. Grant recipients disseminated information, offered education, partnered with health insurance enrollment and provider groups, and encouraged community members to enroll in the Health Insurance Marketplace during the open enrollment period.

Public Programming

The ALA Public Programs Office empowers libraries to create vibrant hubs of learning, conversation, and connection in communities of all types. Grants from the Public Programs Office enable libraries to boost their offerings and infuse their communities with innovative ideas.

In 2018, 50 public libraries were selected for grants to host public programs around the PBS series *The Great American Read*, an eight-part television and online series designed to spark a national conversation about reading and the books that have inspired, moved, and shaped us.

Through ALA's Sara Jaffarian School Library Program Award, school libraries serving grades K–8 are invited to apply for a $5,000 award recognizing outstanding humanities programming in kindergarten through eighth grade. The 2018 winner was Danville (Ark.) Public Schools, for their program "Tales of the Crypt: Danville's Living History."

One hundred libraries nationwide were selected to take part in ALA's Great Stories Club, a national grant program that supports reading and discussion programs for underserved teens. The grantees represented 77 public libraries, 14 school/K–12 libraries, three college/university libraries, two community college libraries, three prison libraries, and one tribal library. They come from 35 states, the District of Columbia, and the Northern Mariana Islands. Working with small groups of teens, grantees will host reading and discussion programs for up to four thematically related books. The titles—selected in consultation with librarian advisors and humanities scholars—are chosen to resonate with reluctant readers struggling with complex issues like academic probation, detention, incarceration, violence, and poverty.

Ninety-five additional libraries were selected to participate in two phases of the Truth, Racial Healing, and Transformation (TRHT) Great Stories Club, an expansion of ALA's long-standing Great Stories Club model that features books to help readers look beneath the surface of racism in America. The TRHT GSC is supported by a grant from the W. K. Kellogg Foundation.

The American Dream Literacy Initiative marked its tenth anniversary. Funded by the Dollar General Literacy Foundation, the American Dream Literacy Initiative offers grants to U.S. public libraries to expand services for adult English language learners (ELL) or adults in need of basic education and workforce development. More than $1.5 million in funding has been distributed to 188 libraries since the program's inception, reaching approximately 25,000 English language learners.

School Libraries

Seeing the need for urgent action to combat cuts in school library funding, staffing, and programming, ALA president Jim Neal hosted a summit in Chicago in May 2018 to work with our nation's library leaders to craft a strategy to advocate for our nation's school libraries.

AASL released a new resource guide to support school librarians addressing challenges related to censorship and patron privacy issues, particularly with LGBTQ+ materials. *Defending Intellectual Freedom: LGBTQ+ Materials in School Libraries* contains resources, links, and activities scaffolded by the *National School Library Standards.*

The North Carolina School Library Media Association (NCSLMA), Tennessee Association of School Librarians (TASL), and Ohio Educational Library Media Association (OELMA) were the first recipients of the AASL Past-Presidents Planning Grant for National School Library Standards. The $2,500 grants, awarded in honor of AASL past presidents, are presented annually to AASL Affiliate organizations for the planning and execution of an event, initiative, or activity focused on the implementation of the *National School Library Standards.*

Two Houston schools extensively damaged by Hurricane Harvey were the recipients of the 2018 catastrophic disaster relief grants offered as part of the American Association of School Librarians' (AASL) Beyond Words: The Dollar General School Library Relief Fund.

AASL added more than 70 concurrent sessions recorded at the AASL National Conference & Exhibition in Phoenix to AASL eCOLLAB, a one-stop shop for on-demand learning that now contains 400 opportunities for professional learning and continues to grow as monthly webinars on the *National School Library Standards* are presented and archived.

AASL announced its 2018 Best Apps and Best Websites for Teaching and Learning at the ALA Annual Conference in New Orleans. The annual lists honor 25 apps and 25 websites that provide enhanced learning and curriculum development for school librarians and their teacher collaborators. These technology resources are chosen for their ability to foster the qualities of innovation, creativity, active participation, and collaboration and for their support of AASL's new *National School Library Standards*.

AASL recognized social media superstars within the school library profession, giving recognitions in eight categories: Sensational Student Voice, Advocacy Ambassador, Tech Troubadour, Program Pioneer, Curriculum Champion, Leadership Luminary, Social Justice Defender, and the newly minted Reader Leader.

Teen Services

YALSA released *Transforming Library Services for and with Teens through Continuing Education* (CE). This report was authored by Linda W. Braun, YALSA CE consultant; Nicole A. Cooke, director of the MS/LIS program at the School of Information Sciences at the University of Illinois at Urbana-Champaign; Denise Lyons, deputy director of Statewide Development at the South Carolina State Library; Sara Ryan, Teen Services Specialist at Multnomah County Library in Portland, Oregon; and Beth Yoke, former YALSA executive director. The report is the result of a year-long national forum that took place from June 1, 2017, to May 31, 2018, and was hosted in partnership with the Chief Officers of State Library Agencies (COSLA) and funded by the Institute of Museum and Library Services (IMLS).

In partnership with COSLA, YALSA implemented a new project, "Transforming Teen Services: A Train the Trainer Approach" from July 1, 2018, through June 30, 2021. The three-year project is funded by a grant from IMLS.

The project brought together state library agency (SLA) youth consultants and frontline library staff from each U.S. state/territory for a robust training program that aims to help them build connected learning (CL), computer science (CS), cultural competence, and other skills so they can better serve and meet the learning needs of youth in their communities.

YALSA also announced its new Innovation in Teen Services Award, which will annually recognize a member who has demonstrated a commitment to creating innovative library services for and with the teens in their community.

In addition, YALSA unveiled its new Doctoral Dissertation Fellowship. Its purpose is to foster research on teens, learning, and libraries, specifically research that aligns with YALSA's National Research Agenda by encouraging and assisting doctoral students in the field with their dissertation research.

United for Libraries

Delaware joined Maryland, Michigan, Nebraska, South Dakota, and Texas in becoming a statewide group member of United for Libraries/ALA.

United for Libraries worked with the ALA Emerging Leaders program to identify possible barriers to service on library boards. The goal of the project, "Beyond Using the Library: Engaging Millennials as Advocates and Civic Library Leaders," is to compile and create tools to help libraries, trustees, foundations, and Friends groups overcome barriers and engage the millennial generation in moving from being the most likely generation of Americans to use public libraries to being active advocates and civic leaders as members of boards of trustees, foundations, and Friends of the Library groups. Feedback from current and past library trustees, Friends, foundation staff/board, and others will be extremely helpful in recognizing common issues that current and past board members encounter, and in the brainstorming on how to alleviate any issues.

Friends of the Library groups and libraries across the country celebrated the 13th annual National Friends of Libraries Week, October 21–27. It offered a twofold opportunity to celebrate Friends—promoting the group in the community, raising awareness, and increasing membership and also giving libraries and boards of trustees the opportunity to recognize the Friends for their help and support of the library.

Programs and Partners

Dollar General Literacy Foundation

ALA and Dollar General Literacy Foundation announced that 20 U.S. public libraries received American Dream Literacy Initiative grants, $10,000 awards to expand services for adult English language learners or adults in need of basic education and workforce development.

In addition, the Dollar General Literacy Foundation has awarded a Youth Literacy grant in the amount of $249,431 to the Association for Library Service to Children (ALSC) and the Young Adult Library Services Association (YALSA). With the funds from Dollar General, YALSA will provide mini-grants to libraries to support literacy focused activities for and with underserved teens, as well as teen summer learning and teen intern programs. Funds will also be used to provide collections of YALSA's Teens' Top Ten nominees to libraries in need and update the Teen Book Finder app and database.

ALSC will use the funds to provide 14 Strengthening Communities through Libraries grants of $5,000 to ALSC members in public libraries to implement STEAM programming during out-of-school time, including after school and seasonal breaks. ALSC will also develop and share supplemental resources that will be made widely available to support the collaborative efforts of libraries their community partners.

FINRA Foundation

RUSA's Financial Literacy Interest Group recently received a three-year grant from the FINRA Foundation to support ongoing programming to better equip libraries to provide valuable financial literacy tools and training to their communities. Grant funds will enable the interest group to provide in-person and online workshops, publish articles, and develop online resources.

Book Club Central

Honorary Book Club Central chair Sarah Jessica Parker selected Wayétu Moore's *She Would Be King* (Graywolf Press) and Sarah Smarsh's *Heartland: A Memoir of Working Hard and Being Broke in the Richest Country on Earth* (Scribner) as her choices for the ALA's Book Club Central.

Health Literacy Toolkit

The National Network of Libraries of Medicine (NNLM) and ALA updated the Libraries Transform Health Literacy Toolkit with brand-new resources to help library professionals raise awareness of how libraries provide trusted health information to their communities.

The free toolkit provides key messages, program ideas, and downloadable marketing materials, including bookmarks and social media graphics, for libraries to use as they promote health literacy during Health Literacy Month (October) and throughout the year. The additions to the toolkit cover a wide-ranging array of health literacy topics including genetics, family history, clinical trials, citizen science projects, customizing care, and student well-being. The toolkit also covers subjects such as aging, nutrition, and chronic illness.

Libraries Ready to Code

The ALA's Libraries Ready to Code (RtC) initiative, sponsored by Google, awarded 250 school and public libraries with $500 in microfunding each to help plan and implement coding activities during Computer Science Education (CS Ed) Week 2018 (December 3–9). The CS Ed Week microfunding came as part of an announcement by ALA and Grow with Google that included the launch of the Libraries Ready to Code website, the expansion of Google's in-person workshops for job seekers and small businesses to libraries in all 50 states, and an additional $1 million investment in funding to libraries. Libraries across America will be able to access the pool of microfunds through ALA to implement digital skills programming. ALA will collaborate with the Public Library Association to administer the new digital skills initiative.

At the 2018 ALA Annual Conference, Libraries Ready to Code released a beta version of the Ready to Code Collection, a website that includes content developed by the 28 grantee cohort libraries through the projects they implemented over the last year.

Promoting Healthy Communities

A new nationwide initiative from PLA and National Network of Libraries of Medicine will increase public library workers' knowledge and skills related to consumer health services. In early 2018, the initiative unveiled a new website for public libraries that gives them easy access to training, tools, and resources for consumer health information, health literacy programming, and more.

Publishing

ALA Editions and ALA Neal-Schuman

ALA Editions and ALA Neal-Schuman publications focus on library education, professional development, advocacy, and programming. Together the two imprints published 53 titles from September 2017 through August 2018. Leading titles from ALA Editions and ALA Neal-Schuman included *National School Library Standards for Learners, School Librarians, and School Libraries*, published in association with the American Association of School Librarians (AASL); *The Librarian's Guide to Homelessness*, by Ryan J. Dowd; the fourth edition of *Fundamentals of Collection Development and Management*, by Peggy Johnson; the fourth edition of *Reference and Information Services*, by Kay Ann Cassell and Uma Hiremath; *LGBTQAI+ Books for Children and Teens*, by Christina Dorr and Liz Deskins; and *63 Ready-to-Use Maker Projects*, by Ellyssa Kroski. ALA Editions and ALA Neal-Schuman contributors have played a substantial role in online continuing education for the profession and are author-experts behind a growing list of course books in print and electronic formats for MLIS and other educational programs.

ALA Graphics

ALA Graphics has been a champion for libraries, literacy, and reading for more than 40 years. Home of the iconic Celebrity READ® Poster Campaign, ALA Graphics is also the source of the unique promotional materials for National Library Week (April), National Library Workers Day (April), Choose Privacy Week (May), Library Card Sign-up Month (September), and Banned Books Week (September), among other events. Recent celebrities who have joined the Campaign include Misty Copeland, John Cena, Constance Wu, and Milo Ventimiglia. Beloved characters such as Harry Potter, The Incredibles, and CatStronauts made their debut on posters and bookmarks, much to the delight of libraries and schools. Matthew Cordell, recipient of the 2018 Caldecott Medal for *Wolf in the Snow*, created original artwork featuring his characters for use by Graphics on a poster and bookmark. In coordination with ALA's Communications and Marketing Office, ALA Graphics offers a range of display materials and bookmarks supporting the Libraries Transform® campaign. In support of the American Association of School Librarians (AASL), ALA Graphics continues to bolster its line of AASL Standards products. Some of Graphics' most popular products focus on helping library patrons and students navigate "fake news" and social networking spaces and improve their research and information literacy skills.

Booklist Publications

Booklist Publications is a multi-platform suite of 19 products and services for librarians and those involved with the library market. In addition to print editions of *Booklist*—for 117 years the chief review publication of the American Library Association—and *Book Links*, a quarterly supplement to *Booklist* that focuses on using children's books in the classroom, Booklist Publications offers Booklist Online, a database of content from the print as well as original content; five e-newsletters covering adult and children's books, YA books, audiobooks, and reference materials, in addition to trends and issues of interest to collection development and readers'-advisory librarians; the *Booklist Reader*, a blog about books and book people delivering news, opinions, and lists; Booklist webinars, sponsor-supported online programs, free to registrants; and *Booklist* live events. In 2017 Booklist Publications began producing custom content for library-market vendors on topics of interest to librarians. *Booklist* is also the sponsor or cosponsor of various ALA media awards, including the Andrew Carnegie Medals for Excellence in Fiction and Nonfiction, the Michael L. Printz Award for outstanding YA literature, and the Odyssey Award for excellence in audiobook production.

American Booksellers Association

333 Westchester Ave., Suite 202, White Plains, NY 10604
915-406-7500
World Wide Web http://www.bookweb.org

Founded in 1900, the American Booksellers Association (ABA) is a national not-for-profit trade organization headquartered in White Plains, New York, that works to help independently owned bookstores grow and succeed.

ABA's core members are key participants in their communities' local economies and culture, and to assist them ABA creates relevant programs; provides education, information, business products, and services; and engages in public policy and industry advocacy. The association actively supports and defends free speech and the First Amendment rights of all Americans. A volunteer board of 11 booksellers governs the association.

At the end of 2018 for the ninth year in a row ABA bookstore membership has grown, with stores operating in more than 2,400 locations. (There has been a 30 percent increase in the number of ABA member bookstores since 2009.) Also, as a channel, independent bookstore sales are up. Overall book sales across indie bookstores for 2018 increased nearly 5 percent over 2017, with a compound annual growth rate of 7.5 percent over the past five years. While not every bookstore or community has seen this growth, the national trends are clear. In addition, nationally in the United States, new stores are opening, established stores are finding new owners, and a new generation is coming into the business as both owner/managers and frontline booksellers. All of this is a result of the fact that indie booksellers remain a resilient and entrepreneurial group.

In 2018 ABA welcomed 96 new indie bookstores that opened for business in 36 states and the District of Columbia. The new stores include a mystery bookstore, a diverse children's bookstore, a community-run book cooperative, and 14 branches of existing businesses. In addition, 28 established ABA member stores were bought by new owners.

For the sixth year in a row, Indies First, a national campaign of activities and events in support of independent bookstores, marked another successful kickoff to the holiday shopping season on Small Business Saturday. Author Jason Reynolds was the spokesperson for the 2018 celebration of Indies First, and he was an especially prominent voice on behalf of indie bookstores, especially via social media. In addition, to support Reynolds' mission of providing children in underserved communities with access to books that reflect their own experiences, ABA and American Express worked together with Simon & Schuster Children's Publishing to make available 20,000 special-edition copies of *Ghost*, the first book in Reynolds' *New York Times* bestselling Track series, to young readers through independent bookstores.

Small Business Saturday sponsor American Express reported that the ninth annual Small Business Saturday kicked off holiday shopping with record levels of reported spending. Spending among U.S. consumers who said they shopped at independent retailers and restaurants reached a record high of an estimated $17.8 billion, with 104 million U.S. consumers shopping or dining at local independently owned businesses that day. In addition, 96 percent of consumers who reported shopping on Small Business Saturday said the day makes them want to patronize local small businesses all year long, not just during the holiday season.

Sales at independent bookstores nationwide were up 1.3 percent in 2018 over 2017 for the week including Small Business Saturday. For IndieCommerce stores, Small Business Saturday generated a more than 50 percent increase in online sales compared to last year; Black Friday sales were up 28 percent, and Cyber Monday sales were up 12 percent.

In December, best-selling author James Patterson announced the names of 333 independent booksellers receiving grants totaling $250,000 as part of his 2018 Holiday Bookstore Bonus Program. Patterson partnered with ABA to distribute the funds, which were awarded to individual booksellers in amounts of $750.

"2018 marks the fifth year I've done this Bookseller Bonus program with the ABA. Along the way, I've spoken to booksellers who've used bonuses to do the things that many of us take for granted—go to the dentist, repair a car, or even buy their family Christmas gifts," said Patterson. "Booksellers make a difference in people's lives every day, and I'm happy to make even a small difference in theirs by giving them a little something more this holiday season."

ABA CEO Oren Teicher said, "James Patterson's extraordinary support of independent booksellers and their work has been generous and sustained. And through his continued funding of holiday bonuses for booksellers he is again demonstrating his earnest commitment to literacy and putting the right book into the hands of young readers. We can't thank him enough!"

Also in 2018, more than 500 indie bookstores nationwide celebrated the fourth Independent Bookstore Day (IBD) on Saturday, April 28, with author appearances, special discounts, activities for all ages, and more. Participation was up from about 400 stores in 2017. Special Independent Bookstore Day merchandise included featured 14 limited-edition items for sale, including Dragons Love Books onesies based on Adam Rubin's *Dragons Love Tacos*, illustrated by Daniel Salmieri (Dial Books); a signed special edition of *Ungrateful Mammals* by Dave Eggers; literary tea towels with quotes from Julia Child and Anthony Bourdain; and a literary map of the universe. Free IBD giveaways included a specially stickered edition of a classic from the Feminism: A Very Short Introduction series from Oxford University Press, and a Llama Llama coloring book activity kit.

In July 2018 independent booksellers across the United States celebrated another year of Find Waldo Local, the shop-local challenge cosponsored by Candlewick Press and the American Booksellers Association. Find Waldo Local, which invites children to pick up a "passport" at any of the 250 participating independent bookstores nationwide, leads participants through a scavenger hunt around their local downtown business district in search of the bespectacled picture-book character Waldo. For every six-inch Waldo standee spotted at a participating business, children earn stamps for their passports that can be used toward fun prizes given out at the host store's final celebration.

In May 2018 PBS aired the first of an eight-part television series, "The Great American Read," hosted by television personality and journalist Meredith Vieira. The series, which picked up again in the fall, aimed to spark a national conversation about books and reading by taking viewers on a journey across the country to uncover the nation's 100 most-loved novels, the people who love them, and their authors. As episodes aired, indie booksellers promoted voting among readers and viewers, put up displays of the best-loved books, and held viewing parties for the series. The series concluded on October 23 by naming Harper Lee's *To Kill a Mockingbird* America's best-loved novel.

Association and Governance

The results of balloting by the bookstore members of ABA to elect four directors to serve on the ABA board were announced in May 2018. Elected to three-year terms (2018–2021) as directors were Kelly Estep of Carmichael's Bookstore in Louisville, Kentucky; Pete Mulvihill of Green Apple Books in San Francisco, California; and Angela Maria Spring of Duende District Bookstore in Washington, D.C. This is the second three-year term on the ABA board for Mulvihill; Estep and Spring have not previously served on the board.

In addition, Bradley Graham of Politics and Prose Bookstore in Washington, D.C., was elected to serve the unexpired period of what would have been ABA president Robert Sindelar's term as a board member.

Continuing on the 11-member board are ABA president Robert Sindelar of Third Place Books, with three locations in the Seattle area; ABA vice president Jamie Fiocco of Flyleaf Books in Chapel Hill, North Carolina; Kenny Brechner of Devaney, Doak and Garrett Booksellers in Farmington, Maine; Kris Kleindienst of Left Bank Books in St. Louis, Missouri; Chris Morrow of Northshire Bookstore in Manchester Center, Vermont, and Saratoga Springs, New York; Christine Onorati of WORD in Brooklyn, New York, and Jersey City, New Jersey; and Annie Philbrick of Bank Square Books in Mystic, Connecticut, and Savoy Bookshop & Café in Westerly, Rhode Island.

Book Awards

In 2018 booksellers at independent bookstores nationwide selected the winners of the 2018 Indies Choice Book Awards and the E. B. White Read-Aloud Awards in eight categories.

The **2018 Indies Choice Book Award Winners**, reflecting the spirit of independent bookstores nationwide, are

- Adult Fiction: *Sing, Unburied, Sing: A Novel* by Jesmyn Ward (Scribner)
- Adult Nonfiction: *Killers of the Flower Moon: The Osage Murders and the Birth of the FBI* by David Grann (Doubleday)
- Adult Debut: *Her Body and Other Parties: Stories* by Carmen Maria Machado (Graywolf Press)
- Audiobook: *Lincoln in the Bardo* by George Saunders, read by Nick Offerman, David Sedaris, George Saunders, and a full cast (Random House Audio)
- Young Adult: *The Hate U Give* by Angie Thomas (Balzer+Bray)

The winners of the **E. B. White Read-Aloud Awards**, reflecting the playful, well-paced language, the engaging themes, and the universal appeal embodied by E. B. White's collection of beloved books, are

- Middle Reader: *Wishtree* by Katherine Applegate (Feiwel & Friends)
- Picture Book: *The Wolf, the Duck, and the Mouse* by Mac Barnett, Jon Klassen (Illus.) (Candlewick)

The **Indie Champion Award** is presented to an author or illustrator booksellers feel understands the importance of independent bookstores to their communities at large and has a strong personal commitment to foster and support the mission and passion of independent booksellers. This year's winner is

- Jason Reynolds

Indie booksellers chose these three classic picture books for induction into the **Picture Book Hall of Fame**.

- *Ada Twist, Scientist* by Andrea Beaty, David Roberts (Illus.) (Harry N. Abrams)
- *I Have a Dream* by Martin Luther King Jr., Kadir Nelson (Illus.) (Schwartz & Wade)
- *We're Going on a Bear Hunt* by Michael Rosen, Helen Oxenbury (Illus.) (Margaret K. McElderry Books)

The **2018 Honor Award** recipients are

- Adult Fiction: *Exit West: A Novel* by Mohsin Hamid (Riverhead Books); *Lincoln in the Bardo: A Novel* by George Saunders (Random House); *Little Fires Everywhere: A Novel* by Celeste Ng (Penguin Press); *Mrs. Caliban* by Rachel Ingalls (New Directions); *Pachinko: A Novel* by Min Jin Lee (Grand Central Publishing)
- Adult Nonfiction: *Hallelujah Anyway: Rediscovering Mercy* by Anne Lamott (Riverhead Books); *Hunger: A Memoir of (My) Body* by Roxane Gay (Harper); *Silence: In the Age of Noise* by Erling Kagge, Becky L. Crook (Trans.) (Pantheon); *Spineless: The Science of Jellyfish and the Art of Growing a Backbone* by Juli Berwald (Riverhead Books); *The Stranger in the Woods: The Extraordinary Story of the Last True Hermit* by Michael Finkel (Knopf)
- Adult Debut: *Fen: Stories* by Daisy Johnson (Graywolf Press); *History of Wolves: A Novel* by Emily Fridlund (Atlantic Monthly Press); *The Leavers: A Novel* by Lisa Ko (Algonquin Books); *The Long Haul: A Trucker's Tales of Life on the Road* by Finn Murphy (W. W. Norton & Company); *Stephen Florida: A Novel* by Gabe Habash (Coffee House Press)
- Audiobook: *American War: A Novel* by Omar El Akkad, read by Dion Graham (Penguin Random House Audio); *The Fact of a Body: A Murder and a Memoir* by Alexandria Marzano-Lesnevich, read by Alexandria

Marzano-Lesnevich (Macmillan Audio); *Hunger: A Memoir of (My) Body* by Roxane Gay, read by Roxane Gay (HarperAudio); *Killers of the Flower Moon: The Osage Murders and the Birth of the FBI* by David Grann, read by Will Patton, Ann Marie Lee, and Danny Campbell (Penguin Random House Audio); *The Ninth Hour* by Alice McDermott, read by Euan Morton (Macmillan Audio)
- Young Adult: *All the Crooked Saints* by Maggie Stiefvater (Scholastic Press); *Dear Martin* by Nic Stone (Crown Books for Young Readers); *Long Way Down* by Jason Reynolds (Atheneum/Caitlyn Dlouhy Books); *Turtles All the Way Down* by John Green (Dutton Books for Young Readers); *When Dimple Met Rishi* by Sandhya Menon (Simon Pulse)

E. B. White Read-Aloud

- Middle Reader: *The Epic Fail of Arturo Zamora* by Pablo Cartaya (Viking Books for Young Readers); *The First Rule of Punk* by Celia C. Pérez (Viking Books for Young Readers); *One Last Word* by Nikki Grimes (Bloomsbury USA Children's Books); *Refugee* by Alan Gratz (Scholastic); *The Stars Beneath Our Feet* by David Barclay Moore (Knopf Books for Young Readers)
- Picture Book: *After the Fall (How Humpty Dumpty Got Back Up Again)* by Dan Santat (Roaring Brook Press); *Alfie (The Turtle That Disappeared)* by Thyra Heder (Harry N. Abrams); *Come With Me* by Holly M. McGhee, Pascal Lemaître (G. P. Putnam's Sons Books for Young Readers); *Dragons Love Tacos 2: The Sequel* by Adam Rubin, Daniel Salmieri (Illus.) (Dial Books); *Escargot* by Dashka Slater, Sydney Hanson (Illus.) (Farrar, Straus and Giroux Books for Young Readers)

Indie Champion Honorees

- Judy Blume
- David Levithan
- Celeste Ng
- Jesmyn Ward
- Jacqueline Woodson

In addition, support and participation continued to grow for ABA's Indies Introduce program, in which panels of independent booksellers select a Winter/Spring and a Summer/Fall list of ten adult titles and ten children's titles as the top debuts of the upcoming publishing season. Publishers once again offered special terms to ABA member bookstores on the selected titles, for which marketing materials were also available from ABA.

Membership Education

The 13th Winter Institute (Wi13), held in Memphis, Tennessee, January 22–25, drew a record number of booksellers, publishers, authors, and international guests.

About 680 booksellers from 370 stores joined more than 130 authors, 96 publisher partners, and 60 international guests who traveled from as far as New Zealand, Denmark, and Guatemala to attend ABA's largest educational event.

With the support of the event's lead sponsor, Ingram Content Group, and publishers large and small, Wi13 provided booksellers with three full days of programming, including keynote addresses and featured speakers, education sessions, publisher/bookseller focus groups, rep picks speed-dating, an ABA Town Hall Meeting, the very popular author reception, and a closing reception featuring authors from small and university presses.

The ABA Town Hall featured an update from the Diversity Task Force and a discussion of numerous topics, including profitability, preorders, and the sustainability of independent bookselling.

Seventy-two booksellers from ABA member stores around the country were awarded scholarships to the Winter Institute in Memphis, funded by a portion of total proceeds raised from publisher sponsorships of the event. Booksellers at all ABA member stores that had not received a scholarship in the last two years were eligible to win a Winter Institute scholarship.

In addition to the recipients of publisher-sponsored scholarships, ABA members attended the institute on scholarships from ABA, the Southern California Independent Booksellers Association, and the Book Industry Charitable Foundation (Binc). Also, Candlewick Press once again awarded a scholarship to a bookseller active in the Candlewick Handselling Indie Recognition Program (CHIRP).

In 2018, during the months of March and April ABA staff traveled around the country to attend the ten regional spring forums. Held in conjunction with the regional bookseller associations, the annual forums are designed to provide an opportunity to share ideas, discuss industry issues, and receive updates on various association projects. Along with an open forum discussion of industry issues, the events featured a new education session, "A Year of Bookstore Profitability."

In May 2018 the annual BookExpo conference and trade show was held at the Javits Convention Center in New York City. In programming organized by ABA, attendees visited publishing houses around New York City for "Meet the Editor," a behind-the-scenes look at the philosophy and process of book editing. BookExpo also held its first-ever grand-opening keynote, featuring Barnes & Noble Chairman Len Riggio.

The 2018 ABA programming at BookExpo included two Publicists Speed Dating sessions. At each, registered ABA member bookstore owners, managers, and event coordinators had the opportunity to meet one-on-one with different publicists to promote their stores and to discover what publicists look for when planning author tours.

The show floor also featured a new interactive exhibit called the Vital Bookstore. The exhibit offered hourly docent-led tours through the display, which was created by Franklin Fixtures in collaboration with Baker & Taylor, to facilitate small-group exploration of physical merchandising strategies and concepts for cafés, children's areas, traditional book spaces, and modern general merchandise areas. In addition, booksellers had the opportunity to take part in a number of small-group discussions on topics such as point-of-sale systems, mixed merchandising, buying for margins, disaster preparedness, leveraging e-books and audiobooks, and more.

In fall 2018 ABA presented the all-new education session "Maximizing Pre-Order Campaigns" at each of the eight fall regional trade shows. The new education session focused on ways to successfully promote and sell pre-orders to become an integral partner to publishers and authors, including new methods developed and tested by ABA's Pre-Orders Task Force of indie stores.

ABA's programming regarding children's bookselling also continued to expand in 2018. The ABC Children's Group at ABA presented the sixth annual Children's Institute in New Orleans, Louisiana, from June 19 to 21. The more than 300 independent booksellers in attendance—as well as many publishers and authors—reflected enthusiasm for greater diversity in books and bookselling and a commitment to making the industry more inclusive.

Throughout 2018 the popularity of ABA's online roundtable discussions, called Marketing Meetups, grew. The twice-monthly conversations among independent booksellers cover a range of topics, including strategies for boosting online sales, summer marketing ideas, bookstore podcasts, frequent buyer programs, co-op advertising, and more.

In 2018 ABA published its annual financial survey of participating independent bookstores, the ABACUS report, in conjunction with Industry Insights of Dublin, Ohio. The report features an expanded range of data; presentation formats, making it easier to evaluate a bookstore's ABACUS results; and a set of online tools. As in previous years, the ABACUS report includes benchmarking comparisons with other businesses based on multiple criteria (such as sales level, store size, and community type) in addition to year-to-year trending information for stores that have reported in previous years. In addition, via a fully secure online dashboard, which offers sophisticated analytical tools not available for past ABACUS surveys, booksellers can run dynamic reports and explore trends across a number of criteria.

Advocacy

ABA's vigorous advocacy efforts on behalf of member bookstores continued during 2018. Among other activities, ABA focused much of its advocacy resources on the growing issue of states and communities giving away millions of dollars in tax subsidies to large retail corporations, growing concerns about antitrust issues, and Amazon's growing market power in many industries, as well as the ongoing sales tax fairness campaign. In order to increase its capacity to address First Amendment issues, ABA promoted Dave Grogan to director of the American Booksellers for Free Expression, Advocacy & Public Policy in February and expanded its advocacy staff.

ABA's advocacy for sales tax fairness continued in 2018 and culminated in June in the U.S. Supreme Court decision in *South Dakota v. Wayfair*, in which the Court upheld a South Dakota economic nexus law requiring out-of-state sellers with 200 sales or $100,000 in revenue from sales in the state to collect and remit sales tax to South Dakota.

While Amazon collects and remits sales tax on remote sales in all states on its direct sales, for the most part it is not required to collect tax on behalf of its third-party sellers that conduct business on Amazon Marketplace. In order to gain insight into the impact of Amazon Marketplace, ABA collaborated with Civic

Economics to release the report *Prime Numbers: Amazon and American Communities* in April. The report includes calculations of uncollected sales tax, displaced jobs, and displaced retail space in 2016, in total and broken down by state. To help booksellers share this information with their lawmakers, ABA created a template letter for booksellers to use to ask their representatives to require third-party marketplaces to collect and remit sales tax.

In July 2018 the Advocates for Independent Business (AIB), a coalition of independent trade associations and businesses that ABA cofounded in 2013, released a new Local Policy Action Toolkit. The toolkit offers independent business owners and retailers tips for engaging with their city officials and advocating for policies that strengthen and grow local businesses. The purpose of the publication is for independent booksellers to use the toolkit to provide policymakers with a clear case for why local, independent businesses matter to their city's well-being and vitality. Nine policies are featured that local governments can implement to better support independent businesses and strengthen their communities.

Beginning in September, the FTC held a series of hearings focused on evaluating antitrust policy and enforcement. ABA submitted written testimony to discuss how Amazon has exploited its dual role as both a marketplace platform and a retailer to inhibit competition. ABA's comments point out that, by undermining the ecosystem of the book industry, Amazon harms its competition and has a chilling effect on the diversity of voices in publishing.

On behalf of more than 80 independent businesses in New York and Virginia, on Wednesday, December 5, the American Booksellers Association sent letters to Governors Andrew Cuomo (New York) and Ralph Northam (Virginia) opposing the massive subsidies the states offered Amazon regarding its site selection of new headquarters locations. The businesses that signed on to the letters include members of ABA, the New Atlantic Independent Booksellers Association, the Southern Independent Booksellers Alliance, and Advocates for Independent Business. They urged the governors to focus on ways the states could support local businesses and asked for meetings with the governors to discuss the matter.

As a member of the Banned Books Week Coalition, ABA participated in coordinating Banned Books Week 2018, which was held from September 23–29. ABA additionally sent out Banned Books Week kits to 500 participating stores. The kits included bookmarks, stickers, counter cards, caution tape, and information about incidents of book censorship in the prior year, all of which helped bookstores with displays, marketing, and messaging. Throughout the year, ABA worked with the National Coalition Against Censorship on a number of challenges to books in schools and libraries.

David Grogan, ABA's director of ABFE, Advocacy and Public Policy, is a board member representative for ABA on the Media Coalition (and now chairperson), a coalition of media groups that work to support free speech, including legal challenges. As part of Media Coalition, ABA challenged a number of laws that would have infringed on the First Amendment rights of bookstores to sell books. ABA is part of the monthly Media Coalition meetings.

In an effort to find new ways to bring the free expression message to a broader, and younger, audience, ABA launched the *Counterspeak* podcast in December. At present, it is a monthly podcast. The first podcast featured Nadine Strossen, former president of the American Civil Liberties Union.

ABA participated in quarterly meetings of the Free Expression Network in Washington, D.C., which included educational panels on issues pertaining to free expression, such as campaign finance reform and social media censorship.

Throughout the year a number of booksellers made use of ABA's free speech hotline to discuss their concerns over protests regarding author events. These protests came from members of the public, from bookstore staff, or via social media. ABA was able to assist booksellers in each of these situations, and in some, booksellers made use of in-store ABA materials regarding controversial author events.

Association of Research Libraries

21 Dupont Circle N.W., Washington, DC 20036
202-296-2296, e-mail arlhq@arl.org
World Wide Web http://www.arl.org

Kaylyn Groves
Senior Writer and Editor

The Association of Research Libraries (ARL) is a nonprofit organization of 124 research libraries in Canada and the United States whose mission is to advance research, learning, and scholarly communication. The Association fosters the open exchange of ideas and expertise, promotes equity and diversity, and pursues advocacy and public policy efforts that reflect the values of the library, scholarly, and higher education communities. ARL forges partnerships and catalyzes the collective efforts of research libraries to enable knowledge creation and to achieve enduring and barrier-free access to information.

ARL's Action Plan 2019–2021 lays out goals and actions in six priority areas: Advocacy and Public Policy; ARL Academy; Data and Analytics; Diversity, Equity, and Inclusion; Innovation; and Scholars and Scholarship.

Below are highlights of the Association's achievements in 2018, many of which were undertaken in partnership with member libraries or other organizations. For links to additional information about these accomplishments, please visit http://www.arl.org/about/arls-key-accomplishments-in-2018.

Advocacy and Public Policy

ARL is the collective voice for research libraries and archives on public policy in the United States and internationally. The Association leads on policy and legal issues that advance sustainable, equitable, and barrier-free access to information and culture while protecting core values of privacy and freedom of expression.

Fair Use/Fair Dealing Week 2018 Highlights Balance in Copyright System

The fifth annual Fair Use/Fair Dealing Week took place February 26–March 2, growing to 153 participating organizations—as well as numerous individuals—celebrating the important and flexible doctrines of fair use and fair dealing worldwide. This year's event was organized by ARL and participants included universities, libraries, library associations, and many other organizations. Sixty ARL member institutions contributed a wide range of resources this year.

Software Preservation Best Practices in Fair Use to Help Safeguard Cultural Record, Advance Research

Code of Best Practices in Fair Use for Software Preservation, released in September, provides guidance on the legality of archiving legacy software to ensure continued access to digital files of all kinds and to illuminate the history of technology. The publication provides librarians, archivists, curators, and others who work to preserve software with a tool to guide their reasoning about when and how to employ fair use.

Two Landmark Laws Passed in United States: Marrakesh Treaty Implementation Act, Geospatial Data Act

After years of advocacy by ARL and many others, the Marrakesh Treaty Implementation Act was signed into law by President Trump on October 9. The Marrakesh Treaty to Facilitate Access to Published Works for Persons Who Are Blind, Visually Impaired, or Otherwise Print Disabled requires countries to ensure minimum copyright limitations and exceptions for the creation and distribution of accessible formats of works and cross-border sharing of these works. Additionally, Senator Orrin Hatch (R-Utah) and Senator Mark Warner (D-Va.) oversaw the passage of the Geospatial Data Act of 2018, which will greatly enhance access by researchers, students, and the public to a vast array of geospatial data, thereby advancing learning and knowledge creation and promoting open and transparent government. Senators Hatch and Warner also led a bipartisan resolution to recognize November 15, 2018, as National GIS Day.

ARL Academy

The ARL Academy shapes and informs leadership practice throughout the research library by advancing professional development. The unified suite of programs empowers ARL library and archive staff with the tools necessary to meet the current and future needs of users. Offerings focus particularly on the challenges of organizational change.

Events Engage 800 Participants in Various Aspects of Research Library Management

In 2018 the ARL Academy offered a virtual Critical Conversation session led by Carol Mandel (NYU) for member representatives to engage one another on user experience. The Academy offered two virtual "On the Edge" discussions—one on artificial intelligence led by Chris Bourg (MIT) and another on learning analytics led by James Hilton (Michigan)—for employees of member institutions. Fifteen member institutions—Alberta; UCLA with Southern California; Delaware; Indiana Bloomington; Iowa State with Iowa; McGill; Penn State; Rice; Rochester with Buffalo, Cornell, and Syracuse; and Yale—hosted ten Library Management Skills Institutes. UC San Diego and Indiana Bloomington each hosted a Digital Scholarship Institute. Four members—Florida, Johns Hopkins, Penn, and Temple—and the Association of Southeastern Research Libraries (ASERL) and the Triangle Research Libraries Network (TRLN) hosted Institutes on Reimagining the Library Liaison.

Leadership Programs Develop Two Cohorts of Research Library Leaders

The 2018–2019 ARL Leadership Fellows cohort participated in the Spring and Fall Association Meetings as well as two Leadership Fellows Institutes, hosted by the University of Iowa and the George Washington University. The 2018–2019 cohort of the Leadership & Career Development Program—for librarians from historically underrepresented racial and ethnic groups—participated in an orientation in Washington, D.C., and their first institute at the Ohio State University.

Publications Explore Outreach, Engagement, Liaison Roles, Liaison Reorganizations

SPEC Kit 361, *Outreach and Engagement* captures a snapshot of how ARL member institutions are defining their outreach and engagement programs, how they are assigning and structuring responsibilities, and how they are measuring the success and impact of their efforts. In *Research Library Issues (RLI)* no. 294, teams from five U.S. and Canadian universities describe their reorganizations and redefinitions of what it means to be a research library liaison with faculty and students.

Data and Analytics

ARL provides data and analytics on research library practices, effectiveness, and impact. The Research and Analytics program aligns ARL's assessment work with the goals and needs of the Association's members. The program's focus on the impact and outcomes of ARL libraries and archives drives and informs data collection and analytics protocols, information dissemination practices, and library assessment.

ARL Releases Annual Salary Survey, ARL Statistics, SPEC Kits, *Research Library Issues* on Demographics

The Association issued the *ARL Annual Salary Survey 2016–2017* and *ARL Statistics 2015–2016* publications in July. The salary survey analyzes data on more than 15,500 professional staff working in the 124 ARL member libraries during 2016–2017. *ARL Statistics, ARL Academic Law Library Statistics,* and *ARL Academic Health Sciences Library Statistics* present information describing the collections, staffing, expenditures, and service activities of the Association's 124 member libraries in 2015–2016. The Assessment program published four SPEC Kits in 2018: *Accessibility and Universal Design* (358), *Library Development* (359), *Learning Analytics* (360), and *Outreach and Engagement* (361). And in *RLI* no. 295, Stanley Wilder (Louisiana State) illustrates recent demographic changes in the professional population of ARL institutions.

ARL Develops Research Library Impact Framework, Launches Pilot Project and Practice Brief Process

In 2018 the ARL Assessment Committee developed a Research Library Impact Framework, a living document to be regularly updated and reprioritized with feedback from the ARL community. The framework will serve as the foundation for the ARL research agenda. In November, ARL sent member representatives a call for expressions of interest in leading and/or participating in a "Research Library Impact" pilot project or in submitting a practice brief. Each pilot project will be an original research study designed to address the research questions identified in the framework. A practice brief is a short document designed to support library professionals with research-based information as they improve their library assessment work.

Library Assessment Conference 2018 Attracts 600 Participants

The seventh biennial Library Assessment Conference: Building Effective, Sustainable, Practical Assessment convened in Houston, Texas, in December. This event advances the growing library assessment community through presentations, workshops, and informal engagement. The 2018 conference was co-sponsored by ARL and the University of Washington Libraries. The University of Houston Libraries and Texas A&M University Libraries hosted the event.

Diversity, Equity, and Inclusion

The Association helps its members develop and sustain diverse, equitable, inclusive, and accessible services, collections, and work environments. ARL's work advances access to economic and social prosperity, encourages full participation in society, and counters the historical lack of access to and underrepresentation of human and material resources that libraries and archives cultivate and steward.

ARL Awards Undergraduates, Graduate Students with Diversity Fellowships, Scholarships

The ARL Fellowship for Digital and Inclusive Excellence (AFDIE) Selection Committee chose 11 undergraduates as 2018–2019 AFDIE Fellows. The AFDIE program introduces undergraduates from a variety of disciplines to digital stewardship and promotes diversification of research library and archives staffs. The ARL/Society of American Archivists (SAA) Mosaic Program Selection Committee accepted three MLIS students from historically underrepresented racial and ethnic groups as 2018–2020 Mosaic Program Fellows. The ARL/SAA Mosaic Program advances much-needed diversification of the archives and special collections professions. Members of the ARL Diversity, Equity, and Inclusion Committee and their designees chose 15 MLIS students to participate in the Initiative to Recruit a Diverse Workforce (IRDW) as 2018–2020 ARL Diversity Scholars. The IRDW helps create a diverse professional community that will better meet the needs of researchers, students, and other constituencies whose demographics and perspectives are quickly evolving.

Two Symposia Advance Diversity, Equity, Inclusion in Research Libraries, Archives

During the American Library Association (ALA) Midwinter Meeting, ARL hosted its 14th Annual Leadership Symposium for participants in ARL's diversity and recruitment programs. The symposium develops leadership skills among participants and provides opportunities for participants to build cohorts and learning communities. The event explores contemporary roles and cultures of research libraries and archives and addresses the realities of working in research and higher education environments, especially for people of color. Additionally, in May ARL and the Association of College & Research Libraries (ACRL) offered the Symposium for Strategic Leadership in Diversity, Equity, and Inclusion. This new symposium aimed to increase understanding and capacity among academic and research library professionals for creating healthy organizations with diverse, equitable, and inclusive climates.

ARL Releases Publication, Statements Promoting Diversity, Equity, Inclusion

In May ARL released *Accessibility and Universal Design*, SPEC Kit 358, an exploration of how ARL member libraries are meeting the accessibility needs of individuals with disabilities. Throughout 2018 ARL also released five statements promoting diversity, equity, and inclusion: "ADA Education and Reform Act Threatens Equity of Access" (February), "ARL Denounces Harassment of Chris Bourg Following Code4Lib Keynote" (March), "ARL Issues Statement on Supreme Court Decision Upholding Travel Ban" (June), "ARL Affirms Support of Civil Rights Protections for Transgender People" (November), and "ARL Condemns Anti-Semitic Attacks" (December).

Innovation

ARL facilitates a culture of innovation within research libraries. The Association helps member representatives build capacity to lead innovative organizations by learning innovative practices and by engaging in an environment that promotes, develops, and shares a culture of innovation.

ARL-CNI Fall Forum Delves into Innovation in Research Libraries

The 2018 Fall Forum, sponsored by ARL and the Coalition for Networked Information (CNI), gathered more than 200 academic and research library leaders in Washington, D.C., on September 27 to explore "Innovation in Research Libraries." The 2018 Julia C. Blixrud Memorial Lecturer, Bernard Banks, spoke about how leaders can create organizational cultures that support productive risk-taking. A panel of university leaders discussed why libraries need to innovate, and a panel of ARL library directors talked about how libraries can encourage innovation. The 2018 recipient of the Julia C. Blixrud Scholarship, Justin Fuhr, shared his impressions of the ARL-CNI Fall Forum in a blog post.

Scholars and Scholarship

ARL catalyzes collective efforts to achieve enduring and barrier-free information. The Association works with the academic and research community to maximize the reach and impact of scholarship; the international library and archives community to advance institutions' financial capacity to support open scholarship through new models; and the ARL membership to support leadership on open scholarship within member institutions.

Press and Library Directors Meet, Release Report, Slides

ARL and the Association of University Presses (AUPresses) hosted the second meeting of press and library directors with reporting relationships (P2L2) in June. The P2L2 Summit focused on shared practices, opportunities, and challenges;

projects; open access sustainability; and the provosts' value of the P2L relationship. The report on the P2L2 Summit and slides from the summit are available on the ARL website.

Toward an Open Monograph Ecosystem (TOME) Convenes Third Annual Meeting, Publishes Report, Slides, Video

TOME, Toward an Open Monograph Ecosystem, is a pilot initiative to advance wide dissemination of scholarship by humanities and humanistic social sciences faculty members through open editions of peer-reviewed and professionally edited monographs. The Association of American Universities (AAU), Association of University Presses (AUPresses), and ARL formally launched TOME in 2017. The TOME Task Force convened its third annual meeting in July to assess TOME's progress, share lessons learned, and determine an action plan to expand participation in the initiative. The report on the third annual TOME meeting and slides from the meeting are available on the ARL website.

ARL Task Force on Wikimedia and Linked Open Data Releases Draft White Paper for Comment

In June 2018 the Association charged a task force to look at Wikidata (the community) and Wikibase (the infrastructure). The task force emerged from several years of discussion between ARL and the Wikimedia Foundation on where the two communities can effectively collaborate. The focus on Wikidata and Wikibase came from two points of alignment in particular: interest in linked open data for both library discovery systems and Wikipedia, and advancing a diversity and inclusion agenda in the cultures of both libraries and Wikimedia. In November the task force circulated a draft white paper for open community comment and will finalize the paper after considering those comments.

The Scholarly Publishing and Academic Resources Coalition

Heather Joseph
Executive Director

21 Dupont Circle N.W., Suite 800, Washington, DC 20036
202-296-2296, e-mail sparc@sparcopen.org
World Wide Web https://www.sparcopen.org

Background and Mission

The Scholarly Publishing and Academic Resources Coalition (SPARC) is a global coalition committed to making Open the default for research and education. SPARC promotes the faster and wider sharing of research outputs and educational materials to increase the impact of research, fuel the advancement of knowledge, and increase the return on research and education investments. SPARC staunchly supports efforts to promote diversity, inclusion, equity, and social justice in and through the library community.

SPARC is a catalyst for action. Supported by 200+ members in the United States and Canada, and with international affiliates active in Africa, Europe and Japan, its pragmatic agenda focuses on collaborating with stakeholders in the global community to encourage new norms, practices, and policies that promote equitable access, sharing, and use of scholarship.

Strategy

To promote the changes in both infrastructure and culture needed to make Open the default in research and education, SPARC's strategy centers on

- Advocating for policies that enable Open practices throughout research and education
- Educating stakeholders on opportunities to change the scholarly communication system
- Incubating projects that promote new models for sharing research outputs and developing educational materials that support the needs of scholars and society

SPARC works to identify shared values and opportunities for action between its library members and stakeholders in the global research and education environment, including faculty and administration, public and private research funders, and the public. SPARC places a premium on empowering students and early career professionals, and actively incorporates collaboration with them across all program areas.

Priorities

SPARC's leadership work is concentrated in three program areas: Open Access, Open Data, and Open Education. Additionally, to maximize progress, SPARC supports efforts that champion intellectual freedom, a free and open Internet, privacy, confidentiality, and equitable copyright and intellectual property policies.

The following were key priorities in 2018.

Conducting Policy Advocacy

SPARC's top priority continued to be to advance policies that promote Open Access to research outputs (including articles and data) and educational materials at the institutional, state, national, and international level. SPARC's advanced this priority by

- Educating key policymakers (including Executive Branch/Administration, U.S. Congress, Canadian Administration, Canadian Parliament, and others) on SPARC's core policy priorities
- Developing strategies to defend against threats to existing policies, as well as proactive strategies to extend/expand policy progress in the United States, Canada, and globally
- Leveraging the Alliance for Taxpayer Access and Right to Research Coalition stakeholder communities to accelerate policy progress
- Working with the media to promote public awareness of the benefits of Open policies
- Working with public and private funders to create and implement Open policies in the United States, Canada, and globally

Advocating for Community Controlled Infrastructure

SPARC concentrated its work on leveraging resources to sustain crucial infrastructure underpinning the scholarly communications ecosystem. In 2018 that work included

- Producing a comprehensive, expert market analysis of the current commercial players in infrastructure across the higher education sector, including a mapping of key areas of vulnerability to this infrastructure (including but not limited to, scholarly communications infrastructure) as well as the identification of specific points of potential community leverage
- Leading research and development efforts on new economic and organizational models for the collective provisioning of Open resources and infrastructure, including support for targeted new investment instruments, and actively collaborating with community efforts to accelerate progress

Promoting Culture Change through Realigning Incentives

SPARC actively promoted the need for realignment of existing reward and incentive structures to advance Open as the default in research and education. SPARC's work to further this priority included

- Leveraging the leadership of research funders and higher education leaders at the University president/provost level to serve as champions and peer-influencers to promote incentive realignment
- Promoting and securing a national convening of these leaders/stakeholders for peer-to-peer discussion and development of strategies to promote adoption of practices and policies rewarding open sharing of research outputs and educational resources
- Encouraging inclusion of rewards/recognition for Open behaviors in evaluation and promotion guidelines
- Promoting exemplars that have made demonstrable progress toward re-aligning rewards
- Supporting research into current evaluation, reward, and incentive structures.
- Presenting webcasts / public programming to increase awareness of critical research culture issues
- Leveraging the OpenCon community to promote culture change within the next generation

Providing Resources to Support Campus Action

SPARC produced and promoted resources that enable our members to take timely and informed actions. SPARC's work to advance this priority included

- Providing members up-to-the-moment updates and analyses of key policy and scholarly communications-related trends and developments
- Issuing action alerts and other opportunities for timely member library participation in advocacy, education, and partnership initiatives
- Delivering tools and resources to support member campus advocacy and education activities (e.g., Connect OER, State Level Policy Trackers, and Declaring Independence.)
- Providing free member campus visits by the SPARC team to promote awareness, education, and advocacy for key program areas
- Convening International Open Access Week as a catalyst for action across the community

Continuing Priorities

Globalization. SPARC continued to expand its presence and programs to reflect and support the global nature of scholarly communications by

- Actively promoting the SPARC brand as a reflection of global presence and activity
- Co-sponsoring meetings outside the United States with partner organizations
- Identifying new opportunities and establishing partnerships with key stakeholders in other global regions

Student and Early Career Researcher Campaign. SPARC promoted the inclusion of students and early career academic professionals in all areas of Open Access by

- Supporting the OpenCon community for students and early career academic professionals
- Empowering local and issue-oriented community building for the next generation through OpenCon satellite events and community calls
- Strengthening joint advocacy efforts to leverage community presence on Open Access, Open Data, Open Education, and related issues
- Maintaining relationships with key national and international organizations representing students and early career academic professionals
- Seeking additional support/partnerships to help strengthen SPARC's community-building efforts to empower the next generation

Open Access Infrastructure Support. SPARC continued its leadership role in promoting digital repositories and open access publishing outlets by

- Supporting academy-based publishing initiatives
- Providing expert consulting services, exploring and supporting transition strategies for subscription-based publishers to move to open-access model
- Contributing to evaluations of potential business models supporting community-wide Open Access infrastructure
- Partnering with key digital repository organizations to promote educational programs of interest to the community
- Participating in workshops and symposia on access issues

Ensuring Organizational Stability and Strength. SPARC continued to place a premium on ensuring that its organizational structure is designed to achieve its mission by

- Deploying flexible employment arrangements to ensure high-level talent can be strategically deployed to meet changing resource needs
- Identifying and capitalizing on opportunities to build internal capacity, via ongoing monitoring of dues structure, grant funding for program support, expanded partnership arrangements, etc.
- Promoting and expanding member retention and recruitment efforts

Program Activities and Outcomes 2018

Policy and Advocacy

- SPARC is regularly invited to represent its community's views in policy forums and consultations ranging from the European Commission to the South African Parliament. Its strong SPARC affiliates in Africa, Europe, and Japan provide it with a network of colleagues and collaborators that strengthens its advocacy presence and reach.
- SPARC led an effort to secure the first-ever federal appropriation to create an Open Textbook Pilot grant program at the U.S. Department of Education. A total of $10 million over two years will fund programs to expand the use of open textbooks at colleges and universities, which are expected to save students multiple times the original investment.
- SPARC worked with a bipartisan coalition of Congressional champions to explicitly add OER as an allowable use of federal Career and Technical Education funds for local and state authorities.
- SPARC provided policy support to member libraries that resulted in the passage of state-level OER legislation in Colorado, Virginia, and Washington.
- SPARC successfully helped lobby for the Congressional passage landmark Open Government Data Act making "Open and Machine Readable" the law of the land.
- SPARC convenes the "Open Research Funders Group," whose members include the Gates, Sloan, Arnold, Arcadia, and Soros Foundations, among others, and provides the group with a forum for regular discussion and opportunities for collaboration in strengthening the open research environment.

Campus Education

- In keeping with its commitment to partnering with the next generation of leaders, SPARC and the Right to Research Coalition hosted the fifth global OpenCon event in Toronto bringing together students and early career academic professionals from around the world and including dozens of SPARC member institutions to catalyze projects to advance Open Access, OER, and Open Data. Since launching in 2014, OpenCon and its satellite events have now reached more than 8,000 individuals across the world.
- SPARC's annual International Open Access Week, a partnership with the international Open Access community, continues to grow in popularity and participation. This year's theme of "Designing Equitable Foundations for Open Knowledge," encouraged the community to focus on increasing equity and inclusion in their efforts to advance open.
- SPARC supported members' local campus efforts by providing free visits by SPARC staff to member campuses, SPARC-sponsored speakers for events, practical guides, talking points, templates, and expert counsel on campus Open Access and Open Education issues.

- SPARC continued to expand online programs to cover hot topics of interest to members, including the launch of a regular repository community call and supporting the Coalition of Open Access Policy Institutions (COAPI) in creating a community call to advance their efforts.
- SPARC provided information and analysis on the growing suite of U.S. federal article- and data-sharing policies to ensure our members stay up-to-date.
- SPARC's suite of active partners continues to expand to deliver effective, cost-effective programs. New partners included Issue Labs, Mozilla, Unpaywall, and ASAPbio.
- SPARC expanded "Connect OER," a comprehensive directory documenting library-centered OER activities and estimates of student savings across more than 100 member campuses.
- SPARC launched the second cohort of its Open Education Leadership Program, which prepares library professionals to continue to serve on the cutting edge of this emerging area.
- SPARC produced a monthly newsletter for members summarizing key happenings and hosted regular webcasts on important topics. It also launched a new "rapid reaction" format to quickly address breaking news items.
- SPARC provided incubation for the Open Access Button, a suite of tools for getting legal, fast, and easy access to research behind paywalls by connecting users with open access copies and working with authors to share their work.

Communication and Media

SPARC is regularly consulted and quoted as an expert source on topics relating to scholarly communication, and its programs have been featured in both the national and trade press, in outlets ranging from NPR to the *Washington Post* to the *Economist* to the *Chronicle of Higher Education*.

Through its website, SPARC highlighted the work of open access champions. SPARC honored the groundbreaking work of both OCSDNet and BCCampus with its 2018 Innovator Awards.

SPARC-ACRL Forums

A major component of SPARC's community outreach occurs at meetings of the American Library Association (ALA) when SPARC works with the Association of College and Research Libraries (ACRL) and its scholarly communication committee to bring current issues to the attention of the community.

In January 2018 the SPARC-ACRL Midwinter forum was held in Colorado and focused on how the library community can reassert its influence to shape the open access publishing landscape. Later in June 2018 at the ALA Annual Meeting in New Orleans, the forum focused on diversity, equity, and inclusion in scholarly communication.

Governance

SPARC is guided by a steering committee. The 2018 committee members were Carolyn Henderson Allen (University of Arkansas), Juan Pablo Alperin (Simon Fraser University), Beth Bernhardt (University of North Carolina–Greensboro) Krista Cox (Association of Research Libraries), Lisa German (University of Houston), Rebecca Graham (University of Guelph), Vivian Lewis (McMaster University), Shilpa Rele (Rowan University), Virginia Steel (UCLA), Xuemao Wang (University of Cincinnati), and Karen Williams (University of Arizona).

Council on Library and Information Resources

1707 L St. N.W., Suite 650, Washington, DC 20036
202-939-4754
World Wide Web http://www.clir.org
Twitter @CLIRNews

Kathlin Smith
Director of Communications

The Council on Library and Information Resources (CLIR) is an independent, nonprofit organization that forges strategies to enhance research, teaching, and learning environments in collaboration with academic and cultural institutions, scholars, specialists, and practitioners. CLIR President Charles Henry leads the 18-member staff and works in close liaison with seven CLIR Distinguished Presidential Fellows.

CLIR is supported by fees from sponsoring institutions, grants from public and private foundations, contracts with federal agencies, and donations from individuals. A list of current sponsors, members, and funders is available at https://www.clir.org/about/current-sponsors-and-funders/.

CLIR's board establishes policy, oversees the investment of funds, sets goals, and approves strategies for their achievement. A full listing of CLIR board members is available at https://www.clir.org/about/governance/.

CLIR's activities in 2018 are described in the following sections.

Initiatives and Partnerships

Digital Library Federation

A program of CLIR, the Digital Library Federation (DLF) is a robust and diverse community of practitioners who advance research, learning, social justice, and the public good through the creative design and wise application of digital library technologies. DLF connects CLIR's vision and research agenda to a network of practitioners working in digital libraries, archives, labs, museums, and elsewhere. Through in-person meetings and year-round working groups, DLF promotes work on standards and best practices; research and data management; practices that open new opportunities for research, teaching, and learning; professional development; the social contexts and impact of digital library work; and community-driven frameworks for policy advocacy.

DLF hosts or facilitates a wide range of activities, which are highlighted below. DLF also maintains resources including a community calendar, jobs board, digitization cost calculator, and digitizing special formats wiki, all available through its website, https://www.diglib.org.

DLF Forum

DLF's annual signature event, the Forum, is open to digital library practitioners from member institutions and the broader community. The Forum provides an opportunity for DLF's advisory committee, working groups, and community members to conduct business and present their work; it also enables community members to share experiences and practices with one another and support a broader level of information sharing among professional staff. The Forum allows DLF to continually review and assess its progress with input from the community at large.

The 2018 DLF Forum in Las Vegas, Nevada, drew some 800 attendees across three events: the first Learn@DLF workshop day, the Forum, and the National Digital Stewardship Alliance's (NDSA) Digital Preservation 2018. Each year, DLF offers Forum fellowships to encourage broad participation and diversity of attendees; in 2018, 24 fellows received support. Many have posted about their experiences at https://www.diglib.org/category/forum.

A Forum highlight was the announcement of the 2018 Community/Capacity Award recipient. The biennial award, which honors constructive, community-minded efforts to build collective capacity in digital libraries and allied fields, was given to Documenting the Now. Documenting the Now develops tools and builds community practices that support the ethical collection, use, and preservation of social media content. More information on the 2018 award is available at https://www.diglib.org/announcing-the-2018-dlf-community-capacity-award-winner/.

Working Groups

DLF hosts 12 working groups, which are typically informal, volunteer-led efforts. A full list is available at https://www.diglib.org/groups/. To assist in these and related efforts, DLF created the Organizer's Toolkit https://wiki.diglib.org/About_DLF_and_the_Organizers%27_Toolkit, which serves as a resource for starting new initiatives or working groups, and facilitating ongoing projects.

Authenticity Project Fellowship Program

In October 2018 DLF announced its partnership with the HBCU Library Alliance for a three-year Authenticity Project. The program will provide mentoring, learning, and leadership opportunities for 45 early- to mid-career librarians from historically black colleges and universities, as well as meaningful frameworks for conversation and collaboration among dozens of additional participants from both organizations from 2019 to 2021.

In each year of the Authenticity Project, fifteen fellows will be matched with two experienced library professionals: an established mentor from an HBCU Library Alliance library or with a strong background in HBCUs, and a "conversation partner" working in an area of the fellow's interest, ideally within a DLF member institution. Fellows will receive full travel, lodging, and registration expenses to the annual DLF Forum and Learn@DLF workshops; access to online discussion spaces and in-person networking opportunities; and opportunities to apply for micro-grant funding to undertake inter-institutional projects of strategic importance across institutions and communities. They will also participate in quarterly facilitated, online networking and discussion sessions.

The Authenticity Project is funded by the Institute of Museum and Library Services. Additional information is available at https://www.diglib.org/opportunities/authenticity-project/.

DLF eResearch Network

Launched in 2014, the annual DLF eResearch Network (eRN) brings together teams from research-supporting libraries to strengthen and advance their data services and digital scholarship roles within their organizations. The core of the network is a curriculum that guides participants through six monthly webinars addressing current topics and strategic methods for supporting and facilitating data services and digital scholarship locally. The eRN culminates in an individualized consultation where participating teams produce strategic agendas and working items for data services and digital scholarship support at their institutions. To date, more than 60 institutions have participated in the eRN.

National Digital Stewardship Alliance (NDSA)

DLF serves as the host institution for the NDSA, a consortium of more than 220 partnering organizations, including universities, professional associations, businesses, government agencies, and nonprofit organizations committed to the long-term preservation of digital information. NDSA activities are organized by three interest groups (Content, Standards and Practices, and Infrastructure), out of which smaller working groups often emerge. NDSA hosts the annual Digital Preservation conference, which, since 2016, has followed the DLF Forum.

Affiliates

Affiliates are institutions or consortia with which CLIR has forged a supportive alliance in pursuit of common goals. In some cases, CLIR or DLF serve as a host institution and fiscal manager for an entire affiliate organization. Examples include NDSA, the International Image Interoperability Framework (IIIF), and the International Internet Preservation Consortium. In other cases, such as DLF's alliance with Taiga or Code4Lib, a major project is hosted for the group, such as communications infrastructure or a conference series. In still other cases, CLIR serves as an incubator for a new idea, such as the Digital Library of the Middle East, event partner (DLF + AMIA Hack Days), or collaborator on pilot projects (as with Jisc).

These partnerships signal CLIR and DLF's commitment to a vision of interdependence, facilitating the integration of services, tools, platforms, and expertise in ways that will reduce costs and create greater efficiencies for the benefit of all. CLIR president Charles Henry provides additional context for these partnerships in his blog, "Affiliates: Models of Interdependency," at https://bit.ly/2VYJ5jr.

Digital Library of the Middle East

CLIR is working with the Qatar National Library, The Antiquities Coalition, Stanford Libraries, and other institutions worldwide to explore the feasibility and undertake technical prototyping of a Digital Library of the Middle East (DLME).

The DLME is envisioned as an internationally shared digital inventory of cultural artifacts that provides detailed descriptions and images of artifacts along with information about the objects' history and provenance. It will ultimately encompass text, video, photographs, archives, manuscripts, 3-D data, and maps illuminating the region's history over 12 millennia, curated by scholars, specialists, and members of the cultures it represents. Records from the DLME will be made publicly available to encourage scholarly discoveries and greater appreciation of the region's rich heritage and living peoples, while helping safeguard fundamentally important expressions of our cultural commonwealth and shared humanity.

In 2018 CLIR received funds from the Andrew W. Mellon Foundation to implement a sustainable, extensible digital library platform and set of curatorial processes to federate records relating to the cultural heritage of the Middle East. The effort, undertaken in collaboration with Stanford University, builds on earlier work funded by the Whiting Foundation to develop a proof of concept released in early 2018. It is available at https://spotlight.dlme.clir.org/library.

More information on the DLME is available at https://dlme.clir.org/.

Leading Change Institute

CLIR and EDUCAUSE hosted the fifth Leading Change Institute (LCI) June 3–8, 2018. LCI aims to prepare and develop the next generation of leaders in libraries, information services, and higher education by engaging those who seek to further develop their skills for the benefit of higher education.

Over six days, participants heard perspectives on the higher education landscape from a wide array of speakers and explored topics ranging from entrepreneurship to leading change through collaboration and creativity. A list of participants from 2018 and previous years is available at https://leadingchangeinstitute.org/alumni/.

Chief Information Officers Group

Since 2002 CLIR has facilitated a semiannual forum of directors of organizations that have merged their library and information technology units on the campuses of liberal arts colleges and small universities. At their meetings and through a listserv, members discuss library and computing issues as an integrated whole. They have explored such topics as organizational models for optimizing success; fostering diversity, equity, and inclusion in merged organizations; information security, compliance, and risk mitigation; and digital scholarship. A list of current members is available at https://www.clir.org/initiatives-partnerships/cios/.

Fellowships and Grants

Digitizing Hidden Special Collections and Archives

Digitizing Hidden Special Collections and Archives is a national grant competition administered by CLIR for digitizing rare and unique content in collecting institutions. Supported by the Andrew W. Mellon Foundation, the program is built on the model of CLIR's Cataloging Hidden Special Collections and Archives program (2008–2014). The program coheres around six core values: scholarship, comprehensiveness, connectedness, collaboration, sustainability, and openness.

Since 2015 Digitizing Hidden Collections has awarded about $4 million annually to institutions holding collections of high value for research, teaching, and learning. A review panel, comprising experts from a range of scholarly and technical disciplines, evaluates proposals and recommends award recipients. Awards range from $50,000 to $250,000 for single-institution projects and $50,000 to $500,000 for collaborative projects. In 2018 CLIR awarded funds to 17 projects,

As part of its Hidden Collections program, CLIR has developed a registry discovery tool (http://registry.clir.org/) to highlight rare and unique library, archival, and museum collections. It features projects funded through CLIR's Cataloging and Digitizing Hidden Special Collections and Archives programs as well as numerous other special collections throughout the United States and Canada.

More information about the program, including a list of funded projects, is available at https://www.clir.org/hiddencollections/.

Recordings at Risk

In 2017 CLIR launched a new national grant program, Recordings at Risk. The program supports the preservation of rare and unique audio, audiovisual, and other time-based media content of high scholarly value through digital reformatting. Funded by the Andrew W. Mellon Foundation, the program has run four competitions to date. CLIR will announce the recipients of a fifth competition in April 2019, at which point the program will have awarded a total of $2.3 million. Grants from the open competitions range from $10,000 to $50,000 and cover costs of preservation reformatting for audio or audiovisual content by qualified external service providers.

Recordings at Risk encourages professionals who may be constrained by limited resources or technical expertise to take action against the threats of media degradation and obsolescence. The program aims to help institutions identify priorities and develop practical strategies for digital reformatting, build relationships with partners, and raise awareness of best practices. More information about the program, including a list of funded projects, is available at https://www.clir.org/recordings-at-risk/.

Postdoctoral Fellowship Program

The CLIR Postdoctoral Fellowship Program offers recent Ph.D. graduates the chance to develop research tools, resources, and services while exploring new career opportunities. CLIR Postdoctoral Fellows work on projects that forge and strengthen connections among library collections, educational technologies, and current research. Launched in 2004, the program has supported 190 fellows at 81 host institutions across the United States, Canada, and overseas.

In June 2018 CLIR announced the award of 22 postdoctoral fellowships. Funds from the Alfred P. Sloan Foundation supported six fellowships in software and research data curation for the sciences and social sciences, and four fellowships in data curation for energy economics—a new area of focus. With funds from the Andrew W. Mellon Foundation, CLIR awarded five fellowships in data curation for Latin American and Caribbean Studies. Individual institutions supported an additional seven fellowships in academic libraries.

In September CLIR received funding from the Mellon Foundation to support two cohorts of Postdoctoral Fellows in Data Curation in African American and African Studies, starting in summer 2019.

All new 2018 fellows attended a summer seminar, hosted at Bryn Mawr College, addressing issues faced by 21st-century libraries, including data and software curation and management. The seminar provided an opportunity for fellows to participate in cohort-building activities. Fellows' supervisors joined the seminar for one day to discuss expectations and establish effective communication strategies.

Additional information about the postdoctoral fellowship program, including a list of current and former fellows, is available at https://www.clir.org/fellowships/postdoc/.

Mellon Dissertation Fellowships

In 2018 CLIR awarded 15 graduate students Mellon Fellowships for Dissertation Research in Original Sources. The fellowship is intended to help graduate students in the humanities and related social science fields pursue doctoral research using original sources and gain skill and creativity in using original source materials in libraries, archives, museums, and related repositories. To date, the program has supported 242 graduate students who have carried out their dissertation research in public and private libraries and archives worldwide. A list of current and past fellowship recipients is available at https://www.clir.org/fellowships/mellon/fellowshiprecipients/.

Rovelstad Scholarship in International Librarianship

Sebastian Galbo, a master's student in library and information science at SUNY Buffalo, was awarded the 2018 Rovelstad Scholarship in International Librarianship. Since its inception in 2003, the annual scholarship has provided travel funds for 16 students enrolled in 15 different library and information science programs across the United States to attend the annual meeting of the World Library and Information Congress. In 2018, the meeting took place in Kuala Lumpur, Malaysia.

The final year of the scholarship, which had been generously funded by Mathilde and Howard Rovelstad, occurred in 2018.

Publications

The Future of Email Archives. A Report from the Task Force on Technical Approaches for Email Archives. August 2018. Available at https://www.clir.org/pubs/reports/pub175/. E-mail is an increasingly important part of the historical record, yet it is particularly difficult to preserve, putting future access to this vast resource at risk. This report presents the findings of a yearlong investigation of the Task Force on Technical Approaches for Email Archives, sponsored by the Andrew W. Mellon Foundation and the Digital Preservation Coalition. The 19-member task force, comprising representatives from higher education, government, and industry, was co-chaired by Christopher Prom, of the University of Illinois at Urbana-Champaign, and Kate Murray, of the Library of Congress. The report looks at what makes e-mail archiving so complex and describes emerging strategies to meet the challenge. The task force proposes a series of short- and long-term actions for community development and advocacy, as well as for tool support, testing, and development.

CLIR Annual Report, 2016–2017. April 2018. Available at https://www.clir.org/pubs/annual/.

CLIR Issues 121–126. Available at https://www.clir.org/pubs/issues/.

Association for Library and Information Science Education

ALISE Headquarters, 4 Lan Drive, Suite 310 Westford, MA 01886
978-674-6190, e-mail office@alise.org
World Wide Web http://www.alise.org

Heidi Julien
President 2018–2019

The Association for Library and Information Science Education (ALISE) is an independent, nonprofit professional association, founded in 1915 as the Association of American Library Schools (AALS). It changed to its current name in 1983 to reflect more accurately the mission, goals, and membership of the association. Its mission is to lead in innovative and high-quality research, teaching, and service for educators and scholars in library and information science and cognate disciplines internationally through engagement, advocacy, and knowledge creation and dissemination.

Membership

Membership is open to individuals and institutions. Personal members can include anyone interested in the objectives of the association, with categories including full-time (faculty member, administrator, librarian, researcher, or other interested individual); new professional (doctoral students as they transition to faculty member status, maximum of three years); part-time/retired (part-time or adjunct faculty, or retired professionals); and student (doctoral or other students, maximum of six years). Institutional members include schools with programs accredited by the American Library Association (ALA) and other U.S. and Canadian schools that offer a graduate degree in library and information science or a cognate field. International affiliate institutional membership is open to any school outside the United States or Canada that offers an educational program in library and information science at the professional level as defined or accepted by the country in which the school is located. Associate institutional membership status is accorded to libraries and organizations other than schools of library and information science.

Structure and Governance

ALISE is constituted of operational groups including the board of directors; committees; the council of deans, directors, and program chairs; school representatives; and special interest groups (SIGs). The association has been managed since October 2018 by McKenna Management, Inc. in Westford, MA, with Cambria Happ as executive director. The board of directors is composed of seven elected officers serving three-year terms. Officers for 2018–2019 were Heidi Julien (University at Buffalo), president; Stephen Bajjaly (Wayne State University), vice-president/president-elect; Dietmar Wolfram (University of Wisconsin–Milwaukee), past president; Heather Moulaison Sandy (University of Missouri), secretary/treasurer; Cecilia Salvatore (Dominican University), director for membership services; Rong Tang (Simmons University), director for external relations; and Nicole Cooke (University of Illinois), director for special interest groups. At the end of the September Annual Conference, Wolfram and Salvatore will conclude their terms of service and two newly elected officers will join the board: a new vice-president/president-elect and a new director for membership services.

The board establishes policy, sets goals and strategic directions, and provides oversight for the management of the association. Face-to-face meetings are held in conjunction with the Annual Conference to focus on policy, planning, programmatic, and other matters. For the remainder of the year, business is conducted through teleconferences, an online collaborative work platform, and e-mail.

Committees play a vital role in carrying out the work of the association. Since fall 2008, an open call for volunteers to serve on committees has been used to ensure broader participation in committee service, with members for the coming year appointed by the vice-president/president-elect for most committees. Principal areas of activity include awards, conference program planning, governance, nominations, research competitions, and tellers. (See https://www.alise.org/alise-committees for a full list.) Each committee is given an ongoing term of reference to guide its work as well as the specific charges for the year. Task forces can be charged to carry out tasks outside the scope of the existing standing committees.

The ALISE Council of Deans, Directors, and Program Chairs consists of the chief executive officers of each ALISE institutional member school. The group convenes at the Annual Conference and discusses issues via e-mail in the interim. Carol Barry (Louisiana State University) serves as the 2018–2019 chair.

Within each institutional member school, a school representative is named to serve as a direct link between the membership and the ALISE board. These individuals communicate to the faculty of their school about ALISE and the association's events and initiatives and provide input on membership issues to the ALISE board.

Special interest groups (SIGs) enable members with shared interests to communicate and collaborate, with a particular emphasis on programs at the Annual Conference. New SIGs are established as areas of interest emerge. Ongoing SIGs, grouped by thematic clusters, are

- *Roles and Responsibilities:* Assistant/Associate Deans and Directors, Doctoral Students, Part-Time and Adjunct Faculty
- *Teaching and Learning:* Curriculum, Distance Education, Innovative Pedagogies
- *Topics and Courses:* Archival/Preservation Education; Gender Issues; Historical Perspectives; Information Ethics; Information Policy; International Library Education; Multicultural, Ethnic, and Humanistic Concerns; Research; School Library Media; Technical Services Education, Youth Services

Communication

Announcements, notifications, and membership updates are posted to the ALISE membership listserv. News and events are published on ALISE's official website (http://www.alise.org). The organization has been actively using its social media accounts including Twitter (@alisehq) and Facebook (https://www.facebook.com/ALISEHQ/) to connect with its members and communities, as well as to post announcements and ALISE-related events in a timely manner.

Publications

The ALISE publications program has four components:

- The *Journal of Education for Library and Information Science* (*JELIS*) is a peer-reviewed quarterly journal edited by John Budd and Denice Adkins. The journal is a scholarly forum for discussion and presentation of research and issues within the field of library and information science (LIS) education. The University of Toronto Press began to serve as the publisher of JELIS in 2018. The journal is open access at a green level. It is indexed in Elsevier's Scopus, among other indexing sources.
- The *ALISE Library and Information Science Education Statistical Report* publishes data collected annually from its institutional members on their curriculum, faculty, students, income and expenditures, and continuing professional education. Members can gain free access to existing reports by logging in on the members-only area of the website.
- The new ALISE Book Series published by Rowman & Littlefield addresses issues critical to Library and Information Science education and research through the publication of epistemologically grounded scholarly texts which are inclusive of regional and national contexts around the world. The series editors are Jaya Raju (University of Cape Town) and Dietmar Wolfram (University of Wisconsin–Milwaukee). Several book projects are underway in 2018–2019.
- The ALISE website is the public face of the association and provides information about the association and news of activities and opportunities of interest to members. It provides login access to the MemberClicks system, where members can access members-only benefits (reports, member directory, etc.), renew membership, register for the conference and webinars, and access other services.

Annual Conference

The ALISE Annual Conference traditionally has been held immediately before the ALA Midwinter Meeting. However, at the February 2018 meeting, a decision was made to move the annual meeting to the fall. Thus, the 2019 conference will be held in Knoxville, on September 24–26, 2019. The conference theme is "Exploring Learning in a Global Information Context." Program co-chairs Diane Kelly (University of Tennessee) and Gary Burnett (Florida State University), with President Julien, are planning the ALISE conference, which will offer the usual presentations, poster sessions, and networking and placement opportunities; along with the unCommons—a gathering place to share, debate, brainstorm, and network. The ALISE Academy will lead off the conference. Conference proceedings are housed by the IDEALS repository (https://www.ideals.illinois.edu/handle/2142/98928).

Professional Development

ALISE offers regular webinars free to members to facilitate virtual engagement with research and other membership interests during the year between conferences. Recent webinar offerings have included "Demystifying the Publication Process," "Accompaniment Pedagogy: Improving Online Small Group Collaboration," and "Foundations of Instructional Design for Online Courses." Persons who are interested in offering a webinar may submit a proposal through the webinar submission web page (http://www.alise.org/webinar-proposals).

A new annual ALISE Leadership Academy was offered for the first time February 7–8, 2019 in Charleston, S.C. The objective of the Academy is to provide the next generation of leadership in library and information science with an opportunity to explore their possible interests in and preparation for leadership roles as chairs, directors, and deans.

Grants and Awards

ALISE supports research and recognizes accomplishments through its grants and awards programs. Research competitions include the ALISE Research Grant Competition, the ALISE / Bohdan S. Wynar Research Paper Competition, the ALISE/ProQuest Methodology Paper Competition, the ALISE / Eugene Garfield Doctoral Dissertation Competition, the ALISE/ABC-CLIO Award for Research Excellence in Young Adult Services, the ALISE/School Library Connection Research Excellence Award, and the ALISE Community conn@CT Mini-Grants. Support for conference participation is provided by the University of Washington Information School Youth Services Graduate Student Travel Award, the Doctoral Student to ALISE Award, the ALISE/Jean Tague Sutcliffe Doctoral Student Research Poster Competition, and the ALISE Diversity Travel Award to the ALISE Annual Conference. This last award was created in collaboration with the ALA Office for Diversity Spectrum Scholarship Program, which created a parallel award, the ALA/ALISE Spectrum Travel Award to ALISE, partially funded by ALISE.

Awards recognizing outstanding accomplishments include the ALISE/Norman Horrocks Leadership Award (for early-career leadership), the ALISE / Pratt-Severn Faculty Innovation Award, the ALISE Service Award, the ALISE Award for Professional Contribution, the ALISE/Connie Van Fleet Award for Research Excellence in Public Library Services to Adults, and the *LJ*/ALISE Excellence in Teaching Award, sponsored by Rowman & Littlefield, in collaboration with *Library Journal.* Winners are recognized at an awards luncheon at the Annual Conference. (For a list of award winners, see http://www.alise.org/awards-grants.)

Collaboration with Other Organizations

ALISE seeks to collaborate with other organizations on activities of mutual interest. ALISE members also serve on committees for various national organizations, including ALA committees and the FEDLINK Network.

ALISE continues to build its international connections, with members serving on the International Federation of Library Associations (IFLA) Standing Committees that address education and research, and support of initiatives to address access to information, including the Lyon Declaration that calls on the United Nations to incorporate information in advancing equity and sustainability in the development of the UN post-2015 millennium goals, which shape policies worldwide. ALISE has been expanding its collaborations with peer organizations including the Association for Information Science and Technology (ASIS&T) and the iSchools group.

Conclusion

ALISE is guided by its strategic plan for 2017–2020 (http://www.alise.org/alise-strategic-plan-2017-2020). The association looks forward to continuing its leading role in LIS education and research.

NASIG

PMB 305, 1902 Ridge Rd., West Seneca, NY 14224-3312
716-324-1859, e-mail info@nasig.org
World Wide Web http://www.nasig.org

Angela Dresselhaus
President 2018–2019

Background and Mission

NASIG is an independent organization working to advance and transform the management of information resources. The organization's goal is to facilitate and improve the distribution, acquisition, and long-term accessibility of information resources in all formats and business models.

There are three key components to NASIG's mission:

- NASIG supports a dynamic community of professionals including, but not limited to, librarians, publishers, and vendors engaging in understanding one another's perspectives and improving functionality throughout the information resources lifecycle with an emphasis on scholarly communications, serials, and electronic resources.
- NASIG provides a rich variety of conference and continuing education programming to encourage knowledge sharing among its members and to support their professional and career development.
- NASIG promotes the development and implementation of best practices and standards for the distribution, acquisition, and long-term accessibility of information resources in all formats and business models throughout their lifecycle. In addition to developing best practices, NASIG supports the development of standards by NISO, an affiliated organization.

Established in 1985, NASIG (formerly the North American Serials Interest Group, Inc.) is an independent organization that promotes communication, information, and continuing education about serials, electronic resources, and the broader issues of scholarly communication. NASIG welcomes anyone interested in the information chain. Inspired by the UKSG (formerly the United Kingdom Serials Group), NASIG held its first conference at Bryn Mawr College in June 1986. The annual conference, usually held in May or June, offers a premier opportunity to meet others representing the diverse interests of the information resources community and to hear speakers who are on the cutting edge of scholarly communication.

Members

Founded on strong professional friendships, NASIG constituents work diligently to maintain that personal spirit, exchange of ideas, and unity of purpose on a volunteer basis. Members include a dynamic group of librarians, publishers, vendors, educators, database producers, library systems representatives, and many others involved in the creation, production, delivery, management, and access of serial information, the scholarly communication process, and emerging technologies.

Organization

NASIG has five administrative officers and six members-at-large who constitute the Executive Board. This team also has liaison responsibilities to standing committees and special working groups. The standing committees are Awards and Recognition, Bylaws, Communications, Conference Planning, Conference Proceedings Editors, Continuing Education, Diversity, Evaluation and Assessment, Membership Services, Mentoring, Newsletter, Nominations and Elections, Program Planning, Site Selection, Standards, and Student Outreach.

Opportunities

The annual conference provides a casual venue for pre-conferences, concurrent sessions, practical workshops, special events, and networking. An emphasis on thoughtful discourse and informality promotes an intensity of purpose not always possible at other conferences.

NASIG also has a strong commitment to continuing education. The organization seeks collaborative endeavors to educate individuals about changes, issues, and future possibilities on the information landscape.

An outstanding awards and grants program encourages students, librarians, and paraprofessionals to attend the annual conference and serve on committees. With awards such as the John Riddick Student Grants, the Marcia Tuttle International Award, the Serials Specialist Award, the Horizon Award, the Champion Award, the John Merriman Joint NASIG/UKSG Award, the Rose Robischon Scholarship, and the Fritz Schwartz Serials Education Scholarship, NASIG supports new and seasoned librarians in their continuing professional development.

Partnerships

NASIG has long recognized the value in collaborating with other associations in the information community and has developed several strategic partnerships to further the goals of both organizations. NASIG is a member of National Information Standards Organization (NISO) and Project COUNTER in recognition of the important role that standards play in the information industry and the valuable input that NASIG members can provide in developing and refining industry standards. NASIG is also a strategic affiliate of the Library Publishing Coalition (LPC). NASIG and LPC not only share a vision for a sustainable and open scholarship environment, but both organizations are actively using the development of best practices and shared expertise to make that vision a reality.

In 2018 NASIG became a member of the International Federation of Library Associations and Institutions (IFLA). NASIG hopes to provide member expertise to IFLA standing committees while also offering NASIG members the opportunity to participate in global discussions on serials, continuing resources, and scholarly communications. NASIG's most long-lasting partnerships are with the library publishing and vendor community who are not only represented in the individual and organizational memberships, but also as conference and award sponsors. In addition to vendor sponsorship of awards, NASIG partners with its sister organization UKSG to provide the John Merriman Joint NASIG/UKSG Award to support a member exchange for each organization's conference every year.

NASIG looks forward to developing additional partners in the active and vibrant information community in the coming years.

Publications and Webinars

NASIG's commitment to the implementation of best practices can be seen in the development and continued revision of the core competencies series. Inspired by the American Library Association's Core Competencies for Librarianship, NASIG has formed task forces to produce the following three core competency documents:

- Core Competencies for Electronic Resources Librarians (approved and adopted by the NASIG Executive Board, July 22, 2013; revised with minor edits by CEC, January 26, 2016)
- Core Competencies for Print Serials Management (approved and adopted by the NASIG Executive Board, May 30, 2015; revised with minor edits by CEC, April 25, 2016)
- Core Competencies for Scholarly Communication Librarians (approved and adopted by the NASIG Executive Board, August 11, 2017)

The core competencies serve as professional development tools on campuses across the information community and have even found their way into the education and intern programs at major library and information science graduate programs, such the University of Toronto's iSchool as discussed in Marlene van Ballegooie and Jennifer Browning's 2018 presentation "Cultivating TALint: Using the Core Competencies as a framework for training future e-resource professionals" (https://www.slideshare.net/NASIG/cultivating-talint-using-the-core-competencies-as-a-framework-for-training-future-eresource-professionals).

In 2018 NASIG's Continuing Education Committee produced two NASIG webinars for practitioners, on CORAL (http://coral-erm.org/) and MarcEdit (https://marcedit.reeset.net/). The committee also collaborated with NISO to provide a two-part webinar series entitled "The Library as Publisher." In collaboration with the NC Serials conference, the committee hosted a free webinar entitled "Joining the Library Profession: Getting Hired, Attending Regional Conferences, and Finding a Mentor." NASIG webinars have reduced rates for NASIG and NISO members, and recordings are made freely available six months after the event.

The proceedings of the 2017 NASIG conference were published in the *Serials Librarian*, volume 74, no. 1–4 (2018). Edited by Paul Moeller, Kristen Wilson, Cindy Shirkey, and Leigh Ann DePope, the proceedings include reports on every session at the conference including pre-conferences and are freely available to NASIG members via the NASIG website after a six-month embargo.

Annual Conference

The 2018 NASIG conference was held from June 8–11 in Atlanta, Georgia, with the theme "Transforming the Information Community." Vision sessions were presented by Soren Auer (director, Technische Informationsbibliothek), Lauren Smith (information specialist, Institute for Research and Innovation in Social Services in Glasgow), and Lisa Macklin (director, research, engagement, and scholarly communications, Emory University), and videos of these sessions were made freely available post-conference. Pre-conference events included day-long workshops on MarcEdit, serials cataloging with RDA and linked data for serials, as well as user groups on CORAL and Alma systems.

In addition to hour-long concurrent sessions, members were also treated to lightning sessions highlighting vendor innovations and upcoming projects, student research, and the great ideas showcase. A variety of structured and unstructured events, including a first-timers mentoring program, create an environment where the information community of practice can learn, network, and socialize to further the professional development of all involved.

The 2019 conference will be held in Pittsburgh, Pennsylvania, June 5–8.

Awards and Grants

NASIG's commitment to the professional development of the information community is displayed in the awards and grants provided to professionals throughout their careers. The Horizon Award supports conference attendance for a promising new information professional, while the Birdie MacLennan Award supports conference attendance for a mid-career professional. The Rose Robischon Scholarship is focused on assisting those professionals who lack funds for conference travel, while the John Merriman Joint NASIG/UKSG Award and the Marcia Tuttle International Grant are both focused on increasing the international experience of NASIG members. The Capstone Award recognizes a professional who has made significant and distinguished contributions to the field of information resource management.

NASIG is committed to developing the next generation of information professionals with free membership for students, reduced registration rates for webinars and conferences, and three awards to support conference attendance. The John Riddick Student Grant, the Fritz Schwartz Education Scholarship, and Mexican Student Grant bring multiple students to the NASIG conference each year. The student NASIG conference experience includes a mentor, an opportunity to present at the Student Showcase, and a number of events to make connections and learn from practitioners in the industry. NASIG also recognizes the talents and contributions of paraprofessionals with the First-Timer Award and the Paraprofessional Specialist Award which provide conference attendance support.

International Reports

International Federation of Library Associations and Institutions

Postal Address: P.O. Box 95312, 2509 CH Den Haag, Netherlands
Visiting Address: Prins Willem-Alexanderhof 5, 2595 BE The Hague, Netherlands
Tel. +31 70 3140884, fax +31 70 3834827, e-mail ifla@ifla.org
World Wide Web http://www.ifla.org

Beacher Wiggins

Director for Acquisitions and Bibliographic Access, Library of Congress
Secretary, IFLA Standing Committee on Acquisition and Collection Development, 2015–2019

Susan R. Morris

Special Assistant to the Director for Acquisitions and Bibliographic Access, Library of Congress
Member, IFLA Standing Committee on Cataloguing, 2015–2019

The International Federation of Library Associations and Institutions (IFLA) is the preeminent international organization representing librarians, other information professionals, and library users. Despite budgetary pressures, throughout 2018 IFLA promoted its four core values: freedom of access to information and expression, as stated in Article 19 of the Universal Declaration of Human Rights; the belief that such access must be universal and equitable to support human well-being; delivery of high-quality library and information services in support of that access; and the commitment to enabling all members of IFLA to participate without regard to citizenship, disability, ethnic origin, gender, geographical location, political philosophy, race, or religion. In 2018 IFLA strove to become a more participatory and inclusive organization while promoting an understanding of libraries as cultural heritage resources that are the patrimony of every nation.

World Library and Information Congress (WLIC): 84th IFLA General Conference and Council, Kuala Lumpur, Malaysia

The World Library and Information Congress / 84th IFLA General Conference and Council attracted more than 3,500 delegates from 110 countries to Kuala Lumpur, Malaysia, August 24–30, 2018. Conference attendance exceeded the 2,939 attendees from 137 countries at the WLIC in Columbus, Ohio, in August 2016, and the 3,100 from 137 countries in Wrocław, Poland, in August 2017. This was the second year since 2013 that conference registrations increased over the previous year.

The conference theme, "Transform Libraries, Transform Society," was supported in a welcoming speech by Malaysia National Committee Chair Dato'

Nafisah Ahmad. Remarks by the mayor of Kuala Lumpur, Tan Sri Haji Mhd Amin Nordin bin Abd Aziz, reinforced the city's warm welcome to its IFLA visitors. The president of IFLA, Glòria Pérez-Salmerón, and Secretary General Gerald Leitner spoke on the IFLA Global Vision. Malaysia's minister of tourism, arts, and culture, Mohamaddin Ketapi, described the connection between Malaysian libraries and society. The keynote address by Tan Sri Dato Sri Mr. Ali Hamsa, chief secretary general to government of Malaysia, highlighted the many ways in which Malaysia's library programs support networks, resource sharing, and information literacy. A videotaped welcome by Prime Minister Tun Dr. Mahathir Bin Mohamad led into a performance by the Istana Budaya dance group.

Seventeen satellite meetings, organized by IFLA sections, offered more detailed discussions on specific topics.

The next World Library and Information Congress will take place in August 2019 in Athens, Greece. The location of the 2020 WLIC is still to be announced. The IFLA Governing Board is committed to continuously improving both the conference experience for participants and the financial security of the organization. Although the exhibitor fees and registration are higher than for most conferences in the library community, WLIC historically has not made money for IFLA, and the custom of convening all registered participants in opening and closing ceremonies limits the number of cities that can host the conference to those with conference halls seating at least 3,000 people. Furthermore, member organizations have commented that it is difficult to send representatives to both the general conference and the numerous specialized satellite meetings that occur at a distance from the general conference site. The increased attendance in Wrocław and Kuala Lumpur therefore was gratifying.

IFLA Global Vision and Current Strategic Plan

The IFLA Global Vision for the coming years was kicked off at the IFLA President's Meeting in Barcelona, Spain, March 2018. Throughout the previous year, IFLA had promoted discussion of its Global Vision through workshops and meetings in Alexandria, Athens, Buenos Aires, Madrid, Singapore, Washington, and Yaounde. Discussions focused on strengthening ties within the library world, identifying future challenges and opportunities, and prioritizing possible actions in response to social change. All members and WLIC conference participants were encouraged to vote for options online by October 16, 2017, and approximately 22,000 individuals from 213 countries voted. In keeping with IFLA's participatory, inclusive identity, the vision has been presented and discussed in 185 workshops for 9,291 participants.

The Global Vision informs the new IFLA Global Strategy with ten strategic opportunities in the areas of intellectual freedom, digital realm, better understanding of our communities' needs, ongoing technological change, better advocacy, communicating libraries' relevance and impact to stakeholders, the spirit of collaboration, need to challenge our current structures and behaviors, maximizing access to the world's documentary heritage, and encouraging younger library professionals. Launch of the Global Strategy is planned for the 2019 WLIC in Athens, after Governing Board approval, which is expected in April 2019. Changes in IFLA governance to accommodate the new strategic plan will be addressed at a December 2019 workshop (funded by external donations), to ensure that a new governance structure is in place before the 2021 IFLA elections.

Currently, IFLA continues its Strategic Plan for the years 2016–2021. The plan, grounded in the four core values, sets forth four strategic directions: libraries in society; information and knowledge; cultural heritage; and capacity building. Whereas the strategic plan for 2010–2015 contained five key initiatives, the new strategic plan is more granular, providing for fifteen key initiatives, each tied to one strategic direction.

Standards

In developing the 2016–2021 Strategic Plan, the IFLA Governing Board reached the determination that IFLA's work in developing and promulgating standards should be more holistic than in the past. Therefore, key initiative 1.4, "Promoting IFLA Standards to support libraries in the provision of services to their communities," is tied to the strategic direction for "libraries in society," rather than the strategic direction for "information and knowledge." The IFLA Committee on Standards developed a new IFLA Standards Procedures Manual, which has been official IFLA guidance since 2014. The Committee on Standards has also issued templates for standards; a standards development proposal form that includes a required work plan; and a standards approval request form. Although IFLA standards continue to be developed within the sections because they are the professional units, the standards are now reviewed by the Committee on Standards and the Professional Committee. Approved standards are endorsed and issued on the IFLA website by the Professional Committee. The new approval procedures continue to evolve.

The definition of "IFLA standard" is quite broad and encompasses conceptual models, formatting codes, rules, guidelines, and best practices, ranging from the 2016 Statement of International Cataloguing Principles to IFLA Guidelines for Library Services to People Experiencing Homelessness. Guidelines maintained by IFLA cover services to many other user groups, disaster preparedness, cataloging, library buildings, and numerous other library topics.

Copyright and Libraries

IFLA advocates vigorously for open access to digital content and for the right of libraries to benefit from fair use and exemptions from copyright restrictions. At the WLIC in Kuala Lumpur, the IFLA Governing Board released a statement on "copyright literacy." Entitled "Accelerating Access," the statement recognized the need for librarians to understand the structure and functions of the copyright system and copyright law in order to carry out their daily work. It presents copyright compliance as an element of ethics for librarians but stresses that continuous improvements to the copyright system are essential to library service.

From the time that the Marrakesh Treaty to Facilitate Access to Published Works for Persons Who Are Blind, Visually Impaired, or Otherwise Print Disabled (Marrakesh Treaty) was first agreed by a diplomatic conference in Marrakesh,

Morocco, in June 2013, IFLA has worked tirelessly to promote the treaty and encourage countries to ratify it. The treaty entered into force in June 2016, when it had been ratified by the requisite twenty countries, but the signatories did not include the United States. The United States finally ratified the treaty on October 9, 2018, when the president signed Public Law No. 115-261. Specifically, P.L. No. 115-261 modifies the limitations and exceptions to federal copyright infringement that allow published works to be reproduced and distributed in accessible formats for individuals with print disabilities. The law makes such limitations and exceptions applicable only to activities in the United States; broadens the scope of published works that may be reproduced and distributed in accessible formats; allows published works in accessible formats to be exported and imported for individuals with print disabilities; and modifies certain terms and definitions to conform with the Marrakesh Treaty. In view of the enormous publishing output of the U.S., this implementation greatly advances libraries' ability to serve print-disabled users throughout the Earth.

Cultural Heritage Disaster Reconstruction

Since 1996 IFLA has been a founding member of the International Committee of the Blue Shield and its successor, the Blue Shield (formed in 2016 by a merger of the International Committee of the Blue Shield and the Association of National Committees of the Blue Shield), to protect cultural property in the event of natural and human disasters. Its current Blue Shield partners are the International Council on Archives, the International Council on Monuments and Sites, and the International Council of Museums. In 2016 IFLA launched its Risk Register for Documentary Cultural Heritage, a repository of information about unique documentary heritage assets deemed to be at risk from natural or human-caused disasters throughout the world. The risk register is confidential, and an IFLA committee authenticates each submission.

Grants and Awards

The Federation continues to work with corporate partners and national libraries to maintain programs and opportunities that would otherwise not be possible, especially for librarians and libraries in developing countries. The Jay Jordan IFLA/OCLC Early Career Development Fellowships provide four weeks of intensive experience, based in OCLC headquarters in Dublin, Ohio, for library and information science professionals from countries with developing economies who are in the early stages of their careers. The Fellows for 2018 were from Ethiopia, Indonesia, Jamaica, Kenya, and Serbia. Since its inception in 2001, the program has supported 90 librarians from countries with developing economies.

Numerous awards and grants encourage travel to the annual IFLA conferences. The IFLA/BibLibre International Marketing Award includes a cash stipend and travel to the conference for three representatives of the winning organizations, who are selected by the IFLA Section on Management and Marketing in collaboration with the corporate sponsor. The Emerald Group sponsored the award from 2008 through 2014. After a hiatus in 2015, the French library systems and services vendor BibLibre made a commitment to sponsor the award from 2016 through 2018. For 2019 PressReader will sponsor the award. In 2018 the first-place winner was the New York Public Library (NYPL) for its 2017 NYC Youth Amnesty project that cleared all NYPL fines through October 2017 for youth and children. The second-place winner was Invercargill, New Zealand, City Libraries and Archives, for its project "Keeping Up with the Librarians." The third-place winner was the National and University Library, Zagreb, Croatia, for the project "Greetings from Zagreb!"

The Dr. Shawky Salem Conference Grant and the Naseej (Arabian Advanced Systems Co.) Conference Grant support conference attendance from Arab countries. Many national library professional associations subsidize travel to the IFLA conference for their members; the Comité français *IFLA* supports travelers from any francophone country. The Chartered Institute of Library and Information Professionals (U.K.), or CILIP, sponsors the Alan Hopkinson Award for conference attendance. In addition, IFLA will be able to waive registration for up to forty first-time conference attendees through its IFLA WLIC Participation Grants, with increased funding through a bequest by the late German librarian Angela Bersekowski.

The IFLA Academic and Research Libraries Section sponsors an annual competition awarding conference registration and travel support for contestants from Africa, Latin America, or the Asia/Pacific region who have not attended a WLIC before. Formerly the De Gruyter/Saur Research Paper Award, this competition has been co-sponsored by Ex Libris and Sage since 2015. The four grant recipients in 2018 were from Bangladesh, Botswana, Nigeria, and Pakistan.

The IFLA Green Library Award recognizes a green or sustainable library project. Sponsored by De Gruyter, this award was designed by the IFLA Environment, Sustainability, and Libraries Special Interest Group. In 2018 it was presented to Foshan Library, Guangdong, China. The Foshan Library's green practice extends from its building's architecture to management and staff's commitment to community education for sustainability.

The IFLA/Systematic Award recognizes a library that best combines innovative architecture with information technology solutions, accounting for digital developments and local culture. The winning library must operate in a building that is newly built or newly repurposed as a library. With an award of $5,000 from Systematic, this is one of IFLA's most generous awards. In 2018 it was presented to the School 7 Library (KopGroep Libraries), the Netherlands. The central library of Austin, Texas, was a runner-up.

Some long-standing awards have sunset or are on hiatus while new sponsors are sought for them. The Rovelstad Scholarship in International Librarianship was administered by the Council on Library and Information Resources (CLIR) to send one U.S. citizen or permanent resident to the WLIC each year from 2003 through 2018; all funds from the Rovelstad gift have been fully expended now. The Open Access Award for initiatives in the area of open access monograph publishing, sponsored by Brill from 2013 through 2015 to bring the winner to the WLIC, was discontinued in 2016. The Student Paper Award, which also supports a library science student's attendance at the WLIC, was not offered in 2017 or 2018. The foundation renewed the program Frederic Thorpe Awards, established in 2003, as the Ulverscroft/IFLA Best Practice Awards and funded three librarians to attend the two-day satellite meeting of the Libraries Serving Persons with Print Disabilities Section, held in Louisville, Kentucky, in conjunction with the 2016 WLIC in Columbus, Ohio. In 2018 the question of continued sponsorship of this award remained undecided.

The IFLA Honorary Fellowships, IFLA Medal, and IFLA Scroll of Appreciation recognize service to IFLA by individuals. In 2018 Sinikka Sipilä, president of IFLA from 2013 to 2015, was named an IFLA Honorary Fellow, considered IFLA's highest individual award, for her work in Finland, Africa, and Asia. The IFLA Scroll of Appreciation was presented to the National Committee for the Kuala Lumpur WLIC in 2018, in keeping with the customary award to each National Committee for the WLIC. In addition, two library leaders received the Scroll of Appreciation in Kuala Lumpur in recognition of their distinguished service to the international library community: Marie Sophie Dibounje Madiba, past director of PAC for Africa, and Karen Latimer, library building consultant and architectural historian. The IFLA Medal was awarded to Buhle Mbambo-Thata, longtime director of the IFLA Africa Regional Office and library director in Zimbabwe and South Africa, and Teresa Hackett for her service to CLM and to European library organizations.

Membership and Finances

IFLA has more than 1,400 members in 150 countries all over the world but has lost about 100 members since 2016. Initially established at a conference in Edinburgh, Scotland, in 1927, it has been registered in the Netherlands since 1971 and has headquarters facilities at the Koninklijke Bibliotheek (Royal Library) in The Hague. Although IFLA did not hold a General Conference outside Europe and North America until 1980, there has since been steadily increasing participation from Asia, Africa, South America, and Australia. The Federation now maintains regional offices for Africa (in Pretoria, South Africa); Asia and Oceania (in Singapore); and Latin America and the Caribbean (in Buenos Aires, Argentina; formerly in Mexico City, Mexico, and Rio de Janeiro, Brazil). The organization has seven official working languages—Arabic, Chinese, English, French, German, Russian and Spanish. It maintains four language centers: for Arabic, in Alexandria, Egypt; for Chinese, in Beijing, China; for the French-speaking communities of Africa, in Dakar, Senegal; and for Russian, in Moscow, Russia. The language centers contribute to more effective communication with their respective language communities by providing translations of IFLA publications and becoming involved in local or regional professional events.

IFLA offers a range of membership categories: international library associations, national library associations, other associations (generally regional or special library associations), institutions, institutional subunits, one-person libraries, school libraries, association affiliates (limited to three consecutive years and open only to national associations with operating budgets of 10,000 Euros or less, to encourage membership in countries with developing economies), personal affiliates, student affiliates, new graduate members, and nonsalaried personal members. Association and institution members have voting rights in the IFLA General Council and IFLA elections and may nominate candidates for IFLA offices. Institutional subunits, one-person libraries, and school libraries have limited voting rights for section elections; association affiliates and personal members do not have voting rights but may submit nominations for any IFLA office, and individuals may run for office themselves. Except for affiliates, membership fees are keyed to the UNESCO Scale of Assessment and the United Nations List of Least Developed Countries, to encourage participation regardless of economic circumstances. Membership dues are quite low, ranging from 50 Euros per year for individual students, recent graduates, and retirees to more than 25,000 Euros per year for the largest national library associations.

Financial reports and the IFLA treasurer's report at the WLIC General Assembly in Kuala Lumpur showed that IFLA's revenue from both conferences and memberships has declined each year since 2014 and that IFLA's reserves are currently lower than required by its bylaws. In a sign of its ongoing commitment to both inclusivity and long-term sustainability, in Kuala Lumpur the voting members voted to reduce affiliate membership fees for individuals by 50 percent, to make it easier for unemployed or retired librarians to participate. Several national library associations protested and tried to postpone the vote on the grounds that IFLA is basically a federation of associations and individuals should participate through their national library associations.

UNESCO has given IFLA formal associate relations status, the highest level of relationship accorded to nongovernmental organizations by UNESCO. In addition, IFLA has observer status with the United Nations, the World Intellectual Property Organization (WIPO), the International Organization for Standardization (ISO), and the World Trade Organization, and associate status with the International Council of Scientific Unions.

Leading corporations in the information industry have formed working relationships with IFLA as Corporate Partners. The Corporate Partners provide financial and in-kind support and in turn gain the opportunity to convey information about their products and services to IFLA members and others who pay attention to IFLA's publications and activities. Several levels of corporate partnership are available. Most prominently, in 2014 OCLC became IFLA's first and sole Platinum Partner, providing extraordinary that continues into 2019. Other corporate partners choose to support IFLA at three exceptional levels—gold, silver, or bronze. Gold Corporate Partners in 2018 were Emerald and Sage Publications. DeGruyter Saur, Elsevier, and Sabinet were Silver Partners, and Bronze Partners were Otto Harassowitz GmbH and Zeutschel GmBh. The Federation's Associate Supporters were Annual Reviews and nbd/biblion. In all, IFLA claims 25 corporate supporters.

The IFLA Foundation (Stichting IFLA) was established in 2007. The Foundation accepts private donations and bequests and also is funded by other IFLA income. It gives funding priority to proposals and projects that promise to have a long-term impact in developing and strengthening IFLA; are clearly related to at least one of IFLA's strategic priorities; and are not likely to be funded by other bodies. The Foundation also occasionally makes grants for attendance at the World Library and Information Conference; the grants are administered by the IFLA headquarters and governance structure rather than directly by the Foundation. The Foundation's Board of Trustees consists of IFLA's president, president-elect, treasurer, and secretary general. The Board of Trustees does not respond directly to requests for Foundation grants, which are considered by IFLA headquarters and other appropriate IFLA units. A related foundation, Stichting IFLA Global Libraries, was established in November 2016 with generous funding from the Bill and Melinda Gates Foundation. Its trustees are the IFLA president, president-elect, and one appointed trustee. Stichting IFLA Global Libraries plans to focus on strengthening the library field and empowering public libraries.

Personnel, Structure, and Governance

The secretary general of IFLA is Gerald Leitner, who took office in summer 2016 after serving as secretary general of the Austrian Library Association. His e-mail address is iflasg@ifla.org. Helen Mandl is the deputy secretary general—succeeding Stuart Hamilton—and also continues as the manager for member services. Her e-mail address is helen.mandl@ifla.org.

At IFLA Headquarters, at the end of 2018 there were three policy and research officers, Tanja Clausen, Ariadna Matas Casadevall, and Esmeralda Moscatelli, with Stephen Wyber as manager for policy and advocacy; and four communications officers, María Violeta Bertolini, May Oostrom Kwok, Mathew Rees, and Louis Takács, with Chris Ridings as IFLA webmaster and information technology officer. Vesna Vuksan is the strategic projects manager, and Esther Doria is the project coordination assistant. Suzanne Reid is the membership officer, Kristine Paberza is the member engagement officer, and Lidia Putziger is the nominations coordinator and administrative officer.

The editor of the quarterly *IFLA Journal* is Steven W. Witt. The journal has a ten-member editorial committee, chaired by Shali Zhang of the University of Montana and reporting to the IFLA Professional Committee, that arranges peer review for articles, monitors quality and consistency, and guides editorial direction. The journal is published by SAGE.

New officers and Board members took office at the close of the 2017 conference in Wrocław. The new president for 2017–2019 is Glòria Pérez-Salmerón, past president of FESABID (Federación Española de Sociedades de Archivística, Biblioteconomía, Documentación y Museística). Pérez-Salmerón's presidential theme is "Libraries: Motors for Change," and she has pledged to align her presidency with IFLA's identity as a participatory, inclusive worldwide body while being mindful of its needs for long-term sustainability. Christine Mackenzie of Melbourne, Australia, past treasurer of IFLA, is president-elect and will become president at the close of the WLIC in Athens in 2019. The new treasurer is Barbara Lison, director of the Stadtbibliothek Bremen, Germany.

Under the revised 2008 IFLA Statutes, the 19 members of IFLA's Governing Board (plus the secretary general, ex officio) are responsible for the Federation's general policies, management, and finance. Additionally, the Board represents the Federation in legal and other formal proceedings. The Board is comprised of the president, president-elect, secretary general (ex officio), up to ten directly elected members, the chair of the Professional Committee, the chairs of each IFLA division, and the chair of the Standing Committee of the Management of Library Associations Section, currently Michael Dowling, director for chapter relations and international relations for the American Library Association. Current members, in addition to Pérez-Salmerón, Mackenzie, Leitner, and Dowling, are Huanwen Cheng (China), Marwa El Sahn (Egypt), Ágnes Hajdu Barát (Hungary), Patrick

Losinski (U.S.), Torbjörn Nilsson (Sweden), Victoria Okojie (Nigeria), Victoria Owen (Canada), Viviana Quiñones (France), and Knud Schulz (Denmark), plus the chairs of the Professional Committee and divisions, named below.

The Governing Board delegates responsibility for overseeing the direction of IFLA between Board meetings, within the policies established by the Board, to the IFLA Executive Committee, which includes the president, president-elect, treasurer, chair of the Professional Committee, and two members of the Governing Board, elected every two years by members of the Board from among its elected members. The secretary general of IFLA is a non-voting member, ex officio, and acts as the Executive Committee's secretary. The current elected Governing Board members of the Executive Committee are Okojie and Owen.

The IFLA Professional Committee monitors the planning and programming of professional activities carried out by IFLA's two types of bodies: professional groups—five divisions, forty-four sections, and special interest groups—and strategic programs (formerly called core programs or core activities). The Professional Committee is composed of one elected officer from each division, plus a chair elected by the outgoing Committee; the president, the president-elect, and the professional support officer (vacant at the end of 2018), who serves as secretary; and the chairs of the CLM and FAIFE committees, and two elected members of the Governing Board, currently Quiñones and Schulz. Raissa Teodori, head of the library, Senato Repubblica Italiana, chairs the Professional Committee.

The five divisions of IFLA and their representatives on the Professional Committee are I: Library Types (Vicki McDonald, Australia); II: Library Collections (Ann Okerson, U.S.); III: Library Services (Maja Zumer, Slovenia); IV: Support of the Profession (Antonia Arahova, Greece); and V: Regions (Sueli Mara Soares Pinto Ferreira, Brazil). The chair of the Copyright and Legal Matters Committee is Evelyn Woodberry (Australia). The chair of the Freedom of Access to Information and Freedom of Expression Committee is Martyn Wade (Scotland). Forty-four sections focus on topical interests, such as Statistics and Evaluation, Library Buildings and Equipment, and Rare Books and Special Collections, or on particular types of libraries or parts of the world.

The six IFLA strategic programs, which replace the former five core activities, are the Library Development Programme (LDP); Preservation and Conservation (PAC); UNIMARC Strategic Programme, which maintains and develops the Universal MARC Format, UNIMARC; Committee on Standards; Free Access to Information and Freedom of Expression (FAIFE); and Copyright and Other Legal Matters (CLM). The PAC, CLM, and FAIFE programs are managed by the IFLA manager for policy and advocacy, Stephen Wyber, and report to the Governing Board, as do UNIMARC and the Committee on Standards. The Library Development Programme, on the other hand, reports to the secretary general. The UNIMARC Strategic Programme has a separate office at the National Library of Portugal in Lisbon.

Two other long-standing IFLA projects are the IFLA website and the IFLA Voucher Scheme, which replaced the IFLA Office for International Lending. The Voucher Scheme enables libraries to pay for international interlibrary loan requests using vouchers purchased from IFLA rather than actual currency or credit accounts. Beginning in 2019 IFLA will charge a handling fee in addition to the voucher cost, but by eliminating bank charges and invoices for each transaction, the voucher scheme continues to reduce the administrative costs of international library loans and allows libraries to plan budgets with less regard to short-term fluctuations in the value of different national currencies. The voucher scheme has also encouraged participating libraries to voluntarily standardize their charges for loans.

To ensure an arena within IFLA for discussion of new social, professional, or cultural issues, the Professional Committee approves the formation of special interest groups for a limited time period. There currently are discussion groups for Access to Information Network/Africa (ATINA); Big Data; Digital Humanities/Digital Scholarship; Environment, Sustainability, and Libraries; Evidence for Global and Disaster Health; LGBTQ (Lesbian, Gay, Bisexual, Transgender, Queer/Questioning) Users; Library and Information Science Education in Developing Countries; Library History; Linked Data; National Information and Library Policy; National Organizations and International Relations; New Professionals; Religions: Libraries and Dialogue; and Women, Information, and Libraries. Special interest groups operate for a maximum period of three years. If there is sufficient interest, a special interest group may then become a permanent IFLA section. The Indigenous Matters Section was established from a special interest group in 2015.

Library and Archives Canada: 2018—A Banner Year

Dr. Guy Berthiaume
Librarian and Archivist of Canada

For Library and Archives Canada (LAC), 2018 was a banner year. As we near the end of the implementation of our Three-Year Plan 2016–2019, we have successfully met our key objectives and even raised the bar for the future. Within the plan, we focused our activities on four clearly identified priorities. What follows highlights some of our achievements within each of the priorities.

To Be an Institution Fully Dedicated to Serving All Our Clients

As the guardians of Canada's national collective memory, we have a very wide base of clients with a great variety of interests. Over and above what we do on a continual basis to serve Canadians, four client groups in particular were the beneficiaries of our initiatives in 2018: military history buffs, the genealogical community, indigenous communities, and Canada's youth.

Indigenous Communities Initiatives

With the guidance of an Indigenous Advisory Circle, we are currently developing two digitization initiatives.

1 Digitizing Indigenous Documentary Heritage

This first initiative is a documentary heritage digitization project, *We Are Here: Sharing Stories*, focusing on increasing online access to LAC's holdings that contain First Nations, Inuit, and Métis Nation related content, including government records, private archives, and published works.

Our goal is to provide free online access to unrestricted digital material through LAC's website and social media. Material to be digitized includes photographs, audiovisual recordings, treaties, indigenous-language dictionaries and lexicons, material related to residential schools, portraits, early journals and observations, and cartographic material.

2 Digitizing Indigenous-language Recordings

This second initiative, *Listen, Hear Our Voices*, is a digitization of indigenous-language recordings project that offers support and expertise to indigenous communities in their efforts to preserve and revitalize First Nations, Métis Nation, and Inuit languages.

Through collaborative approaches, we will offer a variety of services to communities to preserve and provide access to indigenous oral recordings. The digitized recordings come from a variety of sources, such as individuals, community centers or organizations willing to share their recordings for the purpose of language and culture preservation and revitalization, universities, museums, and archival repositories.

Digitization of Canadian Expeditionary Force (CEF) Files

LAC holds the personnel files of the soldiers, nurses, and chaplains who served with the Canadian Expeditionary Force. Five years ago, we set out to make the 620,000-plus files of the LAC Personnel Records of the First World War database available to Canadians free of charge. On August 8, 2018, to mark the 100-year anniversary of the final phase of the First World War, we announced that this monumental digitization project had been completed. As a result, Canadians have unprecedented access to this rich resource and are able to research high-quality digital copies of the CEF files for free anytime and anywhere. Each file contains, on average, 49 images, for a total of over 32 million images, or almost 617 terabytes of scanned information.

Youth Advisory Council

In 2018 LAC convened its first Youth Advisory Council (YAC), which provides guidance to LAC in order to help integrate the youth perspective into the visibility of, access to, and relevance of Canada's documentary heritage. The Council, made up of students and young professionals between the ages of 19 and 25, is a pilot project in 2018–2019. Participants are asked to share their opinions on a variety of issues affecting LAC and Canada's documentary heritage, to provide feedback on specific LAC initiatives, and to help identify opportunities to improve LAC's service delivery and presence.

To Be at the Leading Edge of Archival and Library Science and New Technologies

The scope and complexity of projects we pursued in 2018 have helped to establish LAC as a leader among digitally enabled memory institutions worldwide. In particular, years of consultation and planning have led to the implementation of a new library system and the procurement of a new system to manage our digitally borne acquisitions. At the same time, we continued to move forward with the planning of a second state-of-the-art analog preservation facility.

New Digital Asset Management System

LAC has embarked on a large-scale, multistream initiative to move its extensive collection of digital records to a new digital platform to make it easier for Canadians to access published and archival records of historical and modern-day significance.

The new system, supported by Preservica, a global leader in active digital preservation software, addresses the multistream element of our large-scale digital ingest and preservation initiative. It includes all processes, computer systems, software, and hardware that facilitate digital asset management, allowing bulk ingest of digital records, identification and migration of at-risk files, ingest and updating of metadata, and full text search of digital records.

Library System Renewal

On February 1, 2018, LAC proudly launched *Voilà*, Canada's new national union catalogue. The launch marked the completion of the migration of the national union catalogue holdings from our old system (AMICUS) to OCLC. The new catalogue offers an intuitive interface with modern features for searching published materials located in hundreds of libraries across Canada.

Later in the year, LAC launched *Aurora*, a new interface to access LAC's own published holdings. With *Aurora* and *Voilà*, LAC now offers two easy ways to access Canada's rich published heritage from anywhere in the world. *Aurora* also helps raise awareness of LAC's collections and increase user autonomy for requesting materials. Both *Voilà* and *Aurora* are hosted by OCLC, the world's largest online resource for discovering library materials.

A Second World-Class Preservation Facility

In 2015 Library and Archives Canada received approval to plan and develop a new preservation facility to be constructed adjacent to the existing Preservation Centre in Gatineau, Quebec.

The new facility is a solution to LAC's ongoing and future needs for special-purpose infrastructure that provides appropriate preservation and access space for LAC's analog archival holdings, with a view to building a new state-of-the-art facility to open in 2022.

To Be Proactively Engaged in National and International Networks

Throughout 2018 LAC demonstrated its willingness to collaborate with other memory institutions in Canada to improve accessibility to Canada's documentary heritage. We did this by helping smaller organizations gain access to additional funding and by sustaining a dialogue with our partners in the galleries, libraries, archives, and museum sectors.

The Documentary Heritage Communities Program

Through the Documentary Heritage Communities Program (DHCP), LAC supports Canada's documentary heritage organizations by increasing their capacity to preserve and make their collections accessible. In 2018, for the fourth year running, LAC invested $1.5 million to support the development of Canada's archival, library, and museum communities, and the professional associations that represent them, by increasing their capacity to preserve, provide access to, and promote documentary heritage. Since 2015 LAC has contributed $6 million to support 170 projects in Canada.

National Heritage Digitization Strategy

Documentary heritage is a cornerstone of all democratic societies. It supports economic, social, and legal understanding, and cultural growth, while also fostering innovation to ensure a strong future. Canadian memory institutions are working together to find ways to improve access to digital collections and better preserve our cultural heritage.

The Canadian National Heritage Digitization Strategy (NHDS) covers published and unpublished analog materials of national, regional, and local significance: books, periodicals, newspapers, government records (mandatory for federal records, voluntary for other levels of government), posters, rare books, theses, artifacts, photographs, documentary art, film and video, audio recordings, maps, etc.

Presently, the Digitizing Canadian Collections project is providing $1 million from the private sector to support 21 projects by archives, libraries, and documentary heritage institutions throughout Canada.

Second GLAM Summit at the Royal Ontario Museum

In December 2016 LAC, in conjunction with other galleries, libraries, archives, and museums (GLAMs) in Canada, adopted the Ottawa Declaration. The Declaration was a commitment to move forward based on a shared recognition of how much GLAMs have in common, and the opportunities and benefits of working collaboratively.

Members of the GLAM sector came together at a second Summit, entitled "Taking It to the Next Level," on January 30, 2018. The Summit, hosted at the Royal Ontario Museum in Toronto, brought together practitioners and experts to engage in discussions focused on four themes:

- *Communities.* How can collaboration among GLAMs benefit local communities, as well as provide greater opportunities for building links and fostering community identity?
- *Indigenous Peoples.* How can GLAMs work more closely with indigenous peoples to renew mutual relationships that are based on understanding and respect?
- *Private Sector.* How can GLAMs collaborate with the private sector to encourage greater innovation?
- *Government Priorities.* How can GLAMs work with various levels of government?

To Have Greater Public Visibility

Although 2017 was an exceptional year for LAC's public visibility as a result of Canada's 150 anniversary, in 2018 that visibility increased even further. This was achieved by continuing outreach activities, online and in-person, an innovative project to provide Canadians the opportunity to enhance the search capacity of LAC's collections, and the announcement of the funding for a new joint library facility in partnership with the Ottawa Public Library.

Co-Lab

In April 2018 LAC launched Co-Lab, an online crowdsourcing tool that allows contributors to reveal our history, page by page. The public is invited to transcribe, translate, and describe digitized records in LAC's collection, as well as to tag them with keywords to make them more searchable for users of LAC's website and its new Collection Search tool. By using Co-Lab, Canadians help unveil important parts of our history.

The public can also use the new Collection Search to find the materials that matter most to them and then enhance them in the same way by transcribing, tagging, or translating them. Any digitized image found in the new Collection Search is now available for contribution.

Joint Facility with Ottawa Public Library

The Government of Canada's Budget in 2018 provides $73.3 million over six years to support the construction and ongoing operations of a new joint facility that will house Library and Archives Canada and the Ottawa Public Library. The shared facility will house LAC's reference services, reading rooms, genealogy center, and exhibition gallery. Doors are expected to open in 2024.

Events, Exhibitions, and Tours

LAC promotes Canadian documentary heritage by creating or contributing to exhibitions that enable the public to discover its collection in cultural sites throughout Canada and by hosting public events and seminars. LAC also reaches out to Canadians through the publication of *Signatures*, our biannual magazine.

Exhibitions

- *Hiding in Plain Sight: Discovering the Métis Nation in the Archival Records of Library and Archives Canada* is on display at the Red Deer Museum and Art Gallery from December 15, 2018, to March 10, 2019. Presented by the Alberta Métis Federation and the Red Deer Museum and Art Gallery, the exhibition was developed by Library and Archives Canada in collaboration with the Manitoba Metis Federation and the Métis National Council, with the support of the government of Canada.
- *The Artist's Mirror: Self Portraits* at the Glenbow Museum in Calgary featured self-portraits from the collections of Library and Archives Canada from March 2018 until January 2019. Not until the early Renaissance in the mid-1500s in Europe did artists begin to frequently depict themselves as the primary subject in their work. This surge in self-representation can be attributed, in part, to higher-quality and more readily available mirrors. Here artists are looking deeply at themselves, a practice reflected across a wide variety of media, artistic styles, and time periods.
- *Canada: Who Do We Think We Are?* This exhibition in Ottawa marked the 150th anniversary of Confederation and explored different ideas of

Canadian identity. LAC displayed an exemplary variety of our collective past by way of heraldry, musical recordings, stamps, oil paintings, census documents, and published and unpublished manuscripts.

Events and Seminars

In 2018 Library and Archives Canada hosted more than 45 events including book launches, events to mark significant historical dates, seminars, events with partners, exhibition launches, and conferences. Three examples are

- *Doors Open 2018.* On September 28 and 29, 2018, LAC opened the doors of its preservation center in Gatineau to the public. Over 1,400 visitors came to admire the archival treasures stored within its walls, stroll through its vaults, discover the works of Canadian artists, and find out what experts are doing every day to preserve the vast collection of Library and Archives Canada.
- *Wallot-Sylvestre Seminars.* The seminars provide opportunities for Canadian, and international leaders and strategic thinkers to share their ideas on topics in information science, librarianship, archival science, and history. In March 2018 LAC welcomed Laurence Engel, president of the Bibliothèque Nationale de France, and in September 2018 Jeff James, chief executive and keeper of the National Archives (United Kingdom).
- *Signatures Series.* The Signatures Series features interviews with people who have donated their archives to LAC. In September 2018 LAC hosted former prime minister of Canada, the Right Honourable Brian Mulroney, and in October the Oscar-winning director, screenwriter, actor, and film producer Denys Arcand.

Signatures Magazine

The magazine of Library and Archives Canada seeks to make known and interpret the living cultural, civic, and historical record of Canada as reflected in its documentary heritage. Written and produced by LAC staff, it provides a behind-the-scenes look at our treasures and the technical expertise involved in acquiring, preserving, and supporting access to our history. Two editions were published in 2018: *Signatures 6* (Spring/Summer 2018) on "LAC Serving Canadians" and *Signatures 7* (Fall/Winter 2018) on "Acquisitions."

Tours

In July 2017 LAC introduced 90-minute guided public tours of the LAC Preservation Centre, revealing to the public some of the fascinating treasures that are stored there. Tours in English or French include the vaults, a section devoted entirely to works of art, and the laboratories where LAC conservators and restoration experts work diligently to preserve our fragile heritage.

Social Media and the Web

Highlights from LAC's most popular online features include

- *LAC website.* LAC's website is one of the most popular sites of the government of Canada. It is widely consulted for genealogy and military history information. In 2018 the site was viewed 41,751,478 times by 8,900,369 visitors.
- *LAC Blog.* The combined English and French views for LAC's blog hit 306,538 views in 2018.
- *Flickr.* For 2018 LAC images on its Flickr site got an average of 198,458 views a month. Total image views in 2018: 2,381,503.
- *Podcasts.* LAC's podcast team produced nine episodes in 2018. The popularity of the episodes consistently places LAC's podcasts in the top rankings of the Government and Organizations category on iTunes, and the number of listeners continues to grow with each new episode. In 2018 LAC podcasts had 91,137 listens.
- *Facebook.* In 2018 LAC posted over 650 updates in each language on Facebook. Over 7.5 million people saw these posts. Visitors to the page commented on, liked, and shared our posts over 360,000 times.
- *Twitter.* LAC ended the calendar year with over 63,000 followers on its English and French Twitter accounts (combined). Followers engaged with LAC's tweets almost 80,000 times.
- *Instagram.* In the fall of 2018 LAC launched its Instagram account, which is already gaining considerable traction with 44 posts and more than 3,000 followers.

Conclusion

As one can see, 2018 was a banner year for LAC. Considerable progress took place in numerous spheres. Of note, the implementation of the new library system and the procurement of the digital asset management system will enable LAC to thrive in an increasingly digital environment. Moreover, plans to build a new preservation center and to co-locate in the soon-to-be-built library facility in Ottawa are now solidly in place. LAC's immediate future looks exceptionally bright.

International Board on Books for Young People

Nonnenweg 12, Postfach, CH-4009 Basel, Switzerland
E-mail ibby@ibby.org
World Wide Web http://www.ibby.org

Mingzhou Zhang
President, 2018–2020

Liz Page
Executive Director

The founding of the International Board on Books for Young People (IBBY) was the result of the visionary commitment of Jella Lepman (1891–1970). Born in Stuttgart, Germany, she became a politically active journalist. In 1936 she emigrated with her son and daughter from Nazi Germany to London and became a British citizen, working for the British Foreign Office and the BBC during World War II and, beginning in 1941, for the American Broadcasting Station in Europe.

When the war ended, Lepman was engaged at the American headquarters in Germany as adviser for questions relating to children and young people. Despite a lack of funds, she organized an exhibition of children's illustrations and children's books from 20 countries in Munich in 1946. Three years later, with initial funding from the Rockefeller Foundation, she established the International Youth Library in Munich and was its director until 1957.

In the postwar years, individuals actively engaged in the field of children's literature in many countries became aware of the importance of children's books as a means for promoting international understanding and peace. They realized that children everywhere should have access to books with high literary and artistic standards and thus become enthusiastic and informed readers.

With this vision in mind, Lepman organized a meeting in Munich under the title "International Understanding through Children's Books" in November 1951. The goal of the meeting was the foundation of an international organization to promote children's books. The speeches and discussions at this conference were covered by news media worldwide. The meeting resulted in the establishment of a committee to form the International Board on Books for Young People—IBBY.

The committee met in Munich in 1952 and made a formal declaration of intent. The meeting was chaired by Swiss publisher Hans Sauerländer, and the effort was international in character from the beginning; the meeting included representatives from Austria, Germany, the Netherlands, Norway, Sweden, and Switzerland.

The success of this preparatory work resulted in the establishment of IBBY, which was registered as a nonprofit organization in Switzerland when the new organization's first General Assembly and Congress were held at the Swiss Federal Institute for Technology (ETHZ) in Zurich in October 1953. The congress brought together founding members including the authors Erich Kästner, Lisa Tetzner, Astrid Lindgren, Jo Tenfjord, Fritz Brunner, and Pamela Travers; the Swiss illustrators Alois Carigiet and Hans Fischer; publishers Hans Sauerländer and Bettina Hürlimann; and specialists in reading research including Richard Bamberger.

The initial capital for the founding of IBBY was donated by the Swiss foundation Pro Juventute, and its secretary general, Otto Binder, was elected as IBBY's first president. In the early years IBBY also received support from the International Youth Library. However, the dues from the ten national sections that had joined IBBY by 1956 were not sufficient to establish a permanent office, and IBBY's activities were mainly carried out through donations and voluntary work. The organization of the administration was the task of the acting presidents who served for two-year terms during the first decade. Succeeding Otto Binder were Swedish publisher Hans Rabén (1956–1958), Italian professor of education Enzo Petrini (1958–1960), and Lepman (1960–1962).

A notable professionalization of IBBY and an extension of membership were achieved during the presidency of Bamberger (1962–1966). In addition, the publication of IBBY's quarterly journal, *Bookbird,* edited by Lepman, Bamberger, and Lucia Binder, became a permanent activity at this time. During the presidencies of Slovenian publisher Zorka Persic (1966–1970) and Finnish school principal Niilo Visapää (1970–1974), IBBY grew so large that it was no longer possible to rely entirely on voluntary work. In 1974 a permanent office, the IBBY Secretariat, was established in Basel. Leena Maissen was appointed its director and remained in that post until her retirement in 2003. Currently the post is held by Liz Page.

IBBY is a nonprofit organization that represents an international network of people who are committed to bringing books and children together. The annual dues from the national sections are IBBY's only source of regular income; projects are supported by sponsors. IBBY cooperates with many international organizations and children's book institutions around the world and exhibits at the International Children's Book Fair in Bologna and other international book fairs.

The biennial IBBY Congresses, which have taken place in 26 countries, have become increasingly important meeting points for the worldwide membership, now comprising more than 75 national sections, to share information and experiences.

Mission and Programs

IBBY's mission is

- To promote international understanding through children's books
- To give children everywhere the opportunity to have access to books with high literary and artistic standards
- To encourage the publication and distribution of quality children's books, especially in developing countries
- To provide support and training for those involved with children and children's literature
- To stimulate research and scholarly works in the field of children's literature
- To protect and uphold children's rights as outlined in the United Nations Convention on the Rights of the Child

As part of its mission, IBBY administers two major international awards: the biennial Hans Christian Andersen Award, which is presented to an author and illustrator whose body of works has made lasting contributions to children's literature; and the IBBY-Asahi Reading Promotion Award, which is given biennially to one group or institution whose activities are judged to be making lasting contributions to reading promotion programs for children and young people. Both awards will next be given in 2020.

At the 36th IBBY Congress in Athens in 2018 IBBY signed an agreement with the Shenzhen iRead Foundation to establish the IBBY-iRead Outstanding Reading Promoter Award. The award has been established to encourage a real commitment to the cause of reading promotion in the hope of spreading this dedication to others around the globe. The award will recognize outstanding individuals who are working to promote the expansion and development of children's reading. The first award will be given at the IBBY Congress in 2020.

The IBBY Honour List is a biennial selection of outstanding recently published books, honoring writers, illustrators, and translators from IBBY member countries. An annotated catalog is published for each Honour List selection.

The IBBY Documentation Centre of Books for Young People with Disabilities offers information, consultation, and documentation services for organizations, research workers, teachers, students, librarians, publishers, authors, illustrators, policymakers, and the media who work with young people with special needs. A selective list, Outstanding Books for Young People with Disabilities, is prepared biennially and presented in an annotated catalog. The center is based at the North York Central Library Branch of the Toronto (Canada) Public Library.

Traveling exhibitions of the IBBY Honour List and the Outstanding Books for Young People with Disabilities selections are available from IBBY. Detailed information can be found on the IBBY website (http://www.ibby.org).

IBBY established International Children's Book Day in 1967 to inspire a love of reading and to call attention to children's books. Each year the day is sponsored by an IBBY national section and is celebrated on or around Hans Christian Andersen's birthday, April 2.

The IBBY Yamada workshop and project program relies on its international network to help produce and develop book cultures for children within regions that have special needs and lack support.

IBBY established its Children in Crisis program to provide support for children whose lives have been disrupted by war, civil disorder, or natural disaster. The two main activities supported are the therapeutic use of books and storytelling in the form of bibliotherapy, and the creation or replacement of collections of selected books that are appropriate to the situation. The Sharjah/IBBY Fund for Children in Crisis was active from 2012 to 2016. The fund supported projects in Afghanistan, Iran, Lebanon, Palestine, Pakistan, and Tunisia.

In response to the waves of refugees from Africa and the Middle East arriving on the Italian island Lampedusa, IBBY launched the project "Silent Books, from the world to Lampedusa and back" in 2012. The project involved creating the first library on Lampedusa to be used by local and immigrant children. The second part required creating a collection of silent books (wordless picture books) that could be understood and enjoyed by children regardless of language. These books were collected from IBBY National Sections. The books are deposited at the documentation and research archive in Rome (Palazzo della Esposizioni), while a second set is deposited at the library in Lampedusa and a third makes a traveling exhibition for the IBBY network.

Congresses

IBBY's biennial World Congresses, hosted by different national sections, bring together IBBY members and other people involved in children's books and reading development from all over the world. In addition to lectures, panel discussions, seminars, and book exhibitions, the IBBY Membership Assembly takes place. The presentation of the Hans Christian Andersen Awards, the IBBY-Asahi Reading Promotion Awards, and the IBBY Honour list are highlights of the biennial congresses. The 2020 congress is scheduled for September 5–7 in Moscow, Russia.

IBBY national sections also organize regional conferences to improve communication, networking, and professional exchange, and to strengthen ties of friendship and cooperation between the sections in the region.

Bookbird: A Journal of International Children's Literature is a refereed quarterly journal published by IBBY and is open to any topic in the field of international children's literature. *Bookbird* also has occasional themed issues. Calls for manuscripts are posted on the IBBY website. Regular features include coverage of children's literature studies, IBBY activities, and children's literature awards around the world. *Bookbird* also pays special attention to reading promotion projects worldwide. Its editor works in cooperation with an international editorial review board, guest reviewers, and correspondents who are nominated by IBBY national sections.

IBBY cooperates with several international organizations, including the International Federation of Library Associations and Institutions (IFLA), the International Publishers Association (IPA), and the International Literacy Association (ILA).

IBBY's U.S. National Section

The United States Board on Books for Young People, USBBY, is the U.S. national section of IBBY. It is a nonprofit organization devoted to building bridges of international understanding through children's and young adult books. The Friends of IBBY in the United States was founded in 1976 and became a national section of IBBY in 1984. Membership in USBBY is open to individuals and organizations interested in its mission.

A volunteer board includes USBBY's president, president-elect, past president, recording secretary, treasurer, and 12 directors, four elected and eight appointed, representing the membership as well as the patron organizations that support USBBY, such as ILA, the Children's Book Council (CBC), the American Library Association (ALA), and the National Council of Teachers of English (NCTE).

USBBY offers a forum for those interested in national and international activities relating to children's literature. It publishes a semiannual newsletter for its members, creates an annual list of the most outstanding international literature published or distributed in the United States for children and young adults, maintains an active website, sponsors a biennial regional conference that features speakers of international interest, and cosponsors sessions held at annual conferences of ALA, ILA, and NCTE.

USBBY sponsors the publication of a series of annotated bibliographies of outstanding international literature for young people, the Bridges to Understanding series, published by Scarecrow Press.

It also sponsors the creation of an annual USBBY Outstanding International Books (OIB) list, published yearly in *School Library Journal,* and a bookmark listing the selected titles is distributed via the USBBY website, http://www.usbby.org/list_oibl.html, and at meetings and conferences throughout the year.

The OIB committee selects international books that are deemed most outstanding of those published during the calendar year. Books selected for the list represent the best of children's literature from other countries; introduce American readers to outstanding authors and illustrators from other countries; help American children see the world from other points of view; provide a perspective or address a topic otherwise missing from children's literature in the United States; exhibit a distinct cultural flavor; and are accessible to American readers. Committee members judge the books based on artistic and literary merit, originality or creativity of approach, distinctiveness of topic, uniqueness of origin, and qualities that engage and appeal to children.

USBBY also submits nominations for the Hans Christian Andersen award and prepares a biennial selection of outstanding recently published books for the IBBY Honour List, the Silent Books project, and the IBBY list of Outstanding Books for Young People with Disabilities. In addition, it nominates programs for the IBBY-Asahi Reading Promotion Award.

USBBY's Bridge to Understanding Award formally acknowledges the work of adults who use books to promote international understanding among children. The award was established in memory of Arlene Pillar, an educator who served USBBY as newsletter editor from 1984 until her death in 1990. Organizations eligible for this award include schools, libraries, Scout troops, clubs, and bookstores. The winning program may be a one-time event or an ongoing series that serves children ranging in age from kindergarten through tenth grade. The award carries a prize of $1,000 and a certificate. Recent winners included "Promoting Global Awareness in Second Graders," a project in the Madeira City School District in Cincinnati that involved four second-grade teachers as well as the elementary art, music, library, gym, and computer teachers. The project was described as helping students to "make personal connections to the characters of the books, develop empathy, and relate to other children of the world through literature."

Other USBBY activities include support of IBBY's Hands across the Sea Fund, which gives assistance to underfunded IBBY sections.

USBBY has an active twinning relationship with four other IBBY national sections, allowing USBBY members to know and work closely with specific countries and to internationalize USBBY perspectives. Specific initiatives within the twinning program may include payment of IBBY dues for underfunded national sections; provision of funding to purchase books or other needed resources for classrooms and libraries; providing funding or training for writers, illustrators, editors, librarians, and publishers; facilitating fellowships for writers, illustrators, editors, librarians, and publishers, or persons who want to study children's literature; supporting cultural exchange and visits between members of USBBY and twinning national sections; developing reciprocal website postings of newsletters, information about projects, lists of children's books published in each country, and relevant websites; and including news about twinning partners in "Global Partnerships," a regular column in the USBBY newsletter, *Bridges.* Current USBBY twinning partners are Haiti, Lebanon, Palestine, and El Salvador.

The USBBY Secretariat is at the Center for Teaching through Children's Books at National Louis University, 5202 Old Orchard Road, Suite 300, Skokie, IL 60077. It can be reached by telephone at 224-233-2798, and its e-mail is secretariat@usbby.org, website: http://www.usbby.org. USBBY's executive director is V. Ellis Vance, 5503 N. El Adobe Drive, Fresno, CA 93711-2363, e-mail executive.director@usbby.org.

Part 2
Legislation, Funding, and Grants

Legislation

Legislation and Regulations Affecting Libraries in 2018

Kathi Kromer
Associate Executive Director

Shawnda Hines
Assistant Director, Communications

American Library Association
Washington Office

Following a turbulent year, 2018 brought good news for libraries on several fronts, and marked the close of the 115th Congress. Of the 13,556 bills introduced during this congressional session, 443 became law. Five of these were American Library Association (ALA) priorities, and library advocacy led by ALA's Washington Office played an important role in their passage. For one, funding for the Institute of Museum and Library Services (IMLS) was not only renewed but has increased by $11 million over the past two years, despite being targeted for elimination by the president in his proposed fiscal year (FY) 2018 and 2019 budgets. The Museum and Library Services Act (MLSA) was reauthorized by Congress through 2025, sending a strong signal of support for libraries at the federal level.

Additionally, after more than a decade of work, the Marrakesh Treaty was signed into law; a more library-friendly version of the Music Modernization Act was passed; and public access to government information increased with the passage of the Open Government Data Act. Library advocacy also helped to stall the advancement of proposed legislation that would move authority to appoint the U.S. Register of Copyrights from the Librarian of Congress to the president. Despite these significant wins, several legislative and regulatory issues of concern for libraries were not resolved and are likely remain on the agenda for 2019.

Federal Funding for Libraries

Funding Protected

Early 2018 saw a positive development for libraries when the FY 2018 omnibus spending bill passed by Congress and signed by the president in March included significant increases for several library priority programs. Highlights of the spending bill included a $9 million increase for IMLS, a level $27 million for Innovative Approaches to Literacy (IAL), a $22.1 million increase for the National Library of Medicine (NLM), and a $700 million increase for Title IV, which will open new doors for school library funding. Persistent advocacy efforts by ALA to save federal funding for libraries proved to be a tremendous success and put library programs on a solid footing as Congress began the FY 2019 appropriations cycle.

Nonetheless, as in FY 2018, federal funding for libraries was under threat in the administration's FY 2019 budget proposal, which once again recommended shuttering IMLS and eliminating related programs. For the second year in a row the library community engaged in advocacy to protect this funding.

"Dear Appropriator" letter campaigns in the House and the Senate were again successful as thousands of library advocates responded to ALA's FundLibraries campaign to e-mail, call, or visit their representatives to urge their support for the Library Services and Technology Act (LSTA) and IAL. Additionally, ALA's Public Policy and Advocacy Unit coordinated with United for Libraries to activate Friends groups and worked closely with state chapters and associations, generating over 45 letters to representatives from 15 state chapters as well as from the Chief Officers of State Library Agencies; the American Indian Library Association; and the Association of Tribal Archives, *Libraries*, and Museums. In the House, the LSTA letter led by Rep. Raúl Grijalva (D-Ariz.) was ultimately signed by 136 representatives (the second most ever), an impressive result for only ten days of campaigning. Meanwhile, the FY 2019 House IAL Dear Appropriator Letter received 98 signatures. The FY 2019 Dear Appropriator campaign then continued in the U.S. Senate. Consistent advocacy efforts resulted in a letter in support of the LSTA led by Sens. Jack Reed (D-R.I.) and Susan Collins (R-Maine) and signed by 46 senators. A similar letter in support of the IAL program was signed by 35 senators.

In sum, tireless work by library advocates across the country resulted in strong support from appropriators in the House and Senate for federal library programs. And, in September 2018, the president signed the FY 2019 funding bill for Labor-HHS-Education and Related Agencies that included increases in funding for library programs and level funding for other programs. IMLS received an increase of $2 million to be used for research and administration functions. Increases were also provided for library-relevant programs including NLM, Perkins Career and Technical Education, and Title IV education grants. Level funding was provided for the LSTA, IAL, and Striving Readers Comprehensive Literacy programs. Despite these successes, it is likely that library funding will be targeted once more for elimination by the White House in the FY 2020 budget, and a third straight year of aggressive grassroots action will be necessary.

Museum and Library Services Act (MLSA) Reauthorized through 2025

The library community had a huge win at the close of the 115th Congress with the passage and presidential signing of the MLSA, reauthorizing IMLS and the LSTA through 2025. Although a reauthorization is not a prerequisite for any program to receive funding by congressional appropriations committees, its passage sends a strong signal of support within Congress and will increase IMLS's chances of continuing to get the funding it needs to support libraries across the nation. Working with library champion Sen. Jack Reed (D-R.I.) to introduce the MLSA with bipartisan support, ALA Public Policy and Advocacy staff and members spent much of 2018 urging congressional passage.

The legislation appeared to be on the fast track after the Senate unanimously passed the MLSA in early December, but a last-minute objection from House Republican leaders threatened to undo library efforts. After a week-long, targeted grassroots and grasstops campaign, House leadership relented and allowed the MLSA to be brought to the floor, where it passed overwhelmingly (331-28). The president signed the bill on December 31. Like the previous authorization, which expired in 2016, the bill includes some improvements such as explicit permission to use IMLS funding for disaster preparedness and assistance, as well as provisions to enable more tribal libraries to participate in IMLS grant programs. It also encourages greater use of data-driven tools to measure the impact of library services.

FCC/Telecom Policy

Continued Opposition to the Net Neutrality Rollback

Following the December 2017 vote by the Federal Communications Commission (FCC) to roll back net neutrality rules, which were intended to ensure that all traffic on the Internet was treated equally, libraries joined other advocates in challenging the decision. Within a month of the rollback vote, more than twenty state attorneys general filed lawsuits against the FCC, as did at least one major Internet company and several not-for-profit organizations. Additionally, in 2018 more than 30 states introduced legislation to make net neutrality state law. And, four states—California, Washington, Oregon, and Vermont—passed laws protecting net neutrality.

In the first part of the year, library advocacy was focused at the federal level, where ALA joined other prominent advocacy groups in urging members of Congress to support a Joint Resolution of Disapproval under the Congressional Review Act (CRA). Although the CRA resolution passed a Senate vote in May 2018 (52-47), the measure failed to gain enough votes in the House by the end of the year to block the FCC's rollback of net neutrality rules. Thus, the FCC rollback, which took effect in June 2018, currently remains in effect.

With the most straightforward legislative option diminished, net neutrality advocates focused additional energy on the courts. In August 2018 ALA submitted an amici filing with the U.S. Court of Appeals for the District of Columbia Circuit arguing in support of net neutrality and strong, enforceable rules to protect and preserve the open internet. ALA joined the Association of Research Libraries (ARL) and higher education organizations in support of petitioners in the case of Mozilla Corporation v. Federal Communications Commission and United States of America. The ALA asserted that the FCC's 2017 Order will "imperil the internet's continued operation as a reliable platform for research, learning and information sharing, and that the FCC's decision should be reversed as arbitrary and capricious." In 2019, the net neutrality rollback will likely continue to be challenged through the courts. Two of the big questions to be addressed are, one, whether the

FCC had sufficient reason to change the classification of broadband so shortly following the adoption of the 2015 rules and, two, whether the FCC has the right to preempt states from instituting their own net neutrality laws.

Tribal Libraries and Rural Broadband Are on the Agenda

Several bills relevant to improving broadband access in unserved and underserved areas were introduced to Congress in 2018. Most notably, Rep. Ben Ray Lujan (D-N.Mex.-3) joined with Rep. Markwayne Mullin (R-Okla.-2) to introduce the Tribal Connect Act (H.R. 5661), the House companion bill to the legislation (S. 2205) introduced by Sens. Martin Heinrich (D-N.Mex.) and Dean Heller (R-Nev.) in 2017. Like the Senate bill, the Tribal Connect Act in the House was intended to increase access to E-rate by opening eligibility to tribal libraries which may not currently qualify, establish an E-rate pilot program for tribal anchor institutions where no library currently exists, and direct the FCC to provide additional training and performance goals for tribal broadband access. Both bills were referred to committee in their respective chambers. Other bills supportive of rural broadband included the Rural Broadband Permitting Efficiency Act (S. 604 and H.R. 4824) and the Advancing Innovation and Reinvigorating Widespread Access to Viable Electromagnetic Spectrum (AIRWAVES) Act (S. 1682 and H.R. 4953). While none of these three bills ultimately moved forward to become law, they illustrate that there is support in Congress for taking up broadband access issues.

ALA also advocated for better wireless broadband for rural areas as a charter member of the Broadband Access Coalition. This coalition submitted a proposal to the FCC as well as several filings arguing for new spectrum in the 3.7 GHz frequency band to be opened and shared on favorable economic terms so that companies and communities can provide low-cost broadband to consumers and rural anchor institutions like libraries. Access to broadband was a major campaign issue in several states, including Vermont and Maine, giving weight to the possibility that support for rural and tribal broadband initiatives could advance further in 2019.

E-Rate Anniversary and Administrative Issues

In 2018 ALA cosponsored an E-rate summit and celebration on Capitol Hill. Libraries joined education groups and other longtime advocates to commemorate the twentieth year of this successful bipartisan program connecting libraries and schools to the Internet.

On a more pragmatic level, ALA continued to meet with key FCC staff to discuss the open proceeding on the Category Two process as well as broadband access for tribal communities and barriers to their participation in the E-rate program. Additionally, library representatives raised concerns with the FCC regarding E-rate administration, with particular attention to training for E-rate coordinators and outreach to beginner applicants. ALA also advocated for E-rate applicants denied eligibility due to a faulty FCC form. Subsequently, the FCC directed USAC not to reject E-rate requests for FY 2018 because of changes in the form.

Despite a relatively quiet year on the E-rate front, ALA sees problems on the horizon and is preparing to defend funding for the program in 2019.

Copyright

Legislation Threatens to Undermine the Librarian of Congress

Copyright holders, eager to eliminate the authority of the Librarian of Congress to appoint the Register of Copyrights, lobbied the House in 2017 to pass the Register of Copyrights Selection and Accountability Act (H.R. 1695) to "modernize" the U.S. Copyright Office. The legislation would shift Register appointment power from the Librarian of Congress to the president. The Senate-proposed companion legislation (S. 1010) stalled for months due to jurisdictional concerns raised by the Senate Committee on Rules and Administration, but eventually moved forward. Library advocates strongly opposed the legislation, which they saw as an attempt by the entertainment industry to chip away at authority within the Library of Congress as a start toward the ultimate goal of moving the Copyright Office itself. In response to ALA's calls to action, advocates sent a record number of e-mail messages to the Senate in the waning days of the lame duck session in December 2018, and a floor vote on S. 1010 was successfully delayed. Similar legislation may be reintroduced in the 116th Congress, and library advocates will again be called on to stop it.

In other news, the Library Copyright Alliance continued to challenge the Copyright Alternative in Small-Claims Enforcement (CASE) Act of 2017 (H.R. 3945). This legislation would create a small claims court in the U.S. Copyright Office to adjudicate low-cost infringement cases. The legislation aims to help individual artists with limited funds bring claims of infringement. While the rationale behind the bill is well-intentioned, the small claims court, if created, is unlikely to be used by litigants, who would have to sacrifice traditional benefits and protections of federal court litigation. This bill is likely to be reintroduced in 2019. While the Library Copyright Alliance (LCA) argues that the legislation is not workable, its outcome is not directly consequential to library interests.

Digital Millennium Copyright Act Exemptions Granted

In 2017 the LCA requested exemptions from Section 1201 of the Digital Millennium Copyright Act (DMCA), the provision which allows for circumvention of technological protection measures employed to protect access and use of copyrighted works for purposes of fair use. The decision is made by the Librarian of Congress based on recommendations from the U.S. Copyright Office and National Telecommunications and Information Administration (NTIA) following a rulemaking process held every three years. For the seventh round of 1201 rulemaking, the LCA asked that the exemption to circumvent technology on motion picture and television programming to extract film clips for teaching, research, and scholarship purposes be expanded to include K–12 students for class assignments. Previously, the exemption only applied to faculty, college students, and teachers.

Similarly, the LCA requested and received an expansion of the film clip excerpt rule to also apply to Massive Open Online Courses (MOOCs). These expanded exemptions are renewed for three years. The LCA also received a three-year renewal of the exemptions to circumvent video games for preservation purposes by libraries and archives and to circumvent e-books and e-readers to enable the text-to-speech function for people with print disabilities. The proposals were considered during 2018, with the final rule released in October.

Marrakesh Treaty Signed into Law

After more than a decade of stakeholder advocacy, the Marrakesh Treaty was approved by Congress in 2018 and signed into law. The United States will now join other nations that have ratified the World Intellectual Property Organization (WIPO) international treaty to provide broader access to accessible works for people with print disabilities. The treaty provides a copyright exception—the first ever in an international treaty—for libraries as authorized entities to make copies of entire articles and books accessible for people with print disabilities and distribute those copies across borders. The treaty's ratification by the United States will greatly increase access for English speakers with print disabilities, especially in developing countries, where less than 1 percent of all published print content is accessible. The United States will benefit as well by being able to obtain foreign-language content, especially for Spanish speakers with print disabilities. The international library and print-disabled communities are working with WIPO's Accessible Book Consortium (ABC), a public-private partnership to increase the number of accessible books available, create a searchable database of accessible titles, and facilitate the sharing of copies with the nations that have ratified the Marrakesh Treaty.

Music Modernization Act Passed

The Senate's version of the Music Modernization Act (S. 2334) was passed by the House (H.R. 1551) and signed into law in late 2018. The legislation is intended to make it easier for rights holders to collect royalties when their music is digitally streamed. The Music Modernization Act provides copyright protection for pre-1972 sound recordings bringing them under federal copyright protection rather than individual state law protection. This means that these recordings will be treated in the same way as other protected works—a full set of exclusive rights that includes comprehensive copyright exceptions, including fair use, preservation, and first sale. The legislation also provides a term of copyright. Rather than all pre-1972 sound recordings being protected until 2067, copyright terms will be shorter depending on when the sound recording was first published. This will make it easier for archivists and music librarians who hold large collections of rare and one-of-a-kind collections in their libraries to preserve such sound recordings. Thanks to efforts by the LCA, provisions from legislation introduced by Sen. Ron Wyden (D-Ore.) in May 2018—the Accessibility for Curators, Creators, Educators, Scholars, and Society (ACCESS) to Recordings Act (S. 2933)—ultimately prevailed over competing provisions in the Compensating Legacy Artists for their Songs, Service, and Important Contributions to Society (CLASSICS) Act (S. 2393), which library advocates had opposed.

Digital Content Licensing of E-books Unsettled

Digital content licensing and library access to e-books resurfaced as a frontline issue in 2018. Most notably, in July, Sci Fi/Fantasy publisher Tor (a division of Macmillan) announced that it would begin an embargo on e-book sales of new titles to libraries. Tor cited concerns about the impact of library e-book lending on sales. With the embargo in place, libraries cannot purchase Tor e-books until four months after their on-sale date. At the close of the year, ALA representatives met with several publishing industry players, including Hachette Book Group, Penguin Random House, Macmillan Publishers, Simon & Schuster, HarperCollins, the Book Industry Study Group, and the Authors Guild. One important conclusion from the meetings is that the library community needs to communicate with publishers and other major stakeholders on an ongoing basis, focusing on both near-term issues such as specific e-book licensing terms as well as broader strategic industry issues and relationships.

Government Information

Congressional Research Service Reports Now Available

ALA has long advocated for public access to reports issued by the Congressional Research Service (CRS), a federal agency, housed within the Library of Congress, which prepares public policy research for members of Congress. At long last, the Consolidated Appropriations Act signed by the president in March 2018 included a provision to provide public access to nonconfidential CRS reports. These reports have not been routinely published, but the new provision requires the Library to establish a website to provide free, online public access to them (which it did in September 2018). The new legislation will enable libraries to provide their users with free, authentic copies of these useful public policy reports on a broad range of topics.

OPEN Government Data Act Passed

The year brought more good news for open government advocates when Congress passed library-supported legislation to improve public access to government data. The Open, Public, Electronic, and Necessary (OPEN) Government Data Act was included as part of the Foundations for Evidence-Based Policymaking Act (H.R. 4174). The House had previously passed the bill in November 2017; in December 2018 the Senate passed the bill with amendments. The House and Senate agreed on final text on December 21, and it was signed into law in early 2019. The Act, which codifies and builds on an Obama-administration executive order, will make government data available online in machine-readable formats, as well as discoverable through a federal data catalog.

Modernizing the Federal Depository Library Program

Efforts to modernize the Federal Depository Library Program (FDLP), which falls under Title 44 of the U.S. Code, continued in 2018. The bipartisan FDLP Modernization Act of 2018 (H.R. 5305) was introduced and approved in the first half of the year by the Committee on House Administration. The bill, which aimed to update the FDLP and related programs that provide public access to government information for the digital age, was referred to the House Committee on Oversight and Government Reform. Despite advocacy efforts it did not proceed to the House floor, leaving efforts to modernize the FDLP unfinished. Importantly, however, the legislation was developed with considerable input from the library community, incorporating testimony given by librarians at a series of public hearings in 2017, as well as many of the recommendations sent to the Committee by ALA's Public Policy and Advocacy Unit.

Preparing for the 2020 Census

The 2020 Census will be the first decennial census to provide an online response option, and this new e-government option will undoubtedly bring large numbers of users into libraries. Libraries' role in ensuring a complete count cannot be understated, as Census data is used to determine representation in Congress and allocate billions of dollars in federal funding to states and localities. Significantly, a recent study by the Center for Urban Research at the City University of New York showed that a public library is located within five miles of 99 percent of hard-to-count census tracts. ALA's Public Policy and Advocacy Unit is collaborating with Census Bureau staff, Census stakeholders, and library leaders to ensure libraries are informed about the 2020 Census and can plan for potential demands. ALA is also leading efforts to encourage the Census Bureau and community leaders to include libraries in their preparations and outreach activities. For instance, ALA successfully advocated for language to be included in a Senate Appropriations Committee report encouraging the Census Bureau to collaborate with libraries. In addition, ALA worked with state library and local public library leaders in Providence County, Rhode Island, to inform them about the test taking place there in April 2018, which will be the only full practice run in advance of the 2020 Census. Preparations for the decennial census will continue in the coming year.

Looking Forward to 2019

As in past years, ALA's Public Policy and Advocacy Unit will continue to advocate on key library issues in 2019, including funding for IMLS. ALA will leverage existing relationships with agencies such as the FCC and USAC to protect E-rate funding and improve the program, as well as continue collaboration with the Census Bureau to ensure that libraries are well-positioned to support the 2020 Census efforts. ALA will also continue its coalition work, joining with other advocates to support favorable copyright legislation and the reinstatement of net neutrality.

Funding Programs and Grant-Making Agencies

National Endowment for the Humanities

400 7th St. S.W., Washington, DC 20506
202-606-8400, 800-634-1121
TDD (hearing impaired) 202-606-8282 or 866-372-2930 (toll free)
E-mail info@neh.gov, World Wide Web http://neh.gov

The National Endowment for the Humanities (NEH) is an independent federal agency created in 1965. It is one of the largest funders of humanities programs in the United States.

Because democracy demands wisdom, NEH promotes excellence in the humanities and conveys the lessons of history to all Americans, seeking to develop educated and thoughtful citizens. It accomplishes this mission by providing grants for high-quality humanities projects in six funding areas: education, preservation and access, public programs, research, challenge grants, and digital humanities.

Grants from NEH enrich classroom learning, create and preserve knowledge, and bring ideas to life through public television, radio, new technologies, museum exhibitions, and programs in libraries and other community places. Recipients typically are cultural institutions, such as museums, archives, libraries, colleges and universities, and public television and radio stations, as well as individual scholars. The grants

- Strengthen teaching and learning in the humanities in schools and colleges
- Preserve and provide access to cultural and educational resources
- Provide opportunities for lifelong learning
- Facilitate research and original scholarship
- Strengthen the institutional base of the humanities

For more than a half century, NEH has reached millions of people with projects and programs that preserve and study the nation's culture and history while providing a foundation for the future.

The endowment's mission is to enrich cultural life by promoting the study of the humanities. According to the National Foundation on the Arts and the Humanities Act, "The term 'humanities' includes, but is not limited to, the study of the following: language, both modern and classical; linguistics; literature; history; jurisprudence; philosophy; archaeology; comparative religion; ethics; the history, criticism, and theory of the arts; those aspects of social sciences which have humanistic content and employ humanistic methods; and the study and application of the humanities to the human environment with particular attention to reflecting our diverse heritage, traditions, and history and to the relevance of the humanities to the current conditions of national life."

The act, adopted by Congress in 1965, provided for the establishment of the National Foundation on the Arts and the Humanities in order to promote progress and scholarship in the humanities and the arts in the United States. The act included the following findings:

- The arts and the humanities belong to all the people of the United States.
- The encouragement and support of national progress and scholarship in the humanities and the arts, while primarily matters for private and local initiative, are also appropriate matters of concern to the federal government.
- An advanced civilization must not limit its efforts to science and technology alone, but must give full value and support to the other great branches of scholarly and cultural activity in order to achieve a better understanding of the past, a better analysis of the present, and a better view of the future.
- Democracy demands wisdom and vision in its citizens. It must therefore foster and support a form of education, and access to the arts and the humanities, designed to make people of all backgrounds and wherever located masters of technology and not its unthinking servants.
- It is necessary and appropriate for the federal government to complement, assist, and add to programs for the advancement of the humanities and the arts by local, state, regional, and private agencies and their organizations. In doing so, the government must be sensitive to the nature of public sponsorship. Public funding of the arts and humanities is subject to the conditions that traditionally govern the use of public money. Such funding should contribute to public support and confidence in the use of taxpayer funds. Public funds provided by the federal government ultimately must serve public purposes the Congress defines.
- The arts and the humanities reflect the high place accorded by the American people to the nation's rich culture and history and to the fostering of mutual respect for the diverse beliefs and values of all persons and groups.

What NEH Grants Accomplish

Since its founding, NEH has awarded more than 70,000 competitive grants.

Interpretive Exhibitions

Interpretive exhibitions provide opportunities for lifelong learning in the humanities for millions of Americans. Since 1967 NEH has awarded approximately $310 million in grants for interpretive exhibitions, catalogs, and public programs, which are among the most highly visible activities supported by the endowment. NEH support finances exhibitions; reading, viewing, and discussion programs; Web-based programs; and other public education programs at venues across the country.

Renewing Teaching

Over NEH's history, more than 100,000 high school and college teachers have deepened their knowledge of the humanities through intensive summer study supported by the endowment; tens of thousands of students benefit from these better-educated teachers every year.

Reading and Discussion Programs

Since 1982 NEH has supported reading and discussion programs in the nation's libraries, bringing people together to discuss works of literature and history. Scholars in the humanities provide thematic direction for the discussion programs. Using selected texts and such themes as "Work," "Family," "Diversity," and "Not for Children Only," these programs have attracted more than 2 million Americans to read and talk about what they've read.

Chronicling America

NEH's National Digital Newspaper Program is supporting projects to convert microfilm of historically important U.S. newspapers into fully searchable digital files. Developed in partnership with the Library of Congress, this long-term project ultimately will make more than 30 million pages of newspapers accessible online. For more on this project, visit http://chroniclingamerica.loc.gov.

Stimulating Private Support

About $2 billion in humanities support has been generated by NEH's Challenge Grants program, which requires most grant recipients to raise $3 in nonfederal funds for every dollar they receive.

Presidential Papers

Ten presidential papers projects, from Washington to Eisenhower, have received support from NEH. Matching grants for the ten projects have leveraged millions of dollars in nonfederal contributions.

New Scholarship

NEH grants enable scholars to do in-depth study. Jack Rakove explored the making of the Constitution in his *Original Meanings,* and James McPherson chronicled the Civil War in his *Battle Cry of Freedom.* Projects supported by NEH grants have earned nearly 20 Pulitzer Prizes.

History on Screen

Since 1967 NEH has awarded approximately $310 million to support the production of films for broad public distribution, including the Emmy Award–winning series *The Civil War,* the Oscar-nominated films *Brooklyn Bridge, The Restless Conscience,* and *Freedom on My Mind,* and film biographies of John and Abigail Adams, Eugene O'Neill, and Ernest Hemingway. More than 8 million saw the

April 2010 debut of *The Buddha,* a documentary made for PBS by filmmaker David Grubin, and it has been streamed into hundreds of classrooms nationwide. Over seven successive nights on PBS, more than 33 million people watched Ken Burns's *The Roosevelts* (2014), which chronicles the lives of Teddy, Eleanor, and Franklin.

American Voices

NEH support for scholarly editions makes the writings of prominent and influential Americans accessible. Ten presidents are included, along with such key figures as Martin Luther King, Jr., George C. Marshall, and Eleanor Roosevelt. Papers of prominent writers—among them Emily Dickinson, Walt Whitman, Mark Twain, and Robert Frost—are also available.

Library of America

Millions of books have been sold as part of the Library of America series, a collection of the riches of the nation's literature. Begun with NEH seed money, the 303 volumes published to date include the works of such figures as Henry Adams, Edith Wharton, William James, Eudora Welty, and W. E. B. Du Bois.

The Library of America also received a $150,000 grant for the publication of *American Poetry: The Seventeenth and Eighteenth Centuries* (two volumes) and an expanded volume of selected works by Captain John Smith—a key figure in the establishment of the first permanent English settlement in North America, at Jamestown, Virginia—and other early exploration narratives.

Technical Innovation

NEH support for the digital humanities is fueling innovation and new tools for research in the humanities. Modern 3D technology allows students to visit sites ranging from ancient Egypt to the 1964–1965 New York World's Fair. Spectral imaging was used to create an online critical edition of explorer David Livingstone's previously unreadable field diary of 1871.

Science and the Humanities

The scientific past is being preserved with NEH-supported editions of the letters of Charles Darwin, the works of Albert Einstein, and the 14-volume papers of Thomas Edison. Additionally, NEH and the National Science Foundation have joined forces in Documenting Endangered Languages (DEL), a multiyear effort to preserve records of key languages that are in danger of becoming extinct.

EDSITEment

EDSITEment (http://edsitement.neh.gov) assembles the best humanities resources on the Web, drawing more than 400,000 visitors each month. Incorporating these Internet resources, particularly primary documents, from more than 350 peer-reviewed websites, EDSITEment features more than 500 online lesson plans in all areas of the humanities. Teachers use EDSITEment's resources to enhance lessons and to engage students through interactive technology tools that hone critical-thinking skills.

Federal-State Partnership

The Office of Federal-State Partnership links NEH with the nationwide network of 56 humanities councils, which are located in each state, the District of Columbia, Puerto Rico, the U.S. Virgin Islands, the Northern Mariana Islands, American Samoa, and Guam. Each council funds humanities programs in its own jurisdiction.

Directory of State Humanities Councils

Alabama

Alabama Humanities Foundation
1100 Ireland Way, Suite 202
Birmingham, AL 35205-7001
205-558-3980, fax 205-558-3981
http://www.alabamahumanities.org

Alaska

Alaska Humanities Forum
421 W. 1st Ave., Suite 200
Anchorage, AK 99501
907-272-5341, fax 907-272-3979
http://www.akhf.org

Arizona

Arizona Humanities Council
Ellis-Shackelford House
1242 N. Central Ave.
Phoenix, AZ 85004-1887
602-257-0335, fax 602-257-0392
http://www.azhumanities.org

Arkansas

Arkansas Humanities Council
407 President Clinton Ave., Suite 201
Little Rock, AR 72201
501-320-5761, fax 501-537-4550
http://www.arkansashumanitiescouncil.org

California

Cal Humanities
538 9th St., # 210
Oakland, CA 94607
415-391-1474, fax 415-391-1312
http://www.calhum.org

Colorado

Colorado Humanities
7935 E. Prentice Ave., Suite 450
Greenwood Village, CO 80111
303-894-7951, fax 303-864-9361
http://www.coloradohumanities.org

Connecticut

Connecticut Humanities Council
100 Riverview Center, Suite 270
292 Main Street
Middletown, CT 06457
860-685-2260, fax 860-685-7597
http://cthumanities.org

Delaware

Delaware Humanities
100 W. Tenth St., Suite 509
Wilmington, DE 19801
302-657-0650, fax 302-657-0655
http://dehumanities.org

District of Columbia

Humanities D.C.
925 U St. N.W.
Washington, DC 20001
202-387-8393, fax 202-387-8149
http://wdchumanities.org

Florida

Florida Humanities Council
599 Second St. S.
St. Petersburg, FL 33701-5005
727-873-2000, fax 727-873-2014
http://www.floridahumanities.org

Georgia

Georgia Humanities Council
50 Hurt Plaza S.E., Suite 595
Atlanta, GA 30303-2915
404-523-6220, fax 404-523-5702
http://www.georgiahumanities.org

Hawaii

Hawai'i Council for the Humanities
First Hawaiian Bank Bldg.
3599 Waialae Ave., Room 25
Honolulu, HI 96816
808-732-5402, fax 808-732-5432
http://www.hihumanities.org

Idaho

Idaho Humanities Council
217 W. State St.
Boise, ID 83702
208-345-5346, fax 208-345-5347
http://www.idahohumanities.org

Illinois

Illinois Humanities Council
125 S. Church St., Suite 650
Chicago, IL 60603-5200
312-422-5580, fax 312-422-5588
http://www.ilhumanities.org

Indiana

Indiana Humanities
1500 N. Delaware St.
Indianapolis, IN 46202
317-638-1500, fax 317-634-9503
http://www.indianahumanities.org

Iowa

Humanities Iowa
100 Library, Room 4039
Iowa City, IA 52242-1420
319-335-4153, fax 319-335-4154
http://humanitiesiowa.org

Kansas

Kansas Humanities Council
112 S.W. 6th Ave., Suite 400
Topeka, KS 66603-3895
785-357-0359, fax 785-357-1723
http://www.kansashumanities.org

Kentucky

Kentucky Humanities
206 E. Maxwell St.
Lexington, KY 40508
859-257-5932, fax 859-257-5933
http://www.kyhumanities.org

Louisiana

Louisiana Endowment for the Humanities
938 Lafayette St., Suite 300
New Orleans, LA 70113-1782
504-523-4352, fax 504-529-2358
http://www.leh.org

Maine

Maine Humanities Council
674 Brighton Ave.
Portland, ME 04102-1012
207-773-5051, fax 207-773-2416
http://www.mainehumanities.org

Maryland

Maryland Humanities Council
108 W. Centre St.
Baltimore, MD 21201-4565
410-685-0095, fax 410-685-0795
http://www.mdhumanities.org

Massachusetts

Mass Humanities
66 Bridge St.
Northampton, MA 01060
413-584-8440, fax 413-584-8454
http://www.masshumanities.org

Michigan

Michigan Humanities Council
119 Pere Marquette Drive, Suite 3B
Lansing, MI 48912-1270
517-372-7770, fax 517-372-0027
http://michiganhumanities.org

Minnesota

Minnesota Humanities Center
987 Ivy Ave. E.
St. Paul, MN 55106-2046
651-774-0105, fax 651-774-0205
http://www.mnhum.org

Mississippi

Mississippi Humanities Council
3825 Ridgewood Rd., Room 311
Jackson, MS 39211
601-432-6752, fax 601-432-6750
http://www.mshumanities.org

Missouri

Missouri Humanities Council
The Grand Central Building at Union Station
415 South 18th St., Suite 100
St. Louis, MO 63103
Toll free: 1-800-357-0909
314-781-9660, fax 314-781-9681
http://www.mohumanities.org

Montana

Humanities Montana
311 Brantly
Missoula, MT 59812-7848
406-243-6022, fax 406-243-4836
http://www.humanitiesmontana.org

Nebraska

Nebraska Humanities Council
215 Centennial Mall South, Suite 330
Lincoln, NE 68508
402-474-2131, fax 402-474-4852
http://www.humanitiesnebraska.org

Nevada

Nevada Humanities
1670-200 N. Virginia St.
P.O. Box 8029
Reno, NV 89507-8029
775-784-6587, fax 775-784-6527
http://www.nevadahumanities.org

New Hampshire

New Hampshire Humanities
117 Pleasant St.
Concord, NH 03301-3852
603-224-4071, fax 603-224-4072
http://www.nhhc.org

New Jersey

New Jersey Council for the Humanities
28 W. State St., Suite 6
Trenton, NJ 08608
609-695-4838, fax 609-695-4929
http://www.njhumanities.org

New Mexico

New Mexico Humanities Council
4115 Silver Ave. S.E.
Albuquerque, NM 87108
505-633-7370, fax 505-633-7377
http://www.nmhum.org

New York

Humanities New York
150 Broadway, Suite 1700
New York, NY 10038
212-233-1131, fax 212-233-4607
http://www.humanitiesny.org

North Carolina

North Carolina Humanities Council
320 East 9th St., Suite 414
Charlotte, NC 28202
704-687-1520, fax 704-687-1550
http://www.nchumanities.org

North Dakota

Humanities North Dakota
418 E. Broadway, Suite 8
Bismarck, ND 58501
701-255-3360, fax 701-223-8724
http://www. humanitiesnd.org

Ohio

Ohio Humanities Council
471 E. Broad St., Suite 1620
Columbus, OH 43215-3857
614-461-7802, fax 614-461-4651
http://www.ohiohumanities.org

Oklahoma

Oklahoma Humanities
424 Concord Dr., Suite E
Oklahoma City, OK 73102
405-235-0280, fax 405-235-0289
http://www.okhumanities.org

Oregon

Oregon Council for the Humanities
921 S.W. Washington St., #150
Portland, OR 97205
503-241-0543, fax 503-241-0024
http://www.oregonhumanities.org

Pennsylvania

Pennsylvania Humanities Council
325 Chestnut St., Suite 715
Philadelphia, PA 19106-2607
215-925-1005, fax 215-925-3054
http://www.pahumanities.org

Rhode Island

Rhode Island Council for the Humanities
131 Washington St., Suite 210
Providence, RI 02903
401-273-2250, fax 401-454-4872
http://www.rihumanities.org

South Carolina

South Carolina Humanities
2711 Middleburg Drive, Suite 203
P.O. Box 5287
Columbia, SC 29254
803-771-2477, fax 803-771-2487
http://www.schumanities.org

South Dakota

South Dakota Humanities Council
1215 Trail Ridge Rd., Suite A
Brookings, SD 57006
605-688-6113, fax 605-688-4531
http://sdhumanities.org

Tennessee

Humanities Tennessee
807 Main Street, Suite B
Nashville, TN 37201
615-770-0006, fax 615-770-0007
http://www.humanitiestennessee.org

Texas

Humanities Texas
1410 Rio Grande St.
Austin, TX 78701
512-440-1991, fax 512-440-0115
http://www.humanitiestexas.org

Utah

Utah Humanities
202 W. 300 North
Salt Lake City, UT 84103
801-359-9670, fax 801-531-7869
http://www.utahhumanities.org

Vermont

Vermont Humanities
11 Loomis St.
Montpelier, VT 05602
802-262-2626, fax 802-262-2620
http://www.vermonthumanities.org

Virginia

Virginia Foundation for the Humanities
145 Ednam Drive
Charlottesville, VA 22903-4629
434-924-3296, fax 434-296-4714
http://www.virginiahumanities.org

Washington

Humanities Washington
130 Nickerson Street, Suite 304
Seattle, WA 98109
206-682-1770, fax 206-682-4158
http://www.humanities.org

West Virginia

West Virginia Humanities Council
1310 Kanawha Blvd. East
Charleston, WV 25301
304-346-8500, fax 304-346-8504
http://www.wvhumanities.org

Wisconsin

Wisconsin Humanities Council
3801 Regent St.
Madison, WI 53705
608-262-0706, fax 608-263-7970
http://www.wisconsinhumanities.org

Wyoming

Wyoming Humanities Council
1315 E. Lewis St.
Laramie, WY 82072-3459
307-721-9243, fax 307-742-4914
http://www.thinkwy.org

American Samoa

Amerika Samoa Humanities Council
P.O. Box 5800
Pago Pago, AS 96799
684-633-4870, fax 684-633-4873
http://ashcouncil.org

Guam

Humanities Guahan
222 Chalan Santo Papa
Reflection Center, Suite 106
Hagatna, Guam 96910
671-472-4460, fax 671-472-4465
http://www.humanitiesguahan.org

Northern Marianas Islands

Northern Marianas Humanities Council
P.O. Box 506437
Saipan, MP 96950
670-235-4785, fax 670-235-4786
http://northernmarianashumanities.org

Puerto Rico

Fundación Puertorriqueña de las Humanidades
109 San José St., 3rd floor
Box 9023920
San Juan, PR 00902-3920
787-721-2087, fax 787-721-2684
http://www.fphpr.org

Virgin Islands

Virgin Islands Humanities Council
1829 Kongens Gade
St. Thomas, VI 00802-6746
340-776-4044, fax 340-774-3972
http://www.vihumanities.org

NEH Overview

Division of Education Programs

Through grants to educational institutions and professional development programs for scholars and teachers, this division is designed to support study of the humanities at all levels of education.

Grants support the development of curricula and materials, faculty study programs, and conferences and networks of educational institutions.

Contact: 202-606-8500, e-mail education@neh.gov.

Seminars and Institutes

Grants support summer seminars and institutes in the humanities for college and school teachers. These faculty-development activities are conducted at colleges and universities in the United States and abroad. Those wishing to participate in seminars should submit their seminar applications to the seminar director.

Contact: 202-606-8471, e-mail sem-inst@neh.gov.

Landmarks of American History and Culture

Grants for Landmarks workshops provide support to teachers and community college faculty. These professional development workshops are conducted at or near sites important to American history and culture (such as presidential residences or libraries, colonial-era settlements, major battlefields, historic districts, and sites associated with major writers or artists) to address central themes and issues in American history, government, literature, art history, and related subjects in the humanities.

Contact: 202-606-8463, e-mail landmarks@neh.gov.

Division of Preservation and Access

Grants are made for projects that will create, preserve, and increase the availability of resources important for research, education, and public programming in the humanities.

Support may be sought to preserve the intellectual content and aid bibliographic control of collections; to compile bibliographies, descriptive catalogs, and guides to cultural holdings; and to create dictionaries, encyclopedias, databases, and electronic archives. Applications also may be submitted for education and training projects dealing with issues of preservation or access; for research and development leading to improved preservation and access standards, practices, and tools; and for projects to digitize historic U.S. newspapers and to document endangered languages. Grants are also made to help smaller cultural repositories preserve and care for their humanities collections. Proposals may combine preservation and access activities within a single project.

Contact: 202-606-8570, e-mail preservation@neh.gov.

Division of Public Programs

Public humanities programs promote lifelong learning in American and world history, literature, comparative religion, philosophy, and other fields of the humanities. They offer new insights into familiar subjects and invite conversation about important humanities ideas and questions.

The Division of Public Programs supports an array of public humanities programs that reach large and diverse public audiences through a variety of program formats, including interpretive exhibitions, radio and television broadcasts, lectures, symposia, interpretive multimedia projects, printed materials, and reading and discussion programs.

Grants support the development and production of television, radio, and digital media programs; the planning and implementation of museum exhibitions, the interpretation of historic sites, the production of related publications, multimedia components, and educational programs; and the planning and implementation of reading and discussion programs, lectures, symposia, and interpretive exhibitions of books, manuscripts, and other library resources.

Contact: 202-606-8269, e-mail publicpgms@neh.gov.

Division of Research Programs

Through fellowships to individual scholars and grants to support complex, frequently collaborative research, the Division of Research Programs contributes to the creation of knowledge in the humanities.

Fellowships and Stipends

Grants provide support for scholars to undertake full-time independent research and writing in the humanities. Grants are available for a maximum of one year and a minimum of two months of summer study.

Contact: 202-606-8200, e-mail (fellowships) fellowships@neh.gov (summer stipends) stipends@neh.gov.

Research

Grants provide up to three years of support for collaborative research in the preparation for publication of editions, translations, and other important works in the humanities, and in the conduct of large or complex interpretive studies, including archaeology projects and humanities studies of science and technology. Grants also support research opportunities offered through independent research centers and international research organizations.

Contact: 202-606-8200, e-mail research@neh.gov.

Office of Challenge Grants

Nonprofit institutions interested in developing new sources of long-term support for educational, scholarly, preservation, and public programs in the humanities can be assisted in these efforts by an NEH Challenge Grant. Grantees are required to raise $3 in nonfederal donations for every federal dollar offered. Both federal and nonfederal funds may be used to establish or increase institutional endowments and therefore guarantee long-term support for a variety of humanities needs. Funds also can be used for limited direct capital expenditures where such needs are compelling and clearly related to improvements in the humanities.

Contact: 202-606-8309, e-mail challenge@neh.gov.

Office of Digital Humanities

The Office of Digital Humanities encourages and supports projects that utilize or study the impact of digital technology on research, education, preservation, and public programming in the humanities. Launched as an initiative in 2006, Digital Humanities was made permanent as an office within NEH in 2008.

NEH is interested in fostering the growth of digital humanities and lending support to a wide variety of projects, including those that deploy digital technologies and methods to enhance understanding of a topic or issue; those that study the impact of digital technology on the humanities; and those that digitize important materials, thereby increasing the public's ability to search and access humanities information.

The office coordinates the endowment's efforts in the area of digital scholarship. Currently NEH has numerous programs throughout the agency that are actively funding digital scholarship, including Humanities Collections and Resources, Institutes for Advanced Topics in the Digital Humanities, Digital Humanities Challenge Grants, Digital Humanities Start-Up Grants, and many others. NEH is also actively working with other funding partners in the United States and abroad in order to better coordinate spending on digital infrastructure for the humanities.

Contact: 202-606-8401, e-mail odh@neh.gov.

A full list of NEH grants programs and deadlines is available on the endowment's website at http://www.neh.gov/grants.

Institute of Museum and Library Services

955 L'Enfant Plaza North, S.W., Suite 4000, Washington, DC 20024-2135
202-653-4657, fax 202-653-4600
World Wide Web http://www.imls.gov

Vision and Mission

The vision of the Institute of Museum and Library Services (IMLS) is a nation where museums and libraries work together to transform the lives of individuals and communities. The agency's mission is to advance, support, and empower America's museums, libraries, and related organizations' grant making, research, and policy development.

Overview

IMLS is an independent grant-making agency and the primary source of federal support for the nation's approximately 120,000 libraries and 35,000 museums and related organizations. IMLS helps ensure that all Americans have access to museum, library, and information services. The agency supports innovation, lifelong learning, and cultural and civic engagement, enabling museums and libraries from geographically and economically diverse areas to deliver essential services that make it possible for individuals and communities to thrive. The agency strives to inspire libraries and museums to advance innovation, learning, and civic engagement and to provide leadership through research, policy development, and grant making.

IMLS was created with the passage of the Museum and Library Services Act (MLSA) in 1996, which, as amended, authorizes the agency to award financial assistance; collect data; form strategic partnerships; and advise the president, Congress, and other federal agencies on museum, library, and information services. Federal library programs began in 1956, and the agency has consolidated the federal museum programs dating to 1976. Today it is responsive to the needs and opportunities expressed by communities through their libraries and museums and brings cutting-edge approaches to curating essential information within cities, regions, and the nation.

The agency has an expansive reach across the country and into a large variety of institutions. Its discretionary grants are selected through a highly respected and competitive peer-review process drawing on professionals located across the nation. IMLS builds capacity within the museum and library fields to enable better service to communities and to enhance community decision making by sharing trends and data.

IMLS is led by a director who is a presidential appointee confirmed by the Senate and advised by the National Museum and Library Services Board (NMLSB). The NMLSB is a 23-member advisory body that includes the IMLS

This report was produced by *LBTA* from various sources, including but not limited to information provided by IMLS and/or available on the agency's website. *LBTA* bears sole responsibility for any errors or omissions.

director, the deputy director for libraries, the deputy director for museums, and 20 presidentially appointed individuals with expertise in, or commitment to, library or museum services. Based on its knowledge and experience, the NMLSB advises the IMLS director on general policy and practices and helps with the selections for the National Medal for Museum and Library Service.

In fiscal year (FY) 2018 IMLS's work was enhanced by an additional $9 million congressional appropriation, including a $4.7 million increase to the Grants to States program budget. The agency was also allocated a $3 million budget increase for museum programs: $1.75 million for Museums for America and Museum Empowered Grants for Professional Development, $500,000 for Native American/Native Hawaiian Museum Services, and $750,000 toward Museum Grants for African American History and Culture.

On December 31, 2018, President Trump signed into law the Museum and Library Services Act of 2018 (PL 115-410). Passage of the new MLSA reauthorizes the existing programs and functions of IMLS and provides new authority, including to develop and support new museum, library, and information professionals. [As this report was being finalized, *LBTA* learned that the Trump administration's budget proposal for 2020 has—for the third year running—proposed the elimination of IMLS. For more information see https://bit.ly/2UEzayA as well as the table on page 232 of this volume. And if you support strong federal funding for libraries, please let your congressional representatives know—*Ed.*]

Strategic Goals

As highlighted in *Transforming Communities*, the IMLS Strategic Plan for 2018–2022, the agency's goals are to

1. Promote Lifelong Learning. IMLS supports learning and literacy for people of all ages through museums and libraries.
2. Build Capacity. IMLS strengthens the capacity of museums and libraries to improve the well-being of their communities.
3. Increase Public Access. IMLS makes strategic investments that increase access to information, ideas, and networks through libraries and museums.
4. Achieve Excellence. IMLS strategically aligns its resources and relationships to support libraries and museums nationwide.

Transforming Communities is available for download on the IMLS website at https://www.imls.gov/about-us/strategic-plan.

Scope of Responsibilities

This section provides highlights of IMLS's role in supporting and sustaining America's libraries and museums and the services they provide to citizens, as authorized by the MLSA.

Library Services

IMLS library service programs support the following goals:

- To enhance coordination among federal programs that relate to library and information services
- To promote continuous improvement in library services in all types of libraries in order to better serve the people of the United States
- To facilitate access to resources in all types of libraries for the purpose of cultivating an educated and informed citizenry
- To encourage resource sharing among all types of libraries for the purpose of achieving economical and efficient delivery of library services to the public
- To promote literacy, education, and lifelong learning and to enhance and expand the services and resources provided by libraries, including those services and resources relating to workforce development, 21st-century skills, and digital literacy skills
- To enhance the skills of the current library workforce and to recruit future professionals to the field of library and information services
- To ensure the preservation of knowledge and library collections in all formats and to enable libraries to serve their communities during disasters
- To enhance the role of libraries within the information infrastructure of the United States in order to support research, education, and innovation
- To promote library services that provide users with access to information through national, state, local, regional, and international collaborations and networks

Museum Services

IMLS museum service programs support the following goals:

- To encourage and support museums in carrying out their public service role of connecting society to the cultural, artistic, historical, natural, and scientific understandings that constitute our heritage
- To encourage and support museums in carrying out their educational role
- To encourage leadership, innovation, and applications of the most current technologies and practices to enhance museum services through international, national, regional, state, and local networks and partnerships
- To assist, encourage, and support museums in carrying out their stewardship activities to achieve the highest standards in conservation and care of the cultural, historic, natural, and scientific heritage of the United States to benefit future generations
- To assist, encourage, and support museums in achieving the highest standards of management and service to the public, and to ease the financial burden borne by museums as a result of their increasing use by the public

- To support resource sharing and partnerships among museums, libraries, schools, and other community organizations
- To encourage and support museums as a part of economic development and revitalization in communities
- To ensure that museums of various types and sizes in diverse geographic regions of the United States are afforded attention and support
- To support efforts at the state level to maximize museum resources and services

Library Grants

The IMLS Grants to States program awards population-based formula grants to each State Library Administrative Agency (SLAA) in the 50 States, the District of Columbia, the Commonwealth of Puerto Rico, the U.S. Virgin Islands, American Samoa, Guam, and the Commonwealth of the Northern Mariana Islands. The formula consists of a minimum amount set by law plus a supplemental amount based on population (dependent on annual appropriations). Population data are based on the information available from the U.S. Census Bureau website.

The 2010 Act sets base allotments of $680,000 for states and $60,000 for Pacific Territories. The Act limits administrative costs at the state level to 4 percent and requires a 34 percent match from nonfederal state or local funds. Programs and services delivered by each SLAA support the purposes and priorities set forth in the Library Services and Technology Act (LSTA). SLAAs set goals and objectives for their states regarding the use of Grants to States funds within the statutorily required five-year plan approved by IMLS. These goals and objectives are determined through a planning process that includes statewide needs assessments. States take special precautions to ensure that federal funds do not supplant state investments.

Additional information about the IMLS Grants to States program, including application and submission information, is available at https://www.imls.gov/grants/grant-programs/grants-states.

Support for Pacific Territories and Freely Associated States

Grants to the Pacific Territories and the Freely Associated States (FAS) are sanctioned under a Special Rule, which authorizes a small competitive grants program in the Pacific region and the U.S. Virgin Islands. There are seven eligible entities: Guam (GU), American Samoa (AS), the Commonwealth of Northern Mariana Islands (CNMI), the Federated States of Micronesia (FSM), the Republic of the Marshall Islands (RMI), the Republic of Palau (PW), and the U.S. Virgin Islands (VI).

The funds for this grant program are taken from the allotment amounts for the FAS (FSM, RMI, and PW). The territories (GU, AS, CNMI, VI) receive allotments through the Grants to States program and, in addition, may apply for funds under the competitive program. Up to 5 percent of this program's funding is set aside for Mid-Continent Research for Education and Learning (McREL) to facilitate the grants review process. These projects support the LSTA purposes.

Table 1 / IMLS Library Grant Programs in Budget FY 2018

Grants to States

Program	Number of Awards	Funds Awards	Awardee Match
Grants to States	56	$160,546,768	$82,508,448
Grants to States for Pacific Territories, Freely Associated States and the Virgin Islands	7	$248,818	$78,102*

*Only includes match from the Freely Associated States; no match is required from the territories.

Total for all Discretionary Programs

Number of Applications	Number of Awards	Funds Requested	Funds Awarded	Awardee Match
951	324	$106,713,749	$28,469,000	$7,835,444

By Program

Laura Bush 21st Century Librarian Program

Number of Preliminary Proposals	Number of Full Applications*	Number of Awards	Funds Requested	Funds Awarded	Awardee Match
174	53	42	$39,782,291	$10,000,000	$1,844,957

*National Leadership Grants for Libraries***

Number of Preliminary Proposals	Number of Full Applications*	Number of Awards	Funds Requested	Funds Awarded	Awardee Match
323	187	79	$60,641,949	$13,406,000	$5,021,853

*Laura Bush 21st Century Librarian Program grants and National Leadership Grants for Libraries involve a two-phased, peer-reviewed process: an open round of preliminary proposals, from which selected applicants are invited to submit full applications.

**This program has common interests and so is reflected in both the IMLS Office of Library Services (OLS) and Office of Museum Services (OMS) charts.

*Native American and Native Hawaiian Library Service Programs****

Program	Number of Applications	Number of Awards	Funds Requested	Funds Awarded	Awardee Match
Basic Grants	179	179	$1,844,442	$1,844,442	$0
Enhancement Grants	31	21	$4,079,826	$2,783,317	$846,062
Native Hawaiian	4	3	$585,241	$435,241	$122,572
Total	214	203	$6,509,509	$5,063,000	$968,634

***Matching funds are not required for these programs.

Library Discretionary Grants

Library Services Discretionary Grants Programs include National Leadership Grants, Native American Library Services Basic Grants, Native American Library Services Enhancement Grants, Native Hawaiian Library Services, and the Laura Bush 21st Century Librarian Program. On August 24, 2018, IMLS announced 45 grants totaling $8,155,005 to support libraries across the country. The awards were made through the FY 2018 second cycle of the National Leadership Grants for Libraries Program and the Laura Bush 21st Century Librarian Program.

Use of Funds

SLAAs may use IMLS grant funding for

- Expanding services for individuals of all ages to support such individuals' needs for education, lifelong learning, workforce development, and digital literacy skills
- Establishing or enhancing electronic and other linkages and improved coordination among and between libraries and entities
- Providing training and professional development to enhance the skills of the current library workforce and leadership, and advance the delivery of library and information services; and recruiting future professionals to the field
- Developing public and private partnerships with other agencies and community-based organizations
- Targeting library services to individuals of diverse geographic, cultural, and socioeconomic backgrounds, to individuals with disabilities, and to individuals with limited functional literacy or information skills
- Targeting library and information services to persons having difficulty using a library and to underserved urban and rural communities, including low-income children
- Developing library services that provide access to information through local, state, regional, national, and international collaborations and networks
- Carrying out other activities as described in the State Library Administrative Agency's plan

Museum Grants

To be eligible for an IMLS grant, a museum must

- Be either a unit of state or local government or a private nonprofit organization that has tax-exempt status under the Internal Revenue Code
- Be located in one of the 50 States of the United States of America, the District of Columbia, the Commonwealth of Puerto Rico, Guam, American Samoa, the Virgin Islands, the Commonwealth of the Northern Mariana Islands, the Republic of the Marshall Islands, the Federated States of Micronesia, or the Republic of Palau

- Qualify as either a museum that, using a professional staff, is organized on a permanent basis for essentially educational or aesthetic purposes; owns or uses tangible objects, either animate or inanimate; cares for these objects; and exhibits these objects to the general public on a regular basis through facilities that it owns or operates *or* a public or private nonprofit agency responsible for the operation of a museum applying on behalf of that museum

Museum Discretionary Grants

IMLS offered five major museum grant programs in FY 2018:

1. The Museums for America program supports projects that strengthen individual museums as active resources for lifelong learning, as vital components of livable communities, and as good stewards of the nation's collections.
2. National Leadership Grants for Museums support projects that address critical needs of the museum field and that have the potential to advance practice in the profession so that museums can improve services for the American public. Related organizations—such as museum associations, universities, foundations and nonprofits—can apply for grants in this category.
3. The National Museum of African American History and Culture Act directs the IMLS director to consult with the council and director of the National Museum of African American History and Culture to establish grant opportunities to strengthen African American museums by improving care of collections, developing professional management, or providing internship and fellowship programs.
4. The Native American/Native Hawaiian Museum Services program supports the capacity of federally recognized Native American tribes and organizations that primarily serve and represent Native Hawaiians to enhance museum services to sustain heritage, culture, and knowledge through exhibitions, educational services and programming, professional development, and collections stewardship.
5. Museums Empowered, a special initiative of the Museums for America program, grants support activities for professional development and capacity-building in individual museums. The grant program focuses on four areas of relevant needs in the museum field: Digital Technology, Diversity and Inclusion, Evaluation, and Organizational Management.

Among other grants offered or cosponsored by IMLS in FY 2018 were the Community Catalyst Initiative, Inspire! Grants for Small Museums, and Save America's Treasures. Additionally, IMLS offered two technical assistance programs, two national awards programs, and the Collections Assessment for Preservation program, which works to help small and midsized museums better care for their collections.

Further information about IMLS grants is available at https://www.imls.gov/grants/grant-programs and https://www.imls.gov/grants/grant-programs/grants-states.

Museum and Library Cooperative Agreements

IMLS has numerous cooperative agreements to support and enhance agency priorities and services to the library and museum community. Highlights include

STEMeX Evaluation

As part of a two-year cooperative agreement with IMLS, in FY 2018 the Maine Mathematics and Science Alliance continued to conduct a developmental evaluation of four projects funded through the IMLS STEMeX grant initiative. Led by a scientist with expertise in research and evaluation in informal learning settings such as museums and libraries, the evaluation effort will help build understanding of each awardee's project development processes and research findings as their work unfolds and will lead to the development of a summary document of lessons learned. More about STEMeX follows in the section on Science, Technology, Engineering, and Math.

Measures That Matter

Launched in FY 2018, Measures That Matter is a partnership between Chief Officers of State Library Associations (COSLA) and IMLS that seeks to examine, evaluate, and map the landscape of public library data collection in the United States. The project will develop a Library Data and Outcomes Action Plan with key library stakeholder groups for a more coordinated approach to the collection of public library data nationally. The goal is to build a framework within which outcomes, outputs, and indicators can be drawn upon to consistently and effectively demonstrate the role, value, and impact of public libraries.

Inclusive Internship Initiative: Mentored Internships for Diversity

In FY 2018 the American Library Association's (ALA) Public Library Association (PLA) sponsored a paid, mentored public library internship program for 50 high school juniors and seniors from diverse backgrounds. The Inclusive Internship Initiative (III), with support from IMLS, is a summer-long mentored learning project through which library mentors and interns engage with multiple facets of library life, from administration to programming to user services. Interns are given opportunities to connect with one another and learn from mentors across the country at a library "master class" in Washington, D.C., before returning to their host institutions to develop and execute their summer projects alongside their mentors.

Sustaining and Advancing Indigenous Cultures

The Association of Tribal Archives, Libraries, and Museums (ATALM) provides continuing education programs targeted to the needs of tribal archivists, librarians, and museum staff; and is conducting a survey of tribal archives, libraries, and museums, followed by a report documenting activities, challenges, and needs. Funded activities will contribute to improving the informational, educational, and

Table 2 / IMLS Museum Grant Programs in Budget FY 2018

Total

Number of Applications	Number of Awards	Funds Requested	Funds Awarded	Awardee Match
819	239	$120,064,448	$34,714,990	$38,139,979

By Program

Museums for America

Number of Applications	Number of Awards	Funds Requested	Funds Awarded	Awardee Match
472	133	$70,286,280	$19,931,618	$27,703,523

*Museums Empowered**

Number of Applications	Number of Awards	Funds Requested	Funds Awarded	Awardee Match
110	27	$12,178,449	$2,967,382	$3,476,692

*Museums Empowered is a special initiative of the Museums for America program.

National Leadership Grants for Museums

Number of Applications	Number of Awards	Funds Requested	Funds Awarded	Awardee Match
166	31	$31,753,715	$8,112,990	$4,484,348

*Native American/Native Hawaiian Museum Services Program**

Number of Applications	Number of Awards	Funds Requested	Funds Awarded	Awardee Match
31	22	$2,103,943	$1,472,000	$206,465

* Matching funds are not required for this program.

Museum Grants For African American History And Culture

Number of Applications	Number of Awards	Funds Requested	Funds Awarded	Awardee Match
40	26	$3,742,061	$2,231,000	$2,268,951

cultural programs and services available to the nation's 5.2 million indigenous peoples.

Museums for All

The Association of Children's Museums (ACM) is working with IMLS on a nationwide museum access program for low-income families. Following a successful pilot with children's museums, the signature program is now being expanded to include all types of museums. Museums for All invites electronic benefit transfer cardholders to visit participating museums for free or greatly reduced admission fees year-round. By promoting affordable museum experiences, ACM and IMLS are encouraging families of all backgrounds to visit museums regularly, building lifelong museum habits that bolster the role of museums as community anchors. Since its 2014 launch, Museums for All has served more than 1.5 million visitors nationwide at more than 300 museums of all varieties, representing 45+ states, districts, and territories.

Customized Assessment Program for Small and Midsized Museums

IMLS is working with the Foundation of the American Institute for Conservation of Historic and Artistic Works (FAIC) on a Customized Assessment Program (CAP) designed to improve the care and condition of the nation's collections. The program provides small and midsized museums with partial funding toward a general conservation assessment of an institution's collections, buildings, and building systems, as well as its policies and procedures relating to collections care. Participants who complete the program receive an assessment report with recommendations and further guidance. Eighty institutions were accepted for CAP participation in FY 2018.

StoryCorps

For almost a decade, StoryCorps has worked to record and preserve the stories of IMLS National Medal Winners. With support from IMLS, StoryCorps travels to each medal-winning library and museum to capture the voices of their people and hear about their programs and communities. More about the National Medal for Museum and Library Service appears later in this report. To listen to StoryCorps/IMLS recordings, visit https://storycorps.org/participate/host/institute-for-museum-and-library-services/.

Interagency Collaboration

The Museum and Library Services Act (MLSA) authorizes the IMLS director to support interagency collaboration: initiatives, materials, or technology to support workforce development activities undertaken by libraries; resource and policy approaches to eliminate barriers to fully leveraging the roles of libraries and museums in supporting the early learning, literacy, lifelong learning, digital literacy, workforce development, and education needs of the people of the United States; and initiatives, materials, or technology to support educational, cultural, historical, scientific, environmental, and other activities undertaken by museums.

The MLSA also authorizes the director to coordinate the policies and activities of IMLS with the policies and activities of other agencies and offices of the federal government having interest in or responsibilities for the improvement of museums, libraries, and information services. The statute expressly requires the director to coordinate with other agencies to improve literacy through school libraries and through programs supported by the Head Start and Workforce Investment Acts. It also authorizes the director to ensure that IMLS policies and activities are coordinated with federal programs and activities that increase the capacity of libraries and museums to participate in economic and community development, education and research, improving digital literacy skills, and disseminating health information.

IMLS has a wide range of interagency partnerships, including advancing broadband adoption, coordinating early learning activities, supporting the effective delivery of workforce development services, and distributing federal information impacting the health and well-being of Americans. Examples include

U.S. Citizenship and Immigration Services

IMLS has a memorandum of understanding with the U.S. Citizenship and Immigration Services to provide information and outreach to local libraries and museums to help newly arrived individuals understand the benefits of citizenship and learn how to undertake the citizenship process.

National Book Festival and National Student Poets Program

IMLS has served as a charter sponsor of the Library of Congress's National Book Festival since its inception in 2001. The National Student Poets Program is the nation's highest honor for youth poets, with an annual ceremony hosted in conjunction with the festival. In 2018 IMLS partnered with the Alliance for Young Artists and Writers to honor five outstanding youth poets chosen from among thousands of award-winning student writers. The National Student Poets ceremony was held August 30, 2018, at the Library of Congress's James Madison Memorial Building. The young poets, representing five different regions of the country, read original works as part of a ceremony led by Librarian of Congress Carla Hayden and IMLS Director Kathryn K. Matthew. The poets offered public readings during the National Book Festival on September 1, 2018.

Policy Research, Analysis, Data Collection, and Dissemination

The IMLS director is authorized to conduct policy research, analyses, and data collections annually with SLAAs; national, state, and regional library and museum organizations; and other relevant agencies and organizations. IMLS is further mandated to

- Identify national needs for and trends in museum, library, and information services
- Measure the impact and effectiveness of museum, library, and information services including the impact of federal programs authorized under this chapter
- Identify best practices
- Develop plans to improve museum, library, and information services and to strengthen national, state, local, regional, and international communications and cooperative networks

IMLS provides reliable and objective data and analysis to inform policy decisions. The primary data products maintained by IMLS are the Public Libraries Survey and the State Library Administrative Agency Survey. See the section on IMLS Library Surveys later in this report for further information.

National Medal for Museum and Library Service

The National Medal for Museum and Library Service is the nation's highest honor for institutions that make significant and exceptional contributions to their communities. Since 1994 IMLS has presented the award to institutions that demonstrate extraordinary and innovative approaches to public service, exceeding the expected levels of community outreach. The winners are honored at a National Medal award ceremony held in Washington, D.C., each May.

To learn about the ten libraries and museums honored with the 2018 National Medal, visit https://www.imls.gov/issues/national-initiatives/national-medal-museum-and-library-service/2018-medals.

Strategic Priorities and Initiatives

IMLS initiatives and special programs are designed to help libraries and museums address critical needs, such as stimulating economic development through job training and skill development, facilitating family learning, and sustaining our heritage and community cohesion. Special emphasis is given to community engagement; literacy and early learning; reaching rural residents, veterans, underserved, and other special populations; STEM (Science, Technology, Engineering, and Math) programs; and access to collections, both physical and digital. Pending availability of funding, these efforts will continue in FY 2019.

Community Catalyst Initiative

Many museums and libraries carry out their missions in ways that extend beyond traditional formats and objectives, often serving their cities and towns as enablers of community vitality and co-creators of positive community change. IMLS is helping to identify and support conceptual frameworks and successful approaches that support this type of work through its Community Catalyst Initiative. The initiative calls upon libraries and museums to engage in collaborative arrangements that facilitate and support local community development and economic revitalization. Libraries and museums are encouraged to identify and leverage local assets, along with their own resources and competencies, to achieve greater reach and impact within their communities.

In FY 2018 IMLS entered the second year of grant making through the Community Catalyst Initiative. On August 29, 2018, the agency announced that 12 organizations had been approved to receive $1,567,362 in funding through the program, with an additional $1,811,822 in matching nonfederal funds pledged by the awardees.

Also in August IMLS announced a new study, *Understanding the Social Wellbeing Impacts of the Nation's Libraries and Museums*, based on a year-long project initiated under the Community Catalyst Initiative. The goal of the project is to gain a better understanding on a national level of the conditions under which museums and libraries contribute to quality of life and well-being in the communities they serve. The study will focus on these institutions' essential roles within a community to help them more effectively demonstrate the impact of their programs and services.

Veterans and Military Families

The Community Salute Initiative augments the capacity of libraries and museums to meet the unique and critical needs of the nation's more than 22 million veterans and their military families. Libraries and museums serve veterans by assisting them in building skills, by offering healing resources, and by providing access to employment or training opportunities.

The work to date has examined how libraries and museums are responding to the needs of veterans and their families and identified potential new approaches to provide better and more integrated community-based services for this important constituency. These approaches are grounded in community development/engagement practices as well as insights from policy experts, funders, and service providers for veterans and their families.

IMLS worked with a cooperator, FSG, to produce five resource documents tailored for libraries and museums that provide qualitative and quantitative approaches to help museums and libraries better serve veterans and their families/caregivers. The agency is taking these approaches to local communities for use when they informally convene with veterans' service providers, museums, libraries, and local government representatives.

Science, Technology, Engineering, and Math

Science, Technology, Engineering, and Math (STEM) and making-related programs offered through libraries and museums provide local communities with authentic and contextual learning experiences, tools, and spaces as well as training of formal and informal educators. IMLS continues to fund this area through its regular competitive grant making and also Grants to States funding (through the Library Services and Technology Act). Libraries and museums offer people of all ages and backgrounds mentor-led learning opportunities that spark curiosity and build interest in STEM subjects and career pathways. These opportunities introduce learners who are underrepresented in the STEM workforce to important STEM concepts, skills, and experiences including engaging in authentic scientific practices using new technologies and state-of-the-art equipment.

STEMeX is a program that funds scientists and engineers to deliver inquiry-based STEM programs to children aged 6–10 and their families in museums and libraries, using a variety of techniques such as storytelling, personal histories, and analogies. A key goal of STEMeX is to reach children and families from diverse economic, social, and cultural backgrounds.

IMLS investment in making includes support for a variety of learning spaces in libraries and museums that foster innovation and experimentation through design thinking and project-based learning for people of all ages. IMLS also funds work to advance research and promising practices for makerspaces and maker programming nationwide within networks of institutions. The Making + Learning project, funded by IMLS and led by the Children's Museum of Pittsburgh, developed an innovative and easily adaptable framework and related resources designed to enable museum and library practitioners to better support learning in and through their makerspaces and maker programming. Project leaders conducted interviews and site visits with 50 museums and libraries and held a national convening that informed the design of the framework and tools. A downloadable publication, *Making + Learning in Museums & Libraries: A Practitioner's Guide & Framework,* along with a dedicated website and a Massive Open Online Course (MOOC), provide free tutorials that museum and library professionals can use at any time to facilitate use of the project's suite of tools.

Rural/Small Towns

Through its various grant-making authorities, IMLS reaches across the United States and territories into smaller and rural communities with more dispersed populations. IMLS programs support services for tribal entities and build the capacity of museums of African American history and culture. The need for support in these varied communities is expansive: supporting smaller historic houses or general museums in conserving and cataloging collections; helping tribal archives to collect oral histories and preserve language; enhancing digital literacy skills by training staff at museums and libraries on how to work with their patrons to facilitate job searches and other needs; and launching Open e-Books, which distributes free children's content—millions of current e-books—through eligible libraries, working with publishers and nonprofit organizations.

IMLS sees the need to continue supporting and advancing rural museums and libraries as essential community assets that must be considered as part of community revitalization and cohesion-building efforts. The agency is building relationships with small and rural libraries and cultural institutions and those who work in rural and small communities (e.g., USDA, EPA, extension services) to raise awareness of the value of these institutions. IMLS will continue to explore how better to position these institutions within their local community networks and with local investors.

In addition, IMLS has invested in rural and small communities by supporting basic infrastructure, including access to library- and museum-provided broadband connectivity and helping residents gain digital access to employment information and critical job skills. The Museums for America (MFA), Museum Assessment Program (MAP), and Collections Assessment for Preservation (CAP) programs all offer valuable support to many small museums in rural areas and small towns. Rural public libraries often serve as their communities' sole resource for Internet access, particularly where there are economic barriers to home connections and challenges to accessing high-quality Wi-Fi connections. Public libraries, supported by the Grants to States program (LSTA funding), provide Internet access to Americans who use their public libraries to perform life-changing and life-enhancing tasks in the areas of education, health and wellness, and job training.

Accelerating Promising Practices for Small Libraries

In November 2018 IMLS launched a new special funding initiative, Accelerating Promising Practices for Small Libraries (APP), and began accepting grant applications. This new funding opportunity is designed specifically to strengthen the ability of small and rural libraries, archives, and related organizations to serve their communities, and awards sizes range from $10,000 to $50,000. APP is under the umbrella of National Leadership Grants for Libraries, which supports projects that enhance the quality of library and archives services nationwide by advancing theory and practice.

Capacity Building and Community Engagement

The Museum Assessment Program (MAP), offered to the museum community through a cooperative agreement with the American Alliance of Museums, has been a legacy program that helps museums assess strengths and weaknesses and plan for the future. A MAP assessment requires the museum staff and governing authority to complete a self-study. Following the study, a site visit is conducted by one or more museum professionals, who tour the museum and meet with staff, governing officials, and volunteers and produce a report evaluating the museum's operations, making recommendations, and suggesting resources. Three types of MAP assessments are offered: Organizational, Collections Stewardship, and Community Engagement.

In September 2018 IMLS announced the launch of a new special initiative focused on building the museum field's capacity to connect with teachers and students. Museums for Digital Learning is a two-year cooperative agreement that enables museums to broadly share their digitized collections and other resources with K–12 schools across the country. The project aims to build a suite of innovative digital resources with content spanning STEM, history, arts, culture, and the humanities, providing a broad spectrum of free, easy-to-access, adaptable resources for teachers across disciplines. IMLS envisions all types of museums—art museums, children's museums, botanical gardens, history museums, science museums, zoos, aquaria, and more—contributing content to the pilot platform.

The pilot initiative, funded through an IMLS National Leadership Grant for Museums, will be led by the Indianapolis Museum of Art at Newfields in collaboration with the Field Museum in Chicago, Denver-based History Colorado, and a technical consultant. A team of K–12 teachers will co-create the educational resources using standardized templates, then test the content in their classrooms. A cohort of up to ten additional museums of various sizes, disciplines, and geographic locations will also test and validate both the platform and the educational resources.

Aligning with agency priorities around community engagement and impact, an IMLS grant awarded in 2017 supports development of the Free Library Foundation of Philadelphia's "Skills for Community-Centered Librarianship," a continuing-education program for public librarians. The curriculum is organized around three modules—Outreach, Program Development, and Leadership—and aims to provide training on nine interconnected skills essential for library staff to foster and sustain impactful programming in partnership with their communities. In 2018 the project team worked to develop curriculum materials for four workshops: Building Connections, Effective Communication, Community Engagement, and Program Development. After attending the workshops, participants will work on independent projects to practice their new skills. In September 2020, the foundation intends to make training materials and related webinars freely available online for other library systems to use.

Professional Development

A major focal area for IMLS is empowering library and museum staff members to provide users with opportunities to develop the digital skills they need for better success in such areas as education, workforce development, and civic engagement. Funded projects offer open source curricula, training, tools, and credentials for a library audience to learn Web literacy skills and develop digital competencies. Additionally, online courses with in-person group study sessions facilitated by librarians can cover a range of academic, professional, and personal development subjects. Examples include

- Through a joint cooperative agreement, IMLS is working with the PAST Foundation's National Digital Inclusion Alliance (NDIA) on a pilot project that aims to increase digital inclusion by deploying local digital literacy trainers in five tribal and rural communities. The project is part of a broader effort between IMLS and NDIA-PAST to create more equitable access to online information, as well as digital literacy support and training for all residents and communities, particularly the most disadvantaged.
- Museums Empowered: Professional Development and Capacity-Building Opportunities for Museums is a special initiative within the Museums for America funding program designed to provide professional development and capacity-building opportunities for eligible museums in four areas that enable a museum to address relevant needs of its local communities: Digital Technology, Diversity and Inclusion, Evaluation, or Organizational Management.

IMLS Library Surveys

IMLS manages a federal statistical program that identifies national trends and the public use and effectiveness of museum, library, and information services. The statistical survey programs provide reliable and objective data in a wide variety of formats used by policymakers and practitioners to inform policy decisions. For example, these data are used by policymakers at the state and local levels to compare conditions in libraries of comparable sizes, by researchers to analyze state-of-the-art public librarianship, and by private companies seeking reliable national, state, and local statistics for developing business plans and marketing strategies within the library sector of the economy. These statistical survey programs include

- The Public Libraries Survey, which provides information on key metrics of library health and services across the United States and outlying territories, and tracks trends in libraries. In addition to the long-standing library data collections efforts, IMLS uses other federal data to analyze how public libraries serve their communities and produces a report of overall findings, research briefs highlighting topics of general interest, and a public use data file.
- The State Library Administrative Agency Survey, conducted every two years, which studies the current state and health of state library administrative agencies. IMLS produces a summary report of the overall survey

findings and a public use data file that are used by the chief officers of state library agencies; federal policymakers; government and library administrators at federal, state, and local levels; researchers; and ALA.

For IMLS surveys and data, visit https://www.imls.gov/research-tools/data-collection and see "Highlights of IMLS Public Library Surveys" beginning on page 302 of this volume.

Safety and Disaster Preparedness

During natural disasters, museums and libraries often serve as community resources, gathering places, and providers of information. If their facilities are intact, they can play crucial roles in recovery efforts, including

- Serving as places of physical refuge and sources of Wi-Fi, Internet access, phone access, and electricity
- Providing help, advice, and information about recovery assistance such as registering with FEMA and hosting financial planning seminars
- Serving as safe gathering places during times of crisis, using arts and cultural assets to help with recovery, healing, and resilience building
- Serving as gathering places for FEMA workers, Red Cross workers, and others who require physical headquarters for their relief work
- Serving as sources of volunteer networks that are familiar with community needs
- Serving as partners in creating community plans for emergency preparedness and disaster response

IMLS has made significant investments in strengthening institutional capacity to prepare for and respond to disasters among the nation's museums and libraries. As holders of cultural and natural heritage, these institutions can experience catastrophic losses in times of floods, hurricanes, tornadoes, fires, and human-made disasters, but can also be integral to community efforts to recover and build resiliency. Grant-supported activities have ranged from developing emergency preparedness plans and recovery strategies at institutional or community levels to carrying out conservation surveys, treatment, and environmental improvements relating to affected natural and cultural collections.

IMLS Website and Publications

The IMLS website (www.imls.gov) provides a wealth of information on the agency's activities, including IMLS-sponsored conferences, webinars, publications, and grant programs. Through an electronic newsletter, *Primary Source*, and the *UpNext* blog, IMLS provides information on grant deadlines, success stories, and opportunities.

IMLS is on twitter @US_IMLS and Facebook at https://www.facebook.com/USIMLS.

EveryLibrary

P.O. Box 406, Riverside, IL 60546
312-574-0316, e-mail info@everylibrary.org
World Wide Web http://www.everylibrary.org | action.everylibrary.org | SaveSchoolLibrarians.org

John Chrastka
Executive Director

Founded in December 2012 to address a gap in existing voter outreach and public advocacy about library elections and budget negotiations with municipal funding partners of libraries, EveryLibrary has since expanded its focus to include direct engagement with the public as advocates and activists for library issues, activism about school library budgets and policy issues, and support for partner library organizations' legislative and funding agendas.

EveryLibrary is the first and only nationwide political action committee for libraries. It received its designation from the IRS as a 501(c)4 social welfare organization and is chartered as a nonprofit corporation in the State of Illinois. EveryLibrary's mission statement is "Building voter support for libraries." Its vision statement, and the inspiration for its name, is that "Any library funding issue anywhere should matter to every library everywhere."

Board and Advisors

EveryLibrary is administered by a board of directors and is run by staff. It has no members. Its 2018 board of directors included John Chrastka, president and executive director; Erica Findley, treasurer; Patrick "PC" Sweeney, secretary and political director; Brian D. Hart, J. Turner Masland, Harmony Faust, and Peter Bromberg, directors. EveryLibrary convenes an Advisory Committee of volunteers to provide strategic advice to the board and executive director. In 2018, this committee included Rebekkah Smith Aldrich, K. C. Boyd, Michele Cobb, Kyle K. Courtney, Francine Fialkoff, Dustin Fife, Ed Garcia, Sara Kelly Johns, Oleg Kagan, JP Porcaro, Lindsay Sarin, John Shableski, Ian Singer, Kate Tkacik, and Andrew (Andy) Woodworth. Its 2018 academic intern from Syracuse University was Samantha Marison.

Organizational History—Campaign Focus

As a 501(c)4 organization, EveryLibrary works with library boards and staff on Informational Communications Campaigns and with local citizen ballot committees as they conduct "Get Out the Vote" and "Vote Yes" campaigns for their local library's ballot measure. These library ballot campaigns are either advisory or binding and can include bonds, levies, mill levies, warrant articles, parcel taxes, measures, or other referenda placed before voters by library boards or by municipal councils. EveryLibrary's support includes providing pro bono technical assistance and training to library leaders as well as early campaign financial support and consulting to campaign committees and citizen's groups.

Since 2012 EveryLibrary has helped take 96 libraries to their Election Days, winning over $320 million (aggregated per annum) in 77 of those campaigns. EveryLibrary is funded by individual donors, both monthly and annually, and corporate (vendor) donors. Being able to provide these services for free to libraries and committees allows EveryLibrary to focus on best practices for campaigns rather than revenue generation from direct consulting.

The EveryLibrary Institute

In 2016 the EveryLibrary leadership team created the EveryLibrary Institute, a nonprofit companion organization with a research, training, publishing, and programmatic agenda concerned with the future of library funding. In 2018 the EveryLibrary Institute received its 501(c)3 designation from the IRS.

The EveryLibrary Institute was created to advance a voter- and public-facing research agenda that identifies the messages and tests the techniques that will reverse downward trends in voter perception of libraries. Its training program is designed to improve the political literacy skills of librarians, staff, and boards in public, school, and academic libraries. The EveryLibrary Institute is committed to disseminating its findings, learnings, and best practices for the entire library industry through an open access publishing program. It is aligned with programmatic partner organizations and funders who see school, public, and academic libraries as critical solutions to problems in education, civil society, and community well-being.

The current board of the EveryLibrary Institute is the same as that of EveryLibrary but is considered a caretaker board. This board was responsible for preparing the legal and financial infrastructure required to establish an independent organization. A new board of directors will be elected in early 2019.

While it shares a common mission with EveryLibrary to support library funding, the EveryLibrary Institute is a self-funded organization with independent legal and fundraising mechanisms. It maintains its own website at everylibraryinstitute.org and can be contacted at info@everylibraryinstitute.org. EveryLibrary's work as an independent 501(c)4 will continue unchanged alongside this new companion organization.

Library Ballot Measures—2018

In 2018 EveryLibrary supported 17 campaigns (10 wins, 1 partial win, and 6 losses overall) to establish, renew, or expand funding for operations, collections, programs, services, and staffing, or to issue a bond for construction or remodeling of library facilities. Highlights from the year include helping to establish a new library district in Potomac, Illinois. The library in this town of 646 people was set to close without passage of the new district measure. In Douglas, Massachusetts, EveryLibrary helped the Simon Fairfield Library team campaign win critical funding authorization for their library, town, and schools. This was a quick election having been called for early May; without the win, the library would have closed by the Fourth of July. EveryLibrary helped the Bucyrus, Ohio, library establish its first-ever local levy with a win in May. This was the eighth time in 12 years that the library had attempted to pass a funding increase. In Spokane, Washington, the library system passed a $77 million bond package for two new libraries (co-located with the school district) and system-wide renovations. Spokane Public Library was EveryLibrary's first-ever campaign in 2013, and this was its third Election Day with Spokane.

EveryLibrary provided technical assistance and campaign support to two state school library association partners as they identified state ballot measures which, if passed, would improve funding for school library programs in their state, and to help operationalize their voter-facing outreach campaigns. In Colorado, Amendment 73 would have reindexed the state income tax for educational purposes. In Utah, Question #1 would have established a gas tax to fund education and infrastructure. School library budgets stood to benefit in both cases. While neither measure passed, EveryLibrary was proud to bring its resources and experience to help library leaders in Colorado and Utah build new relationships in the education-funding conversation. This focus on new revenue for education is not common in library advocacy settings because it requires school library stakeholders to join broad-based coalitions outside of libraries. It also places library organizations alongside educational unions and political action committees. As the first and only national political action committee for libraries, EveryLibrary is comfortable in this role.

SaveIMLS.org Campaign

When the Trump administration's fiscal year (FY) 2019 budget was released in February 2018, it again called for the complete elimination of funding for the Institute of Museum and Library Services (IMLS) along with reductions or eliminations to other programs affecting school libraries, humanities, museums, and the arts. EveryLibrary immediately issued a call to action to its network of nearly 250,000 Americans to get involved and contact Congress in support of IMLS and allied programs. Whether they use the library themselves or simply understand that our nation is stronger, more secure, and more successful when other people have access, EveryLibrary's network of engaged, involved, and reachable Americans is a key part of the national advocacy matrix. To enable them to quickly and easily contact Congress requesting support for these key initiatives, EveryLibrary updated its action center at http://saveimls.org/ and activated a national paid advertising campaign to reach beyond librarians. The SaveIMLS.org action center included easy-to-use social sharing tools as well. But the key differentiator—and the reason tens of thousands of Americans from all walks of life have responded over the last two fiscal year campaigns—is the paid advertising and our e-mail list.

SaveSchoolLibrarians.org

Through an ongoing partnership with Follett Learning, EveryLibrary continues to support school library budgets and school librarians through its SaveSchool Librarians.org digital action site. Over 25,000 people have signed up to take direct action on behalf of school libraries and their librarians. This opt-in list of dedicated, accessible library advocates is unique in the school library advocacy ecosystem. Over the first 18 months of the initiative, EveryLibrary has engaged in 23 school and district-level direct actions. The site allows for in-district digital outreach to school boards, superintendents, and principals about funding for positions and programs using petitions and e-mail campaigns.

Another key component of these efforts is EveryLibrary's mission to train and support school librarians facing crises. Through a partnership with the ISTE Librarians Network, it co-hosted a series of "From Advocacy to Activism" training webinars in 2018. The ISTE Librarians Network is the largest special interest group within ISTE. This partnership featured four webinars by EveryLibrary leadership where participants learned from real-world examples of how to fight budget or personnel cuts and turn around the funding conversation.

Speaking, Training, and Publishing

This year, EveryLibrary published Volume 4, Issue 1 of *The Political Librarian* to foster and encourage a new discussion at the intersection of public policy and tax policy for libraries. Authors were T. J. Bliss, Jamie LaRue, John Chrastka, Michelle Boisvenue-Fox, T. J. Lamanna, and John Buschman. Several works from Volume 3, Issue 1 (2017) were featured in a webinar series, including those by Dustin Fife (series editor) and Mary Naylor, Peter Bromberg, and Emily Drabinski. *The Political Librarian* is published irregularly as an open access journal and is hosted online by the Open Scholarship project at Washington University in St. Louis.

The EveryLibrary leadership team was in high demand in 2018 as conference, webinar and seminar speakers, presenters, workshop leaders and keynoters. Their presentational approach is rooted in the data about voter and public perception of libraries and informed by successful advocacy campaigns and direct activism for public and school libraries across the country. Executive Director John Chrastka and Political Director Patrick "PC" Sweeney were invited to keynote the 2018 Annual Conference for CILIP, the Chartered Institute of Library and Information Professionals, in Brighton, England, in July. Their speech and workshop discussed EveryLibrary's unique digital advocacy campaigns at the local level and its approach to reaching and activating the general public for libraries.

One Million Americans for Libraries Campaign

EveryLibrary's "One Million Americans for Libraries" Campaign continues to attract Americans from all walks of life to engage in library advocacy issues. The organization ended the year with nearly 300,000 people on its Facebook page and over 130,000 activists in its database. The "One Million Americans for Libraries" Campaign will be sustained through 2019 to grow the "reachable and activated" list of people from all walks of life who care about libraries and are willing to act when asked. EveryLibrary is committed to sharing its list with other library organizations that participate in coalition work.

Organizational Agenda

EveryLibrary will continue to work in 2019 to fulfill its core mission of building voter support for libraries. It is reasonable to expect that funding and programmatic support for education, social welfare, healthcare, citizen's rights, workforce development, and libraries will continue to be at risk at all levels of government. EveryLibrary's six strategic priorities in 2019 are

- To deepen our efforts to support local library communities that go on the ballot to renew or extend their basic taxpayer-approved funding and cultivate opportunities for libraries that want to enhance services and facilities through municipal budgets or voter approved measures.
- To join and support coalitions that align with the mission of libraries as institutions, that promote and extend the rights and prosperity of the people our libraries serve, and that protect the rights, employment, and pensions of the people who work in all types of libraries.
- To continue to build a unique and extensive network of Americans who believe in the power of libraries to change lives and build communities, and who are ready to become advocates and activists for libraries.
- To support the role of library boards and commissions in governing libraries, making policy, and setting budgets that are responsive to diverse local priorities and create inclusive, prosperous, and vibrant communities.
- To continue to broaden our focus beyond Public Library funding and act in support of School Library programs as effective solutions for some of the biggest problems facing schools and districts around the country. This includes assisting our colleagues in Academic Libraries who need institutional support from their administrations and students.
- To be a leader and a listener in a national discussion about the role that public, academic, and school libraries have in people's lives, and work within the profession and across civil society to find the best ways to preserve, protect, and extend everyone's right to use libraries.

Budget, Donor Transparency, and Reporting

EveryLibrary is entirely supported by individual and library vendor donors. It does not ask for or receive any funding from grant making, philanthropic, or charitable organizations. As an independent 501(c)4, EveryLibrary is ineligible for government grants (federal or state). Individual (personal) donors averaged $47.55 for yearly donation; monthly donors averaged $7.55 per month. Vendor and corporate donors average $7,200 in 2018, and accounts for half of the organization's funding. EveryLibrary's operating budget for 2018 was $295,000 with one-third going to direct campaign expenditures, one-third to salaries and operations, and one-third to growing its organizational reach. To keep costs low, staff and interns collaborate together in a paid co-working space in Brooklyn, New York, and across the country in a "virtual office environment" that has few fixed expenses. Its office environment is supported by G-Suite; Nation Builder hosts its public-facing web pages; and it utilizes PayPal, Stripe, and Act Blue for third-party donation processors.

EveryLibrary puts its donor funding to work in three ways: directly on local library campaigns—for both public libraries and school libraries; on building its national reach as an advocacy organization for libraries; and on staff and projects that run the organization. As the only national 501(c)4 for libraries, it "bundles" small donations from around the country and sends them to local Vote Yes committees where needed.

EveryLibrary provides a high level of transparency about its donations and is one of only a few national political action groups that encourages donors to self-disclose. EveryLibrary voluntarily provides annual financial disclosure information to GuideStar, a large national nonprofit financial clearinghouse and rating service, where it currently holds a "Gold Rate" certification.

President's Budget Proposals to Eliminate Key Agencies, 2017–2020

($ million)

Federally Funded Agency	FY 2017 Enacted Appropriations	FY 2018 President's Budget Proposal	FY 2018 Enacted Omnibus	FY 2019 President's Budget Proposal	FY 2019 Enacted Omnibus	FY 2020 President's Budget Proposal
Institute of Museum and Library Services	$231	Elimination*	$240	Elimination*	$242	Elimination*
IMLS Office of Museum Services	$32	Elimination*	$34.7	Elimination*	$34.7	Elimination*
National Endowment for the Arts	$150	Elimination*	$152.8	Elimination*	$155	Elimination*
National Endowment for the Humanities	$150	Elimination*	$152.8	Elimination*	$155	Elimination*

*President's budget proposal includes minor funds to close the agency.

Part 3
Library/Information Science Education, Placement, and Salaries

Library Employment and Career Advice Resources

Susanne Markgren

Librarians and information professionals have many options and pathways to consider when seeking employment and/or advancement in their careers. In order to secure a professional position in today's diverse landscape, job seekers may need to employ multiple strategies—as well as keep an open mind. This article provides readers with a variety of resources and tools to help prepare them for the first step, or the next step, in a career in libraries, archives, and related fields.

Coverage from the *Library Journal* survey "Placements and Salaries 2018," excerpted immediately following this article, offers a positive outlook for recent graduates. More graduates are finding full-time employment than in the previous year, and there is a resurgence of positions in traditional library settings, as well as continued growth in nontraditional settings. The graduates taking part in the *LJ* survey said that the most helpful job-seeking resource was Indeed.com, which is a change from previous years, where they cited more traditional library-specific sites. They also listed government job sites (city, state, and regional), and ALA's job list as helpful in their job searches. Some of the excellent advice that these graduates provided include networking with peers and established information professionals, gaining work experience (through internships, nonprofessional positions, volunteering, etc.), demonstrating this experience on one's résumé, tailoring cover letters to each position, doing background research on organizations before the interview, and starting the job search well before graduation.

The resources presented in this article have been curated based on popularity, longevity, and influence in the library and information community. All are freely available online, and as with every online information source, users should employ critical analysis and judgment to determine currency, accuracy, and bias based on their individual needs.

The Directory of Organizations in Part 6 of this volume may also prove useful for job seekers. Many of these organizations, institutions, libraries, and associations maintain their own job sites and social media accounts where active job listings can be found.

Organization of the Resources

The resources that follow are organized in two principal sections. The first, "Career Advice Sites and Resources," lists informational websites, useful for those seeking more information and advice on specific areas of librarianship and archive

Susanne Markgren is cofounder, Library Career People, and coauthor, with Tiffany Eatman Allen, of *Career Q&A: A Librarian's Real-Life, Practical Guide to Managing a Successful Career* (Information Today, 2013).

work. Many of these are association sites, some of which have mentoring programs, Q&As, and materials offering guidance on résumé writing, preparing for interviews, and negotiating salaries.

Next find a two-part section of "Job Listings" resources—the first specific to librarians, archivists and information professionals; the second covering a broader range of resources. The selected sites primarily post jobs in the United States, but some also post international opportunities. It is good practice to search a variety of job sites, systematically, to get the best and most comprehensive snapshot of available positions. It's also a good idea to seek out specific libraries, companies, institutions, and associations on social media sites; where available, Twitter handles (@ALA_JobLIST, for instance) have been included at the end of each listing.

Career Advice Sites and Resources

American Association of Law Libraries (AALL)—Career Center

https://www.aallnet.org/careers/career-center
Offers information on careers in law libraries, advice on how to find a job, and access to the *AALL Biennial Salary Survey & Organizational Characteristics* (AALL Salary Survey). @aallnet

American Association of School Librarians (AASL)—Education & Careers

http://www.ala.org/aasl/about/ed
Career and education resources for those seeking to enter or advance in the school library field. Job listing are found at ALA JobLIST. @aasl

American Library Association (ALA) JobLIST—Career Development Resources

http://www.ala.org/educationcareers/employment/career-resources
A wealth of resources from the American Library Association (ALA) to help one prepare for a productive and effective job search as well as enhance career development efforts, including a printable Career Development Resource Guide, and information on the Placement Center and upcoming events and conferences. @ALA_JobLIST and @alaplacement

Association of College and Research Libraries (ACRL)

http://www.ala.org/acrl/
Under the heading "Professional Tools" are useful descriptions of various positions and information on recruitment and retention. Job listings are found at ALA JobLIST. @ALA_ACRL

Bureau of Labor Statistics, U.S. Department of Labor, Occupational Outlook Handbook, Librarians

https://www.bls.gov/ooh/education-training-and-library/librarians.htm
Provides information on librarian jobs and salaries, and insight into the growth and outlook of the profession.

Library Career People

http://librarycareerpeople.com/
A Q&A forum and career development archive of professional guidance and advice for librarians, library staff, and those thinking of entering the profession. @LibCareerPeople

Library Worklife—HR E-News for Today's Leaders

http://ala-apa.org/newsletter/
Offers sections, articles, and advice on salaries, career advancement, recruitment, and more. @alaapa

Medical Library Association (MLA) Career Center

http://www.mlanet.org/p/cm/ld/fid=352
Explore a career in the health sciences or medical profession. Includes information, resources, and connections for students and job seekers alike. @MedLibAssn

MLIS SKILLS AT WORK—A Snapshot of Job Postings for Spring 2018

https://ischool.sjsu.edu/sites/main/files/file-attachments/career_trends.pdf
Prepared annually by the Master's of Library and Information Science (MLIS) online degree program at the San José State University (SJSU) School of Information. @SJSUiSchool

Public Library Association (PLA)—Careers in Public Librarianship

http://www.ala.org/pla/tools/careers
Information and career advice about public librarianship from a leading ALA division. Job listing are found at ALA JobLIST. @ALA_PLA

RBMS—Careers & Scholarships

http://rbms.info/careers-faq/
Advice and resources for those interested in careers in special collections. Maintained by the Rare Books and Manuscripts Section (RBMS) of the Association of College Research Libraries (ACRL), a division of ALA. @RBMSinfo

Job Listings for Librarians, Archivists, and Information Professionals

ALA JobLIST

http://joblist.ala.org | @ALA_JobLIST

American Association of Law Librarians (AALL)—Career Center

https://careers.aallnet.org/jobs/ | @aallnet

Archives Gig

https://archivesgig.wordpress.com/ | @archivesgig

ARLIS/NA JobList

https://www.arlisna.org/professional-resources/arlis-na-joblist | @ARLIS_NA

INALJ

http://inalj.com/ | @INALJ (different states have their own handles)

Library Technology Jobs

https://librarytechnology.org/jobs/

Metropolitan New York Library Council (METRO) Jobs

https://metro.org/jobs/ | @mnylc

NASIG Jobs

http://nasigjobs.wordpress.com/ | @NASIG

Association for Information Science and Technology (ASIS&T) Careers

https://asist-jobs.careerwebsite.com/ | @asist_org

Association of Research Libraries (ARL)—Job/Residency/Internship Listings

http://www.arl.org/leadership-recruitment/job-listings | @ARLnews

Special Libraries Association (SLA) Jobs

https://careers.sla.org/ | @SLAhq

Job Listings *Not Specific to* Librarians, Archivists, and Information Professionals

Higher Education

Chronicle of Higher Education: Vitae

https://chroniclevitae.com/ | @chronicle

HigherEdJobs.com

http://www.higheredjobs.com | @insidehighered

EDUCAUSE Job Posting Service

https://jobs.educause.edu/ | @educause

Government

USAJobs.gov

https://www.usajobs.gov/ | @USAJOBS

Interdisciplinary (mega job sites)

Indeed

https://www.indeed.com/ | @indeed

LinkedIn Jobs

https://www.linkedin.com/jobs/ | @LinkedIn

Monster

https://www.monster.com/ | @Monster

SimplyHired

https://www.simplyhired.com/ | @SimplyHired

Discussion Lists

Job listings are regularly posted and reposted on electronic discussion (e-mail) lists. Many library schools / iSchools and library associations maintain their own discussion lists. The following are lists of lists, maintained by large library organizations.

ALA Electronic Discussion Lists—Index of Lists

http://lists.ala.org/sympa/lists | @ALALibrary

International Federation of Library Associations and Institutions (IFLA)—Mailing Lists

https://www.ifla.org/mailing-lists | @IFLA

Placements and Salaries 2018: Foundations and Futures

Suzie Allard

What's old is new again in this year's job market for newly credentialed librarians. Our snapshot shows placements are resurging in traditional library settings, as well as continuing to gain strength in nontraditional areas that benefit from classic LIS skill sets.

The annual *Library Journal (LJ)* Placements and Salaries survey reveals a healthy job market for graduates of American Library Association (ALA)-accredited LIS master's degree programs. The results suggest that core skills such as cataloging, reference, and collection development are essential in traditional and nontraditional settings alike. Results also reinforce the strength and value of the LIS master's degree, both in preparing graduates to excel in a wide range of placements and in signaling the skills and talents of candidates to potential employers. While there are some hints that salary levels are flattening, there are glimmers of improvement in gender pay inequities and interesting shifts across employment sectors.

Forty-two of the 52 ALA-accredited schools participated in this year's survey. They reported producing a total of 4,389 graduates during calendar year 2017, with 31 percent completing questionnaires about their job search status and experiences.

Graduates predominantly self-reported as female (80 percent), while 18 percent were male, 1 percent were nonbinary or not sure, and about 1 percent declined to answer. The 2017 graduates identified themselves as white/non-Hispanic (76 percent), Asian/Pacific Islander (8 percent), Hispanic/Latino (5 percent), black/African American (4 percent), or more than a single race (4 percent). The gender and ethnic composition of this class was very similar to that of the previous year.

Table 1 / Status of 2017 Graduates

School Region	Number of Schools Reporting	Number of Graduates Responding	Employed in LIS Field	Employed Outside of LIS	Currently Unemployed or Continuing Education	Total Answering	Percentage Employed Full-Time
Northeast	10	296	256	25	7	288	84
Midwest	10	384	213	38	21	272	87
Southeast	9	231	224	17	11	224	84
South Central	9	267	264	38	17	264	90
West	4	189	186	19	12	186	79
Total	42	1,367	1,029	137	68	1,234	85

Table based on survey responses from schools and individual graduates. Figures will not necessarily be fully consistent with some of the other data reported. Tables do not always add up, individually or collectively, since both schools and individuals omitted data in some cases.

Suzie Allard is chancellor's professor, associate dean for research, and director of the Center for Information and Communication Studies at the University of Tennessee College of Communication and Information, Knoxville.

Adapted from *Library Journal*, November 1, 2018.

Table 2 / Placements and Full-Time Salaries of 2017 Graduates by Region

Region	Number of Placements	Number Responding				Low Salary			High Salary			Average Salary				Difference in Average M/F Salary†	Median Salary			
		Women	Men	Non-binary*	All	Women	Men	Non-binary*	Women	Men	Non-binary*	Women	Men	Non-binary*	All		Women	Men	Non-binary*	All
Northeast	269	149	25	7	181	30,000	23,000	41,000	132,500	97,500	92,000	51,867	53,688	58,500	52,375	3.5%	50,000	52,000	56,000	51,224
Southeast	249	116	32	2	150	17,500	30,000	35,995	87,500	145,000	56,000	46,081	52,400	45,998	47,428	13.7	45,000	47,500	45,998	45,000
South Central	196	116	22	2	140	19,500	25,000	42,000	107,500	125,000	105,000	47,676	54,008	73,500	49,040	13.3	45,000	51,400	73,500	45,432
Midwest	243	108	32	4	146	25,000	30,000	33,000	118,000	102,500	75,000	49,831	55,997	50,125	51,205	12.4	47,500	50,000	46,250	48,000
Mountain	52	29	4	1	35	31,000	31,000	53,000	104,000	52,500	53,000	49,820	45,213	53,000	49,532	-9.2	48,000	48,675	53,000	48,880
Pacific	169	69	19	1	90	17,500	33,000	60,000	132,500	112,500	60,000	64,747	78,764	60,000	67,712	21.6	57,500	85,300	60,000	60,000
Canada/Int'l.	21	8	4	1	13	21,000	23,800	70,000	87,500	71,000	70,000	46,050	52,575	70,000	49,900	14.2	39,750	57,750	70,000	47,500
Total	1,199	595	138	18	755	17,500	23,000	33,000	132,500	145,000	105,000	50,797	57,220	57,333	52,152	12.6	48,880	52,250	56,000	50,000

This table represents only salaries reported as full-time. Some data were reported as aggregate without breakdown by gender or region. Comparison with other tables may show different number of placements.

*Includes nonbinary, unsure, and declined to answer gender.

†The nonbinary sample is too small to yield statistically significant results when compared to placements and salaries of other genders. Therefore, all gender comparisons shown are male to female only.

For the third year in a row, the typical graduate was relatively young. The majority were 35 or younger (71 percent). Eleven percent were 46 or older, and the average age was 33.

Full-time, Satisfaction Growing

An increasing number of graduates found full-time positions (85 percent). This is a slight uptick from 2016 and marks the fourth year in a row that full-time employment has exceeded 80 percent. Nine out of ten of these full-time positions are permanent. Only 15 percent of employed 2017 graduates took part-time positions, continuing the declining trend noted last year and down by half from the percentage of 2015 graduates who reported part-time status. The majority of this year's part-timers hold only one position, with 40 percent reported holding two, for an average of 1.5 positions, which is similar to last year. Six percent of graduates reported that they were unemployed compared to 7 percent last year. That's higher than the overall U.S. unemployment rate for the comparable period: about 3.95 percent, according to the U.S. Bureau of Labor Statistics. It's nearly three times higher than the overall 2017 unemployment for holders of a master's degree: 2.2 percent.

More than three in four graduates are satisfied with their full-time job placement (78 percent). The highest levels of satisfaction were expressed by full-time employees of public libraries (84 percent), school libraries (83 percent), special libraries (82 percent) and private industry (82 percent). Government library employees were the least satisfied with their positions (63 percent), a marked decline from last year's 76 percent. Many graduates commented that the source of their satisfaction was achieving the position they aspired to have ("my dream job") and demonstrating their learning from their LIS program. Others noted that they were now in a good "stepping stone" position that would provide experience needed to advance into preferred positions later. Other job characteristics that fueled satisfaction were good pay and benefits, schedule flexibility, camaraderie with coworkers, understanding and capable managers and mentors, and a comfortable setting. Some graduates emphasized interesting and fulfilling work, with challenges and room for growth, but also circumstances that allowed them to be successful and make a positive difference. Several expressed a deep fondness for the users or communities they serve.

Graduates in 2017 who said they were dissatisfied with their job expressed frustration about having to settle for part-time or temporary work, working multiple positions to support themselves, missing benefits, or feeling trapped in a nonprofessional library position or a position outside of LIS. Several noted that they were frustrated by unsuccessful attempts to land a professional LIS position. Many feel underpaid and underemployed and long to put their master's degree to work in a fulfilling environment. Some dissatisfied graduates were employed in professional LIS positions but not in their primary area of interest or expertise. Others had issues with management, coworkers, or insufficient resources. A few dissatisfied individuals mentioned their plans to improve their work life by switching to a more fulfilling position or relocating.

(text continues on page 246)

Table 3 / 2017 Total Graduates and Placements by School*

	Graduates				Employed Full Time				Response	
Schools	Women	Men	Non-binary**	All	Women	Men	Non-binary**	All	No. Rec'd.	Rate
Alabama	59	9	1	69	12	4	—	16	25	36.2%
Albany	24	11	—	35	5	1	1	7	8	22.9
Arizona	34	10	—	44	6	2	—	8	12	27.3
Buffalo	49	14	—	63	7	3	—	10	12	19.0
Catholic*	23	10	—	33	2	2	—	4	6	18.2
Clarion	108	12	—	120	13	1	—	14	23	19.2
East Carolina	63	8	—	71	2	3	—	5	7	90.9
Florida State	76	12	—	88	6		—	6	9	10.2
Hawaii	21	7	—	28	12	3	—	15	22	78.6
Ill. Urbana-Champaign*	—	—	—	242	21	6	1	28	41	16.9
Indiana–Bloomington	66	21	—	87	22	4	—	26	30	34.5
Indiana–Purdue	74	8	—	82	6		—	6	8	90.8
Iowa	31	6	—	37	9	4	2	16	21	56.8
Kentucky	60	25	—	85	15	8	—	23	31	36.5
Long Island	83	21	—	104	6	2	—	8	11	10.6
Louisiana State	43	4	—	47	20	2	1	23	26	55.3
Maryland	62	14	—	76	21	6	2	29	38	50.0
Michigan*	76	48	2	126	58	33	2	93	109	86.5
Missouri	33	10	—	43	8	5	—	13	15	34.9
N.C.–Chapel Hill*	44	22	—	66	—	—	—	—	65	98.5
N.C.–Greensboro	66	23	89	178	13	4	1	18	27	15.2
North Texas	269	95	—	364	32	4	—	36	44	12.1
Oklahoma	47	6	—	53	15	1	—	16	18	34.0
Pratt	52	11	—	63	13	1	—	14	18	28.6
Queens	49	16	—	65	21	5	2	28	33	50.8
Rutgers	80	12	—	92	33	5	1	39	49	53.3
San Jose	422	83	—	505	70	13	1	85	117	23.2
Simmons	229	40	—	269	80	11	4	95	113	42.0
South Carolina	102	14	—	116	26	3	—	30	32	27.6
South Florida	59	22	—	81	10	2	—	12	16	19.8
Southern Mississippi	33	7	—	40	17	2	—	20	22	55.0
St. Catherine	46	10	—	56	16	6	1	23	30	53.6
St. John's	—	—	—	28	10	2	—	12	16	57.1
Syracuse	51	17	—	68	7	2	—	9	13	19.1
Tennessee	46	9	—	55	16	1	1	18	18	32.7
Texas–Austin*	61	29	2	92	32	10	1	43	51	55.4
Texas Women's	144	4	—	148	26	1	—	27	32	21.6
Valdosta State	51	17	—	68	17	7	—	26	31	45.6
Washington	110	15	2	127	25	2	—	28	38	29.9
Wayne State	128	23	2	153	24	4	1	30	34	22.2
Wisconsin–Madison*	73	20	—	93	33	6	2	41	51	54.8
Wisconsin–Milwaukee	105	24	—	129	25	6	1	32	45	34.9
Total	3,252	769	98	4,389	812	187	25	1,032	1,367	31.1%

Tables do not always add up, individually or collectively, due to omitted data from schools and/or individuals.
*Some schools conducted their own survey and provided raw data. Comparison with other tables may show different numbers of placements.
**Includes nonbinary, unsure, and declined to answer gender.

Table 4 / Placements by Full-Time Salary of Reporting 2017 Graduates

Schools	Average Salary				Median Salary			Low Salary			High Salary			Placements			
	Women	Men	Non-binary**	All	Women	Men	Non-binary**	Women	Men	Non-binary**	Women	Men	Non-binary**	Women	Men	Non-binary**	Total Placements
Alabama	43,950	39,500	—	43,208	44,000	39,500	—	21,000	25,000	—	63,000	54,000	—	10	2	—	12
Albany	57,250	—	60,000	58,167	57,250	—	60,000	37,500	—	60,000	77,000	—	60,000	2	—	1	3
Arizona	34,125	55,675	—	41,308	32,750	55,675	—	31,000	49,850	—	40,000	61,500	—	4	2	—	6
Buffalo	52,114	145,000	—	67,595	52,000	145,000	—	46,570	145,000	—	59,000	145,000	—	5	1	—	6
Catholic*	69,000	62,000	—	66,667	69,000	62,000	—	63,000	62,000	—	75,000	62,000	—	2	1	—	3
Clarion	49,188	55,000	—	49,833	44,000	55,000	—	31,200	55,000	—	90,000	55,000	—	8	1	—	9
East Carolina	31,720	48,167	—	44,055	31,720	45,000	—	31,720	36,500	—	31,720	63,000	—	1	3	—	4
Florida State	41,630	—	—	41,630	45,260	—	—	22,500	—	—	53,500	—	—	4	—	—	4
Hawaii–Manoa	48,332	56,559	—	50,800	51,000	62,000	—	23,000	44,400	—	60,324	63,276	—	7	3	—	10
Illinois Urbana-Champaign	50,148	41,028	53,000	49,034	47,500	40,000	53,000	30,000	38,000	53,000	86,000	45,085	53,000	18	3	1	22
Indiana–Bloomington	50,844	48,333	—	50,447	48,750	40,000	—	31,200	30,000	—	104,000	75,000	—	16	3	—	19
Indiana–Purdue	41,750	—	—	41,750	37,250	—	—	32,500	—	—	60,000	—	—	4	—	—	4
Iowa	46,857	43,000	35,995	46,818	42,000	43,000	35,995	36,000	38,000	35,995	57,500	48,000	35,995	7	2	1	11
Kentucky	47,783	47,082	—	47,513	45,732	42,000	—	29,000	37,000	—	75,800	75,000	—	8	5	—	13
Long Island	58,900	90,000	—	64,083	56,000	90,000	—	49,500	90,000	—	77,000	90,000	—	5	1	—	6
Louisiana State	43,511	41,647	105,000	47,121	44,000	41,647	105,000	35,000	37,293	105,000	58,240	46,000	105,000	13	2	1	16
Maryland	51,687	59,522	56,000	53,740	55,000	55,867	56,000	34,000	50,000	56,000	65,000	75,400	56,000	18	6	1	25
Michigan*	70,156	82,500	66,250	73,853	62,500	92,500	66,250	25,000	40,000	57,500	132,500	112,500	75,000	45	21	2	68
Missouri	49,000	48,750	—	48,900	49,500	52,000	—	38,000	33,000	—	59,000	58,000	—	6	4	—	10

N.C.–Greensboro	42,263	41,588	—	42,070	41,000	41,676	—	32,000	32,000	—	60,000	51,000	—	10	4	—	14
North Texas	44,779	54,575	—	46,085	45,750	51,650	—	25,000	48,000	—	60,000	67,000	—	26	4	—	30
Oklahoma	44,181	41,000	—	43,828	47,475	41,000	—	28,500	41,000	—	49,000	41,000	—	8	1	—	9
Pratt	52,164	52,500	—	52,192	52,500	52,500	—	37,000	52,500	—	60,000	52,500	—	11	1	—	12
Queens	53,655	50,000	47,500	52,754	52,000	50,000	47,500	32,000	48,000	47,500	89,696	52,000	47,500	15	3	1	19
Rutgers	52,148	55,610	48,000	52,379	52,000	55,966	48,000	26,000	54,898	48,000	75,000	55,966	48,000	23	3	1	27
San Jose	50,422	63,851	60,000	52,750	48,750	70,000	60,000	30,000	33,000	60,000	92,000	90,000	60,000	47	9	1	58
Simmons	50,141	48,493	66,000	50,567	50,000	53,616	65,000	33,000	23,000	41,000	88,000	61,000	92,000	60	10	3	73
South Carolina*	40,096	36,667	—	39,741	50,000	30,000	—	17,500	30,000	—	70,000	50,000	—	26	3	—	29
South Florida	33,948	39,500	—	35,058	37,391	39,500	—	19,000	37,000	—	48,000	42,000	—	8	2	—	10
Southern Mississippi	38,153	45,200	—	38,982	40,000	45,200	—	19,636	37,400	—	59,000	53,000	—	15	2	—	17
St. Catherine	48,833	44,763	35,000	46,820	48,000	45,833	35,000	27,000	35,910	35,000	90,000	54,000	35,000	12	6	1	19
St. John's	53,232	46,750	—	51,792	51,224	46,750	—	40,000	41,500	—	65,000	52,000	—	7	2	—	9
Syracuse	38,000	50,000	—	40,000	42,000	50,000	—	31,000	50,000	—	42,500	50,000	—	5	1	—	6
Tennessee	48,954	—	42,000	48,458	42,000	—	42,000	32,500	—	42,000	86,000	—	42,000	13	—	1	14
Texas–Austin*	67,797	63,750	—	66,833	65,000	52,500	—	37,000	37,500	—	107,500	125,000	—	32	10	—	42
Texas Women's	43,593	55,000	—	44,112	43,000	55,000	—	19,500	55,000	—	61,500	55,000	—	21	1	—	22
Valdosta State	44,070	51,750	—	46,758	45,000	54,000	—	25,000	35,000	—	63,000	65,000	—	13	7	—	20
Washington	57,559	80,000	—	59,013	52,000	80,000	—	38,000	80,000	—	110,000	80,000	—	22	1	—	24
Wayne State	47,954	57,750	—	49,226	47,500	59,000	—	37,500	45,000	—	60,000	68,000	—	17	4	—	22
Wisconsin–Madison*	49,391	50,250	44,500	49,041	47,800	50,250	44,500	35,900	48,000	33,000	65,000	52,500	56,000	19	2	2	23
Wisconsin–Milwaukee	52,537	46,125	70,000	52,082	47,000	37,250	70,000	32,000	31,000	70,000	118,000	79,000	70,000	13	4	1	18
Total	50,797	57,220	57,333	52,152	48,510	52,500	56,000	17,500	23,000	33,000	132,500	145,000	105,000	606	140	18	768

This table represents placements and salaries reported as full-time. Some individuals or schools omitted information, rendering information unusable.
*Some schools conducted their own survey and provided raw data.
**Includes nonbinary, unsure, and declined to answer gender.

(continued from page 242)

Building on a Professional Past

A majority of graduates reported that LIS is their first career (57 percent). About half indicated that they were already working in a library prior to starting an LIS program. Echoing past results, this year's survey found that 43 percent of the 2017 graduates are now career-changers with professional experience in a different domain.

The most common starter field for these graduates was education (34.7 percent), including those who started in K–12, higher education, adult education, and specialties such as music or math instruction. Business was the next most frequent previous profession (11.6 percent) and included subfields like sales, economics, finance, insurance, and human resources. Communication-related careers were the next largest group (9.4 percent), bundling publishing, writing, journalism, advertising, and video production. Law careers (7.4 percent) were the next most common prelude to LIS studies; this category included attorneys, paralegals, and law enforcement. Those with backgrounds in entertainment and the arts (5.7 percent) formed the next group, including TV, music, theater arts, visual arts, video production, and museums.

Salaries Rise Slightly

The average salary for 2017 graduates employed full-time is $52,152. That's only about 1 percent higher than last year's average, but it does continue the positive trend that began in 2013, and it has risen 17 percent from 2011. The average hourly wage rate held steady at $19.02, representing an annual full-time salary of just under $40,000.

Regional variation in average salary level conformed to the 2016 pattern. The Pacific region produced the highest average regional salary ($67,712), while the Southeast generated the lowest ($47,428), a differential of over $20,000. However,

(text continues on page 250)

Table 5 / Average Salary for Starting Library Positions, 2011–2017

Year	Library Schools Represented	Average Full-Time Starting Salary	Difference in Average Salary	Percentage Change
2011	41	$44,565	$2,009	4.72
2012	41	44,503	-62	-0.14
2013	40	45,650	1,147	2.58
2014	39	46,987	1,337	2.93
2015	39	48,371	1,384	2.95
2016	40	51,798	3,427	7.08
2017	41	52,152	354	0.68

Table 6 / Full-Time Salaries of Reporting Professionals by Primary Job Assignment

Assignment	No. Rec'd.	Percent of Total	Low Salary	High Salary	Average Salary	Median Salary
Access Services	13	2.1	25,000	56,000	44,040	44,000
Administration	32	5.2	21,000	145,000	49,440	45,000
Adult Services	22	3.6	29,000	61,000	46,822	49,925
Archival and Preservation	27	4.4	23,800	75,400	45,214	45,600
Assessment	4	0.7	33,000	60,000	51,750	57,000
Budgeting/Finance	2	0.3	51,000	60,000	55,500	55,500
Children's Services	58	9.5	19,656	60,000	43,266	42,550
Circulation	17	2.8	19,000	51,360	38,498	40,000
Collection Development/ Acquisitions	14	2.3	23,000	71,000	47,748	50,000
Communications, PR, and Social Media	2	0.3	46,000	54,000	50,000	50,000
Data Analytics	13	2.1	45,000	86,000	59,077	55,000
Data Curation and Management	6	1.0	40,000	63,276	49,213	47,500
Digital Content Management	24	3.9	35,000	80,000	51,950	50,000
Emerging Technologies	6	1.0	40,000	60,000	48,833	48,000
Government Documents	4	0.7	38,000	62,000	49,308	48,617
Information Technology	11	1.8	32,000	75,000	52,142	54,000
Knowledge Management	8	1.3	25,000	105,000	62,500	63,500
Market Intelligence/Business Research	2	0.3	55,000	60,000	57,500	57,500
Metadata, Cataloging, and Taxonomy	22	3.6	19,636	95,000	46,499	48,000
Outreach	14	2.3	33,000	75,000	52,439	54,500
Patron Programming	5	0.8	47,500	68,000	57,350	58,000
Public Services	13	2.1	30,000	90,000	46,633	42,000
Records Management	9	1.5	32,000	85,300	55,171	56,000
Reference/Information Services	75	12.2	23,000	67,000	48,199	48,000
School Librarian/School Library Media Specialist	54	8.8	19,500	90,000	51,536	51,416
Solo Librarian	6	1.0	30,000	60,000	42,883	43,150
Systems Technology	8	1.3	40,000	57,900	51,108	50,000
Teacher Librarian	25	4.1	35,000	92,000	53,778	50,000
Technical Services	11	1.8	22,500	65,000	45,473	43,000
Training, Teaching and Instruction	29	4.7	37,400	71,400	52,003	52,000
User Experience/Usability Analysis	4	0.7	46,000	79,000	62,500	62,500
Website Design	2	0.3	50,300	75,000	62,650	62,650
YA/Teen Services	32	5.2	32,000	64,000	44,674	42,400
Other	39	6.4	32,000	118,000	55,803	49,000
Total Answering	613		19,000	145,000	49,248	48,000

This table represents full-time placements reported by primary job assignment.

Some individuals omitted placement information, therefore comparison with other tables may show different numbers of placements and average and median salaries.

Table 7 / Comparison of Full-Time Salaries by Type of Organization and Region

	Total Placements	Low Salary	High Salary	Average Salary	Median Salary
Public Libraries					
Northeast	63	23,000	70,000	47,715	49,000
Southeast	39	24,000	63,000	40,639	38,352
South Central	37	19,656	55,000	40,863	41,000
Midwest	49	29,000	118,000	45,891	42,500
Mountain	8	31,000	55,000	46,966	49,365
Pacific	13	23,000	73,144	51,287	51,000
Canada/Int'l.	1	68,000	68,000	68,000	68,000
All Public	210	19,656	118,000	45,057	44,735
College/University Libraries					
Northeast	48	30,000	64,000	51,900	52,250
Southeast	47	19,000	145,000	48,169	45,000
South Central	34	22,660	82,500	43,812	45,000
Midwest	28	30,000	65,000	48,924	49,000
Mountain	14	35,000	67,000	49,686	49,500
Pacific	20	37,000	67,000	52,301	52,112
Canada/Int'l.	5	21,000	71,400	47,280	42,000
All Academic	196	19,000	145,000	48,942	50,000
School Libraries					
Northeast	25	34,000	90,000	59,880	60,000
Southeast	14	17,500	62,500	43,464	46,000
South Central	30	19,500	75,000	48,921	48,790
Midwest	12	38,000	52,000	45,593	45,500
Mountain	1	33,500	33,500	33,500	33,500
Pacific	10	36,600	92,000	62,310	57,000
Canada/Int'l.	1	26,000	26,000	26,000	26,000
All School	93	17,500	92,000	51,644	50,000
Government Libraries					
Northeast	2	54,000	60,000	57,000	57,000
Southeast	12	38,000	75,000	58,622	57,500
South Central	3	19,636	60,000	46,212	59,000
Midwest	3	45,000	57,998	49,614	45,845
Mountain	1	57,500	57,500	57,500	57,500
Pacific	3	50,000	51,600	50,987	51,360
Canada/Int'l.	1	52,000	52,000	52,000	52,000
All Government	25	19,636	75,000	54,696	57,000
Private Industry					
Northeast	10	32,500	132,500	74,250	69,250
Southeast	8	32,000	87,500	63,738	63,750
South Central	18	25,000	125,000	77,374	85,000
Midwest	26	33,000	102,500	67,135	72,500
Mountain	3	62,500	104,000	81,333	77,500
Pacific	32	57,500	132,500	94,009	93,750
Canada/Int'l.	1	37,500	37,500	37,500	37,500
All Private Industry	98	25,000	132,500	78,372	79,500

Table 7 / Comparison of Full-Time Salaries by Type of Organization and Region

	Total Placements	Low Salary	High Salary	Average Salary	Median Salary
Special Libraries					
Northeast	6	35,000	65,000	51,917	54,500
Southeast	5	42,000	63,000	48,400	45,000
South Central	3	27,000	48,880	36,293	33,000
Midwest	3	43,000	60,000	51,000	50,000
Mountain	1	56,000	56,000	56,000	56,000
Pacific	—	—	—	—	—
Canada/Int'l.	1	70,000	70,000	70,000	70,000
All Special	19	27,000	70,000	49,546	50,000
Archives/Special Collections					
Northeast	7	35,000	61,000	46,286	47,500
Southeast	6	30,000	55,000	42,999	42,500
South Central	2	36,000	51,000	43,500	43,500
Midwest	4	35,000	50,500	44,846	46,941
Mountain	1	40,000	40,000	40,000	40,000
Pacific	2	41,061	45,600	43,331	43,331
Canada/Int'l.	1	23,800	23,800	23,800	23,800
All Archives/Special Collections	23	23,800	61,000	43,428	45,000
Nonprofit Organizations					
Northeast	3	30,000	52,000	39,667	37,000
Southeast	7	30,000	75,800	56,829	60,000
South Central	2	52,500	61,500	57,000	57,000
Midwest	5	25,000	90,000	50,900	42,000
Mountain	1	52,000	52,000	52,000	52,000
Pacific	1	52,500	52,500	52,500	52,500
Canada/Int'l.	—	—	—	—	—
All Nonprofit	19	25,000	90,000	52,095	52,000
Other Organizations					
Northeast	17	33,000	90,000	51,451	46,000
Southeast	8	37,400	81,000	47,267	41,250
South Central	9	37,419	86,000	51,680	50,300
Midwest	16	27,000	86,000	51,813	51,750
Mountain	4	31,000	36,800	32,950	32,000
Pacific	8	33,000	90,000	55,035	57,000
Canada/Int'l.	2	47,500	87,500	67,500	67,500
All Other	64	27,000	90,000	50,844	46,285

This table represents only full-time salaries and all placements reported by type. Some individuals omitted placement information, rendering some information unusable.

(continued from page 246)

the variance among the averages for all regions other than the Pacific is substantially smaller, ranging from $4,947 to $1,612. Surprisingly, the highest individual salary reported in the 2017 survey did not come from the Pacific region but from the Southeast! (This analysis does not account for regional variations in cost of living.)

Gender Gap Narrows

This year brought some improvement in salary disparity by gender. Although the overall average salary for male graduates was 12.6 percent higher than that for females, this differential is about six percentage points lower than in 2016. The contrast in salary level by gender is illustrated most starkly by the range of the data: the lowest full-time salary reported by a woman ($17,500) is $5,500 less than the lowest salary earned by a male graduate. The highest reported salary earned by a man was $145,000, $12,500 above the highest wage paid to a female graduate. Because *LJ* received so few nonbinary responses to the gender question, the sample is too small to yield statistically significant results when compared to placements and salaries of other genders. Therefore, all gender comparisons shown throughout the feature are male to female only. Nonbinary responses are included in the "all" category.

Average salaries for male graduates were higher than for women in all but one region. The most pronounced difference was for the Pacific region, where male salaries were 21.6 percent higher than for female graduates, though this is less than half the size of the largest differential in 2016. The Northeast region exhibited only a small gender salary differential of 3.5 percent but still favored men. The lone exception was the Mountain region, in which male average salaries were 9.2 percent lower than for females.

Variations in average salaries by work settings show many of the expected gender discrepancies but with some movement toward parity. Last year's female graduates working in special libraries are actually making 4.7 percent more than their male counterparts on average. In three other settings, men are earning only slightly more than women (government libraries, 0.6 percent, archives, 1.3 percent; and private industry, 2.3 percent). Echoing last year, the largest pay discrepancy by gender occurred in nonprofits, where male graduates are paid 17.2 percent more than women on average. Men who work in school libraries are earning an average of 12.4 percent more than women. The pay bias favoring men was also exhibited in academic libraries (10.2 percent higher) and public libraries (9.2 percent) in this survey. It is notable that the size of the male-biased pay differential in almost all settings was substantially smaller than for 2016 graduates.

Salaries by Library Type

Salaries earned by 2017 graduates varied depending on work setting. The largest financial rewards came from private industry jobs, with an average annual salary of more than $78,000. This was 41 percent above the average salary level for the next most lucrative setting, government libraries. Nonprofit organizations provided the third-highest average salary ($51,590). Among the more traditional work environments, school libraries yielded the highest average salaries ($51,472), while salaries in special, academic, and public libraries registered in the upper $40,000 range. The average salary for archives/special collections work was the lowest ($43,428) and had dropped about 6 percent from the prior year's survey. This runs counter to the past three surveys, in which public library salaries were the lowest on average.

Public libraries were the largest career destination at some 32 percent of 2017 graduates. The current average salary for public library positions was $45,061. This continues the trend of a modest increase over the past two years. This year's starting full-time salaries in public libraries ranged widely ($19,656–$118,000). The public library average salary was lowest in the Southeast region and 17 percent below that region's overall average. By contrast, the Pacific public library salary was substantially higher than other U.S. regions but compared the least favorably with other organization types in its own area (32 percent lower than the overall Pacific salary average).

On average, male graduates working in public libraries earned 9.2 percent more than females in the class of 2017. This disparity has widened slightly since last year, despite women accounting for 80 percent of this year's public library placements and having the highest individual public library salary reported in this survey ($118,000).

College and university libraries claimed 23 percent of 2017 graduates, equaling the prior year's figure. Their overall average salary was $48,930, an increase of 4.8 percent over 2016. The salary range for academic library positions was unusually wide ($19,000–$145,000). Both the highest and lowest salaries were in the Southeast region. With the exception of the Southeast and Mountain regions, academic library salaries were lower than the overall averages for most sectors. This gap was largest for the Pacific (29.5 percent lower) and South Central (11.9 percent) regions.

Gender-based salary differentials for academic libraries were similar to the findings for public libraries. Although women comprised 81 percent of their hires, male graduates' starting salaries were 10.2 percent higher than women's on average, a larger differential than for 2016 graduates. This effect may have been amplified somewhat by the year's overall top salary being paid to a male graduate in this setting.

School libraries hired 10 percent of the 2017 graduates, down from 13.9 percent in the prior survey. The average full-time salary for this setting was $51,472, 3.3 percent lower than 2016 but within 1 percent of this year's overall average salary. School library salaries ranged from $17,500 (in the Southeast) to $92,000 (in the Pacific region). In the Northeast, school librarians' average salary was 14.6 percent higher than the overall average for that region. However, in all other regions, school librarians' average salary was lower than the overall regional average.

Male graduates filled only 8.4 percent of this year's school library placements, but their salaries were 12.4 percent higher on average than those of female graduates. This is the second-highest gender-based salary differential among all

Table 8 / Full-Time Salaries by Type of Organization and Gender

	Total Placements				Low Salary			High Salary			Average Salary				Difference in male vs. female	Median Salary			
	Women	Men	Non-binary*	All	Women	Men	Non-binary*	Women	Men	Non-binary*	Women	Men	Non-binary*	All		Women	Men	Non-binary*	All
Public Libraries	173	38	3	215	19,656	23,000	41,000	118,000	75,000	56,000	44,324	48,388	48,167	45,061	9.2%	43,000	48,000	47,500	44,800
College/University Libraries	160	32	3	197	19,000	30,000	35,000	82,500	145,000	53,000	48,081	53,004	43,333	48,930	10.2	48,500	50,000	42,000	50,000
School Libraries	86	8	1	95	17,500	41,000	48,000	92,000	90,000	48,000	50,971	57,300	48,000	51,472	12.4	50,000	53,949	48,000	50,000
Government Libraries	20	4	2	26	19,636	38,000	56,000	75,000	70,000	60,000	55,002	55,340	58,000	55,285	0.6	57,000	56,680	58,000	57,000
Private Industry	64	31	4	100	32,000	25,000	33,000	132,500	125,000	105,000	77,676	79,458	76,250	78,094	2.3	77,500	80,000	83,500	78,250
Special Libraries	14	3	2	19	27,000	42,000	65,000	63,000	50,000	70,000	47,813	45,667	67,500	49,546	-4.5	49,440	45,000	67,500	50,000
Archives/Special Collections	19	3	1	23	30,000	23,800	35,995	55,000	61,000	35,995	43,686	44,267	35,995	43,428	1.3	45,000	48,000	35,995	45,000
Nonprofit Organizations	15	4	1	20	25,000	52,500	57,500	90,000	67,000	57,500	49,487	58,000	57,500	51,590	17.2	50,000	56,250	57,500	52,000
Other Organizations	48	16	1	65	27,000	33,000	60,000	90,000	90,000	60,000	51,049	48,977	60,000	50,677	-4.1	45,150	47,750	60,000	46,000

This table represents only full-time salaries and all placements reported by type. Some individuals omitted placement information, rendering some information unusable.
*Includes nonbinary, unsure, and declined to answer gender.

the work settings and the most disparate for a traditional library type. On the positive side, this is less than half the school library gender pay differential for 2016, and this year's top individual salary in this setting was earned by a female graduate.

Archives and special collections employed 5 percent of the 2017 graduates, bouncing back from last year's decline to reach a similar level to 2015. Conversely, the average salary for this organizational type was $43,428 this year, dropping 4.9 percent from 2016. This library type offered the lowest average salary and was 16.7 percent below the overall national average. The salary range for this setting varied from only $23,800 for a single Canadian/International position to a high of $61,000 from the Northeast. Average salaries for archivists were highest in the Northeast and Midwest, although even in those regions, they were still well below their overall regional averages (9.3 percent and 8.3 percent, respectively). It is noteworthy that this work situation involves a relatively high proportion of temporary employment; 46 percent of 2017 graduates working full-time in this setting are temporary.

Only three male graduates were hired into archival positions in 2017, so gender salary comparison is of limited value. The average salary for these male graduates was only 1.3 percent higher than the average salary for females working in this setting, and men were recipients of both the highest and lowest individual salaries paid in this setting.

Government library positions were chosen by 3 percent of 2017 job seekers, who were rewarded with an average salary of $55,285, 6.0 percent above the overall average salary level. Almost half of government placements were in the Southeast. The range of government salaries this year was both narrower and lower ($19,636–$75,000) than for 2016 graduates. However, government library compensation outperformed the overall regional averages in five sectors: Northeast (8.8 percent higher), Southeast (21.2 percent), Mountain (16.1 percent), Canada/International (4.2 percent), and South Central (20.3 percent).

The government library setting came the closest to achieving parity in compensation by gender. The four men hired for government library jobs this year were paid an average salary only $338 higher than the average salary earned by their 20 female counterparts. This is a substantial change from last year's 21.8 percent gender pay differential.

Thirteen percent of this year's graduates accepted full-time positions in private industry and were rewarded with an average annual salary of $78,094, up 6.6 percent from the already generous 2016 level. Private industry was again the most lucrative option for 2017's job seekers, with an average salary 50 percent higher than the overall average. Regional average salaries for private industry were far larger than the overall averages for all regions except Canada/International. The most impressive regional salaries for this work setting were for the Pacific (38.5 percent above the average salary for the region), Mountain (56.5 percent higher), South Central (73.3 percent), Southeast (34.3 percent), and the Northeast (32.2 percent). The salary range for private industry this year was typically broad ($25,000–$132,500), reflecting the wide variety of positions open to LIS graduates in nontraditional environments. The lowest salary level was in the South Central region, while the top salary was present in both the Northeast and the Pacific.

Private industry provided one of the better levels of salary parity by gender, with males earning only 2.3 percent more than women on average.

Special libraries hired 3 percent of the 2017 graduates, at an average salary level of $49,546, a modest 2.5 percent increase over the 2016 salary average for this setting. This was the only work context for which a gender salary disparity favored female graduates; women working in this area earned salaries 4.5 percent higher on average than men received. The salaries for special library hires varied from $27,000 in the South Central region to $70,000 for a single position in the Canada/International category. The special library regional salaries for three regions outperformed their regions' overall average salary levels: Canada/International (40.3 percent higher), Mountain (13 percent), and the Northeast (4.1 percent). No Pacific region hires for this workplace type were made this year. The special libraries category bundles a wide variety of libraries (medical, art, historical, industrial/corporate, nonacademic museum, and others), so regional differences may be overshadowed by other factors.

Nonprofit organizations employed 3 percent of this year's graduates. The average salary for this sector was $51,590, nearly equivalent to the overall average salary earned by the class of 2017. It was, however, a substantial drop of 11.7 percent from last year's average for nonprofit positions and slightly below what the 2015 graduates received. The range of salaries this year was less broad than usual, with a low of $25,000 and a peak of $90,000. Three regions delivered salaries for this work sector that exceeded their overall regional average salary levels: Southeast (26.5 percent higher), South Central (16.2 percent), and Mountain (5 percent). There were no nonprofit placements in the Canada/International region. Following the pattern of 2016, nonprofit organizations displayed the highest level of gender pay disparity; male graduates' average salary was 17.2 percent higher than the average for female hires. However, the size of the gender pay differential this year for nonprofits was down substantially from 29.6 percent for 2016 graduates.

The remaining graduates with full-time employment reported that they work for other types of organizations (4 percent) or a vendor (1 percent). Graduates who work for other kinds of organizations earn an average salary of $50,677, which is 2.8 percent lower than the overall average salary, and down 5.2 percent from last year's average for this employer category. The salary range is from $27,000 (in the Midwest) to $90,000 (present in both the Northeast and Pacific regions). This catch-all category was only the second (with special libraries) in this year's survey to turn the tables on gender pay disparity. The average salary for women graduates who work for other kinds of organizations was 4.2 percent above that of their male counterparts.

Responsibilities

Two standard survey questions explored the range of job assignments for newly hired information professionals. In the first, graduates could select any applicable items from a list of 37 duties. The results confirm that their positions are often multidimensional. Each item was selected by at least 3 percent of graduates. The most-cited assignments were reference and information services (53 percent); collection development and acquisitions (42 percent); outreach (37 percent); patron programming (33 percent); circulation (32 percent); readers' advisory (30 percent); and training, teaching, and instruction (30 percent).

Graduates were also asked to identify their single primary duty. The top four were reference and information services (13 percent), children's services (10 percent), school librarian/school library media specialist (7 percent), and archival and preservation (6 percent). The responses on these two measures are consistent with 2016 results.

Working graduates also provided their full job titles and their assessment of whether their position is in an emerging area of LIS. The most unique titles were Cloud Consultant, Discovery Librarian, Creative Technologies Librarian, User Experience and Digital Scholarship Librarian, Data Indexer, Digital Preservation Librarian, Digital Forensics Lab Assistant, Analyst Collection Workflow Consultant, Digital Asset Librarian, Digital Asset Management Fellow, e-Content Analyst, Open Education Librarian, Data Analytics and Visualization Librarian, Intellectual Property Manager, and Tween Librarian.

Relatively few graduates (14 percent) believed that their job is in an emerging area of LIS practice. Areas mentioned include management and curation of all kinds of digital content, assets, and collections, including data and data sets, and customized database configuration and data transformation. Several graduates mentioned identifying, managing, and providing instruction about new technologies. Many noted scholarly communication activities, including accessioning publications and managing institutional repositories. Other activities included managing technology for user experience testing and artificial intelligence; researcher support through data analysis and visualization/GIS; support of open education resources and access; transitions from physical digital media to cloud-based media and streaming services; metadata and machine auto-indexing; using digital forensics tools for archiving and preservation of digital assets; and automated data risk classification for storage and access.

Some graduates occupy positions that have a traditional title, but their job duties include emergent areas in the field. Some examples are a medical librarian in charge of 3-D printing, a reference assistant who is responsible for digital curation of local history collections, a teen and technology librarian who manages and develops programming for a Maker/innovation space, an outreach librarian who performs digital outreach through social media, and a reference and access services associate who does social media curation.

The Job Search

Some 56 percent of respondents indicated that, upon graduation, they stayed with their employer or in the position they held prior to or while attending the LIS master's program. Of graduates who stayed with the employer, 31 percent indicated that they received a raise after obtaining the degree. Others enjoyed a change in status, being promoted (22 percent) or moving from support to professional staff (21 percent). Gaining tenure eligibility (2 percent) affected only a few. Other circumstances graduates referred to were the ability to apply for better positions, or preparation for later transfers to other organizations. Forty-four percent reported no change in status after getting the degree.

Graduates who were looking for a position with a new employer shared their experiences when conducting their job search. Most began their search four to six months before graduation (an average of 4.7 months). Only 17 percent started looking after graduating. Among graduates seeking new employers, 40 percent were hired in their new professional position prior to graduation. Only 21 percent relocated for their placement, and there was very little difference in the average salary earned by relocators ($49,040) versus those who took positions close to home ($48,884). On average, it took graduates about four months to find their new job, an improvement over the prior year.

Graduates said the most helpful job-seeking resource was Indeed.com (33 percent). Government job websites at the city, state, and regional levels (30 percent) and the ALA online job list (29 percent) were also cited. To a lesser extent, campus job boards and Listservs (15 percent) and the INALJ website (12 percent) helped to inform their searches. Some graduates performed searches directly on the websites of places they might like to work (13 percent). Results for this measure have changed somewhat from last year, with an increase in the relative importance of general job search resources like Indeed and the absence of LIS professional organization sites other than ALA.

LIS Schools and Job Placements

LIS schools connect students with vital information about available openings. A Listserv was the most commonly used channel for disseminating position announcements (87 percent). Many schools also used social media accounts such as Facebook and Twitter to circulate job information (58 percent). Some also spread the word through student organizations or activities (50 percent), or by posting paper announcements in communal areas (45 percent). Only about a third have formal job placement centers or services (32 percent). And only six schools reported that they have a formal mentoring program for their graduates, offering formal links among alumni, students, and employers; mentoring from library staff in corresponding areas of interest; individual career counseling; faculty advisors serving as mentors; and courses about job searching.

Using some combination of these communication channels, 67 percent of LIS schools reported that they shared between 100 and 499 job announcements with their students in the last year. On average, each school made 534 announcements available to students. Some electronic channels such as social media and Listservs may also allow job announcements to reach alumni and other stakeholders. The schools reported that 80 percent of the available positions in libraries in 2017 were full-time. The schools were asked about the relative proportions of announcements for traditional vs. nontraditional placements in 2017; among the schools that addressed this, 39 percent said that the proportion was unchanged from 2016.

Accredited Master's Programs in Library and Information Studies

This list of graduate programs accredited by the American Library Association is issued by the ALA Office for Accreditation. Regular updates and additional details appear on the Office for Accreditation's website at http://www.ala.org/CFApps/lisdir/index.cfm. A total of 139 U.S. and Canadian institutions offering both accredited and nonaccredited programs in librarianship are included in the 72nd edition (2019–2020) of *American Library Directory* (Information Today, Inc.).

Northeast: D.C., Md., Mass., N.J., N.Y., Pa., R.I.

Catholic University of America, School of Arts and Sciences, Dept. of Lib. and Info. Science, 620 Michigan Ave. N.E., Washington, DC 20064. Youngok Choi, chair. Tel. 202-319-5085, fax 319-5574, e-mail cua-slis@cua.edu, World Wide Web http://lis.cua.edu. Admissions contact: Louise Gray. Tel. 202-319-5085, fax 319-5574, e-mail grayl@cua.edu.

Clarion University of Pennsylvania, College of Business Admin. and Info. Sciences, Dept. of Info. and Lib. Science, 210 Carlson Lib. Bldg., Clarion, PA 16214. Linda L. Lillard, chair. Tel. 866-272-5612, fax 814-393-2150, e-mail libsci@clarion.edu, World Wide Web http://www.clarion.edu/libsci. Admissions contact: Michelle Ritzler. Tel. 866-393-2337, e-mail gradstudies@clarion.edu.

Drexel University, College of Computing and Informatics, Dept. of Info. Science, 3141 Chestnut St., Philadelphia, PA 19104-2875. Xia Lin, dept. head. Tel. 215-895-2474, fax 215-895-2494, e-mail istinfo@drexel.edu, World Wide Web http://www.cci.drexel.edu. Admissions contact: Matthew Lechtenburg. Tel. 215-895-1951, e-mail ml333@drexel.edu.

Long Island University, College of Education, Info. and Technology, Palmer School of Lib. and Info. Science, 720 Northern Blvd., Brookville, NY 11548-1300. Thomas D. Walker, dir. Tel. 516-299-2866, fax 516-299-4168, e-mail post-palmer@liu.edu, World Wide Web http://www.liu.edu/palmer. Admissions contact: Amy Ingrilli. Tel. 516-299-2857, e-mail amy.ingrilli@liu.edu.

Pratt Institute, School of Info. and Lib. Science, 144 W. 14 St., New York, NY 10011. Anthony Cocciolo, interim dean. Tel. 212-647-7682, fax 212-367-2492, e-mail infosils@pratt.edu, World Wide Web http://www.pratt.edu/academics/information/. Admissions contact: Quinn Lai. Tel. 212-647-7682, e-mail infosils@pratt.edu.

Queens College, Grad. School of Lib. and Info. Studies, Rm. 254, Rosenthal Lib., 65-30 Kissena Blvd., Flushing, NY 11367-1597. Coleen Cool, chair. Tel. 718-997-3790, fax 718-997-3797, e-mail qc_gslis@qc.cuny.edu, World Wide Web http://sites.google.com/a/qc.cuny.edu/glis. Admissions contact: Roberta Brody. Tel. 718-997-3790, e-mail roberta_brody@qc.edu.

Rutgers University, School of Communication and Info., Dept. of Lib. and Info. Science, New Brunswick, NJ 08901-1071. Ross J. Todd, chair. Tel. 848-932-7602, e-mail mlis@comminfo.rutgers.edu, World Wide Web http://comminfo.rutgers.edu. Admissions contact: Lilia Pavlovsky. Tel. 732-932-7576.

Saint John's University, College of Liberal Arts and Sciences, Div. of Lib. and Info. Science, 8000 Utopia Pkwy., Queens, NY 11439. James Vorbach, dir. Tel. 718-990-1834, fax 718-990-2071, e-mail vorbach@stjohns.edu, World Wide Web http://www.stjohns.edu/dlis. Admissions contact: Michael Crossfox. Tel. 718-990-6200, e-mail dlis@stjohns.edu.

Simmons College, School of Lib. and Info. Science, 300 The Fenway, Boston, MA 02115. Sanda Erdelez, dir. Tel. 617-521-2800, fax 617-521-3192, e-mail gslis@simmons.edu, World Wide Web http://slis.simmons.edu/.

Admissions contact: Kate Benson. Tel. 617-521-2868, e-mail slisadm@simmons.edu.

Syracuse University, School of Info. Studies, 343 Hinds Hall, Syracuse, NY 13244. Caroline Hawthornthwaite, dir. Tel. 315-443-2911, fax 315-443-6886, e-mail ischool@syr.edu, World Wide Web http://www.ischool.syr.edu. Admissions contact: Blythe Bennett. Tel. 315-443-2911, e-mail mslis@syr.edu.

University at Albany, State Univ. of New York, College of Emergency Preparedness, Homeland Security and Cybersecurity, Draper 340, Albany, NY 12222. Philip B. Eppard, chair. Tel. 518-442-5258, fax 518-442-5632, e-mail cehc@albany.edu, World Wide Web http://www.albany.edu/cehc/graduate-programs-cehc.php. Admissions contact: Graduate Admissions. Tel. 518-442-3980, e-mail graduate@albany.edu.

University at Buffalo, State Univ. of New York, Graduate School of Educ., Dept. of Info. Sci, 534 Baldy Hall, Buffalo, NY 14260-1020. Heidi Julien, chair. Tel. 716-645-2412, fax 716-645-3775, e-mail ub-lis@buffalo.edu, World Wide Web http://ed.buffalo.edu/information/academics/masters/library-science.html. Admissions contact: Cory Meyers. Tel. 716-645-2110, e-mail gse-info@buffalo.edu.

University of Maryland, College of Info. Studies, 4105 Hornbake Bldg., College Park, MD 20742. Paul T. Jaeger, MLIS Program co-dir. Tel. 301-405-2033, fax 301-314-9145, e-mail ischooladmission@umd.edu, World Wide Web http://ischool.umd.edu/mlis. Admissions contact: Joanne Briscoe. Tel. 301-405-2038, e-mail ischooladmission@umd.edu.

University of Pittsburgh, School of Computing and Info., Info. Culture and Data Stewardship, 135 N. Bellefield Ave., Pittsburgh, PA 15260. Bruce R. Childers, chair. Tel. 412-624-5230, fax 412-648-7001, e-mail sciadmit@pitt.edu, World Wide Web http://www.sci.pitt.edu. Admissions contact: Shabana Reza. Tel. 412-624-3988, e-mail shabana.reza@pitt.edu.

University of Rhode Island, Grad. School of Lib. and Info. Studies, Rodman Hall, 94 W. Alumni Ave., Kingston, RI 02881. Valerie Karno, dir. Tel. 401-874-2878, fax 401-874-4964, e-mail vkarno@uri.edu, World Wide Web http://www.uri.edu/artsci/lsc.

Southeast: Ala., Fla., Ga., Ky., La., Miss., N.C., S.C., Tenn., P.R.

East Carolina University, College of Educ., Lib. Science Degree Program, Mailstop 172, ECU, Greenville, NC 27858. Lana Kaye Dotson, program coord. Tel. 252-328-4389, fax 252-328-4368, e-mail dotsonl@ecu.edu, World Wide Web http://www.ecu.edu/cs-educ/idp/lsed/index.cfm. Admissions contact: Camilla King. Tel. 252-328-6012, e-mail gradschool@ecu.edu.

Florida State University, College of Communication and Info., School of Info., 142 Collegiate Loop, P.O. Box 3062100, Tallahassee, FL 32306-2100. Lorri Mon, dir. Tel. 850-644-5775, fax 850-644-9763, e-mail lmon@fsu.edu, World Wide Web http://ischool.cci.fsu.edu. Admissions tel. 850-645-3280, e-mail ischooladvising@admin.fsu.edu.

Louisiana State University, College of Human Sciences and Education, School of Lib. and Info. Science, 267 Coates Hall, Baton Rouge, LA 70803. Carol Barry, dir. Tel. 225-578-3158, fax 225-578-4581, e-mail slis@lsu.edu, World Wide Web http://slis.lsu.edu. Admissions contact: LaToya Coleman Joseph. Tel. 225-578-3150, e-mail lcjoseph@lsu.edu.

North Carolina Central University, School of Lib. and Info. Sciences, P.O. Box 19586, Durham, NC 27707. Jon P. Gant, dean. Tel. 919-530-6485, fax 919-530-6402, e-mail slisadmissions@nccu.edu, World Wide Web http://www.nccuslis.org. Admissions contact: Nina Clayton.

University of Alabama, College of Communication and Info. Sciences, School of Lib. and Info. Studies, Box 870252, Tuscaloosa, AL 35487-0252. James Elmborg, dir. Tel. 205-348-2719, fax 205-348-3746, e-mail info@slis.ua.edu, World Wide Web http://www.slis.ua.edu. Admissions contact: Lita Shive. Tel. 205-348-1527, e-mail lmshive@slis.ua.edu.

University of Kentucky, College of Communication and Info., School of Lib. and Info. Science, 320 Little Lib., Lexington,

KY 40506-0224. Jeffrey T. Huber, dir. Tel. 859-257-8876, fax 859-257-4205, e-mail ukslis@uky.edu, World Wide Web http://www.uky.edu/cis/slis. Admissions contact: Will Buntin. Tel. 859-257-3317, e-mail wjbunt0@uky.edu.

University of North Carolina at Chapel Hill, School of Info. and Lib. Science, CB 3360, 100 Manning Hall, Chapel Hill, NC 27599-3360. Gary Marchionini, dean. Tel. 919-962-8366, fax 919-962-8071, e-mail info@ils.unc.edu, World Wide Web http://www.sils.unc.edu. Admissions contact: Lara Bailey.

University of North Carolina at Greensboro, School of Educ., Dept. of Lib. and Info. Studies, 446 School of Educ. Bldg., P.O. Box 26170, Greensboro, NC 27402-6170. Lisa O'Connor, chair. Tel. 336-334-3477, fax 336-334-4120, e-mail lis@uncg.edu, World Wide Web http://soe.uncg.edu/academics/departments/lis. Admissions contact: Nora Bird. Tel. 336-256-1313, e-mail njbird@uncg.edu.

University of Puerto Rico, Info. Sciences and Technologies, P.O. Box 21906, San Juan, PR 00931-1906. Jose Sanchez-Lugo, dir. Tel. 787-763-6199, fax 787-764-2311, e-mail egcti@uprrp.edu, World Wide Web http://egcti.upr.edu. Admissions contact: Migdalia Dávila-Perez. Tel. 787-764-0000 ext. 3530, e-mail migdalia.davila@upr.edu.

University of South Carolina, College of Info. and Communications, School of Lib. and Info. Science, 1501 Greene St., Columbia, SC 29208. R. David Lankes, dir. Tel. 803-777-3858, fax 803-777-7938, e-mail rdlankes@sc.edu, World Wide Web http://www.libsci.sc.edu. Admissions contact: Tel. 803-777-3887, e-mail slisss@mailbox.sc.edu.

University of South Florida, College of Arts and Sciences, School of Info., 4202 E. Fowler Ave., CIS 1040, Tampa, FL 33620. James Andrews, dir. Tel. 813-974-3520, fax 813-974-6840, e-mail si@usf.edu, World Wide Web http://www.usf.edu/si. Admissions contact: Daniel Kahl. Tel. 813-974-8022.

University of Southern Mississippi, College of Educ. and Health Sciences, School of Lib. and Info. Science, 118 College Dr., No. 5146, Hattiesburg, MS 39406-0001. Theresa Welsh, dir. Tel. 601-266-4228, fax 601-266-5774, e-mail slis@usm.edu, World Wide Web http://www.usm.edu/slis. Admissions tel. 601-266-5137, e-mail graduate studies@usm.edu.

University of Tennessee, College of Communication and Info., School of Info. Sciences, 451 Communication Bldg., Knoxville, TN 37996. Diane Kelly, dir. Tel. 865-974-2148, fax 865-974-4967, e-mail sis@utk.edu, World Wide Web http://www.sis.utk.edu, Admissions contact: Tanya Arnold. Tel. 865-974-2858, e-mail tnarnold@utk.edu.

Valdosta State Univ., Dept. of Lib. and Info. Studies, 1500 N. Patterson St., Odum 4600, Valdosta, GA 31698-0133. Linda R. Most, dept. head. Tel. 229-333-5966, fax 229-259-5055, e-mail mlis@valdosta.edu, World Wide Web http://www.valdosta.edu/mlis. Admissions contact: Sheila Peacock.

Midwest: Ill., Ind., Iowa, Kan., Mich., Minn., Mo., Ohio, Wis.

Dominican Univ., School of Info. Studies, 7900 W. Division St., River Forest, IL 60305. Kate Marek, dean. Tel. 708-524-6983, fax 708-524-6657, e-mail sois@dom.edu, World Wide Web http:/sois.dom.edu/. Admissions contact: Catherine Galarza-Espino. Tel. 708-524-6983, e-mail cgalarza@dom.edu.

Emporia State University, School of Lib. and Info. Management, Campus Box 4025, 1 Kellogg Circle, Emporia, KS 66801-5415. Wooseob Jeong, dean. Tel. 620-341-5203, fax 620-341-5233, e-mail sliminfo@emporia.edu, World Wide Web http://emporia.edu/slim. Admissions contact: Kathie Buckman. Tel. 620-341-5065.

Indiana University, School of Informatics, Computing and Engineering, Info. and Lib. Science, Luddy Hall, Suite 2999C, 700 N. Woodlawn Ave., Bloomington, IN 47408. Raj Achayra, dean. Tel. 812-855-2018, fax 812-855-6166, e-mail ilsmain@indiana.edu, World Wide Web http://www.ils.indiana.edu/about/accreditations.html. Admissions contact: Stephanie Smith.

Indiana University–Purdue University Indianapolis, School of Informatics and Computing, Dept. of Lib. and Info. Science, 535 W. Michigan St., IT475, Indianapolis, IN 46202. Andrea Copeland, chair. Tel.

317-278-4636, fax 317-278-7669, e-mail soic@iupui.edu, World Wide Web http://soic.iupui.edu/lis. Admissions e-mail soicapps@iupui.edu.

Kent State University, School of Info., P.O. Box 5190, Kent, OH 44242-0001. Kendra Albright, dir. Tel. 330-672-2782, fax 330-672-7965, e-mail ischool@kent.edu, World Wide Web http://www.kent.edu/ischool/master-library-information-science. Admissions contact: Cheryl Tennant.

Saint Catherine University, Graduate College, School of Business and Professional Studies, MLIS Program/Information Management Department, 2004 Randolph Ave. No. 4125, St. Paul, MN 55105. Anthony Molaro, dean. Tel. 651-690-6802, fax 651-690-8724, e-mail imdept@stkate.edu, World Wide Web https://www2.stkate.edu/mlis/home. Admissions contact: Ashley Wells. Tel. 612-214-0741, e-mail aewells@stkate.edu.

University of Illinois at Urbana-Champaign, School of Info. Science, 501 E. Daniel St., Champaign, IL 61820-6211. Allen Renear, dean. Tel. 217-333-3280, fax 217-244-3302, e-mail ischool@illinois.edu, World Wide Web http://ischool.illinois.edu. Admissions contact: Moises Orozco Villicana. Tel. 217-300-5007, e-mail orozco6@illinois.edu.

University of Iowa, Graduate College, School of Lib. and Info. Science, 3087 Main Lib., Iowa City, IA 52242-1420. David Eichmann, dir. Tel. 319-335-5707, fax 319-335-5374, e-mail slis@uiowa.edu, World Wide Web http://slis.grad.uiowa.edu. Admissions contact: Carol Ives. Tel. 319-335-5709, e-mail carol-ives@uiowa.edu.

University of Michigan, School of Info., 4322 North Quad, 105 S. State St., Ann Arbor, MI 48109-1285. Elizabeth Yakel, sr. assoc. dean. Tel. 734-763-2285, fax 734-764-2475, e-mail umsi.admissions@umich.edu, World Wide Web http://www.si.umich.edu. Admissions contact: Laura Elgas.

University of Missouri, College of Educ., Info. Science and Learning Technologies, 303 Townsend Hall, Columbia, MO 65211. Jenny Bossaller, chair. Tel. 877-747-5868, fax 573-884-0122, e-mail sislt@missouri.edu, World Wide Web http://lis.missouri.edu. Admissions tel. 573-882-4546.

University of Wisconsin–Madison, College of Letters and Sciences, Info. School, 600 N. Park St., Madison, WI 53706. Kyung-Sun Kim, interim dir. Tel. 608-263-2900, fax 608-263-4849, e-mail info@ischool.wisc.edu, World Wide Web http://ischool.wisc.edu. Admissions contact: Tanya Hendricks Cobb. Tel. 608-263-2909, e-mail student-services@slis.wisc.edu.

University of Wisconsin–Milwaukee, School of Info. Studies, P.O. Box 413, Milwaukee, WI 53201. Tomas Lipinski, dean. Tel. 414-229-4707, fax 414-229-6699, e-mail soisinfo@uwm.edu, World Wide Web http://www4.uwm.edu/sois.

Wayne State University, School of Info. Science, 106 Kresge Lib., Detroit, MI 48202. Hermina Anghelesco, interim dir. Tel. 313-577-1825, fax 313-577-7563, e-mail asklis@wayne.edu, World Wide Web http://www.slis.wayne.edu. Admissions contact: Matthew Fredericks. Tel. 313-577-2446, e-mail mfredericks@wayne.edu.

Southwest: Ariz., Okla., Texas

Texas Woman's University, School of Lib. and Info. Studies, P.O. Box 425769, Denton, TX 76204-5438. Ling Hwey Jeng, dir. Tel. 940-898-2602, fax 940-898-2611, e-mail slis@twu.edu, World Wide Web http://www.twu.edu/slis. Admissions contact: Mary Honard. E-mail slis@twu.edu.

University of Arizona, College of Social and Behavioral Sciences, School of Info., 1103 E. Second St., Tucson, AZ 85721. P. Bryan Heidorn, dir. Tel. 520-621-3565, fax 520-621-3279, e-mail si-info@email.arizona.edu, World Wide Web http://www.si.arizona.edu/master-arts-library-and-information-science. Admissions contact: Barb Vandervelde. Tel. 520-621-3567, e-mail barbv@email.arizona.edu.

University of North Texas, College of Info., Dept. of Info. Science, 1155 Union Circle, No. 311068, Denton, TX 76203-5017. Jiangping Chen, chair. Tel. 940-565-2445, fax 940-369-7600, e-mail lis-chair@unt.edu, World Wide Web http://informationscience.unt.edu./master-science. Admissions contact: Toby Faber. Tel. 940-565-2445, e-mail ci-advising@unt.edu.

University of Oklahoma, School of Lib. and Info. Studies, College of Arts and Sciences, 401 W. Brooks, Norman, OK 73019-6032. Susan Burke, dir. Tel. 405-325-3921, fax 405-325-7648, e-mail slisinfo@ou.edu, World Wide Web http://www.slis.ou.edu. Admissions contact: Sarah Connelly.

University of Texas at Austin, School of Info., Suite 5.202, 1616 Guadalupe St., Austin, TX 78701-1213. Eric T. Meyer, dean. Tel. 512-471-3821, fax 512-471-3971, e-mail info@ischool.utexas.edu, World Wide Web http://www.ischool.utexas.edu. Admissions contact: Carla Criner. Tel. 512-471-5654, e-mail criner@ischool.utexas.edu.

West: Calif., Colo., Hawaii, Wash.

San José State University, School of Info., Applied Sciences and Arts, One Washington Sq., San Jose, CA 95192-0029. Sandy Hirsh, dir. Tel. 408-924-2490, fax 408-924-2476, e-mail sjsuischool@gmail.com, World Wide Web http://ischool.sjsu.edu. Admissions contact: Linda Main. Tel. 408-924-2494, e-mail linda.main@sjsu.edu.

University of California, Los Angeles, Graduate School of Educ. and Info. Studies, Dept. of Info. Studies, Box 951520, Los Angeles, CA 90095-1520. Jean-Francois Blanchette, acting chair. Tel. 310-825-8799, fax 310-206-3076, e-mail info@gseis.ucla.edu, World Wide Web http://is.gseis.ucla.edu. Admissions contact: Susan Abler. Tel. 310-825-5269, e-mail abler@gseis.ucla.edu.

University of Denver, Morgridge College of Educ., Research Methods and Info. Science, 1999 E. Evans Ave., Denver, CO 80208-1700. Nicholas Cutforth, chair. Tel. 303-871-3587, fax 303-871-4456, e-mail mce@du.edu, World Wide Web http://www.du.edu/education. Admissions contact: Rachel Riley. Tel. 303-871-2508, e-mail rachel.riley@du.edu.

University of Hawaii, College of Natural Sciences, Lib. and Info. Science Program, 2550 McCarthy Mall, Honolulu, HI 96822. Rich Gazan, chair. Tel. 808-956-7321, fax 808-956-5835, e-mail slis@hawaii.edu, World Wide Web http://www.hawaii.edu/lis.

University of Southern California, Marshall School of Business, 3550 Trousdale Parkway, DML 312, Los Angeles, CA 90089-0183. Gary Shaffer, dept. head. Tel. 213-640-4034, e-mail mmlis.program@marshall.usc.edu, World Wide Web http://librarysciencedegree.usc.edu. Admissions tel. 877-830-8647, e-mail info@librarysciencedegree.usc.edu.

University of Washington, The Information School, 370 Mary Gates Hall, Seattle, WA 98195-2840. Anind Dey, dean. Tel. 206-685-9937, fax 206-616-3152, e-mail ischool@uw.edu, World Wide Web http://ischool.uw.edu. Admissions contact: Tel. 206-543-1794, e-mail mlis@uw.edu.

Canada

Dalhousie University, School of Info. Management, Kenneth C. Rowe Management Bldg., Halifax, NS B3H 4R2. Sandra Toze, dir. Tel. 902-494-3656, fax 902-494-2451, e-mail sim@dal.ca, World Wide Web http://www.sim.management.dal.ca. Admissions contact: JoAnn Watson. Tel. 902-494-2471, e-mail joann.watson@dal.ca.

McGill University, School of Info. Studies, 3661 Peel St., Montreal, QC H3A 1X1. Kimiz Dalkir, dir. Tel. 514-398-4204, fax 514-398-7193, e-mail sis@mcgill.ca, World Wide Web http://www.mcgill.ca/sis. Admissions contact: Kathryn Hubbard. Tel. 514-398-4204 ext. 0742, e-mail sis@mcgill.ca.

University of Alberta, School of Lib. and Info. Studies, Faculty of Education, 3-20 Rutherford S., Edmonton, AB T6G 2J4. Toni Samek, chair. Tel. 780-492-4578, fax 780-492-2430, e-mail slis@ualberta.ca, World Wide Web http://www.slis.ualberta.ca. Admissions contact: Lauren Romaniuk. Tel. 780-492-4140, e-mail slisadmissions@ualberta.ca.

University of British Columbia, School of Lib., Archival, and Info. Studies, Irving K. Barber Learning Centre, Suite 470, 1961 East Mall, Vancouver, BC V6T 1Z1. Luanne Freund, dir. Tel. 604-822-2404, fax 604-822-6006, e-mail ischool.info@ubc.ca, World Wide Web http://www.slais.ubc.ca. Admissions contact: Alynne Pols. Tel. 604-822-2461, e-mail ischool.program@ubc.ca.

Université de Montréal, École de bibliothéconomie et des sciences de l'information, C.P. 6128, Succursale Centre-Ville, Montreal, QC H3C 3J7. Lyne Da Sylva, acting dir. Tel. 514-343-6044, fax 514-343-5753, e-mail ebsiinfo@ebsi.umontreal.ca, World Wide Web http://www.ebsi.umontreal.ca. Admissions contact: Alain Tremblay. Tel. 514-343-6044, e-mail alain.tremblay.1@umontreal.ca.

University of Ottawa, School of Info. Studies, Desmarais Bldg., Ottawa, ON K1N 6N5. Helene Carrier, interim dir. Tel. 613-562-5130, fax 613-562-5854, e-mail esis@uOttawa.ca, World Wide Web http://arts.uottawa.ca/sis/. Admissions contact: Catherine Bernard. Tel. 613-562-5800 ext. 1324, e-mail artsgrad@uottawa.ca.

University of Toronto, Faculty of Info., 140 George St., Toronto, ON M5S 3G6. Wendy Duff, dean. Tel. 416-978-3202, fax 416-978-5762, e-mail inquire.ischool@utoronto.ca, World Wide Web http://www.ischool.utoronto.ca. Admissions contact: Barbara Brown. Tel. 416-978-8589, e-mail barb.brown@utoronto.ca.

University of Western Ontario, Grad. Programs in Lib. and Info. Science, Faculty of Info. and Media Studies, Room 240, North Campus Bldg., London, ON N6A 5B7. Nick Dyer-Whitheford, acting dean; Pam McKenzie, assoc. dean. Tel. 519-661-4017, fax 519-661-3506, e-mail mlisinfo@uwo.ca, World Wide Web http://www.fims.uwo.ca. Admissions contact: Shelley Long.

Library Scholarship Sources

For a more complete list of scholarships, fellowships, and assistantships offered for library study, see *Financial Assistance for Library and Information Studies,* published annually by the American Library Association (ALA). The document is also available on the ALA website at http://www.ala.org/educationcareers/scholarships.

American Association of Law Libraries. (1) Degree Candidates Scholarships are available for individuals studying to become law librarians as either a library or law school student, or to library school graduates seeking an advanced degree in a related field. Preference is given to AALL members, but scholarships are not restricted to members. Applicants with law library experience are also given preference, but it is not required. Evidence of financial need must be submitted. (2) AALL Scholarship is awarded annually to individuals seeking a degree from an accredited library or law school, and who intend to have a career in legal information, or to a library school graduate seeking an advanced degree in a related field; (3) LexisNexis John R. Johnson Memorial Scholarship is awarded annually to individuals seeking a degree from an accredited library or law school, and who intend to have a career in legal information, or to a library school graduate seeking an advanced degree in a related field. (4) George A. Strait Minority Scholarship is awarded annually to college graduates, with library experience, and who are members of a minority group as defined by current U.S. guidelines, and are degree candidates in an accredited library or law school and intend to have a career in law librarianship. (5) Marcia J. Koslov Scholarship supports AALL members who work in a government law library by providing funding to attend continuing education programs. For information, write to AALL Scholarship Committee, 105 W. Adams St., Suite 3300, Chicago, IL 60603.

American Library Association. (1) ALA Century Scholarship of $2,500 that funds services or accommodation for a library school student(s) with disabilities admitted to an ALA-accredited library school. (2) David A. Clift Scholarship of $3,000 to a U.S./Canadian citizen or permanent resident who is pursuing an MLS in an ALA-accredited program. (3) Tom and Roberta Drewes Scholarship of $3,000 to a library support-staff member who is a U.S./Canadian citizen or permanent resident and is pursuing an MLS in an ALA-accredited program. (4) Mary V. Gaver Scholarship of $3,000 to a U.S./Canadian citizen or permanent resident who is pursuing an MLS specializing youth services in an ALA-accredited program. (5) Miriam L. Hornback Scholarship of $3,000 to an ALA or library support staffer who is a U.S./Canadian citizen or permanent resident who is pursuing an MLS in an ALA-accredited program. (6) Christopher Hoy/ERT Scholarship of $5,000 to a U.S./Canadian citizen or permanent resident who is pursuing an MLS in an ALA-accredited program. (7) Tony B. Leisner Scholarship of $3,000 to a library support-staff member who is a U.S./Canadian citizen or permanent resident pursuing an MLS in an ALA-accredited program. (8) Peter Lyman Memorial/SAGE Scholarship in New Media to support a student in an ALA accredited master's program in Library and Information Studies pursuing a specialty in new media. (9) Robert L. Oakley Memorial Scholarship of $1,000 to support research and advanced study for librarians in their early to-mid-careers who are interested and/or active in the fields of intellectual property, public policy, copyright and their impacts on libraries, and the ways libraries serve their communities. (10) W. David Rozkuszka Scholarship of $3,000 to an individual who is currently working with government documents in a library and is working toward a master's degree in library science. (11) Spectrum Scholarship Program is ALA's national diversity and recruitment effort designed to address the specific issue of underrepresentation of critically needed ethnic librarians within the profession while serving as a model for ways to bring attention to larger diversity issues in the future. For information, write to ALA Scholarship Clearinghouse, 50 E. Huron St., Chicago, IL 60611, or see http://www.ala.org/scholarships.

ALA/Association for Library Service to Children. (1) Bound to Stay Bound Books Scholarship provides financial assistance for the education of individuals who intend to pursue an MLS or advanced degree and who plan to work in the area of library service to children. (2) Frederic G. Melcher Scholarship provides financial assistance for individuals who intend to pursue an MLS degree and who plan to work in children's librarianship. For information, write to ALA Scholarship Clearinghouse, 50 E. Huron St., Chicago, IL 60611, or see http://www.ala.org/scholarships.

ALA/Association of College and Research Libraries. The WESS-SEES De Gruyter European Librarianship Study Grant supports research in European studies with an emphasis on librarianship, the book trade, resource documentation, and similar information-science-related topics. €2,500 to cover travel to and from Europe and transportation, room, and board in Europe, for up to 30 consecutive days. Application is electronic only. For information, contact award co-chairs Kristen Totleben at ktotleben@library.rochester.edu or Lana Soglasnova at Svetlana.soglasnova@utoronto.edu or ACRL program officer Chase Ollis at collis@ala.org.

ALA International Relations Committee. Bogle Pratt International Library Travel Fund of $1,000 is given to an ALA personal member to attend their first international conference. Applications should be submitted via e-mail to the ALA International Relations Office, intl@ala.org.

ALA/Library and Information Technology Association. (1) LITA/Christian (Chris) Larew Memorial Scholarship of $3,000 for study in an ALA Accredited Master of Library Science (MLS) program to encourage the entry of qualified persons into the library and information technology field. (2) LITA/OCLC Minority Scholarship of $3,000 to a U.S. or Canadian citizen who is a qualified member of a principal minority group (American Indian or Alaskan native, Asian or Pacific Islander, African American, or Hispanic) for study in an ALA Accredited Master of Library Science (MLS) program who has a strong commitment to the use of automated systems in libraries and plans to follow a career in the library and automation field; (3) LITA/LSSI Minority Scholarship to a U.S. or Canadian citizen who is a qualified member of a principal minority group (American Indian or Alaskan native, Asian or Pacific Islander, African American, or Hispanic) for study in an ALA Accredited Master of Library Science (MLS) program who has a strong commitment to the use of automated systems in libraries and plans to follow a career in the library and automation field. For information, write to ALA Scholarship Clearinghouse, 50 E. Huron St., Chicago, IL 60611, or see http://www.ala.org/scholarships.

ALA/Public Library Association. Demco New Leaders Travel Grant of up to $1,500 for a varying number of PLA Members to enhance their professional development by making possible their attendance at major professional development activities. For information, write to PLA Awards Program, ALA/PLA, 50 E. Huron St., Chicago, IL 60611, or see http://www.ala.org/pla/awards.

American-Scandinavian Foundation. Fellowships (up to $23,000) and grants (up to $5,000) to pursue research, study, or creative arts projects in Denmark, Finland, Iceland, Norway, or Sweden. For information, write to Fellowships and Grants, American-Scandinavian Foundation, 58 Park Ave., New York, NY 10026, or see http://www.amscan.org/fellowships-and-grants/.

Association for Library and Information Science Education (ALISE). (1) ALISE Community conn@CT mini-grants of $750 for ALISE members to address a library and information need of a social justice organization through community engagement (in a collaborative manner). (2) A varying number of research grants totaling $5,000 for members of ALISE. For information, write to ALISE, 4 Lan Drive, Suite 310, Westford, MA 01886.

Association of Bookmobile and Outreach Services (ABOS). (1) The Bernard Vavrek Scholarship of $1,000 to a student who is currently enrolled and has completed at least one semester in a library and/or information science graduate degree program, and who is interested in becoming an outreach/bookmobile librarian. (2) The John Philip Award of $300 to recognize outstanding contributions and leadership by an individual in bookmobile and outreach services. (3) The Carol Hole Conference Attendance Award of three $500 to cover conference registration and a stipend for his/her travel expenses and/or accommodations for a conference. For information, write to Cathy Zimmerman, ABPS Awards Chair, Scott County Library System, 200 N. 6th Ave., Eldridge, IA 52748.

Association of Jewish Libraries. (1) An academic scholarship of $1,000 to a student enrolled or accepted in a graduate school of library and information science. Additionally, free full conference registration is included and encouraged. (2) an academic scholarship of $750 CDN to a student enrolled or accepted in a graduate school of library and information science. Additionally, free full conference registration is included and encouraged. (3) A conference subvention award for attending the Association of Jewish Libraries annual conference. Free full conference registration, travel and (shared) room are included. For information, see http://jewishlibraries.org/student_scholarship.

Association of Seventh-Day Adventist Librarians. The D. Glenn Hilts Scholarship for a member of the Seventh-Day Adventist Church in an ALA-accredited graduate library program or, if attending outside the United States or Canada, a program recognized by the International Federation of Library Associations (IFLA). Recipient must be enrolled as a full-time student and use the scholarship only for tuition and books. For information, write to Heather Rodriguez-James, Chair, ASDAL Scholarship and Awards Committee, Del Webb Memorial Library, Loma Linda University, 11072 Anderson St., Loma Linda, CA 92350.

Beta Phi Mu. (1) The Sarah Rebecca Reed Scholarship consisting of two $2,250 awards for individuals beginning LIS studies at an ALA accredited school. (2) The Frank B. Sessa Scholarship of ten $150 awards for Beta Phi Mu members' continuing education. (3) The Harold Lancour Scholarship of $1,750 for a librarian conducting foreign research. (4) The Blanche E. Woolls Scholarship for School Library Media Service of $2,250 for an individual beginning LIS studies with a concentration in School Library Media. (5) The Eugene Garfield Doctoral Dissertation Scholarship of up to six $3,000 awards for doctoral students who are working on their dissertations in LIS and related fields. For information, write to Beta Phi Mu Honor Society, P.O. Box 42139, Philadelphia, PA 19101, or see https://www.betaphimu.org/scholarships_overview.html.

Canadian Association of Law Libraries. (1) The Diana M. Priestly Scholarship of $2,500 for a student enrolled in an approved Canadian law school or accredited Canadian library school. (2) CALL/ACBD Research Grant of up to $3,000 for research in areas of interest to members and to the association. (3) CALL/ACBD Education Reserve Fund Grants for CALL members to further their education in pursuits that do not fit the guidelines of already established scholarships. (4) The James D. Lang Memorial Scholarship to support attendance at a continuing education program. (5) The Eunice Beeson Memorial Travel Fund to assist members of the Association who wish to attend the annual meeting but, for financial reasons, are unable to do so. (6) Janine Miller Fellowship of $2,500 for one CALL member to attend the Law via the Internet Conference. For information, see https://www.callacbd.ca/Awards.

Canadian Federation of University Women. (1) The Aboriginal Women's Award of $10,000 for studies in specific programs of Law, Medicine, Nurse Practitioner or a Master of in Aboriginal Studies. (2) The Ruth Binnie Fellowship of $6,000 for a student in master's studies that focus on one or more aspect(s) of the field of human ecology / home economics / family and consumer sciences. (3) The Canadian Home Economics Association Fellowship of $6,000 for a student enrolled in a postgraduate program in the field of human ecology/home economics/family and consumer sciences in Canada. (4) the CFUW Memorial Fellowship of $8,000 for a student who is currently enrolled in a master's program in science, mathematics, or engineering in Canada or abroad. (5) The Bourse Georgette LeMoyne award of $5,000 for graduate study in any field at a Canadian university (the candidate must be studying in French). (6) The Elizabeth and Rachel Massey Award of $5,000 for postgraduate studies in the visual arts or in music. (7) The Margaret McWilliams Pre-Doctoral Fellowship of $11,000 for a female student who has completed at least one full year as a full-time student in doctoral-level studies. (8) The 1989 Ecole Polytechnique Commemorative Award of $7,000 (two awards) for graduate studies in any field at the doctoral level and one award of $5,000 for master's study. The applicant must justify the relevance of her work to women. (9) The Linda Souter Humanities Award of $6,000 for a master's or doctoral student studying in the area of the humanities. (10) The Alice E. Wilson Award of $5,000 for four mature students returning to graduate studies in any field after at least three years. For information, write to Fellowships Program Manager, Canadian Federation of University Women, 331 Cooper Street, Suite 502, Ottawa, ON K2P 0G5, Canada, or see http://www.fcfdu.org/fellowshipsawards/listoffellowshipsandawards.aspx.

Chinese American Librarians Association. (1) The Sheila Suen Lai Scholarship of $500 to a Chinese descendant who has been accepted in an ALA-accredited program. (2) The CALA Scholarship of Library and Information Science of $1,000 to a Chinese descendant who has been accepted in an ALA-accredited program. (3) Lisa Zhao Scholarship to engage in professional conferences and development activities and to support and contribute to CALA. Two awards include a $500 Current Students Award open to full-time students enrolled in an ALA-accredited library school, and a $500 New Librarians Award for a current CALA member who graduated from an ALA-accredited library school within the past five years and has been a member of CALA for at least three years. For information, write to Meng Xiong Liu, Clark Library, San Jose State University, 1 Washington Sq., San José, CA 95192-0028.

Council on Library and Information Resources. Mellon Fellowships for Dissertation Research in Original Sources offers up to 15 awards of $2,000 per month for periods ranging from 9–12 months and an additional $1,000 upon participating in a symposium on research in original sources and submitting a report acceptable to CLIR on the research experience. For information, write to the Council on Library and Information Resources, 2221 South Clark Street, Arlington, VA 22202.

Massachusetts Black Librarians' Network. $500 for students of African descent entering an ALA-accredited master's program in library science. For information, write to Massachusetts Black Librarians' Network, P.O. Box 400504, Cambridge, MA 02140.

Medical Library Association. (1) The Cunningham Memorial International Fellowship for health sciences librarians from countries other than the United States and Canada. (2) A scholarship of up to $5,000 for a person entering an ALA-accredited library program, with no more than one-half of the program yet to be completed. (3) A scholarship of up to $5,000 for a minority student studying health sciences librarianship. (4) A varying number of Research, Development, and Demonstration Project Grants of $100 to $1,000 for U.S. or Canadian citizens, preferably MLA members. (5) The Clarivate Analytics/MLA Doctoral Fellowship of $2,000 for doctoral work in medical librarianship or information science. (6) The Librarians without Borders Ursula Poland International Scholarship of $1,000 to fund an international project by a U.S. or Canadian health sciences librarian. For information, write to MLA Grants and Scholarships Coordinator, awards@mlahq.org, or see http://www.mlanet.org/page/awards.

Mountain Plains Library Association. A varying number of grants of up to $600 for applicants who are members of the association and have been for the preceding two years. For information, write to Judy Zelenski, Executive Secretary, MPLA, 14293 W. Center Drive, Lakewood, SD 80228.

Society of American Archivists. (1) The F. Gerald Ham and Elsie Ham Scholarship of $10,000 for up to two graduate students in archival education at a U.S. university that meets the society's criteria for graduate education. (2) The Mosaic Scholarship of $5,000 for up to two U.S. or Canadian minority students enrolled in a graduate program in archival administration. (3) The Josephine Foreman Scholarship of $10,000 for a U.S. citizen or permanent resident who is a minority graduate student enrolled in a program in archival administration. (4) The Oliver Wendell Holmes Travel Award of $1,000 to enable foreign students involved in archival training in the United States or Canada to attend the SAA Annual Meeting. (5) The Donald Peterson Student Travel Award of up to $1,500 to enable graduate students or recent graduates to attend the meeting. (6) The Harold T. Pinkett Minority Student Awards to enable minority students or graduate students to attend the meeting. (7) The Brenda S. Banks Travel Award to recognize and acknowledge individuals of color who have demonstrated professional archival experience and who manifest an interest in becoming active members of the Society of American Archivists. For details, write to Teresa Brinati, Society of American Archivists, 17 N. State St., Suite 1425, Chicago, IL 60607, or see http://www2.archivists.org/governance/handbook/section12.

Special Libraries Association. Leadership Symposium Scholarship of $605 for travel expenses and registration at symposium (value $395) for members who demonstrate a desire and commitment to advance their leadership skills and abilities within SLA units. For information, write to Special Libraries Association, 7918 Jones Branch Dr., Suite 300, McLean, Virginia 22102.

Library Scholarship and Award Recipients, 2018

Compiled by the staff of *Library and Book Trade Almanac*

Scholarships and awards are listed by organization.

American Association of Law Libraries (AALL)

AALL and Thomson Reuters/George A. Strait Minority Scholarship. *Winners:* Jieun Chang, Kelsey Cox, Melissa Eng, Ashley Matthews, Kerri-Ann Rowe, Karen Sanchez, Nam Jin Yoon.

AALL Educational Scholarships. To assist individuals studying to become law librarians with their educational expenses. *Winners:* (law degree candidates with library degrees) Kristopher Turner, Cara Sitton.

AALL Grants. To enable law librarians to participate in professional educational opportunities at the AALL Annual Meeting or to engage in original research on topics important to law librarianship. *Winners:* Mari Cheney, Jennifer Dixon, Deborah Ginsberg, Arnetta Girardeau, Malikah Hall, Deborah Heller, Alisha Hennen, Dennis Kim-Prieto, Sarah Larsen, Mandy Lee, Louis Rosen, Patricia Sayre-McCoy, Melanie Sims, Michele A. L. Villagran.

AALL Hall of Fame Award. Recognizes significant, substantial, and long-standing contributions to the profession and service to the Association. *Winners:* George S. Grossman, Joan S. Howland, Sally H. Wise.

AALL Marcia J. Koslov Scholarship. To an AALL member to finance conference or seminar attendance. *Winner:* To be announced.

AALL Spectrum Article of the Year Award. *Winner:* Lori B. Andrews for "iSpy: Threats to Individual and Institutional Privacy in the Digital World" (May/June 2017).

Joseph L. Andrews Legal Literature Award. *Winners:* Michael Widener and Mark S. Weiner for "Law's Picture Books: The Yale Law Library Collection."

Emerging Leader Award. To recognize newer members who have made significant contributions to AALL and/or to the profession and have demonstrated the potential for leadership and continuing service. *Winners:* Shamika Dalton, Stephen Parks, Allison C. Reeve.

Excellence in Marketing Award. Recognizes outstanding achievement in marketing activities by an individual, group of individuals, library, chapter, special interest section, consortium, caucus, or any other group affiliated with the Association. *Winners:* (brochure) University of North Texas at Dallas College of Law Library for "UNT Dallas Law Library 2016–2017 Academic Year Snapshot"; (campaign) Riverside County (California) Law Library for "National Pro Bono Week 2017 at the Riverside County Law Library"; (newsletter) Law Librarians' Society of Washington, DC (LLSDC) for "Law Library Lights," Vol. 61, No. 2 (Winter 2018); (public relations toolkit) University of North Texas at Dallas College of Law Library for promotional materials and events.

Marian Gould Gallagher Distinguished Service Award. To recognize extended and sustained service to law librarianship. *Winners:* Mark E. Estes, Claire M. Germain, Margaret K. Maes, Victoria K. Trotta.

Innovations in Technology Award. To recognize an AALL member, special interest section, chapter, or library for innovative use of technology in the development and creation of an application or resource for law librarians or legal professionals. *Winners:* Cornell University Law Library, Legal Information Preservation Alliance, Mid-America Law Library Consortium, NELLCO (co-founders) for "LawArXiv."

Law Library Advocate Award. To an AALL member who has been a strong advocate of private law librarianship through service to the SIS, their organization, or the larger legal community and demonstrates outstanding potential for continued service and leadership within the profession. *Winner:* June Liebert.

Law Library Journal Article of the Year. *Winner:* Susan Nevelow Mart for "The Algorithm as a Human Artifact: Implications for Legal [Re]Search."

Law Library Publications Award. *Winners:* (nonprint division) University of North Texas at Dallas College of Law Library for "UNT Dallas College of Law Blog"; (print division) Mary Bilder, Laurel Davis, and Lily Dyer (co-creators), Boston College Law Library, for "Robert Morris: Lawyer & Activist" and University of Wisconsin Law Library (Madison) for "A Decade of University of Wisconsin Law Library READ Posters."

LexisNexis / John R. Johnson Memorial Scholarships. *Winners:* (law degree candidates with library degrees) Kristopher Turner, Cara Sitton; (library degree candidate with law degree) Traci Emerson; (library degree candidates without law degrees) Jeannine Linnane, Pearl McCrea.

LexisNexis Research Fund Grants. *Winners:* Michael Slinger and Sarah C. Slinger for "The Complete Periodical Literature of Law Librarianship: An Annotated Bibliographic Research Database"; Nick Harrell and Scott Uhl for "Search Methods of Legal Scholars"; and Alissa Raasch and Duane A. Strojny for "Learning Outcomes, Assessment, and Skills Teaching in Librarian-Taught Legal Research Courses."

Minority Leadership Development Award. *Winner:* Zanada Joyner, Digital Services Librarian, North Carolina Central University School of Law Library, Durham, NC.

Robert L. Oakley Advocacy Award. To recognize an AALL member who has been an outstanding advocate and has contributed significantly to the AALL policy agenda at the federal, state, local, or international level. *Winner:* Peggy Roebuck Jarrett, head of Collection Development, University of Washington Gallagher Law Library, Seattle, WA.

Bethany J. Ochal Award for Distinguished Service to the Profession. To honor members who have made significant contributions to law librarianship and are nearing the end of their library careers or have recently retired. Jacquelyn J. Jurkins, Multnomah Law Library, Portland, Oregon; Scott G. Burgh, City of Chicago Department of Law Library; Regina L. Smith, Jenkins Law Library, Philadelphia; Maryruth Storer, Orange County (California) Public Law Library.

Volunteer Service Award. Honors volunteers who have made significant contributions to the work of AALL. *Winner:* Edward T. Hart.

American Library Association (ALA)

ABC-CLIO / Greenwood Award for Best Book in Library Literature ($5,000). See "Literary Prizes, 2018" in Part 5.

ALA Excellence in Library Programming Award ($5,000). For a cultural/thematic library program or program series that engages the community in planning, sponsorship, and/or active participation, addresses an identified community need, and has a measurable impact. *Donor:* ALA Cultural Communities Fund. *Winner:* Joliet (Illinois) Public Library for the annual event "Star Wars Day," the largest Disney-approved Star Wars event of its kind in the world.

ALA Honorary Membership. To recognize outstanding contributions of lasting importance to libraries and librarianship. *Honoree:* Carla Hayden, Librarian of Congress.

ALA / Information Today, Inc. Library of the Future Award ($1,500). For a library, consortium, group of librarians, or support organization for innovative planning for, applications of, or development of patron training programs about information technology in a library setting. *Donors:* Information Today, Inc., and IIDA. *Winner:* North Carolina State University Libraries for the active learning-centered Emerging Digital Information Skills workshops.

Hugh C. Atkinson Memorial Award. For outstanding achievement (including risk taking) by academic librarians that has contributed significantly to improvements in library automation, management, and/or development or research. *Offered by:* ACRL, ALCTS, LITA, and LLAMA. *Winner:* Larry P. Alford, chief librarian, University of Toronto.

Carroll Preston Baber Research Grant (up to $3,000). For innovative research that could lead to an improvement in library services to any specified group(s) of people. *Donor:*

Eric R. Baber. *Winner:* Emily Crist, Sean Leahy, and Alan Carbery for "Ecological Momentary Assessment of Student Research Behaviors."

Beta Phi Mu Award ($1,000). For distinguished service in library education. *Donor:* Beta Phi Mu International Library and Information Science Honorary Society. *Winner:* Clara M. Chu, Mortenson Center for International Library Programs, University of Illinois Library at Urbana-Champaign.

Bogle-Pratt International Library Travel Fund Award ($1,000). To ALA members to attend their first international conference. *Donors:* Bogle Memorial Fund and Pratt Institute School of Information and Library Science. *Winner:* Not awarded in 2018.

W. Y. Boyd Literary Award. See "Literary Prizes, 2018" in Part 5.

David H. Clift Scholarship ($3,000). To worthy U.S. or Canadian citizens enrolled in an ALA-accredited program toward an MLS degree. *Winner:* Esther Jones.

Melvil Dewey Medal. To an individual or group for recent creative professional achievement in library management, training, cataloging and classification, and the tools and techniques of librarianship. *Donor:* OCLC. *Winner:* Carla J. Stoffle, School of Information, University of Arizona.

Tom and Roberta Drewes Scholarship ($3,000). To a library support staff member pursuing a master's degree in an ALA-accredited program. *Donor:* Quality Books. *Winner:* Brian DeFelice.

EBSCO/ALA Conference Sponsorship Award ($1,000). To enable librarians to attend the ALA Annual Conference. *Donor:* EBSCO. *Winners:* Jessica Colbert, Michelle Farias, Twanna Hodge, Brenda Killen, Victoria Ogle, Everett Pine, and Marian Royal.

Equality Award ($1,000). To an individual or group for an outstanding contribution that promotes equality in the library profession. *Donor:* Rowman & Littlefield. *Winner:* Alexandra Rivera, University of Michigan Library.

Elizabeth Futas Catalyst for Change Award ($1,000). A biennial award to recognize a librarian who invests time and talent to make positive change in the profession of librarianship. *Donor:* Elizabeth Futas Memorial Fund. *Winner (2018):* Linda Crowe.

Loleta D. Fyan Public Library Research Grant (up to $5,000). For projects in public library development. *Donor:* Fyan Estate. *Winner:* Sarah Strahl for "Food Literacy—A Critical Need at Hillsboro Public Library."

Gale, a Cengage Company, Learning Financial Development Award ($2,500). To a library organization for a financial development project to secure new funding resources for a public or academic library. *Donor:* Gale, a Cengage Company. *Winner:* Charlotte Mecklenburg Library Foundation (North Carolina) for "I Love Our Library . . . Do You?" campaign to broaden the base of support for ongoing sustainability.

Mary V. Gaver Scholarship ($3,000). To a student pursuing an MLS degree and specializing in youth services. *Winner:* Emily Werner.

Ken Haycock Award for Promoting Librarianship ($1,000). For significant contribution to public recognition and appreciation of librarianship through professional performance, teaching, or writing. *Winner:* Susan Roman, dean emerita, Dominican University (Illinois) Graduate School of Library and Information Science.

Miriam L. Hornback Scholarship ($3,000). To an ALA or library support staff person pursuing a master's degree in library science. *Winner:* Keiko Newsom.

Paul Howard Award for Courage ($1,000). To a librarian, library board, library group, or an individual for exhibiting unusual courage for the benefit of library programs or services. *Donor:* Paul Howard Memorial Fund. Awarded biennially. *Winner (2017):* Kansas City (Missouri) Public Library for its long-standing record of bringing a wide variety of speakers to the Kansas City community, many of which cover controversial and thought-provoking messages.

John Ames Humphry/OCLC/Forest Press Award ($1,000). To one or more individuals for significant contributions to international librarianship. *Donor:* OCLC/Forest Press. *Winner:* Dr. Ismail Abdullahi.

Tony B. Leisner Scholarship ($3,000). To a library support staff member pursuing a master's degree. *Donor:* Tony B. Leisner. *Winner:* Theresa Boulrice.

Joseph W. Lippincott Award ($1,500). For distinguished service to the library profession.

Donor: Joseph W. Lippincott III. *Winner:* Sally Gardner Reed.

Peter Lyman Memorial/Sage Scholarship in New Media. To support a student seeking an MLS degree in an ALA-accredited program and pursing a specialty in new media. *Donor:* Sage Publications. *Winner:* Kimberly Nicholson.

James Madison Award. To recognize efforts to promote government openness. Not awarded in 2018.

Schneider Family Book Awards. See "Literary Prizes, 2018" in Part 5.

Scholastic Library Publishing Award ($1,000). To a librarian whose "unusual contributions to the stimulation and guidance of reading by children and young people exemplifies achievement in the profession." *Sponsor:* Scholastic Library Publishing. *Winner:* Christina Dorr.

Lemony Snicket Prize for Noble Librarians Faced with Adversity ($3,000 plus a $1,000 travel stipend to enable attendance at the ALA Annual Conference). To honor a librarian who has faced adversity with integrity and dignity intact. *Sponsor:* Lemony Snicket (author Daniel Handler). *Winner:* Yvonne Cech, library director, Brookfield (Connecticut) Library, and Diana Haneski, library media specialist, Marjory Stoneman Douglas High School, Parkland, Florida.

Spectrum Doctoral Fellowships. To provide full tuition support and stipends to minority U.S. and Canadian LIS doctoral students. *Donor:* Institute of Museum and Library Services. *Winner:* Not awarded in 2018.

Spectrum Initiative Scholarships ($5,000). To minority students admitted to ALA-accredited library schools. *Donors:* ALA and Institute of Museum and Library Services. *Winners:* Spectrum Initiative Scholarships ($5,000). To minority students admitted to ALA-accredited library schools. *Donors:* ALA and Institute of Museum and Library Services. *Winners:* Stephanie Akau, Alejandra Alfaro, Jazmine Applin, Aicha Azzaoui, Xena Becker, Yvette Cabrera, Amalia Castaneda, Indira Chakrabarti, Amanda Chin, Sarah Frances Corona, Elisa Marie Cruz, Lizette De La Mora, Emma De Vera, Jermaine A. Dennis, Jungwon Christina DeVone, Hadeer Elsbai, Sandy Enriquez, Riko Fluchel, Veronica Franco, Nina Lynn Garcia, Gwendolyn Govia, Andrea Guzmán, Cearra N. Harris, Moonyung Kang-Larsen, Timmia Jana King, Heebe-Tee-Tse Lee, Ashley Nicole Long, Amanda V. Lopez, Katherine Sharon Lopez, Liliana Elizabeth Lopez, Patricia Shimano Lyons, Cristian Alejandro Martinez, Cynthia Medrano Torres, Teresa Helena Moreno, Daisy Crystal Muralles, Gina Nortonsmith, Ifeanyichukwu D. Ogamba, Christopher Ortega, Julie J. Park, Jennifer Patino, Nancy Garcia Ramirez, Jena Razor, Kenneth F. Redd, Maya Reid, Elise Riley, Regen Roy, Karen Sánchez, Natasha LeValley Seymour, Yuri Shimoda, Makoroba Sow, Jasmine Sykes-Kunk, Tina Thomas, Heather Posey VanDyne, Melissa Vang, Yer Vang, Julie C. Varee, Brandi Veal, Mallory Elizabeth Walker, Kelli Akemi Yakabu, Pa Ja Yang, Nam Jin Yoon, Babak Akbari Zarin.

Sullivan Award for Public Library Administrators Supporting Services to Children. To a library supervisor/administrator who has shown exceptional understanding and support of public library services to children. *Donor:* Peggy Sullivan. *Winner:* Sara Jones, director of county library services, Marin County (California) Free Library.

H. W. Wilson Library Staff Development Grant ($3,500). To a library organization for a program to further its staff development goals and objectives. *Donor:* H. W. Wilson Company. *Winner:* Western Maryland Regional Library for "Service, Safety, and Security in Western Maryland."

American Association of School Librarians (AASL)

AASL/ABC-CLIO Leadership Grant (up to $1,750). To AASL affiliates for planning and implementing leadership programs at state, regional, or local levels. *Donor:* ABC-CLIO. *Winner:* Alabama School Library Association.

AASL/Baker & Taylor Distinguished Service Award ($3,000). For outstanding contributions to librarianship and school library development. *Donor:* Baker & Taylor. *Winner:* Not awarded in 2018.

AASL Collaborative School Library Award ($2,500). For expanding the role of the library in elementary and/or secondary school education. *Donor:* Upstart. *Winners:* Janine Johnson, Emily Shiller, Kim Moran, Charlsie Vanderrest, and Kelly Hall of Scotts Ridge Middle School, Ridgefield, Connecticut.

AASL Distinguished School Administrators Award ($2,000). For expanding the role of the library in elementary and/or secondary school education. *Donor:* ProQuest. *Winner:* Michael Daria, superintendent, Tuscaloosa (Alabama) City Schools.

AASL/Frances Henne Award ($1,250). To a school library media specialist with five or fewer years in the profession to attend an AASL regional conference or ALA Annual Conference for the first time. *Donor:* ABC-CLIO. *Winner:* Deb Sondall Saetveit.

AASL Innovative Reading Grant ($2,500). To support the planning and implementation of an innovative program for children that motivates and encourages reading, especially for struggling readers. *Sponsor:* Capstone. *Winner:* Judy Deichman, Nottoway Middle School, Crewe, Virginia.

AASL President's Crystal Apple Award. To an individual, individuals, or group for a significant impact on school libraries and students. *Winner:* Denine Toor.

Intellectual Freedom Award ($2,000 plus $1,000 to the media center of the recipient's choice). To a school library media specialist and AASL member who has upheld the principles of intellectual freedom. *Donor:* ProQuest. *Winner:* Not awarded in 2018.

National School Library Media Program of the Year Award ($10,000). For excellence and innovation in outstanding library media programs. *Donor:* Follett Library Resources. *Winner:* Robert E. Lee High School, Springfield, Virginia.

Association for Library Collections and Technical Services (ALCTS)

ALCTS/LBI George Cunha and Susan Swartzburg Preservation Award ($1,250). To recognize cooperative preservation projects and/or individuals or groups that foster collaboration for preservation goals. *Sponsor:* Library Binding Institute. *Winner:* Sandy Nyberg.

ALCTS Presidential Citations for Outstanding Service. *Winners:* Kathy Glennan, Harriet Wintermute, Susan Wynne.

Hugh C. Atkinson Memorial Award. *See under:* American Library Association.

Ross Atkinson Lifetime Achievement Award ($3,000). To recognize the contribution of an ALCTS member and library leader who has demonstrated exceptional service to ALCTS and its areas of interest. *Donor:* EBSCO. *Winner:* Mary Case.

Paul Banks and Carolyn Harris Preservation Award ($1,500). To recognize the contribution of a professional preservation specialist who has been active in the field of preservation and/or conservation for library and/or archival materials. *Donor:* Preservation Technologies. *Winner:* Nancy Kraft.

Blackwell's Scholarship Award. See Outstanding Publication Award.

ProQuest Coutts Award for Innovation in Electronic Resources Management ($2,000). To recognize significant and innovative contributions to electronic collections management and development practice. *Donor:* Coutts Information Services. *Winner:* Joanna Voss.

First Step Award (Wiley Professional Development Grant) ($1,500). To enable librarians new to the serials field to attend the ALA Annual Conference. *Donor:* John Wiley & Sons. *Winner:* Natascha Owens.

Harrassowitz Award for Leadership in Library Acquisitions ($1,500). For significant contributions by an outstanding leader in the field of library acquisitions. *Donor:* Harrassowitz. *Winner:* Lauren Corbett.

Margaret Mann Citation (includes $2,000 scholarship award to the U.S. or Canadian library school of the winner's choice). To a cataloger or classifier for achievement in the areas of cataloging or classification. *Donor:* Online Computer Library Center (OCLC). *Winner:* Bruce Chr. Johnson.

Outstanding Collaboration Citation. For outstanding collaborative problem-solving efforts in the areas of acquisition, access, management, preservation, or archiving of library materials. *Winner:* Big Ten Academic Alliance Cooperative Cataloging Partnership (BTAA CCP).

Outstanding Publication Award ($250). To honor the year's outstanding monograph, article, or original paper in the field of acquisitions, collection development, and related areas of resource development in libraries. *Winner:* Alana Verminski and Kelly Marie Blanchat for the monograph *Fundamentals of Electronic Resources Management* (Chicago: ALA-Neal Schuman, 2017).

Esther J. Piercy Award ($1,500). To a librarian with no more than ten years' experience for contributions and leadership in the field of library collections and technical services. *Donor:* YBP Library Services. *Winner:* Alison M. Armstrong.

Edward Swanson Memorial Best of *LRTS* Award ($250). To the author(s) of the year's best paper published in the division's official journal. *Winners:* Deborah B. Henry and Tina M. Neville for "Repositories at Master's Institutions: A Census and Analysis."

Ulrich's Serials Librarianship Award ($1,500). For distinguished contributions to serials librarianship. *Sponsor:* ProQuest. *Winner:* Susan Davis.

Association for Library Service to Children (ALSC)

ALSC/Baker & Taylor Summer Reading Program Grant ($3,000). For implementation of an outstanding public library summer reading program for children. *Donor:* Baker & Taylor. *Winner:* St. Lucie County (Florida) Library System.

ALSC/Booklist/YALSA Odyssey Award. To the producer of the best audiobook for children and/or young adults available in English in the United States. See Odyssey Award in "Literary Prizes, 2018" in Part 5.

ALSC/Candlewick Press "Light the Way: Library Outreach to the Underserved" Grant ($3,000). To a library conducting exemplary outreach to underserved populations. *Donor:* Candlewick Press. *Winner:* Not awarded in 2018.

May Hill Arbuthnot Honor Lectureship. To an author, critic, librarian, historian, or teacher of children's literature who prepares a paper considered to be a significant contribution to the field of children's literature. *Winner:* Naomi Shihab Nye, "Refreshments Will Be Served: Our Lives of Reading and Writing."

Mildred L. Batchelder Award. See "Literary Prizes, 2018" in Part 5.

Louise Seaman Bechtel Fellowship ($4,000). For librarians with 12 or more years of professional-level work in children's library collections, to read and study at Baldwin Library, University of Florida. *Donor:* Bechtel Fund. *Winners:* Anne Mlod, JoAnna Schofield, and Lisa Von Drasek.

Pura Belpré Award. See "Literary Prizes, 2018" in Part 5.

Bookapalooza Program Awards. To provide three libraries with a collection of materials that will help transform their collection. *Winners:* Chilton/Clanton Public Library, Clanton, Alabama; Mandel Public Library, West Palm Beach, Florida; and Daviess County Library, Gallatin, Missouri.

Bound to Stay Bound Books Scholarships ($7,000). For men and women who intend to pursue an MLS or other advanced degree and who plan to work in the area of library service to children. *Donor:* Bound to Stay Bound Books. *Winners:* Emily Zorea, Lisa Gonzalez, Chelsea Tarwater, and Stephanie Luyt.

Randolph Caldecott Medal. See "Literary Prizes, 2018" in Part 5.

Andrew Carnegie Medal for Excellence in Children's Video. To the U.S. producer of the most distinguished video for children in the previous year. *Sponsor:* Carnegie Corporation of New York. *Winner:* Award suspended.

Carnegie-Whitney Awards (up to $5,000). For the preparation of print or electronic reading lists, indexes, or other guides to library resources that promote reading or the use of library resources at any type of library. *Donors:* James Lyman Whitney and Andrew Carnegie Funds. *Winners:* Heidi Blackburn, "Women in STEM in Higher Education Bibliography"; Nicole Dalmer and Lucia Cedeira for "SEEniors: Visual Representations of Older Age in Illustrated Materials"; Kelly Driftmeyer for "Positive Reinforcement Training: An Annotated Bibliography of Resources for Teachers, Trainers, and Learners"; Natalie Dwigans for "Let Our

Voices Be Heard"; Julie Frye and Arnell Hammond for "Inclusion Solution: A Picture Book Bibliography on Disabilities that Represent Children and Families of Color"; Sara Gonzalez for "Building Makers: An Annotated Bibliography of Maker Resources for Librarians, Schools, and Museums"; Hayley Johnson and Sarah Simms for "Through an Extended Lens: Louisiana, Internment, and the Geography of Chance (A Continuation)"; Janice Krueger and Marilyn Harhai for "Annotated Bibliography in Celebration of the Centennial Anniversaries of Passage and Ratification of the Nineteen Amendment"; Michael Mungin for "The Queer People of Color (QPOC) Film Canon"; Matthew Noe and Alice Jaggers for "Essential Graphic Medicine: An Annotated Bibliography"; Jené Watson for "Lighting Their Paths: 500 Titles for PreK through Middle School Boys"; Lacy Wolfe for "Reading the World: Women Authors in English Translation."

Century Scholarship ($2,500). For a library school student or students with disabilities admitted to an ALA-accredited library school. *Winner:* Reagan Callahan.

Distinguished Service Award ($1,000). To recognize significant contributions to, and an impact on, library services to children and/or ALSC. *Winner:* Steven Herb.

Theodor Seuss Geisel Award. See "Literary Prizes, 2018" in Part 5.

Maureen Hayes Author/Illustrator Visit Award (up to $4,000). For an honorarium and travel expenses to make possible a library talk to children by a nationally known author/illustrator. *Sponsor:* Simon & Schuster Children's Publishing. *Winner:* South Carolina State Library, Columbia.

Frederic G. Melcher Scholarships ($6,000). To two students entering the field of library service to children for graduate work in an ALA-accredited program. *Winner:* Not awarded in 2018.

John Newbery Medal. See "Literary Prizes, 2018" in Part 5.

Penguin Random House Young Readers Group Awards ($600). To children's librarians in school or public libraries with ten or fewer years of experience to attend the ALA Annual Conference. *Donor:* Penguin Young Readers Group and Random House Children's Books. *Winners:* Amanda Chuong, Princeton (New Jersey) Public Library; Patricia Moran, Multnomah (Oregon) County Library; Julie Phoenix, St. Louis (Missouri) County Library; Sarah Walker, Ferguson Library, Stamford, Connecticut.

Robert F. Sibert Medal. See "Literary Prizes, 2018" in Part 5.

Laura Ingalls Wilder Medal. See "Literary Prizes, 2018" in Part 5.

Association of College and Research Libraries (ACRL)

ACRL Academic or Research Librarian of the Year Award ($5,000). For outstanding contribution to academic and research librarianship and library development. *Donor:* YBP Library Services. *Winner:* David W. Lewis, Indiana University–Purdue University Indianapolis University Library.

ACRL/CJCLS Library Resources Leadership Award ($5,000). *Winner:* Not awarded in 2018.

ACRL/CLS Innovation in College Librarianship Award ($3,000). To academic librarians who show a capacity for innovation in the areas of programs, services, and operations; or creating innovations for library colleagues that facilitate their ability to better serve the library's community. *Winners:* Teresa D. Williams, Butler University, Indianapolis, Indiana.

ACRL/DLS Routledge Distance Learning Librarian Conference Sponsorship Award ($1,200). To an ACRL member working in distance-learning librarianship in higher education. *Sponsor:* Routledge/Taylor & Francis. *Winner:* Marcia E. Rapchak, Duquesne University, Pittsburgh, Pennsylvania.

ACRL/EBSS Distinguished Education and Behavioral Sciences Librarian Award. To an academic librarian who has made an outstanding contribution as an education and/or behavioral sciences librarian through accomplishments and service to the profession. *Donor:* John Wiley & Sons. *Winner:* Scott Collard, New York University, New York, New York.

ACRL / STS Oberly Award for Bibliography in the Agricultural or Natural Sciences. Awarded biennially for the best English-language bibliography in the field of agriculture or a related science in the preceding two-year period. *Donor:* Eunice Rockwood Oberly. *Winners (2017):* Frank Scholze and Michael Witt for "re3data.org," a registry of research data repositories.

ACRL/WGSS Award for Career Achievement in Women and Gender Studies Librarianship. *Winner:* Diedre Conkling, Lincoln County (Oregon) Library District.

ACRL/WGSS Award for Significant Achievement in Women and Gender Studies Librarianship. *Winners:* Shirley Lew, Vancouver (British Columbia) Community College, and Baharak Yousefi, Simon Fraser University, Burnaby, British Columbia.

Hugh C. Atkinson Memorial Award. *See under:* American Library Association.

Miriam Dudley Instruction Librarian Award. For a contribution to the advancement of bibliographic instruction in a college or research institution. *Winner:* Sharon Mader, University of New Orleans.

ESS De Gruyter European Librarianship Study Grant (formerly the WESS-SEES De Gruyter European Librarianship Study Grant) (€2,500). Supports research pertaining to European studies, librarianship, or the book trade. *Sponsor:* Walter de Gruyter Foundation for Scholarship and Research. *Winner:* Anna Dysert, McGill University Montreal.

Excellence in Academic Libraries Awards ($3,000). To recognize outstanding college and university libraries. *Donor:* YBP Library Services. *Winners:* (university) Virginia Commonwealth University; (college) SUNY Geneseo; (community college) Naugatuck Valley Community College.

Instruction Section Innovation Award ($3,000). To librarians or project teams in recognition of a project that demonstrates creative, innovative, or unique approaches to information literacy instruction or programming. *Donor:* ProQuest. *Winners:* Trent Brager, University of St. Thomas, Amy Mars, St. Catherine University, and Kim Pittman, University of Minnesota–Duluth, for "23 Framework Things," a free online professional development opportunity that helps librarians engage at their own pace through readings, activities, reflection, and discussion.

Marta Lange / Sage-CQ Press Award. To recognize an academic or law librarian for contributions to bibliography and information service in law or political science. *Donor:* Sage-CQ Press. *Winner:* Allan Scherlen, Appalachian State University, Boone, North Carolina.

Katharine Kyes Leab and Daniel J. Leab American Book Prices Current Exhibition Catalog Awards (citations). For the best catalogs published by American or Canadian institutions in conjunction with exhibitions of books and/or manuscripts. *Sponsor:* Leab Endowment. *Winners:* (electronic exhibitions) University of Alberta's Bruce Peel Special Collections Library; (expensive) Yale University's Beinecke Rare Book and Manuscript Library; (moderately expensive) University of Toronto's Thomas Fisher Rare Book Library; (inexpensive) Georgetown University Library; (brochures) University of Illinois at Urbana-Champaign Library.

Ilene F. Rockman Instruction Publication of the Year Award ($3,000). To recognize an outstanding publication relating to instruction in a library environment. *Sponsor:* Emerald Group. *Winner:* Jennifer E. Nutefall, Santa Clara (California) University Library, for *Service Learning, Information Literacy, and Libraries*.

WESS-SEES De Gruyter European Librarianship Study Grant. See ESS De Gruyter European Librarianship Study Grant.

Association of Library Trustees, Advocates, Friends, and Foundations (ALTAFF). See United for Libraries.

Association of Specialized and Cooperative Library Agencies (ASCLA)

ASCLA Cathleen Bourdon Service Award. To recognize an ASCLA personal member for outstanding service and leadership to the division. *Winner:* Veronda J. Pitchford, Reaching Across Illinois Library System, Burr Ridge, Illinois.

ASCLA Exceptional Service Award. To recognize exceptional service to patients, the homebound, inmates, and to medical, nursing, and other professional staff in hospitals. *Winner:* St. Charles (Minnesota) Public Library, Outreach Services.

ASCLA Leadership and Professional Achievement Award. To recognize leadership and achievement in the areas of consulting, multitype library cooperation, statewide service and programs, and state library development. *Winner:* Greg Pronevitz, executive director, Massachusetts Library System.

Francis Joseph Campbell Award. For a contribution of recognized importance to library service for the blind and physically handicapped. *Winner:* Patricia Herndon, director, Georgia Libraries for Accessible Statewide Services (GLASS), Georgia Public Library Service (GPLS).

KLAS/National Organization on Disability Award for Library Service to People with Disabilities ($1,000). To a library organization to recognize an innovative project to benefit people with disabilities. *Donor:* Keystone Systems. *Winner:* Gwinnett County (Georgia) Public Library for "Removing Barriers" project.

Black Caucus of the American Library Association (BCALA)

BCALA Book Literary Award. *Winners:* (first novelist) Margaret Wilkerson Sexton for *A Kind of Freedm: A Novel* (Counterpoint Press); (poetry) Patricia Smith for *Incendiary Art: Poems* (Northwestern University Press); (fiction) Roxane Gay for *Difficult Women* (Grove/Atlantic); (nonfiction) Lawrence P. Jackson for *Chester B. Himes: A Biography* (W.W. Norton & Co.); (Outstanding Contribution to Publishing Citation) Henry Louis Gates, Jr. for *100 Amazing Facts about the Negro* (Knopf Doubleday).

BCALA E-Book Literary Award. *Winners:* (fiction) Erica Marisa Sandifer for *Sunshine in the Delta* (Palmetto Publishing Group); (poetry) Adisa Ajamu for *The New Lynchings* (CreateSpace Independent Publishing Platform).

BCALA Trailblazer's Award. Presented once every five years in recognition of outstanding and unique contributions to librarianship. *Winners* (2015): Thomas Alford, Mary Biblo.

DEMCO/BCALA Excellence in Librarianship Award. To a librarian who has made significant contributions to promoting the status of African Americans in the library profession. *Winner:* Fayrene Muhammad.

E. J. Josey Scholarship Award. *Winners:* Anicka Austin and Jabez Patterson.

Ethnic and Multicultural Information and Exchange Round Table (EMIERT)

David Cohen Multicultural Award ($300). To recognize articles of significant research and publication that increase understanding and promote multiculturalism in North American libraries. *Donor:* Routledge. *Winners:* Keren Dali and Nadia Caidi for "Diversity by Design" (*Library Quarterly*).

EMIERT Distinguished Librarian Award. Given biennially to recognize significant accomplishments in library services that are national or international in scope and that include improving, spreading, and promoting multicultural librarianship. *Winner:* Not awarded in 2018.

Coretta Scott King Awards. See "Literary Prizes, 2018" in Part 5.

Exhibits Round Table (ERT)

Christopher J. Hoy/ERT Scholarship ($5,000). To an individual or individuals who will work toward an MLS degree in an ALA-accredited program. *Donor:* Family of Christopher Hoy. *Winner:* Samantha Hyde.

Federal and Armed Forces Librarians Round Table (FAFLRT)

Achievement Award. For achievement in the promotion of library and information service and the information profession in the federal government community. *Winner:* Jane Cross, U.S. Marine Band Library and Archives.

Adelaide del Frate Conference Sponsorship Award ($1,000). To encourage library school students to become familiar with federal librarianship and ultimately seek work in federal libraries; for attendance at the ALA Annual Conference and activities of FAFLRT. *Winner:* Stefanie Falco.

Distinguished Service Award (citation). To honor a FAFLRT member for outstanding and sustained contributions to the association and to federal librarianship. *Winner:* Janice Young, U.S. Department of Energy, Office of Scientific and Technical Information.

Rising Stars Initiative. To a FAFLRT member new to the profession in a federal or armed forces library or government information management setting. *Winner:* Not awarded in 2018.

Freedom to Read Foundation

Freedom to Read Foundation Gordon M. Conable Conference Scholarship. To enable a library school student or new professional to attend the ALA Annual Conference. *Winner:* Dovi Mae Patino.

Freedom to Read Foundation Roll of Honor (citation): To recognize individuals who have contributed substantially to the foundation. *Winners:* Doug Archer and Barbara Jones.

Judith Krug Fund Banned Books Week Event Grants ($1,000 to $2,500). To support activities that raise awareness of intellectual freedom and censorship issues during the annual Banned Books Week celebration. *Winners:* Handley Regional Library, Winchester, Virginia; Independence (Kansas) Public Library; James F. Byrnes High School, Duncan, South Carolina; Moreno Valley (California) High School Book Club; Suffolk (Virginia) Public Library.

Gay, Lesbian, Bisexual, and Transgender Round Table (GLBTRT)

Larry Romans Mentorship Award ($1,000). To recognize librarians who, through their sustained mentoring efforts, have made a difference in our profession. *Winner:* Courtney Young.

Stonewall Book Awards. See "Literary Prizes, 2018" in Part 5.

Government Documents Round Table (GODORT)

James Bennett Childs Award. To a librarian or other individual for distinguished lifetime contributions to documents librarianship. *Winner:* Karen M. Russ, University of Arkansas Little Rock.

GODORT-Sponsored ALA Emerging Leader Award. A leadership development program that enables newer library workers from across the country to participate in problem-solving work groups, network with peers, gain an inside look into ALA structure, and have an opportunity to serve the profession in a leadership capacity. *Winner:* Kenya S. Flash.

Bernadine Abbott Hoduski Founders Award. To recognize documents librarians who may not be known at the national level but who have made significant contributions to the field of local, state, federal, or international documents. *Winner:* Marilyn Von Seggern, Washington State University, Pullman.

Margaret T. Lane/Virginia F. Saunders Memorial Research Award. *Winner:* Robert Lopresti, Western Washington University Libraries, for *When Women Didn't Count: The Chronic Mismeasure and Marginalization of American Women in Federal Statistics* (Praeger).

NewsBank/Readex/GODORT/ALA Catharine J. Reynolds Research Grant. To documents librarians for travel and/or study in the field of documents librarianship or an area of study benefiting their performance. *Donor:* NewsBank and Readex Corporation. *Winners:* Hayley Johnson and Sarah Simms, Louisiana State University, for their interactive online research guide about Camp Livingston, Louisiana, and its role in Japanese-American internment.

ProQuest/GODORT/ALA Documents to the People Award. To an individual, library, organization, or noncommercial group that most effectively encourages or enhances the use of government documents in library services. *Winner:* Rosemary L. Meszaros, Western Kentucky University.

Larry Romans Mentorship Award ($1,000). To recognize librarians who, through their sustained mentoring efforts, have made a difference in our profession. *Winner:* Courtney Young.

W. David Rozkuszka Scholarship ($3,000). To provide financial assistance to individuals currently working with government documents in a library while completing a master's program in library science. *Winner:* Susie O'Connor.

Intellectual Freedom Round Table (IFRT)

Gerald Hodges Intellectual Freedom Chapter Relations Award. *Winner:* Nebraska Library Association Intellectual Freedom Roundtable.

John Phillip Immroth Memorial Award for Intellectual Freedom ($500). For notable contribution to intellectual freedom fueled by personal courage. *Winner:* Lindsey Whittington.

Eli M. Oboler Memorial Award. See "Literary Prizes, 2018" in Part 5.

Library and Information Technology Association (LITA)

Hugh C. Atkinson Memorial Award. *See under:* American Library Association.

Ex Libris Student Writing Award ($1,000 and publication in *Information Technology and Libraries*). For the best unpublished manuscript on a topic in the area of libraries and information technology written by a student or students enrolled in an ALA-accredited library and information studies graduate program. *Donor:* Ex Libris. *Winner:* Colby Lewis for "The Open Access Citation Advantage: Does It Exist and What Does It Mean for Libraries?"

LITA/Christian Larew Memorial Scholarship in Library and Information Technology ($3,000). To encourage the entry of qualified persons into the library and information technology field. *Sponsor:* Informata.com. *Winner:* Simone Wagner, Simmons School of Library and Information Science.

LITA/Library Hi Tech Award for Outstanding Communication for Continuing Education in Library and Information Science. To an individual or institution for outstanding communication in library and information technology. *Donor:* Emerald Group. *Winner:* Heather Moulaison Sandy, University of Missouri iSchool.

LITA/OCLC Frederick G. Kilgour Award for Research in Library and Information Technology ($2,000 and expense-paid attendance at the ALA Annual Conference). To bring attention to research relevant to the development of information technologies. *Donor:* OCLC. *Winner:* Richard P. Smiraglia, University of Wisconsin–Milwaukee iSchool.

Library History Round Table (LHRT)

Phyllis Dain Library History Dissertation Award. Given biennially to the author of a dissertation treating the history of books, libraries, librarianship, or information science. *Winner (2017):* Margaret Yu-Yin Hung for "English Public Libraries, 1919–1975: Vocation and Popularisation."

Donald G. Davis Article Award (certificate). Awarded biennially for the best article written in English in the field of U.S. and Canadian library history. *Winner* (2018): Jennifer Burek Pierce, "The Reign of Children: The Role of Games and Toys in American Public Libraries, 1877–1925" (*Information and Culture*). Steven Witt, "Agents of Change: The Rise of International Librarianship and the Age of Globalization" *(Library Trends)*.

Eliza Atkins Gleason Book Award. Presented every third year to the author of a book in English in the field of library history. *Winner* (2016): Dr. Cheryl Knott for *Not Free, Not for All: Public Libraries in the Age of Jim Crow* (University of Massachusetts Press).

Justin Winsor Library History Essay Award ($500). To the author of an outstanding essay embodying original historical research on a significant subject of library history. *Winner (2017):* "The 'Spirit of the Fatherland': German-American Culture and Community in the Library and Archive of the German Society of Pennsylvania, ca. 1887–1920."

Library Leadership and Management Association (LLAMA)

Hugh C. Atkinson Memorial Award. *See under:* American Library Association.

John Cotton Dana Library Public Relations Awards ($10,000). To libraries or library organizations of all types for public relations programs or special projects ended during the preceding year. *Donors:* H. W. Wilson Foundation and EBSCO. *Winners:* Milwaukee (Wisconsin) Public Library for "Library Loud Days" that increased library card registrations by 60 percent, increased circulation by 20 percent, and boosted website unique visitors by 40 percent; Rochester (Minnesota) Public Library for "Summer Playlist," a new summer reading program to encourage more Rochester-area residents to read, explore, create, and connect; San José (California) Public Library for their "2-Step Fine Forgiveness Program," a month-long return amnesty program that resulted in the return of nearly half of all the overdue materials and restored account access to thousands of patrons; DC Public Library for "GoDigital," a campaign to develop an easy-to-use portal where all of the library's digital services and products would be made available; California State University San Marcos Library; for "Brewchive," a special collection to share the story of the craft brewing industry and history in San Diego and support the development of a certificate program in the business of brewery engineering; Arlington Heights (Illinois) Memorial Library for "#beinthecircle," a communications campaign combining traditional marketing with a heightened emphasis on social media and the use of "influencer" marketing to promote the program; Kitsap (Washington) Regional Library for their approach to community engagement in a referendum to increase library funding that went from rejection in 2007 and 2010 to a 65 percent approval in 2016; INFOhio Digital Library for efforts to educate Ohio legislators in an attempt to reinstate funding through the creation of advocacy groups and a detailed communications schedule of weekly updates, messages, legislative visits, and phone calls that resulted in an increase of funding to previous levels.

Library Research Round Table (LRRT)

Jesse H. Shera Award for Excellence in Published Research. For a research article on library and information studies published in English during the calendar year. *Winners:* Not awarded in 2018.

Jesse H. Shera Award for Support of Dissertation Research. To recognize and support dissertation research employing exemplary research design and methods. *Winner:* Not awarded in 2018.

Map and Geospatial Information Round Table (MAGIRT)

MAGIRT Honors Award. To recognize outstanding achievement and major contributions to map and geospatial librarianship. *Winner:* Paige Andrew.

New Members Round Table (NMRT)

NMRT ALA Student Chapter of the Year Award. To an ALA student chapter for outstanding contributions to the association. *Winner:* University of North Carolina at Greensboro.

NMRT Annual Conference Professional Development Attendance Award (formerly the Marshall Cavendish Award) (tickets to the ALA Annual Conference event of the winners' choice). *Winners:* Ann Smith Rushing, University of Southern Mississippi, and Beth Caruso, Atkins Library, University of North Carolina.

NMRT Professional Development Grant. To new NMRT members to encourage professional development and participation in national ALA and NMRT activities. *Winner:* Sarah Gilchrist.

Shirley Olofson Memorial Award ($1,000). To an individual to help defray costs of attending the ALA Annual Conference. *Winner:* Sarah Chestnut, University of North Texas.

Office for Diversity

Achievement in Library Diversity Research Honor. To an ALA member who has made significant contributions to diversity research in the profession. *Winner:* Raymond Pun.

Diversity Research Grants ($2,500). To the authors of research proposals that address critical gaps in the knowledge of diversity issues within library and information science. *Winners:* Stephanie Toliver and Mariah Parker, University of Georgia, for "Black Girls Dreaming: Black Girls Analyzing and Evaluating Speculative Fiction by Black Authors," an examination of the current offerings of speculative fiction for black girls and guidelines for literacy stakeholders and parents seeking to select books that explore creativity; Anthony Bernier, San José State University, for "Searching for First Generation LIS Student Success," an analysis of the experience of first generation masters students enrolled at San José State University's School of Information that will address the gap in various literatures that have omitted the first-generation graduate student experience, both on-campus and virtually; Julie Marie Frye, Indiana University Education Library, and Maria Hasler-Barker, Sam Houston State University, for "Silence or Share: How Bilingual Librarians Use Language to Support or Resist Hegemony/Callar o compartir: cómo los bibliotecarios bilingües emplean el idioma para apoyar o resistir la hegemonía" that investigates the unconscious act of gate-keeping that may happen when librarians are interacting with nonnative English speakers.

Office for Information Technology Policy

L. Ray Patterson Copyright Award. To recognize an individual who supports the constitutional purpose of U.S. copyright law, fair use, and the public domain. *Sponsor:* Freedom to Read Foundation. *Winner:* Not awarded in 2018.

Office for Literacy and Outreach Services (OLOS)

Jean E. Coleman Library Outreach Lecture. *Sponsor:* OLOS Advisory Committee. *Lecturer:* Not awarded in 2018.

Public Library Association (PLA)

Baker & Taylor Entertainment Audio Music/Video Product Grant ($2,500 worth of audio music or video products). To help a public library to build or expand a collection of either or both formats. *Donor:* Baker & Taylor. *Winner:* Autauga Prettville (Alabama) Public Library.

Gordon M. Conable Award ($1,500). To a public library staff member, library trustee, or public library for demonstrating a commitment to intellectual freedom and the Library Bill of Rights. *Sponsor:* LSSI. *Winner:* Wanda Mae Huffaker, Utah Library Association's Intellectual Freedom Committee.

Demco New Leaders Travel Grants (up to $1,500). To PLA members who have not attended a major PLA continuing education event in the past five years. *Winners:* Clare Broyles, cataloging and technical services librarian, Radford (Virginia) Public Library, and Christie Reale, Kannapolis branch manager, Cabarrus County (North Carolina) Public Library.

EBSCO Excellence in Rural Library Service Award ($1,000). Honors a library serving a population of 10,000 or fewer that demonstrates excellence of service to its community as exemplified by an overall service program or a special program of significant accomplishment. *Donor:* EBSCO. *Winner:* Scottsboro (Alabama) Public Library.

Helping Communities Come Together Award recognizes a public library's ability to identify community needs specifically in times of crisis and division, and respond in creative and exemplary ways. *Donor:* The Singer Group. *Winner:* Peoria (Illinois) Public Library.

John Iliff Award ($1,000). To a library worker, librarian, or library for the use of technology and innovative thinking as a tool to improve services to public library users. *Sponsor:* Innovative. *Winner:* District of Columbia Public Library.

Allie Beth Martin Award ($3,000). To honor a public librarian who has demonstrated extraordinary range and depth of knowledge about books or other library materials and has distinguished ability to share that knowledge. *Donor:* Baker & Taylor. *Winner:* Hana Zittel, Denver (Colorado) Public Library.

Charlie Robinson Award ($1,000). To honor a public library director who, over a period of seven years, has been a risk taker, an innovator, and/or a change agent in a public library. *Donor:* Baker & Taylor. *Winner:* Mary Anne Hodel, Orange County (Florida) Library System.

Romance Writers of America Library Grant ($4,500). To a library to build or expand a fiction collection and/or host romance fiction programming. *Donor:* Romance Writers of America. *Winner:* Wallkill (New York) Public Library.

Upstart Innovation Award ($2,000). To recognize a public library's innovative achievement in planning and implementing a creative community service program. *Donor:* Upstart/Demco. *Winner:* Orange County (Florida) Library System.

Public Programs Office

Sara Jaffarian School Library Program Award for Exemplary Humanities Programming ($4,000). To honor a K–8 school library that has conducted an outstanding humanities program or series. *Donors:* Sara Jaffarian and ALA Cultural Communities Fund. *Winner:* Danville (Arkansas) Public Schools.

Reference and User Services Association (RUSA)

Award for Excellence in Reference and Adult Library Services ($1,500). To recognize a library or library system for developing an imaginative and unique library resource to meet patrons' reference needs. *Donor:* Reference USA. *Winner:* Toledo Lucas County (Ohio) Public Library for the "Spending Smarter" page, a one-stop guide for personal finance, investment, and referral information.

BRASS Academic Business Librarianship Travel Award ($1,250). To recognize a librarian new to the field of academic business librarianship and support his or her attendance at the ALA Annual Conference. *Donor:* Business Expert Press. *Winner:* Alison Kalinowsky, University of Pittsburgh.

BRASS Excellence in Business Librarianship Award ($4,000). For distinguished activities in the field of business librarianship *Donor:* Mergent. *Winner:* Chris LeBeau, University of Missouri–Kansas City.

BRASS Research Grant Awards ($2,500). To an ALA member seeking support to conduct research in business librarianship. *Donor:* Emerald Publishing. *Winner:* Stephanie Pitts-Noggle, Champaign (Illinois) Public Library.

BRASS Public Librarian Support Award ($1,250). To support attendance at the ALA Annual Conference of a public librarian who has performed outstanding business reference service. *Donor:* Morningstar. *Winner:* Amilcar Perez, Forest Park (Illinois) Public Library.

BRASS Student Travel Award ($1,250). To enable a student enrolled in an ALA-accredited master's program to attend the ALA Annual Conference. *Donor:* Simply Analytics. *Winner:* Rachel Holder, Indiana University.

Sophie Brody Medal. See "Literary Prizes, 2018" in Part 5.

CODES Zora Neale Hurston Award. To recognize the efforts of RUSA members in promoting African American literature. *Donor:* Harper Collins. *Winner:* Not awarded in 2018.

CODES Louis Shores Award (citation). To an individual, team, or organization to recognize excellence in reviewing of books and other materials for libraries. *Winner:* Ron Charles, editor of the "Book World" column, *Washington Post.*

ETS Achievement Award. To recognize excellence in service to RUSA's Emerging Technologies Section (ETS). *Winner:* Donna Brearcliff, Humanities and Social Sciences Section, Researcher and Reference Services Division, Library of Congress.

HS Genealogy/History Achievement Award ($1,500). To encourage and commend professional achievement in historical reference and research librarianship. *Donor:* ProQuest. *Winner:* Dr. Plummer Alston Jones, Jr., professor of library science, East Carolina University, Greenville.

HS Online History Award. A biennial award to recognize a noteworthy online historical collection, an online tool tailored for the purpose of finding historical materials, or an online teaching aid stimulating creative historical scholarship. *Donor:* ABC-CLIO. *Winner* (2018): Not awarded in 2018.

Learning History Research and Innovation Award ($2,500). To an MLS-degreed librarian from an ALA-accredited school to facilitate and further research relating to history and history librarianship. *Donor:* Gale Cengage. *Winner:* Jennifer McElroy, Minnesota Historical Society.

Margaret E. Monroe Library Adult Services Award ($1,250). To a librarian for his or her impact on library service to adults. *Donor:* NoveList. *Winner:* Kaite Stover, director of readers' services, Kansas City (Kansas) Public Library.

Isadore Gilbert Mudge Award ($5,000). For distinguished contributions to reference librarianship. *Donor:* Credo Reference. *Winners:* Eleanor Mitchell, director of library services, Dickinson College, Carlisle, Pennsylvania, and Sarah B. Watstein, dean, Lemieux Library and McGoldrick Learning Commons, Seattle, University.

RSS Service Achievement Award. To an RSS member who has made either a sustained contribution toward attaining the goals of the Reference Services Section or a single significant contribution that has resulted in a positive impact upon the work of the section. *Winner:* Not awarded in 2018.

John Sessions Memorial Award (plaque). To a library or library system in recognition of work with the labor community. *Donor:* Department for Professional Employees, AFL/CIO. *Winner:* State Historical Society of Iowa.

STARS Mentoring Award ($1,250). To a library practitioner new to the field of interlibrary loan, resource sharing, or electronic reserves, to attend the ALA Annual Conference. *Donor:* Atlas Systems. *Winner:* Guerda Baucicaut, InterLibrary Loan & Reserves Specialist, Borough of Manhattan Community College.

STARS Virginia Boucher Distinguished ILL Librarian Award ($2,000). To a librarian for outstanding professional achievement, leadership, and contributions to interlibrary loan and document delivery. *Winner:* Kurt Munson, Northwestern University Library.

United for Libraries (formerly ALTAFF, Association of Library Trustees, Advocates, Friends, and Foundations)

Trustee Citation. To recognize public library trustees for individual service to library development on the local, state, regional, or national level. *Winner:* Penny Weller and Craig Wilson.

United for Libraries/Baker & Taylor Awards. To recognize library friends groups for outstanding efforts to support their libraries. *Donor:* Baker & Taylor. *Winner:* Friends of the Revenna (Nebraska) Library and Friends of the Shelby Area (Michigan) District Library.

United for Libraries/Gale Outstanding Trustee Conference Grant Award ($850). *Donor:* Gale Cengage Learning. *Winner:* Not awarded in 2018.

United for Libraries Major Benefactors Citation. To individuals, families, or corporate bodies that have made major benefactions to public libraries. *Winner:* Not awarded in 2018.

United for Libraries Public Service Award. To a legislator who has been especially supportive of libraries. *Winner:* Not awarded in 2018.

United for Libraries/SAGE Academic Friend Conference Grant ($850 plus free conference registration). Enables one member of a Friends of the Library group at a college/university library to attend the ALA Annual Conference. *Donor:* SAGE Publishing. *Winner:* Dyanna Black, University of Missouri–Kansas City Friends of the Library.

United for Libraries/Thrift Books Friends Grant ($850 plus free conference registration). Enables one member of a Friends of the Library group at a public library to attend the ALA Annual Conference. *Donor:* Thrift Books. *Winner:* Jennifer Kaminski, Friends of the Daviess County (Kentucky) Public Library.

Young Adult Library Services Association (YALSA)

Baker & Taylor/YALSA Collection Development Grants ($1,000). To YALSA members who represent a public library and work directly with young adults, for collection development materials for young adults. *Donor:* Book Wholesalers, Inc. *Winners:* Savannah Kitchens, Chilton/Clanton (Alabama) Public Library, and Sarah Townsend, Suffolk (Virginia) Public Library.

Baker & Taylor/YALSA Conference Scholarship Grants ($1,000). To young adult librarians in public or school libraries to attend the ALA Annual Conference for the first time. *Donor:* Baker & Taylor. *Winners:* Amy Fowler, Nevins Memorial Library, Methuen, Massachusetts, and Cherity Penington, Shawnee (Oklahoma) Middle School.

Dorothy Broderick Student Scholarship ($1,000). To enable a graduate student to attend the ALA Conference for the first time. *Sponsor:* YALSA Leadership Endowment. *Winner:* Not awarded in 2018.

Margaret A. Edwards Award. See "Literary Prizes, 2018" in Part 5.

Great Books Giveaway (books, videos, CDs, and audiocassettes valued at a total of $40,000). *Winners:* Purvis (Mississippi) High School, Suffolk (Virginia) Public Library System, and Oak Park (Michigan) Public Library.

Frances Henne/YALSA/VOYA Research Grant ($1,000). To provide seed money to an individual, institution, or group for a project to encourage research on library service to young adults. *Donor:* Greenwood Publishing Group. *Winner:* Amelia Anderson and Abigail Phillips.

William C. Morris YA Debut Award. See "Literary Prizes, 2018" in Part 5.

Michael L. Printz Award. See "Literary Prizes, 2018" in Part 5.

YALSA/MAE Award ($500 for the recipient plus $500 for his or her library). For an exemplary young adult reading or literature program. *Sponsor:* Margaret A. Edwards Trust. *Winner:* Morgan Brickey, Arlington (Texas) Public Library.

YALSA Service to Young Adults Outstanding Achievement Award ($2,000). Biennial award to a YALSA member who has demonstrated unique and sustained devotion to young adult services. *Winner* (2018): Mary K. Chelton, Graduate School of Library and Information Studies, Queens College, City University of New York.

Association for Information Science and Technology (ASIS&T)

ASIS&T Award of Merit. For an outstanding contribution to the field of information science. *Winner:* Toni Carbo.

ASIS&T Best Information Science Books. *Winner:* Michael Buckland for *Information and Society.*

ASIS&T New Leaders Award. To recruit, engage, and retain new ASIS&T members and to identify potential for new leadership in the society. *Winners:* Aaron Bowen-Ziechek, Isabelle Dorsch, Blake Hawkins, Rachel Juskuv, Sarah Polkinghorne, Manasa Rath, Ana Roeschley.

ASIS&T ProQuest Doctoral Dissertation Award ($1,000 plus expense-paid attendance at ASIS&T Annual Meeting). *Winner:* Olle Skold for "Documenting Videogame Communities."

ASIS&T Research in Information Science Award. For a systematic program of research in a single area at a level beyond the single study, recognizing contributions in the field of information science. *Winner:* Judit Bar-Ilan.

Clarivate Doctoral Dissertation Proposal Scholarship ($2,000). *Winner:* Sarah Polkinhorne for "Food and Information: Embodied Practices in Everyday Life."

Clarivate Outstanding Information Science Teacher Award ($1,500). To recognize the unique teaching contribution of an individual as a teacher of information science. *Winner:* Crystal Fulton, University College Dublin (Ireland).

James M. Cretsos Leadership Award. To recognize new ASIS&T members who have demonstrated outstanding leadership qualities in professional ASIS&T activities. *Winner:* Devon Greyson.

Watson Davis Award for Service. For outstanding continuous contributions and dedicated service to the society. *Winner:* Not awarded in 2018.

Pratt Severn Best Student Research Paper Award. To encourage student research and writing in the field of information science. *Winner:* Ella Milken Detro for "A Librarian's Guide to Algorithmic Bias."

John Wiley Best *JASIST* Paper Award. *Winners:* Michale Kurtz and Edwin Henneken for "Measuring Metrics—A 40-Year Longitudinal Cross-Validation of Citations, Downloads, and Peer Review in Astrophysics."

Bob Williams History Fund Research Grant Award. *Winner:* Lynne Bowker for "Revealing

One of Information Science and Technology's 'Hidden Figures': How Helmut Felber Brought Information Science Principles to Bear on the Development of Early Term Banks."

Bob Williams History Fund Best Research Paper Award. Winner: Alex Poole for "Harold T. Pinkett and the Lonely Crusade of African American Archivists in the Twentieth Century."

Art Libraries Society of North America (ARLIS/NA)

ARLIS/NA Distinguished Service Award. To honor an individual whose exemplary service in art librarianship, visual resources curatorship, or a related field, has made an outstanding national or international contribution to art information. *Winner:* To be announced.

ARLIS/NA Wolfgang M. Freitag Internship Award ($3,000). To provide financial support for students preparing for a career in art librarianship or visual resource librarianship. *Winner:* Anna Hurwitz.

Melva J. Dwyer Award. To the creators of exceptional reference or research tools relating to Canadian art and architecture. *Winner:* Heather Davis (editor) for *Desire Change: Contemporary Feminist Art in Canada* (McGill-Queens University Press & Mentoring Artists for Women's Art).

Gerd Muehsam Award. To one or more graduate students in library science programs to recognize excellence in a graduate paper or project. *Winner:* To be announced.

Sotheby's Institute of Art Research Awards ($3,000, and an additional $2,000 to the winner's sponsor institution). *Winners:* Jason Kaplan and Caroline Frank for *Der Berliner Kunstmarkt: An Analysis of The Berlin Art Market, 1930–1945*.

George Wittenborn Memorial Book Awards. See "Literary Prizes, 2018" in Part 5.

Asian/Pacific Americans Libraries Association (APALA)

APALA Scholarship ($1,000). For a student of Asian or Pacific background who is enrolled in, or has been accepted into, a master's or doctoral degree program in library and/or information science at an ALA-accredited school. *Winner:* Yer Vang.

APALA Travel Grant ($500). To a U.S. or Canadian citizen or permanent resident enrolled in a master's or doctoral degree program in library and/or information science at an ALA-accredited school, or a professional possessing a master's degree or doctoral degree in library and/or information science, to enable attendance at the ALA Annual Conference. *Winner:* Eunah (Lee) Snyder and Katrina Nye.

Emerging Leaders Sponsorship. To fund participation in the 2014 class of the American Library Association's Emerging Leaders program (ELP). *Winner:* Not awarded in 2018.

Sheila Suen Lai Research Grant. *See under:* Chinese American Librarians Association (CALA).

Association for Library and Information Science Education (ALISE)

ALISE Award for Professional Contribution. *Winner:* Claudia Gollop, University of North Carolina–Chapel Hill.

ALISE Diversity Travel Award ($750 for travel expenses, complimentary registration to the ALISE annual conference, and one-year student membership). To increase diversity in LIS education/research for an individual who wishes to address issues of diversity through doctoral study or teaching. *Winner:* Sangeeta Namdev Dhamdhere.

ALISE/Eugene Garfield Doctoral Dissertation Competition. *Winner:* Rachel Ivy Clarke, Syracuse University, for "It's Not Rocket Library Science: Design Epistemology and American Librarianship."

ALISE/Norman Horrocks Leadership Award. To recognize a new ALISE member who has demonstrated outstanding leadership qualities in professional ALISE activities. *Winner:* Not awarded in 2018.

ALISE/Pratt-Severn Faculty Innovation Award. To recognize innovation by full-time faculty members in incorporating evolving information technologies in the curricula of accredited master's degree programs in library and information studies. *Winner:* Peiling Wang, University of Tennessee.

ALISE/ProQuest Methodology Paper Competition. *Winner:* Lynne Bowker, University of Ottawa, for "Corpus Linguistics: It's Not Just for Linguists!"

ALISE Research Grant Competition (one or more grants totaling $5,000). *Winner:* Lynne Bowker, University of Ottawa, for "Against the Clock: Developing and Testing a Framework for Speed Training in LIS Education."

ALISE Service Award. *Winner:* Louise Spiteri, Dalhousie University.

ALISE/Jean Tague Sutcliffe Doctoral Student Research Poster Competition. *Winners:* (first place) Samantha Kaplan, University of North Carolina–Chapel Hill; (second place) Sarah Al-Mahmoud, Simmons College; (third place) Tracie Kreighbaum, Emporia State University, and Ana Valeska Ndumu, Florida State University.

ALISE/University of Washington Information School Youth Services Graduate Student Travel Award. To support the costs associated with travel to and participation in the ALISE Annual Conference. *Winner:* Elizabeth Mills, University of Washington.

ALISE/Connie Van Fleet Award for Research Excellence in Public Library Services to Adults. To recognize LIS research concerning services to adults in public libraries. *Winner:* Bharat Mehra, University of Tennessee.

ALISE/Bohdan S. Wynar Research Paper Competition. *Winners:* J. Elizabeth Mills, University of Washington; Kathleen Campana, Kent State University; Allyson Carlyle, University of Washington; Bowie Kotrla, Florida State University; Eliza T. Dresang, University of Washington; Ivette Bayo Urban, University of Washington; Janet Capps, independent researcher; Cheryl Metoyer, University of Washington; Erika Feldman, independent researcher; Marin Brouwer, Kent School District; Kathleen Burnett, Florida State University, for "Early Literacy in Library Storytimes Part 2: A Quasi-Experimental Study and Intervention with Children's Storytime Providers."

Doctoral Students to ALISE Grant. To support the attendance of one or more promising LIS doctoral students at the ALISE Annual Conference. *Sponsor:* Libraries Unlimited/Linworth. *Winner:* Sylmari Burgos-Ramirez, Simmons College.

Library Journal/ALISE Excellence in Teaching Award (formerly the ALISE Award for Teaching Excellence in the Field of Library and Information Science Education). *Winner:* Renee Hill, University of Maryland.

OCLC/ALISE Library and Information Science Research Grant Competition. To promote independent research that helps librarians integrate new technologies into areas of traditional competence and contributes to a better understanding of the library environment. *Winners:* Rachel Clarke, Syracuse University, for her work to investigate means for wider, more systematic approaches to promoting diverse reading materials in libraries in order to further encouragement of and advocacy for diverse reading and media consumption, especially by those people who might not otherwise be inclined to pursue such resources; Violeta Trkulja and Juliane Stiller, Humboldt-Universitat zu Berlin, for examining the information seeking behavior of refugee migrants in Germany, while they pursuing a job or a training position, or follow an educational path on the Internet; Alexander Voss and Anna Clements, University of St Andrews, who will perform a study to characterize the adoption of ORCID iDs, the use cases and perceptions of the system among researchers in different research communities, and the barriers to uptake the possible interventions.

Association of Jewish Libraries (AJL)

AJL Scholarships ($1,000). For students enrolled in accredited library schools who plan to work as Judaica librarians. *Winner:* Not awarded in 2018.

Fanny Goldstein Merit Award. To honor loyal and ongoing contributions to the association and to the profession of Jewish librarianship. *Winners:* James P. Rosenbloom, Judaica librarian, Brandeis University.

Life Membership Award. To recognize outstanding leadership and professional contributions to the association and to the profession of Jewish librarianship. *Winner:* Not awarded in 2018.

Association of Research Libraries

ARL Diversity Scholarships (stipend of up to $10,000). To a varying number of MLS students from underrepresented groups who are interested in careers in research libraries. *Sponsors:* ARL member libraries and the Institute of Museum and Library Services. *Winners:* Christina Denise Bush, University of Illinois at Urbana-Champaign; Ben B. Chiewphasa, University of Illinois at Urbana-Champaign; Helen Y. Chu, Rutgers University; Reza Davallow Ghajar, University of British Columbia; Hadeer Elsbai, Queens College, CUNY; Natalia Estrada, Kent State University; Patrice Green, University of South Carolina; Joan Hua, University of Washington; Phillip Thomas MacDonald, University of North Carolina at Chapel Hill; Milton Ricardo Antonio Machuca-Gálvez, Rutgers University; Jamie Lee Morin, University of Toronto; Regen Le Roy, University of Michigan; Janis Joyce Shearer, St. Catherine University; Zakir Jamal Suleman, University of British Columbia; Nam Jin Yoon, University of Washington.

Association of Seventh-Day Adventist Librarians

D. Glenn Hilts Scholarship ($1,500) for a member or members of the Seventh-Day Adventist Church who are enrolled in a graduate library program. *Winners:* Dustin Kelley, University of Illinois; Adaliz Cruz, Simmons University.

Beta Phi Mu

Beta Phi Mu Award. *See under:* American Library Association.

Eugene Garfield Doctoral Dissertation Fellowships ($3,000). *Winners:* Brian Dobreski, Syracuse University, for "Values in Knowledge Organization Standards: A Value Analysis of Resource Description and Access (RDA)"; Jamila Ghaddar, University of Toronto, for "Archives, third world futurities and the making of a global order: UNESCO in the Middle East"; Philipp Jordan, University of Hawaii, for "A Meta-Study and Content Analysis of Science Fiction in Computer Science Research"; Hyoungjoo Park, University of Wisconsin–Milwaukee, for "The Impact of Research Data Sharing and Re-Use on Data Citation in STEM Fields"; Jennifer Pierre, University of California, Los Angeles, for "One Big Digital Family: Examining Social Media and Social Support in the Development of 'At-Risk' Youth"; Mei Zhang, University of Wisconsin–Madison, for "What Counts as a Good Selection? E-book Product Selection in U.S. Academic Libraries."

Harold Lancour Scholarship for Foreign Study ($1,750). For graduate study in a country related to the applicant's work or schooling. *Winner:* Emily Drabinski, Long Island University Library.

Sarah Rebecca Reed Scholarship ($2,250). For study at an ALA-accredited library school. *Winners:* Gloria Acosta, Emporia State University, and Joanna Smith, University of California–Los Angeles.

Frank B. Sessa Scholarship for Continuing Professional Education ($1,500). For continuing education for a Beta Phi Mu member. *Winners:* Alexa Hirsch Lalejini, Pi Lambda Sigma Chapter, Syracuse University; Adriene Galindo, Beta Beta Chapter, Simmons College; Kristin Hall, Beta Beta Xi Chapter, St. Catherine University; James Clark, Beta Phi Chapter, University of South Florida; and Monica Rudzinski, At-Large, Kent State University.

Blanche E. Woolls Scholarship ($2,250). For a beginning student in school library media services. *Winner:* Rebekah Craig, Valdosta State University.

Bibliographical Society of America (BSA)

BSA Fellowships ($1,500–$6,000). For scholars involved in bibliographical inquiry and research in the history of the book trades and in publishing history. *Winners:* (ASECS Fellowship for Bibliographical Studies in the Eighteenth Century) Soren Hammerschmidt, Arizona State University, "Modular Pope: Letters, Portraits, and Recycled Print"; (BSA-Harry Ransom Center Pforzheimer Fellowship in Bibliography) Brett Greatley-Hirsch, University of Leeds, "James Shirley's Hyde Park: A Critical Edition"; (BSA-Pine Tree Foundation Fellowship in Culinary Bibliography) Anny Gaul, Georgetown University, "From 'Master of Cooks' to 'Fundamentals of Cooking': A History of Early Arabic Print Cookbooks"; (BSA-Pine Tree Foundation Fellowship in Hispanic Bibliography) Corinna Zeltsman, Georgia Southern University, "Ink under the Fingernails: Printers and Liberalism in 19th-Century Mexico"; (BSA Short Term Fellowships) Richard Calis, Princeton University, "Early Modern Codicology: The Case of Martin Crusius"; S. C. Kaplan, Rice University, "Se livre est a madame de Bourbon': Agnès de Bourgogne, Duchess of Bourbon (1434–1456) and the Female Cultural Networks of Bourbon and Burgundy in the 15th Century"; Julia Mattison, University of Toronto, "The Circulation of French Manuscripts in England"; and Tali Winkler, University of Chicago, "The Role of Early Modern German Book Fairs in Jewish Economic, Cultural, and Intellectual Life"; (BSA Travel Grant) Alessandro Meregaglia, Boise State University, "Caxton Printers of Idaho and the Development of Regional Publishers in the American West"; (McCorison Fellowship for the History and Bibliography of Printing in Canada and the United States) Simon Rowberry, University of Stirling, "Digital Publishing Before the Web"; (Katharine Pantzer Fellowship in the British Book Trades) Adam Hooks, University of Iowa, "Counting Shakespeare"; (Katharine Pantzer Senior Fellowship in Bibliography and the British Book Trades) Cathleen Baker, University of Michigan (Emerita), "New Research into John Baskerville's Virgil (1757)"; (Reese Fellowship for American Bibliography and the History of the Book in the Americas) Kaja Marczewska, University of Westminster, "Anti-Book and 1970s Self-Publishing Practices in the USA"; (Charles J. Tanenbaum Fellowship in Cartographical Bibliography funded by the Pine Tree Foundation) Chet Van Duzer, independent, "Venturing into Unexplored Bibliographical Territory: Cartographic Cartouches."

William L. Mitchell Prize for Research on Early British Serials ($1,000). Awarded triennially for the best single work published in the previous three years. *Winner (2018)*: Dr. Paul Tankard, *Facts and Inventions: Selections from the Journalism of James Boswell* (Yale University Press).

New Scholars Program. To promote the work of scholars who are new to the field of bibliography. *Winners:* (Malkin New Scholar) Rhae Lynn Barnes, Princeton University, "Darkology: The Hidden History of Amateur Blackface Minstrelsy"; (Pantzer New Scholar) Andrew Keener, Northwestern University, "Printed Plays and Polyglot Books: The Multilingual Textures of Early Modern English Drama"; and Tess Goodman, University of Edinburgh, "Copyright and Christmas: Victorian Publishing Strategies for the Poems of Walter Scott."

St. Louis Mercantile Library Prize in American Bibliography ($2,000). Awarded triennially for outstanding scholarship in the bibliography of American history and literature. *Sponsor:* St. Louis Mercantile Library, University of Missouri, St. Louis. *Winner (2020):* To be announced.

Justin G. Schiller Prize for Bibliographical Work on Pre–20th Century Children's Books ($2,000). A triennial award to encourage scholarship in the bibliography of historical children's books. *Winner* (2016): *Tommy Thumb's Pretty Song-Book: The First Collection of English Nursery Rhymes*, a facsimile edition with a history and annotations by Andrea Immel and Brian Alderson (Cotsen Occasional Press).

Catholic Library Association

Regina Medal. For continued, distinguished contribution to the field of children's literature. *Winner:* Andrea Davis Pinkney and Brian Pinkney.

Chinese American Librarians Association (CALA)

CALA Conference Travel Grant. *Winners:* Yongyi Song, Sharon Yang, Yuan Li, Qi Chen, Lili Li.

CALA Distinguished Service Award. To a librarian who has been a mentor, role model, and leader in the fields of library and information science. *Winner:* Zhijia Shen, East Asia Library, University of Washington.

CALA President's Recognition Award. *Winners:* (individuals) Qi Chen, Guoying Liu, Yongming Wang, Yuan Li, Icy Smith, Sai Deng, Michael Bailou Huang; (teams) Assessment & Evaluation Committee, Awards Committee, Scholarship Committee, Constitution & Bylaws Committee, Web Committee.

CALA Scholarship of Library and Information Science ($1,000). *Winner:* Rongqian Ma, University of Pittsburgh.

Sheila Suen Lai Scholarship ($500). *Winner:* Lanyi Peng, San Jose State University.

Lisa Zhao Scholarship ($500). *Winner:* Amanda Chin, University of Washington.

Coalition for Networked Information (CNI)

Paul Evan Peters Award. Awarded biennially to recognize notable and lasting international achievements relating to high-performance networks and the creation and use of information resources and services that advance scholarship and intellectual productivity. *Sponsors:* Association of Research Libraries, CNI, EDUCAUSE. *Winner (2017):* Herbert Van de Sompel, Research Scientist, Los Alamos National Laboratory.

Paul Evan Peters Fellowship ($5,000 a year for two years). Awarded biennially to a student or students pursuing a graduate degree in librarianship or the information sciences. *Sponsors:* Association of Research Libraries, CNI, EDUCAUSE. *Winners:* Bergis Jules and Laima Augustaitis.

Council on Library and Information Resources (CLIR)

CLIR Postdoctoral Fellowships in Scholarly Information Resources. *Current fellows:* Emily Beagle, Diana Carolina Sierra Becerra, Katie Coburn, Heidi Dodson, Seth Erickson, Jennifer Garcon, Zenobie S. Garrett, Daniel Genkins, Jennifer Isasi, Andrew Meade McGee, Nicté Fuller Medina, Margie Montañez, Smiti Nathan, Hyeongyul Roh, Jonathan Scott, Justin D. Shanks, Hadassah St. Hubert, Rachel Starry, Ana Trisovic, Wendy Hoi Yan Wong, Qian Zhang.

Digitizing Hidden Special Collections and Archives Awards. *Sponsor:* Andrew W. Mellon Foundation. *Winners:* Hennepin County (Minnesota) Library for "Building Minneapolis: Images of the City's Building and Infrastructure from the 20th Century"; Hennepin County Library proposes to digitize and/or describe 40,000 photographs recording the city's houses, buildings, streets, bridges, public events, schools, hospitals, libraries, construction and redevelopment projects, and various infrastructure elements.

Harry Ransom Center at the University of Texas at Austin for "Creating a Digital LGBTQ Collection from the Radclyffe Hall and Una Vincenzo, Lady Troubridge Papers at the Harry Ransom Center"; Indiana Historical Society for "Digitization of Madam C. J. Walker Collections Which Encompass the Life, Work, and Impact of America's First Female African American Self-made Millionaire"; Center for Historic Architecture and Design, University of Delaware for "Digitizing Documentation of the Lost and Disappearing Historic Architecture of the Mid-Atlantic"; American Folklore Society, Indiana University Bloomington Libraries, University of Oregon Archives of Northwest Folklore, and Vermont Folklife Center for "Digitizing Hidden Archival Collections in Folklore Studies"; University of Miami Libraries, Duke University, HistoryMiami Museum, and Digital Public Library of

America for "Digitizing the 'World's Most Experienced Airline': Pan American World Airways Resources at the University of Miami, Duke University, and HistoryMiami and Development of an Aviation Portal"; Yale University for "Digitizing the Yale Babylonian Collection"; Digitizing the Yale Babylonian Collection is a two-year project to image and document ca. 35,000 cuneiform artifacts housed in the Yale Babylonian Collection (YBC) using flatbed scanning, High Dynamic Range Imaging (HDR) and Reflectance Transformation Imagery (RTI). The YBC represents one of the most substantial cuneiform collections in the world, and holds documents of unparalleled historical significance, shedding light on the earliest phases of human history. The aim of the project is to advance the research and education objectives associated with this collection by documenting and disseminating the artifacts through Yale's Discovery portal, through the YBC website, and through the international cuneiform aggregate dissemination portal, Cuneiform Digital Library Initiative (CDLI). The project will make the cuneiform texts—a type of artifact that has been particularly targeted for looting and illicit trade—globally accessible to scholars as well as to the public.

University of Florida, University of Puerto Rico–Rio Piedras, and Digital Library of the Caribbean for "Film on a Boat: Digitizing Historical Newspapers of the Caribbean"; Amistad Research Center, Tulane University, for "Fly on the Wall: Black Natchez by Ed Pincus and David Newman, Film Digitization for Access, 1965 and 1967"; College of Physicians of Philadelphia, Legacy Center, Drexel University College of Medicine, University of Pennsylvania Libraries, Pennsylvania Hospital Historic Collections, Library Company of Philadelphia, American Philosophical Society, Thomas Jefferson University Archives and Special Collections, and Philadelphia Area Consortium of Special Collections for "For the Health of the New Nation: Philadelphia as the Center of American Medical Education, 1746–1868"; Montana State University and Montana State Library for "From the Mountains to the Prairies, From Trout to Dace: Revealing Climate and Population Impacts on Culture, Ecology, and Economy in Montana's Fisheries"; Hawaii State Archives, Hawaiinuiakea School of Hawaiian Knowledge at the University of Hawaii–Manoa, Native Hawaiian Legal Corporation, Awaiaulu Literature Project, Hawaii State Department of Education's Office of Hawaiian Education, Honolulu Museum of Art, Washington Place, and Royal Order of Kamehameha I for "I ali'i no ke ali'i i ke kanaka (A chief is a chief because of the people): Justice and Accountability through Access to the Records of Hawaii's Governments"; College of Wooster, Ohio, "Letters from Harriet Noyes: Missionaries and Women's Education in 19th-Century China"; Center for Jewish History and Museum of Chinese in America for "New York Neighbors: The Shared Jewish and Chinese Immigrant and Refugee Experience"; Bethel Broadcasting, Inc. for "Nutarluki 'Make Them New'"; University of Massachusetts, Amherst, for "Visibility for Disability: Documenting the History of Disability in America and the Growth of the Disability Rights Movement"; Adirondack Historical Association for "Visualizing a Vast Wilderness: Mapping the Adirondack Park through Three Centuries."

Mellon Fellowships for Dissertation Research in Original Sources. *Sponsor:* Andrew W. Mellon Foundation. *Winners:* Jessica Bachman, Carly Boxer, Susan Eberhard, Idriss Fofana, Qian He, Zhuqing Hu, Karin Mei Li Inouye, Adrienn Kacsor, Mallory Matsumoto, Ania Nikulina, Eilin Perez, Ekaterina Pukhovaia, Andrea Rosengarten, Andrew Starling, Antony Wood.

EDUCAUSE

EDUCAUSE Community Leadership Award. *Winner:* James Phelps, director of Enterprise Architecture and Strategy, University of Washington.

EDUCAUSE Leadership Award. To acknowledge leadership in higher education information technology. *Winners:* Richard N. Katz, founder and principal, Richard N. Katz and Associates, and Celeste M. Schwartz, vice president for information technology and chief digital officer, Montgomery County (Pennsylvania) Community College.

EDUCAUSE Rising Star Award. To recognize early-career information technology professionals who demonstrate exceptional achievement in the area of information technology in higher education. *Winner:* Damian M. Doyle, assistant vice president of enterprise infrastructure services, University of Maryland–Baltimore County.

Friends of the National Library of Medicine

Michael E. DeBakey Library Services Outreach Award. To recognize outstanding service and contributions to rural and underserved communities by a practicing health sciences librarian. *Winner:* Julie K. Gaines, Medical Partnership Library, Augusta University and University of Georgia.

Institute of Museum and Library Services

National Medal for Museum and Library Service. For extraordinary civic, educational, economic, environmental, and social contributions ($5,000). *Winners:* Children's Museum of Denver at Marsico Campus; Detroit Historical Society; El Paso Museum of Art; Georgetown (Texas) Public Library, History Museum at the Castle, Appleton, Wisconsin; Orange County (Florida) Library System; Pueblo City-County (Colorado) Library District; Reading (Pennsylvania) Public Library; Rochester (Minnesota) Public Library; University of Oregon's Museum of Natural and Cultural History.

International Association of School Librarians (IASL)

Ken Haycock Leadership Development Grant ($1,000). To enable applicants from any nation to attend their first IASL Annual Conference. *Winner:* Not awarded in 2018.

Jean Lowrie Leadership Development Grant ($1,000). To enable applicants from developing nations to attend their first IASL Annual Conference. *Winner:* Dr. Sarwesh Pareek from Bharatiya Vidya Bhavan Vidyashram Pratapnagar, Jaipur.

Takeshi Murofushi Research Award ($500). For funding a research project, preferably of international interest. *Winner:* Not awarded in 2018.

Diljit Singh Leadership Development Grant ($1,000). To enable applicants from developing nations to attend their first IASL conference. *Winner:* Not awarded in 2018.

International Board on Books for Young People (IBBY)

IBBY-Asahi Reading Promotion Award ($10,000). Awarded biennially to projects that are making a lasting contribution to reading promotion for young people. *Offered by:* International Board on Books for Young People. *Sponsor:* Asahi Shimbun. *Winner:* Les Doigts Qui Rêvent (Reading Fingers), to fill the lack of access to tactile illustrated books for visually impaired children in France, Europe, and the world.

International Federation of Library Associations and Institutions (IFLA)

International Federation of Library Associations and Institutions (IFLA) Honorary Fellowship. For distinguished service to IFLA. *Winner:* Sinikka Sipila.

IFLA Medal. To a person or organization for a distinguished contribution either to IFLA or to international librarianship. *Winner:* Buhle Mbambo-Thata and Teresa Hackett.

Jay Jordan IFLA/OCLC Early Career Development Fellowships. To library and information science professionals from countries with developing economies who are in the early stages of their careers. *Winners:* Patience Alehegn Adane Kinde, Ethiopia; Arnold Mwanzu, Kenya; Boris Denadic, Serbia; Chantelle Richardson, Jamaica; Chandra Pratama Setiawan, Indonesia.

Dr. Shawky Salem Conference Grant (up to $1,900). To enable an expert in library and information science who is a national of an Arab country to attend the IFLA Conference for the first time. *Winner:* Khadija Mohsin Ibrahim, Al Safa Library, Dubai, U.A.E.

Library Journal

DEMCO/*Library Journal* Paralibrarian of the Year Award. *Winner:* Orquidea Olvera, Monterey County (California) Free Libraries.

Gale/*Library Journal* Library of the Year. *Sponsor:* Gale Cengage Learning. *Winner:* San Francisco Public Library.

Library Journal/ALISE Excellence in Teaching Award (formerly the ALISE Award for Teaching Excellence in the Field of Library and Information Science Education). *See under:* Association for Library and Information Science Education (ALISE).

Library Journal Best Small Library in America ($20,000). To honor a public library that profoundly demonstrates outstanding service to populations of 25,000 or less. *Co-sponsors: Library Journal* and the Bill and Melinda Gates Foundation. *Winner:* Madison County (North Carolina) Public Libraries.

Library Journal Librarian of the Year. *Winner:* Lance Werner, Kent District (Michigan) Library.

Library of Congress

Kluge Fellowships in Digital Studies. To promote examination of the impact of the digital revolution on society, culture, and international relations using the library's collections and resources. *Fellow:* Kari Kraus, University of Maryland.

Library of Congress Literacy Awards. *Sponsor:* David M. Rubenstein. *Winners:* (David M. Rubenstein Prize, $150,000, for a groundbreaking or sustained record of advancement of literacy by any individual or entity) Reading Is Fundamental, Washington, DC; (the American Prize, $50,000, for a project developed and implemented successfully during the past decade for combating illiteracy and/or aliteracy) East Side Community School, New York, New York; (the International Prize, $50,000, for the work of an individual, nation, or nongovernmental organization working in a specific country or region) Instituto Pedagógico para Problemas del Lenguaje.

Library of Congress Prize for American Fiction. See "Literary Prizes, 2018" in Part 5.

Medical Library Association (MLA)

Virginia L. and William K. Beatty MLA Volunteer Service Award. To recognize a medical librarian who has demonstrated outstanding, sustained service to the Medical Library Association and the health sciences library profession. *Winner:* Molly Knapp.

Estelle Brodman Award for the Academic Medical Librarian of the Year. To honor significant achievement, potential for leadership, and continuing excellence at midcareer in the area of academic health sciences librarianship. *Winner:* Holly K. Grossetta Nardini.

Clarivet Analytics/Frank Bradway Rogers Information Advancement Award. To recognize outstanding contributions to the application of technology to the delivery of health science information, to the science of information, or to the facilitation of the delivery of health science information. *Sponsor:* Thomson Reuters. *Winner:* Michael R. Kronenfeld.

Lois Ann Colaianni Award for Excellence and Achievement in Hospital Librarianship. To a member of MLA who has made significant contributions to the profession in the area of overall distinction or leadership in hospital librarianship. *Winner:* Edward J. Poletti.

Cunningham Memorial International Fellowships. For health sciences librarians from countries outside the United States and Canada, to provide for attendance at the MLA Annual Meeting and observation and supervised work in one or more medical libraries. *Winner:* Biliamin Oladele Popoola.

Louise Darling Medal. For distinguished achievement in collection development in the health sciences. *Winner:* Not awarded in 2018.

Janet Doe Lectureship. *Winner:* Elaine Russo Martin, FMLA, "Social Justice and the Medical Librarian."

EBSCO/MLA Annual Meeting Grants (up to $1,000). To enable four health sciences librarians to attend the MLA Annual Meeting. *Winners:* Sarah Clarke, Kelsey Leonard Grabeel, Alice Jean Jaggers, and Jessica A. Koos.

Ida and George Eliot Prize. To recognize a work published in the preceding calendar year that has been judged most effective in furthering medical librarianship. *Winners:* Whitney A. Townsend, Patricia F. Anderson, Emily C. Ginier, Mark P. MacEachern, Kate M. Saylor, Barbara Lowther Shipman, and Judith E. Smith.

Carla J. Funk Governmental Relations Award ($500). To recognize a medical librarian who has demonstrated outstanding leadership in the area of governmental relations at the federal, state, or local level, and who has furthered the goal of providing quality information for improved health. *Sponsor:* Kent A. Smith. *Winner:* Julie A. Schneider.

Murray Gottlieb Prize. See Erich Meyerhoff Prize below.

T. Mark Hodges International Service Award. To honor outstanding achievement in promoting, enabling, or delivering improved health information internationally. *Winner:* Not awarded in 2018.

David A. Kronick Traveling Fellowship ($2,000). *Sponsor:* Bowden-Massey Foundation. *Winner:* Erica Lake.

Joseph Leiter NLM/MLA Lectureship. *Winner:* Eric Dishman, "Precision Communications for Precision Health: Challenges and Strategies for Reaching All of Us."

Donald A. B. Lindberg Research Fellowship ($10,000). To fund research aimed at expanding the research knowledge base, linking the information services provided by librarians to improved health care and advances in biomedical research. *Winners:* Sue Yeon Syn and JungWon Yoon, "Investigation of the Impact of Text and Visual Formats on Facebook Health Communication Based on User-Centered Evidence from Eye-Movement Analysis."

Lucretia W. McClure Excellence in Education Award. To an outstanding educator in the field of health sciences librarianship and informatics. *Winner:* Mary Edwards.

John P. McGovern Award Lectureship. *Winner:* William Powers, "Reviving the Human: Libraries in the Age of AI."

Majors/MLA Chapter Project of the Year Award. *Sponsor:* J. A. Majors Co. *Winner:* Mid-Atlantic Chapter—Chapter Diversity Task Force for exploring ways to promote diversity and inclusion in medical librarianship and chapter membership.

Medical Informatics Section Career Development Grant ($1,500). To support a career development activity that will contribute to advancement in the field of medical informatics. *Winner:* Carl Leak.

Erich Meyerhoff Prize (formerly the Murray Gottlieb Prize). For the best unpublished essay on the history of medicine and allied sciences written by a health sciences librarian. *Sponsor:* MLA History of the Health Sciences Section. *Winners:* Vicki F. Croft and Susanne K. Whitaker, "The Role of Accreditation on the Evolution of United States and Canadian Veterinary School Libraries in the Late 19th and 20th Centuries."

MLA Continuing Education Grant ($100–$500). *Winner:* Natalie Clairoux.

MLA Scholarship (up to $5,000). For graduate study at an ALA-accredited library school. *Winner:* Justin Fuhr.

MLA Scholarship for Minority Students (up to $5,000). For graduate study at an ALA-accredited library school. *Winner:* Donna Baluchi.

Marcia C. Noyes Award. For an outstanding contribution to medical librarianship. *Winner:* Ana D. Cleveland.

President's Award. To an MLA member for a notable or important contribution made during the past association year. *Winners:* Task Force to Review MLA's Competencies for Lifelong Learning and Professional Success: Gale G. Hannigan, Paula Raimondo, Christopher Childs, Martha Earl, Kate Kelly, Elizabeth Laera, Susan Lessick, Terri Ottosen, Jodi L. Philbrick, and Caitlin Ann Pike.

Rittenhouse Award. For the best unpublished paper on medical librarianship submitted by a student enrolled in, or having been enrolled in, a course for credit in an ALA-accredited library school or a trainee in an internship program in medical librarianship.

Donor: Rittenhouse Book Distributors. *Winner:* Kelsa Bartley, "A Look at the Use of Mobile Apps in the Self-Management of Diseases."

Music Library Association

Vincent H. Duckles Award. For the best book-length bibliography or other tool in music. *Winner:* Jane Gottlieb for *Music Library and Research Skills (second edition)* (New York; Oxford: Oxford University Press, 2016).

Dena Epstein Award for Archival and Library Research in American Music. To support research in archives or libraries internationally on any aspect of American music. *Winner:* Sheryl Kaskowitz for "Government Song Women: How the Special Skills Division Discovered American Folk Music," and Kendra Preston Leonard for "Melody Magazine and Women Musicians in the Early American Cinema."

Kevin Freeman Travel Grants. To colleagues who are new to the profession to enable them to attend the MLA Annual Meeting. *Winners:* Jessica Abbazio, Memory Apata, Enrique Caboverde, Abby Flanagan, Daniel Ray, and Wendy Wong.

Walter Gerboth Award. To members of the association who are in the first five years of their professional library careers, to assist research-in-progress in music or music librarianship. *Winner:* Not awarded in 2018.

Richard S. Hill Award. For the best article on music librarianship or article of a music-bibliographic nature. *Winner:* Kevin Kishimoto and Tracey Snyder, "Popular Music in FRBR and RDA: Toward User-Friendly and Cataloger-Friendly Identification of Works," *Cataloging & Classification Quarterly*.

MLA Citation. Awarded in recognition of contributions to the profession over a career. *Winner:* Geraldine Ostrove.

Eva Judd O'Meara Award. For the best review published in *Notes*. *Winner:* Daniel Batchelder, review of *Walt Disney's Snow White and the Seven Dwarfs: Master Score*.

A. Ralph Papakhian Special Achievement Award. To recognize extraordinary service to the profession of music librarianship over a relatively short period of time. *Winners:* Judy Tsou and Michael Colby.

National Library Service for the Blind and Physically Handicapped, Library of Congress

Library of the Year Awards ($1,000). *Winner:* (Regional Library of the Year) Colorado Talking Book Library, Denver; (Subregional Library/Advisory and Outreach Center of the Year) Braille and Talking Books at Taylor (Michigan) Community Library.

REFORMA (National Association to Promote Library and Information Services to Latinos and the Spanish-Speaking)

Elizabeth A. Martinez Lifetime Achievement Award. To recognize those who have achieved excellence in librarianship over an extended period of service and who have made significant and lasting contributions to REFORMA and the Latino community. *Winner:* Luis Herrera and Teresa "Tess" Tobin.

REFORMA scholarships (up to $1,500). To students who qualify for graduate study in library science and who are citizens or permanent residents of the United States. *Winners:* (Rose Trevino Memorial Scholarship) *Winner:* To be announced; (REFORMA Scholarship) *Winner:* To be announced.

Arnulfo D. Trejo Librarian of the Year Award. To recognize a librarian who has promoted and advocated services to the Spanish-speaking and Latino communities and made outstanding contributions to REFORMA. *Winner:* Sonia Bautista.

Society of American Archivists (SAA)

C. F. W. Coker Award for Description. To recognize creators of tools that enable archivists to produce more effective finding aids.

Winner: University of California for *Guidelines for Born-Digital Archival Description*.

Distinguished Service Award. To recognize an archival institution, education program, nonprofit organization, or governmental organization that has given outstanding service to its public and has made an exemplary contribution to the archives profession. *Winner:* Council of State Archivists and Society of Southwest Archivists.

Diversity Award. To an individual, group, or institution for outstanding contributions to advancing diversity within the archives profession, SAA, or the archival record. *Winners:* Austin History Center for "Community Archivist Program" and University of North Carolina at Chapel Hill for "Maya from the Margins Archives Project."

Fellows' Ernst Posner Award. For an outstanding essay dealing with a facet of archival administration, history, theory, or methodology, published in *American Archivist. Winner:* Katherine S. Madison, "'Who Lives, Who Dies, Who Tells Your Story': The Use and Representation of Records in Hamilton: An American Musical."

Josephine Forman Scholarship ($10,000). *Sponsor:* General Commission on Archives and History of the United Methodist Church. *Winner:* Krystell Jimenez, University of California, Los Angeles.

Mark A. Greene Emerging Leader Award. To recognize early-career archivists who have completed archival work of broad merit, demonstrated significant promise of leadership, performed commendable service to the archives profession, or have accomplished a combination of these requirements. *Winner:* Harrison Inefuku, Iowa State University.

F. Gerald Ham and Elsie Ham Scholarship ($7,500). To recognize an individual's past performance in a graduate archival studies program and his or her potential in the field. *Winner:* Julie Botnick, University of California, Los Angeles.

Philip M. Hamer and Elizabeth Hamer Kegan Award. For individuals and/or institutions that have increased public awareness of a specific body of documents. *Winner:* Find & Connect eScholarship Research Centre.

Oliver Wendell Holmes Travel Award. To enable overseas archivists already in the United States or Canada for training to attend the SAA Annual Meeting. *Winner:* Tianjiao Qi, China.

J. Franklin Jameson Archival Advocacy Award. For individuals and/or organizations that promote greater public awareness of archival activities and programs. *Winners:* Yvonne Lewis Holley and Brad Meltzer.

Sister M. Claude Lane, O.P., Memorial Award. For a significant contribution to the field of religious archives. *Winner:* Sister Louise Grundish, Sisters of Charity, Greensburg, Pennsylvania.

Waldo Gifford Leland Award. To encourage and reward writing of superior excellence and usefulness in the field of archival history, theory, or practice. *Winner:* Anthony Cocciolo, *Moving Image and Sound Collections for Archivists* (Society of American Archivists) .

Theodore Calvin Pease Award. For the best student paper ($100 and publication in *American Archivist*). *Winner:* Not awarded in 2018.

Donald Peterson Student Travel Award (up to $1,000). To enable a student or recent graduate to attend the SAA Annual Meeting. *Winner:* Jessica Serrao, University of North Carolina at Chapel Hill.

Harold T. Pinkett Student of Color Award. To encourage minority students to consider careers in the archival profession, and to promote minority participation in SAA. *Winners:* Juber Ayala, Rutgers University, and Jessica Tai, University of California, Los Angeles.

Preservation Publication Award. To recognize an outstanding work published in North America that advances the theory or the practice of preservation in archival institutions. *Winner:* Laura McCann, "The Whole Story: News Agency Photographs in Newspaper Photo Morgue Collections" in *American Archivist*.

SAA Fellows. To a limited number of members for their outstanding contribution to the archival profession. *Honored*: Amy Cooper Cary, Donna E. McCrea, Kate Theimer, and Rachel Vagts.

SAA Mosaic Scholarship ($5,000). To minority students pursuing graduate education in archival science. *Winners:* Alexis Recto, University of California, Los Angeles.

SAA Spotlight Award. To recognize the contributions of individuals who work for the good of the profession and of archival collections, and whose work would not typically receive public recognition. *Winner:* B. Bernetiae Reed, project documentarian and oral historian, University of North Carolina at Chapel Hill.

Special Libraries Association (SLA)

SLA Copyright Clearance Center Rising Stars Award. To SLA members in the first five years of membership who demonstrate exceptional promise of leadership. *Winners:* Anya Bartelmann, Caren Torrey, Eric Tans, Willow Fuchs, and Heidi Tebbe.

SLA John Cotton Dana Award. For exceptional support and encouragement of special librarianship. *Winner:* Karen Reczek.

SLA Fellows. *Honored*: Kevin Adams, Elizabeth Brown, Robin Dodge, Elaine Lasda, Kimberly Silk.

SLA Hall of Fame Award. For outstanding performance and distinguished service to SLA. *Winner:* Praveen Kumar Jain.

SLA Presidential Citations. To SLA members for notable or important contributions during the previous year that enhanced the association or furthered its goals and objectives. *Winners:* To be announced.

Rose L. Vormelker Award. To SLA members for exceptional service through the education and mentoring of students and working professionals. *Winner:* David Cappoli.

Theatre Library Association

Brooks McNamara Performing Arts Librarian Scholarship. *Winner:* Jeannie Chen, University of California, Los Angeles.

Louis Rachow Distinguished Service in Performing Arts Librarianship Award. For extraordinary contributions to performing arts. *Winner:* Kenneth Schlesinger, Lehman College, Bronx, New York.

George Freedley Memorial Award. *Winner*: Sarah E. Chinn, *Spectacular Men: Race, Gender, and Nation on the Early American Stage* (Oxford University Press).

Richard Wall Award. See "Literary Prizes, 2018" in Part 5.

Other Awards of Distinction

Robert B. Downs Intellectual Freedom Award. To recognize individuals or groups who have furthered the cause of intellectual freedom, particularly as it affects libraries and information centers and the dissemination of ideas. *Offered by:* Graduate School of Library and Information Science, University of Illinois at Urbana-Champaign. *Sponsor:* Libraries Unlimited/ABC-CLIO. *Winner:* Iowa Library Association.

I Love My Librarian Awards ($5,000, a plaque, and a $500 travel stipend to attend the awards ceremony). To recognize librarians for service to their communities, schools, and campuses. Winners are nominated by library patrons. *Sponsors:* Carnegie Corporation of New York and the *New York Times*. *Winners:* Ginny Blackson, James E. Brooks Library, Central Washington University, Ellensburg, Washington; Joy Bridwell, Stone Child College Library, Box Elder, Montana; Tamara Cox, Wren High School, Piedmont, South Carolina; Nancy Daniel, Western Piedmont Community College Library, Morganton, North Carolina; Jennifer Berg Gaither, Baltimore (Maryland) City College; Terri Gallagher, Community College of Beaver County (Pennsylvania) Library; Paula Kelly, Whitehall Public Library, Pittsburgh, Pennsylvania; Stephanie Hartwell-Mandella, Katonah (New York) Village Library; Linda Robinson, Mansfield (Connecticut) Middle School; Lindsey Tomsu, Algonquin Area (Illinois) Public Library District.

RWA Cathie Linz Librarian of the Year. To a librarian who demonstrates outstanding support of romance authors and the romance genre. *Offered by:* Romance Writers of America. *Winner:* Fran Strober Cassano, North Bellmore (New York) Public Library.

USBBY Bridge to Understanding Award ($1,000). To acknowledge the work of adults who use books to promote international understanding among children. *Offered by:* United States Board on Books for Young People. *Winner:* To be announced.

Women's National Book Association Award. Awarded biennially to a living American woman who derives part or all of her income from books and allied arts and who has done meritorious work in the world of books. *Offered by:* Women's National Book Association (WNBA). *Winners (2017):* Carla Hayden and Louise Erdrich.

Part 4
Research and Statistics

Library Research and Statistics

Number of Libraries in the United States and Canada

Statistics are from the *American Library Directory (ALD) 2019–2020* (Information Today, Inc., 2019). Data are exclusive of elementary and secondary school libraries.

Libraries in the United States

Public Libraries	16,857*
Public libraries, excluding branches	9,616
Main public libraries that have branches	1,432
Public library branches	7,241
Academic Libraries	3,574*
Community college	1,087
Departmental	229
Medical	5
Religious	6
University and college	2,487
Departmental	1,177
Law	194
Medical	228
Religious	250
Armed Forces Libraries	227*
Air Force	62
Medical	3
Army	104
Medical	21
Marine Corps	12
Navy	49
Law	1
Medical	9
Government Libraries	821*
Law	352
Medical	112

Special Libraries (excluding public, academic, armed forces, and government)	4,693*
Law	658
Medical	866
Religious	373
Total Special Libraries (including public, academic, armed forces, and government)	5,874
Total law	1,205
Total medical	1,244
Total religious	805
Total Libraries Counted (*)	26,172

Libraries in Regions Administered by the United States

Public Libraries	19*
Public libraries, excluding branches	9
Main public libraries that have branches	3
Public library branches	10
Academic Libraries	38*
Community college	3
Departmental	1
University and college	35
Departmental	19
Law	3
Medical	3
Religious	1
Armed Forces Libraries	2*
Air Force	1
Army	1
Government Libraries	3*
Law	1
Medical	1
Special Libraries (excluding public, academic, armed forces, and government)	5*
Law	3
Religious	1
Total Special Libraries (including public, academic, armed forces, and government)	14
Total law	7
Total medical	4
Total religious	2
Total Libraries Counted (*)	67

Libraries in Canada

Public Libraries	2,204*
Public libraries, excluding branches	801
Main public libraries that have branches	157
Public library branches	1,403
Academic Libraries	324*
Community college	79
Departmental	15
Religious	1
University and college	245
Departmental	170
Law	16
Medical	15
Religious	32
Government Libraries	166*
Law	25
Medical	4
Special Libraries (excluding public, academic, armed forces, and government)	550*
Law	88
Medical	130
Religious	20
Total Special Libraries (including public, academic, armed forces, and government)	643
Total law	129
Total medical	149
Total religious	69
Total Libraries Counted (*)	3,244

Summary

Total U.S. Libraries	26,172
Total Libraries Administered by the United States	67
Total Canadian Libraries	3,244
Grand Total of Libraries Listed	29,483

Note: Numbers followed by an asterisk are added to find "Total libraries counted" for each of the three geographic areas (United States, U.S.-administered regions, and Canada). The sum of the three totals is the "Grand total of libraries listed" in *ALD*. For details on the count of libraries, see the preface to the 72nd edition of *ALD—Ed.*

Highlights of IMLS Public Library Surveys

The Institute of Museum and Library Services (IMLS) collects and disseminates statistical information about public libraries in the United States and its outlying areas. This article presents highlights from two recent IMLS surveys of public libraries and state library administrative agencies. For more information, see "Institute of Museum and Library Services" in Part 2 of this volume and visit https://www.imls.gov/research-tools/data-collection for the most current and comprehensive IMLS survey data and reports.

Public Libraries

The following are highlights from the IMLS report *Public Libraries in the United States, Fiscal Year 2015.* Based on an annual IMLS public library survey (PLS), the report collected data from 98 percent of public libraries in all 50 U.S. states, the District of Columbia, and outlying territories.

Library Use and Programs

- In fiscal year (FY) 2015 there were 1.39 billion visits to public libraries, or 4.48 visits per person, with an estimated 7.3 items checked out per person.
- Between FY 2009 and FY 2015 library visits per capita decreased by 16.29 percent, with library reference transactions per capita decreasing by 21.16 percent.
- The public accessed reference services at public libraries more than 255 million times in FY 2015.

Collections and Circulation

- Public libraries continued to adapt their collections to modern demands in FY 2015 by adding more e-books and audio and video materials, including both physical units and downloadable items. E-books in public libraries increased from .7 per capita in FY 2014 to 1.07 per capita in FY 2015.
- In FY 2017 2.7 billion materials were circulated in public libraries. Although collection materials increased from 3.78 to 4.28 materials per capita between FY 2014 and FY 2015, with notable increases in e-books and audio materials, total circulation per capita was 7.3 in FY 2015, down from 7.54 in FY 2014.
- The circulation of children's materials declined slightly in FY 2015, to 2.58 per capita compared to 2.67 per capita in FY 2014.

Programs and Attendance

- There were 4.70 million programs offered by public libraries in FY 2015, an increase of almost 1 million over FY 2009. 106.9 million people attended library programs, an increase of more than 20 million over FY 2009.

- In FY 2015 total program attendance per 1,000 people was 341.25; that is, for every 1,000 people in a library service area, approximately 341 patrons attended a public library program.
- Children's and young adults' program offerings make up approximately two-thirds of the total programs reported in the PLS. In FY 2015 public libraries offered 455,612 young adults' programs, or 1.47 programs per 1,000 people, and 2.68 million children's programs, or 8.61 programs per 1,000 people.

Public Access Computers and User Sessions

- In FY 2015 public libraries reported 294,319 public access Internet computers, or 4.73 computers per 5,000 people, and 300.65 million user sessions, or nearly one session per person.
- The number of public access Internet computers in public libraries increased markedly between FY 2011 and FY 2015; however, the number of user sessions per capita decreased slightly from 1.14 sessions per capita to 0.97 sessions per capita over this same period.
- The number of public access Internet computers per 5,000 people varied across locales in FY 2015, with higher availability of computers in public libraries in rural areas than in other locales.
- Public access Internet computer user sessions per capita showed little variation across locales in FY 2015. Libraries serving small populations logged more user sessions per capita than libraries serving larger populations.

Revenue and Expenditures

- In FY 2015 public libraries had $12.4 billion in total revenue, compared to $12.1 billion in FY 2014. Public library revenue per capita in FY 2015 was $39.94, up slightly from $39.77 per capita in FY 2014.
- In FY 2015 public libraries had $11.6 billion in total expenditures, compared to $11.3 billion in FY 2014. Public library expenditures per capita in FY 2015 were $37.38 per capita, very little changed from $37.36 per capita in FY 2014.
- Across all locale types and population sizes, local government revenue constituted the majority of public library operating revenue in FY 2015; however, the proportion of revenue from local government was highest in libraries in cities and suburbs and in libraries serving large populations.
- Across all locale types and population sizes, staff expenditures constituted the majority of all public library operating expenditures in FY 2015. The proportion of staff expenditures relative to other expenditures was similar across locales and population sizes except in libraries that serve small populations, where staff expenditures accounted for more than 25 percent of the total.

- In FY 2015 both operating revenue and expenditures per person increased, continuing the trends that began in FY 2012. However, although the financial health of public libraries has improved steadily over the last three years, both operating revenue and expenditures remain below the levels seen at the start of the Great Recession.

Public Library Staff

- One of the most important assets in public libraries is knowledgeable library staff. There were no marked differences in staffing levels between FY 2015 and FY 2014. In FY 2015, total staff per 25,000 people was 11.19 compared to 11.29 in FY 2014. More than one-third (35 percent) of all paid staff hold the title of librarian, and approximately 68 percent of all librarians have an ALA-MLS.
- Libraries in rural areas had more staff (including librarians) per 25,000 people in FY 2015 compared to libraries in all other locales and the national estimate. However, the percentage of librarians with an ALA-MLS was highest in city libraries (86.65 percent) and lowest in rural libraries (27.85 percent).
- The number of librarians per 25,000 people varied across the states, from highs of 10.54 in New Hampshire and 9.02 in Vermont, to lows of 1.41 in Georgia and 1.78 in Nevada. All but 11 states had three or more librarians per 25,000 people. The total number of library staff per 25,000 people was highest in the District of Columbia (20.18) and lowest in Texas (6.38).

State Library Administrative Agencies

The following are highlights from the IMLS report *State Library Administrative Agencies Survey, Fiscal Year 2016.* Based on a biennial survey, the FY 2016 report was released in October 2017.

Introduction

A State Library Administrative Agency (SLAA) is the official state agency charged with the extension and development of public library services throughout the state. It has the authority to administer state plans in accordance with the provisions of the federal Library Services and Technology Act (LSTA).

Across the 50 states and the District of Columbia, SLAAs are located in various state government agencies and report to different authorities. They coordinate and distribute federal funds from the IMLS Grants to States program in addressing statewide and local needs.

Although all SLAAs coordinate and distribute federal funds authorized by the administration of the LSTA, not all share the same function and role within their respective states. Most SLAAs provide important reference and information services to the state government, administer the state library or serve as the state archives, operate libraries for people who are blind or physically handicapped, and support the State Center for the Book. In some states, the SLAA also may function as the public library at large, providing library services to the general public.

Revenue and Expenditures

- Total reported revenues for the 51 SLAAs across all sources were just over $1 billion in FY 2016.
- Revenues from the federal government for all SLAAs totaled $154.3 million (15 percent), while state revenues totaled $856.2 million (82 percent), and revenues from other sources totaled $33.4 million (3.0 percent).
- Total expenditures for FY 2016 across all SLAAs were $1.03 billion. Most expenditures were in financial assistance to libraries ($663.9 million) and operating expenditures including staffing, collections, and other expenses ($344.2 million), with smaller expenditures allocated to other services ($21.4 million) and capital outlay ($1.4 million).
- A closer review of SLAAs' operating expenditures reveals that 53 percent of all operating expenditures were used to support staffing (salaries and wages and employee benefits), whereas 10 percent were used for collections and 37 percent for other expenses.
- From FY 2012 to FY 2014, just after the recession, SLAA revenues and expenditures both increased modestly (5.0 percent and 2.0 percent, respectively), but both financial indicators subsequently decreased by about 5.0 percent from FY 2014 to FY 2016. In FY 2016, revenues and expenditures were roughly at FY 2012 levels—less than 1.0 percent and 2.0 percent below FY 2012, respectively.

Workforce and Staff Development

- The 51 SLAAs reported nearly 2,633 total full-time staff positions for FY 2016, which was a 6.4 percent decrease from FY 2012.
- A total of 367.5 staff—14 percent of all budgeted full-time equivalent (FTE) staff—was reported within the service of administration, 536.7 budgeted FTEs (20 percent) were reported within library development, and 1,276.3 budgeted FTEs (48 percent) were reported within library services. The remaining 452.3 FTE positions (17 percent) were allocated to other services.

Services

- According to FY 2016 survey data, primary services SLAAs provide to libraries and library cooperatives include consulting, administrative library system support, LSTA statewide grant programs, and LSTA statewide services. Most SLAAs provided each of these services.
- During FY 2016, 49 SLAAs (96 percent) provided some form of consulting services to libraries and library cooperatives, with the most common forms identified as library management or organizational development (96 percent), continuing education (94 percent), youth services (96 percent), technology and connectivity (92 percent), and E-Rate consulting (90 percent).
- Fifty SLAAs provided assistance for continuing education programs to at least one type of library in FY 2016. In addition, 44 SLAAs (86 percent)

reported having statewide reading programs. The most common target audiences for SLAA reading programs were the middle childhood and early childhood groups.

- Thirty-five SLAAs (69 percent) provided some type of literacy program in FY 2016. The most commonly offered literacy program was on digital literacy, offered by 33 SLAAs (65 percent), followed by information literacy and language literacy, both offered by 29 SLAAs (57 percent).
- Operational assistance describes services provided by SLAAs to assist and support the development of libraries or to link libraries to external networks. Although the majority of SLAAs provided assistance in the form of interlibrary loan referral and reference referral services (84 and 82 percent, respectively) in FY 2016, only about half provided cooperative purchasing of materials.
- Coordination and integration of library services include working with the materials, services, and programs designed to meet users' needs. By far, SLAAs provided statewide resource-sharing services more than other coordination and integration services in FY 2016. Statewide resource sharing describes organized efforts to support the sharing of services and materials. Only a small share of SLAAs provided support for coordination on acquisitions using other federal program funds (29 percent).

Library Acquisition Expenditures, 2018–2019: U.S. Public, Academic, Special, and Government Libraries

The information in these tables is taken from the 2019–2020 edition of *American Library Directory* (*ALD*) (Information Today, Inc.). The tables report acquisition expenditures by public, academic, special, and government libraries.

Understanding the Tables

Number of libraries includes only those U.S. libraries in *ALD* that reported annual acquisition expenditures. Libraries that reported annual income but not expenditures are not included in the count. Academic libraries include university, college, and junior college libraries. Special academic libraries, such as law and medical libraries, that reported acquisition expenditures separately from the institution's main library are counted as independent libraries.

The amount in the *total acquisition expenditures* column for a given state is generally greater than the sum of the categories of expenditures. This is because the total acquisition expenditures amount also includes the expenditures of libraries that did not itemize by category.

Figures in *categories of expenditure* columns represent only those libraries that itemized expenditures. Libraries that reported a total acquisition expenditure amount but did not itemize are only represented in the total acquisition expenditures column.

Table 1 / Public Library Acquisition Expenditures

			Category of Expenditures (in U.S. dollars)								
State	Number of Libraries	Total Acquisition Expenditures	Books	Other Print Materials	Periodicals/ Serials	Manuscripts & Archives	AV Equipment	AV Materials	Microforms	Electronic Reference	Preservation
Alabama	12	2,236,455	540,657	12,043	8,311	0	4,700	46,664	0	96,608	20,200
Alaska	9	1,854,186	893,275	17,876	85,635	43,021	0	292,211	500	228,457	6,871
Arizona	18	17,916,716	3,097,993	136,909	93,630	575	0	1,142,420	0	629,884	0
Arkansas	6	614,869	186,063	250	17,563	500	0	39,307	0	42,186	0
California	54	75,712,426	29,378,544	813,498	1,845,789	9,000	43,417	7,711,259	63,972	7,759,850	73,161
Colorado	18	13,946,275	4,232,852	448,462	384,357	0	15,000	2,072,167	0	2,402,184	0
Connecticut	38	18,190,409	2,117,983	8,788	597,157	5,305	8,000	507,582	1,080	872,961	39,362
Delaware	2	71,429	40,000	0	5,000	0	0	0	0	0	0
District of Columbia	0	0	0	0	0	0	0	0	0	0	0
Florida	27	23,405,649	10,626,461	844,731	897,389	0	52,514	3,751,911	39,305	5,252,947	0
Georgia	11	2,162,031	838,643	42,253	72,331	0	2,026	252,210	1,850	231,928	198
Hawaii	1	4,667,509	2,792,035	58,456	136,482	0	0	0	36,042	1,644,494	0
Idaho	7	539,840	116,220	1,736	82	0	0	6,261	0	11,360	0
Illinois	77	49,952,476	10,676,153	11,337	483,470	3,000	34,419	3,109,290	9,046	4,291,160	4,000
Indiana	44	24,493,326	8,956,823	12,000	1,002,172	0	102,737	3,808,726	17,254	5,023,504	0
Iowa	46	4,793,669	1,848,886	52,724	133,326	4,000	12,183	616,255	6,190	474,815	0
Kansas	24	4,716,211	1,093,545	0	118,157	0	4,300	216,305	5,600	103,120	3,600
Kentucky	20	11,826,470	2,414,264	109,345	294,949	0	30,224	953,111	1,400	1,824,467	40,776
Louisiana	8	11,324,168	4,090,386	58,554	436,607	0	175,561	1,543,807	5,582	3,453,102	0
Maine	24	880,742	376,469	1,000	74,754	2,000	5,000	96,153	800	235,535	1,000
Maryland	2	7,791,058	0	0	0	0	0	0	0	0	0
Massachusetts	48	13,269,176	2,719,369	65,903	312,921	0	2,717	852,830	10,734	587,175	700
Michigan	53	24,066,080	4,804,241	176,532	342,534	0	30,000	1,589,496	10,186	1,358,573	1,500
Minnesota	19	78,917,084	1,810,098	64,023	30,213	0	83	352,050	257	418,662	516
Mississippi	5	819,046	471,781	0	80,664	0	0	28,981	26,000	149,093	2,162

Missouri	23	19,054,232	5,047,645	105,000	385,186	0	20,045	2,542,264	32,651	3,531,157	150
Montana	14	1,032,274	433,495	98,472	65,756	200	4,373	140,249	0	100,382	7,302
Nebraska	19	11,416,426	239,519	119,000	19,366	0	47	42,114	440	1,406,775	0
Nevada	4	383,469	123,010	0	12,878	0	0	34,565	0	23,084	894
New Hampshire	33	814,335	451,816	1,031	25,796	0	6,600	118,653	2,600	65,321	400
New Jersey	50	16,040,212	9,711,390	117,114	837,568	500	21,500	1,805,298	71,519	1,343,094	7,306
New Mexico	11	2,824,240	1,497,625	214,972	48,013	0	6,000	310,414	9,013	470,450	0
New York	83	36,990,735	13,871,866	46,147	1,204,579	0	257,754	2,634,920	43,360	2,084,098	4,475
North Carolina	11	6,489,140	1,093,475	50,273	85,732	0	7,000	205,236	1,040	97,064	0
North Dakota	9	1,498,975	510,503	300	45,579	0	0	97,880	2,000	300,005	1,000
Ohio	43	59,257,192	15,249,049	327,227	2,379,865	6,921	48,301	7,752,982	248,835	9,417,867	210,489
Oklahoma	13	13,024,342	4,866,187	4,546	859,468	0	0	2,177,435	4,485	1,900,882	0
Oregon	21	4,998,842	2,451,365	14,862	250,112	0	3,500	984,827	23,489	223,697	3,000
Pennsylvania	45	18,547,088	3,578,902	846,770	699,569	156,260	2,226	2,164,588	170,236	1,213,247	235,005
Rhode Island	7	9,796,968	573,670	71,214	49,291	0	0	144,170	70	861,204	650
South Carolina	9	9,867,343	4,412,258	31,426	114,500	0	0	1,883,855	0	1,042,121	0
South Dakota	10	2,282,158	893,044	15,756	69,051	0	16,846	332,722	2,558	300,537	0
Tennessee	15	55,756,810	23,894,188	276,606	728,857	1,000	2,438,770	8,689,808	0	18,486,096	12,107
Texas	83	51,778,396	8,104,717	303,757	478,942	0	27,223	1,463,144	22,030	1,932,972	34,700
Utah	6	2,023,733	1,127,291	0	9,000	0	0	637,161	0	311,455	0
Vermont	21	503,827	253,971	90	15,169	0	0	79,345	0	30,171	500
Virginia	22	9,801,180	3,839,331	146,792	357,413	41,810	22,043	1,153,834	34,878	1,361,016	1,336,701
Washington	14	4,857,026	1,020,691	56,771	105,003	0	1,975	297,298	622	338,610	400
West Virginia	8	1,313,757	576,420	3,000	69,061	0	0	157,301	13,500	211,131	1,500
Wisconsin	43	5,279,380	2,072,684	75,260	124,064	0	15,952	685,418	2,746	280,107	0
Wyoming	8	837,203	161,233	500	13,360	0	0	58,923	40	13,388	0
Puerto Rico	0	0	0	0	0	0	0	0	0	0	0
Total	1,198	740,636,583	200,178,086	5,863,306	16,506,671	274,092	3,423,036	65,583,400	921,910	84,437,996	2,050,625
Estimated % of Acquisition Expenditures			27.03	0.79	2.23	0.04	0.46	0.86	0.12	11.40	0.28

Table 2 / Academic Library Acquisition Expenditures

State	Number of Libraries	Total Acquisition Expenditures	Category of Expenditures (in U.S. dollars)								
			Books	Other Print Materials	Periodicals/ Serials	Manuscripts & Archives	AV Equipment	AV Materials	Microforms	Electronic Reference	Preservation
Alabama	7	5,342,197	500,768	6,031	2,355,794	0	0	38,322	61,000	1,308,910	29,807
Alaska	2	1,900,000	200,000	20,000	1,600,000	0	0	17,500	2,500	50,000	0
Arizona	3	2,530,626	12,136	0	41,543	0	0	862	0	171,474	0
Arkansas	7	12,509,278	1,291,164	419,834	6,452,380	34,264	2,000	28,472	426,218	1,029,627	9,187
California	35	69,995,763	2,974,187	548,107	5,564,980	2,199	37,081	156,732	26,433	10,288,984	106,675
Colorado	9	17,524,669	1,136,926	24,832	477,205	0	0	119,339	0	5,056,113	27,747
Connecticut	7	10,331,989	956,684	32,628	2,933,898	0	80,000	25,127	0	617,150	13,276
Delaware	2	12,371,806	0	0	0	0	0	0	0	0	0
District of Columbia	2	6,803,069	439,600	110,000	1,803,000	0	0	3,267	34,380	1,409,960	47,000
Florida	13	28,179,259	3,934,296	828,478	12,353,995	0	0	269,559	93,114	10,941,329	132,028
Georgia	14	19,883,297	501,715	2,000	925,072	0	3,098	32,450	4,100	1,268,160	300
Hawaii	0	0	0	0	0	0	0	0	0	0	0
Idaho	2	9,081,145	368,331	54,040	1,886,540	0	0	11,776	0	597,018	24,910
Illinois	24	51,726,562	1,503,982	7,648	3,171,395	0	0	99,524	22,560	2,296,252	80,740
Indiana	14	16,072,880	1,381,814	20,385	4,367,062	0	18	52,740	4,978	2,708,645	23,506
Iowa	13	22,727,460	2,076,359	391,576	5,905,596	0	6,000	52,611	33,353	2,088,548	79,027
Kansas	11	8,097,768	786,698	22,300	6,068,100	3,000	0	47,943	27,314	734,349	39,839
Kentucky	7	16,007,971	492,821	17,945	2,393,688	0	2,886	83,465	38,443	272,628	8,170
Louisiana	7	3,521,753	234,423	2,935	1,374,372	500	0	4,935	36,508	1,243,435	23,182
Maine	3	10,402,740	1,264,860	177,656	7,564,612	0	0	0	53,849	475,000	32,730
Maryland	12	11,562,565	1,513,419	34,648	8,393,702	12,434	0	39,469	6,642	1,370,864	49,919
Massachusetts	12	24,214,255	1,046,711	0	2,503,929	36,000	19,011	75,554	2,810	7,531,627	132,781
Michigan	23	23,247,625	2,204,547	139,140	9,137,421	25,203	1,000	150,103	1,398,525	6,969,418	45,742
Minnesota	10	5,545,824	736,431	10,000	1,715,569	280	53,955	70,981	18,459	766,085	40,401
Mississippi	1	96,040	10,000	0	2,700	0	0	0	0	83,340	0

Missouri	15	12,072,581	521,012	0	2,010,172	8,767	4,120	102,294	115,045	1,049,221	31,576
Montana	1	172,720	69,825	0	74,192	0	0	0	0	0	0
Nebraska	6	15,305,680	423,064	89,831	2,585,387	15,000	0	67,021	66,665	1,258,355	14,160
Nevada	0	0	0	0	0	0	0	0	0	0	0
New Hampshire	0	0	0	0	0	0	0	0	0	0	0
New Jersey	10	60,518,541	1,092,915	0	2,567,365	1,000	0	59,313	0	2,084,030	11,383
New Mexico	4	3,330,114	137,311	0	2,685,913	11,802	0	19,878	16,450	112,334	28,574
New York	35	42,321,287	7,034,978	251,509	10,899,958	29,596	68,871	376,335	53,829	10,997,084	206,545
North Carolina	19	71,566,808	1,023,737	82,542	3,699,115	0	1,106,546	136,814	157,167	1,026,945	13,000
North Dakota	2	2,965,537	365,806	0	2,011,935	0	0	30,752	684	539,766	16,594
Ohio	22	33,367,755	2,203,510	0	4,245,053	927	14,254	144,634	54,688	1,529,770	56,851
Oklahoma	6	4,996,243	187,103	575	1,792,261	1,000	0	26,384	0	2,043,618	9,717
Oregon	8	22,471,431	781,170	0	2,462,941	0	32,779	80,337	0	671,127	18,704
Pennsylvania	22	14,852,232	2,192,716	8,585	5,497,253	1,485	0	181,170	22,486	2,807,010	88,993
Rhode Island	3	1,855,603	439,983	0	925,966	5,840	0	23,270	3,000	450,870	6,674
South Carolina	6	6,381,487	1,021,816	289,130	769,178	20,000	137,300	87,153	60,264	2,450,960	47,510
South Dakota	2	2,615,918	135,096	0	1,710,231	0	718	18,515	2,816	106,460	39,562
Tennessee	10	14,764,961	427,742	0	773,668	0	0	38,858	8,900	895,746	3,613
Texas	29	56,581,104	4,301,924	34,000	15,155,910	5,050	89,327	150,651	67,935	4,846,169	114,525
Utah	3	7,930,967	449,582	0	445,188	0	5,000	35,458	0	206,205	21,249
Vermont	2	1,297,065	228,831	4,240	933,841	524	0	26,937	2,266	95,100	5,326
Virginia	12	27,604,445	3,405,191	0	7,270,706	0	1,970	235,962	12,586	4,996,068	58,327
Washington	10	12,967,417	1,351,931	0	6,599,545	2,000	46,000	187,320	7,900	1,561,261	18,098
West Virginia	9	3,048,850	182,839	975	329,380	6,750	14,300	16,675	51,837	496,352	10,778
Wisconsin	9	10,316,553	457,296	1,964	983,963	1,879	0	95,454	14,256	1,648,338	6,446
Wyoming	0	0	0	0	0	0	0	0	0	0	0
Puerto Rico	5	1,194,297	148,552	7,205	275,499	5,000	3,263	19,302	0	450,913	2,300
Total	490	820,176,137	54,151,802	3,640,739	165,697,173	230,500	1,729,497	3,541,218	3,009,960	101,602,618	1,777,472
Estimated % of Acquisition Expenditures			6.60	0.44	20.20	0.03	0.21	0.43	0.37	12.39	0.22

Table 3 / Special Library Acquisition Expenditures

State	Number of Libraries	Total Acquisition Expenditures	Category of Expenditures (in U.S. dollars)								
			Books	Other Print Materials	Periodicals/ Serials	Manuscripts & Archives	AV Equipment	AV Materials	Microforms	Electronic Reference	Preservation
Alabama	0	0	0	0	0	0	0	0	0	0	0
Alaska	0	0	0	0	0	0	0	0	0	0	0
Arizona	2	5,324	3,500	0	324	0	0	0	0	0	1,000
Arkansas	0	0	0	0	0	0	0	0	0	0	0
California	7	292,261	95,536	0	49,047	600	0	26,438	0	88,359	2,281
Colorado	0	0	0	0	0	0	0	0	0	0	0
Connecticut	1	1,000	0	0	0	0	0	0	0	0	0
Delaware	0	0	0	0	0	0	0	0	0	0	0
District of Columbia	2	71,000	48,000	0	20,000	0	0	0	2,000	0	1,000
Florida	0	0	0	0	0	0	0	0	0	0	0
Georgia	0	0	0	0	0	0	0	0	0	0	0
Hawaii	0	0	0	0	0	0	0	0	0	0	0
Idaho	0	0	0	0	0	0	0	0	0	0	0
Illinois	6	3,298,700	66,300	30,000	86,500	4,000	0	2,200	1,000	66,500	5,200
Indiana	1	86,000	0	0	0	0	0	0	0	0	0
Iowa	1	10,000	0	0	0	0	0	0	0	0	0
Kansas	1	6,000	3,000	0	3,000	0	0	0	0	0	0
Kentucky	0	0	0	0	0	0	0	0	0	0	0
Louisiana	1	18,000	5,000	0	13,000	0	0	0	0	0	0
Maine	0	0	0	0	0	0	0	0	0	0	0
Maryland	1	1,000	500	0	300	100	0	0	0	0	100
Massachusetts	0	0	0	0	0	0	0	0	0	0	0
Michigan	1	12,000	3,000	500	3,600	0	0	400	0	0	0
Minnesota	1	50,000	20,000	5,000	9,000	0	0	0	0	16,000	0
Mississippi	0	0	0	0	0	0	0	0	0	0	0

Missouri	0	0	0	0	0	0	0	0	0	0	0
Montana	0	0	0	0	0	0	0	0	0	0	0
Nebraska	1	800	300	0	500	0	0	0	0	0	0
Nevada	0	0	0	0	0	0	0	0	0	0	0
New Hampshire	2	92,000	16,000	10,000	5,000	20,000	0	0	0	32,000	9,000
New Jersey	3	24,700	10,500	0	2,500	1,500	0	0	0	2,000	5,200
New Mexico	2	11,500	1,000	0	1,000	0	0	0	0	0	500
New York	9	496,879	257,605	0	47,278	0	500	0	0	38,475	151,021
North Carolina	0	0	0	0	0	0	0	0	0	0	0
North Dakota	1	8,098	2,660	0	3,975	0	0	0	0	0	1,463
Ohio	4	630,476	51,390	550	36,817	2,169	0	850	0	25,615	900
Oklahoma	1	160,000	8,000	0	45,000	0	0	0	0	0	0
Oregon	0	0	0	0	0	0	0	0	0	0	0
Pennsylvania	1	106,357	7,108	47,812	5,059	18,351	0	4,671	0	3,322	20,034
Rhode Island	0	0	0	0	0	0	0	0	0	0	0
South Carolina	0	0	0	0	0	0	0	0	0	0	0
South Dakota	1	105,000	0	0	0	0	0	0	0	0	0
Tennessee	0	0	0	0	0	0	0	0	0	0	0
Texas	3	1,582,030	3,030	12,000	2,000	0	0	0	0	805,000	0
Utah	1	75,000	5,000	5,000	10,000	0	5,000	0	0	50,000	0
Vermont	0	0	0	0	0	0	0	0	0	0	0
Virginia	4	183,337	86,409	82	47,060	4,026	0	0	0	44,000	1,740
Washington	1	19,800	7,000	0	10,200	0	0	0	0	0	2,600
West Virginia	0	0	0	0	0	0	0	0	0	0	0
Wisconsin	2	85,500	4,000	0	20,000	0	0	0	0	60,000	0
Wyoming	0	0	0	0	0	0	0	0	0	0	0
Puerto Rico	0	0	0	0	0	0	0	0	0	0	0
Total	61	7,432,762	704,838	110,944	421,160	50,746	5,500	34,559	3,000	1,231,271	202,039
Estimated % of Acquisition Expenditures			9.48	1.49	5.67	0.68	0.07	0.46	0.04	16.57	2.72

Table 4 / Government Library Acquisition Expenditures

State	Number of Libraries	Total Acquisition Expenditures	Category of Expenditures (in U.S. dollars)								
			Books	Other Print Materials	Periodicals/ Serials	Manuscripts & Archives	AV Equipment	AV Materials	Microforms	Electronic Reference	Preservation
Alabama	1	275,000	75,000	0	0	0	0	0	0	200,000	0
Alaska	0	0	0	0	0	0	0	0	0	0	0
Arizona	1	2,012	2,000	0	12	0	0	0	0	0	0
Arkansas	0	0	0	0	0	0	0	0	0	0	0
California	4	539,005	234,264	0	1,442	0	0	0	0	145,582	0
Colorado	0	0	0	0	0	0	0	0	0	0	0
Connecticut	0	0	0	0	0	0	0	0	0	0	0
Delaware	0	0	0	0	0	0	0	0	0	0	0
District of Columbia	0	0	0	0	0	0	0	0	0	0	0
Florida	0	0	0	0	0	0	0	0	0	0	0
Georgia	0	0	0	0	0	0	0	0	0	0	0
Hawaii	0	0	0	0	0	0	0	0	0	0	0
Idaho	0	0	0	0	0	0	0	0	0	0	0
Illinois	0	0	0	0	0	0	0	0	0	0	0
Indiana	0	0	0	0	0	0	0	0	0	0	0
Iowa	0	0	0	0	0	0	0	0	0	0	0
Kansas	1	515,260	26,852	0	396,491	0	0	0	0	85,690	6,227
Kentucky	0	0	0	0	0	0	0	0	0	0	0
Louisiana	2	1,803,887	615,201	0	54,114	0	0	1,000	887	263,521	8,034
Maine	1	380,116	0	0	0	0	0	0	0	0	0
Maryland	1	37,000	5,000	0	32,000	0	0	0	0	0	0
Massachusetts	0	0	0	0	0	0	0	0	0	0	0
Michigan	1	35,000	0	0	0	0	0	0	0	0	0
Minnesota	1	74,500	10,000	0	45,500	0	0	0	0	19,000	0
Mississippi	0	0	0	0	0	0	0	0	0	0	0

Missouri	0	0	0	0	0	0	0	0	0	0	0
Montana	0	0	0	0	0	0	0	0	0	0	0
Nebraska	0	0	0	0	0	0	0	0	0	0	0
Nevada	0	0	0	0	0	0	0	0	0	0	0
New Hampshire	0	0	0	0	0	0	0	0	0	0	0
New Jersey	0	0	0	0	0	0	0	0	0	0	0
New Mexico	0	0	0	0	0	0	0	0	0	0	0
New York	0	0	0	0	0	0	0	0	0	0	0
North Carolina	0	0	0	0	0	0	0	0	0	0	0
North Dakota	0	0	0	0	0	0	0	0	0	0	0
Ohio	0	0	0	0	0	0	0	0	0	0	0
Oklahoma	0	0	0	0	0	0	0	0	0	0	0
Oregon	0	0	0	0	0	0	0	0	0	0	0
Pennsylvania	2	470,000	0	0	0	0	0	0	0	0	0
Rhode Island	0	0	0	0	0	0	0	0	0	0	0
South Carolina	0	0	0	0	0	0	0	0	0	0	0
South Dakota	0	0	0	0	0	0	0	0	0	0	0
Tennessee	0	0	0	0	0	0	0	0	0	0	0
Texas	0	0	0	0	0	0	0	0	0	0	0
Utah	0	0	0	0	0	0	0	0	0	0	0
Vermont	0	0	0	0	0	0	0	0	0	0	0
Virginia	0	0	0	0	0	0	0	0	0	0	0
Washington	0	0	0	0	0	0	0	0	0	0	0
West Virginia	1	650,000	50,000	0	400,000	0	0	0	0	200,000	0
Wisconsin	2	91,000	45,000	0	0	0	0	0	0	36,000	0
Wyoming	0	0	0	0	0	0	0	0	0	0	0
Puerto Rico	0	0	0	0	0	0	0	0	0	0	0
Total	18	4,872,780	1,063,317	0	929,559	0	0	1,000	887	949,793	14,261
Estimated % of Acquisition Expenditures			21.82	0.00	19.08	0.00	0.00	0.02	0.02	19.49	0.29

Year in Architecture 2018: Modern Times

Bette-Lee Fox
Managing Editor, *Library Journal*

Library Spaces That Honor the Past While Moving Full Steam Ahead

There can be a quaintness to restoring old architectural elements, a sense of history regained and legacies appreciated, but this year there is nothing nostalgic or old-fashioned about our compilation of academic and public library building projects, completed between July 1, 2017, and June 30, 2018. They shout "today" and embrace a 21st-century aesthetic even in historic structures.

The Ways of Academe

The David K. Hill Family Library at Harper College, Palatine, Illinois, took a dark half-century-old library and turned it into a light-filled heart of the campus, with window walls extended for an additional 3,500 square feet.

Pepperdine's Payson Library, Malibu, California, honors its Spanish Revival roots but has been remodeled for the demands of digital integration and "diverse learning styles." The New York Public Library's Schomburg Center for Research in Black Culture updated its research and gallery spaces while adding an exterior signage system connecting the community to activities within the building.

The Sterling C. Evans Library at Texas A&M University, College Station, was purpose-built for multifunction, multimedia, and active learning while remaining alert to the need for a quiet study environment.

Public Pride

Anchoring a new commercial district, the Madison Public Library, Alabama, was inspired by historic cotton mills. Corrugated metal, brick, and exposed trusses open up to a large sweep of glass. Public art is a highlight of two LA County branches. "Lady Artesia" by Sonia Romero, in the Artesia Library, is a silk-screened ceramic tile mural symbolizing the area's agricultural and dairy industry roots, while the Los Nietos Library displays Louise Griffin's 3-D mural "Everyday Places."

A reworked senior center is the foundation for the new Hilliard Branch of the Columbus Metropolitan Library (CML), Ohio, with existing structural cross-bracing reimagined as reading nooks and an existing floor opened to create a light well enhanced by a grand staircase.

Adapted from *Library Journal,* November 20, 2018. For the Year in Architecture 2018, *Library Journal* solicited information from public and academic libraries nationwide that had undergone new builds and renovation/addition projects completed between July 1, 2017, and June 30, 2018. The tables that follow comprise complete financial and construction statistics for the library buildings submitted, including Canadian projects.

Another Buckeye library, the Middleburg Heights Branch of the Cuyahoga County Public Library, has the largest number of people with autism in the system's service area. The new design, layout, and color palette are intended to be compatible with how members of this community "experience the world." Sensors prevent extreme sunlight in the space, while the children's section includes interactive items for literacy and motor development.

The George W. Hawkes Downtown Library, Arlington, Texas, has a children's DISCOVER wall interactive art installation with reading nooks, while teens get stadium seating. Leadership in Energy & Environmental Design (LEED) Platinum certified, the Central Library of the Austin Public Library, Texas, encompasses a rooftop butterfly garden, a 350-seat special events area, a cookbook bar and café, a technology petting zoo, and a 200-item-capacity bicycle corral.

The Colby Community Library, Wisconsin, sits on a five-acre lot in the city famous for cheese, with an outdoor amphitheater for programming and performances. There are stained glass windows, a fireplace, and hand-applied magazine ads from the 1930s to 1960s as wall coverings, in addition to a full kitchen in the community room and STEAM (Science, Technology, Engineering, Arts, and Math) activities.

Remodel to Remix

The Columbine Library, Littleton, Colorado, met the Jefferson County Public Library's vision for a 21st-century presence by focusing on the user experience. It also exposed the barrel-vaulted ceiling from the building's initial design.

Along with a world languages collection including Hindi, Telugu, Tamil, and Mandarin, the Sharon Forks Library, Cumming, Georgia, features a Hot Spot room.

The Hamilton East Public Library, Fishers, Indiana, has among its collection a kit library, with supplies and tools for an array of activities, and a maker-in-residence area to support Indiana artists. Renovations to the Anderson Public Library, Indiana, include an early literacy room with computers, a play kitchen, and a nursery gym play structure. As well, there is a Mamava lactation pod for nursing parents. A nursing lounge has also been incorporated into the Richland Library Wheatley, South Carolina.

The Daniel Boone Branch of the St. Louis County Library, Ellisville, Missouri, entertains young patrons with a pneumatic tube maze and an interactive light wall, while teens and business folks have dedicated spaces.

With a nod to what's trending, the Livonia Public Library, New York, remodel encompasses reading nooks for kids, a healthy habits concession area, refinished hardwood floors and wainscoting, and a reading lounge.

For that open airy feel, retractable glass walls are big at the Sycamore Plaza Library, Pickerington, Ohio, as well as the addition to the Franklin Public Library, Massachusetts, which was established with 116 volumes donated by Benjamin Franklin. The Franklin County Library, Winchester, Tennessee, has a STREAM Lab for its patrons.

The Cuero Municipal Library, Texas, added a clock tower entry in keeping with its modified Spanish style, along with a 6,000-square-foot outdoor pavilion. It's all here: classic design, fresh features, meeting the future of libraries.

Table 1 / New Academic Buildings, 2018

Institution	Project Cost	Gross Area (Sq. Ft.)	Sq. Ft. Cost	Constr. Cost	Furniture / Equip. Cost	Book Capacity	Architect
Learning Resource Center, Suffolk County Community College, Brentwood, N.Y.	$30,000,000	78,000	$384.62	$24,000,000	$2,200,000	74,000	ikon.5 architects; Wiedersum Assocs.
University of Arkansas Library Annex, Fayetteville	14,800,000	27,000	425.93	11,500,000	2,000,000	2,000,000	Perry Dean Rogers

Table 2 / Academic Library Buildings, Renovations Only, 2018

Institution	Project Cost	Gross Area (Sq. Ft.)	Sq. Ft. Cost	Constr. Cost	Furniture / Equip. Cost	Book Capacity	Architect
Auraria Library, University of Colorado, Denver	$29,300,000	180,000	n.a.	n.a.	n.a.	n.a.	studiotrope Design Collective
David K. Hill Family Library, Harper College, Palatine, Ill.	27,432,319	107,000	$207.30	$22,180,601	$3,321,158	109,529	Legat Architects
Payson Library, Pepperdine University, Malibu, Calif.	22,400,000	66,554	285.67	19,012,461	3,380,877	150,000	AC Martin
Schomburg Center for Research in Black Culture, New York Public Library	22,300,000	9,000	n.a.	n.a.	n.a.	n.a.	Marble Fairbanks
Bizzell Memorial Library–Zarrow Family Faculty and Graduate Student Center, University of Oklahoma, Norman	8,600,000	24,658	255.50	6,300,000	2,300,000	n.a.	REES Associates, Inc.
Sterling C. Evans Library, Texas A&M University, College Station	7,300,000	72,000	83.33	6,000,000	1,300,000	n.a.	HBM Architects; BRW
Maxine Houghton Wallin Special Collections Research Center, University of Minnesota Libraries–Twin Cities	4,965,000	15,369	205.49	3,158,161	570,343	110,000	Bentz/Thompson/Rietow
John T. Richardson Library, DePaul University, Chicago	4,126,000	28,000	126.78	3,550,000	571,000	73,822	Vasilko Architects
DeWitt Wallace Library, Macalester College, St. Paul	1,841,000	9,937	131.93	1,311,000	303,000	n.a.	HGA

n.a.=not available

Table 3 / Academic Library Buildings, Additions and Renovations, 2018

Institution	Status	Project Cost	Gross Area (Sq. Ft.)	Sq. Ft. Cost	Constr. Cost	Furniture / Equip. Cost	Book Capacity	Architect
Seeley G. Mudd Library, Northwestern University, Evanston, Ill.	TOTAL	$29,000,000	35,500	$656.33	$23,300,000	$1,400,000	30,000	Flad Architects
	NEW	n.a.	n.a.	n.a.	n.a.	n.a.	n.a.	
	RENOVATED	n.a.	n.a.	n.a.	n.a.	n.a.	n.a.	
Alcuin Library, Saint John's University, Collegeville, Minn.	TOTAL	25,786,000	102,248	201.59	20,611,000	2,273,932	515,000	CSNA Architects
	NEW	10,586,000	21,701	419.84	9,111,000	710,780	15,000	
	RENOVATED	15,200,000	80,547	142.77	11,500,000	1,563,152	500,000	
Nash Library and Student Learning Commons, Gannon University, Erie, Pa.	TOTAL	14,608,085	88,017	148.23	13,046,820	1,561,265	230,000	Buehler & Associates
	NEW	1,310,526	5,525	237.19	1,310,526	0	0	
	RENOVATED	13,297,559	82,492	142.27	11,736,294	1,561,265	230,000	

n.a.=not available

Table 4 / New Public Library Buildings, 2018

Community	Pop. ('000)	Code	Project Cost	Const. Cost	Gross Sq. Ft.	Sq. Ft. Cost	Equip. Cost	Site Cost	Other Costs	Federal Funds	State Funds	Local Funds	Gift Funds	Architect
Alabama														
Madison	49	B	$8,670,000	$5,300,000	25,000	$212.00	$750,000	$920,000	$1,700,000	$0	$0	$7,749,000	$921,000	HBM Architects; Fuqua & Partners
Arkansas														
Sherwood	31	B	5,855,014	4,182,756	14,244	293.65	393,246	839,284	439,728	0	0	5,855,014	0	Taggart Architects
California														
Artesia	17	B	10,300,000	7,500,000	10,836	692.14	800,000	Owned	2,000,000	0	0	10,300,000	0	IBI Group
Whittier	9	B	7,000,000	4,800,000	7,040	681.82	500,000	Owned	1,700,000	0	0	7,000,000	0	Emar Studio for Public Architecture
Connecticut														
Oxford	13	M	3,740,000	3,000,000	11,978	250.46	132,000	Owned	608,000	0	0	3,628,000	112,000	Peter Gisolfi Associates
Delaware														
New Castle	12	M	23,565,927	16,879,883	43,000	392.56	1,109,988	3,051,181	2,524,875	0	12,210,106	16,038,739	690,000	Tetra Tech; Perkins + Will
Florida														
Tampa	17	B	9,964,965	4,009,000	16,850	237.93	985,000	305,000	4,665,965	0	500,000	9,464,965	0	Harvard Jolly Architecture
Georgia														
Marietta	756	B	14,050,000	11,900,000	31,000	383.87	1,000,000	600,000	550,000	0	2,000,000	12,050,000	0	CAS Architecture
Hawaii														
Nanakuli	27	B	15,500,000	n.a.	18,000	n.a.	n.a.	Owned	n.a.	0	15,500,000	0	0	CDS International

Kansas														
Wichita	390	M	34,352,605	22,035,211	105,200	209.46	4,015,229	3,425,950	4,876,215	0	0	31,190,000	5,500,000	GLMV Architecture
Kentucky														
Louisville	178	O	15,474,139	11,883,507	38,191	311.16	858,153	1,451,900	1,280,579	0	1,380,000	12,571,900	1,522,239	JRA Architects; MSR Design
Ohio														
Hilliard	100	B	15,074,743	8,875,398	55,000	161.37	973,542	925,000	4,300,803	0	0	15,074,743	0	DesignGroup
Middleburg Hts.	16	B	7,500,000	6,000,000	16,000	375.00	500,000	Owned	1,000,000	0	0	7,500,000	10,000	HBM Architects
Youngstown	25	B	4,375,858	3,512,766	11,514	305.09	539,438	Owned	323,654	0	0	2,695,858	1,680,000	Faniro Architects
South Carolina														
Simpsonville	46	B	9,514,394	6,578,774	28,064	234.42	1,309,922	911,016	714,612	0	0	9,387,385	126,939	McMillan Pazdan Smith; Margaret Sullivan Studio
South Dakota														
Aberdeen	39	M	8,339,178	6,514,200	28,200	231.00	1,040,250	Owned	784,728	0	0	6,239,178	2,100,000	CO-OP Architecture; MSR Design
Texas														
Arlington	392	M	29,082,020	19,044,730	81,228	234.46	3,933,000	Owned	6,104,290	0	0	21,508,465	7,573,555	Dewberry
Austin	968	MS	127,181,971	100,621,800	213,450	471.41	8,380,700	14,425	18,165,046	0	0	127,181,971	0	Lake | Flato; Shepley Bulfinch
Washington														
Tukwila	20	B	8,890,000	6,600,000	10,000	660.00	670,000	550,000	1,070,000	0	0	8,890,000	0	Perkins + Will
Wisconsin														
Colby	7	M	2,200,000	1,700,000	10,600	160.38	300,000	100	199,900	500,000	0	500,000	1,200,000	Cedar Corporation

Symbol Code: B—Branch Library; BS—Branch & System Headquarters; M—Main Library; MS—Main & System Headquarters; S—System Headquarters; O—Combined Use Space; n.a.—not available

Table 5 / Public Library Buildings, Additions and Renovations, 2018

Community	Pop. ('000)	Code	Project Cost	Const. Cost	Gross Sq. Ft.	Sq. Ft. Cost	Equip. Cost	Site Cost	Other Costs	Federal Funds	State Funds	Local Funds	Gift Funds	Architect
California														
Napa	140	MS	$4,230,220	$2,940,098	13,300	$221.06	$526,723	Owned	$763,399	$0	$0	$4,230,220	$0	Noll & Tam Architects
Colorado														
Littleton	135	B	4,200,000	3,348,885	30,000	111.63	485,000	Owned	366,335	0	0	4,176,715	23,285	Humphries Poli Architects
Georgia														
Barnesville	19	B	2,153,865	1,673,865	13,000	128.76	100,000	$200,000	180,000	0	1,380,000	773,865	0	CAS Architecture
Cumming	67	B	7,249,525	5,384,612	39,183	137.42	1,093,464	Owned	771,449	0	2,000,000	5,244,525	5,000	McMillan Pazdan Smith
Illinois														
Elmhurst	45	M	1,406,505	838,995	25,000	33.56	363,000	Owned	204,510	0	0	1,406,505	0	Product Architecture + Design
Indiana														
Anderson	71	MS	471,532	192,383	8,350	23.26	200,727	Owned	78,422	0	0	471,532	0	Kimberly Bolan & Associates
Bloomington	147	M	270,348	37,211	32,000	1.17	220,163	Owned	12,974	0	0	270,348	0	Kimberly Bolan & Associates
Fishers	141	B	690,000	425,000	23,000	18.48	225,000	Owned	40,000	0	0	690,000	0	Kimberly Bolan & Associates
Gary	77	M	5,374,997	4,531,239	50,000	90.62	271,682	Owned	572,076	0	0	5,374,997	0	Forms & Funktion, Inc.
North Vernon	28	M	109,479	31,836	4,100	7.77	67,643	Owned	10,000	0	0	99,479	10,000	Kimberly Bolan & Associates
Massachusetts														
Barrington	16	M	3,097,000	2,010,000	13,450	149.45	400,000	Owned	687,000	0	0	3,097,000	0	Tappé Architects
Franklin	33	M	10,070,909	7,720,466	29,938	257.88	928,377	Owned	1,422,066	0	0	10,500,000	0	LLB Architects
Missouri														
Ellisville	64	B	9,577,872	7,110,502	43,981	161.67	861,228	Owned	1,606,142	0	0	9,577,872	0	Bond Architects
Florissant	24	B	6,359,985	4,909,100	34,519	142.21	561,467	Owned	889,418	0	0	6,359,985	0	Bond Architects
Nebraska														
Norfolk	24	M	8,766,642	6,998,055	38,000	184.16	803,000	Owned	965,587	0	750,000	8,011,904	22,000	Alley Poyner Macchietto
New Jersey														
Holmdel	17	M	2,129,000	1,779,000	16,000	111.19	250,000	Leased	100,000	0	0	2,129,000	0	Arcari + Iovino
Pompton Plains	15	M	358,284	326,170	1,400	232.98	9,614	Owned	22,500	0	0	0	358,284	James P. Cutillo & Associates

New York														
Livonia	8	M	2,100,000	1,866,625	7,500	248.89	99,400	Owned	133,975	0	597,000	1,403,000	100,000	Passero Associates
Port Washington	30	M	2,795,000	2,410,000	5,500	438.19	35,000	Owned	350,000	0	650,000	645,000	1,500,000	Lee H. Skolnick; Stalco Const.
White Plains	55	M	2,603,632	1,567,000	24,499	63.97	400,000	Owned	636,632	0	374,000	1,000,000	1,229,632	Bermello Ajamil & Partners
North Carolina														
Charlotte	50	B	8,000,000	7,164,703	26,711	268.23	n.a.	Owned	n.a.	0	0	8,000,000	0	HBM Architects
Monroe	223	MS	918,444	339,337	23,000	14.76	528,797	Owned	50,310	28,000	0	890,444	0	Kimberly Bolan & Associates
Ohio														
Dayton	460	MS	64,000,000	47,000,000	224,000	209.83	2,600,000	Owned	14,400,000	0	0	64,000,000	0	Group 4 Architecture
Pickerington	15	B	750,000	530,000	4,200	126.19	120,000	Leased	100,000	0	0	0	750,000	Moody Nolan
Springfield	132	MS	3,319,990	3,043,004	7,890	385.68	0	Owned	276,986	0	0	3,319,990	0	McCall Sharp Architecture
South Carolina														
Columbia	15	B	3,177,659	2,091,786	11,094	188.55	502,746	Owned	583,127	0	0	3,111,059	66,600	Boudreaux; McMillan Pazdan; Margaret Sullivan
Columbia	40	B	4,405,745	3,069,745	14,700	208.83	445,000	Owned	891,000	0	0	4,340,745	65,000	Liollio Architecture
Columbia	8	B	1,501,954	893,954	4,100	218.04	260,000	Owned	348,000	0	0	1,501,954	0	Liollio Architecture
Tennessee														
Winchester	42	O	135,981	83,844	11,479	7.30	28,340	Owned	23,797	0	0	23,992	111,989	Mark Bennett
Texas														
Cuero	9	M	2,300,000	2,082,575	13,000	160.20	25,000	Owned	192,425	0	0	2,300,000	0	TSG Architects
Utah														
North Ogden	34	B	5,599,054	4,449,448	24,000	185.40	435,050	Owned	714,556	0	0	5,599,054	0	EDA Architects
Ogden	93	M	16,405,164	13,676,894	60,000	227.95	847,455	Owned	1,880,815	0	0	16,030,164	375,000	EDA Architects
Washington														
Bellevue	141	B	1,040,000	690,000	3,000	230.00	120,000	Owned	230,000	0	0	1,040,000	0	Miller Hull Partnership
Colfax	15	O	550,000	470,000	4,000	117.50	0	80,000	0	0	0	80,000	470,000	Tom Maul Architecture
Shoreline	55	B	688,000	390,000	20,000	195.00	245,000	Owned	53,000	0	0	688,000	0	BuildingWork
Wisconsin														
Milwaukee	75	B	5,655,020	4,173,179	23,000	181.44	344,529	Owned	1,137,312	0	0	5,418,182	236,838	HGA
Canada														
Niagara-on-the-Lake, Ont.	17	M	893,236	465,095	10,000	46.50	388,141	Owned	40,000	151,000	67,200	448,840	226,196	Chamberlain Architect Svcs.

Symbol Code: B—Branch Library; Bs—Branch & System Headquarters; M—Main Library; Ms—Main & System Headquarters; S—System Headquarters; O—Combined Use Space; N.a.—Not Available

Table 6 / Six-Year Cost Summary

	Fiscal 2013	Fiscal 2014	Fiscal 2015	Fiscal 2016	Fiscal 2017	Fiscal 2018
Number of new buildings	27	29	38	33	26	20
Number of ARRs	47	55	54	59	44	37
Sq. ft. new buildings	470,167	717,973	896,195	831,110	616,436	775,395
Sq. ft. ARRs	715,380	1,164,535	1,222,795	1,297,229	1,090,370	936,894
New Buildings						
Construction cost	$139,136,298	$212,257,074	$274,900,907	$257,213,872	$207,532,385	$250,938,025
Equipment cost	16,184,831	34,002,671	26,895,130	37,522,113	21,316,125	28,190,468
Site cost	28,272,719	18,929,131	12,031,896	19,242,482	6,968,634	12,993,856
Other cost	29,983,512	49,676,815	68,193,630	73,601,931	41,281,588	53,008,395
New buildings cost	212,079,360	314,866,191	360,746,279	397,152,182	309,498,732	360,630,814
ARRs cost	145,668,398	260,983,928	311,990,635	237,347,021	299,877,478	193,355,042
Total cost	$357,747,758	$575,850,119	$672,736,914	$634,499,203	$609,376,210	$553,985,856

Symbol Code: ARR—Additions, Renovations, and Remodels

Table 7 / Funding Sources

	Fiscal 2013	Fiscal 2014	Fiscal 2015	Fiscal 2016	Fiscal 2017	Fiscal 2018
Federal, new buildings	$1,000,000	$25,617,538	$475,000	$350,000	$25,260,000	$500,000
Federal, ARRs	1,684,211	6,239,463	1,500,000	2,423,000	0	179,000
Federal, total	$2,684,211	$31,857,001	$1,975,000	$2,773,000	$25,260,000	$679,000
State, new buildings	$9,570,111	$64,563,247	$15,169,766	$15,025,234	$3,994,000	$31,590,106
State, ARRs	2,017,590	19,563,872	5,251,244	2,787,038	18,570,711	5,818,200
State, total	$11,587,701	$84,127,119	$20,421,010	$17,812,272	$22,564,711	$37,408,306
Local, new buildings	$192,466,192	$215,147,978	$331,311,400	$371,719,254	$271,148,486	$314,825,218
Local, ARRs	133,692,708	188,446,449	244,614,937	199,559,402	237,888,791	182,254,371
Local, total	$326,158,900	$403,594,427	$575,926,337	$571,278,656	$509,037,277	$497,079,589
Gift, new buildings	$12,366,431	$13,312,404	$24,430,676	$14,388,312	$10,626,623	$21,435,733
Gift, ARRs	8,996,727	50,361,901	63,353,240	32,636,393	43,448,173	5,549,824
Gift, total	$21,363,158	$63,674,305	$87,783,916	$47,024,705	$54,074,796	$26,985,557
Total—Funds Used	$361,793,970	$583,252,852	$686,106,263	$638,888,633	$610,936,784	$562,152,452

Symbol Code: ARR—Additions, Renovations, and Remodels

Public Library State Rankings, 2016

State	Library visits per capita[1]	Registered users per capita[1]	Total circulation per capita[1,2]	Interlibrary loans received per 1,000 population	Average number public-access Internet computers per stationary outlet
Alabama	3	0.6	4	95	17
Alaska	5	0.5	7	19	11
Arizona	4	0.5	7	59	34
Arkansas	4	0.6	5	10	12
California	4	0.6	5	89	20
Colorado	6	0.7	12	217	25
Connecticut	6	0.5	8	273	19
Delaware	4	0.4	7	881	35
District of Columbia[3]	6	0.6	7	0	38
Florida	4	0.6	6	6	32
Georgia	3	0.4	4	1	23
Hawaii[4]	3	0.7	4	0	11
Idaho	6	0.7	11	107	13
Illinois	6	0.4	9	462	20
Indiana	5	0.6	12	93	20
Iowa	6	0.7	9	131	9
Kansas	5	0.7	10	342	10
Kentucky	4	0.6	7	17	24
Louisiana	4	0.5	5	21	17
Maine	6	0.6	8	472	8
Maryland	5	0.6	10	67	27
Massachusetts	6	0.5	9	972	14
Michigan	5	0.5	8	285	19
Minnesota	4	0.7	9	205	16
Mississippi	3	0.6	3	7	12
Missouri	5	0.6	10	69	14
Montana	4	0.5	6	239	11
Nebraska	5	0.7	8	18	11
Nevada	3	0.5	7	35	16
New Hampshire	5	0.6	8	218	7
New Jersey	5	0.5	6	266	19
New Mexico	4	0.7	6	12	15
New York	5	0.6	7	380	18
North Carolina	3	0.6	5	47	20
North Dakota	3	0.4	6	64	11
Ohio	6	0.8	16	1,034	19
Oklahoma	4	0.6	7	13	15
Oregon	6	0.6	15	1,354	13
Pennsylvania	4	0.4	5	385	13
Rhode Island	5	0.4	6	933	21
South Carolina	3	0.5	5	42	22
South Dakota	5	0.5	8	32	8

State	Library visits per capita[1]	Registered users per capita[1]	Total circulation per capita[1,2]	Interlibrary loans received per 1,000 population	Average number public-access Internet computers per stationary outlet
Tennessee	3	0.5	4	17	20
Texas	3	0.5	5	25	24
Utah	5	0.6	12	17	17
Vermont	6	0.6	8	90	7
Virginia	4	0.6	8	16	22
Washington	5	0.6	12	46	17
West Virginia	3	0.5	4	59	8
Wisconsin	5	0.6	10	1,515	14
Wyoming	6	0.6	8	57	12

State	Public-access Internet computers per 5,000 population	Print materials per capita[1,2]	Current print serial subscriptions per 1,000 population	Audio physical materials per 1,000 population	Video physical materials per 1,000 population
Alabama	5	2	2	93	140
Alaska	8	3	7	188	411
Arizona	6	1	2	91	154
Arkansas	5	2	3	95	192
California	3	2	2	84	135
Colorado	6	2	8	171	245
Connecticut	6	4	6	232	339
Delaware	6	2	4	124	267
District of Columbia[3]	7	3	4	44	225
Florida	4	1	2	94	171
Georgia	5	2	1	52	96
Hawaii[4]	2	2	2	146	118
Idaho	7	3	4	165	245
Illinois	7	3	7	245	291
Indiana	7	4	7	254	356
Iowa	8	4	9	215	348
Kansas	7	4	5	191	368
Kentucky	6	2	4	127	205
Louisiana	6	3	5	103	245
Maine	8	5	8	203	340
Maryland	4	2	3	156	187
Massachusetts	5	5	6	228	302
Michigan	6	3	5	203	268
Minnesota	5	3	5	157	193
Mississippi	5	2	2	70	124
Missouri	5	3	5	176	222
Montana	7	3	4	114	199
Nebraska	9	4	7	155	231
Nevada	2	1	2	113	224

State	Public-access Internet computers per 5,000 population	Print materials per capita[1,2]	Current print serial subscriptions per 1,000 population	Audio physical materials per 1,000 population	Video physical materials per 1,000 population
New Hampshire	6	4	8	221	359
New Jersey	5	3	41	187	262
New Mexico	5	3	4	124	206
New York	5	4	8	183	281
North Carolina	4	2	2	67	82
North Dakota	6	3	5	133	190
Ohio	6	3	9	293	457
Oklahoma	5	2	29	129	181
Oregon	4	3	4	196	266
Pennsylvania	3	2	4	136	159
Rhode Island	7	3	5	147	236
South Carolina	5	2	3	94	154
South Dakota	7	4	6	151	208
Tennessee	4	2	2	94	125
Texas	4	2	2	78	125
Utah	4	2	4	208	221
Vermont	9	5	9	211	353
Virginia	5	2	3	119	157
Washington	4	2	5	151	218
West Virginia	4	3	3	109	176
Wisconsin	6	3	7	260	363
Wyoming	8	4	6	292	383

State	Total paid FTE staff per 25,000 population	Paid FTE librarians per 25,000 population	Paid FTE librarians with an ALA-MLS per 25,000 population	Other paid FTE staff per 25,000 population
Alabama	9	4	2	5
Alaska	12	4	2	8
Arizona	7	2	2	5
Arkansas	10	3	1	7
California	7	2	2	5
Colorado	15	5	3	11
Connecticut	16	8	5	9
Delaware	9	3	2	6
District of Columbia[3]	20	6	6	14
Florida	8	2	2	5
Georgia	6	1	1	5
Hawaii[4]	10	3	3	7
Idaho	14	4	2	10
Illinois	18	7	5	11
Indiana	18	6	4	12
Iowa	14	9	2	6
Kansas	17	7	3	10
Kentucky	13	7	2	6

State	Total paid FTE staff per 25,000 population	Paid FTE librarians per 25,000 population	Paid FTE librarians with an ALA-MLS per 25,000 population	Other paid FTE staff per 25,000 population
Louisiana	14	6	2	8
Maine	15	8	4	7
Maryland	14	5	3	9
Massachusetts	14	7	5	7
Michigan	12	5	3	8
Minnesota	10	4	2	6
Mississippi	7	5	1	2
Missouri	15	4	1	11
Montana	10	5	2	5
Nebraska	13	6	2	8
Nevada	7	2	1	5
New Hampshire	16	10	5	6
New Jersey	13	4	4	9
New Mexico	10	4	2	6
New York	16	6	5	11
North Carolina	8	2	2	6
North Dakota	9	5	2	4
Ohio	20	6	4	14
Oklahoma	12	6	3	6
Oregon	13	4	3	9
Pennsylvania	9	3	2	6
Rhode Island	15	6	5	8
South Carolina	10	3	3	7
South Dakota	12	6	2	6
Tennessee	7	2	1	5
Texas	7	2	2	4
Utah	11	3	2	7
Vermont	15	9	3	6
Virginia	12	3	3	9
Washington	14	3	3	11
West Virginia	9	5	1	4
Wisconsin	13	5	3	8
Wyoming	19	7	3	12

State	Total operating revenue per capita[1]	State operating revenue per capita[1]	Local operating revenue per capita[1]	Other operating revenue per capita[1]	Total operating expenditures per capita[1]
Alabama	22	1	20	2	22
Alaska	59	1	53	3	56
Arizona	27	0	26	1	27
Arkansas	30	2	26	2	27
California	38	0	36	2	37
Colorado	63	0	59	4	56
Connecticut	58	0	49	8	60

State	Total operating revenue per capita[1]	State operating revenue per capita[1]	Local operating revenue per capita[1]	Other operating revenue per capita[1]	Total operating expenditures per capita[1]
Delaware	28	4	22	2	27
District of Columbia[3]	84	0	81	2	83
Florida	29	1	26	1	27
Georgia	19	3	15	1	19
Hawaii[4]	25	23	0	1	24
Idaho	41	1	37	3	38
Illinois	68	3	63	3	64
Indiana	56	3	50	3	52
Iowa	42	1	38	3	40
Kansas	54	2	47	5	52
Kentucky	42	1	39	2	34
Louisiana	53	1	50	1	47
Maine	40	0	29	10	40
Maryland	49	9	35	5	47
Massachusetts	45	1	40	4	47
Michigan	44	1	40	2	39
Minnesota	42	2	36	4	41
Mississippi	19	3	12	3	17
Missouri	47	1	43	3	44
Montana	30	1	28	2	27
Nebraska	38	0	36	2	37
Nevada	33	8	23	2	29
New Hampshire	46	0	43	3	46
New Jersey	55	0	53	2	52
New Mexico	32	2	28	1	30
New York	72	3	60	9	66
North Carolina	22	1	20	1	22
North Dakota	29	2	25	2	28
Ohio	70	33	31	6	64
Oklahoma	38	1	35	2	36
Oregon	63	0	60	3	58
Pennsylvania	23	5	13	5	28
Rhode Island	48	8	33	7	47
South Carolina	30	2	27	1	28
South Dakota	36	0	34	1	34
Tennessee	19	0	18	1	19
Texas	21	0	20	1	21
Utah	36	0	34	1	35
Vermont	42	0	33	9	43
Virginia	35	2	32	1	35
Washington	61	0	58	3	59
West Virginia	22	5	15	2	20
Wisconsin	43	1	38	4	40
Wyoming	58	0	55	3	57

State	Total collection expenditures per capita[1]	Total staff expenditures per capita[1]	Salaries and wages expenditures per capita[1]	Reference transactions per capita[1]
Alabama	2	15	12	1
Alaska	4	38	24	1
Arizona	4	16	11	1
Arkansas	4	17	13	1
California	3	23	15	1
Colorado	7	36	26	1
Connecticut	6	44	34	1
Delaware	2	19	14	0
District of Columbia[3]	5	62	50	1
Florida	3	16	12	1
Georgia	2	13	9	1
Hawaii[4]	3	17	17	0
Idaho	4	24	18	1
Illinois	7	42	32	1
Indiana	7	32	24	1
Iowa	5	28	21	1
Kansas	6	31	24	1
Kentucky	5	21	16	1
Louisiana	5	28	20	1
Maine	4	28	22	1
Maryland	6	34	25	1
Massachusetts	6	33	29	1
Michigan	5	24	18	1
Minnesota	4	26	19	1
Mississippi	1	11	8	0
Missouri	7	26	20	1
Montana	3	19	14	0
Nebraska	5	25	18	1
Nevada	4	20	15	1
New Hampshire	5	34	26	1
New Jersey	5	38	27	1
New Mexico	5	19	14	1
New York	6	48	33	1
North Carolina	2	15	11	1
North Dakota	4	18	14	1
Ohio	9	40	30	2
Oklahoma	5	23	17	1
Oregon	6	38	25	1
Pennsylvania	3	19	14	1
Rhode Island	3	34	25	1
South Carolina	4	19	14	1
South Dakota	4	23	17	0
Tennessee	2	12	9	1
Texas	3	14	10	1

State	Total collection expenditures per capita[1]	Total staff expenditures per capita[1]	Salaries and wages expenditures per capita[1]	Reference transactions per capita[1]
Utah	5	22	16	1
Vermont	4	30	23	1
Virginia	4	24	18	1
Washington	8	40	29	1
West Virginia	3	13	10	0
Wisconsin	4	28	21	1
Wyoming	5	43	30	1

1 Per capita is based on the total unduplicated population of legal service areas. The determination of the unduplicated figure is the responsibility of the state library agency and should be based on the most recent state population figures for jurisdictions in the state.

2 The data element definition changed in FY 2016. Missing data for changed data elements are not imputed until data have been collected systematically for at least three years; therefore, missing data were not imputed in FY 2016.

3 The District of Columbia, although not a state, is included in the state rankings. Special care should be used in comparing its data to state data.

4 Caution should be used in making comparisons with the state of Hawaii, as Hawaii reports only one public library for the entire state.

NOTES: 1. Although the data in these tables come from a census of all public libraries and are not subject to sampling error, the census results may contain nonsampling errors. Additional information on nonsampling error, response rates, and definitions may be found in *Data File Documentation Public Libraries Survey: Fiscal Year 2016.* 2. Tables are derived and condensed from the IMLS Public Libraries Survey, FY 2016. Although the publisher believes the data to be accurate, some elements have been excluded or abridged. Data users are advised to utilize the original, fully annotated IMLS data (Tables 36-48) available at https://www.imls.gov/sites/default/files/fy2016_pls_tables.pdf.

SOURCE: IMLS, Public Libraries Survey, FY 2016. Data users who create their own estimates using data from these tables should cite the Institute of Museum and Library Services as the source of the original data only.

School Library Statistics from NCES, 2015–2016

The National Center for Education Statistics (NCES) conducted its Schools and Staffing Survey (SASS) seven times between 1987 and 2011. Included in the survey's wide-ranging coverage of elementary and secondary education in the United States were statistics on the nation's school libraries / library media centers. SASS has since been redesigned by NCES as the National Teacher and Principal Survey (NTPS), first conducted in 2015–2016. The following two tables from NTPS present the most current NCES data on school libraries / media centers, including numbers and percentages of centers and staff by selected school characteristics, enrollment size, locale, staff type, and more.

For additional information, see "National Center for Education Statistics" in Part 1 of this volume and the NCES library statistics page at https://nces.ed.gov/surveys/libraries/.

Table 1 / Number of schools with a library media center and number of full-time and part-time school technology specialists and librarians/library media specialists, by selected school characteristics, 2015–2016

Selected school characteristic	Total number of schools	Number of schools with a library media center	Number of technology specialists		Number of librarians/library media specialists	
			Full time	Part time	Full time	Part time
All public schools	90,400	82,300	36,700	29,400	56,000	17,600
School classification						
Traditional public	83,500	77,900	33,600	27,500	53,900	16,800
Charter school	6,900	4,400	3,100	1,900	2,100	800
Community type						
City	24,800	21,700	9,300	6,400	14,600	4,300
Suburban	29,100	26,800	12,800	8,700	19,900	5,600
Town	12,200	10,900	5,000	4,300	7,400	2,500
Rural	24,400	22,800	9,600	9,900	14,100	5,200
School level						
Primary	50,400	48,200	14,400	16,300	30,600	12,100
Middle	13,900	13,200	6,200	4,700	9,600	2,500
High	17,900	14,400	11,800	6,000	12,300	1,800
Combined	8,200	6,500	4,300	2,400	3,500	1,200
Student enrollment						
Less than 100	6,500	4,000	700	2,200	500	1,100
100–199	7,300	5,600	1,700	3,100	1,800	2,200
200–499	35,700	33,200	11,400	12,400	20,000	8,900
500–749	22,900	22,100	9,400	6,500	16,700	3,500
750–999	9,200	8,800	5,200	3,200	7,500	1,200
1,000 or more	8,800	8,500	8,300	2,000	9,500	900
Percent of K–12 students approved for free or reduced-price lunches						
0–34	24,500	23,600	12,000	8,700	17,800	5,400
35–49	12,000	11,600	5,000	4,800	7,900	3,100
50–74	18,800	17,900	7,300	5,300	12,300	3,600
75 or more	30,100	26,300	10,200	9,000	16,700	4,900
School did not participate in free or reduced-price lunch program	5,000	2,900	2,000	1,600	1,200	600

NOTE: Detail may not sum to totals because of rounding.

SOURCE: U.S. Department of Education, National Center for Education Statistics, National Teacher and Principal Survey (NTPS), "Public School Data File," 2015–2016.

Table 2 / Number and percentage of public schools with libraries/media centers and average number of staff per library/media center, by staff type and employment status and school level, enrollment size, and locale, 2015–2016

(Standard errors appear in parentheses)

School level, enrollment size, and locale	Schools with libraries/media centers				Average number of staff per library/media center: Librarians or library media specialists				Library media center instructional aides				Library media center noninstructional aides			
	Number		Percent		Full time		Part time		Full time		Part time		Full time		Part time	
Total, all public schools[1]	82,300	(440)	91.0	(0.43)	0.7	(0.01)	0.2	(0.01)	0.3	(0.01)	0.1	(0.01)	0.1	(#)	0.1	(#)
Elementary schools	59,500	(350)	95.4	(0.39)	0.6	(0.01)	0.2	(0.01)	0.3	(0.01)	0.1	(0.01)	0.1	(#)	0.1	(0.01)
Enrollment size																
Less than 150 students	3,200	(300)	81.4	(3.88)	0.2	(0.03)	0.4	(0.05)	0.1 !	(0.03)	0.2	(0.04)	‡	(†)	0.1 !	(0.03)
150 to 499 students	28,700	(560)	95.1	(0.49)	0.6	(0.01)	0.3	(0.01)	0.2	(0.01)	0.2	(0.01)	0.1	(0.01)	0.1	(0.01)
500 to 749 students	18,600	(480)	97.8	(0.42)	0.7	(0.01)	0.2	(0.01)	0.3	(0.02)	0.1	(0.01)	0.1	(0.01)	0.1	(0.01)
750 or more students	9,000	(340)	97.8	(0.61)	0.8	(0.02)	0.2	(0.02)	0.3	(0.02)	0.1	(0.02)	0.1	(0.02)	0.1	(0.01)
Locale																
City	16,500	(210)	92.0	(0.92)	0.6	(0.02)	0.2	(0.02)	0.2	(0.02)	0.1	(0.01)	0.1	(0.01)	0.1	(0.01)
Suburban	21,100	(190)	97.0	(0.60)	0.7	(0.02)	0.2	(0.02)	0.2	(0.01)	0.2	(0.01)	0.1	(0.01)	0.1	(0.01)
Town	7,600	(280)	97.1	(0.69)	0.6	(0.02)	0.2	(0.02)	0.3	(0.02)	0.1	(0.02)	0.1	(0.01)	0.1	(0.01)
Rural	14,300	(320)	96.4	(0.82)	0.6	(0.02)	0.2	(0.02)	0.3	(0.02)	0.1	(0.02)	#	(†)	0.1	(0.01)
Secondary schools	16,300	(410)	82.0	(1.46)	0.8	(0.02)	0.1	(0.01)	0.3	(0.02)	0.1	(0.01)	0.2	(0.01)	0.1	(0.01)
Enrollment size																
Less than 150 students	1,400	(200)	46.0	(5.28)	0.2	(0.06)	0.2	(0.05)	‡	(†)	‡	(†)	‡	(†)	‡	(†)
150 to 499 students	4,600	(260)	77.4	(2.60)	0.6	(0.04)	0.2	(0.03)	0.2	(0.02)	0.1	(0.02)	0.1	(0.02)	0.1	(0.01)
500 to 749 students	2,600	(180)	89.6	(2.22)	0.8	(0.04)	0.2	(0.03)	0.2	(0.03)	0.2	(0.04)	0.1	(0.02)	0.1	(0.02)
750 or more students	7,600	(290)	96.5	(0.81)	1.1	(0.02)	0.1	(0.01)	0.4	(0.03)	0.1	(0.02)	0.3	(0.02)	0.1	(0.01)
Locale																
City	4,200	(220)	79.2	(2.51)	0.8	(0.04)	0.1	(0.02)	0.2	(0.03)	0.1	(0.01)	0.2	(0.03)	#	(†)
Suburban	4,800	(210)	80.9	(2.84)	1.0	(0.03)	0.1	(0.02)	0.3	(0.04)	0.1	(0.03)	0.2	(0.03)	0.1	(0.02)
Town	2,900	(180)	82.9	(3.24)	0.8	(0.03)	0.2	(0.03)	0.3	(0.03)	0.1	(0.02)	0.2	(0.03)	0.1	(0.02)
Rural	4,400	(230)	85.6	(2.42)	0.8	(0.04)	0.2	(0.03)	0.3	(0.03)	0.1	(0.02)	0.1	(0.02)	#	(†)

† Not applicable. | # Rounds to zero. | ! Interpret data with caution. The coefficient of variation (CV) for this estimate is between 30 and 50 percent. | ‡ Reporting standards not met. Either there are too few cases for a reliable estimate or the coefficient of variation (CV) is 50 percent or greater. | [1] Total includes combined elementary/secondary schools, which are not shown separately.

NOTE: Detail may not sum to totals because of rounding.

SOURCE: U.S. Department of Education, National Center for Education Statistics, National Teacher and Principal Survey (NTPS), "Public School Data File," 2015–2016.

Book Trade Research and Statistics

Prices of U.S. and Foreign Published Materials

George Aulisio
Editor, ALA ALCTS Library Materials Price Index Editorial Board

The Library Materials Price Index (LMPI) Editorial Board of the American Library Association's Association for Library Collections and Technical Services' (ALCTS) Publications Committee continues to monitor prices for a range of library materials from sources within North America and other key publishing centers around the world.

The U.S. Consumer Price Index (CPI) increased by 1.9 percent in 2018. The 2018 CPI increase is slightly lower than the previous two years. In both 2017 and 2016, the CPI was 2.1 percent. CPI figures are obtained from the Bureau of Labor Statistics at http://www.bls.gov/.

In 2017, all tables that utilized a base index price increase had their base year reset to 2010. All indexes continue to utilize the 2010 base year. Percent changes in average prices from 2014–2018 are conveniently noted in Chart 1.

	Average Price Percent Change				
Index	**2014**	**2015**	**2016**	**2017**	**2018**
U.S. Consumer Price Index	0.8	0.7	2.1	2.1	1.9
U.S. Periodicals (Table 1)	6.1	6.0	7.1	5.6	5.7
Legal Serials Services (Table 2)	10.4	13.9	9.5	11.7	14.1
Hardcover Books (Table 3)	6.5	3.1	0.4*	4.9*	-11.8
Academic Books (Table 4)	-2.2	1.3	-11.6	16.6	0.0
Academic E-Books (Table 4A)	-8.3	-4.3	-5.2	0.6	5.3
Academic Textbooks (Table 4B)	-7.2	10.5	-3.1	0.3	-3.2
U.S. College books (Table 5)	-1.4	-0.6	3.4	-2.8	-0.6
U.S. Mass market paperbacks (Table 6)	0.6	0.1	2.3*	0.8	0.5
U.S. Paperbacks (Table 7)	5.0	1.1	20.3*	-23.8*	14.9
U.S. Audiobooks (Table 7A)	0.2	-14.7	-16.7*	29.3	14.1
U.S. E-Books (Table 7B)	-9.1	-12.8	36.3*	-20.3*	0.7
+Serials (Table 8)	6.7	5.8	6.0	6.5	5.8
+Online Serials (Table 8A)	7.2	6.4	6.2	5.6	5.8
British academic books (Table 9)	1.0	7.1	9.9	-0.5	7.0

* = figures revised from previous editions based on new data
+Data set changes each year.

U.S. Published Materials

Tables 1 through 7B indicate average prices and price indexes for library materials published primarily in the United States. These indexes are U.S. Periodicals (Table 1), Legal Serials Services (Table 2), U.S. Hardcover Books (Table 3), North American Academic Books (Table 4), North American Academic E-Books (Table 4A), North American Academic Textbooks (Table 4B), U.S. College Books (Table 5), U.S. Mass Market Paperback Books (Table 6), U.S. Paperbacks (Excluding Mass Market) (Table 7), U.S. Audiobooks (Table 7A), and U.S. E-Books (Table 7B).

Periodical and Serials Prices

The U.S. Periodical Price Index (USPPI) (Table 1) was reestablished by Stephen Bosch, University of Arizona, in 2014. The table is updated for 2019 using data supplied by EBSCO Information Services. This report includes 2015–2019 data indexed to the base year of 2010. Table 1 is derived from a selected set of titles that, as much as possible, will remain as the sample base for future comparisons. The data in Table 1 is from a print-preferred list, but over half of the titles in the index are based on online pricing so that the data provides a strong mix of both print and online pricing. Including both print and online pricing makes the data in Table 1 more characteristic of a current academic library's serials collection. The subscription prices used are publishers' list prices, excluding publisher discount or vendor service charges. The pricing data for 2010–2014, the base years for the new USPPI, published in 2014, were created from one single report that pulled pricing information for a static set of titles for the five-year period. The pricing data for 2015–2019 is based on that same sampling of titles but is not an exact match due to changes that occur with serial titles. Between the 2010–2014 and 2015–2019 lists, some titles fell off the list due to pricing not being available, while other titles on the list for which pricing had not been available in 2014 now have pricing available.

The new USPPI treats a little more than 5,900 titles in comparison with the original title list, which covered only about 3,700 titles. The previous versions of the USPPI treated Russian translations as a separate category. Russian translations are no longer a focus of this index and are not tracked as a category. These were once seen as a major cost factor, but this is no longer the case, and therefore their inclusion in or exclusion from the index no longer makes sense. There are Russian translation titles in the index, but they are not reported separately.

The main barrier to creating this index is the difficulty of maintaining the title list and obtaining standard retail pricing for titles on the list. Changes in serials titles due to ceased publication, movement to open access, mergers, combining titles in packages, moving to direct orders, and publication delays are a few of the situations that can affect obtaining current pricing information. The new index retains viable titles from the previous index's title lists and includes new title data. The new titles are the most frequently ordered serials in EBSCO's system. From that list of serials, titles were selected for the new index to ensure that the distribution by subject was similar to the distribution in the original index. There are more titles in the selected title set than the number of titles that produced prices over the past six years. This should allow the current index to be sustainable into the future as titles fall off the list and pricing becomes available for titles that may have been delayed or are no longer in memberships.

The first five years of data, published in 2014, showed consistent price changes across subject areas because price data was a historical look at the prices of the same set of journals. The data for 2015, 2016, 2017, 2018, and 2019 are based on the same sample list but do not reflect an identical list of titles as the data for 2010–2014 due to the issues mentioned above. Across subject areas, the changes in price were less volatile in 2019, but the overall 6.7 percent increase mirrors price changes seen in other pricing studies, which nearly all show close to a 6 percent increase. The 6.7 percent increase in 2019 is higher than the 5.6 percent increase seen in 2018. Also, at the subject level, the sample sizes are smaller, so a few changes can cause a large swing in the overall price for that area. In 2019, price increases were much more consistent across subjects. There was only a variation of 4.6 percent—from 7.9 percent to 3.3 percent. Whereas, in 2018, the variation was over 38 percent—from 30.3 percent to -8 percent.

Direct comparisons between Table 1 and Table 8 should be avoided, especially at the subject level. Both tables show the overall rate of increase in serial prices to be around 6 percent; however, beyond that point, there is little that makes a statistically valid comparison. Table 1 represents journals that reflect the collections of an average library, whereas Table 8 is based on a larger set of data coming from a broad mix of sources. Also, Table 1 contains more trade and popular titles, whereas Table 8 contains more foreign titles, prices for which can be impacted by the strength of the U.S. dollar.

The most important trend seen in the data from Table 1 is that increases in prices have remained constant since the economic recovery began in 2010. Price increases have hovered around 6 percent annually during that time. This year, titles in STM and social science subjects dominate the list of areas with the largest price increases. Technology, education, geography, sociology, engineering, general science, political science, chemistry, and agriculture all showed increases of over 7 percent. Average prices for journals in the science and technology area are still far higher than in other areas, and that trend continues, with the average cost of chemistry journals being $5,420.94 and of physics journals being $4,556.67.

In this price index, as with similar indexes, the accuracy of the average price percent change is closely tied to the number of titles in the sample size. Average price changes are far more volatile when utilizing small data sets. For that reason, drawing conclusions about price changes in subject areas with a limited number of titles is less accurate than for subject areas with greater numbers of titles or with the broader index. For example, technology periodicals went up 7.9 percent this year, but to conclude that all journals in the technology area will increase a like amount is likely incorrect. If a specific inflation figure for a small subject area were needed, it would be better to look at an average over a period of time or the overall number for the price study (6.7 percent) than to use the actual numbers year-by-year. The variation in pricing is too volatile in smaller sample sizes to be comparable on a year-to-year basis. In a small sample size, the change in just one or two titles could easily have a large impact on the overall price for an area.

(text continues on page 342)

Table 1 / U.S. Periodicals: Average Prices and Price Indexes, 2015–2019

Index Base 2010 = 100

Subject	LC Class	Titles	2010 Average Price	2015 Average Price	2016 Average Price	2017 Average Price	2018 Average Price	2019 Average Price	Percent Change 2018–2019	Index
Agriculture	S	227	$579.48	$869.87	$917.17	$965.21	$1,010.10	$1,080.51	7.0%	186.5
Anthropology	GN	52	373.64	410.67	430.54	452.60	481.28	513.38	6.7	137.4
Arts and architecture	N	109	112.39	185.99	194.03	203.33	220.33	227.65	3.3	202.5
Astronomy	QB	28	1,793.08	2,215.78	2,271.32	2,440.59	2,590.81	2,724.23	5.1	151.9
Biology	QH	346	2,053.06	2,831.00	2,990.53	3,161.41	3,341.95	3,537.28	5.8	172.3
Botany	QK	53	1,361.09	1,696.40	1,762.41	1,857.80	1,933.11	2,027.84	4.9	149.0
Business and economics	HA-HJ	463	351.29	507.56	536.48	564.62	597.48	638.82	6.9	181.8
Chemistry	QD	141	3,396.26	4,313.62	4,546.42	4,782.17	5,067.65	5,420.94	7.0	159.6
Education	L	226	354.92	534.20	570.32	606.49	646.23	697.00	7.9	196.4
Engineering	T	529	1,244.39	1,776.02	1,896.25	2,016.24	2,138.20	2,294.50	7.3	184.4
Food science	TX	44	356.17	632.13	652.98	703.23	771.52	815.46	5.7	229.0
General works	A	119	85.84	114.90	119.17	123.16	126.48	134.98	6.7	157.2
Geography	G-GF	81	670.60	1,012.27	1,071.50	1,150.39	1,222.64	1,315.32	7.6	196.1
Geology	QE	69	1,368.79	1,760.87	1,867.29	1,952.57	1,996.47	2,130.96	6.7	155.7
Health sciences	R	801	1,009.55	1,504.94	1,597.55	1,690.55	1,785.62	1,907.29	6.8	188.9

History	C,D,E,F	297	202.39	281.56	296.94	314.82	330.67	353.43	6.9	174.6
Language and literature	P	285	168.12	222.52	232.26	243.37	255.39	269.55	5.5	160.3
Law	K	224	214.01	317.43	333.44	348.43	370.20	386.34	4.4	180.5
Library science	Z	100	290.02	392.44	406.34	430.35	451.86	480.26	6.3	165.6
Math and computer science	QA	337	1,242.13	1,633.23	1,706.31	1,795.13	1,911.87	2,033.50	6.4	163.7
Military and naval science	U,V	28	239.90	366.34	382.17	401.15	421.67	443.60	5.2	184.9
Music	M	52	82.18	143.85	149.93	156.42	163.06	170.99	4.9	208.1
Philosophy and religion	B-BD, BH-BX	206	232.37	303.47	323.23	345.27	356.07	374.29	5.1	161.1
Physics	QC	152	2,845.54	3,690.30	3,880.75	4,062.91	4,271.66	4,556.67	6.7	160.1
Political science	J	90	312.76	605.52	652.78	692.06	733.54	785.77	7.1	251.2
Psychology	BF	114	648.21	982.67	1,057.60	1,116.48	1,193.53	1,276.42	6.9	196.9
Recreation	GV	73	69.79	132.38	148.41	155.55	166.15	176.45	6.2	252.8
Science (general)	Q	91	998.51	1,453.57	1,543.19	1,627.42	1,727.98	1,853.31	7.3	185.6
Social sciences	H	40	351.40	719.19	760.91	802.66	839.64	889.02	5.9	253.0
Sociology	HM-HX	223	482.59	793.57	844.08	893.32	950.79	1,022.16	7.5	211.8
Technology	TA-TT	118	535.73	801.22	842.87	901.45	955.82	1,030.96	7.9	192.4
Zoology	QL	118	1,454.26	1,981.71	2,078.77	2,181.53	2,291.62	2,428.58	6.0	167.0
Totals and Averages		5,836	$843.46	$1,202.20	$1,270.87	$1,342.28	$1,418.89	$1,513.25	6.7%	179.4

Compiled by Stephen Bosch, University of Arizona, based on subscription information supplied by EBSCO Information Services.

(continued from page 339)

The Legal Serials Services Index (Table 2) is compiled by Ajaye Bloomstone, Louisiana State University, using data collected from various legal serials vendors. The base year for this index is 2010. This index presents price data covering the years 2010 through 2019.

Table 2 / Legal Serials Services: Average Prices and Price Indexes, 2010–2018

Index Base: 2010 = 100

Year	Titles	Average Price	Percent Change	Index
2010	217	$1,714.96	3.5%	100.0
2011	217	1,904.69	11.1	111.1
2012	219	2,058.66	8.1	120.0
2013	218	2,241.42	8.9	130.7
2014	219	2,473.44	10.4	144.2
2015	218	2,818.02	13.9	164.3
2016	217	3,085.34	9.5	179.9
2017	218	3,446.12	11.7	200.9
2018	217	3,932.85	14.1	229.3
2019	191	$4,653.97	18.3	271.4

Compiled by Ajaye Bloomstone, Louisiana State University.

As in past years, vendors were asked to provide cost data on particular titles with the assumption that the title or set has been held by a large academic research law library. The cost recorded in the index is intended to be based on the upkeep of titles, not necessarily the cost incurred in purchasing a new set, though sometimes the cost is the same, and sometimes the cost of updates can be more expensive than purchasing a new set. A nuance of legal publishing is that for some of the larger legal publishers, hard prices for a calendar year are not set at the beginning of the calendar year but halfway through, so only gross price estimates may be available in time for publication of this article. In addition to titles issued regularly (e.g., journals and law reviews), legal serials may also be updated throughout the year with both regular and irregular updates or releases, new editions, and new or revised volumes. If a title is updated irregularly, the price for its renewal may increase or decrease from one year to the next, depending on the publisher's plans for keeping the title current. It is noteworthy that although legal serials in print format are still produced, titles seem to be migrating, albeit slowly, to an electronic-only format.

Some prices were provided to the compiler with the caveat "no longer available for new sales." There is also a trend for titles purchased in print to come with an electronic component. For such titles, the purchasing library may have no choice but to accept both formats even if the print is preferred. If one was able to purchase the print format without the electronic component, the cost might conceivably change. This leads one to believe that some titles may cease publication entirely. For instance, if the publication is not to be phased out immediately, then the title might, at some point soon, no longer be available in print. In fact, more than 20 titles used for past years' Table 2 ceased publication for 2019. To compensate for the loss of titles, new titles were added. The new titles added with the intent to match the previous year's cost of the ceased publications plus the average percentage of an increase for the remainder of the titles from 2018 to 2019.

Book Prices

U.S. Hardcover Books (Table 3), U.S. Mass Market Paperback Books (Table 6), U.S. Paperbacks (Excluding Mass Market) (Table 7), U.S. Audiobooks (Table 7A), and U.S. E-Books (Table 7B) are prepared by Narda Tafuri, University of Scranton, and are derived from data provided by book wholesaler Baker & Taylor. Figures for 2016 have been revised from previous editions in order to reflect additional late updates to the Baker & Taylor database. Data for 2016 should now be considered final. The 2017 figures in these tables may similarly be revised in next year's tables and therefore should be considered preliminary. The figures for this edition of *Library and Book Trade Almanac* were provided by Baker & Taylor and are based on the Book Industry Study Group's BISAC categories. The BISAC juvenile category (fiction and nonfiction) is divided into children's and young adult. For more information on the BISAC categories, visit http://www.bisg.org.

The overall average book price saw increases in 2018 except for hardcover books. The overall list prices for hardcover books (Table 3) showed a steep decline of -11.8 percent. Mass market paperback prices (Table 6) and e-book prices (Table 7B) showed insignificant increases of 0.5 percent and 0.7 percent. The price of audiobooks (Table 7A), exhibited an increase of 14.1 percent. Notably, trade paperbacks (Table 7) saw the largest increase, with 14.9 percent.

North American Academic Books (Table 4), North American Academic E-Books (Table 4A), and North American Academic Textbooks (Table 4B) are prepared by Stephen Bosch. In 2017 the base index was set to 2010. The data used for this index are derived from all titles treated by the ProQuest Books (formerly Ingram Content Group–Coutts Information Services) and GOBI Library Solutions in their approval plans during the calendar years listed.

The current version of North American Academic Books: Average Prices and Price Indexes 2015–2018 (Table 4) continues to evolve from previous versions due to changes in the supply of raw data. The index includes e-books as well as paperback editions as supplied by these vendors, and this inclusion of paperbacks and e-books as distributed as part of the approval plans has influenced the prices reflected in the index figures. The index is inclusive of the broadest categories of materials as that is the marketplace in which academic libraries operate, and the index attempts to chart price changes that impact that market. Direct comparisons with earlier published versions will show variations because the number of titles treated, and their average prices have changed. This is especially true for those versions published prior to 2009. Data for the current indexes are supplied by ProQuest Books (formerly Ingram Content Group–Coutts Information Services) and by GOBI Library Solutions from EBSCO (formerly YBP Library Services). For indexes published before 2009, Blackwell Book Services was the data supplier. Blackwell was purchased in 2009 by YBP, and the vendor data used to create the index changed at that time. After 2009 the data came from Ingram/Coutts and YBP.

(text continues on page 352)

Table 3 / Hardcover Books: Average Prices and Price Indexes, 2015–2018

Index Base: 2010 = 100

	2010	2015 Final			2016 Final*			2017 Preliminary			2018 Preliminary		
BISAC Category	Average Price	Volumes	Average Price	Index	Volumes	Average Price	Index	Volumes	Average Price	Index	Volumes	Average Price	Index
Antiques and collectibles	$51.44	136	$96.65	187.9	147	$82.21	159.8	133	$71.63	139.3	105	$71.32	138.7
Architecture	85.52	967	99.89	116.8	951	108.58	127.0	1,002	111.14	130.0	833	94.47	110.5
Art	71.53	1,971	74.12	103.6	2,156	78.01	109.1	2,112	82.92	115.9	2,007	74.87	104.7
Bibles	37.50	168	36.10	96.3	201	41.49	110.6	255	41.31	110.2	248	43.11	115.0
Biography and autobiography	53.41	1,747	47.39	88.7	1,886	50.11	93.8	1,823	49.29	92.3	1,672	45.31	84.8
Body, mind and spirit	36.91	156	30.29	82.1	172	29.11	78.9	188	26.91	72.9	203	25.33	68.6
Business and economics	134.61	4,775	152.81	113.5	4,991	162.97	121.1	5,899	166.64	123.8	4,573	156.37	116.2
Children	24.63	13,136	24.74	100.5	15,195	25.44	103.3	14,947	24.26	98.5	16,562	26.29	106.7
Comics and graphic novels	31.51	685	37.81	120.0	637	39.87	126.5	670	42.03	133.4	656	43.71	138.7
Computers	138.53	990	150.02	108.3	1,105	163.90	118.3	1,280	170.85	123.3	1,133	167.62	121.0
Cooking	30.91	1,256	28.63	92.6	1,205	29.69	96.1	1,212	29.73	96.2	1,144	29.75	96.2
Crafts and hobbies	33.28	170	28.90	86.8	155	31.62	95.0	167	31.86	95.7	185	29.43	88.4
Design	76.59	459	66.07	86.3	438	71.09	92.8	433	66.17	86.4	421	63.47	82.9
Drama	42.91	56	84.48	196.9	111	96.50	224.9	80	105.42	245.7	67	84.24	196.3
Education	117.59	2,235	125.09	106.4	2,957	137.59	117.0	3,680	147.72	125.6	2,567	135.14	114.9
Family and relationships	32.24	210	59.13	183.4	200	52.04	161.4	186	45.87	142.3	217	44.83	139.0
Fiction	32.20	4,455	29.80	92.5	4,912	29.82	92.6	5,275	29.44	91.4	4,828	29.45	91.5
Foreign language study	132.47	289	152.19	114.9	237	126.86	95.8	246	125.62	94.8	250	117.66	88.8
Games	52.07	117	38.21	73.4	169	35.37	67.9	137	47.17	90.6	179	43.84	84.2
Gardening	36.42	123	37.83	103.9	103	33.71	92.5	130	44.43	122.0	121	35.90	98.6
Health and fitness	48.51	408	92.58	190.9	366	77.90	160.6	417	83.21	171.5	332	59.12	121.9
History	82.65	5,792	93.24	112.8	6,477	104.21	126.1	6,223	98.54	119.2	5,812	91.97	111.3
House and home	44.61	109	35.71	80.1	90	36.84	82.6	97	41.48	93.0	98	39.01	87.5

Humor	21.94	295	24.26	110.6	291	21.74	99.1	296	22.21	101.2	343	22.92	104.5
Language arts and disciplines	117.67	1,585	146.32	124.3	1,614	147.61	125.4	1,529	149.59	127.1	1,351	139.94	118.9
Law	174.48	2,248	178.28	102.2	2,449	188.88	108.3	2,563	180.41	103.4	2,394	179.47	102.9
Literary collections	83.49	213	113.14	135.5	241	94.74	113.5	296	100.29	120.1	250	97.12	116.3
Literary criticism	117.63	2,328	123.15	104.7	2,945	128.30	109.1	2,590	127.24	108.2	2,404	123.36	104.9
Mathematics	133.23	1,031	158.84	119.2	1,092	144.11	108.2	1,395	172.04	129.1	1,035	147.15	110.4
Medical	171.13	4,119	185.02	108.1	3,176	183.36	107.1	3,813	195.03	114.0	2,979	179.43	104.9
Music	87.84	569	95.23	108.4	667	100.92	114.9	691	97.85	111.4	596	87.41	99.5
Nature	74.89	467	90.78	121.2	474	98.99	132.2	533	100.39	134.0	411	81.20	108.4
Performing arts	76.27	813	98.38	129.0	869	104.34	136.8	947	117.32	153.8	803	97.51	127.9
Pets	24.66	88	24.97	101.3	111	22.79	92.4	103	27.59	111.9	66	20.13	81.6
Philosophy	108.93	1,532	110.15	101.1	1,680	123.58	113.5	1,680	117.92	108.3	1,583	107.36	98.6
Photography	107.99	913	68.32	63.3	873	68.09	63.1	930	73.67	68.2	793	68.16	63.1
Poetry	40.76	280	46.85	114.9	472	54.15	132.8	309	39.90	97.9	287	36.46	89.4
Political science	110.32	3,139	119.01	107.9	3,491	118.28	107.2	3,928	118.33	107.3	3,396	108.62	98.5
Psychology	109.85	1,420	151.62	138.0	1,383	155.18	141.3	1,849	154.54	140.7	1,439	140.95	128.3
Reference	302.69	359	393.07	129.9	366	262.84	86.8	357	371.61	122.8	338	382.99	126.5
Religion	80.88	2,517	87.31	107.9	2,907	81.06	100.2	2,986	82.07	101.5	2,952	79.20	97.9
Science	192.20	4,251	203.05	105.6	4,057	208.87	108.7	4,609	200.76	104.5	3,915	175.59	91.4
Self-help	27.11	304	27.73	102.3	311	25.17	92.8	353	28.73	106.0	407	25.56	94.3
Social science	100.47	3,829	135.13	134.5	4,188	134.49	133.9	5,771	132.84	132.2	4,513	121.71	121.1
Sports and recreation	41.23	616	52.99	128.5	636	56.52	137.1	642	62.89	152.5	589	53.02	128.6
Study aids	101.54	15	138.63	136.5	20	88.66	87.3	20	106.38	104.8	16	100.15	98.6
Technology and engineering	164.66	3,416	168.57	102.4	3,735	182.84	111.0	4,048	199.05	120.9	3,108	200.03	121.5
Transportation	84.28	293	86.15	102.2	297	68.62	81.4	274	71.81	85.2	277	59.06	70.1
Travel	41.32	208	34.31	83.0	221	39.67	96.0	289	38.54	93.3	477	40.90	99.0
True crime	34.83	67	42.26	121.3	89	35.05	100.6	67	29.45	84.5	84	33.54	96.3
Young adult	35.99	2,056	33.47	93.0	2,290	38.07	105.8	2,398	40.03	111.2	2,108	35.65	99.1
Totals and Averages	$89.54	79,381	$101.62	113.5	85,806	$102.04	114.0	91,858	$107.09	119.6	83,127	$94.45	105.5

Compiled by Narda Tafuri, University of Scranton, from data supplied by Baker & Taylor.

* = figures revised from previous editions based on new data from Baker & Taylor.

Table 4 / North American Academic Books: Average Prices and Price Indexes, 2016–2018

Index Base: 2010 = 100

		2010		2016		2017		2018			
Subject Area	LC Class	Titles	Average Price	Titles	Average Price	Titles	Average Price	Titles	Average Price	Percent Change 2017–2018	Index
Agriculture	S	1,139	$107.44	1,924	$93.24	1,822	$118.71	1,822	$114.09	-3.9%	106.2
Anthropology	GN	609	91.96	750	88.11	788	93.04	788	98.31	5.7	106.9
Botany	QK	260	125.84	472	114.99	437	148.27	437	149.82	1.0	119.1
Business and economics	H	10,916	97.31	13,393	100.65	14,796	106.04	14,796	107.07	1.0	110.0
Chemistry	QD	667	223.03	891	192.72	871	208.69	871	200.68	-3.8	90.0
Education	L	4,688	86.47	6,998	81.60	7,305	88.06	7,305	92.00	4.5	106.4
Engineering and technology	T	6,913	133.45	10,218	130.63	11,603	145.33	11,603	148.15	1.9	111.0
Fine and applied arts	M-N	5,535	57.17	8,201	67.85	8,119	72.22	8,119	77.19	6.9	135.0
General works	A	80	75.60	277	90.18	270	91.78	270	109.68	19.5	145.1
Geography	G	1,144	104.98	1,956	91.15	1,850	129.12	1,850	113.22	-12.3	107.8
Geology	QE	276	114.34	773	72.01	392	117.02	392	123.12	5.2	107.7
History	C-D-E-F	10,079	65.29	15,419	66.25	14,380	74.42	14,380	78.64	5.7	120.5
Home economics	TX	812	44.35	684	62.50	805	75.90	805	60.45	-20.4	136.3
Industrial arts	TT	265	52.60	280	61.49	231	61.02	231	62.68	2.7	119.2
Language and literature	P	19,364	57.31	38,506	44.49	28,485	62.65	28,485	62.36	-0.5	108.8

Law	K	4,596	125.35	6,515	125.82	6,809	125.90	6,809	127.59	1.3	101.8
Library and information science	Z	636	90.18	1,089	92.91	952	114.52	952	110.28	-3.7	122.3
Mathematics and computer science	QA	3,965	103.85	5,260	99.77	5,503	109.25	5,503	113.69	4.1	109.5
Medicine	R	8,679	112.66	11,130	128.72	12,602	133.70	12,602	126.05	-5.7	111.9
Military and naval science	U-V	773	79.99	1,365	70.55	1,213	71.03	1,213	79.21	11.5	99.0
Philosophy and religion	B	7,386	81.75	10,698	79.68	11,985	81.17	11,985	83.89	3.3	102.6
Physical education and recreation	GV	1,788	56.03	4,135	52.53	2,772	68.82	2,772	69.03	0.3	123.2
Physics and astronomy	QB	1,627	128.36	2,414	106.47	2,310	129.35	2,310	143.00	10.6	111.4
Political science	J	3,549	99.70	4,855	97.13	5,486	99.65	5,486	102.70	3.1	103.0
Psychology	BF	1,730	76.65	2,338	89.21	2,946	88.73	2,946	83.32	-6.1	108.7
Science (general)	Q	631	108.4	1,533	82.28	1,034	112.56	1,034	107.42	-4.6	99.1
Sociology	HM	6,666	88.75	9,760	91.28	11,218	92.68	11,218	93.29	0.7	105.1
Zoology	QH, QL-QR	3,029	140.26	5,266	101.49	4,036	137.44	4,036	133.32	-3.0	95.1
Totals and Averages		107,802	$89.15	167,100	$82.99	161,020	$96.76	147,108	$96.73	0.0%	108.5

Compiled by Stephen Bosch, University of Arizona, from electronic data provided by ProQuest (formerly Ingrams Content Group–Coutts Information Services), and GOBI Library Solutions from EBSCO (formerly YBP Library Services). The data represents all titles (includes e-books, hardcover, trade, and paperback books, as well as annuals) treated for all approval plan customers serviced by the vendors. This table covers titles published or distributed in the United States and Canada during the calendar years listed. This index does include paperback editions and electronic books. The inclusion of these items does impact pricing in the index.

Table 4A / North American Academic E-Books: Average Prices and Price Indexes, 2016–2018

Index Base: 2010 = 100

		2010		2016		2017		2018			
Subject Area	**LC Class**	**Titles**	**Average Price**	**Titles**	**Average Price**	**Titles**	**Average Price**	**Titles**	**Average Price**	**Percent Change 2017–2018**	**Index**
Agriculture	S	697	$168.73	841	$120.79	811	$134.35	706	$133.99	-0.3%	79.4
Anthropology	GN	385	109.96	335	109.89	348	101.50	364	104.30	2.8	94.9
Botany	QK	190	175.23	217	147.50	192	163.95	146	174.31	6.3	99.5
Business and economics	H	8,481	102.87	7,256	111.36	7,207	107.35	6,519	117.21	9.2	113.9
Chemistry	QD	521	232.57	492	208.27	416	206.61	388	209.77	1.5	90.2
Education	L	2,852	99.96	3,250	103.77	3,386	89.64	2,839	104.20	16.2	104.2
Engineering and technology	T	4,976	152.33	5,289	148.19	5,281	158.34	4,424	163.46	3.2	107.3
Fine and applied arts	M-N	1,493	83.35	2,267	99.48	2,345	92.74	2,213	101.64	9.6	121.9
General works	A	53	89.13	129	108.05	122	104.47	98	101.13	-3.2	113.5
Geography	G	829	117.83	903	104.27	880	131.75	755	125.77	-4.5	106.7
Geology	QE	178	146.85	248	105.82	158	128.30	148	141.93	10.6	96.6
History	C-D-E-F	5,189	89.42	7,106	79.74	6,406	83.45	5,936	92.25	10.5	103.2
Home economics	TX	211	78.08	292	87.14	306	101.68	293	86.37	-15.1	110.6
Industrial arts	TT	23	46.11	75	79.56	46	82.77	53	93.52	13.0	202.8
Language and literature	P	7,664	103.12	11,792	76.62	10,146	86.05	9,657	90.07	4.7	87.3

Law	K	2,433	147.66	2,730	132.13	2,665	133.25	2,786	139.62	4.8	94.6
Library and information science	Z	387	89.43	488	109.23	371	122.97	376	119.59	-2.7	133.7
Mathematics and computer science	QA	3,000	112.65	2,580	108.73	2,255	114.32	2,092	127.44	11.5	113.1
Medicine	R	6,404	134.60	6,018	161.69	5,699	145.71	5,190	142.45	-2.2	105.8
Military and naval science	U-V	487	105.07	683	80.40	535	78.44	518	89.70	14.3	85.4
Philosophy and religion	B	4,262	110.31	5,433	96.45	5,371	90.54	5,163	96.99	7.1	87.9
Physical education and recreation	GV	791	76.57	1,691	64.07	1,226	76.90	1,161	84.05	9.3	109.8
Physics and astronomy	QB	1,288	147.50	1,233	136.58	1,058	145.19	985	166.71	14.8	113.0
Political science	J	2,638	110.10	2,591	108.47	2,705	103.19	2,690	112.97	9.5	102.6
Psychology	BF	1,062	91.35	1,253	108.22	1,427	92.16	1,343	96.84	5.1	106.0
Science (general)	Q	462	122.51	619	99.59	446	116.94	403	119.28	2.0	97.4
Sociology	HM	4,520	103.73	5,071	106.58	5,366	97.02	4,910	105.57	8.8	101.8
Zoology	QH, QL-QR	2,336	164.82	2,242	134.52	1,739	152.03	1,514	149.98	-1.3	91.0
Totals and Averages		63,812	$116.25	73,124	$108.13	68,913	$108.79	63,670	$114.61	5.3%	98.6

Compiled by Stephen Bosch, University of Arizona, from electronic data provided by ProQuest (formerly Ingrams Content Group–Coutts Information Services), and GOBI Library Solutions from EBSCO (formerly YBP Library Services). The data represent all e-book titles treated for all approval plan customers serviced by the vendors. This table covers titles published or distributed in the United States and Canada during the calendar years listed. It is important to note that e-books that were released in a given year may have been published in print much earlier.

Table 4B / North American Academic Text Books: Average Prices and Price Indexes, 2016–2018

Index Base: 2010 = 100

		2010		2016		2017		2018			
Subject Area	**LC Class**	**Titles**	**Average Price**	**Titles**	**Average Price**	**Titles**	**Average Price**	**Titles**	**Average Price**	**Percent Change 2017–2018**	**Index**
Agriculture	S	49	$115.80	102	$139.39	78	$127.73	64	$136.09	6.5%	117.5
Anthropology	GN	35	90.65	57	118.58	75	111.91	56	91.22	-18.5	100.6
Botany	QK	11	109.52	26	136.29	11	135.13	7	77.83	-42.4	71.1
Business and economics	H	694	121.36	1,155	127.33	1,315	127.15	1,070	117.33	-7.7	96.7
Chemistry	QD	94	134.59	125	173.90	117	185.26	115	151.54	-18.2	112.6
Education	L	271	87.75	448	92.57	497	82.91	418	86.98	4.9	99.1
Engineering and technology	T	744	116.38	1,193	138.76	1,266	140.86	1,039	132.04	-6.3	113.5
Fine and applied arts	M-N	73	93.33	162	103.52	179	93.58	119	95.92	2.5	102.8
General works	A	0	0.00	4	76.42	12	93.92	9	77.86	-17.1	n.a.
Geography	G	78	105.21	132	112.75	130	118.51	106	108.43	-8.5	103.1
Geology	QE	36	117.97	39	134.59	29	123.08	28	141.86	15.3	120.3
History	C-D-E-F	81	81.49	193	85.58	225	76.44	219	95.69	25.2	117.4
Home economics	TX	39	89.52	58	104.28	50	170.20	38	116.56	-31.5	130.2
Industrial arts	TT	14	84.72	19	103.76	19	94.65	14	116.57	23.2	137.6
Language and literature	P	309	77.71	579	85.69	694	86.98	563	81.68	-6.1	105.1

Law	K	242	102.09	483	105.89	456	112.18	484	107.95	-3.8	105.7
Library and information science	Z	19	70.30	48	95.71	37	74.34	45	84.37	13.5	120.0
Mathematics and computer science	QA	683	96.11	1,074	108.71	1,045	115.91	1,072	114.87	-0.9	119.5
Medicine	R	1512	126.75	2,322	144.96	2,336	148.14	1,840	141.32	-4.6	111.5
Military and naval science	U-V	3	122.65	16	93.04	14	104.26	29	106.12	1.8	86.5
Philosophy and religion	B	101	72.13	201	80.97	192	70.29	158	70.07	-0.3	97.1
Physical education and recreation	GV	51	79.39	129	101.28	133	96.52	106	106.38	10.2	134.0
Physics and astronomy	QB	243	107.38	387	122.28	423	129.33	397	140.64	8.7	131.0
Political science	J	110	80.09	208	102.54	255	92.14	232	96.94	5.2	121.0
Psychology	BF	138	95.95	199	117.66	251	113.32	170	119.55	5.5	124.6
Science (general)	Q	33	97.14	60	105.56	78	89.84	66	101.15	12.6	104.1
Sociology	HM	353	86.97	676	103.03	797	101.46	596	102.94	1.5	118.4
Zoology	QH, QL-QR	227	109.82	416	134.37	354	144.31	313	131.79	-8.7	120.0
Totals and Averages		6,243	$107.94	10,511	$121.35	11,068	$121.74	9,373	$117.79	-3.2%	109.1

Compiled by Stephen Bosch, University of Arizona, from electronic data provided by ProQuest (formerly Ingrams Content Group–Coutts Information Services), and GOBI Library Solutions from EBSCO (formerly YBP Library Services). The data represents all textbook titles treated for all approval plan customers serviced by the vendors. This table covers titles published or distributed in the United States and Canada during the calendar years listed.

(continued from page 343)

Over time, the data and the data suppliers have changed due to changes in the industry. When compared with earlier versions, the North American Academic Books Price Index (NAABPI) now contains many more titles in the source data because ProQuest Books treats far more titles in their approval programs than did the former Blackwell Book Services. With recent changes at both ProQuest and GOBI, there have been changes to the annual price data pull for books. Starting in 2016, vendors supplied data in separate files for print, e-books, and textbooks. Before 2016 this was not the case, and this change caused large variations in the numbers of titles in the tables and in the average prices. The data for 2014 were normalized in 2016 to conform to the current sets of data, so the numbers of titles and prices have changed from those published in 2015 and previous years. In the future, this approach to gathering the data, along with separate data files for academic print books, e-books, and textbooks, will improve the consistency of the data, especially for e-books. Another major change in 2017 was that the base index year was moved to 2010 to provide consistency across the various indexes published by the Library Materials Price Index Editorial Board.

The average price increase in 2018 in the North American Academic Books Price Index (Table 4) was flat when rounding to one decimal. Previous years showed large swings in prices, including a 16.6 percent increase in 2017 and a -11.6 percent decrease in 2016. The number of titles decreased over this timeframe, going from 167,364 in 2015 to 147,108 in 2018. Despite the decrease in titles in 2018, the overall growth in available titles as well as increasing prices are pressure points for library budgets. The reason that there was no increase in 2018 was primarily large drops in the number of higher-priced titles. There were approximately 5,000 fewer titles in the upper price ranges. Many of these books are e-books. Since e-books tend to be more expensive than print books, the cost of e-books was a driver in the overall price since there were fewer e-books treated in 2018. E-books now make up about 43 percent of the base table.

The average price of North American academic books in 2018 (Table 4) was unchanged from 2017 when rounding to one decimal. This is mainly due to changes in the number of titles treated in the lower and higher part of the price bands <$60 and $120 and up (see Figure 1). Nearly all price bands showed only modest growth in the number of titles between 2015 and 2017, except for the price band above $120, which showed a large increase. In 2018 the lowest price band, $0–60, and the top band, >$120, showed a very large decrease. This led to average prices remaining flat in 2018. The drop in titles in the upper price bands was due to variance in the number of e-books. Take e-books out of the sample, and the drop in the number of titles in the upper price bands shrinks considerably. See Figure 1.

One thing that stands out when looking at the data by price band is that the highest end of the price bands ($120 and up) continues to have a huge impact on the average cost of books. The impact on pricing from the titles in the $120 and up price band is confirmed when looking at the actual dollar values in groups (i.e., the sum of all prices for titles in the group). The increase in the top end of the index was the main factor in the overall changes in the index for 2015–2017 and in the lack of an increase in 2018. Although the $0–$30 price area has the second largest number of titles, the total cost remains the smallest portion as far as total cost (i.e., the sum of all prices) goes into the index. Again, changes in the number

Figure 1 / Number of Titles in Sample Grouped by Price 2015–2018

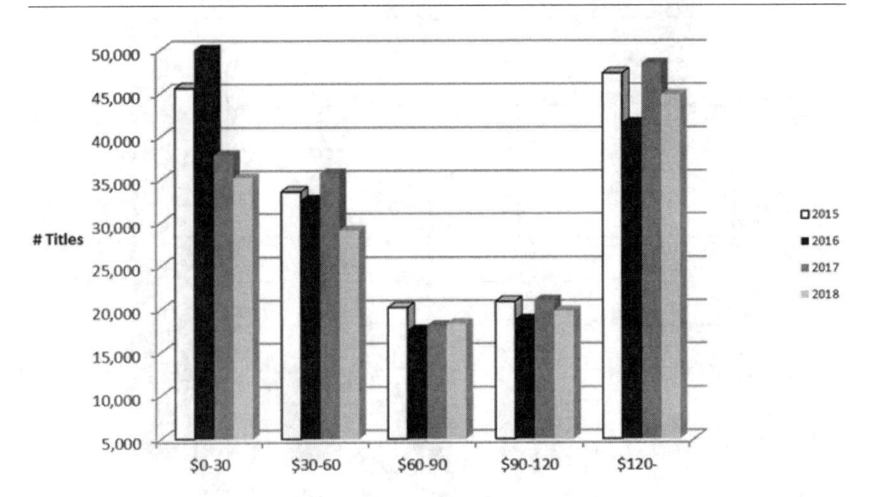

of titles available is a significant driver in increase and decrease, as within the price bands the average price remains constant except for the area with prices over $120, which showed a slight decrease in the overall average price over the past four years. Unlike serials where inflation in price drives higher costs, these data show that changes in the number of titles, not inflationary increases in price, were the primary driver in escalating costs. See Figures 2 and 3.

Table 4A treats e-books as a separate index in order to observe the differences between Table 4 and Table 4A. Currently, many titles are not yet published simultaneously in both print and e-book format, so the number of titles in the e-book index should remain smaller than the broader index. It is safe to say that in the future, the number of titles in the broader index will decline as publishers produce increasing numbers of print-on-demand e-books. Many e-book pricing models add extra charges of as much as 50 to 100 percent to the retail price for multiuser licenses. However, most e-books from aggregators will have multiple pricing models and with the criteria for the supplied data working with the lowest cost license model available, this is a probable factor in keeping the overall prices for e-books lower than expected. The overall price for e-books did show an increase of 5.3 percent in 2018. This is due to changes in the number of titles available in the lower ends of the price bands. Fewer titles in the low end of the price index contributed to an increase in the overall price. The index does show that for the library market, e-books are more expensive than print. Many publishers and e-book aggregators are still adding e-book versions of print books from backlists, and these are showing up in the index. This fact also accounts for the wide swings in numbers of titles in the index from year to year.

In the academic market, the assumption is that e-books are more expensive than their print counterparts. The cheaper versions of e-books available to consumers through such channels as Amazon and the Apple Store are not available to libraries at similar prices, if they are available at all. At best, the academic pricing

Figure 2 / Comparison of Total Costs in Sample Grouped by Price

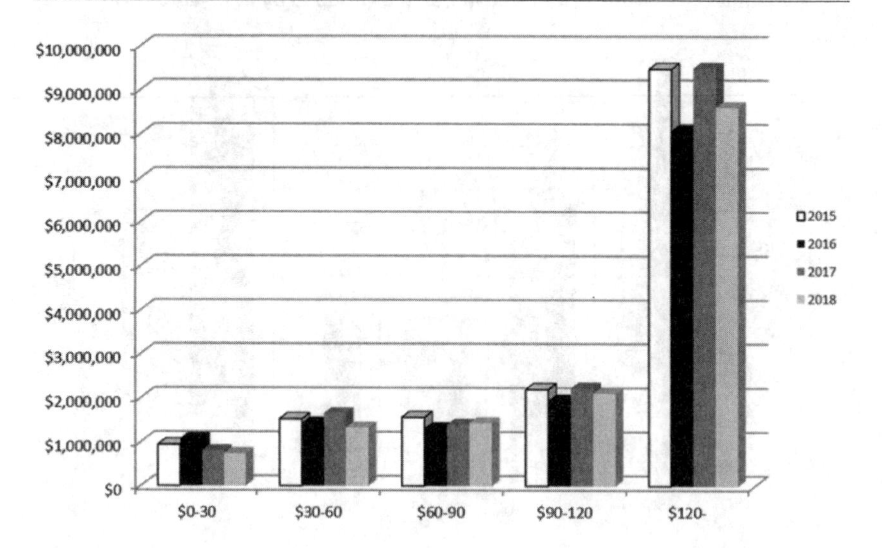

Figure 3 / Comparison of Average Price Grouped by Price Band

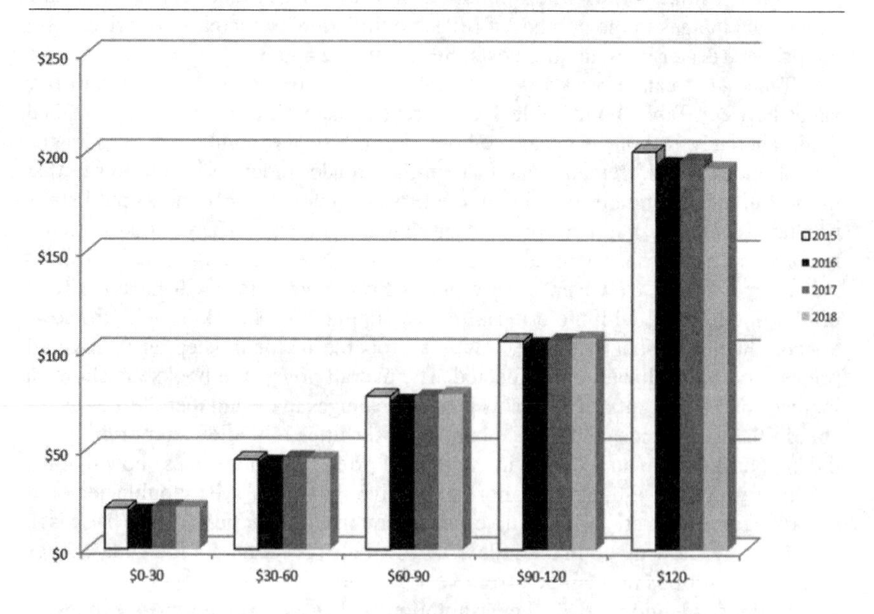

will match the print price for single-user license models, with multiuser models being far more expensive than the print price. The e-book index points out the difference in price: the average price of an e-book in 2018 was $114.61, while the average price for all books was $96.73. The average price of a print book drops to $83.08 when removing e-books from the overall index. The high price for e-books is not surprising, since most pricing models for academic e-books generally charge a higher price than the list print price for access to the e-books. However, over the past two years, it is becoming common practice for single-user licenses to be priced at the same price as print. Responding to customer demands, publishers and vendors offer e-books on multiple platforms with multiple pricing models; consequently, there can be multiple prices for the same title. In these instances, only the first license level, which is normally single-user, is included in the data. Where multiple prices are available for different use models, the lowest price is included in the index. Because electronic access is a major market trend, it is appropriate to have e-books as a separate index. It is also important to note that the e-book market is rapidly changing. The availability of additional pricing models could be a factor in the downward shift in e-book prices. It is important to note that by using the lowest price available for e-books, this approach may be artificially keeping the average price of e-books low for libraries that generally buy multiuser licenses.

The cost of textbooks has been a hot topic on many college campuses. The index for textbooks (Table 4B) documents price changes in this area. The data show that textbooks tend to be more expensive than other types of books, with an average price of $117.79 for textbooks and $96.73 for regular academic books. In 2016 and 2017, the average price of textbooks held roughly flat at around $121, meaning that there was a -3.2 percent decrease in 2018. Based on these figures, average prices look like they have plateaued over the past two years and in 2018 started dropping. This may indicate that textbook publishers are responding to market pressures and scaling back large price increases. However, prices are not yet dropping significantly, and textbooks remain expensive. Pressure on the textbook market from alternative sources such as rental services for either print or electronic versions and resales of used copies may have slowed price increases but have not resulted in an overall significant price drop. E-book versions of textbooks are included in the textbook index, so migration to e-book format does not seem to be lowering costs. This is not much consolation for cash-strapped students. This price index does not include package prices for inclusive access programs.

Overall, price changes vary among subject areas. In 2018 there were several double-digit increases in subject areas, and many areas showed price decreases. This is a normal occurrence. The 2018 data indicate that those areas with the largest increases were not concentrated in specific subject areas but were widely distributed. Overall prices for books in the scientific, technical, and medical (STM) and social science areas are still more expensive than the humanities. STM and social science publishers have tended to be early adopters of e-books and have been publishing e-books for a while. The high average prices in science and the social sciences reflect the availability and higher pricing of e-books in these areas.

It is helpful to remember that price indexes become less accurate at describing price changes the smaller the sample becomes. For example, across Tables 4, 4A, and 4B, "general works" is a small sample showing significant average price swings in 2018; it would be incorrect to conclude that all book prices in those areas increased or decreased at like amounts. In small samples, the inclusion or exclusion of a few expensive items can have a major impact on prices for the category. Because the sample is very small, these titles caused the overall price to jump dramatically.

The U.S. College Books Price Index (Table 5), prepared by Narda Tafuri, contains average price and index number data for the years 2016 through 2018, and the percentage change in price between 2017 and 2018. In 2017, the index base year was reset to 2010. Previous instances of this table have an index base year of 1989.

Data for the index was compiled from 4,718 reviews of books published in *Choice* during 2018. An additional 34 print titles reviewed in *Choice* were omitted from the analysis due to price ($500 or more) or because pricing was only available by contacting the publisher. These books were removed from the analysis so that the average prices were not skewed. This index includes some paperback prices; as a result, the average price of books is less than if only hardcover books were included.

For 2018, the overall average price for books in the humanities, sciences, and social and behavioral sciences (including reference books) was $72.20, a relatively small decrease of -0.6 percent from the average 2017 price of $72.67. Reference books continued to have the highest average price at $146.75. Excluding reference books, the average 2018 book price was $68.68, or a -0.6 percent decrease from the average 2017 price of $69.08.

The average 2018 price for humanities titles increased by 3.2 percent over the previous year. The average price for science and technology titles decreased -8.7 percent, whereas the price for social and behavioral sciences titles increased by 1.1 percent. Since 2010, there has been an overall book price increase of 8.9 percent when reference books are included.

When isolated, the average 2018 price of reference books increased by 9.8 percent over the previous year. The overall price of reference books has seen fluctuations in pricing over the past several years. Compared to 2010, overall price inflation has seen an 8.9 percent increase.

Questions regarding this index may be addressed to the author at narda.tafuri@scranton.edu.

Foreign Prices

As shown in the chart below, in 2018 the U.S. dollar grew in strength against the Canadian dollar (7.9 percent), Euro (4.8 percent), and British pound sterling (5.4 percent), but decreased against the Japanese yen (-2.4 percent).

	12/31/14	12/31/2015	12/31/2016	12/31/2017	12/31/2018
Canada	1.16	1.39	1.35	1.26	1.36
Euro	0.82	0.92	0.95	0.83	0.87
U.K.	0.64	0.68	0.81	0.74	0.78
Japan	119.45	120.42	117.03	112.55	109.85

Data from Bureau of Fiscal Services. U.S. Treasury Department (http://www.fiscal.treasury.gov/fsreports/rpt/treasRptRateExch/treasRptRateExch_home.htm).

(text continues on page 368)

Table 5 / U.S. College Books: Average Prices and Price Indexes, 2016–2018

Index Base: 2010 = 100

	2010		2016				2017				2018				Percent Change
Subject	Titles	Average Price	Titles	Average Price	Indexed to 2010	Indexed to 2015	Titles	Average Price	Indexed to 2010	Indexed to 2016	Titles	Average Price	Indexed to 2010	Indexed to 2017	2017–2018
HUMANITIES	91	$58.99	53	$72.55	123.0	103.0	60	$68.91	116.8	95.0	49	$71.55	121.3	103.8	3.8%
Art and architecture	149	61.69	143	68.61	111.2	104.0	146	66.65	108.0	97.1	118	66.01	107.0	99.0	-1.0
Fine Arts	92	67.13	83	74.43	110.9	107.1	81	58.17	86.7	78.2	54	60.75	90.5	104.4	4.4
Architecture	48	61.53	44	84.94	138.0	93.5	44	77.72	126.3	91.5	37	65.50	106.5	84.3	-15.7
Photography	28	53.02	18	56.50	106.6	100.3	17	58.04	109.5	102.7	10	61.89	116.7	106.6	6.6
Communication	112	59.97	119	77.65	129.5	84.8	101	65.40	109.1	84.2	83	69.52	115.9	106.3	6.3
Language and literature	94	68.66	86	80.92	117.9	105.4	86	77.10	112.3	95.3	61	87.98	128.1	114.1	14.1
African and Middle Eastern	24	62.28	6	49.81	80.0	66.2	10	51.69	83.0	103.8	12	77.33	124.2	149.6	49.6
Asian and Oceanian	24	71.99	18	69.93	97.1	125.4	13	89.30	124.0	127.7	13	76.84	106.7	86.0	-14.0
Classical	24	78.76	26	86.84	110.3	128.0	17	69.69	88.5	80.3	23	93.69	119.0	134.4	34.4
English and American	394	61.96	283	73.29	118.3	108.8	206	69.06	111.5	94.2	201	78.96	127.4	114.3	14.3
Germanic	22	70.36	20	78.94	112.2	108.3	6	75.00	106.6	95.0	21	81.13	115.3	108.2	8.2
Romance	70	59.00	39	64.67	109.6	93.3	42	72.30	122.5	111.8	35	80.88	137.1	111.9	11.9
Slavic	32	35.95	14	75.25	209.3	118.7	10	60.69	168.8	80.7	11	80.00	222.5	131.8	31.8
Other	n.a.	n.a.	n.a.	n.a.	n.a.	n.a.	n.a.	n.a.	n.a.	n.a.	n.a.	n.a.	n.a.	n.a.	n.a.
Performing arts	30	61.97	12	63.10	101.8	109.3	15	75.93	122.5	120.3	9	76.88	124.1	101.3	1.3
Film	130	64.13	96	81.62	127.3	114.9	92	89.34	139.3	109.5	85	82.03	127.9	91.8	-8.2
Music	123	61.01	106	74.51	122.1	114.1	99	71.30	116.9	95.7	85	68.22	111.8	95.7	-4.3
Theater and dance	45	62.38	38	83.52	133.9	105.5	36	88.53	141.9	106.0	23	75.73	121.4	85.5	-14.5
Philosophy	198	63.45	150	70.50	111.1	94.5	162	77.58	122.3	110.0	186	75.81	119.5	97.7	-2.3
Religion	272	57.18	240	61.94	108.3	107.7	192	65.64	114.8	106.0	196	66.42	116.2	101.2	1.2
TOTAL HUMANITIES	2,002	$61.60	1,594	$72.53	117.7	105.0	1,435	$71.20	115.6	98.2	1,312	$73.51	119.3	103.2	3.2
SCIENCE AND TECHNOLOGY	110	$58.09	59	$69.30	119.3	118.3	77	$58.83	101.3	84.9	82	$58.81	101.2	100.0	0.0
History of science and technology	78	54.10	60	53.16	98.3	91.5	51	68.63	126.9	129.1	51	58.41	108.0	85.1	-14.9

Table 5 / U.S. College Books: Average Prices and Price Indexes, 2016–2018 *(cont.)*

Index Base: 2010 = 100

	2010		2016				2017				2018				Percent Change
Subject	**Titles**	**Average Price**	**Titles**	**Average Price**	**Indexed to 2010**	**Indexed to 2015**	**Titles**	**Average Price**	**Indexed to 2010**	**Indexed to 2016**	**Titles**	**Average Price**	**Indexed to 2010**	**Indexed to 2017**	**2017–2018**
Astronautics and astronomy	63	55.58	42	48.65	87.5	101.4	72	57.90	104.2	119.0	50	51.92	93.4	89.7	-10.3
Biology	151	72.74	95	81.12	111.5	105.3	141	63.15	86.8	77.8	76	59.55	81.9	94.3	-5.7
Botany	85	85.09	47	98.08	115.3	102.5	77	69.93	82.2	71.3	63	59.98	70.5	85.8	-14.2
Zoology	121	64.33	88	67.89	105.5	97.6	89	63.05	98.0	92.9	74	60.81	94.5	96.4	-3.6
Chemistry	42	115.42	27	105.31	91.2	143.8	29	121.51	105.3	115.4	21	101.78	88.2	83.8	-16.2
Earth science	102	63.33	103	79.97	126.3	105.4	112	71.36	112.7	89.2	79	66.39	104.8	93.0	-7.0
Engineering	103	88.38	56	113.67	128.6	122.2	86	106.40	120.4	93.6	47	93.51	105.8	87.9	-12.1
Health sciences	146	56.14	121	72.17	128.6	102.7	142	66.61	118.6	92.3	102	66.77	118.9	100.2	0.2
Information and computer science	83	73.50	41	62.78	85.4	117.7	93	63.83	86.8	101.7	59	59.41	80.8	93.1	-6.9
Mathematics	108	61.97	93	67.60	109.1	100.9	107	77.02	124.3	113.9	81	77.71	125.4	100.9	0.9
Physics	50	54.74	36	79.75	145.7	141.1	52	81.59	149.1	102.3	39	69.52	127.0	85.2	-14.8
Sports and physical education	67	54.06	45	83.86	155.1	126.2	78	69.44	128.4	82.8	63	55.41	102.5	79.8	-20.2
TOTAL SCIENCE	1,309	$67.13	913	$75.90	113.1	108.3	1,206	$71.36	106.3	94.0	887	$65.15	97.1	91.3	-8.7
SOCIAL AND BEHAVIORAL SCIENCES	129	$66.32	134	$79.19	119.4	97.7	70	$80.47	121.3	101.6	64	$77.53	116.9	96.3	-3.7
Anthropology	139	63.60	102	81.45	128.1	98.4	115	84.95	133.6	104.3	85	79.38	124.8	93.4	-6.6
Business management and labor	150	58.00	120	54.75	94.4	100.7	122	52.56	90.6	96.0	95	$51.53	88.8	98.0	-2.0
Economics	270	61.16	170	56.26	92.0	83.4	125	63.79	104.3	113.4	114	56.48	92.3	88.5	-11.5
Education	158	62.56	109	74.80	119.6	96.1	24	72.30	115.6	96.7	26	$74.18	118.6	102.6	2.6
History, geography and area studies	154	58.16	95	76.90	132.2	108.9	90	72.33	124.4	94.1	95	66.02	113.5	91.3	-8.7
Africa	38	69.05	30	67.02	97.1	92.4	24	70.34	101.9	105.0	31	$68.20	98.8	97.0	-3.0
Ancient history	49	57.90	45	88.15	152.2	92.1	40	74.73	129.1	84.8	51	86.00	148.5	115.1	15.1
Asia and Oceania	72	60.88	63	64.10	105.3	81.3	63	70.69	116.1	110.3	65	73.55	120.8	104.0	4.0

Central and Eastern Europe	56	66.53	48	69.47	104.4	101.8	50	71.05	106.8	102.3	65	76.17	114.5	107.2	7.2
Latin America and Caribbean	54	59.31	54	68.08	114.8	99.2	60	77.51	130.7	113.9	59	75.24	126.9	97.1	-2.9
Middle East and North Africa	43	65.57	31	75.41	115.0	96.9	51	60.38	92.1	80.1	36	69.60	106.1	115.3	15.3
North America	444	45.50	386	51.15	112.4	102.1	335	50.33	110.6	98.4	343	54.62	120.0	108.5	8.5
United Kingdom	80	69.56	48	83.05	119.4	111.3	66	74.36	106.9	89.5	78	70.68	101.6	95.1	-4.9
Western Europe	138	59.14	108	67.92	114.8	97.8	106	75.01	126.8	110.4	110	85.13	143.9	113.5	13.5
Political science	4	84.36	67	66.96	79.4	136.7	68	58.55	69.4	87.4	60	62.46	74.0	106.7	6.7
Comparative politics	183	66.34	215	73.22	110.4	92.5	186	64.47	97.2	88.0	201	67.63	101.9	104.9	4.9
International relations	213	65.64	151	69.69	106.2	89.8	147	61.87	94.3	88.8	141	61.58	93.8	99.5	-0.5
Political theory	73	56.74	128	72.56	127.9	115.4	118	71.12	125.3	98.0	127	73.98	130.4	104.0	4.0
U.S. politics	253	53.03	201	65.21	123.0	102.8	150	61.03	115.1	93.6	178	63.46	119.7	104.0	4.0
Psychology	126	60.55	61	87.45	144.4	102.1	121	72.33	119.5	82.7	137	71.95	118.8	99.5	-0.5
Sociology	226	60.71	162	78.90	130.0	99.0	182	79.50	131.0	100.8	145	72.71	119.8	91.5	-8.5
TOTAL BEHAVIORAL SCIENCES	3,052	$59.09	2,528	$68.12	115.3	97.2	2,313	$66.58	112.7	97.7	2,306	$67.28	113.9	101.1	1.1
TOTAL GENERAL, HUMANITIES, SCIENCE AND SOCIAL SCIENCE (without Reference)	6,363	$61.53	5,035	$70.92	115.3	101.7	4,954	$69.08	112.3	97.4	4,505	$68.68	111.6	99.4	-0.6
REFERENCE															
General	29	$61.17	37	$102.52	167.6	127.2	20	$101.90	166.6	99.4	19	$154.73	253.0	151.8	51.8
Humanities	128	117.12	72	119.53	102.1	111.8	83	136.80	116.8	114.4	70	132.66	113.3	97.0	-3.0
Science and technology	76	133.19	35	147.98	111.1	123.4	42	110.55	83.0	74.7	34	164.90	123.8	149.2	49.2
Social and behavioral sciences	216	152.91	164	150.84	98.6	103.7	146	142.88	93.4	94.7	90	149.17	97.6	104.4	4.4
TOTAL REFERENCE	449	$133.44	308	$137.39	103.0	115.1	291	$133.66	100.2	97.3	213	$146.75	110.0	109.8	9.8
GRAND TOTAL	6,812	$66.27	5,343	$74.76	112.8	103.4	5,245	$72.67	109.7	97.2	4,718	$72.20	108.9	99.4	-0.6%

Compiled by Narda Tafuri, University of Scranton.

Table 6 / U.S. Mass Market Paperback Books: Average Prices and Price Indexes, 2015–2018

Index Base: 2010 = 100

	2010	2015 Final			2016 Final*			2017 Preliminary			2018 Preliminary		
BISAC Category	Average Price	Volumes	Average Price	Index	Volumes	Average Price	Index	Volumes	Average Price	Index	Volumes	Average Price	Index
Antiques and collectibles	$8.77	n.a.	n.a.	n.a.	n.a.	n.a.	n.a.	n.a.	n.a.	n.a.	n.a.	n.a.	n.a.
Architecture	n.a.	n.a.	n.a.	n.a.	n.a.	n.a.	n.a.	n.a.	n.a.	n.a.	n.a.	n.a.	n.a.
Art	n.a.	n.a.	n.a.	n.a.	n.a.	n.a.	n.a.	n.a.	n.a.	n.a.	n.a.	n.a.	n.a.
Bibles	n.a.	n.a.	n.a.	n.a.	n.a.	n.a.	n.a.	n.a.	n.a.	n.a.	n.a.	n.a.	n.a.
Biography and autobiography	7.51	2	$8.49	113.0	7	$10.71	142.6	5	$9.28	123.6	7	$9.85	131.1
Body, mind and spirit	7.99	n.a.	n.a.	n.a.	2	8.99	112.5	n.a.	n.a.	n.a.	n.a.	n.a.	n.a.
Business and economics	9.32	1	8.99	96.5	n.a.	n.a.	n.a.	1	7.99	85.7	3	8.99	96.5
Children	6.22	204	6.32	101.7	224	6.98	112.2	179	7.14	114.8	230	7.41	119.1
Comics and graphic novels	n.a.	n.a.	n.a.	n.a.	n.a.	n.a.	n.a.	n.a.	n.a.	n.a.	n.a.	n.a.	n.a.
Computers	n.a.	n.a.	n.a.	n.a.	n.a.	n.a.	n.a.	n.a.	n.a.	n.a.	n.a.	n.a.	n.a.
Cooking	n.a.	1	8.99	n.a.	n.a.	n.a.	n.a.	n.a.	n.a.	n.a.	n.a.	n.a.	n.a.
Crafts and hobbies	n.a.	n.a.	n.a.	n.a.	n.a.	n.a.	n.a.	n.a.	n.a.	n.a.	n.a.	n.a.	n.a.
Design	n.a.	n.a.	n.a.	n.a.	n.a.	n.a.	n.a.	n.a.	n.a.	n.a.	n.a.	n.a.	n.a.
Drama	6.30	n.a.	n.a.	n.a.	n.a.	n.a.	n.a.	n.a.	n.a.	n.a.	n.a.	n.a.	n.a.
Education	n.a.	n.a.	n.a.	n.a.	n.a.	n.a.	n.a.	n.a.	n.a.	n.a.	n.a.	n.a.	n.a.
Family and relationships	7.99	1	8.99	112.5	n.a.	n.a.	n.a.	n.a.	n.a.	n.a.	n.a.	n.a.	n.a.
Fiction	6.80	3,234	7.11	104.6	2,998	7.23	106.3	2,754	7.30	107.4	2682	7.26	106.8
Foreign language study	7.08	n.a.	n.a.	n.a.	n.a.	n.a.	n.a.	n.a.	n.a.	n.a.	n.a.	n.a.	n.a.
Games	n.a.	1	7.99	n.a.	2	8.99	n.a.	n.a.	n.a.	n.a.	1	8.50	n.a.
Gardening	n.a.	n.a.	n.a.	n.a.	n.a.	n.a.	n.a.	n.a.	n.a.	n.a.	n.a.	n.a.	n.a.
Health and fitness	7.92	3	8.99	113.5	n.a.	n.a.	n.a.	1	9.99	126.1	4	8.49	107.2
History	9.95	2	9.99	100.4	4	9.49	95.4	5	9.99	100.4	3	9.99	100.4
House and home	n.a.	n.a.	n.a.	n.a.	n.a.	n.a.	n.a.	n.a.	n.a.	n.a.	n.a.	n.a.	n.a.
Humor	n.a.	n.a.	n.a.	n.a.	1	7.99	n.a.	1	9.99	n.a.	2	12.49	n.a.
Language arts and disciplines	13.25	n.a.	n.a.	n.a.	n.a.	n.a.	n.a.	n.a.	n.a.	n.a.	n.a.	n.a.	n.a.

Law	n.a.	n.a.	n.a.	n.a.	n.a.	n.a.	n.a.	n.a.	n.a.	n.a.	n.a.	n.a.	n.a.
Literary collections	5.95	n.a.	n.a.	n.a.	n.a.	n.a.	n.a.	n.a.	n.a.	n.a.	1	4.99	83.9
Literary criticism	7.99	n.a.	n.a.	n.a.	n.a.	n.a.	n.a.	n.a.	n.a.	n.a.	n.a.	n.a.	n.a.
Mathematics	n.a.	n.a.	n.a.	n.a.	n.a.	n.a.	n.a.	n.a.	n.a.	n.a.	n.a.	n.a.	n.a.
Medical	8.99	n.a.	n.a.	n.a.	n.a.	n.a.	n.a.	n.a.	n.a.	n.a.	n.a.	n.a.	n.a.
Music	n.a.	n.a.	n.a.	n.a.	n.a.	n.a.	n.a.	n.a.	n.a.	n.a.	n.a.	n.a.	n.a.
Nature	n.a.	n.a.	n.a.	n.a.	n.a.	n.a.	n.a.	n.a.	n.a.	n.a.	n.a.	n.a.	n.a.
Performing arts	9.99	n.a.	n.a.	n.a.	n.a.	n.a.	n.a.	n.a.	n.a.	n.a.	n.a.	n.a.	n.a.
Pets	7.99	1	9.99	125.0	n.a.	n.a.	n.a.	n.a.	n.a.	n.a.	n.a.	n.a.	n.a.
Philosophy	6.47	1	6.95	107.4	n.a.	n.a.	n.a.	n.a.	n.a.	n.a.	n.a.	n.a.	n.a.
Photography	n.a.	n.a.	n.a.	n.a.	n.a.	n.a.	n.a.	n.a.	n.a.	n.a.	n.a.	n.a.	n.a.
Poetry	7.95	2	6.45	81.1	1	3.99	50.2	n.a.	n.a.	n.a.	n.a.	n.a.	n.a.
Political science	7.97	2	8.47	106.3	n.a.	n.a.	n.a.	1	8.99	112.8	1	9.99	125.3
Psychology	n.a.	n.a.	n.a.	n.a.	n.a.	n.a.	n.a.	n.a.	n.a.	n.a.	1	13.99	n.a.
Reference	7.99	1	7.99	100.0	5	15.70	196.5	n.a.	n.a.	n.a.	n.a.	n.a.	n.a.
Religion	7.99	n.a.	n.a.	n.a.	n.a.	n.a.	n.a.	n.a.	n.a.	n.a.	n.a.	n.a.	n.a.
Science	n.a.	n.a.	n.a.	n.a.	1	13.99	n.a.	n.a.	n.a.	n.a.	n.a.	n.a.	n.a.
Self-help	7.99	n.a.	n.a.	n.a.	n.a.	n.a.	n.a.	n.a.	n.a.	n.a.	6	13.99	175.1
Social science	n.a.	n.a.	n.a.	n.a.	n.a.	n.a.	n.a.	n.a.	n.a.	n.a.	n.a.	n.a.	n.a.
Sports and recreation	7.99	n.a.	n.a.	n.a.	1	9.99	125.0	n.a.	n.a.	n.a.	n.a.	n.a.	n.a.
Study aids	n.a.	n.a.	n.a.	n.a.	n.a.	n.a.	n.a.	n.a.	n.a.	n.a.	n.a.	n.a.	n.a.
Technology and engineering	n.a.	n.a.	n.a.	n.a.	n.a.	n.a.	n.a.	n.a.	n.a.	n.a.	n.a.	n.a.	n.a.
Transportation	n.a.	n.a.	n.a.	n.a.	n.a.	n.a.	n.a.	n.a.	n.a.	n.a.	n.a.	n.a.	n.a.
Travel	n.a.	1	7.99	n.a.	n.a.	n.a.	n.a.	n.a.	n.a.	n.a.	n.a.	n.a.	n.a.
True crime	7.64	13	8.30	108.6	13	8.45	110.6	12	8.41	110.0	7	8.28	108.3
Young adult	8.13	22	9.40	115.6	6	7.99	98.3	8	7.37	90.6	28	11.35	139.6
Totals and Averages	$6.83	3,492	$7.09	103.8	3,265	$7.25	106.1	2,967	$7.31	107.0	2,976	$7.35	107.6

Compiled by Narda Tafuri, University of Scranton, from data supplied by Baker & Taylor.
n.a. = not available
* = figures revised from previous editions based on new data from Baker & Taylor.

Table 7 / U.S. Paperback Books (Excluding Mass Market): Average Prices and Price Indexes, 2015–2018

Index Base: 2010 = 100

	2010	2015 Final			2016 Final*			2017 Preliminary			2018 Preliminary		
BISAC Category	**Average Price**	**Volumes**	**Average Price**	**Index**	**Volumes**	**Average Price**	**Index**	**Volumes**	**Average Price**	**Index**	**Volumes**	**Average Price**	**Index**
Antiques and collectibles	$25.53	126	$33.55	131.4	148	$35.35	138.5	113	$40.09	157.0	88	$40.47	158.5
Architecture	45.31	814	44.20	97.5	785	50.25	110.9	743	48.34	106.7	701	48.93	108.0
Art	38.25	1,680	41.96	109.7	1,830	50.28	131.4	1,636	40.91	106.9	1,636	40.30	105.4
Bibles	38.66	966	40.51	104.8	618	44.05	113.9	716	40.03	103.5	714	45.29	117.1
Biography and autobiography	20.35	2,692	20.40	100.3	2,575	20.25	99.5	2,355	20.44	100.5	2,490	20.49	100.7
Body, mind and spirit	18.03	677	18.20	101.0	728	18.2	101.0	692	17.98	99.7	745	18.17	100.8
Business and economics	69.30	8,946	103.95	150.0	7,065	93.01	134.2	5,720	89.76	129.5	5,996	81.08	117.0
Children	10.42	12,215	15.20	145.9	12,264	14.96	143.6	11,503	16.14	154.9	11,102	12.71	121.9
Comics and graphic novels	16.11	2,043	18.03	111.9	2,153	18.6	115.5	2,059	18.47	114.6	2,300	18.90	117.3
Computers	70.42	2,903	84.97	120.7	4,291	128.17	182.0	2,565	95.30	135.3	3,016	99.87	141.8
Cooking	19.95	1,110	20.41	102.3	1,030	20.82	104.4	914	21.20	106.3	903	20.98	105.2
Crafts and hobbies	19.34	1,103	19.63	101.5	929	19.9	102.9	800	20.38	105.4	661	21.54	111.4
Design	63.98	258	44.92	70.2	254	38.29	59.9	240	40.49	63.3	245	40.58	63.4
Drama	18.95	542	22.79	120.3	522	19.68	103.9	639	22.38	118.1	512	20.55	108.4
Education	42.98	3,989	52.38	121.9	4,589	66.4	154.5	4,502	57.33	133.4	4,065	60.11	139.9
Family and relationships	18.72	674	20.08	107.3	614	22.98	122.7	521	20.95	111.9	566	22.00	117.5
Fiction	17.99	11,041	17.18	95.5	10,791	17.01	94.6	10,103	16.69	92.7	9,867	17.45	97.0
Foreign language study	31.33	1,005	49.25	157.2	856	49.4	157.7	1,004	41.36	132.0	782	42.32	135.1
Games	16.57	766	15.17	91.5	1,831	14.27	86.1	1,260	15.57	94.0	686	17.25	104.1
Gardening	23.45	158	24.97	106.5	124	22.51	96.0	121	22.61	96.4	115	21.65	92.3
Health and fitness	26.95	1,080	32.70	121.3	1,034	36.39	135.0	1,029	30.79	114.2	1,026	30.17	111.9
History	35.79	7,044	40.69	113.7	6,431	39.15	109.4	6,273	37.91	105.9	6,015	38.51	107.6
House and home	21.19	117	20.35	96.1	89	20.15	95.1	98	24.87	117.4	87	22.55	106.4
Humor	14.37	324	15.15	105.4	301	15.42	107.3	298	15.34	106.7	248	15.38	107.0
Language arts and disciplines	64.46	1,762	75.20	116.7	2,313	77.03	119.5	1,645	71.57	111.0	1,435	59.33	92.0

Law	72.07	3,793	86.00	119.3	3,860	87.35	121.2	3,100	81.83	113.5	3,284	88.04	122.2
Literary collections	36.42	343	36.55	100.4	400	33.46	91.9	393	26.60	73.0	417	28.41	78.0
Literary criticism	36.57	1,972	43.85	119.9	2,061	43.32	118.4	1,921	42.31	115.7	1,862	45.63	124.8
Mathematics	86.13	1,033	83.11	96.5	1,565	97.31	113.0	960	77.89	90.4	1,268	99.99	116.1
Medical	90.22	3,743	106.16	117.7	6,442	132.71	147.1	3,528	88.89	98.5	4,261	111.80	123.9
Music	22.83	2,722	25.61	112.2	2,662	30.42	133.3	1,952	28.76	126.0	1,724	27.09	118.7
Nature	37.28	516	31.27	83.9	606	49.37	132.4	563	32.53	87.3	547	39.79	106.7
Performing arts	33.53	955	39.24	117.0	832	38.71	115.5	859	37.67	112.3	861	37.89	113.0
Pets	17.34	150	17.91	103.3	159	20.31	117.1	109	18.17	104.8	110	18.34	105.7
Philosophy	52.66	1,654	44.03	83.6	1,787	55.64	105.7	1,515	41.85	79.5	1,712	48.91	92.9
Photography	31.30	472	38.18	122.0	404	33.86	108.2	412	34.64	110.7	283	34.08	108.9
Poetry	16.73	1,993	17.82	106.5	2,064	17.23	103.0	2,001	17.38	103.9	2,084	17.38	103.9
Political science	41.00	3,865	55.26	134.8	3,952	49.95	121.8	3,760	45.82	111.8	3,716	53.25	129.9
Psychology	47.98	2,292	52.10	108.6	2,240	61.13	127.4	1,939	51.27	106.9	1,903	55.01	114.7
Reference	84.85	720	156.99	185.0	573	156.03	183.9	501	188.19	221.8	447	174.85	206.1
Religion	22.08	7,410	24.55	111.2	6,765	26.32	119.2	6,610	25.86	117.1	6,409	27.10	122.8
Science	116.37	2,654	100.65	86.5	5,449	131.2	112.7	2,457	90.25	77.6	3,904	126.36	108.6
Self-help	17.84	1,038	17.26	96.8	991	17.92	100.4	929	17.53	98.3	1,087	17.06	95.7
Social science	45.05	4,779	51.57	114.5	5,580	56.91	126.3	4,528	47.22	104.8	5,212	55.10	122.3
Sports and recreation	22.30	1,091	25.09	112.5	1,107	24.91	111.7	999	25.60	114.8	885	25.01	112.1
Study aids	49.24	939	43.64	88.6	708	38.6	78.4	581	31.44	63.8	500	43.91	89.2
Technology and engineering	111.20	1,914	113.98	102.5	4,112	139.22	125.2	2,244	99.06	89.1	3,234	140.82	126.6
Transportation	36.26	385	39.52	109.0	531	36.39	100.3	519	38.52	106.2	499	34.66	95.6
Travel	20.93	1,617	21.28	101.7	1,679	21.01	100.4	1,489	21.54	102.9	1,569	20.82	99.5
True crime	20.94	176	18.97	90.6	142	19.53	93.2	166	19.85	94.8	205	19.66	93.9
Young adult	14.86	2,336	20.70	139.3	2,717	25.49	171.5	2,675	18.28	123.0	2,815	17.97	120.9
Totals and Averages	$42.06	114,597	$46.52	110.6	123,553	$55.97	133.1	104,259	$42.66	101.4	106,799	$49.02	116.6

Compiled by Narda Tafuri, University of Scranton, from data supplied by Baker & Taylor.
* = figures revised from previous editions based on new data from Baker & Taylor.

Table 7A / U.S. Audiobooks: Average Prices and Price Indexes, 2015–2018

Index Base: 2010 = 100

	2010	2015 Final			2016 Final*			2017 Preliminary			2018 Preliminary		
BISAC Category	Average Price	Volumes	Average Price	Index	Volumes	Average Price	Index	Volumes	Average Price	Index	Volumes	Average Price	Index
Antiques and collectibles	$36.66	n.a.	n.a.	n.a.	3	$26.66	72.7	3	$33.32	90.9	n.a.	n.a.	n.a.
Architecture	41.24	2	$14.97	36.3	7	25.42	61.6	10	31.49	76.4	2	$22.99	55.7
Art	58.21	8	30.61	52.6	22	16.95	29.1	25	28.82	49.5	16	31.54	54.2
Bibles	43.28	16	37.35	86.3	7	122.85	283.9	6	49.98	115.5	2	49.99	115.5
Biography and autobiography	50.79	1,226	36.61	72.1	1,688	31.87	62.7	1,440	37.45	73.7	1,240	42.77	84.2
Body, mind and spirit	32.98	163	23.60	71.6	148	28.99	87.9	158	29.41	89.2	145	35.86	108.7
Business and economics	49.70	701	29.51	59.4	1,316	27.82	56.0	884	32.15	64.7	788	35.31	71.1
Children	37.80	2,361	39.89	105.5	1,295	34.83	92.2	1,689	31.12	82.3	1,317	36.31	96.1
Comics and graphic novels	n.a.	n.a.	n.a.	n.a.	1	9.99	n.a.	3	8.99	n.a.	n.a.	n.a.	n.a.
Computers	45.00	9	29.77	66.1	30	27.05	60.1	42	28.82	64.1	27	42.32	94.0
Cooking	44.97	21	30.56	68.0	45	32.23	71.7	63	35.24	78.4	60	40.03	89.0
Crafts and hobbies	24.98	3	28.63	114.6	2	27.47	110.0	2	12.99	52.0	3	22.32	89.4
Design	n.a.	1	29.99	n.a.	1	9.99	n.a.	1	9.99	n.a.	6	51.31	n.a.
Drama	33.21	52	29.76	89.6	152	14.36	43.2	60	20.23	60.9	163	18.48	55.6
Education	45.71	26	36.09	78.9	51	40.11	87.7	39	33.48	73.2	40	30.92	67.6
Family and relationships	41.17	157	30.76	74.7	246	29.57	71.8	205	31.78	77.2	181	34.39	83.5
Fiction	50.38	13,094	31.95	63.4	19,260	24.32	48.3	10,985	33.90	67.3	9,892	39.24	77.9
Foreign language study	45.11	137	69.30	153.6	45	110.24	244.4	95	79.58	176.4	98	210.10	465.8
Games	n.a.	1	11.99	n.a.	5	27.99	n.a.	10	40.79	n.a.	5	39.99	n.a.
Gardening	47.82	1	14.99	31.3	2	31.49	65.9	5	26.98	56.4	n.a.	n.a.	n.a.
Health and fitness	43.09	162	40.47	93.9	289	32.62	75.7	289	39.74	92.2	267	38.59	89.6
History	58.07	550	43.41	74.8	1,210	33.47	57.6	903	44.36	76.4	809	47.38	81.6
House and home	n.a.	5	35.79	n.a.	33	38.79	n.a.	40	41.13	n.a.	20	35.98	n.a.
Humor	36.62	108	32.83	89.6	103	27.07	73.9	61	29.85	81.5	95	41.77	114.1
Language arts and disciplines	38.34	20	33.29	86.8	41	30.47	79.5	35	38.16	99.5	29	34.50	90.0

Law	64.49	9	55.11	85.4	41	28.46	44.1	31	42.50	65.9	34	34.16	53.0
Literary collections	52.07	58	40.13	77.1	72	34.98	67.2	45	33.45	64.2	69	43.17	82.9
Literary criticism	42.53	20	43.63	102.6	54	29.32	68.9	32	31.68	74.5	34	41.10	96.6
Mathematics	n.a.	6	36.81	n.a.	8	26.24	n.a.	10	21.49	n.a.	4	26.99	n.a.
Medical	40.13	27	32.39	80.7	24	22.07	55.0	48	34.76	86.6	36	41.68	103.9
Music	35.67	21	30.66	85.9	94	27.55	77.2	136	29.22	81.9	48	36.13	101.3
Nature	41.20	35	31.38	76.2	87	21.69	52.6	63	31.88	77.4	52	35.66	86.5
Performing arts	40.60	79	36.53	90.0	185	37.84	93.2	73	35.08	86.4	95	40.58	99.9
Pets	38.33	17	39.33	102.6	61	39.42	102.9	46	37.77	98.5	29	38.02	99.2
Philosophy	53.05	17	29.04	54.7	135	27.26	51.4	103	23.43	44.2	53	38.02	71.7
Photography	n.a.	n.a.	n.a.	n.a.	2	34.99	n.a.	n.a.	n.a.	n.a.	n.a.	n.a.	n.a.
Poetry	33.59	25	37.22	110.8	24	15.07	44.9	45	22.29	66.4	57	27.10	80.7
Political science	48.04	173	36.92	76.9	404	29.37	61.1	324	37.62	78.3	377	39.14	81.5
Psychology	45.42	106	35.49	78.1	191	28.38	62.5	155	37.39	82.3	161	37.24	82.0
Reference	59.99	4	15.49	25.8	11	23.17	38.6	19	35.36	58.9	8	46.62	77.7
Religion	33.94	950	25.86	76.2	1,243	25.78	76.0	1,248	26.93	79.4	1,109	30.94	91.2
Science	51.89	122	35.31	68.1	193	28.64	55.2	156	33.65	64.9	211	38.90	75.0
Self-help	39.43	286	30.12	76.4	534	32.81	83.2	381	33.61	85.2	435	36.35	92.2
Social science	48.07	122	31.13	64.8	312	25.33	52.7	300	35.15	73.1	321	36.06	75.0
Sports and recreation	48.48	64	34.30	70.7	223	25.98	53.6	145	36.42	75.1	111	38.23	78.9
Study aids	19.41	3	24.97	128.6	2	52.98	272.9	n.a.	n.a.	n.a.	3	41.63	214.5
Technology and engineering	53.33	20	43.13	80.9	82	93.02	174.4	103	101.94	191.2	31	44.76	83.9
Transportation	46.28	9	35.98	77.7	17	32.10	69.4	9	30.21	65.3	10	47.49	102.6
Travel	50.96	26	26.37	51.7	145	17.03	33.4	39	30.91	60.7	32	43.67	85.7
True crime	52.58	111	29.19	55.5	173	33.89	64.5	180	38.98	74.1	189	36.65	69.7
Young adult	44.81	1,714	31.71	70.8	1,742	29.40	65.6	1,452	38.92	86.9	1,098	44.52	99.4
Totals and Averages	$48.00	22,848	$33.27	69.3	32,061	$26.89	56.0	22,196	$34.76	72.4	19,812	$39.67	82.6

Compiled by Narda Tafuri, University of Scranton, from data supplied by Baker & Taylor.
* = figures revised from previous editions based on new data from Baker & Taylor

Table 7B / U.S. E-Books: Average Prices and Price Indexes, 2015–2018

Index Base: 2010 = 100

	2010	2015 Final			2016 Final*			2017 Preliminary			2018 Preliminary		
BISAC Category	Average Price	Volumes	Average Price	Index	Volumes	Average Price	Index	Volumes	Average Price	Index	Volumes	Average Price	Index
Antiques and collectibles	$30.24	154	$12.50	41.4	100	$19.20	63.5	122	$16.75	55.4	142	$9.97	33.0
Architecture	66.57	542	60.93	91.5	438	39.92	60.0	799	21.80	32.8	314	46.67	70.1
Art	41.56	4,913	10.59	25.5	2,663	15.81	38.0	2,300	18.59	44.7	1,276	33.50	80.6
Bibles	6.11	194	8.92	146.0	280	12.26	200.7	2,141	11.86	194.1	405	9.20	150.5
Biography and autobiography	15.47	6,770	15.67	101.3	6,567	20.37	131.7	7,724	17.51	113.2	6,675	20.58	133.0
Body, mind and spirit	13.95	1,344	11.14	79.8	2,114	11.88	85.2	2,440	11.71	83.9	2,812	11.54	82.7
Business and economics	44.82	21,656	23.30	52.0	8,432	47.83	106.7	8,370	40.39	90.1	25,480	49.61	110.7
Children	13.82	19,174	12.37	89.5	16,469	20.79	150.4	24,430	17.46	126.3	24,725	15.60	112.9
Comics and graphic novels	11.39	3,344	8.13	71.4	1,099	9.05	79.5	1,102	11.79	103.5	995	9.18	80.6
Computers	62.09	4,420	64.30	103.6	4,164	72.58	116.9	2,833	81.93	131.9	1,738	52.46	84.5
Cooking	16.79	3,086	12.11	72.1	2,054	15.17	90.4	2,399	13.74	81.9	2,547	14.32	85.3
Crafts and hobbies	17.63	1,269	9.73	55.2	1,103	12.84	72.8	1,111	11.80	66.9	587	14.14	80.2
Design	37.03	145	26.25	70.9	125	24.28	65.6	157	20.54	55.5	120	24.82	67.0
Drama	4.86	1,724	7.58	156.0	1,710	10.32	212.3	1,530	11.87	244.2	1,043	9.71	199.9
Education	45.95	3,574	38.27	83.3	4,505	40.96	89.1	7,387	38.36	83.5	3,216	34.85	75.8
Family and relationships	14.79	1,767	11.22	75.9	1,837	16.37	110.7	1,711	12.80	86.5	2,209	12.58	85.1
Fiction	7.06	88,146	6.22	88.1	62,343	12.71	180.0	71,335	9.93	140.6	78,391	11.65	165.1
Foreign language study	46.68	1,645	20.18	43.2	906	34.71	74.4	1,688	21.73	46.6	2,156	19.31	41.4
Games	12.85	1,246	22.64	176.2	700	9.49	73.9	915	8.64	67.2	1,442	6.82	53.1
Gardening	17.41	307	10.89	62.5	247	13.31	76.5	538	12.12	69.6	287	12.98	74.5
Health and fitness	18.78	2,934	13.79	73.4	2,394	14.83	79.0	2,892	13.59	72.4	2,927	13.77	73.3
History	48.20	10,472	40.49	84.0	9,425	38.50	79.9	12,767	28.60	59.3	8,003	39.26	81.5
House and home	21.57	312	10.26	47.6	246	12.60	58.4	367	14.50	67.2	229	17.27	80.1
Humor	11.15	858	10.64	95.4	1,231	10.15	91.1	794	10.63	95.3	1,099	13.64	122.3
Language arts and disciplines	75.61	1,861	90.30	119.4	1,986	78.29	103.5	2,654	84.93	112.3	2,415	68.09	90.1

Law	112.19	1,747	105.84	94.3	2,168	95.77	85.4	2,375	77.15	68.8	2,049	113.40	101.1
Literary collections	20.27	6,373	5.16	25.5	1,088	18.92	93.3	2,029	13.12	64.7	1,288	13.05	64.4
Literary criticism	87.17	2,926	66.15	75.9	2,672	69.07	79.2	2,856	71.51	82.0	2,560	84.17	96.6
Mathematics	112.32	1,239	84.84	75.5	1,463	85.19	75.8	1,350	53.91	48.0	359	73.01	65.0
Medical	135.71	2,992	103.42	76.2	3,477	110.50	81.4	3,247	84.56	62.3	1,777	65.59	48.3
Music	32.65	1,661	21.53	65.9	1,506	22.35	68.5	2,430	18.07	55.4	2,815	12.96	39.7
Nature	59.48	731	42.19	70.9	780	45.70	76.8	779	39.72	66.8	747	22.83	38.4
Performing arts	32.17	1,329	31.22	97.1	1,763	32.06	99.7	1,794	21.89	68.1	1,829	18.66	58.0
Pets	14.50	292	10.48	72.3	402	12.79	88.2	797	10.51	72.5	421	10.04	69.2
Philosophy	71.43	2,188	57.86	81.0	2,530	45.86	64.2	3,324	32.42	45.4	1,988	37.84	53.0
Photography	27.23	497	17.76	65.2	442	20.52	75.4	493	17.79	65.3	297	19.58	71.9
Poetry	9.54	3,783	6.34	66.5	3,088	8.24	86.3	5,091	8.74	91.6	4,824	7.84	82.2
Political science	59.74	4,026	56.26	94.2	4,153	51.50	86.2	4,735	40.74	68.2	3,189	44.90	75.2
Psychology	56.42	2,169	50.16	88.9	1,951	44.26	78.5	2,612	37.41	66.3	1,725	32.04	56.8
Reference	22.92	3,502	24.66	107.6	4,373	16.72	72.9	2,984	17.15	74.8	1,302	36.87	160.9
Religion	27.81	9,383	20.83	74.9	8,220	23.05	82.9	12,460	18.88	67.9	10,128	22.41	80.6
Science	155.80	3,833	98.18	63.0	3,978	99.79	64.0	5,098	61.83	39.7	1,897	67.74	43.5
Self-help	14.06	4,032	9.69	68.9	3,728	14.21	101.1	5,264	12.24	87.1	5,158	13.42	95.5
Social science	56.83	4,269	55.12	97.0	5,067	49.58	87.2	6,772	39.21	69.0	3,377	39.12	68.8
Sports and recreation	19.22	1,844	17.28	89.9	1,776	17.59	91.5	1,868	17.32	90.1	1,373	19.51	101.5
Study aids	13.94	1,155	11.04	79.2	18,528	30.11	216.0	2,316	33.09	237.4	1,589	19.20	137.7
Technology and engineering	158.44	3,175	119.72	75.6	2,987	128.19	80.9	3,724	79.17	50.0	991	88.82	56.1
Transportation	33.12	324	25.62	77.3	309	23.76	71.7	302	25.80	77.9	330	28.82	87.0
Travel	15.84	3,291	9.50	60.0	2,134	12.86	81.2	2,529	14.61	92.2	1,903	17.45	110.2
True crime	10.37	447	13.57	130.9	474	21.85	210.7	397	19.89	191.8	469	21.56	207.9
Young adult	11.96	5,476	12.30	102.8	5,167	23.82	199.2	5,315	20.72	173.2	5,681	19.21	160.6
Totals and Averages	$41.61	254,541	$22.18	53.3	217,362	$30.24	72.7	243,447	$24.11	58.0	231,299	$24.28	58.3

Compiled by Narda Tafuri, University of Scranton, from data supplied by Baker & Taylor.
* = figures revised from previous editions based on new data from Baker & Taylor.

(continued from page 356)

Serials Prices

Average Price of Serials (Table 8) and Average Price of Online Serials (Table 8A), compiled by Stephen Bosch, provide average prices and percent increases for serials based on titles in select abstracting and indexing products. The serials in this price survey are published in the United States as well as overseas and are indexed in the Clarivate Analytics' (formerly ISI) Arts and Humanities Citation Index, Science Citation Index, and Social Sciences Citation Index, as well as in EBSCO's Academic Search Premier/Ultimate and Masterfile Premier and Elsevier's Scopus. This is the fourth year where titles indexed in Scopus are included in the data. Adding Scopus expands this price survey from about 11,000 titles in 2015 to the current 17,373. The increase in the sample size makes the results more likely to reflect pricing trends accurately.

Tables 8 and 8A cover prices for periodicals and serials for five years, 2015 through 2019. The 2019 pricing is the actual renewal pricing for serial titles indexed in the selected products. These tables were derived from pricing data supplied by EBSCO Information Services and reflect broad pricing changes aggregated from serials indexed in the six major products mentioned above. U.S. Periodicals: Average Prices and Price Indexes (Table 1) is based on price changes seen in a static set of approximately 5,900 serial titles. Average Price of Serials (Table 8) is based on a much broader set of titles, approximately 17,373; however, the titles are not static, so although the table is useful in showing price changes for periodicals it does not rise to the level of a price index. The indexes selected for this price survey were deemed to be representative of serials frequently purchased by academic and public libraries. There are some foreign titles in the indexes, so the scope is broader, and this may give a better picture of the overall price pressures experienced in libraries. Table 8 contains both print and online serials pricing. Table 8A is a subset of the titles treated in Table 8 and contains only online serials pricing.

The most important trend seen in the data in Table 8 is that increases in prices have remained constant since the economic recovery began. Price increases have hovered around 6 percent annually since 2010. For titles with online availability (Table 8A), the rates of increase are very similar, also averaging around 6 percent over the past five years. There is a difference between the average prices for print serials and online serials, so, at least for this set of data, print formats do cost less than their online counterparts. Several large publishers have made online pricing only available through custom quotes, so there is not a standard retail price, and the pricing data are not available for this survey. Consequently, the number of titles covered in the online survey (Table 8A) is less than the number of titles in Table 8.

Another interesting trend is that science subject areas do not dominate the list of subjects with the largest price increases. The subject areas that displayed large increases were quite varied. Military and naval science, education, geology, psychology, technology, political science, recreation, and history saw higher increases than most. Some of these same areas showed the highest increases in the online table (Table 8A), as well. Average prices of journals in the science and technology areas have been far higher than in other areas, and this trend continues, with the average cost of chemistry and physics journals (Table 8) being $4,694.64 and $3,649.23, respectively. Although these STM titles are not inflating at high rates, the impact of a 5 percent increase in a $4,000 title is much higher than a 9 percent increase on a $300 title. Online journals (Table 8A) showed similar average prices for chemistry ($4,839.46) and physics ($3,996.83).

In this price study, as in similar price studies, the data become less accurate at describing price changes as the sample size becomes smaller. For that reason, drawing conclusions about price changes in subject areas with a limited number of titles will be less accurate than for large areas or the broader price survey. Price changes are far more volatile where smaller data sets are used. For example, in Table 8, military and naval science, with 89 titles, showed price changes of 5.8, 4, 4.3, and 9.1 percent between 2015 and 2019. Librarians are encouraged to look at an average price change over the period or the overall number for the price study (6.1 percent) to calculate inflation. Year-to-year price changes in small subject areas are too unstable to be reliable for this purpose.

Foreign Book Prices

British Academic Books (Table 9), compiled by George Aulisio, University of Scranton, indicates the average prices and price indexes from 2015 through 2018. The percent of change in titles and average price is calculated for 2017 to 2018, and the index price shows the percent of change between 2018 and the base year of 2010. This index is compiled using data from GOBI Library Solutions and utilizes prices from cloth editions except when not available. The data also draw from select titles from continental Europe and Africa. The index does not separate more expensive reference titles. Small numbers of titles that include higher-priced reference sets may not be reliable indicators of price changes. This table does not include e-book prices.

Data in the "Totals and Averages" row include the total of the LC Classes profiled in this table, not the total of all books profiled by GOBI Library Solutions. In 2018, total British academic books profiled by GOBI increased to 18,142 titles. This is significant compared to the previous three years, which saw 16,176 titles in 2017, 16,726 titles in 2016, and 16,728 titles in 2015.

In 2018 British academic books experienced a significant overall price increase of 7 percent, bringing the average price for all books profiled to £73.94. The 2018 price increase comes at a time when the United Kingdom's Consumer Price Index saw a relatively high 2.1 percent inflation as of December 2018 (http://www.ons.gov.uk).

Table 9 shows how average prices have increased or decreased in comparison with the 2010 base year. For 2018, the overall index price for all LC subjects profiled in this table is at 146.4 percent. All LC classes listed are currently above their 2010 base prices. The highest increases in comparison with the 2010 base prices are home economics (257.8 percent), sports and recreation (228.6 percent), and psychology (192.7 percent).

The 7 percent average price increase of 2018 is a return to normal after the unusual -0.5 percent average price decrease recorded in 2017. There was an unusually high 9.9 percent increase in 2016 followed by a normal price increase of

(text continues on page 378)

Table 8 / Average Price of Serials, Based on Titles in Select Serial Indexes, 2015–2019

Subject	LC Class	Titles	2015 Average Price	2016 Average Price	Percent Change 2015–2016	2017 Average Price	Percent Change 2016–2017	2018 Average Price	Percent Change 2017–2018	2019 Average Price	Percent Change 2018–2019
Agriculture	S	537	$844.12	$897.39	6.3%	$954.97	6.4%	$1,010.74	5.8%	$1,070.98	6.0%
Anthropology	GN	122	430.85	452.27	5.0	478.12	5.7	524.46	9.7	547.48	4.4
Arts and architecture	N	247	297.12	330.20	11.1	352.04	6.6	373.80	6.2	393.45	5.3
Astronomy	QB	66	1,652.51	1,713.65	3.7	1,807.39	5.5	1,891.13	4.6	1,981.89	4.8
Biology	QH	1,079	2,104.64	2,228.52	5.9	2,356.37	5.7	2,490.96	5.7	2,635.18	5.8
Botany	QK	155	1,323.80	1,382.31	4.4	1,462.76	5.8	1,533.70	4.8	1,624.33	5.9
Business and economics	HA-HJ	1,415	1,051.26	1,120.88	6.6	1,162.39	3.7	1,213.66	4.4	1,280.81	5.5
Chemistry	QD	360	3,882.75	4,064.52	4.7	4,266.06	5.0	4,444.01	4.2	4,694.64	5.6
Education	L	445	617.08	663.38	7.5	705.64	6.4	754.46	6.9	812.06	7.6
Engineering	T	1,649	1,590.41	1,700.02	6.9	1,806.99	6.3	1,917.68	6.1	2,043.65	6.6
Food Science	TX	97	1,110.60	1,174.04	5.7	1,230.58	4.8	1,305.67	6.1	1,374.65	5.3
General works	A	207	205.35	211.05	2.8	220.70	4.6	245.21	11.1	256.56	4.6
Geography	G-GF	280	884.95	943.10	6.6	1,015.00	7.6	1,079.56	6.4	1,151.92	6.7
Geology	QE	220	1,486.60	1,591.49	7.1	1,696.07	6.6	1,802.59	6.3	1,936.79	7.4
Health sciences	R	3,646	1,113.24	1,190.03	6.9	1,263.76	6.2	1,351.38	6.9	1,435.64	6.2
History	C,D,E,F	863	297.28	314.33	5.7	336.50	7.1	358.63	6.6	382.77	6.7
Language and literature	P	973	309.61	325.30	5.1	343.35	5.5	367.42	7.0	388.23	5.7

Law	K	420	435.23	463.97	6.6	488.03	5.2	515.86	5.7	541.28	4.9
Library science	Z	194	727.73	760.10	4.4	788.26	3.7	816.99	3.6	857.89	5.0
Math and computer science	QA	817	1,293.03	1,352.44	4.6	1,420.50	5.0	1,504.89	5.9	1,588.84	5.6
Military and naval science	U,V	89	452.07	478.10	5.8	497.16	4.0	518.64	4.3	565.60	9.1
Music	M	140	222.72	233.89	5.0	250.14	6.9	270.61	8.2	286.27	5.8
Philosophy and religion	B-BD, BH-BX	557	308.69	325.08	5.3	342.48	5.4	361.84	5.7	378.55	4.6
Physics	QC	407	3,011.52	3,141.25	4.3	3,285.10	4.6	3,446.82	4.9	3,649.23	5.9
Political science	J	267	539.15	579.27	7.4	613.57	5.9	657.01	7.1	703.18	7.0
Psychology	BF	282	736.33	786.80	6.9	833.78	6.0	889.76	6.7	954.12	7.2
Recreation	GV	144	357.96	382.71	6.9	408.50	6.7	437.03	7.0	467.02	6.9
Science (general)	Q	211	1,207.42	1,264.27	4.7	1,348.46	6.7	1,406.07	4.3	1,484.48	5.6
Social sciences	H	130	647.28	704.80	8.9	755.97	7.3	802.33	6.1	848.19	5.7
Sociology	HM-HX	709	698.53	743.41	6.4	790.52	6.3	840.38	6.3	896.87	6.7
Technology	TA-TT	348	1,123.13	1,187.92	5.8	1,248.36	5.1	1,304.28	4.5	1,397.56	7.2
Zoology	QL	297	1,170.53	1,272.85	8.7	1,331.33	4.6	1,404.17	5.5	1,464.79	4.3
Totals and Averages		17,373	$1,100.21	$1,167.76	6.1%	$1,233.63	5.6%	$1,305.76	5.8%	$1,384.88	6.1%

Compiled by Stephen Bosch, University of Arizona. Data on serial pricing supplied by EBSCO and is based on titles indexed in EBSCO Academic Search Ultimate, EBSCO Masterfile Complete, Clarivate Analytics (formerly ISI) Arts and Humanities Citation Index, Clarivate Analytics Science Citation Index, Clarivate Analytics Social Sciences Citation Index, and Elsevier's Scopus.

Table 8A / Changes in the Average Price of Online Serials 2015–2019, Based on Titles in Select Serial Indexes

			2015	2016	Percent Change	2017	Percent Change	2018	Percent Change	2019	Percent Change
Subject	LC Class	Titles	Average Price	Average Price	2015–2016	Average Price	2016–2017	Average Price	2017–2018	Average Price	2018–2019
Agriculture	S	264	$990.72	$1,046.23	5.6%	$1,102.71	5.4%	$1,165.63	5.7%	$1,241.24	6.5%
Anthropology	GN	85	484.84	515.88	6.4	543.93	5.4	582.21	7.0	617.92	6.1
Arts and Architecture	N	117	434.71	480.27	10.5	519.31	8.1	550.55	6.0	585.87	6.4
Astronomy	QB	42	1,824.74	1,892.03	3.7	2,011.14	6.3	2,117.99	5.3	2,207.23	4.2
Biology	QH	608	2,004.51	2,121.54	5.8	2,238.78	5.5	2,369.71	5.8	2,510.76	6.0
Botany	QK	96	1,453.69	1,505.53	3.6	1,592.94	5.8	1,665.75	4.6	1,746.08	4.8
Business and Economics	HA-HJ	849	1,360.47	1,486.39	9.3	1,504.56	1.2	1,561.19	3.8	1,642.85	5.2
Chemistry	QD	214	3,864.14	4,080.32	5.6	4,344.84	6.5	4,552.13	4.8	4,839.46	6.3
Education	L	335	709.15	766.99	8.2	815.91	6.4	869.53	6.6	934.14	7.4
Engineering	T	914	1,688.68	1,808.39	7.1	1,908.76	5.6	2,032.98	6.5	2,165.48	6.5
Food Science	TX	50	1,603.14	1,694.78	5.7	1,742.67	2.8	1,839.57	5.6	1,936.88	5.3
General Works	A	68	398.35	413.53	3.8	440.11	6.4	502.54	14.2	523.42	4.2
Geography	G-GF	175	809.67	865.75	6.9	929.43	7.4	994.37	7.0	1,066.01	7.2
Geology	QE	123	1,335.95	1,417.50	6.1	1,511.50	6.6	1,593.61	5.4	1,699.40	6.6
Health Sciences	R	1,830	1,216.98	1,303.11	7.1	1,377.72	5.7	1,470.15	6.7	1,562.99	6.3
History	C,D,E,F	524	357.26	380.53	6.5	410.04	7.8	434.76	6.0	468.38	7.7
Language and Literature	P	571	371.69	394.77	6.2	420.29	6.5	452.91	7.8	482.29	6.5

Law	K	186	581.57	626.17	7.7	660.58	5.5	700.05	6.0	735.63	5.1
Library Science	Z	130	877.58	919.91	4.8	954.29	3.7	982.22	2.9	1,029.99	4.9
Math & Computer Science	QA	583	1,219.68	1,292.13	5.9	1,365.36	5.7	1,460.03	6.9	1,546.15	5.9
Military and Naval Science	U,V	58	504.26	542.65	7.6	577.66	6.5	601.45	4.1	663.67	10.3
Music	M	76	282.95	303.58	7.3	325.60	7.3	355.38	9.1	375.40	5.6
Philosophy & Religion	B-BD, BH-BX	324	384.61	407.70	6.0	432.04	6.0	457.80	6.0	480.86	5.0
Physics	QC	265	3,258.38	3,409.39	4.6	3,578.50	5.0	3,771.17	5.4	3,996.83	6.0
Political Science	J	193	597.34	645.77	8.1	684.41	6.0	735.03	7.4	789.99	7.5
Psychology	BF	181	730.82	790.72	8.2	837.33	5.9	893.18	6.7	962.74	7.8
Recreation	GV	65	675.73	725.97	7.4	786.40	8.3	843.10	7.2	906.12	7.5
Science (general)	Q	126	1,434.72	1,495.41	4.2	1,586.95	6.1	1,649.48	3.9	1,735.84	5.2
Social Sciences	H	79	734.25	801.32	9.1	861.94	7.6	918.13	6.5	968.74	5.5
Sociology	HM-HX	528	773.64	824.87	6.6	876.89	6.3	931.00	6.2	997.60	7.2
Technology	TA-TT	170	1,593.51	1,685.57	5.8	1,748.28	3.7	1,809.38	3.5	1,950.80	7.8
Zoology	QL	170	1,305.92	1,454.18	11.4	1,517.36	4.3	1,598.48	5.3	1,675.75	4.8
Totals and Averages		9,999	$1,199.63	$1,280.00	6.7%	$1,347.53	5.3%	$1,426.30	5.8%	$1,514.71	6.2%

Compiled by Stephen Bosch, University of Arizona. Data on serial pricing supplied by EBSCO and is based on titles indexed in EBSCO Academic Search Ultimate, EBSCO Masterfile Complete, Clarivate Analytics (formerly ISI) Arts and Humanities Citation Index, Clarivate Analytics Science Citation Index, Clarivate Analytics Social Sciences Citation Index, and Elsevier's Scopus.

Table 9 / British Academic Books: Average Prices and Price Indexes, 2015–2018

Index Base: 2010 = 100

		2010		2015		2016		2017		2018			
Subject	LC Class	Titles	Average Price (£)	Titles	Average Price (£)	Titles	Average Price (£)	Titles	Average Price (£)	Titles	Average Price (£)	Percent Change 2017–2018	Index
Agriculture	S	154	£63.97	131	£73.63	142	£77.66	125	£79.66	142	£85.45	7.3%	133.6
Anthropology	GN	154	50.85	92	59.65	148	53.08	121	60.79	150	65.47	7.7	128.7
Botany	QK	45	66.08	21	95.19	19	84.68	27	80.32	30	77.10	-4.0	116.7
Business and economics	H-HJ	1,913	60.54	1,866	75.13	1,897	73.35	1,767	77.80	2,185	84.35	8.4	139.3
Chemistry	QD	96	105.68	72	127.89	57	113.66	47	104.58	58	127.93	22.3	121.1
Education	L	558	52.21	583	68.39	577	179.48	575	78.43	723	77.96	-0.6	149.3
Engineering and technology	T-TS	742	61.84	732	85.51	681	78.93	692	82.39	654	86.12	4.5	139.3
Fine and applied arts	M, N	1,037	35.95	991	50.40	908	51.19	917	53.71	974	59.66	11.1	166.0
General works	A	30	60.03	21	83.47	27	106.91	33	92.37	33	108.43	17.4	180.6
Geography	G-GF, GR-GT	276	65.69	457	72.62	447	75.21	315	87.06	317	86.29	-0.9	131.4
Geology	QE	33	52.28	34	60.87	28	69.53	30	57.36	30	74.38	29.7	142.3
History	C,D,E,F	1,822	42.55	1,835	51.22	1,914	55.21	1,790	54.96	2,051	60.70	10.5	142.7
Home economics	TX	46	30.48	29	85.98	32	67.49	48	83.35	36	78.58	-5.7	257.8
Industrial arts	TT	41	28.47	33	46.11	27	51.62	25	61.26	36	53.10	-13.3	186.5
Language and literature	P	3,987	31.58	3,008	42.33	3,070	46.86	2,902	50.52	3,112	55.95	10.7	177.2

Law	K	1,153	83.10	1,184	85.16	1,117	101.35	1,207	100.34	1,276	101.89	1.6	122.6
Library and information science	Z	100	53.58	114	71.04	106	69.09	98	62.98	93	68.03	8.0	127.0
Mathematics and computer science	QA	207	48.29	172	57.46	188	61.90	186	71.56	195	71.84	0.4	148.8
Medicine	R	1,182	55.12	946	67.52	905	69.56	859	70.12	931	73.90	5.4	134.1
Military and naval sciences	U, V	184	40.95	165	53.43	171	59.75	127	59.93	181	65.54	9.4	160.0
Philosophy and religion	B-BD, BH-BX	1,336	48.17	1,184	56.72	1,098	61.29	1,075	68.74	1,364	73.64	7.1	152.9
Physics and astronomy	QB, QC	214	64.83	185	65.07	179	66.85	167	69.30	206	73.19	5.6	112.9
Political Science	J	737	71.88	819	73.18	827	73.83	802	77.93	787	87.59	12.4	121.9
Psychology	BF	265	39.69	278	69.09	304	73.32	337	72.28	378	76.47	5.8	192.7
Science (general)	Q	60	40.70	53	62.95	62	80.73	71	75.80	82	67.59	-10.8	166.0
Sociology	HM-HX	1,169	58.24	1,281	70.21	1,361	71.40	1,358	73.25	1,649	78.65	7.4	135.0
Sports & Recreation	GV	192	36.76	179	68.49	180	71.38	204	81.24	207	84.02	3.4	228.6
Zoology	QH, QL-QR	382	65.79	263	79.76	254	67.99	271	73.11	262	80.40	10.0	122.2
Totals and Averages		18,115	£50.50	16,728	£63.22	16,726	£69.46	16,176	£69.11	18,142	£73.94	7.0%	146.4

Compiled by George Aulisio, University of Scranton, based on information provided by GOBI Library Solutions.

Table 9 / British Academic Books: Average Prices and Price Indexes, 2014–2017

Index Base: 2010 = 100

		2010		2014		2015		2016		2017			
Subject	**LC Class**	**Titles**	**Average Price (£)**	**Titles**	**Average Price (£)**	**Titles**	**Average Price (£)**	**Titles**	**Average Price (£)**	**Titles**	**Average Price (£)**	**Percent Change 2016–2017**	**Index**
Agriculture	S	154	£63.97	134	£73.28	131	£73.63	142	£77.66	125	£79.66	2.6%	124.5
Anthropology	GN	154	50.85	109	57.63	92	59.65	148	53.08	121	60.79	14.5	119.5
Botany	QK	45	66.08	35	74.78	21	95.19	19	84.68	27	80.32	-5.1	121.6
Business and economics	H-HJ	1,913	60.54	1,911	71.19	1,866	75.13	1,897	73.35	1,767	77.80	6.1	128.5
Chemistry	QD	96	105.68	91	125.67	72	127.89	57	113.66	47	104.58	-8.0	99.0
Education	L	558	52.21	517	64.50	583	68.39	577	179.48	575	78.43	-56.3	150.2
Engineering and technology	T-TS	742	61.84	788	76.69	732	85.51	681	78.93	692	82.39	4.4	133.2
Fine and applied arts	M, N	1,037	35.95	1,009	44.54	991	50.40	908	51.19	917	53.71	4.9	149.4
General works	A	30	60.03	32	72.25	21	83.47	27	106.91	33	92.37	-13.6	153.9
Geography	G-GF, GR-GT	276	65.69	245	67.55	457	72.62	447	75.21	315	87.06	15.8	132.5
Geology	QE	33	52.28	33	59.80	34	60.87	28	69.53	30	57.36	-17.5	109.7
History	C,D,E,F	1,822	42.55	1,725	48.11	1,835	51.22	1,914	55.21	1,790	54.96	-0.5	129.2

Home economics	TX	46	30.48	38	63.79	29	85.98	32	67.49	48	83.35	23.5	273.5
Industrial arts	TT	41	28.47	27	45.43	33	46.11	27	51.62	25	61.26	18.7	215.1
Law	K	1,153	83.10	1,253	88.30	1,184	85.16	1,117	101.35	1,207	100.34	-1.0	120.7
Library and information science	Z	100	53.58	106	69.71	114	71.04	106	69.09	98	62.98	-8.8	117.6
Literature and language	P	3,987	31.58	3,553	38.95	3,008	42.33	3,070	46.86	2,902	50.52	7.8	160.0
Mathematics and computer science	QA	207	48.29	180	54.91	172	57.46	188	61.90	186	71.56	15.6	148.2
Medicine	R	1,182	55.12	1,113	63.10	946	67.52	905	69.56	859	70.12	0.8	127.2
Military and naval sciences	U, V	184	40.95	201	50.67	165	53.43	171	59.75	127	59.93	0.3	146.3
Philosophy and religion	B-BD, BH-BX	1,336	48.17	1,187	52.78	1,184	56.72	1,098	61.29	1,075	68.74	12.1	142.7
Physics and astronomy	QB, QC	214	64.83	161	72.29	185	65.07	179	66.85	167	69.30	3.7	106.9
Political Science	J	737	71.88	794	65.82	819	73.18	827	73.83	802	77.93	5.6	108.4
Psychology	BF	265	39.69	295	63.42	278	69.09	304	73.32	337	72.28	-1.4	182.1
Science (general)	Q	60	40.70	54	57.89	53	62.95	62	80.73	71	75.80	-6.1	186.2
Sociology	HM-HX	1,169	58.24	1,221	64.89	1,281	70.21	1,361	71.40	1,358	73.25	2.6	125.8
Sports & Recreation	GV	192	36.76	170	61.49	179	68.49	180	71.38	204	81.24	13.8	221.0
Zoology	QH, QL-QR	382	65.79	285	79.00	263	79.76	254	67.99	271	73.11	7.5	111.1
Totals and Averages		18,115	£50.50	17,267	£59.05	16,728	£63.22	16,726	£69.46	16,176	£69.11	-0.5%	136.8

Compiled by George Aulisio, University of Scranton, based on information provided by GOBI Library Solutions.

(continued from page 369)
7.1 percent in 2015. There are currently no known reliable indicators for a 2019 industry forecast.

Using the Price Indexes

Librarians are encouraged to monitor publishing industry trends and changes in economic conditions when preparing budget forecasts and projections. The ALA ALCTS Library Materials Price Index (LMPI) Editorial Board endeavors to make information on publishing trends readily available by sponsoring the annual compilation and publication of price data contained in our published tables. The indexes cover newly published library materials and document prices and rates of percent changes at the national and international level. They are useful benchmarks to compare against local costs, but because they reflect retail prices in the aggregate, they are not a substitute for cost data that reflect the collecting patterns of individual libraries, and they are not a substitute for specific cost studies.

Differences between local prices and those found in national indexes arise partially because these indexes exclude discounts, service charges, shipping and handling fees, and other discounts or costs that a library might see. Discrepancies may also relate to a library's subject coverage, its mix of titles purchased—including both current and backfiles—and the proportion of the library's budget expended on domestic or foreign materials. These variables can affect the average price paid by an individual library, although the individual library's rate of increase may not differ greatly from the national indexes.

Closing Note

The LMPI Editorial Board is interested in pursuing studies that would correlate a particular library's costs with the national prices. The group welcomes interested parties to its meeting at ALA Annual. The Library Materials Price Index Editorial Board consists of compilers George Aulisio, Ajaye Bloomstone, Stephen Bosch, and Narda Tafuri. George Aulisio currently serves as editor, and Rachel Fleming, University of Tennessee at Chattanooga, serves as assistant editor.

The LMPI Editorial Board wishes to acknowledge the work of Stephen Bosch, who is retiring in 2019. Stephen has been involved with the LMPI since 2010, and he has assured the board that the impeccable and important tables published in this article will continue after his retirement. The board also congratulates Stephen on receiving the 2019 Ross Atkinson Lifetime Achievement Award. The LMPI Editorial Board agrees that the award is well-deserved!

Book Title Output and Average Prices, 2016–2018

Constance Harbison
Baker & Taylor

Annual book title output in the United States has been generally on the upswing since the Great Recession, although the recovery has been uneven, with data for the two most recent years showing a slight decline. After reaching a high of 216,040 in 2016 (up from 2009's 178,841), revised output figures for 2017 mark a dip to 201,886, followed by further erosion to 196,679 in 2018. However, the 2018 figures may be revised upward as late-arriving materials are added to the database.

The figures for this edition of *Library and Book Trade Almanac* were provided by book wholesaler Baker & Taylor and are based on the Book Industry Study Group's BISAC Subject Headings. Figures for 2016 and 2017 have been revised, reflecting late updates to the Baker & Taylor database. Figures for 2018 are considered preliminary at the time of this report.

For a complete list of current BISAC Subject Headings, visit https://bisg.org/page/bisacedition.

Output by Format and by Category

Revised results for 2017 were mixed. Output of hardcover titles continues to grow steadily; hardcovers priced at less than $81 have moved in a tight range over this period with an increase noted in 2018. Mass market paperbacks have fallen steadily over a decade but appear to be leveling out in 2018. Although the picture for trade paperbacks is less clear, recent figures suggest that output may have hit bottom in 2017. Audiobook output reached a high water mark in 2016, with declining numbers in 2017 and again in 2018; given that the reporting covers physically packaged audiobooks, but not digital downloads, this trend is not surprising.

Output of fiction, a key category, has been uncertain in recent years. Output of hardcover fiction priced at less than $81 had been growing, but 2018 saw lower numbers. Among paperback fiction formats, mass market continues to decline while trade paper is relatively stable. Audiobook fiction output was consistent with the format as a whole, peaking in 2016 followed by significant drops in 2017 and 2018. E-book fiction output appears robust; revised 2017 numbers moved sharply upward from the preliminary figures reported last year, and the category is likely to see a similar jump in 2018.

The important juveniles category is broken down into children's (PreK–6) and young adult (YA; grades 7–12) titles. Overall children's books output has been rising steadily as has production of hardcover books priced at less than $81, but mass market paperbacks remain low while trade paperbacks are relatively stable. Children's e-books have been in a gradual, healthy climb while audiobooks have put up declining numbers in every year but one since 2015.

Overall, YA output has proven unpredictable from year to year, but a continuing decline is evident in the mass market paperback format. YA trade paperbacks and audiobooks have held steady, with YA e-books showing improvement in each of the last three years culminating in 2018.

Table 1 / American Book Production, 2016–2018

BISAC Category	2016	2017	2018
Antiques and Collectibles	295	246	193
Architecture	1,736	1,746	1,536
Art	4,073	3,774	3,661
Bibles	819	971	962
Biography and Autobiography	4,468	4,183	4,169
Body, Mind and Spirit	902	880	948
Business and Economics	12,716	12,334	10,946
Children	27,717	26,664	27,949
Comics and Graphic Novels	2,790	2,729	2,956
Computers	6,069	4,080	4,180
Cooking	2,242	2,127	2,050
Crafts and Hobbies	1,095	970	855
Design	692	673	670
Drama	640	738	581
Education	7,914	8,563	6,840
Family and Relationships	817	707	785
Fiction	18,700	18,130	17,378
Foreign Language Study	1,129	1,282	1,065
Games	2,004	1,398	867
Gardening	227	251	236
Health and Fitness	1,441	1,473	1,390
History	13,000	12,607	11,910
House and Home	179	195	185
Humor	594	595	593
Language Arts and Disciplines	4,157	3,295	2,847
Law	6,466	5,788	5,839
Literary Collections	641	689	669
Literary Criticism	5,033	4,514	4,268
Mathematics	2,866	2,681	2,542
Medical	9,681	7,378	7,272
Music	3,339	2,659	2,334
Nature	1,081	1,099	958
Performing Arts	1,712	1,814	1,667
Pets	270	212	176
Philosophy	3,479	3,199	3,310
Photography	1,278	1,343	1,085
Poetry	2,537	2,310	2,371
Political Science	7,470	7,729	7,124

Psychology	3,776	3,918	3,434
Reference	948	867	786
Religion	9,710	9,602	9,364
Science	9,776	7,362	7,948
Self-Help	1,309	1,284	1,503
Social Science	9,905	10,368	9,835
Sports and Recreation	1,746	1,641	1,476
Study Aids	731	604	519
Technology and Engineering	7,883	6,316	6,372
Transportation	828	794	778
Travel	1,902	1,778	2,047
True Crime	244	245	296
Young Adult	5,013	5,081	4,954
Total	216,040	201,886	194,679

Table 2 / Hardcover Average Per-Volume Prices, 2016–2018

	2016			2017			2018		
BISAC Category	Vols.	$ Total	Prices	Vols.	$ Total	Prices	Vols.	$ Total	Prices
Antiques and Collectibles	147	$12,085.04	$82.21	133	$9,527.24	$71.63	105	$7,489.11	$71.32
Architecture	951	103,258.02	108.58	1,002	111,362.29	111.14	833	78,693.66	94.47
Art	2,156	168,190.52	78.01	2,112	175,118.41	82.92	2,007	150,261.31	74.87
Bibles	201	8,339.78	41.49	255	10,533.22	41.31	248	10,690.43	43.11
Biography and Autobiography	1,886	94,516.06	50.11	1,823	89,847.59	49.29	1,672	75,756.34	45.31
Body, Mind and Spirit	172	5,006.76	29.11	188	5,058.87	26.91	203	5,141.00	25.33
Business and Economics	4,991	813,396.20	162.97	5,899	983,032.83	166.64	4,573	715,063.43	156.37
Children	15,195	386,553.29	25.44	14,947	362,683.38	24.26	16,562	435,345.39	26.29
Comics and Graphic Novels	637	25,399.97	39.87	670	28,162.92	42.03	656	28,671.34	43.71
Computers	1,105	181,106.45	163.90	1,280	218,685.38	170.85	1,133	189,917.61	167.62
Cooking	1,205	35,779.80	29.69	1,212	36,028.46	29.73	1,144	34,031.84	29.75
Crafts and Hobbies	155	4,901.47	31.62	167	5,320.05	31.86	185	5,445.39	29.43
Design	438	31,139.01	71.09	433	28,652.95	66.17	421	26,720.81	63.47
Drama	111	10,711.76	96.50	80	8,433.77	105.42	67	5,644.24	84.24
Education	2,957	406,853.38	137.59	3,680	543,598.74	147.72	2,567	346,896.33	135.14
Family and Relationships	200	10,407.58	52.04	186	8,531.83	45.87	217	9,727.79	44.83
Fiction	4,912	146,466.07	29.82	5,275	155,303.27	29.44	4,828	142,183.74	29.45
Foreign Language Study	237	30,066.13	126.86	246	30,902.98	125.62	250	29,414.31	117.66
Games	169	5,978.16	35.37	137	6,462.80	47.17	179	7,847.67	43.84
Gardening	103	3,471.73	33.71	130	5,775.70	44.43	121	4,343.89	35.90
Health and Fitness	366	28,510.13	77.90	417	34,700.62	83.21	332	19,626.52	59.12
History	6,477	674,977.76	104.21	6,223	613,197.45	98.54	5,812	534,518.74	91.97
House and Home	90	3,315.48	36.84	97	4,023.96	41.48	98	3,823.39	39.01
Humor	291	6,326.20	21.74	296	6,573.73	22.21	343	7,863.24	22.92
Language Arts and Disciplines	1,614	238,243.92	147.61	1,529	228,717.60	149.59	1,351	189,063.29	139.94

Law	2,449	462,565.91	188.88	2,563	462,390.92	180.41	2,394	429,661.16	179.47
Literary Collections	241	22,831.97	94.74	296	29,686.79	100.29	250	24,279.35	97.12
Literary Criticism	2,945	377,852.27	128.30	2,590	329,543.19	127.24	2,404	296,568.96	123.36
Mathematics	1,092	157,369.94	144.11	1,395	240,000.54	172.04	1,035	152,299.12	147.15
Medical	3,176	582,358.53	183.36	3,813	743,668.03	195.03	2,979	534,529.14	179.43
Music	667	67,316.65	100.92	691	67,611.19	97.85	596	52,096.97	87.41
Nature	474	46,921.36	98.99	533	53,507.79	100.39	411	33,371.84	81.20
Performing Arts	869	90,675.64	104.34	947	111,099.22	117.32	803	78,301.97	97.51
Pets	111	2,529.83	22.79	103	2,842.17	27.59	66	1,328.28	20.13
Philosophy	1,680	207,617.76	123.58	1,680	198,103.32	117.92	1,583	169,954.17	107.36
Photography	873	59,441.13	68.09	930	68,514.32	73.67	793	54,047.70	68.16
Poetry	472	25,556.67	54.15	309	12,328.45	39.90	287	10,463.41	36.46
Political Science	3,491	412,918.81	118.28	3,928	464,789.18	118.33	3,396	368,871.60	108.62
Psychology	1,383	214,614.24	155.18	1,849	285,746.03	154.54	1,439	202,820.46	140.95
Reference	366	96,200.36	262.84	357	132,665.39	371.61	338	129,451.40	382.99
Religion	2,907	235,654.53	81.06	2,986	245,060.78	82.07	2,952	233,806.16	79.20
Science	4,057	847,390.43	208.87	4,609	925,322.26	200.76	3,915	687,434.35	175.59
Self-Help	311	7,828.37	25.17	353	10,140.96	28.73	407	10,404.84	25.56
Social Science	4,188	563,236.98	134.49	5,771	766,628.15	132.84	4,513	549,256.85	121.71
Sports and Recreation	636	35,943.73	56.52	642	40,375.12	62.89	589	31,228.18	53.02
Study Aids	20	1,773.13	88.66	20	2,127.65	106.38	16	1,602.44	100.15
Technology and Engineering	3,735	682,917.06	182.84	4,048	805,764.36	199.05	3,108	621,697.38	200.03
Transportation	297	20,380.26	68.62	274	19,675.52	71.81	277	16,359.75	59.06
Travel	221	8,768.09	39.67	289	11,138.36	38.54	477	19,510.52	40.90
True Crime	89	3,119.56	35.05	67	1,972.99	29.45	84	2,817.30	33.54
Young Adult	2,290	87,190.92	38.07	2,398	95,996.37	40.03	2,108	75,149.96	35.65
Total	85,806	$8,755,974.80	$102.04	91,858	$9,836,935.09	$107.09	83,127	$7,851,494.07	$94.45

Table 3 / Hardcover Average Per-Volume Prices, Less than $81, 2016–2018

	2016			2017			2018		
BISAC Category	**Vols.**	**$ Total**	**Prices**	**Vols.**	**$ Total**	**Prices**	**Vols.**	**$ Total**	**Prices**
Antiques and Collectibles	112	$5,499.11	$49.10	102	$4,630.30	$45.40	74	$2,993.22	$40.45
Architecture	480	23,495.74	48.95	488	24,478.97	50.16	500	25,841.47	51.68
Art	1,566	73,165.38	46.72	1,519	70,089.69	46.14	1,459	68,698.91	47.09
Bibles	195	7,139.82	36.61	242	8,898.36	36.77	234	8,579.52	36.66
Biography and Autobiography	1,686	52,118.37	30.91	1,641	50,251.83	30.62	1,532	46,441.57	30.31
Body, Mind and Spirit	165	3,934.81	23.85	181	3,922.87	21.67	199	4,675.07	23.49
Business and Economics	1,429	62,432.61	43.69	1,462	62,211.26	42.55	1,480	62,597.03	42.30
Children	14,775	303,702.52	20.56	14,555	294,020.01	20.20	15,961	330,372.41	20.70
Comics and Graphic Novels	588	18,991.08	32.30	598	19,338.10	32.34	576	18,997.64	32.98
Computers	221	13,451.71	60.87	191	11,446.56	59.93	228	13,791.96	60.49
Cooking	1,182	32,725.11	27.69	1,194	33,120.32	27.74	1,125	31,300.90	27.82
Crafts and Hobbies	151	4,199.47	27.81	162	4,637.08	28.62	182	5,155.39	28.33
Design	343	16,069.09	46.85	334	15,529.15	46.49	317	14,649.36	46.21
Drama	43	1,839.67	42.78	30	1,573.55	52.45	30	1,359.46	45.32
Education	683	34,734.20	50.86	622	30,940.03	49.74	546	28,715.27	52.59
Family and Relationships	159	3,859.60	24.27	156	3,877.07	24.85	175	3,897.97	22.27
Fiction	4,869	139,186.73	28.59	5,243	151,584.17	28.91	4,804	138,697.97	28.87
Foreign Language Study	91	5,331.60	58.59	96	5,257.40	54.76	101	5,669.26	56.13
Games	158	4,648.29	29.42	117	3,834.82	32.78	160	5,255.05	32.84
Gardening	100	3,134.74	31.35	117	3,803.50	32.51	119	4,078.89	34.28
Health and Fitness	252	7,571.99	30.05	281	8,686.36	30.91	252	7,338.40	29.12
History	3,015	133,177.50	44.17	2,935	127,516.92	43.45	2,940	127,561.40	43.39
House and Home	89	3,165.48	35.57	94	3,614.01	38.45	94	3,473.39	36.95
Humor	289	6,106.26	21.13	289	5,710.79	19.76	340	6,878.24	20.23
Language Arts and Disciplines	256	14,569.68	56.91	217	11,874.52	54.72	237	13,146.64	55.47

Law	270	14,724.16	54.53	280	16,089.97	57.46	345	19,271.66	55.86
Literary Collections	144	5,459.69	37.91	165	6,535.42	39.61	153	6,078.39	39.73
Literary Criticism	799	46,530.44	58.24	696	38,706.95	55.61	736	41,223.68	56.01
Mathematics	181	11,298.67	62.42	135	7,735.10	57.30	175	10,076.62	57.58
Medical	279	15,472.82	55.46	313	17,099.21	54.63	285	16,194.52	56.82
Music	297	12,667.79	42.65	309	13,388.58	43.33	301	12,751.49	42.36
Nature	242	8,216.85	33.95	261	9,150.75	35.06	265	9,246.71	34.89
Performing Arts	280	13,112.04	46.83	247	11,225.11	45.45	256	11,161.07	43.60
Pets	110	2,392.33	21.75	97	2,265.43	23.35	66	1,328.28	20.13
Philosophy	422	22,722.37	53.84	459	23,037.47	50.19	532	28,820.96	54.17
Photography	773	36,133.87	46.74	768	34,960.51	45.52	691	30,890.91	44.70
Poetry	373	13,169.82	35.31	276	8,057.90	29.20	266	8,073.66	30.35
Political Science	984	46,693.46	47.45	973	46,662.60	47.96	1,107	52,555.08	47.48
Psychology	253	12,446.23	49.19	287	13,619.85	47.46	323	15,378.73	47.61
Reference	144	4,777.34	33.18	120	3,815.10	31.79	119	3,995.25	33.57
Religion	1,731	61,576.02	35.57	1,750	65,193.69	37.25	1,813	68,653.09	37.87
Science	600	28,999.38	48.33	596	27,459.63	46.07	629	30,124.67	47.89
Self-Help	307	7,347.37	23.93	341	7,961.08	23.35	401	9,554.89	23.83
Social Science	992	52,653.96	53.08	1,044	53,427.50	51.18	1,052	53,464.00	50.82
Sports and Recreation	527	16,526.42	31.36	472	14,148.37	29.98	473	15,138.06	32.00
Study Aids	12	625.48	52.12	11	611.65	55.60	10	618.75	61.88
Technology and Engineering	176	9,567.46	54.36	204	11,460.84	56.18	228	12,540.68	55.00
Transportation	242	10,539.88	43.55	218	10,093.25	46.30	239	10,617.50	44.42
Travel	202	5,622.24	27.83	265	7,602.63	28.69	450	14,671.68	32.60
True Crime	86	2,539.61	29.53	66	1,880.04	28.49	81	2,385.30	29.45
Young Adult	2,156	57,278.04	26.57	2,248	61,800.81	27.49	2,016	53,695.70	26.63
Total	45,479	$1,493,344.30	$32.84	45,467	$1,474,837.08	$32.44	46,677	$1,518,677.72	$32.54

Table 4 / Mass Market Paperbacks Average Per-Volume Prices, 2016–2018

	2016			2017			2018		
BISAC Category	**Vols.**	**$ Total**	**Prices**	**Vols.**	**$ Total**	**Prices**	**Vols.**	**$ Total**	**Prices**
Antiques and Collectibles	n.a.	n.a.	n.a.	n.a.	n.a.	n.a.	n.a.	n.a.	n.a.
Architecture	n.a.	n.a.	n.a.	n.a.	n.a.	n.a.	n.a.	n.a.	n.a.
Art	n.a.	n.a.	n.a.	n.a.	n.a.	n.a.	n.a.	n.a.	n.a.
Bibles	n.a.	n.a.	n.a.	n.a.	n.a.	n.a.	n.a.	n.a.	n.a.
Biography and Autobiography	7	$74.94	$10.71	5	$46.42	$9.28	7	$68.93	$9.85
Body, Mind and Spirit	2	17.98	8.99	n.a.	n.a.	n.a.	n.a.	n.a.	n.a.
Business and Economics	n.a.	n.a.	n.a.	1	7.99	7.99	3	26.97	8.99
Children	224	1,562.63	6.98	179	1,278.14	7.14	230	1,703.48	7.41
Comics and Graphic Novels	n.a.	n.a.	n.a.	n.a.	n.a.	n.a.	n.a.	n.a.	n.a.
Computers	n.a.	n.a.	n.a.	n.a.	n.a.	n.a.	n.a.	n.a.	n.a.
Cooking	n.a.	n.a.	n.a.	n.a.	n.a.	n.a.	n.a.	n.a.	n.a.
Crafts and Hobbies	n.a.	n.a.	n.a.	n.a.	n.a.	n.a.	n.a.	n.a.	n.a.
Design	n.a.	n.a.	n.a.	n.a.	n.a.	n.a.	n.a.	n.a.	n.a.
Drama	n.a.	n.a.	n.a.	n.a.	n.a.	n.a.	n.a.	n.a.	n.a.
Education	n.a.	n.a.	n.a.	n.a.	n.a.	n.a.	n.a.	n.a.	n.a.
Family and Relationships	n.a.	n.a.	n.a.	n.a.	n.a.	n.a.	n.a.	n.a.	n.a.
Fiction	2,998	21,679.92	7.23	2,754	20,112.33	7.30	2,682	19,476.01	7.26
Foreign Language Study	n.a.	n.a.	n.a.	n.a.	n.a.	n.a.	n.a.	n.a.	n.a.
Games	2	17.98	8.99	n.a.	n.a.	n.a.	1	8.50	8.50
Gardening	n.a.	n.a.	n.a.	n.a.	n.a.	n.a.	n.a.	n.a.	n.a.
Health and Fitness	n.a.	n.a.	n.a.	1	9.99	9.99	4	33.96	8.49
History	4	37.96	9.49	5	49.95	9.99	3	29.97	9.99
House and Home	n.a.	n.a.	n.a.	n.a.	n.a.	n.a.	n.a.	n.a.	n.a.
Humor	1	7.99	7.99	1	9.99	9.99	2	24.98	12.49
Language Arts and Disciplines	n.a.	n.a.	n.a.	n.a.	n.a.	n.a.	n.a.	n.a.	n.a.

Law	n.a.	n.a.	n.a.	n.a.	n.a.	n.a.	n.a.	n.a.	n.a.
Literary Collections	n.a.	n.a.	n.a.	n.a.	n.a.	n.a.	1	4.99	4.99
Literary Criticism	n.a.	n.a.	n.a.	n.a.	n.a.	n.a.	n.a.	n.a.	n.a.
Mathematics	n.a.	n.a.	n.a.	n.a.	n.a.	n.a.	n.a.	n.a.	n.a.
Medical	n.a.	n.a.	n.a.	n.a.	n.a.	n.a.	n.a.	n.a.	n.a.
Music	n.a.	n.a.	n.a.	n.a.	n.a.	n.a.	n.a.	n.a.	n.a.
Nature	n.a.	n.a.	n.a.	n.a.	n.a.	n.a.	n.a.	n.a.	n.a.
Performing Arts	n.a.	n.a.	n.a.	n.a.	n.a.	n.a.	n.a.	n.a.	n.a.
Pets	n.a.	n.a.	n.a.	n.a.	n.a.	n.a.	n.a.	n.a.	n.a.
Philosophy	n.a.	n.a.	n.a.	n.a.	n.a.	n.a.	n.a.	n.a.	n.a.
Photography	n.a.	n.a.	n.a.	n.a.	n.a.	n.a.	n.a.	n.a.	n.a.
Poetry	1	3.99	3.99	n.a.	n.a.	n.a.	n.a.	n.a.	n.a.
Political Science	n.a.	n.a.	n.a.	1	8.99	8.99	1	9.99	9.99
Psychology	n.a.	n.a.	n.a.	n.a.	n.a.	n.a.	1	13.99	13.99
Reference	5	78.50	15.70	n.a.	n.a.	n.a.	n.a.	n.a.	n.a.
Religion	n.a.	n.a.	n.a.	n.a.	n.a.	n.a.	n.a.	n.a.	n.a.
Science	1	13.99	13.99	n.a.	n.a.	n.a.	n.a.	n.a.	n.a.
Self-Help	n.a.	n.a.	n.a.	n.a.	n.a.	n.a.	6	83.94	13.99
Social Science	n.a.	n.a.	n.a.	n.a.	n.a.	n.a.	n.a.	n.a.	n.a.
Sports and Recreation	1	9.99	9.99	n.a.	n.a.	n.a.	n.a.	n.a.	n.a.
Study Aids	n.a.	n.a.	n.a.	n.a.	n.a.	n.a.	n.a.	n.a.	n.a.
Technology and Engineering	n.a.	n.a.	n.a.	n.a.	n.a.	n.a.	n.a.	n.a.	n.a.
Transportation	n.a.	n.a.	n.a.	n.a.	n.a.	n.a.	n.a.	n.a.	n.a.
Travel	n.a.	n.a.	n.a.	n.a.	n.a.	n.a.	n.a.	n.a.	n.a.
True Crime	13	109.87	8.45	12	100.88	8.41	7	57.93	8.28
Young Adult	6	47.94	7.99	8	58.92	7.37	28	317.68	11.35
Total	3,265	$23,663.68	$7.25	2,967	$21,683.60	$7.31	2,976	$21,861.32	$7.35

Table 5 / Trade Paperbacks Average Per-Volume Prices, 2016–2018

	2016			2017			2018		
BISAC Category	**Vols.**	**$ Total**	**Prices**	**Vols.**	**$ Total**	**Prices**	**Vols.**	**$ Total**	**Prices**
Antiques and Collectibles	148	$5,231.99	$35.35	113	$4,530.08	$40.09	88	$3,561.47	$40.47
Architecture	785	39,446.49	50.25	743	35,914.41	48.34	701	34,298.65	48.93
Art	1,830	92,008.35	50.28	1,636	66,926.05	40.91	1,636	65,928.30	40.30
Bibles	618	27,221.32	44.05	716	28,662.85	40.03	714	32,336.94	45.29
Biography and Autobiography	2,575	52,149.08	20.25	2,355	48,145.30	20.44	2,490	51,029.60	20.49
Body, Mind and Spirit	728	13,252.29	18.20	692	12,443.91	17.98	745	13,533.77	18.17
Business and Economics	7,065	657,121.98	93.01	5,720	513,433.18	89.76	5,996	486,126.15	81.08
Children	12,264	183,525.45	14.96	11,503	185,611.01	16.14	11,102	141,068.43	12.71
Comics and Graphic Novels	2,153	40,049.01	18.60	2,059	38,024.10	18.47	2,300	43,479.54	18.90
Computers	4,291	549,959.95	128.17	2,565	244,443.01	95.30	3,016	301,216.64	99.87
Cooking	1,030	21,447.45	20.82	914	19,375.93	21.20	903	18,948.21	20.98
Crafts and Hobbies	929	18,486.75	19.90	800	16,302.46	20.38	661	14,238.62	21.54
Design	254	9,726.72	38.29	240	9,717.01	40.49	245	9,940.98	40.58
Drama	522	10,273.66	19.68	639	14,300.86	22.38	512	10,521.78	20.55
Education	4,589	304,709.70	66.40	4,502	258,079.33	57.33	4,065	244,351.40	60.11
Family and Relationships	614	14,107.29	22.98	521	10,913.81	20.95	566	12,453.46	22.00
Fiction	10,791	183,574.98	17.01	10,103	168,574.83	16.69	9,867	172,179.20	17.45
Foreign Language Study	856	42,283.01	49.40	1,004	41,524.72	41.36	782	33,091.03	42.32
Games	1,831	26,134.60	14.27	1,260	19,620.57	15.57	686	11,834.20	17.25
Gardening	124	2,790.72	22.51	121	2,735.45	22.61	115	2,490.07	21.65
Health and Fitness	1,034	37,625.17	36.39	1,029	31,679.12	30.79	1,026	30,950.88	30.17
History	6,431	251,798.30	39.15	6,273	237,809.42	37.91	6,015	231,664.38	38.51
House and Home	89	1,793.31	20.15	98	2,437.02	24.87	87	1,961.78	22.55
Humor	301	4,641.11	15.42	298	4,571.28	15.34	248	3,813.10	15.38
Language Arts and Disciplines	2,313	178,170.54	77.03	1,645	117,728.80	71.57	1,435	85,143.55	59.33

Law	3,860	337,170.62	87.35	3,100	253,670.01	81.83	3,284	289,129.70	88.04
Literary Collections	400	13,385.87	33.46	393	10,454.94	26.60	417	11,847.84	28.41
Literary Criticism	2,061	89,275.24	43.32	1,921	81,275.03	42.31	1,862	84,970.49	45.63
Mathematics	1,565	152,285.93	97.31	960	74,778.43	77.89	1,268	126,782.52	99.99
Medical	6,442	854,918.96	132.71	3,528	313,596.16	88.89	4,261	476,399.45	111.80
Music	2,662	80,981.92	30.42	1,952	56,138.92	28.76	1,724	46,705.85	27.09
Nature	606	29,917.57	49.37	563	18,313.18	32.53	547	21,766.28	39.79
Performing Arts	832	32,207.76	38.71	859	32,355.33	37.67	861	32,625.04	37.89
Pets	159	3,228.91	20.31	109	1,980.16	18.17	110	2,017.04	18.34
Philosophy	1,787	99,422.83	55.64	1,515	63,402.07	41.85	1,712	83,741.31	48.91
Photography	404	13,677.71	33.86	412	14,269.76	34.64	283	9,643.67	34.08
Poetry	2,064	35,572.79	17.23	2,001	34,767.55	17.38	2,084	36,209.71	17.38
Political Science	3,952	197,383.20	49.95	3,760	172,279.08	45.82	3,716	197,888.75	53.25
Psychology	2,240	136,928.89	61.13	1,939	99,420.50	51.27	1,903	104,682.42	55.01
Reference	573	89,407.89	156.03	501	94,285.11	188.19	447	78,156.17	174.85
Religion	6,765	178,039.06	26.32	6,610	170,954.91	25.86	6,409	173,708.05	27.10
Science	5,449	714,905.29	131.20	2,457	221,752.74	90.25	3,904	493,311.48	126.36
Self-Help	991	17,758.47	17.92	929	16,285.85	17.53	1,087	18,548.54	17.06
Social Science	5,580	317,546.78	56.91	4,528	213,796.84	47.22	5,212	287,160.28	55.10
Sports and Recreation	1,107	27,575.49	24.91	999	25,578.05	25.60	885	22,129.82	25.01
Study Aids	708	27,330.11	38.60	581	18,266.30	31.44	500	21,957.45	43.91
Technology and Engineering	4,112	572,456.55	139.22	2,244	222,289.21	99.06	3,234	455,422.02	140.82
Transportation	531	19,320.88	36.39	519	19,992.82	38.52	499	17,295.70	34.66
Travel	1,679	35,280.44	21.01	1,489	32,066.13	21.54	1,569	32,665.29	20.82
True Crime	142	2,772.76	19.53	166	3,294.39	19.85	205	4,029.43	19.66
Young Adult	2,717	69,252.33	25.49	2,675	48,904.58	18.28	2,815	50,573.82	17.97
Total	123,553	$6,915,533.47	$55.97	104,259	$4,447,672.56	$42.66	106,799	$5,235,530.25	$49.02

Table 6 / Audiobook Average Per-Volume Prices, 2016–2018

	2016			2017			2018		
BISAC Category	Vols.	$ Total	Prices	Vols.	$ Total	Prices	Vols.	$ Total	Prices
Antiques and Collectibles	3	$79.97	$26.66	3	$99.97	$33.32	n.a.	n.a.	n.a.
Architecture	7	177.94	25.42	10	314.90	31.49	2	$45.98	$22.99
Art	22	372.79	16.95	25	720.60	28.82	16	504.70	31.54
Bibles	7	859.97	122.85	6	299.86	49.98	2	99.98	49.99
Biography and Autobiography	1,688	53,795.14	31.87	1,440	53,922.00	37.45	1,240	53,040.12	42.77
Body, Mind and Spirit	148	4,289.94	28.99	158	4,647.26	29.41	145	5,199.15	35.86
Business and Economics	1,316	36,608.61	27.82	884	28,419.33	32.15	788	27,827.47	35.31
Children	1,295	45,109.19	34.83	1,689	52,558.77	31.12	1,317	47,824.01	36.31
Comics and Graphic Novels	1	9.99	9.99	3	26.97	8.99	n.a.	n.a.	n.a.
Computers	30	811.63	27.05	42	1,210.61	28.82	27	1,142.60	42.32
Cooking	45	1,450.40	32.23	63	2,220.00	35.24	60	2,402.04	40.03
Crafts and Hobbies	2	54.94	27.47	2	25.97	12.99	3	66.97	22.32
Design	1	9.99	9.99	1	9.99	9.99	6	307.87	51.31
Drama	152	2,182.75	14.36	60	1,213.81	20.23	163	3,011.81	18.48
Education	51	2,045.58	40.11	39	1,305.65	33.48	40	1,236.81	30.92
Family and Relationships	246	7,273.04	29.57	205	6,515.35	31.78	181	6,225.02	34.39
Fiction	19,260	468,428.07	24.32	10,985	372,398.60	33.90	9,892	388,138.70	39.24
Foreign Language Study	45	4,960.80	110.24	95	7,559.92	79.58	98	20,589.99	210.10
Games	5	139.95	27.99	10	407.90	40.79	5	199.95	39.99
Gardening	2	62.98	31.49	5	134.88	26.98	n.a.	n.a.	n.a.
Health and Fitness	289	9,427.60	32.62	289	11,485.03	39.74	267	10,304.84	38.59
History	1,210	40,493.40	33.47	903	40,058.81	44.36	809	38,329.88	47.38
House and Home	33	1,280.23	38.79	40	1,645.10	41.13	20	719.54	35.98
Humor	103	2,788.18	27.07	61	1,821.05	29.85	95	3,967.76	41.77
Language Arts and Disciplines	41	1,249.46	30.47	35	1,335.63	38.16	29	1,000.56	34.50

Law	41	1,166.69	28.46	31	1,317.62	42.50	34	1,161.54	34.16
Literary Collections	72	2,518.69	34.98	45	1,505.22	33.45	69	2,978.76	43.17
Literary Criticism	54	1,583.23	29.32	32	1,013.65	31.68	34	1,397.44	41.10
Mathematics	8	209.93	26.24	10	214.90	21.49	4	107.96	26.99
Medical	24	529.79	22.07	48	1,668.45	34.76	36	1,500.54	41.68
Music	94	2,589.49	27.55	136	3,974.27	29.22	48	1,734.37	36.13
Nature	87	1,887.02	21.69	63	2,008.33	31.88	52	1,854.20	35.66
Performing Arts	185	6,999.76	37.84	73	2,561.17	35.08	95	3,855.00	40.58
Pets	61	2,404.80	39.42	46	1,737.43	37.77	29	1,102.51	38.02
Philosophy	135	3,680.04	27.26	103	2,413.51	23.43	53	2,014.99	38.02
Photography	2	69.98	34.99	n.a.	n.a.	n.a.	n.a.	n.a.	n.a.
Poetry	24	361.62	15.07	45	1,003.03	22.29	57	1,544.57	27.10
Political Science	404	11,865.60	29.37	324	12,190.44	37.62	377	14,756.56	39.14
Psychology	191	5,420.53	28.38	155	5,795.26	37.39	161	5,995.86	37.24
Reference	11	254.87	23.17	19	671.78	35.36	8	372.93	46.62
Religion	1,243	32,041.94	25.78	1,248	33,611.53	26.93	1,109	34,312.07	30.94
Science	193	5,528.17	28.64	156	5,250.00	33.65	211	8,206.88	38.90
Self-Help	534	17,519.92	32.81	381	12,804.88	33.61	435	15,813.83	36.35
Social Science	312	7,902.44	25.33	300	10,544.91	35.15	321	11,574.36	36.06
Sports and Recreation	223	5,793.52	25.98	145	5,280.66	36.42	111	4,243.85	38.23
Study Aids	2	105.95	52.98	n.a.	n.a.	n.a.	3	124.90	41.63
Technology and Engineering	82	7,627.30	93.02	103	10,500.30	101.94	31	1,387.49	44.76
Transportation	17	545.69	32.10	9	271.87	30.21	10	474.91	47.49
Travel	145	2,469.56	17.03	39	1,205.54	30.91	32	1,397.54	43.67
True Crime	173	5,863.49	33.89	180	7,016.45	38.98	189	6,926.53	36.65
Young Adult	1,742	51,221.19	29.40	1,452	56,518.72	38.92	1,098	48,884.79	44.52
Total	32,061	$862,123.75	$26.89	22,196	$771,437.88	$34.76	19,812	$785,910.13	$39.67

Table 7 / E-Book Average Per-Volume Prices, 2016–2018

	2016			2017			2018		
BISAC Category	Vols.	$ Total	Prices	Vols.	$ Total	Prices	Vols.	$ Total	Prices
Antiques and Collectibles	100	$1,919.88	$19.20	122	$2,042.94	$16.75	142	$1,416.09	$9.97
Architecture	438	17,484.22	39.92	799	17,422.09	21.80	314	14,653.76	46.67
Art	2,663	42,110.69	15.81	2,300	42,746.22	18.59	1,276	42,745.63	33.50
Bibles	280	3,432.79	12.26	2,141	25,390.48	11.86	405	3,724.37	9.20
Biography and Autobiography	6,567	133,785.31	20.37	7,724	135,277.31	17.51	6,675	137,389.54	20.58
Body, Mind and Spirit	2,114	25,117.20	11.88	2,440	28,573.37	11.71	2,812	32,459.95	11.54
Business and Economics	8,432	403,302.06	47.83	8,370	338,088.30	40.39	25,480	1,264,176.71	49.61
Children	16,469	342,412.14	20.79	24,430	426,462.63	17.46	24,725	385,645.86	15.60
Comics and Graphic Novels	1,099	9,951.42	9.05	1,102	12,997.08	11.79	995	9,135.14	9.18
Computers	4,164	302,241.86	72.58	2,833	232,094.24	81.93	1,738	91,177.47	52.46
Cooking	2,054	31,160.86	15.17	2,399	32,969.01	13.74	2,547	36,462.15	14.32
Crafts and Hobbies	1,103	14,157.11	12.84	1,111	13,107.32	11.80	587	8,298.75	14.14
Design	125	3,035.19	24.28	157	3,225.12	20.54	120	2,978.90	24.82
Drama	1,710	17,642.04	10.32	1,530	18,156.41	11.87	1,043	10,130.74	9.71
Education	4,505	184,528.98	40.96	7,387	283,373.41	38.36	3,216	112,068.52	34.85
Family and Relationships	1,837	30,064.71	16.37	1,711	21,896.65	12.80	2,209	27,794.37	12.58
Fiction	62,343	792,098.31	12.71	71,335	708,054.27	9.93	78,391	913,559.10	11.65
Foreign Language Study	906	31,449.59	34.71	1,688	36,684.94	21.73	2,156	41,632.40	19.31
Games	700	6,644.52	9.49	915	7,906.92	8.64	1,442	9,837.09	6.82
Gardening	247	3,288.41	13.31	538	6,521.37	12.12	287	3,724.97	12.98
Health and Fitness	2,394	35,502.52	14.83	2,892	39,296.18	13.59	2,927	40,308.50	13.77
History	9,425	362,885.55	38.50	12,767	365,137.47	28.60	8,003	314,194.94	39.26
House and Home	246	3,100.32	12.60	367	5,322.11	14.50	229	3,954.95	17.27
Humor	1,231	12,500.47	10.15	794	8,438.23	10.63	1,099	14,988.83	13.64
Language Arts and Disciplines	1,986	155,485.70	78.29	2,654	225,397.88	84.93	2,415	164,444.87	68.09

Law	2,168	207,627.50	95.77	2,375	183,240.78	77.15	2,049	232,363.87	113.40
Literary Collections	1,088	20,584.33	18.92	2,029	26,611.42	13.12	1,288	16,808.79	13.05
Literary Criticism	2,672	184,563.17	69.07	2,856	204,237.16	71.51	2,560	215,474.34	84.17
Mathematics	1,463	124,635.02	85.19	1,350	72,772.69	53.91	359	26,209.86	73.01
Medical	3,477	384,196.82	110.50	3,247	274,567.54	84.56	1,777	116,547.20	65.59
Music	1,506	33,666.45	22.35	2,430	43,914.92	18.07	2,815	36,480.76	12.96
Nature	780	35,642.95	45.70	779	30,940.58	39.72	747	17,051.82	22.83
Performing Arts	1,763	56,528.28	32.06	1,794	39,274.24	21.89	1,829	34,128.05	18.66
Pets	402	5,142.62	12.79	797	8,377.15	10.51	421	4,226.35	10.04
Philosophy	2,530	116,021.41	45.86	3,324	107,749.29	32.42	1,988	75,230.29	37.84
Photography	442	9,070.89	20.52	493	8,769.21	17.79	297	5,815.58	19.58
Poetry	3,088	25,435.39	8.24	5,091	44,497.36	8.74	4,824	37,811.84	7.84
Political Science	4,153	213,867.68	51.50	4,735	192,921.10	40.74	3,189	143,176.24	44.90
Psychology	1,951	86,356.45	44.26	2,612	97,710.45	37.41	1,725	55,277.28	32.04
Reference	4,373	73,095.50	16.72	2,984	51,174.47	17.15	1,302	48,008.01	36.87
Religion	8,220	189,508.33	23.05	12,460	235,275.25	18.88	10,128	226,918.22	22.41
Science	3,978	396,963.61	99.79	5,098	315,224.50	61.83	1,897	128,500.99	67.74
Self-Help	3,728	52,967.94	14.21	5,264	64,454.60	12.24	5,158	69,223.17	13.42
Social Science	5,067	251,219.85	49.58	6,772	265,525.26	39.21	3,377	132,104.17	39.12
Sports and Recreation	1,776	31,239.84	17.59	1,868	32,358.99	17.32	1,373	26,791.07	19.51
Study Aids	18,528	557,892.82	30.11	2,316	76,640.99	33.09	1,589	30,511.68	19.20
Technology and Engineering	2,987	382,899.40	128.19	3,724	294,823.29	79.17	991	88,016.92	88.82
Transportation	309	7,342.32	23.76	302	7,792.61	25.80	330	9,511.25	28.82
Travel	2,134	27,441.38	12.86	2,529	36,948.06	14.61	1,903	33,206.41	17.45
True Crime	474	10,355.74	21.85	397	7,896.63	19.89	469	10,113.67	21.56
Young Adult	5,167	123,081.72	23.82	5,315	110,103.77	20.72	5,681	109,134.49	19.21
Total	217,362	$6,572,649.26	$30.24	243,447	$5,870,384.26	$24.11	231,299	$5,615,545.92	$24.28

Number of Book Outlets in the United States and Canada

The *American Book Trade Directory* (Information Today, Inc.) has been published since 1915. Revised annually, it features lists of booksellers, wholesalers, periodicals, reference tools, and other information about the U.S. and Canadian book markets. The data shown in Table 1, the most current available, are from the 2019–2020 edition of the directory.

The 12,228 stores of various types shown are located throughout the United States, Canada, and regions administered by the United States. "General" bookstores stock trade books and children's books in a general variety of subjects. "College" stores (both general and specified) carry college-level textbooks. "Educational" outlets handle school textbooks up to and including the high school level. "Mail order" outlets (both general and specified) sell general trade books by mail and are not book clubs; all others operating by mail are classified according to the kinds of books carried.

"Antiquarian" dealers sell old and rare books. Stores handling secondhand books are classified as "used." "Paperback" stores have more than 80 percent of their stock in paperbound books. Stores with paperback departments are listed under the appropriate major classification ("general," "department store," "stationer," and so forth). Bookstores with at least 50 percent of their stock on a particular subject are classified by subject.

Table 1 / Bookstores in the United States and Canada, 2018

Category	United States	Canada
Antiquarian General	436	40
Antiquarian Mail Order	148	6
Antiquarian Specialized	85	1
Art Supply Store	13	1
College General	2,457	127
College Specialized	96	5
Comics	175	23
Computer Software	2	0
Cooking	219	9
Department Store	749	17
Educational	138	22
Federal Sites	305	1
Foreign Language	12	2
General	2,088	434
Gift Shop	80	5
Juvenile	54	11
Mail Order General	43	5
Mail Order Specialized	178	10
Metaphysics, New Age and Occult	100	15
Museum Store and Art Gallery	394	27
Nature and Natural History	31	5

Newsdealer	12	1
Office Supply	6	1
Other	1,647	302
Paperback	23	1
Religious	1,057	89
Self Help/Development	13	4
Stationer	3	2
Toy Store	31	65
Used	353	49
Totals	10,948	1,280

Part 5
Reference Information

Ready Reference

How to Obtain an ISBN

Beat Barblan
United States ISBN/SAN Agency

The International Standard Book Numbering (ISBN) system was introduced into the United Kingdom by J. Whitaker & Sons Ltd. in 1967 and into the United States in 1968 by R. R. Bowker. The Technical Committee on Documentation of the International Organization for Standardization (ISO TC 46) is responsible for the international standard.

The purpose of this standard is to "establish the specifications for the International Standard Book Number (ISBN) as a unique international identification system for each product form or edition of a monographic publication published or produced by a specific publisher." The standard specifies the construction of an ISBN, the rules for assignment and use of an ISBN, and all metadata associated with the allocation of an ISBN.

Types of monographic publications to which an ISBN may be assigned include printed books and pamphlets (in various product formats); electronic publications (either on the Internet or on physical carriers such as CD-ROMs or diskettes); educational/instructional films, videos, and transparencies; educational/instructional software; audiobooks on cassette or CD or DVD; braille publications; and microform publications.

Serial publications, printed music, and musical sound recordings are excluded from the ISBN standard as they are covered by other identification systems.

The ISBN is used by publishers, distributors, wholesalers, bookstores, and libraries, among others, in 217 countries and territories as an ordering and inventory system. It expedites the collection of data on new and forthcoming editions of monographic publications for print and electronic directories used by the book trade. Its use also facilitates rights management and the monitoring of sales data for the publishing industry.

The "new" ISBN consists of 13 digits. As of January 1, 2007, a revision to the ISBN standard was implemented in an effort to substantially increase the numbering capacity. The 10-digit ISBN identifier (ISBN-10) is now replaced by the ISBN 13-digit identifier (ISBN-13). All facets of book publishing are now expected to use the ISBN-13, and the ISBN agencies throughout the world are now issuing only ISBN-13s to publishers. Publishers with existing ISBN-10s need to convert their ISBNs to ISBN-13s by the addition of the EAN prefix 978 and recalculation of the new check digit:

ISBN-10: 0-8352-8235-X
ISBN-13: 978-0-8352-8235-2

When the inventory of the ISBN-10s has been exhausted, the ISBN agencies will start assigning ISBN-13s with the "979" prefix instead of the "978." There is no 10-digit equivalent for 979 ISBNs.

Construction of an ISBN

An ISBN currently consists of 13 digits separated into the following parts:

1. A prefix of "978" for an ISBN-10 converted to an ISBN-13
2. Group or country identifier, which identifies a national or geographic grouping of publishers
3. Publisher identifier, which identifies a particular publisher within a group
4. Title identifier, which identifies a particular title or edition of a title
5. Check digit, the single digit at the end of the ISBN that validates the ISBN-13

For more information regarding ISBN-13 conversion services provided by the U.S. ISBN Agency at R. R. Bowker, LLC, visit the ISBN Agency Web site at http://www.isbn.org, or contact the U.S. ISBN Agency at isbn-san@bowker.com.

Publishers requiring their ISBNs to be converted from the ISBN-10 to ISBN-13 format can use the U.S. ISBN Agency's free ISBN-13 online converter at http://isbn.org/converterpub.asp. Publishers can also view their ISBNs online by accessing their personal account at http://www.myidentifiers.com.

Displaying the ISBN on a Product or Publication

When an ISBN is written or printed, it should be preceded by the letters ISBN, and each part should be separated by a space or hyphen. In the United States, the hyphen is used for separation, as in the following example: ISBN 978-0-8352-8235-2. In this example, 978 is the prefix that precedes the ISBN-13, 0 is the group identifier, 8352 is the publisher identifier, 8235 is the title identifier, and 2 is the check digit. The group of English-speaking countries, which includes the United States, Australia, Canada, New Zealand, and the United Kingdom, uses the group identifiers 0 and 1.

The ISBN Organization

The administration of the ISBN system is carried out at three levels—through the International ISBN Agency in the United Kingdom, through the national agencies, and through the publishing houses themselves. The International ISBN Agency, which is responsible for assigning country prefixes and for coordinating the worldwide implementation of the system, has an advisory panel that represents the International Organization for Standardization (ISO), publishers, and libraries. The International ISBN Agency publishes the *Publishers International ISBN Directory,* which is a listing of all national agencies' publishers with their assigned ISBN publisher prefixes. R. R. Bowker, as the publisher of *Books In Print,* with its extensive and varied database of publishers' addresses, was the obvious place to initiate the ISBN system and to provide the service to the U.S. publishing industry. To date, the U.S. ISBN Agency has entered more than 180,000 publishers into the system.

ISBN Assignment Procedure

Assignment of ISBNs is a shared endeavor between the U.S. ISBN Agency and the publisher. Publishers can apply online through the ISBN Agency's website www.myidentifiers.com. Once the order is processed, an e-mail confirmation will be sent with instructions for managing the account. The publisher then has the responsibility to assign an ISBN to each title, keep an accurate record of each number assigned, and register each title in the *Books In Print* database at www.myidentifiers.com. It is the responsibility of the ISBN Agency to validate assigned ISBNs and keep a record of all ISBN publisher prefixes in circulation.

ISBN implementation is very much market-driven. Major distributors, wholesalers, retailers, and so forth recognize the necessity of the ISBN system and request that publishers register with the ISBN Agency. Also, the ISBN is a mandatory bibliographic element in the International Standard Bibliographical Description (ISBD). The Library of Congress Cataloging in Publication (CIP) Division directs publishers to the agency to obtain their ISBN prefixes.

Location and Display of the ISBN

On books, pamphlets, and other printed material, the ISBN shall be printed on the verso of the title leaf or, if this is not possible, at the foot of the title leaf itself. It should also appear on the outside back cover or on the back of the jacket if the book has one (the lower right-hand corner is recommended). The ISBN shall also appear on any accompanying promotional materials following the provisions for location according to the format of the material.

On other monographic publications, the ISBN shall appear on the title or credit frames and any labels permanently affixed to the publication. If the publication is issued in a container that is an integral part of the publication, the ISBN shall be displayed on the label. If it is not possible to place the ISBN on the item or its label, then the number should be displayed on the bottom or the back of the container, box, sleeve, or frame. It should also appear on any accompanying material, including each component of a multitype publication.

Printing of ISBN in Machine-Readable Coding

All books should carry ISBNs in the EAN-13 bar code machine-readable format. All ISBN EAN-13 bar codes start with the EAN prefix 978 for books. As of

January 1, 2007, all EAN bar codes should have the ISBN-13 appearing immediately above the bar code in eye-readable format, preceded by the acronym "ISBN." The recommended location of the EAN-13 bar code for books is in the lower right-hand corner of the back cover (see Figure 1).

Figure 1 / Printing the ISBN in Bookland/EAN Symbology

Five-Digit Add-On Code

In the United States, a five-digit add-on code is used for additional information. In the publishing industry, this code is used for price information. The lead digit of the five-digit add-on has been designated a currency identifier, when the add-on is used for price. Number 5 is the code for the U.S. dollar, 6 denotes the Canadian dollar, 1 the British pound, 3 the Australian dollar, and 4 the New Zealand dollar. Publishers that do not want to indicate price in the add-on should print the code 90000 (see Figure 2).

Figure 2 / Printing the ISBN Bookland/EAN Number in Bar Code with the Five-Digit Add-On Code

978 = ISBN Bookland/EAN prefix
5 = Code for U.S. $ in the add-on code
2499 = $24.99

90000 means no information

Reporting the Title and the ISBN

After the publisher reports a title to the ISBN Agency, the number is validated and the title is listed in the many R. R. Bowker hard-copy and electronic publications, including *Books in Print; Forthcoming Books; Paperbound Books in Print; Books in Print Supplement; Books Out of Print; Books in Print Online; Books in Print Plus-CD ROM; Children's Books in Print; Subject Guide to Children's Books in Print; Books Out Loud: Bowker's Guide to AudioBooks; Bowker's Complete Video Directory; Software Encyclopedia; Software for Schools;* and other specialized publications.

For an ISBN application and information, visit the ISBN Agency website at www.myidentifiers.com, call the toll-free number 877-310-7333, fax 908-795-3518, or write to the United States ISBN Agency, 630 Central Ave., New Providence, NJ 07974.

The ISSN, and How to Obtain One

U.S. ISSN Center
Library of Congress

In the early 1970s the rapid increase in the production and dissemination of information and an intensified desire to exchange information about serials in computerized form among different systems and organizations made it increasingly clear that a means to identify serial publications at an international level was needed. The International Standard Serial Number (ISSN) was developed and became the internationally accepted code for identifying serial publications.

The ISSN is an international standard, ISO 3297: 2017. The 2017 edition is a minimal revision of the 2007 edition which expanded the scope of the ISSN to cover continuing resources—serials such as journals, magazines, series, and blogs, and such ongoing publications as updating databases, updating loose-leaf services, and certain types of updating websites.

The number itself has no significance other than as a brief, unique, and unambiguous identifier. The ISSN consists of eight digits in Arabic numerals 0 to 9, except for the last ("check") digit, which is calculated using Modulus 11 and uses an "X" in place of the numeral 10 to maintain the ISSN at 8 digits. The numbers appear as two groups of four digits separated by a hyphen and preceded by the letters ISSN—for example, ISSN 1234-5679.

The ISSN is not self-assigned by publishers. Administration of the ISSN is coordinated through the ISSN Network, an intergovernmental organization within the UNESCO/UNISIST program. The ISSN Network consists of national ISSN centers, coordinated by the ISSN International Centre, located in Paris. National ISSN Centers are responsible for registering serials published in their respective countries. Responsibility for the assignment of ISSN to titles from multinational publishers is allocated among the ISSN Centers in which the publisher has offices. A list of these publishers and the corresponding ISSN centers is located on the ISSN International Centre's website, http://www.issn.org.

The ISSN International Centre handles ISSN assignments for international organizations and for countries that do not have a national center. It also maintains and distributes the ISSN Register and makes it available in a variety of products, most commonly via the ISSN Portal, an online subscription database containing full metadata records for each ISSN as well as other features and functionality. In January of 2018, a new ISSN Portal was released that includes free look-up and access to a subset of ISSN metadata. The ISSN Register is also available via Z39.50 access, and as a data file. Selected ISSN data can also be obtained in customized files or database extracts that can be used, for example, to check the accuracy or completeness of a requestor's list of titles and ISSN. Another available ISSN service is OAI-PMH, a customizable "harvesting" protocol through which external applications can automatically and regularly gather new and updated metadata on a defined schedule. The ISSN Register contains bibliographic records corresponding to each ISSN assignment as reported by national ISSN centers. The database contains records for more than 2 million ISSNs.

The ISSN is used all over the world by serials publishers to identify their serials and to distinguish their titles from others that are the same or similar. It is used by subscription services and libraries to manage files for orders, claims, and back issues. It is used in automated check-in systems by libraries that wish to process receipts more quickly. Copyright centers use the ISSN as a means to collect and disseminate royalties. It is also used as an identification code by postal services and legal deposit services. The ISSN is included as a verification element in interlibrary lending activities and for union catalogs as a collocating device. The ISSN is also incorporated into bar codes for optical recognition of serial publication identification and metadata and into the standards for the identification of issues and articles in serial publications. A key use of the ISSN is as an identifier in online systems, where it can serve to connect catalog records or citations in abstracting and indexing databases with full-text journal content via OpenURL resolvers or reference linking services, and as an identifier and link in archives of electronic and print serials.

Because serials are generally known and cited by title, assignment of the ISSN is inseparably linked to the key title, a standardized form of the title derived from information in the serial issue. Only one ISSN can be assigned to a title in a particular medium. For titles issued in multiple media—e.g., print, online, CD-ROM—a separate ISSN is assigned to each medium version. If a major title change occurs or the medium changes, a new ISSN must be assigned. Centers responsible for assigning ISSNs also construct the key title and create an associated bibliographic record.

A significant new feature of the 2007 ISSN standard was the Linking ISSN (ISSN-L), a mechanism that enables collocation or linking among different media versions of a continuing resource. The Linking ISSN allows a unique designation (one of the existing ISSNs) to be applied to all media versions of a continuing resource while retaining the separate ISSN that pertains to each version. When an ISSN is functioning as a Linking ISSN, the eight digits of the base ISSN are prefixed with the designation "ISSN-L." The Linking ISSN facilitates search, retrieval, and delivery across all medium versions of a serial or other continuing resource for improved ISSN functionality in OpenURL linking, search engines, library catalogs, and knowledge bases. The ISSN standard also supports interoperability by specifying the use of ISSN and ISSN-L with other systems such as DOI, OpenURL, URN, and EAN bar codes. ISSN-L was implemented in the ISSN Register in 2008. To help ISSN users implement the ISSN-L in their databases, two free tables are available from the ISSN International Centre's home page: one lists each ISSN and its corresponding ISSN-L; the other lists each ISSN-L and its corresponding ISSNs.

In the United States, the U.S. ISSN Center at the Library of Congress is responsible for assigning and maintaining the ISSNs for all U.S. serial and other continuing resource publications. Publishers wishing to have an ISSN assigned should download an application from the Center's website and mail or e-mail the completed form and other requested materials to the U.S. ISSN Center. Assignment of the ISSN is free, and there is no charge for use of the ISSN.

To obtain an ISSN for a U.S. publication, or for more information about ISSN in the United States, libraries, publishers, and other ISSN users should visit the

U.S. ISSN Center's website, http://www.loc.gov/issn, or contact the U.S. ISSN Center, U.S. Programs, Law, and Literature, Library of Congress, 101 Independence Ave. S.E., Washington, DC 20540-4284 (telephone 202-707-6452, e-mail issn@loc.gov).

For information about ISSN products and services, and for application procedures that non-U.S. parties should use to apply for an ISSN, visit the ISSN International Centre's website, http://www.issn.org, or contact the International Centre at 45 rue de Turbigo, 75003 Paris, France (telephone 33-1-44-88-22-20, e-mail issnic@issn.org).

How to Obtain an SAN

Beat Barblan
United States ISBN/SAN Agency

SAN stands for Standard Address Number. The SAN system, an American National Standards Institute (ANSI) standard, assigns a unique identification number that is used to positively identify specific addresses of organizations in order to facilitate buying and selling transactions within the industry. It is recognized as the identification code for electronic communication within the industry.

For purposes of this standard, the book industry includes book publishers, book wholesalers, book distributors, book retailers, college bookstores, libraries, library binders, and serial vendors. Schools, school systems, technical institutes, and colleges and universities are not members of this industry, but are served by it and therefore included in the SAN system.

The purpose of the SAN is to ease communications among these organizations, of which there are several hundreds of thousands that engage in a large volume of separate transactions with one another. These transactions include purchases of books by book dealers, wholesalers, schools, colleges, and libraries from publishers and wholesalers; payments for all such purchases; and other communications between participants. The objective of this standard is to establish an identification code system by assigning each address within the industry a unique code to be used for positive identification for all book and serial buying and selling transactions.

Many organizations have similar names and multiple addresses, making identification of the correct contact point difficult and subject to error. In many cases, the physical movement of materials takes place between addresses that differ from the addresses to be used for the financial transactions. In such instances, there is ample opportunity for confusion and errors. Without identification by SAN, a complex record-keeping system would have to be instituted to avoid introducing errors. In addition, problems with the current numbering system—such as errors in billing, shipping, payments, and returns—are significantly reduced by using the SAN system. The SAN also eliminates one step in the order fulfillment process: the "look-up procedure" used to assign account numbers. Previously a store or library dealing with 50 different publishers was assigned a different account number by each of the suppliers. The SAN solved this problem. If a publisher prints its SAN on its stationery and ordering documents, vendors to whom it sends transactions do not have to look up the account number, but can proceed immediately to process orders by SAN.

Libraries are involved in many of the same transactions as book dealers, such as ordering and paying for books and charging and paying for various services to other libraries. Keeping records of transactions—whether these involve buying, selling, lending, or donations—entails operations suited to SAN use. SAN stationery speeds up order fulfillment and eliminate errors in shipping, billing, and crediting; this, in turn, means savings in both time and money.

History

Development of the Standard Address Number began in 1968, when Russell Reynolds, general manager of the National Association of College Stores (NACS), approached R. R. Bowker and suggested that a "Standard Account Number" system be implemented in the book industry. The first draft of a standard was prepared by an American National Standards Institute (ANSI) Committee Z39 subcommittee, which was co-chaired by Reynolds and Emery Koltay of Bowker. After Z39 members proposed changes, the current version of the standard was approved by NACS on December 17, 1979.

Format

The SAN consists of six digits plus a seventh *Modulus 11* check digit; a hyphen follows the third digit (XXX-XXXX) to facilitate transcription. The hyphen is to be used in print form, but need not be entered or retained in computer systems. Printed on documents, the Standard Address Number should be preceded by the identifier "SAN" to avoid confusion with other numerical codes (SAN XXXXXXX).

Check Digit Calculation

The check digit is based on *Modulus 11,* and can be derived as follows:

1.	Write the digits of the basic number.	2 3 4 5 6 7
2.	Write the constant weighting factors associated with each position by the basic number.	7 6 5 4 3 2
3.	Multiply each digit by its associated weighting factor.	14 18 20 20 18 14
4.	Add the products of the multiplications.	14 + 18 + 20 + 20 + 18 + 14 = 104
5.	Divide the sum by Modulus 11 to find the remainder.	104 -: 11 = 9 plus a remainder of 5
6.	Subtract the remainder from the Modulus 11 to generate the required check digit. If there is no remainder, generate a check digit of zero. If the check digit is 10, generate a check digit of X to represent 10, since the use of 10 would require an extra digit.	11 - 5 = 6
7.	Append the check digit to create the standard seven-digit Standard Address Number.	SAN 234-5676

SAN Assignment

R. R. Bowker accepted responsibility for being the central administrative agency for SAN, and in that capacity assigns SANs to identify uniquely the addresses of organizations. No SANs can be reassigned; in the event that an organization should cease to exist, for example, its SAN would cease to be in circulation entirely. If an organization using an SAN should move or change its name with no change in ownership, its SAN would remain the same, and only the name or address would be updated to reflect the change.

The SAN should be used in all transactions; it is recommended that the SAN be imprinted on stationery, letterheads, order and invoice forms, checks, and all other documents used in executing various book transactions. The SAN should always be printed on a separate line above the name and address of the organization, preferably in the upper left-hand corner of the stationery to avoid confusion with other numerical codes pertaining to the organization, such as telephone number, zip code, and the like.

SAN Functions

The SAN is strictly a Standard Address Number, becoming functional only in applications determined by the user; these may include activities such as purchasing, billing, shipping, receiving, paying, crediting, and refunding. It is the method used by Pubnet and PubEasy systems and is required in all electronic data interchange communications using the Book Industry Systems Advisory Committee (BISAC) EDI formats. Every department that has an independent function within an organization could have an SAN for its own identification.

For additional information or to make suggestions, write to ISBN/SAN Agency, R. R. Bowker, LLC, 630 Central Ave., New Providence, NJ 07974, call 877-310-7333, or fax 908-795-3518. The e-mail address is san@bowker.com. An SAN can be ordered online through the website www.myidentifiers.com, or an application can be requested by e-mail through san@bowker.com.

Distinguished Books

The Year's Notable Books

The Notable Books Council of the Reference and User Services Association (RUSA), a division of the American Library Association, released its annual list of notable books on January 27, 2019. These titles were selected for their significant contribution to the expansion of knowledge or for the pleasure they can provide to adult readers.

Fiction

Waiting for Eden by Elliot Ackerman (Alfred A. Knopf, a division of Penguin Random House).

Friday Black by Nana Kwame Adjei-Brenyah (Mariner, an imprint of Houghton Mifflin Harcourt).

Washington Black by Esi Edugyan (Alfred A. Knopf, a division of Penguin Random House).

An American Marriage by Tayari Jones (Algonquin Books of Chapel Hill).

The Mars Room by Rachel Kushner (Scribner, an imprint of Simon & Schuster).

The Great Believers by Rebecca Makkai (Viking, a division of Penguin Random House).

Warlight by Michael Ondaatje (Alfred A. Knopf, a division of Penguin Random House).

There There by Tommy Orange (Alfred A. Knopf, a division of Penguin Random House).

The Overstory by Richard Powers (WW Norton & Company, Inc.).

The House of Broken Angels by Luis Alberto Urrea (Little, Brown and Company, a division of Hachette Book Group).

Don't Skip out on Me by Willy Vlautin (Harper Perennial, an imprint of HarperCollins).

Nonfiction

High-Risers: Cabrini-Green and the Fate of American Public Housing by Ben Austen (Harper, an imprint of HarperCollins).

American Prison: A Reporter's Undercover Journey into the Business of Punishment by Shane Bauer (Penguin Press, a division of Penguin Random House).

Frederick Douglass: Prophet of Freedom by David W. Blight (Simon & Schuster).

Rush: Revolution, Madness, and the Visionary Doctor Who Became a Founding Father by Stephen Fried (Crown, a division of Penguin Random House).

Call Me American: A Memoir by Abdi Nor Iftin (Alfred A. Knopf, a division of Penguin Random House).

The Feather Thief: Beauty, Obsession, and the Natural History Heist of the Century by Kirk Wallace Johnson (Viking, a division of Penguin Random House).

Beneath a Ruthless Sun: A True Story of Violence, Race, and Justice Lost and Found by Gilbert King (Riverhead Books, a division of Penguin Random House).

Heavy: An American Memoir by Kiese Laymon (Scribner, an imprint of Simon & Schuster).

Dopesick: Dealers, Doctors, and the Drug Company That Addicted America by Beth Macy (Little, Brown and Company, a division of Hachette Book Group).

The Tangled Tree: A Radical New History of Life by David Quammen (Simon & Schuster).

Rising: Dispatches from the New American Shore by Elizabeth Rush (Milkweed Editions).

Educated: A Memoir by Tara Westover (Random House, a division of Penguin Random House).

Poetry

If They Come for Us: Poems by Fatimah Asghar (One World, a division of Penguin Random House).

American Sonnets for My Once and Future Assassin by Terrance Hayes (Penguin Poets, a division of Penguin Random House).

The Carrying: Poems by Ada Limón (Milkweed Editions).

Best Fiction for Young Adults

Each year a committee of the Young Adult Library Services Association (YALSA), a division of the American Library Association, compiles a list of the best fiction appropriate for young adults ages 12 to 18. Selected on the basis of each book's proven or potential appeal and value to young adults, the titles span a variety of subjects as well as a broad range of reading levels. An asterisk denotes the title was selected as a top ten.

*Acevedo, Elizabeth. *The Poet X* (Harper Teen). 978-0062662804.

Adeyemi, Tomi. *Children of Blood and Bone* (Holt). 978-1250170972.

Albert, Melissa. *The Hazel Wood* (Flatiron Books). 978-1250147905).

*Albertalli, Becky. *Leah on the Offbeat* (Balzer+Bray). 978-0062643803.

Albertalli, Becky and Silvera, Adam. *What if It's Us* (Harper Teen). 978-0062795250.

Arnold, David. *The Strange Fascinations of Noah Hypnotik* (Viking). 978-0425288863.

Barker, Michelle. *The House of One Thousand Eyes* (Annick Press). 978-1773210711.

Barter, Catherine. *Troublemakers* (Carolrhoda Lab). 978-1512475494.

Boecker, Virginia. *The Assassin's Guide to Love and Treason* (Little, Brown Books for Young Readers). 978-0316327343.

Blake, Ashley Herring. *Ivy Aberdeen's Letter to the World* (Little, Brown and Company). 978-0316515467.

Blake, Ashley Herring. *Girl Made of Stars* (HMH Books for Young Readers). 978-1328778239.

Bliss, Bryan. *We'll Fly Away* (Greenwillow Books). 978-0062494276.

*Caletti, Deb. *A Heart in a Body in the World* (Simon Pulse). 978-1481415200.

Clayton, Dhonielle. *The Belles* (Freeform). 978-1484728499.

Cole, Olivia A. *A Conspiracy of Stars* (Katherine Tegen Books). 978-0062644213.

Dao, Julie C. *Forest of a Thousand Lanterns* (Philomel). 978-1524738297.

Daud, Somaiya. *Mirage* (Flatiron). 978-1250126429.

Fleming, Candace, et al. *Fatal Throne: The Wives of Henry VIII Tell All* (Schwartz and Wade). 978-1524716196.

Flores-Scott, Patrick. *American Road Trip* (Holt). 978-1627797412.

Foody, Amanda. *Ace of Shades* (Harlequin Teen). 978-1335692290.

Gilbert, Kelly Loy. *Picture Us in the Light* (Disney-Hyperion). 978-1484726020).

Grimes, Nikki. *Between the Lines* (Nancy Paulsen Books). 978-0399246883.

Hand, Cynthia, Brodi Ashton, and Jodi Meadows. *My Plain Jane* (Harper Teen). 978-0062652775.

Hardinge, Frances. *A Skinful of Shadows* (Amulet Books). 978-1419725722.

Hesse, Monica. *The War Outside* (Little, Brown Books for Young Readers). 978-0316316699.

Hill, Will. *After the Fire* (Sourcebooks Fire). 978-1492669791.

Holczer, Tracy. *Everything Else in the Universe* (G. P. Putnam's Sons). 978-0399163944.

Hutchinson, Shaun David. *The Apocalypse of Elena Mendoza* (Simon Pulse). 978-1481498548.

*Ireland, Justina. *Dread Nation* (Balzer+Bray). 978-0062570604.

*Jackson, Tiffany D. *Monday's Not Coming* (Katherine Tegen Books). 978-0062422675.

Johnson, Maureen. *Truly Devious* (Katherine Tegen Books). 978-0062338051.

Kaplan, Ariel. *We Regret to Inform You* (Knopf Books for Young Readers). 978-1524773700.

*Khorram, Adib. *Darius the Great Is Not Okay* (Dial Books). 978-0525552963.

Killeen, Matt. *Orphan Monster Spy* (Viking). 978-0451478733.

Kisner, Adrienne. *Dear Rachel Maddow* (Feiwel & Friends). 978-1250146021.

Kristoff, Jay. *Lifel1k3* (Knopf Books for Young Readers). 978-1524713928.

Lee, Mackenzi. *The Lady's Guide to Petticoats and Piracy* (Katherine Tegen Books). 978-0062795328.

Legrand, Claire. *Sawkill Girls* (Katherine Tegen Books). 978-0062696601.

Leno, Katrina. *Summer of Salt* (Harper Teen). 978-0062493620.

Lucier, Makiia. *Isle of Blood and Stone* (HMH Books for Young Readers). 978-0544968578.

Mather, Janice Lynn. *Learning to Breathe* (Simon & Schuster Books for Young Readers). 978-1534406018.

McCullough, Joy. *Blood Water Paint* (Dutton Books for Young Readers). 978-0735232112.

McLemore, Anna-Marie. *Blanca and Roja* (Feiwel and Friends). 978-1250162717.

Miller, Samuel. *A Lite Too Bright* (Katherine Tegen Books). 978-0062662002.

*Mills, Emma. *Foolish Hearts* (Holt). 978-1627799379.

Mitchell, Saundra. *All Out: The No-Longer Secret Stores of Queer Teens Throughout the Ages* (Harlequin Teen). 978-1335470454.

Moore, David Barclay. *The Stars Beneath Our Feet* (Knopf Books for Young Readers). 978-1524701246.

*Norton, Preston. *Neanderthal Opens the Door to the Universe* (Disney Hyperion). 978-1484790625.

Nwaubani, Adaobi Tricia. *Buried Beneath the Baobab Tree* (Katherine Tegen Books). 978-0062696724.

Oh, Ellen and Chapman, Elsie (editors). *A Thousand Beginnings and Endings* (Greenwillow Books). 978-0062671158.

Oliver, Lauren. *Broken Things* (Harper Collins). 978-0062224132.

*Plozza, Shivaun. *Frankie* (Flatiron Books). 978-1250142993.

Ramos, Nonieqa. *The Disturbed Girl's Dictionary* (Carolrhoda Lab). 978-1512439762.

Savage, Kim. *In Her Skin* (Farrar, Straus and Giroux). 978-0374308001.

Schwab, Victoria. *City of Ghosts* (Scholastic). 978-1338111002.

Shusterman, Neal and Jarrod. *Dry* (Simon & Schuster BFYR). 978-1481481960.

Smith, Heather. *The Agony of Bun O'Keefe* (Penguin Teen). 978-0143198659.

Stamper, Vesper. *What the Night Sings* (Knopf Books for Young Readers). 978-1524700386.

Steiger, A. J. *When My Heart Joins the Thousand* (Harper Teen). 978-0062656476.

Stone, Nic. *Odd One Out* (Crown). 978-1101939536.

Summers, Courtney. *Sadie* (Wednesday Books). 978-1250105714.

Thomas, Kara. *The Cheerleaders* (Delacorte). 978-1524718329.

Thomas, Leah. *When Light Left Us* (Bloomsbury USA Childrens). 978-1681191812.

Van Draanen, Wendelin. *Wild Bird* (Knopf Books for Young Readers). 978-1101940440.

White, Kiersten. *The Dark Descent of Elizabeth Frankenstein* (Delacorte). 978-0525577942.

Woodson, Jacqueline. *Harbor Me* (Nancy Paulsen). 978-0399252525.

Young, Adrienne. *Sky in the Deep* (Wednesday Books). 978-1250168450.

Zoboi, Ibi. *Pride* (Balzer+Bray). 978-0062564047.

Quick Picks for Reluctant Young Adult Readers

The Young Adult Library Services Association (YALSA), a division of the American Library Association, annually chooses a list of outstanding titles that will stimulate the interest of reluctant teen readers. This list is intended to attract teens who, for whatever reason, choose not to read.

The list includes fiction and nonfiction titles published from late 2017 through 2018. An asterisk denotes the title was selected as a top ten.

*Acevedo, Elizabeth. *The Poet X*. HarperTEEN/HarperCollins. 2018. $17.99. ISBN: 978-0062662804. Xiomara secretly creates poetry to explore her shifting relationship with her Dominican immigrant parents, religion, her body, and chemistry lab partner/crush Aman.

Alexander, Kwame. *Rebound*. Houghton Mifflin Harcourt. 2018. $16.99. ISBN: 978-0544868137. Chuck Bell never liked basketball until a special summer at Grandpa Percy's. The Rebound is the perfect metaphoric title for this prequel to The Crossover.

Andersen, Sarah. *Herding Cats: A Sarah's Scribbles Collection*. Andrews McMeel Publishing. 2018. $14.99. ISBN: 978-1449489786. A compilation of entries from Sarah's popular webcomic *Sarah's Scribbles, Herding Cats* explores topics such as anxiety, online harassment, and obsession with animals with her trademark quirky style.

*Anderson, Laurie Halse and Emily Carroll (Illustrator). *Speak: The Graphic Novel*. Macmillan/Farrar, Straus and Giroux Books for Young Readers. Illus. 2018. $19.99. ISBN: 978-0374300289. An incident at an end-of-summer party leaves Melinda speechless, an outcast, struggling to confront her torment while navigating the pressures of high school. A haunting and invigorating retelling of this award-winning novel that preserves Speak's powerful message.

Bagieu, Penelope. *Brazen: Rebel Ladies Who Rocked the World*. Macmillan/Roaring Brook Press/First Second Books. Illus. 2018. $17.99. ISBN: 978-1626728691. Some of history's most spirited and inspiring women overcome difficult odds in this graphic novel representation of girl power at its best.

Balog, Cyn. *Alone*. Sourcebooks/Sourcebooks Fire. 2017. $17.99. ISBN: 978-1492655473. Seda's mom inherits a creepy old mansion that used to house a live murder mystery show. When a 20-inch snowstorm strands a group of teens there, live murder mystery takes on new meanings.

Blas, Terry, Molly Muldoon, and Matthew Seely (Illustrator). *Dead Weight: Murder at Camp Bloom*. Oni Press. 2018. $19.99. ISBN: 978-1620104811. Summer camp turns deadly when Jesse and Noah are witnesses to a camp counselor's murder by another staff member at their wilderness camp for overweight teens. Jesse and Noah team up with two other campers to solve the case.

Callender, Kheryn. *This Is Kind of an Epic Love Story*. HarperCollins/Balzer+Bray. 2018. $17.99. ISBN: 978-0062820228. Nate doesn't believe in happy endings. When his childhood best friend Oliver moves back to town, he will have to be honest about how he feels and face the consequences once and for all or will lose Ollie all over again.

Carter, Ally. *Not If I Save You First*. Scholastic Press. 2018. $18.99. ISBN: 978-1338134148. Maddie, daughter of the head of the Secret Service, and Logan, the president's son, were best friends until something went horribly wrong at a State event. Six years later, Maddie is living in the Alaskan wilderness when Logan unexpectedly reappears with a mystery assailant hot on his heels.

Cherry, Alison, Lindsay Ribar, and Michelle Schusterman. *The Pros of Cons*. Scholastic Press/Point. 2018. $18.99. ISBN: 978-1338151725. Vanessa, Phoebe, and Callie are attending three different conventions that are being held at the same hotel. A hilarious mix-up brings the three girls together.

Chmakova, Svetlana. *Crush (Berrybrook Middle School)*. Yen Press/JY for Kids. 2018. $11.00. ISBN: 978-0316363242. Jorge is a chill guy just trying to survive middle school. Quiet and thoughtful, he uses his size to protect others. But can he protect himself from developing a massive crush on Jazmine?

Coker, Jessika. *Juniper: The Happiest Fox*. Chronicle Books. 2018. $16.95. ISBN: 978-1452167602. Juniper was a runt fox kit rescued from a fur farm and adopted by an animal rehabilitator whose snaggle-toothed smile has won the hearts of millions on Instagram. This photograph-filled book shares Juniper's story and includes fascinating facts about foxes.

Coles, Jay. *Tyler Johnson Was Here*. Hachette/Little, Brown Books for Young Readers. 2018. $17.99. ISBN: 978-0316440776. Marvin's twin brother, Tyler, goes missing after a party and is later found shot and killed. A video surfaces that depicts Tyler being shot three times as a victim of police brutality, prompting Marvin to find ways to speak up and resist.

Colfer, Eoin, Andrew Donkin, and Giovanni Rigano (Illustrator). *Illegal*. Sourcebooks/Jabberwocky. 2018. $19.99. ISBN: 978-1492662143. Ebo and his brother, Kwame, leave Northern Africa in search of their sister and refuge in Europe. Crossing the blazing desert and rough Mediterranean seas on an inflatable boat carries no guarantee for survival.

Cooner, Donna. *Screenshot*. Scholastic Press/Point. 2018. $9.99. ISBN: 978-0545903998. Ambitious Skye is focused on winning a coveted summer internship with a senator, but someone with a screenshot from an embarrassing video threatens to destroy her perfect social media image.

Crossan, Sarah. *Moonrise*. Bloomsbury YA. 2018. $17.99. ISBN: 978-1681193663. Joe Moon is in a hot Texas town, renting a shabby apartment, trying to find a job, and visiting the "Farm" every day at 2 P.M. to spend as much time as possible with his brother on death row.

Doeden, Matt. *Coming Up Clutch: The Greatest Comebacks, Upsets, and Finishes in Sports History*. Lerner Publishing Group/Millbrook Press. 2018. $34.65. ISBN: 978-1512427561. Doeden shares some of the most exciting moments in sports, from the most remarkable plays to the most heartbreaking mistakes.

Doll, Jen. *Unclaimed Baggage*. Macmillan/Farrar, Straus and Giroux Books for Young Readers. 2018. $17.99. ISBN: 978-0374306069. Doris, Nell, and Grant meet while working at Unclaimed Baggage, a quirky shop that sells long lost luggage and its contents. The friendship they form helps each face their problems, including long-distance love, grief, and alcohol abuse.

Flood, Joe. *Sharks: Nature's Perfect Hunter*. Macmillan/Roaring Brook Press/First Second Books. 2018. $12.99. ISBN: 978-1626727885. This entry in the Science Comics series illuminates everyone's favorite predator with explanations of the diverse types of sharks, their evolutionary history, their habitat, and their behavior.

Friend, Natasha. *How We Roll*. Macmillan/Farrar, Straus and Giroux Books for Young Readers. 2018. $17.99. ISBN: 978-0374305666. New girl in town Quinn has a condition called alopecia that makes her hair fall out. When she meets Nick, a former all-star football player who lost his legs in a snowboarding accident, they help each other find confidence again.

Gratz, Alan. *Grenade*. Scholastic Press. 2018. $17.99. ISBN: 978-1338245691. Fourteen-year-old Hideki is preparing to defend his home island of Okinawa during World War II. Ray is an eighteen-year-old U.S. Marine fighting his first battle. During the Battle of Okinawa, they will discover resilience and compassion as the horrors of war forever change their perspective on humanity.

*Greenwald, Tommy. *Game Changer*. ABRAMS/Amulet Books. 2018. $16.99. ISBN: 978-1419731433. Teddy Youngblood is one of the most talented incoming freshman football players on the team. After an incident at practice that lands Teddy in a coma, his family must fight to figure out what really happened.

Grimes, Nikki. *Between the Lines*. Penguin Random House/Nancy Paulsen Books. 2018. $17.99. ISBN: 978-0399246883. Aspiring reporter Darrian chronicles a semester writing and performing slam poetry in Mr. Ward's class. Each student in the class weaves their own unique story into their poems, learning to trust each other and the creative process along the way.

Hawkins, Rachel. *Royals*. Penguin Random House/G. P. Putnam's Sons. 2018. $17.99. ISBN: 978-1524738235. When her sister becomes engaged to a prince, Daisy is thrust into the spotlight and must learn to be proper, or at least not embarrass her new royal family, which is easier said than done with the prince's scandalous brother around.

Honeybourn, Jennifer. *When Life Gives You Demons*. Macmillan/Feiwel and Friends/Swoon Reads. 2018. $17.99. ISBN: 978-1250158239. Shelby Black just wants to pass geometry, and for her crush to notice her, but her side job as an exorcist-in-training keeps getting in the way. When demons flood her town, she must find a way to stop them.

Keplinger, Kody. *That's Not What Happened*. Scholastic Press. 2018. $18.99. ISBN: 978-1338186529. Leanne ("Lee") is one of a handful of students who survived a school shooting. When another victim's parents prepare to release a book with a false story, Lee has to decide whether to keep what she knows to herself or speak up.

Kim, Heather. *Sweet Revenge: Passive-Aggressive Desserts for Your Exes and Enemies*. Capstone/Switch Press. 2018. $19.95. ISBN: 978-1630790899. Kill your enemies with kindness by baking them desserts with names like "You're Such a Pizza Crap," "The Two of Us Are Toast," and "You're Driving Me Bananas" bacon and banana cupcakes.

Kirby, Jessi. *The Other Side of Lost*. HarperCollins/HarperTEEN. 2018. $17.99. ISBN: 978-0062424242. When her cousin Bri passes away unexpectedly, social media star Mari deletes her profiles and strikes out on the 211-mile hike of the John Muir Trail planned by Bri.

Koblish, Scott. *The Many Deaths of Scott Koblish*. Chronicle Books. 2018. $14.95. ISBN: 978-1452167121. Marvel illustrator Scott Koblish illustrates his own potential demise in a myriad of funny, irreverent, and yet often quite plausible ways as a mechanism for dealing with anxiety.

*Krosoczka, Jarrett. *Hey Kiddo: How I Lost My Mother, Found My Father, and Dealt with Family Addiction*. Scholastic Press/Graphix. 2018. $24.99. ISBN: 978-0545902472. Beloved graphic novel creator Jarrett Krosoczka tells the story of his childhood growing up with a mother addicted to heroin and how his grandparents' support of his passion for art helped him survive.

Mak, Ton. *A Sloth's Guide to Mindfulness*. Chronicle Books. 2018. $14.95. ISBN: 978-1452169460. A roly-poly sloth, beset with anxieties and doubts, walks readers through mindfulness and relaxation techniques.

Maldonado, Torrey. *Tight*. Penguin Random House/Nancy Paulsen Books. 2018. $16.99. ISBN: 978-1524740559. When Bryan's dad introduces him to a boy named Mike, the two bond over comics and superheroes, becoming as close as brothers. But this brotherhood becomes strained when Mike turns to more reckless activities and Bryan must decide whether or not to follow.

McAnulty, Stacy. *The Miscalculations of Lightning Girl*. Penguin Random House/Random House Books for Young Readers. 2018. $16.99. ISBN: 978-1524767570. Twelve-year-old Lucy has just finished her last online high school course after being struck by lightning leaves her with super-genius math skills. But before she officially graduates, her grandmother makes her pass one final test: attending middle school.

McGhee, Alison. *What I Leave Behind*. Simon & Schuster/Atheneum/Caitlin Dlouhy Books. 2018. $17.99. ISBN: 978-1481476560. Sixteen-year-old Will believes that what troubles you must leave you through the soles of your feet, so he walks. In 100 chapters, each 100 words, Will walks the streets of L.A. to cope with unfortunate tragedies haunting his world.

*McNeil, Gretchen. *#MurderTrending*. Disney Book Group/Freeform Books. 2018. $17.99. ISBN: 978-1368010023. In the near future, the prison system has been replaced with a reality TV show—Alcatraz 2.0—that features staged executions of convicted murderers. Dee Guerrera becomes a sensation by accidentally killing one of the executioners—but how long can she survive?

O'Doherty, Carolyn. *Rewind.* Highlights/Boyds Mills Press. 2018. $17.95. ISBN: 978-1629798141. Time spinners may be able to freeze and rewind time, but their own time is short—no time spinner lives past the age of 20. When Alex starts to get sick at just 16, she must decide just what she is willing to do to live a little longer.

Pacat, C. S. and Johanna the Mad (Illustrator) *Fence, vol. 1.* Boom Entertainment/BOOM! Box. 2018. $9.99. ISBN: 978-1684151745. Nicholas is determined to become a world-class fencer like his estranged father. When he starts at Kings Row Boys School, though, he suddenly finds himself in very close quarters with both his nemesis and his father's legitimate son.

Pak, Greg and Takeshi Miyazawa (Illustrator). *Mech Cadet Yu, vols. 1 and 2.* Boom Entertainment/BOOM! Studios. 2018. $14.99. ISBN: 978-1684151950 (vol. 1) and 978-1684152537 (vol. 2). In the near future, humans pair up with sentient robots to fight insectoid aliens. Stanford Yu is chosen by a mech to be its pilot, but in between training, hazing, and another invasion, it's a lot harder than it looks.

*Reynolds, Jason. *Track series (Sunny [vol. 3] and Lu [vol. 4]).* Simon & Schuster/Atheneum/Caitlin Dlouhy Books. 2018. $16.99. ISBN: 978-1481450218 (Sunny) and 978-1481450249 (Lu). Sunny considers himself a murderer, because his mother died giving birth to him. He has been running track to please his dad, but what he really wants is to dance. Coach has the perfect solution. "Lightning" Lu is heading into the track championships as co-captain of his team. When unexpected hurdles come up, he wonders if lightning can really strike twice.

Rhodes, Jewell Parker. *Ghost Boys.* Hachette/Little, Brown and Company. 2018. $16.99. ISBN: 978-0316262286. After a police officer shoots and kills 12-year-old Jerome, Jerome's ghost stays nearby and meets other ghost boys from the past, including Emmett Till.

*Saeed, Aisha. *Amal Unbound.* Penguin Random House/Nancy Paulsen Books. 2018. $17.99. ISBN: 978-0399544682. Amal's dream of becoming a teacher in her small Pakistani village vanishes when she is forced to become an indentured servant to the powerful Khan family to pay off her own family's debt.

Schwab, Victoria. *City of Ghosts.* Scholastic Press. 2018. $17.99. ISBN: 978-1338111002. Ever since she drowned, Cassidy has been able to see ghosts. When Cassidy and her paranormal-hunting parents take a trip to haunted Edinburgh, Scotland, she encounters a ghost who could put her life in danger.

Shen, Ann. *Legendary Ladies: 50 Goddesses to Empower and Inspire You.* Chronicle Books. 2018. $19.95. ISBN: 978-1452163413. Beautiful artwork and single-page descriptions illuminate fifty goddesses from religions around the world, both ancient and modern.

Shipley, Jocelyn. *Impossible.* Orca Book Publishers. 2018. $9.95. ISBN: 978-1459815568. When Jemma runs out to buy diapers, she witnesses a murder that could put both her and her baby girl's lives in danger.

Spalding, Amy. *The Summer of Jordi Perez.* Skyhorse Publishing/Sky Pony Press. 2018. $16.99. ISBN: 978-1510127663. Fashion blogger Abby wins a coveted internship at an L.A. boutique. She and fellow intern Jordi must compete for one paid position, but things get complicated when the two fall for each other.

*Stiefel, Chana. *Animal Zombies!: And Other Blood-Sucking Beasts, Creepy Creatures, and Real-Life Monsters.* National Geographic/NatGeo Kids. 2018. $14.99. ISBN: 978-1426331497. Eye-popping photographs amp up the creepy factor in this fact book of strange and dangerous animals.

*Summers, Courtney. *Sadie.* Macmillan/St. Martin's Press/Wednesday Books. 2018. $17.99. ISBN: 978-1250105714. After the brutal murder of her little sister Mattie, Sadie will stop at nothing to track down the man responsible and bring him to justice.

Ukazu, Ngozi. *Check Please! Book 1: #Hockey.* Macmillan/Roaring Brook Press/First Second. 2018. $23.99. ISBN: 978-1250177957. Eric Bittle vlogs his college days on the university's hockey team including living with straight men, baking epic pies, and crushing on his dreamy captain.

*Wang, Jen. *The Prince and the Dressmaker*. Macmillan/Roaring Brook Press/First Second. 2018. $24.99. ISBN: 978-1626723634. Frances, a talented young dressmaker, is given the chance to be the prince's personal seamstress. What she doesn't expect is what type of clothing Prince Sebastian will request.

Wilde, Jen. *The Brightsiders*. Macmillan/Feiwel and Friends/Swoon Reads. 2018. $16.99. ISBN: 978-1250189714. Emmy King is a bisexual teen rockstar drummer living the good life, until a wild night of partying goes too far. The paparazzi scandalizes Emmy and begins hounding her love life, but they will learn not to mess with the girl in the purple lipstick.

Amazing Audiobooks for Young Readers

Each year a committee of the Young Adult Library Services Association (YALSA), a division of the American Library Association, compiles a list of the best audiobooks for young adults ages 12 to 18. The titles are selected for their teen appeal and recording quality, and because they enhance the audience's appreciation of any written work on which the recordings may be based. While the list as a whole addresses the interests and needs of young adults, individual titles need not appeal to this entire age range but rather to parts of it. An asterisk denotes the title was selected as a top ten.

A Million Junes by Emily Henry, read by Julia Whelan (Listening Library).

Ball Don't Lie by Matt de la Peña, read by Dion Graham (Listening Library).

Benjamin Franklin You've Got Mail by Adam Mansbach and Alan Zweibel, read by Nick Podehl, Tom Parks, and Lauren Ezzo (Brilliance Audio).

Dear Martin by Nic Stone, read by Dion Graham (Listening Library).

Denton Little's Still Not Dead by Lance Rubin, read by Lance Rubin (Listening Library).

**Fantastic Beasts and Where to Find Them* by J. K. Rowling and Newt Scamander, read by Eddie Redmayne (Bloomsbury Children's).

**Flying Lessons and Other Stories*, edited by Ellen Oh, read by various authors (Listening Library).

Genuine Fraud by E. Lockhart, read by Rebecca Soler (Listening Library).

Girls Who Code by Reshma Saujani, read by Reshma Saujani (Listening Library).

Goodbye Days by Jeff Zentner, read by Michael Crouch (Listening Library).

Heartless by Marissa Meyer, read by Rebecca Soler (Macmillan Audio).

**Honor Girl* by Maggie Thrash, read by Ensemble Cast (Dreamscape Media).

Kill All Happies by Rachel Cohn, read by Lauren Ezzo (Dreamscape Media, LLC).

Long Way Down by Jason Reynolds, read by Jason Reynolds (Simon & Schuster Audio).

Once and For All by Sarah Dessen, read by Karissa Vacker (Listening Library).

Patina by Jason Reynolds, read by Heather Alicia Simms (Simon & Schuster Audio).

**Scythe* by Neal Shusterman, read by Greg Tremblay (Audible Studios).

See You In the Cosmos by Jack Cheng, read by Ensemble Cast (Listening Library).

Solo by Kwame Alexander with Mary Rand Hess, read by Kwame Alexander and Randy Preston (Blink YA Books).

Spellslinger by Sebastien de Castell, read by Joe Jameson (Bolinda Audio).

The Beast Is an Animal by Peternelle Van Arsdale, read by Candace Thaxton (Simon & Schuster Audio).

**The Gentleman's Guide to Vice and Virtue* by Mackenzi Lee, read by Christian Coulson (HarperAudio).

**The Hate U Give* by Angie Thomas, read by Bahni Turpin (HarperAudio).

**The Inexplicable Logic of My Life* by Benjamin Alire Sáenz, read by Robbie Daymond (Listening Library).

The Pearl Thief by Elizabeth Wein, read by Maggie Service (Bolinda Audio).

The Sun Is Also a Star by Nicola Yoon, read by Dominic Hoffman, Raymond Lee, and Bahni Turpin (Listening Library).

Turning 15 on the Road to Freedom: My Story of the 1965 Selma Voting Rights March by Lynda Blackmon Lowery, as told to Elspeth Leacock and Susan Buckley, read by Damaras Obi (Listening Library).

Turtles All the Way Down by John Green, read by Kate Rudd (Listening Library).

Undefeated by Steve Sheinkin, read by Mark Bramhill (Listening Library).

Who Killed Christopher Goodman? by Allan Wolf, read by Jesse Lee, Nick Podehl, Lauren Ezzo, Scott Merriman, Scott Lange, Kate Rudd, Will Damron, and Whitney Dykhouse (Candlewick on Brilliance Audio).

The Reading List

Established in 2007 by the Reference and User Services Association (RUSA), a division of the American Library Association, this list highlights outstanding genre fiction that merits special attention by general adult readers and the librarians who work with them.

RUSA's Reading List Council, which consists of 12 librarians who are experts in readers' advisory and collection development, selects books in eight categories: Adrenaline (suspense, thrillers, and action adventure), Fantasy, Historical Fiction, Horror, Mystery, Romance, Science Fiction, and Women's Fiction.

The RUSA website provides more detail on each of the winning titles along with lists of "Read Alikes" and runners-up.

Adrenaline

Safe Houses: A Novel by Dan Fesperman (Borzoi / Alfred A. Knopf, a division of Penguin Random House).

Fantasy

Foundryside: A Novel by Robert Jackson Bennett (Crown, an imprint of Penguin Random House).

Historical Fiction

Between Earth and Sky: A Novel by Amanda Skenandore (Kensington Books).

Horror

The Silent Companions: A Novel by Laura Purcell (Penguin Books, an imprint of Penguin Random House).

Mystery

The Widows of Malabar Hill by Sujata Massey (Soho Crime, an imprint of Soho Press).

Romance

Intercepted by Alexa Martin (Berkley/Jove, an imprint of Penguin Random House).

Science Fiction

The Calculating Stars by Mary Robinette Kowal (Tor, an imprint of Tom Doherty Associates / Macmillan).

Women's Fiction

Stray City: A Novel by Chelsey Johnson (Custom House, an imprint of William Morrow).

The Listen List

Established in 2010 by the Reference and User Services Association (RUSA), the annual Listen List highlights outstanding audiobooks that merit special attention by general adult listeners and the librarians who work with them. Titles are chosen by RUSA's Listen List Council, which annually selects about a dozen audiobooks that may include fiction, nonfiction, poetry, and plays. To be eligible, titles must be available for purchase and circulation by libraries. This year's list recognizes 13 outstanding recordings.

An annotated version of the list on the RUSA website includes more information on each choice and lists additional audiobooks of interest.

An Absolutely Remarkable Thing by Hank Green, narrated by Kristen Sieh and Hank Green (Penguin Audio/Books on Tape).

The Darkest Child by Delores Phillips, narrated by Bahni Turpin (Recorded Books/Griot Audio).

Dear America: Notes of an Undocumented Citizen by Jose Antonio Vargas, narrated by Jose Antonio Vargas (HarperCollins/HarperAudio).

Educated: A Memoir by Tara Westover, narrated by Julia Whelan (Random House Audio/Books on Tape).

A False Report: A True Story of Rape in America by T. Christian Miller and Ken Armstrong, narrated by Helen Huber, T. Christian Miller, and Ken Armstrong (Random House Audio/Books on Tape).

The Feather Thief: Beauty, Obsession, and the Natural History Heist of the Century by Kirk Wallace Johnson, narrated by MacLeod Andrews (Penguin Audio).

The House of Broken Angels by Luis Alberto Urrea, narrated by Luis Alberto Urrea (Hachette Audio/Blackstone Audio).

I Am, I Am, I Am: Seventeen Brushes with Death by Maggie O'Farrell, narrated by Daisy Donovan (Books on Tape).

The Last Black Unicorn by Tiffany Haddish, narrated by Tiffany Haddish (Simon & Schuster Audio).

The Monk of Mokha by Dave Eggers, narrated by Dion Graham (Random House Audio/Books on Tape).

The Secrets Between Us by Thrity Umrigar, narrated by Sneha Mathan (HarperAudio).

The Silence of the Girls by Pat Barker, narrated by Kristin Atherton and Michael Fox (Random House Audio).

The Trauma Cleaner: One Woman's Extraordinary Life in the Business of Death, Decay, and Disaster by Sarah Krasnostein, narrated by Rachel Tidd (Blackstone Audio).

The Alex Awards

The Alex Awards are given to ten books written for adults that have special appeal to young adults ages 12 through 18. The winning titles are selected by a committee of the Young Adult Library Services Association (YALSA), a division of the American Library Association, from among the previous year's publishing. The award is sponsored by the Margaret A. Edwards Trust.

The Black God's Drums by P. Djèlí Clark (Tor, an imprint of Tom Doherty Associates/Macmillan).

The Book of Essie by Meghan MacLean Weir (Alfred A. Knopf, a division of Penguin Random House).

Circe by Madeline Miller (Little, Brown and Company, a division of Hachette Book Group).

Educated: A Memoir by Tara Westover (Random House).

The Girl Who Smiled Beads: A Story of War and What Comes After by Clemantine Wamariya and Elizabeth Weil (Crown, an imprint of Penguin Random House).

Green by Sam Graham-Felsen (Random House).

Home After Dark by David Small, illustrated by the author (Liveright, an imprint of W.W. Norton & Company).

How Long 'Til Black Future Month? by N. K. Jemisin (Orbit, an imprint of Hachette Book Group).

Lawn Boy by Jonathan Evison (Algonquin Books of Chapel Hill, a division of Workman Publishing).

Spinning Silver by Naomi Novik (Del Rey, a division of Penguin Random House).

Outstanding International Books for Young Readers, 2018

The United States Board on Books for Young People (USBBY), the U.S. national section of the International Board on Books for Young People (IBBY), compiles an annual list of books that represent the best in international children's literature. Hundreds of titles originating outside the United States were considered for this year's list.

Grades Pre-K to 2

Buitrago, Jairo. *On the Other Side of the Garden*. Trans. By Elisa Amado. Illus. by Rafael Yockteng. Groundwood Books. Chile.

Chabbert, Ingrid. *A Drop of the Sea*. Trans. from French. Illus. by Guridi. Kids Can Press. France.

Clarke, Maxine Beneba. *Patchwork Bike*. Illus. by Van Thanh Rudd. Candlewick Press. Australia.

Crowther, Kitty. *Stories of the Night*. Trans. by Julia Marshall. Illus. by the author. Gecko Press. Sweden.

de Arias, Patricia. *Marwan's Journey*. Trans. from Spanish. Illus. by Laura Borràs. Minedition. Chile.

Dubuc, Marianne. *Up the Mountain Path*. Illus. by the author. Princeton Architectural Press. Canada.

Gomi, Taro. *I Really Want to See You, Grandma*. Trans. From Japanese. Illus. by the author. Chronicle Books. Japan.

Grant, Shauntay. *Africville*. Illus. by Eva Campbell. Groundwood Books. Canada.

Kaadan, Nadine. *Tomorrow*. Trans. and Illus. by the author. Lantana Publishing. Syria.

Latour, Francie. *Auntie Luce's Talking Paintings*. Illus. by Ken Daley. Groundwood Books. Canada / set in Haiti.

Nilsson, Ulf. *A Case for Buffy*. Trans. by Julia Marshall. Illus. by Gitte Spee. Gecko Press. Sweden.

Sanna, Francesca. *Me and My Fear*. Illus. by the author. Flying Eye Books. UK.

Soundar, Chitra. *Farmer Falgu Goes to the Market*. Illus. by Kanika Nair. Karadi Tales. India.

Grades 3–5

Blexbolex. *Vacation*. Illus. by the author. Enchanted Lion. France.

Duprat, Guillaume. *Eye Spy: Wild Ways Animals See the World*. Trans. by Patrick Skipworth. Illus. by the author. What On Earth Books. France.

Edwards, Nicola. *What a Wonderful Word*. Illus. by Luisa Uribe. Kane Miller. UK.

Gifford, Clive. *The Colors of History: How Colors Shaped the World*. Illus. by Marc-Etienne Peintre. Quarto Publishing. UK.

Green, Shari. *Missing Mike*. Pajama Press. Canada.

Ho, Van and Skrypuch, Marsha Forchuk. *Too Young to Escape*. Pajama Press. Canada / set in Vietnam.

Kacer, Kathy. *The Sound of Freedom*. Annick Press. Canada.

Kinew, Wab. *Go Show the World: A Celebration of Indigenous Heroes*. Illus. by Joe Morse. Tundra Books. Canada.

Lewis, Gill. *A Story Like the Wind*. Illus. by Jo Weaver. Eerdmans Publishing. UK.

Parr, Maria. *Astrid the Unstoppable*. Trans. by Guy Puzey. Illus. by Katie Harnett. Candlewick Press. Norway.

Walters, Eric. *From the Heart of Africa: A Book of Wisdom*. Illus. include original art from African countries. Tundra Books. Canada.

Widmark, Martin. *The House of Lost and Found*. Trans. by Polly Lawson. Illus. by Emilia Dziubak. Floris Books. Sweden.

Wilcox, Merrie-Ellen. *After Life: Ways We Think About Death*. Orca Book Publishers. Canada.

Winter, Ali. *Peace and Me*. Illus. by Mickaël El Fathi. Lantana Publishing. UK.

Grades 6–8

Bailey, Linda. *Mary Who Wrote Frankenstein*. Illus. by Júlia Sardà. Tundra Books. Canada.

Ellis, Sarah. *Dodger Boy*. Groundwood Books. Canada.

First News / Walker Books Ltd. *Voices from the Second World War: Stories of War as Told to Children of Today*. Candlewick Press. UK.

Hargrave, Kiran Millwood. *The Island at the End of Everything*. Alfred A. Knopf. UK / set in the Philippines.

Nielsen, Susin. *No Fixed Address*. Penguin Random House Canada Young Readers. Canada.

Orr, Wendy. *Swallow's Dance*. Pajama Press. Canada.

Smith, Heather. *Ebb & Flow. Kids Can Press*. Canada.

Tregonning, Mel. *Small Things*. Illus. by the author. Pajama Press. Australia.

Williamson, Victoria. *The Fox Girl and the White Gazelle*. Floris Books. Scotland.

Grades 9–12

Barter, Catherine. *Troublemakers*. Carolrhoda Books. UK.

Mills, Jean. *Skating Over Thin Ice*. Red Deer Press. Canada.

Ntshingila, Futhi. *We Kiss Them With Rain*. Catalyst Press. South Africa.

Notable Children's Books

A list of notable children's books is selected each year by the Notable Children's Books Committee of the Association for Library Service to Children (ALSC), a division of the American Library Association. Recommended titles are selected by children's librarians and educators based on originality, creativity, and suitability for children. [See "Literary Prizes, 2018" later in Part 5 for Caldecott, Newbery, and other award winners—*Ed.*]

Younger Readers

All-of-a-Kind Family Hanukkah by Emily Jenkins. Illus. by Paul O. Zelinsky. Random House / Schwartz & Wade.

Alma and How She Got Her Name by Juana Martinez-Neal. Illus. by the author. Candlewick.

Baby Monkey, Private Eye by Brian Selznick and David Serlin. Illus. by Brian Selznick. Scholastic.

A Big Mooncake for Little Star by Grace Lin. Illus. by the author. Little, Brown.

Black Bird Yellow Sun by Steve Light. Illus. by the author. Candlewick.

Blue by Laura Vaccaro Seeger. Illus. by the author. Roaring Brook / Neal Porter.

Bowwow Powwow / Bagosenjige-niimi'idim by Brenda J. Child. Illus. by Jonathan Thunder. Tr. by Gordon Jourdain. Minnesota Historical Society.

The Day You Begin by Jacqueline Woodson. Illus. by Rafael López. Penguin / Nancy Paulsen.

Don't Touch My Hair! by Sharee Miller. Illus. by the author. Little, Brown.

Drawn Together by Minh Lê. Illus. by Dan Santat. Disney/Hyperion.

Dreamers by Yuyi Morales. Illus. by the author. Holiday / Neal Porter.

The Fox on the Swing by Evelina Daciūtė. Illus. by Aušra Kiudulaitė. Tr. by the Translation Bureau. Thames & Hudson.

Fox the Tiger by Corey R. Tabor. Illus. by the author. HarperCollins / Balzer+Bray.

Good Rosie! by Kate DiCamillo. Illus. by Harry Bliss. Candlewick.

Hello Lighthouse by Sophie Blackall. Illus. by the author. Little, Brown.

How Raven Got His Crooked Nose: An Alaskan Dena' ina Fable by Barbara J. Atwater and Ethan J. Atwater. Illus. by Mindy Dwyer. Alaska Northwest.

I Walk with Vanessa: A Story about a Simple Act of Kindness by Kerascoët. Illus. by the authors. Random / Schwartz & Wade.

Imagine! by Raúl Colón. Illus. by the author. Simon & Schuster / Paula Wiseman.

In the Past: From Trilobites to Dinosaurs to Mammoths in More than 500 Million Years by David Elliott. Illus. by Matthew Trueman. Candlewick.

Islandborn by Junot Díaz. Illus. by Leo Espinosa. Dial.

Jerome By Heart by Thomas Scotto. Illus. by Olivier Tallec. Tr. by Claudia Zoe Bedrick and Karin Snelson. Enchanted Lion.

Julián Is a Mermaid by Jessica Love. Illus. by the author. Candlewick

King and Kayla and the Case of the Lost Tooth by Dori Hillestad Butler. Illus. by Nancy Meyers. Peachtree.

Lena's Shoes Are Nervous: A First-Day-of-School Dilemma by Keith Calabrese. Illus. by Juana Medina. Simon & Schuster / Atheneum.

Let the Children March by Monica Clark-Robinson. Illus. by Frank Morrison. HMH.

Mommy's Khimar by Jamilah Thompkins-Bigelow. Illus. by Ebony Glenn. Simon & Schuster / Salaam Reads.

My Beijing: Four Stories of Everyday Wonder by Nie Jun. Illus. by the author. Tr. by Edward Gauvin. Lerner / Graphic Universe.

Night Job by Karen Hesse. Illus. by G. Brian Karas. Candlewick.

A Parade of Elephants by Kevin Henkes. Illus. by the author. Greenwillow.

The Party and Other Stories by Sergio Ruzzier. Illus. by the author. Chronicle.

The Patchwork Bike by Maxine Beneba Clarke. Illus. by Van Thanh Rudd. Candlewick.

The Rough Patch by Brian Lies. Illus. by the author. Greenwillow.
Saturday Is Swimming Day by Hyewon Yum. Illus. by the author. Candlewick.
See Pip Flap by David Milgrim. Illus. by the author. Simon & Schuster/Simon Spotlight.
Thank You, Omu! by Oge Mora. Illus. by the author. Little, Brown.
The Wall in the Middle of the Book by Jon Agee. Illus. by the author. Dial.
You and Me by Rebecca Kai Dotlich. Illus. by Susan Reagan. Creative Editions.

Middle Readers

Ana María Reyes Does NOT Live in a Castle by Hilda Eunice Burgos. Lee & Low/Tu.
All that Trash: The Story of the 1987 Garbage Barge and Our Problem with Stuff by Meghan McCarthy. Illus. by the author. Simon & Schuster/Paula Wiseman.
Aru Shah and the End of Time by Roshani Chokshi. Disney/Hyperion.
The Assassination of Brangwain Spurge by M.T. Anderson and Eugene Yelchin. Illus. by Eugene Yelchin. Candlewick.
Beavers by Rachel Poliquin. Illus. by Nicholas John Frith. HMH.
Between the Lines: How Ernie Barnes Went from the Football Field to the Art Gallery by Sandra Neil Wallace. Illus. by Bryan Collier. Simon & Schuster/Paula Wiseman.
The Book of Boy by Catherine Gilbert Murdock. Greenwillow.
The Brilliant Deep: Rebuilding the World's Coral Reefs by Kate Messner. Illus. by Matthew Forsythe. Chronicle.
Camp Panda: Helping Cubs Return to the Wild by Catherine Thimmesh. HMH.
Can I Touch Your Hair? Poems of Race, Mistakes, and Friendship by Irene Latham and Charles Waters. Illus. by Sean Qualls and Selina Alko. Carolrhoda.
Dragons in a Bag by Zetta Elliott. Illus. by Geneva B. Random.
Edison: The Mystery of the Missing Mouse Treasure by Torben Kuhlmann. Illus. by the author. Tr. by David Henry Wilson. NorthSouth.
The Eye that Never Sleeps: How Detective Pinkerton Saved President Lincoln by Marissa Moss. Illus. by Jeremy Holmes. Abrams.
Finding Langston by Lesa Cline-Ransome. Holiday.
Front Desk by Kelly Yang. Scholastic/Arthur A. Levine.
Game Changers: The Story of Venus and Serena Williams by Lesa Cline-Ransome. Illus. by James Ransome. Simon & Schuster/Paula Wiseman.
Hammering for Freedom by Rita Lorraine Hubbard. Illus. by John Holyfield. Lee & Low.
Knights vs. Dinosaurs by Matt Phelan. Illus. by the author. Greenwillow.
Louisiana's Way Home by Kate DiCamillo. Candlewick.
Marcus Vega Doesn't Speak Spanish by Pablo Cartaya. Viking.
Martin Rising: Requiem for a King by Andrea Davis Pinkney. Illus. by Brian Pinkney. Scholastic.
Memphis, Martin, and the Mountaintop: The Sanitation Strike of 1968 by Alice Faye Duncan. Illus. by R. Gregory Christie. Boyds Mills/Calkins Creek.
Merci Suárez Changes Gears by Meg Medina. Candlewick.
No Small Potatoes: Junius G. Groves and His Kingdom in Kansas by Tonya Bolden. Illus. by Don Tate. Knopf.
Pass Go and Collect $200: The Real Story of How Monopoly Was Invented by Tanya Lee Stone. Illus. by Steven Salerno. Holt/Christy Ottaviano.
Otis and Will Discover the Deep: The Record-Setting Dive of the Bathysphere by Barb Rosenstock. Illus. by Katherine Roy. Little, Brown.
The Parker Inheritance by Varian Johnson. Scholastic/Arthur A. Levine.
Saving Winslow by Sharon Creech. HarperCollins/Joanna Cotler.
The Season of Styx Malone by Kekla Magoon. Random/Wendy Lamb.
So Tall Within: Sojourner Truth's Long Walk toward Freedom by Gary D. Schmidt. Illus. by Daniel Minter. Roaring Brook.
Stella Díaz Has Something to Say by Angela Dominguez. Roaring Brook.
Tiger vs. Nightmare by Emily Tetri. Illus. by the author. First Second.

Thirty Minutes over Oregon: A Japanese Pilot's World War II Story by Marc Tyler Nobleman. Illus. by Melissa Iwai. Clarion.

The Truth as Told by Mason Buttle by Leslie Connor. HarperCollins / Katherine Tegen.

The United States v. Jackie Robinson by Sudipta Bardhan-Quallen. Illus. by R. Gregory Christie. HarperCollins / Balzer+Bray.

What Do You Do with a Voice Like That? The Story of Extraordinary Congresswoman Barbara Jordan by Chris Barton. Illus. by Ekua Holmes. Simon & Schuster / Beach Lane.

When Angels Sing: The Story of Rock Legend Carlos Santana by Michael Mahin. Illus. by Jose Ramirez. Atheneum.

Older Readers

Amal Unbound by Aisha Saeed. Penguin / Nancy Paulsen.

Apollo 8: The Mission that Changed Everything by Martin W. Sandler. Illus. Candlewick.

Attucks! Oscar Robertson and the Basketball Team that Awakened a City by Phillip Hoose. Illus. Farrar.

Be Prepared by Vera Brosgol. Illus. by Vera Brosgol and Alec Longstreth. First Second.

Boots on the Ground: America's War in Vietnam by Elizabeth Partridge. Illus. Viking.

Children of Blood and Bone by Tomi Adeyemi. Holt.

Crash: The Great Depression and the Fall and Rise of America by Marc Favreau. Little, Brown.

The Cruel Prince by Holly Black. Little, Brown.

Ghost Boys by Jewell Parker Rhodes. Little, Brown.

The Girl Who Drew Butterflies: How Maria Merian's Art Changed Science by Joyce Sidman. Illus. HMH.

Harbor Me by Jacqueline Woodson. Penguin / Nancy Paulsen.

Hey, Kiddo: How I Lost My Mother, Found My Father, and Dealt with Family Addiction by Jarrett J. Krosoczka. Illus. by the author. Scholastic / Graphix.

Hurricane Child by Kheryn Callender. Scholastic.

The Hyena Scientist by Sy Montgomery. Illus. by Nic Bishop. HMH.

Illegal by Eoin Colfer and Andrew Donkin. Illus. by Giovanni Rigano. Sourcebooks / Jabberwocky.

Ivy Aberdeen's Letter to the World by Ashley Herring Blake. Little, Brown.

Jazz Owls: A Novel of the Zoot Suit Riots by Margarita Engle. Illus. by Rudy Gutierrez. Atheneum.

Lifeboat 12 by Susan Hood. Simon & Schuster.

The Mad Wolf's Daughter by Diane Magras. Penguin / Kathy Dawson.

March Forward, Girl: From Young Warrior to Little Rock Nine by Melba Pattillo Beals. Illus. by Frank Morrison. HMH.

The Night Diary by Veera Hiranandani. Penguin / Kokila (originally Dial).

Nowhere Boy by Katherine Marsh. Roaring Brook.

The Poet X by Elizabeth Acevedo. HarperTeen.

The Prince and the Dressmaker by Jen Wang. Illus. by the author. First Second.

Rebound by Kwame Alexander. Illus. by Dawud Anyabwile. HMH.

Run for Your Life by Silvana Gandolfi. Tr. by Lynne Sharon Schwartz. Yonder / Restless.

Small Spaces by Katherine Arden. Putnam.

Spooked! How a Radio Broadcast and The War of the Worlds *Sparked the 1938 Invasion of America* by Gail Jarrow. Illus. Boyds Mills / Calkins Creek.

Something Rotten: A Fresh Look at Roadkill by Heather L. Montgomery. Illus. by Kevin O'Malley. Bloomsbury.

Streetcar to Justice: How Elizabeth Jennings Won the Right to Ride in New York by Amy Hill Hearth. Greenwillow.

They Call Me Güero: A Border Kid's Poems by David Bowles. Cinco Puntos.

Tight by Torrey Maldonado. Penguin / Nancy Paulsen.

The Unwanted: Stories of the Syrian Refugees by Don Brown. Illus. by the author. HMH.

All Ages

Imagine by Juan Felipe Herrera. Illus. by Lauren Castillo. Candlewick.

We Are Grateful: Otsaliheliga by Traci Sorell. Illus. by Frané Lessac. Charlesbridge.

Notable Recordings for Children

This annual listing of notable recordings for children available on compact disc (CD) or for digital download (DL) is produced by the Association for Library Service to Children (ALSC), a division of the American Library Association. Recommended titles are chosen by children's librarians and educators on the basis of their originality, creativity, and suitability.

Back to the Land. Hot Peas 'N Butter Records, CD. Gr. PreS+. Packed with energy, this family-friendly recording features a clear, full sound of rousing, folksy songs with environmental messages. Performed by Hot Peas 'N Butter.

Beanstalk Jack. Paper Canoe Co., CD. Gr. K+. Journey into a musical fractured fairy tale of Jack and the Beanstalk with clever lyrics, exuberant musical arrangements, and expert production quality. Performed by an ensemble cast.

Before She Was Harriet by Lesa Cline-Ransome. Live Oak Media. CD and book. Gr. K–3. With a musical score and sound effects carefully tailored to each beautiful spread of the picture book, Sisi Aisha Johnson, January LaVoy, Lisa Renee Pitts, and Bahni Turpin take turns painting scenes from Harriet Tubman's life with their passionate, engaging reading.

Children of Blood and Bone by Tomi Adeyemi. Macmillan Audio. DL. Gr. 7+. Bahni Turpin's powerful narration, voiced through three distinct perspectives, weaves a story of grit and determination in the face of persecution in this epic fantasy.

The Christmasaurus by Tom Fletcher. Listening Library. CD. Gr. 1–4. Paul Shelley's whimsical narration delights with a tale of a dinosaur, a young boy in a wheelchair, and the magic of Christmas.

Du Iz Tak? by Carson Ellis. Weston Woods. CD and book. Gr. PreS–2. With a multigenerational ensemble cast, sound effects, and an expressive musical accompaniment, this simple-text picture book explores the wonders of imagination and creativity in nature. (2019 Odyssey Honor Audiobook.)

Esquivel! Space-Age Sound Artist by Susan Wood. Live Oak Media. CD and book. Gr. K–5. The roo-roo, bzzz, and zowww of instruments jump off the page as Brian Amador's lyrical narration creates a story in stereo-sound about Esquivel's innovative and creative musical career. (2019 Odyssey Honor Audiobook.)

Falu's Bazaar. Falu Music Publishing. CD. Gr. PreS+. A spicy trilingual (English, Hindi, and Gujrati) journey to South Asia features original children's songs with a variety of traditional Indian, Bollywood, and pop instrumentation. Performed by Falu.

For Every One by Jason Reynolds. Simon & Schuster Audio. DL. Gr. 6+. Reynolds performs the speech he wrote prior to his success as a writer, emotionally conveying the shared journey, struggles, and dreams of those who have faced harsh realities.

The Griffin's Feather: Dragon Rider #2 by Cornelia Funke. Atmende Bücher. DL. Gr. 3–6. A fantastical soundscape layered with Marc Thompson and Cornelia Funke's theatrical narration brings listeners along on this epic adventure to save the last Pegasus.

The Journey of Little Charlie by Christopher Paul Curtis. Listening Library. CD. Gr. 5+. Talented storyteller Michael Crouch portrays the tensions of the Pre–Civil War North and South through a wide variety of character voices and tones.

Keep it Real. Aurora Elephant Music. DL. Gr. PreS+. Caspar Babypants entertains listeners of all ages with clever toe-tapping tunes of original songs mixed with remakes, performed in a variety of musical styles.

Lu by Jason Reynolds. Simon & Schuster Audio. DL. Gr. 5+. Guy Lockard brings Lu's competitive nature, attitude, and ego off the page through quick wit, expert pacing, and engaging interpretations of the friends and adults in Lu's life.

Marcus Vega Doesn't Speak Spanish by Pablo Cartaya. Listening Library. CD. Gr. 4+. Seamlessly shifting between Spanish and English, Cartaya reads his own novel about entrepreneurial Marcus Vega searching for his father in his homeland of Puerto Rico with emotion and understanding.

Monstrous Devices by Damien Love. Listening Library. CD. Gr. 4–7. With great aplomb and distinct accents, Allan Corduner throws listeners, along with the main character Alex, into a world in which robots are alive, ancient magical powers can come to life, and Alex's grandfather eats too many sweets.

Nanette's Baguette by Mo Willems. Weston Woods. CD and book. Gr. PreS–2. Trixie Willems, along with Mo and Cher Willems, exuberantly perform the rhyming trials and tribulations of Nanette trying to get a baguette home to her mother.

Nate Expectations by Tim Federle. Simon & Schuster Audio. DL. Gr. 5+. Federle's narration of his own character's return to his small town nails the deadpan humor and sarcasm of Nate's first-person voice.

The Night Diary by Veera Hiranandani. Listening Library. CD. Gr. 4+. Priya Ayyar lends her voice talent to Nisha and other characters in this moving story of a young girl's search for home, identity, and a hopeful future in a tumultuous partitioning of India.

On Bird Hill by Jane Yolen. Live Oak Media. CD and book. Gr. PreS–1. Yolen's narration conveys a sense of exploration, while gentle music and sound effects add to the feeling of wonder in her sparse picture book.

The Parker Inheritance by Varian Johnson. Scholastic Audiobooks. Gr. 3–7. In pursuit of the mysterious Parker inheritance, author Varian Johnson takes readers down a trail of clues spanning three generations of fear and discrimination in the American South. Narrator Cherise Boothe evokes an appropriate sense of time and place with her compelling cast of characters and authentic range of emotions. (2019 Odyssey Honor Audiobook.)

The Poet X by Elizabeth Acevedo. Harper Audio. DL. Gr. 7+. Acevedo performs her original slam poetry novel with expert pacing, nuanced emotion, and a natural blend of English and Spanish to share Xiomara's struggle to discover her place in the world. (2019 Odyssey Honor Audiobook.)

Quidditch Through the Ages by J. K. Rowling. Bloomsbury. CD. Gr. 2+. With timely sound effects and Andrew Lincoln's variety of accents and light tone, even non–Harry Potter fans will be drawn into this humorous "textbook" about a fictional sport.

Rebound by Kwame Alexander. Recorded Books. CD. Gr. 4–8. With rhythmic narration, Ron Butler relates Charlie's emotional journey from sullen to happy as he processes his father's death with help from his grandparents and basketball.

Spin: The Rumpelstiltskin Musical by Neil Fishman and Harvey Edelman. Harper Audio. CD. Gr. 1+. This delightful written-for-audio children's musical combines Jim Dale's grandfatherly narration and a full cast of singing performers to draw the listener into a witty reimagining of the Rumpelstiltskin fairy tale. Read by Jim Dale and an ensemble cast.

Sunny by Jason Reynolds. Simon & Schuster. DL. Gr. 5+. Through deft use of pacing and tone, Guy Lockard captures Sunny's frenetic energy and wika-wika wordplay.

They All Saw a Cat by Brendan Wenzel. Weston Woods. CD and book. Gr. PreS–1. John Lithgow's gentle propulsive narration and a distinct musical accompaniment ferret out the major characteristics of each animal encountered by a cat as it strolls and surveys the world.

Tight by Torrey Maldonado. Listening Library. CD. Gr. 5+. Maldonado's dynamic Brooklyn accent perfectly suits his story of Bryan, as he struggles with finding the right friends, set against the backdrop of the city streets and projects.

We Found a Hat by Jon Klassen. Weston Woods. CD and book. Gr. PreS–2. Ambient sounds and gently strummed guitar music pull listeners into the dry, western, desert setting, while Johnny Heller and Christopher Curry voice two old tortoise friends.

Whichwood by Tahereh Mafi. Listening Library. CD. Gr. 5+. Bronson Pinchot's wry and familiar narration breaks the fourth wall, bringing readers into this darkly humorous fantasy about a young, overworked Mordeshoor, caretaker of the dead.

The Wild Robot Escapes by Peter Brown. Hachette Audio. DL. Gr. 2–7. A plethora of sound effects and Kathleen McInerney's "mechanical" narration set the scene for Roz the robot's episodic odyssey to find her son, Brightbill.

Notable Children's Digital Media

The Association for Library Service to Children (ALSC), a division of the American Library Association, produces this annual list covering a diverse array of digital media for children up to age 14. The Notable Children's Digital Media list recognizes real-time, dynamic, and interactive media content that enables and encourages active engagement and social interaction while informing, educating, and entertaining in exemplary ways.

Artie's Magic Pencil. iOS/Android. PreK. Children join Artie on an interactive and creative drawing adventure as they learn how shapes can combine in a variety of ways to form objects. Downloadable worksheets for continued learning off-screen are also included.

Be Internet Awesome. Internet-based. Elementary, Middle School. Explore the Interland, featuring four challenging games that teach kids the fundamentals of digital safety and citizenship: Be Internet Smart, Be Internet Alert, Be Internet Strong, Be Internet Kind, and Be Internet Brave. Also features educational resources for educators and parents regarding digital safety and citizenship for kids.

Coral Reef. iOS. PreK, Elementary. Part of Tinybop's Explorer's Library series, *Coral Reef* encourages children to learn about marine life and explore the reef ecosystem.

Ed and the Curious Crew at The Royal Children's Hospital. iOS/Android. Elementary, Middle School. Designed by the Royal Children's Hospital in Melbourne, Australia, this app uses videos and games to give kids a behind-the-scenes tour of the hospital and lets kids explore the hospital's different departments and careers.

Hopscotch. iOS. Elementary, Middle School. *Hopscotch* is a visual coding language that allows kids to create their own games and apps via drag and drop. Video tutorials and lesson plans for educators are also available.

Inventioneers. iOS/Android/Amazon/Windows. Elementary, Middle School. Explore physics concepts in a fun, game-based environment. Complete levels to earn additional objects to use in building your own invention.

Khan Academy Kids. iOS. PreK. Whimsical characters guide early learners through a multitude of interactive songs, videos, and activities in the areas of literacy, language, math, and logic. Caregivers can also track their child's progress through a report card feature.

Lexi's World. iOS. PreK, Elementary. This app introduces letters, spelling, typing, and animals to kids. Children discover new words as they interact with *Lexi's World*.

Living Paintings: Thyssen-Bornemisza Museum. iOS/Android. Elementary. Learn about the Thyssen-Bornemisza Museum's most famous works of art through interactive games. Young artists can also upload or create their own masterpieces in the art studio using 20 different colors and four artistic mediums.

Moshi Twilight Sleep Stories. iOS/Android/Amazon. PreK/Parent/Caregiver. Relax into bedtime with calming stories, specifically created to help children drift off to sleep with soothing music, audio effects, and narration.

Nighty Night. iOS. PreK. A calming bedtime app, *Nighty Night* allows children to interact with the short story by turning off lights and putting animals to bed, accompanied by music and narration.

Peek-a-Zoo. iOS. PreK. *Peek-a-Zoo* is a simple-to-use app game that teaches children to recognize emotions and interpret facial expressions by having them answer questions about animated animals.

Play and Learn Science. iOS/Android. PreK, Elementary. With 12 interactive games that can be played in English or Spanish, *Play and Learn Science* by PBS Kids encourages children and caregivers to explore basic earth science, physical science, and life science topics together.

Queer Kid Stuff. Internet-based. PreK, Elementary. Lindsay and co-host Teddy educate children on a variety of LGBTQ+ topics in an entertaining way in this Web series. Printable activity sheets are also included.

RelationShapes. iOS/Android. PreK. Develop visual-spatial reasoning by playing with different shapes and then making meaning out of them using fun stickers and backgrounds.

Space Science Investigations: Plant Growth. iOS. Elementary, Middle School. Designed by NASA, this educational game explores life on the International Space Station and allows users to conduct scientific experiment games revolving around growing plants in space. Features additional information regarding actual plant life experiments in space, as well as an educator's guide.

Top Ten Bestselling Books of 2018

Sources included in this roundup are *Publishers Weekly*, *USA Today*, Barnes and Noble, Amazon, and Goodreads for print books; and Amazon and Apple for digital titles. Library-centric lists include the top adult print book checkouts reported by two major U.S. public library systems—New York Public Library and San Diego County Library—and the top ten most popular library e-books as reported by OverDrive. [Due to varying list selection criteria among the sources, apples-to-apples comparisons are not practicable—*Ed.*]

Print Bestsellers

Publishers Weekly

1. *Becoming.* Michelle Obama.
2. *Magnolia Table: A Collection of Recipes for Gathering*. Joanna Gaines.
3. *Girl, Wash Your Face: Stop Believing the Lies About Who You Are So You Can Become Who You Were Meant to Be.* Rachel Hollis.
4. *Diary of a Wimpy Kid: The Meltdown.* Jeff Kinney.
5. *Fire and Fury: Inside the Trump White House.* Michael Wolff.
6. *The Wonky Donkey.* Craig Smith; art by Katz Cowley.
7. *Fear: Trump in the White House.* Bob Woodward.
8. *Dog Man and Cat Kid.* Day Pilkey.
9. *You Are A Badass: How to Stop Doubting Your Greatness and Start Living an Awesome Life.* Jen Sincero.
10. *The President Is Missing*. James Patterson and Bill Clinton.

USA Today

1. *Becoming.* Michelle Obama.
2. *Fire and Fury: Inside the Trump White House.* Michael Wolff.
3. *Girl, Wash Your Face: Stop Believing the Lies About Who You Are So You Can Become Who You Were Meant to Be.* Rachel Hollis.
4. *Fear: Trump in the White House.* Bob Woodward.
5. *Magnolia Table: A Collection of Recipes for Gathering.* Joanna Gaines.
6. *Diary of a Wimpy Kid: The Meltdown.* Jeff Kinney.
7. *The Wonky Donkey.* Craig Smith; art by Katz Cowley.
8. *The President Is Missing.* James Patterson and Bill Clinton.
9. *A Wrinkle in Time.* Madeleine L'Engle.
10. *12 Rules for Life: An Antidote to Chaos.* Jordan B. Peterson.

Barnes & Noble

1. *Becoming.* Michelle Obama.
2. *Fear: Trump in the White House.* Bob Woodward.
3. *Fire and Fury: Inside the Trump White House.* Michael Wolff.
4. *The Subtle Art of Not Giving a F*ck: A Counterintuitive Approach to Living a Good Life.* Mark Manson.
5. *The President Is Missing.* James Patterson and Bill Clinton.
6. *Girl, Wash Your Face: Stop Believing the Lies About Who You Are So You Can Become Who You Were Meant to Be.* Rachel Hollis.
7. *12 Rules for Life: An Antidote to Chaos.* Jordan B. Peterson.
8. *The Reckoning.* John Grisham.
9. *A Higher Loyalty: Truth, Lies, and Leadership.* James Comey.
10. *The Woman in the Window.* A. J. Finn.

Amazon

1. *Becoming.* Michelle Obama.
2. *Girl, Wash Your Face: Stop Believing the Lies About Who You Are So You Can*

Become Who You Were Meant to Be. Rachel Hollis.
3. *The Wonky Donkey*. Craig Smith; art by Katz Cowley.
4. *Fire and Fury: Inside the Trump White House*. Michael Wolff.
5. *Fear: Trump in the White House*. Bob Woodward.
6. *Last Week Tonight with John Oliver Presents A Day in the Life of Marlon Bundo*. Jill Twiss.
7. *12 Rules for Life: An Antidote to Chaos.* Jordan B. Peterson.
8. *Magnolia Table: A Collection of Recipes for Gathering*. Joanna Gaines.
9. *Whose Boat Is This Boat? Comments That Don't Help in the Aftermath of a Hurricane.* The Staff of the Tonight Show with Stephen Colbert.
10. *The Subtle Art of Not Giving a F*ck: A Counterintuitive Approach to Living a Good Life.* Mark Manson.

Goodreads Most Popular Books Added by Readers

1. *Educated: A Memoir.* Tara Westover.
2. *The Woman in the Window.* A. J. Finn.
3. *Becoming*. Michelle Obama.
4. *The Great Alone.* Kristin Hannah.
5. *Where the Crawdads Sing.* Delia Owens.
6. *An American Marriage*. Tayari Jones.
7. *The Tattooist of Auschwitz*. Heather Morris.
8. *Nine Perfect Strangers*. Liane Moriarty.
9. *The Outsider*. Stephen King.
10. *Still Me*. Jojo Moyes.

Digital Bestsellers

Amazon Kindle Editions

1. *The Handmaid's Tale.* Margaret Atwood.
2. *A Killer's Mind.* Mike Omer.
3. *The 7 Habit of Highly Effective People.* Stephen R. Covey.
4. *Harry Potter and the Sorcerer's Stone.* J. K. Rowling.
5. *Say You're Sorry.* Melinda Leigh.
6. *Beneath a Scarlet Sky.* Mark Sullivan.
7. *Whisper Me This.* Kerry Anne King.
8. *Fire and Fury: Inside the Trump White House*. Michael Wolff.
9. *The Storyteller's Secret*. Sejal Badani.
10. *The King Tides*. James Swain.

Apple Books*

Fiction

1. *The Woman in the Window.* A. J. Finn.
2. *Crazy Rich Asians.* Kevin Kwan.
3. *Little Fires Everywhere.* Celeste Ng.
4. *The Great Alone*. Kristin Hannah.
5. *The Wife Between Us*. Greer Hendricks and Sarah Pekkanen.
6. *The Fallen*. David Baldacci.
7. *The President Is Missing*. James Patterson and Bill Clinton.
8. *Origin*. Dan Brown.
9. *Before We Were Yours*. Lisa Wingate.
10. *Sharp Objects*. Gillian Flynn.

Nonfiction

1. *Fire and Fury: Inside the Trump White House.* Michael Wolff.
2. *Fear: Trump in the White House*. Bob Woodward.
3. *Girl, Wash Your Face: Stop Believing the Lies About Who You Are So You Can Become Who You Were Meant to Be.* Rachel Hollis.
4. *The Subtle Art of Not Giving a F*ck: A Counterintuitive Approach to Living a Good Life.* Mark Manson.
5. *Educated, A Memoir.* Tara Westover.
6. *Becoming*. Michelle Obama.
7. *A Higher Loyalty: Truth, Lies, and Leadership*. James Comey.
8. *12 Rules for Life: An Antidote for Chaos*. Jordan B. Peterson.
9. *The 5 Love Languages: The Secret to Love That Lasts*. Gary Chapman.
10. *You Are A Badass: How to Stop Doubting Your Greatness and Start Living an Awesome Life.* Jen Sincero.

* Apple does not currently publish a combined list of bestselling fiction and nonfiction titles in the Apple Books (formerly iBooks) format.

Top Print and Digital Titles from the Library*

New York Public Library Print Checkouts System-wide

1. *Manhattan Beach.* Jennifer Egan.
2. *Origin*. Dan Brown.
3. *The Handmaid's Tale.* Margaret Atwood.
4. *Sing, Unburied, Sing*. Jesmyn Ward.
5. *Fire and Fury: Inside the Trump White House.* Michael Wolff.
6. *Little Fires Everywhere.* Celeste Ng.
7. *A Gentleman in Moscow*. Amor Towles.
8. *Hillbilly Elegy: A Memoir of a Family and Culture in Crisis*. J. D. Vance.
9. *The Underground Railroad.* Colson Whitehead.
10. *Exit West*. Mohsin Hamid.

San Diego County Library Print Checkouts System-wide / Print

1. *Two Kinds of Truth*. Michael Connelly.
2. *The Rooster Bar*. John Grisham.
3. *The Late Show*. Michael Connelly.
4. *Camino Island*. John Grisham.
5. *The Midnight Line*. Lee Child.
6. *The Woman in the Window*. A. J. Finn.
7. *The Great Alone*. Kristin Hannah.
8. *Y Is for Yesterday*. Sue Grafton.
9. *End Game*. David Baldacci.
10. *Little Fires Everywhere.* Celeste Ng.

OverDrive's Most Popular Library Ebooks

1. *Little Fires Everywhere.* Celeste Ng.
2. *The Great Alone*. Kristin Hannah.
3. *The Woman in the Window.* A. J. Finn.
4. *Before We Were Yours*. Lisa Wingate.
5. *Crazy Rich Asians.* Kevin Kwan.
6. *Origin*. Dan Brown.
7. *Educated, A Memoir.* Tara Westover.
8. *The Handmaid's Tale.* Margaret Atwood.
9. *The Rooster Bar*. John Grisham.
10. *Fire and Fury: Inside the Trump White House.* Michael Wolff.

* Lists include adult fiction and nonfiction checkouts only.

Literary Prizes, 2018

Compiled by the staff of *Library and Book Trade Almanac*

Academy of American Poets Fellowship ($25,000). For outstanding poetic achievement. *Offered by:* Academy of American Poets. *Winner:* Martin Espada.

Jane Addams Children's Book Awards. For children's books that effectively promote the cause of peace, social justice, world community, and equality. *Offered by:* Jane Addams Peace Association. *Winners:* (younger children) Malala Yousafzai for *Malala's Magic Pencil,* illustrated by Kerascoet (Little, Brown Books for Young Readers); (older children) Sara Holbrook for *The Enemy: Detroit, 1954* (Calkins Creek, an imprint of Boyds Mills Press).

Aesop Prize. For outstanding illustrated children's publications utilizing folkloric themes. *Offered by:* American Folklore Society. *Winner:* Jaime Hernandez for *The Dragon Slayer: Folktales from Latin America* (Toon Books).

Agatha Awards. For mystery writing in the method exemplified by author Agatha Christie. *Offered by:* Malice Domestic Ltd. *Winners:* (contemporary novel) Louise Penny for *Glass Houses: A Chief Inspector Gamache Novel* (Minotaur Books); (first novel) Kellye Garrett for *Hollywood Homicide: A Detective by Day Mystery* (Midnight Ink); (historical) Rhys Bowen for *In Farleigh Field* (Lake Union Publishing); (children's/YA) Cindy Callaghan for *Sydney Mackenzie Knocks 'Em Dead* (Aladdin); (nonfiction) Mattias Boström for *From Holmes to Sherlock: The Story of the Men and Women Who Created an Icon* (Mysterious Press); (short story) Gigi Pandian for "The Library Ghost of Tanglewood Inn" (Henery Press).

American Academy of Arts and Letters Award of Merit ($25,000). Given annually, in rotation, for the short story, sculpture, novel, poetry, drama, and painting. *Offered by:* American Academy of Arts and Letters. *Winner:* Marina Adams (painting).

American Academy of Arts and Letters Awards in Literature ($10,000 each). To honor eight writers for exceptional accomplishment in any genre. *Offered by:* American Academy of Arts and Letters. *Winners:* Clare Cavanagh, Mary Gaitskill, Ishion Hutchinson, Marlon James, Kay Redfield Jamison, Rick Moody, Mary Robison, Brenda Shaughnessy.

American Academy of Arts and Letters Blake-Dodd Prize ($25,000). Triennial prize to a nonfiction writer. *Offered by:* American Academy of Arts and Letters. *Winner (2017):* Elizabeth Kolbert.

American Academy of Arts and Letters Benjamin H. Danks Award ($20,000). Triennial prize to an exceptional young writer. *Offered by:* American Academy of Arts and Letters. *Winner (2017):* Jamaal May.

American Academy of Arts and Letters E. M. Forster Award ($20,000). To a young writer from the United Kingdom or Ireland for a stay in the United States. *Offered by:* American Academy of Arts and Letters. *Winner:* Jon McGregor.

American Academy of Arts and Letters Sue Kaufman Prize for First Fiction ($5,000). For a work of first fiction (novel or short stories). *Offered by:* American Academy of Arts and Letters. *Winner:* Emily Fridlund for *History of Wolves* (Atlantic Monthly Press).

American Academy of Arts and Letters Addison M. Metcalf Award ($10,000). To a young writer of fiction, nonfiction, drama, or poetry. *Offered by:* American Academy of Arts and Letters. *Winner (2017):* Safiya Sinclair.

American Academy of Arts and Letters Arthur Rense Poetry Prize ($20,000). Triennial prize to an exceptional poet. *Offered by:* American Academy of Arts and Letters. *Winner (2017):* August Kleinzahler.

American Academy of Arts and Letters Rosenthal Family Foundation Award ($10,000). To a young writer of considerable literary talent for a work of fiction. *Offered by:* American Academy of Arts and Letters. *Winner:* Hannah Lillith Assadi for *Sonora* (Soho Press).

American Academy of Arts and Letters John Updike Award ($10,000). Biennial prize to a writer in mid-career whose work has demonstrated consistent excellence. *Offered by:* American Academy of Arts and Letters. *Winner (2017):* Dana Spiotta.

American Academy of Arts and Letters Harold D. Vursell Memorial Award ($20,000). To a writer whose work merits recognition for the quality of its prose style. *Offered by:* American Academy of Arts and Letters. *Winner:* Atticus Lish.

American Academy of Arts and Letters E. B. White Award ($10,000). To a writer for achievement in children's literature. *Offered by:* American Academy of Arts and Letters. *Winner:* Not awarded in 2018.

American Book Awards. For literary achievement by people of various ethnic backgrounds. *Offered by:* Before Columbus Foundation. *Winners:* Thi Bui, *The Best That We Could Do: An Illustrated Memoir* (Harry N. Abrams); Rachelle Cruz, *God's Will for Monsters* (Inlandia Books); Tommy Curry, *The Man-Not: Race, Class, Genre, and the Dilemmas of Black Manhood* (Temple University Press); Tongo Eisen-Martin, *Heaven Is All Goodbyes* (City Lights); Dana Naone Hall, *Life of the Land: Articulations of a Native Writer* ('Ai Pohaku Press); Kelly Lytle Hernández, *City of Inmates: Conquest, Rebellion, and the Rise of Human Caging in Los Angeles, 1771–1965* (University of North Carolina); Victor LaValle, *The Changeling: A Novel* (Spiegel & Grau); Bojan Louis, *Currents* (BkMk Press at the University of Missouri–Kansas City); Valeria Luiselli, *Tell Me How It Ends: An Essay in Forty Questions* (Coffee House); Cathryn Josefina Merla-Watson and B. V. Olguín, *Altermundos Latin@ Speculative Literature, Film, and Popular Culture* (UCLA Chicano Studies Research Center Press); Tiya Miles, *The Dawn of Detroit: A Chronicle of Slavery and Freedom in the City of the Straits* (The New Press); Tommy Pico, *Nature Poem* (Tin House Books); Rena Priest, *Patriarchy Blues* (MoonPath Press); Joseph Rios, *Shadowboxing: poems & impersonations* (Omnidawn); Sunaura Taylor, *Beasts of Burden: Animal and Disability Liberation* (The New Press); (anticensorship award) Rob Rogers; (editor and publisher award) Charles F. Harris; (lifetime achievement) Sequoyah Guess; (oral literature award) *Heroes Are Gang Leaders*.

American Indian Youth Literature Awards. Offered biennially to recognize excellence in books by and about American Indians. *Offered by:* American Indian Library Association. *Winners (2018):* (picture book) Michaela Goade, illustrator, Johnny Marks, Hans Chester, David Katzeek, Nora Dauenhauer, and Richard Dauenhauer (editors) for *Shanyaak'utlaax: Salmon Boy* (Sealaska Heritage Institute); (middle school) Arigon Starr (editor) featuring the work of Theo Tso, Jonathan Nelson, Kristina Bad Hand, Roy Boney, Jr., Lee Francis IV, Johnnie Diacon, Weshoyot Alvitre, Renee Nejo, and Michael Sheyahshe for *Tales of the Mighty Code Talkers, Volume 1* (Native Realities); (young adult) Lisa Charleyboy and Mary Beth Leatherdale (editors) for *#Not Your Princess: Voices of Native American Women* (Annick Press).

American Poetry Review / Honickman First Book Prize in Poetry ($3,000 and publication of the book). To encourage excellence in poetry and to provide a wide readership for a deserving first book of poems. *Winner:* Jacob Saenz for *Throwing the Crown* (American Poetry Review).

Américas Book Award for Children's and Young Adult Literature. To recognize U.S. works of fiction, poetry, folklore, or selected nonfiction that authentically and engagingly portray Latin America, the Caribbean, or Latinos in the United States. *Sponsor:* Consortium of Latin American Studies Programs (CLASP). *Winners:* Ibi Zoboi for *American Street* (HarperCollins Publishers); Duncan Tonatiuh for *Danza!: Amalia Hernández and el Ballet Folklórico de México* (Abrams Books).

Rudolfo and Patricia Anaya Lecture on the Literature of the Southwest. To honor a Chicano or Chicana fiction writer. *Offered by:* National Hispanic Cultural Center, University of New Mexico. *Winner:* Hector Armienta.

Hans Christian Andersen Literature Award (500,000 Danish kroner, about $90,000). Biennial prize to a writer whose work can be compared with that of Andersen. *Offered by:* Hans Christian Andersen Literary Committee. *Winner (2018):* A. S. Bayatt.

Anthony Awards. For superior mystery writing. *Offered by:* Boucheron World Mystery Convention. *Winners:* Attica Locke for *Bluebird, Bluebird* (Mulholland); (first novel) Kellye Garrett for *Hollywood Homicide* (Midnight Ink); (paperback original) Lori Rader-Day for *The Day I Died* (William Morrow); (Bill Crider Award for novel in a series) Sue Grafton for *Y is for Yesterday* (Kinsey Millhone #25) (A Marian Wood Book); (short story) Hilary Davidson for "My Side of the Matter" from *Killing Malmon* (Down & Out Books); (anthology) Gary Phillips (editor) for *The Obama Inheritance: Fifteen Stories of Conspiracy Noir* (Three Rooms Press); David Grann for *Killers of the Flower Moon: The Osage Murders and the Birth of the FBI* (Doubleday); (online content) Jungle Red Writers.

Asian/Pacific American Awards for Literature. For books that promote Asian/Pacific American culture and heritage. *Sponsor:* Asian/Pacific American Librarians Association (APALA). *Winners:* (adult fiction) Lisa Ko for *The Leavers* (Algonquin Books of Chapel Hill); (adult nonfiction) Eleanor Ty for *Asianfail: Narratives of Disenchantment and the Model Minority* (University of Illinois Press); (young adult) Misa Sugiura for *It's Not Like It's a Secret* (HarperTeen); (children's) Uma Krishnaswami for *Step Up to the Plate, Maria Singh* (Tu Books); (picture book) Bao Phi for *A Different Pond* (Capstone Young Readers).

Audio Publishers Association Awards (Audies). To recognize excellence in audiobooks. *Winners:* (audiobook of the year) *Lincoln in the Bardo* by George Saunders, read by Nick Offerman, David Sedaris, George Saunders, and a full cast; (drama) *Brother Francis: The Barefoot Saint of Assisi* by Paul McCusker, read by over 30 actors including Joseph Timms, Owen Teale, and Geoffrey Palmer; (autobiography/memoir) *Born to Run*, written and read by Bruce Springsteen; (best female narrator) *The Hate U Give* by Angie Thomas, read by Bahni Turpin; (best male narrator) *Born a Crime: Stories from a South African Childhood*, written and read by Trevor Noah; (business/personal development) *Peak Performance* by Brad Stullberg and Steve Magness, read by Christopher Lane; (erotica) *Claim & Protect* by Rhenna Morgan, read by John Lane; (excellence in design) *In Death Limited Collector's Edition* by J. D. Robb, design by Carissa Dreese; (excellence in marketing) *Transform Your Commute Campaign* by Penguin Random House Audio; (excellence in production) *Sherlock Holmes* by Arthur Conan Doyle and Stephen Fry, read by Stephen Fry; (fantasy) *The Strange Case of the Alchemist's Daughter* by Theodora Goss, read by Kate Reading; (fiction) *Eleanor Oliphant Is Completely Fine* by Gail Honeyman, read by Cathleen McCarron; (history/biography) *Loving Vs. Virginia* by Patricia Hruby Powell, read by Adenrele Ojo and MacLeod Andrews; (humor) *Carpet Diem: Or . . . How to Save the World by Accident* by Justin Lee Anderson, read by Matthew Lloyd Davies; (inspirational/faith-based fiction) *Catching the Wind* by Melanie Dobson, read by Nancy Peterson; (inspirational/faith-based nonfiction) *Fire Road: The Napalm Girl's Journey through the Horrors of War to Faith, Forgiveness, and Peace* by Kim Phuc Phan Thi, read by Emily Woo Zeller; (literary fiction and classics) *House of Names* by Colm Toibin, read by Juliet Stevenson, et al.; (middle grade) *See You in the Cosmos* by Jack Cheng, read by Kivlighan de Montebello, Brittany Pressley, Michael Crouch, and a full cast; (multi-voiced performance) *Restart* by Gordon Korman, read by Jonathan Todd Ross, Laura Knight Keating, Ramon de Ocampo, Andy Paris, Suzy Jackson, Graham Halstead, and John Kroft; (mystery) *The Girl Who Takes an Eye for an Eye* by David Lagercrantz, read by Simon Vance; (narration by the author) *Norse Mythology*, written and read by Neil Gaiman; (nonfiction) *American Wolf: A True Story of Survival and Obsession in the West* by Nate Blakeslee, read by Mark Bramhall; (original work) *Romeo and Juliet: A Novel* by David Hewson, read by Richard Armitage; (paranormal) *Curse on the Land: Soulwood, Book 2* by Faith Hunter, read by Khristine Hvam; (romance) *The Duchess Deal* by Tessa Dare, read by Mary Jane Wells; (science fiction) *Provenance* by Ann Leckie, read by Adjoa Andoh; (short stories/collections) *The Language of Thorns: Midnight Tales and Dangerous Magic* by Leigh Bardugo, read by Lauren Fortgang; (thriller/

suspense) *The Fourth Monkey* by J. D. Barker, read by Edoardo Ballerini and Graham Winton; (young adult) *The Hate U Give* by Angie Thomas, read by Bahni Turpin; (young listeners up to age eight) *Trombone Shorty* by Troy "Trombone Shorty" Andrews, read by Dion Graham.

Bad Sex in Fiction Award (United Kingdom). To "draw attention to the crude, badly written, often perfunctory use of redundant passages of sexual description in the modern novel, and to discourage it." *Sponsor: Literary Review. Winner:* James Frey for *Katerina* (Gallery / Scout Press).

Baileys Women's Prize for Fiction (United Kingdom) (formerly the Orange Prize for Fiction) (£30,000). For the best novel written by a woman and published in the United Kingdom. *Winner:* Kamila Shamsie for *Home Fire* (Riverhead Books).

Bancroft Prizes ($10,000). For books of exceptional merit and distinction in American history, American diplomacy, and the international relations of the United States. *Offered by:* Columbia University. *Winners:* Waldo Heinrichs and Marc Gallicchio for *Implacable Foes: War in the Pacific, 1944–1945* (Oxford University Press); Louis S. Warren for *God's Red Son: The Ghost Dance Religion and the Making of Modern America* (Basic Books); Douglas L. Winiarski for *Darkness Falls on the Land of Light: Experiencing Religious Awakenings in Eighteenth-Century New England* (University of North Carolina Press for the Omohundro Institute of Early American History and Culture).

Barnes & Noble Discover Great New Writers Awards. To honor a first novel and a first work of nonfiction by American authors. *Offered by:* Barnes & Noble. *Winners:* (fiction) Paul Howarth for Only Killers and Thieves (HarperCollins); (nonfiction) Kiese Laymon for Scribner).

Mildred L. Batchelder Award. To the American publisher of a children's book originally published in a language other than English and subsequently published in English in the United States. *Offered by:* American Library Association, Association for Library Service to Children. *Winner:* Delacorte Press / Random House Children's / Penguin Random House, for *The Murderer's Ape*, written and illustrated by Jakob Wegelius, translated from the Swedish by Peter Graves.

BBC National Short Story Award (United Kingdom) (£15,000). *Winner:* Ingrid Persaud for "The Sweet Sop."

Pura Belpré Awards. To a Latino/Latina writer and illustrator whose work portrays, affirms, and celebrates the Latino cultural experience in an outstanding work of literature for children and youth. *Offered by:* American Library Association, Association for Library Service to Children. *Winners:* (narrative) Ruth Behar for *Lucky Broken Girl* (Nancy Paulsen / Penguin Random House); (illustration) Juana Martinez-Neal for *La Princesa and the Pea*, written by Susan Middleton Elya (G. P. Putnam's Sons / Penguin Random House).

Helen B. Bernstein Book Award for Excellence in Journalism ($15,000). To a journalist who has written at book length about an issue of contemporary concern. *Offered by:* New York Public Library. *Winner:* Masha Gessen for *The Future Is History: How Totalitarianism Reclaimed Russia* (Riverhead Books).

Black Caucus of the American Library Association (BCALA) Literary Awards. *Winners:* (fiction) Roxane Gay for *Difficult Women* (Grove/Atlantic); (nonfiction) Lawrence P. Jackson for *Chester B. Himes: A Biography* (W. W. Norton & Company); (first novelist award, to acknowledge outstanding achievement in writing and storytelling by a first-time fiction writer) Margaret Wilkerson Sexton for *A Kind of Freedom* (Counterpoint Press); (poetry) Patricia Smith for *Incendiary Art* (Northwestern University Press); (outstanding contribution to publishing citation) Henry Louis Gates, Jr. for *100 Amazing Facts About the Negro* (Knopf Doubleday).

Irma Simonton Black and James H. Black Award for Excellence in Children's Literature. To a book for young children in which the text and illustrations work together to create an outstanding whole. *Offered by:* Bank Street College of Education. *Winner:* Tara Lazar (writer) and Ross MacDonald (illustrator) for *7 Ate 9: The Untold Story* (Disney Hyperion).

James Tait Black Memorial Prize (United Kingdom) (£10,000). To recognize literary excellence in fiction and biography. *Offered by:* University of Edinburgh. *Winners:* (fiction) Eley Williams for *Attrib. and Other Stories* (Influx Press); (biography) Craig Brown for *Ma'am Darling: 99 Glimpses of Princess Margaret* (4th Estate).

James Tait Black Prize for Drama (United Kingdom) (£10,000). *Offered by:* University of Edinburgh in partnership with the National Theatre of Scotland and in association with the Traverse Theatre. *Winner:* Tanika Gupta for *Lions and Tigers.*

Blue Peter Book of the Year (United Kingdom). To recognize excellence in children's books. Winners are chosen by a jury of viewers, ages 8–12, of the BBC television children's program *Blue Peter. Winners:* (best story) Cressida Cowell for *The Wizards of Once* (Hodder Children's Books); (best book with facts) Susan Martineau, for *Real-Life Mysteries*, illustrated by Vicky Barker (B Small Publishing Limited).

Bookseller/Diagram Prize for Oddest Title of the Year. *Sponsor: The Bookseller* magazine. *Winner:* Thomas Götz von Aust for *The Joy of Waterboiling* (Achse Verlag).

Boston Globe/Horn Book Awards. For excellence in children's literature. *Winners:* (fiction and poetry) Elizabeth Acevedo for *The Poet X* (Harper Teen); (nonfiction) Isabel Quintero for *Photographic: The Life of Graciela Iturbide,* illustrated by Zeke Peña (Getty); (picture book) Jillian Tamaki for *They Say Blue* (Abrams).

W. Y. Boyd Literary Award for Excellence in Military Fiction ($5,000). For a military novel that honors the service of American veterans during a time of war. *Offered by:* American Library Association. *Donor:* W. Y. Boyd II. *Winner:* Jeff Shaara for *Frozen Hours: A Novel of Korean War* (Ballantine Books).

Branford Boase Award (United Kingdom). To the author and editor of an outstanding novel for young readers by a first-time writer. *Winners:* Mitch Johnson (author) and Rebecca Hill and Becky Walter (editors) for *Kick* (Usborne).

Bridport International Creative Writing Prizes (United Kingdom). For poetry and short stories. *Offered by:* Bridport Arts Centre. *Winners:* (poetry, £5,000) John Freeman for "Exhibition"; (short story, £5,000) V. Sanjay Kumar for "The Fore Caddy"; (flash fiction, 250-word maximum, £1,000) Tim Craig for "The Grand Finale"; (Peggy Chapman-Andrews Award for a First Novel) Megan Davis for *The Messenger*.

British Book Awards (aka the Nibbies) (United Kingdom). *Offered by: The Bookseller. Winners:* (book of the year) Gail Honeyman for *Eleanor Oliphant Is Completely Fine* (Harper); (fiction) Jon McGregor for *Reservoir 13* (Fourth Estate); (debut) Gail Honeyman for *Eleanor Oliphant Is Completely Fine* (Harper); (crime/thriller) Jane Harper for *The Dry* (Abacus); (children's) (tie) Robert Macfarlane and Jackie Morris for *The Lost Words* (Hamish Hamilton); Angie Thomas for *The Hate U Give* (Walker); (nonfiction) Reni Eddo-Lodge for *Why I'm No Longer Talking to White People about Race* (Bloomsbury); (lifestyle) Jamie Oliver for *5 Ingredients* (Michael Joseph); (audio) Penguin Random House UK Audio for *La Belle Sauvage* by Philip Pullman, narrated by Michael Sheen.

British Fantasy Awards. *Offered by:* British Fantasy Society. *Winners:* (Karl Edward Wagner Award) N. K. Jemisin; (newcomer) Jeanette Ng for *Under the Pendulum Sun* (Angry Robot); (magazine/periodical) *Shoreline of Infinity*, edited by Noel Chidwick; (nonfiction) FT Barbini (editor) for *Gender Identity and Sexuality in Science Fiction and Fantasy* (Luna Press); (comic/graphic novel) Marjorie Liu and Sana Takeda for *Monstress, Vol. 2* (Image Comics); (independent press) Unsung Stories; (artist) Jeffrey Alan Love; (anthology) *New Fears*, edited by Mark Morris (Titan Books); (collection) Joe Hill for *Strange Weather* (Gollancz); (film/television production) *Get Out*, written and directed by Jordan Peele (Universal Pictures); (audio) *Anansi Boys* by Neil Gaiman, adapted by Dirk Maggs (BBC Radio 4); (novella) Ellen Klages for *Passing Strange* (Tor.com); (short fiction) Laura Mauro for "Looking for Laika" in *Interzone* #273; (horror) Victor LaValle for *The Changeling* by (Spiegel & Grau); (fantasy) Jen Williams for *The Ninth Rain* (Headline).

Sophie Brody Medal. For the U.S. author of the most distinguished contribution to Jewish literature for adults, published in the preceding year. *Donors:* Sophie and Arthur Brody Foundation. *Offered by:* American Library Association, Reference and User Services

Association. *Winner:* Ilana Kurshan for *If All the Seas Were Ink: A Memoir* (St. Martin's Press).

Witter Bynner Poetry Fellowships ($10,000). To encourage poets and poetry. *Sponsor:* Witter Bynner Foundation for Poetry. *Winner:* Not awarded in 2018.

Caine Prize for African Writing (£10,000). For a short story by an African writer, published in English. *Winner:* Makena Onjerika for "Fanta Blackcurrant" in *Wasafiri*.

Randolph Caldecott Medal. For the artist of the most distinguished picture book. *Offered by:* American Library Association, Association for Library Service to Children. *Winner:* Matthew Cordell for *Wolf in the Snow* (Feiwel & Friends / Macmillan).

California Book Awards. To California residents to honor books of fiction, nonfiction, and poetry published in the previous year. *Offered by:* Commonwealth Club of California. *Winners:* (fiction) Josh Weil for *The Age of Perpetual Light* (Grove Atlantic); (first fiction) Rachel Khong for *Goodbye, Vitamin* (Henry Holt & Company); (nonfiction) Richard Rothstein for *The Color of Law: A Forgotten History of How Our Government Segregated America* (W. W. Norton & Company); (poetry) Tongo Eisen-Martin for *Heaven Is All Goodbyes* (City Lights Books); (juvenile) Susan Goldman Rubin for *Maya Lin: Thinking with Her Hands* (Chronicle Books); (young adult) Dashka Slater for *The 57 Bus: A True Story of Two Teenagers and the Crime That Changed Their Lives* (Farrar, Straus and Giroux); (contribution to publishing) Obi Kauffman for *The California Field Atlas* (Heyday Books); (Californiana) Robert Aquinas McNally for *The Modoc War* (Bison Books / University of Nebraska Press).

John W. Campbell Award. For the best new science fiction or fantasy writer whose first work of science fiction or fantasy was published in a professional publication in the previous two years. *Offered by:* Dell Magazines. *Winner:* Rebecca Roanhorse for "Welcome to Your Authentic Indian Experience™" (in *Apex Magazine, August 2017*).

John W. Campbell Memorial Award. For science fiction writing. *Offered by:* Gunn Center for the Study of Science Fiction. *Winner:* David Walton for *The Genius Plague* (Pyr).

Andrew Carnegie Medal for Excellence in Fiction and Nonfiction. For adult books published during the previous year in the United States. *Sponsors:* Carnegie Corporation of New York, ALA/RUSA, and *Booklist*. *Winners:* (fiction) Jennifer Egan for *Manhattan Beach* (Scribner); (nonfiction) Not awarded in 2018.

Carnegie Medal (United Kingdom). See CILIP Carnegie Medal.

Center for Fiction First Novel Prize ($10,000). *Offered by:* Center for Fiction, Mercantile Library of New York. *Winner:* Tommy Orange for *There There* (Alfred A. Knopf).

Chicago Folklore Prize. For the year's best folklore book. *Offered by:* American Folklore Society. *Winner:* Jeanne Pitre Soileau for *Yo' Mama, Mary Mack, and Boudreaux and Thibodeaux: Louisiana Children's Folklore and Play* (University Press of Mississippi).

Chicago Tribune Nelson Algren Short Story Award ($3,500). For unpublished short fiction. *Offered by: Chicago Tribune. Winner:* Dustin Hyman for "Church of Pit."

Chicago Tribune Heartland Prize for Fiction ($7,500). *Offered by: Chicago Tribune. Winner:* George Saunders for *Lincoln in the Bardo* (Bloomsbury).

Chicago Tribune Heartland Prize for Nonfiction ($7,500). *Offered by: Chicago Tribune. Winner:* Caroline Fraser for *Prairie Fires: The American Dreams of Laura Ingalls Wilder* (Metropolitan Books).

Chicago Tribune Literary Award. To recognize lifetime achievement of a prominent writer, usually someone with strong connections to the Midwest. *Winner:* Ron Chernow.

Chicago Tribune Young Adult Literary Prize. To recognize a distinguished literary career. *Winner:* David Levithan.

Children's Africana Book Awards. To recognize and encourage excellence in children's books about Africa. *Offered by:* Africa Access, African Studies Association. *Winners:* (young readers) *Baby Goes to Market* by Atinuke, illustrated by Angela Brooksbank (Candlewick); *Mama Africa!* by Kathryn Erskin, illustrated by Charly Palmer (Farrar, Straus and Giroux); *Grandma's List* by Portia Dery, illustrated by Toby Newsome (African Bureau Stories); (older readers) Arushi Raina for *When Morning Comes*

(Tradewinds); (new adult) Imbolo Mbue for *Behold the Dreamers* (Random House).

Children's Literature Legacy Award (formerly the Laura Ingalls Wilder Award). Awarded to an author or illustrator whose books have made a substantial and lasting contribution to children's literature. *Offered by:* American Library Association, Association for Library Service to Children. *Winner:* Jacqueline Woodson.

Cholmondeley Awards for Poets (United Kingdom) (£1,500). For a poet's body of work and contribution to poetry. *Winners:* Vahni Capildeo, Kate Clanchy, Linton Kwesi Johnson, Daljit Nagra, Zoë Skoulding.

CILIP Carnegie Medal (United Kingdom). For the outstanding children's book of the year. *Offered by:* CILIP: The Chartered Institute of Library and Information Professionals (formerly the Library Association). *Winner:* Geraldine McCaughrean for *Where the World Ends* (Usborne).

CILIP Kate Greenaway Medal and Colin Mears Award (United Kingdom) (£5,000 plus £500 worth of books donated to a library of the winner's choice). For children's book illustration. *Offered by:* CILIP: The Chartered Institute of Library and Information Professionals. *Winner:* Sydney Smith for *Town Is by the Sea by Joanne Schwartz* (Walker Books).

Arthur C. Clarke Award. For the best science fiction novel published in the United Kingdom. *Offered by:* British Science Fiction Association. *Winner:* Anne Charnock for *Dreams Before the Start of Time* (47North).

David Cohen Prize for Literature (United Kingdom) (£40,000). Awarded biennially to a living British writer, novelist, poet, essayist, or dramatist in recognition of an entire body of work written in the English language. *Offered by:* David Cohen Family Charitable Trust. *Winner (2017):* Tom Stoppard.

Matt Cohen Award: In Celebration of a Writing Life (C$20,000). To a Canadian author whose life has been dedicated to writing as a primary pursuit, for a body of work. *Offered by:* Writers' Trust of Canada. *Sponsors:* Marla and David Lehberg. *Winner:* David Bergen.

Commonwealth Short Story Prize (United Kingdom) (£5,000). To reward and encourage new short fiction by Commonwealth writers. *Offered by:* Commonwealth Institute. *Winners:* (regional winner, Africa) Efua Traore (Nigeria) for "True Happiness"; (regional winner, Canada and Europe) Lynda Clark (United Kingdom) for "Ghillie's Mum"; (regional winner, Asia) Sagnik Datta (India) for "The Divine Pregnancy of a Twelve-Year-Old Girl"; (regional winner, Caribbean, and overall winner) Kevin Jared Hosein (Trinidad and Tobago) for "Passage"; (regional winner, Pacific) Jenny Bennett-Tuionetoa (Samoa) for "Matalasi."

Costa Book Awards (United Kingdom) (£5,000 plus an additional £25,000 for Book of the Year). For literature of merit that is readable on a wide scale. *Offered by:* Booksellers Association of Great Britain and Costa Coffee. *Winners:* (biography) Bart van Es for *The Cut Out Girl: A Story of War and Family, Lost and Found* (Penguin); (novel) Sally Rooney for *Normal People* (Hogarth); (first novel) Stuart Turton for *The Seven Deaths of Evelyn Hardcastle* (Raven/Bloomsbury); (children's) Hilary McKay for *The Skylarks' War* (Macmillan Children's Books); (poetry) J.O. Morgan for *Assurances* (Penguin).

Costa Short Story Award (United Kingdom). *Winners:* (first place, £3,500) Caroline Ward Vine for "Breathing Water."

Crab Orchard Review Literary Prizes ($2,000 and publication in *Crab Orchard Review*). *Winners:* (Jack Dyer Fiction Prize) May-lee Chai for "Fish Boy"; (John Guyon Literary Nonfiction Prize) Kerry Neville for "Teaching the N-Word"; (Richard Peterson Poetry Prize) Esther Lin for "Cholera Is What My Grandfather Did During the War."

Crime Writers' Association (CWA) Dagger Awards (United Kingdom). *Winners:* (diamond dagger, for significant contribution to crime writing) Michael Connelly; (gold dagger, for best novel) Steve Cavanagh for *The Liar*; (gold dagger, for nonfiction) Thomas Harding for *Blood on the Page*; (Ian Fleming steel dagger, for best thriller) Attica Locke for *Bluebird, Bluebird*; (John Creasey dagger, for best debut crime novel) Melissa Scrivner Love for *Lola*; (CWA historical dagger, for the best historical crime novel) Rory Clements for *Nucleus*; (CWA short story dagger) Denise Mina for "Nemo Me Impune Lacessit" in *Bloody Scotland*; (international dagger, for a work translated into English) Henning Mankell for *After the Fire*; (CWA Dagger in the Library, for a body of work) Martin Edwards; (debut dagger, for a previously unpublished crime writer) Bill Crotty for *The Eternal Life of Ezra Ben Simeon*.

Benjamin H. Danks Award ($20,000). To a promising young writer, playwright, or composer, in alternate years. *Offered by:* American Academy of Arts and Letters. *Winner (2017):* Jamaal May.

Dartmouth Medal. For creating current reference works of outstanding quality and significance. *Donor:* Dartmouth College. *Offered by:* American Library Association, Reference and User Services Division. *Winner:* Theodore Levin, Saida Daukeyeva, and Elmira Köchümkulova for *The Music of Central Asia* (Indiana University Press).

Derringer Awards. To recognize excellence in short crime and mystery fiction. *Sponsor:* Short Mystery Fiction Society. *Winners:* (flash story, up to 1,000 words) Earl Staggs for "Fishing for an Alibi" in *Flash Bang Mysteries*; (short story, 1,001–4,000 words) Robert Lopresti for "The Cop Who Liked Gilbert and Sullivan" in *Sherlock Holmes Mystery Magazine*; (long story, 4,001–8,000 words) David H. Hendrickson for "Death in the Serengeti" in *Fiction River: Pulse Pounders: Andrenaline*; (novelette, 8,001–20,000 words) Brendan DuBois for "Flowing Waters" in *Ellery Queen's Mystery Magazine*; (Edward D. Hoch Memorial Golden Derringer for Lifetime Achievement) John M. Floyd.

Diagram Prize for Oddest Title of the Year. See Bookseller/Diagram Prize for Oddest Title of the Year.

Philip K. Dick Award. For a distinguished science fiction paperback published in the United States. *Sponsor:* Philadelphia Science Fiction Society and the Philip K. Dick Trust. *Winner:* Carrie Vaughn for *Bannerless* (Mariner Books / Houghton Mifflin Harcourt).

Digital Book Awards. To recognize high-quality digital content available to readers as e-books and enhanced digital books. *Sponsor:* Digital Book World. *Winners:* (publisher of the year) Dark Horse; (trade publisher of the year) Macmillan; (children's publisher of the year) Disney Publishing; (educational publisher of the year) A Book Apart; (corporate publisher of the year) NASA; (academic/scholarly publisher of the year) Princeton University Press; (religious publisher of the year) Kube Publishing and LifeWay (tie); (independent publisher of the year) Milkweed Editions; (publishing executive of the year) Jeff Bezos, Amazon and Dominique Raccah, Sourcebooks (tie); (publishing entrepreneur of the year) Matt and Melissa Hammersley, Novel Effect; (publishing commentator of the year) Joanna Penn; (DBW Medal for Leadership in Diversity) Morgan Jerkins; (innovation in accessibility) Amazon Alexa; (best mobile application) Novel Effect; (best Alexa skill: publishing + storytelling) *Short Bedtime Story*, Webguild; (best Google action: publishing + storytelling) *Storycastle*; (best use of blockchain in publishing technology) *Publica*; (best use of AR/VR in publishing) *Devar*; (best use of AR/VR in storytelling) *Supersaurs*; (best marketing campaign) *The President Is Missing*; (best book cover art) *Destruction of Man*; (best use of multimedia in book marketing) *Autonomous Driving: How the Driverless Revolution Will Change the World*; (best use of podcasting in book marketing) Macmillan; (best use of social media in book marketing) *7th Grade Revolution*; (best use of voice assistants in book marketing) Simon & Schuster for Stephen King Library skill; (best use of data in publishing) Biblio/Virtusales; (best agency representation in publishing) Susan Rabiner Literary Agency; (best overall book) *Galdo's Gift: The Boovie*; (best fiction) *Galdo's Gift: The Boovie*; (best nonfiction) *This Will Be My Undoing: Living at the Intersection of Black, Female, and Feminist in (White) America*; (best anthology) *High Growth Handbook*; (best architecture book) *Naturally Animated Architecture*; (best audiobook) *What Happened*; (best business book) *Hit Refresh*; (best children's book) *Galdo's Gift: The Boovie*; (best economics book) *Broken Pie Chart: Five Ways to Build Your Investment Portfolio to Withstand and Prosper in Risky Markets*; (best book of essays) *Feel Free: Essays*; (best fine arts book) *Why Bach? An Audio-Visual Appreciation*; (best health / medical science) *Family Nurse Practitioner Certification Intensive Review, Third*

Edition: Fast Facts and Practice Questions; (best horror book) *Gilchrist: A Novel*; (best how-to book) *Final Cut Pro X 10.4—How It Works*; (best inspirational book) *Grace for the Unexpected Journey*; (best interactive fiction book) *Galdo's Gift: The Boovie*; (best mathematics/science book) *The Book of Why: The New Science of Cause and Effect*; (best poetry book) *The Carrying*; (best political book) *Fire and Fury: Inside the Trump White House*; (best religious book) *Longing For Motherhood*; (best science fiction book) *Artificial Condition*; (best short story collection) *The Love That Dare Not Speak Its Name: Short Stories*; (best social issues book) *This Will Be My Undoing: Living at the Intersection of Black, Female, and Feminist in (White) America*; (best technology book) *Autonomous Driving: How the Driverless Revolution Will Change the World*; (best textbook) *CollegeScope*.

DSC Prize for South Asian Literature ($50,000). To recognize outstanding literature from or about the South Asian region and raise awareness of South Asian culture around the world. *Sponsor:* DSC Limited. *Winner:* Jayant Kaikini for *No Presents Please, translated by* Tejaswini Niranjana (Harper Perennial / HarperCollins India).

Dundee Picture Book Award (Scotland) (£1,000). To recognize excellence in storytelling for children. The winner is chosen by the schoolchildren of Dundee. *Winner:* Michelle Robinson (writer) and Sarah Horne (illustrator) for *School for Little Monsters* (Scholastic).

Educational Writers' Award (United Kingdom) (£2,000). For noteworthy educational nonfiction for children. *Offered by:* Authors' Licensing and Collecting Society and Society of Authors. *Winner:* Cath Senker for *Far from Home: Refugees and Migrants Fleeing War, Persecution and Poverty* (Franklin Watts).

Margaret A. Edwards Award ($2,000). To an author whose book or books have provided young adults with a window through which they can view their world and which will help them to grow and to understand themselves and their role in society. *Donor: School Library Journal. Winner:* Angela Johnson for *Heaven, Looking for Red, The First Part Last*, and *Sweet, Hereafter* (Simon & Schuster Books for Young Readers) and *Toning the Sweep* (Orchard Books).

T. S. Eliot Prize for Poetry (United Kingdom) (£20,000). *Offered by:* Poetry Book Society. *Winner:* Hannah Sullivan for *Three Poems*.

Encore Award (United Kingdom) (£10,000). Awarded for the best second novel. *Offered by:* Royal Society of Literature. *Winners:* (tie) Andrew Michael Hurley for *Devil's Day* (John Murray) and Lisa McInerney for *The Blood Miracles* (John Murray).

European Union Prize for Literature (€5,000). To recognize outstanding European writing. *Sponsors:* European Commission, European Booksellers Federation, European Writers' Council, Federation of European Publishers. *Winners:* (Serbia) Jelena Lengold for "Jasmine and the Death"; (Luxembourg) Jean Back for "European Clouds"; (Luxembourg) Gast Groeber "Current Weather Warning: Predominantly Heavy Fog"; (Romania) Ioana Pârvulescu "A Voice"; (Yugoslav Republic of Macedonia) Lidija Dimkovska for "When I Left Karl Liebknecht."

FIL Literary Award in Romance Languages (formerly the Juan Rulfo International Latin American and Caribbean Prize) (Mexico) ($150,000). For lifetime achievement in any literary genre. *Offered by:* Juan Rulfo International Latin American and Caribbean Prize Committee. *Winner:* Ida Vitale.

Financial Times and McKinsey Business Book of the Year Award (£30,000). To recognize books that provide compelling and enjoyable insight into modern business issues. *Winner:* John Carreyrou for *Bad Blood: Secrets and Lies in a Silicon Valley Startup* (Alfred A. Knopf).

Flaherty-Dunnan First Novel Prize. See Center for Fiction Flaherty-Dunnan First Novel Prize.

Sid Fleischman Award for Humor. See Golden Kite Awards.

ForeWord Reviews Book of the Year Awards ($1,500). For independently published books. *Offered by: ForeWord Reviews* magazine. *Winners:* (editor's choice prize, fiction) Megan Hunter for *The End We Start From* (Grove Press); (editor's choice prize, nonfiction) Sean Sherman and Beth Dooley for *The Sioux Chef's Indigenous Kitchen* (University of Minnesota Press).

E. M. Forster Award ($20,000). To a young writer from England, Ireland, Scotland, or Wales, for a stay in the United States. *Offered by:* American Academy of Arts and Letters. *Winner:* Jon McGregor.

Forward Prizes (United Kingdom). For poetry. *Offered by: The Forward. Winners:* (best collection, £10,000) Danez Smith for *Don't Call Us Dead* (Chatto & Windus); (Felix Dennis Prize for best first collection, £5,000) Phoebe Power for *Shrines of Upper Austria* (Carcanet Press); (best single poem, £1,000) Liz Perry for "The Republic of Motherhood" (Granta).

Josette Frank Award. For a work of fiction in which children or young people deal in a positive and realistic way with difficulties in their world and grow emotionally and morally. *Offered by:* Bank Street College of Education and the Florence M. Miller Memorial Fund. *Winners:* (older readers) Renee Watson for *Piecing Me Together* (Bloomsbury USA Children's).

George Freedley Memorial Award. For the best English-language work about live theater published in the United States. *Offered by:* Theatre Library Association. *Winner:* Sarah E. Chinn for *Spectacular Men: Race, Gender, and Nation on the Early American Stage* (Oxford University Press).

French-American Foundation Translation Prize ($10,000). For a translation or translations from French into English of works of fiction and nonfiction. *Offered by:* French-American Foundation. *Donor:* Florence Gould Foundation. *Winners:* (fiction) Paul Eprile for his translation of *Melville: A Novel* by Jean Giono (New York Review Books) and Howard Curtis for his translation of *The Principle* by Jérôme Ferrari (Europa Editions); (nonfiction) Samuel E. Martin for his translation of *Bark* by Georges-Didi Huberman (MIT Press) and Alison L. Strayer for her translation of *The Years* by Annie Ernaux (Seven Stories Press).

Frost Medal. To recognize achievement in poetry over a lifetime. *Offered by:* Poetry Society of America. *Winner:* Ron Padgett.

Lewis Galantière Award. Awarded biennially for a literary translation into English from any language other than German. *Offered by:* American Translators Association. *Winner (2018):* Sam Taylor for his translation of *The Heart* by Maylis de Kerangal (Farrar, Straus and Giroux).

Galaxy National Book Awards. See Specsavers National Book Awards.

Theodor Seuss Geisel Award. For the best book for beginning readers. *Offered by:* American Library Association, Association for Library Service to Children. *Winner:* Laurel Snyder (author) and Emily Hughes (illustrator) for *Charlie & Mouse* (Chronicle).

David Gemmell Legend Awards for Fantasy. For novels published for the first time in English during the year of nomination. *Winners:* (best novel) Robin Hobb for *Assassin's Fate* (Del Rey); (best newcomer) Nicholas Eames for *Kings of the Wyld* (Orbit); (best cover art) Richard Anderson for *Kings of the Wyld* by Nicholas Eames (Orbit).

Giller Prize (Canada). See Scotiabank Giller Prize.

Gival Press Novel Award ($3,000 and publication by Gival Press). *Winner:* William Orem for *Miss Lucy.*

Giverny Award. For an outstanding children's science picture book. *Offered by:* 15 Degree Laboratory. *Winner:* Anna Forrester (author) and Susan Detwiler (illustrator) for *Bat Count: A Citizen Science Story* (Arbordale Publishing).

Alexander Gode Medal. To an individual or institution for outstanding service to the translation and interpreting professions. *Offered by:* American Translators Association. *Winner:* Siegfried Ramler.

Golden Duck Awards for Excellence in Children's Science Fiction Literature. *See* LITA Excellence in Children's and Young Adult Science Fiction.

Golden Kite Awards. For children's books. *Offered by:* Society of Children's Book Writers and Illustrators. *Winners:* (middle grade fiction) Jack Cheng for *See You in the Cosmos* (Dial Books/Penguin Random House); (nonfiction for older readers) Deborah Heiligman for *Vincent and Theo: The Van Gogh Brothers* (Godwin Books/Henry Holt and Company); (picture book nonfiction) Carole Boston Weatherford for *Schomburg: The Man Who Built a Library* (Candlewick Press); (picture book illustration) Kenard Pak for *Goodbye Autumn, Hello Winter*

(Henry Holt and Company); (picture book text) Carolyn Crimi for *There Might Be Lobsters* (Candlewick Press); (young adult fiction) Elana K. Arnold for *What Girls Are Made Of* (Carolrhoda Lab); (Sid Fleischman Award) Crystal Allen for *The Magnificent Maya Tibbs: The Wall of Fame Game* (Balzer+Bray / HarperCollins).

Governor General's Literary Awards (Canada) (C$25,000, plus C$3,000 to the publisher). For works, in English and French, of fiction, nonfiction, poetry, and for translation. *Offered by:* Canada Council for the Arts. *Winners:* (fiction, English) Sarah Henstra for *The Red Word* (ECW Press); (poetry, English) Cecily Nicholson for *Wayside Sang* (Talonbooks); (drama, English) Jordan Tannahill for *Botticelli in the Fire & Sunday in Sodom* (Playwrights Canada Press); (nonfiction, English) Darrel J. McLeod for *Mamaskatch: A Cree Coming of Age* (Douglas & McIntyre); (young people's literature—text, English) Jonathan Auxier for *Sweep: The Story of a Girl and her Monster* (Puffin Canada / Penguin Random House Canada Young Readers); (young people's literature—illustrated, English) Jillian Tamaki for *They Say Blue* (Groundwood Books); (translation from French to English) Phyllis Aronoff and Howard Scott for *Descent into Night*, translation of *Explication de la nuit* by Edem Awumey (Les Éditions du Boréal); (fiction, French) Karoline Georges for *De synthèse* (Éditions Alto); (poetry, French) Michaël Trahan for *La raison des fleurs* (Le Quartanier); (drama, French) Anne-Marie Olivier for *Venir au monde* (Atelier 10); (nonfiction, French) Frédérick Lavoie for *Avant l'après: voyages à Cuba avec George Orwell* (La Peuplade); (young people's Literature—text, French) Mario Brassard for *Ferdinand F., 81 ans, chenille* (Soulières éditeur); (young people's literature—illustrated, French) Marianne Dubuc for *Le chemin de la montagne* (Comme des géants); (translation from English to French) Lori Saint-Martin and Paul Gagné for *Le Monde selon Barney*, translation of *Barney's Version* by Mordecai Richler (Knopf Canada).

Dolly Gray Children's Literature Awards. Presented biennially for fiction or biographical children's books with positive portrayals of individuals with developmental disabilities. *Offered by:* Council for Exceptional Children, Division on Autism and Developmental Disabilities. *Winners (2018):* (intermediate book) Sally J. Pla for *The Someday Birds* (Harper Collins); (picture book) Julia Finley Mosca (author) and Daniel Rieley (illustrator) for *The Girl Who Thought in Pictures: The Story of Dr. Temple Grandin* (Innovation Press).

Kate Greenaway Medal and Colin Mears Award. See CILIP Kate Greenaway Medal.

Eric Gregory Awards (United Kingdom) (£4,000). For a published or unpublished collection by poets under the age of 30. *Winners:* Zohar Atkins, Victoria Adukwei Bulley, Jenna Clake, Joseph Eastell, Annie Katchinska, Ali Lewis, Stephen Sexton.

Griffin Poetry Prizes (Canada) (C$65,000). To a living Canadian poet or translator and a living poet or translator from any country, which may include Canada. *Offered by:* Griffin Trust. *Winners:* (international) Susan Howe for *Debths* (New Directions); (Canadian) Billy-Ray Belcourt for *This Wound Is a World* (Frontenac House).

Gryphon Award ($1,000). To recognize a noteworthy work of fiction or nonfiction for younger children. *Offered by:* the Center for Children's Books. *Winners:* Doug Wechsler for *The Hidden Life of a Toad* (Charlesbridge).

Dashiell Hammett Prize. For a work of literary excellence in the field of crime writing by a U.S. or Canadian writer. *Offered by:* North American Branch, International Association of Crime Writers. *Winner:* Stephen Mack Jones for *August Snow* (Soho Crime).

R. R. Hawkins Award. For the outstanding professional/scholarly work of the year. *Offered by:* Association of American Publishers. *Winner:* Bloomsbury Publishing for Arcadian Library Online.

Anthony Hecht Poetry Prize ($3,000 and publication by Waywiser Press). For an unpublished first or second book-length poetry collection. *Winner:* Katherine Hollander for *My German Dictionary.*

Drue Heinz Literature Prize ($15,000 and publication by University of Pittsburgh Press). For short fiction. *Winner:* Brad Felver for *The Dogs of Detroit.*

O. Henry Awards. See PEN/O. Henry Prize.

William Dean Howells Medal. In recognition of the most distinguished novel published in the preceding five years. *Offered by:* American Academy of Arts and Letters. *Winner (2015):* William H. Gass for *Middle C* (Vintage).

Hugo Awards. For outstanding science fiction writing. *Offered by:* World Science Fiction Convention. *Winners:* (novel) N. K. Jemisin for *The Stone Sky* (Orbit Books); (novella) Martha Wells for *Every All Systems Red* (Tor.com); (novelette) Suzanne Palmer for "The Secret Life of Bots" (*Clarkesworld*, September 2017); (short story) Rebecca Roanhorse for "Welcome to Your Authentic Indian Experience™" (in *Apex Magazine*, August 2017); (series) Lois McMaster Bujold for World of the Five Gods (Harper Voyage/Spectrum Literary Agency); (related work) Ursula K. Le Guin for *No Time to Spare: Thinking About What Matters* (Houghton Mifflin Harcourt); (graphic story) Marjorie Liu (author) and Sana Takeda (illustrator) for *Monstress, Volume 2: The Blood* (Image); (dramatic presentation, long form) Allan Heinberg (screenplay) and Patty Jenkins (director) for *Wonder Woman* (DC Films/Warner Bros.); (dramatic presentation, short form) Josh Siegal and Dylan Morgan (writers) and Dean Holland (director) for *The Good Place*: "The Trolley Problem" (Fremulon/3 Arts Entertainment/Universal Television).

ILA Children's and Young Adults' Book Awards. For first or second books in any language published for children or young adults. *Offered by:* International Literacy Association. *Winners:* (primary fiction) Corinna Luyken for *The Book of Mistakes* (Dial); (primary nonfiction) Matt Lamothe for *This Is How We Do It: One Day in the Lives of Seven Kids from around the World* (Chronicle); (intermediate fiction) Paul Mosier for *Train I Ride* (HarperCollins Children's); (intermediate nonfiction) Emma Otheguy for *Martí's Song for Freedom* (Lee & Low); (young adult fiction) Julia Walton for *Words on Bathroom Walls* (Random House Children's); (young adult nonfiction) Allison Britz for *Obsessed: A Memoir of My Life with OCD* (Simon & Schuster).

IMPAC Dublin Literary Award (Ireland) (€100,000). For a book of high literary merit, written in English or translated into English; if translated, the author receives €75,000 and the translator €25,000. *Offered by:* IMPAC Corp. and the City of Dublin. *Winner:* Mike McCormack for *Solar Bones* (Canongate Books).

Independent Publisher Book Awards (IPPY). Created to recognize exemplary independent, university, and self-published titles across a wide spectrum of genres. *Sponsor:* Jenkins Group/Independent Publisher Online. *Winners:* (photography) Christopher Felver and the University of New Mexico Press for *Tending the Fire: Native Voices and Portraits*; (popular fiction) Amy Blumenfeld and SparkPress for *The Cast*; (literary fiction) Carole Giangrande and Inanna Publications for *All That Is Solid Melts into Air*; (short story fiction) Louise Marburg and WTAW Press for *The Truth about Me: Stories*; (poetry) Maggie Smith and Tupelo Press for *Good Bones*; (juvenile fiction) A. L. Janney for *The Phantom of New York, Vol. 1: Peter and the Crown* (self-published); (young adult fiction) Renée Veillet and Tellwell for *Rings of Time*; (historical fiction) Erika Mailman and Bonhomie Press for *The Murderer's Maid*.

Indies Choice Book Awards. Chosen by owners and staff of American Booksellers Association member bookstores. *Winners:* (adult fiction) Jesmyn Ward for *Sing, Unburied, Sing: A Novel* (Scribner); (adult nonfiction) David Grann for *Killers of the Flower Moon: The Osage Murders and the Birth of the FBI* (Doubleday); (adult debut) Carmen Maria Machado for *Her Body and Other Parties: Stories* (Graywolf Press); (young adult) Angie Thomas for *The Hate U Give* (Balzer+Bray); (audiobook) *Lincoln in the Bardo* by George Saunders, read by Nick Offerman, David Sedaris, George Saunders, and a full cast (Random House Audio).

International Prize for Arabic Fiction ($50,000 and publication in English). To reward excellence in contemporary Arabic creative writing. *Sponsors:* Booker Prize Foundation, Emirates Foundation for Philanthropy. *Winner:* Ibrahim Nasrallah (Palestine/Jordan) for *The Second War of the Dog*.

Rona Jaffe Foundation Writers' Awards ($30,000 each). To identify and support women writers of exceptional talent in the early stages of their careers. *Offered by:* Rona Jaffe Foundation. *Winners:* Chelsea Bieker, Lisa Chen, Lydia Conklin, Gabriela Garcia, Karen Outen, Alison C. Rollins.

Jerusalem Prize (Israel). Awarded biennially to a writer whose works best express the theme of freedom of the individual in society. *Offered by:* Jerusalem International Book Fair. *Winner (2017):* Karl Ove Knausgaard.

Jewish Book Council Awards. *Winners:* (Jewish Book of the Year) Beate and Serge Klarsfeld for *Hunting the Truth: Memoirs of Beate and Serge Klarsfeld,* translated from the French by Sam Taylor (Farrar, Straus and Giroux); (American Jewish studies) Jack Wertheimer for *The New American Judaism: How Jews Practice Their Religion Today* (Princeton University Press); (autobiography and memoir) Ehud Barak for *My Country, My Life: Fighting for Israel, Searching for Peace* (St. Martin's Press); (biography) Ariel Burger for *Witness: Lessons from Elie Wiesel's Classroom* (Houghton Mifflin Harcourt); (book club award) Ronald H. Balson for *The Girl from Berlin* (St. Martin's Press); (children's literature) Erica S. Perl for *All Three Stooges* (Knopf Books for Young Readers); (contemporary Jewish life and practice) Leon Wiener Dow for *The Going: A Meditation on Jewish Law* (Palgrave Macmillan); (debut fiction) Bram Presser for *The Book of Dirt* (Text Publishing); (education and Jewish identity) Barry Scott Wimpfheimer for *The Talmud: A Biography* (Princeton University Press); (fiction) Michael David Lukas for *The Last Watchman of Old Cairo* (Spiegel & Grau); (history) Ronen Bergman for *Rise and Kill First: The Secret History of Israel's Targeted Assassinations* (Random House); (Holocaust) Omer Bartov for *Anatomy of a Genocide: The Life and Death of a Town Called Buczacz* (Simon and Schuster); (modern Jewish thought and experience) Alan L. Mittleman for *Does Judaism Condone Violence? Holiness and Ethics in the Jewish Tradition* (Princeton University Press); (poetry) Erika Meitner for *Holy Moly Carry Me* (BOA Editions, Ltd.); (scholarship) Marcin Wodziński, cartography by Waldemar Spallek, for *Historical Atlas of Hasidism* (Princeton University Press); (Sephardic culture) Jonathan Decter for *Dominion Built of Praise: Panegyric and Legitimacy Among Jews in the Medieval Mediterranean* (University of Pennsylvania Press); (women's studies) Alice Shalvi for *Never a Native* (Halban Publishers); (writing based on archival material) Rebecca Erbelding for *Rescue Board: The Untold Story of America's Efforts to Save the Jews of Europe* (Penguin Random House/Doubleday).

Sue Kaufman Prize for First Fiction ($5,000). For a first novel or collection of short stories. *Offered by:* American Academy of Arts and Letters. *Winner:* Emily Fridlund for *History of Wolves* (Atlantic Monthly Press).

Ezra Jack Keats Awards. For children's picture books. *Offered by:* New York Public Library and the Ezra Jack Keats Foundation. *Winners:* (new writer award) Derrick Barnes for *Crown: An Ode to the Fresh Cut,* illustrated by Gordon C. James (Agate Bolden/Denene Millner Books); (new illustrator award) Evan Turk for *Muddy: The Story of Blues Legend Muddy Waters* by Michael Mahin (Atheneum Books for Young Readers).

Kerlan Award. To recognize singular attainments in the creation of children's literature and in appreciation for generous donation of unique resources to the Kerlan Collection for the study of children's literature. *Offered by:* Kerlan Children's Literature Research Collections, University of Minnesota. *Winner:* Jennifer Holm and Matthew Holm.

Coretta Scott King Book Awards ($1,000). To an African American author and illustrator of outstanding books for children and young adults. *Offered by:* American Library Association, Ethnic and Multicultural Exchange Round Table (EMIERT). *Winners:* (author) Renee Watson for *Piecing Me Together* (Bloomsbury USA Children's); (illustrator) Ekua Holmes for *Out of Wonder: Poems Celebrating Poets* (Candlewick).

Coretta Scott King/Virginia Hamilton Award for Lifetime Achievement. Given in even-numbered years to an African American author, illustrator, or author/illustrator for a body of books for children or young adults. In odd-numbered years, the award honors substantial contributions through active engagement with youth, using award-winning African American literature for children or young adults. *Winner:* Eloise Greenfield.

Coretta Scott King/John Steptoe Award for New Talent. To offer visibility to a writer or illustrator at the beginning of a career. *Sponsor:* Coretta Scott King Book Award Committee. *Winner:* Kathryn Erskine (author) and Charly Palmer (illustrator) for *Mama Africa! How Miriam Makeba Spread Hope with Her Song* (Farrar, Straus and Grioux) and David Barclay Moore for *The Stars Beneath Our Feet* (Knopf Books for Young Readers).

Kirkus Prize ($50,000). For outstanding fiction, nonfiction, and young readers literature. *Offered by: Kirkus Reviews. Winners:* (fiction) Ling Ma for *Severance* (Farrar, Straus and Grioux); (nonfiction) Rebecca Solnit for *Call Them by Their True Names* (Haymarket Books); (young readers) Derrick Barnes for *Crown: An Ode to the Fresh Cut*, illustrated by Gordon C. James (Agate Bolden/Denene Millner Books).

Lambda Literary Awards. To honor outstanding lesbian, gay, bisexual, and transgender (LGBT) literature. *Offered by:* Lambda Literary Foundation. *Winners:* (lesbian fiction) Carmen Maria Machado for *Her Body and Other Parties: Stories* (Graywolf Press); (gay fiction) John Rechy for *After the Blue Hour* (Grove Press); (bisexual fiction) Barbara Browning for *The Gift* (Coffee House Press); (transgender fiction) Bogi Takács (editor) for *Transcendent 2: The Year's Best Transgender Speculative Fiction* (Lethe Press); (LGBTQ nonfiction) Keeanga-Yamahtta Taylor for *How We Get Free: Black Feminism and the Combahee River Collective* (Haymarket Books); (transgender nonfiction) C. Riley Snorton for *Black on Both Sides: A Racial History of Trans Identity* (University of Minnesota Press); Rosamond S. King for *Rock/Salt/Stone* (Nightboat Books); (gay poetry) C. A. Conrad for *While Standing in Line for Death* (Wave Books); (transgender poetry) Ching-In Chen for *recombinant* (Kelsey Street Press); (lesbian mystery) A. E. Radley for *Huntress* (Heartsome Publishing); (gay mystery) Marshall Thornton for *Night Drop* (CreateSpace Independent Publishing Platform); (lesbian memoir/biography) Alexandria Marzano-Lesnevich for *The Fact of a Body: A Murder and a Memoir* (Flatiron Books); (gay memoir/biography) Chike Frankie Edozien for *Lives of Great Men: Living and Loving as an African Gay Man* (Team Angelica Publishing); (lesbian romance) Yolanda Wallace for *Tailor-Made* (Bold Strokes Books); (gay romance) Laurie Loft for *Love and Other Hot Beverages* (Riptide Publishing); (LGBTQ erotica) Steve Berman for *His Seed: An Arboretum of Erotica* (Unzipped Books); (LGTBQ anthology) Juliana Delgado Lopera for *¡Cuéntamelo! Oral Histories by LGBT Latino Immigrants* (Aunt Lute Books); (LGTBQ children's/young adult) Rebecca Podos for *Like Water* (Balzer+Bray); (LGTBQ drama) Audrey Cefaly for *The Gulf* (Samuel French); (LGTBQ graphic novel) Emil Ferris for *My Favorite Thing Is Monsters* (Fantagraphics); (LGTBQ science fiction/fantasy/horror) Annalee Newitz for *Autonomous* (Tor Books); (LGTBQ studies) Trevor Hoppe for *Punishing Disease: HIV and the Criminalization of Sickness* (University of California Press).

Harold Morton Landon Translation Award ($1,000). For a book of verse translated into English. *Offered by:* Academy of American Poets. *Winner:* David Larsen for *Names of the Lion* by Ibn Khalawayh (Wave Books).

David J. Langum, Sr. Prize in American Historical Fiction ($1,000). To honor a book of historical fiction published in the previous year. *Offered by:* Langum Foundation. *Winner:* Louisa Hall for *Trinity* (Ecco).

David J. Langum, Sr. Prize in American Legal History or Biography ($1,000). For a university press book that is accessible to the educated general public, rooted in sound scholarship, with themes that touch upon matters of general concern. *Offered by:* Langum Foundation. *Winner:* Laura Kalman for *The Long Reach of the Sixties: LBJ, Nixon, and the Making of the Contemporary Supreme Court* (Oxford University Press).

Latner Writers' Trust Poetry Prize (C$25,000) (Canada). To a writer with an exceptional body of work in the field of poetry. *Offered by:* Writers' Trust of Canada. *Sponsor:* Latner Family Foundation. *Winner:* Jordan Scott.

James Laughlin Award ($5,000). To commend and support a second book of poetry. *Offered by:* Academy of American Poets. *Winner:* Geffrey Davis for *Night Angler* (BOA Editions).

Ruth Lilly and Dorothy Sargent Rosenberg Poetry Fellowships ($25,800). To emerging poets to support their continued study and writing of poetry. *Offered by:* The Poetry Foundation. *Winners:* Safia Elhillo, Hieu Minh Nguyen, sam sax, Natalie Scenters-Zapico, and Paul Tran.

Ruth Lilly Poetry Prize ($100,000). To a U.S. poet in recognition of lifetime achievement. *Offered by:* Poetry Foundation. *Winner:* Martin Espada.

Astrid Lindgren Memorial Award (Sweden) (5 million kroner, more than $575,000). In memory of children's author Astrid Lindgren, to honor outstanding children's literature and efforts to promote it. *Offered by:* Government of Sweden and the Swedish Arts Council. *Winner:* Jacqueline Woodson.

LITA Excellence in Children's and Young Adult Science Fiction. *Sponsor:* Library and Information Technology Association. *Winner:* (Golden Duck List for picture books) Katy S. Duffield (author) and K. G. Campbell (illustrator) for *Aliens Get the Sniffles Too! Ahhh-Choo!* (Candlewick); Jon Agee for *Life on Mars* (Dial Books); Kim Griswell (author) and Valeri Gorbachev (illustrator) for *Rufus Blasts Off!* (Sterling Children's Books); Marie Alafaci (author) and Shane McG (illustrator) for *Zelda's Big Adventure* (Clarion Books); Camille Andros (author) and Brianne Farley (illustrator) for *Charlotte the Scientist Is Squished* (Clarion Books); Kim Smith for *E.T. the Extra-Terrestrial: The Classic Illustrated Storybook* (Quirk Books). (Eleanor Cameron List for middle grade books) Will Buckingham (author) and Monica Arnaldo (illustrator) for *Lucy and the Rocket Dog* (Alfred A Knopf); A. S. King for *Me and Marvin Gardens* (Arthur A. Levine Books); Will McIntosh for *Watchdog* (Delacorte Press); Michelle Cuevas for *The Care and Feeding of a Pet Black Hole* (Dial Books); Frank Cottrell Boyce for *Sputnik's Guide to Life on Earth* (Walden Pond Press); Alex Alice for *Castle in the Stars: The Space Race of 1869* (First Second); Katie Slivensky for *The Countdown Conspiracy* (HarperCollins); Kevin Emerson for *Last Day on Mars* (Walden Pond Press); Landry Q. Walker (author) and Keith Zoo (illustrator) for *Crash Course #1* (Penguin Workshop); Nathan Hale for *One Trick Pony* (Amulet Books). (Hal Clement List for young adult books) Amy Ross for *Jek/Hyde* (Harlequin Teen); Ari Goelman for *The Innocence Treatment* (Roaring Brook Press); Claudia Gray for *Defy the Stars* (Little, Brown); Scott Reintgen for *Nyxia* (Penguin Random House); Jon McGoran for *Spliced* (Holiday House); Julia Keller for *Dark Intercept* (Tor Teen); Emily Suvada for *This Mortal Coil* (Simon Pulse); Katie Kennedy for *What Goes Up* (Bloomsbury USA Childrens); Heather Kaczynski for *Dare Mighty Things* (HarperTeen); Gregory Scott Katsoulis for *All Rights Reserved* (Harlequin Teen); Scott Westerfeld (author) and Alex Puvilland (illustrator) for *Spill Zone* (First Second); Mary Weber for *The Evaporation of Soft Snow* (Thomas Nelson).

Locus Awards. For science fiction writing. *Offered by:* Locus Publications. *Winners:* (science fiction) John Scalzi for *The Collapsing Empire* (Tor); (fantasy) N. K. Jemisin for *The Stone Sky* (Orbit); (horror) Victor LaValle for *The Changeling* (Spiegel & Grau); (young adult) Nnedi Okorafor for *Akata Warrior* (Viking); (first novel) Theodora Goss for *The Strange Case of the Alchemist's Daughter* (Saga); (novella) Martha Wells for *All Systems Red* (Tor.com); (novelette) Samuel R. Delany for "The Hermit of Houston" (published in *F&SF* 9-10/17); (short story) Linda Nagata for "The Martian Obelisk" (published by Tor.com 7/19/17); (anthology) Gardner Dozois (editor) for *The Book of Swords* (Bantam); (collection) Ursula K. Le Guin for *Ursula K. Le Guin: The Hainish Novels and Stories* (Library of America); (nonfiction) Alexandra Pierce and Mimi Mondal (editors) for *Luminescent Threads: Connections to Octavia E. Butler* (Twelfth Planet); (art book) Douglas Ellis, Ed Hulse, and Robert

Weinberg (editors) for *The Art of the Pulps: An Illustrated History* (IDW).

London Book Festival Awards. To honor books worthy of further attention from the international publishing community. *Winners:* (spiritual/religious) R. M. L. (Robert M. Levinson) for *The Leper Messiah* (Tellwell Talent); (young adult) Paddy Eger for *Tasman: An Innocent Convict's Struggle for Freedom* (Tendril); (general fiction) Milton Lyles for *The Other Side of Tomorrow* (Story Merchant); (children's) Grant Maloy Smith for *Fly Possum Fly* (Headline Books); (poetry) Kenneth Salzmann for *The Last Jazz Fan and Other Poems* (CreateSpace Independent Publishing Platform); (general nonfiction) Pamela Capone for *The Little Love That Could* (Aha! Press); (business) Richard Newman for *You Were Born to Speak* (self-published); (biography/autobiography/memoir) Elizabeth Katkin for *Conceivability: What I Learned Exploring the Frontiers of Fertility* (Simon & Schuster); (genre-based) Desiree Span for *Oliver and Erica: When Friends Become Lovers* (Amsterdam Publishers); (science fiction) Rita Chapman for *Destiny: Part 2 of the Liberty Saga* (Strategic Book Publishing and Rights Agency); (how-to) Gladys Mezrahi for *Más Wow y Menos Oops* (self-published); (wild card) Kennedy Ross for *He Said It, I Didn't—A Biblical Book Report Brooklyn Style* (self-published); (unpublished) Michael J. Ganas for *Angels in the Balance*.

Elizabeth Longford Prize for Historical Biography (United Kingdom) (£5,000). *Sponsors:* Flora Fraser and Peter Soros. *Winner:* Giles Tremlett for *Isabella of Castile: Europe's First Great Queen* (Bloomsbury).

Los Angeles Times Book Prizes. To honor literary excellence. *Offered by: Los Angeles Times. Winners:* (Art Seidenbaum Award for First Fiction) Jenny Zhang for *Sour Heart* (Lenny/Random House); (biography) Laura Dassow Walls for *Henry David Thoreau: A Life* (University of Chicago Press); (Christopher Isherwood Prize for Autobiographical Prose) Benjamin Taylor for *The Hue and Cry at Our House: A Year Remembered* (Penguin Books); (current interest) Nancy MacLean for *Democracy in Chains: The Deep History of the Radical Right's Stealth Plan for America* (Viking); (fiction) Mohsin Hamid for *Exit West* (Riverhead Books); (graphic novel/comics) Leslie Stein for *Present* (Drawn and Quarterly); (history) Dan Egan for *The Death and Life of the Great Lakes* (W. W. Norton & Company); (mystery/thriller) Joyce Carol Oates for *A Book of American Martyrs* (Ecco); (poetry) Patricia Smith for *Incendiary Art: Poems* (TriQuarterly Books/Northwestern University Press); (science & technology) Robert M. Sapolsky for *Behave: The Biology of Humans at Our Best and Worst* (Penguin Press); (young adult literature) Jason Reynolds for *Long Way Down* (Atheneum/Caitlyn Dlouhy Books).

Amy Lowell Poetry Traveling Scholarship. For one or two U.S. poets to spend one year outside North America in a country the recipients feel will most advance their work. *Offered by:* Amy Lowell Poetry Traveling Scholarship. *Winner:* Molly McCully Brown.

Walter & Lillian Lowenfels Criticism Award. *Offered by:* Before Columbus Foundation. *Winner:* Kellie Jones, *South of Pico: African American Artists in Los Angeles in the 1960s and 1970s* (Duke University).

J. Anthony Lukas Awards. For nonfiction writing that demonstrates literary grace, serious research, and concern for an important aspect of American social or political life. *Offered by:* Columbia University Graduate School of Journalism and the Nieman Foundation for Journalism at Harvard. *Winners:* (Lukas Book Prize, $10,000) Amy Goldstein for *Janesville: An American Story* (Simon & Schuster); (Mark Lynton History Prize, $10,000) Stephen Kotkin for *Stalin: Waiting for Hitler, 1929–1941* (Penguin); (Work-in-Progress Award, $30,000) (tie) Chris Hamby for *Soul Full of Coal Dust: The True Story of An Epic Battle for Justice* (Little, Brown and Company) and Rachel Louise Snyder for *No Visible Bruises: What We Don't Know About Domestic Violence Can Kill Us* (Bloomsbury).

Macavity Awards. For excellence in mystery writing. *Offered by:* Mystery Readers International. *Winners:* (mystery novel) Anthony Horowitz for *Magpie Murders* (Harper); (first mystery) Sheena Kamal for *The Lost Ones* (William Morrow); (nonfiction)

Martin Edwards for *The Story of Classic Crime in 100 Books* (Poisoned Pen/British Library); (short story) Paul D. Marks for "Windward" in *Coast to Coast: Private Eyes from Sea to Shining Sea* (Down & Out Books); (Sue Feder Historical Mystery Award) Rhys Bowen for *In Farleigh Field* (Lake Union Publishing).

McKitterick Prize (United Kingdom) (£4,000). To an author over the age of 40 for a first novel, published or unpublished. *Winner:* Anietie Isong for *Radio Sunrise* (Jacaranda).

Man Booker International Prize (United Kingdom) (£60,000). To the author and translator of a work translated into English. *Offered by:* Man Group. *Winner:* Olga Tokarczuk for *Flights*, translated by Jennifer Croft (Penguin Random House).

Man Booker Prize for Fiction (United Kingdom) (£50,000). For the best novel written in English by a Commonwealth author. *Offered by:* Booktrust and the Man Group. *Winner:* Anna Burns for *Milkman* (Faber & Faber).

Lenore Marshall Poetry Prize ($25,000). For an outstanding book of poems published in the United States. *Offered by:* Academy of American Poets. *Winner:* Craig Morgan Teicher for *The Trembling Answers* (BOA Editions Ltd.).

Somerset Maugham Awards (United Kingdom) (£2,500). For works in any genre except drama by a writer under the age of 35, to enable young writers to enrich their work by gaining experience of foreign countries. *Winners:* Kayo Chingonyi for *Kumukanda* (Chatto Poetry); Fiona Mozley for *Elmet* (JM Originals); Miriam Nash for *All the Prayers in the House* (Bloodaxe).

Addison M. Metcalf Award in Literature ($2,000). Awarded biennially in alternation with the Addison M. Metcalf Award in Art. *Winner (2017):* Safiya Sinclair.

Vicky Metcalf Award for Literature for Young People (C$25,000) (Canada). To a Canadian writer of children's literature for a body of work. *Offered by:* Writers' Trust of Canada. *Sponsor:* Metcalf Foundation. *Winner:* Christopher Paul Curtis.

Midwest Booksellers Choice Awards. *Offered by:* Midwest Independent Booksellers Association. *Winners:* (fiction) Chloe Benjamin for *The Immortalists* (G. P. Putnam's Sons); (nonfiction) Sean Sherman and Beth Dooley for *The Sioux Chef's Indigenous Kitchen* (University of Minnesota Press); (poetry) Danez Smith for *Don't Call Us Dead* (Chatto & Windus); (young adult and middle grade) Margi Preus for *The Clue in the Trees: An Enchantment Lake Mystery* (University of Minnesota Press); (children's picture book) Bao Phi for *A Different Pond*, illustrated by Thi Bui (Capstone).

William C. Morris YA Debut Award. To honor a debut book published by a first-time author writing for teens and celebrating impressive new voices in young adult literature. *Offered by:* American Library Association, Young Adult Library Services Association. *Donor:* William C. Morris Endowment. *Winner:* Angie Thomas for *The Hate U Give* (Balzer+Bray).

Mythopoeic Fantasy Awards. To recognize fantasy or mythic literature for children and adults that best exemplifies the spirit of the Inklings, a group of fantasy writers that includes J. R. R. Tolkien, C. S. Lewis, and Charles Williams. *Offered by:* Mythopoeic Society. *Winners:* (adult literature) John Crowley for *Ka: Dar Oakley in the Ruin of Ymr* (Saga Press); (children's literature) Garth Nix for *Frogkisser* (Scholastic Press); (Mythopoeic Scholarship Award in Inklings Studies) Sørina Higgins (editor) for *The Inklings and King Arthur: J. R. R. Tolkien, Charles Williams, C. S. Lewis, and Owen Barfield on the Matter of Britain* (Apocryphile Press); (Mythopoeic Scholarship Award in Myth and Fantasy Studies) Michael Levy and Farah Mendlesohn for *Children's Fantasy Literature: An Introduction* (Cambridge University Press).

National Book Awards. To celebrate the best in American literature. *Offered by:* National Book Foundation. *Winners:* (fiction) Sigrid Nunez for *The Friend* (Riverhead); (nonfiction) Jeffrey C. Stewart, *The New Negro: The Life of Alain Locke* (Oxford University Press); (poetry) Justin Philip Reed for *Indecency* (Coffee House Press); (young people's literature) Elizabeth Acevedo for *The Poet X* (Harper Teen).

National Book Awards (United Kingdom). See Specsavers National Book Awards.

National Book Critics Circle Awards. For literary excellence. *Offered by:* National Book

Critics Circle. *Winners:* (fiction) Anna Burns for *Milkman* (Graywolf); (nonfiction) Stephen Coll for *Directorate S: The C.I.A. and America's Secret Wars in Afghanistan* (Penguin); (biography) Christopher Bonanos for *Flash: The Making of Weegee the Famous* (Henry Holt and Company); (autobiography) Nora Krug for *Belonging: A German Reckons with History and Home* (Scribner); (poetry) Ada Limon for *The Carrying* (Milkweed); (criticism) Zadie Smith for *Feel Free: Essays* (Penguin); (John Leonard Prize) Tommy Orange for *There There* (Alfred A. Knopf); (Nona Balakian Citation for Excellence in Reviewing) Maureen Corrigan; (Ivan Sandrof Lifetime Achievement Award) Arte Publico.

National Book Foundation Literarian Award for Outstanding Service to the American Literary Community. *Offered by:* National Book Foundation. *Winner:* Doron Weber.

National Book Foundation Medal for Distinguished Contribution to American Letters ($10,000). To a person who has enriched the nation's literary heritage over a life of service or corpus of work. *Offered by:* National Book Foundation. *Winner:* Isabel Allende.

National Translation Awards ($5,000). To honor translators whose work has made a valuable contribution to literary translation into English. *Offered by:* American Literary Translators Association. *Winners:* (prose) Charlotte Mandell, translator from French, for *Compass* by Mathias Enard (New Directions); (poetry) Katrine Øgaard Jensen, translator from Danish, for *Third-Millennium Heart* by Ursula Andkjaer Olsen (Action Books / Broken Dimanche Press).

Nebula Awards. For science fiction writing. *Offered by:* Science Fiction and Fantasy Writers of America (SFWA). *Winners:* (novel) N. K. Jemisin for *The Stone Sky* (Orbit); (novella) Martha Wells for *All Systems Red* (Tor.com); (novelette) Kelly Robson for "A Human Stain" (Tor.com); (short story) Rebecca Roanhorse for "Welcome to Your Authentic Indian Experience™" (in *Apex Magazine*, August 2017); (Ray Bradbury Award for dramatic presentation) Jordan Peele (director and screenwriter) for *Get Out* (Universal Pictures); (Andre Norton Award for young adult science fiction and fantasy) Sam J. Miller for *The Art of Starving* (HarperCollins).

John Newbery Medal. For the most distinguished contribution to literature for children. *Offered by:* American Library Association, Association for Library Service to Children. *Winner:* Erin Entrada Kelly for *Hello, Universe* (Greenwillow).

Nibbies (United Kingdom). See British Book Awards.

Nimrod Literary Awards ($2,000 plus publication). *Offered by: Nimrod International Journal of Prose and Poetry. Winners:* (Pablo Neruda Prize in Poetry) Emma DePanise for "Dry Season" and other poems; (Katherine Anne Porter Prize in Fiction) Sharon Solwitz for "Tremblement."

Nobel Prize in Literature (Sweden). For the total literary output of a distinguished career. *Offered by:* Swedish Academy. *Winner:* Not awarded in 2018.

Eli M. Oboler Memorial Award. Given biennially to an author of a published work in English or in English translation dealing with issues, events, questions, or controversies in the area of intellectual freedom. *Offered by:* Intellectual Freedom Round Table, American Library Association. *Winners (2018):* Robert P. Doyle for *Banned Books: Defending Our Freedom to Read* (Office for Intellectual Freedom, American Library Association).

Flannery O'Connor Awards for Short Fiction. For collections of short fiction. *Offered by:* University of Georgia Press. *Winners:* Colette Sartor for *Once Removed and Other Stories* (University of Georgia Press).

Oddest Book Title of the Year Award. See Bookseller/Diagram Prize for Oddest Title of the Year.

Scott O'Dell Award for Historical Fiction ($5,000). *Offered by: Bulletin of the Center for Children's Books,* University of Chicago. *Winner:* Lauren Wolk for *Beyond the Bright Sea* (Dutton Books for Young Readers).

Odyssey Award. To the producer of the best audiobook for children and/or young adults available in English in the United States. *Sponsors:* American Library Association, ALSC / Booklist / YALSA. *Winner:* Harper Audio for *The Hate U Give* by Angie Thomas, narrated by Bahni Turpin.

Seán Ó Faoláin Short Story Competition (€2,000 and publication in the literary journal *Southword*). *Offered by:* Munster Literature Centre, Cork, Ireland. *Winner:* Louise Crimmins for "How to Pass."

Dayne Ogilvie Prize (C$4,000) (Canada). To an emerging Canadian writer from the LGBT community who demonstrates promise through a body of quality work. *Offered by:* Writers' Trust of Canada. *Winner:* Ben Ladoucer.

Orbis Pictus Award for Outstanding Nonfiction for Children. *Offered by:* National Council of Teachers of English. *Winner:* Jason Chin for *Grand Canyon* (Roaring Brook Press).

Oxford-Weidenfeld Translation Prize. *Winners:* Lisa Dillman for her translation from Spanish of *Such Small Hands* by Andrés Barba (Portobello Books).

PEN Award for Poetry in Translation ($3,000). For a book-length translation of poetry from any language into English, published in the United States. *Offered by:* PEN American Center. *Winner:* Not awarded in 2018.

PEN/Saul Bellow Award for Achievement in American Fiction ($25,000). Awarded biennially to a distinguished living American author of fiction. *Offered by:* PEN American Center. *Winner (2018):* Edmund White.

PEN/Bellwether Prize for Socially Engaged Fiction ($25,000). Awarded biennially to the author of a previously unpublished novel that addresses issues of social justice and the impact of culture and politics on human relationships. *Founder:* Barbara Kingsolver. *Winner (2018):* Katherine Seligman for *If You Knew* (Algonquin).

PEN Beyond Margins Awards. See PEN Open Book Awards.

PEN/Robert W. Bingham Prize ($25,000). To a writer whose first novel or short story collection represents distinguished literary achievement and suggests great promise. *Offered by:* PEN American Center. *Winner:* Jenny Zhang for *Sour Heart* (Lenny).

PEN/Robert J. Dau Short Story Prize for Emerging Writers ($2,000 to 12 writers). To recognize 12 emerging fiction writers for their debut short stories. *Offered by:* PEN American Center. *Winners:* Elinam Agbo for "1983" in *The Baltimore Review*; Lin King for "Appetite" in *SLICE*; Lauren Friedlander for "Bellevonia Beautee" in *The Rumpus*; Alex Terrell for "Black Dog" in *Black Warrior Review*; Grayson Morley for "Brent, Bandit King" in *The Brooklyn Review*; Megan Tucker for "Candidates" in *Washington Square Review*; Cristina Fries for "New Years in La Calera" in *EPOCH*; Celeste Mohammed for "Six Months New" in *New England Review*; Ernie Wang for "Stay Brave, My Hercules" in *McSweeney's*; Maud Streep for "The Crazies" in *One Story*; Ava Tomasula y Garcia for "Videoteca Fin del Mundo" in *Black Warrior Review*; Drew McCutchen for "Zombie Horror" in *The Baltimore Review.*

PEN/Diamonstein-Spielvogel Award for the Art of the Essay ($10,000). For a book of essays by a single author that best exemplifies the dignity and esteem of the essay form. *Winner:* Ursula K. Le Guin for *No Time to Spare: Thinking About What Matters* (Houghton Mifflin Harcourt).

PEN/ESPN Award for Literary Sports Writing ($5,000). To honor a nonfiction book on the subject of sports. *Winners:* Jonathan Eig for *Ali: A Life* (Houghton Mifflin Harcourt).

PEN/ESPN Lifetime Achievement Award for Literary Sports Writing ($5,000). For a writer whose body of work represents an exceptional contribution to the field. *Winner:* David Kindred.

PEN/Faulkner Award for Fiction ($15,000). To honor the year's best work of fiction published by an American. *Winner:* Joan Silber for *Improvement* (Counterpoint Press).

PEN/John Kenneth Galbraith Award for Nonfiction ($10,000). Given biennially for a distinguished book of general nonfiction. *Offered by:* PEN American Center. *Winner (2017):* Matthew Desmond for *Evicted: Poverty and Profit in the American City* (Crown/Penguin Random House).

PEN Grant for the English Translation of Italian Literature ($5,000). *Winner:* Jeanne Bonner for her translation from the Italian of *A Walk in the Shadows* by Mariateresa Di Lascia.

PEN/Heim Translation Fund Grants ($2,000–$4,000). To support the translation of book-length works of fiction, creative nonfiction, poetry, or drama that have not previously appeared in English or have appeared only in an egregiously flawed translation. *Winners:* Janine Beichman, Alexander Dickow,

Emily Drumsta, Lindy Falk van Rooyen, Bruce Fulton and Ju-Chan Fulton, Michael Gluck, Mariam Rahmani, Aaron Robertson, Julia Sanches, Jamie Lee Searle, Brian Sneeden, Ri J. Turner.

PEN/Ernest Hemingway Foundation Award. For a distinguished work of first fiction by an American. *Offered by:* PEN New England. *Winner:* Weike Wang for *Chemistry* (Knopf).

PEN/O. Henry Prize. For short stories of exceptional merit, in English, published in U.S. and Canadian magazines. *Winners:* Lauren Alwan for "An Amount of Discretion" in *The Southern Review;* Jo Ann Beard for "The Tomb of Wrestling" in *Tin House;* Thomas Bolt for "Inversion of Marcia" in *n+1;* Marjorie Celona for "Counterblast" in *The Southern Review;* Youmna Chlala for "Nayla" in *Prairie Schooner;* Dounia Choukri for "Past Perfect Continuous" in *Chicago Quarterly Review;* Viet Dinh for "Lucky Dragon" in *Ploughshares;* Anne Enright for "Solstice" in *The New Yorker;* Brad Felver for "Queen Elizabeth" in *One Story;* Tristan Hughes for "Up Here" in *Ploughshares;* Dave King for "The Stamp Collector" in *Fence;* Jamil Kochai for "Nights in Logar" in *A Public Space;* Jo Lloyd for "The Earth, Thy Great Exchequer, Ready Lies" in *Zoetrope;* Michael Parker for "Stop 'n' Go" in *New England Review;* Mark Jude Poirier for "How We Eat" in *Epoch;* Michael Powers for "More or Less Like a Man" in *The Threepenny Review;* Lara Vapnyar for "Deaf and Blind" in *The New Yorker;* Stephanie A. Vega for "We Keep Them Anyway" in *The Threepenny Review;* Brenda Walker for "The Houses that Are Left Behind" in *Kenyon Review;* Jenny Zhang for "Why Were They Throwing Bricks?" in *n+1.*

PEN/Nora Magid Award ($2,500). Awarded biennially to honor a magazine editor who has contributed significantly to the excellence of the publication he or she edits. *Winners (2017):* Michael Archer and Joel Whitney for *Guernica.*

PEN/Malamud Award. To recognize a body of work that demonstrates excellence in the art of short fiction. *Winners:* Amina Gautier and Joan Silber.

PEN/Ralph Manheim Medal for Translation. Given triennially to a translator whose career has demonstrated a commitment to excellence. *Winner (2018):* Barbara Harshav.

PEN/Nabokov Award for Achievement in International Literature ($50,000). To a writer of any genre and of any nationality for their exceptional body of work. *Winner:* Edna O'Brien.

PEN/Phyllis Naylor Working Writer Fellowship ($5,000). To a published author of children's or young adult fiction to aid in completing a book-length work in progress. *Offered by:* PEN American Center. *Winner:* Vicky Shiefman for *Help Me God, Please Pretty Please* (work in progress).

PEN New England Awards. For works of fiction, nonfiction, and poetry by New England writers or with New England topics or settings. *Winners:* Not awarded in 2018.

PEN New England Henry David Thoreau Prize for Literary Excellence in Nature Writing. *Winner:* Bernd Heinrich.

PEN Open Book Award (formerly PEN Beyond Margins Award) ($5,000). For book-length writings by authors of color, published in the United States during the current calendar year. *Offered by:* PEN American Center. *Winner:* Alexis Okeowo for *A Moonless, Starless Sky: Ordinary Women and Men Fighting Extremism in Africa* (Hachette Books).

PEN/Joyce Osterweil Award for Poetry ($5,000). A biennial award given in odd-numbered years to recognize a new and emerging American poet. *Offered by:* PEN American Center. *Winner (2017):* Natalie Scenters-Zapico for *The Verging Cities* (Center for Literary Publishing/Colorado State University).

PEN/Laura Pels Foundation Awards for Drama ($7,500 and $2,500). To recognize a master American dramatist, an American playwright in mid-career, and an emerging American playwright. *Offered by:* PEN American Center. *Winners:* (master) Luis Alfaro; (mid-career) Sybil Kempson; (emerging) Mike Lew.

PEN/Jean Stein Book Award ($75,000). To recognize a book-length work of any genre for its originality, merit, and impact. *Win-*

ner: Layli Long Soldier for *Whereas* (Graywolf).

PEN/Jean Stein Grant for Literary Oral History ($10,000). For a literary work of nonfiction that uses oral history to illuminate an event, individual, place, or movement. *Winner:* Nyssa Chow for *Still.Life.*

PEN Translation Prize ($3,000). To promote the publication and reception of translated world literature in English. *Winner:* Len Rix, for his translation from the Hungarian of *Katalin Street* by Magda Szabo (NYRB Classics).

PEN/Edward and Lily Tuck Award for Paraguayan Literature ($3,000 author and $3,000 to translator). To the living author of a major work of Paraguayan literature. *Winner:* Javier Viveros for *Fantasmario*, illustrated by Charles DaPonte (Tiempo Ediciones & Contenidos).

PEN/Voelcker Award for Poetry. Given in even-numbered years to an American poet at the height of his or her powers. *Offered by:* PEN American Center. *Winner (2018):* Kamau Brathwaite.

PEN/Jacqueline Bograd Weld Award for Biography ($5,000). To the author of a distinguished biography published in the United States during the previous calendar year. *Offered by:* PEN American Center. *Winner:* John A. Farrell for *Richard Nixon: The Life* (Doubleday).

PEN/E. O. Wilson Literary Science Writing Award ($10,000). For a book of literary nonfiction on the subject of the physical and biological sciences. *Winner:* Lindsey Fitzharris for *The Butchering Art: Joseph Lister's Quest to Transform the Grisly World of Victorian Medicine* (Scientific American/Farrar, Straus and Giroux).

Maxwell E. Perkins Award. To honor an editor, publisher, or agent who has discovered, nurtured, and championed writers of fiction in the United States. *Offered by:* Center for Fiction, Mercantile Library of New York. *Winner:* Ajai Singh "Sonny" Mehta, chairman, Knopf Doubleday Publishing Group and editor in chief, Alfred A. Knopf Publishers.

Phoenix Awards. To the authors of English-language children's books that failed to win a major award at the time of publication 20 years earlier. *Winner:* Elizabeth Partridge for *Restless Spirit: The Life and Work of Dorothea Lange* (Viking).

Edgar Allan Poe Awards. For outstanding mystery, suspense, and crime writing. *Offered by:* Mystery Writers of America. *Winners:* (novel) Attica Locke for *Bluebird, Bluebird* (Hachette/Mulholland Books); (first novel) Jordan Harper for *She Rides Shotgun* (HarperCollins/Ecco); (paperback original) Anna Mazzola for *The Unseeing* (Sourcebooks/Landmark); (fact crime) David Grann for *Killers of the Moon: The Osage Murders and the Birth of the FBI* (Doubleday); (critical/biographical) Lawrence P. Jackson for *Chester B. Himes: A Biography* (W. W. Norton & Company); (short story) John Crowley for "Spring Break" in *New Haven Noir* (Akashic Books); (juvenile) James Ponti for *Vanished!* (Simon & Schuster/Aladdin); (young adult) Jason Reynolds for *Long Way Down* (Simon & Schuster/Atheneum Books for Young Readers); (television episode) Noah Hawley for "Somebody to Love" in *Fargo* (FX Networks/MGM); (Robert L. Fish Memorial Award) Lisa D. Gray for "The Queen of Secrets" in *New Haven Noir* (Akashic Books); (grand master) Jane Langton; William Link; Peter Lovesey; (Raven Award) The Raven Book Store, Lawrence, Kansas; Kristopher Zgorski; (Ellery Queen Award) Robert Pépin; (Mary Higgins Clark Award) Carol Goodman for *The Widow's House* (HarperCollins/William Morrow).

Poets Out Loud Prize ($1,000 and publication by Fordham University Press). For a book-length poetry collection. *Sponsor:* Fordham University. *Winners:* Julia Bouwsma for "Midden"; (editor's prize) Henk Roussow for "Xamissa."

Katherine Anne Porter Award ($20,000). Awarded biennially to a prose writer of demonstrated achievement. *Offered by:* American Academy of Arts and Letters. *Winner (2018):* Noy Holland.

Michael L. Printz Award. For excellence in literature for young adults. *Offered by:* American Library Association, Young Adult Library Services Association. *Winner:* Nina LaCour for *We Are Okay* (Dutton Books for Young Readers).

V. S. Pritchett Memorial Prize (United Kingdom) (£1,000). For a previously unpublished short story. *Offered by:* Royal Society of Literature. *Winner:* Emily Ruth Ford for "Please Be Good to Me."

Pritzker Military Library Literature Award ($100,000). To recognize a living author for a body of work that has profoundly enriched the public understanding of American military history. *Sponsor:* Tawani Foundation. *Winner:* Dennis Showalter.

Prix Aurora Awards (Canada). For science fiction. *Offered by:* Canadian SF & Fantasy Association. *Winners:* (novel) Fonda Lee for *Jade City* (Orbit); (young adult novel) (tie) Fonda Lee for Exo (Scholastic); Elizabeth Whitton for *Houses of the Old Blood* (Kettlescon); (short fiction) Liz Westbrook-Trenholm for "Gone Flying" in *The Sum of Us: Tales of the Bonded and Bound* (Laksa Media Groups); (related work) Susan Forest and Lucas K. Law (editors) for *The Sum of Us: Tales of the Bonded and Bound* (Laksa Media Groups); (graphic novel) Peter Chiykowski for *Rock Paper Cynic* (rockpapercynic.com); (poem/song) Matt Moore for "Heaven Is the Hell of No Choices" in *Polar Borealis*; (artist) Dan O'Driscoll; (visual presentation) *Blade Runner 2049*; (CSFFA Hall of Fame) Candas Jane Dorsey; Dr. Jaymie Matthews; Robert Charles Wilson.

Prix Goncourt (France). For "the best imaginary prose work of the year." *Offered by:* Société des Gens des Lettres. *Winner:* Nicolas Mathieu for *Leurs enfants après eux*.

PROSE Awards. For outstanding professional and scholarly works. *Offered by:* Association of American Publishers. *Winners*: (biological and life sciences) MIT Press for *Language in Our Brain: The Origins of a Uniquely Human Capacity* by Angela D. Friederici; (humanities) Oxford University Press for *Jane Crow: The Life of Pauli Murray* by Rosalind Rosenberg; (physical sciences and mathematics) Cell Press for *CHEM*, Robert D. Eagling (editor-in-chief); (reference) Bloomsbury Publishing for *Arcadian Library Online* by the Arcadian Library/Bloomsbury Publishing; (social sciences) Princeton University Press for *Adaptive Markets: Financial Evolution at the Speed of Thought* by Andrew W. Lo.

Pulitzer Prizes in Letters ($10,000). To honor distinguished work dealing preferably with American themes. *Offered by:* Columbia University Graduate School of Journalism. *Winners:* (fiction) Andrew Sam Greer for *Less* (Lee Boudeaux Books/Little, Brown and Company); (drama) Martyna Majok for *Cost of Living*; (history) Jack E. Davis for *The Gulf: The Making of an American Sea* (Liveright/W. W. Norton & Company); (biography/autobiography) Caroline Fraser for *Prairie Fires: The American Dreams of Laura Ingalls Wilder* (Metropolitan Books); (poetry) Frank Bidart for *Half-light: Collected Poems 1965–2016* (Farrar, Straus and Giroux); (general nonfiction) James Forman, Jr., for *Locking Up Our Own: Crime and Punishment in Black America* (Farrar, Straus and Giroux).

Raiziss/De Palchi Translation Award ($5,000 book award and a $25,000 fellowship, awarded in alternate years). For a translation into English of a significant work of modern Italian poetry by a living translator. *Offered by:* Academy of American Poets. *Winner:* (book award) Anthony Molino for *The Diary of Kaspar Hauser by Paolo Febbraro* (Negative Capability Press).

RBC Bronwen Wallace Award for Emerging Writers (C$10,000) (Canada). For writers under the age of 35 who are unpublished in book form; award alternates each year between poetry and short fiction. *Offered by:* Writers' Trust of Canada. *Sponsor:* Royal Bank of Canada. *Winner:* Maria Riva.

Arthur Rense Poetry Prize ($20,000). Awarded triennially to an exceptional poet. *Offered by:* American Academy of Arts and Letters. *Winner (2017):* August Kleinzahler.

Harold U. Ribalow Prize. For Jewish fiction published in English. *Sponsor: Hadassah* magazine. *Winner:* Carol Zoref for *Barren Island* (New Issues).

Rita Awards. *Offered by:* Romance Writers of America. *Winners:* (first book) Alexis Daria for *Take the Lead* (St. Martin's Press); (short contemporary romance) Kait Nolan for *Second Chance Summer* (self-published); (mid-length contemporary romance) Abigail Strom for *Tell Me* (Montlake); (long contemporary romance) Lexi Ryan for *Falling Hard* (self-published); (erotic) by J. Kenner for *Wicked Dirty* (Martini & Olive Books);

(long historical) Kelly Bowen for *Between the Devil and the Duke* (Grand Central Publishing); (short historical) Catherine Tinley for *Waltzing with the Earl* (Harlequin); (mainstream) Kristan Higgins for *Now That You Mention It* (Harlequin); (inspirational) Kara Isaac for *Then There Was You* (self-published); (paranormal) Stephanie Rowe for *Hunt the Darkness* (self-published); (novella) Brynn Kelly for *Forbidden River* (Harlequin); (suspense) HelenKay Dimon for *The Fixer* (HarperCollins); (young adult) Pintip Dunn for *Seize Today* (Entangled Publishing).

Rita Golden Heart Awards. For worthy unpublished romance manuscripts. *Offered by:* Romance Writers of America. *Winners:* (contemporary) Arianna James for "Thrown"; (short contemporary) Janet Raye Stevens for "Cole for Christmas"; (historical) Scarlett Peckham for "The Duke of Charlotte Street"; (mainstream) Anna Murray for "Birds of a Feather"; (paranormal) Kay Hudson for "Jinn on the Rocks"; (suspense) Pamela Varnado for "Extreme Fear"; (young adult) C. R. Grissom for "Mouthful."

Rogers Writers' Trust Fiction Prize (C$50,000) (Canada). To a Canadian author of a novel or short story collection. *Offered by:* Writers' Trust of Canada. *Sponsor:* Rogers Communications. *Winner:* Kathy Page for *Dear Evelyn* (Biblioasis).

Sami Rohr Prize for Jewish Literature ($100,000). For emerging writers of Jewish literature. *Offered by:* Family of Sami Rohr. *Winner:* Ilana Kurshan for *If All the Seas Were Ink* (St. Martin's).

Rosenthal Family Foundation Award ($10,000). For a work of fiction of considerable literary achievement. *Offered by:* American Academy of Arts and Letters. *Winner:* Hannah Lillith Assadi for *Sonora* (Soho Press).

Royal Society of Literature Benson Medal (United Kingdom). To recognize meritorious works in poetry, fiction, history and belles letters, honoring an entire career. The recipient may be someone who is not a writer but has done conspicuous service to literature. *Winner:* Liz Calder.

Royal Society of Literature Giles St Aubyn Awards for Non-Fiction (United Kingdom). For first-time writers of nonfiction. *Offered by:* Royal Society of Literature. *Winners:* (£10,000) Laurence Blair for *Lost Countries of South America: Travels in a Continent's Past and Present* (The Bodley Head); (£5,000) Lily Le Brun for *Looking to Sea: Britain Through the Eyes of its Artists* (Hodder and Stoughton); (special commendation) Paul Craddock for *Dragon in a Suitcase: A Cultural History of the Art of Transplant* (Fig Tree).

Royal Society of Literature Ondaatje Prize (United Kingdom) (£10,000). For a distinguished work of fiction, nonfiction, or poetry evoking the spirit of a place. *Offered by:* Royal Society of Literature. *Winner:* Pascale Petit for *Mama Amazonica* (Bloodaxe Books).

Saltire Society Scotland Literary Awards. To recognize noteworthy work by writers of Scottish descent or living in Scotland, or by anyone who deals with the work or life of a Scot or with a Scottish problem, event, or situation. *Offered by:* Saltire Society. *Sponsors:* Creative Scotland, the National Library of Scotland, the Scottish Poetry Library, the Scottish Historical Review Trust, Tamdhu Speyside Single Malt Scotch Whisky. *Winners:* (book of the year £5,000, individual categories £2,000) Sue Black for *All That Remains: A Life in Death* (Doubleday); (fiction book of the year) Leila Aboulela for *Elsewhere, Home* (Telegram); (nonfiction book of the year) Sue Black for *All That Remains: A Life in Death* (Doubleday); (research book of the year) Tom Mole for *What the Victorians Made of Romanticism* (Princeton University Press); (poetry book of the year) Jay Whittaker for *Wristwatch* (Cinnamon Press); (history) Les Wilson for *The Drowned and the Saved* (Birlinn); (first book) Mick Kitson for *Sal* (Canongate).

Carl Sandburg Literary Awards. *Sponsor:* Chicago Public Library Foundation. *Winners:* Judy Blume and Neil DeGrasse Tyson; (21st Century Award, for significant recent achievement by a Chicago-area writer) Erika L. Sanchez, author of *Lessons on Expulsion (Graywolf) and I Am Not Your Perfect Mexican Daughter* (Knopf Books for Young Readers).

Schneider Family Book Awards ($5,000). To honor authors and illustrators for books that embody artistic expressions of the disability experience of children and adolescents.

Offered by: American Library Association. *Donor:* Katherine Schneider. *Winners:* (young children) Allen Say for *Silent Days, Silent Dreams* (Arthur A. Levine Books); (middle school) Shari Green for *Macy McMillan and the Rainbow Goddess* (Pajama Press); (teen) Whitney Gardner for *You're Welcome, Universe* (Knopf Books for Young Readers).

Scotiabank Giller Prize (Canada) (C$100,000 first place, C$10,000 to each of the finalists). For the best Canadian novel or short story collection written in English. *Offered by:* Giller Prize Foundation and Scotiabank. *Winner:* Esi Edugyan for *Washington Black* (Patrick Crean Editions / HarperCollins); (finalists) Patrick deWitt for *French Exit* (House of Anansi Press); Eric Dupont for *Songs for the Cold of Heart,* translated by Peter McCambridge (QC Fiction / Baraka Books); Sheila Heti for *Motherhood* (Alfred A. Knopf Canada); Thea Lim for *An Ocean of Minutes* (Viking).

Shamus Awards. To honor mysteries featuring independent private investigators. *Offered by:* Private Eye Writers of America. *Winners:* (hardcover novel) T. Jefferson Parker for *The Room of White Fire* (G. P. Putnam's Sons); (first novel) Kristen Lepionka for *The Last Place You Look* (Minotaur); (original paperback) Richard Zahradnik for *Lights Out Summer* (Camel Press); (short story) Robert S. Levinson for "Rosalie Marx Is Missing" in *Ellery Queen's Mystery Magazine*; (lifetime achievement) Walter Mosley.

Shelley Memorial Award ($6,000 to $9,000). To a poet or poets living in the United States, chosen on the basis of genius and need. *Offered by:* Poetry Society of America. *Winner:* Ntozake Shange.

Robert F. Sibert Medal. For the most distinguished informational book for children. *Offered by:* American Library Association, Association for Library Service to Children. *Winner:* Larry Dane Brimner for *Twelve Days in May: Freedom Ride 1961* (Calkins Creek / Highlights).

Society of Authors Traveling Scholarships (United Kingdom) (£2,500). *Winners:* Jenn Ashworth, Tash Aw, Jessie Greengrass, James Harpur, Sudhir Hazareesingh.

Specsavers National Book Awards (United Kingdom) (formerly the Galaxy National Book Awards, earlier the British Book Awards). *Winners:* (new writer) Adam Kay for *This Is Going to Hurt* (Picador); (autobiography/biography) Dolly Alderton for *Everything I Know About Love* (Fig Tree); (children's) Ben Brooks (author) and Quinton Winter (illustrator) for *Stories for Boys Who Dare to Be Different* (Quercus); (young adult) Scarlett Curtis for *Feminists Don't Wear Pink* (Penguin Children's Books); (crime/thriller) Belinda Bauer for *Snap* (Transworld); (popular fiction) Gail Honeyman for *Eleanor Oliphant Is Completely Fine* (Harper); (popular nonfiction) Adam Kay for *This Is Going to Hurt* (Picador); (international author) Sally Rooney for *Normal People* (Faber & Faber); (food and drink) Yotam Ottolenghi for *Ottolenghi Simple* (Ebury Press); (audiobook) Penguin Audio for *The Order of Time* by Carlo Rovelli, read by Benedict Cumberbatch; (ZBOS Book Club Book of the Year) Adam Kay for *This Is Going to Hurt* (Picador); (UK author) Philip Pullman for *The Book of Dust Vol 1: La Belle Sauvage* (Penguin).

Spur Awards. *Offered by:* Western Writers of America. *Winners:* (contemporary novel) Leo W. Banks for *Double Wide* (Brash Books); (historical novel) Dave Osborne for *The Coming* (Bloomsbury USA); (traditional novel) Jeff Guinn for *Silver City: A Novel of the American West* (G. P. Putnam's Sons); (historical nonfiction) David Grann for *Killers of the Flower Moon: The Osage Murders and the Birth of the FBI* (Doubleday); (contemporary nonfiction) Flannery Burke for *A Land Apart: The Southwest and the Nation in the Twentieth Century* (University of Arizona Press); (nonfiction biography) Jane Little Botkin for *Frank Little and the IWW: The Blood That Stained an American Family* (University of Oklahoma Press); (original mass-market paperback novel) Charles G. West for *Hell Hath No Fury: A John Hawk Western* (Pinnacle); (romance) Gina Welborn and Becca Whitham for *The Promise Bride* (Zebra); (juvenile fiction) Matthew P. Mayo for *Stranded: A Story of Frontier Survival* (Five Star Publishing); (juvenile nonfiction) Mary Gibson Sprague for *Glorious Fourth of July and Other Stories from the Plains* (South Dakota Historical Society Press); (storyteller) Jean Abernethy for *Fergus and the Greener Grass* (Trafalgar Square Books); (short fiction) Rod Miller for "Lost and Found: A Short Story" (Wildside Press); (short nonfiction) Ben Mauk for "States of Decay: A Journey Through America's Nuclear Heartland" (*Harper's Magazine*); (poem) Marleen Bussma for "She Saddles Her Own Horse" (self-published); (song) Jean Prescott and Darrell Arnold for "The Pitchfork Grays" (Line Camp Music); (documentary script) MJ Isakson and Eric Frith for "Down the Fence" (Down the Fence Films); (drama script) Taylor Sheridan for *Wind River* (Acacia Filmed Entertainment/Film 44/Savvy Media/Media Holding); (first nonfiction book) Jane Little Botkin for *Frank Little and the IWW: The Blood That Stained an American Family* (University of Oklahoma Press); (first novel) Leo W. Banks for *Double Wide* (Brash Books).

Wallace Stevens Award ($100,000). To recognize outstanding and proven mastery in the art of poetry. *Offered by:* Academy of American Poets. *Winner:* Sonia Sanchez.

Bram Stoker Awards. For superior horror writing. *Offered by:* Horror Writers Association. *Winners:* To be announced. *Winners (2017)*: (novel) Christopher Golden for *Ararat* (St. Martin's Press); (first novel) Robert Payne Cabeen for *Cold Cuts* (Omnium Gatherum Media); (young adult novel) Kim Liggett for *The Last Harvest* (Tor Teen); (graphic novel) Damian Duffy and Octavia E. Butler for *Kindred: A Graphic Novel Adaptation* (Abrams ComicArts); (long fiction) Stephen Graham Jones for *Mapping the Interior* (Tor.com); (short fiction) Lisa Mannetti for "Apocalypse Then" in *Never Fear: The Apocalypse* (13Thirty Books); (fiction collection) Joe Hill for *Strange Weather* (William Morrow); (screenplay) Jordan Peele for *Get Out* (Universal Pictures, Blumhouse Productions, QC Entertainment); (anthology) Doug Murano for *Behold! Oddities, Curiosities & Undefinable Wonders* (Crystal Lake); (nonfiction) Grady Hendrix for *Paperbacks from Hell: The Twisted History of 70s and 80s Horror Fiction* (Quirk Books); (poetry) Christina Sng *for A Collection of Nightmares* (Raw Dog Screaming Press).

Stonewall Book Awards. *Offered by:* Gay, Lesbian, Bisexual, and Transgender Round Table, American Library Association. *Winners:* (Barbara Gittings Literature Award) Cat Fitzpatrick and Casey Plett (editors) for *Meanwhile, Elsewhere: Science Fiction and Fantasy from Transgender Writers* (Topside Press); (Israel Fishman Nonfiction Award) John Chaich and Todd Oldham for *Queer Threads: Crafting Identity and Community* (Ammo); (Mike Morgan and Larry Romans Children's and Young Adult Literature Award) Dashka Slater for *The 57 Bus: A True Story of Two Teenagers and the Crime That Changed Their Lives* (Farrar, Straus and Giroux) and Brandy Colbert for *Little & Lion* (Little, Brown and Company).

Story Prize ($20,000). For a collection of short fiction. *Offered by: Story* magazine. *Winner:* Lauren Groff for *Florida* (Riverhead Books).

Flora Stieglitz Straus Awards. For nonfiction books that serve as an inspiration to young readers. *Offered by:* Bank Street College of Education and the Florence M. Miller Memorial Fund. *Winner:* (older readers) Bryan Stevenson for *Just Mercy* (Delacorte Press); (younger readers) Yuyi Morales for *Dreamers* (Holiday House).

Theodore Sturgeon Memorial Award. For the year's best short science fiction. *Offered by:* Gunn Center for the Study of Science Fiction. *Winner:* Charlie Jane Anders for "Don't Press Charges and I Won't Sue" in *Global Dystopias* (Boston Review).

Sunburst Awards for Canadian Literature of the Fantastic (C$1,000). *Winners:* (adult) David Demchuk for *The Bone Mother* (Chizine Publications); (young adult) Cherie Dimaline for *The Marrow Thieves* (Dancing Cat Books); (short story) Sandra Kasturi for "The Beautiful Gears of Dying" in *The Sum of Us* (Laksa Media).

Sunday Times EFG Short Story Award (United Kingdom) (£30,000). To an author from any country for an English-language story of 6,000 words or less. *Winner:* Courtney Zoffness for "Peanuts Aren't Nuts."

Tanizaki Junichiro Prize (Japan) (1 million yen, approximately $8,450). For a full-length work of fiction or drama by a professional writer. *Offered by:* Chuokoron-Shinsha, Inc. *Winner:* Tomoyuki Hoshino for *Honō*.

RBC Taylor Prize (formerly the Charles Taylor Prize for Literary Nonfiction) (Canada) (C$25,000). To honor a book of creative nonfiction widely available in Canada and written by a Canadian citizen or landed immigrant. *Offered by:* Charles Taylor Foundation. *Winner:* Tanya Talaga for *Seven Fallen Feathers: Racism, Death and Hard Truths in a Northern City* (Anansi Press).

Sydney Taylor Book Awards. For a distinguished contribution to Jewish children's literature. *Offered by:* Association of Jewish Libraries. *Winners:* (younger readers) Richard Michelson (author) and Karla Gudeon (illustrator) for *The Language of Angels: A Story About the Reinvention of Hebrew* (Charlesbridge); (older readers) Alan Gratz for *Refugee* (Scholastic); (teen readers) Antonio Iturbe for *The Librarian of Auschwitz*, translated by Lilit Thwaites (Henry Holt and Co.).

Sydney Taylor Manuscript Award ($1,000). For the best fiction manuscript appropriate for readers ages 8–13, both Jewish and non-Jewish, revealing positive aspects of Jewish life, and written by an unpublished author. *Winner:* Judith Pransky for *The Seventh Handmaiden.*

Theatre Library Association Award. See Richard Wall Memorial Award.

Dylan Thomas Prize (United Kingdom) (£30,000). For a published or produced literary work in the English language, written by an author under 30. *Offered by:* Swansea University. *Winner:* Kayo Chingonyi for *Kumukanda* (Chatto & Windus).

Thriller Awards. *Offered by:* International Thriller Writers. *Winners:* (hardcover novel) Riley Sager for *Final Girls* (Dutton); (first novel) K. J. Howe for *The Freedom Broker* (Quercus); (paperback original) Christine Bell for *Grievance* (Lake Union); (short story) Zoe Z. Dean for "Charcoal and Cherry" in *Ellery Queen's Mystery Magazine*; (young adult) Gregg Hurwitz for *The Rains* (Tor Teen); (e-book original novel) Sean Black for *Second Chance* (Sean Black); (master) George R. R. Martin; (Silver Bullet) James Rollins; (legend) Robert Gussin and Patricia Gussin.

Thurber Prize for American Humor ($5,000). For a humorous book of fiction or nonfiction. *Offered by:* Thurber House. *Winner:* Patricia Lockwood for *Priestdaddy* (Riverhead).

Tom-Gallon Trust Award (United Kingdom) (£1,000). For a short story. *Offered by:* Society of Authors. *Sponsor:* Authors' Licensing and Collecting Society. *Winner:* Chris Connolly for "The Speed of Light and How It Cannot Help Us."

Betty Trask Prize and Awards (United Kingdom). To Commonwealth writers under the age of 35 for "romantic or traditional" first novels. *Offered by:* Society of Authors. *Winners:* (Betty Trask Prize, £10,000) Omar Robert Hamilton for *The City Always Wins* (Faber); (Betty Trask Awards, £3,000) Sarah Day for *Mussolini's Island* (Tinder Press); Clare Fisher for *All the Good Things* (Viking); Eli Goldstone for *Strange Heart Beating* (Granta); Lloyd Markham for *Bad Ideas\Chemicals* (Parthian); Masande Ntshanga for *The Reative* (Jacaranda).

Kate Tufts Discovery Award ($10,000). For a first or very early book of poetry by an emerging poet. *Offered by:* Claremont Graduate University. *Winner:* Donika Kelly for *Bestiary* (Graywolf).

Kingsley Tufts Poetry Award ($100,000). For a book of poetry by a mid-career poet. *Offered by:* Claremont Graduate School. *Winner:* Patricia Smith for *Incendiary Art: Poems* (Triquarterly).

21st Century Award. To honor recent achievement in writing by an author with ties to Chicago. See Carl Sandburg Literary Awards.

UKLA Children's Book Awards (United Kingdom). Sponsor: United Kingdom Literacy Association. *Winners:* (ages 3–6) Morag Hood for *Colin and Lee Carrot and Pea* (Two Hoots); (ages 7–11) (tie) Elizabeth Laird (author) and Lucy Eldridge (illustrator) for *Welcome to Nowhere* (Macmillan); Martin Brown for *Lesser Spotted Animals* (David Fickling Books); (ages 12–16) Sarah Crossan and Brian Conaghan for *We Come Apart* (Bloomsbury).

Ungar German Translation Award ($1,000). Awarded biennially for a distinguished literary translation from German into English that has been published in the United States. *Offered by:* American Translators Association. *Winner (2017):* Alex Levine for his translation of *Exploratory Experiments: Ampere, Farraday, and the Origins of Electrodynamics* (University of Pittsburgh Press).

John Updike Award ($20,000). Given biennially to a writer in mid-career who has demonstrated consistent excellence. *Offered by:* American Academy of Arts and Letters. *Winner (2017):* Dana Spiotta.

VCU/Cabell First Novelist Award ($5,000). For a first novel published in the previous year. *Offered by:* Virginia Commonwealth University. *Winner:* Hernan Diaz for *In the Distance* (Coffee House Press).

Harold D. Vursell Memorial Award ($20,000). To a writer whose work merits recognition for the quality of its prose style. *Offered by:* American Academy of Arts and Letters. *Winner:* Atticus Lish.

Amelia Elizabeth Walden Award ($5,000). To honor a book relevant to adolescents that has enjoyed a wide teenage audience. *Sponsor:* Assembly on Literature for Adolescents, National Council of Teachers of English. *Winner:* Angie Thomas for *The Hate U Give* (Balzer+Bray).

Richard Wall Memorial Award (formerly the Theatre Library Association Award). To honor an English-language book of exceptional scholarship in the field of recorded performance, including motion pictures, television, and radio. *Offered by:* Theatre Library Association. *Winner:* Steven J. Ross for *Hitler in Los Angeles: How Jews Foiled Nazi Plots Against Hollywood and America* (Bloomsbury USA).

George Washington Book Prize ($50,000). To recognize an important new book about America's founding era. *Offered by:* Washington College and the Gilder Lehrman Institute of American History. *Winner:* Kevin J. Hayes for *George Washington: A Life in Books* (Oxford University Press).

Hilary Weston Writers' Trust Prize for Nonfiction (C$60,000) (Canada). *Offered by:* Writers' Trust of Canada. *Winner:* Elizabeth Hay for *All Things Consoled: A Daughter's Memoir* (McClelland & Stewart).

E. B. White Award ($10,000). For achievement in children's literature. *Offered by:* American Academy of Arts and Letters. *Winner:* Not awarded in 2018.

E. B. White Read-Aloud Awards. For children's books with particular appeal as read-aloud books. *Offered by:* American Booksellers Association/Association of Booksellers for Children. *Winners:* (picture book) Mac Barnett (author) and Jon Klassen (illustrator) for *The Wolf, the Duck, and the Mouse* (Candlewick); (middle readers) Katherine Applegate for *Wishtree* (Feiwel & Friends).

Whiting Writers' Awards ($50,000). For emerging writers of exceptional talent and promise. *Offered by:* Mrs. Giles Whiting Foundation. *Winners:* (poetry) Anne Boyer, Rickey Laurentiis, and Tommy Pico; (fiction) Patty Yumi Cottrell, Brontez Purnell, and Weike Wang; (nonfiction) Esme Weijun Wang; (drama) Nathan Alan Davis, Hansol Jung, and Antoinette Nwandu.

Walt Whitman Award ($5,000). To a U.S. poet who has not published a book of poems in a standard edition. *Offered by:* Academy of American Poets. *Winner:* Emily Skaja for "Brute."

Richard Wilbur Award ($1,000 and publication by University of Evansville Press). For a book-length poetry collection. *Winner:* Ned Balbo for "3 Nights of the Perseids."

Laura Ingalls Wilder Award. See Children's Literature Legacy Award.

Thornton Wilder Prize for Translation ($20,000). To a practitioner, scholar, or patron who has made a significant contribution to the art of literary translation. *Offered by:* American Academy of Arts and Letters. *Winner:* Bill Porter (aka Red-Pine).

Robert H. Winner Memorial Award ($2,500). To a mid-career poet over 40 who has published no more than one book of poetry. *Offered by:* Poetry Society of America. *Winner:* Elizabeth Knapp.

George Wittenborn Memorial Book Awards. To North American art publications that represent the highest standards of content, documentation, layout, and format. *Offered by:* Art Libraries Society of North America (ARLIS/NA). *Winners:* To be announced.

Thomas Wolfe Prize and Lecture. To honor writers with distinguished bodies of work. *Offered by:* Thomas Wolfe Society and University of North Carolina at Chapel Hill. *Winner:* Gillian Welch.

Thomas Wolfe Fiction Prize ($1,000). For a short story that honors Thomas Wolfe. *Offered by:* North Carolina Writers Network. *Winner:* Theresa Dowell Blackinton for "Reunification."

Helen and Kurt Wolff Translator's Prize ($10,000). For an outstanding translation from German into English, published in the United States. *Offered by:* Goethe Institut Inter Nationes, New York. *Winner:* Isabel Fargo Cole for her translation of *Old Rendering Plant* by Wolfgang Hilbig (Two Lines Press).

World Fantasy Awards. For outstanding fantasy writing. *Offered by:* World Fantasy Convention. *Winners:* (novel) (tie) Victor LaVAlle for *The Changeling* (Spiegel & Grau) and Fonda Lee for *Jade City* (Orbit); (novella) EllenKlages for *Passing Strange* (Tor.com); (short fiction) Natalia Theodoridou for "The Birding: A Fairy Tale" in *Strange Horizons*; (anthology) Peter S. Beagle and Jacob Weisman (editors) for *The New Voices of Fantasy* (Tachyon Publications); (collection) Jane Yolen for *The Emerald Circus* (Tachyon Publications); (best artist) Gregory Manchess; (special award, professional) Harry Brockway, Patrick McGrath, and Daniel Olson for *Writing Madness* (Centipede Press); (special award, nonprofessional) Justina Ireland and Troy L. Wiggins for *FIYAH: Magazine of Black Speculative Fiction*; (lifetime achievement) Charles de Lint; Elizabeth Wollheim.

Writers' Trust Engel/Findley Award (C$25,000) (Canada). To a Canadian writer predominantly of fiction, for a body of work. *Offered by:* Writers' Trust of Canada. *Sponsors:* Writers' Trust Board of Directors, Pitblado Family Foundation, and Michael Griesdorf Fund. *Winner:* Alissa York.

Writers' Trust/McClelland & Stewart Journey Prize (C$10,000) (Canada). To a new, developing Canadian author for a short story first published in a Canadian literary journal during the previous year. *Offered by:* Writers' Trust of Canada. *Sponsor:* McClelland & Stewart. *Winner:* Shashi Bhat for "Mute" in *The Dalhousie Review.*

Writers' Trust Shaughnessy Cohen Prize for Political Writing (C$25,000) (Canada). For literary nonfiction that captures a political subject of relevance to Canadian readers. *Offered by:* Writers' Trust of Canada. *Winner:* To be announced. *Winner (2017):* Tanya Talaga for *Seven Fallen Feathers: Racism, Death, and Hard Truths in a Northern City* (House of Anansi).

YALSA Award for Excellence in Nonfiction. For a work of nonfiction published for young adults (ages 12–18). *Offered by:* American Library Association, Young Adult Library Services Association. *Winner:* Deborah Heiligman, *Vincent and Theo: The Van Gogh Brothers* (Henry Holt and Company).

Young Lions Fiction Award ($10,000). For a novel or collection of short stories by an American under the age of 35. *Offered by:* Young Lions of the New York Public Library. *Winner:* Lesley Nneka Arimah for *What It Means When a Man Falls from the Sky* (Riverhead Books).

Young People's Poet Laureate ($25,000). For lifetime achievement in poetry for children. Honoree holds the title for two years. *Offered by:* the Poetry Foundation. *Winner (2017):* Margarita Engle.

Morton Dauwen Zabel Award ($10,000). Awarded biennially, in rotation, to a progressive and experimental poet, writer of fiction, or critic. *Offered by:* American Academy of Arts and Letters. *Winner (2018):* Elaine Scarry.

Zoetrope Short Fiction Prizes. *Offered by: Zoetrope: All-Story. Winners:* (first, $1,000) Miles Greaves for "The Teeth"; (second, $500) Uzma Aslam Khan for "My Mother Is a Lunar Crater"; (third, $250) Gráinne Murphy for "Further West."

Charlotte Zolotow Award. For outstanding writing in a picture book published in the United States in the previous year. *Offered by:* Cooperative Children's Book Center, University of Wisconsin–Madison. *Winners:* Bao Phi for *A Different Pond*, illustrated by Thi Bui (Capstone).

Part 6
Directory of Organizations

Directory of Library and Related Organizations

Networks, Consortia, and Other Cooperative Library Organizations

This list is taken from the current edition of *American Library Directory* (Information Today, Inc.), which includes additional information on member libraries and primary functions of each organization.

United States

Alabama

Alabama Health Libraries Assn., Inc. (AL-HeLa), Lister Hill Lib., Univ. of Alabama, Birmingham 35294-0013. SAN 372-8218. Tel. 205-975-8313, fax 205-934-2230. *Pres.* Becca Billings.

Library Management Network, Inc. (LMN), 2132 6th Ave. S.E., Suite 106, Decatur 35601. SAN 322-3906. Tel. 256-308-2529, fax 256-308-2533. *Secy.* Julia Everett.

Marine Environmental Sciences Consortium, Dauphin Island Sea Laboratory, Dauphin Island 36528. SAN 322-0001. Tel. 251-861-2141, fax 251-861-4646, e-mail disl@disl.org. *Coord.* John Dindo.

Network of Alabama Academic Libraries, c/o Alabama Commission on Higher Education, Montgomery 36104. SAN 322-4570. Tel. 334-242-2211, fax 334-242-0270. *Exec. Dir.* Sheila Snow-Croft.

Alaska

Alaska Library Network (ALN), P.O. Box 23005, Anchorage 99523-0051. SAN 371-0688. Tel. 907-786-0618, e-mail info@aklib.net. *Exec. Dir.* Steve Rollins.

Arkansas

Northeast Arkansas Hospital Library Consortium, 223 E. Jackson, Jonesboro 72401. SAN 329-529X. Tel. 870-972-1290, fax 870-931-0839. *Dir.* Karen Crosser.

California

49-99 Cooperative Library System, c/o Southern California Lib. Cooperative, 248 E. Foothill Blvd., Suite 101, Monrovia 91016. SAN 301-6218. Tel. 626-359-6111, fax 626-283-5949. *Dir.* Diane R. Satchwell.

Bay Area Library and Information Network (BayNet), 1462 Cedar St., Berkeley 94702. SAN 371-0610. Tel. 415-355-2826, e-mail infobay@baynetlibs.org. *Pres.* Brian Edwards.

Califa, 330 Townsend St., Ste. 133, San Francisco 94107. Tel. 888-239-2289, fax 415-520-0434, e-mail califa@califa.org. *Exec. Dir.* Paula MacKinnon.

Consumer Health Information Program and Services (CHIPS), 12350 Imperial Hwy., Norwalk 90650. SAN 372-8110. Tel. 562-868-4003, fax 562-868-4065, e-mail referenceservices@library.lacounty.gov.

Gold Coast Library Network, 3437 Empresa Dr., Suite C, San Luis Obispo 93401-7355. Tel. 805-543-6082, fax 805-543-9487. *Admin. Dir.* Maureen Theobald.

National Network of Libraries of Medicine–Pacific Southwest Region (NN/LM-PSR), Louise M. Darling Biomedical Lib., Los Angeles 90095-1798. SAN 372-8234. Tel. 310-825-1200, fax 310-825-5389, e-mail psr-nnlm@library.ucla.edu. *Dir.* Judy Consales.

Nevada Medical Library Group (NMLG), Barton Memorial Hospital Lib., 2170 South Ave., South Lake Tahoe 96150. SAN 370-0445. Tel. 530-543-5844, fax 530-541-4697. *Senior Exec. Coord.* Laurie Anton.

Northern California Assn. of Law Libraries (NOCALL), 268 Bush St., No. 4006, San Francisco 94104. SAN 323-5777. E-mail admin@nocall.org. *Pres.* Michael Ginsborg.

Northern and Central California Psychology Libraries (NCCPL), 2040 Gough St., San Francisco 94109. SAN 371-9006. Tel. 415-771-8055. *Pres.* Scott Hines.

OCLC Research Library Partnership, 155 Bovet Rd., Suite 500, San Mateo 94402. Tel. 614-764-6000, e-mail oclcresearch@oclc.org. *Exec. Dir.* Rachel Frick.

Peninsula Libraries Automated Network (PLAN), 2471 Flores St., San Mateo 94403-4000. SAN 371-5035. Tel. 650-349-5538, fax 650-349-5089. *Dir., Information Technology* Monica Schultz.

San Bernardino, Inyo, Riverside Counties United Library Services (SIRCULS), 555 W. 6th St., San Bernadino 92410. Tel. 909-381-8257, fax 909-888-3171, e-mail ils@inlandlib.org. *Exec. Dir.* Vera Skop.

San Francisco Biomedical Library Network (SFBLN), San Francisco General Hospital UCSF/Barnett-Briggs Medical Lib., 1001 Potrero Ave., Bldg. 30, 1st Fl., San Francisco 94110. SAN 371-2125. Tel. 415-206-6639, e-mail fishbon@ucsfmedctr.org. *Lib. Dir.* Stephen Kiyoi.

Santa Clarita Interlibrary Network (SCILNET), Powell Lib., Santa Clarita 91321. SAN 371-8964. Tel. 661-362-2271, fax 661-362-2719. *Libn.* John Stone.

Serra Cooperative Library System, Serra c/o SCLC, 248 E. Foothill Blvd., Suite 101, Monrovia 91016-5522. SAN 301-3510. Tel. 626-283-5949. *Exec. Dir.* Diane R. Satchwell.

Southern California Library Cooperative (SCLC), 248 E. Foothill Blvd., Suite 101, Monrovia 91016-5522. SAN 371-3865. Tel. 626-283-5949. *Dir.* Diane R. Satchwell.

Colorado

Colorado Alliance of Research Libraries, 3801 E. Florida Ave., Suite 515, Denver 80210. SAN 322-3760. Tel. 303-759-3399, fax 303-759-3363. *Exec. Dir.* George Machovec.

Colorado Assn. of Law Libraries, P.O. Box 13363, Denver 80201. SAN 322-4325. Tel. 303-492-7535, fax 303-492-2707. *Pres.* Andrea Hamilton.

Colorado Council of Medical Librarians (CCML), P.O. Box 101058, Denver 80210-1058. SAN 370-0755. Tel. 303-724-2124, fax 303-724-2154. *Pres.* Kimberly O'Neill.

Colorado Library Consortium (CLiC), 7400 E. Arapahoe Rd., Suite 75, Centennial 80112. SAN 371-3970. Tel. 303-422-1150, fax 303-431-9752. *Exec. Dir.* Jim Duncan.

Connecticut

Bibliomation, 24 Wooster Ave., Waterbury 06708. Tel. 203-577-4070. *Exec. Dir.* Carl DeMilia.

Connecticut Library Consortium, 234 Court St., Middletown 06457-3304. SAN 322-0389. Tel. 860-344-8777, fax 860-344-9199, e-mail clc@ctlibrarians.org. *Exec. Dir.* Jennifer Keohane.

Council of State Library Agencies in the Northeast (COSLINE), Connecticut State Lib., 231 Capitol Ave., Hartford 06106. SAN 322-0451. Tel. 860-757-6510, fax 860-757-6503. *Exec. Dir.* Timothy Cherubini.

CTW Library Consortium, Olin Memorial Lib., Middletown 06459-6065. SAN 329-4587. Tel. 860-685-3887, fax 860-685-2661. *Libn. for Collaborative Projects* Lorri Huddy.

Hartford Consortium for Higher Education, 31 Pratt St., 4th Fl., Hartford 06103. SAN 322-0443. Tel. 860-702-3801, fax 860-241-1130. *Exec. Dir.* Martin Estey.

Libraries Online, Inc. (LION), 100 Riverview Center, Suite 252, Middletown 06457. SAN 322-3922. Tel. 860-347-1704, fax 860-346-3707. *Exec. Dir.* Alan Hagyard.

Library Connection, Inc., 599 Matianuck Ave., Windsor 06095-3567. Tel. 860-937-8261, fax 860-298-5328. *Exec. Dir.* George Christian.

District of Columbia

Association of Research Libraries, 21 Dupont Circle NW, Suite 800, Washington 20036. Tel. 202-296-2296, fax 202-872-0884. *Exec. Dir.* Mary Lee Kennedy.

Council for Christian Colleges and Universities, 321 8th St. N.E., Washington 20002. SAN 322-0524. Tel. 202-546-8713, fax 202-546-8913, e-mail council@cccu.org. *Pres.* Shirley V. Hoogstra.

District of Columbia Area Health Science Libraries (DCAHSL), P.O. Box 96920, Washington 20090. SAN 323-9918. Tel. 202-863-2518, fax 202-484-1595, e-mail mtaliaferro@aamc.org. *Pres.* Wanda Whitney.

FEDLINK/Federal Library and Information Network, c/o Federal Lib. and Info. Center Committee, 101 Independence Ave. SE, Washington 20540-4935. SAN 322-0761. Tel. 202-707-4800, fax 202-707-4818, e-mail flicc@loc.gov. *Mgr.* Joan Fitts.

Washington Theological Consortium, 487 Michigan Ave. N.E., Washington 20017-1585. SAN 322-0842. Tel. 202-832-2675, fax 202-526-0818, e-mail wtc@washtheocon.org. *Exec. Dir.* Larry Golemon.

Florida

Florida Library Information Network, R. A. Gray Bldg., State Library and Archives of Florida, Tallahassee 32399-0250. SAN 322-0869. Tel. 850-245-6600, fax 850-245-6744, e-mail library@dos.myflorida.com. *Bureau Chief* Cathy Moloney.

Library and Information Resources Network, 7855 126th Ave. N, Largo 33773. Tel. 727-536-0214, fax 727-530-3126.

Midwest Archives Conference (MAC), 2598 E Sunrise Blvd., Suite 2104, Fort Lauderdale 33304. E-mail membership@midwestarchives.org. *Pres.* David McCartney.

Northeast Florida Library Information Network (NEFLIN), 2233 Park Ave., Suite 402, Orange Park 32073. Tel. 904-278-5620, fax 904-278-5625, e-mail office@neflin.org. *Exec. Dir.* Brad Ward.

Panhandle Library Access Network (PLAN), Five Miracle Strip Loop, Suite 8, Panama City Beach 32407-3850. SAN 370-047X. Tel. 850-233-9051, fax 850-235-2286. *Exec. Dir.* Charles Mayberry.

SEFLIN/Southeast Florida Library Information Network, Inc, Wimberly Lib., Office 452, Florida Atlantic Univ., 777 Glades Rd., Boca Raton 33431. SAN 370-0666. Tel. 561-208-0984, fax 561-208-0995. *Exec. Dir.* Jennifer Pratt.

Southwest Florida Library Network (SWFLN), 13120 Westlinks Terrace, Unit 3, Fort Myers 33913. Tel. 239-313-6338, fax 239-313-6329. *Exec. Dir.* Luly Castro.

Tampa Bay Library Consortium, Inc., 4042 Park Oaks Blvd., Suite 430, Tampa 33619. SAN 322-371X. Tel. 813-622-8252, fax 813-628-4425. *Exec. Dir.* Charlie Parker.

Tampa Bay Medical Library Network, Medical Lib., Department 7660, 501 Sixth Ave. South, Saint Petersburg 33701. SAN 322-0885. Tel. 727-767-8557. *Chair* Joshua Brown.

Three Rivers Regional Library Consortium, 176 SW Community Circle, Mayo 32066. Tel. 386-294-3858. *Dir.* Dale Collum.

Georgia

Association of Southeastern Research Libraries (ASERL), c/o Robert W. Woodruff Library, 540 Asbury Circle, Suite 316, Atlanta 30322-1006. SAN 322-1555. Tel. 404-727-0137. *Exec. Dir.* John Burger.

Atlanta Health Science Libraries Consortium, Fran Golding Medical Lib. at Scottish Rite, 1001 Johnson Ferry Rd. NE, Atlanta 30342-1600. Tel. 404-785-2157, fax 404-785-2155. *Pres.* Kate Daniels.

Atlanta Regional Council for Higher Education (ARCHE), 133 Peachtree St., Suite 4925, Atlanta 30303. SAN 322-0990. Tel. 404-651-2668, fax 404-880-9816, e-mail arche@atlantahighered.org. *Pres.* Elizabeth Kiss.

Consortium of Southern Biomedical Libraries (CONBLS), Robert B. Greenblatt, MD Library, 1439 Laney Walker Blvd., Augusta, 30912. SAN 370-7717. Tel. 843-792-8839. *Chair* Brenda Seago.

Georgia Interactive Network for Medical Information (GAIN), c/o Mercer Univ. School of Medicine, 1550 College St., Macon 31207. SAN 370-0577. Tel. 478-301-2515, fax 478-301-2051, e-mail gain.info@gain.mercer.edu.

GOLD Georgia Resource Sharing for Georgia's Libraries (GOLD), c/o Georgia Public Lib. Service, 1800 Century Pl. NE, Suite 150, Atlanta 30345-4304. SAN 322-094X. Tel. 404-235-7128, fax 404-235-7201. *Project Mgr.* Elaine Hardy.

LYRASIS, 1438 W. Peachtree St. N.W., Suite 150, Atlanta 30309. SAN 322-0974. Tel. 800-999-8558, fax 404-892-7879. *CEO* Robert Miller.

Public Information Network for Electronic Services (PINES), 1800 Century Pl. Suite 150, Atlanta 30345-4304. Tel. 404-235-7200. *Prog. Mgr.* Terran McCanna.

Hawaii

Hawaii-Pacific Chapter, Medical Library Assn. (HPC-MLA), Health Sciences Lib., Honolulu 96813. SAN 371-3946. Tel. 808-692-0810, fax 808-692-1244. *Chair* Mabel Trafford.

Idaho

Canyon Owyhee Library Group (COLG), 203 E. Owyhee Ave., Homedale 83628. Tel. 208-337-4613, fax 208-337-4933. *Pres.* Pam Herman.

Cooperative Information Network (CIN), 8385 N. Government Way, Hayden 83835-9280. SAN 323-7656. Tel. 208-772-5612, fax 208-772-2498.

Library Consortium of Eastern Idaho (LCEI), 113 S. Garfield, Pocatello 83204-3235. SAN 323-7699. Tel. 208-237-2192. *Pres.* Marilyn Kamoe.

LYNX Consortium, c/o Boise Public Lib., 715 S. Capitol Ave., Boise 83702-7195. SAN 375-0086. Tel. 208-384-4238, fax 208-384-4025. *Dir.* Kevin Booe.

Illinois

Areawide Hospital Library Consortium of Southwestern Illinois (AHLC), c/o St. Elizabeth Hospital Health Sciences Lib., 211 S. Third St., Belleville 62222. SAN 322-1016. Tel. 618-234-2120 ext. 2011, fax 618-222-4614.

Assn. of Chicago Theological Schools (ACTS), Univ. of St. Mary of the Lake, Mundelein 60060-1174. SAN 370-0658. Tel. 847-566-6401. *Chair* Thomas Baima.

Big Ten Academic Alliance (formerly Committee on Institutional Cooperation), 1819 S. Neil St., Suite D, Champaign 61820-7271. Tel. 217-333-8475, fax 217-244-7127, e-mail btaa@staff.cic.net. *Exec. Dir.* Keith A. Marshall.

Center for Research Libraries, 6050 S. Kenwood, Chicago 60637-2804. SAN 322-1032. Tel. 773-955-4545, fax 773-955-4339. *Pres.* Bernard F. Reilly.

Chicago Area Museum Libraries (CAML), c/o Lib., Field Museum, Chicago 60605-2496. SAN 371-392X. Tel. 312-665-7970, fax 312-665-7893. *Museum Libn.* Christine Giannoni.

Consortium of Academic and Research Libraries in Illinois (CARLI), 100 Trade Center Dr., Suite 303, Champaign 61820. SAN 322-3736. Tel. 217-244-4664, fax 217-244-7596, e-mail support@carli.illinois.edu. *Sr. Dir.* Anne Craig.

Council of Directors of State University Libraries in Illinois (CODSULI), Southern Illinois Univ. School of Medicine Lib., 801 N. Rutledge, Springfield 62702-4910. SAN 322-1083. Tel. 217-545-0994, fax 217-545-0988.

East Central Illinois Consortium, Booth Lib., Eastern Illinois Univ., 600 Lincoln Ave., Charleston 61920. SAN 322-1040. Tel. 217-581-7549, fax 217-581-7534. *Mgr.* Stacey Knight-Davis.

Heart of Illinois Library Consortium, 511 N.E. Greenleaf, Peoria 61603. SAN 322-1113. *Chair* Leslie Menz.

Illinois Heartland Library System, 1704 W. Interstate Dr., Champaign 61822. Tel. 217-352-0047. *Exec. Dir.* Leslie Bednar.

Illinois Library and Information Network (ILLINET), c/o Illinois State Lib., Gwendolyn Brooks Bldg. 300 S. Second St., Springfield 62701-1796. SAN 322-1148. Tel. 217-785-5600. *Dir.* Greg McCormick.

LIBRAS, Inc., North Park Univ., 3225 W. Foster Ave., Chicago 60625-4895. SAN 322-1172. Tel. 773-244-5584, fax 773-244-4891. *Pres.* Rebecca Miller.

Metropolitan Consortium of Chicago, Chicago School of Professional Psychology, 325 N. Wells St., Chicago 60610. SAN 322-1180. Tel. 312-329-6630, fax 312-644-6075. *Coord.* Margaret White.

National Network of Libraries of Medicine–Greater Midwest Region (NN/LM-GMR), c/o Lib. of Health Sciences, Univ. of Illinois at Chicago, 1750 W. Polk St., M/C 763, Chicago 60612-4330. SAN 322-1202. Tel. 312-996-2464, fax 312-996-2226. *Dir.* Kathryn Carpenter.

Network of Illinois Learning Resources in Community Colleges (NILRC), P.O. Box 120, Blanchardville 53516-0120. Tel. 608-523-4094, fax 608-523-4072. *Bus. Mgr.* Lisa Sikora.

System Wide Automated Network (SWAN), 800 Quail Ridge Dr., Westmont 60559. Tel. 844-792-6542. *Exec. Dir.* Aaron Skog.

Indiana

Central Indiana Health Science Libraries Consortium, Indiana Univ. School of Medicine Lib., Indianapolis 46202. SAN 322-1245. Tel. 317-274-8358, fax 317-274-4056. *Officer* Elaine Skopelja.

Consortium of College and University Media Centers (CCUMC), Indiana Univ., 306 N. Union St., Bloomington 47405-3888. SAN 322-1091. Tel. 812-855-6049, fax 812-855-2103, e-mail ccumc@ccumc.org. *Exec. Dir.* Aileen Scales.

Evansville Area Library Consortium, 3700 Washington Ave., Evansville 47750. SAN 322-1261. Tel. 812-485-4151, fax 812-485-7564. *Coord.* Jane Saltzman.

Evergreen Indiana Consortium, Indiana State Lib., 315 W. Ohio St., Indianapolis 46202. Tel. 317-234-6624, fax 317-232-0002. *Coord.* Anna Goben.

Iowa

Polk County Biomedical Consortium, c/o Broadlawns Medical Center Lib., Des Moines 50314. SAN 322-1431. Tel. 515-282-2394, fax 515-282-5634. *Treas.* Elaine Hughes.

Quad City Area Biomedical Consortium, Great River Medical Center Lib., West Burlington 52655. SAN 322-435X. Tel. 319-768-4075, fax 319-768-4080. *Coord.* Sarah Goff.

Sioux City Library Cooperative (SCLC), c/o Sioux City Public Lib., Sioux City 51101-1203. SAN 329-4722. Tel. 712-255-2933 ext. 255, fax 712-279-6432. *Chair* Betsy Thompson.

State of Iowa Libraries Online (SILO), State Lib. of Iowa, Des Moines 50319. SAN 322-1415. Tel. 515-281-4105, fax 515-281-6191. *State Libn.* Michael Scott.

Kansas

Associated Colleges of Central Kansas (ACCK), 210 S. Main St., McPherson 67460. SAN 322-1474. Tel. 620-241-5150, fax 620-241-5153. *Dir.* Cindy Sutton.

Dodge City Library Consortium, c/o Comanche Intermediate Center, 1601 First Ave., Dodge City 67801. SAN 322-4368. Tel. 620-227-1609, fax 620-227-4862.

State Library of Kansas/Statewide Resource Sharing Div., 300 S.W. 10 Ave., Room 312-N., Topeka 66612-1593. SAN 329-5621. Tel. 785-296-3296, fax 785-368-7291. *Dir.* Jeff Hixon.

Kentucky

Appalachian College Assn., 801 Brighton Ave., Richmond 40475. Tel. 859-986-4584, fax 859-986-9549. *Pres.* Beth Rushing.

Assn. for Rural and Small Libraries, 201 E. Main St., Suite 1405, Lexington 40507. Tel. 859-514-9178, e-mail szach@amrms.com. *Pres.* Jet Kofoot.

Assn. of Independent Kentucky Colleges and Universities (AIKCU), 484 Chenault Rd., Frankfort 40601. SAN 322-1490. Tel. 502-695-5007, fax 502-695-5057. *Pres.* Gary S. Cox.

Eastern Kentucky Health Science Information Network (EKHSIN), c/o Camden-Carroll Lib., Morehead 40351. SAN 370-0631. Tel. 606-783-6860, fax 606-784-2178. *Lib. Dir.* Tammy Jenkins.

Kentuckiana Metroversity, Inc., 200 W. Broadway, Suite 800, Louisville 40202. SAN 322-1504. Tel. 502-897-3374, fax 502-895-1647.

Kentucky Medical Library Assn., VA Medical Center, Lib. Services 142D, Louisville 40206-1499. SAN 370-0623. Tel. 502-287-6240, fax 502-287-6134. *Head Libn.* Gene M. Haynes.

Theological Education Assn. of Mid America (TEAM-A), Southern Baptist Theological Seminary, Louisville 40280. SAN 377-5038.

Tel. 502-897-4807, fax 502-897-4600. *Dir., Info. Resources* Ken Boyd.

Louisiana

Health Sciences Library Assn. of Louisiana (HSLAL), 1501 Kings Hwy., Shreveport 71103. SAN 375-0035. Tel. 318-675-5679. *Pres.* Deidra Woodson.

Loan SHARK, State Lib. of Louisiana, 701 N. Fourth St., Baton Rouge 70802. SAN 371-6880. Tel. 225-342-4918, fax 225-219-4725, e-mail ill@state.lib.la.us. *Admin.* Kytara Christophe.

Louisiana Library Network (LOUIS), 1201 N. Third St., Suite 6-200, Baton Rouge 70802. E-mail louisresources@regents.la.gov. *Exec. Dir.* Terri Gallaway.

New Orleans Educational Telecommunications Consortium, 2045 Lakeshore Dr., Suite 541, New Orleans 70122. Tel. 504-524-0350, e-mail noetc@noetc.org. *Dir.* Michael Adler.

Southeastern Chapter of the American Assn. of Law Libraries (SEAALL), c/o Supreme Court of Louisiana, New Orleans 70130-2104. Tel. 504-310-2405, fax 504-310-2419. *Pres.* Michelle Cosby.

Maine

Health Science Library Information Consortium (HSLIC). Disbanded December 2018.

Maryland

Maryland Interlibrary Loan Organization (MILO), c/o Enoch Pratt Free Lib., Baltimore 21201-4484. SAN 343-8600. Tel. 410-396-5498, fax 410-396-5837, e-mail milo@prattlibrary.org. *Mgr.* Emma E. Beaven.

National Network of Libraries of Medicine (NNLM), National Lib. of Medicine, Bldg. 38, 8600 Rockville Pike, Room B1-E03, Bethesda 20894. SAN 373-0905. Tel. 301-496-4777, fax 301-480-1467. *Head, National Network Coordinating Office* Amanda J. Wilson.

National Network of Libraries of Medicine–Southeastern Atlantic Region (NN/LM-SEA), Univ. of Maryland Health Sciences and Human Services Lib., 601 W. Lombard S., Baltimore 21201-1512. SAN 322-1644. Tel. 410-706-2855, fax 410-706-0099, e-mail hshsl-nlmsea@hshsl.umaryland.edu. *Dir.* Mary Tooey.

U.S. National Library of Medicine (NLM), 8600 Rockville Pike, Bethesda 20894. SAN 322-1652. Tel. 301-594-5983, fax 301-402-1384, e-mail custserv@nlm.nih.gov. *Coord.* Martha Fishel.

Washington Research Library Consortium (WRLC), 901 Commerce Dr., Upper Marlboro 20774. SAN 373-0883. Tel. 301-390-2000, fax 301-390-2020. *Exec. Dir.* Mark Jacobs.

Massachusetts

Boston Library Consortium, Inc., 10 Milk St., Suite 354, Boston 02108. SAN 322-1733. Tel. 617-262-0380, fax 617-262-0163, e-mail admin@blc.org. *Exec. Dir.* Susan Stearns.

Cape Libraries Automated Materials Sharing Network (CLAMS), 270 Communication Way, Unit 4E, Hyannis 02601. SAN 370-579X. Tel. 508-790-4399, fax 508-771-4533. *Exec. Dir.* Gayle Simundza.

Central and Western Massachusetts Automated Resource Sharing (C/W MARS), 67 Millbrook St., Suite 201, Worcester 01606. SAN 322-3973. Tel. 508-755-3323 ext. 30, fax 508-755-3721. *Exec. Dir.* Timothy Spindler.

Cooperating Libraries of Greater Springfield (CLGS), Springfield Technical Community College, Springfield 01102. SAN 322-1768. Tel. 413-755-4565, fax 413-755-6315, e-mail lcoakley@stcc.edu. *Coord.* Lynn Coakley.

Fenway Libraries Online, Inc. (FLO), c/o Wentworth Institute of Technology, 550 Huntington Ave., Boston 02115. SAN 373-9112. Tel. 617-989-5032. *Exec. Dir.* Walter Stein.

Massachusetts Health Sciences Libraries Network (MAHSLIN), Lamar Soutter Lib., Univ. of Massachusetts Medical School, Worcester 01655. SAN 372-8293. http://nahsl.libguides.com/mahslin/home. *Pres.* Dan McCloskey.

Merrimack Valley Library Consortium, 4 High St., North Andover 01845. SAN 322-4384. Tel. 978-557-1050, fax 978-557-8101. *Exec. Dir.* Eric C. Graham.

Minuteman Library Network, 10 Strathmore Rd., Natick 01760-2419. SAN 322-4252. Tel. 508-655-8008, fax 508-655-1507. *Exec. Dir.* Susan McAlister.

National Network of Libraries of Medicine–New England Region (NN/LM-NER), Univ. of Massachusetts Medical School, 55 Lake Ave. N., Room S4-241, Worcester 01655. SAN 372-5448. Tel. 800-338-7657, fax 508-856-5977. *Dir.* Elaine Martin.

North Atlantic Health Sciences Libraries, Inc. (NAHSL), Hirsh Health Sciences Lib., 145 Harrison Ave., Boston 02111. SAN 371-0599. Tel. 617-636-3638, fax 617-636-3805. *Chair* Debra Berlanstein.

North of Boston Library Exchange, Inc. (NOBLE), 26 Cherry Hill Drive, Danvers 01923. SAN 322-4023. Tel. 978-777-8844, fax 978-750-8472. *Exec. Dir.* Ronald A. Gagnon.

Northeast Consortium of Colleges and Universities in Massachusetts (NECCUM), Merrimack College, 315 Turnpike St., North Andover 01845. SAN 371-0602. Tel. 978-556-3400, fax 978-556-3738. *Pres.* Richard Santagati.

Northeastern Consortium for Health Information (NECHI), Lowell General Hospital Health Science Lib., 295 Varnum Ave., Lowell 01854. SAN 322-1857. Tel. 978-937-6247, fax 978-937-6855. *Libn.* Donna Beales.

SAILS Library Network, 10 Riverside Dr., Suite 102, Lakeville 02347. SAN 378-0058. Tel. 508-946-8600, fax 508-946-8605, e-mail support@sailsinc.org. *Exec. Dir.* Deborah K. Conrad.

Southeastern Massachusetts Consortium of Health Science (SEMCO), Wilkens Library, 2240 Iyannough Rd., West Barnstable 02668. SAN 322-1873. *Pub. Serv. Coord.* Tim Gerolami.

Western Massachusetts Health Information Consortium, Baystate Medical Center Health Sciences Lib., Springfield 01199. SAN 329-4579. Tel. 413-794-1865, fax 413-794-1974. *Pres.* Susan La Forter.

Michigan

Detroit Area Consortium of Catholic Colleges, c/o Wayne State Univ., Detroit 48202. SAN 329-482X. Tel. 313-883-8500, fax 313-883-8594. *Dir.* Chris Spilker.

Detroit Area Library Network (DALNET), 6th Floor SEL, 5048 Gullen Mall, Detroit 48202. Tel. 313-577-6789, fax 313-577-1231, info@dalnet.org. *Exec. Dir.* Steven K. Bowers.

Lakeland Library Cooperative, 4138 Three Mile Rd. N.W., Grand Rapids 49534-1134. SAN 308-132X. Tel. 616-559-5253, fax 616-559-4329. *Dir.* Carol Dawe.

The Library Network (TLN), 41365 Vincenti Ct., Novi 48375. SAN 370-596X. Tel. 248-536-3100, fax 248-536-3099. *Dir.* James Pletz.

Michigan Health Sciences Libraries Assn. (MHSLA), 1407 Rensen St., Suite 4, Lansing 48910. SAN 323-987X. Tel. 517-394-2774, fax 517-394-2675. *Pres.* Jill Turner.

Mideastern Michigan Library Cooperative, 503 S. Saginaw St., Suite 839, Flint 48502. SAN 346-5187. Tel. 810-232-7119, fax 810-232-6639. *Dir.* Denise Hooks.

Mid-Michigan Library League, 201 N Mitchell, Suite 302, Cadillac 49601-1835. SAN 307-9325. Tel. 231-775-3037, fax 231-775-1749. *Dir.* Sheryl L. Mase.

Midwest Collaborative for Library Services, 1407 Rensen St., Suite 1, Lansing 48910. Tel. 800-530-9019, fax 517-492-3878. *Exec. Dir.* Scott Garrison.

PALnet, 1050 W Bristol Rd., Flint 48507. Tel. 810-766-4070, fax 810-766-2041. *Dir.* Vince Molosky.

Southeastern Michigan League of Libraries (SEMLOL), Lawrence Technological Univ., 21000 W. Ten Mile Rd., Southfield 48075. SAN 322-4481. Tel. 810-766-4070, fax 248-204-3005. *Treas.* Gary Cocozzoli.

Southwest Michigan Library Cooperative, Willard Public Library, 305 Oak St., Battle Creek, 49017. SAN 308-2156. Tel. 269-657-3800, e-mail rhulsey@willard.lib.mi.us. *Dir.* John Mohney.

Suburban Library Cooperative (SLC), 44750 Delco Blvd., Sterling Heights 48313. SAN 373-9082. Tel. 586-685-5750, fax 586-685-5750. *Dir.* Tammy Turgeon.

Upper Peninsula of Michigan Health Science Library Consortium, c/o Marquette Health System Hospital, 580 W. College Ave., Marquette 49855. SAN 329-4803. Tel. 906-225-3429, fax 906-225-3524. *Lib. Mgr.* Janis Lubenow.

Upper Peninsula Region of Library Cooperation, Inc., 1615 Presque Isle Ave., Marquette 49855. SAN 329-5540. Tel. 906-228-7697, fax 906-228-5627. *Treas.* Suzanne Dees.

Valley Library Consortium, 3210 Davenport Ave., Saginaw 48602-3495. Tel. 989-497-0925, fax 989-497-0918. *Exec. Dir.* Randall Martin.

Minnesota

Capital Area Library Consortium (CALCO), c/o Minnesota Dept. of Transportation, Lib. MS155, 395 John Ireland Blvd., Saint Paul 55155. SAN 374-6127. Tel. 651-296-5272, fax 651-297-2354. *Libn.* Shirley Sherkow.

Central Minnesota Libraries Exchange (CMLE), Miller Center, Room 130-D, Saint Cloud 56301-4498. SAN 322-3779. Tel. 320-308-2950, fax 320-654-5131, e-mail cmle@stcloudstate.edu. *Exec. Dir.* Mary Wilkins-Jordan.

Cooperating Libraries in Consortium (CLIC), 1619 Dayton Ave., Suite 204, Saint Paul 55104. SAN 322-1970. Tel. 651-644-3878. *Exec. Dir.* Ruth Dukelow.

Metronet, 1619 Dayton Ave., Suite 314, Saint Paul 55104. SAN 322-1989. Tel. 651-646-0475, fax 651-649-3169, e-mail information@metrolibraries.net. *Exec. Dir.* Ann Walker Smalley.

Metropolitan Library Service Agency (MELSA), 1619 Dayton Ave., No. 314, Saint Paul 55104-6206. SAN 371-5124. Tel. 651-645-5731, fax 651-649-3169, e-mail melsa@melsa.org. *Exec. Dir.* Ken Behringer.

MINITEX, Univ. of Minnesota–Twin Cities, 60 Wilson Library, 309 19th Ave. S, Minneapolis 55455-0439. SAN 322-1997. Tel. 612-624-4002, fax 612-624-4508. *Dir.* Valerie Horton.

Minnesota Library Information Network (MnLINK), Univ. of Minnesota–Twin Cities, Minneapolis 55455-0439. Tel. 800-462-5348, fax 612-624-4508. *Info. Specialist* Nick Banitt.

Minnesota Theological Library Assn. (MTLA), Luther Seminary Lib., 2375 Como Ave., Saint Paul 55108. SAN 322-1962. Tel. 651-641-3447. *Exec. Dir.* Sandra Oslund.

MNPALS, Minnesota State Univ. Mankato, 3022 Memorial Library, Mankato 56001. Tel. 507-389-2000, fax 507-389-5488. *Exec. Dir.* Johnna Horton.

Northern Lights Library Network (NLLN), 1104 7th Ave. S., Box 136, Moorhead 56563. SAN 322-2004. Tel. 218-477-2934. *Exec. Dir.* Kathy Brock Enger.

Prairielands Library Exchange (formerly Southwest Area Multicounty Multitype Interlibrary Exchange—SAMMIE), 1501 State St., Marshall 56258. SAN 322-2039. Tel. 507-532-9013, fax 507-532-2039, e-mail info@sammie.org. *Exec. Dir.* Shelly Grace.

Southeastern Libraries Cooperating (SELCO), 2600 19th St. N.W., Rochester 55901-0767. SAN 308-7417. Tel. 507-288-5513, fax 507-288-8697. *Exec. Dir.* Ann Hutton.

Southwest Area Multicounty Multitype Interlibrary Exchange—SAMMIE. See Prairielands Library Exchange.

Twin Cities Biomedical Consortium (TCBC), c/o Fairview Univ. Medical Center, 2450 Riverside Ave., Minneapolis 55455. SAN 322-2055. Tel. 612-273-6595, fax 612-273-2675. *Mgr.* Colleen Olsen.

Mississippi

Central Mississippi Library Council (CMLC), c/o Millsaps College Lib., 1701 N. State St., Jackson 39210. SAN 372-8250. Tel. 601-974-1070, fax 601-974-1082. *Chair* Stephen Parks.

Mississippi Electronic Libraries Online (MELO), Mississippi State Board for Community and Junior Colleges, Jackson 39211. Tel. 601-432-6518, fax 601-432-6363, e-mail melo@colin.edu. *Dir.* Audra Kimball.

Missouri

Greater Western Library Alliance (GWLA), 5109 Cherry St., Kansas City 64110. Tel. 816-926-8765, fax 816-926-8790. *Exec. Dir.* Joni Blake.

Health Sciences Library Network of Kansas City (HSLNKC), Univ. of Missouri–Kansas City Health Sciences Lib., 2411 Holmes St., Kansas City 64108-2792. SAN 322-2098. Tel. 816-235-1880, fax 816-235-6570. *Pres.* Cindi Kerns.

Kansas City Library Service Program (KC-LSP), 14 W. 10 St., Kansas City 64105.Tel. 816-701-3520, fax 816-701-3401, e-mail kc-lspsupport@kclibrary.org. *Lib. Systems and Service Prog. Mgr.* Melissa Carle.

Mid-America Law Library Consortium (MALLCO), 100 North Tucker Blvd., St. Louis 63101. Tel. 314-977-3449, fax 314-977-3966, e-mail mallcoexecutivedirector@gmail.com. *Exec. Dir.* Corie Dugas.

Mid-America Library Alliance/Kansas City Metropolitan Library and Information Network, 15624 E. 24 Hwy., Independence 64050. SAN 322-2101. Tel. 816-521-7257, fax 816-461-0966. *Exec. Dir.* Mickey Coalwell.

Mobius, 111 E. Broadway, Suite 220, Columbia 65203. Tel. 877-366-2487, fax 541-264-7006. *Exec. Dir.* Donna Bacon.

Saint Louis Regional Library Network, 1190 Meramec Station Rd., Suite 207, Ballwin 63021. SAN 322-2209. Tel. 800-843-8482, fax 636-529-1396, e-mail slrln@amigos.org. *Pres.* Nina O'Daniels.

Western Council of State Libraries, 1190 Meramec Station Rd., Suite 207, Ballwin 63021-6902. Tel. 972-851-8000, fax 636-529-1396.

Montana

Treasure State Academic Information and Library Services (TRAILS), Montana State Univ., P.O. Box 173320, Bozeman 59717. Tel. 406-994-4432, fax 406-994-2851. *Coord.* Pamela Benjamin.

Nebraska

ICON Library Consortium, McGoogan Lib. of Medicine, Univ. of Nebraska, Omaha 68198-6705. Tel. 402-559-7099, fax 402-559-5498. *Exec. Secy.* Mary Helms.

Nevada

Desert States Law Library Consortium, Wiener-Rogers Law Lib., William S. Boyd School of Law, 4505 Maryland Pkwy., Las Vegas 89154-1080. Tel. 702-895-2400, fax 702-895-2416. *Dir.* Jean Price.

Information Nevada, Interlibrary Loan Dept., Nevada State Lib. and Archives, 100 N. Stewart St., Carson City 89701-4285. SAN 322-2276. Tel. 775-684-3360, fax 775-684-3330. *Asst. Admin., Lib. and Development Svcs.* Tammy Westergard.

New Hampshire

GMILCS, Inc., 31 Mount Saint Mary's Way, Hooksett 03106. Tel. 603-485-4286, fax 603-485-4246, e-mail helpdesk@gmilcs.org. *Systems Adminr.* Marilyn Borgendale.

Health Sciences Libraries of New Hampshire and Vermont, Breene Memorial Lib., 36 Clinton St., New Hampshire Hospital, Concord 03246. SAN 371-6864. Tel. 603-527-2837, fax 603-527-7197. *Admin. Coord.* Anne Conner.

Librarians of the Upper Valley Coop. (LUV Coop), c/o Hanover Town Lib., 130 Etna Rd., Etna 03750. SAN 371-6856. Tel. 603-643-3116. *Coord.* Barbara Prince.

Merri-Hill-Rock Library Cooperative, c/o Plaistow Public Lib., 85 Main St., Plaistow 03865. SAN 329-5338. *E-mail* director@plaistowlibrary.com. *Chair* Cab Vinton.

New Hampshire College and University Council, 3 Barrell Court, Suite 100, Concord 03301-8543. SAN 322-2322. Tel. 603-225-4199, fax 603-225-8108. *Pres.* Thomas R. Horgan.

Nubanusit Library Cooperative, c/o Frost Free Lib., 28 Jaffrey Rd., Marlborough 03455. SAN 322-4600. *Chair* Kristin Readel.

Rochester Area Librarians, c/o Ossipee Public Lib., 74 Main St., Ossipee 03814. E-mail opl@worldpath.net. *Chair* Maria Moulton.

New Jersey

Basic Health Sciences Library Network (BHSL), Overlook Hospital Health Science Lib., 99 Beauvoir Ave., Summit 07902. SAN 371-4888. Tel. 908-522-2886, fax 908-522-2274. *Coord.* Pat Regenberg.

Bergen County Cooperative Library System, 810 Main St., Hackensack 07601. Tel. 201-498-7301, fax 201-489-4215, e-mail bccls@bccls.org. *Pres.* Kurt Hadeler.

Bergen Passaic Health Sciences Library Consortium, c/o Health Sciences Lib., Englewood Hospital and Medical Center, 350 Engle St., Englewood 07631. SAN 371-0904. Tel. 201-894-3069, fax 201-894-9049. *Coord.* Lia Sabbagh.

Burlington Libraries Information Consortium (BLINC), 5 Pioneer Blvd., Westampton 08060. Tel. 609-267-9660, fax 609-267-4091, e-mail hq@bcls.lib.nj.us. *Dir.* Ranjna Das.

Health Sciences Library Association of New Jersey (HSLANJ), P.O. Box 12606, Wilmington, DE 19850-2606. Tel. 570-856-5952, fax 888-619-4432, e-mail communications@hslanj.org. *Exec. Dir.* Robb Mackes.

Libraries of Middlesex Automation Consortium (LMxAC), 27 Mayfield Ave., Edison 08837. SAN 329-448X. Tel. 732-750-2525, fax 732-750-9392. *Exec. Dir.* Eileen M. Palmer.

LibraryLinkNJ, New Jersey Library Cooperative, 44 Stelton Rd., Suite 330, Piscataway 08854. SAN 371-5116. Tel. 732-752-7720, fax 732-752-7785. *Exec. Dir.* Kathy Schalk-Greene.

Morris Automated Information Network (MAIN), 16 Wing Dr., Suite 212, Cedar Knolls 07927. SAN 322-4058. Tel. 973-862-4606, fax 973-512-2122. *Exec. Dir.* Phillip Berg.

Morris-Union Federation, 214 Main St., Chatham 07928. SAN 310-2629. Tel. 973-635-0603, fax 973-635-7827. *Exec. Dir.* Karen Brodsky.

New Jersey Health Sciences Library Network (NJHSN), Overlook Hospital Lib., 99 Beauvoir Ave., Summit 07902. SAN 371-4829. Tel. 908-522-2886, fax 908-522-2274. *Lib. Mgr.* Patricia Regenberg.

New Jersey Library Network, Lib. Development Bureau, 185 W. State St., Trenton 08608. SAN 372-8161. Tel. 609-278-2640 ext. 152, fax 609-278-2650. *Admin.* Ruth Pallante.

Virtual Academic Library Environment (VALE), NJEdge/NJIT, 218 Central Ave., GITC 3902, Newark 07102-1982. Tel. 855-832-3343. *Prog. Mgr.* Melissa Lena.

New Mexico

Estacado Library Information Network (ELIN), 509 N. Shipp, Hobbs 88240. Tel. 505-397-9328, fax 505-397-1508.

New Mexico Consortium of Academic Libraries, c/o Donnelly Library, 802 National Ave., Las Vegas. SAN 371-6872. *Pres.* Ruben Aragon. *V.P./Pres.-Elect* Poppy Johnson-Renval.

New Mexico Consortium of Biomedical and Hospital Libraries, c/o Presbyterian Hospital, Robert Shafer Library, 1100 Central Ave., S.E., Santa Fe 87505. SAN 322-449X. Tel. 505-820-5218, fax 505-989-6478. *Co-Pres.* Amanda Okandan.

New York

Academic Libraries of Brooklyn, Long Island Univ. Lib. LLC 517, One University Plaza, Brooklyn 11201. SAN 322-2411. Tel. 718-488-1081, fax 718-780-4057. *Dir.* Ingrid Wang.

Associated Colleges of the Saint Lawrence Valley, SUNY Potsdam, 288 Van Housen Extension, Potsdam 13676-2299. SAN 322-242X. Tel. 315-267-3331, fax 315-267-2389. *Admin. Coord.* Ben Dixon.

Brooklyn-Queens-Staten Island-Manhattan-Bronx Health Sciences Librarians (BQSIMB), 150 55th St., Brooklyn 11220. Tel. 718-630-7200, fax 718-630-8918. *Pres.* Sheryl Ramer Gesoff.

Capital District Library Council (CDLC), 28 Essex St., Albany 12206. SAN 322-2446. Tel. 518-438-2500, fax 518-438-2872. *Exec. Dir.* Kathleen Gundrum.

Central New York Library Resources Council (CLRC), 6493 Ridings Rd., Syracuse 13206-1195. SAN 322-2454. Tel. 315-446-5446, fax 315-446-5590. *Exec. Dir.* Debby Emerson.

CONNECTNY, Inc., 6721 U.S. Highway 11, Potsdam 13676. Tel. 716-930-7752. *Exec. Dir.* Pamela Jones.

Consortium of Foundation Libraries, 32 Old Slip, 24th Fl., New York 10005-3500. SAN 322-2462. Tel. 212-620-4230, e-mail foundationlibraries@gmail.com. *Chair* Susan Shiroma.

Library Assn. of Rockland County (LARC), P.O. Box 917, New City 10956-0917. Tel. 845-359-3877. *Pres.* Carol Connell Connor.

Library Consortium of Health Institutions in Buffalo (LCHIB), Abbott Hall, SUNY at Buffalo, 3435 Main St., Buffalo 14214. SAN 329-367X. Tel. 716-829-3900 ext. 143, fax 716-829-2211, e-mail hubnet@buffalo.edu; ulb-lchib@buffalo.edu. *Exec. Dir.* Martin E. Mutka.

Long Island Library Resources Council (LILRC), 627 N. Sunrise Service Rd., Bellport 11713. SAN 322-2489. Tel. 631-675-1570. *Dir.* Herbert Biblo.

Medical and Scientific Libraries of Long Island (MEDLI), c/o Palmer School of Lib. and Info. Science, Brookville 11548. SAN 322-4309. Tel. 516-299-2866, fax 516-299-4168. *Pres.* Claire Joseph.

Metropolitan New York Library Council (METRO), 599 Eleventh Ave., 8th Fl., New York 10036. SAN 322-2500. Tel. 212-228-2320, fax 212-228-2598, e-mail info@metro.org. *Exec. Dir.* Nate Hill.

New England Law Library Consortium (NELLCO), 756 Madison Ave., Suite 102, Albany 12208. SAN 322-4244. Tel. 518-694-3025, fax 518-694-3027. *Exec. Dir.* Corie Dugas.

Northeast Foreign Law Libraries Cooperative Group, Columbia Univ. Lib., 435 W. 116 St., New York 10027. SAN 375-0000. Tel. 212-854-1411, fax 212-854-3295. *Coord.* Silke Sahl.

Northern New York Library Network, 6721 U.S. Hwy. 11, Potsdam 13676. SAN 322-2527. Tel. 315-265-1119, fax 315-265-1881, e-mail info@nnyln.org. *Exec. Dir.* John J. Hammond.

Rochester Regional Library Council, 390 Packetts Landing, Fairport 14450. SAN 322-2535. Tel. 585-223-7570, fax 585-223-7712, e-mail rrlc@rrlc.org. *Exec. Dir.* Kathleen M. Miller.

South Central Regional Library Council, Clinton Hall, Ithaca 14850. SAN 322-2543. Tel. 607-273-9106, fax 607-272-0740, e-mail scrlc@scrlc.org. *Exec. Dir.* Mary-Carol Lindbloom.

Southeastern New York Library Resources Council (SENYLRC), 21 S. Elting Corners Rd., Highland 12528-2805. SAN 322-2551. Tel. 845-883-9065, fax 845-883-9483. *Exec. Dir.* Tessa Killian.

SUNYConnect, Office of Lib. and Info. Services, Albany 12246. Tel. 518-443-5577, fax 518-443-5358. *Asst. Provost for Lib. and Info. Svcs.* Carey Hatch.

United Nations System Electronic Information Acquisitions Consortium (UNSEIAC), c/o United Nations Lib., New York 10017. SAN 377-855X. Tel. 212-963-3000, fax 212-963-2608, e-mail unseiac@un.org. *Coord.* Amy Herridge.

Western New York Library Resources Council, 4950 Genesee St., Buffalo 14225. SAN 322-2578. Tel. 716-633-0705, fax 716-633-1736. *Exec. Dir.* Sheryl Knab.

North Carolina

North Carolina Community College System, 200 W. Jones St., Raleigh 27603-1379. SAN 322-2594. Tel. 919-807-7100, fax 919-807-7165. *Dir. Lib. Svcs.* Colleen Turnage.

Northwest AHEC Library at Hickory, Catawba Medical Ctr., 810 Fairgrove Church Rd., Hickory 28602. SAN 322-4708. Tel. 828-326-3662, fax 828-326-3484. *Dir.* Karen Lee Martinez.

Northwest AHEC Library Information Network, Wake Forest Univ. School of Medicine, Medical Center Blvd., Winston-Salem 27157-1060. SAN 322-4716. Tel. 336-713-7700, fax 336-713-7701. *Dir.* Mike Lischke.

Triangle Research Libraries Network, Wilson Lib., CB No. 3940, Chapel Hill 27514-8890. SAN 329-5362. Tel. 919-962-8022, fax 919-962-4452. *Exec. Dir.* Lisa Croucher.

Western North Carolina Library Network (WNCLN), c/o Appalachian State Univ., 218 College St., Boone 28608. SAN 376-7205. Tel. 828-262-2774, fax 828-262-3001. *Libn.* Ben Shirley.

North Dakota

Central Dakota Library Network, Morton Mandan Public Lib., Mandan 58554-3149. SAN 373-1391. Tel. 701-667-5365, e-mail mortonmandanlibrary@cdln.info.

Ohio

Assn. of Christian Librarians (ACL), P.O. Box 4, Cedarville 45314. Tel. 937-766-2255, fax 937-766-5499, e-mail info@acl.org. *Pres.* Denise Nelson.

Christian Library Consortium (CLC), c/o ACL, P.O. Box 4, Cedarville 45314. Tel. 937-766-2255, fax 937-766-5499, e-mail info@acl.org. *Coord.* Beth Purtee.

Consortium of Ohio Libraries, P.O. Box 38, Cardington 43315-1116. E-mail Info@info.cool-cat.org. *Chair* Lisa Murray.

Consortium of Popular Culture Collections in the Midwest (CPCCM), c/o Popular Culture Lib., Bowling Green 43403-0600. SAN

370-5811. Tel. 419-372-2450, fax 419-372-7996. *Head Libn.* Nancy Down.

Five Colleges of Ohio, 102 Allen House, Kenyon College, Gambier 43022. Tel. 740-427-5377, fax 740-427-5390, e-mail ohiofive@gmail.com. *Exec. Dir.* Susan Palmer.

Northeast Ohio Regional Library System (NEO-RLS), 1580 Georgetown Rd., Hudson 44236. SAN 322-2713. Tel. 330-655-0531, fax 330-655-0568. *Exec. Dir.* Catherine Hakala-Ausperk.

NORWELD (formerly Northwest Regional Library System), 181½ S. Main St., Bowling Green 43402. SAN 322-273X. Tel. 419-352-2903, fax 419-353-8310. *Exec. Dir.* Arline V. Radden.

OCLC Online Computer Library Center, Inc., 6565 Kilgour Place, Dublin 43017-3395. SAN 322-2748. Tel. 614-764-6000, fax 614-718-1017, e-mail oclc@oclc.org. *Pres./CEO* Skip Pritchard.

Ohio Health Sciences Library Assn. (OHSLA), Medical Lib., South Pointe Hospital, Warrensville Heights 44122. Tel. 216-491-7454, fax 216-491-7650. *Pres.* Mary Pat Harnegie.

Ohio Library and Information Network (OhioLINK), 1224 Kinnear Rd., Columbus 43215. SAN 374-8014. Tel. 614-485-6722, fax 614-228-1807, e-mail info@ohiolink.edu. *Exec. Dir.* Gwen Evans.

Ohio Network of American History Research Centers, Ohio Historical Society Archives-Lib., Columbus 43211-2497. SAN 323-9624. Tel. 614-297-2510, fax 614-297-2546, e-mail reference@ohiohistory.org. *Exec. Dir.* Jackie Barton.

OHIONET, 1500 W. Lane Ave., Columbus 43221-3975. SAN 322-2764. Tel. 614-486-2966, fax 614-486-1527. *Exec. Officer* Nancy S. Kirkpatrick.

Ohio Public Library Information Network (OPLIN), 2323 W. 5 Ave., Suite 130, Columbus 43204. Tel. 614-728-5252, fax 614-728-5256, e-mail support@oplin.org. *Exec. Dir.* Don Yarman.

Serving Every Ohioan Library Center, SEO, 40780 Marietta Rd., Caldwell 43724. SAN 356-4606. Tel. 740-783-5705, fax 800-446-4804. *Dir.* Dianna Clark.

Southeast Ohio and Neighboring Libraries (SWON), 10250 Alliance Rd., Suite 112, Cincinnati 45242. SAN 322-2675. Tel. 513-751-4422, fax 513-751-0463, e-mail info@swonlibraries.org. *Exec. Dir.* Cassondra Vick.

Southeast Regional Library System (SERLS), 252 W. 13 St., Wellston 45692. SAN 322-2756. Tel. 740-384-2103, fax 740-384-2106, e-mail dirserls@oplin.org. *Dir.* Jay Burton.

Southwestern Ohio Council for Higher Education (SOCHE), Miami Valley Research Park, 3155 Research Blvd., Suite 204, Dayton 45420-4015. SAN 322-2659. Tel. 937-258-8890, fax 937-258-8899, e-mail soche@soche.org. *Exec. Dir.* Cassie Barlow.

State Assisted Academic Library Council of Kentucky (SAALCK), 12031 Southwick Lane, Cincinnati 45241. SAN 371-2222. Tel. 800-771-1972, e-mail saalck@saalck.org. *Exec. Dir.* Anne Abate.

Theological Consortium of Greater Columbus (TCGC), Trinity Lutheran Seminary, Columbus 43209-2334. Tel. 614-384-4646, fax 614-238-0263. *Lib. Systems Mgr.* Ray Olson.

Oklahoma

Oklahoma Health Sciences Library Assn. (OHSLA), HSC Bird Health Science Lib., Univ. of Oklahoma, Oklahoma City 73190. SAN 375-0051. Tel. 405-271-2285 ext. 48755, fax 405-271-3297. *Exec. Dir.* Joy Summers-Ables.

Oregon

Chemeketa Cooperative Regional Library Service, 4000 Lancaster Dr. N.E., Rm. 9/136, Salem 97305-1453. SAN 322-2837. Tel. 503-399-5165, fax 503-399-7316, e-mail contact@cclrs.org. *Dir.* John Goodyear.

Library Information Network of Clackamas County (LINCC), 1810 Red Soils Court, #110, Oregon City 97045. SAN 322-2845. Tel. 503-723-4888, fax 503-794-8238. *Lib. System Analyst* Greg Williams.

Orbis Cascade Alliance, 2288 Oakmont Way, Eugene 97401. SAN 377-8096. Tel. 541-246-2470. *Exec. Dir.* Dana Bostrom.

Oregon Health Sciences Libraries Assn. (OHSLA), Oregon Health and Science Univ. Lib., 3181 S.W. Sam Jackson Park Rd., Portland 97239-3098. SAN 371-2176. Tel.

503-494-3462, fax 503-494-3322, e-mail library@ohsu.edu. *Pres.* Jackie Wirz.

Washington County Cooperative Library Services, 111 N.E. Lincoln St., MS No. 58, Hillsboro 97124-3036. SAN 322-287X. Tel. 503-846-3222, fax 503-846-3220. *Mgr.* Eva Calcagno.

Pennsylvania

Berks County Library Assn. (BCLA), Reading Public Lib., Reading 19602. SAN 371-0866. Tel. 610-478-9035, 610-655-6350. *Pres.* Christie Himmelreich.

Central Pennsylvania Consortium (CPC), c/o Franklin & Marshall College, Goethean Hall 101, Lancaster 17604. SAN 322-2896. Tel. 717-358--2896, fax 717-358-4455, e-mail cpc@dickinson.edu. *Interim Pres.* Neil Weissman.

Central Pennsylvania Health Sciences Library Assn. (CPHSLA), Office for Research Protections, Pennsylvania State Univ., 212 Kern Graduate Bldg., University Park 16802. SAN 375-5290. Fax 814-865-1775. *Pres.* Helen Houpt.

Eastern Mennonite Associated Libraries and Archives (EMALA), 2215 Millstream Rd., Lancaster 17602. SAN 372-8226. Tel. 717-393-9745, fax 717-393-8751. *Chair* John Weber.

Greater Philadelphia Law Library Assn. (GPLLA), P.O. Box 335, Philadelphia 19105. SAN 373-1375. *Pres.* Lori Strickler Corso.

HSLC/Access PA (Health Science Libraries Consortium), 3600 Market St., Suite 550, Philadelphia 19104-2646. SAN 323-9780. Tel. 215-222-1532, fax 215-222-0416, e-mail support@hslc.org. *Exec. Dir.* Maryam Phillips.

Interlibrary Delivery Service of Pennsylvania (IDS), c/o Bucks County IU, No. 22, 705 N Shady Retreat Rd., Doylestown 18901. SAN 322-2942. Tel. 215-348-2940 ext. 1625, fax 215-348-8315, e-mail ids@bucksiu.org. *Admin. Dir.* Pamela Dinan.

Keystone Library Network, Dixon Univ. Center, 2986 N. Second St., Harrisburg 17110-1201. Tel. 717-720-4088, fax 717-720-4211. *Coord.* Mary Lou Sowden.

Lehigh Valley Assn. of Independent Colleges, 130 W. Greenwich St., Bethlehem 18018. SAN 322-2969. Tel. 610-625-7888, fax 610-625-7891. *Exec. Dir.* Diane Dimitroff.

Montgomery County Library and Information Network Consortium (MCLINC), 301 Lafayette St., 2nd Fl., Conshohocken 19428. Tel. 610-238-0580, fax 610-238-0581, e-mail webmaster@mclinc.org. *Exec. Dir.* Sharon Moreland-Sender.

National Network of Libraries of Medicine–Middle Atlantic Region (NN/LM-MAR), Univ. of Pittsburgh, 3550 Terrace St., 200 Scaife Hall, Pittsburgh 15261. Tel. 412-684-2065, fax 412-648-1515, e-mail nnlmmar@pitt.edu. *Exec. Dir.* Renae Barger.

Northeastern Pennsylvania Library Network, c/o Marywood Univ. Lib., 2300 Adams Ave., Scranton 18509-1598. SAN 322-2993. Tel. 570-348-6260, fax 570-961-4769. *Exec. Dir.* Catherine H. Schappert.

Northwest Interlibrary Cooperative of Pennsylvania (NICOP), Mercyhurst College Lib., 501 E. 38th St., Erie 16546. SAN 370-5862. Tel. 814-824-2190, fax 814-824-2219. *Archivist/Libn.* Earleen Glaser.

Pennsylvania Academic Library Consortium, 1005 Pontiac Rd., Suite 330, Drexel Hill 19026. Tel. 215-567-1755. *Exec. Dir.* Catherine C. Wilt.

Pennsylvania Library Assn., 220 Cumberland Pkwy, Suite 10, Mechanicsburg 17055. Tel. 717-766-7663, fax 717-766-5440. *Exec. Dir.* Christi Buker.

Philadelphia Area Consortium of Special Collections Libraries (PACSCL), P.O. Box 22642, Philadelphia 19110-2642. Tel. 215-985-1445, fax 215-985-1446, e-mail lblanchard@pacscl.org. *Exec. Dir.* Laura Blanchard.

Southeastern Pennsylvania Theological Library Assn. (SEPTLA), c/o Biblical Seminary, 200 N. Main St., Hatfield 19440. SAN 371-0793. Tel. 215-368-5000 ext. 234. *Pres.* Jenifer Gundry.

State System of Higher Education Library Cooperative (SSHELCO), c/o Bailey Lib., Slippery Rock 16057. Tel. 724-738-2630, fax 724-738-2661. *Coord.* Mary Lou Sowden.

Susquehanna Library Cooperative (SLC), Stevenson Lib., Lock Haven Univ., 401 N. Fairview St., Lock Haven 17745. SAN

322-3051. Tel. 570-484-2310, fax 570-484-2506. *Interim Dir. of Lib. and Info. Svcs.* Joby Topper.

Tri-State College Library Cooperative (TCLC), c/o Rosemont College Lib., 1400 Montgomery Ave., Rosemont 19010-1699. SAN 322-3078. Tel. 610-525-0796, e-mail office@tclclibs.org. *Pres.* Anne Krakow.

Rhode Island

Library of Rhode Island Network (LORI), One Capitol Hill, Providence 02908-5803. SAN 371-6821. Tel. 401-574-9300, fax 401-574-9320. *Chief of Lib. Svcs.* Karen Mellor.

Ocean State Libraries (OSL), 300 Centerville Rd., Suite 103S, Warwick 02886-0226. SAN 329-4560. Tel. 401-738-2200, e-mail support@oslri.net. *Exec. Dir.* Susan Straub.

South Carolina

Charleston Academic Libraries Consortium (CALC), P.O. Box 118067, Charleston 29423-8067. SAN 371-0769. Tel. 843-574-6088, fax 843-574-6484. *Chair* Charnette Singleton.

Partnership Among South Carolina Academic Libraries (PASCAL), 1333 Main St., Suite 305, Columbia 29201. Tel. 803-734-0900, fax 803-734-0901. *Exec. Dir.* Rick Moul.

South Carolina AHEC, c/o Medical Univ. of South Carolina, 19 Hagood Ave., Suite 802, Charleston 29425. SAN 329-3998. Tel. 843-792-4431, fax 843-792-4430. *Exec. Dir.* David Garr.

South Dakota

South Dakota Library Network (SDLN), 1200 University, Unit 9672, Spearfish 57799-9672. SAN 371-2117. Tel. 605-642-6835, fax 605-642-6472. *Dir.* Warren Wilson.

Tennessee

Knoxville Area Health Sciences Library Consortium (KAHSLC), Univ. of Tennessee Preston Medical Lib., 1924 Alcoa Hwy., Knoxville 37920. SAN 371-0556. Tel. 865-305-9525, fax 865-305-9527. *Pres.* Cynthia Vaughn.

Tennessee Health Science Library Assn. (THeSLA), Holston Valley Medical Center Health Sciences Lib., 130 W. Ravine Rd., Kingsport 37660. SAN 371-0726. Tel. 423-224-6870, fax 423-224-6014. *Pres.* Sandy Oelschlegel.

Tenn Share, P.O. Box 331871, Nashville 37203-7517. Tel. 615-669-8670, e-mail execdir@tenn-share.org. *Exec. Dir.* Jenifer Grady.

Tri-Cities Area Health Sciences Libraries Consortium (TCAHSLC), James H. Quillen College of Medicine, East Tennessee State Univ., Johnson City 37614. SAN 329-4099. Tel. 423-439-6252, fax 423-439-7025. *Dir.* Biddanda Ponnappa.

Texas

Abilene Library Consortium, 3305 N. 3 St., Suite 301, Abilene 79603. SAN 322-4694. Tel. 325-672-7081, fax 325-672-7082. *Coord.* Edward J. Smith.

Amigos Library Services, Inc., 4901 LBJ Freeway, Suite 150, Dallas 75244-6179. SAN 322-3191. Tel. 972-851-8000, fax 972-991-6061, e-mail amigos@amigos.org. *Pres./CEO* Alan Kornblau.

Council of Research and Academic Libraries (CORAL), P.O. Box 6733, San Antonio 78212. SAN 322-3213. Tel. 210-710-4475.

Del Norte Biosciences Library Consortium, El Paso Community College, El Paso 79998. SAN 322-3302. Tel. 915-831-4149, fax 915-831-4639. *Coord.* Becky Perales.

Harrington Library Consortium, 413 E. 4 Ave., Amarillo 79101. SAN 329-546X. Tel. 806-378-6037, fax 806-378-6038. *Dir.* Amanda Barrera.

Health Libraries Information Network (Health LINE), 3500 Camp Bowie Blvd. LIB-222, Fort Worth 76107-2699. SAN 322-3299. E-mail dfwhealthline@gmail.com. *Pres.* Michele Whitehead.

Houston Area Library Automated Network (HALAN), Houston Public Lib., 500 McKinney Ave., Houston 77002. Tel. 832-393-1411, fax 832-393-1427, e-mail website@hpl.lib.tx.us. *Chief* Judith Hiott.

Houston Area Research Library Consortium (HARLiC), c/o Univ. of Houston Libs., 114 University Libraries, Houston 77204-2000.

SAN 322-3329. Tel. 713-743-9807, fax 713-743-9811. *Pres.* Dana Rooks.

National Network of Libraries of Medicine–South Central Region (NN/LM-SCR), c/o HAM-TMC Library, 1133 John Freeman Blvd., Houston 77030-2809. SAN 322-3353. Tel. 713-799-7880, fax 713-790-7030, e-mail nnlm-scr@exch.library.tmc.edu. *Dir.* L. Maximillian Buja.

South Central Academic Medical Libraries Consortium (SCAMeL), c/o Lewis Lib.-UNTHSC, 3500 Camp Bowie Blvd., Fort Worth 76107. SAN 372-8269. Tel. 817-735-2380, fax 817-735-5158. *Dir.* Daniel Burgard.

Texas Council of Academic Libraries (TCAL), VC/UHV Lib., 2602 N. Ben Jordan, Victoria 77901. SAN 322-337X. Tel. 361-570-4150, fax 361-570-4155. *Chair* Karen Baen.

TEXSHARE—Texas State Library and Archives Commission, 1201 Brazos St., Austin 78701. Tel. 512-463-5455, fax 512-936-2306, e-mail texshare@tsl.texas.gov. *Dir. and State Libn.* Mark Smith.

Utah

National Network of Libraries of Medicine–MidContinental Region (NN/LM-MCR), Spencer S. Eccles Health Sciences Lib., Univ. of Utah, Salt Lake City 84112-5890. SAN 322-225X. Tel. 801-587-3412, fax 801-581-3632. *Dir.* Jean Shipman.

Utah Academic Library Consortium (UALC), Univ. of Utah, Salt Lake City 84112-0860. SAN 322-3418. Tel. 801-581-7701, 801-581-3852, fax 801-585-7185, e-mail UALCmail@library.utah.edu. *Budget Dir.* Parker M. Dougherty.

Utah Health Sciences Library Consortium, c/o Spencer S. Eccles Health Sciences Lib., Univ. of Utah, Salt Lake City 84112-5890. SAN 376-2246. Tel. 801-585-5743, fax 801-581-3632. *Chair* Jean Shipman.

Vermont

Catamount Library Network, 43 Main St., Springfield 05156. *Mailing Address:* Ten Court St., Rutland 05701-4058. *Pres.* Amy Howlett.

Vermont Resource Sharing Network, c/o Vermont Dept. of Libs., 109 State St., Montpelier 05609-0601. SAN 322-3426. Tel. 802-828-3261, fax 802-828-1481. *Ref. Libn.* Scott Murphy.

Virgin Islands

Virgin Islands Library and Information Network (VILINET), c/o Div. of Libs., Archives, and Museums, Charles W. Turnball Regional Library, 4607 Tutu Park Mall, Saint Thomas 00802. SAN 322-3639. Tel. 340-774-0630, e-mail info@vilinet.net. *Territorial Dir. of Libs., Archives, and Museums* Ingrid Bough.

Virginia

American Indian Higher Education Consortium (AIHEC), 121 Oronoco St., Alexandria 22314. SAN 329-4056. Tel. 703-838-0400, fax 703-838-0388, e-mail info@aihec.org. *Pres./CEO* Carrie Billy.

Lynchburg Area Library Cooperative, c/o Sweet Briar College Lib., P.O. Box 1200, Sweet Briar 24595. SAN 322-3450. Tel. 434-381-6315, fax 434-381-6173. *Dir.* Nan B. Carmack.

Lynchburg Information Online Network (LION), 2315 Memorial Ave., Lynchburg 24503. SAN 374-6097. Tel. 434-381-6311, fax 434-381-6173. *Systems Admin.* Lisa Broughman.

NASA Libraries Information System–NASA Galaxie, NASA Langley Research Center, MS 185-Technical Lib., Two W. Durand St., Hampton 23681-2199. SAN 322-0788. Tel. 757-864-2356, fax 757-864-2375. *Br. Head* Hope R. Venus.

Richmond Academic Library Consortium (RALC), James Branch Cabell Lib., Virginia Commonwealth Univ., 901 Park Ave., Richmond 23284. SAN 322-3469. Tel. 804-828-1110, fax 804-828-1105. *Pres.* Christopher Richardson.

Southside Virginia Library Network (SVLN), Longwood Univ., 201 High St., Farmville 23909-1897. SAN 372-8242. Tel. 434-395-2431, 434-395-2433, fax 434-395-2453. *Dean of Lib.* Suzy Szasz Palmer.

Southwestern Virginia Health Information Librarians, Sentara RMH Virginia Funkhouser Health Sciences Library, 2010 Health Campus Dr., Harrisonburg 22801. SAN

323-9527. Tel. 540-689-1772, fax 540-689-1770, e-mail mdkhamph@sentara.com. *Libn.* Megan Khamphavong.

Virginia Independent College and University Library Assn., c/o Mary Helen Cochran Lib., Sweet Briar 24595. SAN 374-6089. Tel. 434-381-6139, fax 434-381-6173. *Asst. Dir.* Katie Glaeser.

Virginia Tidewater Consortium for Higher Education (VTC), 4900 Powhatan Ave., Norfolk 23529. SAN 329-5486. Tel. 757-683-3183, fax 757-683-4515, e-mail lgdotolo@aol.com. *Pres.* Lawrence G. Dotolo.

Virtual Library of Virginia (VIVA), George Mason Univ., 4400 University Dr., Fenwick 5100, Fairfax 22030. Tel. 703-993-4652, fax 703-993-4662. *Dir.* Anne Osterman.

Washington

Inland NorthWest Health Sciences Libraries (INWHSL), Campus Library, P.O. Box 1495, Spokane 99210-1495. SAN 370-5099. Tel. 509-335-5544. *Chair* Suzanne Fricke.

National Network of Libraries of Medicine–Pacific Northwest Region (NN/LM-PNR), T-344 Health Sciences Bldg., Univ. of Washington, Seattle 98195. SAN 322-3485. Tel. 206-543-8262, fax 206-543-2469, e-mail nnlm@u.washington.edu. *Assoc. Dir.* Catherine Burroughs.

WIN Library Network, Gonzaga Univ., 502 E. Boone Ave., AD 95, Spokane 99258. Tel. 509-313-6545, fax 509-313-5904, e-mail winsupport@gonzaga.edu. *Pres.* Kathleen Allen.

West Virginia

Mid-Atlantic Law Library Cooperative (MALLCO), College of Law Lib., West Virginia Univ., Morgantown 26506-6135. SAN 371-0645. Tel. 304-293-7641, fax 304-293-6020. *Lib. Dir.* Lynn Maxwell.

Wisconsin

Fox River Valley Area Library Consortium (FRVALC), c/o Polk Lib., Univ. of Wisconsin–Oshkosh, 800 Algona Blvd., Oshkosh 54901. SAN 322-3531. Tel. 920-424-3348, 920-424-4333, fax 920-424-2175. *Coord.* Holly Egebo.

Fox Valley Library Council, c/o OWLS, 225 N. Oneida St., Appleton 54911. SAN 323-9640. Tel. 920-832-6190, fax 920-832-6422. *Pres.* Pat Exarhos.

North East Wisconsin Intertype Libraries, Inc. (NEWIL), 515 Pine St., Green Bay 54301. SAN 322-3574. Tel. 920-448-4413, fax 920-448-4420. *Coord.* Jamie Matczak.

South Central Wisconsin Health Science Library Consortium, c/o Fort Healthcare Medical Lib., Fort Atkinson 53538. SAN 322-4686. Tel. 920-568-5194, fax 920-568-5195. *Coord.* Carrie Garity.

Southeastern Wisconsin Health Science Library Consortium, Veterans Admin. Center Medical Lib., Milwaukee 53295. SAN 322-3582. Tel. 414-384-2000 ext. 42342, fax 414-382-5334. *Coord.* Kathy Strube.

Southeastern Wisconsin Information Technology Exchange, Inc. (SWITCH), 6801 North Yates Rd., Milwaukee 53217. Tel. 414-382-6710. *Coord.* Jennifer Schmidt.

Wisconsin Library Services (WILS), 1360 Regent St., No. 121, Madison 53715-1255. Tel. 608-216-8399, e-mail information@wils.org. *Dir.* Stef Morrill.

Wisconsin Public Library Consortium (WPLC), c/o WILS, 1360 Regent St., No. 121, Madison 53715-1255. Tel. 608-216-8399, e-mail information@wils.org. *Dir.* Stef Morrill.

Wisconsin Valley Library Service (WVLS), 300 N. 1 St., Wausau 54403. SAN 371-3911. Tel. 715-261-7250, fax 715-261-7259. *Dir.* Marla Rae Sepnafski.

WISPALS Library Consortium, c/o Gateway Technical College, 3520 30th Ave., Kenosha 53144-1690. Tel. 262-564-2602, fax 262-564-2787. *Chair* Scott Vrieze.

Wyoming

WYLD Network, c/o Wyoming State Lib., 2800 Central Ave., Cheyenne 82002-0060. SAN 371-0661. Tel. 307-777-6333, e-mail support@wyldnetwork.com. *State Libn.* Jamie Marcus.

Canada

Alberta

The Alberta Library (TAL), 6-14, 7 Sir Winston Churchill Sq., Edmonton T5J 2V5. 10707-100 Avenue NW, Suite 700, Edmonton T5J 3M1. Tel. 780-414-0805, fax 780-414-0806, e-mail admin@thealbertalibrary.ab.ca. *CEO* Tim Janewski.

NEOS Library Consortium, Cameron Lib., 5th Fl., Edmonton T6G 2J8. Tel. 780-492-0075, fax 780-492-8302. *Mgr.* Anne Carr-Wiggin.

British Columbia

British Columbia Electronic Library Network (BCELN), WAC Bennett Lib., 7th Fl., Simon Fraser Univ., Burnaby V5A 1S6. Tel. 778-782-7003, fax 778-782-3023, e-mail office@eln.bc.ca. *Exec. Dir.* Anita Cocchia.

Center for Accessible Post-Secondary Education Resources, Langara College Library, 100 W. 49th Ave., Vancouver V5Y 2Z6. SAN 329-6970. Tel. 604-323-5639, fax 604-323-5544, e-mail caperbc@langara.bc.ca. *Dir.* Patricia Cia.

Council of Prairie and Pacific University Libraries (COPPUL), 1958 Main Mall, Rm. 219, Vancouver V6T 1Z2. Tel. 604-827-0578. *Exec. Dir.* Kristina McDavid.

Electronic Health Library of British Columbia (e-HLbc), c/o Bennett Lib., 8888 University Dr., Burnaby V5A 1S6. Tel. 778-782-5440, fax 778-782-3023, e-mail info@ehlbc.ca. *Exec. Dir.* Anita Cocchia.

Northwest Library Federation, 3939 Broadway Ave., Smithers V0J 2N0. *Mailing address:* Box 4722, Smithers V0J 2N0. Tel. 778-883-3445, e-mail director@nwlf.ca. *Dir.* Melissa Sawatsky.

Public Library InterLINK, 5489 Byrne Rd., No 158, Burnaby V5J 3J1. SAN 318-8272. Tel. 604-517-8441, fax 604-517-8410, e-mail info@interlinklibraries.ca. *Operations Mgr.* Rita Avigdor.

Manitoba

Manitoba Library Consortium, Inc. (MLCI), c/o Lib. Admin., Univ. of Winnipeg, 515 Portage Ave., Winnipeg R3B 2E9. SAN 372-820X. Tel. 204-786-9801, fax 204-783-8910. *Chair* Stephen Carney.

Nova Scotia

Maritimes Health Libraries Assn. (MHLA-ABSM), W. K. Kellogg Health Sciences Lib., Halifax B3H 1X5. SAN 370-0836. Tel. 902-494-2483, fax 902-494-3750. *Libn.* Shelley McKibbon.

NOVANET, The Consortium of Nova Scotia Academic Libraries, 120 Western Pkwy., No. 202, Bedford B4B 0V2. SAN 372-4050. Tel. 902-453-2470, fax 902-453-2369, e-mail office@novanet.ca. *Mgr.* Bill Slauenwhite.

Ontario

Canadian Assn. of Research Libraries (Association des Bibliothèques de Recherche du Canada), 203-309 Cooper St., Ottawa K2P 0G5. SAN 323-9721. Tel. 613-482-9344, fax 613-562-5297, e-mail info@carl-abrc.ca. *Exec. Dir.* Susan Haigh.

Canadian Health Libraries Assn. (CHLA-ABSC), 468 Queen St. E., LL-02, Toronto M5A 1T7. SAN 370-0720. Tel. 416-646-1600, fax 416-646-9460, e-mail info@chla-absc.ca. *Pres.* Jeanna Hough.

Canadian Heritage Information Network, 1030 Innes Rd., Ottawa K1B 4S7. SAN 329-3076. Tel. 613-998-3721, fax 613-998-4721, e-mail pch.rcip-chin.pch@canada.ca. *Dir.* Charlie Costain.

Canadian Research Knowledge Network (CRKN), 11 Holland Ave., Suite 301, Ottawa K1Y 4S1. Tel. 613-907-7040, fax 866-903-9094. *Exec. Dir.* Clare Appavoo.

Hamilton and District Health Library Network, c/o St Joseph's Healthcare Hamilton, Sherman Lib., Room T2305, 50 Charlton Ave. E., Hamilton L8N 4A6. SAN 370-5846. Tel. 905-522-1155 ext. 33410, fax 905-540-6504. *Coord.* Karen Dearness.

Health Science Information Consortium of Toronto, c/o Gerstein Science Info. Center, Univ. of Toronto, Toronto M5S 1A5. SAN

370-5080. Tel. 416-978-6359, fax 416-971-2637. *Exec. Dir.* Miriam Ticoll.

Ontario Council of University Libraries (OCUL), 130 Saint George St., Toronto M5S 1A5. Tel. 416-946-0578, fax 416-978-6755. *Exec. Dir.* John Barnett.

Ontario Library Consortium (OLC), c/o Brant Public Lib., 12 William St., Paris M3L 1K7. *Pres.* Kelly Bernstein.

Perth County Information Network (PCIN), c/o Stratford Public Lib., 19 St. Andrew St., Stratford N5A 1A2. Tel. 519-271-0220, fax 519-271-3843, e-mail webmaster@pcin.on.ca. *CEO* Sam Coglin.

Southwestern Ontario Health Libraries and Information Network (SOHLIN), London Health Sciences Centre, London N6A 5W9. Tel. 519-685-8500 ext. 56038. *Pres.* Jill McTavish.

Toronto Health Libraries Assn. (THLA), 3409 Yonge St., Toronto M4N 2L0. SAN 323-9853. Tel. 416-485-0377, fax 416-485-6877, e-mail medinfoserv@rogers.com. *Pres.* Sharon Bailey.

Woodstock Hospital Regional Library Services, Woodstock General Hospital, 310 Juliana Dr., Woodstock N4V 0A4. SAN 323-9500. Tel. 519-421-4233 ext. 2735, fax 519-421-4236. *Libn.* Alanna Marson.

Quebec

Assn. des Bibliothèques de la Santé Affiliées a l'Université de Montréal (ABSAUM), c/o Health Lib., Univ. of Montreal, Montreal H3C 3J7. SAN 370-5838. Tel. 514-343-6826, fax 514-343-2350. *Dir.* Monique St-Jean.

Federal Libraries Consortium (FLC), 550 de la Cite Blvd., Gatineau K1A 0N4. Tel. 613-410-9752, fax 819-934-7539, e-mail fedlibraries consortium.LAC@canada.ca.

Réseau BIBLIO de l'Ouatouais, 2295 Saint-Louis St., Gatineau, Quebec J8T 5L8. SAN 319-6526. Tel. 819-561-6008. *Exec. Gen.* Sylvie Thibault.

Saskatchewan

Consortium of Academic and Special Libraries of Saskatchewan (CASLS), Courthouse, 2425 Victoria Ave., Regina S4P 3M3. Mailing address: P.O. Box 5032, Regina S4P 3M3. *Chair* Melanie Hodges Neufeld.

Library and Information-Industry Associations and Organizations, U.S. and Canada

AIIM—The Association for Information and Image Management

Chair, Ian Story
President and CEO, Peggy Winton
8403 Colesville Rd., Suite 1100, Silver Spring, MD 20910
800-477-2446, 301-587-8202, fax 301-587-2711, e-mail aiim@aiim.org
World Wide Web http://www.aiim.org
European Office: Broomhall Business Centre, Lower Broomhall Farm, Broomhall Ln., Worcester WR5 2NT, UK
Tel. 44-1905-727600, fax 44-1905-727609, e-mail info@aiim.org

Object

AIIM is an international authority on enterprise content management, the tools and technologies that capture, manage, store, preserve, and deliver content in support of business processes. Founded in 1943.

Officers (2019)

Chair Ian Story, Microsoft; *V.Chair* Greg Reid, BDO; *Treas.* Daniel Abdul, United Healthcare Group; *Past Chair* Mark Patrick, Commander U.S. Navy (Ret.); *Memb.-at-Large* Pamela Doyle, PD Squared.

Board Members

Martin Birch, Andrea Chiappe, Dave Jones, Stephen Ludlow, Ed McQuiston, Kramer Reeves, Rand Wacker.

Publication

The Digital Landfill (blog).

American Association of Law Libraries

Executive Director, Vani Ungaper
105 W. Adams St., Suite 3300, Chicago, IL 60603
312-939-4764, fax 312-431-1097, e-mail vungapen@aall.org
World Wide Web http://www.aallnet.org

Our Mission

The American Association of Law Libraries advances the profession of law librarianship and supports the professional growth of its members through leadership and advocacy in the field of legal information and information policy.

Membership

Memb. 4,000. For law librarians and other legal information professionals of any professional sector. Dues (Indiv.) $263; (Ret.) $65; (Student) $65. Year. June–May.

Officers (2019–2020)

Pres. Michelle Cosby, Univ. of Tennessee, Joel A. Katz Law Lib. 1505 W. Cumberland Ave., Knoxville, TN 37916. Tel. 865-974-6728, fax 865-974-6571, e-mail mcosby2@utk.edu; *V.P.* Emily R. Florio, Finnegan, Henderson,

Farabow, Garrett & Dunner, LLP, 901 New York Ave. N.W., Washington, DC 20001-4435. Tel. 202-216-5374, fax 202-408-4400, e-mail emily.florio@finnegan.com; *Secy.* Luis Acosta, Library of Congress, 3910 Montrose Driveway, Chevy Chase, MD 20815. Tel. 202-707-9131, fax 202-707-3585, e-mail laco@loc.gov; *Treas.* Mr. Cornell H. Winston, United States Attorney's Office, 312 N. Spring St. Suite 12, United States Courthouse, Los Angeles, CA 90012-2488. Tel. 213-894-2419, fax 213-894-0141, e-mail Cornell.H.Winston@usdoj.gov; *Past Pres.* Femi Cadmus, Duke Univ.School of Law, J. Michael Goodson Law Lib., P.O. Box 90361, Durham, NC 27708-0361. Tel. 919-613-7115, fax 919-613-7237, e-mail femi.cadmus@duke.edu.

Board Members

Elizabeth G. Adelman. E-mail eadelman@buffalo.edu; Emily M. Janoski-Haehlen. E-mail ejanoskihaehlen@uakron.edu; June Hsiao Liebert. E-mail jliebert@sidley.com; Jean P. O'Grady. E-mail jean.ogrady@dlapiper.com; Karen Selden. E-mail karen.selden@colorado.edu; Jason R. Sowards. E-mail jsowards@nvcourts.nv.gov.

Publications

AALL eNewsletter (mo.).

AALL eBriefing.

AALL Spectrum (bi-mo.; free; nonmemb. $75).

Law Library Journal (q.; digital memb. only; pdf, free; or print, memb. $35, nonmemb. $125).

AALL Biennial Salary Survey & Organizational Characteristics. (biennial; memb. only online; print e-mail orders@aall.org).

Index to Foreign Legal Periodicals (print or online).

AALL White Papers (digital).

Universal Citation Guide.

American Indian Library Association

Executive Director, Heather Devine-Hardy (Eastern Shawnee)
E-mail hhdevine@gmail.com
World Wide Web http://www.ailanet.org

Object

To improve library and information services for American Indians. Founded in 1979; affiliated with American Library Association in 1985.

Membership

Any person, library, or other organization interested in working to improve library and information services for American Indians may become a member. Dues (Inst.) $40; (Indiv.) $20; (Student) $10.

Officers (2018–2019)

Pres. Lillian Chavez; *V.P./Pres.-Elect* George Gottschalk (Muscogee [Creek] Nation]; *Secy.* Aaron LaFromboise (Blackfeet). E-mail alafromboise@bfcc.edu; *Treas.* Liana Juliano; *Past Pres.* Omar Poler (Chippewa); *Membs.-at-Large* Joy Bridwell (Chippewa-Cree), Carlos Duarte, Rhiannon Sorrell (Diné), Ofelia "Liz" Zepeda (Tohono O'odham).

Editorial Board Chair

Newsletter Editor. George Gottschalk.

Publication

AILA Newsletter (bi-ann., electronic and print). *Ed.* George Gottschalk.

American Library Association

Executive Director, Mary W. Ghikas
50 E. Huron St., Chicago, IL 60611
800-545-2433, fax 312-440-9374, e-mail mghikas@ala.org.
World Wide Web http://www.ala.org

Object

The object of the American Library Association shall be to promote library service and librarianship. The mission of the American Library Association (ALA) is to provide leadership for the development, promotion, and improvement of library and information services and the profession of librarianship in order to enhance learning and ensure access to information for all. Founded 1876.

Membership

Memb. (Indiv.) 54,500; (Inst.) 4,000; (Corporate) 175; (Total) 58,826. Any person, library, or other organization interested in library service and librarians. Dues (Indiv.) 1st year, $72; 2nd year, $110; 3rd year and later, $145; (Trustee and Assoc. Memb.) $65; (Lib. Support Staff) $52; (Student) $38; (Foreign Indiv.) $87; (Nonsalaried/Unemployed/Ret.) $52; (Inst.) $175 and up, depending on operating expenses of institution.

Officers (2018–2019)

Pres. Loida A. Garcia-Febo. E-mail loidagarcia febo@gmail.com; *Pres.-Elect* Wanda Kay Brown. Winston-Salem State Univ., Winston-Salem, NC 27110. Tel. 336-750-2446; *Treas.* Susan H. Hildreth, Tel. 206-221-2335; *Past Pres.* James (Jim) Neal, Columbia Univ. E-mail jneal0@columbia.edu.

Divisions

See the separate entries that follow: American Assn. of School Libns.; Assn. for Lib. Collections and Technical Services; Assn. for Lib. Service to Children; Assn. of College and Research Libs.; Assn. of Specialized, Government, and Cooperative Lib. Agencies; Lib. and Info. Technology Assn.; Lib. Leadership and Management Assn.; Public Lib. Assn.; Reference and User Services Assn.; United for Libraries; Young Adult Lib. Services Assn.

Board Members

Tamika Barnes *(2018–2021)*; Trevor A. Dawes *(2017–2020)*; Karen Downing *(2016–2019)*; Ed Garcia *(2018–2021)*; Maria McCauley, Ph.D. *(2018–2021)*; Andrew K. Pace *(2016–2019)*; Lessa Kanani'opua Pelayo-Lozada *(2017–2020)*; Patricia "Patty" M. Wong *(2017–2020)*.

Round Table Chairs

(ALA staff liaison in parenthesis)

Ethnic & Multicultural Information Exchange (EMIERT). Safi S. M. Safiullah (Briana Jarnagin).

Exhibits (ERT). David Lysinger (Paul Graller).

Federal & Armed Forces Libraries (FAFLRT). Kimberly Megginson (Vicky Crone).

Games and Gaming Round Table (GameRT). Brian Mayer (Tina Coleman).

Gay, Lesbian, Bisexual, Transgender Round Table (GLBTRT). Ana Elisa De Campos Salles (Jody Gray).

Government Documents Round Table (GODORT). Hallie Pritchett.

Intellectual Freedom (IFRT). John Mack Freeman (Deborah Caldwell-Stone, Eleanor Diaz, James LaRue, Kristin Pekoll).

International Relations (IRRT). Muzhgan Israfil Nazarova (Delin Guerra).

Learning (LearnRT, formerly CLENERT). Angela Glowcheski (Danielle M. Ponton).

Library Research (LRRT). Amanda L. Folk (Kelsey Henke).

New Members (NMRT). Nicole Spoor (Kimberly L. Redd).
Retired Members. (Danielle M. Alderson).
Social Responsibilities. Diedre Conkling.

Committee Chairs

(ALA staff liaison in parentheses)
Accreditation (Standing). Loretta R. Parham (Karen Lynn O'Brien, Kerri Price).
American Libraries Advisory (Standing). Susan H. Polos (Terra Dankowski, Mary Mackay, Sanhita SinhaRoy, Carrie Smith).
Appointments (Standing). Wanda Kay Brown (JoAnne M. Kempf).
Awards (Standing). Susan L. Jennings (Cheryl Malden).
Chapter Relations (Standing). Julius C. Jefferson, Jr. (Michael Dowling, Donald Wood).
Conference Committee (Standing). Clara Nalli Bohrer (Mary W. Ghikas, Alee Navarro, Lina Zabaneh).
Constitution and Bylaws (Standing). Stephen L. Matthews (JoAnne M. Kempf, Sheryl Reyes).
Diversity, Literacy and Outreach Services (Standing). Martin L. Garnar (Jody Gray, Gwendolyn Prellwitz).
Election (Standing). Satia Marshall Orange (JoAnne M. Kempf, Sheryl Reyes).
Human Resource Development and Recruitment (Standing). Aliqae Geraci (Adriane Alicea, Beatrice Calvin, Kimberly L. Redd, Lorelle R. Swader).
Information Technology Policy Advisory (Standing). George Stachokas (Pamela Yvonne Akins, Sherri Vanyek).
Information Technology Policy Advisory (Office for). Sukrit Goswami.
Literacy (Standing). Kevin Reynolds (Amber Hayes).
Membership (Standing). Christina Rodriques (Ron Jankowski, Lorelle Swader).
Membership Meetings. Holly L. Camino (Marsha Patrice Burgess, Lois Ann Gregory-Wood, Lorelle Swader).
Nominating (Standing). Emmanuel L. Faulkner, Sr. (JoAnne M. Kempf, Sheryl Reyes).
Public and Cultural Programs Advisory (Standing). Janie L. Hermann (Sarah Ostman, Deborah A. Robertson, Brian Russell).
Research and Statistics (Standing). Martha Adkins (Kathy Rosa).
Rural, Native, and Tribal Libraries of All Kinds. (Paulita Aguilar).
Scholarships and Study Grants. Hong Huang (Kimberly L. Redd).
Training, Orientation, and Leadership Development. Libby Holtmann (Kimberly L. Redd, Lorelle R. Swader).

Publications

American Libraries (6x yearly; memb.; organizations in U.S., Canada, and Mexico $74; elsewhere $84; single copy $7.50).
Booklist (22x yearly, with digital edition access to current and past issues of *Book Links* and 24/7 access to *Booklist Online*; U.S. and Canada $169.50; foreign $188).
Library Studies, Issues & Trends report.
Library Technology Reports (8x yearly, online and print $335, non-U.S. $379).
Smart Libraries Newsletter (mo., online and print $99, non-U.S. $109).

American Library Association
American Association of School Librarians

Executive Director, Sylvia Knight Norton (ex officio)
50 E. Huron St., Chicago, IL 60611
312-280-4382, 800-545-2433 ext. 4382, e-mail snorton@ala.org or aasl@ala.org
World Wide Web http://www.aasl.org

Object

The American Association of School Librarians empowers leaders to transform teaching and learning.

Established in 1951 as a separate division of the American Library Association, AASL understands the current realities and evolving dynamics of the school librarian professional environment and is positioned to help members transform learning through school libraries. AASL publishes standards for the profession with the latest, *National School Library Standards for Learners, School Librarians, and School Libraries* (2018), providing a comprehensive approach through integrated frameworks consisting of four domains (Think, Create, Share, Grow) and six Shared Foundations (Inquire, Include, Collaborate, Curate, Explore, Engage).

Membership

Memb. 7,000+. Open to all school librarians, librarians, libraries, interested individuals, and business firms, with requisite membership in ALA.

Board of Directors (2018–2019)

Pres. Kathryn Roots Lewis; *Pres.-Elect* Mary Keeling; *Treas.* Judy Deichman; *Past Pres.* Steven Yates; *Div. Councilor* Diane R. Chen, Lisa Brakel, Maria Cahill, Becky Calzada, Anita Cellucci, Brene Duggins, Sue Heraper, Laura Hicks, Kathy Lester, Erika Long, Ann Morgester, Sarah Searles, Ann Schuster, Wendy Stephens, Phoebe Warmack.

Section Leadership

AASL/ESLS. Elizabeth Burns, Maria Cahill, Lucy Santos Green, Meghan Harper, Stephanie Jones.

AASL/ISS. Anna Brannin, Courtney Lewis, Sarah Ludwig, Elizabeth Nelson, Phoebe Warmack.

AASL/SPVS. Lori Donovan, Erin Downey, Stephanie Ham, Maria Petropulos, Sarah Searles.

Committee Chairs

AASL/ALSC/YALSA Joint Committee on School/Public Library Cooperation. April Witteveen (YALSA).

Alliance for Association Excellence. Judith Deichman.

Annual Conference. Jennifer Anders, Becky Calzada.

Association of American University Presses Book Selection. Dona Helmer.

Awards. Susan Yutzey.

Best Apps for Teaching and Learning. Mary Morgan Ryan.

Best Websites for Teaching and Learning. Sherry Gick.

Bylaws and Organization. Devona Pendergrass.

CAEP Coordinating Committee. April Dawkins, Gail Dickinson.

Induction. Robyn Young.

Leadership Development. Steven Yates.

National Conference. Heather Jankowski, Alice Bryant.

Practice. Jay Bansbach, Eileen Kern.

School Library Month. Shannon DeSantis.

Social Media Recognition. Marifran DeMaine.

Standards Implementation. Jennisen Lucas.

Editorial Board Chairs

Knowledge Quest Editorial Board. Karla Collins.

School Library Research Editorial Board. Melissa Johnston, Mega Subramaniam.

Social Media Editorial Board. Len Bryan.

Task Force Chairs

Presidential Initiative. Bethany Bratney, Casey Rawson.

Vision for Implementing ESSA. Eileen Kern.

Crosswalk. Jay Bansbach.

Open Educational Resources. Lori Donovan.

Public Charter Infographic. Hannah Byrd Little.

Scheduling Position Statement. Ann Martin.

State Standards Workshop. Cassandra Barnett.

Awards Committee Chairs

ABC-CLIO Leadership Grant. Michael-Brian Ogawa.

Affiliate of the Year Award. Mary Jo Richmond.

Collaborative School Library Award. Susan Ballard.

Distinguished School Administrators Award. Susan Hess.

Frances Henne Award. Klaudia Janek.

Innovative Reading Grant. Catherine Evans.

Inspire Collection Development Grant. John Byrnes.

Inspire Disaster Recovery Fund. LeeAnna Mills.

Inspire Special Event Grant. Rebecca Gordon.

Intellectual Freedom Award. Brittany Tignor.

National School Library of the Year Award. Rob Hilliker.

Past-Presidents Planning Grant. Dorcas Hand.

Roald Dahl Miss Honey Social Justice Award. Savannah Sessions.

Ruth Toor Grant for Strong Public Schools Libraries. Hilda Weisburg.

Student Bridge Scholarship. Rachel Altobelli.

Publications

Knowledge Quest (bi-mo.; memb.; nonmemb. $12 per issue; https://knowledgequest.aasl.org). *Ed.* Meg Featheringham. E-mail mfeatheringham@ala.org.

School Library Research (electronic, free, at http://www.ala.org/aasl/slr). *Ed.* Meg Featheringham. E-mail mfeatheringham@ala.org. *Co-Eds.*

American Library Association
Association for Library Collections and Technical Services

Executive Director, Keri Cascio
50 E. Huron St., Chicago, IL 60611
800-545-2433 ext. 5030, fax 312-280-5033, e-mail kcascio@ala.org
World Wide Web http://www.ala.org/alcts

Object

The Association for Library Collections and Technical Services (ALCTS) envisions an environment in which traditional library roles are evolving. New technologies are making information more fluid and raising expectations. The public needs quality information anytime, anyplace. ALCTS provides frameworks to meet these information needs.

ALCTS provides leadership to the library and information communities in developing principles, standards, and best practices for creating, collecting, organizing, delivering, and preserving information resources in all forms. It provides this leadership through its members by fostering educational, research, and professional service opportunities. ALCTS is committed to quality information, universal access, collaboration, and lifelong learning.

Standards—Develop, evaluate, revise, and promote standards for creating, collecting, organizing, delivering, and preserving information resources in all forms.

Best practices—Research, develop, evaluate, and implement best practices for creating, collecting, organizing, delivering, and preserving information resources in all forms.

Education—Assess the need for, sponsor, develop, administer, and promote educational programs and resources for lifelong learning.

Professional development—Provide opportunities for professional development through research, scholarship, publication, and professional service.

Interaction and information exchange—Create opportunities to interact and exchange information with others in the library and information communities.

Association operations—Ensure efficient use of association resources and effective delivery of member services.

Established in 1957; renamed in 1988.

Membership

Memb. 3,800. Any member of the American Library Association may elect membership in this division according to the provisions of the bylaws.

Officers (2018–2019)

Pres. Kristin E. Martin; *Pres.-Elect* Jennifer B. Bowen; *Past Pres.* Mary Beth Thomson.

Board of Directors

Officers; Miranda Henry Bennett, Sunshine Jacinda Carter, Megan Dougherty, Netanel Ganin, Jill Emery, Kelli Getz, Dracine Hodges, Katharine D. Leigh, Mary E. Miller, Brooke Morris-Chott, Julie Mosbo, Bonnie Parks, Julie Reese; Chelcie Juliet Rowell, Deborah A. Ryszka, Jacquie Samples, Erin S. Stalberg, Jacqueline Marie Toce, Kerry Ward.

Committee Chairs

Advocacy and Policy. Paul D. Moeller.

Affiliate Relations. Jacqueline Marie Toce.

Budget and Finance. Miranda Henry Bennett.

Continuing Education. Jeremy J. Myntti, Andrea A. Wirth.

Fundraising. Rachel K. Fischer, Melinda Reagor Flannery.

International Relations. Margaret Mering.

Leadership Development. Laura N. Evans.

Library Materials Price Index Editorial Board. George J. Aulisio, Jr.

LITA/ALCTS Metadata Standards Committee. Michael R. Bolam, Scott A. Opasik.

LRTS Editorial Board. Mary Beth Weber.

Membership. Elyssa M. Gould, Emily Sanford.

Monographs Editorial Board. Susan E. Thomas.

Nominating. Vicki L. Sipe.

Organization and Bylaws. Katharine D. Leigh.

Planning Committee. Katharine D. Leigh.

President's Program. Felicity A. Dykas.

Program. Eleanor I. Cook, Marianne S. Hanley.

Publications. Alison M. Armstrong, Rebecca Kemp Goldfinger.

Standards. Miranda Nixon.

Interest Group Chairs

Access to Continuing Resources. Jessie Lorraine Copeland.

Acquisitions Managers and Vendors. Jared Howland, Lee Sochay.

Authority Control (ALCTS/LITA). Martha Rice Sanders.

Book and Paper. Priscilla Anderson, Kim Knox Norman.

CaMMS Catalog Management. Jeanette Claire Sewell, Vesselina Kirilova Stoytcheva.

CaMMS Cataloging Norms. Paul C. Heyde, Rachel Turner.

CaMMS Competencies and Education for a Career in Cataloging. Bobby Bothmann, Gretchen L. Hoffman.

CaMMS Copy Cataloging. George E. Gottschalk, IV, Anita Kazmierczak.

CaMMS Faceted Subject Access. Lynn Gates, Lucas (Wing Kau) Mak.

Cartographic Resources Cataloging IG (MAGIRT). Tim Kiser.

Catalog Form and Function. Michael J. Monaco.

Cataloging and Classification Research. Sai Deng, Becky Skeen.

Chief Collection Development Officers at Large Research Libraries. Denise Pan.

CMS Collection Development Librarians of Academic Libraries. Ann Roll.
CMS Collection Management in Public Libraries (RUSA Codes). Daniel F. Barden, Holly S. Blosser.
Collection Development Issues for the Practitioner. Kevin Garewal.
Collection Evaluation and Assessment. Natasha A. Cooper, Lisa Leyser Jochelson.
Collection Management and Electronic Resources. Shannon Tharp.
College and Research Libraries. Danielle Lorraine Ostendorf.
Creative Ideas in Technical Services. Timothy Ryan Mendenhall.
Digital Conversion. Stefan Elnabli.
Digital Preservation. Justin Lee Baumgartner, Patrice-Andre Prud'homme.
Electronic Resources. Ellen Derey Safley.
Electronic Resources Management (ALCTS/LITA). Mark A. Beatty, Jenny Levine, Julie Reese.
FRBR. Michele Seikel.
Heads of Cataloging Departments. Angela Jewel Kinney, David A. Van Kleeck.
Linked Library Data (ALCTS/LITA). Craig Allen Boman, Scott Carlson.
MARC Formats Transition. Sherab Chen, Rachel Paul.
Metadata. Anna L. Neatrour.
New Members. Xiping Liu, Rachel Turner.
Newspapers. Brian Geiger.
Preservation Administrators. Beth Doyle, Ann Kearney.
Preservation Metadata. Ilda Cardenas, Marielle Veve.
Promoting Presservation. Kara M. McClurken.
Public Libraries Technical Services. Yu-Lan Margaret Chou, Michael P. Santangelo.
Publisher-Vendor-Library Relations. Ajaye Bloomstone, Carolyn Morris, Maridath Ann Wilson.
Role of the Professional Librarian in Technical Services. Suzhen Chen, Kristin Louise Flachsbart.
Scholarly Communication. Sarah Beaubien.
Technical Services Directors of Large Research Libraries. Paula Sullenger.
Technical Services Managers in Academic Libraries. Shannon Tennant.
Technical Services Workflow Efficiency. TJ Kao, Gina Solares.

Publications

ALCTS News (q.; free; posted at http://www.ala.org/alcts). *Ed.* Chelcie Juliet Rowell.
Library Resources and Technical Services (LRTS) (q.; nonmemb. $100; international $100). Electronic only. *Ed.* Mary Beth Weber, Technical and Automated Services Dept., Rutgers Univ. Libs., 47 Davidson Rd., Piscataway, NJ 08854. E-mail lrseditor@lists.ala.org.

American Library Association
Association for Library Service to Children

Executive Director, Aimee Strittmatter
50 E. Huron St., Chicago, IL 60611
800-545-2433 ext. 2163, fax 312-280-5271, e-mail alsc@ala.org
World Wide Web http://www.ala.org/alsc

Object

The Association for Library Service to Children (ALSC) develops and supports the profession of children's librarianship by enabling and encouraging its practitioners to provide the best library service to our nation's children.

The Association for Library Service to Children is interested in the improvement and extension of library services to children in all types of libraries. It is responsible for the evaluation and selection of book and nonbook library materials and for the improvement of techniques of library service to children from preschool through the eighth grade of junior high school age, when such materials and techniques are intended for use in more than one type of library. ALSC has specific responsibility for

1. Continuous study and critical review of activities assigned to the division.
2. Conduct of activities and carrying on of projects within its area of responsibility.
3. Cooperation with all units of ALA whose interests and activities have a relationship to library service to children.
4. Interpretation of library materials for children and of methods of using such materials with children, to parents, teachers, and other adults, and representation of librarians' concern for the production and effective use of good children's books to groups outside the profession.
5. Stimulation of the professional growth of its members and encouragement of participation in appropriate type-of-library divisions.
6. Planning and development of programs of study and research in the area of selection and use of library materials for children for the total profession.
7. Development, evaluation, and promotion of professional materials in its area of responsibility. Founded in 1901.

Membership

Memb. 4,000. Open to anyone interested in library services to children. Dues in addition to ALA membership (Regular) $50; (Student) $20; (Nonsalaried/Ret.) $35; (Advocate) $25.

Address correspondence to the executive director.

Officers (2019–2020)

Pres. Jamie Campbell Naidoo, School of Lib. and Information Studies, Univ. of Alabama, 541 Gorgas Lib., Box 870252, Tuscaloosa, AL 35487. Tel. 205-348-1518, e-mail naidooalsc@gmail.com; *V.P./Pres.-Elect* Cecilia P. McGowan. E-mail nmcgowanalsc@gmail.com; *Past Pres.* Nina Lindsay, Oakland Public Lib., 125 14th St., Rm. 6, Oakland, CA 94612-4397. Tel. 510-238-6706, e-mail ninaalsc@gmail.com; *Fiscal Officer* Paula Holmes.

Board of Directors

Officers; Julie Dietzel-Glair, Linda L. Ernst; Elisa Gall; Africa S. Hands, Amy E. Koester; Sujei Lugo; Karen Ann MacPherson; Anne Michaud; Sue McCleaf Nespeca; Alena Rivers; Amy E. Sears; Aimee Strittmatter (Ex-Officio);

Committee Chairs

Advocacy and Legislation. Nathaniel D. Halsan, Sarah Okner.

Arbuthnot Honor Lecture 2020. Lisa Von Drasek.

Budget. Gretchen Caserotti.

Building Partnerships. Jackie Cassidy, Hadeal Salamah.

Children and Libraries Editorial Advisory. Anna Haase Krueger.

Children and Technology. Angela Nolet.

Distinguished Service Award. Mary Beth Dunhouse.

Early Childhood Programs and Services. Kimberly Alberts, Stephanie C. Prato.

Education. Rachel Reinwald, Amanda Yother.

Excellence for Early Learning Digital Media. Katie A. Paciga.

Grants Administration. Ariana Augustine Sani Hussain.

Intellectual Freedom. Justin Azevedo, Betsy Boyce Brainerd.

Library Service to Underserved Children and Their Caregivers. Jason Miles Driver, Sr., Erin Lovelace.

Local Arrangements. Eboni R. Njoku.

Managing Children's Services. Laura Koenig.

Membership. Alyx Andrea Campbell.

Nominating and Leadership Development. Andrew Medlar.

Notable Children's Books. Melody R. Frese.

Notable Children's Digital Media. Laura Bos, Alec B. Chunn.

Notable Children's Recordings. Annamarie E. Carlson.

Oral History. Sharon McKellar.

Organization and Bylaws. Julie A. Corsaro, Joanna Ward.

Preconference Planning. Vicky Smith.

Program Coordinating. Michael P. Santangelo.

Public Awareness. Skye Corey, Mary Schreiber.

Quicklists Consulting. Amanda Yuk-Wah Choi, Kimberly Probert Grad.

Charlmae Rollins President's Program. Marianne Martens, Johanna Ulloa Giron.

Scholarships. Heather Acerro.

School-age Programs and Service. Alexa E. Newman.

Special Collections and Bechtel Fellowship. Allison G. Kaplan.

Website Advisory. Roxanne Hsu Feldman, Patrick J. Gall.

Task Force Chairs

Equity, Diversity, and Inclusion (EDI) within ALSC Implementation. Hanna Lee, Kirby McCurti.

National Institute Planning. Marge Loch-Wouters.

Research Agenda. Kathleen Campana, Brooke E. Newberry.

Student Gift Membership. Andrea Vaughn Johnson.

Summer/Out-of-School-Time Learning. Elsa D. Ouvrard-Prettol.

Awards Committee Chairs

Mildred L. Batchelder Award 2020. Lauren Aimonette Liang.

Pura Belpré Award 2020. Maria Xochitl Peterson.

Randolph Caldecott Award 2020. Julie F. Roach.

Theodor Seuss Geisel Award 2020. Jean B. Gaffney.

John Newbery Award 2020. Krishna Grady.

Odyssey Award 2020. Sharon Haupt.

Robert F. Sibert Informational Book Award 2020. Sally L. Miculek.

Publications

ALSC Matters! (q., electronic; memb. Not available by subscription.)

Children and Libraries: The Journal of the Association for Library Service to Children (q.; print and online; memb.; nonmemb. $50; foreign $60).

Everyday Advocacy Matters (q., electronic; memb.).

American Library Association
Association of College and Research Libraries

Executive Director, Mary Ellen K. Davis
50 E. Huron St., Chicago, IL 60611-2795
312-280-2523, 800-545-2433 ext. 2523, fax 312-280-2520, e-mail acrl@ala.org
World Wide Web http://www.ala.org/acrl

Object

The Association of College and Research Libraries (ACRL) leads academic and research librarians and libraries in advancing learning and transforming scholarship. Founded 1940.

Membership

Memb. 11,172. For information on dues, see ALA entry.

Officers (2019–2020)

Pres. Lauren Pressley; *Pres.-Elect* Karen Munro; *Past Pres.* Cheryl A. Middleton, Oregon State Univ., 121 The Valley Lib., Corvallis, OR 97331. Tel. 541-737-8527, e-mail Cheryl.Middleton@oregonstate.edu.

Board of Directors

Officers; Carolyn Henderson Allen, Faye A. Chadwell, April D. Cunningham, Emily Daly, Jeanne R. Davidson, Mary Ellen K. Davis (Ex-Officio), Caroline Fuchs, Kelly Gordon

Jacobsma, LeRoy Jason LaFleur, Beth McNeil, Lori J. Ostapowicz-Critz, Allison Payne, Elois Sharpe.

Committee Chairs

Academic/Research Librarian of the Year Award. Jennifer Leigh Fabbi.
ACRL 2019 Coordinating. Trevor A. Dawes.
ACRL 2019 Chair's Choice. Maggie Farrell, Janice D. Welburn.
ACRL 2019 Colleagues. John P. Culshaw, Julia M. Gelfand.
ACRL 2019 Contributed Papers. Beth McNeil, Lisa M. Stillwell.
ACRL 2019 Innovations. Michael Meth, Willie Miller.
ACRL 2019 Invited Presentations. Orolando Duffus, Nancy J. Weiner.
ACRL 2019 Keynote Speakers. Martin L. Garnar, Courtney L. Young.
ACRL 2019 Local Arrangements. Evan Meszaros, Michelle S. Millet.
ACRL 2019 Panel Sessions. Alyssa Koclanes, Kathy A. Parsons.
ACRL 2019 Poster Sessions. Jose A. Aguinaga, Michelle Demeter.
ACRL 2019 Preconference Coordinating. Peter D. Hepburn, Kimberly Burke Sweetman.
ACRL 2019 Roundtable Discussions Committee. Michael Courtney, Sojourna Jeanette Cunningham.
ACRL 2019 Scholarships. Rachel Besara, Cynthia K. Steinhoff.
ACRL 2019 Virtual Conference. Jodie L. Borgerding, Nicole Tekulve.
ACRL 2019 Workshop Programs. Christopher Cox, Karen E. Downing.
Appointments. Erin L. Ellis.
Hugh C. Atkinson Memorial Award. Angela M. Gooden, Bruce Chr. Johnson, Holly A. Tomren.
Budget and Finance. Carolyn Henderson Allen.
Diversity. Federico Martinez-Garcia, Jr.
Excellence in Academic Libraries Awards. Irene M. H. Herold.
Government Relations. Kevin William Baggett.
Immersion Program. Jennifer L. Corbin.
Leadership Recruitment and Nomination. Amanda R. Peters.
Liaisons Coordinating. Michelle Demeter.
Liaisons Grants. Farzaneh Razzaghi.
Liaisons Training and Development. Susie A. Skarl.
Membership. Jodie L. Borgerding.
Section Membership. Kimberly Tully.
New Roles and Changing Landscapes. Anne M. Grant.
Professional Development. Eric A. Kidwell.
2019 President's Program Planning. Rebecca Kate Miller.
2020 President's Program Planning. Anne-Marie Deitering.
Professional Values. Jill Sodt.
Publications Coordinating. Cassandra Kvenild.
Research Planning and Review. Kathleen Kern.
Research and Scholarly Environment. Yasmeen Shorish.
(Dr. E. J.) Josey Spectrum Scholar Mentor. Tamara Rhodes.
Standards. Kim L. Eccles.
Information Literacy Frameworks and Standards. Amanda Nichols Hess.
Student Learning and Information Literacy. Elizabeth Galoozis.
Value of Academic Libraries. Holly Mercer.

Editorial Board Chairs

Academic Library Trends and Statistics Survey. Georgie Lynn Donovan.
ACRL/LLAMA Interdivisional Academic Library Facilities Survey. Anne Marie Casey, Eric A. Kidwell.
College & Research Libraries. Wendi Arant Kaspar.
College & Research Libraries News. Amanda Dinscore.
Choice. Amanda L. Folk.
New Publications Advisory. Rebecca Miller Waltz.
Publications in Librarianship. Daniel Clark Mack.
RBM. Richard Saunders.
Resources for College Libraries. Neal Baker.

Task Force Chairs

ACRL/ALA/ARL IPEDS. Robert E. Dugan, Jennifer F. Paustenbaugh.

ACRL/RBMS-SAA Joint Task Force to Revise the Statement on Access to Research Materials in Archives and Special Collections Libraries. Elizabeth Call, Michelle Aviva Ganz.

Diversity Alliance. Jon E. Cawthorne.

Impactful Scholarship and Metrics. Rachel Borchardt.

National Survey of Student Engagement (NSSE) Information Literacy Module Review. Mary Jane Petrowski.

Project Outcome for Academic Libraries. Eric George Ackermann.

Status of Academic Librarians Standards and Guidelines Review. Julia M. Gelfand.

Discussion Group Conveners

Assessment. Nancy B. Turner.

Balancing Baby and Book. Laura Bornella.

Continuing Education/Professional Development. Megan R. Griffin.

Copyright. Sara R. Benson, Carla S. Myers.

First-Year Experience. Charissa Powell.

Global Library Services. Ms. Hong Cheng, Daniel Perkins.

Heads of Public Services. William H. Weare, Jr.

Hip Hop Librarian Consortium. Craig E. Arthur.

International Perspectives on Academic and Research Libraries. Raymond Pun.

Leadership. Raymond Pun.

Learning Commons. Diane M. Fulkerson.

Library and Information Science Collections. Rachael Clark, Duncan R. Stewart.

Library Support for Massive Open Online Courses (MOOCs). Kyle Kenneth Courtney.

Media Resources. Steven Dennis Milewski.

MLA International Biography. Daniel P. Coffey.

New Members. Ashley Rosener.

Personnel Administrators and Staff Development. Julie Brewer, Michael A. Crumpton.

Philosophical, Religious, and Theological Studies. Martha Adkins.

Scholarly Communication. Mel DeSart, Lori J. Ostapowicz-Critz.

Student Retention. Quetzalli Barrientos, Holly Jane Luetkenhaus.

Undergraduate Librarians. Jason Kruse, Amy Wainwright.

Interest Group Conveners

Academic Library Services to Graduate Students. Hannah Gascho Rempel.

Academic Library Services to International Students. Leila June Rod-Welch.

Access Services. DaVonne R. Armstrong.

African-American Studies Libns. KYmberly Mieshia Dionne Keeton.

Asian, African, and Middle Eastern Studies Interest Group. Triveni S. Kuchi.

Contemplative Pedagogy. Sara Smith.

Digital Badges. Kelsey O'Brien, Victoria Raish.

Health Sciences. Mary Beth Slebodnik.

History Librarians. Alain J. St. Pierre, Jr.

Image Resources. Tiffany Saulter.

Librarianship in For-Profit Educational Institutions. Adrienne Nicole Sayban.

Library Marketing and Outreach. Sabine Dantus, Joan Petit.

Research Assessment and Metrics. James P. Morris-Knower.

Residency. Kaitlin A. Springmier.

Systematic Reviews and Related Methods. Paul G. Fehrmann, Scott Marsalis.

Technical Services. Erin Finnerty.

Universal Accessibility. Jessica Brangiel.

Virtual Worlds. Valerie J. Hill.

Publications

Choice (12x yearly; $513; Canada and Mexico $551; other international $660). *Ed.* Mark Cummings. Tel. 860-347-6933 ext. 119, e-mail mcummings@ala-choice.org.

Choice Reviews-on-Cards (requires subscription to *Choice* or *Choice Reviews* $576; Canada and Mexico $618; other international $713).

College & Research Libraries (*C&RL*) (6x yearly; open access online-only). *Ed.* Wendi Arant Kaspar.

College & Research Libraries News (*C&RL News*) (11x yearly; memb.; nonmemb. $58; Canada and other PUAS countries $63; other international $68). *Ed.* David Free Tel. 312-280-2517, e-mail dfree@ala.org.

RBM: A Journal of Rare Books, Manuscripts, and Cultural Heritage (s. ann.; $52; Canada and other PUAS countries $58; other international $69). *Ed.* Richard Saunders. Southern Utah Univ., 351 W. University Blvd. Gerrald R. Sherratt Lib., Cedar City, UT 84720-2415. Tel. 435-865-7947, fax 435-865-8152, e-mail rsaunders@suu.edu.

American Library Association
Association of Specialized, Government, and Cooperative Library Agencies

Executive Director, Jeannette P. Smithee
50 E. Huron St., Chicago, IL 60611-2795
800-545-2433, e-mail ascla@ala.org
World Wide Web http://www.ala.org/asgcla

Object

The Association for Specialized, Government, and Cooperative Library Agencies (ASGCLA) enhances the effectiveness of library service by advocating for and providing high-quality networking, enrichment, and educational opportunities for its diverse members, who represent state library agencies, libraries serving special populations, library cooperatives, and library consultants. ASGCLA's members are

- Librarians, library agencies, and staff serving populations with special needs, such as those with sensory, physical, health, or behavioral conditions or those who are incarcerated or detained
- Librarians and staff of state library agencies, and state library consultants—organizations created or authorized by state governments to promote library services
- Library networks and cooperatives, organizations of one or more types of libraries—academic, public, special, or school—that collaborate to maximize the funds available for provision of library services to all citizens; they may serve a community, a metropolitan area, a region, or a statewide or multistate area
- Consultants, independent or contract librarians, as well as those who work outside traditional library settings

Member activity is centered around interest groups.

Membership

Memb. 800+. For information on dues, see ALA entry.

Officers (2018–2019)

Pres. Adam S. Szczepaniak, Jr.; *Pres.-Elect* Sherry Machones; *Secy.* Rhonda K. Gould; *Div. Councilor* Michael A. Golrick; *Staff Liaisons* Ninah Moore, Shuntai Sykes, Melissa Vanyek.

Interest Group Leaders

Alzheimer's and Related Dementias. Tysha Shay.

Armed Forces Librarian. Virginia Sanchez.

Bridging Deaf Cultures @ your library. Alec McFarlane.

Collaborative Digitization. Sandra McIntyre.

Consortial eBooks. Dee Brennan, Veronda Pitchford.

Consortium Management. Tracy Byerly.

Consumer Health Information Librarians. Carrie Banks, Lydia Collins.

Federal Librarian. Lee Lipscomb.

Future of Libraries. Amy Paget.

Library Consultants. Liz Bishoff.

Library Services for Youth in Custody. Camden Eadoin Tadhg.

Library Services to Persons with Print Disabilities. Mark Lee.

LSTA Coordinators. Kathleen Peiffer.
Physical Delivery. Susan Palmer, Greg Pronevitz.
State Library Agencies—Library Development. Shannon White, Wendy Knapp.
State Library Agencies—Youth Services Consultants. Sharon Rawlins.
Tribal Librarians. Lillian Chavez.
Universal Access. Marti Goddard.

For more information on ASCLA interest groups, see https://www.ascladirect.org/interest-groups.

Board Members

Officers; Carrie Scott Banks, Erin Boyington, Tracy Byerly, Vicky L. Crone, Ed Garcia, Michael A. Golrick, Mike L. Marlin, Ninah Moore, Amy Jane Paget, Lily Sacharow, Jeannette Smithee, Stephen H. Spohn, Jr., Shuntai Sykes, Melissa Vanyek, Lance D. Wiscamb, Janice Marie Young.

Committee Chairs

Accessibility Assembly. Reed W. Strege.
Awards. Wendy Cornelisen.
Conference Programming. Lydia N. Collins, Allan Martin Kleiman.
Finance and Planning. Sherry Machones.
Guidelines for Lib. and Information Services for the American Deaf Community. Martha L. Goddard.
Interest Group Coordinating. Jeannette Smithee, Adam S. Szczepaniak, Jr.
Membership. Elizabeth A. Burns.
Nominating. Carson Block.
Online Learning. Anna C. Popp.
President's Program Planning. Jeannette Smithee, Adam S. Szczepaniak, Jr.
Web Presence. Stephanie Irvin.

American Library Association
Library and Information Technology Association

Executive Director, Jenny Levine
50 E. Huron St., Chicago, IL 60611-2795
800-545-2433, x4270, fax 312-280-3257, e-mail lita@ala.org
World Wide Web http://www.lita.org

Object

As the center of expertise about information technology, the Library and Information Technology Association (LITA) leads in exploring and enabling new technologies to empower libraries. LITA members use the promise of technology to deliver dynamic library collections and services.

LITA educates, serves, and reaches out to its members, other ALA members and divisions, and the entire library and information community through its publications, programs, and other activities designed to promote, develop, and aid in the implementation of library and information technology.

Membership

Memb. 2,900. Dues (Reg.) $60; (Nonsalaried/Ret./Earning less than $30,000 per year) $30; (Student) $25; (Org./Corp.) $90.

Officers (2018–2019)

Pres. Bohyun Kim *Pres.-Elect* Emily Morton-Owens; *Past Pres.* Andromeda Yelton.

Board of Directors

Officers; Mark A. Beatty, Tel. 312-280-4268, e-mail mbeatty@ala.org; Lindsay Anne Cronk;

Tabatha Farney; Jodie Gambill; Amanda L. Goodman; Margaret Heller; Christopher Lawton; Jenny Levine, Tel. 312-280-4267, e-mail jlevine@ala.org; Brian Rennick; Evviva R. Weinraub; Berika Williams; *Div. Councillor* Aaron Dobbs.

Committee Chairs

Appointments. Emily Morton-Owens.
Assessment and Research. Kyle Denlinger.
Blog Subcommittee. Cinthya Ippoliti, John Klima.
Bylaws and Organization. Jodie Gambill.
Communications and Marketing. Joel Tonyan.
Diversity and Inclusion. Jennifer C. Brown.
Education. Cinthya Ippoliti.
Financial Advisory. Brian Rennick.
Forum Planning 2019. Christopher Lawton, Berika Williams.
Fundraising. Andromeda Yelton.
LITA/ALCTS Metadata Standards. Michael R. Bolam, Scott A. Opasik.
Membership Development. Robert T. Wilson.
Nominating. Abigail H. Goben.
Program Planning. Natalie Marie DeJonghe.
Publications. Heidi E. Hanson.
Top Technology Trends. Tammy Allgood Wolf.
Web Coordinating. Michael Joseph Paulmeno.

Interest Group Chairs

Altmetrics and Digital Analytics. Mark A. Beatty, Jenny Levine.
Authority Control. Martha Rice Sanders.
Drupal4Lib. Ilana Kingsley.
Electronic Resources Management (LITA/ALCTS). Mark A. Beatty, Jenny Levine, Julie Reese.
E-rate CIPA. Victoria Teal Lovely, Rob Lee Nunez, II.
Heads of Library Technology. Kelly Kobiela, Ray Schwartz.
Imagineering. Dena Heilik.
Instructional Technologies. Lilly Ramin.
Linked Library Data. Craig Allen Boman, Scott Carlson.
Machine and Deep Learning Research. David Lacy.
Maker Technology. Erik Carlson.
MARC Formats Transition. Sherab Chen, Rachel Paul.
New Members. Mark A. Beatty, Jenny Levine.
Open Source Systems. Jacob W. Ineichen.
Patron Privacy Technologies. Mark A. Beatty, Jenny Levine.
User Experience. Mark A. Beatty, Jenny Levine.
Women in Information Technology. Mark A. Beatty, Jenny Levine.

Editorial Board Chairs

LITA Acquisitions Editor Marta Deyrup.
ITAL Editor Ken Varnum.

Awards Committee Chairs

Hugh C. Atkinson Award. Angela M. Gooden, Bruce Chr. Johnson, Holly A. Tomren.
Frederick G. Kilgour Award. Aimee Fifarek.
LITA / Christian Larew Memorial Scholarship. Christopher Lawton.
LITA / Ex Libris Student Writing Award. Lisa Janicke Hinchliffe.
LITA / Library Hi Tech Award. Tod A. Olson.
LITA / Recognizing Excellence in Children's and Young Adult Science Fiction. Mark A. Beatty, Jenny Levine.

Advisory Group Staff Liaisons

Mark A. Beatty, Jenny Levine.

Publication

Information Technology and Libraries (*ITAL*) (open source at http://ejournals.bc.edu/ojs/index.php/ital/issue/current). *Ed.* Ken Varnum. For information or to send manuscripts, contact the editor.

American Library Association
Library Leadership and Management Association

Executive Director, Kerry Ward
50 E. Huron St., Chicago, IL 60611
312-280-5032, 800-545-2433 ext. 5032, fax 312-280-2169
e-mail kward@ala.org
World Wide Web http://www.ala.org/llama

Object

The Library Leadership and Management Association (LLAMA) Strategic Plan sets out the following:

Mission: The Library Leadership and Management Association advances outstanding leadership and management practices in library and information services by encouraging and nurturing individual excellence in current and aspiring library leaders.

Vision: As the foremost organization developing present and future leaders in library and information services, LLAMA provides a welcoming community where aspiring and experienced library leaders and library supporters from all types of libraries can seek and share knowledge and skills in leadership, administration, and management in a manner that creates meaningful transformation in libraries around the world.

Core Values: LLAMA believes advancing leadership and management excellence is achieved by fostering the following values—exemplary and innovative service to and for our members, and leadership development and continuous learning opportunities for our members.

Established in 1957.

Membership

Memb. 3,900+. Dues (indiv.) $50; (Organization) $65; (Student) $15.

Officers (2019–2020)

Pres. Lynn Hoffman, Somerset County Lib. System; *Pres.-Elect* Anne Cooper Moore, Univ. of North Carolina at Charlotte; *Treas.* Susan M. Considine, Fayetteville Free Lib.; *Past Pres.* Pixey A. Mosley, Texas A&M Univ., Tel. 979-862-1086, e-mail pmosley@library.tamu.edu; *Div. Councilor* Rivkah K. Sass, Univ. of Southern California.

Board of Directors

Officers; Audrey Barbakoff, King County Lib. System; Tamika Barnes; Scott P. Muir, Rowan Univ.; Fred Reuland. Tel. 800-545-2433, ext. 5032, e-mail freuland@ala.org; Joseph A. Salem, Jr.; Kerry Ward. Tel. 800-545-2433, ext. 5036, e-mail kward@ala.org.

Committee Chairs

ACRL/LLAMA Interdivisional Committee on Building Resources. Anne Marie Casey, Eric A. Kidwell.
Competencies. Barbara J. Mann.
Content Coordinating. Anne E. Langley.
Continuing Education Development. Marlee Givens.
Innovation Incubator. Cinthya Ippoliti.
Leadership Development Seminar. Kerry Ward.
Membership. Kerry Ward.
Mentoring. Richard R. Guajardo.
Nominating. Kerry Ward.
Program. William Martin Modrow.
Reorganization Implementation. Kerry Ward.

Discussion Group Chairs

Circulation/Access Services. Jane G. Scott.
Emerging Trends. Laura Lillard.
Fiscal and Business Issues. Kenneth E. Flower.
Hot Topics in Assessment. Elizabeth M. Joseph.
LLAMA Dialogue with Directors. Fred Reuland, Kerry Ward.
LLAMA Diversity Officers. Fred Reuland, Kerry Ward.

LLAMA Women Administrators. Jennifer Renee Steinford.

Middle Management. Jeffrey Scott Bullington.

Address correspondence to the executive director.

Publication

Library Leadership and Management (*LL&M*) (open access at https://journals.tdl.org/llm/index.php/llm/index). *Ed.* Joe Salem, Michigan State Univ., e-mail jsalem@msu.edu.

American Library Association
Public Library Association

Executive Director, Barbara A. Macikas
50 E. Huron St., Chicago, IL 60611
312-280-5752, 800-545-2433 ext. 5752, fax 312-280-5029, e-mail pla@ala.org
World Wide Web http://www.pla.org

The Public Library Association (PLA) has specific responsibility for

1. Conducting and sponsoring research about how the public library can respond to changing social needs and technical developments
2. Developing and disseminating materials useful to public libraries in interpreting public library services and needs
3. Conducting continuing education for public librarians by programming at national and regional conferences, by publications such as the newsletter, and by other delivery means
4. Establishing, evaluating, and promoting goals, guidelines, and standards for public libraries
5. Maintaining liaison with relevant national agencies and organizations engaged in public administration and human services, such as the National Association of Counties, the Municipal League, and the Commission on Postsecondary Education
6. Maintaining liaison with other divisions and units of ALA and other library organizations, such as the Association for Library and Information Science Education and the Urban Libraries Council
7. Defining the role of the public library in service to a wide range of user and potential user groups
8. Promoting and interpreting the public library to a changing society through legislative programs and other appropriate means
9. Identifying legislation to improve and to equalize support of public libraries

PLA enhances the development and effectiveness of public librarians and public library services. This mission positions PLA to

- Focus its efforts on serving the needs of its members
- Address issues that affect public libraries
- Commit to quality public library services that benefit the general public

The goals of PLA are

- Advocacy and Awareness: PLA is an essential partner in public library advocacy.
- Leadership and Transformation: PLA is the leading source for learning opportunities to advance transformation of public libraries.
- Literate Nation: PLA will be a leader and valued partner of public libraries' initiatives to create a literate nation.
- Organizational Excellence: PLA is positioned to sustain and grow its resources to advance the work of the association.

Membership

Memb. 8,000+. Open to all ALA members interested in the improvement and expansion of public library services to all ages in various types of communities.

Officers (2018–2019)

Pres. Monique le Conge Ziesenhenne, Palo Alto City Lib., Palo Alto, CA. E-mail monique.leconge@cityofpaloalto.org; *Pres.-Elect* Ramiro S. Salazar, San Antonio Public Lib. San Antonio, TX; *Past Pres.* Pam Sandlian Smith, Anythink Libs., Adams County, CO. E-mail psmith@anythinklibraries.org. *ALA Div. Councilor* Stephanie Chase.

Directors

Officers; Cindy Fesemyer, Michelle Jeske, Richard Kong, Tracy Strobel, Kelvin Watson, Carrie Willson.

Committee Chairs

Advocacy and Strategic Partnerships. Sara Charlton.

Budget and Finance. Clara Nalli Bohrer.

Continuing Education Advisory Group. Anthony James Baltiero.

Digital Literacy. Monica Marie Dombrowski.

Leadership Development. Meaghan O'Connor.

Measurement, Evaluation and Assessment. Linda Hofschire.

Membership Advisory Group. Kimberly Lauren Hagen.

Nominating. Felton Thomas, Jr.

PLA 2020 Conference Committee. Felton Thomas, Jr.

PLA 2020 Annual Conference Program Subcommittee. Juliane Morian.

Public Libraries Advisory. Mary Rzepczynski.

Technology. Henry Miller Bankhead.

Web Content Working Group. Theresa A. Jehlik.

Task Force Chairs

2020 Census Library Outreach and Education Task Force. Larra Clark.

Family Engagement. Clara Nalli Bohrer, Kathleen S. Reif.

Social Worker. Jean Badalamenti, Ms. Leah Esguerra.

Task Force on Equity, Diversity, Inclusion and Social Justice. Richard Kong, Amita Kaur Lonial.

Awards Committee Chairs

Baker & Taylor Entertainment Audio Music/Video Product Award. Sara Pope.

Gordon M. Conable Award Jury. Ashley Janet Brown.

DEMCO New Leaders Travel Grant Jury. Regina Greer Cooper.

EBSCO Excellence in Rural Library Service Award Jury. Helen Rigdon.

John Iliff Award Jury. Anastasia Diamond-Ortiz.

Allie Beth Martin Award Jury. Susan Wray.

Charlie Robinson Award Jury. Luren E. Dickinson.

Romance Writers of America Library Grant Jury. Amelia Zavala Vander Heide.

Singer Group Helping Communities Come Together Award Jury. Sarah Campbell Tansley.

Upstart Innovation Award Jury. Abby Simpson.

Publication

Public Libraries (6x yearly; memb.; nonmemb. $65; Canada and Mexico $75; Int'l. $100. *Ed.* Kathleen Hughes, PLA, 50 E. Huron St., Chicago, IL 60611. E-mail khughes@ala.org.

American Library Association
Reference and User Services Association

Executive Director, Bill Ladewski
50 E. Huron St., Chicago, IL 60611
800-545-2433 ext. 4395, 312-280-4395, fax 312-280-5273, e-mail bladewski@ala.org or rusa@ala.org
World Wide Web http://www.ala.org/rusa

Object

The Reference and User Services Association (RUSA) is responsible for stimulating and supporting excellence in the delivery of general library services and materials, and the provision of reference and information services, collection development, readers' advisory, and resource sharing for all ages, in every type of library.

The specific responsibilities of RUSA are

1. Conduct of activities and projects within the association's areas of responsibility
2. Encouragement of the development of librarians engaged in these activities, and stimulation of participation by members of appropriate type-of-library divisions
3. Synthesis of the activities of all units within the American Library Association that have a bearing on the type of activities represented by the association
4. Representation and interpretation of the association's activities in contacts outside the profession
5. Planning and development of programs of study and research in these areas for the total profession
6. Continuous study and review of the association's activities

Membership

Memb. 3,200+

Officers (2019–2020)

Pres. Ann K. G. Brown; *Pres.-Elect* Elizabeth Marie German; *Secy.* Candice Townsend; *Past Pres.* Chris LeBeau.

Board of Directors

Officers; Jennifer C. Boettcher, Jason Matthew Coleman, Greg Fleming, Megan Gaffney, Ed Garcia, Stephanie J. Graves, Emily Anne Hamstra, Kathleen Kern, Bill Ladewski, Rhea Brown Lawson, Cynthia Robin Levine, Jenny McElroy, Alesia M. McManus, Ninah Moore, Jenny L. Presnell, Christina Pryor, Shuntai Sykes, Melissa Vanyek.

Committee Chairs

Access to Information. Arlene McFarlin Weismantel.

AFL-CIO/ALA Labor. Jane Billinger, Benjamin Scott Blake.

Budget and Finance. Ann K. G. Brown.

Conference Program Coordinating. Cathay Keough, Joseph A. Thompson, Jr.

Membership Engagement. Nancy Housel Abashian.

Nominating. Alesia M. McManus.

President's Program Planning. Teresa Morris.

Professional Development. Stephanie J. Graves.

Professional Resources. Jennifer C. Boettcher.

Volunteer Development. Jason Matthew Coleman.

For more committee rosters, see http://www.ala.org/rusa/contact/rosters.

Task Force Chairs

Professional Competencies for Reference and User Services Librarians. Ninah Moore.

Restructuring Implementation. Bobray J. Bordelon, Jr.

Awards Committee Chairs

Andrew Carnegie Medals for Excellence in Fiction and Nonfiction. Ann K. G. Brown.
Awards Coordinating Committee. Jenny L. Presnell.
Excellence in Reference and Adult Services Award. Suzanne Odom.
Isadore Gilbert Mudge Award. Brian E. Coutts.
Gail Schlachter Memorial Research Grant. David A. Tyckoson.
John Sessions Memorial Award. Heather Howard.
Margaret E. Monroe Library Adult Services Award. Neil Hollands.

Publications

Reference & User Services Quarterly (online only at http://journals.ala.org/index.php/rusq) (memb.). *Ed.* M. Kathleen Kern, Miller Learning Ctr., Univ. of Georgia.
RUSA Update (q., online newsletter, at http://www.rusaupdate.org).

American Library Association
United for Libraries: Association of Library Trustees, Advocates, Friends, and Foundations

Executive Director, Beth Nawalinski
600 Eagleview Blvd., Suite 300, Exton, PA 19341
800-545-2433, ext. 2161, fax 215-545-3821, e-mail bnawalinski@ala.org or united@ala.org
World Wide Web http://www.ala.org/united

Object

United for Libraries was founded in 1890 as the American Library Trustee Association (ALTA). It was the only division of the American Library Association (ALA) dedicated to promoting and ensuring outstanding library service through educational programs that develop excellence in trusteeship and promote citizen involvement in the support of libraries. ALTA became an ALA division in 1961. In 2008 the members of ALTA voted to expand the division to more aggressively address the needs of friends of libraries and library foundations, and through a merger with Friends of Libraries USA (FOLUSA) became the Association of Library Trustees, Advocates, Friends and Foundations (ALTAFF). In 2012 members voted to add "United for Libraries" to its title.

Memb. 5,000. Open to all interested persons and organizations. Dues (prorated to match ALA membership expiration) $55; (student with ALA membership) $20.

Officers (2018–2019)

Pres. Skip Dye; *V.P./Pres.-Elect* Peter Pearson *Secy.* Donna McDonald; *Past Pres.* Steve Laird; *Div. Councilor* Christine Lind Hage.

Board of Directors

Gordon Baker, Paula Beswick, Ned Davis, Alan Fishel, Patricia M. Hogan, Jill Joseph, Gary Kirk, Virginia B. "Ginny" Moore, David Paige, Sarah Jessica Parker, Veronda Pitchford, Libby Post, MaryEllin Santiago, Patricia Glass Schuman, Mark Smith, Kathryn Spindel, Rocco Staino, Marcellus Turner, Dick Waters.

Committee Chairs

Annual Conference Program. Robin Hoklotubbe.
Awards. Camila Alire.
Leaders Orientation. Steve Laird.
Legislation, Advocacy, and Intellectual Freedom. Deborah Doyle.

Newsletter and Website Advisory. Ned Davis.
Nominating. Christine Hage.
PLA Conference Program 2016–2018. Marcellus Turner.

Publications

The Good, the Great, and the Unfriendly: A Librarian's Guide to Working with Friends Groups.
The Complete Library Trustee Handbook.
Even More Great Ideas for Libraries and Friends.
A Library Board's Practical Guide to Self-Evaluation.
A Library Board's Practical Guide to Hiring Outside Experts.
Getting Grants in Your Community
Making Our Voices Heard: Citizens Speak Out for Libraries.

American Library Association
Young Adult Library Services Association

Executive Director, Anita Mechler
50 E. Huron St., Chicago, IL 60611
312-280-4390, 800-545-2433 ext. 4390, fax 312-280-5276,
e-mail amechler@ala.org or yalsa@ala.org
World Wide Web http://www.ala.org/yalsa
YALSA blog http://yalsa.ala.org/blog, The Hub http://yalsa.ala.org/thehub,
Wiki http://wikis.ala.org/yalsa, Twitter http://twitter.com/yalsa
Facebook http://www.facebook.com/YALSA

Object

In every library in the nation, high-quality library service to young adults is provided by a staff that understands and respects the unique informational, educational, and recreational needs of teenagers. Equal access to information, services, and materials is recognized as a right, not a privilege. Young adults are actively involved in the library decision-making process. The library staff collaborates and cooperates with other youth-serving agencies to provide a holistic, community-wide network of activities and services that support healthy youth development. To ensure that this vision becomes a reality, the Young Adult Library Services Association (YALSA)

1. Advocates extensive and developmentally appropriate library and information services for young adults ages 12 to 18
2. Promotes reading and supports the literacy movement
3. Advocates the use of information and digital technologies to provide effective library service
4. Supports equality of access to the full range of library materials and services, including existing and emerging information and digital technologies, for young adults
5. Provides education and professional development to enable its members to serve as effective advocates for young people
6. Fosters collaboration and partnerships among its individual members with the library community and other groups involved in providing library and information services to young adults
7. Influences public policy by demonstrating the importance of providing library and information services that meet the unique needs and interests of young adults
8. Encourages research and is in the vanguard of new thinking concerning the provision of library and information services for youth

Membership

Memb. 5,100. Open to anyone interested in library services for and with young adults. For information on dues, see ALA entry.

Officers

Pres. Crystle Martin. E-mail crystle.martin@gmail.com; *Div. Councilor* Abigail Leigh Phillips. E-mail Abigail.LeighPhillips@gmail.com; *Fiscal Officer* Dora Ho. E-mail dorah2005@gmail.com; *Pres.-Elect* Todd Krueger. E-mail toddbcpl@gmail.com; *Secy.* Franklin L. Escobedo. E-mail adrithian@yahoo.com; *Past Pres.* Sandra Hughes-Hassell. E-mail smhughes@email.unc.edu.

Board of Directors

Officers; Trixie Dantis, Kate Denier, Jane Gov, Derek Ivie, Melissa McBride, Ryan Moniz, Colleen Seisser, Mega Subramaniam, Valerie Tagoe, Josie Watanabe, Dorcas Wong.

Committee Chairs

Advocacy and Activism. Melissa McBride.

Fund and Partner Development. Colleen Seisser.

Leading the Transformation of Teen Services. Derek Ivie.

Publications

Journal of Research on Libraries and Young Adults (q.) (online, open source, peer-reviewed). *Ed.* Denise Agosto. E-mail yalsaresearch@gmail.com.

Young Adult Library Services (YALS) (q.) (online only; memb.; nonmemb. $70; foreign $70). *Ed.* Megan Honig. E-mail yalseditor@gmail.com.

American Theological Library Association

Executive Director, Brenda Bailey-Hainer
300 S. Wacker Dr., Suite 2100, Chicago, IL 60606-6701
888-665-2852 or 312-454-5100, fax 312-454-5505, e-mail bbailey-hainer@atla.com.
World Wide Web http://www.atla.com

Mission

The mission of the American Theological Library Association (ATLA) is to foster the study of theology and religion by enhancing the development of theological and religious libraries and librarianship.

Membership

Dues (Inst.) $100–$1,000; (Indiv. varies, based on income) $35–$181.50; (Student) $35; (Affiliates) $100.

Officers (2018–2019)

Pres. Jennifer Bartholomew, Sacred Heart Seminary and School of Theology, 7335 S. Hwy 100, P.O. Box 429, Hales Corners, WI 53130-0429. E-mail jbartholomew@shsst.edu *V.P.* Stephen Sweeney, Saint John Vianney Theological Seminary, 1300 South Steele St., Denver, CO 80210-2599. E-mail stephen.sweeney@archden.org; *Secy.* Ellen Frost, Perkins School of Theology, Bridwell Lib., P.O. Box 750476, Dallas, TX 75275-0476; *Treas.* Christina Torbert. Univ. of Mississippi; *Past Pres.* Matthew J. Ostercamp, North Park Univ., Brandel Lib., 5114 N. Christiana Ave., Chicago, IL 60625. Tel. 773-244-5580, e-mail mjostercamp@northpark.edu.

Board of Directors

Officers; Suzanne Estelle-Holmer, Shanee' Yvette Murrain, Brad Ost, Matthew Ostercamp, Armin Seidlecki, Michelle Spomer, Matthew Thiesen, Jennifer Ulrich.

Committee Chairs

Conference. Erica Durham.
Diversity, Equity, and Inclusion. Evan Boyd.
Endowment. Sharon Taylor.
Professional Development. Martha Adkins.
Scholarly Communication. Andy Keck.

Publications

Annual Yearbook.
ATLA Newsletter. (mo., online).
ATLA *Summary of Proceedings.*

Archivists and Librarians in the History of the Health Sciences

President, Melissa Grafe
E-mail contact.alhhs@gmail.com
World Wide Web http://www.alhhs.org

Object

The association was established exclusively for educational purposes, to serve the professional interests of librarians, archivists, and other specialists actively engaged in the librarianship of the history of the health sciences by promoting the exchange of information and by improving the standards of service.

Membership

Memb. Approximately 150. Dues $15.

Officers (2018–2019)

Pres. Melissa Grafe, Medical Historical Lib., Harvey Cushing/John Hay Whitney Medical Lib., Yale Univ., New Haven, CT. E-mail melissa.grafe@yale.edu; *Secy.* Dawne Lucas, Health Sciences Lib., Univ. of North Carolina at Chapel Hill. E-mail dawne_lucas@unc.edu; *Treas.* Phoebe Evans Letocha, Alan Mason Chesney Medical Archives, Johns Hopkins Univ., Baltimore, MD. E-mail alhhs.treasurer@gmail.com; *Past Pres.* Rachel Ingold, History of Medicine Collections, Rubenstein Rare Book and Manuscript Lib., Duke Univ., 411 Chapel Dr., Durham, NC. Tel. 919-684-8549, e-mail rachel.ingold@duke.edu. *Membs.-at-Large* Beth DeFrancis Sun, Emily R. Novak Gustainis, Keith C. Mages, John Schleicher.

Committee Chairs

Annual Meeting 2019 Local Arrangements. Judith Wiener.
Annual Meeting 2019 Program. Lisa Mix.
Archivist. Jodi Koste.
Nominating 2019. Stephen Greenberg.
Recruiting. Jonathan Erlen.
Website. Russell Johnson.

Editorial Board Chairs

The Watermark Stephen E. Novak.

Awards Committee Chairs

Joan E. Klein Travel Scholarship. Keith Mages.
Publications Awards 2019. Toby Appel.

Recognition Awards 2019. Emily Gustainis.
Watermark (q.; memb.). *Ed.* Stephen E. Novak. Augustus C. Long Health Sciences Lib., Columbia Univ. E-mail sen13@cumc.columbia.org.

ARMA International

CEO, Jocelyn Gunter
11880 College Blvd., Suite 450, Overland Park, KS 66210
913-444-9174, 844-565-2120, fax 913-257-3855, e-mail headquarters@armaintl.org.
World Wide Web http://www.arma.org

Object

To advance the practice of records and information management as a discipline and a profession; to organize and promote programs of research, education, training, and networking within that profession; to support the enhancement of professionalism of the membership; and to promote cooperative endeavors with related professional groups.

Membership

Approximately 26,000 in more than 30 countries. Annual dues (Professional) $175; (Assoc.) $95. Chapter dues vary.

Officers

Pres. Ryan Zilm, USAA. E-mail ryanzilm.arma@gmail.com; *Pres.-Elect* Bill Bradford, Jagged Peak Energy. Tel. 303-947-4119, e-mail billbradford.arma@gmail.com; *Treas.* Michael Haley, Cohasset Associates. Tel. 908-642-3582, e-mail michaelhaley.arma@gmail.com; *Past Pres.* Ilona Koti, ARK-IGC LLC, Pollock Pines, CA. Tel. 408-705-8253, e-mail ilona.koti@yahoo.com.

Board of Directors

Officers; Susan Goodman, John J. Jablonski, Michelle Kirk, Mark Levin, Ben Robbins, Jason C. Stearns.

Publications

inDEPTH newsletter (bi-mo. memb.)
InfoPro newsletter (mo.)
Information Management (IM) (bi-mo., memb., e-magazine). *Ed.* Nick Inglis. Tel. 913-341-3808, e-mail editor@armaintl.org.
RIM and IG Around the World (mo.)

Art Libraries Society of North America

Executive Director, Nancy Short
7044 South 13th St., Oak Creek, WI 53154
414-908-4954, 800-817-0621, fax 414-768-8001, e-mail n.short@arlisna.org
World Wide Web https://www.arlisna.org

Object

The object of the Art Libraries Society of North America (ARLIS/NA) is to foster excellence in art librarianship and visual resources curatorship for the advancement of the visual arts. Established 1972.

Membership

Memb. 1,000+. Dues (Business Affiliate) $250; (Introductory) $100 (two-year limit); (Indiv.) $150; (Student) $50 (three-year limit); (Ret.) $75; (Unemployed/Bridge) $50. Year. Jan. 1–Dec. 31. Membership is open to all those interested in visual librarianship, whether they be professional librarians, students, library assistants, art book publishers, art book dealers, art historians, archivists, architects, slide and photograph curators, or retired associates in these fields.

Officers (2018–2019)

Pres. Kim Collins, Robert W. Woodruff Lib., Emory Univ., Atlanta, GA. Tel. 404-727-2997, e-mail kcolli2@emory.edu; *V.P./Pres.-Elect* Laura Schwartz, Univ. of Calif., San Diego. Tel. 858-534-1267, e-mail l7schwartz@ucsd.edu; *Secy.* Samantha Deutch, Frick Art Ref. Lib., the Frick Collection, New York, NY. Tel. 212-547-6894, e-mail deutch@frick.org; *Treas.* Doug Litts, Ryerson and Burnham Libs., The Art Institute of Chicago. Tel. 312-443-3671, e-mail dlitts@artic.edu; *Past Pres.* Eumie Imm Stroukoff, Santa Fe, NM. E-mail eistroukoff@gmail.com.

Board Members

Officers; *Editorial Director* Roger Lawson.

Committee Chairs

Advocacy and Public Policy. Serenity Ibsen.
Awards. Karyn Hinkle.
Cataloging Advisory. Andrea Puccio.
Development. Gregory P. J. Most.
Diversity. Amanda Meeks.
Documentation. Samantha Deutch.
Finance. Matthew Gengler.
International Relations. Beverly Mitchell.
Membership. Laurel Bliss.
Nominating. Debbie Kempe.
Professional Development. Karen Stafford.
Strategic Directions. Emilee Mathews.

Editorial Board Chair

Roger Lawson.

Publications

ARLIS/NA Multimedia & Technology Reviews (bi-mo.; memb.). *Eds.* Melanie Emerson, Gabriella Karl-Johnson, Alexandra Provo. E-mail arlisna.mtr@gmail.com.
ARLIS/NA Research & Reports.
ARLIS/NA Reviews (bi-mo.; memb.).
Art Documentation (2x yearly; memb., subscription). *Ed.* Judy Dyki E-mail jdyki@cranbrook.edu
Miscellaneous others (request current list from headquarters).

Asian/Pacific American Librarians Association

Executive Director, Buenaventura "Ven" Basco
P.O. Box 677593 Orlando, FL 32867-7593
407-823-5048, e-mail bbasco@mail.ucf.edu
World Wide Web http://www.apalaweb.org

Object

To provide a forum for discussing problems and concerns of Asian/Pacific American librarians; to provide a forum for the exchange of ideas by Asian/Pacific American librarians and other librarians; to support and encourage library services to Asian/Pacific American communities; to recruit and support Asian/Pacific American librarians in the library/information science professions; to seek funding for scholarships in library/information science programs for Asian/Pacific Americans; and to provide a vehicle whereby Asian/Pacific American librarians can cooperate with other associations and organizations having similar or allied interests. Founded in 1980; incorporated 1981; affiliated with American Library Association 1982.

Membership

Approximately 300. Dues (Corporate) $250; (Inst.) $70; (Lib. Support Staff) $20; (Life) $400; (Personal) $35 (one-year limit); (Ret.) $20 (one-year limit); (Student) $15 (Unemployed) $20. Open to all librarians and information specialists of Asian/Pacific descent working in U.S. libraries and information centers and other related organizations, and to others who support the goals and purposes of the association. Asian/Pacific Americans are defined as people residing in North America who self-identify as Asian/Pacific American.

Officers (2018–2019)

Pres. Paolo Gujilde; *V.P./Pres.-Elect* Alanna Aiko Moore; *Secy.* Annie Pho; *Treas.* Peter Spyers-Duran; *Past Pres.* Dora Ho, Los Angeles Public Lib., 630 W. 5th St., Los Angeles. E-mail dora2005@gmail.com; *Membs.-at-Large* Lana Adlawan, Jaena Rae Cabrera, Rose L. Chou, Anchalee (Joy) Panigabutra-Roberts.

Committee Chairs

Communications and Media. Jaena Rae Cabrera, Molly Higgins.

Constitution and Bylaws. Sheila Garcia.

Family Literacy Focus. Camden Kimura, Samantha Sermeno.

Finance and Fundraising. Ray Pun.

Literature Awards. Dora Ho, Ven Basco.

Membership. Maria (Pontillas) Shackles.

Mentorship. Valeria Molteni, Johana Orellana.

Nominating. Lessa Pelayo-Lozada (EB Liaison).

Program Planning. Andrew Carlos.

Scholarships and Awards. Rebecca Martin.

Publication

APALA Newsletter (2–3x yearly).

Association for Information Science and Technology

Executive Director, Lydia Middleton
8555 16th St., Suite 850, Silver Spring, MD 20910
301-495-0900, fax 301-495-0810, e-mail asist@asist.org
World Wide Web http://www.asist.org

Object

The Association for Information Science and Technology (ASIS&T, formerly the American Society for Information Science and Technology) provides a forum for the discussion, publication, and critical analysis of work dealing with the design, management, and use of information, information systems, and information technology.

Membership

Regular Memb. (Indiv.) 1,100; (Student) 500. Dues (Professional) $140; (Student) $40; (Community Only) $75; (Transitional Professional) $70; (Inst.) $700; (Corporate Patron) $800.

Officers (2018–2019)

Pres. Elaine Toms, Univ. of Sheffield, Sheffield, UK. E-mail e.toms@sheffield.ac.uk; *Pres.-Elect* Clara Chu, Univ. of Illinois at Urbana-Champaign, Urbana, IL. E-mail cmchu@illinois.edu; *Treas.* June Abbas, Univ. of Oklahoma, Norman, OK. E-mail asist@asist.org; *Past Pres.* Lisa M. Given, Swinburne Univ. of Technology, Melbourne, Australia. E-mail lgiven@swin.edu.au.

Board of Directors

Officers; Sarah Buchanan, Timothy Dickey; *Dirs.-at-large* Dania Bilal, Emily Knox, Agnes Mainka, Heather O'Brien, Soo Young Rieh, Abebe Rorissa; *Parliamentarian* Steve Hardin.

Committee Chairs

Awards and Honors. Abebe Rorissa.
Budget and Finance. June Abbas.
Constitution and Bylaws. Debora Shaw.
History. Kathryn La Barre.
Membership. Iris Xie.
Nominations. Lynn Silipigni Connaway.
Standards. Mark Needleman, Timothy Dickey.

Publications

Inside ASIS&T newsletter (bi-mo.).

Periodicals

Journal of the Association for Information Science and Technology. (JASIST) (mo.). Available with ASIS&T membership or from Wiley Blackwell.

Bulletin of the Association for Information Science and Technology (bi-mo.; memb.; online only).

Proceedings of the ASIS&T Annual Meeting. Available from ASIS&T.

Association for Library and Information Science Education

Executive Director, Cambria Happ
ALISE Headquarters, 4 Lan Dr., Suite 310, Westford, MA 01886
978-674-6190, e-mail office@alise.org
World Wide Web http://www.alise.org

Object

The Association for Library and Information Science Education (ALISE) is an independent nonprofit professional association whose mission is to promote excellence in research, teaching, and service for library and information science education through leadership, collaboration, advocacy, and dissemination of research. Its enduring purpose is to promote research that informs the scholarship of teaching and learning for library and information science, enabling members to integrate research into teaching and learning. The association provides a forum in which to share ideas, discuss issues, address challenges, and shape the future of education for library and information science. Founded in 1915 as the Association of American Library Schools, it has had its present name since 1983.

Membership

Memb. 700+ in four categories: Personal, Institutional, International Affiliate Institutional, and Associate Institutional. Dues (Indiv. full-time) $155; (Emerging Professional/Part-Time/Ret.) $85; (Student) $40; (Inst. varies, based on school budget) $400–$2,900 (Inst. Int'l./Assoc.) $350. Personal membership is open to anyone with an interest in the association's objectives.

Officers (2018–2019)

Pres. Heidi Julien, SUNY Buffalo, NY. E-mail heidijul@buffalo.edu; *Pres.-Elect* Stephen Bajjaly, Wayne State Univ. E-mail bajjaly@wayne.edu; *Secy./Treas.* Heather Moulaison Sandy, Univ. of Missouri. E-mail moulaisonhe@missouri.edu; *Past Pres.* Dietmar Wolfram, Univ. of Wisconsin–Milwaukee. E-mail dwolfram@uwm.edu.

Directors

Nicole Cooke, Cecilia Salvatore, Rong Tang.

Publications

Journal of Education for Library and Information Science (*JELIS*) (q.; online only; memb.; nonmemb. $135). *Eds.* John M. Budd and Denice Adkins. E-mail jeliseditor@alise.org.

Knowledge, Skills, and Abilities Survey (KSAs).

Library and Information Science Education Statistical Report (ann.; electronic; memb.; nonmemb. $135).

Association for Rural and Small Libraries

President, Lisa Lewis
5300 Lakewood Rd., Whitehall, Michigan 49461
248-457-5001, e-mail kmasters@arsl.info
World Wide Web http://www.arsl.info
Twitter @RuralLibAssoc

Object

The Association for Rural and Small Libraries (ARSL) was established in 1978, in the Department of Library Science at Clarion University of Pennsylvania, as the Center for Study of Rural Librarianship.

ARSL is a network of people throughout the United States dedicated to the positive growth and development of libraries. ARSL believes in the value of rural and small libraries, and strives to create resources and services that address national, state, and local priorities for libraries situated in rural communities.

Its objectives are

- To organize a network of members concerned about the growth and development of useful library services in rural and small libraries
- To provide opportunities for the continuing education of members
- To provide mechanisms for members to exchange ideas and to meet on a regular basis
- To cultivate the practice of librarianship and to foster a spirit of cooperation among members of the profession, enabling them to act together for mutual goals
- To serve as a source of current information about trends, issues, and strategies
- To partner with other library and non-library groups and organizations serving rural and small library communities
- To collect and disseminate information and resources that are critical to this network
- To advocate for rural and small libraries at the local, state, and national levels

Membership

Dues (Indiv. varies, based on salary) $15–$49; (Inst.) $150; (Business) $200; (Affiliate) $150.

Officers (2018–2019)

Pres. Lisa Lewis, 181 N 9th St., Show Low, AZ 85901. E-mail llewis@showlowaz.gov; *V.P./Pres.-Elect* Jennifer Pearson, Marshall County Memorial Lib., 310 Old Farmington Rd., Lewisburg, TN 37091. E-mail mcmlib@bellsouth.net; *Secy.* Jennie Garner, North Liberty Community Lib., P.O. Box 320, North Liberty, IA 52317. E-mail jgarner@northlibertyiowa.org; *Treas.* Clancy Pool, St. John Lib., 1 E Front St., St. John, WA 99171; *COSLA Appointee* Mary J. Soucie, North Dakota State Lib., 604 East Boulevard Ave., Bismarck, ND 58505-0800. E-mail msoucie@nd.gov; *Past Pres.* Kieran Hixon, Colorado State Lib., P.O. Box 313, Florence, CO 81226. E-mail kieran.hixon@gmail.com.

Board of Directors

Officers; Hope Decker, Julie Elmore, Bailee Hutchinson, Aimee Newberry, Jane Somerville, Kathy Street, Meredith Wickham, Sara Wright, Kathy Zappitello.

Committee Chairs

Advocacy. Mary Soucie.
Conference. Julie Elmore, Judy Calhoun.
Conference Logistics. Tena Hanson, Becky Heil.
Finance. Clancy Pool.
Governance. Sara Wright.

Marketing and Communication. Bailee Hutchinson.
Membership. Kathy Street.
Nominating. Kieran Hixon.
Partnerships. Jennifer Pearson, Kathy Zappitello.

Association of Academic Health Sciences Libraries

Executive Director, Louise S. Miller
2150 N. 107 St., Suite 205, Seattle, WA 98133
206-209-5261, fax 206-367-8777, e-mail office@aahsl.org
World Wide Web http://www.aahsl.org

Object

The Association of Academic Health Sciences Libraries (AAHSL) comprises the libraries serving the accredited U.S. and Canadian medical schools belonging to or affiliated with the Association of American Medical Colleges. Its goals are to promote excellence in academic health science libraries and to ensure that the next generation of health practitioners is trained in information-seeking skills that enhance the quality of health care delivery, education, and research. Founded in 1977.

Membership

Memb. 150+. Full membership is available to nonprofit educational institutions operating a school of health sciences that has full or provisional accreditation by the Association of American Medical Colleges. Full members are represented by the chief administrative officer of the member institution's health sciences library. Associate membership (and nonvoting representation) is available to organizations having an interest in the purposes and activities of the association. For dues information, contact the association.

Officers (2018–2019)

Pres. Judith Cohn, Health Sciences Libs., Rutgers, State Univ. of New Jersey. Tel. 973-972-4353, e-mail judith.s.cohn@rutgers.edu; *Pres.-Elect* Sandra Franklin, Woodruff Health Sciences Ctr. Lib., Emory Univ. Tel. 404-727-0288, e-mail librsf@emory.edu; *Secy./Treas.* Jerry Perry, Arizona Health Sciences Lib., Univ. of Arizona. Tel. 520-626-6121, e-mail jerryperry@email.arizona.edu; *Past Pres.* Paul Schoening, Bernard Becker Medical Lib., Washington Univ. School of Medicine. Tel. 314-362-7080, e-mail paschoening@wustl.edu.

Board of Directors

Officers, Tania Bardyn, Nadine Dexter, Louise S. Miller, Debra Rand.

Committee Chairs

Assessment and Statistic. Matthew Wilcox.
Competency-Based Medical Education. Judy Spak.
Future Leadership. Heidi Heilemann.
New and Developing Health Sciences Libraries. Joanne Muellenbach.
Program and Education. Shannon Jones.
Research Services. Kristi Holmes.
Scholarly Communication. Emily McElroy.

Task Force Chairs

Diversity and Inclusion. Cristina A. Pope.

Association of Christian Librarians

Executive Director, Janelle Mazelin
P.O. Box 4, Cedarville, OH 45314
937-766-2255, fax 937-766-5499, e-mail info@acl.org
World Wide Web http://www.acl.org
Facebook https://www.facebook.com/ACLibrarians
Twitter @ACLibrarians

Object

The mission of the Association of Christian Librarians (ACL) is to strengthen libraries through professional development of evangelical librarians, scholarship, and spiritual encouragement for service in higher education. ACL is a growing community that integrates faith, ministry, and academic librarianship through development of members, services, and scholarship.

Founded 1957.

Membership

Memb. 500+ at about 150 institutions. Membership is open to those who profess the Christian faith as outlined by the association's statement of faith, and are employed at an institution of higher education. Associate memberships are available for nonlibrarians who both agree with ACL's statement of faith and are interested in libraries or librarianship. Dues (Indiv. 1st Year) $40; (Ret. Libn./Lib. School Student) $35; (Varies, based on income) $40–$120.

Officers (2018–2019)

Pres. (2016–2020) Denise Nelson, Point Loma Nazarene Univ.; *V.P. (2017–2019)* Nate Farley, Univ. of Northwestern–St. Paul; *Secy. (2017–2020)* Carol Reid; *Treas. (2008–2019)* Sheila O. Carlblom, Indiana Wesleyan Univ.; *Past Pres. (2012–2016)* Frank Quinn, Point Loma Nazarene Univ., San Diego, CA.

Board Members

Officers; Janelle Mazelin; *Dirs.-at-Large* Robert Burgess, Mark Hanson, Alison Johnson, Alison Jones, Leslie Starasta, Jennifer Walz.

Section Chairs

Bible College. Pradeep Das.

Liberal Arts. Gail Heideman.

Publications

The Christian Librarian. (2x yearly; memb.; nonmemb. $30). *Ed.* Garrett Trott. Corban Univ., Salem, OR.

Christian Periodical Index (q.; electronic).

The Librarian's Manual (English or Spanish; electronic or print; $40).

Library Guidelines for ABHE Colleges and Universities (memb.).

Association of Independent Information Professionals

President, Judith Binder
8550 United Plaza Blvd., Suite 1001, Baton Rouge, LA 70809
225-408-4400, fax 225-408-4422, e-mail office@aiip.org
World Wide Web http://www.aiip.org
LinkedIn https://www.linkedin.com/groups/159756
Twitter @AIIP

Object

Members of the Association of Independent Information Professionals (AIIP) are owners of firms providing such information-related services as online and manual research, document delivery, database design, library support, consulting, writing, and publishing.

The objectives of the association are

- To advance the knowledge and understanding of the information profession
- To promote and maintain high professional and ethical standards among its members
- To encourage independent information professionals to assemble to discuss common issues
- To promote the interchange of information among independent information professionals and various organizations
- To keep the public informed of the profession and of the responsibilities of the information professional

Membership

Memb. 200+. Dues (Full) $200; (Assoc.) $200; (Student) $50; (Supporting) $500; (Ret.) $75; (Emeritus) $50.

Officers (2019–2020)

Pres. Judith Binder, RBSC Research Corp., Research Group; *Pres.-Elect* Jennifer Pflaumer, Paroo; *Secy.* Phyllis Smith, ITK Vector Inc.; *Treas.* Beth Plutchak, Beth Plutchak Consulting LLC; *Past-Pres.* Cindy Shamel, Shamel Info. Svcs.

Board of Directors

Officers; George Puro, Cindy Romaine, Kirsten Smith.

Publications

AIIP Connections (q.).
Member Directory (ann.).
Professional papers series.

Association of Jewish Libraries

President, Dina Herbert
P.O. Box 1118, Teaneck, NJ 07666
201-371-3255, e-mail info@jewishlibraries.org
World Wide Web http://www.jewishlibraries.org
Facebook https://www.facebook.com/jewishlibraries
Twitter @JewishLibraries

Object

The Association of Jewish Libraries (AJL) is an international professional organization that fosters access to information and research in all forms of media relating to all things Jewish. The association promotes Jewish literacy and scholarship and provides a community for peer support and professional development.

AJL membership is open to individuals and libraries, library workers, and library supporters. There are two divisions within AJL: RAS (Research Libraries, Archives, and Special Collections) and SSC (Schools, Synagogues, and Centers). The diverse membership includes libraries in synagogues, JCCs, day schools, yeshivot, universities, Holocaust museums, and the Library of Congress. Membership is drawn from North America and places beyond, including China, the Czech Republic, the Netherlands, Israel, Italy, South Africa, Switzerland, and the United Kingdom.

Goals

The association's goals are to

- Maintain high professional standards for Judaica librarians and recruit qualified individuals into the profession
- Facilitate communication and exchange of information on a global scale
- Encourage quality publication in the field in all formats and media, print, digital, and so forth, and to stimulate publication of high-quality children's literature
- Facilitate and encourage establishment of Judaica library collections
- Enhance information access for all through application of advanced technologies
- Publicize the organization and its activities in all relevant venues: stimulate awareness of Judaica library services among the public at large; promote recognition of Judaica librarianship within the wider library profession; and encourage recognition of Judaica library services by other organizations and related professions
- Ensure continuity of the association through sound management, financial security, effective governance, and a dedicated and active membership

AJL conducts an annual convention in the United States or Canada in late June.

Membership

Memb. 600. Year: Oct. 1–Sept. 30. Dues (Indiv.) $70; (First-year Lib. School Student) Free; (Second/third-year Lib. School Student) $35; (Ret.) $35; (Large Inst.) (Greater than 100 FTE/includes personal membership) $100; (Small Inst.) (100 or fewer FTE/includes 1 personal membership) $75; (Corporate) $70.

Officers

Pres. Dina Herbert, National Archives and Records Admin., Alexandria, VA. E-mail dina.herbert@gmail.com; *V.P./Pres.-Elect* Kathleen Bloomfield, Adat Shalom Reconstructionist Congregation, 1240 Oakmont Rd., Unit 52-i, Seal Beach, CA 90740; *Secy.* Nancy Sack, Univ. of Hawai'i at Manoa, 2550 McCarthy Mall, Honolulu. Tel. 808-956-2648, e-mail sack@hawaii.edu; *Treas.* Holly Zimmerman, AARP, 601 E. St. N.W., Washington, DC 20049. E-mail: hzimmerman@aarp.org; *Past*

Pres. Amalia Warshenbrott. E-mail amaliaima @att.net; *Membs.-at-Large* Rebecca Levitan. E-mail: ralevitan@gmail.com; Daniel A. Scheide. E-mail: dascheide@gmail.com.

Board Members

Officers; Sharon Benamou, Emily Bergman, Michelle Chesner, Joy Kingsolver, Amalia S. Levi, Ellen Share.

Committee Chairs

Accreditation. Shaindy Kurzmann.
Advertising. Jackie Ben-Efraim.
Cataloging. Heidi G. Lerner.
Conference, Local. Jackie Ben-Efraim, Lisa Silverman.
Conference, Organization-Wide. Lisa Silverman.
Conference Stipend. Lenore M. Bell.
Continuing Education. Haim Gottschalk.
Librarianship and Education. Haim Gottschalk.
Member Relations. Heidi Rabinowitz.
Public Relations. Jessica Fink.
Publications. Laura Schutzman.
Web. Sheryl Stahl.

Editorial Board Chairs

AJL News and *AJL Reviews.* Uri Kolodney.
Judaica Librarianship. Rachel Leket-Mor.

Awards Committee Chairs

Groner-Wikler Scholarship. Emily Bergman.
Jewish Fiction Award. Jeremiah Aaron Taub.
Reference and Bibliography Award. Amalia S. Levi.
Student Scholarship. Tina Weiss.
Sydney Taylor Book Award. Rebecca Levitan.
Sydney Taylor Manuscript Competition. Fan and Hyman Jacobs Library.

Publications

AJL Conference Proceedings.
AJL News (q., digital; memb.). *Ed.* Uri Kolodney, Univ. of Texas at Austin. Tel. 512-495-4399, e-mail: kolodney@austin.utexas.edu.
AJL Reviews (q., digital; memb.).
Judaica Librarianship (annual, digital; memb.). *Ed.* Rachel Leket-Mor, Arizona State Univ. Libs. E-mail rachel.leket-mor@asu.edu.

Association of Research Libraries

Executive Director, Mary Lee Kennedy
21 Dupont Circle N.W., Suite 800, Washington, D.C. 20036
202-296-2296, fax 202-872-0884, e-mail arlhq@arl.org
World Wide Web http://www.arl.org

Object

The Association of Research Libraries (ARL) is a nonprofit organization of 124 research libraries in Canada and the United States whose mission is to advance research, learning, and scholarly communication. The Association fosters the open exchange of ideas and expertise, promotes equity and diversity, and pursues advocacy and public policy efforts that reflect the values of the library, scholarly, and higher education communities. ARL forges partnerships and catalyzes the collective efforts of research libraries to enable knowledge creation and to achieve enduring and barrier-free access to information.

Membership

Memb. 124. Membership is institutional. Dues: $30,005 for 2019.

Officers

Pres. Susan Gibbons, Yale Univ.; *V.P./Pres.-Elect* Lorraine Haricombe, Univ. of Texas at

Austin; *Treas.* Diane Parr Walker, Univ. of Notre Dame; *Past Pres.* Mary Ann Mavrinac, Univ. of Rochester.

Board of Directors

H. Austin Booth (ex officio, voting), New York Univ.; Constantia Constantinou, Univ. of Pennsylvania; John Culshaw, Univ. of Iowa; Bob Fox, Univ. of Louisville; Susan Gibbons, Yale Univ.; Lorraine Haricombe, Univ. of Texas at Austin; Mary Lee Kennedy (ex officio, non-voting), ARL; Vivian Lewis, McMaster Univ.; Adriene Lim, Univ. of Oregon; Mary Ann Mavrinac, Univ. of Rochester; Catherine Murray-Rust, Georgia Inst. of Technology; Jennifer Paustenbaugh, Brigham Young Univ.; Diane Parr Walker, Univ. of Notre Dame; Leslie Weir, Univ. of Ottawa.

Advisory Group Chairs

Advocacy and Public Policy Committee. Kevin Smith, Univ. of Kansas.

ARL Academy Advisory Group. Simon Neame, Univ. of Massachusetts, Amherst.

Diversity, Equity, and Inclusion Committee. Beth McNeil, Iowa State Univ.

Finance Committee. Diane Parr Walker, Univ. of Notre Dame.

Governance Committee. John Culshaw, Univ. of Iowa.

Innovation Lab Advisory Group. Xuemao Wang, Univ. of Cincinnati.

Member Engagement and Outreach Committee. David Banush, Tulane Univ.

Membership Committee. Adriene Lim, Univ. of Oregon.

Program Advisory Group. Mary Lee Kennedy, ARL.

Research and Analytics Committee. Steven Mandeville-Gamble, Univ. of California, Riverside.

Publications

ARL Academic Health Sciences Library Statistics (ann.).

ARL Academic Law Library Statistics (ann.).

ARL Annual Salary Survey (ann.).

ARL Statistics (ann.).

Research Library Issues (4x yearly).

ARL Membership

Nonuniversity Libraries

Boston Public Lib.; Center for Research Libs.; Lib. of Congress; National Agricultural Lib.; National Archives and Records Administration; National Lib. of Medicine; New York Public Lib.; Smithsonian Institution Libs.

University Libraries

Alabama; Albany (SUNY); Alberta; Arizona; Arizona State; Auburn; Boston College; Boston Univ.; Brigham Young; British Columbia; Brown; Buffalo (SUNY); Calgary; California, Berkeley; California, Davis; California, Irvine; California, Los Angeles; California, Riverside; California, San Diego; California, Santa Barbara; Case Western Reserve; Chicago; Cincinnati; Colorado, Boulder; Colorado State; Columbia; Connecticut; Cornell; Dartmouth; Delaware; Duke; Emory; Florida; Florida State; George Washington; Georgetown; Georgia; Georgia Inst. of Technology; Guelph; Harvard; Hawaii, Manoa; Houston; Howard; Illinois, Chicago; Illinois, Urbana-Champaign; Indiana, Bloomington; Iowa; Iowa State; Johns Hopkins; Kansas; Kent State; Kentucky; Laval; Louisiana State; Louisville; McGill; McMaster; Manitoba; Maryland; Massachusetts, Amherst; Massachusetts Inst. of Technology; Miami (Florida); Michigan; Michigan State; Minnesota; Missouri, Columbia; Nebraska, Lincoln; New Mexico; New York; North Carolina, Chapel Hill; North Carolina State; Northwestern; Notre Dame; Ohio; Ohio State; Oklahoma; Oklahoma State; Oregon; Ottawa; Pennsylvania; Pennsylvania State; Pittsburgh; Princeton; Purdue; Queen's (Kingston, Ontario); Rice; Rochester; Rutgers; Saskatchewan; Simon Fraser; South Carolina; Southern California; Southern Illinois, Carbondale; Stony Brook (SUNY); Syracuse; Temple; Tennessee, Knoxville; Texas, Austin; Texas A&M; Texas Tech; Toronto; Tulane; Utah; Vanderbilt; Virginia; Virginia Commonwealth; Virginia Tech; Washington; Washington, Saint Louis; Washington State; Waterloo; Wayne State; Western; Wisconsin, Madison; Yale; York.

Association of Vision Science Librarians

Co-Chairs Leslie Holland, Dede Rios
World Wide Web http://www.avsl.org

Object

To foster collective and individual acquisition and dissemination of vision science information, to improve services for all persons seeking such information, and to develop standards for libraries to which members are attached. Founded in 1968.

Membership

Memb. (Indiv.) 150+, (Inst.) 100+.

Leadership Team

Co-Chair Leslie Holland, Southern College of Optometry, Memphis. E-mail lholland@sco.edu; *Co-Chair* Dede Rios, Rosenberg School of Optometry, Univ. of the Incarnate Word, San Antonio. E-mail dmrios1@uiwtx.edu; *Treas.* Elaine Wells, SUNY College of Optometry, Harold Kohn Vision Science Lib., New York. E-mail ewells@sunyopt.edu; *Membership* Trish Duffel, Univ. of Iowa, Dept. of Ophthalmology and Visual Sciences, C. S. O'Brien Lib., Iowa City. E-mail trish-duffel@uiowa.edu; *Archivist* Gale Oren, Univ. of Michigan Kellogg Eye Ctr., John W. Henderson Lib., Ann Arbor. E-mail goren@umich.edu.

Meetings

Annual meeting held in the fall, midyear mini-meeting with the Medical Library Association.

Beta Phi Mu (International Library and Information Studies Honor Society)

Executive Director, Alison M. Lewis
P.O. Box 42139, Philadelphia, PA 19101
267-361-5018, e-mail executivedirector@betaphimu.org or headquarters@betaphimu.org
World Wide Web http://www.betaphimu.org

Object

To recognize distinguished achievement in and scholarly contributions to librarianship, information studies, or library education, and to sponsor and support appropriate professional and scholarly projects relating to these fields. Founded at the University of Illinois in 1948.

Membership

Memb. 40,000. Eligibility for membership in Beta Phi Mu is by invitation of the faculty from institutions where the American Library Association, or other recognized accrediting agency approved by the Beta Phi Mu Executive Board, has accredited or recognized a professional degree program. Candidates must be graduates of a library and information science program and fulfill the following requirements: complete the course requirements leading to a master's degree with a scholastic average of 3.75 where A equals 4 points, or complete a planned program of advanced study beyond the master's degree which requires full-time study for one or more academic years with a scholastic average of 3.75 where A equals 4.0. Each chapter or approved institution is allowed to invite no more than 25 percent of the annual graduating class, and the faculty of participating library schools must attest to their initiates' professional promise.

Officers

Pres. (2017–2020) Elaine Yontz, Dept. of Interdisciplinary Professions, College of Education, East Carolina Univ., Ragsdale 112-Mail Stop 172, Greenville, NC 27858-4353. Tel. 252-737-1150, e-mail yontzm@ecu.edu; *V.P./Pres.-Elect (2018–2021)* Cecelia Brown, School of Lib. and Information Studies, Univ. of Oklahoma, 401 W Brooks, Rm. 120, Norman, OK 73019-6032. Tel. 405-325-3921, e-mail cbrown@ou.edu; *Treas. (2017–2020)* Emily Knox, School of Information Sciences, Univ. of Illinois, 501 E. Daniel St., Champaign, IL 61820. Tel. 217-300-0212, e-mail: knox@illinois.edu; *Past Pres. (2016–2019)* Vicki Gregory, Univ. of South Florida College of Arts and Sciences, 4202 E. Fowler Ave., CIS 2036, Tampa, FL 33620. Tel. 813-974-3520, e-mail gregory@usf.edu; *Dirs.-at-large* Michelle Demeter, Camille McCutcheon.

Directors

Gordon N. Baker, Sheri Ross, Heather Moulaison Sandy, Laura Sanders.

Publications

Beta Phi Mu Scholars Series. Available from Rowman & Littlefield, Publishers, 4501 Forbes Blvd., Suite 200, Lanham, MD 20706. *Ed.* Andrea Falcone. E-mail bpm-series@gmail.com.

Newsletter. *The Pipeline* (biennial; electronic only). *Ed.* Alison Lewis.

Chapters

Alpha. Univ. of Illinois at Urbana-Champaign, School of Info. Sciences; *Gamma.* Florida State Univ., College of Communication and Info.; *Epsilon.* Univ. of North Carolina at Chapel Hill, School of Info. and Lib. Science; *Theta.* c/o Pratt Inst., School of Info.; *Iota.* Catholic Univ. of America, Dept. of Lib. and Info. Science; Univ. of Maryland, College of Info. Studies; *Lambda.* Univ. of Oklahoma, School of Lib. and Info. Studies; *Xi.* Univ. of Hawaii at Manoa, Lib. and Info. Science Program; *Omicron.* Rutgers Univ., Grad. School of Communication, Info., and Lib. Studies; *Pi.* Univ. of Pittsburgh, School of Info. Sciences; *Sigma.* Drexel Univ., College of Computing and Informatics; *Psi.* Univ. of Missouri at Columbia, School of Info. Science and Learning Technologies; *Omega.* San José State Univ., School of Info.; *Beta Beta.* Simmons Univ., School of Lib. and Info. Science; *Beta Delta.* State Univ. of New York at Buffalo, Dept. of Lib. and Info. Studies; *Beta Epsilon.* Emporia State Univ., School of Lib. and Info. Management; *Beta Zeta.* Louisiana State Univ., School of Lib. and Info. Science; *Beta Iota.* Univ. of Rhode Island, Grad. School of Lib. and Info. Studies; *Beta Kappa.* Univ. of Alabama, School of Lib. and Info. Studies; *Beta Lambda.* Texas Woman's Univ., School of Lib. and Info. Sciences; *Beta Mu.* Long Island Univ., Palmer School of Lib. and Info. Science; *Beta Nu.* St. John's Univ., Div. of Lib. and Info. Science-*Beta Xi.* North Carolina Central Univ., School of Lib. and Info. Sciences; *Beta Pi.* Univ. of Arizona, School of Info.; *Beta Rho.* Univ. of Wisconsin at Milwaukee, School of Info. Science; *Beta Phi.* Univ. of South Florida, School of Lib. and Info. Science; *Beta Psi.* Univ. of Southern Mississippi, School of Lib. and Info. Science; *Beta Omega.* Univ. of South Carolina, College of Lib. and Info. Science; *Beta Beta Epsilon.* Univ. of Wisconsin at Madison, School of Lib. and Info. Studies; *Beta Beta Theta.* Univ. of Iowa, School of Lib. and Info. Science; *Pi Lambda Sigma.* Syracuse Univ., School of Info. Studies; *Beta Beta Mu.* Valdosta State Univ., Lib. and Info. Science Program; *Beta Beta Nu.* Univ. of North Texas, College of Info.; *Beta Beta Omicron.* East Carolina Univ., Dept. of Interdisciplinary Professions; *Beta Beta Xi.* St. Catherine Univ., Master of Lib. and Info. Science Program.

Bibliographical Society of America

Executive Director, Erin Schreiner
P.O. Box 1537, Lenox Hill Station, New York, NY 10021
212-452-2710, e-mail bsa@bibsocamer.org
World Wide Web http://www.bibsocamer.org

Object

To promote bibliographical research and to issue bibliographical publications. Organized in 1904.

Membership

Dues (Partner) $80; (Sustaining) $125; (Leadership) $250; (Advancing) $500; (Lifetime) $1,250; (Emerging bibliographers, 35 and under) $25. Year. Jan.–Dec.

Officers

Pres. Barbara A. Shailor, Yale Univ.; *V.P.* Michael T. Ryan, New York Historical Society; *Secy.* Jennifer J. Lowe, Saint Louis Univ.; *Treas.* G. Scott Clemons, Brown Brothers Harriman. E-mail scott.Clemons@bbh.com. *Delegate to the ACLS* David Vander Meulen, Univ. of Virginia; *Webmaster and BibSite Administrator* Donna Sy, Rare Book School.

Council

(2022) Caroline Duroselle-Melish, Ken Soehner, Jackie Vossler; *(2021)* Thomas Goldwasser, Adam G. Hooks, Michael F. Suarez, Nick Wilding; *(2020)* Douglas Pfeiffer, Simran Thadani, Heather Wolfe.

Committee Chairs

Audit. Joan Friedman.
Development. Barbara A. Shailor.
Fellowship. Hope Mayo.
Finance. Jackie Vossler.
International Development and Collaboration Working Group. Nina Musinsky.
Membership Working Group. Elizabeth Ott.
Policy and Procedures Manual Working Group. Joan Friedman.
Program. Sonja Drimmer.
Publications. Douglas Pfeiffer.

Publication

Papers of the Bibliographical Society of America (q.; memb.). *Ed.* David L. Gants, Florida State Univ.

Bibliographical Society of Canada (La Société Bibliographique du Canada)

President, Ruth-Ellen St. Onge
360 Bloor St. W., P.O. Box 19035 Walmer, Toronto, ON M5S 3C9
E-mail secretary@bsc-sbc.ca
World Wide Web http://www.bsc-sbc.ca

Object

The Bibliographical Society of Canada is a bilingual (English/French) organization that has as its goal the scholarly study of the history, description, and transmission of texts in all media and formats, with a primary emphasis on Canada, and the fulfillment of this goal through the following objectives:

- To promote the study and practice of bibliography: enumerative, historical, descriptive, analytical, and textual
- To further the study, research, and publication of book history and print culture
- To publish bibliographies and studies of book history and print culture
- To encourage the publication of bibliographies, critical editions, and studies of book history and print culture
- To promote the appropriate preservation and conservation of manuscript, archival, and published materials in various formats
- To encourage the utilization and analysis of relevant manuscript and archival sources as a foundation of bibliographical scholarship and book history
- To promote the interdisciplinary nature of bibliography, and to foster relationships with other relevant organizations nationally and internationally
- To conduct the society without purpose of financial gain for its members, and to ensure that any profits or other accretions to the society shall be used in promoting its goal and objectives

Membership

The society welcomes as members all those who share its aims and wish to support and participate in bibliographical research and publication. Dues (Reg.) $80; (Student) $35; (Ret.) $50; (Inst.) $100; (Life) $1,000.

Executive Council (2018–2019)

Pres. Ruth-Ellen St. Onge. E-mail president@bsc-sbc.ca; *1st V.P.* Karen Smith. E-mail vice_president_1@bsc-sbc.ca; *2nd V.P.* Christopher Young. E-mail vice_president_2@bsc-sbc.ca; *Secy.* Alexandra Kordoski Carter. E-mail secretary@bsc-sbc.ca; *Assoc. Secy.* Marie-Claude Felton; *Treas.* Tom Vincent. E-mail treasurer@bsc-sbc.ca; *Assoc. Treas.* Meaghan Scanlon; *Past Pres.* Nancy Earle. E-mail past_president@bsc-sbc.ca.

Council

Executive Council; *(2016–2019)* Christopher Doody, Sarah Lubelski, Josée Vincent; *(2017–2020)* Gwen Davies, Hannah McGregor, Annie Murray; *(2018–2021)* Ruth Panofsky, Alison Rukavina, Jennifer Scott.

Committee Chairs

Awards. Sarah Lubelski.

Communications. Christopher Young.

Fellowships. Josée Vincent.

Publications. Geoffrey Little.

Publications

Bulletin (s. ann). *Ed.* Philippe Mongeau.

Papers of the Bibliographical Society of Canada/Cahiers de la Société Bibliographique du Canada (s. ann.). *Ed.* Ruth Bradley-St-Cyr, Univ. of Ottawa, Canada.

Black Caucus of the American Library Association

President, Richard Ashby
P.O. Box 1894, Hyattsville, MD 20788
World Wide Web http://www.bcala.org

Mission

The Black Caucus of the American Library Association (BCALA) serves as an advocate for the development, promotion, and improvement of library services and resources for the nation's African American community and provides leadership for the recruitment and professional development of African American librarians. Founded in 1970.

Membership

Membership is open to any person, institution, or business interested in promoting the development of library and information services for African Americans and other people of African descent and willing to maintain good financial standing with the organization. The membership is currently composed of librarians and other information professionals, library support staff, libraries, publishers, authors, vendors, and other library-related organizations in the United States and abroad. Dues (Lifetime) $500; (Corporate) $200; (Inst.) $60; (Reg.) $45; (Library Support Staff) $20; (Student) $10; (Ret.) $25.

Officers

Pres. Richard Ashby; *V.P./Pres.-Elect* Shauntee Burns-Simpson; *Secy.* Elisa Garcia; *Treas.* Cherese McKnight; *Past Pres.* Denyvetta Davis.

Board Members

Officers; (2018–2020) Elizabeth Jean Brumfield, (2018–2020) Valerie Carter, (2017–2019) Fannie Cox, (2018–2020) Jina DuVernay, (2017–2019) Tiffeni Fontno, (2017–2019) Brian Hart, (2018–2020) Nichelle Hayes, (2018–2020) Tatanisha Love, (2017–2019) Kim McNeil-Capers, (2017–2019) Jerrod Moore, (2017–2019) Fayrene Muhammad, (2018–2020) Jasmine Simmons, (2017–2019) Cyndee Sturgis Landrum.

Committee Chairs

Affiliates. Andrew P. Jackson.
ALA Relations. Trevor Dawes.
Awards. John Page.
Budget and Finance. Sharon Mahaffey.
Constitution and Bylaws. Jos Holman.
Fundraising. BRIAN HART.
History. Sybyl Moses.
International Relations. Eboni M. Henry, Vivian Bordeaux.
Marketing and Public Relations. Jina Duvernay, Shaundra Walker.
Membership. Rudolph Clay, Jr., Fayrene Muhammad.
National Conference. Cyndee Sturgis Landrum, Keith Jemison.
Nomination and Election. Kelvin A. Watson.
President's Advisory. Denyvetta Davis.
Programs. Shauntee Burns, Shannon Jones.
Publications. Jason Alston.
Recruitment and Professional Development. Fannie Cox, Angeline Beljour, Brandy McNeil.
Services to Children and Families of African Descent. Karen Lemmons, Kirby McCurtis.
Technology Advisory. Jerrod Moore, Roosevelt Weeks.

Awards Committee Chairs

Literary Awards. Gladys Smiley Bell.
Dr. E. J. Josey Scholarship. Sylvia Sprinkle-Hamlin.

Publication

BCALA News (3x yearly; memb.). *Ed.* Jason Alston. E-mail jasonalston@gmail.com.

Canadian Association for Information Science (L'Association Canadienne des Sciences de l'Information)

President, Heather Hill
World Wide Web http://www.cais-acsi.ca

Object

To promote the advancement of information science in Canada and encourage and facilitate the exchange of information relating to the use, access, retrieval, organization, management, and dissemination of information.

Membership

Institutions and individuals interested in information science and involved in the gathering, organization, and dissemination of information (such as information scientists, archivists, librarians, computer scientists, documentalists, economists, educators, journalists, and psychologists) and who support Canadian Association for Information Science (CAIS) objectives can become association members.

Officers (2018–2019)

Pres. Heather Hill, Western Univ.; *V.P./Pres.-Elect* Philippe Mongeon, Univ. of Montréal, Pavillon Lionel-Groulx, 3150 Jean-Brillant, Room C-2070, Montréal. Tel. 1-514-343-6111 ext. 1743, e-mail philippe.mongeon@umontreal.ca; *Secy./Treas.* Philippe Mongeon.

Board Members

Officers; *Webmaster* Robyn Stobbs, Univ. of Alberta; *Student Representative* Roger Chabot, Western Univ.; *Ex-Officio Member* Valerie Nesset, Univ. at Buffalo.

Editorial Board Chairs

Canadian Journal of Info. and Lib. Science. Valerie M. Nesset.

Publication

Canadian Journal of Information and Library Science. (q.; memb.; print; online). For nonmember subscription information visit https://utpjournals.press/loi/cjils. *Ed.* Valerie M. Nesset, Graduate School of Education Univ. at Buffalo. E-mail vmnesset@buffalo.edu.

Canadian Association of Research Libraries (Association des Bibliothèques de Recherche du Canada)

Executive Director, Susan Haigh
309 Cooper St., Suite 203, Ottawa, ON K2P 0G5
613-482-9344 ext. 101, e-mail info@carl-abrc.ca
World Wide Web http://www.carl-abrc.ca
Twitter @carlabrc

Membership

The Canadian Association of Research Libraries (CARL), established in 1976, is the leadership organization for the Canadian research library community. The association's members are the 29 major academic research libraries across Canada together with Library and Archives Canada and the National Research Council Canada, National Science Library. Membership is institutional, open primarily to libraries of Canadian universities that have doctoral graduates in both the arts and the sciences. CARL is an associate member of the Association of Universities and Colleges of Canada (AUCC) and is incorporated as a not-for-profit organization under the Canada Corporations Act.

Mission

The association provides leadership on behalf of Canada's research libraries and enhances their capacity to advance research and higher education. It promotes effective and sustainable scholarly communication, and public policy that enables broad access to scholarly information.

Officers (2017–2020)

Pres. Donna Bourne-Tyson, Dalhousie Univ., 6100 Univ. Ave., Halifax, NS. Tel. 902-494-4089, e-mail donna.bourne-tyson@dal.ca; *V.P.* Jonathan Bengtson, Univ. of Victoria, Victoria, BC; *Secy.* Guylaine Beaudry, Concordia Univ., Montréal, PQ; *Treas.* Lesley Balcom (Atlantic Region Representative), Univ. of New Brunswick, Harriet Irving Lib., 5 MacAulay Ln., Fredericton, NB. Tel. 506-458-7056, e-mail lbalcom@unb.ca.

Board of Directors

Larry Alford, Univ. of Toronto, Toronto, Ont. (Ontario Region Representative); Melissa Just, Univ. of Saskatchewan, Saskatoon (Western Region Representative).

Committee Chairs

Advancing Research. Catherine Steeves.
Assessment. Colleen Cook.
Policy. Martha Whitehead.
Strengthening Capacity. Vivian Lewis.

Member Institutions

National Members

Lib. and Archives Canada, National Research Council Canada, National Science Lib.

Regional Members

Univ. of Alberta, Univ. of British Columbia, Brock Univ., Univ. of Calgary, Carleton Univ., Concordia Univ., Dalhousie Univ., Univ. of Guelph, Univ. Laval, McGill Univ., McMaster Univ., Univ. of Manitoba, Memorial Univ. of Newfoundland, Univ. de Montréal, Univ. of New Brunswick, Univ. of Ottawa, Univ. du Québec à Montréal, Queen's Univ., Univ. of Regina, Ryerson Univ., Univ. of Saskatchewan, Université de Sherbrooke, Simon Fraser Univ., Univ. of Toronto, Univ. of Victoria, Univ. of Waterloo, Western Univ., Univ. of Windsor, York Univ.

Catholic Library Association

Executive Director, Bland O'Connor
8550 United Plaza Blvd., Suite 1001, Baton Rouge, LA 70809
225-408-4417, e-mail cla2@cathla.org
World Wide Web http://www.cathla.org

Object

The promotion and encouragement of Catholic literature and library work through cooperation, publications, education, and information. Founded in 1921.

Membership

Memb. 1,000. Dues $25–$500. Year. July–June.

Officers

Pres. N. Curtis LeMay, Univ. of St. Thomas, 2115 Summit Ave., Mail IRL, St. Paul, MN. Tel. 651-962-5451, e-mail nclemay@stthomas.edu; *V.P./Treas.* Jack Fritts. E-mail jfritts@ben.edu; *Past Pres.* Mary Kelleher, Doherty Lib., Univ. of St. Thomas, 3800 Montrose, Houston. Tel. 713-686-4345, e-mail kellehm@stthom.edu.

Board Members

Officers; Elyse Hayes, Pat Lawton, Bland O'Connor, Madison Petty, Cortney Schraut, Kathryn Shaughnessy.

Section Chairs

Academic Libraries, Archives and Library Education. Bro. Andrew J. Kosmowski, SM.

High School and Young Adult Library Services. Eva Gonsalves.

Parish and Community Library Services. Paul Pojman.

Publication

Catholic Library World (q.; memb.; nonmemb. $100 domestic, $125 international). *General Ed.* Sigrid Kelsey. E-mail sigridkelsey@gmail.com.

Chief Officers of State Library Agencies

Executive Director, Timothy Cherubini
201 E. Main St., Suite 1405, Lexington, KY 40507
859-514-9150, fax 859-514-9166, e-mail info@cosla.org
World Wide Web http://www.cosla.org
Twitter @COSLA_US

Object

Chief Officers of State Library Agencies (COSLA) is an independent organization of the chief officers of state and territorial agencies designated as the state library administrative agency and responsible for statewide library development. Its purpose is to identify and address issues of common concern and national interest; to further state library agency relationships with federal government and national organizations; and to initiate cooperative action for the improvement of library services to the people of the United States.

COSLA's membership consists solely of these top library officers, variously designated as state librarian, director, commissioner, or executive secretary. The organization provides a continuing mechanism for dealing with the problems and challenges faced by these officers. Its work is carried on through its members, a board of directors, and committees.

Officers (2018–2019)

Pres. Stacey Aldrich, State Libn., Hawaii State Public Lib. System, 44 Merchant St. Honolulu. Tel. 808-586-3704, e-mail stacey.aldrich@librarieshawaii.org; *V.P./Pres.-Elect* Jennie Stapp, State Libn., Montana State Lib. Tel. 406-444-3116, e-mail jstapp2@mt.gov; *Secy.* Patience Fredericksen, State Libn. and Dir., State of Alaska, Alaska Div. of Libs., Archives and Museums, P.O. Box 110571, Juneau, AK 99801. Tel. 907-465-2911, e-mail patience.fredericksen@alaska.gov; *Treas.* Karen Mellor, Rhode Island Office of Lib. and Information Svcs. One Capitol Hill, Providence. Tel. 401-574-9304, e-mail karen.mellor@olis.ri.gov; *Past Pres.* Sandra Treadway, Libn. of Virginia, Lib. of Virginia, 800 E. Broad St., Richmond, VA 23219. Tel. 804-692-3535, e-mail sandra.treadway@lva.virginia.gov.

Directors

Randy Riley, State Libn., Lib. of Michigan, 702 West Kalamazoo, P.O. Box 30007, Lansing, Michigan 48909. Tel. 517-373-5860, e-mail rileyr1@michigan.gov; Julie Walker, State Libn., Georgia Public Lib. Svcs. Tel. 404-406-4519, e-mail jwalker@georgialibraries.org.

Chinese American Librarians Association

Executive Director, Lian Ruan
E-mail lruan@illinois.edu
World Wide Web http://cala-web.org

Object

To enhance communications among Chinese American librarians as well as between Chinese American librarians and other librarians; to serve as a forum for discussion of mutual problems and professional concerns among Chinese American librarians; to promote Sino-American librarianship and library services; and to provide a vehicle whereby Chinese American librarians can cooperate with other associations and organizations having similar or allied interests.

Membership

Memb. approximately 600. Membership is open to anyone interested in the association's goals and activities. Dues (Reg. $30; (International/Student/Nonsalaried/Overseas) $15; (Inst.) $100; (Affiliated) $100; (Life) $300.

Officers (2018–2019)

Pres. Ying Zhang. E-mail ying.zhang@ucf.edu; *V.P./Pres.-Elect* Fu Zhuo. E-mail zhuof@umkc.edu; *Treas.* Ying Liao. E-mail cairo_liao@hotmail.com; *Past Pres.* Le Yang. E-mail yanglegd@gmail.com.

Board of Directors

Officers; *(2016–2019)* Xiaojie Duan, Jianye He, Yongyi Song, Hong Wu, Hong Miao; *(2017–2020)* Leping He, Weiling Liu, Ping Fu, Ray Pun, Hong Yao; *(2018–2021)* Qi Chen, Michael Huang, Yuan Li, Guoying (Grace) Liu, Minhao Jiang.

Committee Chairs

Assessment and Evaluation. Anna Xiong, Yan He.

Awards. Wenli Gao, Leping He.

Best Book Award. Hilda LoGuan, Li Sun.

Conference Program. Fu Zhuo.

Constitution and Bylaws. Hong Yao.

Election Committee. Weiling Liu.

Finance. Jennifer Zhao.

International Relations. Michael Huang, Yue Li.

Local Arrangement. Andrew Le, Yunshan Ye.
Membership: Min Tong, Lei Jin.
Mentorship Program. Qinghua Xu.
Nominating. Le Yang.
Public Relations/Fundraising. Yuan Li, Le Yang.
Publications. Guoying Liu.
Web Committee. Minhao Jiang, Tiewei Liu, Jingjing Wu.

Editorial Board Chairs

CALA Newsletter. Ray Pun.
International Journal of Librarianship (IJOL) Guoying Liu.

Awards Committee Chairs

Best Book Award. Hilda LoGuan, Li Sun.
Best Service Awards. Leping He, Hanrong Wang.
Conference Travel Grant. Yongyi Song, Wenli Gao.
Scholarship. Yue Li, Daniel Xiao.

Publications

CALA Newsletter (2x yearly; memb.; online). *Eds.* Ray Pun. E-mail raypun101@gmail.com; Yingqi Tang. E-mail tang@jsu.edu.
International Journal of Librarianship (IJoL). Ed. Grace Liu. E-mail gliu@uwindsor.ca.

Coalition for Networked Information

Executive Director, Clifford A. Lynch
21 Dupont Circle, Suite 800, Washington, DC 20036
202-296-5098, fax 202-872-0884, e-mail clifford@cni.org
World Wide Web http://www.cni.org
Facebook https://www.facebook.com/cni.org
Twitter @cni_org
YouTube https://www.youtube.com/user/cnivideo/
Vimeo http://vimeo.com/cni

Mission

The Coalition for Networked Information (CNI) promotes the transformative promise of networked information technology for the advancement of scholarly communication and the enrichment of intellectual productivity.

Membership

Memb. 240+. Membership is institutional. Dues $8,450. Year. July–June.

Staff

Assoc. Exec. Dir. Joan K. Lippincott, 21 Dupont Cir., Suite 800, Washington, DC 20036. Tel. 202-296-5098, e-mail joan@cni.org; *Admin. Asst.* Sharon Adams. E-mail sharon@cni.org; *Systems Coord.* Maurice-Angelo F. Cruz. E-mail angelo@cni.org; *Office Mgr.* Jacqueline J. Eudell. E-mail jackie@cni.org; *Communications Coord.* Diane Goldenberg-Hart. E-mail diane@cni.org.

Steering Committee Members (2018–2019)

John P. Barden, Yale Univ.; Daniel Cohen, Northeastern Univ.; P. Toby Graham, Univ. of Georgia; Harriette Hemmasi, Georgetown Univ.; Mary Lee Kennedy, (ex officio), Assn. of Research Libs.; Clifford A. Lynch (ex officio), Coalition for Networked Info.; Beth Sandore Namachchivaya, Univ. of Waterloo; John O'Brien (ex officio), EDUCAUSE; Sharon P. Pitt, Univ. of Delaware; Jenn Stringer, Univ. of California, Berkeley; Donald J. Waters, Andrew W. Mellon Foundation.

Publication

CNI-Announce (online; subscribe by online form at https://www.cni.org/resources/follow-cni/cni-announce).

Periodic reports (https://www.cni.org/resources/publications/other-publications-by-cni-staff).

Council on Library and Information Resources

President, Charles Henry
2221 S. Clark St., Arlington, VA 22202
E-mail contact@clir.org
World Wide Web http://www.clir.org
Twitter @CLIRnews

Object

In 1997 the Council on Library Resources (CLR) and the Commission on Preservation and Access (CPA) merged and became the Council on Library and Information Resources (CLIR). CLIR is an independent, nonprofit organization that forges strategies to enhance research, teaching, and learning environments in collaboration with libraries, cultural institutions, and communities of higher learning.

CLIR promotes forward-looking collaborative solutions that transcend disciplinary, institutional, professional, and geographic boundaries in support of the public good. CLIR identifies and defines the key emerging issues relating to the welfare of libraries and the constituencies they serve, convenes the leaders who can influence change, and promotes collaboration among the institutions and organizations that can achieve change. The council's interests embrace the entire range of information resources and services from traditional library and archival materials to emerging digital formats. It assumes a particular interest in helping institutions cope with the accelerating pace of change associated with the transition into the digital environment.

While maintaining appropriate collaboration and liaison with other institutions and organizations, CLIR operates independently of any particular institutional or vested interests. Through the composition of its board, it brings the broadest possible perspective to bear upon defining and establishing the priority of the issues with which it is concerned.

Officers

Chair Christopher Celenza, Georgetown Univ.; *Pres.* Charles Henry. E-mail chenry@clir.org; *V.Chair* Buhle Mbambo-Thata, AfLIA–African Lib. and Info. Assns. and Insts.; *Treas.* Guy Berthiaume, Librarian and Archivist of Canada.

Board of Directors

Officers; Michele Casalini, Casalini Libri; Dan Cohen, Northeastern Univ.; Jill Cousins, Hunt Museum; Tess Davis, Antiquities Coalition; Kurt De Belder, Leiden Univ.; Kathlin Fitzpatrick, Michigan State Univ.; Emilie Gordenker, Royal Picture Gallery Mauritshuis; Michael A. Keller, Stanford Univ.; W. Joseph King, Lyon College; Carol Mandel, New York Univ. Div. of Libs.; Max Marmor, Samuel H. Kress Fdn.; Richard Ovenden, Univ. of Oxford; Ingrid Parent, Univ. of British Columbia; Winston Tabb, Johns Hopkins Univ., Sohair Wastawy, Qatar National Lib.; John Price Wilkin, Univ. of Illinois at Urbana-Champaign.

Address correspondence to headquarters.

Publications

Annual Report.

CLIR Issues (bi-mo.; electronic).

EveryLibrary

Executive Director, John Chrastka
P.O. Box 406, 45 E. Burlington St., Riverside, IL. 60546
312-574-5098, e-mail info@everylibrary.org
World Wide Web http://www.everylibrary.org
Facebook https://www.facebook.com/EveryLibrary
LinkedIn https://www.linkedin.com/company/3801587/
Twitter @EveryLibrary

Object

EveryLibrary is a national political action committee for libraries. Organized as a 501(c)4, the organization provides pro bono advising and consulting to libraries about their funding requests, either when it appears on a ballot or through a municipal funding partner. EveryLibrary's mission is to "build voter support for libraries" at all levels of government, and it works to fulfill that mission as a completely donor-supported organization.

Board Members

Peter Bromberg, John Chrastka, Harmony V. Faust, Erica Findley, Brian D. Hart, J. Turner Masland, Patrick "PC" Sweeney.

Publication

The Political Librarian (irreg.; open access). *Ed.* Dustin Fife, E-mail dustin.fife@everylibrary.org.

Federal Library and Information Network

Executive Director, Laurie Neider
Library of Congress, Washington, DC 20540-4935
202-707-4801, e-mail lneider@loc.gov
World Wide Web http://www.loc.gov/flicc
Twitter @librarycongress

Object

The Federal Library and Information Network (FEDLINK) is an organization of federal agencies working together to achieve optimum use of the resources and facilities of federal libraries and information centers by promoting common services, coordinating and sharing available resources, and providing continuing professional education for federal library and information staff. FEDLINK serves as a forum for discussion of the policies, programs, procedures, and technologies that affect federal libraries and the information services they provide to their agencies, to Congress, to the federal courts, and to the public.

Membership

The FEDLINK voting membership is composed of representatives of the following U.S. federal departments and agencies: Each of the national libraries (the Library of Congress, National Agricultural Library, National Library of Education, National Library of Medicine, and the National Transportation Library); each cabinet-level executive department, as defined in 5 U.S.C. § 101; additional departments and agencies (the Defense Technical Information Center; departments of the Air Force, Army, and Navy; Executive Office of the President, Government Accountability Office, General Services Administration, Government Printing Office, Institute of Museum and Library

Services, National Aeronautics and Space Administration, National Archives and Records Administration, National Technical Information Service [Department of Commerce], Office of Management and Budget, Office of Personnel Management, Office of Scientific and Technical Information [Department of Energy], Office of the Director of National Intelligence, and the Smithsonian Institution); the U.S. Supreme Court and the Administrative Office of the U.S. Courts; the District of Columbia; and other federal independent agencies and government corporations.

Officers

Exec. Dir. Laurie Neider. Tel. 202-707-4801, e-mail lneider@loc.gov.

Address correspondence to the executive director.

Publication

FEDLINK Bulletin (bi-wk.; electronic).

Medical Library Association

Executive Director, Kevin Baliozian
65 E. Wacker Place, Suite 1900, Chicago, IL 60601-7298
312-419-9094, fax 312-419-8950, e-mail websupport@mail.mlahq.org
World Wide Web http://www.mlanet.org
Twitter @MedLibAssn

Object

The Medical Library Association (MLA) is a nonprofit professional education organization with nearly 4,000 health sciences information professional members and partners worldwide. MLA provides lifelong educational opportunities, supports a knowledge base of health information research, and works with a global network of partners to promote the importance of high-quality information for improved health to the health care community and the public.

Membership

Memb. (Inst.) 400+; (Indiv.) 3,200+, in more than 50 countries. Dues (Indiv.) $75–$225; (Student) $50; (Int'l.) $150; (Affiliate) $140; (Inst.) $325–$880. Year. Institutional members are medical and allied scientific libraries. Individual members are people who are (or were at the time membership was established) engaged in professional library or bibliographic work in medical and allied scientific libraries or people who are interested in medical or allied scientific libraries. Members can be affiliated with one or more of MLA's more than 20 special-interest sections and its regional chapters.

Officers

Pres. Beverly Murphy, Duke Univ. Med. Ctr.; *Pres.-Elect* Julia Esparza, Louisiana State Univ. HSC; *Secy.* Gurpreet Kaur Rana, Taubman Health Sciences Lib., Univ. of Michigan; *Treas.* Amy Blevins, Indiana Univ. School of Med.; *Past Pres.* Barbara A. Epstein, Univ. of Pittsburgh; *Incoming Treas.* Shannon D. Jones, Med. Univ. of South Carolina; *Incoming Pres.-Elect* Lisa K. Traditi, Univ. of Colorado Anschutz Med. Campus; *Exec. Dir.* Kevin Baliozian. Med. Lib. Assn.

Board of Directors

Officers; Marie T. Ascher, Donna R. Berryman, Keith W. Cogdill, Stephanie Fulton, Sally Gore, Elizabeth R. Lorbeer, Sandra Irene Martin, Melissa Ratajeski, Meredith I. Solomon.

Committee Chairs

Ad Hoc Committee to Review Core Clinical Journals. Andrea M. Ketchum, Michele S. Klein-Fedyshin.
Awards. Meredith I. Solomon.
Books Panel. JoLinda L. Thompson.
Bylaws. Emily Ginier.
Communities Transition Team. Stephanie Fulton, Keith W. Cogdill.
Credentialing. Keydi Boss O'Hagan.
Education Steering. Elizabeth Laera.
Education Annual Programming. Kelli Ham.
Finance. Amy Blevins.
Governmental Relations. Cristina Pope.
Grants and Scholarships. Elizabeth Irish.
Joseph Leiter NLM/MLA Lectureship. Sarah E. Katz.
Librarians Without Borders®. Donna B. Flake.
Membership. Stephanie C. Kerns.
National Program. James Dale Prince, Mellanye J. Lackey.
Nominating. Barbara A. Epstein.
Oral History. Gale A. Oren.
Professional Recruitment and Retention. Kelly Thormodson.
Scholarly Communications. Lilian Hoffecker.

Editorial Board Chairs

JMLA Editor-in-Chief. Katherine Goold Akers.
MLA News Christine Willis.

Task Force Chairs

Annual Meeting Innovation. Kevin Baliozian, Lisa K. Traditi.
Communities Strategic Goal. Rikke Sarah Ogawa.
Diversity and Inclusion. Sandra G. Franklin.
Joint MLA/AAHSL Legislative. Sandra L. Bandy.
Research Imperative. Mary M. Langman.

Awards Committee Chairs

Virginia L. and William K. Beatty Volunteer Service. Heather J Martin.
Estelle Brodman Award for the Academic Medical Librarian of the Year. Charlotte Beyer.
Clarivate Analytics/Frank Bradway Rogers Information Advancement Award. Nita K. Mailander.
Clarivate Analytics/MLA Doctoral Fellowship. Janice Swiatek.
Lois Ann Colaianni Award for Excellence and Achievement in Hospital Librarianship. Alexandria Quesenberry.
Consumer Health Librarian of the Year Award Jury. Lisa Huang.
Louise Darling Medal for Distinguished Achievement in Collection Development in the Health Sciences. Kelly Farrah.
Janet Doe Lectureship. Linda Walton.
Ida and George Eliot Prize. Rebecca Carlson McCall.
Fellows and Honorary Members. Lin Wu.
Carla J. Funk Governmental Relations. Rose L. Turner.
T. Mark Hodges International Service. Gretchen Kuntz.
Majors/MLA Chapter Project of the Year. Latrina Keith.
Lucretia W. McClure Excellence in Education. Cheryl Louise Branche.
Erich Meyerhoff Prize. Stephen J. Greenberg.
Research Advancement in Health Sciences Librarianship Awards Jury. Michelle Kraft.
Rising Stars. Rebecca Raszewski.
Rittenhouse. Ariel FitzGerald Pomputius.
Section Project of the Year. Terrie R. Wheeler.

Grants, Scholarships, and Fellowships Juries

Ysabel Bertolucci MLA Annual Meeting Grant. Lori Snyder.
Naomi C. Broering Hispanic Heritage Grant. Yamila El-Khayat.
Continuing Education. Jaclyn Vialet.
Cunningham Memorial International Fellowship. Ansley Stuart.
Eugene Garfield Research Fellowship. Trey Lemley.
David A. Kronick Traveling Fellowship. Erin R. B. Eldermire.

Donald A. B. Lindberg Research Fellowship. Peace Ossom Williamson.

Librarians Without Borders® Ursula Poland International Scholarship. Beverley A. Wood.

MLA/EBSCO Annual Meeting Grant. Kristen DeSanto.

MLA/HLS Professional Development Grant. Michelle M. Volesko Brewer.

MLA Librarians Without Borders/Elsevier Foundation/Research4Life Grants. Katherine Downton.

MLA/MIS Career Development Grant. Nicole Capdarest-Arest.

MLA Research, Development, and Demonstration Project Grant. Sharon Leslie.

MLA Scholarship. Karen McElfresh.

MLA Scholarship for Minority Students. Adela V. Justice.

Research Training Institute Jury. Melissa L. Rethlefsen.

Publications

Journal of the Medical Library Association (q.; electronic version, free to all through PubMed Central. *Ed.* Katherine G. Akers, Wayne State Univ. E-mail jmla@journals.pitt.edu.

MLA Connect (10x yearly; electronic; memb.). *Ed.* Christine Willis.

Music Library Association

President, Susannah Cleveland
1600 Aspen Commons Suite 100, Middleton, WI 53562
608-836-5825, fax 608-831-8200, e-mail mla@areditions.com
World Wide Web http://www.musiclibraryassoc.org
Facebook https://www.facebook.com/Music.Library.Association
Twitter @musiclibassoc
Vimeo https://vimeo.com/musiclibraryassoc

Object

The Music Library Association provides a professional forum for librarians, archivists, and others who support and preserve the world's musical heritage. To achieve this mission, it

- Provides leadership for the collection and preservation of music and information about music in libraries and archives
- Develops and delivers programs that promote continuing education and professional development in music librarianship
- Ensures and enhances intellectual access to music for all by contributing to the development and revision of national and international codes, formats, and other standards for the bibliographic control of music
- Ensures and enhances access to music for all by facilitating best practices for housing, preserving, and providing access to music
- Promotes legislation that strengthens music library services and universal access to music
- Fosters information literacy and lifelong learning by promoting music reference services, library instruction programs, and publications
- Collaborates with other groups in the music and technology industries, government, and librarianship, to promote its mission and values

Membership

Memb. 1,200+. Dues (Inst.) $175; (Indiv.) $140; (Ret.) $105; (Paraprofessional) $75; (Student) $65. (Foreign, add $10.) Year. July 1–June 30.

Officers

Pres. Susannah Cleveland. E-mail clevels@bgsu.edu; *Secy.* Misti Shaw. E-mail mistshaw@indiana.edu; *Past Pres.* Mark C. McKnight. E-mail mark.mcknight@unt.edu.

Board of Directors

Officers; *Admin. Officer* Tracey Rudnick, *Asst. Admin. Officer* Janelle West; *Membs.-at-Large (2018–2020): Parliamentarian* Rachel Fox Von Swearingen, *Fiscal Officer* Beth Iseminger, *Planning Officer* Bruce J. Evans; *Membs.-at-Large (2019–2021): Asst. Parliamentarian* Kimmy Szeto, *Asst. Fiscal Officer* Anne Shelley, *Asst. Planning Officer* Jonathan Sauceda.

Committee Chairs

Archives and Special Collections. Adriana P. Cuervo.
Awards: Best of Chapters. Carolyn A. Johnson.
Career Development and Services. Emma Dederick, Timothy Sestrick.
Cataloging and Metadata. Tracey Snyder.
Development. Lindsay J. Brown.
Diversity. Joy M. Doan.
Education. Sonia Archer-Capuzzo.
Emerging Technologies and Services. Jonathan Manton.
Finance. Beth Iseminger.
Joint Committee: MLA, MPA, and MOLA. Jane Gottlieb.
Legislation. Kyra Folk-Farber.
Membership. Mallory Sajewski.
Music Library Advocacy. Linda B. Fairtile.
Nominating. Mary D. Brower.
Oral History. Therese Z. Dickman.
Planning. Bruce J. Evans.
Preservation. Treshani Perera.
Program, 2019. Anne E. Shelley.
Program, 2020. Erin Conor.
Public Libraries. Kristine E. Nelsen.
Public Services. Sara J. Manus.
Publications. Liza F. Vick.
Resource Sharing and Collection Development. Stephanie Bonjack.
Web. Kerry C. Masteller.

Publications

Basic Manual Series. *Series Ed.* Kathleen A. Abromeit.
Basic Music Library. *Ed.* Daniel Boomhower.
Index and Bibliography Series (irreg.; price varies). *Ed.* Maristella Feustle.
MLA Newsletter. (6x yearly; memb.). *Ed.* Michelle Hahn.
Music Cataloging Bulletin (mo.; online subscription only, $35). *Ed.* Christopher Holden.
Notes (q.; memb.). *Ed.* Deborah Campana.
Technical Reports and Monographs in Music Librarianship (irreg.; price varies). *Ed.* Jonathan Sauceda.

NASIG

President, Angela Dresselhaus
PMB 305, 1902 Ridge Rd., West Seneca, NY 14224-3312
716-324-1859, e-mail info@nasig.org
World Wide Web http://www.nasig.org
Twitter: @NASIG
Facebook: https://www.facebook.com/groups/2399345882/
Instagram: https://www.instagram.com/nasig_official/
LinkedIn: https://www.linkedin.com/groups/149102/
YouTube: https://www.youtube.com/channel/UCVvnh_CzXS8YgftuvIypTiQ

Vision and Mission

Established in 1985, NASIG is an independent organization working to advance and transform the management of information resources. NASIG's goal is to facilitate and improve the distribution, acquisition, and long-term accessibility of information resources in all formats and business models. There are three key components to the organization's mission:

1. NASIG supports a dynamic community of professionals including, but not limited to, librarians, publishers, and vendors engaging in understanding one another's perspectives and improving functionality throughout the information resources lifecycle with an emphasis on scholarly communications, serials, and electronic resources.
2. NASIG provides a rich variety of conference and continuing education programming to encourage knowledge sharing among its members and to support their professional and career development.
3. NASIG promotes the development and implementation of best practices and standards for the distribution, acquisition and long-term accessibility of information resources in all formats and business models throughout their lifecycle. In addition to developing best practices, NASIG supports the development of standards by NISO, an affiliated organization.

Membership

Memb. 596. For any person, library, or organization interested in information resources and scholarly communication. Dues (Indiv.) $75; (Ret.) $25; (Student) Free; (Lifetime) $1000/one time; (Inst.) $195.

Officers

Pres. Angela Dresselhaus, East Carolina Univ.; *Pres.-Elect* Kristen Wilson, Index Data; *Secy.* Beth Ashmore, North Carolina State Univ.; *Treas.* Jessica Ireland, Radford Univ.; *Past Pres.* Steve Oberg, Wheaton College; *Membs.-at-Large* Karen Davidson, Mississippi State Univ.; Maria Hatfield, WT Cox Info. Svcs.; Lisa Martincik, Univ. of Iowa; Marsha Seamans, Univ. of Kentucky; Steve Shadle, Univ. of Washington; Ted Westervelt, Library of Congress.

Board Members

Officers; *Newsletter Editor-in-chief* Lori Duggan, Indiana Univ. Bloomington; *Marketing and Social Media Coord.* Eugenia Beh (MIT).

Committee Chairs

Archivist. Peter Whiting, Univ. of Southern Indiana.
Awards and Recognition. Jennifer Leffler, Univ. of Colorado.
Bylaws. Derrik Hiatt, Texas A&M Univ.
Communications. Treasa Bane, Univ. of Wisconsin-Baraboo/Sauk County and Rachel Miles, Virginia Tech.
Conference Planning. Denise Novak, Carnegie Mellon Univ. and Pat Roncevich, Univ. of Pittsburgh.
Conference Proceedings Editors. Paul Moeller, Univ. of Colorado Boulder, Cindy Shirkey,

East Carolina Univ., Cecilia Genereux, Univ. of Minnesota Twin Cities and Courtney McAllister, The Citadel.

Conference Coordinator. Anne Creech, Univ. of Richmond.

Continuing Education. Julia Proctor, Pennsylvania State Univ. and Lori Terrill, Black Hills State Univ.

Diversity. Del Williams, California State Univ. Northridge.

Evaluation and Assessment. Esta Tovstiadi, SUNY Potsdam.

Membership Services. Christine Radcliff, Texas A&M Univ.-Kingsville and Char Simser, Kansas State Univ.

Mentoring Group. Xiaoyan Song, North Carolina State Univ.

Newsletter. Lori Duggan, Indiana Univ.

Nominations and Elections. Stephanie Adams, Tennessee Tech Univ.

Program Planning. Maria Collins, North Carolina State Univ.

Registrar. Mary Ann Jones, Mississippi State Univ.

Standards. Jennifer Coombs, Kansas City Public Library.

Student Outreach. Danielle Williams, Univ. of Evansville.

Task Force Chairs

Digital Preservation. Shannon Keller, New York Public Library.

Web-Based Infrastructure Implementation. Paoshan Yue, Univ. of Nevada, Reno.

Publications

Conference Proceedings (currently published in two issues of Serials Librarian).

Core Competencies for Electronic Resources Librarians.

Core Competencies for Print Serials Management.

Core Competencies for Scholarly Communication Librarians.

NASIG Newsletter.

Various NASIGuides.

NASIG Blog.

NASIG Jobs Blog.

Meetings

Annual conference held in the summer. Continuing education events and webinars throughout the year.

National Association of Government Archives and Records Administrators

Executive Director, Johnny Hadlock
444 N. Capitol Street, N.W. Suite 237, Washington, DC 20001
202-508-3800, fax 202-508-3801, e-mail info@nagara.org
World Wide Web http://www.nagara.org
Twitter @InfoNAGARA

Object

Founded in 1984, the National Association of Government Archives and Records Administrators (NAGARA) is a nationwide association of local, state, and federal archivists and records administrators, and others interested in improved care and management of government records. NAGARA promotes public awareness of government records and archives management programs, encourages interchange of information among government archives and records management agencies, develops and implements professional standards of government records and archival administration, and encourages study and research into records management problems and issues.

Membership

Most NAGARA members are federal, state, and local archival and records management agencies. Dues (Org.) $225–$750 dependent on number of contacts; (NARA Employees

Indiv.) $40; (Students/Ret.) $50; (All other Indiv.) $89.

Officers (2018–2019)

Pres. Rebekah Davis, Limestone County Archives, 102 W. Washington St., Athens, AL. Tel. 256-233-6404, e-mail rebekah.davis@limestonecounty-al.gov; *V.P.* Casey Coleman, U.S. Securities and Exchange Commission, Silver Spring, MD. E-mail colemanca@sec.gov; *Pres.-Elect* Jelain Chubb, Archives and Info. Svcs., Texas State Lib. and Archives Commission. E-mail jchubb@tsl.texas.gov; *Secy.* Marissa Paron, Lib. and Archives Canada. E-mail marissa.paron@canada.ca; *Treas.* Bethany Cron, National Archives and Records Admin., Ann Arbor, MI. E-mail bethany.cron@nara.gov; *Past Pres.* Patty Davis, U.S. Dept. of Justice, 950 Pennsylvania Ave. N.W., Washington, DC. Tel. 202-532-6559, e-mail patrice.m.davis@usdoj.gov; *Memb.-at-Large* Jennifer Day, The City of Oklahoma, 200 N. Walker Ave., OKC, OK 73102. E-mail jennifer.day@okc.gov.

Board of Directors

Officers; Jen Haney Conover, Jannette Goodall, Chad Owen, Kristopher Stenson, Kathleen Williams, Galen Wilson, Joyce Wittenberg.

Committee Chairs

Advocacy. Mark Walsh.
Communications. Rebekah Davis.
Membership. Galen Wilson.
Professional Development. Pari Swift.

Publications

Newsletter (q.; memb.; electronic).

National Federation of Advanced Information Services

Executive Director, Marci Granahan
801 Compass Way, Suite 201 Annapolis, MD 21401
443-221-2980, fax 443-221-2981, e-mail mgranahan@nfais.org
World Wide Web http://www.nfais.org
Twitter @NFAISForum

Object

The National Federation of Advanced Information Services (NFAIS) is an international nonprofit membership organization composed of leading information providers. Its membership includes government agencies, nonprofit scholarly societies, private-sector businesses, and libraries. NFAIS is committed to promoting the value of credible, high-quality content. It serves all groups that create, aggregate, organize, or facilitate access to such information. In order to improve members' capabilities and to contribute to their ongoing success, NFAIS provides opportunities for education, advocacy, and a forum in which to address common interests. Founded in 1958.

Membership

Memb. 60. Full members are organizations whose main focus is any of the following activities: information creation, organization, aggregation, dissemination, access, or retrieval. Organizations are eligible for associate member status if they do not meet the qualifications for full membership.

Officers (2018–2019)

Pres. Deanna Marcum, Ithaka S+R; *Pres.-Elect/Treas.* Ryan Bernier, EBSCO; *Secy.* Suzanna Daulerio, ASTM International; *Past Pres.* Mary Sauer-Games, OCLC, Inc.

Board Members

Ghazal Badiozamani, Paula Krebs, Allan Lu, Ann Michael, Steven Petric, Rhonda Ross, Joshua Schnell, Peter Simon, Wayne Strickland.

Staff

Dir. of Professional Development Nancy Blair-DeLeon.

Publications

For a detailed list of NFAIS publications, go to http://www.nfais.org/publications.

National Information Standards Organization

Executive Director, Todd Carpenter
3600 Clipper Mill Rd., Suite 302, Baltimore, MD 21211-1948
301-654-2512, e-mail nisohq@niso.org
World Wide Web http://www.niso.org

Object

The National Information Standards Organization (NISO) fosters the development and maintenance of standards that facilitate the creation, persistent management, and effective interchange of information so that it can be trusted for use in research and learning. To fulfill this mission, NISO engages libraries, publishers, information aggregators, and other organizations that support learning, research, and scholarship through the creation, organization, management, and curation of knowledge. NISO works with intersecting communities of interest and across the entire lifecycle of an information standard. NISO standards apply both traditional and new technologies to the full range of information-related needs, including discovery, retrieval, repurposing, storage, metadata, business information, and preservation.

NISO also develops and publishes recommended practices, technical reports, white papers, and information publications. NISO holds regular educational programs on standards, technologies, and related topics where standards-based solutions can help solve problems. These programs include webinars, online virtual conferences, in-person forums, and teleconferences.

Experts from the information industry, libraries, systems vendors, and publishing participate in the development of NISO standards and recommended practices. The standards are approved by the consensus body of NISO's voting membership, representing libraries, publishers, vendors, government, associations, and private businesses and organizations. NISO is supported by its membership and grants.

NISO is a not-for-profit association accredited by the American National Standards Institute (ANSI) and serves as the U.S. Technical Advisory Group Administrator to ISO/TC 46 Information and Documentation as well as the secretariat for ISO/TC 46/SC 9, Identification and Description.

Membership

Voting Members: 80+. Open to any organization, association, government agency, or company willing to participate in and having substantial concern for the development of NISO standards. Library Standards Alliance Members: 60+. Open to any academic, public, special, or government-supported library interested in supporting the mission of NISO.

Officers

Chair Keith Webster, Dean of Univ. Libs., Carnegie Mellon Univ., 5000 Forbes Ave.,

Pittsburgh. Tel. 412-268-2447, e-mail kwebster@andrew.cmu.edu. *V.Chair* Marian Hollingsworth, Clarivate Analytics, 1500 Spring Garden St., Philadelphia PA 19130. Tel. 215-386-0100, e-mail marian.hollingsworth@clarivate.com; *Treas.* Jabin White, ITHAKA JSTOR, 100 Campus Dr., Suite 100, Princeton, NJ 08154. Tel. 609-986-2224, e-mail jabin.white@ithaka.org; *Past Chair* Chris Shillum, Product Mgmt. Platform and Content, Reed Elsevier, 360 Park Ave. S. New York. Tel. 212-462-1987, e-mail c.shillum@elsevier.com.

Directors

Gerry Grenier, Evan Owens, Wendy Queen, Maria Stanton, Greg Suprock, Miranda Walker, Robert Wheeler.

Committee Chairs

Audit. Evan Owens.
Finance. Jabin White.
Nominating. Todd Carpenter.

Staff

Assoc. Dir. for Programs Nettie Lagace; *Dir. of Content* Jill O'Neill.

Publications

Information Standards Quarterly (back issues available in open access from the NISO website).

NISO Newsline (free e-newsletter released on the first Wednesday of each month; distributed by e-mail and posted on the NISO website).

For additional NISO publications, see the article "NISO Standards" beginning on page 609 of this volume.

NISO's published standards, recommended practices, and technical reports are available free of charge as downloadable PDF files from the NISO website (http://www.niso.org). Hardcopy documents are available for sale from the website.

Patent and Trademark Resource Center Association

President, Dave Zwicky
Reference Department. Univ. of Delaware Library, Newark, DE 19717-5267
World Wide Web http://www.ptrca.org

Object

The Patent and Trademark Resource Center Association (PTRCA) provides a support structure for the more than 80 patent and trademark resource centers (PTRCs) affiliated with the U.S. Patent and Trademark Office (USPTO). The association's mission is to discover the interests, needs, opinions, and goals of the PTRCs and to advise USPTO in these matters for the benefit of PTRCs and their users, and to assist USPTO in planning and implementing appropriate services. Founded in 1983 as the Patent Depository Library Advisory Council; name changed to Patent and Trademark Depository Library Association in 1988; became an American Library Association affiliate in 1996. In 2011 the association was renamed the Patent and Trademark Resource Center Association.

Membership

Open to any person employed in a patent and trademark resource center library whose responsibilities include the patent and trademark collection. Affiliate membership is also available. Dues (Reg.) $65; (Student) $10.

Officers (2018–2019)

Pres. Dave Zwicky, West Lafayette, IN; *Secy.* John Schlipp, W. Frank Steely Lib., Northern Kentucky Univ., Nunn Dr., Highland Heights. Tel. 859-572-5723, e-mail schlippj1@nku.edu; *Treas.* Jim Miller, McKeldin Lib., Univ. of Maryland, Lib. Ln., College Park. Tel. 301-405-9152, e-mail jmiller2@umd.edu; *Past Pres.* Lisha Li, Atlanta, GA; *Div. Representatives (Academic) (2017–2019)* Suzanne Reinman, Stillwater, OK; *(2018–2020)* Siu Min Yu, Houston, TX; *(Public) (2017–2019)* Andrew Maines, Buffalo, NY; *(2018–2020)* Christine Deines, Davenport, IA.

Committee Chairs (2017–2018)

Bylaws. Marian Armour-Gemman.
Conference. Lisha Li.
Database. Jim Miller.
Election. Leena Lalwani.
Membership and Mentoring. Dave Zwicky.
Program (Ad Hoc). Paulina Borrego.
Publications. Suzanne Reinman.

Publication

PTRCA Journal. Electronic at http://ptrca.org/newsletters.

Polish American Librarians Association

President, Ewa Barczyk
P.O. Box 7232, Prospect Heights, IL, 60070-7232
World Wide Web http://palalib.org

Object

The mission of the Polish American Librarians Association (PALA) is to positively affect services provided to library patrons of Polish descent and individuals interested in Polish culture.

The organization's vision is

- To enhance professional knowledge by developing forums for discussion and networks of communication among library staff working with Polish collections and patrons of Polish origin
- To promote understanding and respect among all cultures by expanding the means to access reliable, current information about Polish and Polish American culture
- To promote Polish American librarianship
- To provide opportunities for cooperation with other library associations

Founded in 2009.

Membership

Membership is open to librarians, students of library schools, library support staff, and others who support the vision of PALA. Dues (Reg.) $25; (Support Staff/Student/Ret./Unemployed) $15.

Officers

Pres. Ewa Barczyk, Golda Meir Lib., Univ. of Wisconsin Milwaukee, 2311 E. Hartford Ave., Milwaukee. Tel. 414-412-5456, e-mail ewa@uwm.edu; *Secy.* Paulina Poplawska, New Ulm Public Lib., New Ulm, MN. E-mail ppoplawska@tds.lib.mn.us; *Treas.* Bernadetta Koryciarz, Niles-Maine District Lib., 6960 Oakton St., Niles, IL 60714. Tel. 847-663-6642, e-mail bkorycia@nileslibrary.org; *Past Pres.* Leonard Kniffel, PolishSon.com, 2743 N. Greenview Ave., Chicago. Tel. 773-935-3635, e-mail lkniffel@sbcglobal.net.

Board of Directors

Officers; *Dirs.-at-Large* Iwona Bozek, Karla Marszalik, Krystyna Matusiak, Hanna Przybylski, Ronald V. Stoch.

REFORMA (National Association to Promote Library and Information Services to Latinos and the Spanish-Speaking)

President, Madeline Peña Feliz
P.O. Box 832, Anaheim, CA 92815-0832
E-mail info@reforma.org
World Wide Web http://www.reforma.org

Object

Promoting library services to the Spanish-speaking for nearly 40 years, REFORMA, an affiliate of the American Library Association, works in a number of areas to advance the development of library collections that include Spanish-language and Latino-oriented materials; the recruitment of more bilingual and bicultural professionals and support staff; the development of library services and programs that meet the needs of the Latino community; the establishment of a national network among individuals who share its goals; the education of the U.S. Latino population in regard to the availability and types of library services; and lobbying efforts to preserve existing library resource centers serving the interest of Latinos.

Membership

Memb. 800+. Membership is open to any person who is supportive of the goals and objectives of REFORMA. Dues (Indiv.) $10–$50; (Int'l.) Free; (Life) $450; (Inst.) $100–$250. Year.

Officers (2018–2019)

Pres. Madeline Peña Feliz, Los Angeles Public Lib., 630 West 5th St., Los Angeles, CA 90071. Tel. 213-228-7496, e-mail president@reforma.org; *V.P./Pres.-Elect* Kenny Garcia, California State Univ., Monterey Bay Lib. E-mail vice-president@reforma.org; *Secy.* Ana Campos, Los Angeles Public Lib. E-mail secretary@reforma.org; *Treas.* Gloria Grover, Los Angeles Public Lib., 630 W. Fifth St., Los Angeles, CA 90071. Tel. 213-228-7575, e-mail treasurer@reforma.org; *Past Pres.* Tess Tobin, New York City College of Technology Lib., 300 Jay St., Brooklyn. Tel. 718-260-5499, e-mail past-president@reforma.org; *Memb.-at-Large* Patricia Valdovinos, Los Angeles Public Lib. E-mail at-large-rep@reforma.org; *Chapter Rep.* Manny Figueroa, Queens Lib. E-mail chapter-east-region@reforma.org.

Committee Chairs

Awards. Haydee Hodis.
Education. Michele A. L. Villagran.
Finance. Tess Tobin.
Fundraising. Cynthia Bautista, Sonia Bautista.
International Relations. Ray Pun.
Legislative. Mario Ascencio.
Membership. Adriana Blancart-Hayward.
Mentoring. Antonio Apodaca.
Nominations. Maria Kramer.
Organizational Development and New Chapters. Martha A. Anderson.
Program. Kenny Garcia.
Public Relations. Jesus Espinosa.
Recruitment and Mentoring. Minerva Alaniz.
REFORMA National Conferences Coordinating Committee. Jacqueline Ayala, Loanis Menendez.
Scholarship. Delores Carlito.
Technology. Edwin Rodarte.
Translations. Lupie Leyva.
Webinar: Libbhy Romero, Patty Tarango.

Awards Committee Chairs

Pura Belpré Award. Ramona Caponegro.
Librarian of the Year. Haydee Hodis.

Publication

REFORMA (e-newsletter).

Meetings

General membership and board meetings take place at the American Library Association Midwinter Meeting and Annual Conference and Exhibition.

Society for Scholarly Publishing

Executive Director, Melanie Dolechek
10200 W. 44th Ave., Suite 304, Wheat Ridge, CO 80033-2840
303-422-3914, fax 720-881-6101, e-mail mdolechek@sspnet.org
World Wide Web http://www.sspnet.org
Twitter @ScholarlyPub

Object

To draw together individuals involved in the process of scholarly publishing. This process requires successful interaction of the many functions performed within the scholarly community. The Society for Scholarly Publishing (SSP) provides the leadership for such interaction by creating opportunities for the exchange of information and opinions among scholars, editors, publishers, librarians, printers, booksellers, and all others engaged in scholarly publishing.

Membership

Memb. 1,000+. Open to all with an interest in the scholarly publishing process and dissemination of information. Dues (New Member) $175; (Indiv. Renewal) $190; (Libn.) $85; (Early Career New) $40; (Ret. Renewal) $75; (Student) $40; (Supporting Organization) $1,850; (Sustaining Organization) $4,850; (Intl. Indiv.) $50; (Intl. Early Career) $25; (Intl. Libn.) $25; (Intl. Student); $10. Year. Jan.–Dec.

Officers

Pres. Adrian Stanley, Digital Science; *Pres.-Elect* Angela Cochran, American Society of Civil Engineers; *Secy./Treas.* Byron Laws, Nova Techset; *Past Pres.* Jennifer Pesanelli, FASEB. E-mail jpesanelli@faseb.org; *Membs.-at-Large* Lori Carlin, Hillary Corbett, David Crotty, Robert Harington, Lauren Kane, Elizabeth R. Lorbeer, Alice Meadows, Alison Mudditt, Laura Ricci.

Board of Directors

Officers; *Exec. Dir.* Melanie Dolechek; *Gen. Mgr.* Crystal Stone.

Committee Chairs

Annual Meeting Program. Yael Fitzpatrick, Cason Lynley, Ben Mudrak.
Audit. Emilie Delquie, Lisa Hart.
Career Development. Meredith Adinolfi, Emilie Delquie.
Certification/Training. Helen Szigeti.
Community Engagement. Thomas A. Ciavarella, Bonnie Zavon.
Development. Mike Groth, Paul Yeager.
Education. Tim Cross, Jean P. Shipman, Greg Suprock.
Finance. Philip V. DiVietro, Byron Laws.
Marketing. Marianne Calilhanna, Josh Lancette, Elizabeth L. Ralls.
Membership. Nick Dormer, Keith L. Layson.
Peer Groups. Carol A. Meyer, Jamie Wielgus.
Publications. Sylvia Izzo Hunter, Phill Jones.
Scholarly Kitchen Cabinet. Susan Kesner.

Publication

Learned Publishing (memb.). Published by the Association of Learned and Professional

Society Publishers (ALPSP) in collaboration with SSP.

The Scholarly Kitchen (Moderated blog). *Ed.* David Crotty.

Meetings

An annual meeting is held in late May/early June. SSP also conducts a Librarian Focus Group (January) and the Fall Seminar Series (October).

Society of American Archivists

Executive Director, Nancy P. Beaumont
17 N. State St., Suite 1425, Chicago, IL 60602
312-606-0722, toll-free 866-722-7858, fax 312-606-0728, e-mail saahq@archivists.org
World Wide Web http://www2.archivists.org
Twitter @archivists_org

Object

Founded in 1936, the Society of American Archivists (SAA) is North America's oldest and largest national archival professional association. Representing more than 6,000 individual and institutional members, SAA promotes the value and diversity of archives and archivists and is the preeminent source of professional resources and the principal communication hub for American archivists.

Membership

Memb. 6,200+. Dues (Indiv.) $80 to $325, graduated according to salary; (Assoc. domestic) $115; (Ret.) $77; (Student/Bridge) $55; (Inst.) $340; (Sustaining Inst.) $595.

Officers

Pres. Meredith Evans, Jimmy Carter Presidential Lib. and Museum; *V.P.* Michelle Light, Univ. of Nevada, Las Vegas; *Treas.* Amy Fitch, Rockefeller Archive Ctr.

SAA Council

Members Steven Booth, Courtney Chartier, Melissa Gonzales, Brenda Gunn, Petrina Jackson, Erin Lawrimore, Bertram Lyons, Ricardo Punzalan, Audra Yun; *Ex Officio* Nancy P. Beaumont; *Staff Liaisons* Matt Black, Teresa Brinati, Peter Carlson, Felicia Owens, Rana Salzmann.

Committee Chairs

Appointments. Rachel Onuf.
Awards. Christina Zamon, Jennifer Kinniff.
Diversity. Harrison Inefuku.
Education. Erin Faulder.
Ethics and Professional Conduct. Sarah Keen, Polina Ilieva.
Finance. Amy Fitch.
Host. Jennifer Hecker, Kristy Sorensen.
Membership. Michelle Sweetser.
Nominating. Dominique Luster.
Program. Joyce Gabiola, Rachel Winston.
Public Awareness. Caryn Radick.
Public Policy. Sarah Quigley.
Research, Data, and Assessment. Paul Conway, Jennifer King.
Selection of SAA Fellows. Danna Bell.
Standards. John Bence, Rebecca Wiederhold.

Editorial Board Chairs

American Archivist Christopher Lee.
Publications Board. Christopher Prom.

Task Force Chairs

Research/Data and Evaluation. Melissa Gonzales.
Tragedy Response Initiative. Lisa Calahan.

Working Groups Chairs

Dictionary. Rosemary Flynn.
Intellectual Property. Aprille McKay.

Publications

American Archivist (s. ann.; memb.; nonmemb. "premium" print and online edition $289, online only $239, print only $239). *Ed.* Christopher Lee. Tel. 919-962-7024, e-mail AmericanArchivist@archivists.org; *Reviews Ed.* Bethany Anderson. Tel. 217-300-0908, e-mail ReviewsEditor@archivists.org.
Archival Outlook (bi-mo.; memb.).
In the Loop e-newsletter (bi-wk.).

Software and Information Industry Association

President, Jeff Joseph
1090 Vermont Ave. N.W. Sixth Floor, Washington, DC 20005-4905
202-289-7442, fax 202-289-7097
World Wide Web http://www.siia.net
Twitter @SIIA

The Software and Information Industry Association (SIIA) was formed January 1, 1999, through the merger of the Software Publishers Association (SPA) and the Information Industry Association (IIA).

Membership

Memb. 800+ companies. Open to companies that develop software and digital information content. For details on membership and dues, see the SIIA website, http://www.siia.net.

Officers

Pres. Jeff Joseph, Tel. 202-789-4440.

Senior Staff

Managing Dir., SIPA Nancy Brand; *Senior V.P. and Managing Dir., FISD* Tom Davin; *Managing Dir., Connectiv* Mike Marchesano; *Senior V.P., Global Public Policy* Carl Schonander; *SIIA Pres.* Jeff Joseph.

Board of Directors

Richard Atkinson, Adobe Systems, Inc.; Mark Bohannon, Red Hat, Inc.; Ed Coburn, Cabot Wealth Network; Brendan Desetti, D2L Inc.; Steve Dickey, Cboe Global Markets, Denise Elliott, Kiplinger Washington Editors, Inc.; Heather Farley, Access Intelligence; David Foster, Business Valuation Resources, LLC; Kate Friedrich, Thomson Reuters; Yousaf Hafeez, Capital Markets Development, BT; Meg Hargreaves, CQ Roll Call Group; Bernard McKay, Intuit, Inc.; Chuck Melley, Pearson; Marion Minor, EPG Media and Specialty Info.; Heath Morrison, McGraw-Hill Education; Morris Panner, Ambra Health; Jessica Perry, SHRM (Society for Human Resource Mgmt.); Marcy V. Pike, FIA, Fidelity Investments; Johanna Shelton, Google, Inc.; Sallianne Taylor, Bloomberg L.P.; Ken Wasch, Copyrightlaws.com; Greg A. Watt, WATT Global Media.

Scholarly Publishing and Academic Resources Coalition

Executive Director, Heather Joseph
21 Dupont Circle N.W., Suite 800, Washington, DC 20036
202-296-2296, fax 202-872-0884, e-mail heather@sparcopen.org
World Wide Web https://sparcopen.org
Twitter @SPARC_NA

Object

SPARC, the Scholarly Publishing and Academic Resources Coalition, is a global organization that promotes expanded sharing of scholarship in the networked digital environment. It is committed to faster and wider sharing of outputs of the research process to increase the impact of research, fuel the advancement of knowledge, and increase the return on research investments.

Developed by the Association of Research Libraries, SPARC has become a catalyst for change. Its pragmatic focus is to stimulate the emergence of new scholarly communication models that expand the dissemination of scholarly research and reduce financial pressures on libraries. Action by SPARC in collaboration with stakeholders—including authors, publishers, and libraries—builds on the unprecedented opportunities created by the networked digital environment to advance the conduct of scholarship.

SPARC's role in stimulating change focuses on

- Educating stakeholders about the problems facing scholarly communication and the opportunities for them to play a role in achieving positive change
- Advocating policy changes that advance scholarly communication and explicitly recognize that dissemination of scholarship is an essential, inseparable component of the research process
- Incubating demonstrations of new publishing and sustainability models that benefit scholarship and academe

SPARC is an advocate for changes in scholarly communication that benefit more than the academic community alone. Founded in 1997, it has expanded to represent more than 800 academic and research libraries in North America, the United Kingdom, Europe, and Japan.

Membership

Memb. 200+ institutions. SPARC membership is open to international academic and research institutions, organizations, and consortia that share an interest in creating a more open and diverse marketplace for scholarly communication. Dues are scaled by membership type and budget. For more information, visit SPARC's website at https://sparcopen.org/become-a-member, SPARC Europe at https://sparcopen.org/people/sparc-europe/, SPARC Japan at http://www.nii.ac.jp/sparc, or SPARC Africa at https://sparcopen.org/people/sparc-africa/.

Staff

Dir., Open Educ. Nicole Allen. E-mail nicole@sparcopen.org; *Senior Consultant* Raym Crow. E-mail crow@sparcopen.org; *Dir. of Operations* Shawn Daugherty. E-mail shawn@sparcopen.org; *Exec. Dir.* Heather Joseph. E-mail heather@sparcopen.org; *Programs and Operations Assoc.* Stacie Lemick. E-mail stacie@sparcopen.org; *Asst. Dir., Right to Research Coalition* Joseph McArthur. E-mail joe@righttoresearch.org; *Open Educ. Coord.* Mo Nyamweya. E-mail mo@sparcopen.org; *Dir. of Programs and Engagement* Nick Shockey. E-mail nick@sparcopen.org; *Instructor, Open Educ. Leadership Program* Tanya Spilovoy. E-mail leadership@sparcopen.org; *Consultant* Greg Tananbaum. E-mail greg@sparcopen.org; *Open Educ. Ambassador* Camille Thomas. E-mail camille@sparcopen.org.

Steering Committee

Beth Bernhardt, H. Austin Booth, Krista Cox, Regina Gong, Rebecca Graham, Jennifer Grayburn, Rachel J. Harding, Heather Joseph, Joy Kirchner, Vivian Lewis, Shilpa Rele, Steven Escar Smith, Virginia Steel, Karen Williams.

Special Libraries Association (SLA)

Executive Director, Amy Lestition Burke
7918 Jones Branch Drive, Suite 300, McLean, VA 22102
703-647-4900, fax 703-506-3266, e-mail aburke@sla.org.
World Wide Web https://www.sla.org
Twitter @SLAhq

Mission

The Special Libraries Association promotes and strengthens its members through learning, advocacy, and networking initiatives.

Strategic Vision

SLA is a global association of information and knowledge professionals who are employed in every sector of the economy. Its members thrive where data, information, and knowledge intersect, and its strategic partners support SLA because they believe in the association's mission and the future of its members. SLA's goal is to support information professionals as they contribute, in their varied and evolving roles, to the opportunities and achievements of organizations, communities, and society.

Membership

Memb. 9,000+ in 75 countries. Dues (Org.) $750; (Indiv.) $100–$200; (Student / Intl. / Salary less than $18,000 income per year) $50; (Ret.) $100.

Officers (2019)

Pres. Hal Kirkwood, Univ. of Oxford, Oxford, U.K. E-mail kirkwoodhal@gmail.com; *Pres.-Elect* Tara Murray, Pennsylvania State Univ., University Park, PA. E-mail tem10@psu.edu; *Treas.* Bill Noorlander, BST America, New York, NY. E-mail bill.noorlander@bstamerica.com; *Past Pres.* Roberto Sarmiento, Northwestern Univ., Evanston, IL. E-mail sarmiento@northwestern.edu.

Directors

Zena Applebaum, Hildy Dworkin, Amy Jankowski, Barbara Kern.

Board of Directors

Directors; Officers; *Chapter Cabinet Chair* Valerie Perry; *Chapter Cabinet Chair-Elect* Robin Dodge; *Past Chapter Cabinet Chair* Emma Davidson; *Div. Cabinet Chair* Alex Grigg Dean; *Div. Cabinet Chair-Elect* Jill Konieczko; *Past Div. Cabinet Chair* Laura Walesby.

Committee Chairs

Annual Conference Advisory Council. Jeff Bond.
Awards and Honors. Tom Rink.
Finance. Willem Noorlander.
Governance and Strategy. Tara Murray.
Nominating. Jill Strand.

Publication

Information Outlook (bi-mo.; memb., nonmemb. $240/yr.). *Ed.* Stuart Hales. E-mail shales@sla.org.

Theatre Library Association

President, Francesca Marini
c/o New York Public Library for the Performing Arts
40 Lincoln Center Plaza, New York, NY 10023
E-mail theatrelibraryassociation@gmail.com
World Wide Web http://www.tla-online.org/
Twitter @theatrelibassn

Object

To further the interests of collecting, preserving, and using theater, cinema, and performing arts materials in libraries, museums, and private collections. Founded in 1937.

Membership

Memb. 300. Dues (Indiv.) $50; (Student/Non-salaried) $25; (Inst.) $75; (Sustaining) $150. Year. Jan.–Dec.

Officers

Pres. Francesca Marini, Cushing Lib., Texas A&M Univ. E-mail fmarini@library.tamu.edu; *V.P.* Diana King, Univ. of California, Los Angeles. E-mail diking@library.ucla.edu; *Exec. Secy.* Laurie Murphy, New York Univ., Bobst Lib., 70 Washington Sq. South, New York. Tel. 212-998-2603, e-mail laurie.murphy@nyu.edu; *Treas.* Beth Kattelman, Ohio State Univ. E-mail kattelman.1@osu.edu; *Past Pres.* (ex officio) Colleen Reilly, Houston Community College. E-mail colleen.reilly@hccs.edu.

Board of Directors

(2017–2019) Felicity Ann Brown, Selena Chau, Kathryn Hujda, Helice Koffler, Charlotte Price; *(2018–2020)* Suzanne Lipkin, David Nochimson, Joseph Tally; *(2019–2021)* Matt DiCintio, Rachel Smiley, Dale Stinchcomb, Scott Stone.

Committee Chairs

Conference Planning. Diana King.
Membership. Matt DiCintio.
Nominating. Helice Koffler.
Publications. Joseph Tally.
Strategic Planning. Diana King.
Website Editorial. Eric Colleary, Charlotte Price.
Ad Hoc on Libraries. Diana King (TLA), Wade Hollingshaus (ASTR).

Awards Committee Chairs

Book Awards. Suzanne Lipkin, Annemarie van Roessel.

Publications

Broadside Archive (digital back issues). *Ed.* Angela Weaver *(2008–2014).*
Performing Arts Resources (occasional) see http://www.tla-online.org/publications/performing-arts-resources/performing-arts-resources-volumes/ for links to subscription and https://www.proquest.com/products-services/iipa_ft.html for database from ProQuest.

Urban Libraries Council

President and CEO, Susan Benton
1333 H St. N.W., Suite 1000 West, Washington, DC 20005
202-750-8650, e-mail info@urbanlibraries.org
World Wide Web http://www.urbanlibraries.org
Facebook https://www.facebook.com/UrbanLibrariesCouncil/
Twitter @UrbanLibCouncil

Object

Since 1971 the Urban Libraries Council (ULC) has worked to strengthen public libraries as an essential part of urban life. A member organization of North America's leading public library systems, ULC serves as a forum for research widely recognized and used by public- and private-sector leaders. Its members are thought leaders dedicated to leadership, innovation, and the continuous transformation of libraries to meet community needs.

ULC's work focuses on helping public libraries to identify and utilize skills and strategies that match the challenges of the 21st century.

Membership

Membership is open to public libraries and to corporate partners specializing in library-related materials and services. The organization also offers associate memberships. Annual membership dues for libraries are based on the size of a library's operating budget (local + state).

Officers (2018–2019)

Chair Rhea Brown Lawson; *V.Chair/Chair-Elect* Vickery Bowles; *Secy./Treas.* Richard Reyes-Gavilan; *Past Chair* Michael Sherrod; *Memb.-at-Large* C. Mary Okoye.

Board Members

Jill Bourne, Janet Hutchinson, John W. Laney, William (Bill) H. Meadows, Michael Meyer, Brandon Neal, Skye Patrick, Mary Blankenship Pointer, Jesus Salas, Rebecca Stavick, Mary J. Wardell.

State, Provincial, and Regional Library Associations

The associations in this section are organized under three headings: United States, Canada, and Regional. Both the United States and Canada are represented under Regional associations.

United States

Alabama

Memb. 1,200. Publication. *ALLA COMmunicator* (q.).

Pres. Carrie Steinmehl, Hoover Public Lib., 200 Municipal Dr., Hoover 35216. Tel. 205-444-7748, e-mail carries@bham.lib.al.us; *Pres.-Elect* Jessica Hayes, Auburn Univ. at Montgomery, P.O. Box 244023, Montgomery 36124-4023. Tel. 334-244-3814, e-mail jhayes11@aum.edu; *Secy.* Paula Webb, Univ. of South Alabama, 5901 USA Dr. North, Mobile 36688. Tel. 251-461-1933, e-mail pwebb@southalabama.edu; *Treas.* Karen Preuss, Montgomery City-County Public Lib., P.O. Box 1950, Montgomery 36102-1950. Tel. 334-240-4300, e-mail kpreuss@mccpl.lib.al.us; *Memb.-at-Large* (Central Alabama) Jeff Graveline, Univ. of Alabama at Birmingham, Mervyn H. Sterne Lib., SL 172, 1720 2nd Ave S., Birmingham 35294-0014. Tel. 205-934-6364, e-mail jgraveli@uab.edu; (North Alabama) Laura Pitts, Scottsboro Public Lib., 1002 South Broad St., Scottsboro 35768. Tel. 256-574-4335, e-mail laurap@scottsboro.org; (South Alabama) Wendy Congairdo, Thomas B. Norton Public Lib., 221 W. 19th Ave., Gulf Shores 36542. Tel. 251-968-1176, e-mail wcongiardo@hotmail.com. *Past Pres.* Sonya Jordan, Mountain Brook High School, 3650 Bethune Dr., Mountain Brook 35223. Tel. 205-414-3800 ext. 7619, e-mail jordans@student.mtnbrook.k12.al.us; *Assn. Admin.* (ex-officio) Angela Moore, Alabama Lib. Assn., 6030 Monticello Dr., Montgomery 36117. Tel. 334-414-0113, e-mail allibraryassoc@gmail.com.

Address correspondence to the administrator.

Alabama Lib. Assn., 6030 Monticello Dr., Montgomery 36117. Tel. 334-414-0113, e-mail allibraryassoc@gmail.com.

World Wide Web http://allanet.org.

Alaska

Memb. 450+. Publication. *Newspoke* (q.) (online at http://akla.org/newspoke).

Pres. Robert Barr. E-mail Robert.Barr@juneau.org; *Pres.-Elect* Deborah Rinio. E-mail northernlightslibrarian@gmail.com; *Secy.* Paul Adasiak. E-mail pfadasiak@alaska.edu; *Treas.* Rebecca Moorman. E-mail rmoorman@alaska.edu; *Conference Coords.* Robert Barr. E-mail Robert.Barr@juneau.org, Freya Anderson. E-mail freya.anderson@alaska.gov; *ALA Representative* Lorelei Sterling. E-mail lsterling@alaska.edu; *PNLA Representative* Julie Niederhauser. E-mail Julie.niederhauser@alaska.gov; *Past Pres.* Erin Hollingsworth. E-mail Erin.Hollingsworth@nsbsd.org.

Address correspondence to the secretary, Alaska Lib. Assn., P.O. Box 81084, Fairbanks 99708. E-mail akla@akla.org.

World Wide Web http://www.azla.org.

Arizona

Memb. 1,000. Term of Office. Nov.–Nov. Publication. *AzLA Newsletter* (6x yearly).

Pres. Michelle Simon, Pima County Public Lib., 101 N. Stone Ave. Tucson 85701. Tel. 520-594-5654, e-mail michesimon54@gmail.com; *Secy.* Amber Kent, Casa Grande Public Lib., 449 N. Drylake St., Casa Grande 85122. Tel. 520 421-8710, e-mail AKent@casagrande az.gov; *Treas.* Rene Tanner, Arizona State Univ., Tempe. Tel. 480-965-7190, e-mail rene.tanner@asu.edu; *Northern Regional Representative* Martha Baden; *Central Regional Representative* Erin Lorandos; *Southern Regional Representative* Hanna Stewart; *ALA Councilor* Dan Stanton; *MPLA Representative* Amadee Ricketts; *Past Pres.* Gina Macaluso, Univ. of Arizona School of Information, 1103 E. 2nd St., Tucson. Tel. 520-621-5220, e-mail ginamacaluso@email.arizona.edu.

Address correspondence to Arizona Lib. Assn., 1645 W. Valencia Rd. #109-432

Tucson 85746. Tel. 602-614-2841, e-mail admin@azla.org.

World Wide Web http://www.azla.org.

Arkansas

Memb. 600. Publication. *Arkansas Libraries* (4x yearly).

Pres. Jil'Lana Heard, Lake Hamilton Junior High, 281 Wolf St., Pearcy 72035. Tel. 501-767-2731, e-mail jillana.heard@lhwolves.net; *Pres.-Elect* Crystal Gates, William F. Laman Public Libr. System, 2801 Orange St., North Little Rock 72114. Tel. 501-771-1995, e-mail crystal.gates@lamanlibrary.org; *Secy.* Jessica Riedmueller, Univ. of Central Arkansas, 201 Donaghey Ave., Conway 72035. Tel., 501-450-5233, e-mail jriedmueller@uca.edu *Treas.* Lynn Valetutti, Arkansas State Lib., 900 W. Capitol Ave., Suite 100, Little Rock 72201. Tel. 501-682-2840, e-mail lynn@library.arkansas.gov; *ALA Councilor* Lacy Wolfe, Henderson State Univ., 1100 Henderson St., Box 7541, Arkadelphia 71999. Tel. 870-230-5322, e-mail wolfel@hsu.edu; *Past Pres.* Dean Covington, Univ. of Central Arkansas, 201 Donaghey Ave., Conway 72035. Tel. 501-450-5202, e-mail dcovington@uca.edu.

Address correspondence to Arkansas Lib. Assn., P.O. Box 3821, Little Rock 72203. Tel. 501-313-1398, e-mail info@arlib.org.

World Wide Web http://arlib.org.

California

Memb. 2,500. Publication. CLA *Insider* (memb.; online).

Pres. Michelle Perera, Pasadena Public Lib. E-mail mperera@cityofpasadena.net; *V.P./Pres.-Elect* Hillary Theyer, Torrance Public Lib. E-mail HTheyer@torranceca.gov; *Secy.* Stephanie Beverage, Huntington Beach Public Lib. E-mail Stephanie.Beverage@surfcity-hb.org; *Treas.* Derek Wolfgram, Redwood City Public Lib., E-mail dwolfgram@redwoodcity.org; *Past Pres.* Dolly Goyal, San Mateo County Libs. E-mail goyal@smcl.org.

Address correspondence to California Lib. Assn., 1055 E. Colorado Blvd., 5th Floor, Pasadena 91106. Tel. 626-204-4071, e-mail info@cla-net.org.

World Wide Web http://www.cla-net.org.

Colorado

Pres. Tammy Sayles, Pikes Peak Lib. District. E-mail tjsmlis@gmail.com; *V.P./Pres.-Elect* Ryan F. Buller, Univ. of Denver. E-mail Ryan.Buller@du.edu; *Secy.* Anne Holland, Space Science Institute. E-mail aholland@spacescience.org; *Treas.* Mike Varnet, Pikes Peak Lib., 1175 Chapel Hills Dr., Colorado Springs 80920. Tel. 719-884-9700, e-mail mvarnet@ppld.org; *Past Pres.* Carol Smith, Colorado School of Mines, Arthur Lakes Lib. E-mail cesmith@mines.edu.

Address correspondence to Colorado Assn. of Libs., P.O. Box 740905, Arvada 80006-0905. Tel. 303-463-6400, fax 303-458-0002, e-mail cal@cal-webs.org.

World Wide Web World Wide Web http://www.cal-webs.org.

Connecticut

Memb. 1,000+. Term of Office. July–June. Publication. *CLA Today* (6x yearly; online). E-mail editor@ctlibrarians.org.

Pres. Kate Byroade, Cragin Memorial Lib., 8 Linwood Ave., Colchester 06415. Tel. 860 537-5752, e-mail kbyroade@colchesterct.gov; *V.P./Pres.-Elect* Lisa Karim, Simsbury Public Lib., 725 Hopmeadow St., Simsbury. Tel. 860-658-7663, fax 860-658-6732, e-mail lkarim@simsburylibrary.info; *Recording Secy.* Catherine Potter, East Hartford Public Lib., 840 Main St., East Hartford 06108; Tel. 860-290-4333, e-mail cpotter@easthartfordct.gov; *Treas.* Kristina Edwards, Central Connecticut State Univ., Elihu Burritt Lib., New Britiain. Tel. 860-832-2073, e-mail kedwards@ccsu.edu; *Past Pres.* Glenn Grube, Avon Free Public Lib., 281 Country Club Rd. Avon 06001. Tel. 860-673-9712, e-mail ggrube@avonctlibrary.info.

Address correspondence to Connecticut Lib. Assn., 234 Court St., Middletown 06457. Tel. 860-346-2444, fax 860-344-9199, e-mail cla@ctlibrarians.org.

World Wide Web http://ctlibraryassociation.org.

Delaware

Memb. 200+. Publication. *DLA Bulletin* (q.; online). E-mail Nicole.Ballance@lib.de.us.

V.P. Alison Wessel, DHSS Lib, Delaware Dept. of Health and Social Svcs., Herman M. Holloway Sr. Health and Social Svcs. Campus, 1901 N. DuPont Hwy., New Castle 19720. Tel. 302-255-2986, e-mail alisonwessel.dla@gmail.com; *Secy.* Adrienne Johnson, Wilmington Univ. Lib., 320 DuPont Hwy., New Castle 19720. Tel. 302-295-1177, e-mail adrienne.m.johnson@wilmu.edu; *Treas.* Joel Rudnick, Delaware Technical Community College, Owens Campus, P.O. Box 630, 21179 College Dr., Georgetown 19947. Tel. 302-259-6199, e-mail rudnick.dla@gmail.com; *ALA Councilor* Lauren Wallis, Univ. of Delaware Morris Lib. Tel. 302-831-3763, e-mail lwallis@udel.edu; *Delaware State Libn.* Annie Norman, Delaware Div. of Libs., 121 Martin Luther King Jr. Blvd. N., Dover 19901. Tel. 302-257-3001, fax 302-739-6787, e-mail annie.norman@state.de.us; *President, Friends of Delaware Libs.* Kay Bowes. E-mail kaybowes@gmail.com; *Past Pres.* Michelle Hughes, Dover Public Lib., 35 Loockerman Plaza, Dover 19901. Tel. 302-736-7079, fax 302-736-5087, e-mail michelle.hughes@lib.de.us.

Address correspondence to Delaware Lib. Assn., c/o Delaware Division of Libs., 121 Martin Luther King Jr. Blvd. N., Dover 19901. E-mail dla@lib.de.us.

World Wide Web http://dla.lib.de.us.

District of Columbia

Memb. 300+. Term of Office. July–June. Publication. *Capital Librarian* (mo., online).

Pres. Nicholas Brown. E-mail president@dcla.org; *V.P.* Tracy Sumler. E-mail vice_president@dcla.org; *Secy.* Leah Castaldi. E-mail secretary@dcla.org; *Treas.* Heather Wiggins. E-mail treasurer@dcla.org; *ALA Councilor* Richard Huffine. E-mail ala_councilor@dcla.org; *Past Pres.* Candice Townsend. E-mail past_president@dcla.org.

Address correspondence to District of Columbia Lib. Assn., Union Station, 50 Massachusetts Ave. N.E., P.O. Box 1653 Washington, DC 20002.

World Wide Web http://www.dcla.org.

Florida

Memb. (Indiv.) 1,000+. Publication. *Florida Libraries* (s. ann.).

Pres. Sarah Hammill, Florida Intl. Univ. E-mail hammills@fiu.edu; *V.P./Pres.-Elect* Eric Head, Citrus County Lib. System. E-mail eric.head@citruslibraries.org; *Secy.* Tina Neville, Univ. of South Florida, St. Petersburg. E-mail neville@mail.usf.edu; *Treas.* Donna Vazquez, Florida Gulf Coast Univ. E-mail devazque@fgcu.edu; *State Libn.* Amy Johnson, Division of Lib. and Info. Svcs. E-mail Amy.Johnson@dos.myflorida.com; *ALA Councilor* Sara Gonzalez, Orange County Lib. System; *Past Pres.* Robin Shader, Northwest Regional Lib., Tel. 850-522-2109, e-mail rshader@nwrls.com; *Exec. Dir.* Lisa O'Donnell. Tel. 850-270-9205, e-mail lisa@flalib.org.

Address correspondence to the executive director.

Florida Lib. Assn., 541 E. Tennessee St., #103, Tallahassee 32308. Tel. 850-270-9205, e-mail admin@flalib.org.

World Wide Web http://www.flalib.org.

Georgia

Memb. 800+. Publication. *Georgia Library Quarterly* (q., online). *Ed.* Virginia Feher, Univ. of North Georgia. E-mail virginia.feher@ung.edu.

Pres. Jennifer Lautzenheiser, Middle Georgia Regional Lib., 1180 Washington St., Macon 31208. Tel. 478-744-0880, e-mail lautzenheiserj@bibblib.org; *1st V.P./Pres.-Elect* Laura Burtle, Georgia State Univ. Lib., 100 Decatur St. S.E., Atlanta 30303. Tel. 404-413-2706, e-mail lburtle@gsu.edu; *2nd V.P.* Oscar Gittemeier, Atlanta-Fulton Public Lib., Tel. 404-730-1826, e-mail oscar.gittemeier@fultoncounty.gov; *V.P. Marketing and Branding* Amanda Roper, Chattanooga State Community College, 4501 Amnicola Hwy. Chattanooga, TN 37406. E-mail amanda.l.addison@gmail.com; *Secy.* Amy Eklund, Gwinnett County Public Lib., 1001 Lawrenceville Hwy. Lawrenceville 30046. Tel. 770-822-4522, e-mail amypeklund@hotmail.com; *Treas.* Ben Bryson, Marshes of Glynn Libs., 208 Gloucester St., Brunswick 31520. Tel. 912-279-3735, e-mail bbryson@glynncounty-ga.gov.

Address correspondence to the president.

Georgia Lib. Assn., P.O. Box 30324, Savannah 31410. Tel. 912-999-7979, e-mail membership.gla@gmail.com.

World Wide Web http://gla.georgialibraries.org.

Hawaii

Memb. 250. Publication. *HLA Newsletter* (q., online).

Pres. Sharrese Castillo, Wahiawa Public Lib. E-mail sharrese.c.c@gmail.com; *V.P./Pres.-Elect* Michael Aldrich, BYU Hawaii. E-mail michael.aldrich@byuh.edu; *Secy.* Jessica Hogan. E-mail jessica.hogan@librarieshawaii.org; *Treas.* Joy Oehlers, Kapi'olani Community College Lib., 4303 Diamond Head Rd., Honolulu 96816. Tel. 808-734-9352, e-mail aichin@hawaii.edu; *Past Pres.* Gwen Sinclair. Univ. of Hawai'i at Manoa Lib. E-mail gsinclai@hawaii.edu.

Address correspondence to Hawai i Lib. Assn., P.O. Box 4441, Honolulu 96812-4441. E-mail hawaii.library.association@gmail.com.

World Wide Web http://hawaiilibraryassociation.weebly.com.

Idaho

Memb. 420. Term of Office. Oct.–Oct.

Pres. Katherine Lovan, Middleton Public Lib., Middleton. E-mail klovan@mymiddletonlibrary.org and LeAnn Gelskey, Hailey Public Lib., Hailey. E-mail leanngelskey@gmail.com; *V.P./Pres.-Elect* Erin Downey, Boise School District. Tel. 208-854-4110, e-mail erindowney.ila@gmail.com; *Secy.* Beverley Richmond, Priest Lake Public Lib., 28769 Idaho 57, Priest Lake 83856. Tel. 208-443-2454, e-mail plplibrary@hotmail.com; *Treas.* Jane Clapp, Boise State Univ. E-mail janeclapp.ila@gmail.com; *Membership Committee Chair* Cindy Bigler, Soda Springs Public Lib. E-mail sspl@sodaspringsid.com.

Address correspondence to Idaho Lib. Assn., 4911 N. Shirley Ave., Boise 83703.

World Wide Web http://idaholibraries.org.

Illinois

Memb. 3,500. Publication. *ILA Reporter* (bi-mo.; online).

Pres. Cynthia L. Fuerst, Vernon Area Public Lib. District; *V.P./Pres.-Elect* Molly Beestrum, Northwestern Univ. Libs.; *Treas.* Brian Shepard, Indiana Trails Public Lib. District; *ALA Councilor* Jeannie Dilger, Palatine Public Lib. District; *Past Pres.* Melissa Gardner, Palatine Public Library District; *Exec. Dir.* Diane Foote. E-mail dfoote@ila.org.

Address correspondence to the executive director. Illinois Lib. Assn., 33 W. Grand Ave., Suite 401, Chicago 60654-6799. Tel. 312 644-1896, fax 312 644-1899, e-mail ila@ila.org.

World Wide Web http://www.ila.org.

Indiana

Indiana Lib. Federation. Memb. 2,000+. Publications. *Focus on Indiana Libraries* (mo.; memb.). *Communications Mgr.* Tisa M. Davis, 941 E. 86th St., Suite 260, Indianapolis 46240. Tel. 317-257-2040, ext. 104, fax 317-257-1389, e-mail askus@ilfonline.org.

Pres. Susie Highley, Indiana Middle Level Education Assn., 11025 E. 25th St., Indianapolis 46229. Tel. 317-894-2937; *Pres.-Elect* Leslie Sutherlin, South Dearborn Community Schools, 5770 Highlander Pl., Aurora 47001. Tel. 812-926-3772; *Secy.* Kelly Ehinger, Adams Public Lib. System, 128 S. 3rd St., Decatur 46733. Tel. 260-724-2605; *Treas.* Michael Williams, Indianapolis Public Lib., 40 E. Saint Clair St., Indianapolis 46204. Tel. 317 275-4302; *ALA Councilor* Beth Munk, Kendallville Public Lib., 221 S. Park, Kendallville 46755 Tel. 260-343-2022; *Past Pres.* Edra Waterman, Hamilton East Public Lib., 1 Library Plaza, Noblesville 46060. Tel. 317-770-3202, e-mail ewaterman@hepl.lib.in.us; *Exec. Dir.* Lucinda Nord. Tel. 317-257-2040, ext. 101, e-mail exec@ilfonline.org.

Address correspondence to Indiana Lib. Federation, 941 E. 86 St., Suite 260, Indianapolis 46240. Tel. 317-257-2040, fax 317-257-1389, e-mail askus@ilfonline.org.

World Wide Web http://www.ilfonline.org.

Iowa

Memb. 1,500. Publication. *Catalyst* (bi-mo., online).

Pres. Dan Chibnall, Drake Univ., 2507 University Ave., Des Moines 50311. Tel. 515-271-2112, e-mail dan.chibnall@drake.edu; V.P./Pres.-Elect Mara Strickler, Algona Public Lib., Tel. 515-295-5476, e-mail mstrickler@algona.lib.ia.us; Secy. Misty Gray, State Lib. of Iowa, 3501 Harry Langdon Blvd, Suite 190, Council Bluffs 51503. Tel. 712-299-8767, e-mail misty.gray@iowa.gov; Treas. Thomas Kessler, Univ.

of Northern Iowa, Rod Lib., Cedar Falls 50613-3675. Tel. 319-277-3106, e-mail thomas.kessler@uni.edu; ALA Councilor Samantha Helmick, Burlington Public Lib., Tel. 319-753-1647, e-mail shelmick@burlington.lib.ia.us; Past Pres. Michael Wright, Dubuque County Lib. District, 5290 Grand Meadow Dr., Asbury 52002. Tel. 563-582-0008, e-mail michaelw@dubcolib.lib.ia.us.

Address correspondence to Iowa Lib. Assn., 6919 Vista Dr., West Des Moines 50266. Tel. 515-282-8192.

World Wide Web http://www.iowalibraryassociation.org.

Kansas

Kansas Lib. Assn. Memb. 1,500. Term of Office. July–June. Publication. *Kansas Libraries!* (6x yearly; online). E-mail kilbmag@gmail.com.

Pres. Laura Littrell, Kansas State Univ., Lib. Planning and Assessment, 1117 Mid-Campus Drive North, 314A Hale Lib., Manhattan 66506. Tel. 785-532-5467, e-mail laurlit@k-state.edu; *1st V.P.* Robin Newell, Emporia Public Lib., 110 E. Sixth Ave., Emporia 66801. Tel. 620-340-6464, e-mail newellr@emporialibrary.org; *2nd V.P.* Meagan Zampieri, Hays Public Lib. E-mail mzampieri@hayslibrary.org; *Secy.* Bethanie O'Dell, Emporia State Univ. E-mail bodell1@emporia.edu; *Treas.* Diana Weaver, Basehor Community Lib., 1400 158th St., Basehor 66007. Tel. 913-724-2828, e-mail dweaver@basehorlibrary.org; *Exec. Secy.* George Seamon, Northwest Kansas Lib, System, #2 Washington Sq.; Norton 67654. Tel. 785-877-5148, e-mail director@nwkls.org; *Parliamentarian* Dan Ireton Kansas State Univ. E-mail dli6873@k-state.edu.

Address correspondence to the president. Kansas Lib. Assn., Northwest Kansas Lib. System, 2 Washington Sq., Norton 67654. Tel. 785-877-5148.

World Wide Web http://www.kslibassoc.org.

Kentucky

Memb. 1,600. Publication. *Kentucky Libraries* (q.). *Ed.* Robin Harris, Law Lib., Brandeis School of Law, Univ. of Louisville, Louisville, 40292-0001, Tel. 502-852-6083, e-mail robin.harris@louisville.edu.

Pres. Debbra Tate, Kentucky State Univ., Blazer Lib., 400 E. Main St., Frankfort 40601. Tel. 502-597-6862, e-mail president@klaonline.org; *Pres.-Elect* Kandace Rogers, Sullivan Univ., 2355 Harrodsburg Rd., Lexington 40504. Tel. 859-514-3359, e-mail krogers@sullivan.edu; *Secy.* Mark Adler, Paris-Bourbon County Lib., 701 High St., Paris, 40361. Tel. 859-987-4419, x103, e-mail madler@bourbonlibrary.org; *Past Pres.* Tara Griffith, Barren County Schools, 507 Trojan Trail, Glasgow 42141. Tel. 270-202-2547, e-mail tara.griffith@barren.kyschools.us; *Exec. Dir.* John Tom Underwood, Kentucky Lib. Assn., 5932 Timber Ridge Drive, Unit 101, Prospect 40059. Tel. 502-223-5322, fax 502-223-4937, e-mail info@kylibasn.org.

Address correspondence to the executive director.

Kentucky Lib. Assn., 5932 Timber Ridge Dr., Suite 101, Prospect 40059. Tel. 502-223-5322, fax 502-223-4937, e-mail info@kylibasn.org.

World Wide Web http://www.klaonline.org.

Louisiana

Memb. 1,000+. Term of Office. July–June. Publication. *Louisiana Libraries* (q.). *Ed.* Celise Reech-Harper, Assoc. Dir., Beauregard Parish Lib., 205 South Washington Ave., DeRidder 70634. Tel. 337-463-6217 ext. 22, e-mail celise@beau.org.

Pres. Catherine A. Smith. Tel. 318-603-6374, e-mail catlib2000@yahoo.com; *1st V.P./Pres.-Elect* Sonnet Ireland. Tel. 504-390-6834, e-mail sonnet.ireland@yahoo.com; *2nd V.P.* Megan Lowe. Tel. 318-362-9911, e-mail meganwlowe@gmail.com; *Secy.* Christopher Achee. Tel. 225-647-3955, e-mail cachee@state.lib.la.us; *ALA Councilor* Vivian McCain. Tel. 318-513-5508, e-mail vmccain@mylpl.org; *Parliamentarian* Charlene Picheloup. Tel. 337-229-4701, e-mail crpeachy@yahoo.com; *Past Pres.* Patricia Brown. Tel. 318-357-6263, e-mail brownpa@nsula.edu; *Exec. Dir.* Bland O'Connor. Tel. 225-922-4642, fax 225-408-4422, e-mail office@llaonline.org.

Address correspondence to Louisiana Lib. Assn., 8550 United Plaza Blvd., Suite 1001, Baton Rouge 70809. Tel. 225-922-4642, 877-550-7890, fax 225-408-4422, e-mail office@llaonline.org.

World Wide Web http://www.llaonline.org.

Maine

Maine Lib. Assn. Memb. 950. Publication. *MLA to Z* (q., online). E-mail mlatozeditor@gmail.com.

Pres. Alisia Revitt, Maine InfoNet, UMaine, 5784 York Village, Suite 58, Orono 04469. Tel. 207-370-8286, e-mail mla.alisiarevitt@gmail.com; *V.P.* Jennifer Alvino, Windham Public Lib., 217 Windham Center Rd., Windham 04062. Tel. 207-892-1908, e-mail jaalvino@windhammaine.us; *Secy.* Lisa Shaw, Maine State Lib., 145 Harlow St., Bangor 04401. Tel. 207-947-8336 ext. 114, e-mail lisa.m.shaw@maine.gov; *Treas.* Michael Dignan, Paris Public Lib., 37 Market Sq., Paris 04291-1509. Tel. 207-743-6994, e-mail mdignan@paris.lib.me.us; *Memb.-at-Large* Cadence Atchinson. E-mail catchinson@une.edu; Kate Wing. E-mail katemwing@gmail.com; *ALA Councilor* Kara Reiman, Walker Memorial Lib., 800 Main St., Westbrook 04092. Tel. 207-854-0630 ext. 4, kreiman@westbrook.me.us; *Past Pres.* Bryce Cundick, Mantor Lib., Univ. of Maine at Farmington, 116 South St., Farmington 04938-1998. Tel. 207-778-7224, e-mail mla.brycecundick@gmail.com. *Exec. Dir. and Archivist* Jenna Blake Davis. Tel. 207-730-3028, e-mail mainelibrary@gmail.com.

Address correspondence to executive director, Maine Lib. Assn., 93 Saco Ave., Old Orchard Beach 04064. Tel. 207-730-3028, e-mail mainelibrary@gmail.com.

World Wide Web http://mainelibraries.org.

Maryland

Maryland Lib. Assn. Memb. 1,000+. Term of Office. July–July. Publication. *The Crab* (q., memb., online). *Ed.* Annette Haldeman. E-mail annette.haldeman@mlis.state.md.us.

Pres. Joseph Thompson, Carroll County Public Lib., 1100 Green Valley Rd., New Windsor 21776. Tel. 443-293-3131, fax 410-386-4509, e-mail jthompson@carr.org; *V.P./Pres.-Elect* Andrea Berstler, Wicomico Public Libs., 122 S. Division St., Salisbury 21801. Tel. 410-749-3612, fax 410-548-2968, e-mail aberstler@wicomico.org; *Secy.* Mary Anne Bowman, St. Mary's County Public Lib., 23250 Hollywood Rd., Leonardtown 20650. Tel. 301-475-2846 ext. 1015, fax 410-884-4415, e-mail mabowman@stmalib.org; *Treas.* Patty Sundberg, Carroll County Public Lib., 705 Ridge Ave., Mount Airy 21771. Tel. 410-386-4470 ext. 4402, e-mail sundberg@carr.org; *ALA Councilor* David Dahl, Univ. of Maryland. Tel. 301-314-0395, e-mail ddahl1@umd.edu; *Conference Dir.* Tiffany Sutherland, Calvert Lib. Tel. 410-535-0291, e-mail tsutherland@calvertlibrary.info; *Past Pres.* Denise Davis, Cecil County Public Lib., 301 Newark Ave., Elkton 21921-5441. Tel. 443-745-2000, fax 410-996-1055, e-mail ddavis@ccplnet.org; *Exec. Dir.* Margaret Carty, Maryland Lib. Assn., 1401 Hollins St., Baltimore 21223. Tel. 410-947-5090, e-mail mcarty@mdlib.org.

Address correspondence to Maryland Lib. Assn., 1401 Hollins St., Baltimore 21223. Tel. 410-947-5090, fax 410-947-5089, e-mail mla@mdlib.org.

World Wide Web http://www.mdlib.org.

Massachusetts

Massachusetts Lib. Assn. Memb. (Indiv.) 1,000; (Inst.) 100.

Pres. William L. Adamczyk, Milton Public Lib., 476 Canton Ave., Milton 02186. Tel. 617-698-5757, e-mail wadamczyk@ocln.org; *V.P.* Esmé E. Green, Goodnow Lib., 21 Concord Rd., Sudbury 01776. Tel. 978-440-5515, e-mail greene@sudbury.ma.us; *Secy.* Noelle Boc, Tewksbury Lib., 300 Chandler St., Tewksbury 01876. Tel. 978-640-4490, e-mail nboc@tewksburypl.org; *Treas.* Jennifer Pike. Gleason Public Lib., 22 Bedford Rd., Carlise 01741. Tel. 978-369-4898, e-mail treasurer@masslib.org; *Past Pres.* Alexander Lent, Peabody Institute Lib. of Danvers, 15 Sylvan St., Danvers 01923. Tel. 978-774-0554.

Address correspondence to Massachusetts Lib. Assn. P.O. Box 813, Carlisle 01741. Tel. 781-698-7764, e-mail manager@masslib.org.

World Wide Web http://www.masslib.org.

Michigan

Memb. 1,200+.

Pres. Kristin Shelley, East Lansing Public Lib.; *Pres.-Elect* Michelle Boisvenue-Fox, Kent District Lib.; *Treas.* Richard Schneider, Muskegon District Lib., 4845 Airline Rd., Unit 5, Muskegon 49444. Tel. 231-737-6248, e-mail rschneider@madl.org; *ALA Councilor* Jennifer Dean; *State Libn.* (ex-officio) Randy Riley; *Past Pres.* Steven Bowers, Detroit Area Lib. Network (DALNET); *Exec. Dir.* (ex-officio) Gail Madziar. Tel. 517-394-2774, ext. 224, e-mail gmadziar@milibraries.org.

Address correspondence to the executive director.

Michigan Lib. Assn., 3410 Belle Chase Way, Suite 100, Lansing 48911. Tel. 517-394-2774, e-mail MLA@milibraries.org.

World Wide Web http://www.milibraries.org.

Minnesota

Memb. 1,100. Term of Office. (*Pres., Pres.-Elect*) Jan.–Dec. Publication. *Roundup* (mo., online).

Pres. Kirsten Clark, Univ. of Minnesota Libs.; *Pres.-Elect* Patti Bross, Lake City Public Lib.; *Secy.* Lisa Motschke, St. Paul Public Lib.; *Treas.* Jonathan Carlson, College of Saint Benedict/Saint John's Univ.; *Memb.-at-Large* Tasha Nins, Hennepin County Lib.; *ALA Chapter Councilor* Hannah Buckland, Hennepin County Lib.; *Past Pres.* Ryan McCormick, Great River Regional Lib. E-mail mcco0303@email.arizona.edu; *Interim Exec. Dir.* Dara Rudick. E-mail mla@management-hq.com.

Address correspondence to the executive director.

Minnesota Lib. Assn., 400 S. 4th St., Suite 754E, Minneapolis 55415. Tel. 612-294-6549, e-mail mla@management-hq.com.

World Wide Web http://www.mnlibraryassociation.org.

Mississippi

Memb. 625. Term of Office. Jan.–Dec. Publication. *Mississippi Libraries* (q.). *Ed.* Tina Harry. E-mail tharry@olemiss.edu.

Pres. Sarah Crisler-Ruskey, Harrison County Public Lib. System. Tel. 228-539-0110; *V.P.* Mary Beth Applin, Hinds Community College. Tel. 601-857-3380; *Secy.* Victoria Penny, Northwest Mississippi Community College. Tel. 662-562-3278; *Treas.* Jennifer Wann, Bolivar County Lib. System. Tel. 662-843-2774 ext. 102, e-mail jwann@bolivar.lib.ms.us; *ALA Councilor* Ellen Ruffin, McCain Lib. and Archives. Tel. 601-266-4349; *Past Pres.* Sarah Mangrum, Univ. Libs. (USM). Tel. 601-266-4251, e-mail sarah.rials@usm.edu; *Admin.* Paula Bass, P.O. Box 13687, Jackson 39236-3687. Tel. 601-981-4586, e-mail info@misslib.org.

Address correspondence to the administrator.

Mississippi Lib. Assn., P.O. Box 13687, Jackson 3923-3687. Tel. 601-981-4586, e-mail info@misslib.org.

World Wide Web http://www.misslib.org.

Missouri

Memb. 800+. Term of Office. Jan.–Dec. Publication. *MO INFO* (bi-mo.).

Pres. Erin Gray, Springfield-Greene County Lib. E-mail mlapresident@molib.org; *Pres.-Elect* Cindy Dudenhoffer, Central Methodist Univ.; *Secy. and Memb.-at-Large* Jamie Emery, Saint Louis Univ.; *Treas. and Memb.-at-Large* Susan Wray, Mid-Continent Public Lib.; *Memb.-at-Large* Jenny Bossaller, Meredith McCarthy, Jennifer Parsons, Christina Prucha. *Treas.-Elect and Member-at-Large* Steve Campbell, Scenic Regional Lib.; *ALA Councilor* Stephanie Tolson, St. Charles Community College; *Past Pres.* April Roy, Kansas City Public Lib. E-mail aprilroy@kclibrary.org.

Address correspondence to the president.

Missouri Lib. Assn. 1190 Meramec Station Rd., Suite 207, Ballwin, 63021-6902. E-mail mlapresident@molib.org.

World Wide Web http://www.molib.org.

Montana

Memb. 600. Term of Office. July–June. Publication. *Focus* (bi-mo.). *Eds.* Alice Ebi Kestler and Sarah Creech. E-mail mlaFOCUSeditor@gmail.com.

Pres. Elizabeth Jonkel, Missoula Public Lib., 301 E. Main, Missoula 59802. Tel. 406-721-2665, e-mail ejonkel@missoula.lib.mt.us; *V.P./Pres.-Elect* Mary Anne Hansen, MSU-Bozeman Lib., 1510 S. Grand Ave, Bozeman 59715; *Secy./Treas.* Megan Stark, UM-Missoula Lib., 32 Campus Dr., Missoula 59812; *Past Pres.* Lisa Mecklenberg Jackson, Montana Innocence Project, 120 Southridge Dr., Missoula 59803; *Exec. Dir.* Debbi Kramer,

Montana Lib. Assn., Inc., 33 Beartooth View Dr., Laurel 59044. Tel. 406-579-3121, e-mail debkmla@hotmail.com.

Address correspondence to the executive director. Montana Lib. Assn. E-mail debkmla@hotmail.com.

World Wide Web http://www.mtlib.org.

Nebraska

Term of Office. Jan.–Dec.

Pres. Rebecca McCorkindale. E-mail nlapres@gmail.com; *Pres.-Elect* Michael Straatmann. E-mail nlapresidentelect@gmail.com; *Secy.* Bailey Halbur. E-mail nlasecretary@gmail.com; *Treas.* Matt Kovar. E-mail nlatreasurer@gmail.com; *ALA Councilor* Micki Dietrich. E-mail mdietrich@omahalibrary.org; *Past Pres.* Andrew Cano, Univ. of Nebraska–Lincoln. E-mail nlapastpresident@gmail.com; *Exec. Dir.* Creative Association Management.

Address correspondence to the executive director.

Nebraska Lib. Assn., P.O. Box 21756, Lincoln 68542-1756. E-mail nlaexecutivedirector@nebraskalibraries.org.

World Wide Web https://nebraskalibraries.org.

Nevada

Memb. 450. Term of Office. Jan.–Dec. Publication. *Nevada Libraries* (q.). *Ed.* Tam Anderson, Las Vegas-Clark County Lib. District. E-mail andersont@lvccld.org.

Pres. Jeff Scott, Washoe County Lib. System. E-mail jscott@washoecounty.us; *Treas.* Joy Gunn, Henderson Libs. E-mail jgunn@hendersonlibraries.com; *Finance* Marco Veyna-Reyes, Las Vegas-Clark County Lib. District. E-mail marco.nla.financechair@gmail.com *Past Pres.* Soraya Silverman-Montoya, Las Vegas–Clark County Lib. District. E-mail nlapresidentsorayasilverman@gmail.com; *Exec. Secy.* Seungyeon Yang-Peace, Las Vegas-Clark County Lib. District. E-mail sueyangpeace@gmail.com.

Address correspondence to the executive secretary.

World Wide Web http://www.nevadalibraries.org.

New Hampshire

Memb. 700.

Pres. Christine Friese, Portsmouth Public Lib., 175 Parrott Ave., Portsmouth 03801. Tel. 603-766-1703, e-mail president@nhlibrarians.org; *V.P./Pres.-Elect* Amy Lappin, Lebanon Public Libs., 80 Main Str., West Lebanon 03784, Tel. 603-298-8544, e-mail amy.lappin@leblibrary.com; *Secy.* Sarah St. Martin Manchester City Lib., 405 Pine St., Manchester 03104. Tel. 603-624-6550, ext. 3343, e-mail sstmartin@manchesternh.gov; *Treas.* Deann Hunter, Laconia Public Lib., 695 Main St., Laconia 03246. Tel. 603-524-4775, e-mail dhunter@laconialibrary.org; *Treasurer-Elect* Kim Gabert, Wadleigh Memorial Lib., 49 Nashua Street, Milford 03055. Tel. 603-249-0645, e-mail kgabert@wadleighlibrary.org; *ALA Councilor* Lori Fisher, Baker Free Lib., 509 South St., Bow 03304. Tel. 603-224-7113, e-mail lori@bakerfreelib.org *Past Pres.* Sylvie Brikiatis, Nesmith Lib., 8 Fellows Rd., Windham 03087. Tel. 603-432-7154, e-mail SBrikiatis@NesmithLibrary.org.

Address correspondence to New Hampshire Lib. Assn., c/o New Hampshire State Lib., 20 Park St., Concord 03301-6314. E-mail nhlaexecutive@googlegroups.com.

World Wide Web http://nhlibrarians.org.

New Jersey

Memb. 1,800. Term of Office. July–June. Publication. *New Jersey Libraries NEWSletter* (q.). E-mail newsletter_editor@njlamembers.org.

Pres. Leah Wagner, Monroe Township Lib. (Middlesex). E-mail lwagner@monroetwplibrary.org *1st V.P./Pres.-Elect* Tonya Garcia, Long Branch Public Lib. E-mail tgarcia@lbpl@gmail.com; *2nd V.P.* Nancy Weiner, William Paterson Univ. E-mail weinern@wpunj.edu; *Secy.* Maureen Donohue, Middlesex Public Lib. E-mail mdonohue@middlexlibrarynj.org; *Treas.* Amy Babcock-Landry, Livingston Public Lib. E-mail babcock-landry@livingston.bccls.org; *ALA Councilor* Jayne Beline, Parsippany Lib. E-mail Jayne.Beline@parsippanylibrary.org; *Past Pres.* Michael Maziekien, Cranford Public Lib. E-mail maziekiennjla@gmail.com; *Exec. Dir.* Patricia Tumulty, New Jersey Lib. Assn., P.O. Box 1534, Trenton

08607. Tel. 609-394-8032, fax 609-394-8164, e-mail ptumulty@njla.org.

Address correspondence to the executive director.

New Jersey Lib. Assn., P.O. Box 1534, Trenton 08607. Tel. 609-394-8032, fax 609-394-8164.

World Wide Web http://www.njla.org.

New Mexico

Memb. 550. Term of Office. Apr.–Apr. Publication. *NMLA Newsletter* (bi-mo., online). *Ed.* Robyn Gleasner. E-mail newsletter@nmla.org.

Pres. John Sandstrom. E-mail jsand713@nmsu.edu; *V.P./Pres.-Elect* David Cox. E-mail spiriteagle75@aol.com; *Secy.* Sarah Obenauf. E-mail secretary@nmla.org; *Treas.* Bridget O'Leary Storer. E-mail treasurer@nmla.org; *Members-at-Large* Cordelia Hooee. E-mail clhooee@gmail.com, Ron Gonzales. E-mail rgonzales@grantsnm.gov, Sharon Jenkins. E-mail djenkins@nmsu.edu, Katherine Skinner. E-mail katherineskinner@ruidoso-nm.gov, *ALA-APA Councilor* Elizabeth Titus. E-mail etitus@lib.nmsu.edu.

Address correspondence to New Mexico Lib. Assn., P.O. Box 26074, Albuquerque 87125. Tel. 505-400-7309, fax 505-544-5740, e-mail contact@nmla.org.

World Wide Web http://nmla.org.

New York

Memb. 4,000. Term of Office. Nov.–Nov. Publication. *The eBulletin* (6x yearly, online).

Pres. Michelle Young, Clarkson Univ.; *Pres.-Elect* Jen Cannell, Capital Region BOCES; *Treas.* Cassie Guthrie, Greece Public Lib.; *Treas.-Elect* Roger Reyes, Suffolk Coop. Lib. System; *ALA Chapter Councilor* Jennifer Ferriss, Saratoga Springs Public Lib.; *Past Pres.* Tim Burke, Upper Hudson Lib. System. Tel. 518-437-9880, e-mail tim.burke@uhls.lib.ny.us; *Exec. Dir.* Jeremy Johannesen, New York Lib. Assn., 6021 State Farm Rd., Guilderland 12084. Tel. 518-432-6952, fax 518-427-1697, e-mail director@nyla.org.

Address correspondence to the executive director.

New York Lib. Assn., 6021 State Farm Rd., Guilderland 12084. Tel. 518-432-6952, fax 518-427-1697, e-mail info@nyla.org.

World Wide Web http://www.nyla.org.

North Carolina

Memb. 1,100. Term of Office. Oct.–Oct. Publication. *North Carolina Libraries* (1–2x yearly, online). *Ed.* Ralph Scott. E-mail scottr@ecu.edu.

Pres. Michael A. Crumpton, Walter Clinton Jackson Lib., Univ. of North Carolina–Greensboro, 320 College Ave., Greensboro 27412. Tel. 336-256-1213, e-mail macrumpt@uncg.edu; *V.P./Pres.-Elect* Lorrie Russell, High Point Public Lib., 901 Main St., High Point 27262. Tel. 336-883-3644, e-mail ncla.vicepresident@gmail.com; *Secy.* Denelle Eads, UNC Charlotte, Atkins Lib., 9201 University City Blvd., Charlotte 28223-0001. Tel. 704-687-1165, e-mail deads@uncc.edu; *Treas.* Siobhan Loendorf, Catawba County Lib., 115 West C St., Newton 28658. Tel. 828-465-8292, e-mail nclatreasurer@gmail.com; *Treas.-Elect* Amy Harris, Univ. of North Carolina–Greensboro, P.O. Box 26170, Greensboro 27412-0001. Tel. 336-256-0275, e-mail a_harri2@uncg.edu; *ALA Councilor* Lynda Kellam, UNC Greensboro / Walter Clinton Jackson Lib., P.O. Box 26170, Greensboro 27412. Tel. 336-303-8104, e-mail lmkellam@uncg.edu; *Past Pres.* Rodney Lippard, Univ. of South Carolina Aiken, 471 University Pkwy. Aiken 29801. Tel. 919-923-7716, e-mail rodneyl@usca.edu.

Address correspondence to the executive assistant.

North Carolina Lib. Assn., 265 East Chester Dr., Suite 133, #364, High Point 27262. Tel. 919-839-6252, fax 888-977-3143, e-mail nclaonline@gmail.com.

World Wide Web http://www.nclaonline.org.

North Dakota

Memb. (Indiv.) 300+. Term of Office. Sept.–Sept. Publication. *The Good Stuff* (q.). *Ed.* Marlene Anderson, Bismarck State College Lib., P.O. Box 5587, Bismarck 58506-5587. Tel. 701-224-5578, e-mail marlene.anderson@bismarckstate.edu.

Pres. Margaret (Maggie) Townsend, Legacy High School. E-mail president@ndla.info; *Pres.-Elect* Traci Lund, Divide County Public Lib. E-mail dcl@nccray.net; *Secy.* Eric Stroshane, North Dakota State Lib. E-mail estroshane@nd.gov; *Treas.* Aaron Stefanich, Grand Forks Public Lib., 2110 Lib. Cir., Grand Forks

58201. Tel. 701-772-8116, e-mail aaron.stefanich@gflibrary.com; *ALA Councilor* Laurie L. McHenry, Univ. of North Dakota–Thormodsgard Law Lib. E-mail laurie.mchenry@email.und.edu; *Past Pres.* Stephanie Kom, State Historical Society of North Dakota. E-mail sbaltzerkom@nd.gov.

Address correspondence to the president.

North Dakota Lib. Assn., 604 E. Boulevard Ave., Bismarck 58505.

World Wide Web http://www.ndla.info.

Ohio

Memb. 2,700+. Term of Office. Jan.–Dec. Publication. *OLC News* (online).

Chair Kacie Armstrong, Euclid Public Lib., Tel. 216-261-5300, e-mail kacie.armstrong@euclidlibrary.org; *V.Chair/Chair-Elect* Cheryl Kuonen, Mentor Public Lib., Tel. 440-255-8811, e-mail cheryl.kuonen@mentorpl.org; *Secy./Treas.* Paula Brehm-Heeger, Public Lib. of Cincinnati and Hamilton County. Tel. 513-369-6941, e-mail paula.brehm-heeger@cincinnatilibrary.org; *Immediate Past Chair* Nicholas Tepe, Athens County Public Libs. Tel. 740-753-2118, e-mail ntepe@myacpl.org; *ALA Councilor* Meg Delaney, Toledo Lucas County Public Lib., Tel. 419-259-5333, e-mail meg.delaney@toledolibrary.org; *Dir. of Comms.* Angie Jacobsen, Ohio Lib. Council, 1105 Schrock Rd., Ste. 440, Columbus, OH 43229. Tel. 614-410-8092, e-mail ajacobsen@olc.org.

Address correspondence to the director of communications.

Ohio Lib. Council, 1105 Schrock Rd., Suite 440, Columbus 43229. Tel. 614-410-8092.

World Wide Web http://www.olc.org.

Oklahoma

Memb. (Indiv.) 1,000; (Inst.) 60. Term of Office. July–June. Publication. *Oklahoma Librarian* (bi-mo.).

Pres. Stacy Schrank; *V.P./Pres.-Elect* Lisa Wells; *Secy.* Jackie Kropp; *Treas.* Susan Urban; *ALA Councilor* Sarah Robbins; *Past Pres.* Linda Pye.

Address correspondence to Oklahoma Lib. Assn., 1190 Meramec Station Rd., Suite 207, Ballwin, MO 63021-6902. Tel. 800-843-8482, fax 636-529-1396, e-mail ola@amigos.org.

World Wide Web http://www.oklibs.org.

Oregon

Memb. (Indiv.) 1,000+. Publications. *OLA Hotline.* (bi-w.). E-mail olahotline@olaweb.org; *OLA Quarterly.* (q.) *Ed.* Charles Wood. E-mail wuchakewu@gmail.com.

Pres. Esther Moberg, Seaside Public Lib. E-mail olapresident@olaweb.org; *V.P./Pres.-Elect* Elaine Hirsch, Lewis & Clark College, Watzek Lib. E-mail olavp@olaweb.org; *Secy.* Kathy Street, Oregon Trail Lib. District. E-mail kstreet@otld.org; *Treas.* Lori Wamsley, Mt. Hood Community College Lib. E-mail olatreasurer@olaweb.org; *Memb.-at-Large* Forrest Johnson, Linn Benton Community College Lib. E-mail fjohnso5@g.emporia.edu; *ALA Representative* Danielle Jones, Multnomah County Lib. E-mail daniellej@multco.us; *Past Pres.* Buzzy Nielsen, Crook County Lib. E-mail olapastpresident@olaweb.org.

Address correspondence to Oregon Lib. Assn., P.O. Box 3067, La Grande 97850. Tel. 541-962-5824, e-mail ola@olaweb.org.

World Wide Web http://www.olaweb.org.

Pennsylvania

Memb. 1,900+. Term of Office. Jan.–Dec. Publication. *PaLA Bulletin* (q.).

Pres. Denise Sticha, Berks Co. Public Libs. E-mail denise.sticha@berks.lib.pa.us; *1st V.P.* Michele Legate; *2nd V.P. (2019 Erie Conference)* Paula Collins, Clearfield Co. Public Lib. E-mail pcollins@clearfieldcountylibrary.org; *2nd V.P. (2020 Kalahari)* Slyvia Orner; *3rd V.P.* Sheli Pratt-McHugh, Univ. of Scranton. E-mail michelle.mchugh@scranton.edu; *Treas.* Leslie Christianson, Marywood Univ. E-mail lchristianson@maryu.marywood.edu, gregory@lycoming.edu; *ALA Councilor* Rob Lesher, Dauphin County Lib. System. Tel. 717-234-4961, e-mail rlesher@dcls.org; *Past Pres.* Tina Hertel, Muhlenberg College. Tel. 484-664-3550, e-mail thertel@muhlenberg.edu; *Exec. Dir.* Christi Buker. Pennsylvania Lib. Assn., 220 Cumberland Pkwy., Suite 10, Mechanicsburg 17055. Tel. 717-766-7663, e-mail christi@palibraries.org.

Address correspondence to the executive director.

Pennsylvania Lib. Assn., 220 Cumberland Parkway, Suite 10, Mechanicsburg 17055. Tel. 717-766-7663, fax 717-766-5440.

World Wide Web http://www.palibraries.org.

Rhode Island

Memb. (Indiv.) 350+; (Inst.) 50+. Term of Office. June–June. Publication. *RILA Bulletin* (6x yearly). *Ed.* Rachael Juskuv, Bryant Univ. Tel. 401-232-6291. E-mail rilabulletin@gmail.com.

Pres. Kieran Ayton, Rhode Island College, 600 Mt. Pleasant Ave., Providence, 02908. Tel. 401-456-9604, e-mail kayton@ric.edu; *V.P.* Julie Holden, Cranston Public Lib. E-mail julieholden@cranstonlibrary.org; *Secy.* Chelsea Watts, CCRI Newport. E-mail secretary@rilibraries.org; *Treas.* Beatrice Pulliam, Providence Public Lib. E-mail bpulliam@provlib.org; *Memb.-at-Large* Lisa Perry, East Providence Public Lib. E-mail lperry@eplib.org; David Meincke, Johnson and Wales Univ. Lib. E-mail dmeincke@jwu.edu; *ALA Councilor* Jack Martin, Providence Public Lib. E-mail jmartin@provlib.org; *Past Pres.* Aaron Coutu, Cumberland Public Lib., 1464 Diamond Hill Rd., Cumberland 02864. Tel. 401-333-2552 ext. 128, e-mail acoutu@cumberlandlibrary.org.

Address correspondence to Rhode Island Lib. Assn., P.O. Box 6765, Providence 02940.

World Wide Web http://www.rilibraries.org.

South Carolina

Memb. 350+. Term of Office. Jan.–Dec. Publication. *South Carolina Libraries* (s.-ann., online). *Ed.* Brent Appling, Univ. of South Carolina. Tel. 803-777-0994, e-mail applingm@mailbox.sc.edu.

Pres. Amanda Stone, South Carolina State Lib., 1500 Senate St., Columbia 29201. Tel. 803-734-4816, e-mail astone@statelibrary.sc.gov; *1st V.P.* Nathan Flowers, Francis Marion Univ., 4822 E. Palmetto St., Florence 29506. Tel. 843-661-1306, e-mail nflowers@fmarion.edu; *2nd V.P.* Michelle Rubino, Greenville Technical College Libs., 506 S. Pleasantburg Dr., Bldg. 102, Greenville 29607. Tel. 864-236-6439, e-mail michelle.rubino@gvltec.edu; *Secy.* Amanda Reed, Richland Lib., 1431 Assembly St., Columbia 29201. Tel. 803-929-3457, e-mail areed@richlandlibrary.com. *Treas.* Steven Sims, Francis Marion Univ., 4822 E. Palmetto St., Florence 29506. Tel. 843-661-1299, e-mail ssims@fmarion.edu; *ALA Councilor* Kevin Reynolds, Wofford College, 429 North Church St., Spartanburg 29303. Tel. 864-597-4300, e-mail reynoldsjk@wofford.edu; *Past Pres.* Jimmie Epling, Darlington County Lib. System, 204 N. Main St., Darlington 29532. Tel. 843-398-4940 ext. 303, e-mail jimmie.epling@darlington-lib.org; *Exec. Secy.* Donald Wood, South Carolina Lib. Assn., P.O. Box 1763, Columbia 29202. Tel. 803-252-1087, fax 803-252-0589, e-mail scla@capconsc.com.

Address correspondence to the executive secretary.

South Carolina Lib. Assn., P.O. Box 1763, Columbia 29202. Tel. 803-252-1087, e-mail scla@capconsc.com.

World Wide Web http://www.scla.org.

South Dakota

Memb. (Indiv.) 450+; (Inst.) 60+. Publication. *Book Marks* (q.). *Ed.* Kelly Henkel Thompson, 1200 W. Univ. Ave., Box 918, Mitchell 57301. Tel. 605-995-2677, e-mail bookmarkssd@gmail.com.

Pres. Maria Gruener, Watertown Regional Lib., Watertown. E-mail mgruener@watertownsd.us; *V.P./Pres.-Elect* Ashia Gustafson, Brookings Public Lib., Brookings. E-mail agustafson@cityofbrookings.org; *Recording Secretary* Kim Bonen, K. O. Lee Aberdeen Public Lib., Aberdeen. E-mail kbonen@g.emporia.edu; *Exec. Secy./Treas.* Audrea Buller, Lennox Community Lib., Lennox. E-mail SDLibraryAssociation@gmail.com; *ALA Councilor* Lisa Brunick, Augustana Univ., Sioux Falls. E-mail lisa.brunick@augie.edu; *Past Pres.* Mary Francis, Dakota State Univ., Madison. E-mail mary.francis@dsu.edu.

Address correspondence to the executive secretary.

South Dakota Lib. Assn., P.O. Box 283, Lennox 57039. Tel. 605-214-8785.

World Wide Web http://www.sdlibraryassociation.org.

Tennessee

Memb. 600+. Term of Office. July–June. Publications. *Tennessee Libraries* (q.; online). *Ed.* Sharon Holderman, Tennessee Tech Univ. Lib.

E-mail sholderman@tntech.edu; *TLA Newsletter* (q.; online). *Ed.* Holly Mills. E-mail hcmills@tntech.edu.

Pres. Jeffie Nicholson. E-mail jeffienicholson@williamsoncounty-tn.org; *V.P./Pres.-Elect* Jill Rael. E-mail jhistoryfinder@gmail.com; *Recording Secy.* Sean Hogan. E-mail hogand@apsu.edu; *Past Pres.* Richard Groves, Williamson County Lib., 1314 Columbia Ave., Franklin 37064. E-mail richardpgroves@gmail.com. *Exec. Dir.* Annelle R. Huggins, Tennessee Lib. Assn., P.O. Box 241074, Memphis 38124-1074. Tel. 901-485-6952, e-mail arhuggins1@comcast.net.

Address correspondence to the executive director.

Tennessee Lib. Assn., P.O. Box 241074, Memphis 38124-1074. Tel. 901-485-6952, e-mail arhuggins1@comcast.net.

World Wide Web http://tnla.org.

Texas

Memb. 6,500+. Term of Office. Apr.–Apr. Publications. *Texas Library Journal* (q.), *Ed.* Wendy Woodland. E-mail wendyw@txla.org, *TLACast* (6–8x yearly; online).

Pres. Jennifer LaBoon, Fort Worth ISD; *Pres.-Elect* Cecilia Barham, North Richland Hills Public Lib.; *Treas.* Edward Melton, Harris County Public Lib.; *Rep.-at-Large* Daniel Burgard, Univ. of North Texas Health Science Ctr.; Christina Gola, Univ. of Houston; Janice Newsum, Houston ISD; Martha (Marty) Rossi, ESC—20. *ALA Councilor* Mary Woodard, Mesquite ISD; *Past Pres.* Ling Hwey Jeng, Texas Woman's Univ. School of Lib. and Information Studies; *Exec. Dir.* Dana Braccia, Texas Lib. Assn., 3355 Bee Cave Rd., Ste. 401, Austin 78746-6763. Tel. 512-328-1518 ext. 151, e-mail danab@txla.org.

Address correspondence to the executive director.

Texas Lib. Assn., 3355 Bee Cave Rd., Suite 401, Austin 78746-6763. Tel. 512-328-1518, fax 512-328-8852, e-mail tla@txla.org.

World Wide Web http://www.txla.org.

Utah

Memb. 650. Publication. *Utah Libraries News* (q.; online). *Ed.* Mindy Hale. E-mail mindynhale@gmail.com.

Pres. Rebekah Cummings, J. Willard Marriott Lib., Univ. of Utah. Tel. 801-581-7701, e-mail rebekah.cummings@utah.edu; *V.P.* Vern Waters, South Jordan Lib. E-mail vwaters@slcolibrary.org; *Treas.* Javaid Lal, 15 N. Temple, Salt Lake City 84150. E-mail JLal@ula.org; *Memb.-at-Large* Shawn Bliss. E-mail snbliss@utah.gov; Emily Darowski. E-mail emily_darowski@byu.edu; Xiaolian Deng. E-mail xdeng@slcolibrary.org; Joe Everett. E-mail jeverett@familysearch.org; Kim Fong. E-mail kfong@murray.utah.gov; Daniel Mauchley. E-mail dmauchley@duchesne.utah.gov; Adriana Parker. E-mail adriana.parker@utah.edu; *ALA Chapter Councilor* Pamela Martin. E-mail pamela.martin@usu.edu; *Past Pres.* Dan Compton, Summit County Lib., 1885 W. Ute Blvd., Park City 84098. Tel. 435-615-3947, e-mail dcompton@summitcounty.org; *Exec. Dir.* Barbara Hopkins, Canyons School District, 9150 S. 500 W., Sandy 84070. Tel. 801-826-5095, e-mail barbaraw.hopkins@gmail.com.

Address correspondence to the executive director.

World Wide Web http://www.ula.org.

Vermont

Memb. 400. Publication. *VLA News* (q.). *Ed.* Janet Clapp, Rutland Free Lib., 10 Court St., Rutland. Tel. 802-773-1860, e-mail jclappmls@gmail.com or vermontlibrariesnews@gmail.com.

Pres. Cindy Weber, Stowe Free Lib., 90 Pond St., Stowe 05672. Tel. 802-253-6145, e-mail vermontlibrariespresident@gmail.com; *V.P./Pres.-Elect* Amy Olsen, Lanpher Memorial Lib., 141 Main St., Hyde Park 05655. Tel. 802-888-4628, e-mail vermontlibrariesvicepresident@gmail.com; *Secy.* Kelly McCagg, Burnham Memorial Lib. 898 Main St., Colchester 05446. Tel. 802-264-5661, e-mail kmccagg@colchestervt.gov; *Treas.* Susan Smolinsky, Peacham Lib., 656 Bayley Hazen Rd., Peacham 05862. Tel. 802-592-3216, e-mail vermontlibrariestreasurer@gmail.com; *ALA Councilor* Marti Fiske, Dorothy Alling Memorial Lib., 21 Library Ln., Williston 05495. Tel. 802-878-4918, e-mail marti@williston.lib.vt.us; *Past Pres.* Margaret Woodruff, Charlotte Public Lib., 115 Ferry Rd.,

Charlotte 05445. Tel. 802-425-3864, e-mail vermontlibrariespastpresident@gmail.com.

Address correspondence to Vermont Lib. Assn., P.O. Box 803, Burlington 05402.

World Wide Web http://www.vermontlibraries.org.

Virginia

Memb. 950+. Term of Office. Oct.–Oct. Publication. *Virginia Libraries* (ann.). *Ed.* Virginia (Ginny) Pannabecker, Virginia Tech. E-mail vpannabe@vt.edu.

Pres. Jessica Scalph, Haymarket Gainesville Community Lib., 14870 Lightner Rd. Haymarket. Tel. 703 792-8702, e-mail jscalph@pwcgov.org; *Pres.-Elect* Jennifer Resor-Whicker, Radford Univ., McConnell Lib., P.O. Box 6881, Radford 24142. Tel. 540-831-5691, e-mail jrwhicker@radford.edu; *2nd V.P.* Adrian L. Whicker, Roanoke County Public Lib. System, 6303 Merriman Rd., Roanoke 24018. Tel. 540-777-8776, e-mail awhicker@roanokecountyva.gov; *Secy.* Kayla Payne, Staunton Public Lib. *Treas.* Cori Biddle, Bridgewater College Lib., 402 E. College St., Bridgewater 22812. Tel. 540-828-5415, e-mail cstrickl@bridgewater.edu; *ALA Councilor* Samantha Thomason, Central Rappahannock Regional Lib., 1201 Caroline St., Fredericksburg 22401. Tel. 540-372-1144, e-mail sthomason@crrl.org; *Past Pres.* Todd D. Elliott, Portsmouth Public Lib., 601 Court St., Portsmouth 23704. Tel. 757-393-8365, e-mail elliottt@portsmouthva.gov; *Exec. Dir.* Lisa Varga, Virginia Lib. Assn., P.O. Box 56312, Virginia Beach 23456. Tel. 757-689-0594, e-mail vla.lisav@cox.net.

Address correspondence to the executive director.

Virginia Lib. Assn., P.O. Box 56312, Virginia Beach 23456. Tel. 757-689-0594, fax 757-447-3478, e-mail vla.lisav@cox.net.

World Wide Web http://www.vla.org.

Washington

Memb. (Indiv.) 742, (Inst.) 47. Publications. *Alki: The Washington Library Association Journal* (3x yearly, online). *Ed.* Di Zhang, Seattle Public Lib. E-mail alkieditor@wla.org.

Pres. Rhonda Gould, Walla Walla County Rural Lib. District. E-mail rhondag@wwrurallibrary.com; *V.P./Pres.-Elect* Emily Keller, Univ. of Washington Libs. Tel. 206-685-2660, e-mail emkeller@uw.edu;

Treas. Kim Hixson, Yakima Valley Libs. E-mail khixson@yvl.org; *ALA Councilor* Steven Bailey, King County Lib. System; *Past Pres.* Craig Seasholes, Seattle Public Schools, Tel. 206-854-7956, e-mail wlacraig@gmail.com; *Exec. Dir.* Kate Laughlin, Washington Lib. Assn., P.O. Box 33808, Seattle 98133. Tel. 206-823-1138, e-mail kate@wla.org.

Address correspondence to the executive director.

Washington Lib. Assn., P.O. Box 33808, Seattle 98133. Tel. 206-823-1138, e-mail info@wla.org.

World Wide Web http://www.wla.org.

West Virginia

Memb. 650+. Publication. *West Virginia Libraries* (6x yearly). *Ed.* Kaity Carson. Tel. 304-295-7771, e-mail kaity@viennapubliclibrary.org.

Pres. Megan Hope Tarbett, Putnam County Library, 4219 State Route 34, Hurricane 25526. Tel. 304-757-7308, e-mail megan.tarbett@putnam.lib.wv.us; *1st V.P./Pres.-Elect* Heather Campbell-Shock. West Virginia Lib. Commission, 1900 Kanawha Blvd., Charleston 25305. Tel. 304-558-2069, e-mail Heather.S.Campbell@wv.gov; *2nd V.P.* Todd Duncan, South Charleston Public Lib., 312 4th Ave., South Charleston 25303. Tel. 304-744-6561, e-mail todd@scplwv.org; *Secy.* Jessica McMillen, WVU Libs., P.O. Box 6069, 1549 University Ave., Morgantown 26506. Tel. 304-293-0312, e-mail jessica.mcmillen@mail.wvu.edu; *Treas.* Brian Raitz, Parkersburg and Wood County Public Lib., 3100 Emerson Ave., Parkersburg 26104. Tel. 304-420-4587 ext. 501, fax 304-420-4589, e-mail wvlibrarydude@gmail.com; *ALA Councilor* Majed Khader, Marshall Univ., 1625 Campbell Dr., Huntington 25705. Tel. 304-696-3121, fax 304-696-5219, e-mail khader@marshall.edu; *Past Pres.* Brenna Call, Vienna Public Lib., 2300 River Rd., Vienna 26105. Tel. 304-295-7771, e-mail brenna@viennapubliclibrary.org; *Exec. Dir.* Kelly Funkhouser, Morgantown Public Lib., West Virginia Lib. Assn., P.O. Box 1432, Morgantown 26507. Tel. 304-291-7425, e-mail wvlaexdir@gmail.com.

Address correspondence to the president.

World Wide Web http://www.wvla.org.

Wisconsin

Memb. 1,900. Term of Office. Jan.–Dec. Publication. *WLA eNewsletter* (3–4x yearly; online).

Pres. Scott Vrieze. E-mail vriezes@uwstout.edu; *Secy.* Desiree Bongers, Ripon Public Lib., Ripon. Tel. 920-748-6160, e-mail dbongers@riponlibrary.org; *Treas.* Katharine Clark; *ALA Councilor* Sherry Machones. E-mail smachones@northernwaters.org; *Past Pres.* Marge Loch-Wouters. E-mail lochwouters@gmail.com; *Exec. Dir.* Plumer Lovelace III, Wisconsin Lib. Assn., 4610 S. Biltmore Ln., Madison 53718. Tel. 608-245-3640, e-mail lovelace@wisconsinlibraries.org.

Address correspondence to Wisconsin Lib. Assn., 4610 S. Biltmore Ln., Madison 53718. Tel. 608-245-3640, e-mail wla@wisconsinlibraries.org.

World Wide Web http://wla.wisconsinlibraries.org.

Wyoming

Memb. 450+. Term of Office. Oct.–Oct. Publication. Newsletter (ann.; August).

Pres. Kate Mutch, Natrona County Lib. Tel. 307-237-4935 ext. 111, e-mail kmutch@natronacountylibrary.org; *V.P.* Abby Beaver, Wyoming State Lib. Tel. 307-777-5913, e-mail abby.beaver@wyo.gov; *ALA Councilor* Janice Grover-Roosa, Western Wyoming Community College; *Past Pres.* Katrina Brown, Sheridan College Mary Brown Kooi Lib. Tel. 307-675-0221, e-mail kbrown@sheridan.edu; *Exec. Secy.* Laura Grott (ex-officio), P.O. Box 1387, Cheyenne 82003. Tel. 307-632-7622, e-mail lauragrott@gmail.com.

Address correspondence to the executive secretary.

Wyoming Lib. Assn., P.O. Box 1387, Cheyenne 82003.

World Wide Web http://www.wyla.org.

Canada

Alberta

Memb. 500. Term of Office. May–April.

Pres. Norene Erickson, MacEwan Univ. E-mail president@laa.ca; *1st V.P.* Briana Ehnes, Red Deer Public Lib. E-mail 1stvicepresident@laa.ca; *2nd V.P.* Céline Gareau-Brennan, Univ. of Alberta. E-mail 2ndvicepresident@laa.ca; *Treas.* Louisa Robison, Service Alberta. E-mail treasurer@laa.ca; *Past Pres.* Deb Cryderman, Camrose Public Lib. E-mail pastpresident@laa.ca; *Exec. Dir.* Christine Sheppard, 80 Baker Cres. N.W., Calgary T2L 1R4. Tel. 403-284-5818, 877-522-5550, e-mail info@laa.ca.

Address correspondence to the executive director.

Lib. Assn. of Alberta, 80 Baker Cres. N.W., Calgary T2L 1R4. Tel. 403-284-5818, 877-522-5550.

World Wide Web http://www.laa.ca.

British Columbia

Memb. 750+. Term of Office. April–April. Publication. *BCLA Perspectives* (q.; online). E-mail perspectives@bcla.bc.ca.

Pres. Shirley Lew, Vancouver Community College Lib.; *V.P./Pres.-Elect* Chris Middlemass, Vancouver Public Lib.; *Recording Secy.* Danielle LaFrance, Vancouver Public Lib.; *Treas.* Stephanie Kripps, Vancouver Public Lib.; *Past Pres.* Anne Olsen, Univ. of British Columbia, Koerner Lib.; *Exec. Dir.* Annette DeFaveri, British Columbia Lib. Assn., 900 Howe St., Suite 150, Vancouver V6Z 2M4. Tel. 604-683-5354 or 888-683-5354, fax 604-609-0707, e-mail execdir@bcla.bc.ca.

Address correspondence to the executive director.

British Columbia Lib. Assn., 900 Howe St., Suite 150, Vancouver V6Z 2M4. Tel. 604-683-5354, e-mail bclaoffice@bcla.bc.ca.

World Wide Web http://www.bcla.bc.ca.

Manitoba

Memb. 500+. Term of Office. May–May.

Pres. Kerry Macdonald. E-mail president@mla.mb.ca; *Secy.* Kathleen Williams. E-mail secretary@mla.mb.ca; *Treas.* Kelly Murray; *Past Pres.* Alix-Rae Stefanko.

Address correspondence to Manitoba Lib. Assn., 606-100 Arthur St., Winnipeg R3B 1H3. Tel. 204-943-4567, e-mail secretary@mla.mb.ca.

World Wide Web http://www.mla.mb.ca.

Ontario

Memb. 5,000+. Publications. *Open Shelf* (mo., multimedia). *Ed.* Martha Attridge Bufton; *The Teaching Librarian* (3x yearly; memb.). *Ed.* Caroline Freibauer. E-mail teachinglibrarian@outlook.com.

Pres. Richard Reid, Durham District School Board. E-mail richard.reid@ddsb.ca; *V.P./Pres.-Elect* Andrea Cecchetto, Markham Public Lib. E-mail acecch@markham.library.on.ca; *Treas.* Janneka Guise, Univ. of Toronto. E-mail jan.guise@utoronto.ca; *Past Pres.* Kerry Badgley, North Grenville Public Lib. Board. E-mail Kerry.Badgley@canada.ca; *Exec. Dir.* Shelagh Paterson, Ontario Lib. Assn. E-mail spaterson@accessola.com.

Address correspondence to Ontario Lib. Assn., 2 Toronto St., Toronto M5C 2B6. Tel. 416-363-3388 or 866-873-9867, fax 416-941-9581 or 800-387-1181, e-mail info@accessola.com.

World Wide Web http://www.accessola.com.

Quebec

Memb. (Indiv.) 100+. Term of Office. May–April. Publication. *ABQLA Bulletin* (3x yearly). *Ed.* Maria Ressina.

Pres. Katherine Hanz. E-mail katherine.hanz@mcgill.ca; *V.P.* Eamon Duffy; *Treas.* Anne Wade. E-mail wada@education.concordia.ca; *Past Pres.* Julian Taylor. E-mail jtaylorqclib@gmail.com.

Address correspondence to the president.

World Wide Web http://www.abqla.qc.ca.

Saskatchewan

Memb. 200+.

Pres. Alison Jantz, Saskatoon Theological Union, Univ. of Saskatchewan, Saskatoon. Tel. 306-270-1532, e-mail akj175@campus.usask.ca or Alison.Jantz@usask.ca; *V.P. Membership and Pubns.* Linda Winkler, Univ. of Regina. E-mail linda.winkler@uregina.ca; *V.P. Advocacy and Development* Tony Murphy, Wapiti Regional Lib., 145 12 St. E., Prince Albert S6V 1B6. Tel. 306-953-4750, e-mail director@wapitilibrary.ca; *Treas.* Brad Doerksen, Dr. John Archer Lib., Univ. of Regina, 3737 Wascana Pkwy., Regina S4S 0A2. Tel. 306-337-2927, e-mail brad.doerksen@uregina.ca; *Memb.-at-Large* Lindsay Baker, Wapiti Regional Lib., 145 12th St. E., Prince Albert S6V 1B7. Tel. 306-953-4761, e-mail commservices@wapitilibrary.ca; Alan Kilpatrick. E-mail akilpatrick@lawsociety.sk.ca; Lukas Miller, Lib., Regina General Hospital, Regina, Saskatchewan Health Authority, 1440 14th Ave., Regina S4P 0W5. Tel. 306-766-4142, e-mail lukas.miller@saskhealthauthority.ca; Nina Verishagen, Saskatchewan Polytechnic Lib., 1130 Ldylwyld Dr., Saskatoon. Tel. 306-659-4425, e-mail nina.verishagen@saskpolytech.ca; *Past Pres.* Gwen Schmidt, Saskatoon Public Lib.; *Exec. Dir.* Dorothea Warren Saskatchewan Lib. Assn., #15 – 2010 7th Ave. Regina S4R 1C3. Tel. 306-780-9413, fax 306-780-9447, e-mail slaexdir@sasktel.net.

Address correspondence to the executive director.

Saskatchewan Lib. Assn., #15 – 2010 7th Ave., Regina S4R 1C3. Tel. 306-780-9413, fax 306-780-9447.

World Wide Web http://www.saskla.ca.

Regional

Atlantic Provinces: N.B., N.L., N.S., P.E.I.

Memb. (Indiv.) 320+; (Inst.) Publication. *APLA Bulletin* (4x yearly). *Eds.* Katherine Felix, Marc Harper, Margaret Vail. E-mail bulletin@apla.ca.

Pres. Patricia Doucette, Holland College, Prince Edward Island. Tel. 902-566-9350, e-mail president@apla.ca; *V.P./Pres.-Elect* Trecia Schell, Pictou-Antigonish Regional Lib. E-mail president-elect@apla.ca; *V.P. Membership* Carolyn DeLorey, Angus L. Macdonald Lib., St. Francis Xavier Univ., Antigonish, NS. Tel. 902-867-2343, e-mail membership@apla.ca; *Secy.* Cynthia Holt, Council of Atlantic Univ. Libs./Conseil des bibliothèques universitaires de l'Atlantique (CAUL-CBUA). E-mail caholt1@gmail.com; *Treas.* Maggie Neilson, Acadia Univ., Vaughan Memorial Lib., Room 420, 50 Acadia St., Wolfville, NS B4P 2R6. Tel. 902-585-1718, e-mail maggiejean.neilson@acadiau.ca; *Past Pres.* Kathryn Rose, Queen Elizabeth II Lib., Memorial Univ. of Newfoundland. Tel. 709-864-3139, e-mail past-president@apla.ca.

Address correspondence to Atlantic Provinces Lib. Assn., Kenneth C. Rowe Mgt. Bldg., Dalhousie Univ., 6100 University Ave., Suite 4010, P.O. Box 15000, Halifax, NS B3H 4R2. E-mail contact@apla.ca.

World Wide Web http://www.apla.ca.

Mountain Plains: Ariz., Colo., Kans., Mont., Neb., Nev., N.Dak., N.Mex., Okla., S.Dak., Utah, Wyo.

Memb. 700. Term of Office. Oct.–Oct. Publications. *MPLA Newsletter* (6x yearly, online). *Ed.* Melanie Argo, Madison Public Lib., 209 E. Center, Madison, SD 57042. Tel. 605-256-7525, e-mail editor@mpla.us.

Pres. Leslie H. Langley, Southeastern Public Lib., System, Wister Public Lib., 101 Caston Ave., Wister, OK 74966. Tel. 918-655-7654, fax 918-655-3267, e-mail president@mpla.us; *V.P./Pres.-Elect* Stephen Sweeney, St. John Vianney Seminary, Cardinal Stafford Lib., 1300 South Steele St., Denver, CO 80210. Tel. 303-715-3192, fax 303-715-2037, e-mail vice president@mpla.us; *Recording Secy.* Brenda Hemmelman, South Dakota State Lib., 800 Governors Dr., Pierre, SD 57501. Tel. 605-773-5075, fax 605-773-6962, e-mail secretary@mpla.us; *Past Pres.* Mickey Coalwell, Lib. Systems and Services, LLC, 7134 McGee St., Kansas City, MO 64114. Tel. 816-804-0942, e-mail pastpresident@mpla.us; *Exec. Secy.* Judy Zelenski, 14293 West Center Dr., Lakewood, CO 80228. Tel. 303-985-7795, e-mail exec secretary@mpla.us.

Address correspondence to the executive secretary.

Mountain Plains Lib. Assn., 14293 West Center Dr., Lakewood, CO 80228. Tel. 303-985-7795, e-mail execsecretary@mpla.us.

World Wide Web http://www.mpla.us.

New England: Conn., Maine, Mass., N.H., R.I., Vt.

Memb. (Indiv.) 650+. Term of Office. Nov.–Oct. Publication. *NELA News* (blog).

Pres. Susan Edmonds, Milford Town Lib., Milford, MA. Tel. 413-323-5925, ext. 102, e-mail president@nelib.org; *V.P.* Jennifer Bruneau, Boylston Public Lib., Boylston, MA. Tel. 413-323-5925, ext. 103, e-mail vice-president@nelib.org; *Secy.* Lucinda Walker, Norwich Public Lib., Norwich, VT. Tel. 413-323-5925, ext. 106. E-mail secretary@nelib.org; *Treas.* Bernie Prochnik, Bath Public Lib., Bath, NH. Tel. 413-323-5925, ext. 105, e-mail treasurer@nelib.org; *Senior Director* Jean Canosa-Albano, Springfield City Libr., Springfield, MA. Tel. 413-323-5925, ext. 108, e-mail director-sr@nelib.org; *Junior Director* Emily Weiss, Bedford Public Lib., Bedford, NH. Tel. 413-323-5925, ext. 107, e-mail director-jr@nelib.org; *Past Pres.* Debbi Dutcher, Maxfield Public Lib., Loudon, NH. Tel. 413-323-5925, ext. 104, e-mail past-president@nelib.org; *Admin.* Robert Scheier. NELA Office. 55 N. Main St., Unit 49, Belchertown, MA 01007. Tel. 413-323-5925, ext. 100, e-mail library-association-administrator@nelib.org.

Address correspondence to the administrator. New England Lib. Assn., 55 N. Main St., Unit 49, Belchertown, MA 01007. Tel. 413-323-5925, e-mail rlibrary-association-administrator @nelib.org.

World Wide Web http://www.nelib.org.

Pacific Northwest: Alaska, Idaho, Mont., Ore., Wash., Alberta, B.C.

Memb. 170+. Term of Office. Aug.–Aug. Publication. *PNLA Quarterly. Eds.* Samantha Schmehl Hines, Peninsula College, Port Angeles, WA. Tel. 360-417-6275, e-mail shines@pencol.edu or pqeditors@gmail.com.

Pres. Jenny Grenfell, North Mason Timberland Lib., Belfair, WA. Tel. 360-275-3232, e-mail ktfjen@gmail.com; *1st V.P. / Pres.-Elect* Tori Koch, Billings Public Lib., Billings, MT. Tel. 406-657-8295, e-mail kocht@ci.billings.mt.us; *2nd V.P. / Membership Chair* Jay Peters, Coquitlam Public Lib., 575 Poirier St. Coquitlam BC V3J 6A9. Tel. 604-937-4148 ext. 4248, e-mail jpeters@coqlibrary.ca; *Secy.* Sheree West, Spokane County Lib. District, Spokane, WA. Tel. 509-893-8412, e-mail swest@scld.org; *Treas.* Lisa Fraser, PNLA, P.O. Box 1032, Bothell WA 98041. Tel. 425-369-3458, e-mail lgfraser@kcls.org; *Past Pres.* Rick Stoddart, Univ. of Idaho Lib., Moscow, ID. Tel. 208-885-2504, e-mail rstoddart@uidaho.edu.

Address correspondence to Pacific Northwest Lib. Assn., P.O. Box 1032, Bothell WA 98041.

World Wide Web http://www.pnla.org.

Southeastern: Ala., Ark., Fla., Ga., Ky., La., Miss., N.C., S.C., Tenn., Va., W.Va.

Memb. 500. Publication. *The Southeastern Librarian (SELn)* (q.). *Ed.* Perry Bratcher, 503A Steely Lib., Northern Kentucky Univ., Highland Heights, KY 41099. Tel. 859-572-6309, fax 859-572-6181, e-mail bratcher@nku.edu.

Pres. Tim Dodge, Auburn Univ. Libs., Auburn, AL. E-mail president@selaonline.org; *Pres.-Elect* Melissa Dennis, Univ. of Mississippi, University, MS. E-mail president.elect@selaonline.org; *Secy.* Crystal Gates, William F. Laman Public Lib., North Little Rock, AR. E-mail secretary@selaonline.org; *Treas.* Beverly James, Greenville County Lib. System, Greenville, SC. E-mail treasurer@selaonline.org; *Archivist* Camille McCutcheon, Univ. of South Carolina Upstate, Spartanburg, SC. E-mail archivist@selaonline.org; *Past Pres.* Linda Suttle Harris, Univ. of Alabama at Birmingham.

Address correspondence to Southeastern Lib. Assn., Admin. Services, P.O. Box 30703, Savannah, GA 31410. Tel. 912-999-7979, e-mail selaadminservices@selaonline.org.

World Wide Web http://selaonline.org.

State and Provincial Library Agencies

The state library administrative agency in each of the U.S. states will have the latest information on its state plan for the use of federal funds under the Library Services and Technology Act (LSTA). The directors and addresses of these state agencies are listed below.

United States

Alabama

Nancy Pack, Dir., Alabama Public Lib. Svc., 6030 Monticello Dr., Montgomery 36117. Tel. 334-213-3900, fax 334-213-3993, e-mail npack@apls.state.al.us. World Wide Web http://statelibrary.alabama.gov.

Alaska

Patience Frederiksen, Dir., Alaska State Lib., P.O. Box 110571, Juneau 99811-0571. Tel. 907-465-2911, fax 907-465-2151, e-mail patience.frederiksen@alaska.gov. World Wide Web http://library.state.ak.us.

Arizona

Holly Henley, State Libn. and Dir. of Lib. Svcs., Arizona State Lib., Archives and Public Records, 1700 W. Washington, 7th Fl., Phoenix 85007. Tel. 602-542-6200, World Wide Web http://www.azlibrary.gov.

Arkansas

Carolyn Ashcroft, State Libn., Arkansas State Lib., 900 W. Capitol, Suite 100, Little Rock 72201. Tel. 501-682-1526, e-mail carolyn@library.arkansas.gov. World Wide Web http://www.library.arkansas.gov.

California

Greg Lucas, State Libn., California State Lib., P.O. Box 942837, Sacramento 94237-0001. Tel. 916-323-9759, fax 916-323-9768, e-mail csl-adm@library.ca.gov. World Wide Web http://www.library.ca.gov.

Colorado

Nicolle Davies, Asst. Commissioner, Colorado State Lib., 201 E. Colfax Ave., Denver 80203-1799. Tel. 303-866-6733, fax 303-866-6940, e-mail davies_n@cde.state.co.us. World Wide Web http://www.cde.state.co.us/cdelib.

Connecticut

Kendall F. Wiggin, State Libn., Connecticut State Lib., 231 Capitol Ave., Hartford 06106. Tel. 860-757-6510, fax 860-757-6503, e-mail kendall.wiggin@ct.gov. World Wide Web http://www.ctstatelibrary.org.

Delaware

Annie Norman, Dir., Delaware Division of Libs., 121 Martin Luther King Jr. Blvd. N., Dover 19901. Tel. 302-257-3001, fax 302-739-6787, e-mail annie.norman@delaware.gov. World Wide Web http://libraries.delaware.gov.

District of Columbia

Richard Reyes-Gavilan, Exec. Dir., District of Columbia Public Lib., 1990 K St. N.W., Washington, DC 20006. Tel. 202-727-1101, fax 202-727-1129, e-mail rrg@dc.gov. World Wide Web http://www.dclibrary.org.

Florida

Amy L. Johnson, Div. Dir., Division of Lib. and Info. Svcs., R.A. Gray Bldg., 500 S. Bronough St., Tallahassee 32399-0250. Tel. 850-245-6600, fax 850-245-6622, e-mail info@dos.myflorida.com. World Wide Web http://dos.myflorida.com/library-archives/.

Georgia

Julie Walker, State Libn., Georgia Public Lib. Svc., 1800 Century Pl., Suite 580, Atlanta 30345. Tel. 404-235-7140, e-mail jwalker@georgialibraries.org. World Wide Web http://www.georgialibraries.org.

Hawaii

Stacy Aldrich, State Libn., Hawaii State Public Lib. System, Office of the State Libn., 44 Merchant St., Honolulu 96813. Tel. 808-586-3704, fax 808-586-3715, e-mail stlib@librarieshawaii.org. World Wide Web http://www.librarieshawaii.org.

Idaho

Ann Joslin, State Libn., Idaho Commission for Libs., 325 W. State St., Boise 83702. Tel. 208-639-4166, fax 208-334-4016, e-mail ann.joslin@libraries.idaho.gov. World Wide Web http://libraries.idaho.gov.

Illinois

Greg McCormick, Dir., Illinois State Lib., 300 S. Second St., Springfield 62701-1796. Tel. 217-785-5600, fax 217-785-4326, e-mail islinfo@ilsos.net. World Wide Web http://www.cyberdriveillinois.com/departments/library/home.html.

Indiana

Jacob Speer, State Libn., Indiana State Lib., 315 W. Ohio St., Indianapolis 46202. Tel. 317-232-3675, e-mail jspeer@library.in.gov. World Wide Web http://www.in.gov/library.

Iowa

Michael Scott, State Libn., State Lib. of Iowa, 1112 E. Grand Ave., Des Moines 50319-0233. Tel. 800-248-4483, fax 515-281-6191, e-mail Michael.Scott@iowa.gov. World Wide Web http://www.statelibraryofiowa.org.

Kansas

Eric Norris, State Libn., Kansas State Lib., Capitol Bldg., 300 S.W. 10th Ave., Rm. 312-N, Topeka 66612. Tel. 785-296-5466, e-mail eric.norris@ks.gov. World Wide Web http://www.kslib.info.

Kentucky

Terry Manuel, Commissioner, Kentucky Dept. for Libs. and Archives, 300 Coffee Tree Rd., P.O. Box 537, Frankfort 40602-0537. Tel. 502-564-8303, e-mail terry.manuel@ky.gov. World Wide Web http://www.kdla.ky.gov.

Louisiana

Rebecca Hamilton, State Libn., State Lib. of Louisiana, 701 N. 4th St., P.O. Box 131, Baton Rouge 70821-0131. Tel. 225-342-4923, fax 225-219-4804, e-mail rhamilton@crt.state.la.us. World Wide Web http://www.state.lib.la.us.

Maine

James Ritter, State Libn., Maine State Lib., 64 State House Sta., Augusta 04333-0064. Tel. 207-287-5600, fax 207-287-5624, e-mail james.ritter@maine.gov. World Wide Web http://www.maine.gov/msl/.

Maryland

Irene M. Padilla, State Libn., Maryland State Lib., 22 S. Calhoun St., Baltimore 21223. Tel. 667-219-4800, fax 667-219-4798, e-mail md.statelibrary@maryland.gov. World Wide Web https://www.marylandlibraries.org/.

Massachusetts

James Lonergan, Dir., Massachusetts Board of Lib. Commissioners, 98 N. Washington St., Suite 401, Boston 02114-1933. Tel. 617-725-1860 ext.. 222, fax 617-725-0140, e-mail james.lonergan@state.ma.us. World Wide Web http://mblc.state.ma.us.

Michigan

Randy Riley, State Libn., Lib. of Michigan, 702 W. Kalamazoo St., P.O. Box 30007, Lansing 48909-7507. Tel. 517-335-1517, e-mail rileyr1@michigan.gov. World Wide Web http://www.michigan.gov/libraryofmichigan.

Minnesota

Jennifer R. Nelson, Dir. of State Lib. Services, Minnesota State Lib. Agency, Div. of State Lib. Svcs., MN Dept. of Educ., 1500 Hwy. 36 W., Roseville 55113. Tel. 651-582-8791, fax 651-582-8752, e-mail mde.lst@state.mn.us. World Wide Web https://education.mn.gov/MDE/dse/Lib/sls/index.htm.

Mississippi

Hulen Bivins, Exec. Dir., Mississippi Lib. Commission, 3881 Eastwood Dr., Jackson 39211. Tel. 601-432-4039, e-mail hbivins@mlc.lib.ms.us. World Wide Web http://www.mlc.lib.ms.us.

Missouri

Robin Westphal, State Libn., Missouri State Lib., 600 W. Main St., P.O. Box 387, Jefferson City 65101. Tel. 573-526-4783, e-mail robin.westphal@sos.mo.gov. World Wide Web http://www.sos.mo.gov/library.

Montana

Jennie Stapp, State Libn., Montana State Lib., 1515 E. 6th Ave., P.O. Box 201800, Helena, 59620-1800. Tel. 406-444-3116, fax 406-444-0266, e-mail jstapp2@mt.gov. World Wide Web http://msl.mt.gov.

Nebraska

Rodney G. Wagner, Dir., Nebraska Lib. Commission, 1200 N St., Suite 120, Lincoln 68508-2023. Tel. 402-471-4001, fax 402-471-2083, e-mail rod.wagner@nebraska.gov. World Wide Web http://www.nlc.nebraska.gov.

Nevada

Tod Colegrove, Admin., Nevada State Lib. and Archives, 100 N. Stewart St., Carson City 89701. Tel. 775-684-3410, fax 775-684-3311, e-mail tcolegrove@admin.nv.gov. World Wide Web http://nsla.nv.gov/.

New Hampshire

Michael York, State Libn., New Hampshire State Lib., 20 Park St., Concord 03301. Tel. 603-271-2397, e-mail michael.york@dncr.nh.gov. World Wide Web http://www.state.nh.us/nhsl.

New Jersey

Mary Chute, State Libn., New Jersey State Library, an affiliate of Thomas Edison State Univ., P.O. Box 520, Trenton 08625-0520. Tel. 609-278-2640 ext. 101, fax 609-278-2652, e-mail mchute@njstatelib.org. World Wide Web http://www.njstatelib.org.

New Mexico

Eli Guinnee, State Libn., New Mexico State Lib., 1209 Camino Carlos Rey, Santa Fe 87507-5166. Tel. 505-476-9762, e-mail Eli.Guinnee@state.nm.us. World Wide Web http://www.nmstatelibrary.org.

New York

Liza Duncan, Principal Libn., New York State Lib., Cultural Educ. Ctr., 222 Madison Ave., Albany 12230. Tel. 518-474-5946, fax 518-486-5786, e-mail Liza.Duncan@nysed.gov. World Wide Web http://www.nysl.nysed.gov/.

North Carolina

Timothy G. Owens, State Libn., State Lib. of North Carolina, Administrative Section, 4640 Mail Svc. Ctr., Raleigh 27699-4600; 109 E. Jones St., Raleigh 27601. Tel. 919-814-6784, fax 919-733-8748, e-mail timothy.owens@ncdcr.gov. World Wide Web http://statelibrary.ncdcr.gov.

North Dakota

Mary J. Soucie, State Libn., North Dakota State Lib., 604 E. Boulevard Ave., Dept. 250, Bismarck 58505-0800. Tel. 701-328-4654, fax 701-328-2040, e-mail msoucie@nd.gov. World Wide Web http://ndsl.lib.state.nd.us/.

Ohio

Beverly Cain, Agency Dir. and State Libn., State Lib. of Ohio, 274 E. First Ave., Suite 100, Columbus 43201. Tel. 616-644-6843, e-mail bcain@library.ohio.gov. World Wide Web http://www.library.ohio.gov/.

Oklahoma

Melody Kellogg, Dir., Oklahoma Dept. of Libs., 200 N.E. 18th St., Oklahoma City 73105-3298. Tel. 405-521-2502, fax 405-525-7804, World Wide Web http://www.odl.state.ok.us.

Oregon

Caren Agata, Interim State Libn., State Lib. of Oregon, 250 Winter St., N.E., Salem 97301. Tel. 503-378-5030, fax 503-585-8059, e-mail caren.agata@state.or.us. World Wide Web https://www.oregon.gov/Library.

Pennsylvania

Glenn Miller, Deputy Secy. of Educ., Commissioner of Libs., and State Libn., State Lib. of Pennsylvania, Forum Bldg., 607 South Dr., Harrisburg, PA 17120-0600. Tel. 717-787-2646, fax 717-772-3265, e-mail ra-edocldepty secty@pa.gov. World Wide Web http://www.statelibrary.pa.gov.

Rhode Island

Karen Mellor, Chief of Lib. Services, Rhode Island Office of Lib. and Info. Svcs., One Capitol Hill, Providence 02908. Tel. 401-574-9304, fax 401-574-9320, e-mail karen.Mellor@olis.ri.gov. World Wide Web http://www.olis.ri.gov.

South Carolina

Leesa M. Aiken, Dir., South Carolina State Lib., 1500 Senate St., Columbia 29201. Tel. 803-734-8668, fax 803-734-8676, e-mail laiken @statelibrary.sc.gov. World Wide Web http://www.statelibrary.sc.gov.

South Dakota

Daria Bossman, State Libn., South Dakota State Lib., MacKay Bldg., 800 Governors Dr., Pierre 57501. Tel. 605-773-3131, option 6, fax 605-773-6962, e-mail daria.bossman@state.sd.us. World Wide Web http://library.sd.gov/.

Tennessee

Charles A. Sherrill, State Libn. and Archivist, Tennessee State Lib. and Archives, 403 7th Ave. N., Nashville 37243. Tel. 615-741-7996, fax 615-532-9293, e-mail chuck.sherrill@tn.gov. World Wide Web http://www.tennessee.gov/tsla/.

Texas

Mark Smith, Dir. and Libn., Texas State Lib. and Archives Commission, 1201 Brazos St., Austin 78701; P.O. Box 12927, Austin 78711-2927. Tel. 512-463-6856, fax 512-463-5436, e-mail msmith@tsl.state.tx.us. World Wide Web http://www.tsl.state.tx.us.

Utah

Colleen Eggett, State Libn., Utah State Lib. Div., 250 N. 1950 W., Suite A, Salt Lake City 84116-7901. Tel. 801-715-6770, fax 801-715-6767, e-mail ceggett@utah.gov. World Wide Web http://library.utah.gov/.

Vermont

Jason Broughton, State Libn., Vermont State Lib., 60 Washington St., Suite 2, Barre, VT 05641. Tel. 802-636-0040, e-mail jason.broughton@vermont.gov. World Wide Web https://libraries.vermont.gov/state_library.

Virginia

Sandra Gioia Treadway, Libn. of Virginia, Lib. of Virginia, 800 E. Broad St., Richmond 23219-8000. Tel. 804-692-3535, fax 804-692-3556, e-mail sandra.treadway@lva.virginia.gov. World Wide Web http://www.lva.virginia.gov/.

Washington

Cindy Aden, State Libn., Washington State Lib., Office of the Secretary of State, Point Plaza E., 6880 Capitol Blvd., Tumwater 98501; P.O. Box 42460, Olympia 98504-2460. Tel. 360-704-5276, e-mail cindy.aden@sos.wa.gov. World Wide Web http://www.sos.wa.gov/library.

West Virginia

Karen Goff, Exec. Secy., West Virginia Lib. Commission Cultural Ctr., Bldg. 9, 1900 Kanawha Blvd. E., Charleston 25305. Tel. 304-558-2041 ext. 2084, fax 304-558-2044, e-mail karen.e.goff@wv.gov. World Wide Web http://www.librarycommission.wv.gov/.

Wisconsin

Kurt Kiefer, Asst. State Superintendent, Div. for Libs. and Tech., Wisconsin Dept. of Public Instruction, Div. for Libs. and Tech., 125 S.

Webster St., Madison 53703; P.O. Box 7841, Madison 53707-7841. Tel. 608-266-2205, fax 608-267-9207, e-mail kurt.kiefer@dpi.wi.gov. World Wide Web http://dpi.wi.gov.

Wyoming

Jamie Markus, State Libn., Wyoming State Lib., 2800 Central Ave., Cheyenne 82002. Tel. 307-777-5914, e-mail jamie.markus@wyo.gov. World Wide Web http://library.wyo.gov/.

American Samoa

Justin H. Maga, Territorial Libn., Feleti Barstow Public Lib., Box 997687, Pago Pago 96799. Tel. 684-633-5816, fax 684-633-5823, e-mail justinmaga@gmail.com. World Wide Web https://www.americansamoa.gov/feleti-barstow-public-library.

Federated States of Micronesia

Rufino Mauricio, Dir., Office of National Archives, Culture, and Historic Preservations, PS173, Palikir, Pohnpei State 96941. Tel. 691-320-2343-6922, fax 691-320-5632, e-mail hpo@mail.fm. World Wide Web http://www.fsmgov.org.

Guam

Sandra Stanley, Admin. Officer, Guam Public Lib. System, 254 Martyr St., Hagatna 96910-5141. Tel. 671-475-4765, fax 671-477-9777, e-mail sandra.stanley@guampls.guam.gov. World Wide Web http://gpls.guam.gov/.

Northern Mariana Islands

Erlinda Naputi, State Lib. Dir., CNMI Joeten-Kiyu Public Lib., Insatto St., Beach Rd., Susupe, P.O. Box 501092, Saipan 96950. Tel. 670-235-7316, fax 670-235-7550, e-mail ecnaputi@gmail.com. World Wide Web http://cnmilib.org.

Palau

Sinton Soalalai, Chief, Div. of School Mgt., Palau Ministry of Educ., P.O. Box 7080, Koror 96940. Tel. 680-488-2570, fax 680-488-2380, e-mail ssoalablai@palaumoe.net. World Wide Web http://palaugov.org/division-of-chool-management.

Puerto Rico

Aixamar Gonzalez-Martinez, Acting Dir., Lib. and Info. Svcs. Program, Puerto Rico Dept. of Educ., P.O. Box 190759, San Juan 00919-0759. Tel. 787-773-3564, fax 787-753-6945, e-mail gonzalezmai@de.pr.gov. World Wide Web website not available.

Republic of the Marshall Islands

Amenta Matthew, Exec. Dir., Alele Museum, Lib., and National Archives, P.O. Box 629, Majuro 96960. Tel. 011-692-625-3372, fax 011-692-625-3226, e-mail alele@ntamar.com. World Wide Web http://alelemuseum.tripod.com/Index.html.

U.S. Virgin Islands

Arlene Pinney-Benjamin, Acting Dir., The Division of Libraries, Archives and Museums, c/o Florence Williams Public Lib., 1122 King St. Christiansted, St. Croix 00820. Tel. 340-773-5715, fax 340-773-5327, e-mail arlene.benjamin@dpnr.vi.gov. World Wide Web http://www.virginislandspubliclibraries.org/usvi/.

Canada

Alberta

Diana Davidson, Dir., Alberta Public Lib. Svcs., Municipal Affairs, 8th Fl., 10405 Jasper Ave., Edmonton T5J 4R7. Tel. 780-415-0284, fax 780-415-8594, e-mail diana.davidson@gov.ab.ca or libraries@gov.ab.ca. World Wide Web http://www.municipalaffairs.alberta.ca/alberta_libraries.cfm.

British Columbia

Mari Martin, Dir., Libs. Branch, Ministry of Educ., P.O. Box 9831, Stn. Prov. Govt., Victoria V8W 9T1. Tel. 250-886-2584, fax 250-953-4985, e-mail Mari.Martin@gov.bc.ca. World Wide Web https://www2.gov.bc.ca/gov/content/education-training/administration/community-partnerships/libraries.

Manitoba

Dir., Public Lib. Services, Manitoba Dept. of Sport, Culture, and Heritage, 300-1011 Rosser Ave., Brandon R7A OL5. Tel. 204-726-6590, fax 204-726-6868, e-mail pls@gov.mb.ca. World Wide Web http://www.gov.mb.ca/chc/pls/index.html.

New Brunswick

Sylvie Nadeau, Exec. Dir., New Brunswick Public Libs., Provincial Office, 570 Two Nations Crossing, Suite 2, Fredericton E3A 0X9. Tel. 506-453-2354, fax 506-444-4064, e-mail Sylvie.NADEAU@gnb.ca. World Wide Web http://www2.gnb.ca/content/gnb/en/departments/nbpl.html.

Newfoundland and Labrador

Andrew Hunt, Exec. Dir., Provincial Info. and Lib. Resources Board, 48 St. George's Ave., Stephenville A2N 1K9. Tel. 709-643-0900, fax 709-643-0925, e-mail ahunt@nlpl.ca. World Wide Web http://www.nlpl.ca.

Northwest Territories

Brian Dawson, Territorial Libn., Northwest Territories Public Lib. Svcs., 75 Woodland Dr., Hay River X0E 1G1. Tel. 867-874-6531, fax 867-874-3321, e-mail brian_dawson@gov.nt.ca. World Wide Web http://www.nwtpls.gov.nt.ca.

Nova Scotia

Dir., Provincial Lib., Nova Scotia Provincial Lib., 6016 University Ave., 5th Fl., Halifax B3H 1W4. Tel. 902-424-2457, fax 902-424-0633, e-mail nspl@novascotia.ca. World Wide Web https://library.novascotia.ca.

Nunavut

Ron Knowling, Mgr., Nunavut Public Lib. Svcs., P.O. Box 270, Baker Lake X0C 0A0. Tel. 867-793-3353, fax 867-793-3360, e-mail rknowling@gov.nu.ca. World Wide Web http://www.publiclibraries.nu.ca.

Ontario

Rod Sawyer, Ontario Government Ministry of Tourism, Culture, and Sport, 401 Bay St., Suite 1700, Toronto M7A 0A7. Tel. 416-314-7627, fax 416-212-1802, e-mail rod.sawyer@ontario.ca. World Wide Web http://www.mtc.gov.on.ca/en/libraries/contact.shtml.

Prince Edward Island

Kathleen Eaton, Dir., Education, Early Learning and Culture, Public Lib. Svc., Public Lib. Svc. of Prince Edward Island, 89 Red Head Rd., Morell C0A 1S0. Tel. 902-368-4784, fax 902-894-0342, e-mail keeaton@gov.pe.ca. World Wide Web http://www.library.pe.ca.

Quebec

Jean-Louis Roy, CEO, Bibliothèque et Archives Nationales du Québec (BAnQ), 2275 rue Holt, Montreal H2G 3H1. Tel. 800-363-9028 or 514-873-1100, e-mail pdg@banq.qc.ca. World Wide Web http://www.banq.qc.ca/portal/dt/accueil.jsp.

Saskatchewan

Alison Hopkins, Provincial Libn./Exec. Dir., Provincial Lib. and Literacy Office, Ministry of Educ., 409A Park St., Regina S4N 5B2. Tel. 306-787-2972, fax 306-787-2029, e-mail alison.hopkins@gov.sk.ca. World Wide Web http://www.education.gov.sk.ca/provincial-library/public-library-system.

Yukon Territory

Melissa Yu Schott, Dir., Public Libs., Community Development Div., Dept. of Community Svcs., Government of Yukon, P.O. Box 2703, Whitehorse Y1A 2C6. Tel. 867-335-8600, e-mail Melissa.YuSchott@gov.yk.ca. World Wide Web https://yukon.ca.

State School Library Media Associations

Alabama

Children's and School Libns. Div., Alabama Lib. Assn. Memb. 600+. Publication. *CCSLD Handbook* (online, memb.).

Chair Laura Tucker, Homewood Public Lib., 1721 Oxmoor Rd., Homewood 35209. Tel. 205-332-6600, e-mail ltucker@bham.lib.al.us; *Chair-Elect* Jennifer Powell, Tarrant High School. E-mail powell.jennifer@tarrant.k12.al.us; *Secy.* Daniel Tackett, Vestavia Hills Lib. in the Forest. E-mail dtackett@bham.lib.al.us.

Address correspondence to Alabama Lib. Assn., 6030 Monticello Dr., Montgomery 36117. Tel. 334-414-0113, e-mail allibraryassoc@gmail.com.

World Wide Web https://www.allanet.org/children-s-and-school-librarian-s-division-csld-.

Alaska

Alaska Assn. of School Libns. Memb. 100+. Publication. *The Puffin* continuing basis online at http://akasl.org/puffin-news. Submissions e-mail akasl.puffin@gmail.com.

Pres. Janet Madsen. E-mail akasl.presidentelect@gmail.com; *Secy.* Jessica Tonnies; *Co-Treas.* Laura Guest, Audrey Drew, e-mail akasltreasurer@gmail.com; *Past Pres.* Jill Gann, Kenai Central High School and Kenai Middle School, KPBSD. E-mail akasl.president@gmail.com.

Address correspondence to Alaska Assn. of School Libns., P.O. Box 101085, Anchorage 99510-1085.

World Wide Web http://www.akasl.org.

Arizona

Teacher-Libn. Div., Arizona Lib. Assn. Memb. 1,000. Term of Office. Jan.–Dec.

Pres. Jean Kilker, Maryvale High School, 3415 N. 59th Ave., Phoenix 85033. Tel. 602-764-2134, e-mail jkilker@phoenixunion.org.

Address correspondence to the chairperson.

World Wide Web http://www.azla.org/?page=TLD.

Arkansas

Arkansas Assn. of School Libns., div. of Arkansas Lib. Assn.

Chair Daniel Fouts II, Osceola High School, 2800 W. Semmes Ave., Osceola 72370. Tel. 870-563-1863, e-mail dfouts@glaucus.org; *Past Chair* Sloan Powell, Raymond and Phyllis Simon Middle School, 1601 Siebenmorgan Dr., Conway 72032. E-mail powells@conwayschools.net.

Address correspondence to e-mail arasl.chair@gmail.com.

World Wide Web https://arasl.weebly.com.

California

California School Lib. Assn. Memb. 1,200+. Publications. *CSLA Journal* (2x yearly). *Ed.* Mary Ann Harlan, San Jose State Univ. E-mail maryann.harlan@sjsu.edu; *CSLA Newsletter* (10x yearly, memb., via e-mail).

(State Board)

Pres. Kathleen Sheppard, Los Angeles Unified School Dist. E-mail krsheppard814@gmail.com; *Pres.-Elect* Katie McNamara, Bakersfield Unified School Dist., Fresno Pacific Univ. E-mail Katie_McNamara@kernhigh.org; *Secy.* Terri Brown, Fort Miller Middle, Fresno Unified School Dist., 2847 Beverly Ave., Clovis 93611. E-mail tbrown411@gmail.com; *Treas.* Lori Stevens, Riverside Poly High School, 5450 Victoria Ave., Riverside 92506. E-mail lstevens@rusd.k12.ca.us; *Past Pres.* Renée Ousley-Swank, Curriculum Frameworks and Instructional Resources Div., California Dept. of Educ., 1430 N St., Sacramento 95814-5901. Tel. 916-319-0449, e-mail ROusleySwank@cde.ca.gov.

Address correspondence to California School Lib. Assn., 6444 E. Spring St., No. 237, Long Beach 90815-1553. Tel./fax 888-655-8480, e-mail info@csla.net.

World Wide Web http://www.csla.net.

Colorado

Colorado Assn. of School Libs. Memb. 250+.

Co-Pres. Terri Brungardt, Widefield School District 3. E-mail brungardtt@wsd3.org;

Co-Pres. Tiah Frankish, Adams 12 Five Star Schools. E-mail fra008000@adams12.org; *Co-Secy.* Katherine Kates, Academy Dist. 20. E-mail k_kates@hotmail.com; *Membs.-at-Large* Rachel Budzynski, University Schools. E-mail rbudzynski@universityschools.com; Amy Hawkins-Keeler, Widefield High School. E-mail keelera@wsd3.org; *Legislative Rep.* David Sanger, CAL Legislative Committee. E-mail dsanger401@aol.com; *Past Pres.* Molly Gibney. E-mail mgibney@comcast.net.

Address correspondence c/o Colorado Assn. of Libs., P.O. Box 740905, Arvada 80006-0905. Tel. 303-463-6400.

World Wide Web https://cal-webs.org/Colorado_Association_of_School_Libraries.

Connecticut

Connecticut Assn. of School Libns. (formerly Connecticut Educ. Media Assn.). Memb. 500+. Term of Office. July–June.

Pres. Barbara Johnson, E-mail bjohnson@ctcasl.org; *V.P.* Melissa Thom. E-mail joyful learning@melissathom.com; *Recording Secy.* Jenny Lussier. E-mail jlussier13@gmail.com; *Treas.* Jody Pillar, E-mail treasurer@ctcasl.org.

Address correspondence to the president. P.O. Box 166, Winchester Center 06094.

World Wide Web https://casl.wildapricot.org.

Delaware

Delaware Assn. of School Libns., div. of Delaware Lib. Assn. Memb. 100+. Publications. *DASL Newsletter* (online; irreg.); column in *DLA Bulletin* (2x yearly).

Pres. Kim Read, St. George's Technical High School, 555 Hyatt's Corner Rd., Middletown 19709. Tel. 302-449-3360, e-mail kim.read@nccvt.k12.de.us; *V.P./Pres.-Elect* Katelynn Scott, Alfred G. Waters Middle School, 1235 Cedar Lane Rd., Middletown 19709. Tel. 302-449-3490 ext. 2134, e-mail katelynn.scott@appo.k12.de.us; *Secy.* Jennifer O'Neill, Heritage Elementary, 2815 Highlands Ln., Wilmington 19808. Tel. 302-454-3424 ext. 131, e-mail jennifer.oneill@redclay.k12.de.us; *Treas.* Harry Robert Brake, Woodbridge High School, 14712 Woodbridge Rd., Greenwood 19950. Tel. 302-232-3333 ext. 3375, e-mail harry.brake@wsd.k12.de.us; *Past Pres.* Rachel West, Appoquinimink Community Lib.

651 N. Broad St., Middletown 19709. Tel. 302-378-5588, e-mail lrwest@nccde.org.

Address correspondence to the president, c/o Delaware Lib. Assn., Delaware Division of Libs., 121 Martin Luther King Jr. Blvd. N., Dover 19901.

World Wide Web http://dla.lib.de.us/divisions/dasl/.

District of Columbia

District of Columbia Assn. of School Libns. Memb. 8. Publication. *Newsletter* (4x yearly).

Address correspondence to DC Assn. of School Libns., 330 10th St. N.E., Washington, DC 20002. Tel. 301-502-4203, e-mail contact dcasl@gmail.com.

World Wide Web http://dcasl.weebly.com.

Florida

Florida Assn. for Media in Educ. Memb. 1,400+. Term of Office. Nov.–Oct. Publication. *Florida Media Quarterly* (q.; memb.). *Ed.* Okle Miller. E-mail okle.miller@gmail.com.

Pres. Julie Hiltz, E-mail juliehiltz@gmail.com; *Pres.-Elect* Lorraine Stinson. E-mail Lorraine.Stinson@stjohns.k12.fl.us; *Secy.* Debbie Tanner; *Treas.* Amelia Zukoski. E-mail Amelia.Zukoski@stjohns.k12.fl.us; *Parliamentarian* Sandra McMichael. E-mail sandymc@bellsouth.net. *Past Pres.* Andrea Parisi. E-mail andrea.parisi@ocps.net.

Address correspondence to FAME, P.O. Box 941169, Maitland 32794-1169. Tel. 863-585-6802, e-mail FAME@floridamediaed.org.

World Wide Web http://www.floridamediaed.org.

Georgia

Georgia Lib. Media Assn. Memb. 700+.

Pres. Holly Frilot. E-mail president@glma-inc.org; *Pres.-Elect* Martha Bongiorno; *Secy.* Julie Pszczola; *Treas.* Lora Taft. E-mail treasurer@glma-inc.org; *Past Pres.* Jennifer Helfrich.

Address correspondence to Georgia Lib. Media Assn. P.O. Box 148, Waverly Hall 31831. E-mail info@glma-inc.org.

World Wide Web http://www.glma-inc.org.

Hawaii

Hawaii Assn. of School Libns. Memb. 145. Term of Office. June–May. Publication. *HASL Newsletter* (3x yearly). *Newsletter Chair* Jenny Yamamoto, Leilehua High School. E-mail myhaslnews@gmail.com.

Co-Pres. Imelda Amano, Manoa Elementary (Ret.); *Co-Pres.* Meera Garud, Hawai'i P-20 Partnerships for Education; *V.P. Programming* Denise Sumida, Pearl Harbor Elementary; *V.P. Membership* Maricar Kawasaki, Makalapa Elementary; *Recording Secy.* Elodie Arellano, Ahuimanu Elementary; *Treas.* Caroline Lee, Waipahu Intermediate School;

Address correspondence to Hawaii Assn. of School Libns., P.O. Box 894752, Mililani 96789. E-mail hasl.contactus@gmail.com.

World Wide Web https://haslhawaii.weebly.com.

Idaho

School Libs. Services and Consulting, Idaho Commission for Libs.

School Library Action Planning Committee: School Library Consultant Jeannie Standal. Tel. 208-639-4139, e-mail jeannie.standal@libraries.idaho.gov; Kit Anderson, Teton High School, Teton School Dist.; Dennis Hahs, West Ada School Dist.; Lynn Johnson, Mountain View School Dist.; Kiersten Kerr, Coeur d'Alene School Dist.; Susan Tabor-Boesch, Wood River Middle School, Blaine County Schools.

Address correspondence to Jeannie Standal, 325 W. State St., Boise 83702. Tel. 208-639-4139, fax 208-334-4016, e-mail jeannie.standal@libraries.idaho.gov.

World Wide Web https://libraries.idaho.gov/school-libraries.

Illinois

Assn. of Illinois School Lib. Educators. Memb. 1,000. Term of Office. July–June. Publications. Newsletter (4x yearly). *Ed.* David P. Little. E-mail dplittleretired@gmail.com.

Pres. Mary Morgan Ryan, Northern Suburban Special Education Dist, Highland Park. E-mail president@aisled.org; *Pres.-Elect* Anna Kim, Chappell Elementary, Chicago. E-mail preselect@aisled.org; *Secy.* Dawn Scuderi, Lemont High School, Lemont. E-mail secretary@aisled.org; *Treas.* Christy Semande, Canton USD #66, Canton. E-mail treasurer@aisled.org; *Past Pres.* Jacob Roskovensky, Charleston High School, Charleston. E-mail pastpres@aisled.org; *Exec. Secy.* Becky Robinson. E-mail execsecretary@aisled.org.

Address correspondence to the Assn. of Illinois School Lib. Educators. P.O. Box 1326, Galesburg 61402-1326. Tel. 309-341-1099, fax 309-341-2070, e-mail execsecretary@aisled.org.

World Wide Web https://www.aisled.org.

Indiana

Assn. of Indiana School Library Educators (AISLE), affiliation of the Indiana Lib. Federation (ILF).

Chair Diane Rogers, Ben Davis 9th Grade Ctr. Tel. 317-988-7577; *V.Chair* Chad Heck, MSD Pike Township. Tel. 317-347-8673; *Secy.* JoyAnn Boudreau, Hamilton Southeastern Intermediate/Junior High. Tel. 317-594-4120; *Treas.* Michael Williams, Indianapolis Public Lib., 40 St. Clair St., Indianapolis 46204. Tel. 317-275-4302; *Advisory Board Membs.* Jennifer Longgood, Northwestern High School. Tel. 765-438-7151; Sarah Bardwell, Southwest Dubois School Corp. Tel. 812-683-2217; Kathleen Rauth, Center for Inquiry at 2. Tel. 317-226-4202; *Past Chair* Tara White, Elkhart Community Schools. Tel. 574-262-5869; *Exec. Dir. ILF* Lucinda Nord, 941 East 86th St., Suite 260, Indianapolis 46240. Tel. 317-257-2040, ext. 101.

Address correspondence to AISLE, c/o Indiana Lib. Federation, 941 E. 86 St., Suite 260, Indianapolis 46240. Tel. 317-257-2040, fax 317-257-1389, e-mail askus@ilfonline.org.

World Wide Web https://www.ilfonline.org/page/AISLE.

Iowa

Iowa Assn. of School Libns., div. of the Iowa Lib. Assn. Memb. 180+. Term of Office. Jan.–Jan.

Pres. Katy Kauffman, Ankeny. E-mail TL katykauffman@gmail.com; *V.P./Pres.-Elect* Jenahlee Chamberlain, Cedar Rapids. E-mail jenahlee.chamberlain@gmail.com; *Secy./Treas.*

Jen Keltner. E-mail kaseyjenkeltner@gmail.com; *Membs.-at-Large* Miranda Kral, Michelle Kruse, Jill Hofmockel; *Past Pres.* Sarah Staudt, Mason City. E-mail slstaudt@gmail.com.

Address correspondence to the president.

World Wide Web http://www.iasl-ia.org.

Kansas

Kansas Assn. of School Libns. Memb. 600.

Pres. Martha House. E-mail mhouse@cgrove417.org; *Pres.-Elect* Tonya Foster. E-mail tonya_foster@cox.net; *Secy.* Rachel Hodges. E-mail hodgesrac@gmail.com; *Treas.* Brenda Lemon. E-mail blemon@473mail.net; *Past Pres.* Marla Wigton. E-mail marla.wigton510@gmail.com.

Address correspondence to the president.

World Wide Web http://www.ksschoollibrarians.org.

Kentucky

Kentucky Assn. of School Libns. (KASL), section of Kentucky Lib. Assn. Memb. 600+. Publication. *KASL Blog.* (blog) http://www.kaslblog.com/.

Pres. Lori Hancock. E-mail lhancock@thelexingtonschool.org; *Pres.-Elect* Emily Northcutt. E-mail emily.northcutt@franklin.kyschools.us; *Secy.* Sam Northern. E-mail samuel.northern@simpson.kyschools.us; *Treas.* Fred Tilsley. E-mail ftilsley@windstream.net; *Past Pres.* Amanda Hurley. E-mail amanda.hurley@fayette.kyschools.us.

Address correspondence to the president.

World Wide Web http://www.kasl.us.

Louisiana

Louisiana Assn. of School Libns., section of Louisiana Lib. Assn. Memb. 230. Term of Office. July–June. Publication. *LASL Newsletter* (3x yearly).

Pres. Tiffany Whitehead. E-mail librariantiff@gmail.com; *1st V.P./Pres.-Elect* Kim Adkins. E-mail kwadkins@caddoschools.org; *2nd V.P.* Amanda Blanco. E-mail arblanco@lpssonline.com; *Secy.* Stephanie Wilkes. E-mail stephaniecwilkes@gmail.com.

Address correspondence to Louisiana Assn. of School Libns., c/o Louisiana Lib. Assn., 8550 United Plaza Blvd., Suite 1001, Baton Rouge 70809. Tel. 225-922-4642, fax 225-408-4422, e-mail office@llaonline.org.

World Wide Web http://laslonline.weebly.com.

Maine

Maine Assn. of School Libs. Memb. 200+.

Pres. Amanda Kozaka, Cape Elizabeth Middle School. E-mail akozaka@capeelizabethschools.org; *Pres.-Elect* Jennifer Stanbro, Skillin Elementary, South Portland; *Secy.* Cathy Potter, Falmouth Middle School, Falmouth; *Past Pres.* Tina Taggart, Foxcroft Academy, 975 W. Main St., Dover-Foxcroft 04426. E-mail tina.taggart@staff.foxcroftacademy.org.

Address correspondence to the president. Maine Assn. of School Libs., c/o Maine State Lib., 64 State House Station, Augusta 04333-0064. E-mail maslibraries@gmail.com.

World Wide Web http://www.maslibraries.org.

Maryland

Maryland Assn. of School Libns. (formerly Maryland Educ. Media Organization). Publication. Newsletter (mo.; online).

Pres. Brittany Tignor, Snow Hill High School, Worcester County Public Schools. E-mail BDHulme-Tignor@worcesterk12.org; *Pres.-Elect* April Wathen, G. W. Carver Elementary, St. Mary's County Public Schools. E-mail aawathen@smcps.org; *Secy.* Stacey Kahler, Westminster West Middle School, Carroll County Public Schools. E-mail slkahle@carrollk12.org; *Treas.* Jenifer Lavell, Thomas Johnson Middle School, Prince George's County Public Schools. E-mail jenifer.lavell@pgcps.org; *Membs.-at-Large* Marianne Fitzgerald; Amanda Lanza; *Delegate* Marcia Porter, Lockerman Middle School, Caroline County Public Schools. E-mail porter.marcia@ccpsstaff.org; *MSDE Rep.* Laura Hicks. E-mail laura.hicks@maryland.gov; *Past Pres.* Emmanuel Faulkner, The Historic Samuel Coleridge-Taylor Elementary, Baltimore County Public Schools. E-mail EFaulkner@bcps.k12.md.us.

Address correspondence to Maryland Assn. of School Libns. E-mail maslmaryland@gmail.com.

World Wide Web http://maslmd.org.

Massachusetts

Massachusetts School Lib. Assn. Memb. 800. Publication. *MSLA Forum* (irreg.; online). *Eds.* Katherine Steiger, Reba Tierney.

Pres. Carrie Tucker, East Bridgewater Jr./Sr. High School. E-mail ctucker@maschoolibraries.org; *Secy.* Jennifer Dimmick, Newton South High School. E-mail jdimmick@maschoolibraries.org; *Treas.* Jennifer Varney, MLKing, Jr. School, Cambridge. E-mail jvarney@maschoolibraries.org; *Exec. Dir.* Kathy Lowe, Massachusetts School Lib, Assn., P.O. Box 658, Lunenburg 01462. E-mail klowe@maschoolibraries.org.

Address correspondence to the executive director. Massachusetts School Lib. Assn., P.O. Box 658, Lunenburg 01462.

World Wide Web http://www.maschoolibraries.org.

Michigan

Michigan Assn. for Media in Educ. Memb. 1,200. Publication. *Media Matters!* newsletter (mo.). *Eds.* Beverly Banks. E-mail beverlybanks@wlcsd.org and Jonathan Richards. E-mail jrichards@vanburenschools.net.

Pres. Cynthia Zervos, F., Bloomfield Hills Schools, Way Elementary, 765 W. Long Lake, Bloomfield Hills 48302. E-mail cynthia.zervos@mimame.org; *Pres.-Elect* Cat Kerns, Saginaw Township Community Schools, 3460 N. Center Rd., Saginaw 48603. Tel. 989-799-5790 ext. 8080, e-mail ckerns@mimame.org; *Secy.* Alexa Hirsh Lalejini. E-mail ahirsch@mimame.org; *Treas.* Lisa Kelley, Rochester Community Schools, University Hills, 600 Croydon, Rochester Hills 48309. Tel. 248-726-4404, e-mail lkelley@mimame.org; *Past Pres.* Klaudia Janek, International Acad., 1020 East Square Lake Rd., Bloomfield Hills 48304. Tel. 248-341-5925, e-mail kjanek@mimame.org; *Exec. Secy.* Teri Belcher. E-mail tbelcher@mimame.org.

Address correspondence to MAME, 1407 Rensen, Suite 3, Lansing 48910. Tel. 517-394-2808, fax 517-492-3878, e-mail mame@mimame.org.

World Wide Web http://www.mimame.org.

Minnesota

Info. and Technology Educators of Minnesota (ITEM) (formerly Minnesota Educ. Media Organization). Memb. 400+. Term of Office. July–June.

Pres. Tammi Wilkins, Duluth Public Schools. E-mail tammi.wilkins@isd709.org; *Co-Pres.-Elect* Sara Florin, Centennial Public Schools; *Co-Pres.-Elect* Kim Haugo, Osseo Public Schools; *Secy.* Sally Kimmes, Osseo Public Schools. E-mail Sally.kimmes@gmail.com; *Treas.* Dawn French, Saint Paul Public Schools; *Past Co-Pres.* Lisa Gearman, Chaska High School. E-mail gearmanl@district112.org; *Past Co-Pres.* Sara Swenson, Edina High School. E-mail sara.swenson@edinaschools.org.

Address correspondence to Info. and Technology Educators of Minnesota (ITEM), P.O. Box 130555, Roseville 55113. Tel. 651-771-8672, e-mail admin@mnitem.org.

World Wide Web http://mnitem.org.

Mississippi

School Lib. Section, Mississippi Lib. Assn. Memb. 1,300.

Address correspondence to School Lib. Section, Mississippi Lib. Assn., P.O. Box 13687, Jackson 39236-3687. Tel. 601-981-4586, e-mail info@misslib.org.

World Wide Web http://www.misslib.org/page-1818448.

Missouri

Missouri Assn. of School Libns. Memb. 1,000. Term of Office. July–June.

Pres. Jennifer Millikan, St. Joseph's Academy. E-mail jmillikan@stjosephacademy.org; *1st V.P.* Amy Hertzberg, Nevada Middle School, Nevada R-V School Dist. E-mail ahertzberg@nevada.k12.mo.us; *2nd V.P.* Kirsten Shaw, Martin Warren Elementary, Warrensburg School Dist. E-mail kshaw@warrensburgr6.org; *Secy.* Lisa Newton, Clarkton C-4 School Dist. E-mail lnewton@clarktonschools.org; *Treas.* Rebecca Parker, Border Star Montessori, Kansas City Public Schools. E-mail treasurer@maslonline.org; *AASL Affiliate Assembly Delegate* Victoria Jones, Wydown Middle School, School Dist. of Clayton. E-mail victoriajones@claytonschools.net; *Past Pres.* Mernie Maestas, Boone

Trail Elementary, Wentzville R-IV School Dist. E-mail pastpresident@maslonline.org.

Address correspondence to Missouri Assn. of School Libns., P.O. Box 2107, Jefferson City 65102. Tel. 573-893-4155, fax 573-635-2858, e-mail info@maslonline.org.

World Wide Web http://www.maslonline.org.

Montana

School Lib. Div., Montana Lib. Assn. Memb. 200+.

Co-Chair Angela Archuleta, Lewistown Junior High School/Lewis & Clark Elementary, 914 W. Main St., Lewistown 59457. Tel. 406-546-3774, e-mail angela.archuleta@lewistown.k12.mt; *Co-chair* Erin Regele, Billings West HS Lib., 2201 St. Johns Ave., Billings 59102. *MLA Exec. Dir.* Debbi Kramer, 33 Beartooth View Dr., Laurel 59044. Tel. 406-579-3121, e-mail debkmla@hotmail.com.

Address correspondence to the Montana Lib. Assn. executive director.

World Wide Web http://www.mtlib.org/governance/sld.

Nebraska

Nebraska School Libns. Assn. Memb. 300+. Term of Office. July–June. Publication. *NSLA News* (blog; mo.).

Pres. Courtney Pentland. E-mail mrspentland@gmail.com; *Pres.-Elect* Cynthia Stogdill. E-mail cynstogdill@gmail.com; *Secy.* Crys Bauermeister. E-mail cbauermeister@gmail.com; *Treas.* Mandy Peterson. E-mail mandy.peterson@schuylercommunityschools.org; *Past Pres.* Angie Richeson. E-mail angierichesons@gmail.com. *Exec. Secy.* Kim Gangwish. E-mail contactnsla@gmail.com.

Address correspondence to the executive secretary.

World Wide Web http://www.neschoollibrarians.org.

Nevada

Nevada School and Children Libns. Section, Nevada Lib. Assn. Memb. 120.

Chair Susan Thurnbeck, Las Vegas–Clark County Lib. Dist. E-mail thurnbecks@lvccld.org; *Past Chair* Larry Johnson, Las Vegas–Clark County Lib. Dist.; *Exec. Secy. NLA* Sue (Seungyeon) Yang-Peace, Las Vegas-Clark County Lib. Dist. E-mail sueyangpeace@gmail.com.

Address correspondence to the executive secretary, Nevada Lib. Assn.

World Wide Web http://nevadalibraries.org/Handbook-NSCLS.

New Hampshire

New Hampshire School Lib. Media Assn. Memb. 250+. Term of Office. July–June. Publication. *NHSLMA Newsletter* (irreg.; online).

Pres. Caitlin Bennett, Londonderry Middle School, Londonderry. E-mail caitlin.annie.bennett@gmail.com; *V.P.* Karen Abraham, Laconia High School. E-mail vice-president@nhslma.org; *Recording Secy.* Katie Gadwah, John Stark Regional High School, Weare. E-mail nhslma@gmail.com; *Treas.* Helen Burnham, Lincoln Street School, Exeter. E-mail hburnham@sau16.org; *Conference Chair* Justine Thain, Hooksett School Dist., Hooksett. E-mail jthain.nhslma@gmail.com; *Past Pres.* Rachel Hopkins, Salem High School, Salem. E-mail rachel.hopkins@comcast.net.

Address correspondence to the president, NHSLMA, P.O. Box 418, Concord 03302-0418. E-mail nhslma@gmail.com.

World Wide Web http://nhslma.org.

New Jersey

New Jersey Assn. of School Libns. (NJASL). Memb. 1,000+. Term of Office. Aug. 1–July 31. Publication. *Bookmark Newsletter* (mo.; memb.). *Ed.* Casey Schaffer. E-mail bookmark@njasl.org.

Pres. Christina Cucci. E-mail president@njasl.org; *Pres.-Elect* Jill Mills. E-mail Presidentelect@njasl.org; *V.P.* Beth Thomas. E-mail vp@njasl.org; *Recording Secy.* Christine Halstater. E-mail secretary@njasl.org; *Treas.* Jean Stock, Larchmont Elementary, 301 Larchmont Blvd., Mt. Laurel 08054. Tel. 856-273-3700 ext.17508, e-mail treasurer@njasl.org; *Membs.-at-Large* Amy Gazelah, Kim Zito. E-mail membersatlarge@njasl.org. *Past Pres.* Lisa Bakanas, Cherokee High School, 120 Tomlinson Mill Rd., Marlton 08053. Tel. 856-983-5140 ext. 2357, e-mail pastpresident@njasl.org.

Address correspondence to recording secretary, New Jersey Assn. of School Libns., P.O. Box 1460, Springfield 07081.

World Wide Web http://www.njasl.org.

New York

Section of School Libns., New York Lib. Assn. Memb. 800+. Term of Office. Nov.–Oct. Publication. *School Library Update* (3x yearly; memb.; online).

Pres. Charlie Jennifer Kelly. E-mail charlieakajennykelly@gmail.com; *Pres.-Elect* Tara Thibault-Edmonds. E-mail tthibault-edmonds@rondout.k12.ny.us; *Secy.* Gail Brisson. E-mail Gail.brisson@gmail.com; *Treas.* Anne Paulson. E-mail anneppaulson@gmail.com; *V.P. of Conferences* Michelle Miller. E-mail mmiller@mwcsd.org; *V.P. of Communications* Heather Turner. E-mail hturner@fabiuspompey.org; *Past Pres.* Penny Sweeney. E-mail psweeney@liverpool.k12.ny.us.

Address correspondence to New York Lib. Assn., 6021 State Farm Rd., Guilderland 12084. Tel. 518-432-6952, fax 518-427-1697, e-mail info@nyla.org.

World Wide Web https://www.nyla.org/max/4DCGI/cms/review.html?Action=CMS_Document&DocID=136&MenuKey=ssl.

North Carolina

North Carolina School Lib. Media Assn. Memb. 1,000+. Term of Office. Nov.–Oct.

Pres. Bitsy Griffin, Old Town Global Academy, 3930 Reynolda Rd., Winston-Salem 27106. Tel. 336-703-4283, e-mail bitsygriffin@ncslma.org; *Pres.-Elect* Laura Long. E-mail lauralong@ncslma.org; *Secy.* Colleen Pinyan. E-mail colleenpinyan@ncslma.org; *Treas.* Jennifer Abel, North Henderson High School, 35 Fruitland Rd., Hendersonville 28792. Tel. 828-697-4500, e-mail jenniferabel@ncslma.org; *Past Pres.* Brene Duggins, Oak Grove High School, 3507 Midway School Rd., Winston-Salem 27107. Tel. 336-474-8280, e-mail breneduggins@ncslma.org.

Address correspondence to the president. 514 Daniels St., #130 Raleigh 27605.

World Wide Web http://www.ncslma.org.

North Dakota

School Lib. and Youth Svcs. Section, North Dakota Lib. Assn. Memb. 100.

Chair Allison Radermacher, Ellendale Public School. E-mail aradermacher@ellendale.k12.nd.us.

Address correspondence to the North Dakota Lib. Assn. 604 E. Boulevard Ave., Bismarck 58505.

World Wide Web http://www.ndla.info.

Ohio

Ohio Educ. Lib. Media Assn. Memb. 1,000.

Pres. Deb Logan, Pleasant Local Schools. E-mail deb.jd3logan@gmail.com; *V.P.* Brandi Young, South-Western City School Dist., Westland High School. E-mail b.nicole.young@gmail.com; *Secy.* Jamie Davies, Dublin City Schools, Eli Pinney Elementary. E-mail jdaviesoelma@gmail.com; *Treas.* Joey Fabian, Cuyahoga County Public Lib. E-mail jfabian41@gmail.com; *Past Pres.* Kelly Silwani, Olentangy Local Schools. E-mail krs1614@gmail.com.

Address correspondence to Ohio Educ. Lib. Media Assn., 1737 Georgetown Rd., Suite B, Hudson 43236. Tel. 330-615-2409, fax 1-800-373-9594, e-mail OELMA@neo-rls.org.

World Wide Web http://www.oelma.org.

Oklahoma

Oklahoma School Libns. Div., Oklahoma Lib. Assn. Memb. 200+.

Chair Amanda Kordeliski. E-mail oksl@oklibs.org; *Chair-Elect* Cathy Benge; *Past Chair* Kelsey Gourd, Lakeview Elementary, 3310 108th Ave. N.E., Norman 73026. E-mail kgourd@norman.k12.ok.us.

Address correspondence to the chairperson, School Libs. Div., Oklahoma Lib. Assn., 1190 Meramec Station Rd., Suite 207, Ballwin, MO 63021-6902. Tel. 800-843-8482, fax 636-529-1396.

World Wide Web http://www.oklibs.org/?page=OKSL.

Oregon

Oregon Assn. of School Libs. Memb. 600. Publication. *Interchange* (3x yearly). *Coord.*

Ed. Dana Berglund. E-mail interchange@oasl.olaweb.org.

Pres. Stuart Levy. E-mail president@oasl.olaweb.org; *Pres.-Elect* Laurie Nordahl. E-mail presidentelect@oasl.olaweb.org; *Secy.* Jenny Takeda. E-mail secretary@oasl.olaweb.org; *Treas.* Chris Myers. E-mail treasurer@oasl.olaweb.org; *Membs.-at-Large* Jean Gritter. E-mail region2@oasl.olaweb.org; Kate Weber. E-mail listserv@oasl.olaweb.org; *Past Pres.* Paige Battle. E-mail pastpresident@oasl.olaweb.org.

Address correspondence to the president, OASL, c/o Oregon Lib. Assn., P.O. Box 3067, La Grande 97850. Tel. 541-962-5824, e-mail president@oasl.olaweb.org.

World Wide Web http://www.olaweb.org/oasl-home.

Pennsylvania

Pennsylvania School Libns. Assn. Memb. 800+. Publication. *PSLA Pulse* (blog).

Pres. Allison Mackley, Derry Township School Dist. E-mail amackley@psla.org; *Pres.-Elect* Cathi Fuhrman, Hempfield School Dist. E-mail cfuhrman@psla.org; *V.P.* Robin Burns, Salisbury Township School Dist. E-mail rburns@psla.org; *Secy.* Allison Burrell, Bloomsburg Area School Dist. E-mail aburrell@psla.org; *Treas.* Erika Rhodeside. E-mail pslatreasurer@gmail.com; *Past Pres.* Jennifer Bates. E-mail jbates@psla.org.

Address correspondence to the president.

World Wide Web http://www.psla.org.

Rhode Island

School Libns. of Rhode Island (formerly Rhode Island Educ. Media Assn.). Memb. 350+. Publication. *SLRI Update* (irreg.; online).

Pres. Lisa Girard. E-mail SLRI.prez@gmail.com; *V.P.* Deanna Brooks. E-mail SLRI.viceprez@gmail.com; *Secy.* Lisa Casey. E-mail SLRI.secretary@gmail.com; *Treas.* Jillian Waugh. E-mail SLRI.treasurer@gmail.com; *Past Pres.* Sarah Hunicke.

Address correspondence to the president. School Libns. of Rhode Island, P.O. Box 470, East Greenwich 02818.

World Wide Web http://www.slri.info.

South Carolina

South Carolina Assn. of School Libns. Memb. 900. Term of Office. July–June. Publication *The SCASL Messenger* (q., online, memb.). *Ed.* Anya Bonnette. E-mail anya.bonnette@ocsd5.net.

Pres. Heather Thore. E-mail president@scasl.net; *Pres.-Elect* Pamela Williams. E-mail president.elect@scasl.net; *Secy.* Susan Myers. E-mail secretary@scasl.net; *Treas.* Camillia Harris; *Past Pres.* Cathy Jo Nelson.

Address correspondence to South Carolina Assn. of School Libns., P.O. Box 2442, Columbia 29202. Tel./fax 803-492-3025.

World Wide Web http://www.scasl.net.

South Dakota

South Dakota School Lib. Media Section, South Dakota Lib. Assn. Memb. 140+. Term of Office. Oct.–Sept.

Chair Kimberly Darata, Douglas School Dist. E-mail Kimberly.Darata@k12.sd.us; *Past Chair* Laura Allard, Memorial Middle School, 1401 S. Sertoma Ave., Sioux Falls 57106. E-mail laura.allard@k12.sd.us.

Address correspondence to the chairperson. South Dakota School Lib. Media Section, South Dakota Lib. Assn., P.O. Box 283, Lennox 57039. Tel. 605-214-8785.

World Wide Web http://www.sdlibraryassociation.org/page/Sections.

Tennessee

Tennessee Assn. of School Libns. Memb. 450. Term of Office. Jan.–Dec. Publication. *TASL Talks* (wk.; blog).

Pres. Jennifer Sharp, Overton High School, 4820 Franklin Rd., Nashville 37220. E-mail jennifer.sharp.tasl@gmail.com; *Pres.-Elect* Vicki Winstead, Vance Middle School, 815 Edgemont Ave., Bristol 37620. E-mail vcwinstead.tasl@gmail.com; *Secy.* Lindsey Kimery, Woodland Middle School, 1500 Volunteer Pkwy., Brentwood 37027. E-mail LindsKAnderson@gmail.com; *Treas.* Elizabeth Shepherd, Discovery School, 1165 Middle TN Blvd., Murfreesboro 37130. E-mail eshepherd78@gmail.com; *Past Pres.* Blake Hopper, Powell Valley Elementary, 323 Hopper Circle, Speedwell 37870. E-mail blake.hopper.tasl@gmail.com.

Address correspondence to the president. P.O. Box 11185, Murfreesboro 37129.

World Wide Web http://www.tasltn.org.

Texas

Texas Assn. of School Libns., div. of Texas Lib. Assn. Memb. 4,500+. Term of Office. Apr.–Mar.

Chair Nancy Jo Lambert. E-mail LambertN@friscoisd.org; *Chair-Elect* Richelle O'Neil. E-mail RGONeil@garlandisd.net; *Secy.* Liza Zinkie. E-mail librarianzee6@gmail.com; *Councilor* Susi Grissom; *Alternate Councilor* JoAnn Reed; *Past Chair* Kate DiPronio. E-mail Ktlee523@gmail.com; *TLA Exec. Dir.* Dana Braccia. E-mail danab@txla.org.

Address correspondence to the chairperson. TLA, 3355 Bee Cave Rd., Suite 401, Austin 78746. Tel. 512-328-1518, fax 512-328-8852.

World Wide Web http://www.txla.org/groups/tasl.

Utah

Utah Educ. Lib. Media Assn. Memb. 500+. Publication. *UELMA Works* (q.). *Ed.* Liz Petty. E-mail elisabethapetty@outlook.com.

Pres. Ann Riding, North Davis Junior High, 835 S. State St., Clearfield 84015. Tel. 801-402-6500, e-mail board@uelma.org; *Pres.-Elect* Emily DeJong, Salt Lake School Dist. E-mail board@uelma.org; *Secy.* Stephanie MacKay, Centennial Jr. High; *Past Pres.* Lorraine Wyness, Taylorsville High School, 5225 S. Redwood Rd., Taylorsville 84123. Tel. 385-646-8949, e-mail board@uelma.org; *Exec. Dir.* Davina Sauthoff. Tel. Wasatch Junior High, 3750 South 3100 E., Salt Lake City 84109. Tel. 435-512-6809, e-mail executivedirector@uelma.org.

Address correspondence to the executive director.

World Wide Web http://www.uelma.org.

Vermont

Vermont School Lib. Assn. (formerly Vermont Educ. Media Assn.). Memb. 220+. Term of Office. May–May.

Co-Pres. Martine Larocque Gulick. E-mail mgulick@ewsd.org; *Co-Pres.* Caitlin Classen. E-mail cclassen@ewsd.org; *Pres.-Elect* Deb Ehler-Hansen. E-mail vermonthan1@gmail.com; *Secy.* Susan Monmaney. E-mail vslasecretary@gmail.com; *Treas.* Megan Sutton. E-mail msutton@acsdvt.org; *Past Pres.* Donna Sullivan-Macdonald. E-mail dmacdonald@sbschools.net.

Address correspondence to the president.

World Wide Web https://vsla.wildapricot.org.

Virginia

Virginia Assn. of School Libns. (VAASL) (formerly Virginia Educ. Media Assn. [VEMA]). Memb. 1,200. Term of Office. Nov.–Nov. Publication. *VAASL Voice* (q.; memb.).

Pres. Kendel Lively. E-mail President@vaasl.org; *Pres.-Elect* Patrice Lambusta. E-mail PresidentElect@vaasl.org; *Secy.* Jannelle Jampole. E-mail secretary@vaasl.org; *Treas.* Trish Branscome. E-mail Treasurer@vaasl.org; *Past Pres.* Laurie Bolt. E-mail PastPresident@vaasl.org; *Exec. Dir.* Margaret Baker. E-mail executive@vaasl.org.

Address correspondence to the executive director, P.O. Box 2015, Staunton 24402-2015. Tel. 540-416-6109, e-mail executive@vaasl.org.

World Wide Web http://vaasl.org.

Washington

School Lib. Div., Washington Lib. Assn. (formerly Washington Lib. Media Assn.). Memb. 700+. Term of Office. Apr.–Apr.

Chair Ann Hayes-Bell. E-mail ann.hayes.bell@k12.shorelineschools.org; *V.Chair/Chair-Elect* Marian Royal, Seattle School Dist. E-mail mbroyal@seattleschools.org; *Past Chair* Marianne Costello. E-mail costellom1@mac.com.

Address correspondence to the Washington Lib. Assn. P.O. Box 33808, Seattle 98133. Tel. 206-823-1138, e-mail info@wla.org.

World Wide Web http://www.wla.org/school-libraries.

West Virginia

School Lib. Div., West Virginia Lib. Assn. Memb. 50. Term of Office. Nov.–Nov.

Chair Leigh Ann Hood, East Park Elementary, 805 Pittsburgh Ave., Fairmont 26554. Tel. 304-534-0927, e-mail lahood@k12.wv.us; *Past*

Chair Lynda Suzie Martin, Brookhaven Elementary, 147 Estate Dr., Morgantown 26508. Tel. 304-282-0147, e-mail librarynbct@gmail.com.

Address correspondence to the chairperson.

World Wide Web http://www.wvla.org.

Wisconsin

Wisconsin Educ. Media and Technology Assn. Memb. 800+.

Pres. Michele Green, New London; *V.P.* Micki Uppena; *Pres.-Elect* Raquel Rand; *Secy.* Peg Billing, Tomahawk; *Treas.* Pamela Hansen; *Past Pres.* Heidi Catlin, School Dist. of Rhinelander, 665 Coolidge Ave., Suite B, Rhinelander 54501. Tel. 715-365-9747.

Address correspondence to WEMTA, 6000 Gisholt Dr. #200, Madison 53713 Tel. 608-501-3408, e-mail wemta@wemta.org.

World Wide Web http://www.wemta.org.

Wyoming

School Lib. Interest Group (formerly Teacher-Libn. Interest Group), Wyoming Lib. Assn. Memb. 100+.

Chair Connie Hollin, Guernsey-Sunrise School (K–12). Tel. 307-836-2733, e-mail chollin@gsviking.org.

Address correspondence to the chairperson.

World Wide Web https://wyla.org/School-Library-Interest-Group.

International Library Associations

International Association of Law Libraries

Jeroen Vervliet, President
P.O. Box 5709, Washington, DC 20016
E-mail j.vervliet@ppl.nl
World Wide Web http://www.iall.org

Object

The International Association of Law Libraries (IALL) is a worldwide organization of librarians, libraries, and other persons or institutions concerned with the acquisition and use of legal information emanating from sources other than their jurisdictions and from multinational and international organizations.

IALL's purpose is to facilitate the work of librarians who acquire, process, organize, and provide access to foreign legal materials. IALL has no local chapters but maintains liaison with national law library associations in many countries and regions of the world.

Membership

More than 400 members in more than 50 countries on five continents.

Officers

Pres. Jeroen Vervliet, Peace Palace Lib., Carnegieplein 2, 2517 KJ The Hague, Netherlands. Tel. 31-70-302-4242, e-mail j.vervliet@ppl.nl; *V.P.* Barbara Garavaglia, Univ. of Michigan Law Lib., Ann Arbor 48109-1210. Tel. 734-764-9338, fax 734-764-5863, e-mail bvaccaro@umich.edu; *Secy.* David Gee, Institute of Advanced Legal Studies, Univ. of London, 17 Russell Sq., London WC1B 5DR, UK. Tel. +44 (0)20 7862 5822, fax +44 (0)20 7862 5770, e-mail David.Gee@sas.ac.uk; *Treas.* Kurt Carroll, Lib. of Congress, Washington, DC 20540. Tel. +1 202-707-1494, e-mail kcarr@loc.gov.

Board of Directors

Daniel Boyer, Nahum Gelber Law Lib., McGill Univ.; Lily Echiverri, Univ. of the Philippines, Quezon City; Michel Fraysse, Université de Toulouse 1 Capitole Libs.; Ryan Harrington, UNCITRAL Law Lib., Vienna International Centre; Kerem Kahvecioglu, Istanbul Bilgi Univ., Sisli, Istanbul; Petal Kinder, High Court of Australia, Canberra; Gloria Orrego-Hoyos, Law School, Univ. de San Andrés, Buenos Aires.

Publications

International Journal of Legal Information (*IJLI*) (3x yearly; memb.).
IALL Newsletter (3x yearly; memb.).

International Association of Music Libraries, Archives, and Documentation Centres

Anders Cato, Secretary-General
Gothenburg University Library, P.O. Box 210, SE 405 30 Gothenburg, Sweden
Tel. 46-31-786-4057, cell 46-703-226-092, fax 46-31-786-40-59, e-mail secretary@iaml.info
World Wide Web http://www.iaml.info

Object

The object of the International Association of Music Libraries, Archives, and Documentation Centres (IAML) is to promote the activities of music libraries, archives, and documentation centers and to strengthen the cooperation among them; to promote the availability of all publications and documents relating to music and further their bibliographical control; to encourage the development of standards in all areas that concern the association; and to support the protection and preservation of musical documents of the past and the present.

Membership

Memb. approximately 1,700 in about 40 countries worldwide.

Officers

Pres. Stanislaw Hrabia, Uniwersytet Jagiellonski, Kraków. E-mail president@iaml.info; *V.P.s* Jane Gottlieb, The Juilliard School, New York; Joseph Hafner, McGill Univ., Montréal; Balázs Mikusi, National Széchényi Lib., Budapest; Rupert Ridgewell, British Lib., London; *Secy.-Gen.* Pia Shekhter, Gothenburg Univ. Lib., Box 210, SE 405 30 Gothenburg. Tel. 46-31-786-40-57, e-mail secretary@iaml.info; *Treas.* Thomas Kalk, Stadtbüchereien Düsseldorf. E-mail treasurer@iaml.info; *Past Pres.* Barbara Dobbs Mackenzie, *Répertoire International de Littérature Musicale* (*RILM*), New York.

Publication

Fontes Artis Musicae (q.; memb.). *Ed.* James P. Cassaro, Univ. of Pittsburgh, B-30 Music Bldg., Pittsburgh, PA 15260. Tel. 412-624-4131, e-mail fontes@iaml.info.

Professional Branches

Archives and Music Documentation Centres. *Chair* Marie Cornaz, Bibliothèque Royale de Belgique, Brussels. E-mail archives@iaml.info.

Broadcasting and Orchestra Libraries. *Chair* Sabina Benelli, Teatro alla Scala, Milan. E-mail broadcasting-orchestra@iaml.info.

Libraries in Music Teaching Institutions. *Chair* Charles Peters, William & Gayle Cook Music Lib., Indiana Univ., Bloomington. E-mail teaching@iaml.info.

Public Libraries. *Chair* vacant. *V.Chair* Carolyn Dow, Polley Music Lib., Lincoln City Libs., Lincoln, Neb. E-mail public-libraries@iaml.info.

Research Libraries. *Chair* Thomas Leibnitz. Musiksammlung der Österreichischen Nationalbibliothek, Vienna. E-mail research-libraries@iaml.info.

Subject Sections

Audio-Visual Materials. *Chair* Jonathan Manton, Yale Univ., New Haven. E-mail ajustice@usc.edu.

Bibliography. *Chair* Stefan Engl, Österreichische Nationalbibliothek, Vienna. E-mail bibliography@iaml.info.

Cataloguing and Metadata. *Chair* Frédéric Lemmers, Bibliothèque royale de Belgique, Brussels. E-mail cataloguing@iaml.info.

Service and Training. *Chair* Anna Pensaert, Cambridge Univ. Lib., Cambridge. E-mail service@iaml.info.

International Association of School Librarianship

Jill Hancock, Executive Director
65 E. Wacker Place, Suite 1900, Chicago, IL 60601
e-mail iasl@mlahq.org
World Wide Web http://www.iasl-online.org

Mission and Objectives

The mission of the International Association of School Librarianship (IASL) is to provide an international forum for those interested in promoting effective school library programs as viable instruments in the education process. IASL also provides guidance and advice for the development of school library programs and the school library profession. IASL works in cooperation with other professional associations and agencies.

Membership is worldwide and includes school librarians, teachers, librarians, library advisers, consultants, education administrators, and others who are responsible for library and information services in schools. The membership also includes professors and instructors in universities and colleges where there are programs for school librarians, and students who are undertaking such programs.

The objectives of IASL are to advocate the development of school libraries throughout all countries; to encourage the integration of school library programs into the instruction and curriculum of the school; to promote the professional preparation and continuing education of school library personnel; to foster a sense of community among school librarians in all parts of the world; to foster and extend relationships between school librarians and other professionals in connection with children and youth; to foster research in the field of school librarianship and the integration of its findings with pertinent knowledge from related fields; to promote the publication and dissemination of information about successful advocacy and program initiatives in school librarianship; to share information about programs and materials for children and youth throughout the international community; and to initiate and coordinate activities, conferences, and other projects in the field of school librarianship and information services.

Founded 1971.

Membership

Approximately 825.

Officers

Pres. Katy Manck, Independent Book Reviewer, Gilmer, Tex. E-mail katyroo@gmail.com or Katy.Manck@gmail.com; *V.P. Assn. Operations* Mihaela Banek Zorica, Univ. of Zagreb, Faculty of Humanities and Social Sciences, Dept. of Information Sciences, Zagreb, Croatia. E-mail mbanek@ffzg.hr; *V.P. Assn. Relations* Albert Boekhorst, Brasil, Netherlands. E-mail albertkb@gmail.com; *V.P. Advocacy and Promotion* Patricia Carmichael, Queensland, Australia. E-mail isabell.rina@gmail.com or iasl.giggle.it@gmail.com; *Treas.* Jennifer Branch-Mueller, Univ. of Alberta, Canada. E-mail jbranch@ualberta.ca.

Regional Board of Directors

Jerry Mathema, Africa; Shyh-Mee Tan, Asia; Annie Tam, East Asia; Tom Adamich, North America; Paulette Stewart, Latin America/Caribbean; Vanja Jurilj, Europe; Sevgi Arioglu, North Africa/Middle East; Susan La Marca, Oceania; Zakir Hossain, International Schools.

Publications

School Libraries Worldwide (http://www.iasl-online.org/publications/slw/index.html), the association's refereed research and professional journal (online only; 2x yearly; memb.).

IASL Newsletter (http://www.iasl-online.org/publications/newsletter.html) (print; 3x yearly; memb.).

International Association of Scientific and Technological University Libraries (IATUL)

Anne Horn, President
World Wide Web http://www.iatul.org

Object

The main object of the International Association of Scientific and Technological University Libraries (IATUL) is to provide a forum where library directors and senior managers can meet to exchange views on matters of current significance and to provide an opportunity for them to develop a collaborative approach to solving problems. IATUL also welcomes into membership organizations that supply services to university libraries, if they wish to be identified with the association's activities.

Membership

260 in 60 countries.

Officers

Pres. Anne Horn, Univ. of Sheffield, UK. E-mail a.horn@sheffield.ac.uk; *V.P.* Charles Eckman, Univ. of Miami, USA. E-mail ceckman @miami.edu; *Secy.* Lucille Webster, Durban Univ. of Technology, South Africa. E-mail webster@dut.ac.za; *Treas.* Howard Amos, Univ. of Otago Lib., New Zealand. E-mail howardamos@otago.ac.nz.

Board Members

Officers: Jill Benn, Univ. of Western Australia, Perth. Donna Bourne-Tyson, Dalhousie Univ., Canada. Lars Egeland, Oslo Metropolitan Univ., Norway; J. K. Vijaykumar, King Abdullah University of Science and Technology, Saudi Arabia. Anna Walek, Gdańsk University of Technology, Poland.

Publication

IATUL Conference Proceedings (at http://iatul.org/conferences/pastconferences/) (ann.).

International Council on Archives

Anthea Seles, Secretary-General
60 rue des Francs-Bourgeois, 75003 Paris, France
Tel. 33-1-40-27-63-06, fax 33-1-42-72-20-65, e-mail ica@ica.org
World Wide Web http://www.ica.org

Object

The mission of the International Council on Archives (ICA) is to establish, maintain, and strengthen relations among archivists of all lands, and among all professional and other agencies or institutions concerned with the custody, organization, or administration of archives, public or private, wherever located. Established 1948.

Membership

Approximately 1,900 in nearly 200 countries and territories

Officers

Pres. David Fricker, Australia; *V.P.s* M. Normand Charbonneau, Canada; Henri Zuber, France; *Secy.-Gen.* Anthea Seles, France.

Board Members

Hamad Bin Mohammed Al-Dhawyani, Oman; Opeta Alefaio, Fiji; Azemi Abdul Aziz, Malaysia; Françoise Banat-Berger, France; Alexander Lukas Bieri, Switzerland; Caroline Brown, UK; Paola Caroli, Italy; Margaret Crockett, France; Yonten Dargye, Bhutan; Abdulla A. Kareem El Reyes, UAE; Charles Farrugia, Malta; Emilie Gagnet Leumas, USA; Tim Harris, UK; Jeff James, UK; Takeo Katoh, Japan; Paul Lihoma, Malawi; Gustavo Castaner Marquadt, Belgium; Matthias Massode, Benin; Jean-Paul Nenga Mukanya, Congo; Yolanda Cagigas Ocejo, Spain; Rocio Pazmiño, Ecuador; Vilde Ronge, Norway; Günther Schefbeck, Austria; Fina Sola i Gasset, Spain; David Sutton, UK; Rita Tjien-Fooh, Suriname; Amatuni Virabyan, Armenia; Kelvin L. White, USA; Ian E. Wilson, Canada; Lara Wilson, Canada; Atakilty Assefa Asgedom (ex officio), Ethiopia.

Publications

Comma (print and online; 2x yearly, memb.).

Flash (online only; 2x yearly; memb.).

ICA e-newsletter (online only; mo.).

Conference Papers and Proceedings.

International Federation of Film Archives (Fédération Internationale des Archives du Film)

Michael Loebenstein , Secretary-General
Secretariat, 42 rue Blanche, B-1060 Brussels, Belgium
Tel. 32-2-538-30-65, fax 32-2-534-47-74, e-mail info@fiafnet.org
World Wide Web http://www.fiafnet.org

Object

Founded in 1938, the International Federation of Film Archives (FIAF) brings together not-for-profit institutions dedicated to rescuing films and any other moving-image elements considered both as cultural heritage and as historical documents.

FIAF is a collaborative association of the world's leading film archives whose purpose has always been to ensure the proper preservation and showing of motion pictures. Almost 90 member archives in more than 50 countries collect, restore, and exhibit films and cinema documentation spanning the entire history of film.

FIAF seeks to promote film culture and facilitate historical research, to help create new archives around the world, to foster training and expertise in film preservation, to encourage the collection and preservation of documents and other cinema-related materials, to develop cooperation between archives, and to ensure the international availability of films and cinema documents.

Officers

Pres. Frédéric Maire; *Secy.-Gen.* Michael Loebensten; *Treas.* Jon Wengström. *V.P.s* Cecilia Cenciarelli, Michal Brigant, Iris Elezi.

Address correspondence to Christophe Dupin, Senior Administrator, FIAF Secretariat. E-mail c.dupin@fiafnet.org.

Publications and Databases

FIAF Bulletin Online.

FIAF Directory.

FIAF International Index to Film Periodicals database. (ProQuest).

International Index to Film Periodicals database. (OVID).

International Index to Television Periodicals database.

Journal of Film Preservation. Ed. Elaine Burrows. E-mail jfp.editor@fiafnet.org.

Treasures from the Film Archives database.

Extensive selection of books through the FIAF Bookshop.

International Federation of Library Associations and Institutions

P.O. Box 95312, 2509 CH The Hague, Netherlands
Tel. 31-70-314-0884, fax 31-70-383-4827, e-mail ifla@ifla.org
World Wide Web http://www.ifla.org

Object

The object of the International Federation of Library Associations and Institutions (IFLA) is to promote international understanding, cooperation, discussion, research, and development in all fields of library activity, including bibliography, information services, and the education of library personnel, and to provide a body through which librarianship can be represented in matters of international interest. IFLA is the leading international body representing the interests of library and information services and their users. It is the global voice of the library and information profession. Founded 1927.

Officers

Pres. Glòria Pérez-Salmerón, Federación Española de Sociedades de Archivística, Biblioteconomía, Documentación y Museística, Spain; *Pres.-Elect* Christine Mackenzie, freelance librarian, Australia; *Treas.* Barbara Lison, Stadtbibliothek Bremen, Germany; *Past Pres.* Donna Scheeder, Library Strategies International, USA; *Secy.-Gen.* Gerald Leitner (ex officio), Netherlands.

Governing Board

Huanwen Cheng (China), Marwa El Sahn (Egypt), Ágnes Hajdu Barát (Hungary), Patrick Losinski (USA), Torbjörn Nilsson (Sweden), Victoria Okojie (Nigeria), Victoria Owen (Canada), Viviana Quiñones (France), Knud Schulz (Denmark), plus the chairs of the IFLA Professional Committee and divisions.

Publications

IFLA Annual Report.
IFLA Journal (4x yearly).
IFLA Trend Reports.
IFLA Professional Reports.
IFLA Publications Series.
IFLA Series on Bibliographic Control.
Global Studies in Libraries and Information (irreg. series).
Access and Opportunity for All: How Libraries Contribute to the United Nations 2030 Agenda.

American Membership

Associations

American Lib. Assn., Assn. for Lib. and Info. Science Educ., Assn. of Research Libs., Chief Officers of State Lib. Agencies, Medical Lib. Assn., Special Libs. Assn., Urban Libs. Council, Chinese American Libns. Assn., Polish American Lib. Assn.

Institutional Members

More than 100 libraries and related institutions are institutional members or consultative bodies and sponsors of IFLA in the United States (out of a total of more than 1,000 globally), and more than 100 are individual affiliates (out of a total of more than 300 affiliates globally).

International Organization for Standardization

Sergio Mujica, Secretary-General
ISO Central Secretariat, Chemin de Blandonnet 8, CP 401
1214 Vernier, Geneva, Switzerland
Tel. 41-22-749-01-11, fax 41-22-733-34-30, e-mail central@iso.org
World Wide Web http://www.iso.org

Object

Founded in 1947, the International Organization for Standardization (ISO) is a worldwide federation of national standards bodies that currently comprises members from 164 countries and 785 technical committees and subcommittees working on various aspects of standards development. The object of ISO is to promote the development of standardization and related activities in the world with a view to facilitating international exchange of goods and services, and to developing cooperation in the spheres of intellectual, scientific, technological, and economic activity. The scope of ISO covers international standardization in all fields except electrical and electronic engineering standardization, which is the responsibility of the International Electrotechnical Commission (IEC). The results of ISO technical work are published as international standards.

Officers

Pres. John Walter, Canada; *Pres.-Elect* Eddy Njoroge, Kenya; *V.P. (Policy)* Scott Steedman, UK; *V.P. (Technical Management)* Sauw Kook Choy, Singapore; *Secy.-Gen.* Sergio Mujica, Chile; *Treas.* Dominique Christin, Switzerland.

Technical Work

The technical work of ISO is carried out by groups of experts collaborating worldwide, representing every imaginable sector, from soaps to spacecraft, from MP3 to coffee. Among its technical committees are

ISO/TC 46—Information and documentation (Secretariat, Association Française de Normalization, 11 ave. Francis de Pressensé, 93571 La Plaine Saint-Denis, Cedex, France). Scope: Standardization of practices relating to libraries, documentation and information centers, indexing and abstracting services, archives, information science, and publishing.

ISO/TC 37—Language and terminology (Secretariat, Standardization Administration of China, No. 9 Madian Donglu, Haidian District, Beijing 100088, China). Scope: Standardization of descriptions, resources, technologies and services related to terminology, translation, interpreting, and other language-based activities in the multilingual information society.

ISO/IEC JTC 1—Information technology (Secretariat, American National Standards Institute, 1899 L St. NW, 11th Fl., Washington, DC 20036). Scope: Standardization in the field of information technology.

ISO Annual Report.

ISOfocus (6x yearly).

Extensive selection of titles on the ISO website (https://www.iso.org/publication-list.html).

Foreign Library Associations

The following is a list of regional and national library associations around the world. A more complete list can be found in *International Literary Market Place* (Information Today, Inc.).

Regional

Africa

Standing Conference of Eastern, Central, and Southern African Lib. and Info. Assns. (SCECSAL), c/o Uganda Library and Information Assn., P.O. Box 25412, Kampala. Tel. 256-704-885-246, e-mail secretariat@ulia.org.ug. World Wide Web https://www.ulia.org.ug/SCECSAL.php.

The Americas

Assn. of Caribbean Univ., Research, and Institutional Libs. (ACURIL), P.O. Box 21337, San Juan, Puerto Rico 00931. Tel. 787-612-9343, e-mail executivesecretariat@acuril.org, World Wide Web https://acuril.org. *Pres.* Monique Alberts; *Exec. Secy.* Luisa Vigo-Cepeda.

Seminar on the Acquisition of Latin American Lib. Materials (SALALM), c/o SALALM Secretariat, Latin American Lib., 422 Howard Tilton Memorial Lib., Tulane Univ., 7001 Freret St., New Orleans, LA 70118-5549. Tel. 504-247-1366, fax 504-247-1367, e-mail salalm@tulane.edu, World Wide Web https://www.salalm.org. *Exec. Dir.*. Hortensia Calvo. E-mail hcalvo@tulane.edu.

Asia

Congress of Southeast Asian Libns. (CONSAL), # Razathingaha Road, Nearby Razathingaha Circle, Uottra Thiri TSP, Naypyitaw, Myanmar. Tel. 95 67 418427, fax 95 67 418426, e-mail: info@consalxvii.org, World Wide Web http://consal.org.

The Commonwealth

Commonwealth Lib. Assn. (COMLA), c/o University of the West Indies, Bridetown Campus, Learning Resource Center, P.O. Box 64, Bridgetown, Barbados. Tel. 246-417-4201, fax 246- 424-8944, e-mail watsone@uwichill.edu.bb, World Wide Web http://isis.uwimona.edu.jm/. *Pres.* Elizabeth Watson.

U.K. Library and Archives Group on Africa (SCOLMA), c/o Sarah Rhodes, Bodleian Social Science Lib., Univ. of Oxford, Manor Rd. Bldg., Manor Rd., Oxford OX1 3UQ, England. Tel. 01865-277162, World Wide Web http://scolma.org. *Chair* Lucy McCann. *Secy.* Sarah Rhodes.

Europe

European Bureau of Library, Information and Documentation Associations (EBLID), c/o EBLIDA Secretariat, Koninklijke Bibliotheek (National Library of the Netherlands), Prins Willem-Alexanderhof 5, 2595 BE, The Hague. Tel.: 31 (0) 70 3140137, e-mail eblida@eblida.org, World Wide Web http://www.eblida.org. *Dir.* Guiseppe Vitiello.

Ligue des Bibliothèques Européennes de Recherche (LIBER) (Assn. of European Research Libs.), P.O. Box 90407, 2509 LK The Hague, Netherlands. Tel. 31-70-314-07-67, fax 070-314-01-97, e-mail liber@kb.nl, World Wide Web http://www.libereurope.eu. *Pres.* Jeannette Frey. *V.P.* Julien Roche. *Secy.-Gen.* John MacColl. *Exec. Dir.* Astrid Verheusen.

National

Argentina

ABGRA (Asociación de Bibliotecarios Graduados de la República Argentina) (Assn. of Graduate Libns. of Argentina), Parana 918, 2do Piso, C1017AAT Buenos Aires. Tel. 54-11-4811-0043, fax 54-11-4816-3422, e-mail info@abgra.org.ar, World Wide Web http://www.abgra.org.ar. *Pres.* Gloria Priore.

Australia

Australian Lib. and Info. Assn., Box 6335, Kingston, ACT 2604. Tel. 61-2-6215-8222, fax 61-2-6282-2249, e-mail enquiry@alia.org.au, World Wide Web http://www.alia.org.au. *CEO* Sue McKerracher. E-mail sue.mckerracher@alia.org.au.

Australian Society of Archivists, P.O. Box 576, Crows Nest, NSW 1585. Tel. 612-9431-8644, e-mail office@archivists.org.au, World Wide Web http://www.archivists.org.au. *Pres.* Julia Mant; *V.P.* Andrea McKinnon-Matthews.

National and State Libs. Australia (NSLA), State Lib. Victoria, 328 Swanston St., Melbourne VIC 3000. Tel. 03 8664 7512, e-mail nsla@slv.vic.gov.au, World Wide Web https://www.nsla.org.au. *Chair* Kate Torney. *Exec. Officer* Barbara Lemon.

Austria

Österreichische Gesellschaft für Dokumentation und Information (Austrian Society for Documentation and Info.), c/o Österreichische Computer Gesellschaft OCG, Wollzeile 1, 1010 Vienna. E-mail office@oegdi.at, World Wide Web http://www.oegdi.at. *Chair:* Gerhard Frohlich.

Vereinigung Österreichischer Bibliothekarinnen und Bibliothekare (VOEB) (Assn. of Austrian Libns.), Universitätsbibliothek Graz, Universitätsplatz 3, 8010 Graz. E-mail voeb@ub.tuwein.ac.at, World Wide Web http://www.univie.ac.at/voeb/php. *President* Werner Schlacher. E-mail werner.schlacher@uni-graz.at.

Bangladesh

Bangladesh Assn. of Libns., Info. Scientists and Documentalists (BALID), House # 67/B (3rd floor), Road # 9/A, Dhanmondi, Dhaka-1209, Bangladesh. E-mail balidbd@gmail.com, info@balidbd.org. *Chair* Dr. Mizra Mohd Rezaul Islam.

Barbados

Lib. Assn. of Barbados, P.O. Box 827E, Bridgetown, Barbados. E-mail milton@uwichill.edu.bb.

Belgium

Archief- en Bibliotheekwezen in België (Belgian Assn. of Archivists and Libns.), Royal Library of Belgium, Boulevard de l'Empereur 2, 1000 Brussels. Tel. 2-519-53-93, fax 2-519-56-10, e-mail abb@kbr.be, World Wide Web http://www.archibib.be.

Assn. Belge de Documentation/Belgische Vereniging voor Documentatie (Belgian Assn. for Documentation), 4 Boulevard de l'Empereur, 1000 Bruxelles. Tel. 2-675-58-62, fax 2-672-74-46, e-mail abdbvd@abd-bvd.be, World Wide Web http://www.abd-bvd.be. *Pres.* Guy Delsaut. E-mail guy.delsaut@skynet.be; *Secy.-Gen.* Michele Orban. E-mail michele.orban@gmail.com.

Association des Professionales des Bibliothéques Francophones de Belgique (APBFB), Rue Nanon 98, 5002 Namur. Tel. 32-472-94-12-05, e-mail info@apbfb.be, World Wide Web http://www.apbfb.be. *Pres.* Françoise Dury.

Association Professionnelle des Bibliothécaires et Documentalistes. See Association des Professionales des Bibliothéques Francophones de Belgique (APBFB).

Vlaamse Vereniging voor Bibliotheek-, Archief-, en Documentatiewezen (Flemish Assn. of Libns., Archivists, and Documentalists), Statiestraat 179, B-2600 Berchem, Antwerp. Tel. 3-281-44-57, e-mail vvbad@vvbad.be, World Wide Web http://www.vvbad.be. *Coord.* Jessica Jacobs. E-mail jessica.jacobs@vvbad.be.

Belize

Belize National Lib. Service and Info. System (BNLSIS), P.O. Box 287, Princess Margaret Dr., Belize City. Tel. 501-223-4248, fax 501-223-4246, e-mail nls@btl.net, World Wide Web http://www.nlsbze.bz.

Bolivia

Centro Nacional de Documentación Científica y Tecnológica (National Scientific and Technological Documentation Center), Av. Mariscal Santa Cruz 1175, Esquina c Ayacucho, La Paz. Tel. 02-359-583, fax 02-359-586, e-mail iicndct@huayna.umsa.edu.bo, World Wide Web http://www.bolivian.com/industrial/cndct.

Bosnia and Herzegovina

Drustvo Bibliotekara Bosne i Hercegovine (Libns. Society of Bosnia and Herzegovina), Zmaja od Bosne 8B, 71000 Sarajevo. Tel. 33-275-5325, fax 33-212-435, e-mail nubbih @nub.ba, World Wide Web http://www.nub.ba. *Pres.* Ismet Ovcina. E-mail ured.direktora@nub.ba.

Botswana

Botswana Lib. Assn., Box 1310, Gaborone. Tel. 267-732-31047, e-mail secretary@bla.org.bw, World Wide Web http://www.bla.org.bw. *Pres.* Peter Mazebe II Mothataesi Sebina. E-mail president@bla.org.bw.

Brunei Darussalam

Persatuan Perpustakaan Negara Brunei Darussalam (National Lib. Assn. of Brunei), c/o Class 64 Lib., SOASC, Jalan Tengah, Bandar Seri Begawan BS8411. Fax 2-222-330, e-mail pobox.bla@gmail.com, World Wide Web http://bruneilibraryassociation.wordpress.com.

Cameroon

Assn. des Bibliothécaires, Archivistes, Documentalistes et Muséographes du Cameroun (Assn. of Libns., Archivists, Documentalists, and Museum Curators of Cameroon), BP 12092, Yaoundé. Tel. 237-2-22-22-28-98, e-mail abadcameroun@gmail.com, World Wide Web http://www.abadcam.sitew.com. *Pres.* Alim Garga. E-mail a_garga @yahoo.fr.

Chile

Colegio de Bibliotecarios de Chile (Chilean Lib. Assn.), Avda. Diagonal Paraguay 383, Torre 11, Oficina 122, 6510017 Santiago. Tel. 2-222-5652, e-mail cbc@bibliotecarios.cl, World Wide Web http://www.bibliotecarios.cl.

China

China Society for Lib. Science, 33 Zhongguancun Nandajie, Hai Dian District, Beijing 100081. Tel. 86-10-8854-4114, fax 86-10-6841-7815, e-mail webmaster@nlc.gov.cn, World Wide Web http://www.nlc.gov.cn.

Colombia

Asociación Colombiana de Bibliotecólogos y Documentalistas (Colombian Assn. of Libns. and Documentalists), Calle 21, No. 6-58, Oficina 404, Bogotá D.C. Tel. 1-282-3620, fax 1-282-5487, e-mail secretaria@ascolbi.org, World Wide Web http://www.ascolbi.org. *Pres.* Leonardo Ramirez O.

Congo (Republic of)

Assn. des Bibliothécaires, Archivistes, Documentalistes et Muséologues du Congo (ABADOM) (Assn. of Librarians, Archivists, Documentalists, and Museologists of Congo), BP 3148, Kinshasa-Gombe. E-mail bernardakondzo72@gmail.com.

Croatia

Hrvatsko Knjiznicarsko Drustvo (Croatian Lib. Assn.), c/o National and Univ. Lib., Hrvatske bratske zajednice 4, 10 000 Zagreb. Tel./fax 1-615-93-20, e-mail hkd@nsk.hr, World Wide Web http://www.hkdrustvo.hr. *Pres.* Dijana Machala. *Secy.* Andreja Tominac.

Cuba

Asociación Cubana de Bibliotecarios (ASCUBI) (Lib. Assn. of Cuba), P.O. Box 6670, Havana. Tel. 7-555-442, fax 7-816-224, e-mail ascubi@bnjm.cu, World Wide Web http://ascubi.blogspot.com/. *Chair* Margarita Bellas Vilariño. E-mail ascubi@bnjm.cu.

Cyprus

Kypriakos Synthesmos Vivliothicarion (Lib. Assn. of Cyprus), c/o Pedagogical Academy, P.O. Box 1039, Nicosia. E-mail kebepcy@gmail.com, World Wide Web http://kebep.blogspot.com.

Czech Republic

Svaz Knihovniku a Informacnich Pracovniku Ceske Republiky (SKIP) (Assn. of Lib. and Info. Professionals of the Czech Republic), National Library of the Czech Republic, Mariánské náměstí 190/5, 110 00 Prague

1. Tel. 420-221-663-379, fax 420-221-663-175, e-mail skip@nkp.cz, World Wide Web http://skip.cz. *Chair* Mgr. Roman Giebisch.

Denmark

Arkivforeningen (Archives Society), v/Ingrid Nostberg, Vestfoldmuseene IKS, Department Vestfoldarkivet, 3205 Sandefjord. Tel. 958 21 501, e-mail post@arkivarforeningen.no, World Wide Web http://www.arkivarforeningen.no. *Deputy Chair* Ingrid Nostberg.

Danmarks Biblioteksforening (Danish Lib. Assn.), Vartov, Farvergade 27D, 1463 Copenhagen K. Tel. 3325-0935, fax 3325-7900, e-mail db@db.dk, World Wide Web http://www.db.dk. *Dir.* Michel Steen-Hansen. E-mail msh@db.dk.

Danmarks Forskningsbiblioteksforening (Danish Research Lib. Assn.), c/o University of Southern Denmark, Studiestræde 6, 1455 Copenhagen K. Tel. 45-4220-2177, e-mail secretariat@dfdf.dk, World Wide Web http://www.dfdf.dk. *Pres.* Bertil Dorch. E-mail bfd@bib.sdu.dk.

Dansk Musikbiblioteks Forening (Assn. of Danish Music Libs.), c/o Helene Olsen, Sundby Library, Jemtelandsgade 3, Copenhagen S. E-mail sekretariat@dmbf.nu, World Wide Web http://www.dmbf.nu. *Chair* Ojvind Harkamp. E-mail ojvnid@dragoer.dk.

Kommunernes Forening for Paedagogiske Laeringscentre (Municipal Association of Educational Learning Centers—KFPLC), The Old Town Hall, Industrivej 2, 4683 Ronnede. Tel. 33-11-13-91, e-mail kfplc@kfplc.dk, World Wide Web http://www.kfplc.dk. *Chair* Michael Nohr. *Mgr.* Gitte Frausing. E-mail gf@ksbf.dk.

Ecuador

Asociación Ecuatoriana de Bibliotecarios (Ecuadoran Lib. Assn.), c/o Casa de la Cultura Ecuatoriana, Casillas 87, Quito. E-mail asoecubiblio@gmail.com.

El Salvador

Asociación de Bibliotecarios de El Salvador (ABES) (Assn. of Salvadorian Libns.), Járdines de la Hacienda Block D pje, 19 No. 158, Ciudad Merliot, Antiguo Cuscatlán, La Libertad. Tel. 503-2534-8924, fax 523-2228-2956, e-mail abeselsalvador@gmail.com.

Finland

Suomen Kirjastoseura (Finnish Lib. Assn.), Runeberginkatu 15 A 6, 00100 Helsinki. Tel. 44-522-2941, e-mail info@fla.fi, World Wide Web http://www.fla.fi. *Exec. Dir.* Rauha Maarno. E-mail rauha.maarno@fla.fi.

France

Association des Archivistes Français (Assn. of French Archivists), 8 rue Jean-Marie Jego, 75013 Paris. Tel. 1-46-06-39-44, fax 1-46-06-39-52, e-mail secretariat@archivistes.org, World Wide Web http://www.archivistes.org.

Association des Bibliothécaires Français (Assn. of French Libns.), 31 rue de Chabrol, F-75010 Paris. Tel. 1-55-33-10-30, fax 1-55-30-10-31, e-mail info@abf.asso.fr, World Wide Web http://www.abf.asso.fr. *Chair* Alice Bernard; *Gen. Secy.* Chantal Ferreux.

Association des Professionnels de l'Information et de la Documentation (Assn. of Info. and Documentation Professionals), 25 rue Claude Tillier, 75012 Paris. Tel. 06-81-39-82-14, e-mail adbs@adbs.fr, World Wide Web http://www.adbs.fr. *Pres.* Danielle DuFour-Coppolani.

Germany

Arbeitsgemeinschaft der Spezialbibliotheken (Assn. of Special Libs.), c/o Wissenschaftskolleg zu Berlin—Bibliothek, Wallotstr. 19, 14193 Berlin. Tel. 030-89001-144, fax 030-89001-400, e-mail geschaeftsstelle@aspb.de, World Wide Web http://aspb.de. *Chair* Kirsten Schoof. E-mail kirsten.schoof@aesthetics.mpg.de.

Berufsverband Information Bibliothek (Assn. of Info. and Lib. Professionals), Gartenstr. 18, 72764 Reutlingen. Tel. 7121-3491-0, fax 7121-3004-33, e-mail mail@bib-info.de, World Wide Web http://www.bib-info.de. *Chair* Ing. Ute Engelkenmeier.

Deutsche Gesellschaft für Informationswissenschaft und Informationspraxis eV (German Society for Information Science and

Practice eV), Windmühlstr. 3, 60329 Frankfurt-am-Main. Tel. 69-43-03-13, fax 69-490-90-96, e-mail mail@dgi-info.de, World Wide Web http://www.dgi-info.de. *Pres.* Marleis Ockenfeld.

Deutscher Bibliotheksverband eV (German Lib. Assn.), Fritschestr. 27–28, 10585 Berlin. Tel. 30-644-98-99-10, fax 30-644-98-99-29, e-mail dbv@bibliotheksverband.de, World Wide Web http://www.bibliotheks verband.de. *Dir.* Barbara Schleihagen.

VdA—Verband Deutscher Archivarinnen und Archivare (Assn. of German Archivists), Woerthstr. 3, 36037 Fulda. Tel. 661-29-109-72, fax 661-29-109-74, e-mail info@vda.archiv.net, World Wide Web http://www.vda.archiv.net. *Chair* Ralf Jacob.

Verein Deutscher Bibliothekare eV (Society of German Libns.), Univ. Lib. Erlangen-Nürnberg, Universitatsstrasse 4, 91054 Erlangen. Tel. 09131-85-22150, e-mail geschaeftsstelle@vdb-online.org, World Wide Web http://www.vdb-online.org. *Chair* Konstanze Söllner, e-mail chairman@vdb-online.org.

Ghana

Ghana Lib. Assn., Box GP 4105, Accra. Tel. 244-17-4930, e-mail info@gla-net.org, World Wide Web http://gla-net.org. *Pres.* Samuel B. Aggrey.

Greece

Enosis Hellinon Bibliothekarion (Assn. of Greek Libns.), Skoufa 52, P.O. Box 10672, Athens. Tel./fax 210-330-2128, e-mail info@eebep.gr, World Wide Web http://www.eebep.gr. *Pres.* Alexandra Papazoglou. *Secy.* Eva Semertaki.

Guyana

Guyana Lib. Assn., c/o Department of Public Information, Area 'B' Homestretch Ave., D'Urban Park, Georgetown. Tel. 592-226-6715, fax 592-227-4052, e-mail info@dpi.gov.gy, World Wide Web https://dpi.gov.gy/tag/guyana-library-association/.

Hong Kong

Hong Kong Lib. Assn., GPO Box 10095, Hong Kong, China. E-mail hkla@hkla.org, World Wide Web http://www.hkla.org. *Pres.* Diana Chan. E-mail president@hkla.org. *Secy.* Wong Hoi Yan Wendy. E-mail membership@hkla.org.

Hungary

Magyar Könyvtárosok Egyesülete (Assn. of Hungarian Libns.), H-1054, Hold u 6, Budapest. Tel./fax 1-311-8634, e-mail mke@oszk.hu, World Wide Web http://www.mke.info.hu. *Chair* Dr. Ágnes Hajdu; *Secy. Gen.* Judit Gerencsér.

Iceland

Upplysing—Felag bokasafns-og upplysingafraeoa (Information—The Icelandic Lib. and Info. Science Assn.), Mailbox 8865, 128 Reykjavík. Tel. 354-864-6220, e-mail upplysing@upplysing.is, World Wide Web http://www.upplysing.is. *Chair* Oddfrídur Steinunn Helgadóttir. E-mail formadur@upplysing.is.

India

Indian Assn. of Special Libs. and Info. Centres, P-291, CIT Scheme 6M, Kankurgachi, Kolkata 700-054. Tel. 33-2362-9651, e-mail iaslic@vsnl.net, World Wide Web http://www.iaslic1955.org.in. *Pres.* Jatindra Nath Satpathi; *Gen. Secy.* Sajal Kanti Goswami.

Indian Lib. Assn., A/40-41, Flat 201, Ansal Bldg., Mukerjee Nagar, New Delhi 110009. Tel./fax 11-2765-1743, e-mail dvs-srcc@rediffmail.com, World Wide Web http://www.ilaindia.net. *Pres.* Shabahat Husain. E-mail shabahat12@rediffmail.com; *Gen. Secy.* Pardeep Rai. E-mail raipardeep@gmail.com.

Indonesia

Ikatan Pustakawan Indonesia (Indonesian Lib. Assn.), c/o National Library, Jalan Salemba Raya 28.A, Central Jakarta, 10430. Tel. (021) 3900944, World Wide Web http://ipi.web.id. *Chair* Dedi Junaedi.

Ireland

Cumann Leabharlann na hEireann (Lib. Assn. of Ireland), c/o 138–144 Pearse St., Dublin 2. E-mail honsecretary@libraryassociation.ie, World Wide Web http://www.library/association.ie. *Pres.* Philip Cohen. E-mail president@libraryassociation.ie. *Secy.* Eimear McGinn. E-mail honsecretary@library association.ie.

Israel

Israeli Center for Libs., 22 Baruch Hirsch St., P.O. Box 801, 51108 Bnei Brak. Tel. 03-6180151, fax 03-5798048, e-mail meida@gmail.com or icl@icl.org.il, World Wide Web http://www.icl.org.il. *CEO* Zvika Mier. E-mail zvika@icl.org.il.

Italy

Associazione Italiana Biblioteche (Italian Lib. Assn.), Biblioteca Nazionale Centrale, Viale Castro Pretorio 105, 00185 Rome RM. Tel. 6-446-3532, fax 6-444-1139, e-mail segreteria@aib.it, World Wide Web http://www.aib.it.

Jamaica

Lib. and Info. Assn. of Jamaica, P.O. Box 125, Kingston 5. Tel./fax 876-927-1614, e-mail liajapresident@yahoo.com, World Wide Web http://www.liaja.org.jm. *Pres.* Viviene Kerr-Williams. E-mail vskwilliams@gmail.com.

Japan

Info. Science and Technology Assn., 1-11-14, Shinkawa, Chuo-ku, Tokyo 104-0033. Tel. 81-3-6222-8506, fax 81-3-6222-8107, e-mail infosta@infosta.or.jp, World Wide Web http://www.infosta.or.jp.

Nihon Toshokan Kyokai (Japan Lib. Assn.), 1-11-14 Shinkawa, Chuo-ku, Tokyo 104 0033. Tel. 3-3523-0811, fax 3-3523-0841, e-mail info@jla.or.jp, World Wide Web http://www.jla.or.jp.

Senmon Toshokan Kyogikai (Japan Special Libs. Assn.), c/o Japan Lib. Assn., Bldg. F6, 1-11-14 Shinkawa Chuo-ku, Tokyo 104-0033. Tel. 3-3537-8335, fax 3-3537-8336, e-mail jsla@jsla.or.jp, World Wide Web http://www.jsla.or.jp.

Jordan

Jordan Lib. and Info. Assn., P.O. Box 6289, Amman 11118. Tel./fax 00962-64629412, World Wide Web http://www.jila.org. *Pres.* Omar Al-Jaradat.

Kenya

Kenya Assn. of Lib. and Info. Professionals (formerly Kenya Lib. Assn.), Buruburu, P.O. Box 49468-00100 Nairobi. Tel. 20-733-732-799, e-mail info@kenyalibraryassociation.or.ke, World Wide Web http://www.kenya libraryassociation.or.ke.

Korea (Democratic People's Republic of)

Lib. Assn. of the Democratic People's Republic of Korea, c/o Grand People's Study House, P.O. Box 200, Pyongyang. E-mail korea@korea-dpr.com.

Korea (Republic of)

Korean Lib. Assn., San 60-1, Banpo-dong, Seocho-gu, Seoul 137-702. Tel. 2-535-4868, fax 2-535-5616, e-mail license@kla.kr, World Wide Web http://www.kla.kr.

Laos

Association des Bibliothécaires Laotiens (Lao Lib. Assn.), c/o Direction de la Bibliothèque Nationale, Ministry of Educ., BP 704, Vientiane. Tel. 21-21-2452, fax 21-21-2408, e-mail bailane@laotel.com.

Latvia

Latvian Libns. Assn., c/o Latvian National Lib., Mukusalas iela 3, Riga, LV-1423. Tel. 67806100, fax 67280851, e-mail lnb@lnb.lv, World Wide Web http://www.lnb.lv.

Lebanon

Lebanese Lib. Assn., P.O. Box 13-5053, Beirut 1102 2801. Tel. 1-786-456, e-mail kjaroudy@lau.edu.lb, World Wide Web http://www.llaweb.org. *Pres.* Randa Chidiac. E-mail randachidiac@usek.edu.lb.

Lesotho

Lesotho Lib. Assn., Private Bag A26, Maseru 100. Tel. 213-420, fax 340-000, e-mail info@lla.co.ls, World Wide Web https://lla.org.ls. *Pres.* Kubelo Tsiki.

Lithuania

Lietuvos Bibliotekininku Draugija (Lithuanian Libns. Assn.), Gedimino pr. 51, Vilnius, LT-01504. Tel. 370-5-231-8585, e-mail lbd.sekretore@gmail.com, World Wide Web http://www.lbd.lt. *Chair* Jolita Stephonaitiene. E-mail jolita.stephonaitiene@lnb.lt.

Luxembourg

Association Luxembourgeoise des Bibliothécaires, Archivistes, et Documentalistes (ALBAD) (Luxembourg Assn. of Libns., Archivists, and Documentalists), c/o National Lib. of Luxembourg, BP 295, L-2012 Luxembourg. Tel. 352-621-46-14-15, World Wide Web http://www.albad.lu. *Pres.* Estelle Beck. E-mail presidence@albad.lu. *Secy. Gen.* Bernard Linster. E-mail secretarie@albad.lu.

Malawi

Malawi Lib. Assn., c/o Univ. Libn., P.O. Box 429, Zomba. Tel. 524-265, fax 525-255, World Wide Web http://www.mala.mw. *Pres.* Gift Kadzamira.

Malaysia

Persatuan Pustakawan Malaysia (Libns. Assn. of Malaysia), P.O. Box 12545, 50782 Kuala Lumpur. Tel./fax 3-2694-7390, e-mail pustakawan55@gmail.com, World Wide Web http://ppm55.org. *Pres.* Dato 'Nafisah binti Ahmad. E-mail nafisah@pnm.gov.my.

Mali

Association Malienne des Bibliothécaires, Archivistes et Documentalistes (Mali Assn. of Libns., Archivists, and Documentalists) (AMBAD), BP E4473, Bamako. Tel. 20-29-94-23, fax 20-29-93-76, e-mail dnambko@afribone.net.ml.

Malta

Malta Lib. and Info. Assn. (MaLIA), c/o Univ. of Malta Lib., Msida MSD 2080. E-mail info@malia-malta.org, World Wide Web https://www.facebook.com/malia.malta/. *CEO* Cheryl Falzon.

Mauritania

Association Mauritanienne des Bibliothécaires, Archivistes, et Documentalistes (Mauritanian Assn. of Libns., Archivists, and Documentalists), c/o Bibliothèque Nationale, BP 20, Nouakchott. Tel. 525-18-62, fax 525-18-68, e-mail bibliothequenationale@yahoo.fr.

Mauritius

Mauritius Lib. Assn., Quatre Bornes, Mauritius 230. Tel. 230 5769 7392, fax 454-9553, e-mail mauritiuslibassociation@gmail.com, World Wide Web https://www.facebook.com/Mauritius-Library-Association-MLA-142991592578201/.

Mexico

Asociación Mexicana de Bibliotecarios (Mexican Assn. of Libns.), Angel Urraza 817-A, Colonia Del Valle, Benito Juárez, Mexico DF, CP 03100. Tel. 55-55-75-33-96, e-mail correo@ambac.org.mx, World Wide Web http://www.ambac.org.mx. *Pres.* Marisela Castro Moreno; *V.P.* Brenda Cabral Vargas.

Myanmar

Myanmar Lib. Assn., Room 003, Diamond Jubilee Hall, Yangon University, Yangon, Myanmar. Tel. 95-9-420728446, e-mail libraryassociation@mlamyanmar.org, World Wide Web http://myanmarlibraryassociation.org. *Pres.* Daw Ah Win.

Namibia

Namibia Information Workers Assn., P.O. Box 308, Windhoek. Tel. 264-8148-10713, e-mail niwaassociation@gmail.com, World

Wide Web http://www.niwa-namibia.org. *Chair* Elizabeth Matheus.

Nepal

Nepal Lib. Assn., KVPL, Bhrikuti Mandap, Kathmandu. Tel. 01-4221163, e-mail nepal libraryassociation@gmail.com, World Wide Web http://www.nepallibraryassociation.org. *Pres.* Indraprasad Adhikari. *Secy.* Reshma Dangol.

The Netherlands

KNVI—Koninklijke Nederlandse Vereniging van Informatieprofessionals (Royal Dutch Association of Information Professionals), Ambachtsstraat 15, 3861 RH Nijkerk. Tel. 033-2473427, e-mail info@knvi.nl, World Wide Web http://knvi.nl. *Pres.* Paul Baak; *Pres.* Wouter Bronsgeest.

New Zealand

New Zealand Lib. Assn. (LIANZA), P.O. Box 1467, Wellington 6140. Tel. 027-347-5326, e-mail officeadmin@lianza.org.nz, World Wide Web http://www.lianza.org.nz. *Pres.* Paula Eskett; *Exec. Dir.* Ana Pickering.

Nicaragua

Asociación Nicaraguense de Bibliotecarios y Profesionales Afines (ANIBIPA) (Nicaraguan Assn. of Libns.), Bello Horizonte, Tope Sur de la Rotonda 1/2 cuadra abajo, J-11-57, Managua. Tel. 277-4159, e-mail anibipa@hotmail.com. World Wide Web https://www.facebook.com/ANIBIPA.

Nigeria

National Lib. of Nigeria, Central Business District, P.M.B. 1 Garki—Abuja, 900001. Tel. 09-234-6773, e-mail info@nln.gov.ng, World Wide Web http://www.nln.gov.ng. *Chair* Zaynab Alkhali.

Norway

Arkivar Foreningen (Assn. of Archivists), IKA Møre og Romsdal, Postbox 1073 City Center 6001 Ålesund. Tel. 936 56 026, e-mail post@arkivarforeningen.no, World Wide Web http://www.arkivarforeningen.no/. *Deputy Chair* Ingrid Nostberg.

Norsk Bibliotekforening (Norwegian Lib. Assn.), Universitetsgata 14, 0164 Oslo. Tel. 23 24 34 30, e-mail nbf@norskbibliotekforening.no, World Wide Web https://norskbibliotekforening.no/. *Dir.* Mariann Schjeide. *Gen. Secy.* Ann Berit Hulthin. E-mail abh@norskbibliotekforening.no.

Panama

Asociación Panameña de Bibliotecarios (Lib. Assn. of Panama), c/o Biblioteca Interamericana Simón Bolivar, Estafeta Universitaria, Panama City. E-mail biblis2@arcon.up.ac.pa, Tel. 507-6527-1904, World Wide Web https://www.facebook.com/asociacionpanamenabibliotecarios/info.

Paraguay

Asociación de Bibliotecarios Graduados del Paraguay (Assn. of Paraguayan Graduate Libns.), Facultad Politécnica, Universidad Nacional de Asunción, 2160 San Lorenzo. Tel. 21-585-588, e-mail abigrap@pol.una.py, World Wide Web http://www.pol.una.py/abigrap.

Peru

Asociación Peruana de Archiveros y Gestores de la Información (Peruvian Assn. of Archivists and Info. Managers), Av. Manco Capac No. 1180, Dpto 201, La Victoria, Lima. Tel. 51-934-182079, e-mail contactos@archiverosdelperu.org, World Wide Web http://archiverosdelperu.org/. *Pres.* Ricardo Arturo Moreau Heredia.

Philippines

Assn. of Special Libs. of the Philippines, c/o Goethe-Institut Philippinen, G/4-5/F Adamson Centre, 121 Leviste St., Salcedo Village, 1227 Makati City. Tel. 2-840-5723, e-mail aslplibrarians@gmail.com, World Wide Web https://aslplibrarians.org. *Pres.* Brian Lloyd Dayrit.

Philippine Libns. Assn., Room 301, National Lib. Bldg., T. M. Kalaw St., 1000 Ermita, Manila. Tel. 525-9401. World Wide Web http://plai.org.ph. *Pres.* Michael Pinto.

Poland

Stowarzyszenie Bibliotekarzy Polskich (Polish Libns. Assn.), al Niepodleglosci 213, 02-086 Warsaw. Tel. 22-608-28-24, e-mail biuro@sbp.pl, World Wide Web http://www.sbp.pl. *Dir.* Anna Grzecznowska. E-mail a.grzecznowska@sbp.pl; *Secy.* Małgorzata Dargiel-Kowalska. E-mail m.dargiel-kowalska@sbp.pl.

Portugal

Associação Portuguesa de Bibliotecários, Arquivistas e Documentalistas (Portuguese Assn. of Libns., Archivists, and Documentalists), Praca Dr. Nuno Pinheiro Torres 10-A, 15500 246 Lison. Tel. 21-816-19-80, fax 21-815-45-08, e-mail bad@bad.pt, World Wide Web http://www.apbad.pt.

Puerto Rico

Sociedad de Bibliotecarios de Puerto Rico (Society of Libns. of Puerto Rico), Apdo 22898, San Juan 00931-2898. Tel./fax 787-764-0000, World Wide Web http://www.sociedadbibliotecarios.org.

Russia

Rossiiskaya Bibliotechnaya Assotsiatsiya (Russian Lib. Assn.), 18 Sadovaya St., St. Petersburg 191069. Tel./fax 812-110-5861, e-mail rba@nlr.ru, World Wide Web http://www.rba.ru. *Exec. Secy.* Trushina Irina Aleksandrovna.

Senegal

Association Sénégalaise des Bibliothécaires, Archivistes et Documentalistes (Senegalese Assn. of Libns., Archivists, and Documentalists), BP 2006, Dakar RP, Université Cheikh Anta Diop, Dakar. Tel. 77-651-00-33, fax 33-824-23-79, e-mail asbadsn@gmail.com, World Wide Web http://www.twitter.com/asbadsn. *Pres.* Thierno Kandji.

Serbia and Montenegro

Jugoslovenski Bibliografski Informacijski Institut, Terazije 26, 11000 Belgrade. Tel. 11-2687-836, fax 11-2687-760.

Sierra Leone

Sierra Leone Assn. of Archivists, Libns., and Info. Scientists, 7 Percival Street, Freetown. Tel. 022-220-758.

Singapore

Lib. Assn. of Singapore, National Lib. Board, 100 Victoria St., No. 14-01, Singapore 188064. Tel. 6332-3255, fax 6332-3248, e-mail lassec@las.org.sg, World Wide Web http://www.las.org.sg. *Pres.* Samantha Ang Seok Hian. E-mail president@las.org.sg.

Slovenia

Zveza Bibliotekarskih Druötev Slovenije (Union of Assns. of Slovene Libns.), Turjaöka 1, 1000 Ljubljana. Tel. 1-2001-176, fax 1-4257-293, e-mail info@zbds-zveza.si, World Wide Web http://www.zbds-zveza.si. *Pres.* Sabina Fras Popovic. E-mail sabina.fras-popovic@mb.sik.si.

South Africa

Lib. and Info. Assn. of South Africa, P.O. Box 1598, Pretoria 0001. Tel. 27 (0) 12-328-2010, 27 (0) 12-323-4912, fax 27 (0) 12 323 1033, e-mail liasa@liasa.org.za, World Wide Web http://www.liasa.org.za. *Mgr.* Annamarie Goosen. E-mail manager@liasa.org.za.

Spain

Federación Española de Archiveros, Bibliotecarios, Museólogos y Documentalistas (ANABAD) (Spanish Federation of Assns. of Archivists, Libns., Archaeologists, Museum Curators, and Documentalists), de las Huertas, 37, 28014 Madrid. Tel. 91-575-1727, fax 91-578-1615, e-mail anabad@anabad.org, World Wide Web http://www.anabad.org. *Pres.* José María Nogales Herrera.

Sri Lanka

Sri Lanka Lib. Assn., Sri Lanka Professional Centre 275/75, Stanley Wijesundara Mawatha, Colombo 7. Tel./fax 11-258-9103, e-mail slla@slltnet.lk, World Wide Web http://www.slla.org.lk. *Pres.*

S. Arulanantham, e-mail sriarul91@gmail.com; *Gen. Secy.* Sevwandi Jayasinghe. E-mail meghajayasinghe@gmail.com.

Sweden

Foreningen for Archiv & Informationsforvaltening (Society of Archives and Records Management in Sweden—FAI), c/o Foreningshuset Sedab AB, Timber Road 26, 120 30 Stockholm. Tel. 08-121 513 21, e-mail info@fai.nu, World Wide Web https://fai.nu. *Pres.* Katarina Ekelof.

Svensk Biblioteksförening (Swedish Lib. Assn.), Oxtorgsgrand 2, 111 57 Stockholm. Tel. 08-545-132-30, fax 8-545-132-31, e-mail info@svbib.se, World Wide Web http://www.biblioteksforeningen.se. *Pres.* Johanna Hansson.

Svensk Förening för Informationsspecialister (Swedish Assn. for Info. Specialists), Box 2001, 135 02 Tyresö. E-mail info@sfis.nu, World Wide Web http://www.sfis.nu. *Chair* Elisabeth Hammam Lie.

Svenska Arkivsamfundet (Swedish Archival Society). See Foreningen for Archiv & Informationsforvaltening (Society of Archives and Records Management in Sweden—FAI).

Switzerland

Bibliothek Information Schweiz / Bibliothèque Information Suisse / Biblioteca Informazione Swizzera / Library Information Switzerland (BIS), Bleichemattstrasse 42, 5000 Aarau. Tel. 41-62-823-19-38, fax 41-62-823-19-39, e-mail info@bis.ch, World Wide Web http://www.bis.ch.

Verein Schweizer Archivarinnen und Archivare (Assn. of Swiss Archivists), Schweizerisches Bundesarchiv, Büro Pontri GmbH, Solohurnstr. 13, Postfach CH-3322, Urtenen Schönbühl. Tel. 41-31-312-26-66, fax 41-31-312-26-68, e-mail info@vsa-aas.ch, World Wide Web http://www.vsa-aas.org. *Pres.* Claudia Engler.

Taiwan

Lib. Assn. of the Republic of China (LAROC), 20 Zhongshan South Rd., Taipei 10001. Tel. 2-2361-9132, fax 2-2370-0899, e-mail lac@msg.ncl.edu.tw, World Wide Web http://www.lac.org.tw.

Tanzania

Tanzania Lib. Assn., P.O. Box 33433, Dar es Salaam. Tel./fax 255-744-296-134, e-mail info@tla.or.tz, World Wide Web http://www.tla.or.tz.

Thailand

Thai Lib. Assn., 1346 Songkhon 5 Road (between Sri Burapha Road 8-9), Klong Chan, Bang Kapi, Bangkok 10240. Tel. 02-734-9022, fax 02-734-9021, e-mail tla2497@gmail.com, World Wide Web http://tla.or.th.

Trinidad and Tobago

Lib. Assn. of Trinidad and Tobago, P.O. Box 1275, Port of Spain. Tel. 868-687-0194, e-mail latt46@gmail.com, World Wide Web http://www.latt.org.tt. *Pres.* Juliet Glenn-Callender.

Tunisia

Association Tunisienne des Documentalistes, Bibliothécaires et Archivistes (Tunisian Assn. of Documentalists, Libns., and Archivists), c/o Directorate General of Communication, Prime Minister, Casbah, 1020 Tunis.

Turkey

Türk Kütüphaneciler Dernegi (Turkish Libns. Assn.), Necatibey Cad Elgun Sok 8/8, 06440 Kizilay, Ankara. Tel. 312-230-13-25, fax 312-232-04-53, e-mail tkd.dernek@gmail.com, World Wide Web http://www.kutuphaneci.org.tr. *Pres.* Ali Fuat Kartal.

Uganda

Uganda Lib. and Info. Assn., P.O. Box 25412, Kampala. Tel. 256-704-885-246, e-mail secretariat@ulia.org.ug. World Wide Web https://www.ulia.org.ug/. *President* Sarah Kaddu.

Ukraine

Ukrainian Lib. Assn., a/c 62, Kiev, 03057. Tel. 380-44-383-14-32, e-mail info@ula.org.ua,

World Wide Web http://www.uba.org.ua. *Exec. Dir.* Soshynska Yaroslava.

United Kingdom

Archives and Records Assn., UK and Ireland (formerly the Society of Archivists), Prioryfield House, 20 Canon St., Taunton TA1 1SW, England. Tel. 1823-327-077, fax 1823-271-719, e-mail societyofarchivists@archives.org.uk, World Wide Web http://www.archives.org.uk. *Chief Exec.* John Chambers; *Chair* Karl Magee.

Bibliographical Society, Institute of English Studies, Senate House, Malet St., London WC1E 7HU, England. E-mail admin@bibsoc.org.uk, World Wide Web http://www.bibsoc.org.uk. *Pres.* Margaret Ford. E-mail president@bibsoc.org.uk.

Chartered Institute of Lib. and Info. Professionals (CILIP), 7 Ridgmount St., London WC1E 7AE, England. Tel. 20-7255-0500, fax 20-7255-0501, e-mail info@cilip.org.uk, World Wide Web http://www.cilip.org.uk. *Pres.* David Stewart; *V.P.* Judy Broady-Preston.

School Lib. Assn., 1 Pine Court, Kembrey Park, Swindon SN2 8AD, England. Tel. 1793-530-166, fax 1793-481-182, e-mail info@sla.org.uk, World Wide Web http://www.sla.org.uk. *Pres.* Chris Riddell; *Chair* Leslie Martin; *Dir.* Allison Tarrant.

Scottish Lib. and Info. Council, 175 W. George St., Glasgow G2 2LB, Scotland. Tel. 141-202-2999, e-mail info@scottishlibraries.org, World Wide Web http://www.scottishlibraries.org. *Chair* Ian Ruthven.

Society of College, National, and Univ. Libs. (SCONUL) (formerly Standing Conference of National and Univ. Libs.), 94 Euston St., London NW1 2HA, England. Tel. 20-7387-0317, fax 20-7383-3197, e-mail info@sconul.ac.uk, World Wide Web http://www.sconul.ac.uk. *Exec. Dir.* Ann Rossiter.

Uruguay

Agrupación Bibliotecológica del Uruguay (Uruguayan Lib. and Archive Science Assn.) and Asociación de Bibliotecólogos del Uruguay (Uruguayan Libns. Assn.), Eduardo V. Haedo 2255, CP 11200, Montevideo. Tel. 2409-9989, e-mail abu@adinet.com.uy, World Wide Web http://www.abu.net.uy. *Pres.* Victor Aguirre Negro.

Vietnam

Hôi Thu-Vien Viet Nam (Vietnam Lib. Assn.), National Lib. of Vietnam, 31 Trang Thi, Hoan Kiem, 10000 Hanoi. Tel. 4-3825-5397, fax 4-3825-3357, e-mail info@nlv.gov.vn, World Wide Web http://www.nlv.gov.vn. *Dir.* Ba Kuieu Thuy Nga.

Zambia

Lib. and Info. Assn. of Zambia., P.O. Box 32379, 10101 Lusaka. *Tel.* 260-9650-24914, e-mail liaz@zambia.co.zm, World Wide Web https://zambia.co.zm/.

Zimbabwe

Zimbabwe Lib. Assn., ZimLA Midlands Branch, P.O. Box 1521, Gweru. Tel. 263-773-568-837, e-mail information@zimla.org.zw, World Wide Web http://zimla.org.zw. *Pres.* Shadreck Ndinde. *Pres.-Elect* Jerry Mathema.

Directory of Book Trade and Related Organizations

Book Trade Associations, United States and Canada

For more extensive information on the associations listed in this section, see the annual edition of *Literary Market Place* (Information Today, Inc.).

AIGA—The Professional Assn. for Design (formerly American Institute of Graphic Arts), 233 Broadway, Suite 1740, New York, NY 10279. Tel. 212-807-1990, fax 212-807-1799, e-mail general@aiga.org, World Wide Web http://www.aiga.org. *Interim CEO* Barry Barese; *Interim CFO* Anthony Graziano; *Dir. of Exec. Office* Amy Chapman.

American Book Producers Assn. (ABPA), 23 Waverly Place, Suite 6-B, New York, NY10003. Tel. 917-620-9440, fax 212-675-1364, e-mail office@ABPAonline.org, World Wide Web http://www.abpaonline.org. *Pres.* Richard Rothschild; *V.P./Treas.* Nancy Hall; *Admin.* Michael Centore.

American Booksellers Assn., 333 Westchester Ave. Suite S202, White Plains, NY 10604. Tel. 800-637-0037, fax 914-417-4013, e-mail info@bookweb.org, World Wide Web http://www.bookweb.org. *Pres.* Robert Sindelar, Third Place Books, 17171 Bothell Way NE, Lake Forest Park, WA 98155-4204. Tel. 206-366-3309, e-mail rsindelar@thirdplacebooks.com; *V.P./Secy.* Jamie Fiocco, Flyleaf Books, 752 Martin Luther King Blvd., Chapel Hill, NC 27514. Tel. 919-942-7936, e-mail jamie@flyleafbooks.com. *CEO* Oren Teicher. E-mail oren@bookweb.org.

American Literary Translators Assn. (ALTA), University of Arizona, Esquire Building #205, 1230 N. Park Ave., Tucson, AZ 85721. World Wide Web http://www.utdallas.edu/alta. *Exec. Dir.* Elisabeth Jaquette. E-mail elisabeth@literarytranslators.org.

American Printing History Assn., Box 4519, Grand Central Sta., New York, NY 10163-4519. World Wide Web http://www.printinghistory.org. *Pres.* Haven Hawley; *Treas.* David Goodrich; *Board Secy.* Virginia Bartow; *Exec. Secy.* Lyndsi Barnes. E-mail secretary@printinghistory.org.

American Society for Indexing, 1628 E. Southern Ave., No. 9-223, Tempe, AZ 85282. Tel. 480-245-6750, e-mail info@asindexing.org, World Wide Web http://www.asindexing.org. *Pres.* Devon Thomas. E-mail president@asindexing.org; *V.P./Pres.-Elect* Jennifer Spanier. E-mail presidentelect@asindexing.org; *Exec. Dir.* Gwen Henson. E-mail gwen@asindexing.org.

American Society of Journalists and Authors, 355 Lexington Ave., 15th Fl., New York, NY 10017-6603. Tel. 212-997-0947, fax 212-937-2315, e-mail asjaoffice@asja.org, World Wide Web http://www.asja.org. *Pres.* Milt Toby. E-mail president@asja.org; *V.P.* Janine Latus. E-mail vicepresident@asja.org; *Exec. Dir.* Holly Koenig.

American Society of Media Photographers, P.O. Box 1810, Traverse City, MI 49685-1810. Tel. 877-771-2767, fax 231-946-6180, e-mail asmp@vpconnections.com, World Wide Web http://www.asmp.org. *Chair* Luke Copping. E-mail president@asmp.org; *V.Chair* Marianne Lee. E-mail lee@asmp.org; *Exec. Dir.* Tom Kennedy. E-mail kennedy@asmp.org.

American Society of Picture Professionals, 201 E. 25 St., No. 11C, New York, NY 10010. Tel.

516-500-3686, e-mail director@aspp.com, World Wide Web http://www.aspp.com. *Pres.* Cecilia de Querol. E-mail president @aspp.com; *Exec. Dir.* Darrell Perry. E-mail director@aspp.com.

American Translators Assn., 225 Reinekers Lane, Suite 590, Alexandria, VA 22314. Tel. 703-683-6100, fax 703-683-6122, e-mail ata@atanet.org, World Wide Web http://www.atanet.org. *Pres.* Ted R. Wozniak; *Secy.* Karen Tkaczyk; *Treas.* John M. Milan; *Exec. Dir.* Walter W. Bacak, Jr. E-mail walter@atanet.org.

Antiquarian Booksellers Assn. of America, 20 W. 44 St., No. 507, New York, NY 10036-6604. Tel. 212-944-8291, fax 212-944-8293, World Wide Web http://www.abaa.org. *Pres.* Vic Zoschak; *V.P./Secy.* Brad Johnson; *Treas.* Peter Blackman; *Exec. Dir.* Susan Benne. E-mail sbenne@abaa.org.

Assn. Media and Publishing, 1090 Vermont Ave., N.W., 6th Fl., Washington, DC 20005-4905. Tel. 646-568-1309, World Wide Web http://www.siia.net/amp. *Pres.* Larry Hoffer; *V.P.* Christina Folz; *Exec. Dir.* Mike Marchesano. Tel. 646-568-1309, e-mail ExecutiveDirector@associationmediaand-publishing.org.

Assn. of American Publishers, 455 Massachusetts Ave. N.W., Suite 700, Washington, DC 20001. Tel. 202-347-3375, fax 202-347-3690, World Wide Web http://www.publishers.org. *Pres./CEO* Maria A. Pallante. E-mail ceo@publishers.org. *Chair* Tim Bozik; *V.Chair* John Sargent; *Treas.* W. Drake McFeely.

Assn. of American University Presses, 1412 Broadway, Suite 2135, New York, NY 10018. Tel. 212-989-1010, fax 212-989-0275, e-mail info@aaupnet.org, World Wide Web http://aaupnet.org. *Pres.* Jennifer Crewe, Columbia Univ. Press; *Pres.-Elect* Kathryn Conrad, Univ. of Arizona Press; *Treas.* Robbie Dircks, Univ. Washington Press; *Exec. Dir.* Peter Berkery. Tel. 917-288-5594, e-mail pberkery@aaupnet.org.

Assn. of Canadian Publishers, 174 Spadina Ave., Suite 306, Toronto, ON M5T 2C2. Tel. 416-487-6116, fax 416-487-8815, e-mail admin@canbook.org, World Wide Web http://www.publishers.ca. *Pres.* Glenn Rollans, Brush Publishing, Edmonton; *V.P.* Melissa Pitts, University of British Columbia Press, Vancouver; *Treas.* Semareh Al-Hillal, Kids Can Press, Toronto; *Exec. Dir.* Kate Edwards. Tel. 416-487-6116 ext. 2340, e-mail kate_edwards@canbook.org.

Audio Publishers Assn., 333 Hudson Street Suite 503, New York, NY 10013. Tel. 646-688-3044, e-mail info@audiopub.org; World Wide Web http://www.audiopub.org. *Pres.* Linda Lee; *V.P.* Amy Metsch; *V.P., Member Communications* Robin Whitten; *Secy.* Janet Benson; *Treas.* Anthony Goff; *Exec. Dir.* Michele Cobb. E-mail mcobb@audiopub.org.

Authors Guild, 31 E. 32 St., 7th Fl., New York, NY 10016. Tel. 212-563-5904, fax 212-564-5363, e-mail staff@authorsguild.org, World Wide Web http://www.authorsguild.org. *Pres.* Doug Preston; *V.P.* Monique Truong; *Secy.* Rachel Vail; *Treas.* Peter Petre. *Exec. Dir.* Mary Rasenberger.

Book Industry Study Group, 232 Madison Ave., Suite 1400, New York, NY 10016. Tel. 646-336-7141, e-mail info@bisg.org, World Wide Web http://bisg.org. *Chair* Maureen McMahon, Kaplan Publishing; *V. Chair* Peter Balis, John Wiley & Sons; *Secy.* Kempton Mooney, Nielsen Book; *Treas.* Fran Toolan, Firebrand Technologies; *Exec. Dir.* Brian O'Leary. Tel. 646-336-7141 ext. 12. e-mail brian@bisg.org.

Book Manufacturers' Institute (BMI), P.O. Box 731388, Ormand Beach, FL 32173. Tel. 386-986-4552, fax 386-986-4553, World Wide Web http://www.bmibook.org. *Pres.* James H. Fetherston, Worzalla Publishing Company; *Exec. Dir./Secy.* Matthew J. Baehr; *V.P./Pres.-Elect* Joseph H. Upton, Edwards Brothers Malloy; *Treas.* David McCree, LSC Communications.

Bookbuilders of Boston, 115 Webster Woods Lane, North Andover, MA 01845. Tel. 781-378-1361, fax 419-821-2171, e-mail office@bbboston.org, World Wide Web http://www.bbboston.org. *Pres.* Iris Febres. E-mail iris.febres@bbboston.org; *1st V.P.* Josh Garstka. E-mail josh.garstka@bbboston.org; *2nd V.P.* Margaret Rosewitz. E-mail margaret.rosewitz@bbboston.org; *Treas.* James Taylor. E-mail james.taylor@bbboston.org; *Clerk* Laura Rodriguez. E-mail laura.rodriguez@bbboston.org.

Bookbuilders West. See Publishing Professionals Network.

Canadian International Standard Numbers (ISNs) Agency, c/o Lib. and Archives

Canada, 395 Wellington St., Ottawa, ON K1A 0N4. Tel. 866-578-7777 (toll-free) or 613-996-5115, World Wide Web http://www.bac-lac.gc.ca/eng/services/isbn-canada/Pages/isbn-canada.aspx.

Canadian Printing Industries Assn., 3-1750 The Queensway, Suite 135, Toronto, ON M9C 5H5, World Wide Web http://www.cpia-aci.ca. *Chair* Richard Kouwenhoven. E-mail rkouwenhoven@hemlock.com; *Admin.* Tracey Preston. Tel. 866-244-3311, e-mail tpreston.opia@on.aibn.com.

CBA: The Assn. for Christian Retail (formerly Christian Booksellers Association), 9240 Explorer Drive, Suite 200, Colorado Springs, CO 80920. Tel. 719-265-9895, fax 719-272-3510, e-mail info@cbaonline.org, World Wide Web http://www.cbaonline.org.

Children's Book Council, 54 W. 39 St., 14th Fl., New York, NY 10018. Tel. 917-890-7416, e-mail cbc.info@cbcbooks.org, World Wide Web http://www.cbcbooks.org. *Exec. Dir.* Carl Lennertz.

Christian Booksellers Association. See CBA: The Assn. for Christian Retail.

Community of Literary Magazines and Presses, 154 Christopher St., Suite 3C, New York, NY 10014. Tel. 212-741-9110, e-mail info@clmp.org, World Wide Web http://www.clmp.org. *Co-chairs* Nicole Dewey, Gerald Howard; *Exec. Dir.* Mary Gannon. E-mail mgannon@clmp.org.

Copyright Society of the USA, 1 E. 53 St., 8th Fl., New York, NY 10022. Tel. 212-354-6401, World Wide Web http://www.csusa.org. *Pres.* Glenn Pudelka; *V.P./Pres.-Elect* Naomi Jane Gray; *Secy.* Theodore Cheng; *Treas.* Casey M. Chisick; *Exec. Dir.* Kaitland E. Kubat.

Educational Book and Media Assn. (formerly Educational Paperback Assn.), P.O. Box 3363, Warrenton, VA 20188. Tel. 540-318-7770, e-mail info@edupaperback.org, World Wide Web http://www.edupaperback.org. *Pres.* Joyce Skokut; *V.P.* Nancy Stetzinger; *Treas.* Bryan Thompson; *Exec. Dir.* Brain Gorg.

Evangelical Christian Publishers Assn., 9633 S. 48 St., Suite 140, Phoenix, AZ 85044. Tel. 480-966-3998, fax 480-966-1944, e-mail info@ecpa.org, World Wide Web http://www.ecpa.org. *Pres./CEO* Stan Jantz; *Chair* Byron Williamson; *V.Chair* David Moberg; *Secy.* Cory Verner; *Treas.* Tim Murphy.

Graphic Artists Guild, 31 West 34th St., 8th Fl., New York, NY 10001. Tel. 212-791-3400, e-mail admin@graphicartistsguild.org, World Wide Web http://www.graphicartistsguild.org. *Pres.* Lara Kisielewska. E-mail president@graphicartistsguild.org; *Admin. Dir.* Paula Hinkle. E-mail membership@graphicartistsguild.org.

Great Lakes Independent Booksellers Assn., c/o Exec. Dir., 250 Woodstock Ave, Clarendon Hills, IL 60514. Tel. (630) 841-8129, e-mail larry@gliba.org, World Wide Web http://www.gliba.org. *Pres.* Susan Thomas, Coffee Tree Books, 159 E Main St., Morehead, KY 40351. Tel. 606-784-8364, e-mail coffeetreebooks@hotmail.com. *Exec. Dir.* Larry Law.

Guild of Book Workers, 521 Fifth Ave., New York, NY 10175. Tel. 212-292-4444, e-mail communications@guildofbookworkers.org, World Wide Web http://www.guildofbookworkers.org. *Pres.* Bexx Caswell. E-mail president@guildofbookworkers.org; *V.P.* Brien Beidler. E-mail vicepresident@guildofbookworkers.org; *Secy.* Rebecca Smyrl. E-mail secretary@guildofbookworkers.org.; *Treas.* Laura Bedford. E-mail treasurer@guildofbookworkers.org.

Horror Writers Assn., P.O. Box 56687, Sherman Oaks, CA 91413. E-mail hwa@horror.org, World Wide Web http://www.horror.org. *Pres.* Lisa Morton. E-mail president@horror.org; *V.P.* John Palisano. E-mail vp@horror.org; *Secy.* Becky Spratford. E-mail secretary@horror.org; *Treas.* Leslie Klinger. E-mail treasurer@horror.org; Admin. Brad Hodson. E-mail admin@horror.org.

Independent Book Publishers Assn. (formerly PMA), 1020 Manhattan Beach Blvd., Suite 204, Manhattan Beach, CA 90266. Tel. 310-546-1818, fax 310-546-3939, e-mail info@ibpa-online.org, World Wide Web http://www.ibpa-online.org. *Chair* Brook Warner, She Writes Press; *Treas.* Ian Lamont, i30 Media; *Secy.* Elizabeth Turnbull, Light Messages; *CEO* Angela Bole. E-mail angela@ibpa-online.org.

International Standard Book Numbering U.S. Agency, 630 Central Ave., New Providence, NJ 07974. Tel. 877-310-7333, fax 908-219-0188, e-mail isbn-san@bowker.com, World Wide Web http://www.isbn.org. *Dir., Identifier Svcs.* Beat Barblan.

Jewish Book Council, 520 Eighth Ave., 4th Fl., New York, NY 10018. Tel. 212-201-2920, fax 212-532-4952, e-mail jbc@jewishbooks.org, World Wide Web http://www.jewishbookcouncil.org. *Pres.* Jane Weitzman; *V.P.s* Joy Greenberg, Carol Levin, Lenore J. Weitzman; *Secy.* Elisa Spungen Bildner; *Treas.* William Daroff; *Exec. Dir.* Naomi Firestone-Teeter.

Library Binding Institute / Hardcover Binders International, see Book Manufacturers' Institute (BMI).

Midwest Independent Publishers Assn. (MIPA), P.O. Box 7132, St. Paul, MN 55107-0132. Tel. 651-917-0021, World Wide Web http://www.mipa.org. *Pres.* Suzzanne Kelley, North Dakota State Univ. Press, Tel. 701-231-6848, e-mail president@mipa.org; *V.P.* Peter Liptak, Exile Press. Tel. 612-392-2805, e-mail vicepresident@mipa.org; *Treas.* Jennifer Baum, Scribe Publishing. Tel. 248-259-0090, e-mail treasurer@mipa.org.

Miniature Book Society. Tel. 619-226-4441, e-mail member@mbs.org, World Wide Web http://www.mbs.org. *Pres.* Jim Brogan; *Secy.* Gail Faulkner; *Treas.* Cathie Abney.

Minnesota Book Publishers' Roundtable. E-mail information@publishersroundtable.org, World Wide Web http://www.publishersroundtable.org. *Pres.* Carla Valdez, Coffee House Press, 837 Glenwood Ave., Minneapolis, MN 55405. E-mail laura@wiseinkpub.com; *V.P.* Lauren Kukla. E-mail lauren@mightymedia.com; *Secy.* Elizabeth Dingmann Schneider. E-mail e.schneider@redlineeditorial.com; *Treas.* Erik Gilg, 401 2nd Ave. N., Suite 310, Minneapolis, MN 55401. E-mail erik.gilg@quarto.com.

Mountains and Plains Independent Booksellers Assn., 2105 Union Drive, Lakewood, CO 80215. Tel. 720-272-0805, fax 970-484-0037, e-mail info@mountainsplains.org, World Wide Web http://www.mountainsplains.org. *Pres.* Nicole Sullivan, BookBar Bookstore, 4280 Tennyson St., Denver, CO 80212. Tel. 720-443-2227, e-mail info@bookbardenver.com; *Vice Pres.* Christopher Green, The Bookworm of Edwards, 295 Main St., Unit C-101, Edwards, CO 81632. Tel. 970-926-7323, e-mail inventory@bookwormofedwards.com; *Treas.* Amanda Sutton; *Secy.* Phoebe Gaston. E-mail phoebe@booktravelerswest.com.com. *Exec. Dir.* Heather Duncan. E-mail heather@mountainsplains.org.

MPA—The Assn. of Magazine Media (formerly Magazine Publishers of America), 757 Third Ave., 11th Fl., New York, NY 10017. Tel. 212-872-3700, e-mail mpa@magazine.org, World Wide Web http://www.magazine.org. *Chair* Tom Harty. *Pres./CEO.* Linda Thomas Brooks. E-mail lthomasbrooks@magazine.org.

National Assn. of College Stores, 500 E. Lorain St., Oberlin, OH 44074-1294. Tel. 800-622-7498, 440-775-7777, fax 440-775-4769, e-mail info@nacs.org, World Wide Web http://www.nacs.org. *Pres.* Chad M. Schreier; *Pres.-Elect* Steve Westenbroek; *CEO* Robert A. Walton. E-mail rwalton@nacs.org.

National Book Foundation, 90 Broad St., Suite 604, New York, NY 10004. Tel. 212-685-0261, fax 212-213-6570, e-mail nationalbook@nationalbook.org, World Wide Web http://www.nationalbook.org. *Chair* David Steinberger, Perseus Books Group; *V.Chair* Morgan Entrekin, Grove/Atlantic; *Secy.* Calvin Sims; *Treas.* W. Drake McFeely; *Exec. Dir.* Lisa Lucas. E-mail llucas@nationalbook.org.

National Coalition Against Censorship (NCAC), 19 Fulton St., Suite 407, New York, NY 10038. Tel. 212-807-6222, fax 212-807-6245, e-mail ncac@ncac.org, World Wide Web http://www.ncac.org. *Dirs.* Jon Anderson, Michael Bamberger, Joan E. Bertin, Judy Blume, Susan Clare, Tim Federle, Chris Finan, Eric M. Freedman, Martha Gershun, Robie Harris, Phil Harvey, Michael Jacobs, Emily Knox, Chris Peterson, Larry Siems, Emily Whitfield; *Exec. Dir.* Chris Finan. E-mail chris@ncac.org.

New Atlantic Independent Booksellers Assn. (NAIBA), 2667 Hyacinth St., Westbury, NY 11590. Tel. 516-333-0681, fax 516-333-0689, e-mail naibabooksellers@gmail.com, World Wide Web http://www.newatlanticbooks.com. *Pres.* Bill Reilly, The River's End Bookstore; *V.P.* PK Sindwani, Towne Book Center and Café; *Secy.-Treas.* Donna Fell, Sparta Books; *Exec. Dir.* Eileen Dengler. E-mail NAIBAeileen@gmail.com.

New England Independent Booksellers Assn. (NEIBA), 1955 Massachusetts Ave., #2, Cambridge, MA 02140-1405. Tel. 617-547-3642, fax 617-547-3759, e-mail beth@neba.org,

World Wide Web http://www.newengland books.org. *Pres.* Laura Cummings, White Birch Books, North Conway, NH; *V.P.* John LeDonne, Gibson's Bookstore, Concord, NH; *Treas.* Courtney Flynn, Trident Booksellers and Cafe, Boston, MA; *Exec. Dir.* Beth Ineson. E-mail beth@neba.org.

New York Center for Independent Publishing (formerly the Small Press Center), c/o General Society of Mechanics and Tradesmen Lib., 20 W. 44 St., New York, NY 10036. Tel. 212-764-7021, e-mail info@nycip.org, World Wide Web http://nycip.wordpress.com.

Northern California Independent Booksellers Assn., 651 Broadway, 2nd Fl., Sonoma, CA 95476. Tel. 415-561-7686, fax 415-561-7685, e-mail info@nciba.com, World Wide Web http://www.nciba.com. *Pres.* Michael Barnard; *Treas.* Melinda Powers; Secy. Carolyn Hutton. *Exec. Dir.* Calvin Crosby. E-mail calvin@nciba.com.

PEN American Center, Div. of International PEN, 588 Broadway, Suite 303, New York, NY 10012. Tel. 212-334-1660, fax 212-334-2181, e-mail pen@pen.org, World Wide Web http://www.pen.org. *Pres.* Jennifer Egan; *Exec. V.P.* Markus Dohle; *V.P.s* Masha Gessen, Tracy Higgins; *Secy.* Ayad Ahktar; *Treas.* Yvonne Marsh; *CEO* Susanne Nossel. E-mail snossel@pen.org.

Publishers Marketing Assn. (PMA). See Independent Book Publishers Assn.

Publishing Professionals Network (formerly Bookbuilders West), c/o Postal Annex, 274 Redwood Shores Parkway, Box 129, Redwood City, CA 94065-1173. E-mail operations@pubpronetwork.org, World Wide Web http://pubpronetwork.org. *Pres.* David Zielonka. E-mail david.zielonka@cengage.com; V.P. Brenda Ginty. E-mail gintybrenda@gmail.com; *Secy.* Mimi Heft. E-mail mimi.heft.design@gmail.com; *Treas.* Barbara Fuller. E-mail barbara@editcetera.com.

Romance Writers of America, 14615 Benfer Rd., Houston, TX 77069. Tel. 832-717-5200, e-mail info@rwa.org, World Wide Web http://www.rwa.org. *Pres.* HelenKay Dimon. E-mail hkdimon@aol.com; *Pres.-Elect* Carolyn Jewell. E-mail carolyn@carolynjewell.com; *Secy.* Renee Ryan. E-mail secretary@rwa.org; *Treas.* Nan Dixon. E-mail treasurer@rwa.org. *Exec. Dir.* Allison Kelley. E-mail allison.kelley@rwa.org.

Science Fiction and Fantasy Writers of America, P.O. Box 3238, Enfield, CT 06083-3238. World Wide Web http://www.sfwa.org. *Pres.* Cat Rambo. E-mail president@sfwa.org; *V.P.* Erin M. Hartshorn. E-mail erin.hartshorn@sfwa.org; *Secy.* Curtis C. Chen. E-mail curtis.chen@sfwa.org; *CFO* Nathan Lowell. E-mail cfo@sfwa.org; *Exec. Dir.* Kate Baker. E-mail office@sfwa.org.

SIBA (formerly Southern Independent Booksellers Alliance), 3806 Yale Ave., Columbia, SC 29205. Tel. 803-994-9530, fax 309-410-0211, e-mail info@sibaweb.com, World Wide Web http://www.sibaweb.com. *Exec. Dir.* Wanda Jewell. E-mail wanda@sibaweb.com; Asst. Exec. Dir. Linda-Marie Barrett, E-mail lindamarie@sibaweb.com.

Society of Children's Book Writers and Illustrators (SCBWI), 4727 Wilshire Blvd., Suite 301, Los Angeles, CA 90010. Tel. 323-782-1010, e-mail scbwi@scbwi.org, World Wide Web http://www.scbwi.org. *Exec. Dir.* Lin Oliver. E-mail linoliver@scbwi.org; Assoc. Exec. Dir. Sarah Baker, E-mail sarahbaker@scbwi.org.

Society of Illustrators (SI), 128 E. 63 St., New York, NY 10065. Tel. 212-838-2560, fax 212-838-2561, e-mail info@societyillustrators.org, World Wide Web http://www.societyillustrators.org. *Pres.* Tim O'Brien; *Exec. Secy.* Leslie Cober-Gentry; *Exec. Dir.* Anelle Miller. E-mail anelle@societyillustrators.org.

Southern Independent Booksellers Alliance. See SIBA.

Western Writers of America, c/o Candy Moulton, 271 CR 219, Encampment, WY 82325 Tel. 307-329-8942, e-mail wwa.moulton@gmail.com, World Wide Web http://www.westernwriters.org. *Pres.* Nancy Plain; *V.P.* Chris Enss; *Exec. Dir., Secy./Treas.* Candy Moulton.

Women's National Book Assn., P.O. Box 237, FDR Sta., New York, NY 10150. Tel. 866-610-WNBA (9622), e-mail info@wnba-books.org, World Wide Web http://www.wnba-books.org. *Pres.* Jane Kinney-Denning, e-mail nationalpresidentWNBA@gmail.com; Pres., Rachelle Yousuf; *V.P.s/Presidents-Elect*, Natalie Obando-Desai, Bebe (Sarah) Brechner; *Secretary* Linda Rosen; *Treas.* Christine Sikule.

International and Foreign Book Trade Associations

For Canadian book trade associations, see the preceding section, "Book Trade Associations, United States and Canada." For a more extensive list of book trade organizations outside the United States and Canada, with more detailed information, consult *International Literary Market Place* (Information Today, Inc.), which also provides extensive lists of major bookstores and publishers in each country.

International

African Publishers' Network, c/o Ghana Book Publishers Association, Bureau of Ghana Languages Building, Kawukudi Culture, P.O. Box Lt 471, Laterbiokorshie, Accra, Ghana. Tel. 233-30-291-2764, 233-20-911-5191, e-mail info.africanpublishers@gmail.com, World Wide Web http://www.african-publishers.net/. *Acting Exec. Dir.* Ernest Oppong.

Afro-Asian Book Council, 212, Shahpur Jat, New Delhi—110 049, India. Tel. 91-11-26493326, fax 91-11-41752055, e-mail info@aabookcouncil.org, World Wide Web http://www.aabookcouncil.org/. *Secy.-Gen.* Ramesh Mittal. E-mail rkmittal@dkagencies.com; *Dir.* Pranav Gupta. E-mail pgprintsindia@gmail.com.

Centro Regional para el Fomento del Libro en América Latina y el Caribe (CERLALC) (Regional Center for Book Promotion in Latin America and the Caribbean), Calle 70, No. 9-52, Bogotá, Colombia. Tel. 571-518-70-70, e-mail libro@cerlalc.com, World Wide Web http://www.cerlalc.org. *Dir.* Marianne Ponsford.

Federation of European Publishers, Chaussee d'lxelles 29/35, Box 4, 1050 Brussels, Belgium. Tel. 32-2-770-11-10, fax 32-2-771-20-71, e-mail info@fep-fee.eu, World Wide Web http://www.fep-fee.eu. *Pres.* Rudy Vanschoonbeek; *Dir.* Anne Bergman-Tahon.

International Board on Books for Young People (IBBY), Nonnenweg 12, Postfach CH-4009, Basel, Switzerland. Tel. 41-61-272-29-17, fax 41-61-272-27-57, e-mail ibby@ibby.org, World Wide Web http://www.ibby.org. *Exec. Dir.* Elizabeth Page.

International League of Antiquarian Booksellers (ILAB), c/o Rue Toepffer 5, Case postale 499, 1211 Geneva 12, Switzerland. E-mail secretary@ilab.org, World Wide Web http://www.ilab.org. *Pres.* Sally Burdon; *Gen. Secy.* Stewart Bennett.

International Publishers Assn. (Union Internationale des Editeurs), 23 ave. de France, CH-1202 Geneva, Switzerland. Tel. 41-22-704-1820, fax 41-22-704-1821, e-mail info@internationalpublishers.org, World Wide Web http://www.internationalpublishers.org. *Pres.* Hugo Setzer; *Secy.-Gen.* José Borghino.

STM: The International Assn. of Scientific, Technical, and Medical Publishers, Prama House, 267 Banbury Road, Oxford OX2 7HT, England. Tel. 44-0-1865-339-321, fax 44-0-1865-339-325, e-mail info@stm-assoc.org, World Wide Web http://www.stm-assoc.org. *CEO* Michael Mabe.

National

Argentina

Cámara Argentina del Libro (Argentine Book Assn.), Av. Belgrano 1580, 4 piso, C1093AAQ Buenos Aires. Tel. 54-11-4381-8383, fax 54-11-4381-9253, e-mail cal@editores.org.ar, World Wide Web http://www.editores.org.ar.

Fundación El Libro (Book Foundation), Yrigoyen 1628, 5 piso, C1089AAF Buenos Aires. Tel. 54-11-4370-0600, fax 54-11-4370-0607, e-mail fundacion@el-libro.com.ar, World Wide Web http://www.el-libro.org.ar. *Pres.* Maria Theresa Carbano; *Admin. Dir.* José Gutiérrez Brianza.

Australia

Australian and New Zealand Assn. of Antiquarian Booksellers (ANZAAB), P.O. Box 1610, Carindale, Brisbane, QLD 4152. E-mail admin@anzaab.com, World Wide Web http://www.anzaab.com. *Contact* Jorn Harbeck.

Australian Booksellers Assn., 828 High St., Unit 9, Kew East, Vic. 3102. Tel. 3-9859-7322, fax 3-9859-7344, e-mail mail@aba.org.au, World Wide Web http://www.booksellers.org.au. *CEO* Robbie Egan.

Australian Publishers Assn., 60/89 Jones St., Ultimo, NSW 2007. Tel. 2-9281-9788, e-mail apa@publishers.asn.au, World Wide Web http://www.publishers.asn.au. *Chief Exec.* Michael Gordon-Smith.

Austria

Hauptverband des Österreichischen Buchhandels (Austrian Publishers and Booksellers Assn.), Grünangergasse 4, A-1010 Vienna. Tel. 43-1-512-15-35, fax 43-1-512-84-82, e-mail office@hvb.at, World Wide Web http://www.buecher.at. *Mgr.* Gustav Soucek.

Verband der Antiquare Österreichs (Austrian Antiquarian Booksellers Assn.), Grünangergasse 4, A-1010 Vienna. Tel. 1-512-1535-14, e-mail sekretariat@hvb.at, World Wide Web http://www.antiquare.at.

Belarus

National Book Chamber of Belarus, 31a V Horuzhei Str., Rm. 707, 220002 Minsk. Tel. 375-17-288-67-15, fax 375-17-283-29-60, e-mail palata@natbook.org.by, World Wide Web http://natbook.org.by. *Dir.* Ivanova Elena Vitalievna. E-mail elvit@natbook.org.by.

Belgium

Boek.be (formerly Vlaamse Boekverkopersbond, Flemish Booksellers Assn.), Te Buelaerlei 37, 2140 Borgerhout. Tel. 03-230-89-23, fax 3-281-22-40, World Wide Web http://www.boek.be/over-boekbe.

Vlaamse Uitgevers Vereniging (Flemish Publishers Assn.). See Boek.be.

Bolivia

Cámara Boliviana del Libro (Bolivian Book Chamber), Calle Capitan Ravelo No. 2116, 682 La Paz. Tel. 2-211-3264, e-mail cabolib@entelnet.bo, World Wide Web http://www.cabolib.org.bo.

Brazil

Cámara Brasileira do Livro (Brazilian Book Assn.), Rua Cristiano Viana 91, Pinheiros-Sao Paulo-SP, CEP: 05411-000. Tel./fax 11-3069-1300, e-mail cbl@cbl.org.br, World Wide Web http://www.cbl.org.br. *Pres.* Vitor Tavares da Silva Filho.

Sindicato Nacional dos Editores de Livros (Brazilian Publishers Assn.), Rue da Ajuda 35-18 andar, 20040-000 Rio de Janeiro-RJ. Tel. 21-2533-0399, fax 21-2533-0422, e-mail snel@snel.org.br, World Wide Web http://www.snel.org.br. *Pres.* Marcos de Veiga Pereira.

Chile

Cámara Chilena del Libro AG (Chilean Assn. of Publishers, Distributors, and Booksellers), Av. Libertador Bernardo O'Higgins 1370, Oficina 501, Santiago. Tel. 2-672-0348, fax 2-687-4271, e-mail prolibro@tie.cl, World Wide Web http://www.camlibro.cl.

Colombia

Cámara Colombiana del Libro (Colombian Book Assn.), Calle 35, No. 5A 05, Bogotá. Tel. 57-1-323-01-11, fax 57-1-285-10-82, e-mail camlibro@camlibro.com.co, World Wide Web http://www.camlibro.com.co. *Exec. Chair* Enrique González Villa; *Secy.-Gen.* Manuel José Sarmiento Ramírez.

Czech Republic

Svaz ceských knihkupcu a nakladatelu (Czech Publishers and Booksellers Assn.), Fugnerovo nameisti 1808/3, Prague 2, 120 00. Tel. 420-227-660-644, e-mail sckn@sckn.cz, World Wide Web http://www.sckn.cz. *Exec. Secy.* Marcela Turečková. E-mail tureckova@sckn.cz.

Denmark

Danske Boghandlerforening (Danish Booksellers Assn.), Slotsholmsgade 1 B, 1216 Copenhagen K. Tel. 45-32-54-2255, fax 45-32-54-0041, e-mail ddb@bogpost.dk, World Wide Web http://www.boghandlerforeningen.dk. *Chair* Helle Busck Fensvig; *Dir.* Bo Dybkær

Danske Forlæggerforening (Danish Publishers Assn.), Stock Exchange, Slotsholmsgade 1, 1217 Copenhagen K. Tel. 45-33-15-66-88, e-mail info@danskeforlag.dk, World Wide Web http://www.danskeforlag.dk. *Dir.* Ulrik Huilshoj. E-mail ulrikhuilshoj@gmail.com.

Ecuador

Cámara Ecuatoriana del Libro, N29-61 Eloy Alfaro and England, 9th Floor, Quito. Tel. 593-2-2553311, fax 593-2-2553314, e-mail info@celibro.org.ec, World Wide Web http://celibro.org.ec. *Pres.* Vicente Velásquez Guzmán.

Egypt

General Egyptian Book Organization (GEBO), P.O. Box 235, Cairo 11511. Tel. 2-257-75367, e-mail walaakotb@gebo.gov.eg, World Wide Web https://www.gebo.gov.eg.

Estonia

Estonian Publishers Assn., Roosikrantsi 6-207, 10119 Tallinn. Telephone 372-644-9866, fax 372-617-7550, e-mail kirjastusteliit@eki.ee, World Wide Web http://www.estbook.com. *Managing Dir.* Kaidi Urmet. E-mail kirjastusteliit@eki.ee.

Finland

Kirjakauppaliitto Ry (Booksellers Association. of Finland), Eteläranta 10, 00130 Helsinki. Tel. 040-689-9112, e-mail toimisto@kirjakauppaliitto.fi, World Wide Web http://www.kirjakauppaliitto.fi. *Managing Director* Laura Karlsson. E-mail laura.karlsson@kirjakauppaliitto.fi.

Suomen Kustannusyhdistys (Finnish Book Publishers Assn.), Unioninkatu 11, FI-00130 Helsinki. Tel. 358 9 22877252, World Wide Web http://www.kustantajat.fi/en. *Pres.* Pasi Vainio; *Dir.* Sakari Laiho. E-mail sakari.laiho@Kustantajat.fi.

France

Bureau International de l'Edition Française (BIEF) (International Bureau of French Publishing), 115 blvd. Saint-Germain, F-75006 Paris. Tel. 01-44-41-13-13, fax 01-46-34-63-83, e-mail info@bief.org, World Wide Web http://www.bief.org. *Dir. Gen.* Nicolas Roche. *New York Branch* French Publishers Agency, 30 Vandam Street, Suite 5A, New York, NY 10013. Tel./fax 212-254-4540, World Wide Web http://frenchpubagency.com.

Cercle de la Librairie (Circle of Professionals of the Book Trade), 35 rue Grégoire-de-Tours, F-75006 Paris. Tel. 01-44-41-28-00, fax 01-44-41-28-65, e-mail commercial@electre.com, World Wide Web http://www.electre.com.

Syndicat de la Librairie Française, Hotel Massa, 38 rue du Faubourg Saint-Jacques, F-75014 Paris. Tel. 01-53-62-23-10, fax 01-53-62-10-45, e-mail contact@syndicat-librarie.fr, World Wide Web http://www.syndicat-librairie.fr. *Admin. Secy.* Anne Criulanscy. E-mail a.criulanscy@syndicat-librairie.fr.

Syndicat National de la Librairie Ancienne et Moderne (SLAM) (National Assn. of Antiquarian and Modern Booksellers), 4 rue Gît-le-Coeur, F-75006 Paris. Tel. 01-43-29-46-38, fax 01-43-25-41-63, e-mail slam-livre@wanadoo.fr, World Wide Web http://www.slam-livre.fr. *Pres.* Herve Valentin; *Secy.-Gen.* Pierre Prevost.

Syndicat National de l'Edition (SNE) (National Union of Publishers), 115 blvd. Saint-Germain, F-75006 Paris. Tel. 01-44-41-40-50, fax 01-44-41-40-77, World Wide Web http://www.sne.fr. *Pres.* Vincent Montagne.

Germany

Börsenverein des Deutschen Buchhandels e.V. (Stock Exchange of German Booksellers), Braubachstr. 16, 60311 Frankfurt-am-Main. Tel. 49-69-1306-0, fax 49-69-1306-201, e-mail info@boev.de, World Wide Web http://www.boersenverein.de. *Gen. Mgr.* Alexander Skipis.

Verband Deutscher Antiquare e.V. (German Antiquarian Booksellers Assn.), Geschäftsstelle, Seeblick 1, 56459 Elbingen. Tel. 49-0-6435-90-91-47, fax 49-0-6435-90-91-48, e-mail buch@antiquare.de, World Wide Web http://www.antiquare.de. *Chair* Sibylle Wieduwilt. E-mail s.wieduwilt@antiquare.de.

Hungary

Magyar Könyvkiadók és Könyvterjesztök Egyesülése (Assn. of Hungarian Publishers and Booksellers), Kertész u. 41. I / 4, 1073 Budapest. Tel. 06-1-343-2536, e-mail mkke@mkke.hu, World Wide Web http://www.mkke.hu. *Pres.* Gál Katalin; *Dir.* Gergely Péterfy.

Iceland

Félag Islenskra Bókaútgefenda (Icelandic Publishers Assn.), Baronsstig 5, 101 Reykjavik. Tel. 511-8020, fax 511-5020, e-mail fibut@fibut.is, World Wide Web http://www.fibut.is. *Chair* Heidar Ingi Svannsson.

India

Federation of Indian Publishers, Federation House, 18/1C Institutional Area, Aruna Asaf Ali Marg, New Delhi 110067. Tel. 11-2696-4847, fax 11-2686-4054, e-mail fippresident@gmail.com, World Wide Web http://www.fiponline.org. *Exec. Dir.* Shri. Ramesh K. Mittal.

Indonesia

Ikatan Penerbit Indonesia (Assn. of Indonesian Book Publishers), Jl. Kalipasir 32, Cikini Jakarta Pusat 10330. Tel. 21-3141-907, e-mail sekretariat@ikapi.org, World Wide Web http://www.ikapi.org. *Secy.* Novi Arsianti.

Ireland

Publishing Ireland/Foilsiu Eireann (formerly CLÉ: The Irish Book Publishers' Assn.), 63 Patrick St., Dun Laoghaire, Co Dublin. Tel. 353-1-639-4868, e-mail info@publishingireland.com, World Wide Web http://www.publishingireland.com. *Mgr.* Stephanie Lawless. E-mail stephanie@publishingireland.com.

Israel

Book Publishers' Assn. of Israel, 29 Carlebach St., 67132 Tel Aviv. Tel. 3-561-4121, fax 3-561-1996, e-mail info@tbpai.co.il, World Wide Web http://www.tbpai.co.il. *Chair* Benny Trioaks.

Italy

Associazione Italiana Editori (Italian Publishers Assn.), Corso di Porta Romana 108, 20122 Milan. Tel. 2-89-28-0800, fax 2-89-28-0860, e-mail info@aie.it, World Wide Web http://www.aie.it. *Pres.* Ricardo Franco Levy.

Associazione Librai Antiquari d'Italia (Antiquarian Booksellers Assn. of Italy), via Discipilini 32, Riva del Garda (TN) 38066. E-mail alai@alai.it, World Wide Web http://www.alai.it. *Pres.* Mario Giupponi.

Japan

Antiquarian Booksellers Assn. of Japan, Kokusai Hamamatsucho Bldg., 9th Floor, 1-9-18 Kaigan, Minato-ku, Tokyo, 105-0022. Tel. 81-3-6367-6070, fax: 81-3-6367-6196, e-mail abaj@abaj.gr.jp, World Wide Web http://www.abaj.gr.jp.

Japan Assn. of International Publications (formerly Japan Book Importers Assn.), 1-1-13-4F Kanda, Jimbocho, Chiyodak-ku, Tokyo 101-0051. Tel. 3-5479-7269, fax 3-5479-7307, e-mail office@jaip.jp, World Wide Web http://www.jaip.jp. *Exec. Dir.* Mark Gresham.

Japan Book Publishers Assn., 5th Fl., Shuppan-Club Bldg. 1-32, Kanda-Jimbocho, Chiyoda-ku, Tokyo,101-0051. Tel. 81-0-3-6273-7065, fax 81-0-3-6811-0959, e-mail research@jbpa.or.jp, World Wide Web http://www.jbpa.or.jp. *Pres.* Masahiro Oga.

Kenya

Kenya Publishers Assn., P.O. Box 42767, Nairobi 00100. Tel. 254-020-2635498, e-mail info@kenyapublishers.org, World Wide Web http://www.kenyapublishers.org. *Chair* Lawrence Njagi.

Korea (Republic of)

Korean Publishers Assn., Samchungro 6, Sogang-dong, Jongro-gu, Seoul 03062. Tel. 735-2701-4, fax 2-738-5414, e-mail webmaster@kpa21.or.kr, World Wide Web http://eng.kpa21.or.kr. *Chair* Yoon Cheol-ho.

Latvia

Latvian Publishers' Assn., Baznicas iela 37-3, LV-1010 Riga. Tel./fax 67-217-730, e-mail lga@gramatizdeveji.lv, World Wide Web http://www.gramatizdeveji.lv. *Exec. Dir.* Dace Pugacha.

Lithuania

Lithuanian Publishers Assn., Germany 18A, LT 01130, Vilnius. Tel. 370-675-75692, fax 370-670-32287, e-mail info@lla.lt, World Wide Web http://www.lla.lt. *Pres.* Remigijus Jokubauskas; *Exec. Dir.* Rūta Elijošaityte-Kaikarė.

Malaysia

Malaysian Book Publishers' Assn., No. 7-6, Block E2, Jl PJU 1/42A, Dataran Prima, 47301 Petaling Jaya, Selangor. Tel. 3-7880-5840, fax 3-7880-5841, e-mail info@mabopa.com.my, World Wide Web http://www.mabopa.com.my. *Pres.* Ishak Hamzah.

Mexico

Cámara Nacional de la Industria Editorial Mexicana (Mexican Publishers' Assn.), Holanda No. 13, Col. San Diego Churubusco, Deleg. Coyoacan, 04120 Mexico DF. Tel. 155-56-88-20-11, fax 155-56-04-31-47, e-mail contacto@caniem.com, World Wide Web http://www.caniem.com. *Pres.* Carlos Anaya Rosique. E-mail presidencia@caniem.com.

The Netherlands

KVB—Koninklijke Vereeniging van het Boekenvak (Royal Society for the Book Trade), P.O. Box 12040, AA Amsterdam-Zuidoost. Tel. 20-624-02-12, fax 20-620-88-71, e-mail info@kvb.nl, World Wide Web http://www.kvb.nl. *Dirs.* M. K. J. David and A. Schroën.

Nederlands Uitgeversverbond (Royal Dutch Publishers Assn.), Postbus 12040, 1100 AA Amsterdam. Tel. 20-430-9150, fax 20-430-9199, e-mail info@mediafederatie.nl, World Wide Web https://mediafederatie.nl. *Chair* Derk Haank; *Dir.* Peter Stadhouders. E-mail pstadhouders@mediafederatie.nl.

Nederlandsche Vereeniging van Antiquaren (Netherlands Assn. of Antiquarian Booksellers), Notendijk 7, 4583 SV Terhole. Tel. 31-0-114-3142-09, fax 31-0-114-e-mail info@nvva.nl, World Wide Web http://www.nvva.nl. *Chair* Gert Jan Bestebreurtje; *Secy.* Peter Everaers.

Nederlandse Boekverkopersbond (Dutch Booksellers Assn.), Postbus 32, 3720 AA Bilthoven. Tel. 30-228-79-56, fax 30-228-45-66, e-mail info@boekbond.nl, World Wide Web http://www.boekbond.nl. *Dir.* Anne Schroën. E-mail schroen@boekbond.nl.

New Zealand

Booksellers New Zealand, P.O. Box 25033, Featherston Street, Wellington 6146. Tel. 4-472-1908, fax 4-472-1912, e-mail info@booksellers.co.nz, World Wide Web http://www.booksellers.co.nz. *CEO* Lincoln Gould. E-mail lincoln.gould@booksellers.co.nz.

Nigeria

Nigerian Publishers Assn., 1st Floor Premium House, Opp. Evans Brothers (Nig. Publishers) Ltd., Jericho, GPO Box 2541, Dugbe, Ibadan, Oyo States. Tel. 234-803-917-7779, e-mail nigerianpublishers@ymail.com, World Wide Web http://www.nigerianpublishers.com. *Pres.* Adedapo Gbadega.

Norway

Norske Bokhandlerforening (Norwegian Booksellers Association), Sehesteds gate 6, 0164 Oslo. Tel. 47-22-39-68-00, e-mail firmapost@bokhandlerforeningen.no, World Wide Web http://www.bokhandlerforeningen.no. *Chief Exec. Officer* Trine Stensen. E-mail trine@bokhandlerforeningen.no.

Norske Forleggerforening (Norwegian Publishers Assn.), Sehesteds gate 6, 0164 Oslo. Tel. 22-00-75-80, fax 22-33-38-30, e-mail dnf@forleggerforeningen.no, World Wide Web http://www.forleggerforeningen.no. *Chair* Tom Harald Jenssen; *Managing Dir.* Kristenn Einarsson.

Peru

Cámara Peruana del Libro (Peruvian Publishers Assn.), Av. Cuba 427, Jesús María, Apdo. 10253, Lima 11. Tel. (511) 265-0735, fax (511) 265-0735, e-mail cp-libro@cpl.org.pe, World Wide Web http://www.cpl.org.pe. *Pres.* Jose Carlos Alvarino Ordonez. E-mail jcalvarino@hotmail.com.

Philippines

Philippine Educational Publishers Assn., Phoenix Building, 927 Quezon Ave., Quezon City. Tel. (632) 376-4041 local 334, fax (632) 376-4031, e-mail pepasecretariat@gmail.com. World Wide Web https://www.pepa.org.ph. *Pres.* Jose Paolo M. Sibal.

Poland

Polish Society of Book Editors, Holy Cross 30, lok 156, 00-116 Warsaw. Tel. 22-407-77-30, fax 22-850-34-76, e-mail ptwk@ptwk.pl, World Wide Web http://www.wydawca.com.pl. *Dir.* Maria Kuisz.

Władze Stowarzyszenia Księgarzy Polskich (Assn. of Polish Booksellers), ul. Świętokrzyska 14, 00-050 Warsaw. Tel./fax 0-22-827-93-81, e-mail skp@ksiegarze.org.pl, World Wide Web http://www.ksiegarze.org.pl. *Chair* Tadeusz Prześlakiewicz; *Gen. Secy.* Katarzyna Balicka-Więckowska.

Portugal

Associação Portuguesa de Editores e Livreiros (Portuguese Assn. of Publishers and Booksellers), Av. dos Estados Unidas da America 97, 6 Esq., 1700-167 Lisbon. Tel. 21-843-51-80, e-mail geral@apel.pt, World Wide Web http://www.apel.pt.

Russia

Assn. of Book Publishers of Russia, 101000, Lubyanka, Luchnikov per., D.4, p. 1, Moscow. Tel. 7-926-900-85-27, e-mail askibook@gmail.com, World Wide Web http://www.aski.ru.

Rossiiskaya Knizhnaya Palata (Russian Book Chamber), Zvezdny boulevard 17, building 1, 129085, Moscow. Tel. 495-688-96-89, fax 495-688-99-91, e-mail info@bookchamber.ru, World Wide Web http://www.bookchamber.ru.

Singapore

Singapore Book Publishers Assn., 1003 Bukit Merah Central #-3-05, Singapore 159836. Tel. 65-6225-5770, e-mail info@singaporebookpublishers.sg, World Wide Web http://www.singaporebookpublishers.sg. *Pres.* Peter Schoppert. E-mail schoppert@nus.edu.sg.

Slovenia

Zdruzenie Zaloznikov in Knjigotrzcev Slovenije Gospodarska Zbornica Slovenije (Assn. of Publishers and Booksellers of Slovenia), Dimičeva 13, SI-1504 Ljubljana. Tel. 386-1-5898-000, fax 386-1-5898-100, e-mail info@gzs.si, World Wide Web http://www.gzs.si/eng. *Pres.* Boštjan Gorjup; *Gen. Mgr.* Sonja Šmuc.

South Africa

Publishers Assn. of South Africa (PASA), P.O. Box 18223, Wynberg 7824. Tel. 21-762-9083, fax 21-762-2763, e-mail pasa@publishsa.co.za, World Wide Web http://www.publishsa.co.za. *Chair* Steve Cillier; *Exec. Dir.* Mpuka Radinku.

South African Booksellers Assn. (formerly Associated Booksellers of Southern Africa), P.O. Box 870, Bellville 7535. Tel. 21-945-1572, fax 21-945-2169, e-mail saba@sabooksellers.com, World Wide Web http://sabooksellers.com. *Pres.* Guru Redhi. E-mail Redhi@iafrica.com.

Spain

Federación de Gremios de Editores de España (Federation of Spanish Publishers Assns.), Calle de Cea Bermúdez 44, 28003 Madrid. Tel. 91-534-51-95, fax 91-535-26-25, e-mail fgee@fge.es, World Wide Web http://www.federacioneditores.org. *Pres.* Miguel Barrero; *Secy.* Antonio María Ávila.

Sri Lanka

Sri Lanka Book Publishers Assn., No. 3G 12C, BMICH Office Complex, Block 04, Bauddhaloka Mawatha, Colombo. Tel. 0094-112-696-821, e-mail bookpub@sltnet.lk, World Wide Web http://www.bookpublishers.lk. *Pres.* Vijitha Yapa.

Sweden

Svenska Förläggareföreningen (Swedish Publishers Assn.), c/o Svenska Publisher AB, Kungstensgatan 38, 2 tr, 113 59 Stockholm.

Tel. 8-736-19-40, e-mail info@forlaggare.se, World Wide Web http://www.forlaggare.se. *Chair* Eva Gedin.

Switzerland

Swiss Booksellers and Publishers Association (SBVV), Limmatstrasse 111, Postfach 8031, Zürich. Tel. 44-421-36-00, fax 44-421-36-18, e-mail info@sbvv.ch, World Wide Web https://www.sbvv.ch. *CEO* Dani Landolf. E-mail dani.landolf@sbvv.ch.

Thailand

Publishers and Booksellers Assn. of Thailand, 83/159 Moo Chinnakhet 2, Ngam Wong Wan Rd., Tungsonghong Lak Si, Bangkok 10210. Tel. 2-954-9560-4, fax 02-954-9565-6, e-mail info@pubat.or.th, World Wide Web http://www.pubat.or.th. *Pres.* Suchada Hassakun.

Uganda

Uganda Publishers Assn., P.O. Box 7732, Kampala. Tel. 256-41-270370, fax 256-41-348224.

United Kingdom

Antiquarian Booksellers Assn., 6 Bell Yard, London WC2A 2JR, England. Tel. 44-0-20-7421-4681, fax 44-0-20 7421-4641, e-mail admin@aba.org.uk, World Wide Web http://www.aba.org.uk. *Pres.* Roger Treglown; *Secy.* Camilla Szymanowska.

Assn. of Learned and Professional Society Publishers, Egale 1, 80 St Albans Road, Watford, Hertfordshire WD17 1DL England. Tel. 44 (0)1245 260571, e-mail admin@alpsp.org, World Wide Web http://www.alpsp.org. *Interim Chief Exec.* Wayne Sime.

Booktrust, G8 Battersea Studios, 80 Silverthorne Road, Battersea, London SW8 3HE, England. Tel. 020 7801 8800, e-mail query@booktrust.org.uk, World Wide Web http://www.booktrust.org.uk. *Pres.* Michael Morpurgo; *Chief Exec.* Diana Gerald.

Publishers Assn., 50 Southwark Street, London SE1 1UN, England. Tel. 44 0 20 7378 0504, e-mail mail@publishers.org.uk, World Wide Web http://www.publishers.org.uk. *Pres.* Peter Phillips.

Scottish Book Trust, Sandeman House, Trunk's Close, 55 High St., Edinburgh EH1 1SR, Scotland. Tel. 131-524-0160, e-mail info@scottishbooktrust.com, World Wide Web http://www.scottishbooktrust.com. *Chair* Keir Bloomer.

Welsh Books Council (Cyngor Llyfrau Cymru), Castell Brychan, Aberystwyth, Ceredigion SY23 2JB, Wales. Tel. 1970-624-151, fax 1970-625-385, e-mail info@wbc.org.uk, World Wide Web http://www.cllc.org.uk. *Chief Exec.* Helgard Krause.

Uruguay

Cámara Uruguaya del Libro (Uruguayan Publishers Assn.), Colón 1476, Apdo. 102, 11000 Montevideo. Tel. 2-916-93-74, fax 2-916-76-28, e-mail gerencia@camaradellibro.com.uy, World Wide Web http://www.camaradellibro.com.uy. *Pres.* Alvaro Risso.

Venezuela

Cámara Venezolana del Libro (Venezuelan Publishers Assn.), Av. Andrés Bello, Centro Andrés Bello, Torre Oeste 11, piso 11, of. 112-0, Caracas 1050. Tel. 212-793-1347, fax 212-793-1368, e-mail cavelibrocgeneral@gmail.com, World Wide Web http://www.cavelibro.org.ve.

Zambia

Booksellers and Publishers Assn. of Zambia, P.O. Box 51109, 10100 Lusaka. E-mail dongo.banda@gmail.com.

Zimbabwe

Zimbabwe Book Publishers Assn., P.O. Box 3041, Harare. Tel. 4-773-236, fax 4-754-256.

National Information Standards Organization (NISO)

NISO, the National Information Standards Organization, a nonprofit association accredited by the American National Standards Institute (ANSI), identifies, develops, maintains, and publishes technical standards to manage information in today's continually changing digital environment. NISO standards apply to both traditional and new technologies and to information across its whole lifecycle, from creation through documentation, use, repurposing, storage, metadata, and preservation. The following listing includes NISO standards of interest to readers of *Library and Book Trade Almanac.*

Content and Collection Management

ANSI/NISO Z39.2-1994 (R2016)	Information Interchange Format ISBN 978-1-937522-70-4
ANSI/NISO Z39.14-1997 (R2015)	Guidelines for Abstracts ISBN 978-1-937522-44-5
ANSI/NISO Z39.18-2005 (R2010)	Scientific and Technical Reports—Preparation, Presentation, and Preservation ISBN 978-1-937522-21-6
ANSI/NISO Z39.19-2005 (R2010)	Guidelines for the Construction, Format, and Management of Monolingual Controlled Vocabularies ISBN 978-1-937522-22-3
ANSI/NISO Z39.23-1997 (S2015)	Standard Technical Report Number Format and Creation ISBN 978-1-937522-45-2
ANSI/NISO Z39.29-2005 (R2010)	Bibliographic References ISBN 978-1-937522-26-1
ANSI/NISO Z39.32-1996 (R2012)	Information on Microfiche Headers ISBN 978-1-937522-29-2
ANSI/NISO Z39.41-1997 (S2015)	Placement Guidelines for Information on Spines ISBN 978-1-937522-46-9
ANSI/NISO Z39.43-1993 (R2017)	Standard Address Number (SAN) for the Publishing Industry ISBN 978-1-937522-75-9

ANSI/NISO Z39.48-1992 (R2009)	Permanence of Paper for Publications and Documents in Libraries and Archives ISBN 978-1-937522-30-8
ANSI/NISO Z39.71-2006 (R2011)	Holdings Statements for Bibliographic Items ISBN 978-1-937522-31-5
ANSI/NISO Z39.73-1994 (R2012)	Single-Tier Steel Bracket Library Shelving ISBN 978-1-937522-32-2
ANSI/NISO Z39.74-1996 (R2012)	Guides to Accompany Microform Sets ISBN 978-1-937522-40-7
ANSI/NISO Z39.78-2000 (R2018)	Library Binding ISBN 978-1-937522-86-5
ANSI/NISO Z39.84-2005 (R2010)	Syntax for the Digital Object Identifier ISBN 978-1-937522-34-6
ANSI/NISO Z39.85-2012	The Dublin Core Metadata Element Set ISBN 978-1-937522-14-8
ANSI/NISO Z39.86-2005 (R2012)	Specifications for the Digital Talking Book ISBN 978-1-937522-35-3
ANSI/NISO Z39.96-2019	JATS: Journal Article Tag Suite, version 1.2 ISBN 978-1-937522-89-6
ANSI/NISO Z39.98-2012	Authoring and Interchange Framework for Adaptive XML Publishing Specification ISBN 978-1-937522-07-0
ANSI/NISO Z39.102-2017	STS: Standards Tag Suite ISBN 978-1-937522-78-0
ANSI/NISO/ISO 12083-1995 (R2009)	Electronic Manuscript Preparation and Markup ISBN 978-1-880124-20-8

Standards for Discovery to Delivery

ANSI/NISO Z39.19-2005 (R2010)	Guidelines for the Construction, Format, and Management of Monolingual Controlled Vocabularies ISBN 978-1-937522-22-3
ANSI/NISO Z39.50-2003 (S2014)	Information Retrieval (Z39.50) Application Service Definition and Protocol Specification ISBN 978-1-937522-42-1
ANSI/NISO Z39.83-1-2012	NISO Circulation Interchange Part 1: Protocol (NCIP), version 2.02 ISBN 978-1-937522-03-2

ANSI/NISO Z39.83-2-2012	NISO Circulation Interchange Protocol (NCIP) Part 2: Implementation Profile 1, version 2.02 ISBN 978-1-937522-04-9
ANSI/NISO Z39.85-2012	The Dublin Core Metadata Element Set ISBN 978-1-937522-14-8
ANSI/NISO Z39.87-2006 (R2017)	Data Dictionary—Technical Metadata for Digital Still Images ISBN 978-1-937522-76-6
ANSI/NISO Z39.88-2004 (R2010)	The OpenURL Framework for Context-Sensitive Services ISBN 978-1-937522-38-4
ANSI/NISO Z39.89-2003 (S2014)	The U.S. National Z39.50 Profile for Library Applications ISBN 978-1-937522-43-8
ANSI/NISO Z39.99-2017	ResourceSync Framework Specification ISBN 978-1-937522-73-5

Business Information

ANSI/NISO Z39.7-2013	Information Services and Use: Metrics and Statistics for Libraries and Information Providers—Data Dictionary ISBN 978-1-937522-15-5
ANSI/NISO Z39.93-2014	The Standardized Usage Statistics Harvesting Initiative (SUSHI) Protocol ISBN 978-1-937522-47-6

Preservation and Storage

ANSI/NISO Z39.32-1996 (R2012)	Information on Microfiche Headers ISBN 978-1-937522-29-2
ANSI/NISO Z39.48-1992 (R2009)	Permanence of Paper for Publications and Documents in Libraries and Archives ISBN 978-1-937522-30-8
ANSI/NISO Z39.73-1994 (R2012)	Single-Tier Steel Bracket Library Shelving ISBN 978-1-937522-32-2
ANSI/NISO Z39.78-2000 (R2018)	Library Binding ISBN 978-1-937522-86-5

In Development / NISO Initiatives

NISO develops new standards, reports, and best practices on a continuing basis to support its ongoing standards development program. NISO working groups are currently developing or exploring the following:

- Collection Description Specification (NISO Z39.91-200x)
- Criteria for Indexes (NISO Z39.4-201X)
- Digital Bookmarking and Annotation (NISO Z39.97-201x)
- Information Retrieval Service—Description Specification (NISO Z39.92-200x)
- Information Services and Use Metrics & Statistics for Libraries and Information Providers—Data Dictionary (NISO Z39.7-201x)
- Permanence of Paper for Publications and Documents in Libraries and Archives (ANSI/NISO Z39.48-201x)
- Scientific and Technical Reports—Preparation, Presentation, and Preservation (ANSI/NISO Z39.18-2005 [R201x])
- Standard Interchange Protocol (SIP) (NISO Z39.100-201x)
- Standards-Specific Ontology (SSOS) (NISO Z39.103.201x)

NISO Recommended Practices

A Framework of Guidance for Building Good Digital Collections, 3rd ed., 2007
ISBN 978-1-880124-74-1

NISO RP-2005-01	Ranking of Authentication and Access Methods Available to the Metasearch Environment ISBN 978-1-880124-89-5
NISO RP-2005-02	Search and Retrieval Results Set Metadata ISBN 978-1-880124-88-8
NISO RP-2005-03	Search and Retrieval Citation Level Data Elements ISBN 978-1-880124-87-1
NISO RP-2006-01	Best Practices for Designing Web Services in the Library Context ISBN 978-1-880124-86-4
NISO RP-2006-02	NISO Metasearch XML Gateway Implementers Guide ISBN 978-1-880124-85-7
NISO RP-6-2012	RFID in U.S. Libraries ISBN 978-1-937522-02-5
NISO RP-7-2012	SERU: A Shared Electronic Resource Understanding ISBN 978-1-937522-08-7
NISO RP-8-2008	Journal Article Versions (JAV) ISBN 978-1-880124-79-6
NISO RP-9-2014	KBART: Knowledge Bases and Related Tools ISBN 978-1-937522-41-4

NISO RP-10-2010 Cost of Resource Exchange (CORE) Protocol
ISBN 978-1-880124-84-0

NISO RP-11-2011 ESPReSSO: Establishing Suggested Practices Regarding Single Sign-On
ISBN 978-1-880124-98-7

NISO RP-12-2012 Physical Delivery of Library Resources
ISBN 978-1-937522-01-8

NISO RP-14-2014 NISO SUSHI Protocol: COUNTER-SUSHI Implementation Profile
ISBN 978-1-937522-45-2

NISO RP-15-2013 Recommended Practices for Online Supplemental Journal Article Materials
ISBN 978-1-937522-12-4

NISO RP-16-2013 PIE-J: The Presentation and Identification of E-Journals
ISBN 978-1-937522-05-6

NISO RP-17-2013 Institutional Identification: Identifying Organizations in the Information Supply Chain
ISBN 978-1-937522-11-7

NISO RP-19-2014 Open Discovery Initiative: Promoting Transparency in Discovery
ISBN 978-1-937522-42-1

NISO RP-20-2014 Demand Driven Acquisition of Monographs
ISBN 978-1-937522-44-5

NISO RP-21-2013 Improving OpenURLs Through Analytics (IOTA): Recommendations for Link Resolver Providers
ISBN 978-1-937522-18-6

NISO RP-22-2015 Access License and Indicators
ISBN 978-1-937522-49-0

NISO RP-23-2015 Protocol for Exchanging Serial Content (PESC)
ISBN 978-1-937522-66-7

NISO RP-24-2019 Transfer Code of Practice, version 4.0
ISBN 978-1-937522-90-2

NISO RP-25-2016 Outputs of the NISO Alternative Assessment Project
ISBN 978-1-937522-71-1

NISO Technical Reports

NISO TR01-1995 Environmental Guidelines for the Storage of Paper Records
by William K. Wilson
ISBN 978-1-800124-21-5

NISO TR02-1997 Guidelines for Indexes and Related Information Retrieval Devices
by James D. Anderson
ISBN 978-1-880124-36-X

NISO TR03-1999	Guidelines for Alphabetical Arrangement of Letters and Sorting of Numerals and Other Symbols by Hans H. Wellisch ISBN 978-1-880124-41-6
NISO TR04-2006	Networked Reference Services: Question/Answer Transaction Protocol ISBN 978-1-880124-71-0
NISO TR-05-2013	IOTA Working Group Summary of Activities and Outcomes ISBN 978-1-937522-17-9
NISO TR-06-2017	Issues in Vocabulary Management ISBN 978-1-937522-79-7

Other NISO Publications

The Case for New Economic Models to Support Standardization
by Clifford Lynch
ISBN 978-1-880124-90-1

The Exchange of Serials Subscription Information
by Ed Jones
ISBN 978-1-880124-91-8

The Future of Library Resource Discovery
by Marshall Breeding
ISBN 978-1-937522-41-4

Information Standards Quarterly (*ISQ*) [NISO quarterly open access magazine]
ISSN 1041-0031

Internet, Interoperability and Standards—Filling the Gaps
by Janifer Gatenby
ISBN 978-1-880124-92-5

Issues in Crosswalking Content Metadata Standards
by Margaret St. Pierre and William P. LaPlant
ISBN 978-1-880124-93-2

Making Good on the Promise of ERM: A Standards and Best Practices Discussion Paper
by the ERM Data Standards and Best Practices Review Steering Committee
ISBN 978-1-9357522-00-1

Metadata Demystified: A Guide for Publishers
by Amy Brand, Frank Daly, and Barbara Meyers
ISBN 978-1-880124-59-8

The Myth of Free Standards: Giving Away the Farm
by Andrew N. Bank
ISBN 978-1-880124-94-9

NISO Newsline [free monthly e-newsletter]
ISSN 1559-2774

NISO Working Group Connection (free quarterly supplement to Newsline)

Patents and Open Standards
by Priscilla Caplan
ISBN 978-1-880124-95-6

The RFP Writer's Guide to Standards for Library Systems
by Cynthia Hodgson
ISBN 978-1-880124-57-4

Streamlining Book Metadata Workflow
by Judy Luther
ISBN 978-1-880124-82-6

Understanding Metadata: What Is Metadata, and What Is It For?: A Primer
by Jenn Riley
ISBN 978-1-937522-72-8

Up and Running: Implementing Z39.50: Proceedings of a Symposium Sponsored by the State Library of Iowa
edited by Sara L. Randall
ISBN 978-1-880124-33-8

Z39.50: A Primer on the Protocol
ISBN 978-1-880124-35-2

Z39.50 Implementation Experiences
ISBN 978-1-880124-51-2

NISO standards are available online at http://www.niso.org/publications/standards.

Recommended Practices, Technical Reports, White Papers, and other publications are available on the NISO website at http://www.niso.org/publications.

For more information, contact NISO, 3600 Clipper Mill Rd., Suite 302, Baltimore, MD 21211. Tel. 301-654-2512, fax 410-685-5278, e-mail nisohq@niso.org, World Wide Web http://www.niso.org.

Calendar, 2019–2027

This listing contains information on association meetings and promotional events that are, for the most part, national or international in scope. State and regional library association meetings are also included. To confirm the starting or ending date of a meeting, which may change after *Library and Book Trade Almanac* has gone to press, contact the association directly. Addresses of library and book trade associations are listed in Part 6 of this volume.

For information on additional book trade and promotional events, see *Literary Market Place* and *International Literary Market Place,* published by Information Today, Inc., and other library and book trade publications such as *Library Journal, School Library Journal*, and *Publishers Weekly*. The American Library Association (ALA) keeps an online calendar at http://www.ala.org/conferences events/planning-calendar. An Information Today events calendar can be found at http://www.infotoday.com/calendar.shtml.

2019

June

3–5	Specialized Information Publishers Assn.	Washington, DC
10–13	Assn. of Christian Librarians	Marion, IN
11–13	Assn. of American University Presses	Detroit, MI
14–18	Special Libraries Assn.	Cleveland, OH
17	Assn. of Jewish Libraries	Woodland Hills, CA
18–20	Assn. of Canadian Publishers Annual Meeting	Toronto, ON
19–23	Seoul International Book Fair	Seoul, South Korea
20–25	American Library Assn. Annual Conference	Washington, DC
20–25	American Assn. of School Librarians @ ALA	Washington, DC
26–28	Assn. of European Research Libraries (LIBER)	Dublin, Ireland

July

7–12	IEEE International Symposium on Information Theory	Paris, France
13–16	American Assn. of Law Libraries (AALL)	Washington, DC
16–17	Computing Conference	London, UK
17–23	Hong Kong Book Fair	Hong Kong
18–20	National Assn. of Government Archives and Records Administrators (NAGARA)	St. Paul, MN

July 2019 *(cont.)*

18–21	Comic-Con International	San Diego, CA
31–Aug. 6	Society of American Archivists	Austin, TX

August

7–9	Pacific Northwest Library Assn.	Spokane, WA
8–9	Wyoming Library Assn.	Cheyenne, WY
10–26	Edinburgh International Book Festival	Edinburgh, UK
21–23	International Symposium on Information Management and Big Data	Lima, Peru
21–25	Beijing International Book Fair	Beijing, China
24–30	International Federation of Library Assns. (IFLA) General Conf. and Assembly	Athens, Greece

September

4–8	Moscow International Book Fair	Moscow, Russia
19–20	Minnesota Library Assn.	Prior Lake, MN
19–21	Colorado Assn. of Libraries	Loveland, CO
25–27	North Dakota Library Assn.	West Fargo, ND
25–27	South Dakota Library Assn.	Spearfish, SD
25–27	Ohio Library Council	Cincinnati, OH
26–29	Gothenburg Book Fair	Gothenburg, Sweden
27–29	Arkansas Library Assn. / Southeastern Library Association	Hot Springs, AR
30–Oct. 1	Maine Library Association	Newry, ME

October

2–4	Idaho Library Assn.	Nampa, ID
2–4	Iowa Library Assn. / Nebraska Library Assn. / Nebraska School Library Assn.	La Vista, NE
2–4	Missouri Library Assn.	Kansas City, MO
8–10	International Conference of Indigenous Archives, Libraries, and Museums	Temecula, CA
8–11	Wisconsin Library Assn.	Wisconsin Dells, WI
9–11	Georgia Libraries Conference	Macon, GA
9–11	South Carolina Library Assn.	Columbia, SC
10–13	International Literacy Assn.	New Orleans, LA
13–16	Pennsylvania Library Assn.	Erie, PA
15–16	Internet Librarian International	London, UK
15–18	North Carolina Library Assn.	Winston-Salem, NC
16–18	West Virginia Library Assn.	Shepherdstown, WV

16–20	Frankfurt Book Fair	Frankfurt, Germany
19–23	Assn. for Information Science and Technology (ASIS&T)	Melbourne, Australia
20–22	New England Library Assn.	Groton, CT
20–27	Belgrade International Book Fair	Belgrade, Serbia
21–23	Internet Librarian	Monterey, CA
21–25	International Assn. of School Librarianship (IASL)	Dubrovnik, Croatia
22–24	Illinois Library Assn.	Tinley Park, IL
22–25	Mississippi Library Assn.	Jackson, MS
23–25	Kansas Library Assn.	Overland Park, KS
23–25	Virginia Library Assn.	Norfolk, VA
24–25	Kentucky Library Assn.	Bowling Green, KY
24–26	California Library Assn.	Pasadena, CA
24–27	Helsinki Book Fair	Helsinki, Finland
24–27	Krakow International Book Fair	Krakow, Poland
30–Nov. 1	New Mexico Library Assn./Mountains Plains Library Assn.	Albuquerque, NM

November

2–10	Istanbul Book Fair	Istanbul, Turkey
3–5	Indiana Library Federation	Indianapolis, IN
3–7	International Conference on Information and Knowledge Management (CIKM)	Beijing, China
5–7	KM World	Washington, DC
6–10	Buch Wien International Book Fair	Vienna, Austria
7–8	Arizona Library Assn.	Tucson, AZ
13–16	New York Library Assn.	Saratoga Springs, NY
14–16	American Assn. of School Librarians (AASL) National Conference	Louisville, KY
19–20	Streaming Media West CA	Huntington Beach,
20–25	Salon du Livre de Montréal	Montreal, QC
28–29	Bibliographical Society of Australia and New Zealand	Melbourne, Australia
30–Dec. 8	Guadalajara International Book Fair	Guadalajara, Mexico

December

15–18	International Conference on Information Systems (ICIS)	Munich, Germany

2020

January

7–10	Hawaii International Conference on System Sciences	Maui, HI
24–28	American Library Assn. Midwinter Meeting	Philadelphia, PA
24–28	American Assn. of School Librarians (AASL) @ ALA Midwinter Meeting	Philadelphia, PA

February

25–29	Public Library Assn.	Nashville, TN

March

10–12	London Book Fair	London, UK
24–27	Texas Library Assn.	Houston, TX
30–Apr. 2	Tennessee Library Assn.	Knoxville, TN
31–Apr. 2	Computers in Libraries	Arlington, VA

April

15–17	Wisconsin Assn. of Academic Libraries	Milwaukee, WI
29–May 1	Wisconsin Assn. of Public Libraries	Oshkosh, WI

June

25–30	American Library Assn. Annual Conference	Chicago, IL
25–30	American Assn. of School Librarians @ ALA	Chicago, IL

July

11–14	American Assn. of Law Libraries (AALL)	New Orleans, LA

September

30–Oct. 2	South Dakota Library Assn.	Aberdeen, SD

October

1–3	Assn. of Library Service to Children (ALSC) National Institute	Minneapolis, MN
6–8	West Virginia Library Assn.	Davis, WV
14–18	Frankfurt Book Fair	Frankfurt, Germany
18–21	Pennsylvania Library Assn.	Mount Pocono, PA
20–22	Illinois Library Assn.	Springfield, IL
21–23	New Mexico Library Assn.	Albuquerque, NM

25–27	New England Library Assn.	Manchester, NH
27–30	Wisconsin Library Assn.	Green Bay, WI

November

4–7	New York Library Assn.	Saratoga Springs, NY

December

13–16	International Conference on Information Systems (ICIS)	Hyderabad, India

2021

January

22–26	American Library Assn. Midwinter Meeting	Indianapolis, IN
22–26	American Assn. of School Librarians (AASL) @ ALA Midwinter Meeting	Indianapolis, IN

April

14–17	Assn. of College and Research Libraries	Seattle, WA
20–23	Texas Library Assn.	San Antonio, TX

June

24–29	American Library Assn. Annual Conference	Chicago, IL
24–29	American Assn. of School Librarians @ ALA	Chicago, IL

July

17–20	American Assn. of Law Libraries (AALL)	Cleveland, OH

September

29–Oct. 1	South Dakota Library Assn.	Pierre, SD

October

12–14	Illinois Library Assn.	Peoria, IL
17–20	Pennsylvania Library Assn.	Monroeville, PA
20–24	Frankfurt Book Fair	Frankfurt, Germany
21–24	American Assn. of School Librarians (AASL) National Conference	Salt Lake City, UT

November

3–6	New York Library Assn.	Syracuse, NY

December 2021

12–15	International Conference on Information Systems (ICIS)	Austin, Texas

2022

January

21–25	American Library Assn. Midwinter Meeting	San Antonio, TX
21–25	American Assn. of School Librarians (AASL) @ ALA Midwinter Meeting	San Antonio, TX

April

25–28	Texas Library Assn.	Fort Worth, TX

June

23–28	American Library Assn. Annual Conference	Washington, DC
23–28	American Assn. of School Librarians @ ALA	Washington, DC

October

19–23	Frankfurt Book Fair	Frankfurt, Germany

December

11–14	International Conference on Information Denmark Systems (ICIS)	Copenhagen,

2023

January

27–31	American Library Assn. Midwinter Meeting	New Orleans, LA
27–31	American Assn. of School Librarians (AASL) @ ALA Midwinter Meeting	New Orleans, LA

March

15–18	Assn. of College and Research Libraries	Pittsburgh, PA

April

19–22	Texas Library Assn.	Austin, TX

June

22–27	American Library Assn. Annual Conference	Chicago, IL
22–27	American Assn. of School Librarians @ ALA	Chicago, IL

July

16–19	American Assn. of Law Libraries	Denver, CO

October

18–22	Frankfurt Book Fair	Frankfurt, Germany
19–21	American Assn. of School Librarians (AASL) National Conference	Tampa, FL

2024

February

9–13	American Library Assn. Midwinter Meeting	Denver, CO
9–13	American Assn. of School Librarians (AASL) @ ALA Midwinter Meeting	Denver, CO

April

16–19	Texas Library Assn.	San Antonio, TX

June

27–July 2	American Library Assn. Annual Conference	San Diego, CA
27–July 2	American Assn. of School Librarians @ ALA	San Diego, CA

2025

April

1–4	Texas Library Assn.	Dallas, TX
2–5	Assn. of College and Research Libraries	Minneapolis, MN

June

26–July 1	American Library Assn. Annual Conference	Philadelphia, PA
26–July 1	American Assn. of School Librarians @ ALA	Philadelphia, PA

October

16–19	American Assn. of School Librarians (AASL) National Conference	St. Louis, MO

2026

March

30–Apr. 2	Texas Library Assn.	Houston, TX

June

25–30	American Library Assn. Annual Conference	Chicago, IL
25–30	American Assn. of School Librarians @ ALA	Chicago, IL

2027

January

22–26	American Library Assn. Midwinter Meeting	Philadelphia, PA

March

30–Apr. 2	Texas Library Assn.	Dallas, TX

April

7–10	Assn. of College and Research Libraries	Portland, OR

June

24–29	American Library Assn. Annual Conference	New Orleans, LA
24–29	American Assn. of School Librarians @ ALA	New Orleans, LA

Acronyms

A

AACR2. Anglo-American Cataloging Rules
AAHSL. Association of Academic Health Sciences Libraries
AALL. American Association of Law Libraries
AASL. American Association of School Librarians
AAU. Association of American Universities
ABA. Acquisitions and Bibliographic Access Directorate
ABA. American Booksellers Association
ABC. Accessible Book Consortium
ABOS. Association of Bookmobile and Outreach Services
ABPA. American Book Producers Association
ACL. Association of Christian Librarians
ACM. Association of Children's Museums
ACRL. Association of College and Research Libraries
AFSIC. Alternative Farming Systems Information Center
AgLaw. Agricultural Law Information Partnership
AGLINET. Agricultural Libraries Network
AgNIC. Agriculture Network Information Collaborative
AGRICOLA. AGRICultural On-Line Access
AIB. Advocates for Independent Business
AIGA. Professional Association for Design (formerly American Institute of Graphic Arts)
AIIM. Association for Information and Image Management
AIIP. Association of Independent Information Professionals
AILA. American Indian Library Association
AILI. FEDLINK American Indian Libraries Initiative
AJL. Association of Jewish Libraries
ALA. American Library Association
ALCTS. Association for Library Collections and Technical Services
ALHHS. Archivists and Librarians in the History of the Health Sciences
ALIC. Archives Library Information Center
ALISE. Association for Library and Information Science Education
ALS. Academic Libraries Survey
ALSC. Association for Library Service to Children
ALTA. American Literary Translators Association
ALTAFF. Association of Library Trustees, Advocates, Friends, and Foundations (now United for Libraries)
ANSI. American National Standards Institute
APALA. Asian/Pacific American Librarians Association
APP. Accelerating Promising Practices for Small Libraries
ARL. Association of Research Libraries
ARLIS/NA. Art Libraries Society of North America
ARSL. Association for Rural and Small Libraries
ASCLA. Association of Specialized and Cooperative Library Agencies
ASERL. Association of Southeastern Research Libraries
ASGCLA. Association of Specialized, Government, and Cooperative Library Agencies
ASI. American Society for Indexing
ASIS&T. Association for Information Science and Technology
ATALM. Association of Tribal Archives, Libraries, and Museums

ATLA. American Theological Library Association
AUPresses. Association of University Presses
AVSL. Association of Vision Science Librarians
AWIC. Animal Welfare Information Center

B

BCALA. Black Caucus of the American Library Association
Binc. Book Industry Charitable Foundation
BISAC. Book Industry Study Group
BISAC. Book Industry Systems Advisory Committee
BMI. Book Manufacturers' Institute
BSA. Bibliographical Society of America

C

CAIS. Canadian Association for Information Science
CALA. Chinese American Librarians Association
CAP. Collections Assessment for Preservation
CAP. Customized Assessment Program
CARL. Canadian Association of Research Libraries
CBA. Association for Christian Retail (formerly Christian Booksellers Association)
CBC. Children's Book Council
CDO. Collection Development Office
CGP. Catalog of U.S. Government Publications
CHLA. Canadian Health Libraries Association
C&I. Cataloging and indexing
CIP. Cataloging in Publication
CLA. Catholic Library Association
CLENERT. See Learning Round Table
CLIR. Council on Library and Information Resources
CMO. ALA Communications and Marketing Office
CNI. Coalition for Networked Information
COAPI. Coalition of Open Access Policy Institutions
COSLA. Chief Officers of State Library Associations
CRKN. Canadian Research Knowledge Network
CRO. ALA Chapter Relations Office
CRO. Congressional Relations Office
CRS. Congressional Research Service
CUI. Controlled unclassified information

D

DEL. Documenting Endangered Languages
DHCP. Documentary Heritage Community Program
DLF. Digital Library Federation
DLME. Digital Library of the Middle East
DMCA. Digital Millennium Copyright Act
DTIC. Defense Technical Information Center

E

ECLS. Early Childhood Longitudinal Study
EDI. Equity, diversity and inclusion
ELS. Education Longitudinal Study
EMIERT. Ethnic and Multicultural Information and Exchange Round Table
ERA. Electronic Records Archives
ERDC. U.S. Army Engineer Research and Development Center Library
ERIC. Education Resources Information Center
eRN. DLF eResearch Network
ERT. Exhibits Round Table
ESLS. Educators of School Librarians Section of AASL

F

FAB. FEDLINK Advisory Board
FAFLRT. Federal and Armed Forces Librarians Round Table
FAIC. Foundation of the American Institute for Conservation of Historic and Artistic Works
FAME. Florida Association for Media in Education
FCCC. Fostering Creative Community Connections
FDLP. Federal Depository Library Program

FEDLINK. Federal Library and Information Network
FESABID. Federación Española de Sociedades de Archivística, Biblioteconomía, Documentación y Museística
FIAF. International Federation of Film Archives
FINRA. Financial Industry Regulatory Authority
FLC. Federal Libraries Consortium (Canada)
FNIC. Food and Nutrition Information Center
FOIA. Freedom of Information Act
FRCs. Federal Records Centers
FSRIO. Food Safety Research Information Office
FTRF. Freedom to Read Foundation

G

GameRT. Games and Gaming Round Table
GLAMS. Galleries, libraries, archives, and museums
GLBTRT. Gay, Lesbian, Bisexual, and Transgendered Round Table
GODORT. Government Documents Round Table
GPO. Government Publishing Office

H

HBCU. Historically Black Colleges and Universities
HRDR. ALA Office for Human Resource Development and Recruitment

I

IACs. Information Analysis Centers
IAL. Innovative Approaches to Literacy
IALL. International Association of Law Libraries
IAML. International Association of Music Libraries, Archives and Documentation Centres
IASL. International Association of School Librarianship
IATUL. International Association of Scientific and Technological University Libraries
IBBY. International Board on Books for Young People
ICA. International Council on Archives
ICIS. International Conference on Information Systems
IFLA. International Federation of Library Associations and Institutions
IFRT. Intellectual Freedom Round Table
IIBD. Independent Bookstore Day
III. Inclusive Internship Initiative
ILAB. International League of Antiquarian Booksellers
ILA. International Literacy Association
ILL. Interlibrary loan
IMLS. Institute of Museum and Library Services
INALJ. Information professionals finding and sharing jobs
IPA. International Publishers Association
IRDW. Initiative to Recruit a Diverse Workforce
IR. Institutional repositories
IRO. ALA International Relations Office
IRRT. International Relations Round Table
ISBD. International Standard Bibliographical Description
ISBN. International Standard Book Number
ISNs. Canadian International Standard Numbers
ISO. International Organization for Standardization
ISOO. Information Security Oversight Office
ISS. Independent School Section of AASL
ISSN. International Standard Serial Number

J

JCLC. National Joint Conference of Librarians of Color
JELIS. *Journal of Education for Library and Information Science*

L

LAC. Library and Archives Canada
LARC. Library and Research Center
LCA. Library Copyright Alliance
LC. Library of Congress
LCI. Leading Change Institute

LearnRT. Learning Round Table (formerly CLENERT)
LEED. Leadership in Energy and Environmental Design
LHC. Lister Hill Center for Biomedical Communications
LHRT. Library History Round Table
LIBER. Association of European Research Libraries
LIS. Library and information science
LITA. Library and Information Technology Association
LJ. *Library Journal*
LLAMA. Library Leadership and Management Association
LMPI. Library Materials Price Index
LPC. Library Publishing Coalition
LRRT. Library Research Round Table
LRTS. *Library Resources and Technical Services*
LSCM. Library Services and Content Management
LSTA. Library Services and Technology Act

M

MAGIRT. Map and Geospatial Information Round Table
MAP. Museum Assessment Program
MFA. Museums for America
MLA. Medical Library Association
MLA. Music Library Association
MLIS. Master of Library and Information Science
MLSA. Museum and Library Services Act
MMLIS. Master of Management in Library and Information Science
MOOCs. Massive Open Online Courses
MPA. Association of Magazine Media (formerly Magazine Publishers of America)

N

NAABPI. North American Academic Books Price Index
NAC. National Archives Catalog
NAGARA. National Association of Government Archives and Records Administrators
NAIBA. New Atlantic Independent Booksellers Association
NAL. National Agricultural Library
NALDC. National Agricultural Library Digital Collection
NALT. National Agricultural Library Thesaurus
NANP. National Digital Newspaper Program
NARA. National Archives and Records Administration
NASIG. formerly North American Serials Interest Group
NBRII. National Bibliographic Records Inventory Initiative
NCAC. National Coalition Against Censorship
NCBI. National Center for Biotechnology Information
NCES. National Center for Education Statistics
NCTE. National Council of Teachers of English
NDC. National Declassification Center
NDSA. National Digital Stewardship Alliance
NEH. National Endowment for the Humanities
NEIBA. New England Independent Booksellers Association
NFAIS. National Federation of Advanced Information Services
NHDS. National Heritage Digitization Strategy
NHPRC. National Historical Publications and Records Commission
NIH. National Institutes of Health
NISIC. National Invasive Species Information Center
NISO. National Information Standards Organization
NLE. National Library of Education
NLM. National Library of Medicine
NLS. National Library Service for the Blind and Physically Handicapped
NLWD. National Library Workers Day
NMLSB. National Museum and Library Services Board
NMRT. New Members Round Table
NNLM. National Network of Libraries of Medicine

NTIS. National Technical Information Service
NTPS. National Teacher and Principal Survey
NTRL. National Technical Reports Library

O

OAI. Open archives initiative
OCLC. Online Computer Library Center
ODLOS. Office for Accreditation, the Office for Diversity, Literacy and Outreach Services
ODLOS. Office for Diversity, Literacy and Outreach Services
OFR. National Archives' Office of the Federal Register
OGIS. Office of Government Information Services
OIB. USSBY Outstanding International Books
OIF. Office for Intellectual Freedom
OLA. Office for Library Advocacy
OLOS. Office for Literacy and Outreach Services
OPEN. Open, Public, Electronic, and Necessary Government Data Act

P

PALA. Polish American Librarians Association
PLA. Public Library Association
PPO. Public Programs Office
PRD. Preservation Reformatting Division
PTRCA. Patent and Trademark Resource Center Association

R

RBMS. Rare Books and Manuscripts Section
RDA. Resource Description and Access
RDS. Research data services
REFORMA. National Association to Promote Library and Information Services to Latinos and the Spanish-Speaking
RIC. Rural Information Center
RIM. Research information management
RtC. Libraries Ready to Code
RUSA. Reference and User Services Association

S

SAA. Society of American Archivists
SAN. Standard Address Number
SASS. Schools and Staffing Survey
SIBA. formerly Southern Independent Booksellers Alliance
SIIA. Software and Information Industry Association
SLA. Special Libraries Association
SLAA. State Library Administrative Agency
SLHE. *Standards for Libraries in Higher Education*
SLM. School Library Month
SPARC. Scholarly Publishing & Academic Resources Coalition
SPVS. Supervisors Section of AASL
SSP. Society for Scholarly Publishing
STEAM. Science, Technology, Engineering, Arts, and Math
STEM. Science, Technology, Engineering, and Mathematics

T

TCJA. Tax Cuts and Jobs Act
TOME. Toward an Open Monograph Ecosystem
TPS. Teaching with Primary Sources
TRHT GSC. Truth, Racial Healing, and Transformation Great Stories Club
TRLN. Triangle Research Libraries Network

U

UELMA. Utah Educational Library Media Association
UKSG. formerly the United Kingdom Serials Group
ULC. Urban Libraries Council
USAIN. United States Agricultural Information Network
USBBY. United States Board on Books for Young People

USPPI. U.S. Periodical Price Index

W

WAIC. Water and Agriculture Information Center
WIPO. World Intellectual Property Organization
WLIC. World Library and Information Congress

Y

YAC. Youth Advisory Council
YALSA. Young Adult Library Services Association

Index

Note: Page numbers followed by "f" and "t" represent figures and tables respectively. The Directory of Organizations (Part 6) is not included in the index.

A

D

E

I

M

O

V

W

Y